P9-BJR-860

Contemporary
Literary Criticism

Guide to Gale Literary Criticism Series

For criticism on	Consult these Gale series
Authors now living or who died after December 31, 1959	*CONTEMPORARY LITERARY CRITICISM (CLC)*
Authors who died between 1900 and 1959	*TWENTIETH-CENTURY LITERARY CRITICISM (TCLC)*
Authors who died between 1800 and 1899	*NINETEENTH-CENTURY LITERATURE CRITICISM (NCLC)*
Authors who died between 1400 and 1799	*LITERATURE CRITICISM FROM 1400 TO 1800 (LC)* *SHAKESPEAREAN CRITICISM (SC)*
Authors who died before 1400	*CLASSICAL AND MEDIEVAL LITERATURE CRITICISM (CMLC)*
Black writers of the past two hundred years	*BLACK LITERATURE CRITICISM (BLC)*
Authors of books for children and young adults	*CHILDREN'S LITERATURE REVIEW (CLR)*
Dramatists	*DRAMA CRITICISM (DC)*
Hispanic writers of the late nineteenth and twentieth centuries	*HISPANIC LITERATURE CRITICISM (HLC)*
Native North American writers and orators of the eighteenth, nineteenth, and twentieth centuries	*NATIVE NORTH AMERICAN LITERATURE (NNAL)*
Poets	*POETRY CRITICISM (PC)*
Short story writers	*SHORT STORY CRITICISM (SSC)*
Major authors from the Renaissance to the present	*WORLD LITERATURE CRITICISM, 1500 TO THE PRESENT (WLC)*

ISSN 0091-3421

Volume 98

Contemporary Literary Criticism

Excerpts from Criticism of the Works
of Today's Novelists, Poets, Playwrights,
Short Story Writers, Scriptwriters, and
Other Creative Writers

Deborah A. Stanley
EDITOR

Jeff Chapman
Pamela S. Dear
Jeff Hunter
Daniel Jones
John D. Jorgenson
Jerry Moore
Polly A. Vedder
Thomas Wiloch
Kathleen Wilson
ASSOCIATE EDITORS

GALE

DETROIT • NEW YORK • TORONTO • LONDON

STAFF

Deborah A. Stanley, *Editor*

...an, Pamela S. Dear, Jeff Hunter, Daniel Jones,
...Jorgenson, Jerry Moore, Polly A. Vedder,
Thomas Wiloch, and Kathleen Wilson, *Associate Editors*

Tracy Arnold-Chapman, John P. Daniel, Christopher Giroux,
Joshua Lauer, Janet Mullane, Patricia Onorato, Annette Petrusso,
Linda Quigley, and Janet Witalec, *Contributing Editors*

Susan Trosky, *Permissions Manager*
Margaret A. Chamberlain, Maria Franklin, and Kimberly F. Smilay, *Permissions Specialists*
Edna Hedblad, Michele Lonoconus, Maureen A. Puhl, and Shalice Shah, *Permissions Associates*
Sarah Chesney and Jeffrey Hermann, *Permissions Assistants*

Victoria B. Cariappa, *Research Manager*
Julia C. Daniel, Tamara C. Nott, Michele P. LaMeau, Tracie A. Richardson,
Norma Sawaya, Sean R. Smith, and Cheryl L. Warnock, *Research Associates*
Laura C. Bissey and Alfred A. Gardner I, *Research Assistants*

Mary Beth Trimper, *Production Director*
Deborah L. Milliken, *Production Assistant*

Barbara J. Yarrow, *Graphic Services Manager*
Sherrell Hobbs, *Macintosh Artist*
Randy Bassett, *Image Database Supervisor*
Robert Duncan and Mikal Ansari, *Imaging Specialists*
Pamela Reed, *Photography Coordinator*

Library of Congress Catalog Card Number 76-46132
ISBN 0-7876-1062-3
ISSN 0091-3421

Printed in the United States of America
10 9 8 7 6 5 4 3 2 1

Contents

Preface vii

Acknowledgments xi

Preface

A Comprehensive Information Source
on Contemporary Literature

amed "one of the twenty-five most distinguished reference titles published during the past twenty-five years" by *Reference Quarterly,* the *Contemporary Literary Criticism (CLC)* series provides readers with critical commentary and general information on more than 2,000 authors now living or who died after December 31, 1959. Previous to the publication of the first volume of *CLC* in 1973, there was no ongoing digest monitoring scholarly and popular sources of critical opinion and explication of modern literature. *CLC,* therefore, has fulfilled an essential need, particularly since the complexity and variety of contemporary literature makes the function of criticism especially important to today's reader.

Scope of the Series

CLC presents significant passages from published criticism of works by creative writers. Since many of the authors covered by *CLC* inspire continual critical commentary, writers are often represented in more than one volume. There is, of course, no duplication of reprinted criticism.

Authors are selected for inclusion for a variety of reasons, among them the publication or dramatic production of a critically acclaimed new work, the reception of a major literary award, revival of interest in past writings, or the adaptation of a literary work to film or television.

Attention is also given to several other groups of writers-authors of considerable public interest—about whose work criticism is often difficult to locate. These include mystery and science fiction writers, literary and social critics, foreign writers, and authors who represent particular ethnic groups within the United States.

Format of the Book

Each *CLC* volume contains about 500 individual excerpts taken from hundreds of book review periodicals, general magazines, scholarly journals, monographs, and books. Entries include critical evaluations spanning from the beginning of an author's career to the most current commentary. Interviews, feature articles, and other published writings that offer insight into the author's works are also presented. Students, teachers, librarians, and researchers will find that the generous excerpts and supplementary material in *CLC* provide them with vital information required to write a term paper, analyze a poem, or lead a book discussion group. In addition, complete bibliographical citations note the original source and all of the information necessary for a term paper footnote or bibliography.

Features

A *CLC* author entry consists of the following elements:

■   The **Author Heading** cites the author's name in the form under which the author has most commonly published, followed by birth date, and death date when applicable. Uncertainty as to a birth or death date is indicated by a question mark.

■ A **Portrait** of the author is included when available.

■ A brief **Biographical and Critical Introduction** to the author and his or her work precedes the excerpted criticism. The first line of the introduction provides the author's full name, pseudonyms (if applicable), nationality, and a listing of genres in which the author has written. To provide users with easier access to information, the biographical and critical essay included in each author entry is divided into four categories: "Introduction," "Biographical Information," "Major Works," and "Critical Reception." The introductions to single-work entries—entries that focus on well known and frequently studied books, short stories, and poems—are similarly organized to quickly provide readers with information on the plot and major characters of the work being discussed, its major themes, and its critical reception. Previous volumes of *CLC* in which the author has been featured are also listed in the introduction.

■ A list of **Principal Works** notes the most important writings by the author. When foreign-language works have been translated into English, the English-language version of the title follows in brackets.

■ The **Excerpted Criticism** represents various kinds of critical writing, ranging in form from the brief review to the scholarly exegesis. Essays are selected by the editors to reflect the spectrum of opinion about a specific work or about an author's literary career in general. The excerpts are presented chronologically, adding a useful perspective to the entry. All titles by the author featured in the entry are printed in boldface type, which enables the reader to easily identify the works being discussed. Publication information (such as publisher names and book prices) and parenthetical numerical references (such as footnotes or page and line references to specific editions of a work) have been deleted at the editor's discretion to provide smoother reading of the text.

■ Critical essays are prefaced by **Explanatory Notes** as an additional aid to readers. These notes may provide several types of valuable information, including: the reputation of the critic, the importance of the work of criticism, the commentator's approach to the author's work, the purpose of the criticism, and changes in critical trends regarding the author.

■ A complete **Bibliographical Citation** designed to help the user find the original essay or book precedes each excerpt.

■ Whenever possible, a recent, previously unpublished **Author Interview** accompanies each entry.

■ A concise **Further Reading** section appears at the end of entries on authors for whom a significant amount of criticism exists in addition to the pieces reprinted in *CLC*. Each citation in this section is accompanied by a descriptive annotation describing the content of that article. Materials included in this section are grouped under various headings (e.g., Biography, Bibliography, Criticism, and Interviews) to aid users in their search for additional information. Cross-references to other useful sources published by Gale Research in which the author has appeared are also included: *Authors in the News, Black Writers, Children's Literature Review, Contemporary Authors, Dictionary of Literary Biography, DISCovering Authors, Drama Criticism, Hispanic Literature Criticism, Hispanic Writers, Native North American Literature, Poetry Criticism, Something about the Author, Short Story Criticism, Contemporary Authors Autobiography Series,* and *Something about the Author Autobiography Series.*

Other Features

CLC also includes the following features:

- An **Acknowledgments** section lists the copyright holders who have granted permission to reprint material in this volume of *CLC*. It does not, however, list every book or periodical reprinted or consulted during the preparation of the volume.

- Each new volume of *CLC* includes a **Cumulative Topic Index,** which lists all literary topics treated in *CLC, NCLC, TCLC,* and *LC 1400-1800.*

- A **Cumulative Author Index** lists all the authors who have appeared in the various literary criticism series published by Gale Research, with cross-references to Gale's biographical and autobiographical series. A full listing of the series referenced there appears on the first page of the indexes of this volume. Readers will welcome this cumulated author index as a useful tool for locating an author within the various series. The index, which lists birth and death dates when available, will be particularly valuable for those authors who are identified with a certain period but whose death dates cause them to be placed in another, or for those authors whose careers span two periods. For example, Ernest Hemingway is found in *CLC,* yet F. Scott Fitzgerald, a writer often associated with him, is found in *Twentieth-Century Literary Criticism.*

- A **Cumulative Nationality Index** alphabetically lists all authors featured in *CLC* by nationality, followed by numbers corresponding to the volumes in which the authors appear.

- An alphabetical **Title Index** accompanies each volume of *CLC*. Listings are followed by the author's name and the corresponding page numbers where the titles are discussed. English translations of foreign titles and variations of titles are cross-referenced to the title under which a work was originally published. Titles of novels, novellas, dramas, films, record albums, and poetry, short story, and essay collections are printed in italics, while all individual poems, short stories, essays, and songs are printed in roman type within quotation marks; when published separately (e.g., T. S. Eliot's poem *The Waste Land),* the titles of long poems are printed in italics.

- In response to numerous suggestions from librarians, Gale has also produced a **Special Paperbound Edition** of the *CLC* title index. This annual cumulation, which alphabetically lists all titles reviewed in the series, is available to all customers and is typically published with every fifth volume of *CLC*. Additional copies of the index are available upon request. Librarians and patrons will welcome this separate index: it saves shelf space, is easy to use, and is recyclable upon receipt of the next edition.

Citing *Contemporary Literary Criticism*

When writing papers, students who quote directly from any volume in the Literary Criticism Series may use the following general forms to footnote reprinted criticism. The first example pertains to material drawn from periodicals, the second to material reprinted in books:

[1]Alfred Cismaru, "Making the Best of It," *The New Republic,* 207, No. 24, (December 7, 1992), 30, 32; excerpted and reprinted in *Contemporary Literary Criticism,* Vol. 85, ed. Christopher Giroux (Detroit: Gale Research, 1995), pp. 73-4.

[2]Yvor Winters, *The Post-Symbolist Methods* (Allen Swallow, 1967); excerpted and reprinted in *Contemporary Literary Criticism,* Vol. 85, ed. Christopher Giroux (Detroit: Gale Research, 1995), pp. 223-26.

Suggestions Are Welcome

The editors hope that readers will find *CLC* a useful reference tool and welcome comments about the work. Send comments and suggestions to: Editors, *Contemporary Literary Criticism,* Gale Research, Penobscot Building, Detroit, MI 48226-4094.

Acknowledgments

The editors wish to thank the copyright holders of the excerpted criticism included in this volume and the permissions managers of many book and magazine publishing companies for assisting us in securing reproduction rights. We are also grateful to the staffs of the Detroit Public Library, the Library of Congress, the University of Detroit Mercy Library, Wayne State University Purdy/Kresge Library Complex, and the University of Michigan Libraries for making their resources available to us. Following is a list of the copyright holders who have granted us permission to reproduce material in this volume of *CLC*. Every effort has been made to trace copyright, but if omissions have been made, please let us know.

COPYRIGHTED EXCERPTS IN *CLC*, VOLUME 98, WERE REPRODUCED FROM THE FOLLOWING PERIODICALS:

Agenda, v. 4, Autumn, 1966 for a review of "No Voyage" by Wallace Kaufman. Reproduced by permission of the author.—*The American Book Review,* v. 15, October-November, 1993. © 1993 by *The American Book Review.* Reproduced by permission.—*The American Scholar,* Winter, 1993. Copyright © 1993 by the United Chapters of the Phi Beta Kappa Society. Reproduced by permission.—*The American Spectator,* v. 26, February, 1993. Copyright © *The American Spectator* 1993. Reproduced by permission.—*The Atlantic Monthly,* v. 270, August, 1992 for "Joe Mitchell's Secret" by Roy Blount, Jr. Copyright 1992 by The Atlantic Monthly Company, Boston, MA. Copyright © 1992 by Roy Blount. Reproduced by permission of International Creative Management, Inc.—*Belles Lettres: A Review of Books by Women,* v. VI, Summer, 1991. Reproduced by permission.—*The Bloomsbury Review,* v. 10, May-June, 1990 for an interview with Mary Oliver by Eleanor Swanson; v. 10, May-June, 1990 for a review of "House of Light" by Eleanor Swanson; v. 15, July-August, 1995 for a review of "A Poetry Handbook" by Thomas R. Smith. Copyright © 1990, 1995 by Owaissa Communications Company, Inc. 1990. All reproduced by permission of the respective authors.—*Book World—The Washington Post,* May 17, 1991. © 1991 Postrib Corp. Reproduced courtesy of the *Chicago Tribune* and *The Washington Post.*—*Bucknell Review,* v, XXI, Spring, 1973. Copyright © by *Bucknell Review* 1973. Reproduced by permission of Associated University Presses.—*Chicago Tribune,* February 10, 1991. © copyrighted 1991, Chicago Tribune Company. All rights reserved. Reproduced with permission.—*The Christian Science Monitor,* v. 52, May 12, 1960. © 1960, renewed 1988 The Christian Science Publishing Society. All rights reserved. Reproduced by permission from *The Christian Science Monitor.*—*Cinema,* n. 34, 1974 for "Dorothy Arzner" by Gerald Peary. Reproduced by permission of Gerald Peary./ n. 34, 1974 for "Dorothy Arzner Interview" by Gerald Peary and Karyn Kay. Reproduced by permission of Gerald Peary and Karyn Kay.—*CLA Journal,* v. XIX, June, 1976. Copyright, 1976 by The College Language Association. Reproduced by permission of The College Language Association.—*Colloquia Germanica,* v. 10, April, 1976-77 for "Nelly Sachs" by Lawrence L. Langer. © A. Francke AG Verlag Bern, 1976. All rights reserved. Reproduced by permission of the author.—*The Columbia Forum,* v. IV, Winter, 1975. Reproduced by permission.—*Commentary,* v. 36, October, 1963 for "The New Yorker & Hannah Arendt" by Irving Howe. Copyright © 1963, renewed 1991 by the American Jewish Committee. All rights reserved. Reproduced by permission of the publisher and the Literary Estate of Irving Howe.—*The Commonweal,* v. LXXVIII, September 20, 1963. Copyright © 1963 Commonweal Publishing Co., Inc. Reproduced by permission of Commonweal Foundation.—*Contemporary Literature,* v. 30, Spring, 1989. © 1989 by the Board of Regents of the University of Wisconsin System. Reproduced by permission of The University of Wisconsin Press.—*Dimension,* v. 1, 1968. © 1968 by Dimension. Reproduced by permission.—*Drama Survey,* v. 3, Fall, 1963 for "Clifford Odets and the American Family" by Michael J. Mendelsohn. Copyright 1963, renewed 1991 by The Bolingbroke Society, Inc. Reproduced by permission of the author.—*Encounter,* v. LII, March, 1979 for "Re-Reading Hannah Arendt" by Walter Laqueur. © 1979 by the author. Reproduced by permission of the author.—*English Journal,* v. 59, February, 1970 for "A Study of the Allusions in Bradbury's 'Fahrenheit 451'" by Peter Sisario. Copyright © 1970 by the National Council of Teachers of English. Reproduced by permission of the publisher and author.—*Essays in Literature,* v. 5, Fall, 1978. Copyright 1978 by Western Illinois University. Reproduced by permission.—*Extrapolation,* v. 32, Winter, 1991. Copyright 1991 by The Kent State University Press.

PHOTOGRAPHS AND ILLUSTRATIONS APPEARING IN *CLC*, VOLUME 98, WERE RECEIVED FROM THE FOLLOWING SOURCES:

Hannah Arendt

1906-1975

German-born American philosopher, journalist, editor, and translator.

The following entry provides criticism of Arendt's work. For further information on her life and career, see *CLC*, Volume 66.

INTRODUCTION

A distinguished political philosopher and cultural historian, Arendt directed her writing towards the analysis of modern political movements, most notably of the events and circumstances that led to the rise of totalitarianism and to the ubiquitous sense of personal, social, and political alienation in the twentieth century. Arendt maintained that political activity expresses what is most valuable in human endeavor and argued that individuals achieve a sense of purpose and meaning through active participation in decision-making processes concerning social change or the preservation of ideas. Her reputation as a profound and independent philosophical analyst of political systems began with the publication of *The Origins of Totalitarianism* (1951), but her best-known and most controversial book is *Eichmann in Jerusalem* (1963), which blends reports of the 1962 trial of Nazi war criminal Adolf Eichmann with observations about Nazism and anti-Semitism. The work also suggests a Jewish complicity in Germany's atrocities during World War II. Ever ready to apply philosophical thought to current events, Arendt examined a broad range of topics—racism, war and revolution, culture and the life of the mind, the nature of evil, the social effects of technology—yet her main concerns were twofold: the problem of political evil in the twentieth century and the dilemma of the Jew in the contemporary world. "Twenty years after her death [her admirers] see her desire for a 'new politics' of collective action vindicated by the revolutions of 1989," remarked Tony Judt, "and her account of modern society in general and totalitarianism in particular confirmed by the course of contemporary history."

Biographical Information

Born October 14, 1906, in Hannover, Germany, to erudite Jewish parents active in social causes, Arendt spent her childhood in Konigsberg, her father's ancestral home. She studied philosophy, theology, and Greek under instruction from three leading contemporary German philosophers: Martin Heidegger, with whom she had a brief liaison, at Marburg University; Edmund Husserl at Freiburg University; and Karl Jaspers at Heidelberg University. Heidegger's ideas strongly

influenced Arendt's own thought, and Jaspers directed her doctoral dissertation on St. Augustine's concept of love, which was published in 1929. Forced out by rising anti-Semitic sentiments, Arendt fled in 1933 to Paris, where she worked with Jewish orphans and refugees and completed her first book, a biography of an eighteenth-century Berlin salon hostess, *Rahel Varnhagen* (1958). In 1940 Arendt married Heinrich Blucher, an art historian. The two moved to New York, where Arendt served as research director for the Conference of Jewish Relations from 1944 to 1946 and as chief editor of Schocken Books from 1946 to 1948. She became a naturalized U.S. citizen in 1950 and received a Guggenheim Fellowship in 1952. During this time Arendt established herself as an incisive political commentator by writing essays and reviews for *Aufbau* (*Construction*), an emigre newspaper, and secured her reputation with the publication of *The Origins of Totalitarianism* and *The Human Condition* (1958). Following her appointment as the first woman professor at Princeton University in 1959, Arendt later lectured for the Committee on Social Thought at the University of Chicago from 1963 to 1967, when she joined the graduate faculty at the New School for Social Research. *Eichmann in Jerusalem,* which first appeared as a series of articles in *The New Yorker,* generated furor over Arendt's comments about German Jews, and Arendt lost many friends despite her efforts to reply to her critics. Arendt voiced her response to the revolutionary zeal of 1960s in *On Revolution* (1963), *Men in Dark Times* (1968), *On Violence* (1970), and *Crises of the Republic* (1972). Arendt died suddenly of a heart attack on December 4, 1975, in New York City.

Major Works

The Origins of Totalitarianism, Arendt's first major publication, analyzes the historical circumstances that fostered the development of fascist ideology in twentieth-century German and Russian society, tracing its roots to anti-Semitism and nineteenth-century imperialism. Closely related to *Origins, The Human Condition* outlines Arendt's views on the public realm or *vita activa* of human activity, interpreting the causes of personal and social alienation in terms of the nature of labor, work, and action. Her posthumous *The Life of the Mind* (1978), a proposed three-volume study of the elementary mental activities of thinking, willing, and judging, of which only the volumes "Thinking" and "Willing" were published, treats the private realm or *vita comtemplativa,* analyzing the processes of the mind and their effects on action. Arendt's belief that political activity was the noblest of human endeavors expressed itself in the highly controversial *Eichmann in Jerusalem,* which suggests that the failure of Jews to act against the policies of Nazi Germany actually enabled the state to proceed with the Holocaust; though never intending to exculpate Eichmann's guilt, Arendt showed that he was not a mere evil madman, but rather someone who had developed an inability to think. Her other book-length studies include *On Revolution,* which is a comparative analysis of the American and French revolutions, and *On Violence,* which argues that violence is a reaction to a lack of power. Some of Arendt's best work is found in essays she wrote for a variety of periodicals and later collected in such volumes as *Men in Dark Times,* which contains biographical sketches of her personal heroes; *Crises of the Republic,* which offers her observations on the civil rights movement, the anti-war movement, and the Watergate scandal; *The Jew as Pariah* (1978), which collects pieces on Jewish themes; and *Essays in Understanding* (1995), which features the writings of her early career.

Critical Reception

Arendt's writings provoked widespread debate among political scientists, sociologists, and historians, who in turn generated a wealth of contradictory commentary on a variety of subjects; at the same time their influence has proved extraordinary, extending even to the American judicial system. (*The Origins of Totalitarianism* has been cited in several court decisions protecting the rights of displaced persons and expatriates.) "To some she represented the worst of 'Continen-

tal' philosophizing. . . . For such critics her insights into the woes of the century are at best derivative, at worst plain wrong," observed Judt, who added, "Others . . . find her a stimulating intellectual presence; her refusal to acknowledge academic norms and conventional categories of explanation, which so frustrates and irritates her critics, is precisely what most appeals to her admirers." The paradoxical reception of Arendt's work derives in part from ambiguities detected in the works themselves, which have provided fodder for both her supporters and detractors. Margaret Canovan, for instance, detected a "serious inconsistency" between the "elitist" and the "democratic" aspects of Arendt's political thought, while such critics as Sheldon S. Wolin, George Kateb, and John Sitton, contrary to prevalent analyses of her work in terms of totalitarianism, have scrutinized her writings for indications of her attitudes toward democratic government. Although the hostility that greeted *Eichmann in Jerusalem* has subsided, the volume continues to fascinate readers. Walter Laqueur, for example, reevaluated the question of "whether, in fact, [Arendt] was misunderstood and injustice done to her"; Tony Seibers analyzed the book in terms of its affinities to literary elements of storytelling; and Barry Clarke examined Arendt's representation of the "banality of evil" in the personality of Eichmann. In addition, numerous comparative analyses of Arendt's writings and those of other philosophers—from Jean-Jacques Rousseau and Immanuel Kant to Walter Benjamin and Heidegger—further illuminated her own ideas. "[Arendt] made a good many little errors, for which her many critics will never forgive her," admitted Judt. "But she got the big things right, and for this she deserves to be remembered."

PRINCIPAL WORKS

Der Liebsgriff bei Augustin: Versuch einer philosophischen Interpretation (dissertation) 1929
The Origins of Totalitarianism (philosophy) 1951
The Human Condition (philosophy) 1958
Rahel Varnhagen: The Life of a Jewess (biography) 1958
Between Past and Future: Six Exercises in Political Thought (philosophy) 1961
Eichmann in Jerusalem: A Report on the Banality of Evil (journalism) 1963
On Revolution (philosophy) 1963
Men in Dark Times (philosophy) 1968
On Violence (philosophy) 1970
Crises of the Republic (philosophy) 1972
The Jew as Pariah: Jewish Identity and Politics in the Modern Age (philosophy) 1978
The Life of the Mind. 2 vols. (philosophy) 1978
Lecture's on Kant's Political Philosophy (lectures) 1982
Hannah Arendt—Karl Jaspers: Correspondence, 1926-1969 (letters) 1992

Between Friends: The Correspondence of Hannah Arendt and Mary McCarthy, 1949-1975 (letters) 1995
Essays in Understanding, 1930-1954 (essays) 1995

CRITICISM

Denis Donoghue (essay date May 1962)

SOURCE: "After Reading Hannah Arendt," in *Poetry* (Chicago), Vol. 100, No. 2, May, 1962, pp. 127-30.

[*In the following essay, Donoghue relates "the profound, humane reflections" in Arendt's works to contemporary poetry, noting that he "had the disturbing impression that she had far more to say—more of humane relevance—than any ten contemporary poets."*]

I first read Hannah Arendt in *Partisan Review,* a classic essay on Hitler's concentration camps. The essay was free from hysteria, violence, vituperation; there was only the violence within—Wallace Stevens's great phrase—animating the prose; no "rhetoric". I had not thought much about the camps; they were not part of my weather. I was eleven when the War started and no one took me aside to tell me about "original" guilt, categorical responsibility, and my share thereof. So after a few days or weeks the essay faded, I economized on emotional expenditure—*Hiroshima Mon Amour* is at least half-true—and went on my way, such as it was. Then after several years I read *The Origins of Totalitarianism* and now, very recently, *The Human Condition.* These books are operations performed upon the modern conscience in the hope, even now, of giving it a second chance. Perhaps if we could be made to see what we're doing, we might quit and begin again.

One of the most disturbing implications in Hannah Arendt's books is that there are facts, situations, events with which the human imagination cannot cope. I had always assumed that the imagination was good enough for anything, and I had been delighted by Stevens's picture of reality and the imagination in dynamic poise, the violence within grappling with that other violence which is its occasion, its challenge. Dynamic accord; reality and the imagination equal and inseparable. But Hannah Arendt is right; the human imagination is dazed by the reality of the concentration camps; it staggers, doubts its own evidence, lurches in torpor or hysteria. It cannot disclose the real.

I had always assumed that reality is "there", outside the self, a nexus of people, values, things, and events to be apprehended with faith and good-will by the senses, the intelligence, and the imagination. Growing up in a Christian context I acquired a dim but pervasive notion that human life is sacred, that nothing is trivial or absurd, that a modest object

like a table is good for holding things and somehow "valid" because it brings people together. I had not thought much about it. I still adhere to this rough-and-ready notion of reality because I have not encountered a better one. But *The Origins of Totalitarianism* and *The Human Condition* document its practical failure in the modern world. "Modern man, when he lost the certainty of a world to come, was thrown back upon himself and not upon this world; far from believing that the world might be potentially immortal, he was not even sure that it was real." He resents "everything given, even his own existence"; he resents the fact "that he is not the creator of the universe and himself". The self is now the only reality. Hence the beautiful dynamic poise of reality and the imagination is a delusion; the only reality is each man's transaction with himself.

I knew a little of this before reading Hannah Arendt, but I thought it a philosophical causerie rather than the glum, faithless axiom of our lives. I knew nothing of its connexion with totalitarianism, imperialism, anti-Semitism and the local motives which conspire with those realities. The evidence is beyond dispute. But what can we do? Most of Hannah Arendt's sentences are indicative rather than optative, but a certain persuasion is implicit: I shall describe it, adding a few marginal notes. We must try to dissolve our resentment and be grateful for the gift of life itself; we must re-establish human rights as rights to the human condition independent of any inborn human dignity; we must sponsor in ourselves and others attitudes of reverence, respect, *volo ut sis,* mutual responsibility. We must certify the revelatory character of human action, thought, choice, and sufferance. We must know what we are doing. We must think. (Perhaps thought would be enough; with good-will.)

> **One of the most disturbing implications in Hannah Arendt's books is that there are facts, situations, events with which the human imagination cannot cope.**
>
> —*Denis Donoghue*

Our occasion is literary. I remind myself of this with a certain embarrassment because while reading Hannah Arendt I had the disturbing impression that she had far more to say—more of humane relevance—than any ten contemporary poets. In comparison with her mind most of the literary minds on current exhibition seemed thin, slack, frivolous. This impression came more in sorrow and dismay than in anger. It may be faithless, even chimerical, but let it stand. At least our topic is clear: what is the relation—assuming some relation—between contemporary poetry and the profound, humane reflections of Hannah Arendt? If there is a moral circle of reference she is close to its centre. The easy answer is that of course several modern poets have written about such matters: Richard Eberhart, Karl Shapiro—lots of people. John Wain: remember that thing about Major Weatherley. Yes, this is fine, but obviously not the point. The record of modern poetry is inadequately given as x poems about Belsen plus y poems about Hungary plus z poems about Eichmann. We should rephrase the question: what is the function of poetry in a world dominated by mindless, automatic, aggressive, self-obsessed forces? Most poems are, deep down, essays in self-indulgence; this has probably always been true, and the amount of frivolous poetry in print today is great and will be greater; but good poems manage to get written and published. The function of these poems is probably the same as it has always been, except that the occasion is more urgent, and if they have any contribution to make to human survival then please hurry up. The first duty of the poet is to stay in office. His "office" is to keep the lines open, to hold fast to the imagination even if it should fail, even if it is not enough; to hold out against the lure of disintegration and mindlessness; to "show" that the real is not our invention; to re-build, so far as he may, a human community. Above all, to speak out for the value, the sacredness, of human life; life itself, from first to last, not just the moments in the rose-garden when the pool fills with light, but the whole thing. I once saw two aeroplanes crashing a hundred feet above the center of a small town in Ireland, and the event seemed significant, though I didn't know what it signified. I also saw a film-star named Carole Landis in the same town, and a few weeks later someone told me she had killed herself; and this, too, seemed significant and I didn't know what it signified. Significance can be black, white, red, or even colorless. Everybody stumbles into a rose-garden and sometimes the roses are black; and I didn't have enough faith or enough understanding to know that the stretches of time between spectacular deaths are also significant though they may often seem to Mr. Eliot and others (including me) the merest "waste sad time". Martin Buber knows this and speaks beautifully. The poet who makes the whole of time and place seem valid will probably change the course of history not at all; his entire work will not be as influential as Mr. Khrushchev's dearest whim. But Mr. Eliot was right: the poetry does not matter. Purify the source. The rest is not our business.

To test my dismay, after reading Hannah Arendt I read Elizabeth Bishop, a poet in whom the realities of Belsen, Buchenwald, Hungary, and Angola do not disclose themselves to the eye of the beholder. She has a poem about catching a fish and having certain thoughts and then letting the fish go. I had always enjoyed that poem, even though I was embarrassed by the gush of "rainbow, rainbow, rainbow" at the end. Reading it in a new "context of feeling", I find that the thoughts she has while holding on to the wretched fish are full of self-regard, claiming a wealth of tender insight denied to the rest of fishermen. On the other hand at least her fish is a fish and not some awful symbol; and I believe in those five pieces of fish-line, and I am delighted that they are five because that is what the count came to and not because five is some awful mystic number. And Miss Bishop's feeling, however girlish and self-aware, is generous. This is a messy report and I don't apologize for the mess. I didn't learn as much from Miss Bishop's poem as from Miss Arendt's observations on Disraeli; but if the world survives it will continue to need generous feeling, and Miss Bishop will help to make it human.

Irving Howe (essay date October 1963)

SOURCE: "'The New Yorker' & Hannah Arendt," in *Commentary,* Vol. 36, No. 4, October, 1963, pp. 318-19.

[*In the following essay, Howe denounces the* New Yorker's *refusal to print rebuttals to Arendt's arguments in* Eichmann in Jerusalem, *which made its debut in the magazine as a controversial series of articles.*]

Some months ago, shortly after James Baldwin published in the *New Yorker* his now famous article about the Negroes, there appeared a mildly satiric comment upon it in the *New Republic*. The author of this comment elaborated upon the incongruity between Baldwin's passionate outcry and the sumptuous advertisements surrounding it. At the time I found this mildly irritating, for it seemed very much the sort of thing that highbrows—include me, too—might say without reflection, a kind of pat and automatic criticism based on a pat and automatic opposition to mass culture. After all, Baldwin had reached far more people than if his article had appeared in some little magazine; he had been paid far better than any of these magazines could possibly pay him; and the *New Yorker,* I was convinced, had not tried to censor his views. Why then complain? Wasn't it another instance of highbrow sour grapes? What if Baldwin's *cri de coeur* was flanked by ads for sleek minks and noiseless racing cars? Intellectual intransigence, I lectured myself, can too easily decline into mere snobbism and self-righteousness.

Etc.

Then, a few months later, when Hannah Arendt published in the *New Yorker* her equally famous articles about the Eichmann case, I found myself troubled once more, and this time with far greater urgency than after the Baldwin article. But I could not locate the source of my trouble: was it merely the reflex of a highbrow at seeing the *New Yorker* venture upon one of its regular expeditions into The Serious? Or could it be a not very admirable envy at seeing a respected intellectual break into the prosperity and publicity the *New Yorker* brought with it?

Miss Arendt's articles roused in me such strong sentiments of disagreement that for the moment I put aside the problem of their appearance in the *New Yorker.* Time went by, and most of what had to be said in criticism of her articles was said by Marie Syrkin, Lionel Abel, and Norman Podhoretz; so that, in my mind, I could turn back to the feeling of resentment I had had upon first seeing them in the pages of the *New Yorker.*

The solution to my problem was first suggested by Marie Syrkin. How many *New Yorker* readers, she burst out in a conversation, had ever before cared to read anything of the vast literature about Jewish resistance, martyrdom, and survival during World War II? How many would ever read anything about it again? And how many—she continued—would ever know that a notable Jewish historian, Dr. Jacob Robinson, had discovered a large number of factual errors in those articles?

For the *New Yorker* does not print polemics, rebuttals, or qualifying comments. I gather that a number of communications were sent to it concerning the errors in Miss Arendt's articles, but that only one brief correction was printed. The *New Yorker* speaks out, *ex cathedra,* upon occasion: it recognizes the presence of History: and that, one gathers, is that. Hiroshima—John Hersey. Negroes—James Baldwin. Jews—Hannah Arendt. The magazine secures what it takes to be the leading authority or the most interesting writer (but alas, the two are not always the same) to work up a subject; and there it stops. Precisely why it will not print rebuttals or running exchanges I don't know; but I imagine that the answer would be something like this: "Polemics, arguments, that's the sort of thing little magazines do, it's incestuous, you know, what Abel said about Rosenberg's article as qualified by Hook—you know, it's all sort of grubby. . . ."

No doubt; often enough it *is* grubby. Replies and counter-replies; charges and refutations. These fill the intellectual journals, and who does not become impatient with them? Who doesn't sooner or later throw up his hands and say, "Let them bash each other's heads in. . . ."

But who stops to think what our intellectual life would be without precisely these exchanges?

Let me cite an example, which concerns an article less likely to rouse passion than that of Miss Arendt. There recently appeared in *Partisan Review* an essay by Lionel Trilling, "The Fate of Pleasure," which I take to be a full-scale attack on the modernist outlook in thought and literature. As such, it rouses in me an urge to argument and reply; and I know that if I were to write a reasonably competent answer to Mr. Trilling,

Partisan Review would print it and invite Mr. Trilling to rebut. Probably I won't get down to writing this reply, since other obligations will distract me, and in any case I suspect that someone else, similarly aroused by the essay, may at the very moment be preparing to attack it. As an experienced hand, Mr. Trilling must surely expect something of the kind to happen, and I am sure he would join me in saying that this is precisely the way things should be. It is part of what we mean by a free and sustained intellectual life.

Now let's return to Hannah Arendt and the *New Yorker.* Her articles raised issues of the utmost gravity, for they contained charges against the European Jews, their institutions and leaders, which are certain to rouse the deepest emotions among those of us who—Jews who by an accident of geography—survive. These articles reached a mass audience almost certainly unequipped to judge them critically, a mass audience that would never see Lionel Abel's devastating critique or even hear that Dr. Robinson had prepared a point-by-point refutation. For the *New Yorker,* as for the whole cultural style it represents, the publication of Miss Arendt's articles disposed, in effect, of the issue: there was nothing more for it to say or allow to be said in its columns, except to defend Miss Arendt in a lugubrious editorial against those who had presumed to notice that she wrote with insufficient scholarship or humane sympathies. One suspects that, for the *New Yorker,* it would have been tiresome to keep returning to "the same old thing."

But returning to "the same old thing" is the essence of the intellectual life.

Now one can hardly blame the *New Yorker* for not opening its pages to debate on this or any other issue. It has never claimed to be a serious intellectual journal; only a few of its intellectual friends have made that claim. Nor am I concerned here with the propriety of Miss Arendt publishing her articles in its pages. I am concerned with something far more important: the social meaning, the objective consequences, of their appearance in the *New Yorker.*

Hundreds of thousands of good middle-class Americans will have learned from those articles that the Jewish leadership in Europe was cowardly, inept, and even collaborationist; that the Jewish community helped the Nazis achieve their goal of racial genocide; and that if the Jews had not "cooperated" with the Nazis, fewer than five to six million Jews would have been killed. No small matter: and you will forgive some of us if we react strongly to this charge. But the *New Yorker* will not accept in its columns the refutations of highly responsible and scholarly opponents of Miss Arendt. These, it might be remembered, are scholars who have worked their way through—as it is not clear that Miss Arendt has—the primary sources in Yiddish, Polish, and Hebrew. As far as the *New Yorker* is concerned, Miss Arendt has the first, the last, the only word. One would surmise that its editors regard Miss Arendt's articles as "literature," quite as they might regard Baldwin's article. A terrific piece, a great story: you don't argue with literature.

What we face here, then, is a difficult problem: a problem in social controls, in the nature of modern journalism and the peculiar powers it enjoys, in the new forms of mass culture that flourish in our sophisticated age.

J. M. Cameron (review date 6 November 1969)

SOURCE: "Bad Times," in *New York Review of Books,* Vol. XIII, No. 8, November 6, 1969, pp. 4, 6, 8-9.

[*In the following excerpt, Cameron highlights ambiguities in Arendt's political writings, tracing their genesis to the "peculiar character" of twentieth-century culture.*]

Thinkers who are original and profound often mask their ideas in a style, not so much of prose as of thought, that is opaque to all but the most determined reader. This is obvious in the work of, say, Kant; and opacity of style may produce those long-lasting ambiguities that provide rich material for the work of the commentator. If Miss Arendt's work survives—and it is surely more likely to survive than that of most other contemporary writers on politics—we may well find that the darkness of her thought attracts a multitude of commentators.

It is not even clear that the most polemical of her works, *Eichmann in Jerusalem,* has a central and controlling argument. What were execrated by the work's enemies were not what may be its central theses, for these they did not understand nor try to understand. (One thesis was, I believe, that thinking one is in the right entails that there is such a thing as being in the right; and that men who think they are in the right in killing the innocent are not thereby exculpated; on the contrary, a man who believes in his heart that he acts rightly in killing a man because he is a Jew or a bourgeois or a Communist is much worse than a man who acts out of fear or sloth, knowing in his heart that what he does is monstrously wicked. Sincerity is not a virtue and is not even admirable as such.) They raised questions about the nature and truth of the illustrative material, a diversion that could not have been indulged so easily had the central arguments been clearer.

But *could* they have been clearer? My own formulation of one of them could easily be challenged; and even if I am roughly right, this one is hard for contemporary men to take. Out of the mouths of our babes and sucklings come the notions that moral judgments express features of dispensable culture patterns, that what all men do is what they must do, that the category of punishment is a relic of barbarism. If the children are corrupt, it is we who are the sophistical agents of corruption.

When, therefore, a notable scourge of sophistry, or one who would be this, to wit, Miss Arendt, arises, we are tempted to think she too is a sophist or to talk about something else. But there she is, blocking the road, stubborn, Gothic, simple where we look to find the complexity, complex where we expect platitudes, an admirer of many styles of thought and life and yet, surely, in the end a pessimist, a defender of reaction, one who aches with nostalgia for a dead political order. These are immediate possible responses to Miss Arendt's work. Certainly, it is work to which no one can remain indifferent. What gives it its power and its measure of truth is a question worth asking, for if we can go some distance toward answering it her work will become more available; and, given the soundness of our intuition that here is an important writer, to make her work more available will be a service to the public.

What lies behind almost all Miss Arendt's writing on politics seems to be the conviction that in a deep way, hard to be grasped and harder to be expressed, our own period is a great turning point in the history of the human race. It is still possible to think and write about the phenomena of our period in such a way as to quite miss this point. This is because we think those categories which will do for the understanding of the history and institutions of the period between, say, the fifth century B.C. and the day before yesterday are suitable for speaking about our own day. This, she argues, is a mistake, not, of course, a total mistake, for there are some things in our social life that belong, still, to the past as well. But it is to risk missing the point: about totalitarianism, about the consequences—and nature—of contemporary science and technology, about the nature of evil in our period. She not only argues that the traditional categories won't do; she also maintains that the new categories of the new social sciences won't do either, for to understand the peculiar character of our period it is necessary also to understand the past. This Weber may have done; but the incapacity and shallowness of the later schools of sociology are themselves signs of the terrible crisis through which we move.

The peculiar character of our period is an opportunity as well as an affliction. In *Between Past and Future* she speaks of our time as a kind of gap, not of course a gap in historical time, for this would make no sense, but a gap constituted by our capacity to think reflectively of our present and to reach into the past and anticipate the future. This capacity to transcend historical time and thus constitute a gap is something that belongs to men as such and has been exercised in all periods; but the gap we constitute presents us with agonizing problems, for the tradition that has since the ancient world determined our ways of thinking about public affairs is dead, and we are therefore like men who have to learn a new language. Intellectually, perhaps, the break comes with Marx, but it is made final not so much by speculation as by actions and happenings.

. . . . neither the twentieth-century aftermath nor the nineteenth-century rebellion against tradition actually caused the break in our history. This sprang from a chaos of mass-perplexities on the political scene and of mass opinions in the spiritual sphere which the totalitarian movements, through terror and ideology, crystallized into a new form of government and domination. Totalitarian domination as an established fact, which in its unprecedentedness cannot be comprehended through the usual categories of political thought . . . has broken the continuity of Occidental history.

This break does give us, it is argued, a special opportunity, one that men have not enjoyed for a very long time. We are able "to look upon the past with eyes undistracted by any tradition, with a directness which has disappeared from Occidental reading and hearing ever since Roman civilization submitted to the authority of Greek thought." Such a thesis is characteristic of Miss Arendt's boldness; but it is also an instance of what is puzzling in what she writes.

What is proposed, "To look upon the past with eyes undistracted by any traditions," seems at first to set before us a difficult but possible task; but on reflection what is proposed seems not so much hard as overwhelmingly strange. What would it be to look upon the past in the way prescribed? Certainly, to look upon the past with understanding entails attention, and careful attention, to the traditions which are a part of its tissue. Would such attention count as distraction? Again, even if we grant the central assertion that in important ways we are in our day presented with radically new phenomena, we need to be aware of traditional ways of thinking and feeling in order to demonstrate the novelty of this or that phenomenon.

What lies behind almost all Miss Arendt's writing on politics seems to be the conviction that in a deep way, hard to be grasped and harder to be expressed, our own period is a great turning point in the history of the human race.

—*J. M. Cameron*

Above all, the past weighs upon the mind of the living, whether or not we perceive this weighing as a nightmare, to echo Marx in *The Eighteenth Brumaire,* simply through the language we use. In their denseness, their complexity, the hidden signs of their genesis discovered by the philologist and lexicographer, our languages give us the essence of the human past. The recognition of this is one of Vico's greatest claims to

eminence. The very character of thought and discourse robs Miss Arendt's proposal of sense. And of course she herself pays not the slightest attention to this proposal.

This is one instance of a difficulty Miss Arendt's work offers to a special kind of reader, what one might call the donnish reader. Other instances could be given, above all from those passages in which she professes to be offering an exegesis of passages from classic writers. I choose two examples, one from Descartes, the other from Marx.

In *The Human Condition* and again in *Between Past and Future* she tells us that (I quote from the latter) "the fundamental experience underlying Cartesian doubt was the discovery that the earth, contrary to all direct sense experience, revolves round the sun." This is quite without support in the text of Descartes. It is perfectly clear in both the *Discourse* and the *Meditations* that the "experience" underlying the resolve to go in for systematic doubt is that of the contrast between the lack of coherence in the conclusions of the philosophers and the coherence of mathematics. Descartes lived in a period of mathematical progress and of philosophical stagnation. Again, all the medieval thinkers knew perfectly well that the question about the adequacy of the Ptolemaic hypothesis was a question about whether or not it "saved the appearances." It did not follow from its saving the appearances that it was true. The success of the heliocentric theory can only be a tiny constituent, and an unimportant one, in the profound social and intellectual crisis of the sixteenth and seventeenth centuries. So far as astronomy had a causal role in the crisis, the idea of the infinity of space (Pascal brings this out) and the idea that superlunar as well as sublunar substances are subject to change and decay were of far greater significance. Finally, even the young Descartes was far too sharp ever to have thought that the observation of apparent motion in one body from a point on another body showed the observer which body is "really" in motion. Indeed, there is an excellent discussion of just this point in the *Principles.*

My difficulty over some of the things Miss Arendt appears to be saying about Marx can perhaps best be put by stating what seems to me to be the point of the more important Theses on Feuerbach and then asking the reader to reflect upon what is said on e.g., pp. 21-25 of *Between Past and Future*.

Marx is concerned in the Theses on Feuerbach with two problems between which he sees connections: first, the epistemological problem of the relation between the observer and the world; secondly, how, if materialism is true and men are shaped by circumstances and education, can we hope to change society and ourselves, that is, how is this logically possible? Lucien Goldmann has shown how close Marx is here to the *il faut parier* of Pascal and also how close to Kant; and to Augustine (*credo ut intelligam*) and therefore to

Descartes. In the fifth thesis Marx argues against Feuerbach that sense perception has a practical and intentional, not merely contemplative, character; it is an active apprehension of the world for the sake of certain ends prescribed by the nature of man-in-the-world. The contemplative model has a paralyzing effect when we come to questions of practice, and men look upon the determining forces of society in a state of trance-like passivity. How men are to transcend this heavy world is not a matter for theological reflection. They must act, not as men who strike out convulsively and blindly, for such conduct exactly exemplifies socially determined conduct, but as men who stake everything on the truth of their judgments as to how they can make the future. Of course, the enterprise could come to nothing—or to catastrophe, which is the same thing. But *il faut parier*. There is no alternative to this. *Vous êtes embarqué*. Not to wager is just to lay another kind of bet.

Set against these considerations what Miss Arendt says about the last of the Theses ("The philosophers have only interpreted the world differently; the point is, however, to change it"). She writes of this that "in the light of Marx's thought, one could render [it] more adequately as: The philosophers have interpreted the world long enough; the time has come to change it." This is surely an impossible interpretation of this fragment saved from oblivion by Engels.

A last donnish query to Miss Arendt, before I go on to praise her. Why does she think our ability to initiate and control the process of nuclear fission and fusion is a sign that for the first time we can now "make nature" in the way in which hitherto we have been able to "make history"? (This is asserted in connection with a discussion of Vico's view that we can understand history in a way we cannot understand nature, since we are the makers of history, God is the maker of nature.) I have puzzled over this for a long time without being able to see just what she has in mind. She argues to this effect in *The Human Condition* and repeats the argument in *Between Past and Future,* so she evidently thinks it very important; and of course, in the way she puts it—natural forces are spoken of as having been "let loose, unchained"—there is the strong suggestion that we are now confronted with demonic forces that we can no longer control, that we are in fact in the position of the sorcerer's apprentice.

Now, I would not wish to deny what is here implied. My difficulty is with the premise of her argument. For example, I want to know why the invention of agriculture or the domestication and selective breeding of animals, things without which civilization would not have grown, does not count as "making nature." Miss Arendt's answer appears to be that in all earlier technological processes we were imitating and making use of natural forces; now, with nuclear fission and fusion, we are "initiating" new natural processes.

I can make no sense of this argument. In so far as any techno-logical process can be rightly termed an "imitation" of a natural process, and there is something difficult about this concept, then nuclear processes can be so termed. If, for example, it is argued that the selective breeding of animals and plants is an imitation of the evolutionary process of natural selection, then nuclear processes are imitations of what goes on in, for example, the sun. Producing a bulldog or a Jersey cow seems a tranquil, undramatic kind of thing. It is the result of the application of rules of thumb. The dog and the cow merge into the human landscape. Nuclear processes presuppose very advanced mathematics and industrial techniques themselves inconceivable without an advanced mathematical culture. Their results are dramatic and sometimes horrible: a city is destroyed, a mountain moved, the genetic code of animals and plants disturbed for generations. There is no doubt about the contrast. What is questionable is the additional charge, so to speak, Miss Arendt wishes to give to her account of what is happening by the groundless, as it seems to me, arguments that we now "make nature" where formerly we could make only history. In any acceptable sense of making nature we have been doing this ever since we passed out of the stage of food-gathering and hunting.

What I have so far tried to bring out can be put in this way. Miss Arendt is able to describe, often brilliantly and with great perception and sensitiveness, some of the macroscopic features of our present culture and is able to set these against what is always an interesting, though sometimes capricious, account of the history of European culture. But with a kind of impatience she insists on adding to her excellent accounts and analyses arguments that won't stand up and a willful exegesis of the classic writers. This weakens and obscures the main drift of her arguments, necessarily intricate enough, and provides footholds for those who wish to attack her out of malice or through a sectarian spirit; and sometimes it produces an intolerable obscurity.

Nous sommes les derniers. Péguy's cry could very well have served for the epigraph to *Between Past and Future*. Indeed; there is a certain affinity of intellectual temper and of emotional concern between Miss Arendt and Péguy. For both the fate of the Jews is the central mystery of the modern world. It is in their attitudes to Israel (the spiritual family, that is) that men show what they are and invite judgment. For both the attitude to the Jews is fateful: the attitude of the French to the condemnation of Dreyfus; the attitude of Europe and the United States to the Final Solution. Equally, they are both concerned with the bad faith and the intellectual confusions of those who come down on the right side when it is no longer dangerous to do so. Both link the peculiar anti-Semitism of modern times, believed by shallow thinkers to be a survival from the Middle Ages, with the general character of the modern world.

Nous sommes les derniers. Péguy would illustrate this by

contrasting the world of his childhood, the world of decent and laborious poverty in the home where chairs were made and repaired, a world already dying when he was a child, with the world of mass democracy. He believed that the former was continuous with the Middle Ages and the world of antiquity and was, despite all its injustices and cruelties, even in these injustices and cruelties, a human world. Miss Arendt's general thesis in **Between Past and Future** is not unlike this; and the elegiac tone that pervades, in **Men in Dark Times,** her studies of individual figures, Rosa Luxemburg, John XXIII, Hermann Broch, Arthur Benjamin, to pick out the best, provides a suitable obbligato to the argument of the former book.

In older versions of the English puppet show of Punch, at the end of the play Punch cries out: The Devil is dead, we may all do as we like. In a brilliant characterization of totalitarianism Miss Arendt shows us that it is in this Punch-like way that the European drama, or at least an episode, ended.

> ... the totalitarian phenomenon, with its striking anti-utilitarian traits and its strange disregard for factuality, is based in the last analysis on the conviction that everything is possible—and not just permitted, morally or otherwise. . . . The totalitarian systems tend to demonstrate that action can be based on any hypothesis and that, in the course of constantly guided action, the particular hypothesis will become true, will become actual, factual reality. The assumption which underlies consistent action can be as mad as it pleases; it will always end in producing facts which are then "objectively" true.

Madness in politics and the propagation of convenient fictions, these are not novelties in human history. After all, the eighth and ninth books of Plato's *Republic* contain very plausible sketches of Stalin and Hitler. What is new is the total inversion of rationality to the point where even those who for the time stand outside the fringes of the absolutely mad nevertheless find it "interesting," "a point of view." "No doubt," they say, "there has been much exaggeration; it may not literally be true that plotters lighted a bonfire under the window of the aged Maxim Gorky to bring on his bronchitis; all the same, there must have been a plot of some kind." Or (between 1933 and 1939): "No one deplores more than I do the excesses of the Nazis, but no doubt there is some exaggeration, and we must not overlook Herr Hitler's remarkable solution to the unemployment problem." *Et patati et patata.*

Such idiocies are not the fruit of propaganda only; they are induced by the very structure of the totalitarian regime (one hesitates to use of it the term "state" or "society"). This Miss Arendt shows in another remarkable passage.

> In contradistinction to both tyrannical and authori-

tarian regimes, the proper image of totalitarian rule and organization [is] the structure of the onion, in whose center, in a kind of empty space, the leader is located. . . . All the extraordinarily manifold parts of the movement; the front organizations, the various professional societies, the party membership, the party bureaucracy, the elite formations and police groups, are related in such a way that each forms the facade in one direction and the center in another, that is, plays the role of normal outside world for one layer and the role of radical extremism for another. The great advantage of this system is that the movement provides for each of its layers, even under conditions of totalitarian rule, the fiction of a normal world along with a consciousness of being different from and more radical than it. . . . The onion structure makes the system organizationally shock-proof against the factuality of the real world.

This is a distillation of what is set out with more complexity in what is certainly her greatest book, **The Origins of Totalitarianism,** q.v., as the footnotes say.

Miss Arendt is able to describe, often brilliantly and with great perception and sensitiveness, some of the macroscopic features of our present culture and is able to set these against what is always an interesting, though sometimes capricious, account of the history of European culture.

—J. M. Cameron

Is there comfort or consolation or reassurance for us in these "Dark Times"? One thinks here of Wittgenstein's words, written in 1945, in the Foreword to the *Philosophical Investigations.* "It is not impossible that it should fall to the lot of this work, in its poverty and in the darkness of this time, to bring light into one brain or another—but, of course, it is not likely." Of course, just this heroic persistence, not in the conviction that truth is great and that it will prevail, but simply in the conviction that truth is great, is for those fortunate enough to be its witnesses or its audience consolation in itself.

Miss Arendt wishes to drive us into a dilemma, in the belief that the excruciating experience of thinking our way through it will produce a way of overcoming it that neither she nor anyone else can now provide. The dilemma is this. In recent centuries men have come to believe that in an important if obscure sense classical antiquity provides us with examples of human greatness and virtue, a greatness and a virtue necessarily connected with the social and political institutions that protected and nourished them. The problem is to restore this *humanitas* within a totally different social context. This is a problem over which Machiavelli and the Jacobins were tormented: how to restore *humanitas* in the form of republican virtue. The form taken by the revolutions of modern times is, then, an attempt to bring back *humanitas;* but, with the possible exception of the American Revolution, they have failed in this, ending in restoration or tyranny. If revolution cannot bring back greatness and virtue in political affairs, then perhaps nothing can. Here is the dilemma. We cannot but respond to the signs under which revolution is conducted; but we can no longer believe in the possibility of bringing about what would alone justify revolution.

> Authority as we once knew it, which grew out of the Roman experience of foundation and was understood in the light of Greek political philosophy, has nowhere been re-established, either through revolutions or through the even less promising means of restoration, and least of all through the conservative moods and trends which occasionally sweep public opinion. For to live in a political realm with neither authority nor the concomitant awareness that the source of authority transcends power . . . means to be confronted anew, without the religious trust in a sacred beginning and without the protection of traditional and therefore self-evident standards of behavior, by the elementary problems of human living-together.

Whether or not we are really within this dilemma is another question. Miss Arendt herself ispuzzled by the impossibility of bringing the American Revolution under the same description as the French.

Perhaps we may end with a question out of Machiavelli and Hume. Machiavelli argues that Christianity, though unfortunately "true," robs men of their civic virtue. It encourages what Hume would call the monkish virtues, meekness and humility, for example, and its sacrifice is unbloody (the comparison is with the bloody sacrifices of the old law and of the pagan rites, and perhaps with the games in the arena) and thus debilitating. Gibbon advances the same thesis in a vulgarized and flippant form. Hume, in *The Natural History of Religion,* argues that monotheism, just because it treats the universe as a single systematic whole, is the only religion one can take seriously and as therefore possibly true; but its consequences, dogmatism, fanaticism, and persecution, are appalling. But polytheism, intellectually absurd and an obstacle to the scientific understanding of the world, issues in tolerance and other social virtues.

Here is another dilemma not unconnected with that outlined by Miss Arendt. All the dilemmas have some resemblance to the dilemmas set out in Dostoevsky's fable of the Grand Inquisitor. But how *could* we expect to get out of such a di-

lemma? Neither intellectual power nor force nor the two in combination can do this for us. Pascal, a great framer of dilemmas and paradoxes, would say that we cannot expect the three orders, *l'ordre des corps, l'ordre des esprits, l'ordre de la charité* (Brunschvicg 793), to come together; for the absolute realization of charity, that is, Jesus Christ, is, from the world's point of view, invisible. The sign of his glory is his humility, the sign of his richness his poverty, the sign of his rule over men its invisibility; and the sign of Divine power, his resurrection, is *secret,* not an event within the order of the world.

Something has gone badly wrong here. We have, it is true, a stick with which to beat the utopians; but they are scarcely worth beating. But can we really conceive that the world is so arranged that the laborer is necessarily cheated of his reward and that modest solutions to the problem of how men are to live together are always defective? This would imply that the world is ruled by wicked demons. We may believe, with Miss Arendt, that men often let the demons loose and suffer on this account; but we also believe that evil is self-destructive. This even shows itself when its contrary seems to be demonstrated, as in those scenes of which we know when children went to their death crying out the great *Hear, O Israel* in obedience to the instruction of their mothers. It is clear enough who are the victors and who the vanquished here. To see here only the triumph of evil is to miss the sense of human life.

Philip Green (review date 7 May 1972)

SOURCE: "Crises of the Republic," in *New York Times Book Review,* May 7, 1972, pp. 27-8.

[*In the review below, Green comments on the "astonishing" insight Arendt brought to her writings, despite "those occasional lapses from which no truly serious work of the intellect is ever wholly free."*]

In a recent essay not reprinted in this collection, Hannah Arendt has written that "thinking" isinherently an antisocial and subversive activity, a quiet enemy to all established versions of right and order. The truly independent thinker is never finally at ease with the customs and institutions of his (or her) times, but rather is continually and relentlessly probing for the soft spots in a society's self-image; attacking the difference between appearance and reality, what is and what ought to be. Thinking scorns all "isms," convenient fictions masking the truth about the imperfections of a social order— or of its revolutionary opposite; the thinker is not an ideologue but a philosopher.

Those who enjoy their social criticism in small doses only, or who like to believe that the political ideas of others are lies but theirs are the truth ("you are an oppressor, I am a liberator"), can never quite be happy with thinking in this sense.

And few of the people who have been deeply engaged in the political life of our age can be happy with Hannah Arendt, for there is virtually no panacea for the political diseases of this age that she has not subjected to the subversion of thought. Socialism and capitalism, anarchism and élitism, imperialism, and "third-world" revolutionism, student rebellion and adult repression, have all been shorn of their glossy facades by Arendt's practice of philosophy unalloyed by partisan interest; and that is still happening in these latest essays (all of which have recently appeared in *The New York Review of Books*).

> **Miss Arendt is talking about us as well as others when she writes that "(the) defiance of established authority, religious and secular, social and political, as a worldwide phenomenon may well one day be accounted the outstanding event of the last decade."**
>
> —*Philip Green*

Thus the reader who searches here for some sympathetic variant of "radicalism," "liberalism," or "conservatism" will be disappointed. Anyone, though, who doubts the worthiness of our own status quo, and is inspired by the most fundamental criticisms of it, will find at least as much to be grateful for in the work of Hannah Arendt as in that of any recent political thinker: for what she has constructed over the past several decades is nothing less than the most radical challenge of all to the entire course of our modern political history.

In such influential works as *The Origins of Totalitarianism, Between Past and Future, Eichmann in Jerusalem, On Revolution,* and *Men in Dark Times,* Miss Arendt has returned again and again to a set of interrelated themes: that the unrestrained, "value-free," individualistic secularism of the modern world has gradually undermined the bases of legitimate authority, of any meaningful affective relationship between man and the state; that the illusion of liberal "freedom" has often been purchased at the cost of devaluing real political participation by the people; that the bureaucratic organization of modern societies permits the most hideous of evils to be accomplished by the most ordinary of men; that the "mass societies" of our era "can no longer be controlled, let alone governed." (**"Thoughts on Politics and Revolution"**). All of this, finally, is summed up in a phrase that reappears throughout her writing: "the crisis of modern times," a crisis which, brought about by the lack of opportunities for humane and creative action by the mass of men and women, leads to the opposite kind of (pseudo-) action, to war and repression.

Miss Arendt's latest essays on this grand theme are particularly interesting for two reasons. First, in the 1950's it was possible for those Americans who noticed her work at all, to write off her perception of permanent crisis as the misapprehension of a refugee from European horrors, whose view of the twentieth century as a blasted heath was poetic but of little relevance to Americans. That kind of dismissal is no longer possible. *These* essays are, in large part, about, as she says, the **Crises of the Republic;** Miss Arendt is talking about us as well as others when she writes that "(the) defiance of established authority, religious and secular, social and political, as a worldwide phenomenon may well one day be accounted the outstanding event of the last decade."

Second, it is likely that those unfamiliar with the traditions of "political philosophy" think of it as an abstract and slippery subject, producing grand generalizations but shedding little light on worldly matters. It is true that to maintain the stance of a detached, speculative thinker sometimes strains one's ability to observe mundane affairs accurately. In Miss Arendt's case, for example, her account of Communism (in *Origins*) as an uprising of the classless masses has never been persuasive; *Eichmann in Jerusalem* indeed contains errors of scholarship (though none that affect her basic argument about the way in which modern bureaucracy produces "banal" evil); historians have quarreled with her interpretation of both the French and American revolutions (in *On Revolution*). And yet, in the end it is astonishing how much insight into the daily events of our political history is contained in those books, and especially in these recent essays.

In particular, the essay **"Lying in Politics: Reflections on the Pentagon Papers"** is worth the closest attention. Miss Arendt's treatment of the Pentagon Papers is unique. Her denunciation of mindlessness and duplicity in government—of (in a phrase she borrows from Senator Fulbright) "the arrogance of power"—is combined with a politely savage critique of those social scientists who, possessing (in her words) their own "arrogance of mind," lent their talents to provide the underpinnings of that duplicity. But both the arrogance of power and the arrogance of mind are merely two related versions of the same disease she has discussed before; of a modern attitude that refuses to recognize any natural limits on what the aggressiveness of science and power can accomplish. The world, in her phrase, is "defactualized," and nothing in the political universe is seen as so "real" that the clever and the mighty cannot restructure it at will. We thought, that is, that we could do anything to anybody, which was stupid; and we were willing to try, which was brutal and immoral: and those two kinds of folly are really one and the same, an inability to see that there is a real factual *and* moral human universe beyond what we ourselves construct as the targets for our weaponry or our propaganda. Thus, in other words, we are back with Miss Arendt's permanent theme of the absence of true authority, and the substitution for it of the sheer will to dominate: a theme now both sharpened and deepened by being located in this concrete historical instance.

The other essays as well develop this basic theme in an immediate historical context. In **"Civil Disobedience"** her argument is that the question, to obey or not to obey, is not a "moral" question but a "factual" one; or rather, that there are no "moral" questions separate from what is actually happening. People in large numbers disobey because they have to, not because they are willfully conscientious; and the problem is not how to repress them, but how to reconstruct our politics so that they do not *have* to disobey; so that real authority again exists: "Representative government itself is in a crisis today, partly because it has lost, in the courseof time, all institutions that permitted the citizens' actual participation, and partly because it is now gravely affected by the disease from which the party system suffers: bureaucratization and the two parties' tendency to represent nobody except the party machines."

On Violence (which has been previously published in what is now an obsolete paperback edition) makes a similar point. The violence of authorities or rebels occurs when legitimate authority no longer exists, and we know that legitimate authority no longer exists when large-scale violence occurs; the question is not whether one *ought* to be violent, but what can be done to restore the situation in which it makes sense to be nonviolent. Again, the crisis of our time is that such a restoration is now necessary in so large a part of even the "democratic" world; and at the moment it is not forthcoming.

The subtlety and attention to detail with which these and related points are pursued can hardly be more than hinted at here. As before, too, the grand swath that Miss Arendt cuts through the weedy ideologies around her leaves some confusions of its own in its wake. In particular, one wonders with whom comparison is being made, and on what grounds, in the remark that "(as) distinguished from other countries, this republic . . . may still be in possession of its traditional instruments for facing the future with some measure of confidence." Here and elsewhere in her writings, the Cassandra of the twentieth century seems a little like Pollyanna where America is concerned. But there is so much to grapple with, and learn from in those writings, that one accepts those occasional lapses from which no truly serious work of the intellect is ever wholly free.

Lore Dickstein (review date 24 November 1974)

SOURCE: A review of *Rahel Varnhagen*, in *New York Times Book Review*, November 24, 1974, pp. 27, 30.

[*In the following review, Dickstein objects to the dispassionate narrative tone and the lack of psychoanalysis of the subject in* Rahel Varnhagen, *especially since "the reader . . . would have expected more from so brilliant a theorist."*]

[*Rahel Varnhagen: The Life of a Jewish Woman*] was written more than 40 years ago and the woman it deals with lived more than 170 years ago, but the story of Rahel Varnhagen survives the passage of time. Rahel Varnhagen was one of the more renowned "salon Jewesses" of Berlin at the turn of the 19th century. Her charm and brilliance not only reflected the cultural awakening of her time, but influenced it: she was a strong proponent of the Romantic movement in Germany and the originator of the Goethe cult. In this biography by Hannah Arendt, the distinguished political philosopher and cultural historian, the focus is on Rahel's problems of identity—who she was and where she belonged. Although Arendt's presentation is flawed, the life of this Jewish woman who was cursed with living in interesting times has a gripping fascination and resonance for us today.

Rahel Levin Varnhagen was born in Berlin in 1771, the daughter of a wealthy Jewish merchant. She lived through a period of great social and political upheaval—the French Revolution, the riseand fall of Napoleon, the consolidation of the feudal German states and the rise of German nationalism. The turn of the 19th century—the time of Rahel's adulthood—witnessed a reaction to the precepts of the Enlightenment and the upsurge of the Romantic movement. It was the time of Schleiermacher, Schlegel, Humboldt, Novalis, Fichte, Hegel and Goethe. Rahel's life was directly affected by these events (though she was an apolitical person) and as a "salon Jewess" she knew a great many of the major figures.

The situation of the German Jews during this period is an intriguing and baffling anomaly. The Jew was a disenfranchised person; he had no political rights and was excluded from large areas of the German economy. But the ideals of the Enlightenment, which proclaimed all men part of a common humanity regardless of nationality, rank or birth, had its effect on German intellectual society. It created a magical moment in history when what mattered was not one's place in society (and the society was a highly structured one), but one's unique personality. For a short period of time, from the late 1780's until the French occupation began in 1806, a mixed cosmopolitan society existed in Berlin. The Jewish salons, precisely because they were on the fringe of the social structure, became the common meeting ground for people from all levels of German society.

For those "exceptional" Jews who had money or education—or for the lucky few who had both—this was a period of great social mobility. One by one they were allowed assimilation into the mainstream of German society. Their acceptance was short-lived (it ended abruptly with the nationalistic reaction to Napoleon's invasion), but for many German Jews assimilation meant their only chance for survival. For Rahel

Varnhagen it became the obsession of her life: "The Jew must be extirpated from us; that is the sacred truth, and it must be done even if life were uprooted in the process."

For the enlightened Jewish women of Berlin the way out of the ghetto and into German society was by marriage—preferably to a gentile of high standing. Such a marriage was possible only if one possessed either beauty or money—ideally both; Rahel Varnhagen had neither (what was left of her father's money had gone to her brothers). While her garret on Jägerstrasse was considered the most brilliant cosmopolitan salon in Berlin and Rahel talked to and was discussed by practically every important figure in Berlin's intellectual circles, her personal life was desperately unhappy. Rahel considered her Jewishness a personal tragedy; she felt herself, in Arendt's words, "born in the wrong place, assigned by history to a doomed world." It is Rahel's sense of being destined to be unhappy, to remain a pariah all her life, that is the real tragedy of her life.

What Rahel in her political innocence—and a great many enlightened Jews of her time—did not understand was that they could never be accepted as equal members of German society. The blind, desperate attempts at assimilation, which were just barely feasible before the reaction against Napoleon set in, continued well into a period of rampant German nationalism and its accompanying antagonism toward the French, toward women and of course Jews. But Rahel could never come to terms with society's judgment of her. Despite her wish to "be like the others"—she belatedly changed her last name to Robert in 1810, long after it was possible for her to pass, and converted as Antonie Friederike when she married the gentile Karl August Varnhagen in 1814—her sense of herself remained always Rahel Levin, Jewess.

Rahel's struggle toward assimilation and the conflict she experienced thereby is the most fascinating aspect of Arendt's book. Because marriage was the only means of social acceptance open to her, Rahel's various affairs and liaisons provide the most revealing glimpses into her life and the world she lived in.

For four years, between 1796 and 1800, at the height of German cosmopolitanism and tolerance, Rahel was engaged to Count Karl von Finckenstein, a nobleman she had met in her salon. Finckenstein represented everything Rahel felt excluded from—he belonged to society by birth. But within the confines of Rahel's salon, where what mattered was one's brilliance and articulateness. Finckenstein had little to show for himself but his title. Rahel's attempts to draw him into her intellectual circle were disastrous—he felt himself rightly outclassed. He ultimately withdrew to his family, to the ancestral ties that gave him a standing in a world he knew; he broke with Rahel because she threatened his very existence.

Rahel's second engagement came soon after the break with Finckenstein. Between 1800 and 1802 Rahel was engaged and passionately in love with the secretary of the Spanish legation, Don Raphael d'Urquijo. Since he was a foreigner, Rahel thought Urquijo would be without the prejudices of German society. But Urquijo had prejudices of his own: women occupied a subordinate place in the world he came from and Rahel's amorous aggressiveness and her friendships with other men infuriated him. Urquijo was Rahel's "beautiful object" (we gather he was a very attractive, sensual man), but she became a kind of fascinating monster to him—and he dropped her. Rahel's reaction to this second jilting is the anguished cry of a woman who has lost more than a lover: "I sold myself out to him, gave him—this is no cliché; accursed that I am, I have experienced it—gave him my whole heart." Rahel had also lost her entrée into society; the moment in history when it was at all possible for her to assimilate had passed her by.

By the time Rahel met Karl August Varnhagen in 1808 she was depressed, poor, and still a pariah—a single, 40-year-old Jewish woman. The days of the Jewish salon were over: "At my 'tea table' . . . I sit with nothing but dictionaries. . . . Never have I been so alone. Absolutely. Never so completely and utterly bored." Varnhagen, a man 14 years younger than she and without charm, rank, money, education or a future, became Rahel's last chance for assimilation. Rahel educated and cultivated him; in gratitude he idolized her, collected, her letters and diaries, noted down every word she uttered. (If not for Varnhagen's efforts, we would know little of Rahel's life.) Varnhagen eventually made a name for himself as a war correspondent and minor diplomat and even managed to dig up a noble ancestor, adding "von Ense" to his name.

Varnhagen rescued Rahel, gave her social respectability, but it is not clear whether she ever really loved him. What we do know is that she never really felt she belonged, not even as Frau Friederike Varnhagen von Ense. On her deathbed Rahel said, by Varnhagen's account: "The thing which all my life seemed to me the greatest shame, which was the misery and misfortune of my life—having been born a Jewess—this I should on no account now wish to have missed." Rahel's attempts to become someone else, to assimilate and "be like the others" ultimately failed because she could in the end only be herself.

Arendt tells Rahel's story dispassionately; she stands outside and "narrate[s] the story of Rahel's life as she herself might have told it." Rahel does tell her own story extremely well: her letters and diaries, which Arendt quotes extensively, are revelations of a genuinely sensitive, intelligent person. Arendt must have been highly selective; from what we can gather, there is rich literary treasure in the German archives (volumes and volumes of material about Rahel and her circle are listed in the bibliography). In addition, Arendt presents only Rahel Varnhagen the person; her role in the culture of her day is not explored in depth. Yet this book is not psycho-history; in the preface Arendt expresses a marked distaste for the "pseudo-scientific apparatus" of psychoanalytic or inter-pretive biography, "that modern form of indiscretion in which the writer attempts to penetrate his subject's tricks and as-pires to know more than the subject knew about himself or was willing to reveal." Accordingly, she does not evaluate or explore Rahel's motivations. This is a serious loss for the reader; we want to know more, and would have expected more from so brilliant a theorist.

One assumes that this book, which was written in 1933 and first appeared in England only in 1957, has been resurrected in this country because of the current interest in "lost women," women who were important historical figures but never made it into the history books. But to present this book to the Ameri-can public more or less as it was written 40 years ago is a disservice. The book alludes to the political events and his-torical figures of Rahel's time as if they were familiar, acces-sible landmarks; they may be in Germany, but they are not well known to the general American audience.

My objection is not only to Arendt's reticence as narrator, but also with the translation, which adheres too closely to the author's original German formulations. For example, the reader finds himself occasionally muddling through a sen-tence like this: "From another place in the world she would be thrown into the stream again, only apparently untrue, in truth obeying the consistent principle, the objective pattern of her life which she had called 'the business'; only appar-ently true, in truth yielding, despite all memories, to new re-alities, open and ready to accept every new chance." These are faults of omission, and while they need not diminish the impact and fascination of Rahel Varnhagen's story, they do prevent the book from being a major work. The material is all there; it needs only to be fleshed out.

It is one of the ironies of history that Arendt wrote most of this book just before fleeing Nazi Germany in 1933, exactly 100 years after Rahel Varnhagen's death. The author does not attempt to draw any parallels between her own rejection by another, more virulent Germany and Rahel's own politi-cal situation. But the reader can speculate on the reverbera-tions Rahel's life had for Hannah Arendt, herself a Jewish woman in Germany.

Mary McCarthy (essay date 22 January 1976)

SOURCE: "Saying Good-by to Hannah," in *New York Review of Books,* Vol. XXII, Nos. 21-22, January 22, 1976, pp. 8, 10-11.

[*Below, McCarthy eulogizes Arendt, emphasizing her person rather than her ideas.*]

Her last book was to be called **The Life of the Mind** and was intended to be a pendant to **The Human Condition** (first called *The Vita Activa*), where she had scrutinized the triad of labor, work, and action: man as *animal laborans, homo faber,* and doer of public deeds. She saw the mind's life, or *vita contemplativa,* as divided into three parts also: thinking, will-ing, and judging. The first section, on thinking, was finished some time ago. The second, on willing, she finished just be-fore she died, with what must have been relief, for she had found the will the most elusive of the three faculties to grapple with. The third, on judging, she had already sketched out and partly written; though the literature on the subject was sparse (mainly Kant), she did not expect it to give her much diffi-culty.

I say "her last book," and that is how she thought of it, as a final task or crowning achievement, if she could only bring it off—not only filling in the other side of the tablet of human capacities but a labor of love in itself for the highest and least visible of them: the activity of the mind. If she had lived to see the book (two volumes, actually) through the press, no doubt she would have gone on writing, since her nature was expressive as well as thoughtful, but she would have felt that her true work was done.

She would have executed a service or mission she had been put into the world to perform. In this sense, Hannah, I be-lieve, was religious. She had heard a voice such as spoke to the prophets, the call that came to the child Samuel, girded with a linen ephod in the house of Eli, the high priest. One can look on this more secularly and think that she felt herself indentured, bound as though under contract by her particular endowments, given her by Nature, developed in her by her teachers—Jaspers and Heidegger—and tragically enriched by History. It was not a matter of self-fulfillment (the idea would have been laughable or else detestable to Hannah) but of an injunction laid on all of us, not just the talented, to follow the trajectory chance and fate have launched us on, like a poet keeping faith with his muse. Hannah was not a believer in slavish notions of one's "duty" (which may be why she had so much trouble with the section on the will) but she was responsive to a sense of calling, vocation, including that of the citizen to serve the common life. She was also a very private person, and I think (though we never spoke of it) that **The Life of the Mind** was a task she dedicated to the memory of Heinrich, a kind of completion and rounding out of *their* common life.

Heinrich Bluecher, her husband and friend, was the last of her teachers. Though he was only ten years older than she, in their intellectual relationship there was something fatherly, indulgent, on his side, and pupil-like, eager, approval-seeking, on hers; as she spoke, he would look on her fondly, nodding to himself, as though luck had sent him an unimaginably bright girl student and tremendous "achiever," which he himself, a philosopher in every sense, was content, with his pipes and cigars, not to be. He was proud of her and knew she would go far, to peaks and ranges he could discern in the distance, and calmly sat back, waiting for her to find them.

For her, Heinrich was like a pair of corrective lenses; she did not wholly trust her vision until it had been confirmed by his. While they thought alike on most questions, he was more a "pure" philosophic spirit, and she was more concerned with the *vita activa* of politics and fabrication—the fashioning of durable objects in the form of books and articles; neither was much interested in the biological sphere of the *animal laborans*—household drudgery, consumption of goods; though both were fond of young people, they never had any children. When he died, late in 1970, quitesuddenly, though not as suddenly as she, she was alone. Surrounded by friends, she rode like a solitary passenger on her train of thought. So *The Life of the Mind,* begun in those bleak years, was conceived and pondered for (and she must have hoped *with*) Heinrich Bluecher, not exactly a monument but something like a triptych or folding panel with the mysterious will at the center. Anyway, that is what I guess, and she is not here to ask.

I spoke of a crowning achievement, but Hannah was not in the least ambitious (absurd to connect her with a "career"); if there was some striving for a crown, it was in the sense of a summit toward which she had labored in order to be able to look around, like an explorer, finishing the last stages of an ascent alone. What would be spread out before her were the dark times she had borne witness to, as a Jewess and a displaced person, the long-drawn-out miscarriage of a socialist revolution, the present perils of the American Republic, in which she had found a new political home in which to hang, with increasing despondency, the ideas of freedom she had carried with her, but also the vast surveyor's map of concepts and insights, some inherited from a long philosophical tradition and some her own discoveries, which, regarded from a high point, could at least show us where we were.

In the realm of ideas, Hannah was a conservationist; she did not believe in throwing anything away that had once been thought. A use might be found for it; in her own way, she was an enthusiastic recycler. To put it differently, thought, for her, was a kind of husbandry, a humanizing of the wilderness of experience—building houses, running paths and roads through, damming streams, planting windbreaks. The task that had fallen to her, as an exceptionally gifted intellect and a representative of the generations she had lived among, was to apply thought systematically to each and every characteristic experience of her time—*anomie,* terror, advanced warfare, concentration camps, Auschwitz, inflation, revolution,

school integration, the Pentagon Papers, space, Watergate, Pope John, violence, civil disobedience—and, having finally achieved this, to direct thought inward, upon itself, and its own characteristic processes.

The word "systematically" may be misleading. Despite her German habits, Hannah was not a system-builder. Rather, she sought to descry systems that were already *there,* inherent in the body of man's interaction with the world and with himself as subject. The distinctions made by language, from very ancient times, indeed from the birth of speech, between *this* and *that* (e.g., work and labor, public and private, force, power, and violence), reveal man as categorizer, a "born" philosopher, if you will, with the faculty of separating, of finely discriminating, more natural to his species than that of constructing wholes. If I understood her, Hannah was always more for the Many than for the One (which may help explain her horrified recognition of totalitarianism as a new phenomenon in the world). She did not want to find a master key or universal solvent, and if she had a religion, it was certainly not monotheistical. The proliferation of distinctions in her work, branching out in every direction like tender shoots, no doubt owes something to her affection for the scholastics but it also testifies to a sort of typical awe-struck modesty before the world's abundance and intense particularity.

But I do not want to discuss Hannah's ideas here but to try to bring her back as a person, a physical being, showing herself radiantly in what she called the world of appearance, a stage from which she has now withdrawn. She was a beautiful woman, alluring, seductive, feminine, whichis why I said "Jewess"—the old-fashioned term, evoking the daughters of Sion, suits her, like a fringed Spanish shawl. Above all, her eyes, so brilliant and sparkling, starry when she was happy or excited, but also deep, dark, remote, pools of inwardness. There was something unfathomable in Hannah that seemed to lie in the reflective depths of those eyes.

She had small, fine hands, charming ankles, elegant feet. She liked shoes; in all the years I knew her, I think she only once had a corn. Her legs, feet, and ankles expressed quickness, decision. You had only to see her on a lecture stage to be struck by those feet, calves, and ankles that seemed to keep pace with her thought. As she talked, she moved about, sometimes with her hands plunged in her pockets like somebody all alone on a walk, meditating. When the fire laws permitted, she would smoke, pacing the stage with a cigarette in a short holder, inhaling from time to time, reflectively, her head back, as if arrested by a new, unexpected idea. Watching her talk to an audience was like seeing the motions of the mind made visible in action and gesture. Peripatetic, she would come abruptly to a halt at the lectern, frown, consult the ceiling, bite her lip, pensively cup her chin. If she was reading a speech, there were always interjections, asides, like the footnotes that peppered her texts with qualifications and appendices.

There was more than a touch of the great actress in Hannah. The first time I heard her speak in public—nearly thirty years ago, during a debate—I was reminded of what Bernhardt must have been or Proust's Berma, a magnificent stage diva, which implies a goddess. Perhaps a chthonic goddess, or a fiery one, rather than the airy kind. Unlike other good speakers, she was not at all an orator. She appeared, rather, as a mime, a thespian, enacting a drama of mind, that dialogue of me-and-myself she so often summons up in her writings. Watching her framed in the proscenium arch, we were not far from the sacred origins of the theater. What she projected was the human figure as actor and sufferer in the agon of consciousness and reflection, where there are always two, the one who says and the one who replies or questions.

> **In the realm of ideas, Hannah was a conservationist; she did not believe in throwing anything away that had once been thought.**
>
> —*Mary McCarthy*

Yet nobody could have been farther from an exhibitionist. Calculation of the impression she was making never entered her head. Whenever she spoke in public, she had terrible stage fright, and afterward she would ask only "Was it all right?" (This cannot have been true of the classroom, where she felt herself at ease and among friends.) And naturally she did not play roles in private or public, even less than the normal amount required in social relations. She was incapable of feigning. Though she prided herself as a European on being able to tell a lie, where we awkward Americans blurted out the truth, in fact there was a little hubris there. Hannah's small points of vanity never had any relation to her real accomplishments. For example, she thought she knew a good deal about cooking and didn't. It was the same with her supposed ability to lie. Throughout our friendship, I don't think I ever heard her tell even one of those white lies, such as pleading illness or a previous engagement, to get herself out of a social quandary. If you wrote something she found bad, her policy was not to allude to it—an unvarying course of action that told you louder than words what she thought.

What was theatrical in Hannah was a kind of spontaneous power of being seized by an idea, an emotion, a presentiment, whose vehicle her body then became, like the actor's. And this power of being seized and worked upon, often with a start, widened eyes, "Ach!" (before a picture, a work of architecture, some deed of infamy), set her apart from the rest of us like a high electrical charge. And there was the vibrant, springy, dark, short hair, never fully gray, that sometimes from sheer force of energy appeared to stand bolt upright on her head.

I suppose all this must have been part of an unusual physical endowment, whose manifestation in her features and facial gestures was the beauty I spoke of. Hannah is the only person I have ever watched *think*. She lay motionless on a sofa or a day bed, arms folded behind her head, eyes shut but occasionally opening to stare upward. This lasted—I don't know—from ten minutes to half an hour. Everyone tiptoed past if we had to come into the room in which she lay oblivious.

She was an impatient, generous woman, and those qualities went hand in hand. Just as, in a speech or an essay, she would put everything in but the kitchen stove, as if she could not keep in reserve a single item of what she knew or had happened that instant to occur to her, so she would press on a visitor assorted nuts, chocolates, candied ginger, tea, coffee, Campari, whiskey, cigarettes, cake, crackers, fruit, cheese, almost all at once, regardless of conventional sequence or, often, of the time of day. It was as if the profusion of edibles, set out, many of them, in little ceremonial-like dishes and containers, were impatient propitiatory offerings to all the queer gods of taste. Someone said that this was the eternal Jewish mother, but it was not that: there was no notion that any of this fodder was good for you; in fact most of it was distinctly bad for you, which she must have known somehow, for she did not insist.

She had a respect for privacy, separateness, one's own and hers. I often stayed with her—and Heinrich and her—on Riverside Drive and before that on Morningside Drive, so that I came to know Hannah's habits well, what she liked for breakfast, for instance. A boiled egg, some mornings, a little ham or cold cuts, toast spread with anchovy paste, coffee, of course, half a grapefruit or fresh orange juice, but perhaps that last was only when I, the American, was there. The summer after Heinrich's death she came to stay with us in Maine, where we gave her a separate apartment, over the garage, and I put some thought into buying supplies for her kitchen—she liked to breakfast alone. The things, I thought, that she would have at home, down to instant coffee (which I don't normally stock) for when she could not be bothered with the filters. I was rather pleased to have been able to find anchovy paste in the village store. On the afternoon of her arrival, as I showed her where everything was in the larder, she frowned over the little tube of anchovy paste, as though it were an inexplicable foreign object. "What is that?" I told her. "Oh." She put it down and looked thoughtful and as though displeased, somehow. No more was said. But I knew I had done something wrong in my efforts to please. She did not wish to be *known,* in that curiously finite and, as it were, reductive way. And I had done it to show her I knew her—a sign of love, though not always—thereby proving that in the last analysis I did not know her at all.

Her eyes were closed in her coffin, and her hair was waved back from her forehead, whereas *she* pulled it forward, sometimes tugging at a lock as she spoke, partly to hide a scar she had got in an automobile accident—but even before that she had never really bared her brow. In her coffin, with the lids veiling the fathomless eyes, that noble forehead topped by a sort of pompadour, she was not Hannah any more but a composed death mask of an eighteenth-century philosopher. I was not moved to touch that grand stranger in the funeral parlor, and only in the soft yet roughened furrows of her neck, in which the public head rested, could I find a place to tell her good-by.

Robert Lowell (essay date 13 May 1976)

SOURCE: "On Hannah Arendt," in *New York Review of Books,* Vol. XXII, No. 8, May 13, 1976, p. 6.

[*In the following essay, Lowell reminisces about his relationship with Arendt and his impressions on reading her works.*]

Hannah Arendt was an oasis in the fevered, dialectical dust of New York—to me, and I imagine to everyone who loved her. We met in the late Fifties or early Sixties in Mary McCarthy's apartment. She seemed hardly to take her coat off, as she brushed on with purpose to a class or functional shopping. In her hurry, she had time to say to me something like "This is an occasion," or more probably, "This is a meeting." I put the least intention into her words, but later dared telephone her to make a call. The calls were part of my life as long as I lived in New York—once a month, sometimes twice.

I was overawed. Years earlier Randall Jarrell had written me in Holland that if I wanted to discover something big and new, I would read Hannah Arendt's *Origins of Totalitarianism.* Randall seldom praised in vain, but my Dutch intellectual friends, as usual embarrassingly more into whatever was being written in America, were ahead of me, and were discussing *Origins* with minds sharpened by the Dutch Resistance, a hatred of Germany, and a fluency with German philosophers. I felt landless and alone, and read Hannah as though I were going home, or reading *Moby Dick,* perhaps for the second time, no longer seeking adventure, but the voyage of wisdom, the tragedy of America.

Writing when Stalin was still enthroned and the shade of Hitler still unburied, Hannah believed with somber shrewdness, like Edmund Burke, that totalitarian power totally corrupts. Compared with Melville, however, she might seem an optimist about America. *Origins,* like many of her books, is apparently a defense of America, one that overstates and troubles us by assuming that we must be what we declared ourselves

to be in our Revolutionary and post-Revolutionary beginnings. Her dream, it is both German and Jewish, now perhaps seems sadly beyond our chances and intentions. Yet the idea is still true, still taunting us to act. What is memorable, and almost uniquely rare and courageous in a thinker, is that Hannah's theory is always applied to action, and often to immediate principles of state. Her imperatives for political freedom still enchant and reproach us, though America has obviously, in black moments one thinks almost totally, slipped from those jaunty years of Harry Truman and the old crusade for international democracy. We couldn't know how fragile we were, or how much totalitarianism could ameliorate, bend, adulterate itself, and succeed.

Hannah's high apartment house high on the lower Hudson always gave me a feeling of apprehension, the thrill, hesitation, and helplessness of entering a foreign country, a north German harbor, the tenements of Kafka. Its drabness and respectability that hid her true character also emphasized her unfashionable independence. On my first visit, I blundered about a vacant greenish immensity unable to find the name of any owner. Then I ran through the small print cards, uniform as names in a telephone book, that filled a green brass plaque camouflaged to lose itself in the dark green hall. No Arendt; then I found what I was seeking: *Blucher 12a.* It was inevitable for Hannah to use her husband's name for domestic identification. The elevator was brusque and unhurried; through my ineptitude, it made false premature stops. A vehemently not-Hannah German woman appeared and gave me advice that sent me to the top of the building. Did another lady dart out shouting wrong directions? So it seemed, but memories magnify. Later when my arrivals were errorless though gradual, it seemed an undeserved rescue to find Hannah in her doorway and ready to kiss me.

Once inside, the raw Hudson, too big for New York, was chillingly present, but only in a window at an angle and raised several feet above the floor. We almost had to stand to see it, and it was soon lost in the urgency of conversation. I sometimes had an architectural temptation to cut away the unalterable window.

How many fine views have given me comfort by their nearness, yet were only taken in by chance over a typescript or the head of a friend. How unconsciously Hannah held the straying mind. Though a philosopher in every heartbeat of her nervous system, she belonged, like all true thinkers, to culture and literature. Coming to America in early middle age, she had the pluck not only to learn English but to write it with a power of phrase and syntax that often made her a master, the strongest theoretical writer of her age. Phrasing, syntax, and vehemence—her finest sentences are a wrenching then a marriage of English and German, of English instantness and German philosophical discipline. She translated many of her books into German, but I imagine if she had written in

German and let someone else translate her into English her freshness, nerve, and actuality would have suffered a glaze, a stealing of her life.

Because I once failed to speak out, yet was stirred almost to hysteria by the smearing reception of Hannah's book *Eichmann in Jerusalem,* I want to take it up now, yet evade what is beyond my non-Jewish limitation. I read her book innocently in *The New Yorker* before the anger of faction could accumulate and burst. I was astonished to discover a new kind of biography, a blueprint of a man flayed down to his abstract moral performance, no color, no anecdote, nothing kept that would support a drawing or even a snapshot—yet a living kicking anatomy, Eichmann's X-ray in motion. It was a terrifying expressionist invention applied with a force no imitator could rival, and to a subject too sordid for reappraisal. The book's lesson seemed to be that given the right bad circumstances, Eichmann is still in the world. I have never understood why Hannah's phrase the banality of evil excited such universal polemic. She wasn't writing of Attila or Caesar, but Eichmann. The Eichmann who managed the railroading of thousands, perhaps millions, to their death camps was an appallingly uninteresting man both in his criminal efficiency and in his irrelevant pedantry and evasions while on trial for his life. Since Hannah has written, who has dreamed of painting Eichmann as colorful? Hannah's rage against Eichmann's mediocrity was itself enraging.

It was far more so when she turned with the same heat against the rhetoric and windowdressing of the Eichmann trial in Israel; and far more still when she said that certain Jews, themselvesmartyrs, cooperated in the destruction of other Jews. Who can expound the sober facts? Must not justice allow that Hannah Arendt, where she was wrong, wrote with the honest foolhardiness of a prophet? Perhaps her warnings to us to resist future liquidation are too heroic to live with, for nearly all of us are cowards if sufficiently squeezed by the hand of the powerful.

No society is more acute and overacute at self-criticism than that of the New York Jews. No society I have known is higher in intelligence, wit, inexhaustible willingness to reason, bicker, tolerate, and differ. When Hannah's *Eichmann* was published, a meeting was summoned by Irving Howe and Lionel Abel, normally urbane and liberal minds. The meeting was like a trial, the stoning of an outcast member of the family. Any sneering overemphasis on Hannah, who had been invited but was away teaching in Chicago, was greeted with derisive clapping or savage sighs of amazement. Her appointed defenders drifted off into unintelligibly ingenious theses and avoided her name. When her tolerance was eloquently and unfavorably compared with Trotsky's, Alfred Kazin walked self-consciously to the stage and stammered, "After all Hannah didn't kill any Jews." He walked off the stage laughed at as irrelevant and absurd. His was the one voice for the defense. I

admire his bravery, and wish I had dared speak. Half my New York literary and magazine acquaintance was sitting near, yet their intensity was terrifying, as if they were about to pick up chairs.

Hannah did other portraits, genial, penetrating, good-humored ones, and had an unlikely genius for the form, as if the universal could win in a contest for hunting down particulars. How Disraeli and Clemenceau shine in her *Origins of Totalitarianism*. A subtle, relentless search for truth animates her essays on Rosa Luxemburg, Brecht, and Auden.

My meetings with Hannah were most often alone and at four in the afternoon. They had the concentrated intimacy of a tutorial. Large nuts were spread out on the table, the ashtrays filled, the conversation rambled through history, politics, and philosophy, but soon refreshed itself on gossip, mostly about people one liked, the dead and still living. Hannah made crushingly laconic sentences, but narrow slander, even of one's enemies, bored her. She thought and breathed within boundaries, ones held with such firm belief that she could function safely with almost torrential carelessness. She used to talk with merry ease, revising my definitions and her own, as if haphazard words could be as accurately attuned as writing. Yet all was warm, casual, and throwaway. It seems immoral to remember her epigrams I used to repeat, her acuteness and good temper seemed to inspire me to make sense beyond my custom.

I felt so much at home, I used to bring her poems. Rhythms with meaning would delight her, but she was quick to find obscurities and uncouth, pretentious generalizations. Mostly the poems were a device to diversify our talk about history, politics, and persons. I tried not to overstay, but sometimes I left in the dark and was late for supper—so cooling and kind was her affection, a parenthesis in the unjust blur of ordinary life.

Margaret Canovan (essay date February 1978)

SOURCE: "The Contradictions of Hannah Arendt's Political Thought," in *Political Theory,* Vol. 6, No. 1, February, 1978, pp. 5-26.

[*Below, Canovan investigates Arendt's major works, discerning "a contradiction between democratic and elitist attitudes on the one hand, and an uncertainty about the relation of her political thought to practice on the other."*]

Hannah Arendt's political thought is baffling even to the most sympathetic reader. It is baffling not only because of her fondness for questioning our established certainties, and not only because her political values are strange and shocking to us, but most importantly because her thought is riven by a deep

and serious inconsistency and confused by a persistent uncertainty of stance.

The serious inconsistency lies between what may for the sake
of brevity be called Arendt's elitist and her democratic aspects. She can be read as one of the most radical of demo-
crats. Her political ideal is a vision of ancient Athens, a polity
in which there were neither rulers nor ruled, but all citizens
were equal within the agora, acting among their peers. She
asserts that every man is a new beginning, and is capable of
acting in such a way that no one, not even he himself, can
know what he may achieve. She cites again and again the
revolutionary situations in which the people have sprung spontaneously into action, and she shares Jefferson's desire to
perpetuate that revolutionary impulse by means of direct
democratic participation. However, if Arendt in some moods
can seem preeminently the theorist of participatory democracy, she can also be read as an elitist of almost Nietzschean
intensity. She attributes totalitarianism largely to the rise of
"mass society"; she expresses contempt not only for the activity of labouring but for the characteristic tastes and dispositions of labourers; and she shows what is, for a modern
political thinker, a truly astonishing lack of interest in the
social and economic welfare of the many, except in so far as
the struggle to achieve it poses a threat to the freedom of the
few.

The starkest expression of this contrast between the two sides
of her thought might at first sight appear to be her image of
the *polis* in *The Human Condition,* where she makes very
clear the opposition between the brilliant, sunlit world of the
free and equal citizens in the agora, and the dark, miserable,
degraded lives of the slaves, whose toil is the price of their
masters' glory. Her contrast echoes Rousseau's defiant paradox in *The Social Contract,* where, opposing representation
of the citizens, he acknowledged that it had been easier for
the ancient Greeks to dispense with representation and to act
on their own behalf, because they had slaves to do the work.
Rousseau added,

> What? Is freedom to be maintained only with the
> support of slavery? Perhaps. The two extremes meet.
> Everything outside nature has its disadvantages, civil
> society more than all the rest. There are some situa-
> tions so unfortunate that one can preserve one's free-
> dom only at the expense of someone else; and the
> citizen can be perfectly free only if the slave is abso-
> lutely a slave.

There are certainly many echoes in Arendt's writings of
Rousseau's paradox, and her insistence on the *costs* of freedom is part of her stress on the fragile, unnatural quality of
human goods. Neither the good state, nor anything else of
supreme human worth, is given to us by nature, and all that
man achieves must be achieved by violating and disrupting

nature's order. However, the contradiction between Arendt's
elitist and democratic sides goes much deeper than this
hardsaying about the historical interrelations between freedom and slavery, and is much more difficult to make sense
of. It is exemplified in *The Human Condition* not by the
flaunting paradox of the polis, in which freedom among the
masters rests upon slavery for the labourers, but rather by a
chapter on "The Labor Movement," which cuts uncomfort-
ably across the argument of the book. For, having heaped
contempt upon labouring and those who labour, Arendt then
acknowledges that in the politics of the nineteenth and twentieth centuries, most of those who have engaged in what she
recognises as political action have in fact been labourers:

> The incapacity of the *animal laborans* for distinc-
> tion and hence for action and speech seems to be
> confirmed by the striking absence of serious slave
> rebellions in ancient and modern times. No less strik-
> ing, however, is the sudden and frequently extraor-
> dinarily productive role which the labor movements
> have played in modern politics. From the revolutions
> of 1848 to the Hungarian revolution of 1956, the
> European working class, by virtue of being the only
> organised and hence the leading section of the people,
> has written one of the most glorious and probably
> the most promising chapter of recent history. [*The
> Human Condition*]

It is this favourable judgement upon political action by ordinary working people, repeated again and again in her comments on modern revolutions, that is really hard to reconcile
with Arendt's elitist side. For the contradiction between demo-
crat and elitist in her work is not to be easily resolved as a
desire for democracy among an elite of free men, raised above
the need for labour and above the tastes of mass society. It is
a serious and unresolved contradiction which allows her work
to be read in two incompatible ways.

In the course of a long and illuminating discussion of Marx's
inconsistencies, Arendt once remarked, "Such fundamental
and flagrant contradictions rarely occur in second-rate writers; in the work of the great authors they lead into the very
center of their work" [*The Human Condition*]. I wish to argue that the contradiction between democratic and elitist views
in Arendt's writings is a contradiction of this kind, to be taken
seriously and explored. Furthermore, I hope that an exploration of it will throw some light on another of the difficulties
which her readers encounter. I said earlier that besides the
deep and serious inconsistency in her thought, her readers
were troubled by a persistent uncertainty in her stance. I mean
by this the problem of what relation, if any, she meant her
political thinking to have to the political realities of the present
day. Was she purely a political moralist? One of the long line
of those who have condemned the faults of their own time in
a spirit of despair, and depicted utopias rather to point the

contrast than to propose amendments? Or was she a more familiar type among modern political thinkers, one who hopes to influence politics in the future and whose schemes can therefore be fairly criticised if they are wildly impracticable?

The relation of Arendt's political thought to modern political practice is again somewhat reminiscent of Rousseau, who oscillated between moralistic utopianism and rejection of all modern politics on the one hand, and practical commitment (even to the extent of writing constitutions for Poland and Corsica) on the other. *The Human Condition* in particular seems consciously utopian in its appeal from a corrupt modern world to a totally different order. It is in accord with this utopian atmosphere that Arendt leaves her central concept of Action as imprecise and unrelated to current conditions as Rousseau leaves the General Will.

However, it is clear from Arendt's later writings that she does not regard Action as the exclusive property of a vanished age, whether the age of Athens or the more recent age of the American Revolution. She recognises authentic political action in spontaneous popular uprisings of various kinds, from the Hungarian Revolution to the Civil Rights Movement and the anti-Vietnam war demonstrations in America. Furthermore, when she proposes a political system of self-federating councils as an alternative to parliamentary democracy, as she does so often, she is perfectly serious about her proposal.

It might perhaps be argued (and, as we shall see, there is a good deal to be said for this view) that her political ideal was initially cast in utopian form because experience, in the days of Hitler and Stalin, had led her justly to despair of modern politics; whereas, from the dawning of the Hungarian Revolution onwards, signs of hope appeared that made a new foundation of political freedom increasingly plausible. The difficulty with this interpretation is that her descriptions of the council system, *ex hypothesi* the fruit of her reconciliation with the present, strike most readers as utopian in the pejorative sense. If she did indeed intend this system of direct popular participation in politics to be taken seriously as an alternative to party politics, she ought to have made a much more serious case for it, and to have tried to answer the many objections that can be raised against it. We shall be considering these objections at a later stage of the argument. For the moment, our concern is simply with the baffling oscillation between concrete political proposals and utopian irresponsibility in her treatment of the subject.

We have identified two serious problems at the heart of Hannah Arendt's political thought: a contradiction between democratic and elitist attitudes on the one hand, and an uncertainty about the relation of her political thought to practice on the other. The present article makes no claim to solve these problems in the sense of making them disappear (certainly not by resolving them into a higher consistency, in the manner of Rousseau-interpretation). In some ways, indeed, a detailed examination of her inconsistencies can only make her *more* baffling, by forcing the reader to recognise contradictions where his instinct in reading Arendt will be to seize on one side of her thought and to ignore the other. However, I hope that the investigation will eventually lead us to understand in some degree how she could be so inconsistent, and also to recognise that these defects in her thought are bound up closely with its very considerable virtues. Meanwhile, let us look briefly at her major works.

The first edition of *The Origins of Totalitarianism,* originally entitled *The Burden of Our Time,* was published in 1951, and Arendt tells us that the manuscript was finished in 1949, four years after the death of Hitler and four years before the death of Stalin. In the "Preface" to the first edition she said:

> We no longer hope for an eventual restoration of the old world order with all its traditions, or for the reintegration of the masses of five continents who have been thrown into a chaos produced by the violence of wars and revolutions and the growing decay of all that has still been spared.

What is interesting for our present purposes is not only the (scarcely surprising) near despairat the appalling state of modern politics which is manifested in the book, but also the role played in Arendt's account of totalitarianism by the "masses." This is not to suggest that her book is a simple, mass society explanation of totalitarianism. On the contrary, her argument is enormously intricate and complex. Nevertheless, it is quite evident that she was greatly influenced by the tradition of mass society theory, with its inbuilt elitist bias of distrust for the common people. She lays great stress upon the mass support the totalitarian regimes received, and develops some of the traditional themes of the mass society theorists to explain this. For instance, she speaks of masses being the result of the sheer numbers of modern populations, pressing upon men and breaking down their sense of the worth of individual human beings, and she repeats the familiar assertion that it was the breakdown of the old class structure that, by destroying social order, turned men into a mass.

It is not clear what precisely she means by the "breakdown of classes." However, she does say two things that distinguish her theory from the more conservative branches of the mass society tradition. First, she emphasises that the "mass" which made totalitarianism possible was recruited from *all* classes, not simply from the emancipated lower orders. Second, she says that the breakdown of classes is not to be equated with that "equality of conditions" which de Tocqueville had observed a hundred years before in the United States:

> The masses, contrary to prediction, did not result from growing equality of condition, from the spread of

general education and its inevitable lowering of standards and popularization of content. (America, the classical land of equality of condition and of general education with all its shortcomings, knows less of the modern psychology of masses than perhaps any other country in the world.)

Instead of identifying the masses with the lower orders, indeed, Arendt stresses that totalitarian movements received particularly enthusiastic support from that very intellectual elite on whom nineteenth-century prophets of mass society had relied to defend civilised values against the mob.

Therefore, in this first edition of *Totalitarianism,* while Arendt's fear and distrust of the modern masses is evident, there is as yet no suggestion that it is characteristic of these masses to be labourers. This particular theme was introduced only into the second edition, as an offshoot of another train of thought, the reflections (published in the same year) on *The Human Condition*. And the clearest possible illustration of the central inconsistency in Arendt's political thought is that this new underpinning for her mass society theory, this new condemnation of the labourers as natural fodder for totalitarianism, was introduced into the second edition cheek by jowl with an "Epilogue" prompted by the Hungarian uprising of 1956 and expressing Arendt's new faith in the people and their capacity for action. It would seem that even before her early reflections on totalitarianism had been completely articulated, they were already overtaken by the events that drove her thought in a different direction.

Arendt's picture of *The Human Condition,* with its exaltation of Action and its denigration of Labour, is a familiar though disturbing one. In some ways her perspective is radically egalitarian, in that she insists that every man is a new beginning, and that no one can know a man's potential until he has acted. However, she claims unequivocally that the free life of action flourished when the labourer was enslaved and production for consumption despised, and she asserts that in the modern age, the emancipation of the labourer and the new dignity accorded to production have resulted in the loss of Action, the destruction of the public World, and the subordination of all human life to the low values of the labourer. Her strictures are harsh: she says, for instance, that "the spare time of the *animal laborans* is never spent in anything but consumption, and the more time left to him, the greedier and more craving his appetites." Elsewhere, she refers to "the *animal laborans,* whose social life is worldless and herdlike and who therefore is incapable of building or inhabiting a public, worldly realm." She reinforces this later when she denies that labourers are capable of the experience of "plurality," of equality and distinction at the same time, which makes possible action among one's peers.

One of the signs of strain in Arendt's thought is that this line

of argument leads her into precisely the kind of materialistic explanation of the modern world of which she is, at other times, such a keen opponent. In spite of her attacks on the materialistic determinism of the ideologies, Marxist or Nazi, she comes close in *The Human Condition* to saying that man *is* what he does for a living, and that the ultimate cause of the deficiencies of the modern world lies in the technological changes which have elevated labouring from misery to respectability.

With the notable exception of the chapter on "The Labor Movement" (to which we shall return), *The Human Condition* shows Arendt at her most elitist and most utopian, demonstrating a haughty and distant contempt for the vulgarity of the modern world. However, this is only one side of her thought. The oddity of her position is revealed by the second edition of *The Origins of Totalitarianism,* (published in the same year), in which, on the one hand, she capped her theory of mass society with her contemptuous view of labour, and, on the other hand, rejoiced at the same time over the capacity of ordinary working people for action, as demonstrated in Hungary in 1956. Let us look at this contradiction in more detail.

The second edition of *Totalitarianism* contains a new chapter on "Ideology and Terror" (first published in 1953, before the Hungarian Revolution—which is probably significant), in which she connected the theory of mass society which she had used in the first edition with her newly articulated theory of Labour. As we have seen, her original text had specifically dissociated masses from any particular social class. Now, however, she connected the masses with the activity of labouring. Maintaining, with de Tocqueville, that it is the isolation of men from one another that makes tyranny possible, she claimed that this isolation becomes particularly ominous when craftsmanship is replaced by labour, so that the dominated individual is not even in a secure and creative relationship with the material world: "a tyranny over 'labourers' . . . would automatically be a rule over lonely, not only isolated, men and tend to be totalitarian."

She even says, on the same page, that "uprootedness and superfluousness which have been the curse of modern masses since the beginning of the industrial revolution" have produced the loneliness that makes support for totalitarian movements possible—seemingly implying a materialist determinism that makes totalitarianism a necessary and inevitable outcome of technological change. This lapse into materialist determinism is, however, sharply at variance with her usual emphasis upon the capacity of man to act freely and unexpectedly, and it was the latter side of her thought that was apparently confirmed in practice by the Hungarian Revolution of 1956.

In her many comments upon it, and notably in the "Epilogue"

attached to this same edition of *The Origins,* Arendt stressed above all the spontaneity and unexpectedness of this popular uprising. Certainly her own theories up to that time would not have led one to expect it. Evidently, it was not true that mass society and totalitarianism disabled men from political action, nor that political concerns are the preserve of an elite of nonlabourers—for Arendt stressed that the revolution had received universal support in Hungary, and that the aims of its supporters, workers as well as students, had been political rather than social or economic. The one aspect of her theory which the event confirmed was that, indeed, every man is a new beginning, no one can know what he may do, and that therefore political theories are always liable to be torn apart by events. Arendt herself emphasized this:

> Events, past and present—not social forces and historical trends, not questionnaires and motivation research, nor any other gadgets in the arsenal of the social sciences—are the true, the only reliable teachers of political scientists. . . . Once such an event as the spontaneous uprising in Hungary has happened, every policy, theory and forecast of future potentialities needs re-examination.

The events of 1956 made a deep and lasting impression upon Hannah Arendt, and tore a great rent in the web of her thought (although, as we have seen, there were some strains and tangles there already). From 1956 on, by no means simply or straightforwardly, but recognisably nevertheless, her theory shifts away from the view of modern men as mass men with only the labourer's consciousness, toward seeing them as people capable of political action, and away from a view of action itself as something lost since the Greeks, toward seeing it as an ever-present possibility.

The strains involved in this shift can be seen in *The Human Condition* itself, published two years after the Hungarian uprising, and particularly in the chapter on "The Labor Movement," which bears all the signs of being an afterthought. While the general tenor of the book has been to suggest that action is the preserve of an elite and that labour unfits a man for it, Arendt suddenly inserts a chapter pointing out that the chief representatives of political action in the last two centuries have been the European working class. Furthermore, these despised labourers have even invented a new form of polity—the system of people's councils. Arendt acknowledges "This apparently flagrant discrepancy between historical fact—the political productivity of the working class—and the phenomenal data obtained from an analysis of the laboring activity," and provides a rather lame explanation designed to show that such political activity by the workers is only a temporary phenomenon. Such tactics, however, cannot entirely bridge the gulf between the two distinct viewpoints that are to be found, by 1958, struggling for supremacy in Arendt's thinking. On the one hand we have the older, more familiar

perspective of the critic of modern mass society, offering pessimistic analyses of the labouring mentality and of totalitarian politics, and using for contrast a utopian image of elite action in a long dead polis. On the other hand, strengthened by the experience of the Hungarian Revolution, we have the believer in the constant possibility of unexpected political action, not only among an elite of some kind but among ordinary people, and the proponent of direct democracy by means of people's councils. Let us follow the continuing relations between these two voices in Arendt's reflections *On Revolution*.

Of Hannah Arendt's long books, *On Revolution* is the one in which formal organisation is least apparent. The argument is rambling and digressive, as if it were an accurate report of the process of thinking itself. Filled with both fascinating discussions and infuriating arbitrariness, the book is focussed on the American Revolution, and particularly upon an attempt to recall to mind the political experience of the American revolutionaries—an experience obscured by theories drawn from the quite different experience of the French Revolution. To cram into a nutshell what is in fact an exceedingly tortuous argument, we can say that Arendt maintains that the point of the American Revolution was the attempt to found public freedom, not just to secure civil liberties and no taxation without representation, but to establish lasting institutions which would provide a public realm in which men could act politically. The French Revolution was, according to her account, similarly concerned with public freedom in its early stages, but was rapidly deflected by the irruption into politics of the social question, the problem of the hopeless misery of the Parisian masses, and the compassion for their misery which led the Jacobins to justify tyranny in the interests of social betterment. The foundation of freedom in America was possible not only because (owing to the unprecedented prosperity of the country) the pressure of misery was not inescapable, as it was in Europe, but also because the Founding Fathers' enthusiasm for liberty was not diluted by irrelevant compassion for the poor, which might have tempted them to pervert political means to social ends.

For most of the book Arendt makes an explicit contrast between the few, who are capable of politics and the love of freedom because they have property and leisure, and the many, who are cursed by poverty and misery, subject to the constant necessity of bodily toil and suffering and who are therefore a threat to free politics. They pose such a threat for a number of reasons: because they will try to degrade politics into the accomplishment of mere physical welfare; because they are a mass, incapable of plurality; above all, because they cannot comprehend or enjoy the exalted passion for public action, since their tastes are circumscribed by physical wants. The image that is conjured up, as in *The Human Condition,* is of a small aristocracy of free men of noble disposition, constantly defending their free politics against the mass of ignoble slaves who make that freedom possible. Indeed, Arendt even says toward the end of [*On Revolution*]:

> The fact that political 'elites' have always determined the political destinies of the many and have, in most instances, exerted a domination over them, indicates . . . the bitter need of the few to protect themselves against the many, or rather to protect the island of freedom they have come to inhabit against the surrounding sea of necessity.

The impression of a kind of inherited distinction between the noble and the base is strengthened when Arendt refers to developments in America since the Revolution. For surely the mass of the population now possess not only that bare minimum which, at the time when the Republic was founded, raised them above the absolute tyranny of need, but even affluence and leisure comparable to that of many of the Founding Fathers themselves. Should not the many, then, bequalified to participate in politics? But in fact, Arendt suggests that the distinction between the free and those subject to necessity is more than a matter of simple affluence.

> When, in America and elsewhere, the poor became wealthy, they did not become men of leisure whose actions were prompted by a desire to excel, but succumbed to the boredom of vacant time.

It seems that the labouring mentality is a hereditary curse, for Arendt even blames what she takes to be the perversion of American political traditions, the loss of concern for political freedom amidst the frantic pursuit of affluence, on the influx of poor immigrants from Europe:

> For abundance and endless consumption are the ideals of the poor; they are the mirage in the desert of misery.

A great deal of *On Revolution,* therefore, like a great deal of Hannah Arendt's previous books, seems to be concerned with arguing that political freedom, which is the all-important glory of human existence, is possible only among an aristocratic leisured class undisturbed by compassion for their serfs, and that it has been lost in the modern age because increasing equality of condition has given politics into the hands of the poor and lowly. Such a position, while unattractive (at any rate to most British and American readers), would be consistent. But Arendt is not consistent. Not only is the elitist position contradicted by other writings from the same period as *On Revolution,* but in the final chapter of the book itself, precisely the same inconsistency appears that we have already noticed in her previous writings. Having designated politics as the preserve of the leisured class, beyond the understanding of the poor, she goes on to express enthusiasm for direct participatory democracy, and to cite case after case where its

organs—councils of various kinds—have sprung up spontaneously amongst those very people whom she has condemned to political oblivion.

The first instance of such a spontaneous generation of popular spaces for political action occurred, by her own account, in that first French Revolution which was overwhelmed and deflected from political freedom by the pressure of the poor. Not surprisingly, Arendt's discussion here is extremely ambivalent. She describes the Parisian Commune and the spontaneously generated popular societies both as "mighty pressure groups of the poor" and as "the germs . . . of a new type of political organization, of a system which would permit the people to become Jefferson's 'participators in government'." Similarly, she attributes Robespierre's suppression of these popular societies to two quite different motives. On the one hand, she claims, he was defending the Republic, the space of public freedom, against the pressure of misery and necessity; but on the other, he was crushing genuine public action and the spontaneous impulse to federate local councils, in the interests of party rule over a centralised state.

Arendt maintains that similar councils were spontaneously formed among ordinary people in many subsequent revolutions—1870-1871 in France, in 1905 and 1917 in Russia, in 1918-1919 in Germany, and in 1956 in Hungary. She stresses that those who engaged in this activity were "infinitely more interested in the political than in the social aspect of revolution"—apparently in spite of the fact that these were not leisured aristocrats but ordinary people. Councils of this sortbecame her political ideal, recommended enthusiastically on many occasions. Let us look in more detail at what she had in mind.

> **It is quite evident that Arendt was greatly influenced by the tradition of mass society theory, with its inbuilt elitist bias of distrust for the common people.**
>
> **—*Margaret Canovan***

The system she proposes is a nationwide network of small, face-to-face gatherings, on the lines of the Workers' Councils, Soldiers' Councils, Neighbourhood Councils, and Student Councils that have sprung up in the revolutions. It is of the essence of such a system that it should not be organised bureaucratically from above, but should be generated by the people themselves. Once these tiny political spaces have been constituted, they will naturally federate among themselves, sending deputies, whose personal qualities they trust, up to higher level councils.

Arendt makes it quite clear that the purpose of such a political system, and the reason why she favours it, is not that it would represent the *interests* of the many better than is done by existing representative governments, but that it would extend to the many—indeed to anyone who chose to take part in it—the inestimable blessing of political action. As she has stressed all along, "political freedom, generally speaking, means the right to be a 'participator in government', or it means nothing." The regularity with which such councils have sprung up spontaneously in revolution after revolution only to be crushed by the bureaucratic parties, seems to her to indicate that her own passion for public freedom is shared by the people in general (even, as we have remarked, by "labourers").

In the course of her discussion of the council system, Arendt eventually confronts the question of the existence of an elite. She explicitly contrasts her own ideal with the modern rationale of representative government, according to which the party system provides for "government of the people *by an elite sprung from the people.*" Her comments are interesting. She objects to the term elite because it implies:

> an oligarchic form of government, the domination of the many by the rule of a few. From this, one can only conclude—as indeed our whole tradition of political thought has concluded—that the essence of politics is rulership and that the dominant political passion is the passion to rule or to govern. This, I propose, is profoundly untrue.

On the contrary, her claim is that the true political passion is not the desire to rule, but the desire to *act* among one's equals.

Nevertheless, she is willing to accept that her council system would give rise to a political elite just as much as parliamentary government does:

> the political way of life has never been and never will be the way of life of the many, even though political business, by definition, concerns . . . all citizens. Political passions—courage, the pursuit of public happiness, the state of public freedom, an ambition that strives for excellence . . . are out of the ordinary in all circumstances.

What, then, is the difference? It appears to lie in the different types of elite that the two systems would select. In parliamentary systems politics has become a career, so that the criteria for selection are professional rather than political. The kinds of men who emerge from the processes of intraparty struggles and the need to sell themselves to the electorate are not those with the authentic talent for political action. In the revolutionary councils, on the contrary, the elite "selected themselves": those who cared about public affairs took it upon

themselves to act, and chose from among themselves the deputies for the higher councils. This kind of self-constituted elite seems to Arendt preferable to the present political elites of party politicians, and she spells out the implications quite clearly:

> The joys of public happiness and the responsibilities for public business would then become the share of those few from all walks of life who have a taste for public freedom and cannot be 'happy' without it. Politically, they are the best, and it is the task of good government and the sign of a well-ordered republic to assure them of their rightful place in the public realm. To be sure, such an 'aristocratic' form of government would spell the end of general suffrage as we understand it today.

Those who were not sufficiently interested in public business to join in fully would simply be left out.

On Revolution was published in 1963. Seven years later, after a period which saw intense political activity in America in which Arendt was deeply interested, she repeated in almost identical terms her hopes for the replacement of parliamentary government by this council system, and of universal representation by a "true political elite" of those who wished to participate. It is clear, therefore, that these must be regarded as serious and considered views on Arendt's part, and the problems they raise, in terms of both democratic elitism and of utopian irresponsibility, must be confronted.

As far as the problem of democracy versus elitism is concerned, Arendt's ideal of the council system may be said to represent a partial reconciliation of the two conflicting sides of her thought. Her ideal of participatory democracy is in principle open to absolutely everyone; but as a matter of fact, only the natural political elite will concern themselves with politics and run it as they please. What is *not* clear is whether she expects members of this new political elite to be equally distributed among all social classes (as her account of the revolutionary councils would suggest) or whether, in accordance with her own theories, she expects them to be members of those classes who are furthest from labour and the dispositions it fosters.

But if the council idea provides a reconciliation of sorts between her democratic and elitist aspects, it makes ten times more obvious than before the uneasy relation between utopianism and pragmatism in her thought. If the council system is intended as a serious suggestion for political reform (and the tone in which Arendt wrote about it makes it impossible to regard it as anything else), then objections and difficulties crowd in upon it, objections to which Arendt seems to have devoted no attention at all. It is, to say the least, unfair of her to accuse the student left of leaving their slogan of "participatory democracy" at a "declamatory stage," whenher own proposals are so completely undefended.

One obvious problem concerns what her councils would actually *do*. Within them, citizens are to concern themselves with public affairs—but one of the points on which Arendt is most insistent, throughout her writings, is that politics is something separate and distinct from administration, the management of social and economic affairs, the organization of the welfare of the people. She remarks in *On Revolution* that "the fatal mistake of the councils" that have sprung up in revolutions "has always been that they themselves did not distinguish clearly between participation in public affairs and administration or management of things in the public interest." Similarly, she denies that it is the business of men in politics to represent either interests (as British and American parties and pressure groups do) or ideologies (after the manner of the continental parties).

All sorts of objections suggest themselves. Where is the line between politics and administration to be drawn? Along the lines of the distinction between ministers and civil servants in Britain? But, after all, according to Arendt most of the so-called politics of a country like Britain is not politics at all, but national housekeeping. What *are* the new political elite to concern themselves with? And above all, while they are exercising their new-found freedom of action, who is to carry on the ordinary business of government, the management of the economy, and the representation of interests? What is to become of the interests and welfare of those who do not choose to enter the public arena, perhaps because they are too old, too ill, overburdened with work, or too inarticulate? Perhaps even more crucial, what are the political elite to live on? For if they are paid salaries, they will surely turn into professional politicians, while if they are not, only students, the rich, and the unemployed will be able to join in.

The objections that can be raised against Arendt's council system are exasperatingly obvious. What is baffling is not only that she should have made so little attempt to answer any of them, but also that she should have thought such a utopian system obviously preferable to the system of representative democracy existing, for instance, in America. For although she had suggested in *On Revolution* that the spirit of political action that animated the Founding Fathers had been lost even in America itself, she recognised the political upheavals and student movements of the 1960s as a resurgence of authentic political action. The generation of the Civil Rights Movement and the anti-Vietnam war demonstrations seemed to her to have rediscovered "what the eighteenth century had called 'public happiness'," the determination to act and change things, and the joy that comes from action. Is there, we might ask, anything fundamentally wrong with a political system in which such action can not only take place, but succeed?

Arendt's thought is baffling. It is baffling that a thinker of such intellectual power should be so inconsistent; that a woman with such a profound sense of the worth of every human being (and, moreover, one who had meditated deeply on totalitarianism and genocide) should be so elitist; that an observer of politics who insisted so strongly upon responding to events as they happen, and upon preferring common sense to theories, should put forward such a wildly utopian political scheme. There are no simple explanations for these lapses, but I think that it may perhaps help us to understand how Arendt came to fall into them if we reflect a little upon one of her comments on the American student movement.

Having been asked by an interviewer for her views on the student movement, Arendt praised its rediscovery of the joys of action, but recognised that it was in danger of collapsing into ideological fanaticism and destructiveness. She went on, however:

> The good things in history are usually of very short duration, but afterward have a decisive influence on what happens over long periods of time. Just consider how short the true classical period in Greece was, and that we are in effect still nourished by it today.

Perhaps this (thoroughly existentialist) insight into the fundamental significance of rare events may help us to understand a little better both the distortions and the strengths of Arendt's political thought.

First of all, Arendt's remark illustrates the sense which possessed her throughout her thinking of the *fragility* of the good things in human life. And even more fragile and easily destroyed than the great works of man's hands are the great deeds of which they are capable. Again and again she stressed that the significant points in human history are rare, unpredictable, easily destroyed, and easily forgotten. It was this sense of the precariousness and fragility of human greatness that led her to take a view of history and politics utterly opposed to that of the social scientists. It led her also to watch out for and to celebrate gladly contemporary instances of significant action, whether in Hungary in 1956 or in America in the 1960s. And it was surely this same sense of the desperate fragility of action that made her cling to the council system, that chimerical scheme for institutionalising action—although, in view of her remarks about the rapid degeneration of human things, she must surely have realised that such councils would quickly degenerate also. (Once again, she reminds us of Rousseau's combination of a chimerical determination to institutionalise the General Will, and a bitter awareness that any possible state would quickly become corrupt.)

However, if it was her sense of the rarity and fragility of great deeds that led her to desperately utopian schemes for institutionalising greatness, the same insight should surely have led her to make a crucial distinction that is sadly lacking in her thought. The distinction is that between what one may call *normal* politics and *extraordinary* politics, and it is unfortunate that the same concern for rare events that gave her unparalleled insight into extraordinary politics should have led her to overlook normal politics altogether. Her theory of politics as the unexpected, unpredictable actions of a few free men is an excellent account of what happens in extraordinary political situations. Not only in revolutions, but also in less dramatic cases of extraordinary politics, from the Civil Rights Movement to the ecological movements active at present, it is certainly true that a few people, caring more for public affairs than for their private interests, *do* take upon themselves the burden of action, *do* display courage, *do* create a public space and show themselves to be a self-constituted elite. It is certainly true that such extraordinary politics is the concern of the few. It may well even be true that those few tend not to be engaged in productive labour (for a variety of reasons which need not include Arendt's theories about the baseness of the labouring mentality). What is surely crucial, however, is to recognise that extraordinary politics of this kind, with the informality, unpredicatability, pure political passion, and elitism that are inseparable from it, is something exceptional and can never be a complete substitute for the more mundane politics of interests which Arendt despises.Attempts to institutionalise spontaneity, like attempts to make revolution permanent, are self-defeating. All that can be done by way of institutionalising extraordinary politics is to establish those rights of freedom of speech, publication, and assembly that allow citizens to engage, if they so choose, in this kind of action alongside the ordinary, mundane politics of national housekeeping.

By the time that Arendt was writing about the student movement, it ought surely to have been obvious that the Western democracies *do* provide spaces for political action for any citizens who care to take advantage of them. Besides defending his interests through the machinery of voting and party government, a citizen can if he chooses join with others to create a new political space and start a new political process, which may (like the anti-Vietnam war demonstrations) have remarkable results. Why did Arendt not recognise this? Why did she continue to insist that the representative system ought to be replaced by an obviously utopian attempt at institutionalising extraordinary politics? Only a conjectural answer can be given to this question, but I suspect that there are two reasons. In the first place, her extreme preference for the extraordinary, for those "good things in history" which are usually "of short duration," blinded her to the solid virtues of the ordinary politics of interests. Second, she continued to interpret politics in America in the 1960s, to some extent, in terms of an inherited theory of mass society and its political dangers. As we saw earlier, she had never subscribed to this theory without qualification, but it left her with a residual

fear of representative democracy, which seems to have made impossible for her a truly realistic assessment of the strengths of the American political system.

It is ironic that there should be this element of inflexibility in her thought in view of her own theories about the nature of thinking. We have quoted her remarks on the short duration of the good things in history in order to explain her concentration on extraordinary rather than ordinary politics, but the same passage can also serve us as a guide to what, by her account, is the point of political thinking—not to solve abstract problems, but to reflect upon truly significant political events. As she remarked in the course of a profound discussion of this question in the "Preface" to **Between Past and Future**:

> my assumption is that thought itself arises out of incidents of living experience and must remain bound to them as the only guideposts by which to take its bearings.

The paradox here is that thought always lags behind actions and events. In her early attempts to make sense of her desperate experience of the modern world, Arendt had denied the deterministic ideologies and had asserted that every man is a new beginning, and the spontaneous, unforeseeable action is the human capacity par excellence. When, against all expectation, the Hungarian Revolution broke out, it was at one and the same time a confirmation of her view of man, a new starting point upon which to base new thinking—*and* an event that rendered much of her previous theory obsolete. The same Hungarian rising which confirmed her belief in the capacity of men for spontaneous political action, disproved her theories of the effect on man of labour and of totalitarian rule. Similarly, the American student movements of the 1960s, while confirming her views about the power which citizens in action can generate and the joys they can find in such action, disproved her belief that the United States had lost its revolutionary spirit and thatmodern representative democracy was a degenerate political system which ought to be replaced by councils.

It is perhaps in the light of such reflections that we should consider Arendt's inconsistencies: for much (if not all) of her inconsistency should surely be seen as the breaks between different strata of theory, laid down in the wake of different political experiences. In particular, the political changes of her time led her from a deep distrust of the modern masses (entirely justified in view of her experiences as a Jew in Germany), complemented by the dream of an elitist utopia, toward a greatly increased faith in the people and their political capacities, and a greater willingness to see political action as something that happens in the present, not just in the utopian past. This shift was by no means complete, as we have seen. Arendt continued to the end to talk in terms of mass society, even when this involved impossible distinctions between the people and the masses; while her notion of the council system seems an uneasy halfway house between the pure utopianism of **The Human Condition** and a fully realistic recognition of the spaces for political action that are available to the citizens of modern liberal states.

Her work remained flawed, in other words, because, like any writer, she could not remain completely true to her own principle of rethinking everything in the wake of each new event. While her inconsistencies need to be recognised, however, it is important not to make too much of these defects in her thought. For much of the worth of her thinking lies precisely in the qualities that led her into inconsistency: on the one hand, her responsiveness to the new and unexpected in politics, and on the other, her unceasing endeavour to make sense of the world, to "think what we are doing."

Walter Laqueur (essay date March 1979)

SOURCE: "Re-reading Hannah Arendt," in *Encounter*, Vol. LII, No. 3, March, 1979, pp. 73-79.

[*In the essay below, Laqueur addresses the questions of why Arendt wrote* Eichmann in Jerusalem, *why it provoked controversy, and "whether, in fact, she was misunderstood and injustice done to her."*]

Few books in living memory have stirred up more bitter controversy than Hannah Arendt's **Eichmann in Jerusalem,** published in 1964. The controversy still continues as the introduction to a recent collection of Mrs Arendt's "Jewish" essays shows [**The Jew as Pariah**], albeit without the acrimony of the earlier debate. The editor clearly believes that Mrs Arendt was misunderstood by her critics. The republication of these essays inevitably raises the question what made Mrs Arendt write the book, what it was that provoked so much criticism and whether, in fact, she was misunderstood and injustice done to her.

Hannah Arendt, thirty-five years of age at the time, arrived in the United States in 1941, having escaped from France. Her main intellectual interests had been philosophy and modern literature. She had written a doctoral dissertation on the concept of love in the work of St Augustine; her first articles, published in pre-Hitler Germany, were on Rilke's *Duino Elegies* and onKierkegaard. She belonged to a generation and a milieu that was basically unpolitical but which had developed a passionate interest in politics—in the widest sense—following Hitler's rise to power and the outbreak of the Second World War. Soon after her arrival in the United States she began to publish articles, first in New York's German-language weekly *Der Aufbau*, later in other periodicals. Her early journalistic work in the USA has been almost entirely ne-

glected (or forgotten) yet it provides essential clues to the genesis of the book that created such a furore two decades later.

What emerged from these articles was that Hannah Arendt always had doubts about Zionism and that gradually she came to believe that Herzl had been a crackpot; that Zionism was a chauvinistic, fanatical and hysterical phenomenon, and that it had never been a popular movement. At the same time she insisted on the establishment of a Jewish army to fight Nazism "for the glory and the honour of the Jewish people"— this was the theme of her very first article in the United States and of many that were to follow. Her demand was based on something like a neo-Bundist ideology. An army is usually the function of a state—except perhaps in the case of Prussia, where according to an old saying, the state was a mere appendage of the army. But since Hannah Arendt did not want a state for the Jews, her demand for an army was curious, to say the least. She was at this time very much preoccupied with the fate of the Jews in Europe and, above all, with Jewish resistance. Thus a report published in *Aufbau* about the "*Musterghetto* Theresienstadt" provided an occasion to develop a theory to explain Nazi policy towards the Jews. Jews are tolerated, and sometimes even protected, where their presence will create anti-Semitism among the local population; they will be deported from regions which are not anti-Semitic. Jews are deported from areas where their very presence could lead to resistance. ("If Mrs Mueller in Germany sees that her neighbour, Mrs Schmidt, behaves decently to Mrs Cohn, she knows that she must not be afraid of Mrs Schmidt—she may even talk openly to Mrs Schmidt.") An ingenious theory no doubt—but quite wrong. On another occasion, writing on the "part of the Jewish partisans in the European uprising", Hannah Arendt noted that the European Jews were not doomed: the Jews of Europe no longer faced a separate fate if they refused to accept it. (*"Die Gesetzmaessigkeiten des fuedischen Sonderschicksals verloren immer ihre Gueltigkeit wenn Juden sich weigerten, es als Schicksal zu akzeptieren."*) Or to put it into more simple language: The Jews did not have to die if they did not want to die. A small minority of Jewish millionaires and scoundrels had acted as traitors, but a very substantial part of the people had chosen the road of armed struggle. She wrote about a hundred thousand Jewish partisans in Poland, ten thousand in France—fighting the Nazis in the streets, fields, and forests. . . .

Even before the War ended Hannah Arendt gave her mind to the question of guilt, noting that the number of those responsible and guilty among the Germans was relatively small. Hence the conclusion that there was no political method for dealing with German mass crimes; "where all are guilty, nobody in the last analysis can be judged." Even in a murder camp, Mrs Arendt noted, everyone, whether directly active or not, was forced to take part in one way or another in the workings of the machine—"that is the horrible thing."

This in brief outline was the origin of the concept of "the Banality of Evil." (I recently came across it in Joseph Conrad's preface to *Under Western Eyes,* written well before the First World War; but it may have been used before.)

Hannah Arendt was fearful of the great opportunities that would exist in Europe after the War for the re-emergence of an international fascist organisation. The arch evil of our time had been defeated but not completely eradicated—except in the areas under immediate Russian influence, where the "forces of yesterday" had been destroyed once and forever.

I have concentrated on the issues that have a direct bearing on the controversy of the early 1960s. A reading of Hannah Arendt's political journalism shows that she was more often wrong than right both in her analysis and predictions. There was always an inclination on her part to exaggerate as well as to generalise and to be original on the basis of a slender factual basis. She had considerable intelligence but little common sense and apparently no political instinct—she was a philosophical not a political animal.

The case of Theresienstadt is an extreme case in point. The obvious explanation provided in *Aufbau,* that of a *Musterghetto,* was quite right, which is more than can be said about the theories about "selective deportation." Again, the fears of a great revival of fascism after the War are psychologically understandable; but they were not at all borne out by subsequent events. The fact that she had so often been wrong did not ever shake Hannah Arendt's confidence in her own judgment. In one of her very last essays she wrote that "Anti-Communism" was "at the root of all theories in Washington—in sheer ignorance of all pertinent facts. . . ." This from the woman who had been one of the most influential architects of the concept of Totalitarianism, who had explained in *The Burden of our Time* that Nazi Germany and Soviet Russia were "two essentially identical systems." True, Mrs Arendt later retracted this; after the Hungarian revolt in 1956 (which deeply influenced her) she wrote that the closed system of the Soviet Union was no longer "totalitarian" in the strict sense of the term; one of the reasons given was the food supplies sent to the Hungarians, another . . . the flowering of the arts in the Soviet Union! Mrs Arendt had fundamentally exaggerated in 1951, and then again after 1956 without, however, incurring lasting damage either to her self-confidence or to her reputation.

There was a general tendency during the War and indeed for quite a few years after to overrate the importance (and the numerical strength) of Jewish resistance in Europe. The same is true, incidentally, with regard to War-time resistance in general—excepting only Yugoslavia. I have dealt with this topic in a recent study (*Guerrilla*); all that need be said in this context is that resistance was physically possible only in a very few countries. The dramatic reports about tens and hundreds of thousands of *maquis,* Jewish or non-Jewish, were of course sheer fantasy. Thus, seen in retrospect, European Jews did not live up to Mrs Arendt's expectations as fighters for the glory and honour of their people; as a result they were punished, for if they had fought, they (or at least many of them) would have survived; since most of them did not fight, five or six millions were killed. Mrs Arendt found mitigating circumstances for non-Jews—since everyone in a murder-camp was forced to take part in the working of the machine. She did not make such allowances for her fellow Jews.

Hannah Arendt attended the Eichmann trial as a journalist, and her account was published in five instalments in *The New Yorker* magazine in late spring of 1963. It became a *succès de scandale* from the first moment. Some critics were shocked by the medium chosen by Mrs Arendt—a witty weekly, entertaining, frivolous, intellectually pretentious and quite unserious. An investigation into mass murder set out among Peter Arno's cartoons, the advertisements for Cadillacs and Oldsmobiles, Beefeater gin and holidays in Bermuda—a little bit of Holocaust, a little bit of Tiffany and Saks Fifth Avenue—it was quite a remarkable mixture. Others complained about her style, the snide remarks, the flippancy and superciliousness—and its concomitant: the heartlessness. Yet others pointed to the unfortunate tendency on the part of the author throughout her book to use terms that were emotionally highly charged, and to apply a double yardstick.

Thus, when Gideon Hausner (the chief Israeli prosecutor) asked some of the survivors of the death camps why they had not offered armed resistance, Mrs Arendt expressed indignation about cruel and foolish questions of this kind. But her own critique of the Jewish leadership rested precisely on the same basis: Those who did not fight were guilty. Again, any form of contact between Jewish leaders and the Nazis, even when the aim was to make the emigration of Jews possible, or to save lives, was "collaboration" as far as Dr Arendt was concerned. But the term "collaboration" in the context of the Second World War has a certain connotation of which the author was no doubt quite aware. If she believed that Jews should *not* have talked to the Nazis *under any circumstances,* she should have said so. But she did not, and for this reason the indiscriminate use of the term was irresponsible. A German critic was taken aback by the fact that Dr Arendt had singled out two Germans who had resisted—one was the right-wing writer Reck Malleczewen, the other the liberal-existentialist philosopher Karl Jaspers. Reck Malleczewen had died in a concentration camp, but there is no known evidence that Professor Jaspers (although his books were censored and his Jewish wife was in hiding) ever "resisted", in the Arendt-heroical sense, the *Gestapo* state. Why then was he singled out? Because he was Hannah Arendt's teacher in Heidelberg to whom she remained devoted to the end of his life (he died in Basel in 1969).

This little episode is revealing: while in no way central to Hannah Arendt's arguments, it was typical of her approach to history. But it has yet another aspect which, to the best of my knowledge, has not so far been noted: the curious resemblance between master and disciple. Both were philosophers, both felt from time to time obliged to comment on politics, frequently on a high pitch, bordering on excitements and obsessions—from which their philosophical writings were quite free. Thus Jaspers, during the height of the Cold War, emerges as an advocate of West Germany's nuclear rearmament. In the 1960s, on the other hand, he published a treatise (*The Future of Germany*) in which he demonstrated that West Germany was well on the way towards abolishing parliamentary democracy and, to all intents and purposes, to becoming "fascist" again. This book was published in the United States with a preface by Hannah Arendt in which she stated that "politically [this is] the most important book to appear after the Second World War. . . ." Had Hannah Arendt really believed this, she would certainly have published at least an article in the same vein. She did not, which surely suggests that she had reservations. But filial piety nevertheless prevailed over intellectual integrity.

The most detailed and ambitious, but in many respects least effective reply to Hannah Arendt was the late Jacob Robinson's *And the Crooked Shall be Made Straight,* a book of more than 400 pages published in 1965. The late Dr Robinson probably knew all there was to know about the factual background and with his jurist's training he was also an expert on the legal implications of War Crime trials. His technique in the book was that of the lawyer who wishes to discredit a hostile witness by showing that he is not really master of the subject. And so he relentlessly subjected every word of Dr Arendt to critical examination, pointing out that the correct spelling of a certain *SS-Obergruppenfuehrer* should be Hanns (not Hans)—as if mistakes of this kind necessarily disqualified her from commenting on *SS* policy. Dr Robinson's book was a case of overkill; he demonstrated that Dr Arendt had indeed committed many mistakes, partly in view of a cavalier attitude to facts, partly perhaps out of genuine ignorance. She knew, after all, neither Hebrew nor Yiddish, neither Polish nor Russian; and most of the relevant literature was at the time in these languages. She had to rely basically on Professor Raoul Hilberg's book (a book on the Nazis, not on the Jews) and on what she learned during the day-to-day proceedings of the Eichmann trial. But Robinson's book, hastily written, also contained factual mistakes; it failed to tackle important issues; it was inconsistent, claiming at one and the same time that much further study was needed on "collaboration" and that there had been no collaboration and treason at all among the Jews. Above all, Dr Robinson, in the light of his background, training and interests, was quite obviously the wrong person to "refute" Hannah Arendt—immersed in questions of plodding detail, he could not possibly follow her to the rarified heights of abstraction where the moral

philosopher indulges herself in virtuoso turns, but where Dr Robinson would be quite lost.

I should mention in passing my own involuntary involvement in the affair. I had reviewed Dr Robinson's book at the time and had noted its shortcomings. This produced an irate reply from Hannah Arendt, far longer than the original review. It dealt largely with Dr Robinson's book rather than my review which mainly served as a "peg" for her rejoinder. My review had been more moderate than most, and there had been no anger in it. But Mrs Arendt was far from satisfied. She was at the time already something of a cult figure among the New York City intelligentsia. She did not mind being attacked, but she evidently disliked not being taken very seriously as a student of contemporary Jewish history. And so she imputed to the reviewer sinister motives: Mr Laqueur, she implied, was dependent on Dr Robinson, a vassal jumping to the aid of his seigneur. My relations with the late Dr Robinson were neither close, nor (for a variety of reasons) friendly. Hannah Arendt, who did not know me at all, could not possibly know about my relations, if any, with Dr Robinson; and yet she was quite ready to assume the worst, to insinuate and incriminate. Her reaction greatly intrigued me, even though I knew of course that statements made in the heat of polemics should not be taken too seriously nor remembered for too long. Hannah Arendt was certainly at the time in a state of near panic (as her writings show), firmly convinced that the Elders of Zion had conspired to "get her."

Hannah Arendt's main arguments are well known and can be summarised therefore in briefest outline. Eichmann was guilty and deserved to be executed, but he was an idealist in a perverted way. He had no criminal intent; he was basically a normal human being acting under the pressure of a totalitarian régime for which he was not personally responsible. Hence the conclusion that justice was not done in Jerusalem. It was the wrong court condemning him for the wrong reasons. He should have been hanged as *hostis generis humani;* rather than *hostis Judaeorum*. Dr Arendt attributed to this distinction enormous importance; I failed to see the crucial significance of this issue at the time, and I am afraid I have not become any wiser in the years between. Far more important are the charges she made against Jewish leaders and their responsibility for the catastrophe. Without their active collaboration ("mere compliance would not have been enough") the destruction of so many millions of Jews would not have been possible—"there would have been either complete chaos or an impossibly severe drain on German manpower." The "ghetto police", Mrs Arendt reported, was an instrument in the hands of the murderers; the actual work of killing in the extermination centres was usually in the hands of Jewish commandos, who also dug the graves and extinguished the traces of mass murder, and had built the gas chambers in the first place. Thus Jewish cooperation put an end to the clear-cut division (in Camus' phrase) between "victims and executioners." There was a moral collapse among the victims. The leadership, almost without exception, cooperated in one way or another, for one reason or another, with the Nazis. If the Jewish people had been unorganised and leaderless, there would have been chaos, and plenty of misery, but the total number of victims would hardly have been between five and six million. Hence the conclusion that this role of the Jewish leaders in the destruction of their own people is undoubtedly the darkest chapter of the whole dark story.

Some of these allegations are true; some are wrong; most are only half true. There is no reason to assume that if the Jewish people had been "leaderless", the Nazis would have found the killing more difficult or even impossible. It has frequently been pointed out that the extermination proceeded quite smoothly even where there were no "Jewish Councils"—or where the "Jewish Councils" were not required to collaborate with the Nazis in the preparation for the final solution, *die Endlösung*. Nor is it true that the division between executioners and victims was obliterated. But even if resistance would not have meant survival, this still leaves the painful issue of "Jewish appeasement."

Hannah Arendt's condemnation of appeasement is basically correct as a rule of political behaviour when dealing with enemies of this kind. It is inexplicable how Dr Robinson could possibly write in 1965 that "there is no evidence that the motivation in accepting and maintaining membership in the *Judenraete* was not generally honourable." There was a great deal of such evidence. But there was no conspiracy of silence, no deliberate attempt to whitewash villains or to make heroes out of doubtful characters—as Mrs Arendt seems to have believed: she saw herself, no doubt, as a champion of truth which had been suppressed too long. There was a certain reluctance to deal systematically with the most tragic subject of all—for the very same reason that there has been reluctance in every European country (including the neutral ones)—to come to terms with the many manifestations of "collaboration" in the Nazi era. The Jewish case was different, to be sure, because Frenchmen or Dutchmen had a certain freedom of choice. They did not *have* to collaborate. (A recent French writer notes, *"le collaborationisme n'était pas une fatalité. Un Louis Marin ou un Louis Vallon adhéraient en 1939 aux mêmes partis qu'un Philippe Henriot ou un Marcel Déat . . ."*) The Jews did not have to collaborate either; but the alternative was considerably more unpleasant.

There had been books and articles, countless autobiographies and memoirs on the "Jewish Councils" in Poland (by Philip Friedman and others); in Holland (by Abel Herzberg and others); in Theresienstadt (by H. G. Adler); and elsewhere. Professor Hilberg's book, which had many harsh things to say about the Jewish reaction, had already appeared; and it was Hannah Arendt's main source. The facts were known but they had not fully registered (even though, as in the famous Kastner

trial, the basic issues had been discussed). If many of the facts referred to in Hannah Arendt's book had been known for a long time, what made so many people so angry about *Eichmann in Jerusalem*? And why, then, did the book become a *cause célébre*?

Her series of articles, and the book that subsequently emerged were of course far more widely read than the scholarly articles or monographs dealing with the same subject. The scholars (among whom there were, and are, quite a few not less extreme than Hannah Arendt in their condemnation of collaboration) were more cautious in stating their conclusions, not because they were "afraid", but because they were more aware of the complexity of the situation; the horrendous pressures under which the "Jewish Councils" had been acting. Hannah Arendt's book on the other hand, was impressionistic and subjective; there was her usual tendency towards exaggeration. She attacked without discrimination the *entire* Jewish leadership in Europe and made some exceedingly silly remarks which she probably later regretted (the reference to Leo Baeck as the "Jewish Fuehrer"—without quotation remarks). She attacked Zionists for their collaboration with the Nazis (referring to the organisation of illegal immigration) and also because of certain ideological similarities, real or imaginary. Thus she antagonised all Zionists and pro-Zionists.

> **The Eichmann controversy did not do any lasting harm to Hannah Arendt's reputation. On the contrary, at the time of her death she was widely thought to be one of the most original and influential of thinkers.**
>
> *—Walter Laqueur*

But this, again, does not explain the vehement reactions triggered off by her book. The most telling criticism came from non-Zionists (such as Eva Reichmann) or anti-Zionists, or Zionists such as Ernst Simon, Martin Buber and Gershom Scholem who had belonged to *Brith Shalom* which stood for Arab-Jewish collaboration and which had been actively supported by Hannah Arendt. Her attitude towards Zionism was by no means as consistent as commonly believed: while she supported *Ichud,* she also had sympathies for Menachem Begin's *Irgun Zyai Leumi,* which (in her view) attracted the most decent and idealist elements. This apparent paradox is not difficult to explain. Dr Arendt hated "conciliators" and "appeasers" (such as Chaim Weizmann); she always had a weakness for those who fought and resisted. She belonged to those intellectuals about whom it has been said that *ils n'aiment que les trains qui partent*—the direction of the departure is always a secondary consideration.

Hannah Arendt was bitterly attacked precisely because she was held in such high esteem by many of her contemporaries. This, in a way, was quite unfair; for she had, after all, not made her name as a contemporary historian. She had moved very far from her national Jewish enthusiasm of 1942-43, but no one expected that she would want deliberately and unnecessarily to cause offence and pain. Hannah Arendt's attitude towards her people (her personal "Jewish problem") was complex; and there is little doubt that this had a bearing on the writing of this book. (Sooner or later, someone more familiar with this aspect than the present writer will deal with this element in the affair.)

Hannah Arendt was mainly attacked not for *what* she said, but for *how* she said it. She was at once highly intelligent and exceedingly insensitive. She would not, or could not, discriminate, see the nuances, and this in a context in which nuances were all-important. She certainly had the intellectual equipment to deal with the subject: but not the temperament. She was one of the cleverest writers of her generation; but the Holocaust is a subject in which cleverness can be a positive disadvantage. Her memory was selective: when she wrote about Eichmann, she had forgottenalmost all she had ever written about the "human condition" in a Totalitarian State. The Holocaust is a subject that has to be confronted in a spirit of humility; whatever Mrs Arendt's many virtues, humility was not among them. "Judge not, that ye be not judged"— but Hannah Arendt loved to judge, and was at her most effective in the role of *magister humanitatis,* invoking moral pathos. And thus she rushed in where wiser men and women feared to tread, writing about extreme situations which she in her life had never experienced, an intellectual by temperament always inclined to overstatement, most at ease when dealing with abstractions, at her weakest when analysing real people in concrete situations. The constellation was as unfortunate as the result predictable.

The Eichmann controversy did not do any lasting harm to Hannah Arendt's reputation. On the contrary, at the time of her death (in 1975) she was widely thought to be one of the most original and influential of thinkers. She was an erudite and brilliant woman; she wrote well; her ideas appealed to Left and Right alike—an almost unique case of the time. Even her confusion seemed attractive in the Manhattan of the 1960s. The fact that her political comments and her historical *obiter dicta* were often wrong was quite immaterial. One can easily think of professional politicians being wrong most of the time; they seem not to be worse off as a result; in politics it is far more damaging to be right at the wrong time.

Nor should it be forgotten that she had made her name as a political philosopher, not as a political journalist. True, Hannah

Arendt's political philosophy has also baffled admirers and critics alike. One of them (a highly sympathetic commentator) admitted that most of what she had written about Totalitarianism had been wrong, but still her book was a "considerable work of art, vivid and enthralling, intensely reflective. Even when it fails as history it succeeds as reflection. . . ." It is certainly true that when *The Origins of Totalitarianism* appeared it was more enthusiastically welcomed by literary figures than by students of history and politics.

The romantic streak in Hannah Arendt has been noted by many. Perhaps *Eichmann in Jerusalem* too should be treated aesthetically rather than as historical analysis? If so, it may well remain one of the few works of art inspired by that trial.

There still is a last paradox: the relationship between the political philosopher and the political journalist. Is a political philosopher reliable who can be trusted only on the level of abstraction? I have been assured that there is only a tenuous link between these two activities. A great art historian is not necessarily the best expert to establish the provenance or authenticity of a painting.

It has been argued—(by Leni Yahil among others) that it was the merit of Hannah Arendt's book to provide fresh impetus to the study of the *Judenrat* phenomenon and, more generally speaking, the issue of "collaboration." This is, I believe, only partially correct. Even before *Eichmann in Jerusalem* appeared there had been a great deal of comment on the subject. Solomon Bloom had written a memorable essay on Rumkovski and the Lodz Ghetto as far back as 1949; Friedmann had written on Gens (of the Vilna Ghetto) and Merin; N. Blumenthal on Bialistok; and there were many more studies both for the general public and of a more specialised character. Two of the most important books on the "Jewish Councils" appeared in 1965 and 1972 respectively (Presser's*Ondergang* and I. Trunk's *Judenrat*). During the last fifteen years there have been more specialised studies on the "Jewish Councils" in Holland, in Hungary (Braham), in Theresienstadt (L. Rothkirchen) and, above all, in Poland. Following the publication of the Czerniakov diaries, there has been much illuminating comment on the *Judenrat* phenomenon. Some writers have recently tried to draw an interim balance, comparing the findings of various studies. Most of this work, I suggest, would have been done in any case; and thus the impact of the "controversy" consists mainly in having compelled her contemporaries to rethink the whole issue of Jewish collaboration and resistance during the Second World War.

I doubt whether anyone basically changed his views as a result. There are some (e.g. Dvorzhetzki and Eisenbach) who see the *Judenrat* virtually without exception in a negative light. N. Blumenthal in his investigation of the Lublin *Judenrat* reaches the conclusion that not all were "criminals and traitors", but that even those who were not, objectively served as "Nazi tools." Others (such as Z. A. Braun, Weiss, and Kaplinski) maintain that a wholesale condemnation of the *Judenrat* distorts history. They argue that there were enormous differences between conditions in one ghetto and another, that in a few the *Judenrat* closely collaborated with the resistance, that in some (perhaps twenty per cent according to Trunk) the German orders were carried out with excessive zeal and no attempt was made to circumvent and sabotage them; and that in most places the general strategy was to gain time. Yehuda Bauer has noted that if the advancing Red Army had reached Lodz a few months earlier, then Rumkovski, the "King" of the local ghetto, would have entered the annals of Jewish history as a hero, and not as a traitor. It is also true that one has to differentiate between the period before the deportations started (when the *Judenrat* engaged in the administration of the ghetto) and the time thereafter when Jewish leaders actively participated in the selection of the victims who were to be sent to the extermination camps.

So it is that fifteen years after the "Arendt controversy" we are no nearer to a consensus than before, and it is quite likely that there never will be agreement; partly because (as has been noted) conditions varied so much from place to place, partly also because there are genuine differences of opinion with regard to what could have been expected from Jewish communities facing the Nazi terror machine. If in many cases "mitigating circumstances" can be found—even if some leaders in fact behaved heroically—the *Judenrat* phenomenon, as a whole, has acquired a negative connotation; and rightly so. From the moment that the "Jewish Councils" were used by the Nazis to help in the "Final Solution", their action became indefensible. True, it can always be argued that they acted to prevent worse from happening: but this argument has been heard too often.

Why was there so little resistance? The question deeply bothered Hannah Arendt and most contemporaries. The answer is in many ways obvious. Given the isolation of the Jews, the demographic structure of the Jewish communities, the lack of psychological and organisational preparation, the hostility of the non-Jewish population in Eastern Europe, the lack of arms, the unsuitability of the surrounding terrain, there could not have been much resistance—certainly not successful resistance.

But could there have been more resistance than there was? And why did Jews let themselves beslaughtered like sheep? Hannah Arendt was doubly shocked—partly because during the War she had imagined that there *had* been a great deal of resistance—only to find out later that this had not been the case. But she was also by temperament one of the intellectuals who had great admiration for men or women of action (preferably intellectuals who were also doers—such as Rosa Luxemburg—even if the results were disastrous). The meek-

ness of the Jews seemed intolerable in retrospect. She looked for a scapegoat, and she found it in the "Jewish leadership."

Sixty years before Hannah Arendt published her book, the greatest modern Hebrew poet, after the Kishinev pogrom (1903), wrote his *Ba'ir Ha'hariga* (In the City of Slaughter):

> Great is the sorrow and great is the shame—and which
> of the two is greater, answer thou, O son of man. . . .
> The grandsons of the Maccabeans—they ran like
> mice, they hid themselves like bed-bugs and died the
> death of dogs wherever found.

Bialik's indictment was far stronger than Hannah Arendt's, but there were no irate reviews, no protests, no refutations. His poem, unlike Hannah Arendt's book, influenced a whole generation.

Was it because Arendt's book, pretending to be an objective historical account, contained much that was unfair or untrue? I do not think that this was the main reason, for her book also contained much that was true. His contemporaries felt that Hayyim Nahman Bialik's attack was born out of agony. Hannah Arendt's reproaches were those of an outsider, lacking identification; they were almost inhumanly cold and they were based on a profound ignorance of the historical realities. They were never adequately reflected in her philosophical abstractions, and were, in part at least, rooted in an aesthetical approach. The situation was not comparable to the Irish 1916 Easter Rising which William Butler Yeats welcomed for its "terrible beauty." There was no beauty in the Holocaust and no real hope in desperate Jewish convulsions. A tragic uprising like the Warsaw Ghetto revolt was not for the living but a gesture for posterity.

Berel Lang (essay date Summer 1988)

SOURCE: "Hannah Arendt and the Politics of Evil," in *Judaism,* Vol. 37, No. 3, Summer, 1988, pp. 264-75.

[*In the following essay, Lang explains how the relation between personal conscience or religious commitment and public or civic life informs Arendt's conception of modern totalitarianism.*]

In the 20th century the position of the German Jewish community was to be one of unusual complexity, of powerful ironies and, ultimately, of great disruption and pain. On the one hand, the ideals nourished by the Enlightenment, emerging in the last part of the 18th Century, and represented in Germany by such figures as Kant, Lessing, and Goethe, had spoken eloquently about the dignity of man, about the principles of civic equality and the inalienable rights shared by all persons. The hopeful statements of these ideals, and the political changes which accompanied them, produced a strong sense of identification on the part of German Jews in the life of their country. By the beginning of the 20th Century, and still more obviously by the time of the first World War, German Jews had a tradition of actively contributing to German culture—in literatureand the arts, in the natural and social sciences, in politics. If one extends this brief survey to German as a language and not only to Germany as a political entity, the achievements loom even larger—since we would make room, then, as the present century unfolded, also for the Vienna of Freud and the Prague of Franz Kafka.

And yet, of course, notwithstanding the principles announced by the Enlightenment, despite the achievements of the German-Jewish community and the will of many of its members to identify themselves as Germans, the nation and the culture resisted their integration, first in small ways, and then much more purposefully. Why this process went in the direction it did is not the focus of the discussion here, except for the fact that *its* background is also responsible for the extraordinary ambivalence—cultural, religious, ideological, psychological—which came to effect the 20th century German Jewish community—and then, too, the thought of Hannah Arendt, which is to be considered here. Moses Mendelssohn, the most prominent Jewish spokesman for the German Enlightenment, answered the question of how the Jews of Germany could live up to ideals of emancipation and yet remain Jews, by endorsing the recommendation that they should attempt to be Jews in their homes and Germans in the street. But this was more easily said than done—as we recall now in the common parody of the statement which asserted that the Jews turned out to be Germans in their homes and Jews only in the street (that is, in the eyes of the Germans). This parody is something of an exaggeration, no doubt, but there was enough truth in it to attest to the continuing ambiguity between the public and the private lives of the Jews of Germany. To be sure, the strains between the public and the private, between civic life and private conscience, have been problems in the 20th century not only for Judaism but for other religions as well—(and among Jews elsewhere, too, not only for those in Germany). But in an age when religious identity of every kind would be challenged, there was, for the Jew, the additional problem of discovering what public role he would be *allowed* even if he were willing to give up his private or religious commitments. The question of the relation between personal conscience or religious commitment, on the one hand, and a public or civic life, on the other, was, we shall see, a constant preoccupation of Hannah Arendt; it was also a factor in her conception of modern totalitarianism which was the basis for her view of what is referred to here as the "politics of evil."

There is perhaps no more pointed example of the conflicting alternatives between a public and a private self as they appeared to 20th century German Jewry than in the family history of one of its most intriguing and best-known offspring, Gershom Scholem, who, in his writings about Jewish mysticism, would substantially alter the understanding of Jewish religious history. Like in the story recited in the Passover Hagaddah, there were in the Scholem household, located in middle-class Berlin at the turn of the century, four sons. Of these, Gershom was the youngest. Early in his life and almost entirely on his own initiative, Gershom identified himself with the Jewish tradition, undertook to study Hebrew and the classical texts, and became a Zionist. For such non-conformity, his father, when Gershom was about 20, forced him to leave the family home and cut off relations with him (these relations were later, but only shakily, restored). Gershom emigrated to Palestine in 1923, took a position in the National Library and then in the newly-founded Hebrew University—and the rest of his story is known. Gershom's eldest brother had before this joined the family printing business and, in the process of becoming a man of affairs, had also become an ardent German patriot. After the Nazis took power, in 1938, he emigrated to Australia—but he would, thirty years later and even after everything that had occurred in theintervening years, *still* describe himself as a German nationalist. The next-to-eldest brother more or less accepted the values of the Scholem parents themselves: conservative politically and liberal with respect to Judaism, stopping just short of full assimilation. The third brother, Werner, who was closest in age to Gershom, chose to join the Communist Party and was eventually elected to the Reichstag as a deputy of the Party. In his arguments with Gershom the Zionist, it was Werner's view that the so-called Jewish Question was, in fact, a human question—that the status of the Jews in Germany (indeed, of Jews any place in the world) was an issue not of maintaining Jewish identity, but of achieving universal social justice. This brother was killed by the Nazis in Buchenwald in 1940. Four brothers—four very different conceptions of Jewish identity and four different destinies—in the face of what had been, after all, a single and common starting point.

I would add to this brief family survey a reference to two other items that Gershom Scholem himself notes in his autobiography. The first of these is an incident that he relates. At the age of fourteen, he received the gift of a photograph of Theodore Herzl from his non- or (in the case of his father) anti-Zionist parents. There was for him, first, the oddity of this gift as it came to him from them—it was his parents' Christmas gift to him. The second item is his report that, to the best of his knowledge, despite his father's emphasis on the identity of German Jews as Germans and despite his father's standing in the business community which brought him many acquaintances in the sociable city of Berlin—never once had a non-Jew entered the family home. So much, one might say, for the hope that the Jews might appear to the *Germans* as Germans.

Hannah Arendt's family history, which began in Kant's city of Königsberg, was not as dramatic or as symptomatic as Scholem's—although, since the names of Hannah Arendt and Gershom Scholem have now been mentioned together, this brief parenthesis of social history should also be completed after a sharp exchange of letters between them following the publication of Arendt's book on the Eichmann trial. Scholem, who had been a friend of Arendt's, never spoke to her again.

I mention these anecdotes instead of moving directly to discuss the "politics of evil" both for themselves and also for a purpose—and this is to suggest that Arendt's reflections on the modern history of evil involve much the same ambivalence (verging at times on inconsistency) that we find in the details of her history and in many of her writings but, especially, those that have Judaism and Zionism as their subjects. Arendt is, it seems to me, basically an ironical writer, continually asserting that what seems to be the case often turns out to be exactly its opposite, that even what appears to be the most monstrous evil may, in fact, be something else. As for many passionate ironists, this tendency often leaves both her and her readers, when we ask about her basic commitments, in a quandary. It is not unusual that we should find the life or biography of a philosopher embodied in his or her thinking—and, in many ways, Arendt seems, in her writing as well as in her life, to personify the history—in a sense, also the end—of German Jewry. She would never, *did never,* question or doubt her identification as a Jew. But how to translate that identification into an *identity* was constantly weighted for her with ambiguities; these do not resolve themselves even now when we are in a position to reflect on her life and thought as a whole.

This same tendency to ambiguity and irony plays a central role in Arendt's discussion of what she claims to be the new form which evil assumes in the 20th century, in the new explanations we find there of how evil comes to exist and of how it does its work. To be sure, in one form or other these issues have a long history in religion and philosophy as well as in everyday life—but we can, I believe, discover in Arendt's thinking a coherent and valuable response to such questions. The trail begins here about mid-point in her writings and then extends backward and forward to other of her books. The mid-point I refer to is her report on the trial of Adolf Eichmann—***Eichmann in Jerusalem: A Report on the Banality of Evil***. Arendt's analysis of the Eichmann trial has usually been read and interpreted—and—criticized—as if it were quite independent of her other writings; but it is only by relating this book to those other writings that we can understand her position on the nature—and sometime "banality"—of evil. This does not mean that Arendt's conclusions on this issue are adequate or even that they are consistent—and critics have attacked her on both those counts. But even allowing for such criticism, her account sheds an unusual and valuable light on totalitarianism, a form of political organi-

zation which was, in her view, a unique phenomenon, an invention of the 20th century and, finally, also, a new development in the history of evil. Even the term which she uses to designate that evil—its "banality"—has newly entered the language.

Arendt's report of the trial of Eichmann, a report which appeared in 1963, originally as a series of articles in the *New Yorker* and then, soon afterward, as a volume became a center of controversy as soon as it was published, although it should also be recalled that the strongest reactions to the book were *not* directed at its provocative title. The main protests took issue with a less prominent theme—her discussion of the role, during the Holocaust, of the Jewish communal structures, in particular the Jewish councils or *Judenräte*. It was Arendt's contention that the Nazis were abetted in their design by these Jewish communal organizations—in part by specific decisions which the Councils and their leaders made, in part by the very *existence* of the Councils. By their decisions in response to Nazi dictates—Arendt claimed—the councils, in effect, collaborated with the Nazis; by their very existence, they encouraged passivity and the illusion of hope at a time when what should have been encouraged was precisely the opposite of these.

Arendt was not the first writer to make these charges, but she was undoubtedly the most influential one to have done so, and her accusation gained in emphasis by its appearance in connection with the trial of a man whose inculpation in the events of the Holocaust was undeniable. The reaction to Arendt's rather brief comments on this topic was proportionately harsh; and it seems clear now, in light of the evidence, that, in the charges she made, Arendt was guilty at least of oversimplification—for example, that what she characterized as the universal reaction of the Jewish communities to the Nazi threat was, in fact, far from uniform. But the inadequacy of her account on this point is less relevant for the moment than the fact that her position here was part of a more general view that she held of the "politics of evil"—a view which attempted to describe what happened to the individual and his moral character—and to communities—under the weight of totalitarianism. In order to see *this* development, however, we have to turn to the more central theme of Arendt's book on the Eichmann trial—that is, to her conception of the "banality of evil" as she applied that phrase to Eichmann and, by implication, to many others.

About this theme of her book, too, the reaction to Arendt's formulation was severe—and here, also, it seems she invited this reaction. To describe the role of a central figure in the Holocaust as banal seems unavoidably to diminish both the enormity of what occurred in the Holocaust itself and the culpability of those responsible for it. Arendt did not, as she herself pointed out, agree with these implications—but she was obviously willing to risk them, and the reason for this was the unusual conception of evil that she located in the person and actions of Eichmann.

One thing which the trial in Jerusalem had made quite clear, in Arendt's opinion, was what Eichmann was *not*. If we ordinarily mean by evil the acts of a person who, like Iago in Shakespeare's *Othello,* moves at every turn to cause suffering and then, having succeeded, takes pleasure in that result, someone who commits himself to evil as a principle—this was not the Eichmann who was revealed at his trial, even on the strongest arguments of the prosecution, The charge that evil had been chosen knowingly, chosen for the sake of evil itself, simply did not match up with the acts of the man in the glass booth in Jerusalem, even after taking into account all of the evidence against him. Here was a man who repeatedly insisted that the scenes which he observed in his trips to the camps of the East were repugnant to him; who claimed— evidently with the expectation of being believed—that, notwithstanding the terrible history of which he had been part, he, "personally," had nothing against Jews. Here was a man who would cite Kant's Categorical Imperative to justify his own obedience to the order given for the Final Solution: If he had disobeyed those orders, so Eichmann's version of Kant went, every soldier would be justified in disobeying whatever orders he happened to object to.

There are undoubtedly various ways of understanding a person who had done what Eichmann had done (and what he freely admitted to having done) in organizing the deportation of hundreds of thousands of Jews but who would, on the other hand, express the views just mentioned. Arendt's conception of the banality of evil is one such judgment, although here, too, it is important to understand what she means by the phrase and what she does not mean by it. The term "banality" sometimes refers to what is common or commonplace—and readers who interpret the phrase in this way take it to mean that Eichmann had acted "commonly"—that is, not much differently from the way other people would have acted had they been in his place. This interpretation brings Arendt dangerously close to asserting that Eichmann's failings, even if we judge them as crimes, were, after all, only human—that there is, perhaps, a similar potential for evil in every human being and, thus, finally, that there was nothing unusual about Eichmann himself. And *this* conclusion, if it does not absolve Eichmann, certainly diminishes the weight of the charges against him.

But there is an alternate reading of "banality" which, it seems to me, comes closer to Arendt's intention—and which also underlies her conception of the politics of evil. If calling evil "banal" means that a person acts as he does because although as a human being he *might* have thought clearly about what he was doing but did not; that he only echoed disconnected ideas or ideals which he had taken over from others without understanding them; that he did not think enough about what

he was doing to recognize what its consequences would be, or that the so-called principles on which he was choosing to act were self-contradictory; if, in other words, the evil-doer was a "hollow man," emptied of whatever it is that distinguishes human beings as human—*then* the result of this would be the banality, the sheer mechanical thoughtlessness, of theevil-doer.

This, it seems to me, is, indeed, Arendt's judgment of Eichmann who could not, or at least would not, think about what he was doing. He was not, in these terms, irrational or mad—it was, rather, a matter of being non-rational, of looking human but not quite *being* human. The surest evidence of this for Arendt was the fact that Eichmann seemed unable to recognize a connection between himself and other human beings; he could not put himself in the place of others, that act of moral imagination which is a condition for moral judgment of any kind. How else, Arendt argues, could someone see no inconsistency between sending hundreds of thousands of people to their deaths and continuing to believe that he had nothing "personal" against them? Arendt finds this banality epitomized—it is at this point in her book that she first introduces the phrase the "banality of evil"—in Eichmann's last words, uttered only a short time before he was to be hanged. Even at that hour, she emphasizes, he remained the captive of words he had heard but had not thought. In his speech, he praises Germany, the country he had served; Austria, his native land; and Argentina, the country which provided him with a refuge after the war, until he was seized there by the Israeli agents. He would, he says, with a lack of self-consciousness that verges on unconsciousness—"never forget them."

It seems to me that this is about as far as we can go in understanding what Arendt intended by her phrase, the "banality of evil"—although, again, saying this does not mean that no objections can be raised against the view itself. When Arendt asserts that Eichmann was "thoughtless," a "caricature," a "clown" (it is also to these characteristics that she attributes the "banality")—it seems unlikely that anyone reflecting on the Holocaust would ordinarily associate those terms with the world that Eichmann had inhabited. In speaking in this way of Eichmann, Arendt ignores certain important distinctions—and she also, at a deeper level, places unusual weight on the power of thinking or reason itself—as if the capacity to think would suffice, by itself, to prevent the occurrence of evil. Was it only because Eichmann did not know how to think that he did what he did? How much of evil-doing even outside the Holocaust would that explain?

These last questions bring us closer to the "politics of evil" and, indeed, to the problem of evil more generally. Arendt's critics objected to her conception of the "banality of evil" because it seemed to diminish Eichmann's responsibility— and the same objection would apply to a view of evil as the product of thoughtlessness. In everyday life, if someone does not intend to do something, if a person acts accidentally or when he intends to do something else, if he acts without thinking—then we would ordinarily agree that his responsibility for what he does is diminished. At an extreme, for people who are insane or for young children, we excuse them for all responsibility whatever. The history of ethical thinking as a whole is, in fact, sharply divided between two contradictory views of the relation between knowledge and moral responsibility. On one side in this dispute we find a so-called "rationalist" view of ethics, according to which reason and knowledge are all-powerful. For ethical thinkers in this tradition—for example, Plato—no one never does evil knowingly or intentionally, no one ever *wants* to do wrong. If people knew that what they were doing was evil, this knowledge, by itself, would compel them to avoid it. Thus, when someone does wrong, he does it because he believes that what he is doing is good, not evil. He may be mistaken about that, of course, but then, too, he acts out of ignorance. And if someone acts out of ignorance, his responsibility is considerably diminished;at most, he is responsible for not knowing something he should have known, and this responsibility does not apply in every case.

This may seem a very mild explanation of the phenomenon of evil—as can be seen from the contrasting view which is vividly represented in the western religious traditions, in a radical form in Christianity and, somewhat more moderately, in Judaism. Here the claim is made that it is, indeed, possible to know something to be wrong and to do it anyway (this, it has been argued, is precisely the capacity which Adam and Eve acquired by their first disobedience). Knowledge by itself, on these accounts, does not avert evil-doing, since the *will* to do evil is also a factor. Thus, ignorance may *sometimes* explain why wrongs are done, but not always—and when we find that someone who does wrong knew what he was doing—or if he didn't know, that he *should* have known—he is, to that extent, responsible both for what he did and for its consequences.

It seems clear that Arendt's view of Eichmann and the banality of evil is committed to the first of these two alternatives: Eichmann, in her judgment, simply did not think, perhaps he did not even have the capacity to think, about what he was doing—and the implications of her stress on this is that if he *had* thought about it he would have acted differently, or at least that whatever evil he did would not have been banal. Even holding this, however, believing that in some sense Eichmann did not know what he was doing, Arendt holds that Eichmann should have been punished as he was, concluding finally that there was no alternative.

Now it might be objected that there is an inconsistency here— that Arendt's explanation of why Eichmann did what he did contradicts the judgment that she passes on him. It is not clear

to me how Arendt would have responded to this criticism; but of more basic importance in any event, it seems to me, is the fact that Arendt's ambiguous judgment of Eichmann is, itself, part of a larger view of the politics of evil that Arendt had begun to develop long before the Eichmann trial. Seen against *that* background, in fact, Eichmann appears as an example of a new *kind* of evil-doer, one which comes into existence with 20th century totalitarianism. For with that development, Arendt claims, we discover a new stage in the moral history of mankind: something changes in the character of evil, for its agents and even for its victims. Thus, her writings that describe this change also become pertinent to the attempt to understand, or, at least, represent, Eichmann.

In 1951, Arendt published what for many of her readers remains her most important book, *The Origins of Totalitarianism.* It was her most sustained response to the phenomenon of Nazism which had been brought to an abrupt end only a few years before, and which before that had radically disrupted Arendt's own life. In 1933, she left Germany for France; she was able to find work there mainly on behalf of various Jewish organizations, but after the Nazi invasion of France she was briefly in an internment camp. At the beginning of 1941, she came to the United States where she would live for the rest of her life, and where she soon began work on *The Origins of Totalitarianism.* Characteristically, her analysis of Nazism attempted to place that phenomenon in the context of a broader historical background, first by relating it to the history of anti-Semitism, and then by considering it as only one instance of the totalitarianism which was, for her, an innovation of the 20th century. She recognized, of course, that there had beendictatorial and repressive governments before this century, and that there had also been many instances of cruelty by individuals acting in the name of governments. What was distinctive for her about totalitarianism, which was epitomized for her in the concentration camps of the Nazis (and, also, she added, in the Russian Gulag), was one feature in particular: that here, for the first time, appeared an idea of evil which called for the extinction of man as an individual. Other forms of repression had been intended to intimidate people, to convert them to other doctrines or beliefs or even to destroy them. But in totalitarianism, according to Arendt, we find for the first time an *ideal* that the individual was to be eliminated as an individual: he was to become only an appendage, subordinate to a larger historical purpose. "Totalitarianism," she writes, "strives not toward despotic rule over men, but toward a system in which men are superfluous." That this "superfluity of man," the elimination of the individual person should be held as a principle— or, even, for that matter, as a possibility—was, in Arendt's view, something that even the extreme instances of barbarism in the past had not discovered. Moreover, this principle affects everyone caught up in the net of totalitarianism, its perpetrators as well as its victims. It may seem odd to consider the agents of totalitarianism under the same heading as we do its victims, but Arendt was prepared to go this far as well: in totalitarianism, as in many other systems of evil, the perpetrator himself also was affected, if not in the same *terms,* but equally fundamentally. At its extreme, totalitarianism obliterates individual freedom and reason on both sides: the superfluity of man, in other words, becomes a general principle, encompassing the system as a whole and everyone caught up by it.

It is to this aspect of totalitarianism—which comes into existence only as recent means of social organization and recent means of technology make it possible—that the phrase used here, the "politics of evil," refers. For what Arendt implies here is not just that one form of political expression represents evil to a degree beyond the capacity of any single system *or* individual; it is, in effect, the epitome of evil. The most radical expression of evil, in other words, is political and not simply moral (meaning by the latter, the decisions or acts of an individual like Iago or even Satan)—and we can understand how Arendt reaches this conclusion. Before the 20th century, it was reasonable to assume that the control of individual conscience or freedom rested finally, for better *or* for worse, in the hands of individuals acting on their own. But for totalitarianism as a system, evil is intrinsic, not something separately decided on; as a system, furthermore, it is more effective in accomplishing the goals of evil than any individual decisions or acts could be, no matter how monstrous. Evil which traditionally has been associated with individual decisions and acts, turns out, in the lesson taught by the 20th century, to be political rather than moral.

How, then, do we come back from the politics of evil to the banality of evil? But remember again Arendt's characterization of Eichmann's banality—for we see him now as exemplifying what she has described as the effects of totalitarianism. Eichmann, who was himself the *agent* of totalitarianism, abetting the work of the death camps which were its fullest expression, was also an expression or symptom, in some perverse sense also a victim, of that political form. He was, himself, superfluous as a human being, retaining the appearance of a person, but lacking the capacity for freedom and reason that were, for Arendt, essential to the definition of any such being. Arendt goes so far as to claim that totalitarianism had produced a change not only in how people acted toward each other, but in human nature itself, in what man was. This was an extremeclaim which has in turn itself been disputed by her critics—but it is by understanding its extremity that we now also understand her account of Eichmann and the banality of evil.

To be sure, the fact that the account I have given finds connections among quite separate parts of Arendt's thinking does not mean that those connections (even if the formulation here were accepted) are not also open to question. When Arendt describes the phenomenon of Nazism simply as an instance of totalitarianism in general, or when she equates the Nazi death camps with the Russian Gulag—it may well seem that she overlooks important differences. And, again, the question arises of whether 20th century totalitarianism is, indeed, the innovation that she says it is, either in the history of politics or in the history of evil: it has been argued, on the other side, that genocide itself is not peculiar to the 20th century. There remain, finally, the questions which her account of totalitarianism raises about the issue of guilt and responsibility. If Eichmann acted as he did because of the expression of totalitarianism as a political form, in what sense was he—or anyone else—responsible for what was done? And how does one explain the fact that some Germans avoided, or in a few cases even resisted, being caught up in the killing operations of the Nazis?

These are all compelling questions, and it is not clear to me how Arendt would have answered them or, indeed, if she could answer them. But there is at least one side of her account which Arendt extends consistently and constantly—and this is the connection that she emphasizes between politics and the public life, on the one hand, and the moral life of the individual, on the other. It is not surprising, in fact, that, for Arendt, politics should engender the most extreme form of evil—for, at the other end of the spectrum, it is politics that makes goodness possible in the first place. This discussion began with certain references to the distinction between their public and their private lives that generations of German Jews had taken as an ideal. Arendt did not deny that there could or should be differences—a space—between these two domains, but it was much more important for her that there should be a basic consistency between them, with the public life assuring the means that make the private life of judgment and thought possible. The reason why, in her view, the Enlightenment of the Eighteenth Century failed, notwithstanding its high-minded promises of the rights and dignity of man, was the same reason that the Enlightenment also came to be inculpated in the origins of totalitarianism: the political structures required to assure those rights had never been set up. The political structures which *had* evolved could not guarantee to minorities the rights that the idealistic rhetoric had spoken about—because the structure did not allow minorities to speak in their own voice.

> **Arendt remains one of only a very few writers willing even to try to characterize evil in the form that it took during the Holocaust.**
>
> *—Berel Lang*

In this sense, although Arendt did not apply the term to herself, she was, in contemporary terms, a conservative. It was, for her, only the individual communal unit or council, even the much-maligned nation—in any event, a unit that was the expression of a particular not a universal voice—that would assure the rights of particular citizens and their particular interests. On this basis, when she considered the question of Zionism, Arendt argued for the need, and then for the legitimacy, of the State of Israel. The Jews had lived, she contended, as a "Pariah" people, as outcasts. The basic character of their existence in Europe was what she called Jewish "worldlessness," a condition in which they had no public life—or at least no *assurance* of such a life. And for these liabilities, the State of Israel was a solution—although, as history was to turn out, her conception of the political structures and policies that Israel *should* adopt was sharply at odds with the directions in which Israel went. From the same arguments used to endorse a balance between the private and the public life, moreover, came her opposition to the idea of a world government which would, in her view, overpower the private domain; it would be, she wrote, "the worst tyranny imaginable" [*Lectures on Kant's Political Philosophy*]. If governments did not have limits, they would be unwilling to express the particular interests of the diverse groups of their citizens.

Obviously, these views of Arendt's are open to dispute. But however we judge them in themselves, one conclusion which seems undeniable follows from them collectively—and this is her claim for the necessary relation between political structures and the moral life of the individual. In some sense, to be sure, this relation is obvious: *of course,* our social or political surroundings have consequences for what we are, or do, as individuals. And, of course, the domain of private belief or conscience cannot simply be replaced by the public one. But Arendt's point goes deeper than these, as it attempts to show what the connections between the two are, how they work. Even here, of course, there is room for disagreement—as is also, and more emphatically, true for her study of Eichmann. But notwithstanding such possibilities, it is worth remarking that Arendt remains one of only a very few writers willing even to try to characterize evil in the form that it took during the Holocaust. There have been studies and biographies aplenty of Nazi leaders, and there have been attempts, on the other side, to analyze figures in the Holocaust who were morally exemplary. But few studies other than hers have attempted to analyze the events of the Holocaust as the evil which virtually everyone agrees appears there.

Thus, notwithstanding the criticism that has been directed against other aspects of Arendt's work, her conception of the relation between politics and the life of the individual, between the public domain and private conscience, and, eventually between good and evil, remains. She continually revised her position on the details of these relations; in her later writings, the balance she had seen between the public and the

private domains shifted much more strongly in the direction of the private (her last book, still being written when she died in 1975, was titled, *The Life of the Mind*). But one might think of this shift, too, as only another swing of the pendulum, not as an attempt to settle her last word on the subject. Arendt, I have suggested, was more given to ambivalence or irony than to last words, anyway. This was, itself, her most basic commitment: that, for anyone who thought independently, there *would* always be another word to be said. This does not mean that it is impossible to judge between good and evil—and, indeed, I have been suggesting that it is here, in her account of totalitarianism and the politics of evil, that Arendt's contribution to that judgment developed. Her account of the politics of evil reflected the conflict between the private and public domains which had affected her own life as it did the lives of almost every European Jew in the first half of the 20th century. It hardly needs to be pointed out that the same conflict, in only slightly different terms, continues in the present as well.

Jean Bethke Elshtain (essay date Fall 1989)

SOURCE: "Hannah Arendt's French Revolution," in *Salmagundi*, Vol. 84, Fall, 1989, pp. 203-12.

[*In the essay below, Elshtain discusses Arendt's interpretation of the revolutionary tradition, focusing on her "construction of the French and American revolutions as prototypes of 'successful' revolutions."*]

Of the Chinese students with their worker and peasant allies, massed by the tens of thousands in Tiananmen Square in defiance of martial law, it can be said that Hannah Arendt would have loved it. Their actions are "spontaneous" in the sense that they could not have reasonably been predicted. Their rhetoric is cast in the language of freedom. A papier mache representation of the Statue of Liberty makes its appearance in Shanghai. A student in Beijing quotes Lincoln's Gettysburg Address. Whatever the eventual outcome of these momentous events, they seem to fit Arendtian specifications for "people's power" as against those revolutionary actions she lamented. By turning to the language of American liberty, rather than seizing upon the terrible tropes which identify revolution with the seizure of power and identify power with a monopoly of the means of violence, the Chinese students join Arendt's elite (and, for the most part, doomed) company in the genuine revolutionary tradition whose "treasure" we have lost.

That company includes the spontaneous councils, or soviets, of 1905 and, again, 1917 until they were crushed by the Bolsheviks; 1918 and 1919 in Germany, "when, after the defeat of the army, soldiers and workers in open rebellion constituted themselves into *Arbeiter-und-Soldatenräte*, demanding, in Berlin, that this *Rätesystem* become the foundation stone of the new German constitution, and establishing, together with the Bohemians of the coffee houses, in Munich in the spring of 1919, the short-lived Bavarian *Räterepublik*"; and, finally, "the autumn of 1956, when the Hungarian Revolution" produced a council system in Budapest. To this list from her 1963 work, **On Revolution,** Arendt would surely add Solidarity in Poland (prior to its crushing in December, 1981), whose rhetoricians and theorists included in their ranks a number who looked specifically to Arendt for inspiration. What is this revolutionary tradition, so easily crushed by those who aim to centralize, to forge unity in and through a sovereign state? And how is it that the American republic, on Arendt's reading, came closer to creating genuine bodies politic than the French Revolution which, until recently, dominated revolutionary imagery, symbolism and aspiration?

Before I turn specifically to Arendt's construction of the French and American revolutions as prototypes of "successful" revolutions—successful in the sense that they led to the establishment of a new order, although Arendt laments the success of the French prototype—it may be well to note that Arendt's arguments today are less startling than they were in 1963. We have been deluged in the past several years with retrospectives on the French Revolution. Within France, a bevy of scholars now openly condemn the Revolution, or at least challenge its worshipful enthusiasts. Albert Camus has been vindicated. For it was Camus who dared to take on the revolution in *The Rebel,* and who suffered terribly as a consequence.

If Arendt, in 1963, could be seen as inspiration for free-speech movements and local revolts, Camus in 1951 was blasted, excommunicated from French intellectual life by Sartre and his minions in *Les Temps Modernes*. Castigating the received Marxist interpretation of the French Revolution as an instance of a class war and a glorious example of justifiable revolutionary violence, Camus warned against treating the proletariat as a "mystique," against the attempt by Saint-Just and Robespierre and, later, Marx and Lenin, to fit the world into a theoretical frame underscored by the substitution of a deified notion of the "will of the people" for God himself, against a passion for unity which must see any opposition whatever as treason. Ironically, the dynamics Camus exposed, a kind of ideological automatic pilot, led to his own condemnation by the Marxist left whose stake in controlling revolutionary interpretation was great.

It is curious that Arendt does not refer to Camus. We know, from other references, that she was familiar with his work. Perhaps she did not wish to be drawn into the hopeless morass of postwar European ideological struggle, dominated in France by Marxist discourse whether in the form of straight Stalinist apologias or baroque Sartrian constructions which drew upon Arendt's own teacher, Heidegger. Whatever the reason, Arendt and Camus are of one mind in warning against

revolution understood as the complete overthrowing of all that has gone before and the establishment of a new regime of total virtue and justice that requires violence to achieve its ends. This scenario, they believe, can have but one result: reinforcing the power of the state. They share as well what might be called a rhetorical conception of politics. Arendt describes the "political sphere of life" as one in which "speech rules supreme." Camus stresses "le dialogue" as the form man's sociability takes when it appears as politics.

Both, following Nietzsche, track the seductive power of the master-slave dialectic as a politics of *resentment* that can see in political action only a picture of who rules and who obeys. Finally, Camus and Arendt renounce the claims of politics to aspire to the absolute, and each—Camus is by far more candid in this—suggests that the death of God (and the beheading of his symbolic representative, the King, in the French revolution) unleashed new possibilities for terror by relocating all human meaning and purpose in historic necessity, in a supposedly inexorable law of historic logic. The terrors of twentieth century totalitarianisms flow directly from this momentous shift.

In the background lurks none other than Edmund Burke, at least for Arendt. In his defense of rights guaranteed by custom and history, in contrast to "the new-fangled idea of the rights of man" celebrated by Thomas Paine and valorized by Robespierre, "Burke was right and Paine was wrong." Burke's arguments, she insists, are "neither obsolete nor 'reactionary.'" For Burke recognized that by reducing politics to nature and granting human rights prepolitical status, the French Declaration of the Rights of Man unleashed a vision of entitlements without limit. Rather than putting brakes on the engine of government, or the "locomotive of history" (as the Marxists like to think of it), the generic Rights of Man as a species trait, an ontological given, plunges politics into the vortex of dangerously unlimited claims from necessity.

Always careful to distinguish the "rights of freedom and citizenship" from "the rights of life," Arendt regrets the "fateful misunderstanding" of the French that one can found a government on a vision of generic rights and natural human equality, with all depending on the proposition that"man is good outside society, in some fictitious original state . . . ." Unlike the French revolutionaries, the American founders were "realistic," knowing that human beings will always fall short and that the "only reasonable hope for a salvation from evil and wickedness at which men might arrive even in this world and even by themselves, without any divine assistance," must be the imperfect working of government. Mindful of human limits, the American revolutionaries shored up means to check the urge to unlimited power. Their new government promised not salvation through the instantiation on this earth of a monument to man's prepolitical goodness, but partial redemption from the worst that human beings can conjure up to violate one another. Burke's opposition to those he called the "new fanatics of popular arbitrary power" and his repudiation of the deadly notion of historic necessity, including its all or nothing propositions, are reflected in provocative, perplexing, and, at points murky and elusive ways, in Arendt's commentary.

Arendt specializes in the startling, in drawing sharp contrasts, in ruffling all sorts of feathers, in letting the chips fall where they may. Here is an example of a statement that pleased almost no one: "The sad truth of the matter is that the French Revolution, which ended in disaster, has made world history, while the American Revolution, so triumphantly successful, has remained an event of little more than local importance." Celebrants of the French revolution will dispute its disastrousness. Defenders of American revolutionary virtue will contest her assertion of its insignificance in the worldwide scale of things. No doubt her judgement about the American revolution's impact would have to be amended in light of the events of the past several decades, at least somewhat, but her assessment of the French catastrophe would hold firm. Her case against the French revolution revolves around the use of violence, the social question, the organic metaphor of a body politic, and theories of historic teleology or necessity.

With little fanfare in the way of gruesome statistics, Arendt builds her case against revolutions as a domain of violence. Elaborating on the terrible power of mimesis in politics and history, she laments the conviction that "in the beginning was a crime." The problem of beginnings is obviously relevant to "the phenomenon of revolution," she notes, and that "such a beginning must be intimately connected with violence seems to be vouched for by the legendary beginnings of our history as both biblical and classical antiquity report it: Cain slew Abel, and Romulus slew Remus; violence was the first beginning and, by the same token, no beginning could be made without using violence, without violating." Because a revolution, by definition, folds back upon itself as a return to, or recurrence of, a previous point in time, that revolutionaries should emulate representations of prior beginnings is unsurprising. That a mimetic politics of violence should result is additionally unsurprising if one has embraced the proposition that "in the beginning was a crime."

Wrapping themselves in the mantle of previous beginnings, seeking in violence a negative antithesis of generative qualities associated with the divine, the French were adamant about the necessary role of violence in re-configuring human affairs. Their own favored beginning was Rome. The slaying of one, Remus, made possible the triumph of the other, Romulus. The end of the *ancien regime* and the killing of any and all who either embodied it (the aristocrats) or held the slightest reservations about the total defeat of the old, the absolute triumph of the new in their heart of hearts—this and

this only held forth the promise, indeed was imbedded in the premise, of a new and more glorious Rome.

Dependent on memories from antiquity, "the French hommes de lettres who were to make the Revolution" pursued extreme theoretical abstractions to terrible concrete conclusions. Their "conscious thoughts and words stubbornly returned, again and again, to Roman language, drawn upon to justify revolutionary dictatorship." Oddly, the various metaphors "in which the revolution is seen not as the work of men but as an irresistible process, the metaphors of stream and torrent and current, were still coined by the actors themselves, who, however drunk they might have become with the wine of freedom in the abstract, clearly no longer believed that they were free agents." Prisoners of history, the makers of the French revolution plunged headlong into an orgy of repetitive destruction.

The evidence on the pervasiveness and centrality of violence to the French Revolution is clear and Arendt's thesis of historic repetition and the seductions of mimesis helps to explain its otherwise inexplicable festivals of bloodletting. A number of current critics compare these eighteenth century events to the Stalinist terror of the 1930's, an inescapable analogy in light of Bolshevik repetition of earlier revolutionary constructions. The slide into Terror is marked by the massacres of revolutionary prisoners in September, 1792, the bloody civil war—genocide some now call it—in the Vendée, the triumph of the dictatorship of the Committee of Public Safety. The rights of man were suspended and, according to Eugene Weber, between 1792-1794 alone, tens of thousands were imprisoned and seventeen thousand guillotined. "One representative in the rebellious West, Jean-Baptiste Carrier, turned the Loire river into a 'national bathtub', drowning prisoners in batches of hundreds and reporting back to Paris: 'We shall turn France into a cemetary rather than fail in her regeneration.'" Simon Schama quotes Saint Just: "Those who would make revolutions in the world, those who want to do good in this world must sleep only in the tomb." This, he notes, is "the very clay from which Leninism was to be shaped."

Bad violence, good violence. The good is authentically revolutionary. For Marx and Engels the French conquest of Algeria ("a fortunate fact for the progress of civilization"), the American war against the "lazy Mexicans," and any and all Germanic attacks against Slavic peoples on the grounds that Slavs "lacked the historic requisites for independence," are no more appropriately lamented than the rising of the sun. For these and other instances of good violence bear the seeds of a great and finally irresistible historic teleology. Engels put the dialectical mission of peoples not destined for historic triumph quite pithily: their task is "to perish."

When the "objective conditions" were ripe for the Bolshevik Revolution, Arendt argues, what Lenin and his comrades drew upon was a rhetoric and a teleology forged from lessons "presumably learned from the French Revolution" which implicated them in "the self-imposed compulsion of ideological thinking . . . The trouble has always been the same: those who went into the school of revolution learned and knew beforehand the course a revolution must take." It must defeat open enemies. Then it must ferret out and destroy hidden enemies. To do this it must centralize power, enhance the police, create a layer of spies and functionaries. It must liquidate. Finally, it must forfeit some of its own. This is "the great drama of history," a "grandiose ludicrousness" turned deadly, Arendt submits, for its automatic adherence to "the call of historic necessity." Unless knowingly broken, the cycle repeats itself. Thus the Bolsheviks justified their terror by reference to theviolence of 1792-94. In turn, interpretations of the French Revolution in the twentieth century, at least until recently, were dominated by Russian revolutionary events of 1917 which further "illustrated the necessity of the dictatorship and of terror."

To seek to eliminate poverty as a political project is to embrace the notion that human freedom consists in the wholesale liberation from necessity, or so Arendt contends.

—Jean Bethke Elshtain

Although mimesis carries much of the weight of Arendt's argument as she assays the horrors of the French Revolution, contrasting them unfavorably with the by-far less violent course of the American war for independence, she also, controversially, locates French obsession with "the social question" as a key reason for their descent into terror, absolutism, and ultimate refashioning and strengthening of the centralized machinery of state sovereignty. Several themes are at work: conceptions of the body politic as a unity driven by one will; the abdication of freedom before the dictates of material necessity; the boundlessness of revolutionary sentiments which run roughshod over particular persons in favor of a wholly abstract pity. Arendt has been taken to task repeatedly for her apparent indifference to poverty and suffering. This criticism seems to me misplaced. Hers, instead, is a critique of *representation,* of how it is that poverty, construed as an avoidable condition, too easily lends itself to process thinking, on the one hand, and its corollary, the boundlessness of abstract representation, on the other.

To seek to eliminate poverty as a political project is to embrace the notion that human freedom consists in the wholesale liberation from necessity, or so Arendt contends. If acute misery places human beings under the "absolute dictate of

their bodies," complete liberation from embodiment, from any and all dictates of necessity, is an abdication of the very possibility of freedom which can only be known through its contrast to that over which we do not have complete control. Liberation from "the fetters of scarcity" as the *raison d'etre* of revolution virtually guarantees the loss of any possibility for public freedom. Here Arendt generally loses her reader. Is she really so insouciant concerning the horrors of poverty? The answer is no. But it is clear that she is wary of treating scarcity and want as preeminently political concerns. They too readily lend themselves to cheap sentiment and a politics of manipulation.

This is the way it works. Revolutionary virtue is identified with the welfare of *le peuple,* construed not in their distinctness and plurality but as a mass entity and spectacle. A "will to raise compassion to the rank of the supreme political passion and of the highest political virtue" follows. But "the people" are deemed abject and silent by definition. They require spokesmen. They require champions. 'We' must promulgate measures in 'their' behalf. The word 'will' is brought into play. If the will is to have political efficacy, "if it is to function at all," it "must indeed be one and indivisible." A robust notion of organic unity—one people, one will—is devised. But this will is unstable. It must be shored up. The "unifying power of the common national enemy" without serves to reify the boundaries of *la nation une et indivisible.*

But having construed the problem the revolution is meant to solve in boundless, essentially material terms, the dynamic set in motion restlessly seeks other targets. If the innocent mass of people are by definition 'good' then their enemies, within and without, embody evil.Robespierre's "terror of virtue" appears on the revolutionary stage: absolute ends require means without limit. Revolutionary pity is boundless in its representational force so long as the suffering, the *toujours malheureux,* are departicularized, faceless, a mass. Distinguishing this abstract pity, the boundlessness of sentiments, from genuine compassion, Arendt writes: "For compassion, to be stricken with the suffering of someone else as though it were contagious, and pity, to be sorry without being touched in the flesh, are not only not the same, they may not even be related." One feels compassion, or comprehends it, only in and through the particular. The moment one generalizes, this specificity is lost and the will to power of representational pity comes into play: hence Robespierre's glorification of the poor. The more they suffered the more his power increased and the quest for a revolutionary absolute could be justified.

Pity *for* is not the same as solidarity *with.* Those who pity develop an "unhappy thirst for power" and gain "a vested interest in the existence of the weak." Abstract pity invites cheap sentiment, Manichean absolutism, and confounds any possibility for genuine political freedom. Writes Arendt: "Since the days of the French Revolution, it has been the boundlessness of their sentiments that made revolutionaries so curiously insensitive to reality in general and to the reality of persons in particular, whom they felt no compunctions in sacrificing to their 'principles', or to the course of history, or to the cause of revolution as such." Virtue without limits is evil and poverty lends itself all too readily to this construction of virtue. Opponents are turned out as traitors. Plurality gives way to 'massification.' Hypocrites must be hunted down and crushed. The Reign of Terror and the Reign of Virtue are one.

The real poor, in their human distinctness, are lost. The abstract poor appear on stage in and through representations that guarantee, indeed turn on, their continued political invisibility. They cannot be seen and heard directly and distinctly—only as shadowy occasions for the ministrations of others. To say, with the French revolutionaries, that all power resides in the people and that the people are all who suffer is to understand power as a "natural force whose source and origin lay outside the political realm." By contrast, and distinguishing violence from power, the American revolutionaries rejected the notion of an irrefutable and irreducible general will of "the people," insisting instead that power comes into being when "people . . . get together and bind themselves through promises, covenants, and mutual pledges; only such power, which rested on reciprocity and mutuality, was real power and legitimate. . . ."

Although falling short of Arendt's authentic revolutionary dream of self-constituted multiple bodies politic, the American revolutionaries at least appreciated what Arendt calls "the grammar of action." Action, she writes, is "the only human faculty that demands a plurality of men." Added to this is "the syntax of power: that power is the only human attribute which applies solely to the worldly in-between space by which men are mutually related. . . ." These—action and power—"combine in the act of foundation by virtue of the making and the keeping of promises, which in the realm of politics, may well be the highest human faculty." In colonial America, prior to the revolution, in townships and provinces, counties and cities, and notwithstanding the "numerous differences amongst themselves," the colonists, building on over a century of "covenant-making," were able to win a war against England, and perhaps more important, to combat their own tendencies towards the clarity of theoretical abstraction which always comes at the expense of "political factuality and experience."

True freedom, these Americans understood, is the presence of others in a free-domain, a public space, in which interlocutors engage one another as political equals. A people can be "one" only in foreign affairs. In domestic affairs they must remain distinct: thus Jefferson. Embracing human nature in its singularity, Americans sought (though, finally, they failed) to abolish "sovereignty within the body political of the re-

public" in line with their insight "that in the realm of human affairs sovereignty and tyranny are the same." Often perceived as cranky or hopelessly idealistic, Arendt's brief against sovereignty is in fact another feature of her campaign against mimesis. For national sovereignty, Jean Bodin's *majestas* which he translated into *souveraineté,* demands "undivided centralized power," replicating the terrible majesty of Sovereign God himself.

The American Revolution came closer to realizing this ideal than any other, Arendt insists, but she is clearly disappointed that the multiple "bodies politic" of the colonial era were allowed to wither as a more European style nation-state came into focus and finally triumphed (or so I argue) in World War I.

What the American revolution continues to offer to would-be revolutionaries everywhere is the example of a combined concern to create something new and to insure stability. In modernity we have split these concerns: one is considered progressive, the other conservative. This is stupid, Arendt suggests, but all too predictable given our tendency to mime the opposites deeded us by the French Revolution, including the categories "right" and "left" themselves. With Lincoln, she proclaims that, as the times demand it, we must "think anew and act anew, we must disenthrall ourselves." To be disenthralled is not to be altogether disinherited. A truly revolutionary political project must put together what others have put asunder, must both order human energies and unlock the great potential of authentic human power, the possibilities of coming together, of solidarity *with* particularity.

Alas, what America seems to have made manifest in this century is a space within which human beings in their private capacities can seek almost unlimited material gratification. This is not genuine republican happiness. For no one can be happy, and no one truly free—here Arendt echoes Jefferson—unless he or she experiences "public freedom" by participating in and sharing in public power. The bourgeois flourishes; the citizen withers. That is the sad denouement of the American story. But better this by far than the seductive grandeur of the convulsive revolutionary violence and the absolutist conceptions it leaves behind.

Those who spend their apprenticeships "in the school of past revolutions" are likely to fall into mimesis. So claims Arendt. Those, instead, who seek out the "lost treasure" of the genuine revolutionary tradition have the chance of giving birth to something new. But these latter swim against an awesome, repetitive tide. "It was nothing more or less than this hope for a transformation of the state, for a new form of government that would permit every member of the modern egalitarian society to become a 'participator' in public affairs, that was buried in the disasters of twentieth-century revolutions." Maybe *Solidarnosc* and Tiananmen Square will help us to rewrite this tale and Arendt's revolutionary hopes, in contrast to the ossified and grotesque apologias for bloodletting and terror that continue to emanate from the spokesmen for the bankrupt revolutionary tradition Arendt deplores. The bracing language of public freedom nowechoes in new and unexpected places.

Tobin Siebers (essay date Summer 1992)

SOURCE: "The Politics of Storytelling: Hannah Arendt's *Eichmann in Jerusalem*," in *Southern Humanities Review*, Vol. 26, No. 3, Summer, 1992, pp. 201-11.

[*In the following essay, Siebers analyzes* Eichmann in Jerusalem *in terms of memory and judgment—qualities largely absent in twentieth-century culture but inherent to storytelling.*]

Few modern events have stirred the need for recollection and judgment more than the Holocaust. As time and witnesses pass on, however, its memory grows more dim, and legally speaking the atrocities of Nazi anti-Semitism have remained for the most part unjudged. The trial of Adolf Eichmann and the Nuremberg Trials assume great historical significance because they provided concrete occasions for recollecting and judging. The Eichmann trial in particular created a kind of chain reaction of judgment: the judgment of Eichmann gave way to the judgment of anti-Semitism, of Israel, of the Jewish victims, and of the lawyers and the reporters at the trial. The trial also provided an occasion for a multitude of victims to recount their tales of suffering. The judgment of Eichmann welded participants into a chain of responsibility, in which each person was linked to others in the act of judging and recollecting.

This phenomenon is itself rare, if we follow Hannah Arendt's assessment of the modern world. Arendt describes the modern epoch as one little interested in remembrance and afraid of passing judgment. To judge is to subsume a particular experience under a general rule. But people in the modern age hesitate to perform the calculation that requires them to create a general rule to account for a particular event. Rather, they remain suspended between the love of facts and the love of preexisting categories of thinking. They prefer information and formulas to the act of judging and the need to remember; and since information offers little to the experience of memory, and formulas defeat judgment, modern individuals risk losing the ability to learn from experience. Experience is lost between fact and formula. "Unfortunately," Arendt complains, "it seems to be much easier to condition human behavior and make people conduct themselves in the most unexpected and outrageous manner than it is to persuade anybody to learn from experience; that is, to start thinking and judging instead of applying categories and formulas which are deeply ingrained in our minds but whose basis of experience has long been forgotten and whose plausibility resides

in their intellectual consistency rather than in their adequacy to actual events" [*The Listener* (6 August 1964)].

To have experience, we must judge. But to judge, we must first imagine and remember, and in a way that resists the mechanical repetition of facts and the easy pattern of formulas. Memory and judgment join in their need to tell an individual story. Stories are richer than simple facts and deeper than the preconceived patterns and cultural myths used to impose order on individual experience, and the value of storytelling for cognition thereby surpasses the contributions of history and philosophy. But to tell a story is not easy in the modern world. On the one hand, capitalism speeds up existence. It imposes commercial myths upon us and fractures our stories with its information and advertisements. On the other hand, the rise of totalitarianism works toconfound both memory and judgment; according to Arendt, the death camps were made possible only because the totalitarian system stole the power of judgment from both victims and victimizers. Totalitarianism does not want its story to be told; it relies on secrets and condemns its victims to oblivion.

In Hannah Arendt's eyes, the trial of Eichmann in Jerusalem brought about a collision of the many forces defining modernity, and she saw it as an opportunity to confront the modern condition [in ***Eichmann in Jerusalem***]. Her report on the trial is really a political treatise that attempts to describe what can be learned from Eichmann's story. More specifically, she resists modernity by trying to tell the story of Eichmann on trial in a way that passes judgment on the act of judging itself as well as in a way that defeats those forces working to obliterate memory.

Arendt's task, however, was complicated by the nature of modern thought and national movements. The Nazi movement and Israeli politics collided in the Eichmann trial, and Arendt became caught in the middle. Indeed, the trial became a situation in which people struggled not to be caught in the middle; but Arendt fought for what everyone else feared. She wanted to be precisely in the middle. Her desire to be in the thick of the conflict was partly polemical, but it also derived from her views about memory, storytelling, and judgment. The middle was the vantage point from which she could best tell the story of Eichmann in Jerusalem and render judgment on him. For the act of judging seeks not only to create a general rule to account for particular experience, but also to imagine the situations of other people. Judging, like any form of understanding, involves first reconciling oneself to the existence of the person or the event that one is judging. It is a matter, Arendt argues, of trying "to be at home in the world" [*Partisan Review* 20, No. 4 (1953)].

But who would want to be at home in Eichmann's world, and is it possible to judge a man who has no judgment? Is it possible to sympathize with a person who is incapable of showing sympathy? Finally, how can we understand someone who has no understanding? Judging and memory require human company, but Eichmann cut himself off from the chain of sympathy and responsibility necessary to human beings. Both judging and memory require that a story be told, but Eichmann's story could be told only with the greatest difficulty, because telling a story requires that a listener or reader be open to the story. The great test of a story is its ability to attract people who desire to become the next teller of the tale, so that the experience of the story cannot be separated from its passing from person to person. That no one wanted to listen to Eichmann's story in the first place, and that no one wanted to recount it, means that no one wanted either to know or to judge the man. In a sense, people wanted only to forget him.

Recent work on the Holocaust explains just how fragile are both judgment and memory; neither the desire to remember nor the desire to judge protects them in a climate that deliberately perverts them. We know that Hitler saw it as a disgrace to be a jurist, and we have all heard about the impossible choices imposed upon people in the camps and the ghettos. Arendt argues that the Nazis consistently confounded the act of judgment by forcing their victims to choose the lesser of two evils. If we are confronted by two evils, the argument went, we are required to choose the lesser one, because it is irresponsible to refuse the choice. Unfortunately, this logic made decision itself impossible by allowing only those choices most abhorrent to the victim. It also encouraged those who chose the lesser evil to forget that they had in fact chosen evil. Indeed, the Nazis persecuted their victims by confronting them with evil and tempting them to feel responsibility for crimes that they had no freedom to choose. The totalitarian argument of the lesser evil remains, according to Arendt, "one of the mechanisms built into the machinery of terror and crimes."

For a long time, our only means of facing this machinery of terror and crime was to repeat in nightmarish fashion the very images that the Nazis had created. The result was a kind of Jewish gothic, a catalogue of images and terrors, which represented the camps as the ultimate experience of modern horror. These images were replayed in the media first to inform the public of Nazi crimes and then for entertainment value; the Holocaust has now evolved into a dramatic source used to boost television ratings and to sell automobiles and soft drinks. The memory of the Holocaust has been eroded by repeating plots and making stereotypes of both victimizers and victims. Consequently, those who believe that the experience of the Holocaust has value for the future must discover new ways of introducing us to the events. Claude Lanzmann's epic film *Shoah,* for example, deliberately avoids familiar gothic images by asking people to tell their stories and to stand where they once stood. He forges a link in memory and judgment between the past and present without

using the artificial drama now associated with the Holocaust. His film makes the point in images, which others have made in argument, that the Holocaust is not a single event but a word in which the personal experience of a multitude of sufferers resonates.

Neither memory nor judgment is served by a Jewish gothic that requires fate or history to arrange an eternal combat between anti-Semite and Jew. Hannah Arendt learned this lesson in Jerusalem, to her utter surprise. She went there with everyone else expecting to catch the horrible specter of Hitler dancing in Eichmann's eyes. What she found was banality. Arendt portrays Eichmann first and foremost as a bureaucrat, and in that image of evil she moves ahead of her time. It was not acceptable in 1961, at least not outside Marxist circles, to portray evil in the character of the functionary, but today we understand and accept the image. The fact that our fictions and moral codes now turn to the character of the businessman to represent vice reveals that we have all come to accept what Arendt called the banality of evil. In a reversal of some proportions, however, we tend increasingly to stress the radical evil of that figure, rather than its baseness, thereby undercutting Arendt's idea of banality and creating a stereotype as dangerous as any other.

But Arendt did not describe Eichmann as a functionary to reveal the radical nature of evil; she found evil in that form only because Eichmann was a functionary who had succumbed to evil. Given her idea of judgment, Arendt's only choice as a reporter at the trial was to try to tell the story of this Eichmann. The choice made her into his involuntary biographer, a situation whose irony did not escape her. Just as an Israeli lawyer could not be expected to defend Eichmann without risking personal harm, a Jew could not be expected to tell his story to the world without inciting the Jewish community to anger. That Arendt chose to tell that story and not relinquish her Jewishness is a tribute to both her courage and her foolishness, for some may doubt whether the story was worth all the personal woe that befell her. The tranquility of her work was invaded by hatred. The company of fellow intellectuals was driven beyond her reach. She lost friends to tell the story of an enemy.

Clearly, Hannah Arendt believed that Eichmann's story should be told, but we may ask why. The answer again turns on Arendt's opinion that the story was a valuable experience from which to learn something about how human beings think. Of the Holocaust, Arendt once said, "in such things there is nothing but *Einzelfälle* [particular cases]." Eichmann's case fits that description as well, being part of the Holocaust. As Arendt saw it, the Eichmann trial held only one story, and she could not translate it into another one, no matter how ignoble it seemed. To tell another story would in fact be a form of forgetting Eichmann. Arendt saw too well the temptation to be like Eichmann: to become a person who has stopped thinking. It is easy to forget someone who has stopped thinking, but that is the greatest danger. Arendt's book takes the unexpected form of Eichmann's biography precisely because of this threat. Eichmann's story concerns one man being tried in one city, and Arendt had to emphasize its particular nature or risk losing her hold on the politics of the situation.

Indeed, that there are nothing but particular cases in the Holocaust has extraordinary political repercussions. It is precisely the particular that totalitarianism struggles to erase as it applies its generalizing and ideological rhetoric. The immediate response to it often succumbs to the temptation to meet its totalizing movement with another one, thereby becoming only a mirror image of the enemy. Arendt therefore criticizes both the press and the prosecution for presenting the Eichmann case as a model for thinking about fate, history, or anti-Semitism in general: there is "no system on trial," she concludes, "no history or historical trend, no 'ism', antisemitism for instance, but a person; and if the defendant happens to be a functionary, he stands accused precisely because even a functionary is still a human being, and it is in this capacity that he stands trial. . . . If the defendant were permitted to plead either guilty or not guilty as representative of a system, he would indeed become a 'scapegoat.'"

Arendt's report, then, focuses on the obstacles to judgment and remembrance created by Eichmann's own stories and by the stories told about him by lawyers, politicians, and other reporters. The latter stories, always prompted by special interests, amount to a form of static that interferes at every turn with the real story of Eichmann's life. Arendt describes the television broadcasts of the trial as being interrupted by "real-estate advertising" and the outbursts, apparently "spontaneous," of the lawyers, complaining about Eichmann's lies. She also criticizes the prosecuting attorney for his showmanship. To the stories of genuine suffering told by the victims, she opposes the prosecutor's staging of the event. In his estimation, the trial should tighten its focus on the crimes of the German people against humanity, on anti-Semitism as a phenomenon, or on racism as such. Again and again, he tries to transform the trial into a history lesson on eternal anti-Semitism from Pharaoh to the present. History becomes, in his words, "the bloodstained road traveled by this people," the Jews, and assumes the character of a path necessary to accomplish their destiny. In ***The Origins of Totalitarianism,*** Arendt attacks similar descriptions of Jewish history because they blunt the seriousness of anti-Semitism and conceive of matters human in the most inhuman terms by placing a supernatural view of history above the concept of individual responsibility. Furthermore, in the report on the trial, Arendt complains that such general pictures evade the problem of Eichmann's evil, replacing it with dramas of large and tragic proportions written in the name of such abstractions as destiny and history. These dramas are easy to repeat and to re-

member, but they have little to do with individual human experience.

Similarly, David Ben-Gurion incited Arendt's anger because he announced beforehand those lessons that the trial should teach to "Jews and Gentiles, to Israelis and Arabs, in short, to the whole world." A lesson, or a moral, may come of a story, but if the lesson is told before the story, the story risks not being told. Ben-Gurion's lessons were clear, but Arendt doubted whether they were part of the story. Rather, Ben-Gurion had committed "the sin of trying to make a story come true," to borrow Arendt's remarks on Isak Dinesen, "of interfering with life according to a preconceived pattern, instead of waiting patiently for the story to emerge . . ." [***Men in Dark Times***]. For Ben-Gurion, the trial was supposed to demonstrate that the "Jews had always faced a 'hostile world'" and to implicate the world in the murder of six million Jews: "Let world opinion know this, that not only Nazi Germany was responsible for the destruction of six million Jews of Europe." In a sense, the trial could come to an end only when it had uncovered the Eichmann in every one of us.

No doubt, collective guilt is a powerful political device, but it risks clouding judgment, and it does not serve memory very well because it believes in no particular experience. "Morally speaking," Arendt argues, "it is hardly less wrong to feel guilty without having done something specific than it is to feel free of guilt if one is actually guilty of something." Both actions destroy judgment. Finally, if Eichmann were only one more anti-Semite in the hostile world of eternal anti-Semitism, how could he be judged? His guilt would serve in that case only as a symbol for a collective guilt spread so thin as to have no meaning at all.

In Arendt's opinion, the prosecution's image of Eichmann impeded his exposure to judgment by representing him as a symbol for metaphysical dramas of history and fate. But what distressed her more was the uncanny similarity between this image and Eichmann's own view of himself. For Arendt, Eichmann was, above all else, a man who had stopped thinking. He had adopted the most cliché expressions to describe his life and motivations; he grew elated when he spoke of himself and his destiny, lifted, as it were, by his own petard. Now Arendt discovered that others described not only the defendant but themselves in the same language.

Arendt's commentary on this language is sustained, but her major point may be easily rehearsed and briefly illustrated. Her analysis is, in my opinion, one of the most successful characterizations of "the politics of interpretation" in existence, and it is leaps and bounds ahead of anything being written today under the aegis of either deconstruction or the new historicism. She demonstrates again and again that both Eichmann and those speaking on behalf of the Jewish people used a gothic language of destiny and superhuman agency to interpret themselves. Eichmann confessed that "officialese" was his only language, but his confession was only partially true. He was equally well versed in the cliché language of Destiny, History, and Movement. He described himself as a "bearer of secrets," whose hard-luck story it was to be sacrificed to the gods of misfortune. He was, moreover, swallowed by history and its grandiose events: "everything went wrong, my personal affairs as well as my years-long efforts to obtain land and soil for the Jews. I don't know, everything was as if under an evil spell . . . ." And as if history and destiny were not sufficient causes for his woes, Eichmann blamed the Nazi movement for his bad luck: "The subject of a good government is lucky, the subject of a bad government is unlucky. I had no luck." "I am not the monster I am made out to be," he lamented. "I am the victim of a fallacy."

> **[Arendt went to Jerusalem] expecting to catch the horrible specter of Hitler in Eichmann's eyes. What she found was banality.**
>
> —*Tobin Siebers*

Eichmann represents himself not only as a victim but as an exemplary victim, a special victim unlike any other. He views himself not as ordinary but as radical; he is a person of the kind destined to convey ultimate meanings. Indeed, Eichmann begins his memoirs by suggesting that his destiny flies above the human world and that his form is a mere envelope containing more powerful forces: "Today . . . I begin to lead my thoughts back to the nineteenth of March of the year 1906, when at five o'clock in the morning I entered life on earth *in the aspect of a human being*" (emphasis mine). The trial merely provides Eichmann with the proof of his destiny by setting him apart and marking him with the seal of a unique fate, and he gladly offers himself as a symbol to the world on behalf of the Jews: I propose, he exclaims, "to hang myself in public as a warning example for all anti-Semites on this earth." Here, then, is a man who believes himself victimized by history, fate, and international politics, but who seems all too willing to accept his martyrdom, if only it has the proper symbolic consequences and furthers his own notoriety. So misunderstood by the world in his own eyes, Eichmann simultaneously exculpates himself and offers himself as a symbol of guilt, hoping to achieve through these means an even greater power and agency in world affairs.

The prosecution and press, quite naturally, represented Eichmann as a monster, rather than as a buffoon, and they began repeating his eerie and otherworldly images of himself. He was "a perverted, sadistic personality" and "a man obsessed with a dangerous and insatiable urge to kill." Arendt is also guilty to some extent of repeating Eichmann's rhetoric when she describes him as enigmatic and thought-defying, for Eichmann would have liked to be considered "thought-defying." But, more disturbing, the prosecution and government press releases applied Eichmann's rhetoric of victimization and his sense of martyrdom to the Jewish people as well. Eichmann, when most elated, described himself as a martyr to his idea, and claimed fascination with the "Jewish question" because he saw in the Jews fellow idealists. An idealist, according to Eichmann, lived for an idea and was prepared to sacrifice for that idea everything and everyone. Eichmann's martyr complex was revealed in his fervent desire to die for his idea and in his elation before the executioner; but, in fact, the comparison between Jewish idealism and his own was perverse in the extreme, and so too was the rhetoric at the trial that represented the victims of the Holocaust either as fulfilling some grand destiny or as martyrs to the cause of Israel. The Jews were rarely martyrs, properly speaking, because they did not sacrifice themselves for an idea. Indeed, they were permitted neither the power nor the dignity of having an idea. Rather, they were sacrificed for the ideas of their murderers. They were killed simply because they were. The Nazis worked for the most obvious political reasons to eliminate the possibility of martyrdom, and only a recuperative history, designed to restore dignity and power to the Jewish state, could represent the victims as martyrs to history. Although such revisionary histories lend cohesion to state politics, and are valuable in that respect, they risk masking the fundamentally human and helpless nature of the Jewish victims.

The trial, then, did not sufficiently allow people of flesh and blood to emerge; rather, it concealed them in a garb of theatrical making, designed to summon political generalities, grandiose movements, and fateful plots. Nor did the trial allow the stories of the victims to have their full impact. Perhaps more threatening than the nature of political theater at the trial was its influence on individual testimony. As the trial became more of a stage, Arendt concludes, the events grew more tragic in the dramatic sense, but they were inevitably less personal, individual, and human. "As witness followed witness and horror piled upon horror," Arendt explains, the people "sat there and listened in public to stories they would hardly have been able to endure in private, when they would have had to face the storyteller." The fourth wall of the stage imposed itself between witness and audience, making the stories more bearable but blunting their ability to communicate as well as their essentially human character.

Arendt understands that stories exist only in communications from person to person, because an essential ingredient of any story is the bond created between speaker and listener or writer and reader. Her account of Zindel Grynszpan's testimony focuses on the inherent power of his story and the directness of its telling. Grynszpan recounts a day in his life in the autumn of 1938, when he and his family were deprived of German nationality and expelled to Poland. Some twelve thousand Jews were processed that day by the Germans and driven to the train station through the streets, black with people shouting, "*Juden raus* to Palestine." From the station, they were transported to the Polish border, and there the S.S. drove them like beasts for over a mile until they crossed the border and were interned by the Polish authorities in a village of six thousand—twelve thousand added to six thousand, and the majority had not eaten in four days. Arendt emphasizes that Grynszpan's story did not even remotely resemble a "dramatic moment," but it conveyed nevertheless, through its shining honesty, the needless destruction of his twenty-seven years of life in less than twenty-four hours.

A story's objective is to convey human experience, but its silences and the speaker's inability to continue are equally parts of the storytelling experience, and in the case of the catastrophic events of the Holocaust, the storyteller's own emotional fragmentation may be the most powerful communication of the events. One of the most moving and memorable scenes of Claude Lanzmann's film concerns Abraham Bomba's story about cutting women's hair in the gas chambers. He tries to tell the story of a friend, a good barber, who saw his wife and his sister come into the death chamber. The women did not know that they were there to die, and the barber could not tell them. He tried to cut their hair more slowly, a minute longer, a second longer, just to hug and kiss them, because he knew that he would never see them again. Abraham Bomba breaks down when he tries to tell the story. He turns from the camera and covers his face with his hands. The story stops and starts, interrupted this time not by noise, commercials, or political announcements but by the force of the story itself, by its own rhythms and the emotions dictating its form in a face-to-face encounter between human beings.

It is crucial to stress that Abraham Bomba's story does not fail precisely because it stops and starts. For in Bomba's emotional interruptions resides the story's humanity. It is equally crucial to recognize that the trial did not fail in Arendt's eyes, despite all the obstacles to judgment and memory, for these obstacles were put in place by human hands. The stories of Abraham Bomba and Adolf Eichmann stand at perverse extremes; but both are integral to the experience of the Holocaust, if it is to be remembered and judged, if its stories are to be told. Both stories require a form of patience, although of a very different kind: we must be willing to pass the story from teller to teller, to have the patience both to listen to the story and to retell it. Storytelling engages the patient art of thinking, for thinking is an act of imagining from the standpoint of someone else—an act, therefore, fundamentally of conversation and communication. It implies the idea of a tradition and the desire to be at home and among others in the human community, but it is too rare in our day. The Nazi movement did all that it could to crush our patience with these stories, and

now our modern urge to rush through life demands that we shorten our stories or transform them into blockbusters.

Both of these forces, called modern by Arendt, would seem to condemn the story of the Holocaust to oblivion. But, fortunately, oblivion is not so easily attained. "Nothing human is that perfect," Arendt writes, "and there are simply too many people in the world to make oblivion possible."

That we continue to tell these stories is, humanly speaking, all that judgment and memory require of us.

Richard A. Shweden (review date 20 September 1992)

SOURCE: "Dialogue Amid the Deluge," in *The New York Times*, Vol. CXLIV, No. 49977, September 20, 1992, pp. 1, 53-4.

[*Below, Shweden reviews* Hannah Arendt—Karl Jaspers: Correspondence, 1926-1969, *concluding that "it is a privilege to enter [Arendt's and Jaspers'] studies."*]

The correspondence begins at the University of Heidelberg in 1926, in the years before what now might be called the "ethnic cleansing" of the German universities and the Holocaust. It starts with a skeptical query from a 19-year-old German Jewish student, Hannah Arendt, to her German and non-Jewish professor, Karl Jaspers, about the impossibility of learning anything from history. It ends 43 years later, six years before Arendt's death in 1975, with the student delivering a eulogy for "the greatest educator of all time" and declaring him "the conscience of Germany."

Hannah Arendt—Karl Jaspers: Correspondence, 1926-1969, edited by Lotte Kohler and Hans Saner and translated by Robert Kimber and Rita Kimber, is not a volume of letters between Plato and Socrates. Yet, on a scale just slightly below the immortals, it permits the reader an intimate and ennobling view of the scholarly life. The student and the teacher lived in the age of the deluge in Heidelberg, Munich and Berlin, not in the age of Pericles. Their dialogues are about nationalism, citizenship, ethnic identity and the moral responsibilities of intellectuals in the contemporary world.

The student, Hannah Arendt, the political historian, social philosopher and journalist, fled Germany in 1933 on her way to becoming one of the great itinerant intellectuals of our century. She describes herself in one letter as having "an open mind for temporary arrangements." Arendt was a scholarly nomad who, under the protection of various academic titles—today's lecturer, this year's fellow, professor for the spring quarter—migrated among intellectual centers at Oberlin College, Princeton, Wesleyan, Harvard, Bard College, Columbia, the University of Chicago, the New School for Social

Research and the University of California, Berkeley. She offered seminars and courses on such subjects as "Basic Moral Propositions From Socrates to Nietzsche" and "Political Theory From Machiavelli to Marx." She was the author of several influential books: *The Human Condition, The Life of the Mind, On Revolution, The Origins of Totalitarianism*. She spoke with an authoritative voice about Nazism, Israel, ethnic identity and other aspects of Jewish existence.

She was also an interim reporter for *The New Yorker* who covered the trial of Adolf Eichmann in Israel in 1961 and then wrote the controversial essay *Eichmann in Jerusalem*. She argued that there was no "demonic profundity" to Eichmann's character, that the Nazi who was in charge of the "final solution" was an ordinary and rather uninteresting bureaucrat who had no particular hatred of Jews and was in possession of a normal conscience. She advertised a terrible truth, "the banality of evil": the motives that move human beings in administrative bureaucracies to commit atrocities are themselves average or commonplace, like the desire for promotion.

When Arendt left Germany, she moved to Paris and then to Manhattan. New York City became home base for her breathless wanderings between academic water holes and other forums for moral reflection on the political events and activities of the mid-20th century—the Holocaust, Zionism, Palestine, McCarthyism, Korea, Indochina, the Cuban missile crisis, the assassination of President John F. Kennedy, the student protests of the 1960's. She was constantly on the move, traveling to Europe and Israel, meeting with publishers, on tour on the lecture circuit, dashing off letters and memos, reading and writing in taxicabs. "Alienation and rootlessness," she wrote to her professor, "if we will only understand them aright, make it easier to live in our time."

Karl Jaspers, her professor, lived a more settled life. He was a philosopher and psychiatrist who is sometimes credited with having coined the term "existentialism," although he remarked that "the 'existentialists' consider me a kind of old-fashioned theologian." As a young scholar, Jaspers wrote prolifically about an "axial age" in human history (800 B.C.-200 B.C.) when the most important thoughts worth thinking were first thought. His *magnum opus* is a three-volume work called *The Great Philosophers* (1957). He was a college student at the turn of the century, yet he lived long enough to have received a letter from Arendt about the student protests in Paris in May 1968, in which she wrote, "It seems to me that children in the next century will learn about the year 1968 the way we learned about the year 1848."

Between 1921 and 1937 Jaspers taught at the University of Heidelberg and kept company with Martin Heidegger and other German existentialists, until he was dismissed by the Nazi regime. He and his wife, Gertrud Mayer, a Jew, sat out the war, in Germany, in silence, but as soon as the war was over he began writing about "German guilt." In 1948 he moved to Basel, Switzerland, a city so pristine and cloistered that Jaspers described it as "a last island in the flood."

Basel was a suitable home for Jaspers, who appears in these letters as the most appealing of philosopher-kings. He would write to Arendt, "Oh, if only you were sitting here so we could talk!" and "I'd like to talk with you for hours, for days on end." She would make her pilgrimage to that medieval city that was "spared in the Thirty Years' War," armed with a long list of items for discussion, from Plato to galley proofs.

Jaspers lectured about Kant and Spinoza and pondered the essential nature of the German and Jewish tribes. He worried that the creation of Israel marked the beginning of the end of the greatness of the Jewish people, which he associated with their role as wanderers, and he thought Israel would act like any other state. In 1933, shortly before Arendt departed from Germany. Jaspers had written to his young student, "I find it odd that you as a Jew want to set yourself apart from what is German." In 1947 he proclaimed, "I will never subscribe to a concept of Germanness by which my Jewish friends cannot be Germans or by which the Swiss and the Dutch, Erasmus and Spinoza and Rembrandt and Burckhardt, are not Germans." In 1959 he still wanted to claim Arendt as a German who happened to be a Jew. He appointed her the executor of all translations of his work into English.

The circle of scholars, intellectuals, artists and writers surrounding Arendt and Jaspers embraces two centuries and some legendary personalities. Jaspers was himself a student of Max Weber, one of the founders of modern sociology. He dined at Weber's house. He was present at the funeral of Weber's sister.

Through this volume of letters one has a glimpse of the personal side of a network of teachers, friends and associates that extends from Weber to such contemporary figures as Randall Jarrell, Robert Lowell, Alfred Kazin, Eric Hoffer, Mary McCarthy, Leon Bostein, the president of Bard College, and Gerhard Casper, the president of Stanford University. Arendt and Jaspers seemed to know and develop similar opinions about almost every major German and French intellectual of the century. Martin Heidegger, Edmund Husserl, Thomas Mann, Karl Mannheim, Theodor Adorno, Paul Tillich, Jean-Paul Sartre, Albert Camus. Their opinions are not always flattering.

Heidegger is the bete noire of the correspondence. Intellectuals are not supposed to be bureaucrats, and Arendt seemed to judge them by a different standard. She held it against Heidegger that, as rector of the University of Freiburg, he dutifully followed superior orders from the National Socialist Government and forbade the philosopher Edmund Husserl, a Jew, from entering the philosophy building. In 1933 Heidegger, who believed that philosophy was a sacramental activity and that true philosophizing could only be done in German or in Greek, broke off his friendship with Jaspers, and there was suspicion it was because Jaspers was married to a Jew.

Here is one snippet, Jaspers on Heidegger in 1949: "Two and a half years ago he was experimenting with 'existence' and distorted everything thoroughly. Now he's experimenting more seriously, and, again, that doesn't leave me unconcerned." The philosopher and sociologist Theodor Adorno, another dark figure in these letters, is described by Arendt as a "repulsive" human being who tried unsuccessfully to go along with the Nazis (he later wrote a book called *The Authoritarian Personality*). Nineteen thirty-three was a moment of truth, and some very fancy people did not pass the test.

Arendt and Jaspers lost touch with each other during the war years. After 1945 they wrote frequently. If a letter didn't arrive in four weeks, it was "long overdue." If it didn't arrive in five weeks, it was a "scandal." A typical letter from either, announcing itself as "written in haste," contained a mix of philosophy, politics, gossip, opinions, candid, criticism, editorialbusiness, travel plans, discussions about health and updates on writing projects, awards, academic appointments.

Arendt and Jaspers were bored, and apologetic, whenever they had to get down to business (royalty payments, copyright agreements), and the reader who does not care about phlebitis, the arrival of the potted blue hyacinths or what it says on a University of Chicago Press contract will find some of the letters tedious. The philosophy, the politics, the gossip and the opinions, however, are well worth the tedium of an argument about how best to abridge and translate yet another of Jaspers's fat books.

Arendt and Jaspers admired the United States as a bastion against a deluge of totalitarianism and "genealogical investigations," a deluge that Arendt seemed to expect with every downturn in political fortunes—the election of Dwight Eisenhower over Adlai Stevenson, the Red scare, the assassination of President Kennedy. In her letters she is outspoken about America's intellectuals, its universities and its political institutions. About Sidney Hook, the philosopher, who told her "that it was un-American to quote Plato." About the political theorist Leo Strauss: "He is a convinced orthodox atheist. Very odd. A truly gifted intellect. I don't like him." About Berkeley, where "the students are the donors of the future and therefore considerably more important than the professors." About Princeton, where the students "didn't even know that there had ever been such a thing as Austria-Hungary." Again about Princeton: "The idea of speaking here, of all places, about the concept of revolution has something ineffably comical about it."

Arendt conceived of the United States as a place where the melting pot was not even an ideal, and that is what she liked about it. For her, America had no national tradition. She described the United States as "an a-national republic . . . in which nationality and state are not identical." Social separation was permitted, and there was thick ethnicity, but it had no political or legal significance. People weren't trying to disenfranchise you just because they didn't want you in their club. Truth was obligated "to go about in the guise of opinion." The state did not define reality.

She and Jaspers shared "a deep-seated prejudice" against government projects and administrative "solutions" to social problems. Where there was government there was bureaucracy, and where there was bureaucracy there was the banality of evil, and little room for dialogue and sensible reasons. No bureaucrat says, "I'd like to talk with you for hours, for days on end."

It seems clear from these letters that the idea of "the banality of evil" is as much Jaspers's notion as it is Arendt's. As early as Oct. 19, 1946, he urges on her the view that "a guilt that goes beyond all criminal guilt inevitably takes on a streak of 'greatness'—of satanic greatness—which is, for me, as inappropriate for the Nazis as all the talk about the 'demonic' element in Hitler and so forth. It seems to me that we have to see these things in their total banality."

He cautions her, as well, to beware of "the false inhuman innocence of the victims." Arendt replies that she finds his view "half-convincing. . . . We have to combat all impulses to mythologize the horrible." Fifteen years later, in ***Eichmann in Jerusalem,*** she set off an uproarby documenting how "Eichmann was not Iago and not Macbeth" and how respectable Jewish society in Europe helped organize its own demise. The reaction made her feel B'nai B'rith was out to destroy her reputation. "I'm amazed," she wrote, "and never expected anything like this, and I can see, too, that it's downright dangerous." It seems to be Jaspers's brow from which the banality of evil originally sprung, full-blown.

Arendt's father had died when she was 6, and she was an only child. Jaspers had no children. Throughout her life Arendt addressed Jaspers as "Lieber Verehrtester" (Dear Honored One) and found it difficult to bring herself to say the word "Karl." It took her 10 years to honor Jaspers's repeated requests for a picture of her husband, whom she referred to impersonally in these letters as "Monsieur" and whom she kept very much out of the picture, until Jaspers was nearly 80 years old. Arendt was married to Heinrich Blucher, a non-Jewish German whom she had met in Paris in the 1930's. Blucher taught philosophy at Bard College and the New School. Arendt and Jaspers refer to him as the "identical twin of Socrates." Jaspers, of course, was the fraternal twin. Arendt once wrote from America to her professor that "psychoanalysis has become a downright plague here or, more correctly, a madness." Undoubtedly, those who are psychodynamically inclined will have a field day with some of the idealizations in the letters.

A far better day can be had appreciating the wisdom of these two towering intellectuals whose lives were defined by their confrontations with the great ideas and events of history and by their dialogues with each other. It is a privilege to enter their studies.

Tony Judt (review date 6 April 1995)

SOURCE: "At Home in This Century," in *New York Review of Books,* Vol. 42, No. 6, April 6, 1995, pp. 9-14.

[*In the review below, Judt finds that both* Essays in Understanding *and* Between Friends *provide a better understanding of Arendt herself, demonstrating that "it becomes a little easier to see just what holds together the various parts of her oeuvre and why they provoke such diverse and powerful responses."*]

Hannah Arendt died twenty years ago, leaving a curious and divided legacy. To some she represented the worst of "Continental" philosophizing: metaphysical musings upon modernity and its ills unconstrained by any institutional or intellectual discipline and often cavalierly unconcerned with empirical confirmation. They note her weakness for a phrase or an *aperçu,* often at the expense of accuracy. For such critics her insights into the woes of the century are at best derivative, at worst plain wrong. Others, including the many young American scholars who continue to study and discuss her work, find her a stimulating intellectual presence; her refusal to acknowledge academic norms and conventional categories of explanation, which so frustrates and irritates her critics, is precisely what most appeals to her admirers. Twenty years after her death they see her desire for a "new politics" of collective public action vindicated by the revolutions of 1989, and her account of modern society in general and totalitarianism in particular confirmed by the course of contemporary history. Both sides have a point, though it is sometimes difficult to remember that they are talking about the same person.

In fact, and despite the broad range of topics covered in her writings, Hannah Arendt was throughout her adult life concerned above all with two closely related issues: the problem of political evil in the twentieth century and the dilemma of the Jew in the contemporary world. If we add to this the special difficulty she experienced in acknowledging the distinctive place of Germany in the story she tried to tell—a difficulty of which she was not, it seems to me, always fully aware— we have grasped the central threads of all her writings, even those that seem at first reading most abstracted from such

concerns. It does not follow from this that Arendt's various works can be reread in this light as a single, continuous, coherent theoretical undertaking—she is every bit as diffuse and muddled as her critics claim; but if we understand her main historical concerns against the background of her own obsessions, it becomes a little easier to see just what holds together the various parts of her oeuvre and why they provoke such diverse and powerful responses.

The central place in all of Arendt's thinking of the problem of totalitarianism seems obvious. In a 1954 piece, **"Understanding and Politics,"** reprinted in Jerome Kohn's useful and very well-edited collection of her early essays, she stakes out her territory without ambiguity: "If we want to be at home on this earth, even at the price of being at home in this century, we must try to take part in the interminable dialogue with the essence of totalitarianism." As she would later express it in her **"Thoughts about Lessing,"** the "pillars of the best-known truths" lie shattered today, and the first task of the survivors is to ask how this happened and what can be done. That her own attempt to make sense of the age would not endear her to everyone was something she anticipated as early as 1946, well before the appearance of *The Origins of Totalitarianism*: "Those few students," she wrote in "The Nation," " . . . who have left the field of surface descriptions behind them, who are no longer interested in any particular aspect nor in any particular new discovery because they know that the whole is at stake, are forced into the adventure of structural analyses and can hardly be expected to come forward with perfect books."

Origins is, indeed, not a perfect book. Nor is it particularly original. The sections on imperialism lean heavily on the classic work *Imperialism,* by J. L. Hobson, published in 1905, and on Rosa Luxemburg's Marxist account in *The Accumulation of Capital* (1913). Luxemburg's version was particularly appealing to Arendt because of its emphasis on the self-perpetuating (and self-defeating) nature of capitalist expansion, a characteristic which Arendt then transposed onto totalitarianism; but she also found the general Marxist approach congenial, less for its broader historical claims, which she dismissed and indeed associated with the totalitarian phenomenon itself, than for Marxism's attack on bourgeois philistinism and its adulation of the proletariat. She felt some affinity with both of these prejudices. She borrowed widely, and with rather less acknowledgment, from the works of Franz Neumann and Franz Borkenau, exiles like herself who had in large measure anticipated her account of the Nazi and Soviet states. Her debt to Boris Souvarine, a disillusioned French Trotskyist who published in 1935 a brilliant and prescient study of Stalin, is, however, openly and generously recognized, though her enduring nostalgia for a certain lost innocence of the left prevented her from endorsing Souvarine's root-and-branch inclusion of Lenin in his condemnation of the Soviet enterprise.

The enduring importance of Arendt's major work thus rests not upon the originality of its contribution but on the quality of its central intuition. What Arendt understood best, and whatbinds together her account of Nazism and her otherwise unconnected and underdeveloped discussion of the Soviet experience, was the psychological and moral features of what she called totalitarianism.

By breaking up and taking over all of society, including the whole governing apparatus itself, totalitarian regimes dominate and terrorize individuals from within. The arbitrary and apparently irrational, anti-utilitarian nature of life under such regimes destroys the texture of shared experience, of reality, upon which normal life depends and disarms all attempts by reasonable men to understand and explain the course of events. Hence the tragic failure of outsiders to perceive the danger posed by totalitarian movements, and the lasting inability of commentators to grasp the enormity of the events they were witnessing. Instead of admitting what Arendt called the "utter lunacy" of Stalinism or Nazism, scholarly and other analysts looked for some firm ground of "interest" or "rationality" from which to reinsert these developments into the familiar political and moral landscape.

In the case of Nazism they thus missed the central place of genocide. Far from being just another exercise in mass violence, the plot to eliminate whole peoples and categories of people represented the ultimate in the control and dismantling of the human person and was thus not extraneous to the meaning of the regime but the very basis of it. Similarly, the Stalinist era was not a perversion of the logic of Historical Progress but its very acme—evidence of the infinite malleability of all experience and reality at the service of an idea.

It is not necessary to endorse this account in all its detail to understand that Arendt had it essentially right. At the time and for many years afterward she was assailed by historians, political scientists, and others for the excessively moral, even metaphysical quality of her approach, for her conflation of very different social experiences into a single story, and for her neglect of a variety of factors and (in the Soviet case) "achievements" that might moderate her interpretation. As Eric Hobsbawm remarked in a review of *On Revolution,* historians and others would be "irritated, as the author plainly is not, by a certain lack of interest in mere fact, a preference for metaphysical construct or poetic feeling . . . over reality."

Most of all, of course, many of her readers could not understand, much less endorse, the merging of German and Russian regimes into a single type. They quite correctly noted her annoying habit of attributing to totalitarian regimes, even to Hitler and Stalin themselves, a sort of ideological self-awareness, as though they themselves knew that they were engaged in making their own ideological predictions (about the Jewish "problem" or the inevitability of class conflict)

come true; Arendt admitted as much many years later in a September 1963 letter to Mary McCarthy, where she concedes that "the impact of ideology upon the individual may have been overrated by me [in the *Origins*]."

Since then, however, historians, essayists, and dissidents have done much to illustrate and confirm her account. Her emphasis upon the centrality of terror, which seemed disproportionate when she first proposed it, now sounds almost commonplace. As Arendt expressed it, terror executes on the spot the death sentence supposedly pronounced by Nature upon races and persons, or else by History upon classes, thus speeding-up "natural" or "historical" processes. Hercriticism of the Jacobins, in *On Revolution,* for aiming at a Republic of Virtue and installing instead a reign of terror, offended many at the time for its cavalier unconcern with the classic accounts and interpretations of the French Revolution, Marxist and liberal alike. It now sounds like a benign anticipation of the historical consensus espoused by François Furet and other scholars, notably in their appreciation of terror not as an extraneous political device but as the primary motor and logic of modern tyranny.

Hannah Arendt was throughout her adult life concerned above all with two closely related issues: the problem of political evil in the twentieth century and the dilemma of the Jew in the contemporary world.

—Tony Judt

If Hannah Arendt understood something that so many others missed (and continue to miss, to judge from certain strains in modern German social historiography), it was because she was more concerned with the moral problem of "evil" than with the structures of any given political system; as she put it in **"Nightmare and Flight,"** first published in 1945 and reprinted in the *Essays,* "The problem of evil will be the fundamental question of postwar intellectual life in Europe—as death became the fundamental question after the last war."

It is telling to discover from Kohn's collection that she was an avid and careful reader of some of the great antimodern Catholic writers—in a 1945 essay on **"Christianity and Revolution"** she discusses not only Charles Péguy and Georges Bernanos but also and less predictably G. K. Chesterton. In our post-Christian world, discussion of Evil has a curious, anachronistic feel, rather like invoking the Devil; even when modern students of murderous regimes acknowledge the value of describing them as evil they have been reluctant to invoke the term in any explanatory capacity. But Arendt suffered no such inhibitions, which is why, long before her controversial essay on Eichmann, she engaged the matter of evil head-on. It was not sufficient, she wrote in a 1953 response to Eric Voegelin's criticism of *Origins,* to treat the totalitarian criminals as "murderers" and punish them accordingly. In a world where murder had been accorded the status of a civic duty, the usual moral (and legal) categories will not suffice. The following year she developed the point further in **"Understanding and Politics"**: "The trouble with the wisdom of the past is that it dies, so to speak, in our hands as soon as we try to apply it honestly to the central political experiences of our time. Everything we know of totalitarianism demonstrates a horrible originality which no farfetched historical parallels can alleviate."

This observation isn't very helpful for lawyers (Arendt was trying to account for what she saw as the failure of the Nuremberg Trials), but it does account for her resort to the notion of "banality" when she came to address the problem of Eichmann. Her earlier inclination had been to describe the evil quality of totalitarianism as something utterly "radical"; but Karl Jaspers and others had noted the risk entailed here of making Nazism in particular seem somehow unique and thus, in an awful way, "great." As she thought about the matter more, she developed a rather different line of reasoning: in various essays and later in *The Human Condition* and *The Life of the Mind* she argues that evil comes from a simple failure to *think.*

If this implies that evil is a function of stupidity, then Arendt is merely indulging a tautology of her own making. Moreover, since she nowhere suggests that goodness is a product (or description) of intelligence, she probably did not mean to be taken too seriously. After all, as Mary McCarthy pointed out in a letter of June 1971, if, e.g., Eichmann truly "cannot think" then he is just a monster. But if he has a "wicked heart" then he is exercising some freedom of choice and is thus open to moral condemnation in the usual way. Here, as elsewhere, we do well not to make of Arendt too consistent a thinker.

However, as an account of a certain sort of evil person Arendt's idea was suggestive. In a 1945 essay, **"Organized Guilt and Universal Responsibility,"** she quotes an interview with a camp official at Majdanek. The man admits to having gassed and buried people alive. Then: Q. "Do you know the Russians will hang you?" A. "(Bursting into tears) Why should they? What have I done?" As she commented, such people were just ordinary jobholders and good family men. Their deeds may be monstrous, evidence in Arendt's words of "the bankruptcy of common sense," but the officials themselves are quite simply stupid, ordinary, everyday persons—in short, banal. There is something frustratingly, terrifyingly plausible about this observation. It rings true not just for Eichmann, but for other more recently prominent characters as well—Klaus Barbie or Paul Touvier—and thus suggests something important about the totalitarian state and its servants.

When Arendt came under attack for proposing this characterization it was in part because she did so too soon, as it were, but also because she attached it to a series of provocative and controversial remarks on the other subject that obsessed her, Jews.

In order to understand the complexities of Arendt's relationship to her own, and other people's, Jewishness, it is crucial to remember that she was, after all, a German Jew. Like the German-speaking Jews of Prague, Vienna, and other cities of the old Empire, the Jews of Germany were different from the Jews of the East, and they knew it and felt it. They were educated and cultivated in German, steeped in German *Bildung,* and quite lacked the difficult and frequently distant relationship to the dominant language and culture that shaped Jewish experience in Russia, Poland, and elsewhere in East-Central Europe. They certainly knew that they were Jews and that their non-Jewish German neighbors and fellow citizens knew they were Jewish; but this did not diminish their identification with the idea of German-ness. In the words of Moritz Goldstein, writing in 1912 and quoted with approval by Arendt in her essay on Walter Benjamin, "our relationship to Germany is one of unrequited love" [*Men in Dark Times*]. As she wrote of Rahel Varnhagen, the subject of one of her first books, "Abroad, her place of origin was called Berlin; in Berlin it was called Judengasse."

This deep sense of her own Germanness is invoked by Margaret Canovan, among others, to account for the care Arendt took in her study of totalitarianism to divert attention away from the distinctively *German* sources of Nazism and make of it a general "Western" or "modern" deviation. This seems likely; Arendt never really confronted the fact that the worst persecutions, of Jews in particular, in the modern era took place in Germany. As late as 1964, while enjoying herself with some German interviewers, she admitted to Mary McCarthy that "in my youth, I used to be rather lucky with German *goiim* (never, incidentally, with German Jews) and I was amused to see that some of my luck still holds."

She also had some of the characteristic German prejudices of her youth, notably with respect to the less fortunate peoples to the south and east; in a piece dating from 1944 she scornfully dismissed the European émigré press in the US, "worrying their heads off over the pettiest boundary disputes in a Europe thousands and thousands of miles away—such as whether Teschen belongs to Poland or Czechoslovakia, or Vilna to Lithuania instead of to Poland!" No "Ost-Jud" would have missed the significance of these disputes. Of the Ost-Juden themselves, Arendt wrote dismissively in *The Origins of Totalitarianism:*

These East European conditions, however, although they constituted the essence of the Jewish mass question, are of little importance in our context. Their political significance was limited to backward countries where the ubiquitous hatred of Jews made it almost useless as a weapon for specific purposes.

This almost snobbish, High German quality also contributed to her troubled relations with American Jewry; as William Barrett put it, "one part of her never quite assimilated to America." With her classical education and memories of youth in Königsberg and student days in Marburg and Heidelberg, she probably found many of the American Jews she met, intellectuals included, rather philistine if not positively autodidacts. They in turn could not grasp how one might be so assertively and proudly Jewish and yet (and above all) German at the same time. For she most certainly was Jewish. The titles of the closing chapters of **Rahel Varnhagen** give the clue: "Between Pariah and Parvenu" and "One Does Not Escape Jewishness."

This unambiguous identity did not of course preclude a certain distance from Jewishness—far from it; Arendt was always most critical of her own world and its tragic political myopia. In **Rahel Varnhagen** she notes that "the Berlin Jews considered themselves exceptions. And just as every anti-Semite knew his personal exceptional Jews in Berlin, so every Berlin Jew knew at least two eastern Jews in comparison with whom he felt himself to be an exception." In her essay on Rosa Luxemburg, another exceptional Jewish woman with whom she felt a close affinity, she makes the same point in a different key: "While the self-deception of assimilated Jews consisted in the mistaken belief that they were just as German as the Germans, just as French as the French, the self-deception of the intellectual Jews consisted in thinking that they had no 'fatherland,' for their fatherland actually was Europe" [**Men in Dark Times**].

Her critical distance from official Zionism was consistent with such attitudes. Hannah Arendt had become Zionist in Germany, had passed through a neo-Zionist phase in which she was drawn to bi-nationalism in Palestine, and was never anti-Israel; as she wrote to Mary McCarthy in December 1968, "Any real catastrophe in Israel would affect me more deeply than almost anything else." But she was quite firmly anti-nationalist, Jewish or any other kind; hence the impossibility of her position for many American Jews, who could not readily imagine a strong secular Jewish consciousness divorced from any sympathy for the "national solution." Moreover her deeply held belief, as much aesthetic as political, in the need to separate the private from the public meant that she found something distasteful (and perhaps a little "oriental"?) in the confident political style and self-promotion of many of the leading figures in North American Jewry, including certain intellectuals of her own acquaintance.

It was this cultural abyss, as much as the substance of the work, that explains the otherwise absurd furor over **Eichmann in Jerusalem**. At thirty years' distance the book seems much less controversial. Copious research on the *Judenräte*, the Jewish Councils of Nazi-dominated Europe, suggests what should have been obvious at the time: Arendt knew little about the subject, and some of her remarks about Jewish "responsibility" were insensitive and excessive, but there is a troubling moral question mark hanging over the prominent Jews who took on the task of administering the ghettos. She was not wrong to raise the matter, nor was she mistaken in some of her judgments; but she was indifferent, perhaps callously so, to the dilemmas Jews faced at the time, and was characteristically provocative, even "perverse" (as the historian Henry Feingold put it) in insisting on the powers of the Jewish leaders and neglecting to call due attention to their utter helplessness and, in many cases, their real ignorance of the fate that awaited the Jews.

If the Councils were in one sense the heirs to older self-governing bodies of existing Jewish communities and thus responsible for eliding the distinction between running Jewish life and administering Jewish death, they were also the chosen device of the Nazis for pursuing their own policies. Here as elsewhere it was Nazi policy to make others do their work for them, and while it is almost certainly the case that utter noncooperation would have made things infinitely harder for the Germans, the same observation applies all the more forcibly to the relative compliance of locally appointed non-Jewish authorities in occupied France, Belgium, the Netherlands, and elsewhere.

Arendt made things worse for herself by inserting her controversial but brief comments on this subject into a text that not only introduced the notion of "banality"—such that Jews seemed to become "responsible," Germans merely "banal"—but also criticized Israel for having staged a "show trial" and chosen to emphasize "crimes against the Jewish people" instead of "crimes against humanity." The irony is that the Eichmann Trial *was* a show trial—much as the more recent Barbie and Touvier trials in France were show trials, not in the sense of being rigged but in their primarily pedagogical function. The guilt of the accused in all these cases was never in question. Ben-Gurion was less interested in establishing Eichmann's responsibility, or even in extracting revenge, than in educating a new generation about the past sufferings of the Jews, and thereby further strengthening the foundations of the still fragile Jewish state.

Arendt was thus raising fundamental questions about memory, myth, and justice in the postwar world. Her critics, like Lionel Abel and Norman Podhoretz, could score "debater's points" as Mary McCarthy scornfully put it in a sympathetic letter, but they had not a clue about what she was trying to accomplish, and probably still don't. Like so many others in the initial postwar decades they were dependent on what Karl Jaspers called "life-sustaining lies," though he too could not help chiding his former student for her naiveté in failing to notice "that the act of putting a book like this into the world is an act of aggression" against just such lies. Today, with much of Europe taken up with issues of guilt, memory, past responsibility, "gray zones" of compliance and collaboration, and the problem of individual and collective retribution, Arendt's concerns are once again central.

Compared with these matters, Arendt's properly philosophical and theoretical legacy is lightindeed. This might have come as no surprise to her—in a conversation with Günter Gaus, reprinted in the *Essays,* she renounced any claim to being a "philosopher." Her critics would agree; Stuart Hampshire once wrote, "She seems to me to be inaccurate in argument and to make a parade of learned allusion without any detailed inquiry into texts." One senses a constant tension between a residual duty on Arendt's part to undertake philosophy and a natural preference (and gift) for political and moral commentary and what she called intellectual *action.* It is tempting to see this as a tension between Heidegger and Jaspers, the dominant intellectual influences upon her. At her worst she could lapse considerably toward Heidegger; in Judith Shklar's words, "Philosophy was for both of them an act of dramatizing through word play, textual associations, bits of poetry, and other phrases from their direct experiences." It was "passionate thinking" [*Partisan Review* 50, No. 1 (1983)]. She would slip into phrases like "world alienation," and even in a letter to McCarthy from February 1968, could write like this: "I have a feeling of futility in everything I do. Compared to what is at stake everything looks frivolous. I know this feeling disappears once I let myself fall into that gap between past and future which is the proper temporal *locus* of thought. . . ."

In many of Arendt's ventures into theory, the dominant impression is one of confusion. Categories tumble over one another, their meaning unclear and variable. "She rambles on in the style of an essayist who freely associates one remembered quotation, or fragment of an idea with another until it becomes time to stop" (Hampshire again). Her habit of tracing concepts genetically, which in the case of political ideas takes her back to Plato, is particularly unhelpful when applied to abstractions and mental categories like "thinking" and "willing." One is not surprised to learn, in a 1954 letter to Mary McCarthy, that she finds Hume "not so interesting." McCarthy herself, an affectionate and admiring friend and reader, chided Arendt over the rather misty quality of the argument in her essay on Lessing:

> There are wonderful thoughts in the Lessing speech but sometimes they have to be sensed, rather than clearly perceived, through a fog of approximative translation, e.g., "humanity," "humaneness," "hu-

manitarianism," which are occasionally treated as synonymous and occasionally not.

It was not the translator's fault. Arendt may or may not have been confused, but she is certainly confusing and it does her little service to pretend otherwise. At times she seems to be evincing an innocent nostalgia for the lost world of the ancient *polis,* at others she is displaying sympathy for a sort of syndicalist collectivism (while finding its nearest contemporary incarnation, the Israeli kibbutz, "rule by your neighbors" and not very appealing). She invokes the distinction between ancient (participatory) liberty and the modern (private) kind with an apparent preference for the former; yet she was unshakably against conflating the private and the public and thought that modern American "social" legislation—for example desegregation of schools—could be dangerous just because it sought to blur the distinction.

The Human Condition, her most finished piece of theoretical writing, boils down to a single, albeit powerful, idea: that we have lost the sense of public space, of acting in concert, and have instead become slaves to a vision of human life that consists of a curious combination of "making"—the error of placing *homo faber* at the center of political theory—and "History," the dangerous belief in fate and determined outcomes to which she attributed so many of the woes of our age. These are worthy insights, albeit a touch unreflectively communitarian, and it isn't difficult to see why each new generation of students thinks it has found in Hannah Arendt a trenchant critic of its times. But taken together they are in some conflict, and in any case offer neither a conceptually all-embracing nor a historically rich account of how we got where we are. They also propose no practically applicable solution to any particular political or social problem.

That is because Arendt herself was not setting out to construct any such all-embracing accounts or solutions. Most of her writings were initially conceived as separate lectures, essays, or articles, the forms at which she excelled. They are nearly all, in the proper sense of the word, occasional pieces, designed to respond to a particular event or to address a crisis or problem. And since most of the events in Arendt's world, and all of the crises and problems, returned in due course to the issue of totalitarianism, its causes and consequences, her contributions to modern thought have to be understood as variations on a single theme: we live in the midst of a political crisis whose extent we have yet fully to grasp, and we must act (by thought and by deed) so as to minimize the risk of repeating the experiences of our century. The first need is to recapture—or at least see the virtue of trying to recapture—the old republican qualities of civility, moderation, public discourse, and the like. This isn't a bad starting point for modern political theory—and once again Arendt came early to a position since adopted by many others. But it is, after all, only a starting point.

I have suggested that Hannah Arendt was at her best in short bursts, when she was commenting, appraising, criticizing, or merely thinking aloud on some issue of contemporary significance. Indeed some of the essays in the Kohn collection, notably an unpublished paper from 1950 or 1951 called **"The Eggs Speak Up,"** seem to me among the best pieces she ever wrote and should put an end to a certain image of Arendt as a "theorist" of the cold war, or even an intellectual precursor of "neo-conservatism." It thus comes as no surprise that her long correspondence with Mary McCarthy, published for the first time in its entirety, should be such a pleasure. The letters are not particularly intimate or self-revelatory on Arendt's part, but they do show a relaxed and warm side of her; she seemed to feel that McCarthy was one of the few people who saw what she was about (of *Eichmann in Jerusalem* she tells McCarthy that "you were the only reader to understand what otherwise I have never admitted—namely that I wrote this book in a curious state of euphoria").

She also demonstrates rather more human feeling than her correspondent could sometimes muster; following a series of highly emotional letters from Mary McCarthy in 1960 about the new love in her life (her future husband, James West) and the irritating difficulties posed by various ex-spouses and children from past marriages, it is left to Arendt to bring her friend down to earth with a gentle bump:

> Please don't fool yourself: nobody ever was cured of anything, trait or habit, by a mere woman, though this is precisely what all girls think they can do. Either you are willing to take him "as is" or you better leave well enough alone. What is going to happen to these poorchildren? To add to the shock of parental separation the shock of separating them from each other seems a bit unwise. But how can one judge without knowing anything[?].

When Mary McCarthy seemed vexed that Hannah Arendt continued to maintain friendly relations with Bowden Broadwater, the husband whom McCarthy was abandoning, Arendt chided her:

> The fact is that you brought him into my life, that without you he never would have become—not a personal friend which, of course, he is not—but a friend of the house, so to speak. But once you placed him there you cannot simply take him away from where he is now. As long as he does not do something really outrageous which he has not done so far and really turns against you which he has not done either, I am not going to sit in judgment. . . . You say you cannot trust him. Perhaps you are right, perhaps you are wrong, I have no idea. But it strikes me that you can forget so easily that you trusted him enough to be married to him for fifteen years.

The age difference between them was not great (Arendt was born in 1906, McCarthy in 1912), but one is never in any doubt who was the mature woman, who the precocious girl.

The tone of the correspondence is not always serious. Predictably, there is much gossip, some of it funny. Arendt had no time for most French intellectuals, notably those in fashion. In 1964 she wrote to McCarthy, "I have just finished reading *Les Mots*—and was so disgusted that I was almost tempted to review this piece of highly complicated lying . . . I am going to read les confessions of Simone—for their gossip value, but also because this kind of bad faith becomes rather fascinating." A few months later she provides a follow-up report:

> This [De Beauvoir's *Force of Circumstance*] is one of the funniest books I read in years. Incredible that no one has taken that apart. Much as I dislike Sartre, it seems he is punished for all his sins by this kind of a cross. Especially since her unwavering true love for him is the only mitigating circumstance in the "case against her," really quite touching.

McCarthy, of course, was past mistress at this sort of thing; when in 1966 the Parisian *Nouvel Observateur* ran the headline "Est Elle Nazie?" over its excerpts from *Eichmann in Jerusalem,* she described it as "a sales promotion stunt, coated over with 'anti-fascist' piety," which is about right. A couple of years later the editor, Jean Daniel, sought unsuccessfully to make amends: "Daniel opposed it, I gather. But then he ought to have resigned. To say that here [Paris] is of course ludicrous. No French intellectual would ever resign on a point of principle unless to associate himself with another clique."

If the pair were prejudiced against French intellectuals, others come off little better. McCarthy gives a wonderfully acerbic report of a London dinner party in 1970, full of "silly zombies," from which she reports a remark by Sonia Orwell, as recalled by Stephen Spender, to illustrate the depths of British snobbery: "Auschwitz, oh dear, *no!* That person was never in Auschwitz. Only in some very *minor* death camp." Arendt's prejudices come into play at a rather more rarefied level. Of Vladimir Nabokov she writes in 1962: "There is something in [him] which I greatly dislike. As though he wanted to show you all the time how intelligent he is. And as though he thinks of himself in terms of 'more intelligent than.' There is something vulgar in hisrefinement." In the same letter she replies to McCarthy's request for her views on *The Tin Drum:* "I know the Grass book but could never finish it. In my opinion, mostly second-hand, derivative, *outré* but with some very good parts in it."

The most savage comments are, however, reserved for the New York intellectual scene. Philip Rahv's "Marxist assurance" is compared by McCarthy to conversation with "some fossilized mammoth"; the "PR [*Partisan Review*] boys" in general get short shrift, except "Danny Bell," whom Arendt grudgingly concedes "is the only one who has got a conscience that bothers him once in a while. He is also a bit more intelligent than the others." Of the editor of *The New Yorker,* whose office in 1956 had pressed her for more details in a piece she had written, Mary McCarthy comments: "Shawn is really a curious person; he's a self-educated man and he assumes that everybody, like his own former untaught self, is eager to be crammed with information. A sentence larded with dates and proper names fills him with gluttonous delight—like a *boeuf à la mode.*"

McCarthy could be serious; her intermittent comments on Richard Nixon, from the 1959 "kitchen debate" with Khrushchev to a timely reminder from 1974 that the much eulogized late president was also a crook, are well taken, and she was a gifted scene setter, whether traveling in Sicily or describing a European dinner party with the wives of dead writers ("We had a party yesterday . . . It was full of widows, like *Richard III*"). But in the later correspondence there enters a morbid, even mildly paranoid tone. She doesn't understand why her books get such a poor reception and feels abandoned by her friends. After one attack on her in 1974 she wrote to Arendt: "I can't help feeling, though I shouldn't, that if one of my friends had been in *my* place *I* would [have] raised my voice. This leads to the conclusion that I am peculiar, in some way that I cannot make out; *indefensible,* at least for my friends" (all emphases in original). Even Arendt comes under suspicion—"Something is happening or has happened to our friendship . . . The least I can conjecture is that I have got on your nerves." Whether or not this was the case is unclear—Arendt was much too well bred to say anything in reply. But the somewhat brittle texture of McCarthy's gifts and her fundamentally narcissistic personality may have begun to grate a little. There is a distinctly cooler tone in Arendt's last letters, many of which were dictated.

Whereas there is something ultimately rather monotonous in McCarthy's end of the correspondence, caustic and self-regarding, Arendt's letters have a more measured and cosmopolitan tone. She never tells McCarthy of her own personal dilemmas, for example her frustrations in continuing her long relationship with Heidegger. But a long description from August 1972 of the ambiance at the Rockefeller Center for writers and artists in Bellagio, Italy, not only captures brilliantly the luxuriant, sybaritic, unworldly mood of the retreat, but also nails down some of its comic contradictions, which appear to have changed not at all:

> Now imagine this place filled, but by no means crowded, with a bunch of scholars, or rather professors, from all countries, . . . almost all of them rather mediocre (and this is putting it charitably) with their wives, some of them are plain nuts, others play the

piano or type busily the nonmasterworks of their husbands.

She writes perceptive and balanced comments on the student events of 1968 (in France and the US), in contrast to McCarthy who completely misread what was happening and assured Arendt in June of that year that De Gaulle had "made a mistake in his rapid veer to the Right; he will scare the middle voter whom he was *hoping* to scare with his anti-Communist rhetoric." (In fact De Gaulle and his party scored a huge electoral victory two weeks later by virtue of that very rhetoric.) On the whole it seems fair to conclude that whereas Mary McCarthy's letters, however entertaining, are rather ephemeral, the contributions by Arendt have a weightier texture and can still be read with profit as a commentary on her times.

Like the *Essays,* moreover, they also help us understand Hannah Arendt herself a little better. While she may indeed have been, in McCarthy's words, "a solitary passenger on her train of thought," she was not altogether alone on her journey through the twentieth century. Her elective affinity might have been with the great Germans, past and present, but her true community lay elsewhere, as her friendships and acquaintances suggest. She was born in Königsberg, a city on the geographical periphery of the culture of which it was at the same time a center. This gives her more in common than she may have realized with contemporary writers born in other vulnerable cities at once central and peripheral— Vilna, Trieste, Danzig, Alexandria, Algiers, even Dublin— and accounts for her membership in a very special and transient community, that twentieth-century republic of letters formed against their will by the survivors of the great upheavals of the century.

These lost cosmopolitan communities, in which Germans, Jews, Greeks, Italians, Poles, French, and others lived in productive disharmony, were torn from their roots in the First World War and obliterated in the Second and during its aftermath. This shared experience accounts for Arendt's understanding of Moritz Goldstein's "unrequited love" (the very phrase also used by Milosz in his account in *The Captive Mind* of Polish intellectuals' longing for a disappearing West), and for her instinctive affinity with Albert Camus. They were all "chance survivors of a deluge," as she put it in a 1947 dedication to Jaspers, and wherever they ended up, in New York, Paris, or Rome, they were constrained, like Camus's Sisyphus, to push the boulder of memory and understanding up the thankless hill of public forgetting for the rest of their lives.

In Arendt's case the responsibility, as she felt it, was made heavier by a conscientious, and perhaps distinctively Jewish, refusal to condemn modernity completely or to pass a curse upon the Enlightenment and all its works. She certainly understood the temptation, but she also saw the danger. The tendency to treat Western liberal democracy as somehow "shallow," already present in the appeal of "Eastern" solutions before 1914, has revived twice over in our own time. On the first occasion, in the Sixties, Arendt's response was unambiguous: the struggle against the deceptive charms of what we would now call cultural relativism was for her a matter of moral courage, of exercising what she called judgment. In a letter to Jaspers in December 1963 she reflected that "even good and, at bottom, worthy people have, in our time, the most extraordinary fear about making judgments. This confusion about judgment can go hand in hand with fine and strong intelligence, just as good judgment can be found in those not remarkable for their intelligence." Hannah Arendt was not afraid to judge, and be counted.

For the recent resurfacing of the critical attitude toward the Englightenment, notably in certain Central European circles seduced by the post-Heideggerian notion that the soulless,technological, "fabricating" society of our century is an outgrowth of the Godless *hubris* of the French Enlightenment and its successors, Arendt herself bears some indirect responsibility. It is the very woolliness of her thoughts on these matters that has lent them to just such interpretations, and her reluctance to distance herself definitively from her former lover and mentor did not help. But she would never have made the mistake of supposing that the end of communism promised some sort of definitive success for its opponents, or that the responsibilities of various strands in Western thought for the woes of our time thereby disqualified the Western tradition as a whole. She made a good many little errors, for which her many critics will never forgive her. But she got the big things right, and for this she deserves to be remembered.

FURTHER READING

Biography

Ettinger, Elzbieta. *Hannah Arendt/Martin Heidegger.* New Haven: Yale University Press, 1996, 139 p.

> Brief account of Arendt's relationship with Heidegger.

McCarthy, Mary. "Hannah Arendt and Politics." *Partisan Review* LI (1984/1985): 729-38.

> Recollects the significance of politics in Arendt's public and private life.

Young-Bruehl, Elizabeth. *Hannah Arendt: For Love of the World.* New Haven: Yale University Press, 1982, 563 p.

> Bio-critical study gathered from oral and print sources. Includes chronological bibliography and appendices on Arendt's genealogy, the German texts of her poems, and a synopsis of her doctoral dissertation.

Criticism

Benhabib, Seyla. "Judgment and the Moral Foundations of Politics in Arendt's Thought." *Political Theory* 16, No. 1 (February 1988): 29-51.

> Argues that Arendt's "characterization of [political] action through the categories of plurality, natality, and narrativity" provide an analytic framework in which judgment is a moral faculty in contradistinction to Arendt's view of judgment as "the most political" of cognitive faculties.

Canovan, Margaret. "Arendt, Rousseau, and Human Plurality in Politics." *Journal of Politics* 45, No. 2 (May 1983): 286-302.

> Compares and contrasts Arendt's and Jean-Jacques Rousseau's political thought, detecting the implication that "the proper role of political philosophy is much more limited than often is believed."

Clarke, Barry. "Beyond the Banality of Evil." *British Journal of Political Science* 10,No. 4 (October 1980): 417-39.

> Examines Arendt's conception of the "banality of evil" in Kantian terms in order to clarify the evil Eichmann represents.

Dossa, Shiraz. "Hannah Arendt on Eichmann: The Public, the Private and Evil." *Review of Politics* 46, No. 2 (April 1984): 163-82.

> Argues that Arendt's representation of Eichmann makes sense "on the peculiar terrain of her political theory and particularly in terms of the public-private distinction which lies at the core of this theory."

———. "Human Status and Politics: Hannah Arendt on the Holocaust." *Canadian Journal of Political Science* 11, No. 2 (June 1990): 309-23.

> Examines the relationship between politics and humanism in Arendt's writing.

Gottsegen, Michael J. *The Political Thought of Hannah Arendt.* Albany: State University of New York Press, 1994, 311 p.

> Traces the development of Arendt's mature political thought (1958-1975) and reveals an "action-ideal" conceptual framework that informs her entire canon.

Habermas, Jurgen. "Hannah Arendt's Communications Concept of Power." *Social Research* 44, No. 1 (Spring 1977): 3-24.

> Traces the development of Arendt's communications concept of power back to classical Greek philosophy.

Heather, Gerard P., and Matthew Stolz. "Hannah Arendt and

the Problem of Critical Theory." *Journal of Politics* 41, No. 1 (February 1979): 2-22.

> Suggests that Arendt embodied the mode of thought signified by the phrase "the school of public life itself," rather than the "Critical Theorists," who merely pursue "a fusion of theory and praxis" without achieving it.

Hinchman, Lewis P. and Sandra K. "In Heidegger's Shadow: Hannah Arendt's Phenomenological Humanism." *Review of Politics* 46, No. 2 (April 1984): 183-211.

> Places Arendt's political theory in the context of German phenomenology and *Existenz* philosophy, focusing on points of contact between Arendt and Martin Heidegger.

Honohan, Iseult. "Arendt and Benjamin on the Promise of History: A Network of Possibilities or One Apocalyptic Moment?" *CLIO* 19, No. 4 (Summer 1990): 311-30.

> Compares and contrasts Walter Benjamin's and Arendt's theories of history, concluding that "while Benjamin makes historical understanding *almost* self-sufficient, Arendt's approach retains political action as a source of meaning complementary to historical understanding."

Jacobitti, Suzanne. "Hannah Arendt and the Will." *Political Theory* 16, No. 1 (February 1988): 53-76.

> Explains Arendt's concept of the will and its relation to free action.

Jay, Martin. "Hannah Arendt: Opposing Views." *Partisan Review* XLV, No. 3 (1978): 348-68.

> Examines Arendt's oeuvre in context of the political existential tradition.

Kateb, George. "Arendt and Representative Democracy." *Salmagundi* 60 (Spring/Summer 1983): 20-59.

> Explores Arendt's reticence toward representative democracy and discusses other theoretical arguments that tend to disparage representative democracy as a legitimate political system.

————. *Hannah Arendt: Politics, Conscience, Evil.* Totowa, N.J.: Rowman & Allanheld, 1983, 204 p.

> Critical overview of Arendt's works, focusing on her theory of modern democracy.

————. "Death and Politics: Hannah Arendt's Reflections on the American Constitution." *Social Research* 54, No. 3 (Fall 1987): 605-28.

> Sketches Arendt's thinking on the American Constitution, noting "she helps us see it again with fresh eyes."

Knauer, James T. "Motive and Goal in Hannah Arendt's Concept of Political Action." *American Political Science Review* 74, No. 3 (September 1980): 721-33.

> Demonstrates that Arendt's concept of political action has been misread by critics, then reveals the relationship between instrumentality and meaning in political action.

McKenna, George. "Bannisterless Politics: Hannah Arendt and Her Children." *History of Political Thought* V, No. 11 (Summer 1984): 333-60.

> Contends that "Arendt's radicalism is an irresponsible, empty radicalism. . . and the reason for its derelictions stems form the concept of freedom which underlies most of Arendt's later writing—a freedom so lacking in limits or restraints as to amount to a form of wilfulness."

Morgenthau, Hans. "Hannah Arendt on Totalitarianism and Democracy." *Social Research* 41, No. 1 (Spring 1977): 127-31.

> Discusses the significance of Arendt's contributions to political philosophy.

Schwartz, Benjamin I. "The Religion of Politics." *Dissent* 17, No. 2 (March/April 1970): 144-61.

> Contrasts the public and private sides of Arendt's concept of political action.

Sitton, John. "Hannah Arendt's Argument for Council Democracy." *Polity* XX, No. 1 (Fall 1987): 80-100.

> Analyzes Arendt's argument for council democracy, demonstrating how some of her conceptions obscured "her comprehension of the actual historical experiences of council democracy."

Whitfield, Stephen J. *Into the Dark: Hannah Arendt and Totalitarianism.* Philadelphia: Temple University Press, 1980, 338 p.

> Argues that *The Origins of Totalitarianism* and *Eichmann in Jerusalem* comprise "the most convincing single effort to grasp the meaning of the German and Russian regimes of the 1930s and 1940s."

Wolin, Sheldon S. "Hannah Arendt: Democracy and the Political." *Salmagundi* 60 (Spring-Summer 1983): 3-19.

> Explores the origins of "the antidemocratic strain" in Arendt's thought, but detects a shift to "a leftward position" in her later writings.

Young-Bruehl, Elisabeth. "Reflections on Hannah Arendt's *The Life of the Mind.*" *Political Theory* 10, No. 2 (May 1982): 277-305.

> Analysis of the two completed volumes comprising *The Life of the Mind*—"Thinking" and "Willing"—in an attempt to point the way to "Judging," the never written volume of the proposed trilogy.

Additional coverage of Arendt's life and career is contained in the following sources published by Gale Research: *Contemporary Authors,* Vols. 17-20R and 61-64; *Contemporary Authors New Revision Series,* Vol. 26; *Contemporary Literary Criticism,* Vol. 66; and *Major Twentieth Century Writers.*

Dorothy Arzner
1897-1979

American director and screenwriter.

INTRODUCTION

One of the few women to direct a substantial number of mainstream Hollywood films, Arzner directed or played a significant role as co-director or editor in the making of over twenty movies from the 1920s through the 1940s. Louise Heck-Rabi has stated that the "undisputed achievement of Dorothy Arzner is that she was the only woman director of films in Hollywood who linked the silent and sound moviemaking eras." Often featuring strong female leads, Arzner's films confronted sexist stereotypes and typically dealt with women struggling to obtain sexual equality in their marriages, relationships, and careers. As a director at such prominent studios as Paramount and RKO, Arzner had the opportunity to work with many of the best-known female film stars of the period, including Rosalind Russell, Lucille Ball, Claudette Colbert, Joan Crawford, and Katharine Hepburn. Since the early 1970s, Arzner's films, particularly *Merrily We Go to Hell* (1932) and *Dance, Girl, Dance* (1940), have been a favorite topic among feminist film critics.

Biographical Information

Arzner was born in San Francisco, California, in January 1897. Her birth records were destroyed in the fire following the San Francisco earthquake of 1906; according to a popular anecdote, she sought to define herself as a thoroughly modern woman of the twentieth century by listing her "official" date of birth as 1900. Following the earthquake, Arzner and her family moved to Los Angeles, where her father, Louis Arzner, became the owner of a well-known Hollywood restaurant. After graduating from high school, Arzner studied medicine at the University of Southern California but left before finishing her degree. In 1919 she obtained a position as a typist at what would later become Paramount studios. Arzner impressed her employers and was soon promoted through the ranks, becoming script supervisor, cutter, and eventually editor. A major turning point in her career occurred in 1922 when she created the bullfight scenes in *Blood and Sand* from stock footage and close-ups of Rudolph Valentino, thus saving the studio a tremendous sum. Some of Arzner's other early credits as an editor include work on director James Cruze's films *The Covered Wagon* and *Old Ironsides*. Arzner's directorial debut came in 1927 with the farce *Fashions for Women,* starring Esther Ralston. Arzner directed three other silent films: the two comedies *Ten Modern Commandments* (1927) and *Get Your Man* (1927) and *Manhattan Cock-*

tail (1928). Her first "talkie" was *The Wild Party* (1929). After completing several more films for Paramount, including *Honor among Lovers* (1931) and *Merrily We Go to Hell,* Arzner left to become a freelance director. Among her most successful later films are *Christopher Strong* (1933), starring Katharine Hepburn, and *Craig's Wife* (1936), which featured Rosalind Russell. Arzner's last feature film was the war movie *First Comes Courage* (1943); she contracted pneumonia during the film's final stages and subsequently retired from directing. After leaving Hollywood Arzner developed the first filmmaking course at the Pasadena Playhouse and later taught for four years at UCLA during the 1960s. Among her students at UCLA was widely-known contemporary director Francis Ford Coppola. In 1975 she was honored by the Directors Guild of America. Arzner died in October 1979.

Major Works

Arzner's career as a director spanned two decades, but all of her work focused on a single theme: women's efforts and abilities to control their own fate in a world of self-centered and chauvinistic men. Prime examples of this theme are *Fash-*

ions for Women, Arzner's directorial debut, in which a cigarette girl achieves fame in the Parisian fashion world by manipulating men; *Sarah and Son* (1930), the story of a young immigrant mother who must regain custody of her son from an influential family; and *Christopher Strong,* which depicts aviator Lady Cynthia Darrington's illicit love affair with an older, married man. Arzner used several constructions to develop her theme of women's self-determination. In *Dance, Girl, Dance* and *Working Girls* (1931), for instance, Arzner juxtaposed two types of women in similar situations. The first type (a dancer named Bubbles played by Lucille Ball in *Dance, Girl, Dance* and the older sister May in *Working Girls*) attempts to gain wealth and power by attaching herself to a man who appears to possess these attributes. The second, stronger type (Joan, a woman who strives to be a professional ballerina in *Dance, Girl, Dance,* and June, the younger but more mature sister in *Working Girls*) seeks self-determination and self-fulfillment as the key to success. In *Working Girls* May has an affair with a Harvard student who does not truly love her, and she becomes pregnant. It is only through the efforts of June that the student is forced to marry May, while June is free to marry the man she loves. In *Dance, Girl, Dance* Joan is freed from a string of humiliations at the hand of her rival, the vamp Bubbles, by the attentions of a man who offers to train her as a serious dancer. Arzner also considered the complex relationship between gender and class, the similarities and differences in expectations and roles of women in different economic strata in several of her films. For instance, in *The Bride Wore Red* (1937) two wealthy men disagree about what makes a woman high class: Count Armalia claims it is clothes; Rudi Pal believes it is breeding. The Count appears to be correct as he successfully turns a cabaret singer into a socialite who wins Pal's marriage proposal, but after her deception is revealed, she marries a poor postman whom she loves and who truly values her. The plot of *Anybody's Woman* (1930) is similar: a poor chorus girl marries a wealthy lawyer while he is drunk, but she cannot find acceptance among his small-town friends. In other movies, such as *Fashions for Women* and *Get Your Man,* Arzner's heroines experience little personal sacrifice as they arrive at economic success through the manipulation of men. A final theme in Arzner's films is that of women who sacrifice themselves to solve problems beyond their control; suicide is a popular end for Arzner's heroines. In *Christopher Strong* Darrington kills herself while attempting to set an altitude record rather than tell Strong that she is pregnant. Darrington can face neither destroying Strong's family nor imprisoning herself in the traditional roles of mother and wife. In *Nana* (1934), the screen depiction of Emile Zola's novel of the same title, Nana kills herself rather than face her betrayal of her lover. Finally, in *First Comes Courage* Arzner depicts a woman, Nicole, in the Norwegian underground who marries a Nazi in order to gain information. Although she is in love with an Allied officer, Nicole refuses to leave Norway even after her husband is killed. In each of these films the prob-

lems the heroines face are created by society: confining gender roles in the first two movies and the perils of war in the last. Even in suicide, however, the women determine their own fate.

Critical Reception

Critical and popular reaction to Arzner's films at the time of their release was generally favorable. *Craig's Wife,* for example, was praised for its artistic merit, and a critic for the *Motion Picture Daily* described it as a "radical departure from the regular run film merchandise." *Christopher Strong,* which Sam Goldwyn described as "the best picture of the year," likewise received favorable notices. Scholarly reaction to Arzner's works, which underwent a revival in the 1970s, has centered on the courage and initiative of her female heroines, the limitations women suffer in their relationships with men, and the ways in which Arzner succeeded in expressing the feminine point of view. Though Arzner consistently denied having any feminist intentions, numerous critics have found evidence of feminist themes in her films' form and structure, plays on stereotypes, and use of ironic reversals. Commentators have noted that both *Merrily We Go to Hell* and *Christopher Strong* present contradictions and a refusal to reach closure in such a way as to call patriarchal ideologies into question, while *Dance, Girl, Dance* focuses the viewer's attention on the problematic position that the female characters occupy as members of a male-dominated society. As Claire Johnston has argued: "To understand the real achievement of [Arzner's] work, it is necessary to locate it within the constraints imposed by the Hollywood studio system and in relation to the patriarchal ideology of classic Hollywood cinema."

PRINCIPAL WORKS

The Red Kimono (screenplay) [adapted from a story by Adela Rogers St. John] 1925
Fashions for Women (film) 1927
Get Your Man (film) 1927
Ten Modern Commandments (film) 1927
Manhattan Cocktail (film) 1928
The Wild Party (film) 1929
Anybody's Woman (film) 1930
Behind the Makeup (film) [with Robert Milton] 1930
Charming Sinners (film) [with Robert Milton] 1930
*"The Vagabond King" (film sequence) 1930
Sarah and Son (film) 1930
Honor among Lovers (film) 1931
Working Girls (film) 1931
Merrily We Go to Hell (film) 1932
Christopher Strong (film) 1933
Nana (film) 1934
Craig's Wife (film) 1936
The Bride Wore Red (film) 1937

The Last of Mrs. Cheyney (film) [with Richard Boleslavsky] 1937
Dance, Girl, Dance (film) 1940
First Comes Courage (film) 1943

*This film sequence was one of several by different directors included in *Paramount on Parade,* which was released in 1930.

CRITICISM

Gerald Peary (essay date 1974)

SOURCE: "Dorothy Arzner," in *Cinema,* No. 34, 1974, pp. 2-9.

[*In the following essay, Peary centers on* Christopher Strong, *praising Arzner's directorial and cinematic skills as he remarks on the film's characters and themes.*]

Dorothy Arzner's **Christopher Strong** is ripe for discovery, staking its most persuasive claim to recognition at that juncture of "auteur" aesthetics and progressive politics (sexual politics, that is) so rarely encountered in the American cinema. Furthermore, it is a significant Katharine Hepburn film, this, her second movie after *A Bill of Divorcement;* for it is at RKO in 1933, under the mature, even wise directorial tutelage of Ms. Arzner, that the youthful Hepburn first utilizes her noblest attributes—her independence, unconventionality, resilience, physical prowess, athletic skill—all in the services of the feminist philosophy.

As Lady Cynthia Darrington, world-champion aviatrix (a character reminiscent of Amelia Earhart), Hepburn demonstrates with the certitude of an Isadora Duncan that a woman's true happiness comes through intense, front-seat participation in an exciting profession. In **Christopher Strong** it is flying planes, breaking world's records, competing and winning in the world of men. Conversely, the same happiness can be squandered away, the talented woman's life wasted, if she should misdirect this energy toward some egocentric man, such as **Christopher Strong**'s titular hero, actually non-hero.

Christopher Strong, though the name of Gilbert Frankau's source novel, is a pointedly ironic title for Arzner's movie. The picture isn't finally about Strong, but is much more deeply concerned with the women surrounding the man—Elaine, his wife; Monica, his daughter; Cynthia, his mistress. Nor is Christopher "strong" in any true sense, for beneath his carefully lived-in identities as stalwart citizen-politician, morally righteous British gentleman, doting husband and father, exists a weak, unscrupulous coward. He desperately holds tight to two women, wife and lover, and willingly wrecks both of their lives so that he never will feel unwanted or alone.

Strong is played with standard anxiety and self-flagellation by the eternally tormented Colin Clive. The character reminds more than a bit of [Francois] Truffaut's spineless, lost husband in *La Peau Douce,* who shuttles unhappily between a middle-class wife and his airplane stewardess mistress, but pays for his identity crisis as shotgun victim to his wife's Medea-like rage.

Arzner, however, avoids the militant feminist temptations of the Truffaut-type ending, for her Elaine Strong would never kill her husband. No matter what his transgressions, she would always forgive him. Nor does Arzner allow herself to fantasize an even more incredible *Jules et Jim* type conclusion, with Cynthia taking Christopher for one last airplane ride and then crashing down with both of them in a glorious dual murder-suicide.

In the sometimes misogynist movie world of Truffaut, scorned women become furies and wreak dreadful revenge on the men who have hurt them. But in the real world outside of movie theatres, with which Dorothy Arzner deals, men of a type like Christopher Strong dabble in adultery and tend to get away with it. At the end of the movie, a pregnant, unmarried Cynthia kills herself on a solo flight. Sir Christopher Strong, reunited with Lady Strong, heads for a vacation voyage to New York.

For those critics fervently seeking out fresh directorial faces to bolster their auteur pantheons, Dorothy Arzner belatedly suits their purposes to perfection—thirty long years since her movie retirement. Along with Rowland Brown (and perhaps MGM's erratic but talented George Hill), Arzner appears as one of the few shining originals of the early sound era whose works remain to be excavated and properly explicated. Not only is Dorothy Arzner a bit of a visual stylist (sometimes, as in **Working Girls** [Paramount, 1931] on the prime level of Brown), but she is a director firmly committed to expressing her personal concerns in the body of her films.

Furthermore, for those picky students of the movies on the brink of anti-auteurism, who are concerned beyond the simple existence of personal themes with the *quality* of these themes, Dorothy Arzner also offers a refreshing, contemporary vision. Those who grow tired of Hawksian male camaraderie and back-slapping horseplay infantilism as the paradigm of what movies should be about might look instead to Ms. Arzner, and not only to **Christopher Strong**.

From her first feature, **Fashions for Women** in 1927, with Esther Ralston as an enterprising cigarette girl who makes her way upward in the fashion world by duping the foolish male designers, Arzner sides time and again in her productions with her dashing, flashy women-on-the-go characters against the hollow, conceited male animals who try to run women's lives into the ground (and literally succeed sometimes, as with the plane crash demise of Hepburn's Cynthia in *Christopher Strong*). But while never suppressing the ardour of her support for the strong, independent women in her films, Dorothy Arzner succeeds further, and much more nobly, by expanding her horizons to equal support for all manifestations of womanhood.

The final testimonial of Arzner's earnest feminism goes beyond her undeniably exciting portrayals of the most obviously admirable and heroic of women. Most impressive is her astounding lack of elitism, her genuine concern and empathy with the Shavian "womenly women" who also populate her movies—the repressed, conservative females who live in the shadows of their all-demanding men. Kate Millet's *Three Lives* are opened up into many lives, those of every woman to walk with honor through a Dorothy Arzner film.

Telephoned recently at her West Coast home, 73-year old Ms. Arzner sniffed at the waves of faddish attention directed her way since "the women's lib stuff broke." She has been through at least part of it before—long years ago, during her Hollywood directorial employment. Film writers even then invariably alluded to her freak status as a woman film director when reviewing her pictures, though not always in the admiring tone of articles today.

Even the more sympathetic critics took her directing only half-seriously, converting the female novelty into a subject of human interest for their columns. But other more hostile writers felt compelled to pick apart her capability. "Whether this story is exactly the type of yarn for Miss Arzner is questionable," wrote an anonymous newspaperman (Mordaunt Hall?) for *The New York Times* by way of greeting *Fashions for Women* into the theatres. This critic tried to balance his review in selecting out one of Arzner's attributes for praise: "She undoubtedly has an eye for attractive costumes . . ."

Ms. Arzner brushed aside this condescending male stereotyping with little trouble, creating for herself a respected career as a Paramount director, making nine films at the studio between 1927 and 1932. Normally these featured volatile and vital women in the leads, including the two pictures, *Get Your Man* (1927) and *The Wild Party* (1929) with Clara Bow. By 1930, Dorothy Arzner was left as the only woman still directing in Hollywood,—a status, though not necessarily a desirable one, without change through the end of her time in movies in 1943.

Beginning with *Christopher Strong* (1933) at RKO, Arzner became an independent, moving with characteristic skill among the various studios over the next decade before her retirement. Her best received film was *Craig's Wife* (1935) with Rosalind Russell at Columbia. Her greatest work is the totally unheralded *Dance, Girl, Dance* (1940) at RKO, pitting tough chorine, Lucille Ball, against a touching,

Cinderella-like Maureen O'Hara, with Maria Ouspenskaya utilized brilliantly as their dance teacher mentor, the rare case that her screen characterization honored her real-life identity as master acting teacher of the Stanislavski school.

Ms. Arzner made approximately fourteen pictures (there are several debated titles), before quitting the movies. Later she undertook a second career with equal honor, as a professor in the UCLA film school. No less a person than director Francis Ford Coppola is indebted for her work with him while he was a student and also for her friendship. As he commented in a recent interview, "I was at UCLA film school from about 1960 to 1962, and I barely had two friends at the time . . . It was very lonely . . . One of my directing teachers was Dorothy Arzner, and she was always very sweet to me and encouraging. She was one of the better influences."

If one principle remembrance of *Christopher Strong* is the vibrant, devil-may-care image Katharine Hepburn's Cynthia Darrington, smiling with all the confidence of the world under her pilot's helmet, another equally stirring, affecting memory is of poor little rich wife, Elaine Strong (played abnormally well by the sometimes cloying Billie Burke under Arzner's direction), sitting in a tight ball in her lonely living room, staring emptily at the floor. She is afraid to interrupt her cad of a husband, Christopher Strong, who is thousands of miles away, though really only in the next room, *his* room. While he composes another oratorical gem to be delivered in Parliament, while he listens to the radio for news of the publicized flights of his lover, Elaine Strong does nothing, for she sees herself as nothing, now that her husband rejects her.

Elaine is anti-social, inhibited, afraid to express any positive emotions, a puritan, and an impossible prig. She clings tenaciously to her husband, snubs Cynthia, and constantly criticizes her daughter, while incapable of understanding any of them, especially when they seek out adventures in their lives. But even at her most painful and exasperating, Elaine is never treated by Arzner with the slightest derision. Her obsessed behavior has its reasons, which Arzner makes certain are understood, letting Elaine be seen without masks or defenses, in the quiet private moments which tend to forgive her public fumblings. For example, when Strong and Cynthia kiss for the first time, Arzner shoots the scene in long-shot, through the horrified eyes of Elaine, watching from the balcony above. And the camera stays with her as she retreats into her room and falls sobbing and profoundly alone onto her previously unthreatened marriage bed.

While Elaine Strong virtually becomes abandoned by her wandering spouse, all is neither so rosy on the second female front. Christopher Strong, in almost vampiric fashion, has begun to prey on another robust, vulnerable female victim— the proud and virginal Cynthia Darrington, professional aviatrix and heroine of British school girls. As Strong's will begins to dominate, Cynthia's cherished independence slips away. She sacrifices all to her new lover-gallant, clipping her flying wings to reign as second woman and mistress in his crowded life. She trades in her pilot's gear and aggressive, mannish strut for quiet afternoons of upper class intrigue in high heels, long dress, and mink coat. She and Strong hold hands and whisper love across roadhouse tables, whenever he can slip away from his wife.

But Cynthia becomes bored and itchy at last, finally bursting out in impassioned soliloquy, proclaiming her desires to be free (much as with the sudden eloquence of Maureen O'Hara's fiery "anti-man" speech toward the conclusion of Arzner's later *Dance, Girl, Dance*): "I want to fly again, Chris, I'm getting soft," Cynthia pleads with him. "I have nothing to do all day but wait for your telegrams saying you can't come. I want to go up again. I want to break records. I want to train hard. I want to get up at dawn. I want to smell the fields and the morning air."

Christopher Strong does not even hear her. All he can comment is, "Well, what do women do who can't fly?" The obvious answer is that they sit home sadly and unhappily as his own wife. But such realization is beyond either the care or comprehension of Strong, whose all-consuming chauvinism (there is no more accurate word to describe it) varies in form from solipsistic unconsciousness at best to moments of pure, calculated villainy. There is no sequence in *Christopher Strong* quite so treacherous as that in which Cynthia is lulled into quitting her profession. Strong convinces her to abandon flying at her most trusting, unguarded moment: while they are in bed together making love.

Director Arzner avoids here the contemporary wrath of the Hays office with the utmost delicacy and discretion. While the sound track buzzes with low, incoherent voices conversing in obvious intimacy, the screen shows only a hand, Cynthia's hand, leaning backwards and playing with the objects on a night table—a clock announcing 3 AM, a lamp. The voices become distinct. A soothing Lothario keeps urging, "Give it up. Give it up." And finally a female voice answers softly, "I'll give it up." Out goes the light.

Dorothy Arzner appears to imply here an indictment of the deceitful strategies of men in general through the abstract, disassociated methods of this scene. In the exact language (and also physical situation) appropriate for seduction, the off-screen man and woman are wrestling rhetorically over the woman's soul, her professional identity. In terms of the actual story at hand, Arzner seems to suggest that the same smooth approach which Strong probably used to end Cynthia's virginity, he now utilizes for a second intrusion, almost forced entry, into her private person. When Cynthia flicks out the lamp on this intricate little playlet, symbolically she puts out

the "light" on her life. This is what it ultimately means to succumb to Christopher Strong.

Cynthia had always been her most content in the exclusive world of adventuring men. She is most deliriously happy in the whole movie while lunching with her male co-pilot and mechanic in a restaurant dive. They rub elbows and plot her next flight on a map stretched out on the counter, sharing together the joyful esprit de corps traditionally the exclusive domain of male camaraderie.

(It would be nice to believe that Arzner's single, eye-level shot of this scene constitutes a visual parody of the Hawksian male paradise, although the vision of Howard Hawks hardly was not articulated in 1933 outside of his films themselves. Dorothy Arzner shows three pro "pals" huddled together in the most uncharacteristically sparse RKO setting of napkins, ketchup bottle, and a bare wall, contrasting completely with the plush English country manor decor designed by Van Nest Polglase for the rest of the sequences. Yet this absolutely functional, ascetic surrounding is exactly the type fitted for the Hawksian all-American heroes—pragmatic, without beauty, the *Ceiling Zero* aviator world of hamburgers eaten over the counter before leaping back into the plane.)

Not only is Dorothy Arzner a bit of a visual stylist . . . , but she is a director firmly committed to expressing her personal concerns in the body of her films.

—*Gerald Peary*

Cynthia has never felt so intimately democratic and relaxed among her own sex, partly because she is not accustomed to their company, partly because other women tend to appraise her, both positively and negatively, exclusively in terms of her unique aviatrix role. For autograph-seeking schoolgirls, she is a not-quite-mortal source of adulation: "You are our hero at school. You give us courage and everything." For middle-aged traditionalists like Elaine Strong, Cynthia is perceived as a freakish, tomboyish enigma and a bit of a threat: "I can't bear to watch that young girl do all those dangerous things in the air."

There is little wonder that Cynthia tends to stick with her male companions; while Elaine hobbles dutifully to church, Cynthia takes to the tennis courts for a refreshing match of equals against Christopher Strong. And it seems inevitable later, with her relationship to Strong disintegrating and threatening to end forever, that Cynthia seeks solace back at her original place of comfort, the airport, where she is discovered shaking hands with her mechanic as in old times in the early morning air.

Cynthia climbs once more into the cockpit of a plane and takes off for a solo flight. Her official object is to break the world's altitude record, which she accomplishes easily. But more important are deeply personal needs to soar again through the air, to regain her professional identity and self-respect, to recapture the daring spirit of her fast-disappearing youth. Flying represents freedom and aspiration; now it is extended to mean rebellion against every restraint on her being in the last several years with Strong, also a bold antidote to her own errors in judgment which have left Cynthia without friends, lovers, or occupation, reduced to a woman's dress and, in the near future, maternity clothes. Cynthia Darrington has become, in effect from her grounding, a second Elaine Strong.

Why does Cynthia not only break the altitude record but take her own life in the process? There is no clear answer, only the complex web of increasingly claustrophobic circumstances alluded to above, these topped by the one dire fact which will not go away: Cynthia is pregnant and unmarried in a pre-abortion era and seems certain to remain so. Strong has muttered platitudes about his "duty" to marry her if she ever were to have a baby, but such strained nobility obviously is repugnant to Cynthia. She does not even tell him the new development. Besides, as his relationship with Cynthia is losing its dynamism, Christopher Strong looks to be easing his way back into the favor of his wife and rehabilitating his formerly exemplary existence. Cynthia is left to swim for herself, or to sink.

Does Cynthia plan her suicide from the beginning of her final voyage as a dramatic conclusion to her enterprise—a kind of heroic gesture of death and apotheosis? The answer only can be guessed from interpretation of the largely ambiguous visual clues in the sequence. There is no assistance in the form of verbalized intentions, as Cynthia, in the grand stoic tradition, remains absolutely mute throughout the finale.

It seems possible to infer that Cynthia starts her voyage knowing only for sure that she will fly again, but without a definite plan of suicide (though she has given serious thought to this possibility, as evidenced in an earlier elliptic message from her hand, "Courage conquers even death.") Yet as the plane soars higher and higher, Cynthia's attention shifts dangerously away from managing her flight to recapitulating in her mind the troubles overwhelming her—these, unfortunately without obvious solutions. There is a sudden impulse to end it all, swiftly carried to its terrible conclusion. Cynthia rips off her oxygen mask in the thinnest altitudes. The plane reverses course, plummets nose first into the ground far below, annihilating itself in flames and also the person within.

The unsettling power of this climactic scene is impossible to pinpoint completely. It derives partly from the grim aura of immutability clouding over the events, evoked in the aural-visual combination of somnolent, droning airplane motor sounds monopolizing the sound track and the sight of the altimeter needle methodically rising upward, doggedly claiming as its territory the lower right-hand corner of the frame. Cynthia is wedged quite literally between the two mechanisms in many of the shots, as the well-oiled infernal machine unfeelingly pushes ahead on a path toward Cynthia's death. Not that she loses her will completely, but rather she appears to be nudged along hypnotically the way of the fatal decision.

Though orchestration of this scene is most important, brilliantly integrated in the metronome-like montage, the key ingredient to the chilling effectiveness of the conclusion finally is the magical power of Katharine Hepburn at its center. Hepburn's performance in *Christopher Strong* has been maligned rather unfairly by such an unlikely source of malice as gentleman George Cukor, though critic Joseph McBride's terse dismissal of the characterization in *Film Comment* as "wildly erratic" does contain at least a modicum of truth. Hepburn's love scenes opposite Colin Clive often are phony to the core, the most amateurish posturing in the [Greta] Garbo vein. But these sequences out of control are only part of the story, as even McBride's pungent remark does suggest. There are times in *Christopher Strong* when Hepburn is touching and honest, with the lightest, most easygoing manner. And there are still further moments when Hepburn's still raw talent is pushed into areas so revealing or inner states of feeling, so completely true that they are without parallel on screen. Such a scene is the final one, where Hepburn's Lady Cynthia Darrington becomes immortalized.

The credit goes back to Dorothy Arzner, who avoids throughout *Christopher Strong* the standard pitfall of almost every director to work with Hepburn—that is, whenever in doubt, cut in to her finely carved, eternally photogenic face. Unlike the predictable Hepburn-adoring male directors, Arzner cares primarily about her main character Cynthia, whose activities show perfectly well in medium or long shot; she is concerned only very secondarily with the intrinsic beauties of the lovely actress playing the part. There are extreme closeups of Hepburn, but they are infinitely fewer than usual and dramatically motivated, far different from the aesthetic-erotic digressions, the exercises in photography, which interrupt the usual Hepburn vehicle.

Arzner's stingy strategy is never to waste the Katharine Hepburn face, but to hold back almost indefinitely its amazing dramatic utility. The tease is quite unbearably tense, for even in the minute prior to her death, Hepburn has her visage buried underneath an oxygen mask, a baroque protuberance shielding the film audience from an intimate, fond farewell to Cynthia Darrington. Arzner denies a glamorous death for her leading star, neither allowing her to speak nor be seen, gambling all for the final moment of dramatic impact and succeeding.

There is only one minute part of Cynthia Darrington which Arzner leaves unveiled, to give forth cues to the changing mood of the scene—Cynthia's eyes. And it is here that actress Hepburn is so tremendous, for somehow, in peering out through the window of her goggles, the most harrowing, heart-breaking transition is communicated: from impassive resolve to severe depression, sadness, desperate claustrophobia, the sudden lunging to escape by death.

At first Hepburn's eyes stare toughly ahead, then they begin to soften into thought, then they become melancholy, correspondent with Cynthia's life flashing by in a montage of dissolves projected on the cockpit window. The eyes well with tears. Then, as the altimeter pushes higher and higher and the plane shoots vertically upward into the dangerous altitudes, the eyes open up wide with fright, darting nervously to the side, peering out the window into the celestial clouds. Finally they radiate an insane terror, the time of madness when anything can happen. And it does, as Cynthia flings off the mask, and the bare face of Katharine Hepburn bursts forth, pushed out by Arzner to be looked on quickly and memorized. For in seconds this remarkably beautiful woman with features of an immortal will destroy herself.

Speaking probably for most Hollywood directors, Howard Hawks (again) often has expressed disgust at the idea of showing suicides in his movies. For him, a real hero (translation: a real man) would not kill himself. But Dorothy Arzner, while probably as enamored of valor and personal courage as Hawks, remains free and above this hard-line, masculine view of suicide. She realizes that ending one's own life is often an immensely difficult and extraordinary act, as it is with at least two of her heroines.

When the flighty, spoiled title character of Arzner's *Nana* (Goldwyn, 1934) shoots herself because she can not choose judiciously between her warring lovers, her heroine is vindicated through this act of spontaneous bravery. Nana, in taking her own life, must be noticed and respected. What is true for Nana is thricefold the case for *Christopher Strong*'s Cynthia, whose suicide is one of the few cases in the history of the cinema that this essentially anti-tragic act manages to evoke a tragic response from an audience—the death of John Barrymore by gassing in *Dinner at Eight,* Jean Gabin leaping from a train in [Jean] Renoir's *La Bete Humaine* are two other rare examples which come to mind. And there is the most deservedly famous suicide of all, James Mason's grandiose walk into the ocean at the end of Cukor's *A Star Is Born.*

The death gesture in *Christopher Strong* finally is so diffi-

cult to accept, so deeply sad, because of the total waste of a valuable life. Even Cynthia grasps this. There is the most poignant moment of all, when she tries feebly to reverse herself, to thrust her mask back onto her face and live. Too late.

Though Cynthia dies alone, unobserved, and without apparent influence on the lives of the other characters within the movie, *Christopher Strong* is saved from a final mood of distress and pessimism by a simple fact: an audience has watched the incidents and can learn from them. Undeniably, there is "meaning" and relevance to be discovered in Cynthia's demise, perhaps in particular to women.

Cynthia Darrington's shortcoming, her "tragic flaw," so to speak, is an inability to reconcile her professional needs and aspirations with her personal, emotional life as a woman. But Cynthia's failings imply no universal despair, for Cynthia is only one. A beneficiary of the lesson in *Christopher Strong* could succeed and do it all—becoming an outstanding aviatrix and a terrific, happy lover, too, or whatever.

Or, as Cynthia Darrington's real-life counterpart, Amelia Earhart, once explained of the dangerous flights which would lead to her own untimely death: "Please know that I am quite aware of the hazards. I want to do it because I want to do it. Women must try to do things as men have tried. When they fail, their failure must be but a challenge to others." A sentiment that Ms. Dorothy Arzner will share exactly.

Dorothy Arzner with Gerald Peary and Karyn Kay (interview date 1974)

SOURCE: "Dorothy Arzner Interview," in *Cinema,* No. 34, 1974, pp. 10-17.

[*In the following interview, Arzner discusses her career and the people with whom she worked in the film industry.*]

The following interview was conducted over several months by mail between Wisconsin and California. Questions were posed, answers supplied, then more questions surfaced from the previous answers. Dorothy Arzner personally read over the "final print" and made corrections and additional comments; so, hopefully in the best sense of the term, this ends as an "authorized interview."

Because Ms. Arzner is busily at work completing an ambitious historical novel (based on the early settling of Los Angeles) she found it impossible to detail adequately her film career. Very generously she allowed a personal visit to her California desert home for additional information. The addendum to the interview is based upon conversations during that meeting (with thanks to Joseph McBride for his questions on that occasion).

[Peary and Kay:] How did you decide on a film career?

[Arzner:] I had been around the theatre and actors all my life. My father, Louis Arzner, owned a famous Hollywood restaurant next to a theatre. I saw most of the fine plays that came there—with Maude Adams, Sarah Bernhardt, David Warfield, etc., etc., ad infinitum. D. W. Griffith, Mary Pickford, Douglas Fairbanks, Mack Sennett, and all of the early movie and stage actors came to my Dad's restaurant for dinner. I had no personal interest in actors because they were too familiar to me.

I went to the University of Southern California and focused on the idea of becoming a doctor. But with a few summer months in the office of a fine surgeon and meeting with the sick, I decided that was not what I wanted. I wanted to be like Jesus—"Heal the sick and raise the dead," instantly, without surgery, pills, etc.

All thoughts of University and degrees in medicine were abandoned. Even though I was an "A" student and had a fairly extensive education—I had taken courses in History of Art and Architecture—I became a so-called "Drop Out." Since I was not continuing in my chosen career, I only thought of work to do and independence from taking money from my Dad.

This was after the World War and everything was starting to bounce—even the infant picture studios. An appointment was made for me to meet William DeMille. He was told I was an intelligent girl. There had been a serious flu epidemic, so workers were needed. It was possible for even inexperienced people to have an opportunity if they showed signs of ability or knowledge.

Could you describe this meeting?

There I was standing before William DeMille saying, "I think I'd like a job in the movies." William DeMille: "Where do you think you'd like to start?" Answer: "I might be able to dress sets." Question: "What is the period of this furniture?"—meaning his office furniture. I did not know the answer, but I'll never forget it—"Francescan." He continued: "Maybe you'd better look around for a week and talk to my secretary. She'll show you around the different departments."

That sounded interesting enough to me. I watched the four companies that were working, particularly that of Cecil DeMille. And I remember making the observation, "If one was going to be in this movie business, one should be a director because he was the one who told everyone else what to do. In fact, he was the 'Whole Works.'"

However, after I finished a week of observation, William DeMille's secretary told me that typing scripts would enlighten me to what the film to be was all about. It was the blueprint for the picture. All the departments, including the director's, were grounded in the script. So I turned up at the end of the week in William DeMille's office. He asked, "Now where do you think you'd like to start?" I answered, "At the bottom." He looked penetratingly serious as a school teacher might, then barked, "Where do you think the bottom is?!" I meekly answered, "Typing scripts." "For that, I'll give you a job."

I was introduced to the head of the Typing Department. I was told I'd be given the first opening, but I had my doubts. Weeks went by. I took a job in a wholesale coffeehouse, filing orders and working the switchboard. It was through that switchboard that the call came from Ruby Miller, the Typing Department head. I was making twelve dollars a week. I said, "What's the salary?" "Fifteen dollars a week for three months, then Sixteen-Fifty." So for three dollars more a week I accepted the movie job. And that is how I started at Paramount, then called The Famous Players-Lasky Corporation.

How did you become a cutter and editor?

At the end of six months I went from holding script to cutter, and a good cutter is also an editor, working in conjunction with the director and producer, noting the audience reaction when preview time comes. I was assigned to Realart Studio, a subsidiary of Paramount. I cut and edited fifty-two pictures while chief editor there. I also supervised and trained negative cutters and splicers.

Did Realart have its own stages and crews independent of Paramount? What kinds of films were made there?

Realart Studio was equipped fully—cameramen, set designers, writers, and I was the only editor. It was a small studio with four companies and four stars: Bebe Daniels, Margarite Clark, Wanda Hamley, and Mary Miles Minter. One picture a week was started there and finished in four weeks. It would be eight reels when finished, and called a "program picture." In those days, pictures played for a week in theatres, and the cost of the ticket was thirty to fifty cents. At the end of the week there was another picture.

So much for Realart Studio. I was recalled to the parent company, Paramount, to cut and edit *Blood and Sand* with [Rudolph] Valentino as star, with Lila Lee and Nita Naldi. Fred Niblo was the director. June Mathis was the writer, having gained much fame and authority from guiding and writing *The Four Horsemen of the Apocalypse* to enormous success. It was a "Big Picture"—hundreds of thousands of feet of film, twenty-three reels in the first tight cut, finally brought down to twelve.

What were the physical circumstances is editing at this time?

There were no movieolas or machinery. Everything was done by hand. The film was read and cut over an 8" x 10" box set in the table, covered with frosted glass and a light bulb underneath. The film pieces were placed over a small sprocketted plate, overlapped, and scraped about 1/16th", snipped with glue, and pressed by hand.

Were scenes shot simultaneously from several angles to help your editing?

No, films were shot normally with one camera, except for large spectacular scenes.

Do you feel that editors were paid decent wages before unionization?

For the time, I was paid very well. I never had any complaints. If you were a good editor, you asked a reasonable rate.

Had you done any shooting on Blood and Sand?

Yes, I filmed some shots for the bullfights.

Were there special instructions in editing Valentino's scenes so as to preserve the glamor?

There were no special instructions. The glamor was all on the film, put there by the writer and director, both of superior experience.

What other movies were made with James Cruze?

Then came *The Covered Wagon,* another "super-colossal" picture made 85 miles from a railroad in the "wilds of Utah." We used five tribes of Indians, and oxen were broken to the yoke. I stayed with Cruze through several pictures (*Ruggles of Red Gap,* with Eddy Horton, *Merton of the Movies,* and a number of others), until I left to write scripts for independent companies, like Harry Cohn's Columbia. Then Cruze asked me to work on *Ironsides,* another "Big Picture." He wanted me to write the shooting script, stay on the deck of the ship with him, keep the script, cut and edit—all of which I did for more salary.

Could you talk a little about Cruze, a director known today almost only by name?

It would take too long to tell you about James Cruze. He was one of the "Big Directors," but he didn't exploit himself. He saved Paramount from bankruptcy, and he was one of the finest, most generous men I knew in the motion picture business. He had no prejudices. He valued my ability and told people I was his right arm.

Were you about to walk out on Paramount to direct pictures at a minor studio when given your directoral chance in 1927?

Yes, I was going to leave Paramount after *Ironsides.* I had been writing scripts for Columbia, then considered a "poverty row" company. Harry Cohn made pictures for eight and ten thousand dollars and I was writing scripts for five hundred dollars apiece. But I had told Jack Bachman, Cohn's production man, that the next script I wanted to direct or "No Deal." When I finished *Ironsides,* I had an offer to write and direct a film for Columbia.

It was then I closed out my salary at Paramount and was about to leave for Columbia. It was late in the afternoon. I decided I should say 'goodbye' to someone after seven years and much work: B. P. Schulberg. (I had previously written a shooting script for Ben Schulberg when he had a small independent company. He had been short of cash and couldn't pay, so I told him to take it and pay me when he could, which he did later. It was "bread on the waters" because soon after he was made production head of Paramount when we were about to start *Ironsides.*)

But Mr. Schulberg's secretary told me he was in conference. So I went out to my car in the parking lot, had my hand on the door latch, when I decided after so many years I was going to say 'goodbye' to *someone* important and not just leave unnoticed and forgotten. The ego took over. I had a feeling of high good humor.

So I returned and asked the secretary if she minded if I waited for the conference to be over. She did mind. Mr. Schulberg would not see anyone. It was late then, and he had told her not to make any more appointments. Just about then Walter Wanger passed in the hall. He was head of Paramount's New York studio on Long Island. And, as he passed, I called out, "Oh, you'll do!" He responded, "What's that?" And I told him, I was leaving Paramount after seven years, and I wanted to say goodbye to someone *important*.

"Come into my office, Dorothy." I followed him, and when he sat down behind his desk, I put out my hand and said, "Really, I didn't want a thing, just wanted to say goodbye to someone important. I'm leaving to direct." He turned and picked up the intercom and said, "Ben—Dorothy's in my office and says she's leaving." I heard Ben Schulberg say, "Tell her I'll be right in." Which he was in about three minutes.

"What do you mean you're leaving?" "I've finished *Ironsides.* I've closed out my salary, and I'm leaving." "We don't want you to leave. There's always a place in scenario department for you." "I don't want to go into the scenario department. I'm going to direct for a small company." "What company?" he asked. "I won't tell you because you'd probably spoil it for me." "Now Dorothy, you go into our scenario department and later we'll think about directing." "No, I know I'd never get out of there." "What would you say if I told you that you could direct here?" "Please don't fool me, just let me go. I'm going to direct at Columbia." "You're going to direct here for Paramount." "*Not unless* I can be on a set in two weeks with an 'A' picture. I'd rather do a picture for a small company and have my own way than do a 'B' picture for Paramount."

With that he left saying, "Wait here." He was back in a few moments with a play in his hand. "Here. It's a French farce called *The Best Dressed Woman in Paris.* Start writing the script and get yourself on the set in two weeks. New York is sending Esther Ralston out to be starred. She has made such a hit in *Peter Pan,* and it will be up to you."

So, there I was a writer-director. It was announced in the papers the following day or so: "Lasky Names Woman Director."

What was your directing training prior to **Fashions for Women?**

I had not directed anything before. In fact I hadn't told anyone to do anything before. I had observed several directors on the set in the three years that I held script and edited: Donald Crisp, Jim Cruze, Cecil DeMille, Fred Niblo, Herbert Blache and Nazimova. I kept script on one Nazimova picture, *The Secret Doctor of Gaya,* directed by the husband of the "directress" Madam Blache, but I don't recall meeting her.

Who championed your cause at Paramount? Adolph Zukor? Were you given trouble because you were a woman?

Ben Schulberg, Jim Cruze, Walter Wanger. Adolph Zukor was in New York where the pictures were distributed and had little to do with the making of movies. No one gave me trouble because I was a woman. Men were more helpful than women.

Could you talk about Esther Ralston, star of **Fashions for Women,** *but a forgotten star today. Was she the same type as Clara Bow, another of your leads?*

Esther Ralston was not the same type as Clara Bow—just the opposite. She was blonde, tall, and more of a showgirl type— very beautiful. Clara was a redheaded gamine, full of life and vitality with the heart of a child.

The aggressive character that Ralston played in **Fashions for Women,** *Lola, seems like the kind of character of many of your women. Do you agree?*

No, I do not think Esther as Lola was like other women in my pictures. You would have to see Nancy Carroll, Clara Bow,

Katharine Hepburn, Ruth Chatterton, Anna Sten in *Nana,* Merle Oberon in *First Comes Courage*.

You made the first movies with Ruth Chatterton. Wasn't she an unlikely movie star—a bit older and more mature than most leading ladies?

Ruth Chatterton was a star in the theatre. When talkies came to Paramount, they signed the stage actresses as many of the silent stars fell by the wayside. She was a good actress.

Did you affect her career?

Yes, I certainly affected it. When I made Ruth Chatterton's first motion picture at Paramount, *Sarah and Son,* it broke all box office records at the Paramount theatre in New York. Chatterton became known to the press as "The First Lady of the Screen."

Why did Ruth Chatterton move over to Warner Brothers?

Warners offered her everything an actress could desire— choice of story, director, cameraman, etc., including a salary greater than Paramount.

You made a series of Paramount pictures with Fredric March. Was this coincidence or did you ask to work together again and again?

I took Fredric March from the stage in *The Royal Family* and cast him in **The Wild Party.** I guess my pictures gave him a good start, and I liked his work, so I cast him as the lead in **Sarah and Son, Merrily We Go to Hell,** and **Honor Among Lovers**.

In 1930 you began making movies with Robert Milton. Could you explain the nature of your collaboration?

Robert Milton was a fine stage director, but he didn't know the camera's limitations or its expansions. Because I did know the technique so well, I was asked to help him. I co-directed **Behind the Makeup,** then I was called in to complete **The Constant Wife,** which he had started with Ruth Chatterton. I don't believe I took screen credit on it. I merely helped with technical work. He directed the performances. I blocked the scenes for camera and editing.

Didn't you direct one part of Paramount on Parade? *What was the idea behind this extravaganza?*

"The Vagabond King" was the part I directed. *Paramount on Parade* was an innovative type picture made mainly to exploit Paramount and its directors and stars and to show off the studio.

Paramount was the greatest studio, with more theatres and more big pictures than any others until the Depression. Its Hollywood plant was one block square, on Sunset Boulevard and Vine.

Were you given a choice of technical crew when directing at Paramount?

Yes, I had the cameramen, assistants, costume and set designers I liked best. A director had his, or her, crew that stayed from one picture to another. I made my assistant cameraman, Charles Lang, my first cameraman. Adrian and Howard Greer did clothes for me.

Honor Among Lovers *was one of the first Ginger Rogers films. Did you discover her? Was her famous "stage mother" found on the set during shooting?*

Ginger Rogers was a star in *Girl Crazy* in the theatre. I saw her and liked her and requested her for a small part in **Honor Among Lovers**. Paramount gave me about everything I wanted after **Sarah and Son** and **Anybody's Woman,** so I imagine they offered her much money. She could also continue playing in *Girl Crazy* at the same time. I never saw her mother.

Honor Among Lovers *ends with Julia, the married woman, going on an ocean voyage with a man not her husband. Was this unorthodox ending your choice? Was there pressure to have Julia finish the movie in the arms of her husband?*

I collaborated in the writing of **Honor Among Lovers,** which I made for Paramount in New York. As audiences were ready for more sophistication, it was considered the smartest high comedy at the time.

No, there was no pressure regarding the script. I had very little interference with my pictures. Sometimes there were differences in casting, sets or costumes, but usually I had my way. You see, I was not dependent on the movies for my living, so I was always ready to give the picture over to some other director if I couldn't make it the way I saw it. Right or wrong. I believe this was why I sustained so long—twenty years.

Why the title **Merrily We Go to Hell?**

The movie was made during the overboard drinking era during Prohibition. Freddy March played a drunken reporter with whom a socialite, Sylvia Sidney, fell in love. The title was his philosophy. He made Sylvia laugh when she was bored with the social life of her class. You would have to know the times to judge, "Why the title?"

You were at Paramount at the same time as Marlene Dietrich and Mae West. Did you ever wish to make a movie with either of them?

Yes, I always wanted to make a picture with Marlene. There was a wonderful script called *Stepdaughters of War*. I'd worked on it for months for Chatterton, but when she signed with Warners it had to be called off. Much later, we were planning it again with Dietrich. It was to be a big anti-war picture showing the tragedies of war and how war makes women hard and masculine. When the World War broke out with Nazi Germany, it was called off again.

Could you describe your contract at Paramount? Did you have special clauses giving you control over certain phases of production?

I was under contract to Paramount for three years at a time, paid by the week. I ended with a two year contract, including choice of story. I never had to worry about control over phases of the production. The departments were geared to give a director what he wanted, if he knew exactly what he wanted.

Why then did you leave Paramount?

Paramount changed by 1932. When I left there was a complete change of executives. In fact, they were so fearful of the success of **Merrily We Go to Hell** that they spoke of shelving it. I begged them to release it, I was so sure of its success. A year later they were asking me, "Make another **Merrily We Go to Hell,**" but by that time I wanted to freelance.

You were working already on **Christopher Strong?**

Yes, David Selznick asked me to do a film at RKO, which he headed at the time. It was to be an Ann Harding picture, but she was taken out due to contractual difficulties. So I chose to have Katharine Hepburn from seeing her about the studio. She had given a good performance in *Bill of Divorcement* but now she was about to be relegated to a Tarzan-type picture. I walked over to the set. She was up a tree with a leopard skin on! She had a marvelous figure; and talking to her, I felt she was the very modern type I wanted for **Christopher Strong**.

Did you pay special attention to directing Billie Burke in this movie? It seems the best acting performance of her career. In fact you seem more interested in all the women characters than in Christopher Strong. Is this true?

Yes, I did pay special attention to getting a performance from Billie Burke. But I was more interested in Christopher Strong, played by Colin Clive, than in any of the women characters. He was a man "on the cross." He loved his wife, and he fell in love with the aviatrix. He was on a rack. I was really more sympathetic with him, but no one seemed to pick that up. Of course, not too many women are sympathetic about the torture the situation might give to a man of upright character.

What was your relationship with **Christopher Strong**'s *scriptwriter, Zoe Akins, who had also written* **Sarah and Son, Anybody's Woman,** *and* **Working Girls** *for you at Paramount in 1931? What did Slavko Vorkapitch contribute to the movie?*

My collaboration with Zoe Akins was very close. I thought her a fine writer. Vorkapitch did the montage of the around-the-world flight, when Cynthia (Katharine Hepburn) was met by Chris in San Francisco and their affair was consummated. Incidentally, **Christopher Strong**'s story was not based on Amelia Earhart. It came from an English novel based upon the life of Amy Lowell, who did make the around-the-world flight and also broke the altitude record in her time.

Why do you think Cynthia killed herself? Did you consider other endings?

No, there was no other ending. Cynthia killed herself because she was about to have an illegitimate child. The picture was set in England. We had not accepted so easily the idea of an illegitimate child. In the boat scene, she asked, "Do you love me, Chris?" His answer: "Call it love, if you like." This was from a tortured man who deeply loved his wife and child, but fell in love with the vital, young and daring aviatrix.

Wasn't there a moment when Cynthia tried to save her own life by putting the oxygen mask back on her face after she had ripped it off?

No, Cynthia did not try to save her life. If you remember, she looked back over the whole affair seen through superimpositions as she flew to break the altitude record. Suicide was a definite decision.

How would you evaluate this movie?

Christopher Strong was one of the favorite of my pictures at the time, although I was always so critical of my own works that I could hardly consider any one a favorite. I always saw too many flaws. I was grateful, however, when they were considered so successful.

Some sources have credited you with making an RKO film, The Lost Squadron, *usually listed as directed by George Archainbaud. Did you work on this film?*

No, I had nothing to do with George Archainbaud or *The Lost Squadron.*

All articles about your career say that you were the only woman director in Hollywood at this time. But another woman,

Wanda Tuchock, co-directed a movie called Finishing School, *at RKO in 1933. Were you aware of this? Did you know her?*

I vaguely remember Wanda Tuchock was publicized as a woman director, but I paid so little attention to what anyone else was doing. I never was interested in anyone else's personal life. I was focused on my own work, and my own life.

How did you become involved with **Nana** *at Goldwyn Studio? How was Anna Sten picked to play the lead? Were you satisfied with the completed film?*

Goldwyn chose me to do *Nana* because, when he returned from a trip to Europe, he saw **Christopher Strong** and thought it the best picture of the year. He picked Anna Sten wanting a star to vie with Dietrich and Garbo. It wasn't that I would like to have shot *Nana* differently. I wanted a more important script. But Goldwyn wouldn't accept any script at all until he finally handed me about the fiftieth attempt.

Why did you choose Rosalind Russell for the lead in **Craig's Wife?**

I did not want an actress the audience loved.

They would hate me for making her Mrs. Craig. Rosalind Russell was a bit player at MGM, brilliant, clipped, and unknown to movie audiences. She was what I wanted.

Was **Craig's Wife** *an expensive picture to produce? Was it profitable for Columbia?*

No, *Craig's Wife* was not a high-budget picture. To make it, I told Harry Cohn I would give him an "A" picture for "B" picture money. He fell for that. It was not one of the biggest successes when it was released. But it got such fine press that, over the long run, it was released several times and stood high on Columbia's Box Office list.

Were you also producer of **Craig's Wife?**

I was not the producer, although the whole production was designed by me. Outside of the development of the script, enormously protected from Harry Cohn's interference, Eddie Chodrov was the supervising producer.

Did the playwright, George Kelly, involve himself in the production? Didn't you differ with him on interpretation?

George Kelly had nothing to do with making the picture. I did try to be as faithful to his play as possible, except that I made it from a different point of view. I imagined Mr. Craig was dominated somewhat by his mother and therefore fell in love with a woman stronger than he. I thought Mr. Craig should be down on his knees with gratitude because Mrs. Craig made a man of him.

When I told Kelly this, he rose to his six foot height, and said, "That is *not my* play. Walter Craig was a sweet guy and Mrs. Craig was an SOB." He left. That was the only contact I had with Kelly.

Molly Haskell (essay date 28 April 1975)

SOURCE: "Women in Pairs," in *Village Voice,* April 28, 1975, pp. 77-8.

[*In the following essay, Haskell discusses* Dance, Girl, Dance *and* First Comes Courage, *arguing that Arzner is "the only director who consistently scrutinizes women who have priorities other than marriage and the family."*]

It obviously came as a shock to [Sigmund] Freud and other Oedipally-inclined artists and thinkers, to emerge from the coddled experience of their own mothers to find that other women—those who, perhaps, as little girls, resented having had to give up piano lessons so their brothers could study or wanted something more out of life than little genius/sons to dote on. Most of these artists and thinkers didn't struggle with the problem as honorably (though inadequately) as Freud did. The question What is a Woman? still carries the assumption—and desperate hope—that there is some one thing that is a woman. And, as far as our cultural artifacts and attitudes go, there is.

Otherwise why else would female impersonation, as opposed to male impersonation, be big business? Because there is such a *thing,* identifiable by a set of external, playable mannerisms, as a woman, and no such *thing* as a man. Beyond the limits imposed by haberdashery—the neutral costume itself suggesting that the emphasis is elsewhere—the idea of a man is as unlimited as the ocean. He is a fireman, a wrestler, a writer; he is a person, an essence; he is everything except those "delicious" outward gestures of femininity upon which the female impersonator builds his routine to universal recognition, and by which womanhood is reduced to a set of physical characteristics that are the trivialized mirror opposite of serious, superior man. The impersonator ignores the characteristics that women share with men and seizes upon the extremes of sexual artifice. By the same token, if the names of Gloria Steinem or Bella Abzug or Billie Jean King come up in a conversation men will immediately discuss them not as professionals but sexually, according to the degree to which they are, or are not, fitting members of their sex.

A woman will go for hours or days without thinking of herself as a "woman" . . . and then she begins to worry if there's something wrong with her. And so she continues to impale herself on the fictive contradiction between "real woman-

hood" and the aspirations of a career. Bette Davis gave the dilemma its classic articulation as Margo Channing in *All About Eve.* She's in the stalled car, talking to Celeste Holm; it's the moment when she is feeling contrite over her behavior to Eve Harrington, but before Eve's deceit is revealed. ". . . funny business, a woman's career," she muses. "The things you drop on your way up the ladder, so you can move faster. You forget you'll need them again when you go back to being a woman. That's one career all females have in common—whether we like it or not—being a woman."

Eve's putative womanliness, the qualities to which Margo is referring—kittenish youth, flattery, flirtatiousness, submission, deference, ultra-femininity—take on sublime irony when Eve's treachery is unveiled, and her "femininity" is exposed as a shabby masquerade, an external, "transvestite" performance of womanhood.

This should stand as the final commentary on the myth of "woman," and yet I'm not sure that [director Joseph] Mankiewicz means it to invalidate Margo's melancholy previous speech. Bette Davis herself echoes this eulogy for a lost womanhood in her autobiography, *A Lonely Life.* But her idealization of marriage and the family, her mental picture of "the little woman" is the nostalgia of someone—an actress—who has never been there, or hasn't been there long enough for the charm of the "role" to wear off.

What is wrong, after all, with the kind of "woman" that Margo has been: temperamental and bitchy, to be sure, but kind and loyal (the kind of solid qualities that are always missing from the camp Margo) and gloriously intelligent. Her one lapse—her trust in Eve—is a function of her generosity.

It is when the trappings of femininity are just that—gestures divorced from an ego, a sense of self, as they were in Eve's, but not in Margo's, case, that they become fodder for the impersonator, or abstractable into the patterns of unreality that [Jean] Genet plays with in *The Maids.* By his original intention that the characters be played by boys, Genet was acknowledging the artificiality of the *idea* of femininity—the idea being more interesting to him, because purer, than real femininity—but also confirming its origin as a male fantasy. He is concerned, as [Jean-Paul] Sartre says in the introduction that has always seemed to me more interesting than the play itself, with presenting "to us femininity without women."

The current English production, an offering of the American Film Theatre, has followed the example of previous productions in choosing to have the roles of Claire, Solange, and Madame played by women: respectively, Susannah York, Glenda Jackson, and Vivien Merchant. If there has ever been a time when Genet's 1947 play could have its proper cast—adolescent boys whose sex would not be concealed but kept constantly before the audience by virtue of a placard—the time is now. There is, perhaps, an *ostensible* relevance in having them played by women—since women are themselves in the process of examining the masks of femininity they themselves wear. But this is the one level of fabrication, and psychology, that interests Genet not at all. Social roles, yes, particularly the mistress-servant one, with all its erotic, neurotic, sado-masochistic, and homosexual implications; and the endless inversions of what Sartre calls the "whirligig," the game of intellectual defoliation that proceeds until one arrives at nothing—not a "real," [Samuel] Beckett-like nothing, however, but a nothing concealed within yet another gesture of theatrical bravura.

To make a film of so quintessentially theatrical an enterprise no doubt struck the makers of this one—Christopher Miles, director; Robert Enders, producer; Minos Volankis, adapter—as a supreme challenge, but they have met it with compromise. Thinking, apparently, to add with the camera one more layer of masquerade, they have made the play seem a flailing prisoner of film, closeted against its will. Tensions relax and dissipate in the baroque apartment that is treated like a stage in the round, photographed occasionally from the flies. Neither quite women, nor quite female impersonators, Glenda Jackson and Susannah York, white-faced and grandiloquently petulant, are kept leagues apart by an unseen referee so that sensual potential is deferred for a theatrical pay-off that is never realized.

The play seemed flat in English, and I was struck with the realization that the French language and milieu are even more important to the stylized ciphers of Genet than to the characters of realistic drama. The French bourgeoisie provides the minimal but crucial social grounding in which relationships, beginning with the tyrannical one between mistress and servant, determine behavior and—and this is Genet's point—preclude individuality. Oddly enough, what makes Glenda Jackson the redeeming figure in the film is not her formidable assurance and sense of pitch, but the "Frenchness" she brings to the apparently competent but cowardly Solange.

In Bergman's *Persona,* one of my favorites which I caught again at the Carnegie Hall Cinema retrospective, there is a remarkably similar situation. Two women, sisters by virtue of their physical affinity, are locked in a struggle for domination, the "apparently stronger" (Liv Ullmann's rigid mute) intimidating the "weaker." But like Claire in *The Maids,* Bibi Andersson's childlike and simple nurse turns out to have the resilience, the humility, and strength to survive and grow. It is her employer who collapses when confronted with personal truths. One reason I've always liked *Persona* is that the opposition between the intellectual and the instinctive person, usually divided between man and woman in Bergman's films, here does not follow a sexual polarity. The two women form a complete "world," without reference to man as cre-

ator or master. Unlike *Hour of the Wolf,* where Ullmann is the indestructible earth mother whom [Max von] Sydow's tortured artist worships and flees, neither character in *Persona* is the archetypal Woman, yet both are womanly.

Perhaps the most exciting pair of female opposites in American cinema occurs in Dorothy Arzner's **Dance, Girl, Dance,** in which Maureen O'Hara's ballerina and Lucille Ball's burlesque queen are pitted against each other in a photo-finish struggle between High and Low Art, hard work and sex appeal, and two different kinds of women, without either of which the world would be immeasurably the poorer. (This film and Arzner's **First Comes Courage,** shown recently on a double bill at the Bleecker Street, are now available for bookings.)

There are other Hollywood films about women, about camaraderie among women, about career women, many of them more stylistically distinguished than Arzner's films, but she is the only director who consistently scrutinizes women who have priorities other than marriage and the family and destinies that take precedence over love.

Dance, Girl, Dance, is a crazy, audacious film that darts from one situation to another without warning, relying on its strong central conflict to hold it together. It begins with a group of nightclub dancers, under the unlikely tutelage of Maria Ouspenskaya, being fired from a night club in the midwest and forced to hitch back to New York. The opposition—Lucille Ball's luscious vamp versus O'Hara's shy romantic—is established at the outset through their differing reactions to a playboy who woos them both.

Finally reassembled back in New York, the girls (minus Ball, or "Bubbles," who is still en route) try to put together a hula number under the unelectrified gaze of a saturnine, cigar-smoking producer. It is only when Bubbles arrives, and aims a few bumps and grinds straight for the lecher's libido, that the contract is signed.

Ouspenskaya shakes her head over the chances of her prima protegee, without "oomph" in a vulgar world.

"I could learn it," says O'Hara.

"You don't learn oomph," says Ouspenskaya, "you're born with it."

Bubbles, born with an oversupply (and Ball is wonderful—warm, smart, sexy, and totally in command of her commodities) becomes the star of a burlesque show. To help out O'Hara financially, she takes her on in the humiliating role of stooge. O'Hara comes on first, on toe and in tulle, and under the boos and catcalls of the mostly-male audience, builds up anticipation for Ball.

The moment of truth—and for a contemporary audience it is electrifying—comes when O'Hara, who can stand the abuse no longer, turns on her audience and rips into them, calling them a bunch of dirty old men who wouldn't know what to do with a woman who was any closer to them than the apron of the stage. And, she reminds them, don't think you're fooling your wives!

This is a characteristic Arzner moment: a "career" woman's declaration of independence which also encompasses a sympathy with, and respect for, the wife. Arzner bridges the gap between the different kinds of women she depicts and the different worlds they live in. Like Ouspenskaya, she loves both Bubbles and O'Hara, and never views them as opposites of judgmental, virgin-versus-whore dichotomy as most men would. Her compassion extends even to her men, but her privileged moments are those shared by women: the final scene, after their scuffle, when O'Hara and Ball have been brought to court, and a look passes between them that signals rapport, and Ball's realization that O'Hara was fighting her not over a man but over a principle.

Arzner's films move forward with the jerky unpredictability of a vision not quite resolved into a style. Without rationalization, I think we might see this as an expression of the discomfort of a woman who feels herself an artist in an alien land, but is nevertheless trying, always, to bridge the gap: between Hollywood and her artistic aspirations; between the romantic conventions and her own feminist sensibility.

Arzner was an A student with an extensive education in art and architecture, and a surgical career ahead of her, when she left the University of Southern California (in 1920 at age 20) and got herself a job in the film industry. Starting at Famous Players-Lasky (later to become Paramount Pictures), she worked her way up from the bottom, always with the full intention of becoming a director.

From typing and editing she became for awhile James Cruze's assistant, and then threatened to leave Paramount if she weren't given a directorial assignment. She was. It was an adaptation of a French farce, called *Fashions for Women*.

Among the 17 films she made in Hollywood—and she was the only woman directing there during most of those years—she made: *The Wild Party* (Paramount's first sound film, with Clara Bow); *Christopher Strong* (with Katharine Hepburn as the aviatrix who commits suicide rather than compromise her love—or her career); *Craig's Wife* (a striking interpretation of the George Kelly play, which launched Rosalind Russell as a star); and *Dance, Girl, Dance. First Comes Courage* in 1943 was her last film. She had been sick with pneumonia and had apparently become exasperated with the bureaucratic tangles and commercial constraints of the film industry. She taught filmmaking at UCLA for awhile (Francis

Ford Coppola was one of her students). She is now writing a novel, and gently refusing attempts to draw her further into the public eye as a champion of feminism before it was the fashion for women.

In *Dance, Girl, Dance,* Maureen O'Hara embodies the artistic principle, but in other films, most notably *Craig's Wife* and *First Comes Courage,* it is Arzner as director (working through costume, set design and editing) who forces a "high art" motif on material which resists such upgrading. The most bombastic, but interesting all the same, is *First Comes Courage,* a 1943 war film in which Merle Oberon plays a spy for the Norwegian underground.

Only such a grandiose design (Oberon's monumental impassivity, the severe black and white in which she is dressed for her choice of mission over lover) could explain the lack of feeling for behavioral nuance and ambiguity in the presentation of the villain (Carl Esmond) and the relations between Oberon and Brian Aherne, but the film falls short of the awesome without providing intermediate dividend. Even the usual fascination of role reversal—Esmond's love for Oberon taking precedence over his political commitment, while hers for Aherne must come second—is diluted by the necessity, according to war-film formula, of showing him a coward.

True to Arzner, the most moving character in the film is a woman, a nurse, who assists Oberon and refuses to denounce her even when her own family is threatened. And the most moving scene is the one in which they embrace in a rapture of mutual understanding that transcends war, and that will nourish each of them in their lonely women's destinies in a way that romantic love never can.

And so for all you multitudinous feminists who are supposedly dancing at the altar of Leni Riefenstahl (who *are* you, anyway?), I recommend Arzner as a less problematic first choice. For here are some films that surpass anything that has been done since, by men or women, in picturing (within the conventions of the Hollywood film!) woman's difficult and heroic struggle to wrest her soul from the claims attached to it from the time she was born. And if, in the continuing Linnaean revisions and reclassifyings of film history, extra points are not granted for that, then we are certainly using the wrong grade book.

Pam Cook (essay date 1975)

SOURCE: "Approaching the Work of Dorothy Arzner," in *The Work of Dorothy Arzner: Towards a Feminist Cinema,* edited by Claire Johnston, British Film Institute, 1975, pp. 9-18.

[*In the essay below, Cook discusses narrative structure in*

Arzner's films as it relates to a "critique of patriarchal ideology."]

The films of Dorothy Arzner provide us with an opportunity to investigate a range of film texts made within a production system already in the late 20s and early 30s highly articulated in terms of the dominant ideology of classic Hollywood cinema. There is no doubt that Arzner made complex and interesting films of great relevance to women now in our struggle for our own culture; but the point is not to claim for her a place in a pantheon of 'best Hollywood directors', since the positing of any such pantheon would ignore the complexity of the relationship between ideology and the production of film texts. In looking again at some of Arzner's films, then, we are looking at a body of work produced within the constraints of a studio system heavily determined by economic and ideological factors (*Nana,* in spite of the potential interest of the story, remains little more than a vehicle for Anna Sten, Goldwyn's protegée and hoped-for box-office answer to Dietrich and Garbo, relentlessly photographed in soft-focus by Gregg Toland). Our object will be to define some strategies for a critique of patriarchal ideology in general.

To approach the films in this way is not to try to elevate them to the status of masterpieces, nor simply to regard them as objects worthy of study, but instead to see them as texts (complex products demanding an active reading in terms of the contradictions at work in them), which are produced within a system of representation which tries to fix the spectator in a specific closed relationship to the film. Thus we are attempting to take from Arzner's films some ideas which will open out the problem of the place of women within that system.

Stephen Heath in an article on Brecht remarks:

> Classic film is finally less a question of *mise-en-scène* than of *mise-en-place,* and anything that disturbs that place, that position, the fictions of myself and my 'Reality' can only be theoretical, the theatralisation of representation in its forms: film theatre, critical cinema, a cinema of crisis and contradiction. ('Lessons from Brecht', *Screen* Vol. 15, No. 2, Summer 1974.)

In the history of classic cinema this *'mise-en-place'* has been articulated in response to the demands of patriarchal ideology, with specific consequences for the place of women in representation; for in this structure the place of woman is defined as the locus of 'lack', an empty space which must be filled in the working through of man's desire to find his own place in society. The use of female stereotypes, modified only slightly to meet the demands of changing fashion, has contributed to the propagation of myths of women which relate primarily to the desires of men. The role of women in the film narrative can be seen to perform a similar function: to bring into play the desire of the male protagonists. While there is no doubt that there are progressive elements in many Hollywood films (for example, those of [Douglas] Sirk or [John] Ford) which posit the idea of female desire, nevertheless ultimately these films operate a closure on the possibilities of the working through of this desire (*i.e.,* of articulating and satisfying desire through phantasy). The films of Dorothy Arzner are important in that they foreground precisely this problem of the desire of women caught in a system of representation which allows them at most the opportunity of playing on the specific demands that the system makes on them.

This concept of play permeates every level of the texts: irony operates through the dialogue, sound(s), music, through a play on image, stereotype and gesture and through complex patterns of parallels and reversals in the overall organisation of the scenes. Perhaps the most exemplary film in this sense is *Dance, Girl, Dance,* which has often been acclaimed by feminist critics as a work of major importance. However, it would be a mistake to read the film in 'positive' terms as representing the progress of its heroine to 'maturity' or 'self-awareness'. The value of the film lies not in its creation of a culture-heroine with whom we can finally and fully identify, but in the ways in which it *displaces* identification with the characters and focuses our attention on the problematic position they occupy in their world. A positive reading of the film would imply a conclusion which would be a final closure of the film's contradictions; but this ignores the complexity of the film's structure of reversals. When Judy O'Brien finally turns on her audience in fury and in her long speech fixes them in relation to *her* critical look at them it does indeed have the force of a 'pregnant moment.' The place of the audience *in* the film and the audience *of* the film is disturbed, creating a break between them and the ideology of woman as spectacle, object of their desire. The shock-force of the moment is emphasised by the embarrassment of the audience in the film, and the silence which follows the speech. However, in another masterly reversal, the moment is upended as the enthusiastic clapping of the woman in the audience (Steve Adams' secretary, whose relationship to her boss is depicted in the film as, ironically, one of friendly but almost complete oppression of her by him) escalates into a standing ovation, thus re-locating Judy's speech *as* a performance. The cat-fight between Judy and Bubbles which follows almost immediately takes place on the stage to the accompaniment of music from the burlesque orchestra which resembles the music used for *Tom and Jerry* cartoons. This has the double force of condensing the girls' conflict of desires, and by presenting that conflict as sexually exciting for the cheering, cat-calling audience, calls into question the processes by which women's desires are presented as a spectacle for consumption. In this way our identification with Judy's inspiring words is displaced into an awareness of the continuing process of contradictions at work in the struggle with ideology.

Similarly in the court-room sequence which follows, Judy in the dock speaks with confidence and self-assurance about herself and her relationship to the other people in the film, much to the admiration of her audience and the fair-minded and liberal judge. However, we next see Judy at Steve Adams' dance academy where she finally discovers his identity and the real reason for his pursuit of her—her ability as a dancer. Even as Judy tries to assert her independence in the conversation with Steve which ends the film, the ground is pulled from under her.

> STEVE: *The Judge and I decided* you were in no mood to take favours.
> JUDY: I'm still in no mood. . . .
> STEVE: Now listen to me *you silly child.* You've had *your own way* long enough—now you're going to listen to me . . .
> STEVE (to the dancing instructor): She was born with more than any dancer we've got and she knows less. *It's our job to teach her all we know.* (My italics.)

Judy's moment of triumphant independence becomes a thing of the past as she collapses into Steve's arms *in tears.*

> JUDY: When I think how easy it might have been I could laugh.
> STEVE: Go ahead and laugh, Judy O'Brien.

In this final ironic reversal Judy 'gets what she wants' at the expense of any pretensions to 'independence' she had. Again, by displacing our expectations of identification with Judy's positive qualities into a recognition of the weakness of her position within male-dominated culture, the film's ending opens up the contradictions inherent in that position (our position) thus encouraging us as spectators to recognise the all-important problematic of the difficulties of the working through of female desire under patriarchy.

Without doubt **Dance, Girl, Dance** provides the clearest example, by its play on stereotypes and reversals, of ironic method, especially as it foregrounds the contradiction between women's desire for self-expression and culture, and the cultural processes which articulate a place for woman as spectacle. However, further examples of Arzner's concern with playing with formal elements to conceptualise women's position in ideology can be found in another earlier film. **Merrily We Go To Hell,** made in 1932, displays the seeds of the method which is so rigorously and economically articulated in **Dance, Girl, Dance** in 1940. This is not to suggest that we can formulate a coherent and exhaustive method to apply to all Arzner films. What follows is a tentative enquiry into some of the ways in which this early post-silent comedy treats the problem of the relationship of the spectator to the forms whereby classic cinema represents the place of woman.

> **The value of [Dance, Girl, Dance] lies not in its creation of a culture-heroine with whom we can finally and fully identify, but in the ways in which it *displaces* identification with the characters and focuses our attention on the problematic position they occupy in their world.**
>
> **—Pam Cook**

Merrily We Go To Hell tells the story of an insecure young heiress, Joan Prentice (Sylvia Sidney), whose stern and upright father owns a food-processing business, and who falls in love with a penniless journalist and would-be playwright, Gerry Corbett (Fredric March), who drinks heavily to forget his failure and his broken affair with a successful actress. Joan decides to marry Gerry, in spite of her father's resistance to the idea on the grounds of Gerry's unreliability. Gerry agrees to the marriage despite his fears that his continuing obsession with Claire, the actress, will prevent him from making a go of it.

Meaning is created in the film through the play of oppositions: the 'strength' of Joan's father is contrasted with Gerry's 'weakness' and inability to control his own actions. Similarly Joan's lack of confidence about her identity contrasts sharply with Claire's self-possession and ability to control her 'audience' through a highly articulated image of female sexuality. The conflict of desires between the four protagonists provides the motivation for what happens in the film, but the progress of the narrative and the final reconciliation of Joan and Gerry is complicated on several levels.

The structure of the narrative is episodic: there is no smooth flow from one scene to another, and each scene demands to be read in itself for the meanings it creates. In this way we are constantly distanced from a desire to follow the 'destiny' of the characters in any transparent or linear fashion. Rather we are led in a series of uneven 'events' to question the 'inevitable Truth' of the narrative and to look at the situations in which the protagonists find themselves. By 1932 the codes of suspense were well established in Hollywood cinema. Intercutting of sequences and shots to provide an illusion of simultaneous action had been extensively used in the silent cinema not only to create comedy but also in psychological/social drama, where identification with the central character and the final *dénouement* of the story were essential to the representation of Truth. It is significant therefore that Arzner's film presents its story in a succession of tableaux, where the organisation of meanings within each scene takes precedence over the smooth forward-flow of a narrative which would give an impression of Reality. An example from the film might be the opening scene.

The film opens with an image of Fredric March (Gerry) alone in half-darkness crouched behind a barricade of whisky bottles from which position he is drunkenly and only half-aloud enacting an imaginary battle with the 'horrible people' at the 'horrible party' he is attending. The camera draws back to show us that he has withdrawn to a balcony from which he can see the party—through a brightly-lit window. A couple dancing move into view through the window and seem to begin an argument. Gerry shows an interest in the scene, and we are taken in closer to find Sylvia Sidney (Joan) struggling violently with the sexual advances of a very large, very drunk man. She breaks away and rushes out onto the balcony, unaware of Gerry's presence or the fact that he has been watching with interest and amusement.

In these first few seconds notions of watcher/watched, fear of and inability to cope with sexual demands, innocence, flight and withdrawal are quickly established. The rest of the scene takes place almost entirely on the balcony and is concerned with depicting the nature of the relationship between Gerry and Joan and Joan's place within it. Joan describes herself as 'stupid' and a 'nobody', but when she tells Gerry her name he immediately connects her with 'Prentice Products' and points out a neon advertising sign on the sky-line, thus placing *her* as a product. In the face of her self-negation he emphasises her class status (courtesy of her father), her 'niceness' ('I think you're *swell*') and her need to give (the 'gingerbread and *crème-de-menthe*' song links Joan's wealth with her quality of mothering sexuality). Gerry creates Joan's 'image' for her.

Joan's escort intervenes to take her home, and in spite of her obvious pleasure in Gerry's company she leaves passively to get her coat. Gerry, after a small quarrel with Joan's friend, becomes involved in more drinking with his own friends, and when Joan comes out onto the balcony again to say goodbye we are given a subjective shot in which Gerry's vision is totally blurred—he can't see her at all, and when he asks who she is, she replies 'Oh, nobody'. From this description it can be seen that the scene is circular in structure, and that although we are given certain expectations as to what might happen next (Joan asks Gerry to tea the next day) it is rather the processes at work in the relationship between Gerry and Joan that occupy our attention, through the use of irony on the level of dialogue and image.

The next scene, showing Joan at home with her father, does not follow on easily from the first, but sets out to show a different situation: the relationship between Joan and her father in which she is depicted as child-like and over-indulged. In the first scene it is Gerry who occupies this child-like position vis-à-vis Joan. Thus by means of parallels which are

also contrasts the film sets up tensions on the formal level which act as distancing mechanisms to create new meanings.

The film uses basically two forms of narrative interruption: the 'gag' and the 'pregnant moment'. Both can operate at the level of a small section of a scene, or incorporate a whole scene, but they both serve to introduce elements of discontinuity into the narrative.

An example of the short gag comes at the end of the wedding scene when Gerry places the metal corkscrew on Joan's hand instead of the ring. As she opens her hand the screw is pointing inwards, towards the soft palm of the hand. She laughs, but the vicious connotations of that image create a shock-effect on the level of the meaning of their relationship and her place in it.

A long gag is used in the scene where Gerry first arrives at Joan's house, late for his tea appointment. He meets Joan's father at the door and after their initial curt encounter follows Mr Prentice into the house, practically running to keep up with the long, stern strides of the older man. Left alone, Gerry becomes interested in a picture on the far wall and has to make his way across the highly polished floor by stepping on his handkerchief so he won't lose his balance. Joan finds him there, they sit down to talk, and Gerry extends the gag as they get up to leave by expressing his insecurity again in terms of always having been used to 'places with sawdust on the floor'. The gag does nothing to further the flow of the narrative, rather it arrests it, along with any expectations we may have of the future happiness of the two protagonists.

Dance, Girl, Dance makes use of the gag as a strategy of intervention at the level of the place of the spectator in relation to the film spectacle. The burlesque show sequence plays the position of the film-audience against that of the audience *in* the film to produce a shift in meaning. We see Bubbles performing a mock striptease. From the position of the burlesque audience we watch as the wind-machine threatens to tear off all her clothes, and she hides behind a tree on the stage. The excitement of the burlesque audience is intense as Bubbles' clothes come flying onto the empty stage. The film-audience is suddenly given a privileged shot of Bubbles behind the tree, fully clothed, while the burlesque audience can still be heard whistling and shouting. In that moment our position as spectators of the spectacle is shifted, the mechanism of the phantasy structure within which Bubbles and her burlesque audience are operating is made explicit, and we are made to take a distance on our own place within the ideology of illusionism as it constructs the fictions of our Reality for us.

The force of the pregnant moment is that it works against the complex unity of the text by opening up the whole area of representation to the question of desire and its articulation. In

Merrily We Go To Hell we see Joan at her engagement party waiting for Gerry to arrive before she announces their forthcoming marriage. The party is well under way, except for the marked absence of Gerry. Joan's father comes to the top of the stairs, the camera behind him as he dominates the party below. Cut to Joan dancing with her friend Gregg. They are chatting and move towards a large mirror on the far side of the room from the stairs and dance before it for a moment before Joan suddenly becomes aware of the 'image' of her father on the stairs, looking at her, reflected in the mirror. She stands for some seconds gazing at her own reflection in the mirror and the 'image' of her father in the background before she moves across the room to talk to him. She seems fascinated, held in a fixed relation to the 'image' in the mirror, and as *we* are faced with that image of fascination we are aware of a tension between desire and the patriarchal Law.

It has already been pointed out by Karyn Kay and Gerald Peary that the narrative structure of *Dance, Girl, Dance* comprises a system of repetition and reversal, and the scenes quoted above describing the reversals which follow Judy O'Brien's speech to the burlesque audience are a good example of this method. In *Merrily We Go To Hell* we can detect a similar structure of repetition/reversal based on the oppositions rejection/pursuit and flight/reconciliation. This form of reversal is another way of disturbing the linear flow of the narrative: we are pulled backwards and forwards in a play between memory and anticipation which defeats any final closure of contradictions.

In *Merrily We Go To Hell* this system is important to the central problematic: in the absence of any code of action of her own, Joan is forced to emulate the actions of others. This point is forcibly made in the scene immediately following the mirror-image sequence described above. Joan's father complains irritably about Gerry's absence, because he 'can't stand for her to be humiliated'. Joan is called outside, where she finds Gerry in a taxi lying in a foetal position, in a drunken stupor. She becomes very upset and repeats her father's words: 'He can't do this to me' . . . 'I can't stand the humiliation'. She takes her car and drives wildly into the night in an attempt to escape the intolerable pressure of contradictory demands from her father and Gerry. As she is 'torn', so the mechanisms which attempt to fix her place are pulled apart.

The scene of final reconciliation between Gerry and Joan is an example of the use of ironic reversal to open up contradictions rather than present a closure in which the destiny of the characters is sealed and given as a fixed Truth. Joan is in hospital after the death of her baby. In the darkness of the hospital room she mistakes Gerry at first for her father. Then as he kneels to put his head on her breast and declares his love for her, she puts her arms around him and murmurs 'Gerry, my baby, my baby' as the film ends. The image of

reconciliation, unity, plenitude is shot through with connotations of death, loss and absence. The entire text of the film is cracked open as the workings of ideology in the construction of female desires is exposed.

The use of stereotypes in classic Hollywood cinema is generally recognised as serving a double function. As Panofsky has suggested the use of a limited set of signs based on genre conventions in early cinema was intended to help the audience read the narration of the film more easily. They were given a set of fixed recognition points so that they felt comfortable in relation to the film. However, as cinema developed, we can see from the fact that male stereotypes changed much more rapidly than female stereotypes that the use of stereotypes has a specific ideological function: to represent man as inside history, and woman as eternal and unchanging, outside history. It is this representation of myths of women as a-historical that Arzner's films seek to question. By demonstrating that the fixed female stereotypes are actually a focus of contradictions for women her films cause reverberations within sexist ideology which disturb our place within it. As the myths are disengaged from ideology, the transparency of the myths is destroyed and they are recognised as constructs within representation.

Dance, Girl, Dance uses the standard stereotypes of Vamp/Straight Girl to demonstrate the operation of myth at every level of the film. Judy's position as stooge in Bubbles' act is only the logical extreme of her problem throughout the film: caught in her 'image' of a 'nice girl with class' she is also a stooge in her relationships with the rest of the girls in Madame Basilova's dancing troupe, and in her relationship with Jimmie, and finally with Steve Adams. Because the burlesque show is a logical extreme it is the point at which we can most clearly see the mechanisms of ideology at work. Bubbles controls her audience by offering them an 'image' of female sexuality which operates on the level of phantasy—an 'image' which parodies myths of women as child-like yet sexually provocative and sophisticated through the use of song and gesture. Judy's box-office value as a stooge is to stimulate the demand for Bubbles' brand of 'oomph'. The function of her performance is to increase the desire of the burlesque audience by postponing satisfaction of that desire, through her presentation of herself as spiritual, sexually innocent, dedicated to an art which transcends sexuality. By showing that both these 'images' fulfil specific demands for the burlesque audience, the film causes us to question the function of Judy's dream of dancing the 'Morning Star' ballet, which is only the other side of the coin of her burlesque performance. Judy's desires are totally compatible with the laws of sexist ideology, for as the 'Urban Ballet' sequence clearly shows (its structure is parallel, in reverse, to the burlesque show) myths of the innocence of women, whether idealised and spiritual or sexually provocative, exist at all levels of representation. By demonstrating the specific place of these myths within male-dominated culture Arzner's film denaturalises them.

Judy O'Brien's problem with her 'nice-girl image', her contradictory desire to please others and yet fulfil her own dream, has a precedent in the form of Joan's struggle in *Merrily We Go To Hell*. This film also uses the Vamp/Straight Girl stereotypes to point up contradictions on the level of ideology, and Joan also has her 'moment of truth' when she confronts Gerry with his obsession with Claire's 'image' as she is about to leave him. The problematic of the 'nice-girl image' is presented as a problem on the level of the working through of desire. The role of the 'nice-girl' is to suppress her own desires in favour of those of the male. Yet Arzner's 'nice-girls' are shown as having desires which conflict with those of the male, at the same time as they desire to please the male. It is at this point of tension between desire and ideology in the problematic of woman as subject and object of desire that the myth breaks down, for the 'nice-girl' is impelled by her contradictory desires to explore the possibilities open to her on the level of the 'image', only to find that those possibilities are limited by factors which are outside her control.

It is on the level of the 'image' that *Merrily We Go To Hell* explores this problem. When Joan describes herself as a 'nobody' to Gerry when they first meet, she is in effect offering him an empty page on which he may write his own description of her, which he proceeds to do by placing her first as her father's daughter (a child), then as a provider of loving support (the 'gingerbread and *crème-de-menthe*' song), then as a 'nice-girl' ('I think you're swell'). All aspects of this 'image' are brought into play during the film—Gerry refers to Joan more than once as 'the finest of Prentice Products', and his repetition of 'I think you're swell' continues until it is finally emptied of all significance except its ideological function (in the scene where Joan leaves him) of maintaining the image for himself after it has clearly been discarded by Joan. On the visual level Joan as a 'nice-girl' appears gift-wrapped in her wedding gown as the ideal of innocence (the place of the corkscrew gag in puncturing this image has already been noted). Joan the housewife dresses plainly and does the darning while her husband struggles creatively with his typewriter, summing up ironically his view of marriage: 'Mrs Gerry Corbett, you're Mrs Simon Legree.' (As Gerry characterises himself as a slave in relation to his wife, the shot of Joan's hands darning his sock denies us the possibility of accepting his description of her as 'Mrs Simon Legree', *i.e.,* a slave driver; by use of this irony the contradictions of the 'image' which Gerry gives Joan, contradictions which make the marriage a problem for her, are made explicit.) Again, Joan the cook is found in the kitchen dressed in a shapeless apron, apparently happy in her supportive role (the counterpart to this is Vi's bitter speech about her own failure as a wife). However, when Joan is confronted by an elegant and sophisticated Claire at the office of Gerry's agent, her own place

begins to seem threatened; her 'image' becomes problematic.

Joan's problem with her place *vis-à-vis* Gerry's relationship with Claire is also formulated at the level of the 'image'. After the second meeting between Joan and Gerry when he confesses his unhappy love-affair, Gerry is shown talking to a photograph of Claire which depicts her as sexually provocative: 'I've met a girl who's just the opposite of your lovely fleshly self.' The same photograph of Claire appears later in the newspaper, which causes the fight between Gerry and the gossip-columnist over his motives for marrying Joan. In Gerry's play Claire represents a sexually experienced woman who can manipulate the demands of male ideology to make men do what she wants. Claire is public property, and it is in the tension between the place of woman as public and private property that Joan is caught. Faced with this contradiction and the prospect of losing Gerry, Joan abandons her 'nice-girl image' for that of the sophisticated and promiscuous wife, public property, a 'new identity' which is posed as problematic precisely because it is presented *as* an 'image' *articulated* in response to the demands of male ideology.

The scene which perhaps most clearly emphasises a preoccupation with the function of the image in 'holding representation at a distance' is the scene in which Gerry and Claire enact a mock love-scene in front of imaginary film cameras as Joan looks on. Gerry and Claire are framed in the doorway as they kiss, their enthusiastic audience of friends applauding. We see the 'scene' at first from behind Joan, and watch with her as the mock-kiss becomes 'real' and the mock-directors are forced to shout 'Cut!'. As Gerry and Claire become aware of Joan's presence they look towards her and in a reverse shot we now see Joan (from behind Gerry) framed in the doorway in her turn, transformed into the 'image' of an embittered, frustrated woman. This reversal, by implicating us in the pleasure/pain aspect of our voyeuristic relationship to the film, nevertheless holds off identification by reminding us that we are engaged in a process of fabricating images. This intervention prevents us from accepting the film on any level as Reality. *Merrily We Go To Hell,* by operating a process of montage of interventions, asserts the text as a process of dialectical play between image and narrative, and by implicating us in that process *as* spectators calls into question the forms of cinematographic representation through which ideology attempts to fix our place for us. From this concern in Arzner's films with the potential displacement-effect of the friction of image and diegesis, and the montage of interventions of ironic reversals and narrative interruptions, we can learn much about the possibility of our own intervention as feminist critics and film-makers in patriarchal ideology.

Julia Lesage (essay date 1982)

SOURCE: "The Hegemonic Female Fantasy in *An Unmar-*

ried Woman and *Craig's Wife*," in *Film Reader,* No. 5, 1982, pp. 83-94.

[In the following excerpt, Lesage examines Arzner's depiction of marriage in Craig's Wife.*]*

Hegemony is a term in Marxist theory used by Antonio Gramsci to describe the complex ways that the dominant, most powerful class (in our era, the bourgeoisie) maintains control over ideas. The term originally derives from the Greek and was used to describe Athens' prestige and influence over the other Greek city states. The concept of hegemony is most useful if seen as operating on two interrelated and mutually reinforcing levels: the institutional and the psychological. The dominant class has the power to write history and impose norms because it controls and directs economic, state, cultural, scientific, religious, educational, etc., institutions. In this sense, the health care system or the educational system not only deliver material services but are also ideological systems. In the cultural sphere, some institutions are tied directly to the state (e.g., public education) and some indirectly through grants (Northwestern University). Even the independent arts depend on institutions for funding and exhibition and shape their products accordingly. Furthermore, certain major institutions comprise generally agreed upon systems for conducting personal affairs, and these shape women's lives directly, namely the institutions of marriage, the family, and heterosexuality. Such institutions are not located in a place but have great normative force and are both enacted and protected by law.

If in the U.S. in the 1980s all these institutions foster an ideology that promotes the outlook of white middle class males, no one is surprised. Most of the narrative arts of our era—novels, plays, films, television programs—are devoted to working out the conflicts and contradictions of the bourgeoisie in terms understandable and acceptable to its male members. For example, both *Kramer vs. Kramer* and *Ordinary People* demonstrate that men need to be more emotional and loving and caring. Since women's liberation has supposedly robbed women of such qualities, these two male melodramas imply that if men get rid of the woman in the house, they can grow into what they need and want to be. The two films abolish the married couple in favor of the boys.

Women in the U.S. also live under bourgeois patriarchal hegemony and they do so complexly. The concept of hegemony lets us consider how we as women are exposed to, use, sometimes enjoy and sometimes reject the cultural products and the dominant ideas around us. We grow up in a world of received notions and attitudes, around which we shape our emotional life. If we can analyze hegemony in terms of institutional compulsion or the way that institutions structure choices, we can also analyze how our desires and emotions often lead us to choose or settle for commonly held ideas about what our life as women should be. The narrative arts, especially those set in the domestic sphere, e.g., novels, melodramas, and sex comedies, present scenarios that depict, often conservatively, what our choices, contradictions, and conflicts are. For example, sex comedies, particularly the kind seen at suburban dinner theaters, either involve traditional Oedipal seduction or swapping marital partners but keeping the couple intact; sexual love always finally inheres in the couple. Paul Mazursky's *Blume in Love* and *Bob and Carol and Ted and Alice* represent films of this type, presumably "in tune" with modern mores but with very old comic scenarios. Only with difficulty can we imagine rewriting those scenarios on entirely different terms.

I use the term "hegemonic female fantasy" to describe a phenomenon I have observed in novels, melodramas, television situation comedies, soap operas, and advertisements—that is, in the narrative arts that deal directly with the sphere institutionally and emotionally relegated to women: the domestic sphere. Out of each narrative a notion about women emerges. The characters' desires and needs make up much of the content of their speeches and are the "stuff" that impel the action. But each narrative also has ways to contain and limit its consideration of women's desires and needs: through what is not allowed, through negative example characters, through the connotative manipulation of the mise-en-scène, or through a narrative progression that shows certain kinds of conflicts and resolutions as more important than others. The hegemonic female fantasy is an historical creation—a visible projection in our fictions at any given date of how women are socially, by consensus, defined.

That we like the fictions—at least in part, at least some of them—is inevitable. Fiction also offered our parents narrative scenarios which structured *their* notions of what family life would and should be like. We rebel against some facets of the scenario (to stop going to church was youth's big rebellion in my twenties) but not against all. Furthermore, the hegemonic fantasy put forth by artistic fiction itself changes with history both to express and to contain ongoing changes already being felt in women's lives.

I use the term hegemonic female fantasy in the sense of a daydream that we women could muster up for ourselves, but one that would be pretty socially acceptable. It is the safe fantasy—one we all hold in certain aspects, and certainly the one propagated culturally. For me personally, Diahann Carroll in Richard Rogers' play *No Strings* expressed the hegemonic female fantasy most cogently when she sang, "All I want is lots of money, a nice position, and loads of lovely love." In the 80s the hegemonic fantasy indicates that women should "fulfill their potential," but also that they should find and value a deep emotional experience with an appropriate man. Lesbian love, promiscuity in a senior citizens' home, total dedication to discovering a new virus, serving as an officer in a revolutionary army, or having a bevy of lovers 20 years younger than oneself—these are clearly roles of women that the hegemonic female fantasy has not embraced. The hegemonic fantasy flattens out both the contradictions in women's lives and women's options. It sets out a few issues which are treated as the key issues, and it deals with those issues in a socially acceptable and often predictable way. The artistic tactics for making the conflicts and their resolutions acceptable, for making the fantasy hegemonic or mainstream, are worth attending to in close detail, for they have much to teach us about the interconnections between the narrative arts, ideology, and what we want. . . .

Dorothy Arzner's feature films, particularly *Craig's Wife, Christopher Strong, Dance Girl Dance,* and *Working Girls,* provide useful contrasting examples to the previous type of "optimistic" film. Arzner often looks at the negative hegemonic fantasy about What Women Want; she chooses to go deep into such a fantasy and through it. What are the negative hegemonic female fantasies—both held socially about us and also partially internalized by us? Woman is goldbrick, grasping, calculating. Woman is adulteress, emotionally brittle loner, homebreaker, or manipulator. In reality, we know what a woman must do for economic security. Women gossip about what a woman must do to land Her Man (and keep him and get what she wants from him, etc.). What would we women like from men? That is, what are our common fantasies about what men could bestow? In contrast, what do we realistically expect from them? Generations of women have shared and passed on a body of subcultural lore about these issues.

Within that lore, women's fantasy scenarios serve the function of reality-testing and are often tried out in practice as adaptive strategies imaginatively forged by an oppressed group. However, within mainstream culture, the existence of that "lore" and its wisdoms is usually acknowledged only pejoratively. A grasping woman is depicted as killing love and men's initiative through her craving for security. Or else, in a staple of patriarchal melodrama, the woman sacrifices herself and forgoes her needs totally for those of the children and the Man. In contrast, Arzner's films show the women characters carefully weighing a number of elements: money, social position, personal achievement, emotional integrity, companionship, security, and love. In Arzner's world money and social position very clearly shape the choices the women characters can and do make. And for a woman to choose economic and social independence over love, in Arzner's eyes, is an understandable, if not always joyous choice.

Examining one Arzner film, *Craig's Wife,* in greater detail will demonstrate more clearly this woman director's narrative strategy for presenting an unpleasant fantasy about women and going into that fantasy in depth. The commonly-held fantasy Arzner deals with in *Craig's Wife* is this: mar-

riage is a bargain struck between a man and a woman and reflects the woman's maneuvering for power. A wife does not expect passion or even sexual satisfaction. What she gets is social position and a house. The house is her turf, her domain, a material world in which the organization and the day to day operation is under her control. Often this fantasy enters a film as a given, an element shaping the male protagonist's life—as in *Rebel Without a Cause,* where James Dean strips the plastic covers off the living room furniture and denounces his father, seen wearing an apron, for accepting a submissive role. In *Craig's Wife* such a fantasy about a wife who lives only for her house takes up the film's entire narrative development.

This is a hegemonic female fantasy for middle class women; certainly that marriage was a bargain in which a woman earned social position and a house was a hegemonic fantasy my mother implicitly passed on to me. The unpleasant side of this fantasy, of course, is that the woman may care more for her social standing and her furnishings than for the people with whom she lives. Because she was promised, as her marriage right, control of the domestic sphere, she may also try to extend that control over the household members' lives. This notion indeed represents a *hegemonic* fantasy, for both its promises and its denigrating aspects form part of our general cultural lore telling us what to expect from middle class American family life.

Craig's Wife depicts Harriet Craig as living only for control over her home and shows her as receiving her come-uppance. Arzner's film enacts the bad fantasy completely. Called to her dying sister's bedside, Harriet Craig returns home after several days, insisting that her unwilling niece Ethel come back with her so the young woman's mother could "get more rest." While Harriet was gone, her husband Walter visited an old friend, Fergus Passmore; the following day Fergus' name appears in the newspaper as having committed suicide after he killed his unfaithful wife. Harriet manipulates Walter to protect their reputation; in so doing, she makes her attitudes toward him and their marriage clear, and in this way she rids him of his romantic illusions about her. This provides the dramatic mechanism for him to leave her, saying as he goes: "You married a house. I'll see to it that you have it always."

In the original misogynist play by George Kelly, written in 1925, Harriet offers Ethel a complete exposition of how to insure one's well-being within marriage. This lengthy exchange comes early in the play just after Ethel says she is engaged to a college professor of "romance languages." Harriet's lines in the play reveal a key way that the hegemonic female fantasy is often manipulated within mainstream ideology, particularly how conservative voices can utilize women's fantasies to serve reaction against women's social gains. It works like this: Exactly the opposite motives are assigned to women characters than real women would have within the social sphere (a recent example is the secretary-protagonists' use of sado-masochistic gear to truss up the boss in *Nine to Five,* as if what women wanted was to torment bosses sexually rather than just to get equitable working conditions). In the play *Craig's Wife,* Kelly's pejorative use of the word *independence,* repeated various times, indicates that his dialogue stands as an ideological reaction to women's gaining the right to vote in the U.S. in 1920. Harriet's argument to Ethel in the play goes like this: for women, romance is foolish and impractical. Once snared in romantic love, women are "obliged to revert right back to the almost primitive feminine dependence and subjection they've been trying to emancipate themselves from for centuries" (note how Kelly directly borrows from feminist rhetoric). Harriet tells her niece that she gained financial independence "as the result of another kind of independence; and that is the independence of authority—*over* the man I married" (emphasis Kelly's). Kelly's ideological counter-attack against women's emancipation uses the tactic here of making Harriet seem unnatural, for she seeks to overturn the Great Chain of Natural Hierarchies. Kelly makes it seem "unnatural" that Harriet should self-consciously and from the start oppose a husband's authority. (Similarly Mazursky had to reintegrate the independent woman into the heterosexual couple as soon as possible, i.e., as soon as she was capable of sexual arousal after her divorce.)

In the play Harriet tells Ethel that the key to having security, economic and social "protection," and a home was to "secure their permanence" by manipulating a man's idealism and romantic attitude toward marriage. As in the [Ronald] Reagan era, the conservative position may start out paying lip service to the rhetoric of progressive gains ("equal rights," "social welfare," etc.) but soon reveals in its diction its law-and-order, militaristic stance ("protection," "authority," "securing their permanence"). Phyllis Schlafly is a master of such tactics—for example, she recently declared to the press that sexual harassment does not really pose a threat to working women because women who are chaste in their appearance, who do not provoke trouble, do not get harassed. For the woman who received such formulae from her culture, she is expected to protest defensively: "But I'm a good girl (wife, mother, lover, woman). I always try to _____ (act sincerely and honestly, be good, avoid overt displays of sexuality, keep my eyes cast down, visibly disappear so I won't get noticed and get in trouble)." The power of Kelly's, and Schlafly's, attack on women's independence is that they understand and can adapt previously accepted, i.e., hegemonic, fantasies both men and women hold about women's roles. Hegemonic fantasies about what women are or should be are often manipulated in mainstream cultural pronouncements so that the woman—even if she clings to only socially acceptable desires—is often held to blame for her own socially inferior position and for both her own oppression and that of

others. Kelly's play *Craig's Wife* offers an excellent demonstration of how blame-the-victim ideology works.

Arzner's film does not do this. The film cuts down Harriet's discussion with Ethel to the lines cited below. Here Harriet still is manipulative but, as a woman, she speaks both realistically and consciously of her social role as "homemaker." The dilemma of love in marriage (Does marriage kill love?) is laid out with all its sides sympathetically presented, just as such contradictions exist within the hegemonic fantasy held about middle-class marriage.

> Harriet: Did it ever occur to you that love is a liability in marriage? I saw to it that my marriage was emancipation for me. I had no private fortune or special training, Ethel. The only road to independence for me was through the man I married. I married to be independent.
> Ethel: Independent of your husband, too?
> Harriet: Independent of everyone.
> Ethel: Walter adores you. He's the most trustworthy man in the world.
> Harriet: I don't have to trust him. I know where he is and what he does. If I don't like it, he doesn't do it anymore.
> Ethel: It doesn't strike me as honest.
> Harriet: Dear Ethel, if the woman is the right kind of woman, it's better that the destiny of the home be in her hands than her husband's.

As the film *Craig's Wife* completely develops the bad fantasy of the manipulative wife, not only does it explain the causes for Harriet's behavior, but the film's ending, in fact, leaves Harriet well off. She has the house, now all to herself. She has received a telegram announcing her sister's death, and this news opens her up to emotional life through the direct and cathartic experience of grief. And she has for a neighbor a warm, sympathetic widow who lives alone and who has just stopped by to leave off flowers and thus hears about the sister's death. Harriet had previously rejected this neighbor's visits as intrusive, yet now with the breakdown of her previous, rigid domestic routine, the film's final mise-en-scène leaves it open for us to assume that the neighbor, an emotionally willing source of support, will return. For me, it seemed that in the conclusion of the film Arzner refers to another (usually very well-hidden) aspect of middle class women's fears and dreams: the men will die off early with heart attacks or go off with younger women, etc., but then the older women will have the fine consolation of each other, their gardens, their mutual companionship, and their homes.

That this development is *desirable* for a middle-aged woman, or at least a pleasant hegemonic fantasy, is reinforced by what happens to the other middle-aged women characters in the film, all of whom are developed morefully than in the play. Harriet had harassed both her housekeeper, Mrs. Harold, and her husband's aunt, his mother's sister who lives with the Craigs—Miss Austin. In a gratifying fantasy resolution to both women's problems, Miss Austin finally explains to her nephew Walter how Harriet has manipulated him all these years, and then she invites Mrs. Harold to accompany her around the world as her traveling companion. The maid and the maiden aunt have never had Harriet's opportunity to get a house, to establish "homes" as middle class wives. Their future, as the film envisions it, is a pleasant fantasy about class solidarity among older women who can and will opt for independence, companionship, and expanded horizons. Walter had had two mothers living with him—his aunt and his wife. At the end of the film he finally asserts his "manly" independence—principally by messing up Harriet's immaculate parlor and then moving out. At the same time, both Harriet and his aunt are now free of him, and the film gives no indication that emotionally either will miss him. In her frustration, Miss Austin first confronted Harriet and then old Walter that the only reason she had stayed with the Craigs all these years was because of a deathbed promise to her *sister* to take care of him—bonding between women having kept her there. In the course of the film she explains to Walter several times how Harriet has removed him from his friends and has him completely under control and socially isolated. In contrast to Walter and Harriet's fate, Miss Austin finally declares, "I'll travel around the world so I won't become little. These are the rooms of the dying and the laid out."

Only when Walter could understand the manipulative aspects of romance couldhe become an independent adult. The hegemonic fantasy gratifications promised by marriage, with all their illusory and limiting aspects, exist in men's minds, too. After all, as Harriet says in her *realpolitik,* marriage is a bargain. A man fools himself who does not want to see what it really means to have A Wife: a servant, an ego-tender, a domestic organizer, an arranger of leisure and sexual desire. If a woman manipulates a man for economic security, the myth of romance and the need for A Wife often keep a man emotionally a child.

The hegemonic fantasy about the wife who invests all her emotional energy into maintaining her social position and home, which were her marriage-right, has many negative connotations. As in *Ordinary People* or "Rip Van Winkle" or medieval pageant plays, she becomes equated with the castrating bitch, the phallic woman, the devil's wife. Because of the woman's drive for control over it, the domestic sphere itself seems civilizing, inhibiting, and castrating (What does it inhibit? Male adventure, duty, comradeship, etc.). In such a guise, the castrating wife—or the domestic sphere—even appears in contemporary film theory, as in the following discussion by Geoffrey Nowell-Smith about melodrama as a genre:

It (melodrama) often features women as protagonists, and where the central figure is a man there is regularly an impairment of his "masculinity". . . . In so far as activity remains equated with masculinity and passivity with femininity, the destiny of the characters whether male or female, is unrealisable; he or she can only live out the impairment ("castration") imposed by the law.

Such an interpretation of melodrama strongly contrasts with Arzner's own interpretation of the sexual political situation at the end of *Craig's Wife,* where, through her negative example, the phallic woman has given her weakling husband for the first time in his life some "balls." According to Arzner, she designed the "whole production" of *Craig's Wife,* which differed as follows from George Kelly's work:

I did try to be as faithful to his (Kelly's) play as possible, except that I made it from a different point of view. I imagined Mr. Craig was dominated somewhat by his mother and therefore fell in love with a woman stronger than he. I thought Mr. Craig should be down on his knees with gratitude because Mrs. Craig made a man of him.

When I told Kelly this, he rose to his six-foot height and said, "That is *not my* play. Walter Craig was a sweet guy and Mrs. Craig was an SOB." He left. That was the only contact I had with Kelly.

Craig's Wife also utilizes the three other ways of dealing with fantasy gratifications and punishments which I found in *An Unmarried Woman,* but they do not stylistically define the film. However, such elements do reinforce Arzner's stylistic and thematic strategy of exploring women's condition in depth. If a conflict and its resolution are mentioned, they are not dropped (as with Patty's discussion of abortion and marijuana in *An Unmarried Woman*), but are taken up again and the causes of the conflict sympathetically explored. For example, *Craig's Wife* early shows us Mrs.Passmore deceiving her husband, but later, in discussing Fergus Passmore's murdering her, Walter Craig defends her: "She fell in love with Fergus and then fell in love with someone else." Ordinarily in narrative film, such a social scandal may be introduced so as to provide the occasion for the major characters to confront each other, but rarely are the villain's (villainess') motives in that secondary incident explored.

Second, denigrating connotations in reference to the female characters are allowed in *Craig's Wife,* but these connotations are not just presented as givens; rather they are pushed and explored. The flowery neighbor, effusive and gushy, is shown to feel lonely without a "house full of children" and responds sympathetically to Harriet's grief. The connotation "effusive" gives way to "motherly" to "warmly concerned."

Similarly, at the film's opening, as Miss Austin dines with her nephew, she seems to be the meddling older woman, at least in part. In that, in seeming to need to control her surrogate son's life and to accept his economic largess, she stands as Harriet's double, but an older, more beneficent motherly version. As the film progresses, this connotation of her character gives way to a far richer vision of both her role in Walter's life and the options she herself has.

Finally, there are a few fantasy gratifications that the film just lets stand. In particular, Ethel is rescued by her fiancé, who takes off work from the college where he teaches, travel to Ethel's side just because Ethel's aunt would not let him talk to the young woman on the phone. Two aspects of such a fantasy fulfillment are worth mentioning. First, it is pure fantasy because the fiancé seemingly faces no economic constraints from his job, his position in the public sphere, which would keep him from taking off work to pursue love. Second, rescue by a male is one of the major hegemonic female fantasies, and Arzner lets it stand—for the ingenue. Arzner does the same thing at the end of *Dance Girl Dance,* only with a father-figure rescuer instead. As in *An Unmarried Woman,* when a fantasy fulfillment is presented as Total, it reaffirms that mainstream culture would encourage young women to wish. Arzner does not directly challenge the fantasy of the male rescuer, but she uses other tactics to underscore that it is, in fact, an unlikely resolution if economic and social considerations are also weighed.

In *An Unmarried Woman* the characters give speeches which pass on in one way or another received ideas and established knowledge, both "what everyone knows" and what is commonly attributed to certain types of persons and situations. In this way the characters' speeches both are appropriate for the type of person speaking and build that characterization. Erica and her women friends' speeches distill, usually in an ideological way, current notions about love, women, and sexuality. The speeches also create a portrait of a "modern" woman, Erica, whose ideas and dilemmas then have resonance with many of the spectators' ideas and dilemmas. Similarly, in *Craig's Wife,* much of the dialogue is directly about "the rules of the game." In both films other elements affect how we react to the direct discussion of social coding within the dialogue. Such elements include how the narrative episodes are structured and paced, how much and what kind of "attention" is paid, visually and audially, to certain aspects of the characterization, and when and why such cinematic "attention" is withheld.

Viewers are not dumb for watching soap operas, for getting caught up in melodrama's conflicts, for the narrative arts that deal with the domestic sphere treat things which people need to think about. There are, structurally, many tensions generated in the nuclear family because of its relation to capitalist production and commodification, and we use fiction, especially melodramatic fiction, to explore these tensions. The very concept of "family" is heavily ideological and contains so many contradictions that it may be impossible to satisfactorily mediate the desires aroused by the concept (and by our primary emotional experiences in families) and the reality of what "family" means in women's daily lives. The woman character is placed structurally within these narratives so as to represent the contradictions between dependence and autonomy, between love and money, that all women are thrust into under capitalism. We are forced both symbolically and in our relations to bridge the gap between society's emotional norms (romance, motherhood, fidelity, loyalty, sacrifice, caring, etc.) and its realities which contradict those norms.

Women's space, both economically and socially, remains identified with the domestic sphere. This is true cross-culturally. In contrast stands the realm of public life and official political, institutional, and symbolic power. In our own culture, as Rayna Rapp writes:

> . . . the concept of the family is a socially necessary illusion which simultaneously expresses and masks recruitment to relations of production, reproduction, and consumption—relations that condition different kinds of household bases in different class sectors. Our notions of the family absorb the conflicts, contradictions, and tensions that are actually generated by those material, class-structured relations that households hold to resources in advanced capitalism. In sum, "family" as we understand (and misunderstand) the term is conditioned by the exigencies of household formation, and serves as a shock-absorber to keep households functioning.

As I have pointed out, the narrative arts, especially melodrama, deal with the historical reality that women are enmeshed in in four general ways. Each way can and usually does recoup the discussion of the conflict in terms acceptable to the bourgeois patriarchy. If the conflict is mentioned, perhaps indicating a solution, but then the topic dropped from consideration, it becomes a matter of out-of-sight, out-of-mind. A resolution may be both indicated and denigrated; this is the most common way to deal with a "sticky" problem, letting the viewer know, "Of course you do not want that." Or fulfillment may be openly granted, especially to women characters, and then contained. (In this way, *Coming Home* was the first Hollywood film I saw which indicated that women might prefer some form of sex other than fucking, but then oral sex could be depicted as the preferred form of sex only if offered by a paraplegic man.) Finally, fulfillments will be allowed that reaffirm the patriarchal order.

A narrative text allows for much projection on the reader/viewer's part, allows for a multiplicity of readings. However, across texts such as novels, ads, situation comedies, soap operas, melodramas—all the narrative arts which commonly deal with the domestic sphere—an image of what it is that women are supposed to be or want emerges. I call this the hegemonic female fantasy. It is both in our heads and imposed on us. In terms of the cultural products we receive, it is a bourgeois patriarchal creation. Inside our heads, it is something we use, something we react to or against, and something that limits us. The feminist movement, especially in its cultural wing, has created counter fantasies, other options, other ways of regarding both our past and our current situation. And it is dialectically in the interaction between feminists developing new concepts as part of a movement for social change and the actual fact of revolutionary change that a whole new hegemonic female fantasy might emerge.

Barbara Koenig Quart (essay date 1988)

SOURCE: "Antecedents," in *Women Directors: The Emergence of a New Cinema*, Praeger, 1988, pp. 17-36.

[*In the following excerpt, Quart comments on the female characters in* Christopher Strong, Sarah and Son, *and* Dance, Girl, Dance, *arguing that the "Arzner heroine is . . . a self-determined woman."*]

Feminist scholarly attention continues to return to and circle in fascination around the narratives of the two women who alone worked as directors in classic Hollywood cinema. Although their films largely appear to conform to the mainstream patriarchal ideology (though in very different degrees and ways), imaginative efforts have been made by reading them "against the grain" to find underlying tensions created by their directors' femaleness—even visually conveyed defiances, disguised as compliance.

In America, again only Dorothy Arzner survived the transition from silents to sound, and alone directed until 1944, retiring when *she* chose to. Arzner, whose father's restaurant in Los Angeles brought her into early contact with the stars, started out wanting to be a medical student, and ended up directing seventeen features in the course of her career. While she saw from the very start that "[i]f one was going to be in the movie business, one should be a director," she pragmatically began in filmmaking with typing scripts, then serving as a film cutter, an unusually gifted editor, a writer of stories. And where many of the kinds of women who were directors in the years after WWI were put in the newly created scenario departments of the 1920s, Arzner refused that, insisting on directing, as she also later insisted—with the same strong-mindedness—on taking full responsibility for her films, with the final decisions and the final cut hers.

At the same time the uneasiness of her situation may be suggested by the fact that she was "the total professional, per-

haps rarely went out on an innovative limb, but she never botched a film, lost her temper with colleagues, and could always be counted on for a clear and sleekly competent package." Other kinds of uneasiness are suggested by stories of her comportment on the set, her habitual solemnity, her "non-talking direction": the very low voice in which she spoke, her practice of having others shout her orders to actors and crew, at a nod or signal from her. In a 1936 newspaper article entitled "Hollywood's Only Woman Director Never Bellows Orders Herself," the reporter tellingly notes:

> Practically all successful directors are dominant people who know when to do a bit of outright bullying, and how. Players might not take kindly to bullying from a woman; they'd call it nagging. And so there's only one woman director in Hollywood.

(The act of directing appears to have been even more charged for [Ida] Lupino: "I don't believe in wearing the pants. . . . You don't tell a man, actors, crews. You suggest to them. Let's try something crazy here. That is, if it's comfortable for you, love.")

Arzner makes the uneasiness explicit when she speaks of needing to make a box-office success with each picture.

> I knew if I failed in that, I would not have the kind of fraternity men had one for another to support me. No one was handing me wonderful stories to make. I was usually having actors' first starring roles, and naturally they were only concerned with their own lives.

Given her own force it is not surprising that Arzner's work—however artificial some of it may look to us now—is marked by strong-willed independent central women characters, and the kinds of strong actresses who could portray them. These she had a remarkable ability to recognize when they were unknown—Rosalind Russell and Sylvia Sidney, among them—and of course Katharine Hepburn, whose career was importantly advanced by *Christopher Strong,* though it has been pointed out that Arzner is not credited with this.

The woman pilot heroine of *Christopher Strong* (1933) is a strikingly bold creation, the young and just beginning Katharine Hepburn with her purposeful strides, her brusque talk of enormously ambitious feats, the extraordinarily alert and direct look she gives to the world and to her married lover as well. The schizoid nature of female social conditioning is particularly apparent in the heroine's shift of costume from down-to-business leggings, jodhpurs, mannishly cut flying jackets—to dazzlingly slinky gowns and flower-bestrewn wraps. Arzner clearly felt she needed to reassure her audience that this "new woman" is still recognizably a "real woman" for all the bold courageously ambitious self-sufficiency that would suggest otherwise.

Flight as a metaphor for freedom and transcendence is as stirring in this film as in Larisa Shepitko's *Wings* four and a half decades later. The kind of gusto and love of her work that Arzner herself voiced about the various phases of her moviemaking career, she puts into Lady Cynthia Darrington's relation to flying as well. As opposed to *Craig's Wife* (1936), made from a hit Broadway play whose author, George Kelly, felt only hostility to the woman at its center, *Christopher Strong*—its script a collaboration between Arzner and a woman screenwriter she worked frequently with before and after this film, Zoe Akins—is entirely supportive of its heroine. The camera is enchanted with her, her strikingly free physical movements whether she is leaning back on both elbows or sprawled with a leg positioned in unladylike but graceful casualness, a fire often blazing behind her in token of her passionate intensity. She not only is in the driver's seat of the car, her passenger the man she comes to love—but of the plane, *she* taking *him* aloft.

Links between women are also striking, Cynthia's with the Strong daughter Monica, and with her lover's wife, played by Billie Burke, with whom she shares long exchanges of looks in very tight closeup in a final sequence of the film. Arzner truly does show "genuine empathy with the 'womanly women' who also populate her movies—the repressed, conservative females who live in the shadows of the world." Links between women, even women in extreme conflict, appear in as early an Arzner film as *Sarah and Son* (1930), where two mothers vie for a son, born to one, raised by the other. Though the woman who has raised the boy has been deceitful, in a crucial final scene she invites the other to join her—ready to share—when the barely conscious boy calls for Mother. (This is also a film striking for the numbers of women involved in its shaping.)

Though Hepburn's character bows out to the angel-of-the-house wife, the way she does so, even her final suicidal flight, is an active recordbreaking feat of the kind that makes her convincing as a revered model for the bold young women in the film. Pauline Kael, certainly not known as a feminist, is understandably and revealingly fascinated by Hepburn/Cynthia's other act of self-sacrifice, her agreeing to comply with her lover's request, as soon as they sleep together, that she not fly in an important match.

> There were many movies in the thirties in which women were professionals and the equals of men, but I don't know of any other scene that was so immediately recognizable to women of a certain kind as *their* truth. It was clear that the man wasn't a bastard, and that he was doing this out of anxiety and tenderness—out of love, in his terms. Nevertheless the heroine's acquiescence destroyed her. There are probably few women who have ever accomplished anything beyond the care of a family who haven't in

> one way or another played that scene. . . . It is the intelligent woman's primal post-coital scene, and it's on film; probably it got there because the movie was written by a woman, Zoe Akins, and directed by a woman, Dorothy Arzner.

The theme may not be unique to Arzner, but the shading is crucial, the attention drawn to the man's request, and the sense we are given of what is lost. (This offers an interesting comparison with Lupino's *Hard, Fast, and Beautiful,* and the giving up of a tennis championship there. Lupino's interviews—not to speak of her films—indicate her own profound conflicts about conventional gender roles. Arzner's relation to work is far less ambivalent than Lupino's, her male figures mostly straw men, and the concessions made to them finally less important on the deepest level, because less internalized.) Although it is true at the same time that Cynthia's narrative function demands "that she ultimately bring/restore [both couples in the film] to monogamy," the patriarchal discourse seems to me not to triumph here.

Though *Dance, Girl, Dance* (1940) too is placed within Hollywood (and patriarchal) conventions, dancer heroine Judy's (Maureen O'Hara's) breaking off her performance for a direct accusatory confrontation of the male audience is "a return of scrutiny" in what is assumed to be a "one-way process," with the "effect of directly challenging the entire notion of woman as spectacle." Equally telling is the grossness in various contexts of the male spectator; and the sympathetic motherly "director" play by Mme. Ouspenskaya, who is authoritative and full of contempt for the Hollywood scene and for the gross male who has the power to say yes or no. Arzner is clearly ambivalent about the vital, glamorous vulgarity of Bubbles, the Lucille Ball showgirl—but the scorn for Hollywood implicit in the film, and for the need to be a flesh peddler to survive there, is doubtless something Arzner herself felt in no small part, in this next to last of her films, close to her retirement. Ouspenskaya's heavily male coded clothes and appearance, her mannishly worn hair, are strikingly like those of Arzner herself in many photographs of her.

Arzner truly does show "genuine empathy with the 'womanly women' who also populate her movies—the repressed, conservative females who live in the shadows of the world."

—*Barbara Koenig Quart*

This Ouspenskaya mother figure is unequivocally fine. While the males in the film are ciphers or fools, the ties between the women are what are really important in the film. So is work, for its own sake as opposed to the leering crude agent under whose male gaze the group performs. There is a powerful sense of female solidarity: Madame watches out for her girls, and Adams' (Ralph Bellamy's) woman secretary supports Judy and is the first to clap with understanding of Judy's speech to the audience. The Arzner heroine is indeed a self-determined woman, who insists "on initiating and carrying out her own projects and pursuing her own desires, rather than taking her place as part of the projects of men and as object of their desires"—whatever conventional capitulations to patriarchy Arzner felt compelled to have her make in the final sequence.

When Arzner retired, Lupino had not yet begun, and for some years no women directors were working in America. Muriel Box, however, was getting her filmmaking career underway in England, a director whose name recurs in that country as often and in the same way as Dorothy Arzner's does here, and whose films were capable without being distinctive. But Box's casual account of how she happened to become a director is worth including here because it makes clear yet again how women's situations cross national boundaries: "I am often asked: When did you first begin to direct films? . . . I give the year as 1950 or my age as forty-five. Neither is strictly true. Both refer to my entry as a director only into feature films; I started with documentaries much earlier. . . . My chance to direct in the documentary field would not have come but for the scarcity of male directors in wartime."

Judith Mayne (essay date 1994)

SOURCE: "Working Girls," in *Directed by Dorothy Arzner,* Indiana University Press, 1994, pp. 93-111.

[In the excerpt below, Mayne focuses on issues of work and social class in the lives of women from four of Arzner's films: Working Girls, Nana, The Bride Wore Red, *and* First Comes Courage.*]*

Contemporary interest in Arzner's career and her work has focused largely on how she, as a woman director in Hollywood, conveyed women's lives, desires, and experiences on screen. Arzner's work did indeed focus primarily on women's lives, women's friendships, and women's communities. But women are never identified in a simple or isolated way in Arzner's work. For instance, I suggested earlier in this book that Arzner's screenplay for *The Red Kimono* is indicative of her commitment not only to the exploration of the connections between women, but to those connections as they are shaped and complicated by social class. In this chapter I will examine how the attention to social class and women's lives is foregrounded in four of Arzner's films—*Working Girls* (1931), *Nana* (1934), *The Bride Wore Red* (1937), and *First Comes Courage* (1943). As the title of this chapter indicates, each is concerned with women's working lives.

It is significant that the attention to social class, in Arzner's films, is given especially to working women. To be sure, in early films like *Get Your Man* (1927), American and European definitions of social class are juxtaposed, with attendant differences in sexual morality. Clara Bow's character exploits these differences to her benefit, as if to suggest that the brash, entrepreneurial attitude towards love that she embodies is symptomatic of an approach to social mores quite different from the European aristocratic values with which she clashes. More typically, however, it is through jobs and careers that women's encounters with social class occur. *Sarah and Son* and *Dance, Girl, Dance* use women's careers on stage to explore the differing class associations of vaudeville versus opera (in *Sarah and Son*) and burlesque versus ballet (in *Dance, Girl, Dance*). In *Honor among Lovers,* the obstacles to romance between Julia (Claudette Colbert) and Jerry (Fredric March) are specifically those of social class, since Julia's status as Jerry's secretary puts her outside the wealthy circles in which he circulates.

As coincidence would have it, the four films discussed here have something besides the working girl in common. They were perhaps the largest failures in Arzner's career. By "failure" I do not mean that the films were artistic failures, although in two cases this is true—*Nana* and *The Bride Wore Red* are less interesting than Arzner's other films. More important, these four films marked low points in Arzner's career, and all were failures commercially. While I think *First Comes Courage* is better than many critics (including Arzner herself) allow, it was Arzner's last film, and the project that precipitated her departure from Hollywood. The biggest commercial flop of Arzner's career was *Working Girls,* a film worthy of the kind of attention that *Dance, Girl, Dance* and *Christopher Strong* have received.

By grouping together four failed works, I am not necessarily suggesting that flops occurred whenever Arzner turned her attention to social class; attention to the intersections of class and gender is common in most of her films. In these four works, the working girl is portrayed through and against the conventions of romance, and the connection of "work" and "romance" is often awkward. As a result, the conventions of Hollywood romance are defamiliarized, even to the point of appearing downright silly. This foregrounding of the limitations of Hollywood romance may account for some of the perceived limitations of these films by the critics and audiences of the time.

Working Girls was the third of four films on which Arzner and screenwriter Zoë Akins collaborated. The film was, for all intents and purposes, shelved by Paramount; it never had a national release and received virtually no studio publicity. It never had a general release and is available only in archival prints to this day. This is unfortunate, since this film is one of Arzner's most significant achievements, and it is the most successful of her collaborations with Akins. Stylistically, it is daring and innovative.

Working Girls tells the tale of two sisters, May and June Thorpe, who come to New York City from Rockville, Indiana, determined to make careers for themselves as "working girls." The ambiguity of the film's title is never addressed directly in the film. But the double meaning of "working girl," in its innocent literal sense and in its acquired sense that women who worked outside the home were morally suspect (eventually the term "working girl" became a code for "prostitute"), is evident throughout. The two sisters must learn, simultaneously, the sexual politics of both work and romance. May and June move into the Rolfe House, a boardinghouse for single, working girls like themselves, i.e., women from rather poor backgrounds who have few available funds. The sisters go to work: they get jobs and boyfriends. As in all of Arzner's films featuring communities of women, strong bonds exist among the women who share the living quarters. Yet Arzner gently parodies such institutions. Miss Johnstone, the administrator of the home, is as busy shutting windows to keep out the sounds of music and partying across the way as she is taking care of business; one of the boarders remarks sarcastically that hearing music is supposed to be bad for their morals.

One of the most interesting developments in the film is the change that separates the two sisters as the film progresses. At the beginning of the film, they are virtually interchangeable, an effect emphasized by the similar coloring, makeup, and dress of the two actresses. The only significant difference is that May, the older of the two, seems a bit more mature and reasonable than her younger sister, June. As the film progresses, their dress changes considerably, with one sister becoming more frilly and feminine (and more irresponsible in her relationships with men), and the other more severe, butch, and businesslike (like Arzner herself, one is tempted to note), and much more astute in her relationships with men.

June interviews for a job as a research assistant to Von Schrader, a German scholar, and when he makes clear that he is looking for someone more educated, she calls her sister in, and May gets the job. June sets out to find herself a more frivolous job as a model, but she is snobbily rejected. June begins to pay more attention to her dress and appearance, and she finds a job at a telegraph station in a hotel. Her first two customers become the romantic leads for June and her sister; one is a wealthy Harvard man (who sends a telegram to an ex-girlfriend), and the other is a saxophone player, who quickly invites June to have dinner with him.

Boyd Wheeler, the Harvard man, soon meets May in a shoe store. Unbeknownst to May, he is on the rebound (which June knows because of the telegram he sent); May and Boyd begin a romance. June is suspicious of the liaison precisely be-

cause of the class differences between them. Meanwhile, Kelly, the saxophone player, showers June with gifts. In the film's early scenes, June appears to be the more frivolous sister. Yet as the film progresses, she proves to be the wiser and more practical one. She is never swept off her feet by Kelly in the way that May is by Wheeler, and June's undisguised interest in material things makes her appear not so much naive and superficial as cunning and straightforward. Most important, June does not do what May does, namely, sleep with her boyfriend.

The question of premarital sex is presented in the film less as a moral issue than a practical one. May becomes pregnant, but in the meantime Wheeler has returned to Louise, his former sweetheart—a woman, none too coincidentally, of his own social background. June takes charge of the situation. First, she goes to May's employer, the German scholar, who had let May go when he became aware of his attraction to her and her lack of interest in him. June begs him to give May back her job, and he agrees. Shortly after May begins to work again, she accepts the marriage proposal he had made six months before, and he, confused and in a moment of weakness, agrees. When June discovers that her sister is pregnant with Wheeler's child, she is the one who breaks the news to the German scholar. June's job proves once again to be an asset, since she discovers through a telegram that Wheeler sends to sweetheart Louise that their engagement has ended, at her request. Once June has this information, she proceeds with her plan to force Wheeler to marry her sister.

One might expect that the intersecting working lives and romantic lives of the two sisters would conclude on this note— May with Wheeler in a curious but necessary cross-class marriage made possible mostly by June, who is more appropriately paired with Kelly, the musician. However, there is a twist to this symmetry; June and the German scholar fall in love, as if to suggest yet another cross-class fantasy, one involving education and learnedness as much as wealth (Wheeler may be a Harvard man, but he is never seen at work, and he is drunk most of the time).

The changing fortunes of the two sisters are represented by their changes in appearance. As I've mentioned, the two women are dressed identically at the beginning of the film, and during the first few scenes it is difficult to tell them apart in terms of appearance. However, as the film progresses, June begins to dress in a less frilly, stereotypically "feminine" way, while May, who without her sister's direction would be virtually lost, becomes the more feminine dresser. The contrast in dress is made most strikingly in the decisive scene of the shift in power between the two sisters, when June tends to her ill sister in their room at Rolfe House. June wears a uniform that tends to be associated, in all of Arzner's films, with independence and autonomy (not to mention with Arzner's own style of dress): a suit and tie, with a beret. The difference between the two sisters, at this point, is not just one of clothing, for May's pregnancy becomes quite clear to her sister (and to the audience) during this scene.

A common preoccupation in Arzner's films is the contrast not only between individual women, but also between communities exclusively composed of women and mixed communities of men and women. In *Working Girls,* this contrast takes shape as a movement back and forth from Rolfe House, where men are permitted only in the reception area (and are gawked at by the residents), to the working world; the contrast is also evoked by the juxtaposition of Rolfe House and the unidentified, but supposedly dangerous, community that exists within earshot—from which music and dancing are heard. Interestingly, the working world from which Rolfe House provides a refuge is defined from the outset more in terms of the male/female interactions that it enables than in terms of work in any classic sense of the word. Indeed, the only really traditional concept of a women's work force occurs during the credits of the film, where we see women in silhouette at typewriters, and it is perhaps no coincidence that this abstraction of women in the work force never really finds a concrete match in the film. The work situations that May and June find for themselves are unusual. May goes to work for the German scholar, whose office and home are one, and June finds it odd that home and workplace should thus be combined. June's job in the telegraph office is not a typical work environment, in that she has unusual autonomy—not to mention access to vital plot information! In both cases, the women's jobs are immediately defined in terms of their romantic lives—the scholar proposes to May, and June's first few minutes on the job introduce her to her sister's future husband and her own romantic companion for most of the film.

Working Girls seems to establish contrasts (like romance/work) only to collapse them. Try as Mrs. Johnstone might to keep the noise and accompanying festivities at bay by closing the windows, the inhabitants of Rolfe House nonetheless create their own fun, whether by disobeying the rules of the house or by creating a female world of laughter and dance. Similarly, the worlds of home and paid labor, for women, are never separate. This intersection of seemingly opposing spheres finds, in *Working Girls,* a stunning representation in a scene that is among the most effective and gorgeous in any of Arzner's works. May and June have had a busy day of finding work and finding male companions. The doors of Rolfe House lock at midnight, and unless a girl has signed out for the night, missing the deadline means certain expulsion. June returns five minutes before midnight, in a taxi, from her evening spent with Kelly, who has showered her with presents. At three minutes until midnight, May arrives with Mr. Wheeler, the Harvard man, to whom she already affectionately refers as "Big Frog" (he calls her "Little Frog").

The elevator in Rolfe House shuts down at 11 P.M., so the two sisters must climb up several flights of stairs to their room. Virtually all communication in the film is observed by others, and this scene is no exception, as Loretta, the elevator operator, functions here (as she often does in the film) as a witness. After they have been let into the building by Loretta, the two sisters begin to mount the four flights of stairs to the room they share. From a long shot of the two women about to mount the stairs, the camera moves forward to frame them more closely, and follows their movements up the stairs. Striking effects of light and dark frame them as they climb, exhausted. Visually, the pair are in a state of suspension, their movement upwards at once an ironic reminder of both their aspirations and their limitations. They live in a home that forces the women to climb stairs after 11 P.M.; their fatigue is a reminder of the contrast between the taxi (June) and the personal automobile (May) that have brought them to the door and the institutional surroundings they call home. Yet they are moving upwards, mirroring their own desires to come to the big city and make their fortunes.

Although June and May are still dressed quite similarly, if not identically, their first full day in the city has already produced a significant difference between them. June is loaded down with packages, gifts from Kelly—from candy and perfume to an umbrella and overshoes—while May has nothing. Although May is the older sister, this extended walk up the stairs marks the first shift in their relationship, wherein June is defined as the more astute and the more mature. Their conversation about men reveals an almost startling cynicism and wisdom on June's part and foreshadows how she will prove to be both more clever than her sister and her sister's protector.

June tells May that Mr. Kelly warned her that "a lot of these swell guys think any girl that works is fair game; and you're so darned soft. . . ." May is quick to point out that this Mr. Kelly is a new acquaintance as surely as Boyd Wheeler is, to which June replies: "Don't you worry about me not knowing how to say no. I even know how to say no and yes at the same time—which is something you'll never learn." May insists that she doesn't want to learn such a thing, and the remainder of the film will demonstrate how saying "no and yes at the same time" is indeed what separates the two sisters. May is drawn to Wheeler's wealth and the fact that he is a Harvard man, but June points out that all she managed to get from him was a meal, whereas her saxophone player showered her with gifts.

The difference between the two sisters is identified specifically in terms of their understanding of class. June tells her sister that she doesn't want her "running around with somebody who thinks [she's] not in his class." When May suggests that she may well marry Boyd Wheeler some day, June exclaims, "Gosh, what a fool I've raised for a sister!" May

may well be the older sister, but June is quickly assuming the role of wiser, more experienced sibling.

May doesn't pay the price for her naiveté, since June ensures that the cross-class marriage her sister dreamed of occurs, even if not in quite the same terms May had imagined. But for June, there is a most curious pay-off. When she goes to Von Schrader to tell him that May is marrying someone else, he quickly falls in love with her. When June interviewed with Von Schrader for the job that eventually went to May, her lack of education andgeneral knowledge was pointedly observed by the German scholar. Yet by the conclusion of the film, these two are paired. The pairing is suggested in a peculiar way, because Kelly enters the frame of June and Von Schrader just as she is telling the European that she needs a lot of petting. Kelly's exclamation is the last line of the film: "Why June, you always told me you didn't like petting!" Framed between the two men, June seems to be demonstrating her ability to say "no and yes at the same time," as if to suggest that the "work" of managing relationships requires a precise and finely honed script. Indeed, June's role in *Working Girls* embodies both sharp observations on the complex nature of women's work and a fantasy of women's power to shape the world around them.

If June demonstrates the ability to say "no and yes at the same time," *Working Girls* also demonstrates Arzner's unique ability to say the same to the conventions of Hollywood cinema. *Working Girls* explores the stakes, for women, of binary opposites, ranging from home/workplace, to romance/work, to gender/class. It is impossible to neatly separate one term from the other in this film. The scene of May and June climbing the staircase in Rolfe House provides a stunning mise-en-scène of what might be called a threshold space, literally and figuratively. The vision of *Working Girls* is profoundly ambivalent, in that it is impossible to make clear and absolute distinctions between different realms, and also in the sense that the film both celebrates and critiques how women's work comprises so many complex variables. Arzner's own position as a working girl may have been vastly different from that of May or June, but her own relationship to the Hollywood cinema comprised complex variables as well.

I don't know if Lizzie Borden chose the title of her 1986 film *Working Girls* in conscious homage to Arzner's film, but there are some striking parallels between the two works. In both cases, however different the points of emphasis (Borden's film is about a group of prostitutes who work in a middle-class bordello), being a "working girl" means understanding economics in sexual as well as business terms. In addition, the bordello in Borden's film is presented in some of the same ways as Rolfe House in Arzner's film—a female community where women manage to create a utopian space despite the imposition of rules. Arzner had censorship problems with *Working Girls,* undoubtedly due in part to the direct approach

to May's pregnancy and June's more savvy approach to the relationship between sex and money. The only film in which Arzner directly addresses prostitution is *Nana,* the film for which she was hired to replace another director, and which Samuel Goldwyn intended as a starring vehicle for Russian actress Anna Sten.

I hesitate to make too much of the script adapting Émile Zola's novel to the screen (the final film departs so sharply from the novel that the credits read "suggested by Zola's novel"). Arzner's habit was to work closely with the writer, and to have a writer on the set at all times, and the conditions of production of *Nana* would appear to have made this difficult. However, in the case of *Dance, Girl, Dance,* where Arzner was similarly brought in to manage a project begun by someone else, Arzner's own changes to the already existing script resulted in what is perhaps her most successful and personal film. *Nana* is not one of Arzner's great successes, but some elements of the screenplay are suggestive of Arzner'spreoccupations in other films. Most obviously, the relationship between Nana and Satin is foregrounded from the outset of the film. In Zola's novel, the relationship between the two women (first as fellow prostitutes, later as lesbian lovers) is important, but certainly not as central as in the film. Hence, in what is recognizable as a typical Arzner touch, Nana is defined from the outset as part of a community of women, and the friendship between her and Satin is a constant in the film.

Nana is a working girl in the tradition of the female leads of *Sarah and Son* and *Dance, Girl, Dance;* in these works the world of performance is intimately connected to that of sex. Nana's working life combines prostitution and the stage, and the two worlds are forever intertwined. Unlike the two other films in which women performers are central, here the central opposition is between "sex work" understood in two different ways: literally (as a prostitute) and figuratively (as a performer). Indeed, some of the most interesting moments in the film occur when there is deliberate ambiguity between performance and sexuality.

Nana is introduced in the film as a poor woman, scrubbing floors under the watchful eyes of a married couple; Nana's mother has just died and Nana cannot afford to buy a tombstone for her grave. To the man she exclaims: "It's men who make women whatever they are. I don't know what I'll be— but I won't be weak. And I won't be poor." Titles announce that a year has passed, and Nana enters a café in the company of Satin and Mimi, the three of them clearly coded as prostitutes (or "common women," as a man whom Nana eventually humiliates puts it).

Nana's display sparks the interest of Greiner, an impresario, and he sends a man to Nana who tells her that Greiner "has made more women . . ." Nana interrupts him: "Made them *what?*" "Made them famous," the man continues. "Oh," Nana replies, "now he interests me." Nana's humiliation of a potential client catches the impresario's eye, and the play on the word "made" suggests the interdependence, in the film, of Nana's work and her sexuality. To anyone familiar with Émile Zola's novel, this is hardly stunning news. But the film *Nana* functions in a more interesting way as a "reading" of Zola in Nana's relationships with other women. Zola's novel begins with theatre-goers—virtually all male—discussing the new discovery, Nana. Bordenave, the theatre manager, abruptly corrects anyone who refers to the space as a theatre—"You mean my brothel!" he interrupts, a virtual rhythmic cadence throughout the opening chapter. When Nana finally appears on stage, she is first laughed at and then recognized as a remarkable spectacle. The power of this "man-eater" (as Zola calls her) is measured by her hypnotic, mesmerizing effect on the male spectators. Hence, Zola's novel plays on absolute gender distinctions—male/female, onlooker/performer.

In the film, however, and in keeping with the foregrounding of Nana's connection with Satin, Nana's appearances on stage are less absolutely defined in terms of a female performer versus a male onlooker. To be sure, attention is drawn in the film to the expectations of the male audience vis-à-vis Nana, but equal attention is drawn to two other spectators, Satin and Mimi. These two fellow prostitutes have visited the theatre regularly, trying to see their friend, but each time they are told that Nana doesn't want to see them. Meanwhile, Nana expresses concern about her two friends. When Nana finally comes on stage, the male members in the audience are appropriately dazzled by her performance (and a rather odd performance it is; despite the fact that Goldwyn wanted to make Sten a star in her own terms, her stage performance in *Nana* is like a bad imitation of Marlene Dietrich). They are not, however, the only spectators; Satin and Mimi have taken their seats in the balcony and impatiently (and angrily) await the arrival of the friend they think has betrayed them. ("When does our lady of the sewers come on?" one asks the other.) Mimi and Satin are moved to tears by Nana's performance, and shots of their reactions to their friend onstage provide an interesting counterpoint to the reactions of the male members of the audience.

Much attention has been paid, in feminist film theory, to the polarity of the gaze in classical cinema—where man is "bearer of the look," to use Laura Mulvey's phrase, and woman its object—and in particular to those situations, like Nana onstage, which epitomize the absolute division between woman as object and man as subject. I have always found Zola's novel also to be a stunning demonstration of this process, and it is perhaps one of many non-coincidences that Zola's influence on the cinema has been noted by many filmmakers and theorists alike. But in Arzner's *Nana*, there is no absolute polarity, no rigid opposition, between woman as performer and man as onlooker, since women in the audi-

ence are active spectators and impassioned onlookers. Indeed, reaction shots of the women are as fully a part of the continuity established in this scene as shots of the men are.

This is, I believe, one of the distinctive features of how "women's work" is presented in Arzner's films, particularly women's work onstage. There is no simplistic division between the male gaze and the female object, and women are active and complex subjects, regardless of what they are subject of or subjected to. It is significant in this context that the most famous scene in any of Arzner's films, Judy's speech to the audience in *Dance, Girl, Dance,* may address the audience as male, but the audience we actually see is not exclusively male. For in *Dance, Girl, Dance,* as in *Nana,* the working world of women is just that, and not a rarefied sphere where women exist only as victims or only as objects of male pleasure.

Unfortunately, however, this "reading" of Zola, and of some of the conventions of classical cinema, demonstrated in the foregrounding of the friendships among Nana, Mimi and Satin, and in the presentation of Nana's performance as one eagerly consumed by women as well as men, is not sustained in *Nana*. The film becomes centered on a conflict between two men, both of whom are supposedly ruined by their contact with Nana. In Zola's novel, Nana dies of smallpox, and she is surrounded by a circle of fellow prostitutes as she dies. Meanwhile, in the street, men are gathered, drawn both by her death and by the announcement of war. A rigid boundary line separates the world of men from the world of women in the novel; the men dare not enter the room, where Nana's death and disfigurement are described by Zola in stunningly repulsive detail. In the film, Nana dies by her own hand, clearly an easy, and not particularly satisfying, out. Instead of the sustained exploration of the intersections between gender, work, and performance that one might expect, given the beginning of the film and its representation of women in the theatre, the film moves towards a conclusion of tired clichés of the ruined woman who sacrifices herself. The spectacle of Nana's suicide cannot erase, however, the stunning mise-en-scène of the stage, where Nana's status as a working girl combines the pleasures and dangers of the look with the exploitation and delight of performance.

Even in a film that is ultimately disappointing, like *Nana,* there are elements suggestive of Arzner's unique touch and her ability to draw, even from material seemingly resistant to such inflections, complicated and complex portraits of women's lives. *The Bride Wore Red* was, for Arzner, an unsatisfying film. While the film echoes the preoccupations that are much more extensively developed in other films, *The Bride Wore Red* does focus, somewhat more explicitly than other films directed by Arzner, on the importance of costume and performance to any notion of female identity; and thus the notion of women's work, in this film, includes the realms of fashion and self-presentation.

The plot of *The Bride Wore Red* is based on a practical joke. Two wealthy men are spending the evening gambling in a nightclub, and engage in a discussion about the evidence of class and good breeding. Using the image of a roulette wheel, one (Count Armalia) insists that chance decides who is rich and who is poor, while the other (Rudi Pal) insists that breeding accounts for absolute distinctions. In order to make his point, Armalia insists that the two men go to the seediest club they can find. Joan Crawford, playing Anni, a barmaid, becomes the concrete manifestation of Armalia's wager. Count Armalia, who argues in favor of the "performative" quality of social class, offers her a large sum of money and an all-expense-paid vacation if she will pose as a member of the aristocracy. She agrees and departs for Terrano, where she soon charms another wealthy man—none other than Rudi, the man with whom her benefactor made his original bet. Count Armalia's words to Rudi prove to be prophetic; describing Anni, he says, "Have her properly washed, dressed and coiffured, and you wouldn't be able to tell her from your fiancée."

With her new identity, Anni (now Anne Vivaldi) arrives at the train station and meets Giulio, the local postman and the film's embodiment of peasant purity. Indeed, the opposition of high class and low class is displaced, as the film progresses, by the opposition of city and country. As coincidence would have it, the maid assigned to Anni in the hotel is her old friend from the bar, Maria, who has found true happiness in the country. The film shows the poor—whether maids like Maria or postmen like Giulio—as more attuned to the values of the simple, nature-bound life. The process of the film will be to demonstrate to Anni that what she really desires is a life with Giulio, not with Rudi. Her encounter with the wealthy at the resort may make her long for the riches that Rudi can offer, but it also makes her long for a life in closer touch with nature, neatly represented by Giulio.

Anni wins Rudi's affections away from Maddelena, his fiancée. In a twist typical of Arzner, Maddelena is one of the wealthy, but possesses none of their hypocrisy or arrogance, thus complicating the simple division between upper and lower classes. One of Arzner's preferred actresses, Billie Burke, plays the role of wife to Maddelena's father. As is typical for Burke, she is frilly and feminine, but there is a dry, almost acidic side to her portrayal of the suspicious and cynical woman of the world.

In order to make sure that Rudi proposes to her, Anni extends her stay at the hotel. In the meantime, Contessa di Meina (Burke) wires Armalia, supposedly a close friend of Anne Vivaldi's family, to inquire about Anne. His response—specifying the ruse and Anni's real status as a "cabaret girl"—gets lost when Giulio, carrying the telegram to the hotel, is met by Anni, and they kiss. But when Giulio discovers that Anni plans to marry Rudi, he threatens to deliver the copy of the telegram kept in the office. And this he does, during the farewell dinner for Anni and Rudi. Once her charade is discovered, Anni leaves the hotel and meets Giulio; having acknowledged her true feelings for him, Anni accepts his offer of marriage, and the film ends.

Performance is central to *The Bride Wore Red,* and even though the performance is not so literal or explicit as in *Nana,* the film nonetheless emphasizes from beginning to end the extent to which women's identities—sexual as well as class—depend upon performance. And women's social class also determines what kind of sexual performance is expected of them. Crawford's Anni is introduced through her performance of a song at the bar, and when she is introduced to the count she immediately assumes her status as an object to be consumed; indeed, she asks of the count if he has come to "stare at animals in the zoo." The central performance that she undertakes in the film, of course, is her attempt to act like a "lady." Two particular elements are significant here: her assumption of arrogant speech with servants, and her entrances in different types of clothing down the staircase of the hotel.

When Anni arrives at Terrano, Giulio offers to take her to the hotel in his cart, and she questions whether he should expect a lady to accept. When Anni arrives in her room, the maid enters and asks Anni if she would like her clothes unpacked. Just as Anni is basking in the luxury of being waited upon, she recognizes her old friend Maria. The assumption of wealth is equated with artifice, which comes as no surprise; but the film demonstrates the performative aspect of such speech by drawing on one of Arzner's preferred themes—female community and friendship. Indeed, even though Anni's relationship with Giulio is meant to be her passage to true self-discovery, she appears far more honest, frank, and direct with Maria. During one striking exchange between the two women, Maria wears one of Anni's costumes, making the "quotation" of artifice an important aspect of their relationship.

Similarly, Anni is assisted in her performance by one of the waiters, who subtly instructs her how to eat properly. Later, when she is about to depart with Rudi, she thanks the servant and tells him—in her best aristocratic tone—that a large check will be sent to him later. He informs her that this is not necessary, and that his cousin (virtually everyone in Terrano seems to be a cousin of Giulio) asked him to watch out for her. Still later, when Anni leaves the hotel in disgrace, only this servant continues to treat her like a "lady"—by opening the door for her after others refuse.

If the film contrasts Anni's "authentic" speech with her "performed" speech, in virtually every case the performed speech occurs in public places, while the authentic speech occurs either behind closed doors or in the expanses of forest that surround the hotel, but which are portrayed as quite distant from the social world the hotel represents. Similarly, the entrances Anni makes down the hotel staircase are public performances. Three such entrances occur. It is not surprising that dress is central to each entrance; what is interesting are the different and complex inflections that dress acquires. The title of the film refers to Anni's dream dress, a red, sequined evening gown, which is one of her first purchases once she is endowed by Count Armalia. But when she wants to wear it the first night at the hotel, Maria dissuades her, convinced that it is more appropriate to the seedy club where they knew each other when. Instead, Anni wears an outfit that is demure and excessive at the same time—a white dress with a veil, flowers in her hair, and a fan which she holds before her face. Anni receives the attentions of the crowd, presumably because she is distinctive, yet still one of them.

On the evening of her farewell dinner, once Anni has managed to get a marriage proposal from Rudi, she decides to wear her red dress. As she descends the stairs she once again is the object of attention (shades of Bette Davis wearing a red dress to the ball in *Jezebel*!). Maria advised her not to wear the dress when Anni arrived at the hotel. Now, however, Anni assumes that since she is about to become Rudi's wife, she no longer has to worry about following conventions; she can flaunt them. The dress does indeed provoke a reaction, as if to suggest that Anni always treads a fineline between being acceptable and outrageous, and in more general terms to suggest that the class identity she seeks is a function of appearance. The red dress signifies simultaneously Anni's desire for and her exclusion from the very values to which she aspires.

The complexity of "appearances" achieves yet another dimension when Anni comes down the stairs one final time to the notice of the crowd, at the film's conclusion, when her deception has been revealed. She wears a nondescript black cape—nondescript in the sense that it does not suggest one particular class affiliation; and it is indeed so nondescript that it could be worn by virtually anyone in the film, working-class or aristocratic. Once Anni and Giulio are reunited, she takes off the cloak to reveal a peasant costume that she wore to the "festa"—a carnivalesque celebration in which everyone dresses in supposed authentic peasant garb. Oddly, then, Anni adopts a costume from the most elaborate performance of the film to claim her authentic self. The film suggests not only that gender and class, for women, are equally a function of dress, of appearance; it also suggests, obliquely, that there is virtually no such thing as a female identity that does not rely on costume, staging, and performance. Whatever authentic identity Anni captures at the film's conclusion, it is an identity manufactured by the kind of women's work that keeps the illusions of performance alive.

Several times in the course of Arzner's career she was asked to finish films that others had begun. Her final film, *First Comes Courage,* marked the first time that another director had to finish a film she had started. Arzner became quite ill during the production of the film, and Charles Vidor finished it. As discussed earlier, for reasons having to do with more than her health, this was Arzner's last film as director.

First Comes Courage is set in Norway in 1942, and tells the story of Nicole Larsen (Merle Oberon), an Allied spy who receives her information by virtue of her romance with a German Nazi stationed in Norway, Major Paul Dichter (Carl Esmond). Dichter knows there is a leak somewhere, and a visiting Nazi has suspicions about Nicole. She passes on her information through bogus visits to an eye doctor, who then transmits her information by embedding it in eyeglass lenses. A message that suspicions are forming about Nicole reaches Allied officer Allan Lowell (Brian Aherne), who has been transferred to field service in order to assist the Norwegian underground by wiping out Nazi strongholds. Most of the film takes place as an alternation between Lowell, preparing for and executing his plans in the Norwegian town where Nicole lives, and Nicole, attempting to divert suspicion from herself while continuing to amass information. That a relationship exists between Lowell and Larsen is made evident through cross-cutting, although the specific nature of the relationship is made clear only when he is captured by the Nazis.

> **Even in a film that is ultimately disappointing, like *Nana,* there are elements suggestive of Arzner's unique touch and her ability to draw, even from material seemingly resistant to such inflections, complicated and complex portraits of women's lives.**
>
> **—*Judith Mayne***

Allan has come to the Norwegian village to preside over a bomb attack and to eliminate a key Nazi. After he is captured, Nicole must develop a ruse in order to help him escape from the hospital where he recuperates after the shooting that killed his companion. She is advised by the eye doctor to take Rose Lindstrom, a nurse at the hospital, into her confidence. Withsome hesitation, Nicole does so, and the two are able to move Lowell, dressed in a Nazi uniform, to Nicole's house.

Interestingly (and typically for Arzner), Rose's intervention occurs at just the moment when Nicole sees Allan for the first time and discovers that her comrade is also her lover from the past. The relationship that has been, throughout the film, the basis of spatial opposition, established only through cross-cutting, is now fully a part of the present tense of the film, a function of a single dramatic space. Nicole's alliance with Rose is significant for two reasons. First, Nicole must endanger her cover as a traitor in order to save Lowell, and second, this risk occurs in an alliance with another woman who functions, however briefly, as an indication of the strength of female bonding.

Indeed, for a brief moment, the highly anticipated reunion of Allan and Nicole is overshadowed by the alliance between the two women. Rose is blonde; she is a large, heavy-set woman, whose physical appearance contrasts markedly with the delicate brunette figure of Merle Oberon. The contrast between the two women plays on the butch (Rose)/femme (Nicole) imagery that appears frequently in portrayals of women in Arzner's films. Rose proves, as well, to be as un-wavering in her strength as Nicole; when she is questioned by the Nazis, once she is suspected of having assisted in Lowell's escape, she refuses to break. Molly Haskell assesses the relationship between the two women: "True to Arzner, the most moving character in the film is a woman, a nurse, who assists Oberon and refuses to denounce her even when her own family is threatened. And the most moving scene is the one in which they embrace in a rapture of mutual under-standing that transcends war, and that will nourish each of them in their lonely women's destinies in a way that roman-tic love never can."

The bombing and assassination are to go ahead as planned, and as coincidence would have it, Dichter has planned for Nicole to become his bride on that very day. Dichter is in-creasingly uncomfortable with the suspicions cast his way about Nicole, and he feels his marriage to her will displace those suspicions. For Nicole, the marriage offers yet another opportunity to have more access to information. The wed-ding goes off as planned, and it is an odd ceremony, indeed—the couple march down an aisle of Nazis and wed beneath a Nazi flag, their hands joined over a copy of *Mein Kampf*. But Dichter has discovered the truth about Nicole; he passed false information about a munitions factory only to her, and it was bombed shortly after, thus proving her identity as a spy. He tells Nicole that she will die in a fake accident, but Allan appears on the scene to kill him before he can execute his plan.

Meanwhile, the raid is going off as planned, and both Dichter and Von Elser (the suspicious Nazi) are killed, while Allan and Nicole emerge unscathed. Allan tries to convince Nicole to return to England, but she insists that she must stay in Norway, particularly now that she has the additional status of widow of a Nazi officer. After a final kiss, Nicole disappears into the forest, while Allan rejoins the Allies, who are about

to sail off. As he departs, a final series of match shots situates the two of them as they smile while the distance between them grows.

To be sure, Nicole Larsen is a different kind of working girl than May and June, Nana, or Anni; the profession of spying is hardly like those of research assistant or telegraph operator (*Working Girls*), prostitute (*Nana*), or cabaret singer (*The Bride Wore Red*). But Larsen's career as a spy is presented in ways remarkably similar to Arzner's other films preoccupied with women's work. Larsen's work involves a performance with her Nazi informer, where the typical activities of wom-anhood—companionship and dress, not to mention grace and charm under pressure—become, for her, strategic means to acquire information. The audience is informed of Nicole's true identity almost immediately in the film, since the first scene finds her walking down the town street to the friendly greeting of a Nazi and the bitter reprimand of a townswoman, only to enter the eye doctor's shop where, in the darkened room, he shines a light in her eyes and her true identity is revealed. Hence, from here on in, virtually all of Nicole's performance is recognized as a ruse, a disguise.

Where *First Comes Courage* differs from Arzner's other work is in the mythic heroism attributed to Nicole. Her work is that of a patriot, not just that of a woman trying to survive. But even here, *First Comes Courage* functions as an interesting grid through which to read other films about women and work. Nicole has two stirring speeches in the film, one in which she confronts the Nazi whom she marries out of her devotion to the cause, and another in which she tells Allan, her true love, that she cannot leave with him and forsake her activities in Norway. When Dichter tells Nicole that he knows she is a spy, she expresses contempt for him and denounces his weak-ness (all along he has been more concerned about his own safety than the principles he supposedly cares about); this revelation of her contempt makes her performances as a de-voted companion even more impressive.

Nicole's most impassioned speech comes at the film's con-clusion. Throughout the film there has been an interesting role reversal, to the extent that Nicole occupies fully and com-fortably the position of "hero," with Allan in much more of a supporting role (although he kills Dichter, Nicole had previ-ously saved Allan's life). After the success of the raid and the death of the Nazis, it is Allan who tries to convince Nicole that she should retreat to safety, and Nicole who insists upon the need to continue to fight.

There are curious echoes, in the final moments of the film, of a far more successful film released in the same year as *First Comes Courage*—*Casablanca*. The final encounter between Rick (Humphrey Bogart) and Ilsa (Ingrid Bergman) is one of the best-known scenes in American film, from Rick's insis-tence that Ilsa depart with her husband, rather than stay with him, to his famous remark that "it doesn't take much to see that the problems of three little people don't amount to a hill of beans in thiscrazy world. Someday you'll understand that." At the conclusion of *First Comes Courage,* Allan says to Nicole that she has "done more than any woman could be expected to do." She tells him: "I'll quit when you quit." He insists that "we're not saying goodbye again ever." While the words may not be as classic as Bogart's "hill of beans," Nicole's reply to Allan rings familiar: "Oh but darling it isn't that kind of world any more. People don't dance and laugh and ski, as we once used to." I am not suggesting that any allusion to *Casablanca* is deliberate (the films were in production at approximately the same time), but rather that the mythic qualities associated with love and war, which find perhaps their most classic expression in *Casablanca,* are both cited and turned around in *First Comes Courage.* For in Arzner's film, Nicole expresses views that are more typically expressed by male heroes. Put another way, then, *First Comes Courage* twists the gender conventions of the war/spy genre, and in the process, celebrates women's work, not *as* love and romance, nor as a *substitute* for love and romance, but as what makes everything else possible.

Russell Cousins (essay date 1995)

SOURCE: "Sanitizing Zola: Dorothy Arzner's Problematic *Nana,*" in *Literature Film Quarterly,* Vol. 23, No. 3, 1995, pp. 209-15.

[*In the following essay, Cousins analyzes Arzner's adaptation of* Nana *and concludes that Arzner's film "exposes the pernicious effects . . . of patriarchy" and challenges normative views on male-female relationships.*]

Nana, Zola's best-selling novel about a Second Empire harlot-cum-actress, has attracted successive generations of filmmakers. Two French directors turned the tale into memorable vehicles for their own actress wives. In 1926, Jean Renoir made the most notable of the silent versions with Catherine Hessling in the title role, while in 1955, Christian Jaque directed a lavish cinema-scope spectacle featuring Martine Carol. More recent exploitive Italian and Swedish adaptations have traduced Zola's indictment of debauchery into sexually explicit accounts of Nana's affairs.

The only Hollywood version of Zola's novel was made in 1934 by pioneering female director Dorothy Arzner. Despite the renewal of interest in her films and, in particular, in her depiction of determined women, relatively little attention has been paid to her screen version of Zola's tale of the powerful slumland prostitute who exacts a terrible price from her aristocratic clients. The film deserves more detailed consideration, however, not only as an inchoate expression of proto-feminist positions, but as a case study of the circum-

stances that conditioned this sanitized adaptation of the celebrated French naturalist text.

Given the structures of the Hays Code, a screen version of *Nana* was likely to be a risky business, but for producer Samuel Goldwyn, Zola's rags-to-riches story of a vaudeville actress appeared an ideal launch vehicle for his new star-to-be, Anna Sten. Such were the compromises required to bring Zola's frank account of Second Empire decadence to the screen that the final bowdlerized adaptation bore scant resemblance to the original, andboth Zola's heirs and French cinema critics protested at Hollywood's emasculated treatment.

Before analyzing Arzner's reworking, a consideration of the production problems is desirable. With a screenplay by Justus Mayer, Leo Brinski, and Harry Wagstaff Gribble and a theme song by Richard Rodgers and Lorenz Hart, Goldwyn promised a less sordid, more romantic version of Zola's down-to-earth novel. Direction was initially entrusted to the experienced George Fitzmaurice, but with over half the film completed, a dissatisfied Goldwyn ordered a fresh start with Dorothy Arzner as a replacement director. The abandoned footage appears to have been too close to Zola for the producer's comfort, and several redraftings of the screenplay were required before final approval. Some of the script changes can be deduced from accounts of the original film's progress. Whereas the Fitzmaurice version included Nana's violent lover, Fontan, and had scenes with Nana as "the street brat, then as the greedy, reckless youngster starting as a demimondaine of the boulevards, the woman dodging the police," these elements have no place in Arzner's film.

If establishing an acceptable script was the first problem, working with Goldwyn's Ukrainian actress came a close second. The producer had convinced himself that in Anna Sten he had discovered the new Garbo or the new Dietrich. For over two years he groomed her as the new Hollywood glamor girl. However, the star's thick accent and poor command of English tested both Fitzmaurice and Arzner during filming, and repeated retakes were necessary.

Rarely could Goldwyn's judgment have been more awry than in his promotion of Sten. The mistaken belief that the actress could be molded by Hollywood was compounded by the choice of *Nana* as a launch vehicle. A moment's reflection would have confirmed the naturalist text as fundamentally unsuitable. True, the novel tells of a woman with captivating sex appeal, but neither the earthy, destructive traits in Nana's bisexual personality, nor the sexually explicit character of Zola's descriptions lend themselves to the promotion of a desirable, but essentially unavailable, screen goddess. Even with a sanitized script, *Nana* remained a tricky venture.

The action of Zola's novel is set in the decadent Paris of the

Second Empire. Nana, the wayward daughter of Gervaise Coupeau, has graduated from prostitution to theatrical stardom. Weak on talent but strong on sex appeal, she becomes a free-spending, free-wheeling courtesan who shamelessly ruins successive lovers. Respectable families are destroyed, wealthy financiers beggared, and powerful men humbled. Capriciously, she reverts to rough street trade, has a lesbian relationship, then a passionate affair with a sadistic actor. Following a successful return to the stage, she becomes a national celebrity when the horse named after her triumphs over foreign opposition at Longchamp. After a total eclipse and travel abroad, she returns to Paris only to die hideously from smallpox contracted from her son. Simultaneously, the declaration of war against Prussia heralds the demise of the Second Empire with which she had been so closely identified.

In his depiction of Nana, Zola breaks with the sentimental tradition of the kind-hearted woman of pleasure so dear to the Romantics. Nana is a hard-nosed, destructive whore. As a moralist, Zola sought to demonstrate through Nana's rise the moral bankruptcy of a self-indulgent society given to sexual license, and, in a celebrated image of a gilded fly spreading disease from the gutters throughout society, he presents his heroine as an instrument of working class revenge. The tone is uncompromising, the detail explicit.

The film's story line is necessarily simplified to achieve not only a manageable screen narrative, but also to remain within the bounds of the Hays Code. Nana's numerous secondary lovers, for example, are telescoped into the lecherous Archduke and the impresario, Greiner, who is himself a conflation of the theater director, Bordenave, and the Jewish financier, Steiner. Understandably, the racial stereotyping of the impresario is omitted. Narrative economy is also achieved by representing Nana's repeated theatrical appearances and social activities as single episodes. Given that lesbianism was to be banished from the screen, Mme. Robert and Laure de Piédefer are accorded no more than a passing reference, while Nana's sapphic intimacies with Satan are transmuted into a vague allusion by Arzner's disgruntled Satin. Again, since the depiction of male brutality toward women was taboo, the sadistic Fontan has no role in the film.

Zola's readers may regret more substantial changes in plot development and characterization which severely diminish the scope of the author's thesis and the aesthetic richness of his novel. The omission of Nana's rival actress, Rose Mignon, truncates treatment of the theater, while the elimination of the journalist, Fauchery, entails a double loss. His absence deprives Sabine Muffat of an adulterous affair, and the consequent removal of his newspaper article depicting Nana as the golden fly robs the narrative of its *mise en abyme* sophistication. The film also denies Nana motherhood and, more significantly, depicts her as choosing to take her own life rather

than falling a victim to her son's smallpox. Jettisoned, too, is her affair with the racehorse owner, Vandeuvres, and with this go the Longchamp scenes and her ruined lover's dramatic death in his burning stables. Muffat is spared the humiliation of imitating a dog to please Nana, but with this is lost Zola's illustration of proletarian revenge on French aristocracy. The novel's surrogate moral voices are also abandoned in the omission of Muffat's religious friend, Venot, and the pious widow, Mme. Hugon. Her absence follows from the simplified plot in which Georges Hugon becomes André Muffat's younger brother, thus concentrating Nana's pernicious influence in a single aristocratic household. Georges himself is an amalgam of Zola's two Hugon brothers and, unlike his literary counterpart, does not commit suicide.

The general edulcoration of the story line not only deprives the film of episodes and characters that illustrated unpalatable moral realities, but also curtails the broader critical thrust of Zola's narrative, namely the exposure of widespread corruption and decadence in Second Empire France. The Goldwyn product was essentially intended as a variant of the well-tried formula in which true love, that between Nana and Georges, is thwarted by the social conventions it seeks to deny. Even within the potential straitjacket of a romantic screenplay specifically evolved to satisfy Goldwyn and the Hays Office, Arzner reworks the theme to leave the stamp of her own distinctively subversive ideological inflection.

Throughout her films, Arzner depicts women struggling to define themselves, in their own terms, within a patriarchal society that implicitly denies them their discrete identity and, therefore, their authenticity. Her heroines face acute dilemmas, for, in asserting this difference and challenging patriarchal discourse, they risk an uncomfortable ostracism, whereas conformity with male-determined roles and attitudes, however demeaning, is rewarded. As Claire Johnston writes:

> Patriarchal culture is presented as the dominant force imprisoning women in de-humanizing images, and it is for this reason that the struggle of Arzner's heroines is predominantly waged against cultural definitions of women, of images they are supposed to adhere to without, however, being able to escape them finally because the penalty for doing so would be isolation.

In her version of *Nana,* Arzner articulates her position through the dislocating interplay of three competing discourses: the dominant patriarchal, the burgeoning female, and the disruptive romantic. Normalizing patriarchal discourse affirms established male and female role models, and upholds traditional morality through family structures. Subverting these assumptions is the muted, often defensively ironic, voice of female discourse. Directly challenging the patriarchal value system is romantic discourse that prioritizes relationships above social hierarchiesand their related power structures. For Arzner, *Nana* becomes an ideological battleground.

Whereas Zola introduces Nana through her sensational stage debut, Arzner foregrounds her protagonist as a disadvantaged female determined to succeed where her mother, Gervaise, had failed. Nana defends her dead mother as a victim of patriarchal society, and rejects poverty and powerlessness as inevitable conditions of her own existence: "My mother was not bad, she was weak. It's men who make women whatever they are. I don't know what I'll be, but I won't be weak and I won't be poor."

Nana's articulation of the baleful influence exerted by men in women's lives counterposes the complacency of her mistress who has unreflectively internalized patriarchal attitudes. For her, as for the males in the film, there are "good" women and "bad" women—there are virgins and whores. With this introduction. Arzner presents Nana's challenge to such assumptions.

At the essentially male domain of the Café of the Seven Trout, Nana is exposed to the dehumanizing, gender stereotyping to which women are subjected. As unaccompanied females, Nana and her companions, Mimi and Satin, are typecast as "common women." An oafish, drunken soldier is the first to exhibit crude patriarchal behavior. In turn, patronizing and aggressive, he pesters Nana, but has no answer to her assertiveness and mocking tongue:

> NANA. Oh, what a nuisance you are! Go away please . . .
> SOLDIER. No common woman has ever dared . . . A woman who sits about in cafés must not insult . . .
> NANA. Oh, I understand you soldier, I understand you so well. You see it was wrong of us to speak to you at all. Women of our kind have so little to do with soldiers.
> SOLDIER. I'm inclined to overlook it because of your eyes.

Nana's response is to push the soldier into a fountain, and the spontaneous applause around the café validates for the viewer her principled stand against demeaning male assumptions.

The powerful impresario, Greiner, presents Nana with her next challenge. She is prepared to see her new admirer, but only on her terms: "Tell the great Greiner I shall be pleased to meet him here, or not at all." Such unconventional, "virile" behavior brings the impresario to her table. Again, Nana brilliantly counters his sexual flattery:

> GREINER. May I observe you have a lovely mouth. There is so much to a woman's mouth.
> NANA. I know that. I have to fill it three times a day.

The scenes at the café raise important ideological issues: the female right to social independence and to sexual choices. In their attitude to Nana, both the soldier ("your eyes") and Greiner ("your mouth") betray the patriarchal assumption that the female body exists, not in itself and for itself, but essentially to serve the male. Nana's unabashed self-confidence, her quick-witted rejoinders, and her role-reversal treatment of the male as merely the sexual toy her victims fondly imagined her to be place her in the image of the most memorable Hollywood vamp of the thirties, Mae West.

> **Throughout her films, Arzner depicts women struggling to define themselves, in their own terms, within a patriarchal society that implicitly denies them their discrete identity and, therefore, their authenticity.**
>
> *—Russell Cousins*

The gender issue is explored from a different perspective in Nana's stage debut. Here Nana-the-actress unashamedly presents herself as an object to be admired. She has initiated the action, it is on her terms, and she rejoices in her power. The camera frames the actress from the predominantly male audience's perspective, but, more significantly, records the viewers' excitement and subjection in Nana's reverse angle point-of-view shots.

Nana has been empowered by her stage triumph and, although she can exploit male sexual fantasies to her advantage, she is constantly under pressure to defend her independence. Each captivated male will assume possession; Nana will insist on her freedom. Her relationship with Greiner illustrates the point. At the theater he bluntly asserts his power and does not take kindly to Nana's only weapon, an ironical, punning rejoinder:

> GREINER. I am the potter, you are the clay. I will do the modelling.That is quite clear, eh?
> NANA, So, I am to be you and you are to be me.
> GREINER, You are to be what I make you!

His subsequent failure to keep Nana to himself ends in a torrent of abuse. His "angel" has reverted to "the whore": "You slime of the streets . . . you alley cat. I took you from the streets. I made your name the best known in Paris. . . . To betray Greiner is to cut your theatrical throat. You'll go back to the park bench where your revenue is assured."

Through the love affair between Nana and Georges, Arzner demonstrates the conflict between the conformity of patriarchal positions and the iconoclastic nature of romantic ideology. André Muffat is cast as the archetypal advocate of patriarchal attitudes; Nana and Georges as the dangerous subversives. André, borrowing the discarded Fauchery's description of Nana in the novel, denigrates her as "a gilded fly . . . that's hatched in the gutter and carries poison." She is an Eve figure, a temptress who "is all physical." Dismayed at Georges's liaison with Nana, André considers it his duty to save his younger brother from perdition. Ignoring Georges's (irrational) protestation of love, André assumes the (rational) language of honor, responsibility, and moral rectitude:

> Our house bears a fine name and we should both respect it. . . . You talk like a child, not like a grown man and a soldier. There can't be love for a woman like that. . . . You're incapable of thinking clearly or acting sanely. . . . I love you too much to see you wreck yourself as you aredoing.

Georges, in his love for such a woman, has clearly sinned against tribal tenets; he has let the male side down and will be posted abroad.

André cannot accept that Nana's relationship with Georges is based on mutual love. He mistakenly believes that Nana can be bought off, for, in his gallery of female stereotypes, Nana is the sexual adventuress out for financial gain: "You didn't think. . . . I'd let him wreck his life with a woman like you! Your reputation is too well known; you attract, you seduce, you destroy."

Arzner's Nana, however, refutes this cliched patriarchal definition, and, rounding on her self-appointed judge, she points out that he is himself the victim of such attitudes. For Nana, André has denied himself his own freedom by his unquestioning acceptance of such values and has thus condemned himself to an emotionally stunted, unauthentic life:

> NANA. All your life you have tried to be what you are not.
> ANDRE. All my life I have been what I am.
> NANA. That's what I say. You would crucify him [Georges] for what you have never known.
> ANDRE. I never wished for a woman like you.
> NANA. You have! Your mind has lied to you all these years. You hypocrite.

Once again it is Nana who emerges from the confrontation with dignity, andher reading of André is validated when he eventually returns to her as a subservient lover, no more sure of his "possession" than was Greiner. Ironically, having chastised his bachelor brother for betraying family honor, André, the family man, now betrays the values that previously governed his life. In his new ranking of emotions above duty, he concedes, in a back-handed compliment to Nana, a lowering of his standards:

> I love you, that repays me for everything. . . . No man in Paris ever gave up more for a woman . . . I don't mean money . . . I mean everything I lived for . . . My code, my standards they have all been lowered. My pride has gone and I don't care . . . as long as I can have you.

Nana, too, sacrifices her integrity by becoming André's mistress. Her relationship with Georges had brought a new sense of personal worth, and an awareness of values that transcended those of an exploitive patriarchal society. Her fierce rejection of André's financial bribe, her spirited separation from Greiner, and her refusal of a theatrical manager "who asked too much" signal this evolution. However, the strength of her new-found self-respect is eroded when, treacherously deprived of Georges's letters, she believes herself forgotten. Facing poverty, she trades herself against André's promise of a stage part. Her need for public approval is evident in her expectation of "wonderful people clapping their hands and loving me." For her new paymaster she feels nothing, and for herself only contempt: "I don't love you. Nothing can repay me for what I have done." As she mockingly addresses André's portrait she reveals that, in her self-disgust,she has internalized the male concept of "bad" women: "The good Muffat. The holy Muffat. The Muffat who hated bad women, but learned to love one." The irony now, however, is also directed against herself, and her apology confirms her poor self-image: "I'm sorry. I was rotten anyhow." The declaration of war, which brings the two military brothers face to face, seals her fate. The man she loves, but whom she has betrayed, squares up to the man who "owns" her. Whereas in the novel it is a love-stricken Georges who takes his own life, here it is Nana, overwhelmed by feelings of guilt and worthlessness, who turns a gun on herself: "Listen Georges. This is best . . . I could never bring happiness to you. I never brought happiness to anyone, not even to myself. You see I was born all wrong. Now I can go, and I'm glad I am going, very glad."

This pained self-awareness of Arzner's Nana marks her a very different creature than Zola's unthinking creature of nature. The author's hard-nosed prostitute, created as a corrective to the idealized view of the good-hearted whore, is redeemed in the Hollywood film version to possess precisely those virtues of generosity, dignity, and understanding her literary creator had sought to deny.

Should Nana's suicide be seen as a happy release from an impossible dilemma? a "generous sacrifice?" a "sudden burst of patriotism and self-denial?" an "act of spontaneous bravery . . . which must be noticed and respected?" a "gross misrepresentation of the author's intended image?" Whatever the construction placed on Nana's death, the logic of the narrative.locates the origins in her unhappy, and unresolved, relationshipwith a patriarchal society that constantly denied her freedom and independence. Her repeated negative self-assessments, the internalized judgments of the dominant ideology, chart her ultimate sense of failure to impose alternative female-centered values. A valiant failure, nonetheless, and a defeat that does not legitimate the destructive conditioning of patriarchy that has also marred the lives of Georges and André. If the death of Nana proves anything at all, it confirms the need to rethink the discredited attitudes that have brought about such tragedies.

In the context of the Arzner/Goldwyn *Nana,* Hollywood's silver screen serves not only as a means to reflect projected images, but also as a screen that filters, that removes the gritty substance of Zola's naturalist text to leave a sufficiently anodyne version to satisfy the Hays Code. This sanitized innocence is, however, illusory. By subverting the bowdlerized material she inherited, Arzner exposes the pernicious effects—for male and female alike—of patriarchy, and proposes far more challenging concepts about the male-female relationship than either Goldwyn or the men from the Hays Office could ever have imagined.

FURTHER READING

Biography

Mayne, Judith. *Directed by Dorothy Arzner.* Bloomington: Indiana University Press, 209 p.
> Biographical and critical overview of Arzner's life and career,focusing on the relationship between her lifestyle, her films, and her image as a lesbian.

Criticism

Coleman, John. "Eva's Secret." *New Statesman and Society* 99, No. 2570 (20 June 1980): 943-44.
> Reviews a number of films, including a revival of *Christopher Strong,* of which he says that "time has pushed this to a pinnacle of camp."

Doty, Alexander. "Whose Text Is It Anyway?: Queer Cultures, Queer *Auteurs,* and Queer Authorship." *Quarterly Review of Film and Video* 15, No. 1 (1993): 41-54.
> Analyzes the work of George Cukor and Arzner in relation to gay and lesbian culture.

Haskell, Molly. *From Reverence to Rape: The Treatment of Women in the Movies.* New York: Holt, Rinehart and Winston, 1974, 388 p.
> Surveys the depiction of women in film from the early twentieth century through the early 1970s. Haskell com-

ments briefly on several of Arzner's films, including *Christopher Strong, Craig's Wife,* and *Dance, Girl, Dance.*

———. "Women Directors: Toppling the Male Mystique." *American Film* 1, No. 8 (June 1976): 18-23.
> Remarks on several female directors, including Arzner, whose films,Haskell argues, "focus on subversively demanding heroines who speak their minds, pursue careers, and find satisfaction in . . . female friendships."

Heck-Rabi, Louise. "Dorothy Arzner: An Image of Independence." In *Women Filmmakers: A Critical Reception,* pp. 72-93. Scarecrow Press: 1984.
> Survey of Arzner's works and career.

Johnston, Claire, ed. *The Work of Dorothy Arzner.* London: British Film Institute, 1975, 34 p.
> Contains two essays on Arzner, an interview, and a filmography.

McBride, Joseph. "'Hey, a Broad Is Gonna Direct!' Opened Dorothy Arzner's Career." *Variety* 277 (5 February 1975): 7, 32.
> Covers a tribute to Arzner sponsored by the Directors Guild of America. The article contains numerous comments on Arzner's career from notables in the film industry.

Petro, Patrice. "Feminism and Film History." *Camera Obscura,* No. 22 (January 1990): 8-28.
> Examines numerous approaches to film history and critiques several works on feminist film history. Petro uses Arzner's *Christopher Strong* and *Dance, Girl, Dance* as examples in her discussion.

Rosen, Marjorie. "Epilogue: Feminist Footholds in Filmmaking." In *Popcorn Venus: Women, Movies & the American Dream,* pp. 367-80. New York: Coward, McCann & Geoghegan, 1973.
> Briefly summarizes Arzner's career as a director and popular reaction to it.

Shrage, Laurie. "Feminist Film Aesthetics: A Contextual Approach." In *Aesthetics in Feminist Perspective,* edited by Hilde Hein and Carolyn Korsmeyer, pp. 139-49. Indiana University Press, 1993.
> Focuses on the depiction of marriage and the treatment of mistresses in *Christopher Strong.*

Slide, Anthony. "Dorothy Arzner." In *Early Women Directors,* pp. 92-101. New York: Da Capo Press, 1984.
> Remarks on the three silent films that Arzner directed: *Fashions for Women, Ten Modern Commandments,* and *Get Your Man.*

Smith, Sharon. "In the Thirties: Dorothy Arzner." In *Women Who Make Movies,* pp. 19-24. New York: Hopkinson and Blake, 1975.
    Briefly summarizes Arzner's career.

Fahrenheit 451
Ray Bradbury

American short story writer, novelist, scriptwriter, poet, dramatist, nonfiction writer, editor, and children's writer.

The following entry presents criticism on Bradbury's novel *Fahrenheit 451* (1953). For further information about Bradbury's life and works, see *CLC,* Vols. 1, 3, 10, 15, and 42.

INTRODUCTION

Among Bradbury's most influential and widely read works, *Fahrenheit 451* (1953) describes the impact of censorship and forced conformity on a group of people living in a future society where books are forbidden and burned. (The title refers to the temperature at which book paper catches fire.) The novel was written during the era of McCarthyism, a time when many Americans were maliciously—and often falsely—accused of attempting to subvert the United States government. This was also the period of the Cold War and the moment when television emerged as the dominant medium of mass communication. Within this context, *Fahrenheit 451* addresses the leveling effect of consumerism and reductionism, focusing on how creativity and human individuality are crushed by the advertising industry and by political ideals. Traditionally classified as a work of science fiction, *Fahrenheit 451* showcases Bradbury's distinctive poetic style and preoccupation with human subjects over visionary technology and alien worlds, thereby challenging the boundaries of the science fiction genre itself. The social commentary of *Fahrenheit 451,* alternately anti-utopian, satirical, and optimistic, transcends simple universal statements about government or world destiny to underscore the value of human imagination and cultural heritage.

Plot and Major Characters

Fahrenheit 451, a revision and expansion of Bradbury's 56-page novella "The Fireman," consists of a series of events and dialogue divided into three parts. Together the story traces the emotional and spiritual development of Guy Montag, a twenty-fourth century "fireman" who, unlike his distant predecessors, is employed to *start* fires rather than extinguish them. Under government mandate to seek out and eradicate all books—in Montag's world, book ownership is a crime punishable by death—Montag and his colleagues answer emergency calls to burn the homes of people found to be in possession of books. The first and longest part of the novel, "The Hearth and the Salamander," opens with Montag happily fueling a blaze of burning books. This event is followed

by a period of gradual disillusionment for Montag and then by Montag's abrupt renunciation of his profession. Montag's surprising reversal is induced by several events, including his chance meeting and interludes with Clarisse McClellan, a teenage girl whose childlike wonderment initiates his own self-awareness; the bizarre attempted suicide of his wife Mildred and Montag's reflections upon their sterile relationship; and Montag's participation in the shocking immolation of a woman who refuses to part with her books. During this last episode, Montag instinctively rescues a book from the flames and takes it home, adding it to his secret accumulation of other pilfered volumes. The strain of his awakening conscience, exacerbated by Mildred's ambivalence and by news of Clarisse's violent death, drives Montag into a state of despair. When he fails to report to work, Captain Beatty, the fire chief, becomes suspicious and unexpectedly visits Montag at home to offer circumspect empathy and an impassioned defense of the book burners' mission. Beatty's monologue establishes that the firemen were founded in 1790 by Benjamin Franklin to destroy Anglophilic texts. Beatty also claims that book censorship reflects public demand and the naturally occurring obsolescence of the printed word, which has been supplanted by the superior entertainment of multimedia technology. The scene closes with Beatty's exit and Montag among his books, professing his intent to become a reader. The second and shortest part of the novel, "The Sieve and the Sand," continues Montag's progressive rebelliousness and ends in his inevitable discovery. After an afternoon of reading with Mildred, who quickly becomes agitated and returns to the diversion of her television "family," Montag contacts Faber, a retired English professor he once encountered in a public park. At Faber's apartment Montag produces a stolen Bible. Faber then equips Montag with an electronic ear transmitter to maintain secret communication between them. Invigorated by Faber's complicity, Montag returns home and rashly attempts to reform Mildred and her two friends, Mrs. Phelps and Mrs. Bowles, as they sit mesmerized by images in the television parlor. His patronizing effort at conversation, along with his recitation of Matthew Arnold's "Dover Beach," drive the women out of the house and leave Montag in open defiance of the state. Montag retreats to the firehouse, where he is greeted coolly and goaded by Beatty with literary quotations alluding to Montag's futile interest in books and learning. The scene ends with a minor climax when Beatty, Montag, and the firemen respond to an alarm that leads directly to Montag's own house. The third and final part of the work, "Burning Bright," completes Montag's break from society and begins his existence as a fugitive, enlightened book lover. When the fire squad arrives at his home, Montag obediently incinerates the house and then turns his flamethrower on Beatty to protect Faber, whose identity is jeopardized when Beatty knocks the transmitter from Montag's ear and confiscates it. As he prepares to flee, Montag also destroys the Mechanical Hound, a robotic book detector and assassin whose persistence and infallibility represent the terrifying fusion of bloodhound and computer. Following a dramatic chase witnessed by a live television audience, Montag evades a second Mechanical Hound and floats down a nearby river, safely away from the city. He emerges from the water in an arcadian forest, where he encounters a small band of renegade literati who, having watched Montag's escape on a portable television, welcome him among their ranks. Through conversation with Granger, the apparent spokesperson for the book people, Montag learns of their heroic endeavor to memorize select works of literature for an uncertain posterity. Safe in their wilderness refuge, Montag and the book people then observe the outbreak of war and the subsequent obliteration of the city. The novel concludes with Granger's sanguine meditation on the mythological Phoenix and a quotation from Book of Ecclesiastes.

Major Themes

Fahrenheit 451 reflects Bradbury's lifelong love of books and his defense of the imagination against the menace of technology and government manipulation. Fire is the omnipresent image through which Bradbury frames the dominant themes of degradation, metamorphosis, and rebirth. As a destructive agent, fire is employed by the state to annihilate the written word. Fire is also used as a tool of murder when turned on the book woman and on Beatty, and fire imagery is inherent in the flash of exploding bombs that level civilization in the final holocaust. The healing and regenerative qualities of fire are expressed in the warming fire of the book people, a startling realization for Montag when he approaches their camp, and in Granger's reference to the Phoenix, whose resurrection signifies the cyclical nature of human life and civilization. Through Beatty, Bradbury also posits the unique cleansing property of the flames—"fire is bright and fire is clean"—a paradoxical statement that suggests the simultaneous beauty and horror of fire as an instrument of purification. Montag's irresistible urge to read and his reaction to the desecration of the physical text establish the book as the central symbol of human achievement and perseverance. Thus literature, rather than Montag, can be said to represent the true hero of the novel. However, Bradbury contrasts the sanctity of the printed word with the equal vitality of oral tradition, particularly as cultivated by the book people but also as anticipated by Faber's earlier intent to read to Montag via the ear transmitter. Throughout *Fahrenheit 451* Bradbury expresses a pronounced distrust for technology. The various machines in the novel are depicted as chilling, impersonal gadgets of mechanized anti-culture or state control—namely the ubiquitous thimble radios and television walls, the invasive stomach pumper that revives Mildred, roaring warplanes, and the Mechanical Hound. Considered in its historical context, the novel is both a reflection of mainstream American fears in the 1950s—mainly of the Cold War and the threat of communist world domination—and Bradbury's satire of this same society. Taking aim at the negative power of McCarthy-era anti-intellectualism, a superficial consumer culture, and the perceived erosion of democratic ideals, Bradbury assumes cloaked objectivity in the novel to project the fragile future of the American Dream. Written less than a decade after the end of the Second World War, the specter of book burning and thought control also recall the recent reality of Adolf Hitler's fascist regime. At its most dystopian, *Fahrenheit 451* evokes an intense atmosphere of entrapment, evidenced in Montag's alienation, Mildred's dependency on drugs and television, Faber's reclusion and impotency, and Clarisse's inability to survive. Bradbury's prophetic vision, however, ultimately evinces confidence in the redemptive capacity of mankind, displayed by the survival of the book people and the miraculous inner transformation of Montag.

Critical Reception

While *Fahrenheit 451* is considered one of Bradbury's most effective prose works, the novel has been faulted for its sentimental evocation of culture and "highbrow" literary aspirations. Bradbury's justification of intellectual pursuit as a virtuous and humane ideal, with reading portrayed as a heroic act in itself, has been labelled romantic and elitist. Since Bradbury does not refute Captain Beatty's version of the firemen's history or his convoluted rationale for censorship, critics have claimed that the novel has the effect of positioning intellectuals against the masses, rather than the individual against the state. The totalitarian state is thereby implicitly exonerated by blaming the masses for the book's decline, while intellectuals in the form of the book people are entrusted with saving and repopulating the world. Thus it has been suggested that Bradbury's defense of humanity expresses little faith in the masses. In addition, many of the novel's high-culture allusions are considered too esoteric for the general reader, as with a reference to "Master Ridley," an obscure sixteenth-century martyr, or overly simplistic, as exemplified by Granger's involved exposition of the Phoenix myth. The shifting dystopian-utopian structure of *Fahrenheit 451*, drawing frequent comparison to Aldous Huxley's *Brave New World* (1932) and George Orwell's *Nineteen Eighty-Four* (1949), remains the subject of critical attention as the source of both inconsistency and subtlety in the novel. Praised for its engaging narrative, concise presentation, and pounding intensity, *Fahrenheit 451* embodies Bradbury's effective blending of popular science fiction and serious literature.

PRINCIPAL WORKS

Dark Carnival (short stories) 1947

The Martian Chronicles (short stories) 1950

The Illustrated Man (short stories) 1951

Fahrenheit 451 (novel) 1953

The Golden Apples of the Sun (short stories) 1953

The October Country (short stories) 1955

Moby-Dick (screenplay) 1956

Dandelion Wine (novel) 1957

A Medicine for Melancholy (short stories) 1959

The Day It Rained Forever (short stories) 1959

R is for Rocket (juvenilia) 1962

Something Wicked This Way Comes (novel) 1962

The Machineries of Joy (short stories) 1964

The Wonderful Ice-Cream Suit (drama) 1965

S is for Space (juvenilia) 1966

I Sing the Body Electric! (short stories) 1969

Old Ahab's Friend, and Friend to Noah, Speaks His Piece: A Celebration (poetry) 1971

When Elephants Last in the Dooryard Bloomed: Celebrations for Almost Any Day in the Year (poetry) 1973

Zen and the Art of Writing, and the Joy of Writing (essays) 1973

Long After Midnight (short stories) 1976

Where Robot Mice and Robot Men Run Round in Robot Towns: New Poems, Both Light and Dark (poetry) 1977

The Last Circus, and The Electrocution (short stories) 1980

A Memory for Murder (short stories) 1984

Death Is a Lonely Business (novel) 1985

The Coffin (television play) 1988

The Toynbee Convector (short stories) 1988

A Graveyard for Lunatics: Another Tale of Two Cities (novel) 1990

The Smile (novel) 1991

Yestermorrow: Obvious Answers to Impossible Futures (essays) 1991

Green Shadows, White Whale (novel) 1992

Long After Midnight (prose) 1996

Quicker Than the Eye (novel) 1996

CRITICISM

Everett T. Moore (review date May 1961)

SOURCE: "A Rationale for Bookburners: A Further Word From Ray Bradbury," in *ALA Bulletin*, Vol. 55, No. 5, May, 1961, pp. 403-4.

[*In the following review, Moore presents commentary on the themes of conformity and censorship in* Fahrenheit 451.]

"'The bigger your market, Montag, the less you handle controversy, remember that!'"

It is Captain Beatty speaking, explaining meticulously how it got started—this job of the firemen of the future, in Ray Bradbury's *Fahrenheit 451*. It is the story of the firemen who answer alarms not to put out fires, but to start them.

"'Magazines became a nice blend of vanilla tapioca. Books, so the damned snobbish critics said, were dishwater. No *wonder* books stopped selling, the critics said. But the public knowing what it wanted, spinning happily, let the comic books survive. And the three-dimensional sex magazines, of course. There you have it, Montag. It didn't come from the government down. There was no dictum, no declaration, no censorship, to start with, no! Technology, mass exploitation, and minority pressure carried the trick, thank God.'"

In *Fahrenheit 451*, first published in 1953, Bradbury's imagined future was one that seemed to have come about almost painlessly. If there had been those who resisted the soothing tide of conformity most of them were now comfortably out of the way. "'We're the Happiness Boys, the Dixie Duo, you and I and the others,' says Beatty. 'We stand against the small tide of those who want to make everyone unhappy with conflicting theory and thought. We have our fingers in the dike. Hold steady. Don't let the torrent of melancholy and drear philosophy drown our world.'"

"'You always dread the unfamiliar,' Beatty explained. 'Surely you remember the boy in your own school class who was exceptionally "bright," did most of the reciting and answering while the others sat like so many leaden idols, hating him. And wasn't it this bright boy you selected for beatings and tortures after hours? Of course it was. We must all be alike. Not everyone born free and equal, as the Constitution says, but everyone *made* equal. Each man the image of every other; then all are happy, for there are no mountains to make them cower, to judge themselves against. So! A book is a loaded gun in the house next door. Burn it. Take the shot from the weapon. Breach man's mind. Who knows who might be the target of the well-read man? Me? I won't stomach them for a minute.'"

We recently asked Mr. Bradbury if the future of civilization would look any less bleak to him if he were writing his book today. His answer was as follows:

"When I wrote my novel *Fahrenheit 451* during the years from 1949 to 1953, we were living at the heart of what is known now as the McCarthy era. We were very close to panic and wholesale bookburning. I never believed we would go all out and destroy ourselves in this fashion. I have always believed in the power of our American society to rectify error without having to resort to destruction. Sometimes it takes a long time to swing the pendulum back in the direction of sanity. But the pendulum did swing. McCarthy *is* dead, and the era that carried his name buried with him.

"Still," Mr. Bradbury added, "I feel that what I had to say in *Fahrenheit 451* is valid today and will continue to be valid here and in other countries in other years."

> When I wrote my novel *Fahrenheit 451* during the years from 1949 to 1953, we were living at the heart of what is known now as the McCarthy era. We were very close to panic and wholesale bookburning. I never believed we would go all out and destroy ourselves in this fashion.
>
> —*Ray Bradbury*

Mr. Bradbury referred to a scene in *Fahrenheit 451* which epitomizes the attitude of the bookburners. It is the one from which we have already quoted, in which his fireman hero, Guy Montag, suddenly realizing that for years he had been destroying the mind of his community, pleads illness and does not report for work. The fire chief, Beatty, comes to visit Montag, and, says Mr. Bradbury, "to talk him back to 'health'" with the following rationale:

"'When did it all start, you ask, this job of ours, how did it come about, where, when? Well, I'd say it really got started

around about a thing called the Civil War. Even though our rule book claims it was founded earlier. The fact is we didn't get along well until photography came into its own. Then— motion pictures in the early Twentieth Century. Radio. Television. Things began to have *mass*.

"'And because they had mass, they became simpler,' said Beatty. 'Once, books appealed to a few people, here, there, everywhere. They could afford to be different. The world was roomy. But then the world got full of eyes and elbows and mouths. Double, triple, quadruple population. Films and radios, magazines, books leveled down to a sort of paste-pudding norm, do you follow me?'

'I think so.'

'Picture it. Nineteenth-century man with his horses, dogs, carts, slow motion. Then, in the Twentieth Century, speed up your camera. Books cut shorter. Condensations. Digests. Tabloids. Everything boils down to the gag, the snap ending.

"Classics cut to fit fifteen-minute radio shows, then cut again to fill a two-minute book column, winding up at last as a ten- or twelve-line dictionary résumé. I exaggerate, of course. The dictionaries were for reference. But many were those whose sole knowledge of *Hamlet* (you know the title certainly, Montag; it is probably only a faint rumor of a title to you, Mrs. Montag) whose sole knowledge, as I say, of *Hamlet* was a one-page digest in a book that claimed: *now at last you can read all the classics; keep up with your neighbors.* Do you see? Out of the nursery into the college and back to the nursery; there's your intellectual pattern for the past five centuries or more.'"

Mr. Bradbury adds, in passing, that the Russians, thinking he had written an exclusive criticism of McCarthyism in the U.S.A., pirated *Fahrenheit 451* a few years ago. Published and sold in an edition of some 500,000 copies, the authorities suddenly discovered he meant tyranny over the mind at any time or place.

"In sum," he says: "Russia, too. The novel has now gone underground, I hear. Which makes me, I gather, the *clean* Henry Miller of the Soviets."

Peter Sisario (essay date February 1970)

SOURCE: "A Study of the Allusions in Bradbury's *Fahrenheit 451*," in *English Journal*, Vol. 59, No. 2, February, 1970, pp. 201-5, 212.

[*In the following essay, Sisario examines the source and significance of literary allusions in* Fahrenheit 451 *and considers their didactic potential for the beginning student of literature.*]

Ray Bradbury's *Fahrenheit 451* is more than just a readable and teachable short novel that generates much classroom discussion about the dangers of a mass culture, as Charles Hamblen points out in his article "Bradbury's *Fahrenheit 451* in the Classroom." It is an excellent source for showing students the value of studying an author's use of specific allusions in a work of fiction. While writing excellent social criticism, Bradbury uses several directquotations from works of literature, including the Bible; a careful analysis of the patterning of these allusions shows their function of adding subtle depth to the ideas of the novel.

Fahrenheit 451 is set five centuries from now in an anti-intellectual world where firemen serve the reverse role of setting fires, in this case to books that people have been illegally hoarding and reading. Literature is banned because it might potentially incite people to think or to question the status quo of happiness and freedom from worry through the elimination of controversy. "Intellectual" entertainment is provided by tapioca-bland television that broadcasts sentimental mush on all four walls. The novel, first written in a shorter version for a science-fiction magazine in 1950 and published as a novel three years later, concerns itself with one fireman, Guy Montag, who commits the heresy of questioning his role and seeks to learn why books are considered dangerous.

If we take this imaginary world of the twenty-fourth century as a commentary of our contemporary society, we can interpret the novel on one level as the often-heard argument that mass media, as evidenced by television and popular magazines, are reducing our society to very mediocre tastes. The mass media must keep watering down the intellectual level of its material as it attempts to reach an increasingly larger and intellectually diversified audience. Bradbury takes this problem to an extreme to show the potential effects of such a course on our culture. Television spans four walls, soap operas and sentimentality abound, and books, the carriers of ideas, are burned.

But if we look more closely at the novel, noting specifically the literary and Biblical allusions, we see a deeper message in the novel than simply the warning that our society is headed for intellectual stagnation. The literary allusions are used to underscore the emptiness of the twenty-fourth century, and the Biblical allusions point subtly toward a solution to help us out of our intellectual "Dark Age." Bradbury seems to be saying that the nature of life is cyclical and we are currently at the bottom of an intellectual cycle. We must have faith and blindly hope for an upward swing of the cycle. This concept of the natural cycle is most explicitly stated by Bradbury through the character of Granger:

> And when the war's over, some day, some year, the books can be written again, the people will be called

in, one by one, to recite what they know, and we'll set it up in type until another Dark Age, when we might have to do the whole thing over again.

The major metaphor in the novel, which supports the idea of the natural cycle, is the allusion to the Phoenix, the mythical bird of ancient Egypt that periodically burned itself to death and resurrected from its own ashes to a restored youth. Through the persona of Granger, Bradbury expresses the hope that mankind might use his intellect and his knowledge of his own intellectual andphysical destruction to keep from going through endless cycles of disintegration and rebirth.

This image of the Phoenix is used in the novel in association with the minor character Captain Beatty, Montag's superior. As an officer, Beatty has knowledge of what civilization was like before the contemporary society of the novel. In an attempt to satisfy Guy's curiosity and hopefully to quell any further questioning, Beatty relates to Guy how the twentieth century began to decline intellectually, slowly reaching the point in future centuries of banning books, schools stopped teaching students to think or to question and crammed them with factual data in lieu of an education. Psychological hedonism became the most positive virtue; all questioners and thinkers were eliminated. It is crucial that Beatty wears the sign of the Phoenix on his hat and rides in a "Phoenix car." He has great knowledge of the past yet ironically and tragically does not know how to use his knowledge, treating it only as historical curiosity. He is interested only in keeping that status quo of uninterrupted happiness and freedom from worry. He imparts his knowledge only to firemen who are going through the inevitable questioning he feels all firemen experience. He tells Guy that fiction only depicts an imaginary world, and all great ideas are controversial and debatable; books then are too indefinite. Appropriately, Beatty is burned to death, and his death by fire symbolically illustrates the rebirth that is associated with his Phoenix sign. When Guy kills Beatty, he is forced to run off and joins Granger; this action is for Guy a rebirth to a new intellectual life.

Bradbury employs several specific literary quotations to illustrate the shallowness of Guy's world. By using references to literature, Bradbury carries through a basic irony in the book: he is using books to underscore his ideas about a world in which great books themselves have been banned.

After Beatty has given Guy a capsule history of how the world reached the anti-intellectual depths of the twenty-fourth century, Guy goes to a book he has concealed but has not yet had the courage to read. He reads several pages; then Bradbury has him quote the following passage:

> It is computed, that eleven thousand persons have at several times suffered death rather than submit to break their eggs at the smaller end.

The quotation is from the first book of Swift's *Gulliver's Travels,* "A Voyage to Lilliput." At the point of the quotation Gulliver has learned of a long-standing feud in Lilliput, between those who have traditionally broken their eggs at the larger end, and the edict of the King, ordering all subjects to break their eggs at the smaller end because a member of the royal family had once cut his finger breaking the larger end. The struggle between being reasonable and being saddled to tradition even to the point of ridiculous suicide is perhaps what Bradbury is after here. The twenty-fourth century is just as saddled to the status quo, and Bradbury has been careful to point out the dangers of intellectual deadness. The example from Lilliput is an excellent one for him to choose, since it represents an absurd situation taken to a gross exaggeration, a basic device of satire.

As Guy and his wife read on, a quotation is taken directly from Boswell's *Life of Johnson:*

> We cannot tell the precise moment when friendship is formed. As in filling a vessel drop by drop, there is at last a drop which makes it run over; so in a series of kindnesses there is at last one which makes the heart run over.

Guy makes the point that this quote brings to his mind the girl next door, Clarisse McClellan, who was labelled a "time bomb" by Beatty because she was a sensitive, observant person who questioned society, and was consequently eliminated by the government. Montag made an emotional attachment to Clarisse, an attachment that was sincere and true in a world hostile to honesty. It was his relationship with Clarisse that was for Guy the first "drop"; she started his questioning of the status quo, and subsequent events after her death made Guy think and question more and more seriously, until he completely breaks away from his diseased society at the end of the novel.

Guy continues to read, and quotes again from Boswell, this time from a letter to Temple in 1763: "That favourite subject, Myself." Curiously enough, Guy's wife Mildred, who has not received any inspiration from this secret reading session, says that she understands this particular quote. Her statement is juxtaposed against Guy's saying that Clarisse's favorite subject wasn't herself, but others. He realizes the truth of the statements he has been reading from authors who wrote hundreds of years ago; his wife can only understand the literal level of one statement, the one reflecting the self-interest of her society.

The only other direct quote Bradbury employs from literature comes in the second part of the book, and serves to underscore the emptiness of the world that the three preceding quotes have shown. After Guy returns from having visited Faber, he talks with his wife and two of her friends. The con-

versation of the women reflects the shallowness of the women's thinking, since they are the products of this empty culture. Their discussion of politics, for example, has to do with voting for a candidate for president because he was better looking than his opponent. Guy has a book of poetry with him, and Mildred's visitors are shocked that he has a book. In a scene reminiscent of the banquet in *Macbeth,* Guy's wife attempts to cover for him by telling the women that firemen are allowed to bring books home occasionally to show their families how silly books are. Guy reads from Matthew Arnold's "Dover Beach"; the last two stanzas are quoted, and the last one is particularly apt, since it shows two lovers looking at what appears to be a happy world, but recognizing the essential emptiness that exists:

> Ah, love, let us be true
> To one another! for the world, which seems
> To lie before us like a land of dreams,
> So various, so beautiful, so new,
> Hath really neither joy, nor love, nor light,
> Nor certitude, nor peace, nor help for pain;
> And we are here, as on a darkling plain
> Swept with confused alarms of struggle And flight,
> Where ignorant armies clash by night.

Guy's world, too, rests on happiness, a happiness of psychological comfort and freedom from controversy, but Guy is finding that beneath the exterior is a vast emptiness, a "darkling plain."

Thus far, we have seen how Bradbury has used several allusions to literature to describe the situation of the contemporary world of the novel. It might be wise at this point to note an historical reference made, one that serves to underscore some basic ideas in the book.

Early in the book, when Guy is first beginning to undergo doubts, he and his squad are called to the home of a woman discovered owning books. The woman refuses to leave her home, choosing to die in the flames with her books. On the way back to the firehouse, Guy, shaken by the experience, mentions to Beatty the last words of the woman, "Master Ridley." Beatty—and note again that he has the knowledge—tells Guy that the woman was referring to Nicholas Ridley, Bishop of London in the sixteenth century, who was arrested as a heretic because he allowed dissenters to speak freely. He was burned at the stake with fellow heretic Hugh Latimer, who spoke the words to Ridley that the woman in the novel alludes to as her last words: "We shall this day light such a candle, by God's grace, in England, as I trust shall never be put out." These words recall the Phoenix idea of rebirth by fire, since the woman's death proves to be an important factor in Guy's decision to investigate books. The words are ironic in the sense that the intellectual candle in Montag's world is burning rather dimly at the time, but the words are at the same time a fine statement of the indestructibility of questioners and thinkers in any society.

There are four specific Biblical allusions in the novel, and an examination of them shows that they both support the idea of the natural cycle and contribute to Bradbury's solution to helping us out of, or rather avoiding, the type of world pictured by the literary allusions. This solution would be the natural philosophical outlook that would be held by those who believe in a natural cycle to life and are in the midst of the bottom of a cycle: one must wait and have faith, since things will eventually improve.

Two of the Biblical allusions that support the idea of a philosophical faith in the renewal of cycles are the references to the Lilies of the Field (Matthew 6:28) and to the Book of Job. Saint Matthew's parable of the Lilies illustrates that God takes care of all things and we need not worry; the Lilies don't work or worry, yet God provides for them. This submission to faith, this feeling that God will provide all in due course is also affirmed by the reference to the Book of Job, one of the strongest statements of faith in the face of adversity in Western culture. Both of these references come at significant points in the novel. The allusion to the Lilies of the Field comes as Guy is on his way to see Professor Faber. The Lilies are juxtaposed in zeugma-like style with Denham's Dentifrice, an advertisement Guy sees on the subway train. Both flash through his head and form an excellent contrast: the faith and submission of the Lilies and the artificiality and concern with facades of the contemporary advertisement jingle. After his clandestine meeting with Faber, at which the professor agrees to help Guy learn about books and plan for the future, Guy gets a message from Faber through the small earplug he wears to keep in contact with the teacher. The message simply says, "The Book of Job," in a sense reminding Guy that he must have faith, for the going will be rough on his new venture.

The two other Biblical allusions come at the end of the novel, when Guy has joined Granger and his colleagues. This group of men memorizes great works of our culture as a means of preserving ideas until literature is once again permitted. Guy is assigned to read and memorize the Book of Ecclesiastes, the Old Testament book that asserts the need to submit to the natural order of things. The only direct quotation from Ecclesiastes comes from Chapter Three, the well-known chapter that echoes the natural cycle idea in its opening line, "To everything there is a season . . ." The line comes to Guy as the men trudge along in Canterbury-like procession away from the destroyed city, each man being required to recite aloud from his assigned work in order to bolster their spirit and comradeship. Guy thinks first of some phrases from

Ecclesiastes, appropriately enough, "A time to break down, and a time to build up," and "A time to keep silence and a time to speak." Another quote then comes to Guy, this one from the Book of Revelations, which Guy had told Granger he partially remembered:

> And on either side of the river was there a tree of life, which bore twelve manner of fruits, and yielded her fruit every month; And the leaves of the tree were for the healing of nations (22:2).

This last book of the New Testament, also known as the Book of the Apocalypse, tells us that a victory of God is certain, but that much struggle must come first; we must have faith and endure before we can enjoy the fruits of victory. The lines Bradbury has Guy recall not only reinforce the idea of a cyclical world, but also give us a key to Bradbury's hope that "the healing of nations" canbest come about through a rebirth of man's intellect. We must use our minds to halt the endless cycles of destruction by warfare and rebirth to a world of uneasy peace and intellectual death. The twelve tribes of Israel wandering in the desert seeking a new nation can be recalled here as Montag, Granger, and the others wander away from the city with hope that their new world will soon be established.

The novel provides a "good story" to be sure, yet the teacher can also use *Fahrenheit 451* as a way of illustrating the difference between a good plot that makes a book readable and a carefully structured work of literature.

—Peter Sisario

The literary and Biblical references cited form a pattern at first describing the intellectual "darkling plain" of the twenty-fourth century and then of future hope and guarded optimism through passively waiting. There are countless references to the names of great books and writers, all of whom were noted for major ideas. The many specific lines quoted on pages 94-97 constitute a special case worth noting, since Bradbury does not employ these passages in the same way in which the other literary quotes are used. On these pages, Beatty tells Guy of a dream he had in which he and Guy were engaged in a verbal duel about the value of books, and for each point Guy makes by citing a quote, Beatty refutes him with another quote. Again, Beatty's phenomenal knowledge is shown, as well as his tragic attitude toward the use of ideas and the value of dissent and controversy. Practically all of the lines cited on these four pages are from authors who were writing several centuries ago, men like Shakespeare, John Donne, and Robert Burton, perhaps showing Bradbury's affirmation of the timelessness of great ideas.

Fahrenheit 451 can serve the teacher in several ways in the classroom other than a study of the allusions. The use of reference works such as *Bartlett's Familiar Quotations* and the *Concordance* to the Bible could be taught by having students find the sources of specific quotations. Some of the major quotes could form excellent writing assignments wherein students might be asked to show the relation of a particular quote to some of the major ideas in the book.

By studying the patterning of specific quotations in this novel, students can be made more aware of the need to read more closely and more intelligently. The novel provides a "good story" to be sure, yet the teacher can also use *Fahrenheit 451* as a way of illustrating the difference between a good plot that makes a book readable and a carefully structured work of literature.

George Edgar Slusser (essay date 1977)

SOURCE: *"Fahrenheit 451,"* in *The Bradbury Chronicles*, The Borgo Press, 1977, pp. 52-4.

[*In the following excerpt, Slusser explores the development of* Fahrenheit 451, *focusing on how it differs from its source, Bradbury's novella "The Fireman."*]

Fahrenheit 451 is an expansion of the 56-page novella "**The Fireman.**" The latter is not a good story: it is the kind of Bradbury most readers never see. How did the author rework this material into a classic? *Fahrenheit* is two and a half times longer. Yet it has essentially the same number of episodes. "**The Fireman**" consists almost entirely of events and discussion; these are strung out in tedious fashion. Bradbury rearranges the original elements. As he does so, he tightens the story in order to expand it in new directions. *Fahrenheit* deepens the social and natural contexts. In this matrix, new intricacies of character, and more profound personal relationships, are shaped.

Both versions begin *in media res*, but in quite different ways. The novella opens in the firehouse. Montag is already asking questions: how would it feel to have firemen burning *our* houses and *our* books? The alarm follows—the old woman immolates herself. Here is Montag's visible moment of fall: "his hand closed like a trap" on a book. He goes home to his wife, begins to examine his life. We learn he has been taking books home all along. Bradbury must explain Montag's strange actions: the firehouse, the books. To offset a clumsy beginning, he resorts to clumsier flashbacks. Here Clarisse comes in. Perhaps the people moving in next door had been the start of his new awareness: "One night (it was so long ago) he had gone out for a walk."

The first scene of *Fahrenheit* is his meeting with Clarisse. A man comes home from a routine day, and confronts the unusual. Confused, he passes on to his house, and finds his wife dying of an overdose of sedatives. In "**Fireman,**" this was a remembered detail. It becomes a striking scene: two macabre medics come with their "electric-eyed snake" and pump her out. Montag is stunned: "Strangers . . . take your blood. Who *were* those men?" Questions are yanked from him by these extraordinary happenings. Now the flow of time loosens. There is the first scene at the firehouse, and interludes with Clarisse. Suddenly she is there no more. Time contracts. We have the alarm—the old woman burns. Once again, Montag is driven; he seizes the book, going home to collapse. If he rebels, it is passively, stalling the world as he gropes for answers. This rhythm of constriction and release continues all across the narrative. The changes in the order of sequences are highly significant. Montag is no longer a man instantly aware, immediately in revolt. Clear issues are transformed into atmosphere and vague oppressions. During the first scene of "**Fireman,**" the radio blares: war may be declared any minute. Now there is no mention, although planes are constantly in the sky. To create mood, the role of the Mechanical Hound is expanded. In the novella, it appears only during the chase. Now it is present from the start. It is in a niche at the firehouse; as Montag passes it stirs—later it will haunt and harry him. The Hound becomes his guilt and nemesis. Montag's fall plunges deep into some unconscious past. Those other books behind the grate were taken before: to what end? Only now does he begin to explore their meaning. He will not grasp it at all until the very last. Captain Beatty has long suspected something, and tuned the Hound to him. Like the war that frames it, the drama that now surfaces is something long stirring in the depths of things. In "**Fireman,**" Montag is made too immediately aware (Clarisse shows him the rain: "Why, it's *wine!*"), too critical for a man in his situation—a fireman emerging from cultural night.

And the issues are also too clear in this tale. In *Fahrenheit*, they purposely become opaque: either the figures are not aware of them, or their complexities of character make words and actions ambiguous. The earlier Millie had a stand—books are for "professors and radicals." In the novel, she has become a zombie, befuddled and forlorn, less a mouthpiece for reactionary ideas than a slave to her "parlor" of illusion. In "**Fireman,**" the Captain is simply the enemy, a servant of law and order. Beatty, however, is a complex, twisted being—a scourge of books who speaks exclusively in quotes. His cat and mouse game, Montag realizes, is suicidal—"Beatty had wanted to die!" Faber's role too is altered. His meeting with Montag, in "**Fireman,**" was merely the excuse for discussion. The hero wants to start a "revolution," to plant books in firemen's houses all across the nation. Faber tells him this is folly—the whole civilization has to fall before anything can be done. This is a key idea in *Fahrenheit*. But it is not said outright; rather it is implied in the futile gropings of the characters, men who hardly understand their own motivations, let alone have any clear social purpose. When Montag, later, does plant one book, it is a hopeless gesture. Faber is both afraid and ineffectual. Out of their meeting comes no revolutionary plan, only human contact. Bradbury adds another device here—the "seashell" radio. Montag has not asked Faber to help him, as much as "to teach him." Now a guiding voice goes with him. This too is ineffectual; over Faber's admonitions, Montag explodes, and recites poetry to his wife's friends, betraying himself. But two beings are linked: in this fragmented world, it is a start.

Changes in the final scene help reshape *Fahrenheit*. The crucial moment is the rebirth, in Montag's mind, of *Ecclesiastes*. He had tried to memorize it before, and had despaired. Now, as the city falls, as he holds to the earth "as children do," it floods back. Earlier, he had plunged into the dark river, emerging into real nature: the fire of the sun, rather than man's perverted fire. The Mechanical Hound is replaced by a deer. But nature's darkness is also overwhelming. His dream of the hayloft—"a glass of milk, an apple, a pear"—is drowned in immensity: "Too much land!" He is saved by the campfire—flame that warms not burns. Once more, as with Faber, the paltry spark of human companionship is the merest beginning. In **"Fireman"** there is no evocation of nature, and little of this complex fire imagery. Montag's final triumph is sapped when characters discuss the faculty of "eidetic" memory. He tries to recall the Bible and can't; he is told to relax—"it will come when you need it." Bradbury shapes this rough skeleton into an extended statement of lyrical force. Indeed, if the early story seeks toexpose, *Fahrenheit* mourns—the didactic tale has become elegy. Again there is the confused seeker after knowledge, again we see a world where excessive tolerance ironically leads to suppression of inquiry. The individual is powerless before the holocaust. Like the boy in **"The Smile,"** he can only snatch away a fragment to preserve. Thought destroys, but memory abides. These last men do not interpret their books. Out of some strange fear of the old sin of pride, they are reduced to being the books, memorizing them one by one, and reciting them when needed. The tradition of oral history has come full circle.

John Colmer (essay date 1978)

SOURCE: "Science Fiction," in *Coleridge to Catch-22,* St. Martin's Press, 1978, pp. 197-209.

[*In the following excerpt, Colmer assesses* Fahrenheit 451 *as a work of social criticism, citing shortcomings in the novel's sentimentality and high-culture allusions.*]

Fahrenheit 451 takes its place in a long line of works concerned with the survival of language and the written word, since it not only presents a future in which there is constant war or threat of war but one where there is no legitimate place for books. The infamous burning of the books in Nazi Germany provides the historical model for Bradbury's fictional projection. On this model, he imagines a future society in which reading and the possession of books are anti-social activities and therefore must be eradicated.

The curious title is based on the scientific notion that Fahrenheit 451 is 'the temperature at which book-paper catches fire and burns', and the first paragraph of the book describes the special pleasure of seeing things burn. 'It was a special pleasure to see things eaten, to see things blackened and changed.' Since the meaning of the whole book centres on the character called Montag, it is necessary to establish his function as a fireman and to introduce explanations for his abnormality, his deviation from accepted behaviour. Bradbury introduces his first bit of verbal play in explaining Montag's function in this future society. He is a fireman. Whereas, in our society, a fireman extinguishes fires, in Bradbury's a fireman extinguishes books. He destroys them with fire. A far less successful fictional invention is the character, Clarisse McClellan, the seventeen-year-old social misfit, who likes 'to smell things and look at things, and sometimes stay up all night, walking, and watching the sun rise'. In many ways a sentimental device to represent the natural values and interpersonal relationships that have been lost, she also serves as an effective contrast to Montag's wife, Mildred, who is completely adapted to a life of drug-taking and passive consumption of 'sound thro' little seashells, thimble radios in the ears, and T.V., or rather wall entertainment'. Bradbury himself wrote:

> In writing the short novel *Fahrenheit 451* I thought I wasdescribing a world that might evolve in four or five decades. But only a few weeks ago, in Beverly Hills one night, a husband and wife passed me, walking their dog. I stood staring after them absolutely stunned. The woman held in one hand a small cigarette package-sized radio, its antenna quivering. From this sprang tiny copper wires which ended in a dainty cone plugged in her right ear. There she was, oblivious to man and dog, listening to far winds and whispers and soap opera cries, sleepwalking, helped up and down curbs by a husband who might just as well not have been there.

When Mildred takes an overdose, Bradbury describes the two machines that restore her to normality. The operator of one could look into the soul of the person, as the machine pumped out all the poisons accumulated with the years. The other machine 'pumped all the blood from the body and replaced it with fresh blood and serum'. The invention is an extrapolation from present psychiatric and medical practice to reinforce the notion that human beings have ceased to be regarded as individual personalities and have been reduced to the level of things or controllable processes. This is one of the fairly peripheral bits of social documentation. Less peripheral is the detail that relates to the wall TV, especially the contrast between the mindless mush that Mildred and her neighbours enjoy, and the effect on them of two passages from Matthew Arnold's *Dover Beach*. The women cannot help being moved by Arnold's lines, but one of them, Mrs Bowles, condemns poetry and Montag roundly:

> I've always said, poetry and tears, poetry and sui-cide and crying and awful feelings, poetry and sick-ness; *all* that mush! Now I've had it proved to me. You're nasty, Mr Montag, you're *nasty*.

The trouble with Montag, of course, is that he has discovered the value of books. He keeps some hidden away behind the ventilator grille. And the reader realises that it is only a mat-ter of time before he is discovered. Bradbury develops a cer-tain amount of suspense and drama through Mildred's fears, through the poker-face duels between Montag and the fire chief Beatty, and through the ominous sounds outside Montag's door. One of the most effective minor climaxes in *Fahrenheit 451* occurs when the firemen are called out and Montag finds, to his horror, that the address they have been sent to destroy books is his own.

> **It must be admitted that Bradbury is more successful in creating the horror of mechanised anti-culture than in evoking the positive and continuing power of literature and civilisation. The burning scenes have intense power and the pursuit of Montag by the Mechanical Hound, especially in the last section of the book, is in the best tradition of Gothic pursuit; mysterious, but relentless.**
>
> **—*John Colmer***

It must be admitted that Bradbury is more successful in cre-ating the horror of mechanised anti-culture than in evoking the positive and continuing power of literature and civilisation. The burning scenes have intense power and the pursuit of Montag by the Mechanical Hound, especially in the last sec-tion of the book, is inthe best tradition of Gothic pursuit; mysterious, but relentless. By comparison, the evocation of culture is either laboured or sentimental. It is laboured, be-cause Bradbury cannot rely on his readers picking up his al-lusions. He therefore has to explain laboriously; for instance, the fact that Ridley was one of the Oxford martyrs of 1555 who was burnt at the cross as a martyr to truth. In case the relevance of the words spoken by the woman burnt up by the Mechanical Hound is missed, Bradbury supplies an explana-tory recapitulation a few pages later:

They said nothing on their way back to the firehouse. Nobody looked at anyone else. Montag sat in the front seat with Beatty and Black. They did not even smoke their pipes. They sat there looking out of the front of the great salamander as they turned a corner and went silently on.

'Master Ridley,' said Montag at last.

'What?' said Beatty.

'She said, "Master Ridley." She said some crazy thing when we came in the door. "Play the man," she said, "Master Ridley." Something, something, something.'

'We shall this day light such a candle, by God's grace, in England, as I trust shall never be put out,' said Beatty. Stoneman glanced over at the Captain, as did Montag, startled.

Beatty rubbed his chin. 'A man named Latimer said that to a man named Nicholas Ridley, as they were being burnt alive at Oxford, for heresy, on October 16, 1555.'

The idea of culture is embarrassingly false in the interview with Faber, who then becomes Montag's better self, through the minute transistor that he carries around with him and which acts as his mechanical conscience. It is painfully folksy in the whole section relating to Montag's meeting with Granger and his greenwoods exiles, each of whom has memorised a great book or part of a book. The theme here is the independence of culture from physical objects, but the notion of a revived oral culture is not developed very far in this piece of pre-McLuhan fiction. Most painful of all are Granger's recollec-tions of his artist grandfather's philosophy of individualism. Putting Christmas-cracker sentiments into the mouths of a now dead grandfather does not make them any less trite.

The image of fire undergoes a double transformation in the last part of the book. What had been the destroyer of culture before becomes the centre of civilised life, as Granger and his exiles gather round the camp fire. Finally, the fire that has destroyed nations in the international conflict is seen as a Phoenix. Bradbury provides a characteristically popular ex-planation through Granger.

There was a silly damn bird called a Phoenix back beforeChrist; every few hundred years he built a pyre and burned himself up.

A writer who has to explain all his allusions and symbols for the benefit of lowbrow readers is at a considerable disadvan-tage. But a writer who resorts to condescending explanations like this one probably repels both highbrow and lowbrow readers alike.

When in doubt how to end, there is nothing like putting in a Biblical passage to achieve spurious prophetic power. With the evidence of widespread destruction everywhere, the reader is reminded that there is a time to break down and a time to build up, and Montag recalls a passage from the Bible:

> And on either side of the river was there a tree of life, which bore twelve manner of fruits, and yielded her fruit every month; And the leaves of the tree were for healing of the nations.

Books create diversity and harmony, that is the final message of *Fahrenheit 451*. It is an intensely serious work of popular Science Fiction but it is flawed by sentimentality and meretricious appeals to high culture.

Wayne L. Johnson (essay date 1980)

SOURCE: "Machineries of Joy and Sorrow," in *Ray Bradbury,* Frederick Ungar Publishing Company, 1980, pp. 85-8.

[*In the following excerpt, Johnson provides concise analysis of plot, theme and elements of fantasy and social criticism in* Fahrenheit 451.]

Fahrenheit 451 is one of only two novels Bradbury has written. The other is *Something Wicked This Way Comes.* (*Dandelion Wine* and *The Martian Chronicles* are often referred to as novels, but they are really collections of separate stories unified by theme and specially written bridge passages.) *Fahrenheit 451* is a short novel, an expansion of a story, **"The Fireman,"** originally published in *Galaxy*. The book is about as far as Bradbury has come in the direction of using science fiction for social criticism. Actually, the premise of the book is rather farfetched—that firemen in some future state no longer fight fires but set them, having become arms of a political program aimed at stamping out all literature. This purging of the written word, particularly of the imaginative sort, is found in other stories, most strikingly in **"Pillar of Fire"** and **"The Exiles."** But in these other stories the tone is clearly that of a fantasy. *Fahrenheit 451* is realistic in tone, but keeps such a tight focus on the developing awareness of fireman Guy Montag that we can successfully overlook the improbability of his occupation. In fact, the very improbability of Montag's work allows Bradbury to maintain a certain detachment in the book, so that basic themes such as freedom of speech, the value of imagination, the authority of the state, individualism versus conformity, and soon, can be developed and explored without becoming either too realistic or too allegorical.

> **[The] very improbability of Montag's work allows Bradbury to maintain a certain detachment in the book, so that basic themes such as freedom of speech, the value of imagination, the authority of the state, individualism versus conformity, and so on, can be developed and explored without becoming either too realistic or too allegorical.**
>
> **—*Wayne L. Johnson***

In the course of the book, Montag goes through what today might be called consciousness raising. He begins as a loyal fireman, burning what he is told to burn, progresses through a period of doubts and questioning, and ends up rebelling against the system and doing his part to keep man's literary heritage alive. But the bones of the plot do little to convey the feeling of the book. Bradbury's world here seems much closer to the present than the future—not so much in terms of its overall structure as in terms of its more intimate details. Some of the characterizations—Montag's wife, given over to drugs and mindless television; Clarisse, an archetypal hippie or flower child; and the old woman, who defies the firemen by pouring kerosene over her books and her own body before striking a match—might have been drawn from the turbulent political events of the sixties. It is almost necessary to remind oneself that *Fahrenheit 451* was published in 1953.

Many of Bradbury's pet themes are to be found in the novel. Metamorphosis is a major theme of the story, for in the course of it Montag changes from book-burner to living-book. Montag the fireman is intensely aware of the power of fire: "It was a special pleasure to see things eaten, to see things blackened and *changed*." He himself is changed every time he goes out on a job: "He knew that when he returned to the firehouse, he might wink at himself, a minstrel man, burnt-corked, in the mirror."

Machines are of crucial importance. Overall, the book traces Montag's flight from the dangerous mechanical world of the city to the traditional haven of the country. Montag at first feels comfortable with machines, especially his flame-throwing equipment. The first time Montag meets Clarisse he views the scene in mechanical terms: "The autumn leaves blew over the moonlit pavement in such a way as to make the girl who was moving there seem fixed to a gliding walk, letting the motion of the wind and leaves carry her forward." But many mechanical things are repellent to Montag, particularly the equipment the medical technicians use on his wife after she has taken an overdose of sleeping pills: "They had two machines, really. One of them slid down your stomach like a black cobra down an echoing well looking for all the old water and the old time gathered there."

Montag's particular mechanical enemy is the fire station's Mechanical Hound, more like a huge spider, actually, with its "bits of ruby glass and . . . sensitive capillary hairs in the Nylon-brushed nostrils . . . that quivered gently, gently, its eight legs spidered under it on rubber-padded paws." As Montag becomes more fascinated with books and nearer to betrayal of his duties as a fireman, the hound becomes more suspicious of him. The hound is then symbolic of the relentless, heartless pursuit of the State.

When Montag finally flees the city, he must first cross a mechanical moat, a highway 100 yards across on which the "beetle" cars seem to take pleasure in using pedestrians for target practice. Other machines Montag grows to hate are the radio and television that reduce their audience, Montag's wife, for one, into listless zombies.

But *Fahrenheit 451* is not primarily a work of social criticism. Its antimachine and antiwar elements are there primarily as background for Montag's spiritual development. It is interesting that this development seems to be in the direction of social outcast. Granted that Montag's society has its evils, but at the end of the book we are not so sure that Montag will be completely happy with his new-found friends, the book people. What we are sure of is that Montag has entrenched himself as nay-sayer to a society that has become hostile and destructive toward the past. Montag joins the book people whose task, as Granger puts it, is "remembering." But even as he does so, he promises himself that he will one day follow the refugees from the bombed-out city, seeking, though this is not stated, perhaps his wife, perhaps Clarisse. Most of the book people are like the old man in **"To the Chicago Abyss,"** essentially harmless, using their talents for remembering things to aid their society in whatever way they can. But Montag may perhaps be too rigid an idealist, having rejected his former society with the same vehemence as he once embraced it. Like Spender in ***The Martian Chronicles,*** Montag has committed murder to maintain his freedom and the integrity of his vision. Unlike Spender, but like many of Bradbury's other outsiders and misfits, Montag has successfully achieved a truce or stalemate with a world hostile to his individuality. At the end of ***Fahrenheit 451,*** Montag's future can go either way; toward reintegration with a new, less hostile society, or toward a continuing, perpetual alienation.

John Huntington (essay date July 1982)

SOURCE: "Utopian and Anti-Utopian Logic: H. G. Wells and His Successors," in *Science Fiction Studies,* Vol. 9, No. 2, July 1982, pp. 122-46.

[*In the following excerpt, Huntington considers the dystopian-utopian structure of* Fahrenheit 451 *and comments on the paradoxical symbolism of the book as both cultural and technological achievement.*]

Montag, the protagonist of [***Fahrenheit 451***], like Graham [of H. G. Wells's *When the Sleeper Wakes*], D-503 [of Yevgeny Zamyatin's *We*], and Winston Smith [of George Orwell's *1984*], is a man coming to consciousness and attempting the overthrow or reformation of the closed, totalitarian, futuristic world he valued at the start. As in the other novels we have looked at, here too a woman is the inspiration for the change of mind. As in the other works, the act of seeing beyond the present is at least in part an act of recovery of a lost tradition: Graham is a revolutionary because he retains 19th-century sentiments of justice which the future world claims to have outgrown; D-503 and Winston Smith find an alternative to the totalitarian state in the antique parts of civilization. And Montag rediscovers books, which the future society has banned. Other similarities might be traced, but my point in sketching the by now conventional situation is not to estimate the extent of Bradbury's debt to the tradition, but to establish a broad common background against which we can understand the different way Bradbury's images function logically.

In ***Fahrenheit 451*** the future is bad because people, denied the rich traditional culture contained in books and imaged by nature, have become unstimulated and unstimulating. The dystopian world is in large part conveyed in terms of the denial of positives. Firechief Beatty's defense of the bookless future is essentially that of the Grand Inquisitor, with the important change that the mass's fear of freedom is seen to be a historical phenomenon, a failure of education. In the past, so the ironic argument goes, people were capable of freedom, but because of technology and the triumph of a debased mass culture they have lost their ability to choose and their joy in freedom. Beatty's argument seems to be the author's; in Montag's wife we see heavily done exactly the mindlessness, the need for booklessness that Beatty defends. Beatty argues that mass culture is necessarily simple and, therefore, inevitably a decline from our own élite culture based on books, and in much of its satire the novel supports him. Where the novel makes Beatty clearly an ironic spokesman to be refuted is not in his characterization of the masses and what they want, but in his inadequate appreciation of the sensitive few who are capable of freedom.

The novel expresses this vision of freedom with images of sentimentalized nature (Clarisse rhapsodizes about the smell of leaves, the sight of the man in the moon), the recollection of the small, mid-western town (the front porch and the rocking chair become symbols of freedom), some tag ends of 1930s' romanticizing of Depression survival, and an unquestioning admiration for books. This cluster poses an absolute pole around which accrues all good and in relation to which all movement away is bad. The dystopian and utopian possibilities in the novel are thus represented by separate clusters of images and ideas that the novel finds unambiguous and leaves unchallenged.

What needs emphasis here is the extent to which Bradbury's novel preserves the dystopian-utopian structure by ignoring the implications of its own imagery. The author advises his audience that they must preserve books to prevent the horror he imagines, but he never questions the values implicit in the books. When the new age is accused of serious flaws—unhappiness, fear, war, and wasted lives—there is no sense that the age of books may have also suffered from such problems. At the end, in his vision of a wandering group of book-people Bradbury invokes an idealized hobo mystique, but with little sense of the limits and tragedy of such a life.

In such a simple system of good and bad values, mediation produces horror rather than thought. Nature is good and technology is bad, but the ultimate terror is a mixture of the two, a kind of symbolic miscegenation. When Montag finally makes his break from the technological future he is pursued by a "mechanical hound," a terrifying figure which combines the relentlessness of the bloodhound with the infallibility of technology. In Bradbury's vision the hound is most terrifying for being both alive and not alive.

The threat the hound poses for the imagery system of the novel is put to rest the moment Montag escapes him, and the clear opposition between technology and nature that Clarisse has preached strongly reasserts itself. Montag hears a whisper, sees "a shape, two eyes" in the forest and is convinced it is the hound, but it turns out to be a deer, not just harmless, but afraid of him. Nature is submissive and controllable, while technology is predatory and threatening. This important refuge then leads to a sequence of reversals. Montag sees a fire in the woods and for the first time in his life realizes that fire need not be destructive, that in providing warmth it can be benign. And this perception leads to a moment of trance in which Montag resees himself:

> How long he stood he did not know, but there was a foolish and yet delicious sense of knowing himself as an animal come from the forest, drawn by the fire. He was a thing of brush and liquid eye, of fur and muzzle and hoof, he was a thing of horn and blood that would smell like autumn if you bled it out on the ground.

I take it that this reduction of the human to animal parts is somehow consoling and ennobling. Like all the nature images in this novel, the purple rhetoric obscures true perception, but nevertheless the revelation is there and the blurred but central symbolic transformation of the novel is complete:

Montag has escaped the urban world of destructive technology and joined the nurturing forest world. By rescuing fire for the good, natural side, he has enabled the novel to convert dystopia into utopia.

> **Montag has escaped the urban world of destructive technology and joined the nurturing forest world. By rescuing fire for the good, natural side, he has enabled the novel to convert dystopia into utopia.**
>
> —*John Huntington*

The interesting difficulty is where do books fit into this simple opposition? Since Gutenberg the book has been a symbol of technological progress. Bradbury partly counters this meaning of his symbol by reducing his pastoral, not to paper books, but to humans who remember books. Thus the replication and general availability that are books' virtues, but which the novel has seen as the instruments of the mass-culture that has ruined the world, are denied. We have the *idea* of the book without the *fact* of its production. Then, by becoming a general symbol of the past now denied, the book becomes a symbol for all old values, but this symbolism brings up two difficulties. First, whatever good books have propagated, they have also preached the evils that have oppressed the world. The very technology that the novel finds threatening would be impossible without books. Second, books can readily inspire a repressive and tradition-bound pedantry which, while anti-technological, is also against nature.

Through most of *Fahrenheit 451* Bradbury simply ignores these potential problems with his symbol; but in the final pages, in an act of renunciation that is surprising given the values the novel has promulgated, the moral vision retreats from its main symbolism. The memorizers of books are about to move out of the forest to give succor to the cities that have just been bombed; and Granger, the leader of the bookish hoboes, says:

> Hold onto one thought: you're not important. You're not anything. Some day the load we're carrying with us may help someone. But even when we had the books on hand, a long time ago, we didn't use what we got out of them. We went right on insulting the dead. We went right on spitting on the graves of all the poor ones who died before us. We're going to meet a lot of lonely people in the next week and the next month and the next year. And when they ask us what we're doing, you can say, We're remembering. That's where we'll win out in the long run. And some day we'll remember so much that we'll build the big-

gest steamshovel in history and dig the biggest grave of all time and shove war in and cover it up.

The vagueness, ambiguity, and misdirection of this passage confuse what Granger is saying; but in the technological imagery of the last line and in the attack on the previously sentimentalized past, in the recognition that books have done little to make life better, this paragraph implies a renunciation of the values the novel has been, however naïvely, building. But perhaps it is also, finally, an awareness of a true opposition, of an irony that gets beyond the simple sentimentalisms of much of the novel. Though one may have doubts as to how to take it, one way would be to see here a titanic revision of values, a deep questioning of the pieties that have inspired Montag and Clarisse. In line with such a reading we should observe that one of the books Montag remembers is *Ecclesiastes:* perhaps this is an allusion to the Preacher's famous words against the vanity of life, and particularly the vanity of books. But, then, to read it this way would be to suppose that Bradbury is attempting anti-utopian thought, and that seems unlikely.

Bradbury's novel is in the tradition of utopian prose put forth by Wells himself in his later romances. Whatever political differences we might discover between Wells's sane, organized, post-cometsocieties and Bradbury's nomadic society in nature, we can see that they both depend on an imagery which ignores contradiction. Such utopian thought is incompatible with the basic logical techniques of Well's earlier work. It marks an evasion of the pressure of contradiction. It attempts to bring about conviction not by thought, but by the emotive power of rhythmic prose, the attractiveness of pretty images, the appeal to hope which will treat doubt as merely regretful cynicism. Such utopian images have an honored place, but they belong to a genus quite unlike the anti-utopian investigations that mark Wells's greatest scientific romances.

George R. Guffey (essay date 1983)

SOURCE: "*Fahrenheit 451* and the 'Cubby-Hole Editors' of Ballantine Books," in *Coordinates: Placing Science Fiction and Fantasy,* edited by George E. Slusser, Eric S. Rabkin, and Robert Scholes, Southern Illinois University Press, 1983, pp. 99-106.

[*In the following essay, Guffey explores Bradbury's indictment of censorship in some of his early short stories and comments on the bowdlerization of* Fahrenheit 451 *for high school readers.*]

In April 1975 on the campus of the University of California at Santa Barbara, Ray Bradbury delighted an assembled audience with an uninhibited speech entitled "How Not to Burn a Book; or, 1984 Will Not Arrive." At one point in his wide-ranging presentation he reflected on the emotions which have typically impelled his fiction. "Sometimes I get angry and write a story about my anger. Sometimes I'm delighted and I write a story about that delight. Back in the Joseph McCarthy period a lot of things were going on in my country that I didn't like. I was angry. So I wrote a whole series of short stories."

One of those short stories, **"Usher II,"** was first published in 1950. The hero of **"Usher II"** is William Stendahl, a wealthy lover of fantastic literature and an embittered enemy of censorship and book burning. At one time on Earth, Stendahl had been the proud owner of fifty thousand books, but the Bureau of Moral Climates, in league with the Society for Prevention of Fantasy, had destroyed his beloved library. Amongst the works burned were those of Edgar Allan Poe. "All of his books," Stendahl tells the architect he has hired to re-create the House of Usher, "were burned in the Great Fire. That's thirty years ago—1975. . . . They passed a law. Oh, it started very small. In 1950 and '60 it was a grain of sand. They began by controlling books of cartoons and then detective books . . . , one way or another, one group or another, political bias, religious prejudice, union pressures; there was always a minority afraid of something, and a great majority afraid of the dark. . . . Afraid of the word 'politics' (which eventually became a synonym for Communism among the more reactionary elements . . . and it was worth your life to use the word!), and . . . the print presses trickled down from a great Niagara of reading matter to a mere innocuous dripping of 'pure material.'"

To gain a measure of revenge against the psychologists, sociologists, politicians, and moralists responsible for the burning of his books, Stendahl has built on Mars a letter-perfect imitation of Poe's original House of Usher and has invited many of his own persecutors to a very special kind of housewarming. Over the course of the story, Stendahl lures his antagonists one by one into traps inspired by Poe's macabre stories. One miscreant is killed by a robot ape and stuffed up a chimney; one is beheaded by an enormous razor-sharp pendulum; one is prematurely buried; and, in the climactic scene, the worst of the lot is mortared-up forever in a cellar beneath that melancholy and dreary house. His revenge complete, a jubilant Stendahl helicopters away from Usher II, as the great house breaks apart and sinks slowly into the dark tarn surrounding it.

Approximately a year after the publication of **"Usher II,"** Bradbury broadened his attack on censorship. In a novella entitled **"The Fireman,"** he depicted a future society in which most kinds of books had been banned. The hero of this story is Guy Montag, a fireman. Ironically, in this heavily regimented world of the future, firemen no longer extinguish fires. Their primary duty is to start them. More specifically, their main occupation is the burning of books. At one point in the story, Leahy, a fire chief, delivers a short lecture on the recent history of expurgation and censorship.

> Picture it. The 19th Century man with his horses, dogs, and slow living. You might call him a slow motion man. Then in the 20th Century you speed up the camera. . . . Books get shorter. Condensations appear. Digests. Tabloids. Radio programs simplify. . . . Great classics are cut to fit fifteen minute shows, then two minute book columns, then two line digest resumes. Magazines become picture books. . . . Technology, mass exploitation, and censorship from frightened officials did the trick. Today, thanks to them, you can read comics, confessions, or trade journals, nothing else. All the rest is dangerous. . . . Colored people don't like *Little Black Sambo*. We burn it. White people don't like *Uncle Tom's Cabin*. Burn it, too. Anything for serenity.

In spite of repeated warnings from Leahy, Montag becomes more and more fascinated by books and by reading. Eventually he is found out, and his small collection of books is burned. Angry and frustrated, he kills Leahy and flees to the open countryside. There, in a hobo camp, he meets a band of fugitives who have devoted their lives to the judicious memorization and communication of uncensored versions of the great classics. For years these "living books" have patiently awaited an inevitable, cataclysmic world war which will destroy all the oppressive bureaucracies inhibiting the free flow of ideas. At the end of the story, this long-awaited war comes, leveling the seats of government and, presumably, thereby making the world again safe for the dissemination of uncensored books.

Bradbury's rage against censorship and book burning reached its fullest and most eloquent expression in 1953 when he expanded "TheFireman" to novel length and published it under the new title *Fahrenheit 451*. During the following quarter of a century, *Fahrenheit 451* was reprinted at least forty-eight times by Ballantine. In 1979 Bradbury discovered for the first time that, ironically, *Fahrenheit 451* had in the past itself been systematically censored by its publisher.

At his insistence, the novel has recently been reset and republished, with a spirited Author's Afterword. In that afterword Bradbury emphasizes his continuing problems with publishers wishing both to reprint his popular stories and at the same time edit them for young readers. For example, his frequently anthologized story **"The Fog Horn"** was, he says, recently the proposed object of such treatment: "Two weeks ago my mountain of mail delivered forth a pipsqueak mouse of a letter from a well-known publishing house that wanted to reprint my story **'The Fog Horn'** in a high school reader. In my story, I had described a lighthouse as having, late at night, an illumination coming from it that was a 'God-Light.'

Looking up at it from the view-point of any sea-creature one would have felt that one was in 'the Presence.' The editors had deleted 'God-Light' and 'in the Presence.'" But worst of all was what Ballantine had in the past, without permission, actually done to *Fahrenheit 451:* "Over the years, some cubby-hole editors at Ballantine Books, fearful of contaminating the young, had, bit by bit, censored some 75 separate sections from the novel. Students, reading the novel which, after all, deals with censorship and book-burning in the future, wrote to tell me of this exquisite irony. Judy-Lynn Del Rey, one of the new Ballantine editors, is having the entire book reset and republished . . . with all the damns and hells back in place."

Bradbury's rage against censorship and book burning reached its fullest and most eloquent expression in 1953 when he expanded "The Fireman" to novel length and published it under the new title *Fahrenheit 451*. During the following quarter of a century, *Fahrenheit 451* was reprinted at least forty-eight times by Ballantine. In 1979 Bradbury discovered for the first time that, ironically, *Fahrenheit 451* had in the past itself been systematically censored by its publisher.

—*George R. Guffey*

Collation of a copy from the first printing of the novel in October 1953 with a copy from the forty-fourth printing in August 1977 reveals that by that date fifty-two pages of *Fahrenheit 451* had been completely reset and that, in the process, ninety-eight nonauthoritative, substantive changes had been made in the text. Most of those changes, as Bradbury in his afterword suggest, simply involved the deletion of expletives or oaths. For example, the Ballantine editors at one place in the book altered "'Jesus God,' said Montag. 'Every hour so many damn things in the sky! How in hell did those bombers get up there!'" to "'Every hour so many things in the sky!' said Montag. 'How did those bombers get up there!'"

But many of the changes made by the Ballantine editors fall into other categories. Nudity in the boudoir, no matter how abstractly described, troubled them. "His wife stretched on the bed, uncovered and cold" became merely "His wife stretched on the bed." And parts of the body, particularly that innocuous depression we call "the navel," seem also to have offended them. They altered "All the minor minor minorities with their navels to be kept clean" to "All the minor minor minorities with their ears to be kept clean." Wherever possible, references to the consumption of alcohol were muted. For example, the passage "Did we have a wild party or something? Feel like I've a hangover. God, I'm hungry" was altered to read: "Did we have a party or something? Feel like I've a headache. I'm hungry." In another instance, "Are you drunk?" became "Are you ill?"

Space will not permit an exhaustive account of the kinds of changes *Fahrenheit 451* suffered at the hands of the Ballantine editors, but I must, before moving on, call attention to at least two other examples. At one point in the book, Montag angrily says to his wife's superficial, narcissistic friend: "Go home and . . . think of the dozen abortions you've had, go home and think of that and your damn Caesarian sections, too." The Ballantine editors removed from the passage both the word "damn" and the reference to abortion, leaving only "Go home and . . . think of that and your Caesarian sections, too." Finally, at another point in the action, a vigorously delivered speech culminates in an emphatic, effective vulgarism. "'To hell with that,' he said, 'shake the tree and knock the great sloth down on his ass.'" Under the scalpel of the Ballantine editors, the passage died, leaving behind this poor, shriveled carcass. "He said, 'shake the tree and knock the great sloth down.'"

Although in the afterword to the 1979 corrected edition of *Fahrenheit 451* Bradbury indicated that his novel had, "over the years," been censored "bit by bit," my own research suggests that the excisions and revisions we have been examining were the result of more concentrated efforts. Evidently, Bradbury is unaware (or has forgotten) that, in January 1967, *Fahrenheit 451* was for the first time published in the Ballantine Bal-Hi series. Comparison of my copy from the fifth Bal-Hi printing of October 1968 with my copy of the first Ballantine printing of October 1953 demonstrates that all the variants we have been considering were in actuality the result of revisions made for this special high school paperback series. In addition, comparison of the texts of the fourth printing of October 1963, the seventh printing of September 1966, and the thirtieth printing of July 1972 with the first printing of October 1953 indicates that, although Ballantine was publishing a revised version of the book in its Bal-Hi series, from 1967 to 1973 an uncensored version of the novel was simultaneously being sold to the general public.

According to the copyright page of the corrected 1979 edition, the tenth and last printing of the Bal-Hi version of the novel occurred in October 1973. After 1973, instead of continuing to publish theunexpurgated and unrevised text of the first printing of October 1953, Ballantine, with no warning whatever to potential readers, published, until taken to task by Bradbury himself in 1979, only the revised text prepared for the Bal-Hi series. The text of my own copy from the fortieth printing of December 1975, although in no way labeled

so, is identical to the bowdlerized text of my copy from the fifth Bal-Hi printing (as is the text of my copy from the forty-fourth printing of August 1977).

To understand Ballantine's treatment of *Fahrenheit 451* during the latter half of the 1960s, we must be conscious of the intense social and political pressures brought to bear on publishers of textbooks during the late 1950s and the early 1960s. In 1958, for example, E. Merrill Root published his *Brainwashing in the High Schools,* an assault on eleven textbooks, which, in his view "parallel[ed] the Communist line." Inspired by Root's opening thrust, the Daughters of the American Revolution in 1958 began to compile a list of "unsatisfactory" texts, and a year later, in 1959, began to distribute it. By 1963, the advocates of censorship had widened their offensive. In that year in their influential book, *The Censors and the Schools,* Jack Nelson and Gene Roberts, Jr., wrote: "A vice-president of McGraw-Hill says all publishers must be wary in their treatment of birth control, evolution . . . , sex education, and minority groups." "In some parts of the United States," Nelson and Roberts added, "it is worth a teacher's job to put modern novels such as J. D. Salinger's *The Catcher in the Rye* or George Orwell's *1984* on a classroom reading list."

Although librarians and teachers fought back, the pressure for censorship increased. "The pressure of censorship is a growing part of school life today," wrote Professor Lee A. Burress, Jr., in 1965, the year the first book in the Ballantine Bal-Hi series was evidently published. "If articles on censorship in education journals," he continued, "constitute a reliable index, teachers are much more concerned today than thirty years ago. When *Education Index* commenced publication in 1929, one article a year on censorship was published. In the most recent issues of *Education Index,* there are lengthy bibliographies on censorship." Burress cites numerous recent examples of capricious and ridiculous censorship in his own state of Wisconsin, including actions against Dostoevski's *Crime and Punishment,* for allegedly containing "too much profanity," and the magazine *Today's Health,* for dealing with "the birth of a baby."

Although self-appointed censors presented real problems for publishers of school texts during the 1960s, the rewards were great for those who managed to produce "acceptable" books. Especially lucrative, according to article after article in *Senior Scholastic* and *The Library Journal* during that period, was the growing market for paperback. It was for this increasingly lucrative market that the Bal-Hi series was apparently designed.

A number of important questions now naturally come to mind: What were the titles of the other books published in the Bal-Hi series?Were the other books in the Bal-Hi series, like Bradbury's *Fahrenheit 451,* bowdlerized in order to assure their marketability? And, if bowdlerized, did they, as in the case of *Fahrenheit 451,* eventually replace uncensored versions of the same titles in the regular Ballantine line? All these questions are, I think, well worth answering.

Jack Zipes (essay date 1983)

SOURCE: "Mass Degradation of Humanity and Massive Contradictions in Bradbury's Vision of America in *Fahrenheit 451,*" in *No Place Else: Explorations in Utopian and Dystopian Fiction,* edited by Eric S. Rabkin, Martin H. Greenberg, and Joseph D. Olander, Southern Illinois University Press, 1983, pp. 182-98.

[*In the following essay, Zipes examines inconsistencies in Bradbury's sociopolitical criticism of post-World War II America in* Fahrenheit 451.]

Perhaps it is endemic to academic criticism of science fiction to talk in abstractions and haggle over definitions of utopia, dystopia, fantasy, science, and technology. Questions of rhetoric, semiotic codes, structure, motifs, and types take precedence over the historical context of the narrative and its sociopolitical implications. If substantive philosophical comments are made, they tend to be universal statements about humanity, art, and the destiny of the world. Such is the case with Ray Bradbury's *Fahrenheit 451*. As a result, we hear that the novel contains a criticism of "too rapid and pervasive technological change" within a tradition of "humanistic conservatism." Or, it is actually "the story of Bradbury, disguised as Montag and his lifelong affair with books" and contains his major themes: "the freedom of the mind, the evocation of the past; the desire for Eden; the integrity of the individual; the allurements and traps of the future." One critic has interpreted the novel as portraying a "conformist hell." Another regards it as a social commentary about the present which levels a critique at "the emptiness of modern mass culture and its horrifying effects."

All these interpretations are valid because they are so general and apparent, but they could also pertain to anyone or anything that lived in a "little how town." Their difficulty is that they form abstractions about figures already extrapolated from a particular moment in American history, and these abstractions are not applied to the particular moment as it informs the text, but to the universe at large. Thus, *Fahrenheit 451* is discussed in terms of the world's problems at large when it is essentially bound to the reality of the early 1950s in America, and it is the specificity of the crises endangering the fabric of American society which stamp the narrative concern. The McCarthy witch hunts, the Cold War, the Korean War, the rapid rise of television as a determinant in the culture industry, the spread of advertisement, the abuse of technology within the military-industrial complex, the frustration and violence of the younger generation, the degradation of the

masses—these are the factors which went into the making of *Fahrenheit 451* as an American novel, and they form the parameters of any discussion of the dystopian and utopian dimensions of this work.

> *Fahrenheit 451* is discussed in terms of the world's problems at large when it is essentially bound to the reality of the early 1950s in America, and it is the specificity of the crises endangering the fabric of American society which stamp the narrative concern.
>
> —*Jack Zipes*

Bradbury is an eminently careful and conscious writer, and he always has specific occurrences and conditions in mind when he projects into the future. In *Fahrenheit 451,* he was obviously reacting to the political and intellectual climate of his times and intended to play the sci-fi game of the possible with his readers of 1953. Obviously this game is still playable in 1983 and may continue to appeal to readers in the future. It depends on the author's rhetorical ability to create a mode of discourse which allows him to exaggerate, intensify, and extend scientific, technological, and social conditions from a current real situation to their most extreme point while convincing the reader that everything which occurs in the fantasy world is feasible in the distant future. Belief in reality is at no time expected to be suspended. On the contrary, the reader is expected to bear in mind the reality of his/her situation to be able to draw comparisons and appropriate correspondences with the fictional correlates which are projections not only of the author's imagination but of the probabilities emanating from the social tendencies of the author's environment. Thus, in *Fahrenheit 451* specific American problems of the early 1950s are omnipresent and are constantly projected into the future, estranged, negated, and finally exploded in the hope that more positive values might be reborn from the ashes in phoenix-like manner. *Fahrenheit 451* is structured around fire and death as though it were necessary to conceive new rituals and customs from the ashes of an America bent on destroying itself and possibly the world. Bradbury's vision of America and Americans assumes the form of the sci-fi game of the possible because he wants it to be played out in reality. That is, the ethical utopian rigor of the book imbues the metaphorical images with a political gesture aimed at influencing the reader's conscience and subsequent behavior in society. While Bradbury obviously takes a position against the mass degradation of humanity, there are curious massive contradictions in his illumination of social tendencies which make his own position questionable. Let us try to recast the discursive mode of the narrative in light of the sociopolitical context of Bradbury's day to see what he perceived in the social tendencies of the 1950s and what alternative paths he illuminated in anticipation of possible catastrophes.

First, a world about Montag and his situation at the beginning of the novel. As a law-enforcer, Montag symbolizes those forces of repression which were executing the orders of McCarthy supportersand the conservative United States government led by General Dwight D. Eisenhower, John Foster Dulles, and J. Edgar Hoover. He is not a simple law officer but belongs to the special agency of liquidation and espionage, similar to the FBI and CIA. Moreover, he is an insider, who at thirty years of age has reached full manhood and is perhaps at his most virile stage. This is exactly why he was created and chosen by Bradbury. At thirty, as we know from real life and from numerous other novels of the twentieth century, Montag is also entering a critical stage and is most susceptible to outside influences. Therefore, he is perfect for initiating the game of the possible. Montag likes his job. He gets pleasure out of burning, and his virility is closely linked to "the brass nozzle in his fists, with this great python spitting its venomous kerosene upon the world." We first encounter Montag in a fit of orgasm, idealistically fulfilling his mission of purging the world of evil books. The image of book-burning, the symbolic helmet, the uniform with a salamander on the arm and a phoenix disc on his chest suggest a situation of the past, namely the Nazis, swastikas, and book-burning of the 1930s. But it is not far from the realm of possibility in the early 1950s of America that Montag as an American fireman might be pouring kerosene over books and burning them. The censorship of books which dealt with socialism, eroticism, and sexuality in the early 1950s made the extension of Montag's actions conceivable for Bradbury and his readers. Indeed, *Fahrenheit 451* begins with an acceptable statement for the silent 1950s in America which demanded a silence to all dissent: "It was a pleasure to burn." Here male identity is immediately associated with liquidation and destruction, with dictatorial power. Bradbury plays with the unconscious desires of the American male and extends them into the future as reality while at the same time he immediately questions that reality and machoism through Montag's misgivings.

The narrative thread of the American male vision of 1950 hangs on Montag's piecing together what has made him into the man he is at age thirty so that he can pursue a more substantial and gratifying life. This means that he must undo social entanglements, expose his understanding to the world, and burn in a different way than he does at the beginning of the narrative. His sight is our sight. His possibilities are our possibilities. His discourse with the world is ours. What he does in the future corresponds to the tasks set for us in the 1950s which may still be with us now. Though not exactly a *Bildungsroman, Fahrenheit 451* is a novel of development in that Montag undergoes a learning experience which lends

the book its utopian impetus. Let us consider the main stages of Montag's learning experiences because they constitute Bradbury's angry critique of America—and here we must remember that Bradbury was writing about the same time as the Angry Young Generation in England and the Beat Generation in America, groups of writers who rejected the affluence and vacuousness of technological innovation in capitalist societies.

The first phase of Montag's learning experience is initiated by Clarisse McClellan, who makes him wonder why people talk and why hedoes not pay attention to small things. The name Clarisse suggests light, clarity, and illumination, and Montag must be enlightened. His own ability to discuss, see, feel, and hear has been muted. He is unconscious of his own history and the forces acting on him. Clarisse infers that his consciousness has been stunted by the two-hundred-foot-long billboards, the parlour walls, races, and fun parks, all of which she avoids because they prevent her from being alone with her own thoughts. Thus, she illuminates the way Montag must take not only for his own self-questioning but for the reader's own questioning of the consciousness industry in America. Bradbury wants to get at the roots of American conformity and immediately points a finger at the complicity of state and industry for using technology to produce television programs, gambling sports games, amusement parks, and advertising to black self-reflection and blank out the potential for alternative ways of living which do not conform to fixed national standards. As Bradbury's mouthpiece, Clarisse wonders whether Montag is actually happy leading a death-in-life, and Montag quickly realizes that he is not happy when he enters his sterile and fully automatic house. He proceeds to the room where his wife Mildred is ostensibly sleeping and senses that "the room was cold but nonetheless he felt he could not breathe. He did not wish to open the curtains and open the french windows, for he did not want the moon to come into the room. So, with the feeling of a man who will die in the next hour for lack of air, he felt his way toward his open, separate, and therefore cold bed." The image of death is fully impressed upon him when he becomes aware that his wife has attempted suicide. This is startling, but what is even more startling for Montag is the mechanical, indifferent way the operators treat his wife with a machine that revives her by pumping new blood into her system. Moreover, he becomes highly disturbed when the pill given to his wife by the operators makes her unaware the next morning that she had tried to take her own life. Montag witnesses—because Clarisse has made him more sensitive—the manner in which technology is being used even in the field of medicine to deaden the senses while keeping people alive as machines. He is part of the deadening process. In fact, dead himself he now begins to rise from the ashes like the phoenix. He is testing wings which he never thought he had.

Clarisse is his first teacher, the one who teaches him how to fly. For one intensive week he meets with Clarisse, who instructs him through her own insight and experience why and how the alleged antisocial and disturbed people may have a higher regard for society and be more sane than those who declare themselves normal and uphold the American way of life. Bradbury attacks the American educational system through Clarisse's description of classes in school which are centered on mass media and sports and prevent critical discussion. Schooling is meant to exhaust the young so that they are tame, but the frustration felt by the young is then expressed in their "fun" outside the school, which always turns to violence. Communication gives way to games of beating up people, destroying things, and playing games like chicken. Clarisse admits that she is "'afraid of children my own age. They kill each other.Did it always used to be that way? My uncle says no. Six of my friends have been shot in the last year alone. Ten of them died in car wrecks. I'm afraid of them and they don't like me because I'm afraid.'" But it is not simply fear that cannot be shown in public but all kinds of feelings. Form has subsumed emotions and substance, dissipated humanity, so that the medium has become the message. Art has become abstract, and people are identified with the things they own. They themselves are to be purchased, used, and disposed of in an automatic way.

Montag's life was in the process of becoming a permanent fixture in a system of degradation, but it was fortunately upset by Clarisse for a week. And she upsets it again by disappearing. Despite her disappearance, she has already served an important purpose because Montag is now somewhat more capable of learning from his own experiences, and he moves into his second phase. Significantly it begins with his entering the firehouse where he will start doubting his profession. The mood is set by the firemen playing cards in the tidy, polished firehouse, idling away the time until they can destroy, and the "radio hummed somewhere. . . . war may be declared any hour. This country stands ready to defend its—'" Throughout the novel, war lurks in the background until it finally erupts. The obvious reference here is to the Cold War and the Korean War which might lead to such an atomic explosion as that which occurs at the end of the book. Again the media spread one-sided news about the nation's cause, driving the people hysterically to war instead of convincing them to seek means for communication and co-existence.

Montag gradually learns how the government manipulates the masses through the media, shows of force, and legal measures to pursue its own ends. His first lesson is quick and simple when he discusses a man who was obviously sane but was taken to an insane asylum because he had been reading books and had built his own library. Captain Beatty remarks: "'Any man's insane who thinks he can fool the Government and us.'" Montag's next lesson comes from his direct experience of witnessing a woman destroy herself because her books are burned by the firemen. This incident causes Montag to

bring a book back to his own house and to question what it is in books that would make a woman want to stay in a burning house. For the first time in his life he realizes that human effort and feelings go into the making of a book, and he resolves, despite a warning visit from Beatty, to pursue an experiment with his wife so that they can understand why their lives are in such a mess. Beatty had already attempted to give a false historical explanation of how firemen had been organized by Benjamin Franklin to burn English-influenced books. This time he tries a different ploy by placing the responsibility on the people and arguing that the different ethnic minority and interest groups did not want controversial subjects aired in books. This led to vapid and insipid publications. "'But the public, knowing what it wanted, spinning happily, let the comic-books survive. And the three-dimensional sex-magazines, of course. There you have it, Montag. It didn't come from the Government down. There was no dictum, no declaration, no censorship, to start with, no! Technology, mass exploitation, andminority pressure carried the trick, thank God. Today, thanks to them, you can stay happy all the time, you are allowed to read comics, the good old confessions, or trade-journals.'"

Thus, in Beatty's view—one which, incidentally is never contradicted by Bradbury—the firemen are keepers of peace. He cynically argues that the profession of firemen had to expand to keep the people happy and satisfy their complaints. This is why it conducts espionage and has a computerized system to keep track of each and every citizen in the United States. Yet, despite Beatty's explanation, Montag is firm in his resolution, for he suspects that there is more to Beatty's analysis than meets the eye. Intuitively he recalls Clarisse's discussion about her uncle and the front porches which were eliminated from people's homes because the architects (i.e., the government) did not want people to be active, talking, and communicating with one another. This is why it has become so important for him to talk to his wife and share the experiment in reading with her. However, she has been too conditioned by the television parlour games and by the seashell in her ear—the electronic waves which broadcast music and programs to prevent her thinking. Therefore, Montag is now forced to seek help from Faber, a retired English professor, who had been dismissed from the last liberal arts college because the humanities had in effect been dismissed from the educational system.

By establishing contact with Faber, whose name connotes maker or builder, Montag enters into his third stage of learning experience and begins to assume command of his own destiny. Faber teaches him that the alienation and conformity in society have not been caused by machines but by human beings who have stopped reading of their own accord, and that too few resisted the trend toward standardization and degradation of humanity—including himself. However, Montag gives him hope and courage. So he decides to begin subversive activities with a printer and to set up a communication system with Montag which will depend on the fireman's initiative. He gives Montag a green bullet through which they can communicate and plan their activities without being observed. Here technology is employed to further emancipatory and humanistic interests. The green bullet will also allow Faber to share his knowledge with Montag so that the latter will begin to think for himself. After a violent outburst at home which he knows will end his relationship with Mildred for good, Montag knows that he has made a complete rupture with his former life and recognizes the significance of his relationship with Faber. "On the way downtown he was so completely alone with his terrible error that he felt the necessity for the strange warmness and goodness that came from a familiar and gentle voice speaking in the night. Already, in a few short hours, it seemed that he had known Faber a lifetime. Now he knew that he was two people, that he was above all Montag, who knew nothing, who did not even know himself a fool, but only suspected it. And he knew also that he was the old man who talked to him and talked to him as the train was sucked from one end of the night city to the other one on a long sickening gasp of motion." From this point on Montag moves toward regaining touch with his innermost needs and desires, and he will not be sucked into anything. He avoids the trap set for him by Beatty and burns his real enemies for the first time. His flight from the claws of the mechanical hound, which represents all the imaginative technological skills of American society transformed into a ruthless monster and used to obliterate dissenting humanity, is like the flight of the phoenix born again. Not only is Montag a new person, but he also invigorates Faber, who feels alive for the first time in years. It is a period of war on all fronts, a period of destruction and negation which is reflective of the Cold War, the Korean War, and the oppressive political climate of the 1950s. Yet, there are signs that a new, more humane world might develop after the turmoil ends.

Montag's last phase of learning is a spiritual coming into his own. He escapes to the outside world and follows the abandoned railroad track which leads him to a man whose name, Granger, indicates that he is a shepherd. Granger takes him to the collective of rebels, who are largely intellectuals. Here Bradbury suggests—as he does in many of his works—that the anti-intellectual strain in America forces most intellectuals to take an outsider position from which it is difficult to influence people. The tendency in America is to drive forward without a humanistic intellectual core. Still, Montag learns that certain intellectuals have not abandoned the struggle to assert themselves and still want to assume a responsible role *within* society. Granger informs him:

> "All we want to do is keep the knowledge we think
> we will need, intact and safe. We're not out to incite
> or anger anyone yet. For if we are destroyed, the
> knowledge is dead, perhaps for good. We are model

citizens, in our own special way; we walk the old tracks, we lie in the hills at night, and the city people let us be. We're stopped and searched occasionally, but there's nothing on our persons to incriminate us. The organization is flexible, very loose, and fragmentary. Some of us have had plastic surgery on our faces and fingerprints. Right now we have a horrible job; we're waiting for the war to begin and, as quickly, end. It's not pleasant, but then we're not in control, we're the odd minority crying in the wilderness. When the war's over, perhaps we can be of some use in the world."

By the end of his adventures, there is very little that Montag can learn from his mentors anymore. That is, he will undoubtedly continue to share their knowledge, but he, too, has become an imparter of knowledge. He takes the world into himself and becomes at one with it. The notions of the Book of Ecclesiastes are carried by him, and he will spread its humanistic message to help heal the rifts in the world. There is a suggestion at the end of the novel that the American society is largely responsible for the wars and destruction brought upon itself. A time has come, a season, Montag envisions, for building up. He is no longer a fireman but a prophet of humanity. The dystopian critique gives way to a utopian vision.

In their book on science fiction, Robert Scholes and Eric Rabkin state that "dystopian fiction always reduces the world to a 'State,' and presents us with the struggles of an individual or a small group against that State." Later they amplify this statement by maintaining that "most twentieth-century writers have seen no way to get beyond the enslavement of technology, and we thus find a series of distinguished dystopias (like Huxley's *Brave New World,* 1932) that predict a dismal future for humanity. Some writers, however, have tried to get beyond this doom by postulating psychic growth or an evolutionary breakthrough to a race of superpeople. These tactics, of course, presume the possibility of a basic change in human nature; they do not so much see a way beyond technology as around it." In *Fahrenheit 451,* Bradbury depicts the struggle of the individual against the state, or individualism versus conformity. In the process, despite the overwhelming powers of state control through mass media and technology, he has his hero Montag undergo a process of rehumanization. That is, Montag must shed the influences of the state's monopoly of the consciousness industry and regain touch with his humanistic impulse. In this regard, Bradbury follows the postulates of dystopian fiction as outlined by Scholes and Rabkin. However, there is a curious twist to the "humanistic" impulse of Bradbury which accounts for great contradictions and quasi-elitist notions of culture in *Fahrenheit 451*.

Bradbury does not locate the source of destruction in the state, class society, or technology, but in humankind himself. He has remarked that "machines themselves are empty gloves. And the hand that fills them can be good or evil. Today we stand on the rim of space, and man, in his immense tidal motion, is about to flow out toward far new worlds . . . but he must conquer the seed of his own self-destruction. Man is half-idealist, half-destroyer, and the real and terrible fear is that he can still destroy himself before reaching for the stars. I see man's self-destructive half, the blind spider fiddling in the venomous dark, dreaming mushroom-cloud dreams. Death solves all, it whispers, shaking a handful of atoms like a necklace of dark beads." This is all rather poetic and virtuous, but it is also naive and simplistic because Bradbury, while recognizing the awesome power and tentacles of the state in *Fahrenheit 451,* shifts the blame for the rise of totalitarianism and technological determination onto man's "nature," as if there were something inherent in the constitution of humankind which predetermines the drives, wants, and needs of the masses. Both Beatty and Faber serve as Bradbury's mouthpiece here, and they depict a history in which the masses are portrayed as ignorant, greedy, and more interested in the comfort provided by technology than in creativity and humanistic communication. As we know, Beatty maintains that the different ethnic and minority groups had become offended by the negative fashion in which the mass media depicted them. Thus the machines and the mass media were compelled to eliminate differences and originality. The mass strivings of all these different groups needed more and more regulation and standardization by the state. Thus, individualism, uniqueness, and a critical spirit had to be phased out of the socialization process. Books had to be banned, and the mass media had to be employed to prevent human beings from critical deliberation and reflection.

This analysis exonerates the state and private industry from crimes against humanity and places the blame for destructive tendencies in American society on the masses of people who allegedly want to consume and lead lives of leisure dependent on machine technology. Bradbury portrays such an existence as living death, and only intellectuals or book-readers are capable of retaining their humanity because they have refused to comply with the pressures of "democracy" and the masses who have approved of the way in which the state uses technological control and provides cultural amusement. Faber makes this point even clearer than Beatty: "'The whole culture's shot through. The skeleton needs melting and reshaping. Good God, it isn't as simple as just picking up a book you laid down half a century ago. Remember, the firemen are rarely necessary. The public itself stopped reading of its own accord.'" Faber equates human beings with "squirrels" racing about cages and calls them the "solid unmoving cattle of the majority."

The dystopian constellation of conflict in *Fahrenheit 451* is not really constituted by the individual versus the state, but the intellectual versus the masses. The result is that, while Bradbury does amply reflect the means and ways the state endeavors to manipulate and discipline its citizens in the United States, he implies that the people, i.e., the masses, have brought this upon themselves and almost deserve to be blown up so that a new breed of book-lovers may begin to populate the world. (This is also suggested in *The Martian Chronicles* and such stories as "**Bright Phoenix**.") This elitist notion ultimately defeats the humanistic impulse in Bradbury's critique of mass technology and totalitarianism because he does not differentiate between social classes and their vested interests in America, nor can he explain or demonstrate from a political perspective—and essentially all utopian and dystopian literature is political—who profits by keeping people enthralled and unconscious of the vested power interests.

True, the quality of culture and life in the America of the 1950s had become impoverished, and machines loomed as an awesome threat since a military-industrial complex had been built during World War II and threatened to instrumentalize the lives of the populace. Nor has the quality been improved, or the threat diminished. But this deplorable situation is not due, as Bradbury would have us believe, to the "democratic" drives and wishes of the masses. Such basic critiques of society and technology as Herbert Marcuse's *One-Dimensional Man,* William Leiss's *The Domination of Nature,* and Harry Braverman's *Labor and Monopoly Capital* have shown that mass conformity has its roots in relations of private property and capital, not in the "nature" of humankind. In particular, Braverman provides an apt analysis of the degradation of work and life in the twentieth century. He focuses clearly on the problem which concerns Bradbury, yet which is distorted in the dystopian projection of *Fahrenheit 451:*

> The mass of humanity is subjected to the labor process for the purposes of those who control it rather than for any general purposes of 'humanity' as such. In thus acquiring concrete form, the control of humans over the labor process turns into its opposite and becomes the control of the labor process over the mass of humans. Machinery comes into the world not as the servant of 'humanity,' but as the instrument of those to whom the accumulation of capital gives the *ownership* of the machines. The capacity of humans to control the labor process through machinery is seized upon by management from the beginning of capitalism as the *prime means whereby production may be controlled not by the direct producer but by the owners and representatives of capital.* Thus, in addition to its technical function of increasing the productivity of labor—which would be a mark of machinery under any social system—machinery also has in the capitalist system the func-

tion of divesting the mass of workers of their control over their own labor. It is ironic that this feat is accomplished by taking advantage of the great human advance represented by the technical and scientific developments that increase human control over the labor process. It is even more ironic that this appears perfectly 'natural' to the minds of those who, subjected to two centuries of this fetishism of capital, actually see the machine as an alien force which subjugates humanity.

It might be argued that Bradbury has no sense of irony. Certainly his depiction of conformity and neo-fascism in America lacks subtle mediations, and thus the potential of his utopian vision wanes pale at the end of *Fahrenheit 451*. In fact, it is debatable whether one can call his ending utopian since it is regressive—it almost yearns for the restoration of a Christian world order built on good old American front porches. A group of intellectuals who memorize books are to serve as the foundation for a new society. There is a notion here which borders on selective breeding through the cultivation of brains. Moreover, it appears that the real possibility for future development is not in human potential but in the potential of books. That is, the real hero of *Fahrenheit 451* is not Montag but literature. This accounts for a certain abstract dehumanization of the characters in Bradbury's novel: they function as figures in a formula. They are sketchily drawn and have less character than the implied integrity of books. In essence, Bradbury would prefer to have a world peopled by books rather than by humans.

This becomes even more clear when we regard Francois Truffaut's film adaptation of *Fahrenheit 451*. Truffaut maintained that

> the theme of the film is the love of books. For some this love is intellectual: you love a book for its contents, for what is written inside it. For others it is an emotional attachment to the book as an object. . . . On a less individual and intimate level, the story interests me because it is a reality: the burning of books, the persecution of ideas, the terror of new concepts, these are elements that return again and again in the history of mankind . . . . In our society, books are not burnt by Hitler or the Holy Inquisition, they are rendered useless, drowned in a flood of images, sounds, objects. And the intellectuals, the real ones, the honest ones, are like Jews, like the Resistance; if you're a thinker in the world of objects, you're a heretic; if you're different, you're an enemy. A person who creates a crisis in society because he acknowledges his bad conscience—the living proof that not everyone has betrayed in exchange for a country house, for a car, or for a collection of electronic gadgets—he is a man to eliminate along with his books.

Though Truffaut's interpretation of Bradbury's novel is informed by his French consciousness and experience of fascism and the Resistance, he extends the basic theme of the novel to its most logical, universal conclusion. From the very beginning of the film, the heroes are the books themselves, and all of Truffaut's changes highlight the significance of the books. For instance they are always prominent in each frame in which they appear, and the characters are dwarfed by them in comparison. The people are less human, sexual, and alive than in Bradbury's novel. The divisions between good and evil become blurred so that all human beings without distinction share in the guilt for the mass degradation of humanity. The same actress plays Clarisse and Mildred; Montag becomes more ambivalent as a moral protagonist while his adversary Beatty becomes more sympathetic. The defenders of the books are not noble creatures, and, even in the last frame where people actually become books themselves, they are less significant than the literature and do not seem capable of communication. Annette Insdorf has pointed out that

> Truffaut's film explores the power of the word—but as a visual more than an oral entity. In a sense, the main characters are the books themselves. Truffaut even noted that he could not allow the books to fall out of the frame: "I must accompany their fall to the ground. The books here are characters, and to cut their passage would be like leaving out of frame the head of an actor." During the book-burning, close-ups of pages slowly curling into ashes look almost like fists of defiance. As in *The Soft Skin,* he suggests that the written word can capture and convey emotional depths, while the spoken is doomed to skim surfaces. The stylistic analogue to this sentiment can be found in the film's subordination of the dialogue to visual expression.

While it is true that both Bradbury and Truffaut desire to show that behind each book there is a human being, their obsession with books and literature leads them away from exploring the creative potential of people themselves, who are portrayed both in the novel and film as easily manipulated and devoid of integrity. In the film, the settings and costumes are both futuristic and contemporary, and they evoke a suburban, anonymous atmosphere. Conformity is the rule, and the landscape is frozen and sterile. Strange as it may seem, the book-lovers or exiles do not seem capable of breaking through the homogenized barren setting and congealed human relations. Again, this is due to Truffaut's adherence to the basic assumptions of Bradbury's critique, which retains its elitist notions and can only display frustration and contradictions. What is lacking in both novel and film is a more comprehensive grasp of the forces which degrade humanity and the value of literature. The dystopian constellation does not illuminate the path for resistance or alternatives because it obfuscates the machinations of the power relations of state and private industry which hinder humans from coming into their own. Bradbury in particular exhibits no faith in the masses while trying to defend humanity, and the dystopia which he constructs does not shed light on concrete utopian possibilities.

In Ernst Bloch's study of concrete utopias reflected by literature, he discusses the important notion of *Vor-Schein,* or anticipatory illumination, which is crucial for judging the social value of the imaginative conception. The symbols and chiffres of a literary work must illuminate the tendencies of reality and at the same time anticipate the potential within reality if they are seriously concerned with projecting the possibility for realizing concrete utopias, those brief moments in history such as the French Revolution, the Paris Commune, the October Revolution in Russia, etc., when actual models for egalitarian government and non-exploitative social relations were allowed to take form. The latent possibilities for such concrete utopias must be made apparent through the work of art, and their truth value depends on whether the artist perceives and captures the tendencies of the times. In discussing Bloch's philosophical categories and their significance for science fiction, Darko Suvin discusses anticipatory illumination in terms of the novum, "the totalizing phenomenon or relationship deviating from the author's and implied reader's norm of reality." Suvin maintains that "the most important consequence of an understanding of SF as a symbolic system centered on a novum which is to be cognitively validated within the narrative reality of the tale and its interaction with reader expectations is that the novelty has to be convincingly explained in concrete, even if imaginary terms, that is, in terms of the *specific* time, place, agents, and cosmic and social totality of each tale."

Like Bloch, Suvin uses this notion of novum to clarify the political and ethical function of utopian literature. The artistic depiction of social tendencies and the novum always indicates willy-nilly the actual possibilities for putting into practice new and alternative forms of human comportment which might enable humankind to emancipate itself from alienating and oppressive conditions. Bloch regards both life and art as a process with utopia serving as a beacon, illuminating those elements and moments which can bring to life what-has-not-been-realized:

> The lonely island, where utopia is supposed to lie, may be an archetype. However, it creates a stronger effect through ideal figures of a sought-after perfection, as free or ordered development of the contents of life. That is, the utopian function should essentially hold to the same line as the utopias themselves: the line of concrete mediation with an ideal tendency rooted in thematerial world, as mentioned before. In no way can the ideal be taught and reported through mere facts. On the contrary, its essence depends on its strained relationship to that which has become

merely factual. If the ideal is worth anything, then it has a connection to the process of the world, in which the so-called facts are reified and fixed abstractions. The ideal has in its anticipations, if they are concrete, a correlate in the objective contents of hope belonging to the latent tendency. This correlate allows for *ethical ideals as models, aesthetic ones as anticipatory illuminations which point to the possibility of becoming real.* Such ideals which are reported and delivered through a utopian function are then considered altogether as the content of a humanely adequate, fully developed self and world. Therefore, they are—what may here be considered in the last analysis as a summary or simplification of all ideal existence—collectively inflexions of the basic content—the most precious thing on earth.

Though Bradbury is idealistic, ethical, and highly critical of reified conditions in the America of the 1950s, the utopian function in *Fahrenheit 451* is predicated on a false inflexion of tendencies and contradictions in American society. The novum is not a true novelty allowing for qualitatively changed human relationships and social relations. Montag's learning experience reflects Bradbury's confused understanding of state control, education, private industry, and exploitative use of the mass media. Since he does not dig beneath the people and facts as they are, he cannot find the utopian correlate which points to realizable possibilities in the future. It is a far-fetched dream to have book-lovers and intellectuals as the progenitors of a new society, especially when they have an inaccurate notion of what led the "bad old" society to become fascist and militaristic. The ethical and aesthetic ideals in Bradbury's narrative are derived from an indiscriminate and eclectic praise of books per se. Despite his humanitarian intentions, Bradbury's hatred for the machine and consumer age, its effect on the masses, and the growing deterioration of the cultural level through the mass media led him to formulate romantic anticapitalist notions from an elitist point of view. Thus, what becomes significant about Bradbury's attempt to depict utopian possibilities for humankind individualized like a phoenix rising from the fire is his own contradictory relationship to America.

There is an acute tension between the intellectual and the majority of people in America. There is a disturbing element in the manner by which dissent and doubt are often buried in standard patriotic rhetoric in America. Yet, there are just as many intellectuals and book-lovers, often called mandarins, who upheld the formation of the military-industrial complex in the 1940s and 1950s, as there are those who dissented. To love a book or to be an intellectual is not, as Bradbury would have us believe, ideally ethical and humane. Writing at a time when the military-industrial complex was being developed and received the full support of the university system, Bradbury overlooked the interests of private corporations and complicitous network of intellectuals and book-lovers who havecreated greater instrumental control of the masses. Such an oversight short-circuits the utopian function of his books, and he remains blind to the intricacies of control in his own society. Books are not being burned with "1984" around the corner. Books are proliferating and being distributed on a massive scale. They are being received and used in manifold ways just as are the mass media such as television, film, radio, video—and not by a solid mass of cattle. The struggles of minority groups and women for equal rights and alternate technology and ecology point to certain massive contradictions which underlie the premise of *Fahrenheit 451*. If there is a utopian vision in Bradbury's novel, then it is based on a strange love of humanity and will surely never be concretized unless by books themselves.

William F. Touponce (essay date 1984)

SOURCE: "Reverie and the Utopian Novel," in *Ray Bradbury and the Poetics of Reverie: Fantasy, Science Fiction, and the Reader,* UMI Research Press, 1984, pp. 79-110.

[*In the following essay, Touponce examines the utopian construct and social criticism of* Fahrenheit 451 *through extensive analysis of dialectic; historical and psychological effect; and reader response.*]

Although the utopian novel addresses itself to a reader, literary criticism has been primarily concerned with the author's point of view, paying little attention to how the reader might be affected. One notable exception to this rule is Richard Gerber's *Utopian Fantasy,* which brings out the important role of reader expectation in such works. In following the theme of the utopian traveller in the evolution of utopian fiction since the end of the nineteenth century, he notes that the general aesthetic problem of utopian literature—how to present us with a society already made—inevitably involves the reader in a search for the past history of the society, what he calls the "utopian past."

If the writer of utopia could express the ideas of his hypothetical model of society directly in the experience of his characters, Gerber explains, he could dispense with the argumentative essays—the exposition of utopian life and passages of undigested social theory that often mar the attempt to create an effective utopian novel. But in practice this is nearly impossible to avoid. The new world is simply too unfamiliar. And the creator of a fictional utopia has to present us with a new construct that must be explained to the reader much as the naturalist writer explained society to his readers, but without the initial familiarity of the latter's scenes.

For the nineteenth century, Gerber points to the example of William Morris's *News from Nowhere* as being typical of how

the past is hardly ever made a dramatic problem. As in most utopian novels of this century, historical accounts or discussions of how the utopian society came to be are usually placed in a central part where afamiliar repertoire of characters engage one another. Usually, the stranger or utopian wise man (Old Hammond in Morri's novel) meet and discuss all the important questions connected with the subject. Gerber argues that few utopian novels of this sort are successful at making the society come alive for the reader because of the reader's position in the historical account—he is being passively informed rather than actively searching for the meaning of the utopian past for himself. These discursive passages, Gerber concludes, inevitably slow down the pace of the reader's exploration and discovery so that the reader is barely made to feel what it would be like to live in such a utopia. This last requirement Gerber takes to be the historical task of the utopian tradition and the uppermost desire of utopian authors throughout the historical period his book encompasses.

Gerber also observes what happens to the reader's role in twentieth century utopian fiction, where an assimilation of techniques from the modern novel enables utopian writers to effect their desire for a complete society on the reader with more direct means than didactic arguments and discussions. The imaginary journey with its functional type, the pseudonaive traveller who reminds us of the unreality of the utopian world by his very presence in it, gives way to a new kind of plot which he terms "completely utopian action." In this type of story (Gerber lists Orwell's *1984* and Huxley's *Brave New World* as examples) the historical account has been effectively absorbed into the structure of the novel. Interest centers in the utopian characters and their existential problems which are directly presented (we might say through the system of perspectives that Iser has outlined as the underlying structure of the novel). More importantly, the reader is acquainted with the utopian world by means of an initial shock or surprise (a defamiliarization, we might say) instead of a gradual transition. This surprise enables the utopian writer to attain the closest possible connection with the reader's present-day reality. The reader must of necessity try to familiarize himself with his estranged surroundings (by projecting images into the text). In this manner, and by individual strategies which we need not examine here, *1984* and *Brave New World* bring the reader to actively imagine the utopian society for himself: "At last the utopian writer's aim has been achieved: utopia has come alive, the reader becomes a citizen of the imaginary world."

This traditional desire to achieve the effect of an imaginary society goes along with Gerber's system of aesthetic values in utopian fantasy. Gerber proposes a series of touchstones for the successful utopian novel which can easily be integrated into Iser's theory. Gerber says that in general the reader must feel the presence of a consistently worked-out fundamental hypothesis, first by giving it imaginative reality and then by following it through all its ramifications. Furthermore, the utopian novel must present us with a society worked out in *suggestive* detail. The narrative must work on the reader's imagination with more than just statistics, arguments, or discussions. If there is any satire implicit in the contrast of the two societies (the reader's and theone presented in the book,) it cannot be merely didactic: the reader must feel it for himself. Most importantly for Gerber, the novel's imaginary society should seem to be alive, and we should be made to feel what it would be like to live in such a utopia (utopia must be given full ontological status as an imaginative reality—not written off by the author as just a "fantasy" as W. R. Irwin's study would seem to indicate). And finally, Gerber's aesthetic value system requires that after reading a negative utopia (dystopia or anti-utopia) the reader should be thoroughly and experientially dissatisfied with the present state of society: he will have worked out for himself through the exercise of his own utopian imagination the meaning of the novel's latent social criticism.

Beyond this modicum of expectation, we should refrain at the outset from imposing any abstract generic schemes on our reading of *Fahrenheit 451,* for those critics who have not done so have been led by their preconceptions to derive false interpretations from a true response. A good case in point is John Huntington's recent study of utopian and anti-utopian logic in the novel. Huntington claims that the novel moves from dystopia to utopia, from negative to positive without evoking any critical positions in between, and he thinks that this is a deep structural contradiction which cannot be mediated except in a "blurred" fashion (imagery and evocation rather than true thought): "The dystopian and utopian possibilities in the novel are thus represented by separate clusters of images that the novel finds unambiguous and leaves unchallenged." Indeed, in this view of the text, mediation produces horror rather than thought. Nature is good and technology is bad, but the ultimate horror is a mixture of the two, the mechanical hound, which combines the relentlessness of the bloodhound with the infallibility of technology.

But if both possibilities depend on systems of imagery that ignore contradictions, Huntington goes on to note the very presence of contradiction in the novel's central symbol:

> The interesting difficulty is where do books fit into this simple opposition? Since Gutenberg the book has been a symbol of technological progress. Bradbury counters this meaning of his symbol by reducing his pastoral, not to paper books, but to humans who remember books. Thus the replication and general availability that are books' virtues, but which the novel has seen as the instruments of the mass-culture that has ruined the world, are denied. We have the *idea* of the book without the *fact* of its production. Then, by becoming a general symbol of the past

now denied, the book becomes a symbol for all old values, but this symbolism brings up two difficulties. First, whatever good books have propagated, they have also preached the evils that have oppressed the world. The very technology that the novel finds threatening would be impossible without books. Second, books can readily inspire a repressive and tradition-bound pedantry which, while anti-technological, is also against nature.

One wonders how Huntington could have arrived at this awareness of contradictions if the novel in fact so studiously avoids them. Thus Huntington is confused by the end of the novel where he sees the moral vision of the novel and its ideal of radiant literacy made subject to a "titanic revision of values." But to read it this way would be to suppose that Bradbury is attempting anti-utopian thought, which he admits seems unlikely. These difficulties are the result of genre theory, narrowly conceived. If Huntington had remained true to his actual experience of reading, instead of trying to impose an abstract scheme on it, he would have been led to discover the complex dialectical process by which the social criticism of the novel is effected and to a clearer perception of its themes. On the oneiric level, mediations are everywhere suggested, and as we will show later they evoke anything but horror.

The reader's search for the meaning and significance of utopia is in essence the subject of the book, as should be obvious from the fact that the protagonist, Montag the fireman, is caught up as a reader himself in the very contradictions Huntington mentions. This is what makes the book's portrayed world so dramatic and easily realized (quite apart from the fact that fire itself easily and dramatically brings about the phenomena of a fantastic world). Its main hypothesis—that technology, mass culture, and minority pressure brought about the world we see portrayed in the novel—is indeed made concrete for the reader *because* of the very contradictions of books. I do not mean that *Fahrenheit 451* is contradictory in the sense that it refutes its own hypothesis, but only that it does not deny the negative and contradictory values of books themselves. Why this negative value needs to be preserved is something we can now elaborate on.

Fahrenheit 451 makes vivid for the reader the whole problematic course of Western enlightenment that culminated in technology and the positivistic processes of thought its worldwide dominance have brought about. In order to know nature objectively we in a sense misrecognize or forget ourselves as part of nature. The price of progress is brought about by a kind of oblivion, like that of a surgical operation on our bodies during which we were unconscious or anesthetized. Consciousness once more restored, we find it difficult to bridge the gap between our present and our past: "The loss of memory is a transcendental condition for science. All objectification is a forgetting." The disenchantment of nature and myth brings about a certain triumph of man over his fears, but by defining man in opposition to nature it sets up a program for domination and so reverts to barbarism and mythic repetition. Thus like the phoenix symbol used in the novel, history in *Fahrenheit 451* appears to go in cycles. The irony seems to be that the capacity to know and represent the world to ourselves is the measure of our domination of it, but domination—power and knowledge—are the things most often represented. Language itself (as that of Fire Chief Beatty in the novel) is used deceitfully as a tool for domination: "The capacity of representation is the vehicle of progress and regression at the same time."

It is understandable then that this dialectical process is represented in *Fahrenheit 451* as a fantastic reversal of the real world. Firemen who should control fires (perhaps the ultimate symbol of technology in the novel) are lighting them instead. The reader is at first surprised by this when the novel opens immediately with a scene of house burning or arson in which Montag takes pleasure in burning books, and it sets him off on his quest for understanding the relationship between this fantastic world and his own. It is also therefore a contradiction within the imagery system of the dystopian world itself, for how can the technological world be represented by natural imagery? It seems that we must find a non-alienating way to represent the demands of unrecognized nature. Fire in this world can only be ironic enlightenment.

The principles of this false enlightenment are made apparent to the reader by the book's vitriolic attack on mass culture, which turns out to be a permanent denial of pleasure despite the power it displays and promises. No modern utopian novel insists more than *Fahrenheit 451* on the nonidentity of culture and society. The book struggles at every point to double or split the reader's forced and false identification with the society which has nurtured him. It compels the reader to discover for himself the passivity of the subject in mass culture, his loss of critical autonomy and freedom, and the general decline of negative critical forces in society—forces which could lead to a critique of existing conditions if not to utopia. This splitting constantly happens to Montag in his readings and is dramatized especially in the second part of the novel. It is here that the book registers a deeply felt fear that mass culture is threatening to collapse art as an autonomous realm of utopian freedom into the mere mechanical reproduction and repetition of the economic base. Why are books banned in this society? The reader discovers with Montag that they are the only thing left which harbors the forces of negation or principles through which the world around us could be made to appear false and alienating (what the implied author obviously thinks is the case). As the utopian wise man Faber says, books show the pores in the face of life, its gaps and discontinuities.

But what role does reverie have in the novel? This only emerges clearly in the third part of the novel when Montag has escaped the city. The third part of Bradbury's hypothesis is realized here. It was minority pressure which combined with the other two forces which eventually led to the need for everyone to be the same—to narcissism, in short. People must be mirror images of each other which means that they never have any real contact with a world outside themselves. And advertising and other media techniques are bent on artificially stimulating the consumption of grandiose images of the self within the city itself. This psychological theme is very prominent in *Fahrenheit 451,* and it is surprising that no critic has made much of it since Kingsley Amis twenty years ago.

Amis argued that the lesson to be drawn from *Fahrenheit 451* is not only that a society could be devised that would frustrate active virtues, nor even that these could eventually be suppressed, butthat there is in all kinds of people something that longs for this to happen. This need presupposes not some kind of overt political action (indeed, no violent military takeover or class struggle is indicated in the novel), but a tendency in human behavior that could be reinforced if certain tendencies presently at work in society were not corrected or mitigated. Analyzing a scene from *Fahrenheit 451* in which Mildred, Montag's wife, is near suicide from a drug overdose and is listening only to the noise of an electronic Seashell, he concludes that it demonstrates to him a "fear of pleasure so overmastering that it can break down the sense of reality or at least the pattern of active life, and break them down in everyone, not merely in the predisposed neurotic." Now, it is the experience of reverie in the third part of the novel which connects us to a real natural world (an arcadian utopia, in fact) outside the narcissism of the city. The reader rediscovers through a long water-reverie, which is the exact opposite of Mildred's, the archetypes of utopian satisfaction. We experience with Montag a non-alienating relationship to nature, and this experience of the imaginary, of another world not based on domination, enables us to effect an oneiric criticism of technological society.

It is Bradbury's strategy to link initially the experience of reverie and world with Clarisse, Montag's teenage neighbor. Montag knows that all books that are works of art are connected with her in some way, for she awakens in him the desire to read (to create an imaginary world). But we must also be given some distance from this experience of the imaginary if we are to effect social criticism. To identify completely with a character in a novel or play, as Madame Bovary and Don Quixote do, to become the book, is romantic madness and Faber tells Montag so in the book's central section. This sort of narcissism is resisted early in the book; the reader is repeatedly split, and we should therefore not be surprised at the end when Granger, the leader of the book people, tells Montag that he is not important, but the book he remembers is. Books must preserve their independent, autonomous and negative character, if they are to aid us in transforming basic impulses in the personality such as narcissism. Works of art, therefore, by representing deprivation as negative retract, as it were, the prostitution of the utopian impulse by the culture industry and rescue by mediation what was denied: "The secret of aesthetic sublimation is its representation of fulfillment as a broken promise. The culture industry does not sublimate; it represses." In Bradbury's novel media are not mediations unless they have some historical content to transform in the first place. Books are the repositories of that content, the novel's utopian past.

So Bradbury's novel is itself negative in representing utopia as a broken promise and pessimistic to the extent that utopian alternatives seem to be preserved nowhere else than in the damaged lives of cultural outsiders. Yet it must be that Bradbury believes that social freedom is inseparable from enlightened thought, from remembering the mistakes of the past and not from forgetting them, because he holds out the promise that after this new Dark Age man may begin again. At the end of *Fahrenheit 451* books are no longersymbols of technological progress—of power and knowledge—but rather of wisdom.

Yet it must be that Bradbury believes that social freedom is inseparable from enlightened thought, from remembering the mistakes of the past and not from forgetting them, because he holds out the promise that after this new Dark Age man may begin again. At the end of *Fahrenheit 451* books are no longer symbols of technological progress—of power and knowledge—but rather of wisdom.

—William F. Touponce

Roughly, that is the course of the reader's discovery in the novel. It remains to be shown in detail how the reader builds up an understanding of these themes by means of a repertoire of patterns serving an overall strategy through which the world of *Fahrenheit 451* is presented. As previously mentioned, there are two opposed imagery systems in the novel. They have been isolated and independently studied by thematic criticism, as has the elaborate system of allusions and quotations in the novel. They are in fact two different modes of fantasy, one leading to existential and reflexive use of the imagination in which the self can represent a world to itself in a non-alienated fashion, the other undermining the self's ability to conceive of anything outside of a fragmented dream. Together they constitute the poles of the suspended system

of equivalences that the reader activates in reading the novel, which unfolds in a dialectical three-part structure as I have indicated.

In a first reading, and not by reading selectively to illustrate the imaginative and moral values of the novel, as we will do in a moment, the reader of *Fahrenheit 451* is immediately struck by the fact that the implied author has chosen to select and "depragmatize" a certain mode of fantasy as representing the dominant ideological systems of the fifties. Why, the reader asks, has this one been chosen and not another? Specifically, why is Montag's job (which is supposedly so important to the maintenance of order) treated as a carnival, and why is he a kind of clown? Why is happiness and not freedom the ideal of this society?

This simultaneous evocation and depragmatization of images representing the "culture industry" (*Kulturindustrie*—the term is Theodor Adorno's) leads the reader to project acts of consciousness into the text under conditions very different from that in which he experiences these media in real life. The reader thereby discovers deficiencies or contradictions inherent in such a system. The selection and intensification of Freudian fantasy (perhaps best exemplified by his book *The Interpretation of Dreams,* which discusses the unconscious processes involved in the dream's staging and representation of fulfilled desire) by the repertoire brings the reader to discover a destructive core of narcissism pervading the world of the novel, and by direct implication, the society around him.

I find that Christopher Lasch's *The Culture of Narcissism* (1979) simplifies but still gets at the essential criticism that Bradbury's reader has to enact. Lasch's point is that people in the "society of the spectacle" (and by that he means the specific social and economic environment of the post-World War II period) have lost the experience of real satisfaction because of the fabrication of so many pseudo-needs by industrial civilization. Uninterrupted advertising transmitted by mass media uses Freudian images of utopian satisfaction not so much to create desire (which in Freud's system is related to a lost object anyway) as to activate anxiety about one's self-image. Indeed, the similarities are so striking in so many details that I am tempted to agree with French post-structuralist thinkers such as Louis Marin who argue that at a determined moment of history, utopian textual practice sketches or schematizes unconsciously, by the spatial plays of its internal differences (non-congruences), the empty places (topics) which will be filled by the concepts of social theory in a later phase of history. To write a utopia is to *indicate* what cannot yet be *said* within the available language.

But this would be to deconstruct my own phenomenological project, perhaps the subject for a future book, but hardly compatible with my view here of the temporal unfolding of meaning for the reader of *Fahrenheit 451,* which, as in all fantasy based on reverie, exists in a realm between the unspeakable and the conceptually spoken, the realm of the poetic word. It would also be to deny that the utopian novel can effect critical thought in the reader, is more than a "neutralization" of society's contradictions. For the moment it is best to bracket the relationship between social theory and literature, although Bradbury's book did appear at a time when many studies purported to analyse the psychological impact of social changes on character structure: Eric Fromm's "market-oriented personality," or William H. Whyte's famous "organization man" being two obvious examples. It may be, as Lasch says, that these social theorists mistook the bland surface of American sociability for the deeper reality, which he believes was the creation of a narcissistic personality amenable to social domination, but such arguments, interesting as they are in themselves, would take us too far afield.

In any case Bradbury does lay bare the hidden violence and emptiness of this sort of personality. The reader cannot organize the image-sequences of the programmed fantastic (or so I term the fantasy of the telescreens) which represents the world of appearances, into a coherent experience. Furthermore, we are made aware by a constant ironic switching of character perspectives that the self-mastery and happiness preached by the advocates of this mode of fantasy is completely false. Their inner selves are exposed as chaotic and impulse-ridden. Both Fire Chief Beatty and Mildred are deeply suicidal.

Once the reader discovers that Freudian fantasy has been selected to personify negative trends in our society (especially advertising and debased romantic fantasies, "the Clara Dove five-minuteromance"), he is also led, through the activation of his own archetypal imagination in reverie, to seek out and consider solutions to the problems raised by the programmed fantastic. This is tied together with Montag's search for the utopian past, as I have mentioned, and his readings produce a system of allusions and quotations which guide us in this process by stimulating, however briefly, the experience of the imaginary, the promise of a world of meaning that can only be given through literature. Thus both modes of fantasy converge on the problem of utopia through a process of coherent deformation, a reciprocal projection and contrast of images drawn from both systems.

The search for answers to the utopian past is, as Gerber indicates, an aspect of plot which needs to be integrated into the experience of the main character. *Fahrenheit 451* accomplishes this through its strategies. In particular, the experience of literacy as a new psychic faculty is organized by a theme-and-horizon strategy which now foregrounds and now allows to be part of the background the reading of forbidden books. This strategy controls the dialectical contradictions experienced by Montage, who goes from being a burner of books curious about what they contain, to a Promethean reader

who wants to redeem all culture, to a chastened man who assumes responsibility for his existence, and, by resolutely committing himself to memorize a part of the Bible, for the healing of others. The plot of *Fahrenheit 451,* if we wanted to discuss it apart from the demands of signification made on the reader, is not simply an inversion from positive to negative or vice-versa. The mediations go from ignorance to knowledge and from knowledge to its enunciation as the novel ends.

Despite the apparent oppositional arrangement of the repertoire, which would seem to require that the text set norms against one another by showing up the deficiencies of each norm when viewed from the standpoint of the others, in a process of reciprocal negation and continual conflict, in actuality the strategy embodied in *Fahrenheit 451* is much simpler, closer to what Iser terms the counterbalancing arrangement, and to the traditional utopian novel. In this arrangement the elements of the repertoire allotted to different perspectives form a very definite hierarchy. Qualities and defects of the perspectives are clearly graded. The hero represents the principal perspective through which a catalogue of norms is unfolded. In *Fahrenheit 451* Montag is intended to be an effective counterbalancing visualization of that which the society of spectacles seems to exclude—an exemplary concern for the rights of others and a world outside the self. Nevertheless, the norms of the culture industry take place in a context of negated and negating perspectives—a context quite different from the system out of which they were selected. This is tantamount to saying that the reader becomes aware of the influences and functions they perform in real life. And Clarisse, a minor character by objective standards because she disappears early in the novel, is in essence the inspirational anima figure of Montag's quest. She represents those imaginative values he lacks and which he must acquire. Otherwise the social norms and imaginative values of the repertoireare assigned to perspectives that are subtly undermined. Those characters attracted to fantasy-spectacle (Mildred and Fire Chief Beatty) have complexes which reveal a hidden ontological insecurity which they have not consciously faced. Even Faber's ideal of radiant literacy is undercut, but self-consciously by himself.

What this amounts to saying is that the reader must pay special attention to the oneiric level of the text, the transcendental vantage point which eventually he must build up in order to have a coherent aesthetic response to the text's world and from which the events and characters are to be imagined. Nowhere is this more necessary than in the case of the mechanical hound and the sense of uneasiness it is intended to provoke. This feeling of uneasiness or uncanniness is linked to the oneiric strategy of making the reader become aware of the nonidentity of society and culture. The reader must be doubled or made self-conscious of it. Treated objectively (as Huntington and W. R. Irwin seem to do) the hound represents another character perspective, a failed mediation, or the dragon on Montag's quest. On the oneiric level of significance, however, it is the embodiment of the uncanny return of our existential problems that we have attempted to banish with the use of technology. It represents also the history of repressed nature which follows its own underground logic: "It was like a bee come home from some field where the honey is full of poison wildness, of insanity and nightmare, its body crammed with that overrich nectar . . ."

Huntington says that mediation in this novel produces only horror, which is a true response on the affective level, but it is also a contradiction or negation or mediation because the reader wants to know why technology is represented by alienated natural imagery. Interpreted in a dialectical-historical fashion, these images yield up their truth and cognitive value: this is not the utopian nectar of the gods on Olympus, offering eternal bliss, but that of some dark underworld; it is surely not wisdom or spiritual riches either, but the representation of the productivity and abundance of nature gone awry. What is "that overrich nectar"? The obedient activity of dominated nature, the bee, produces only poison for us by some process that is now mysterious. Like a nightmare it seems alien to conscious life, and cannot be integrated into it. Yet the bee has come home to its hive, our society, and is familiar to us. The material imagination aids us in understanding the oneiric level of significance here, which is much more than metaphor, and in transforming historical content. Thus the reader's response has to be both cognitive and sublimative; he is doubled or split by the initial uncanniness, but in responding he must make full use of his humanity.

W. R. Irwin's response to the novel is interesting in this regard, for he reports that the mechanical hound evokes no uneasiness in him and that the reader is not doubled. Irwin's rhetoric of fantasy, *The Game of the Impossible,* argues that the reader's role in any fantasy text is a kind of "dual participation" because fantasy is a demonstrational narrative dominated by intellectual persuasion. The reader is persuaded by the author's rhetoric to accept an "anti-fact" which is then developed by intellectual play. But the reader must be kept continuously aware that he is engaged with the impossible as a factitious reality—there can be no surprises or ambiguities about the rules of the game of the impossible (Irwin's theory is in fact the exact logical opposite of Todorov's). The reader "must feel at all times intellectually 'at home' in the narrative and yet maintain his sense of intellectual alienation as a means of reflecting on the displaced real." According to Irwin, *Fahrenheit 451* is not a fantasy because its narrative does not deal with the impossible and does not evince utopian thinking that asserts and plays with the idea of an impossible society. Incredibly, Irwin bases these conclusions not on an analysis of the reader's role in *Fahrenheit 451,* or even on a consideration of what the generic role of the reader is in utopian fantasy, but on the supposed science-fiction *content* of the novel.

Science fiction, he says, while it may deal with the improbable, does not assert "the thing which is not." After summarizing the plot of the novel he goes on to affirm:

> My point is that all the devices by which tyranny is secured either exist at present or may be foreseen as probable technological developments of the near future. Even the Mechanical Hound puts no strain on belief; it is a not very daring instance of the malevolent robot. And we are all used to robots. I feel safe in saying that no machine that possesses super-animal or superhuman capabilities can prompt a reader to say "impossible."

Quite apart from the fact that this analysis cannot be made to agree with Irwin's own normative statement that "to define a genre by its material content alone is a mistake," one senses in the background and from his disparagement of reverie in general the presence of a non-dialectical Aristotelian logic with its categories of probable, improbable and impossible. This sort of logic cannot deal with dialectical contradiction or the Freudian logic of the uncanny. Irwin reports that he "feels safe" in his response to the mechanical hound, but also that the narrative did not make him feel at home while engaging in a game of contradictory credences (in other words, this is science fiction, not fantasy; but we are all familiar with robots). Again one wonders whether a true response has been falsified by the imposition of a foreign logical scheme. The recognition that we are the source of strangeness, and that we cannot escape our existential problems by the use of technology and representational logic, constitutes an uncanny feeling to say the least.

In what follows I shall be concerned only to point out instances of the reader's developing response to the oneiric level of the text. Limitations of space forbid my giving a narrative reading as in previous chapters.

In part I, "The Hearth and the Salamander," the main events are the opening scene of arson, already mentioned, Montag's meeting with Clarisse, Mildred's attempted suicide, our first encounter with the mechanical hound, another fire in which an old woman chooses to die with her books (and during which Montag steals a volume), Clarisse's disappearance, Montag's subsequent illness or alienation from his work, and Beatty's attempt to win him back through a defense of utopia. It ends with Montag's decision to find out for himself whether books contain anything worth dying for.

How are these events and characters to be imagined? To begin with, the title of this section is clearly ironic, for houses in this future society have all been "fireproofed." There is no possibility for a fireside reverie in which man might find repose in centering his consciousness on a specific object. The landscape is instead infested with a cold mythical beast, the fire engine/Salamander that "spits its venomous kerosene upon the world." Montag is also a part of this landscape, and his complex emerges in the following lines: ". . . his hands were the hands of some amazing conductor playing all the symphonies of blazing and burning to bring down the tatters and charcoal ruins of history." One critic has called it a "Nero complex" and I see no reason to change this designation. Besides, it provides a useful semantic index for the reader in later contexts where the complex is being transformed. In the second part, where Montag learns from Faber that books are a counter force to man's narcissism, he is told that books exist to remind us "'. . . what asses and fools we are. They're Caesar's praetorian guard, whispering as the parade roars down the avenue. Remember, Caesar, thou art mortal.'" And in the third part, Granger further tells Montag to forget security, to see the world outside himself that is more fantastic than any dream made or paid for in the factories of the culture industry, to hate the Roman named Status Quo.

The first step towards the transformation of this complex is Montag's meeting with Clarisse on a moonlit sidewalk on his way home from work. Ostensibly happy and adjusted to his work and society, a minstrel man, Montag is gently divided against himself during their encounter:

> He saw himself in her eyes, suspended in two shining drops of bright water, himself dark and tiny, in fine detail, the lines about his mouth, everything there, as if her eyes were two miraculous bits of violet amber that might capture and hold him intact. Her face, turned to him now, was fragile milk crystal with a soft and constant light in it. It was not the hysterical light of electricity but—what? But the strangely comfortable and rare and gently flattering light of the candle. One time, as a child, in a power-failure, his mother had found and lit a last candle and there had been a brief hour of rediscovery, of such illumination that space lost its vast dimensions and drew comfortably around them, and they, mother and son alone, transformed, hoping that the power might not come on again too soon . . .

Himself reflected in minuscule in the miraculous water of Clarisse's eyes, in fine aesthetic detail, Montag is given a tranquil affirmation of his being. The material imagination is present here in amber, the scented hardened fossil resin "wept"from trees. This substance is naturally miraculous because it preserves fossils and time. Montag can see himself in the heart of matter, transparent, in tact, and living (unlike the melted tallow skin of his false face which comes later). The amber is oneirically appropriate for Clarisse (and her object reveries), expressing her love and knowledge of the natural world and the past. But more significantly, a world of intersubjectivity is granted here: in the instantaneous moment of the image, which usually inaugurates reverie, Montag re-

discovers a dimension of consciousness lost to this society which paradoxically is saturated with image-spectacles (so much so that he wears a fiery permanent smile on his face, as if he were being recorded and simultaneously transmitted to an unseen audience—another aspect of narcissism). On the level of reflexive reading indicated here, this passage shows us what a reverie text can do, namely, mirror the process of intersubjectivity in reading, of that moment when we feel another consciousness enclosing ours.

Furthermore, this reassuring act of consciousness is tied to our experience of childhood in subtle ways. Husserl, the founder of phenomenology as the eidetic science of the possible structures of consciousness, argued that the first formal act (*der erste Aktus*) that constitutes the child *as* child is an act of empathy stemming from the felt awareness of the other (usually the mother's face or glance) and the subsequent communicating and working with the other. Husserl suggests that through the act of empathy the child comes to see itself as appearing for the other, in the other's surrounding world, and, at the same time, the child comes to see the other as appearing for the child, in the child's life-world. For Husserl, the mirroring structure of the glance is founded on the recognition of the other as an entity existing independently of the child, though supporting him. It is an act of consciousness that opens also new possibilities of love and empathic being, possibilities of transcendence towards a common horizon, instead of the infinite repetition of the same. Such phenomenological interrelatedness gives rise, he says, "to an infinite reciprocal 'mirroring' . . . an unlimited reiteration which is a potentiality for levels of empathy." Thus Montag is brought back to his childhood and the security of reverie in a single instant.

This movement of consciousness is clarified and developed when Montag searches for an equivalent to the soft constant light of Clarisse's face and discovers the memory of a utopian past in a reverie towards childhood that is the opposite of the fantasy world of the programmed fantastic (here represented by the hysterical light of electricity). The light of her face is not the hysterical light of electricity, but the generic light of *the* candle, the light of reverie texts, a humanized light lacking in this technologically oriented society. That light which is strangely comfortable and gently flattering (already the candle speaks poetically and we can imagine an admiring glance between self and world) assures the reader that he is going to discover in this passage the shadings of an ontology of well-being, or reverie. The candlelight which gathers dispersed being around the dreamerawakens the reflexive dimension of consciousness lost to this society: reading.

By leaving the end of his last sentence blank and in suspension, "hoping that the power might not come on again too soon . . . ," Bradbury structures a gap which the reader has to fill in with his own imagination of what the mother and son *did.* after they lit the candle and space lost its vast dimensions, drawing comfortably around them in humanized reverie. In that brief hour of rediscovery where the mother and son are transformed, I imagine they are reading, perhaps even a book of fairy tales. And as Bachelard indicates in a book devoted entirely to a philosophic meditation on reveries of the candle flame, the lifting force of this vertical-tending reverie is the most liberating of all, especially when it dreams of another possible world above the prosaically horizontal, or in the case of the programmed fantastic, circular, life. In oneiric terms, the candle flame is both strange and comfortable because it allows for shadows (indeed, shadows seem part of its valiant struggle to be) and for the unconscious mind under the beneficial influence of the anima to make the candle flame's struggle for illumination and its frail vertical existence into our own because of our own desire for transcendence. The flames of hell are certainly transforming, but they belong properly to the fantastic, not to the delicate penumbral ontology of Bachelardian reverie where the values of the dream and reality can be freely explored.

So the oneiric level of significance discovered by Montag in his reverie of the candle's flame is very much the opposite of the on/off logic of the light switch which controls the source of illumination in these "fire-proofed" houses. Our only role in technological illumination is to be the mechanical subject of a mechanical gesture. "We have entered in the era of administered light," Bachelard says of our loss of the ability to make the light of candles and lamps our own through reverie, humanizing the world and making ourselves at home in it. Bradbury would seem to agree, for mother and son are very much at home in the solitude of the candle flame. Having gathered our reverie of verticality around us, and having glimpsed with Montag the possibility of transcendence of his situation, we can well understand their hopeful consciousness that the lights will not come on again too soon and destroy the beneficial influence of reading in anima.

If I seem to stress Clarisse unduly, it is because her perspective is held up as one of the ideals of the novel, at least initially. Her reveries in which consciousness intimately touches the reality of the material universe offset the erosion of Montag's capacity to dream. Through his encounters and talks with her he rediscovers the power of reading in anima (and later, when he begins to read more resolutely, he realizes that "These men have been dead a long time, but I know their words point, one way or another, to Clarisse.") Although she is presumed dead early in the novel, her spirit returns in the third section when Montag is finally able to represent a utopian experience to himself.

A gentle hunger and curiosity, a desire to look at things as epiphanies of a marvelous reality, pervades the presence in the novel of this anima figure. Obviously she has a very deep sympathy with nature. When Montag first meets her out walking one enchanted moonlit night, the leaves and the wind seem to carry her forward like a wood spirit along the sidewalk. Her unique slender face is wholly outward-looking, nourishing itself on things. Furthermore she constantly probes Montag's identification with his job by asking him questions ("Do you ever *read* any of the books you burn?"), shocks him with her knowledge of the past (firemen once put out fires instead of lighting them) and of the present (how advertising billboards have been made two hundred feet long so that speeding drivers can read them, whereas grass is a green blur, cows are brown blurs). She lives surrounded by a loving family in a house brightly lit at night where Montag can hear human conversation weaving its magic spell.

Bachelard tells us that the subject in reverie is astonished to receive the image, astonished and awakened. When Montag's capacity for reverie is awakened, it is always Clarisse's face (her very name is a simulacrum of reflected light) that will guide him: "The girl's face was there, really quite beautiful in memory: astonishing, in fact." But her own reveries are object reveries, a simple faithfulness to the familiar object. Bachelard says that in object reveries we learn to dream near things and explore our attachment to the world. Clarisse tries to stimulate these reveries in Montag. She leaves a bouquet of late autumn flowers on his porch, or a handful of chestnuts in a little sack or some autumn leaves neatly pinned to a sheet of white paper and thumbtacked to his door. Although her reveries are not the complexly layered structures of consciousness that Montag will develop in his long water reverie, she can do things with a common dandelion flower that reveal Montag's inner being. Her consciousness is infused with objects of the world: there seems to be no distance between them and her, so faithful and welcoming is her glance. Clarisse is truly one of Bachelard's dreamers of looking (*rêveurs du regard*) who can raise objects to a level of poetic existence, and therefore of human existence.

In addition to awakening wonder in the contemplation of the ordinary itself (we are told her face is "fragile milk-crystal," a seemingly commonplace object but evoking at the same time a recognition of it as an exceptional phenomenon, a cool stillness in a world of fiery conflagrations) Clarisse does three things for Montag. First of all, Montag receives from her gaze not a narcissistic mirror image, but a tranquil affirmation of his existence, which is also an act of empathy and a genuine intersubjective relation with an other. Second, she awakens in him an other experience of temporality, an ontological sensitization to the future. The girl's simple wonder at the things of this world (her pale surprise, the narrator says) make her fore-sighted in a utopian sense. Third, she contributes to the level of reflexive reading in the text by stimulating Montag's reading in anima. The second and perhaps most utopian of these accomplishments emerges inthe following passage, where the narrative mode creates the effect of a strange mental process (reverie) suddenly intruding into Montag's mind:

Montag shook his head. He looked at a blank wall. The girl's face was there, really quite beautiful in memory: astonishing in fact. She had a very thin face like the dial of a small clock seen faintly in a dark room in the middle of the night when you waken to see the time and see the clock telling you the hour and the minute and the second, with a white silence and a glowing, all certainty and knowing what it has to tell of the night passing swiftly on toward further darknesses, but moving also toward a new sun.

"*What?*" asked Montag of that other self, the subconscious idiot that ran babbling at times, quite independent of will, habit, and conscience.

Here we can observe a penumbral reverie forming in Montag's mind, beginning with the astonishment of the image (the girl's face in memory), then moving on to a search for an equivalent to that astonishment, a clock seen in the middle of the night upon awakening, and then onward to a sequence where technological segments of time (hours, minutes, seconds) are more and more minutely divided, until only a durational flow, a continuous pulse of experiential time, remains. Montag awakens to discover a new consciousness of time as sustaining the forms of life instead of destroying them. The clock's face is a white silence and a glowing. Like the moon in Montag's long water reverie in the novel's concluding section, it shines by reflected light, not burning time, but telling us where we are. Compensating Montag for a lack in his conscious mind, Clarisse enables him to project unconscious feminine values. An image received from the anima puts Montag's mind in a state of continuous reverie; it is a time fully experienced and filled, disclosing to Montag an inexhaustible reserve of latent life. As Bachelard says, the clock of the feminine runs continuously in a duration that slips peacefully away, but the masculine clock is composed of technological segments, jerks of time, so many projects and ways of not being present to oneself.

One has the sense here also of being guided by the anima figure, because the feminine clock is certain of what it tells Montag: the darkness of the night will get darker, but there is no need for despair; we are also moving toward a new sun. We feel reassured in this strange new experience of time. Montag's reverie begins in memory (perhaps a memory of childhood, of awakening from a nightmare), but opens up to the future, toward not-yet-being, a pattern of consciousness which splits Montag from his identification with his social mask or persona. It lays down the temporal pattern of Montag's utopian longings.

On the oneiric level, meaning is constituted here by Montag's questioning "*'What'?*" directed towards that "other self," the archetypal shadow, which he has taken previously to be a fool butwhich he will want to educate through reading. Prior to this scene, Clarisse and Montag walk together for perhaps five minutes of objective clock time, yet now that time seems immense and numinous to him. The narrator says that her slender figure throws an "immense shadow" on the stage of his imagination. Indeed, it is clear that she reveals to him *his* shadow, without which he would be a one-dimensional man, his shadow which represents the large undiscovered part of himself that this society has repressed and excluded. In the Jungian development of individuation, the persona is the counterpart to the shadow, and its original existence is prompted to a large extent by the need to repress material inconsistent with the social environment. Until he meets Clarisse, Montag's ego is largely fused with his persona as a fireman, but the anima intervenes between these two figures and allows him to deal with his shadow in a manageable and integrative way, although not without a certain amount of anguish when the desire for illumination, expressed as a candle flame, becomes opaque and consciousness thickens into the substance of unhappiness:

> He felt his smile slide away, melt, fold over and down on itself like a tallow skin, like the stuff of a fantastic candle burning too long and now collapsing and now blown out. Darkness. He was not happy. He said the words to himself. He recognized this as the true state of affairs. He wore his happiness like a mask and the girl had run off across the lawn with the mask and there was no way of going to knock on her door and ask for it back.

Here Montag is beginning to make the transition from identification with society to open rebellion against it. His unhappiness is further deepened by his discovery of Mildred's attempted suicide. She is Clarisse's opposite, a true victim of consumer culture. Inwardly, she is a frightened child in despair about ever knowing reality. Outwardly, however, she is an advertising man's dream, addicted to novelty, gadgets, and anxiety-easing pills, Her hair is burnt by chemicals to a brittle straw, her body thin as a praying mantis from dieting. Montag's relationship to her is always "mediated" by some desiring-machine of the media. At night she lies in bed with the little Seashells (remember Johnny Bishop, our other dreamer of the sea, and how he escaped the adult world?) or thimble radios, tamped tight in her ears, "and an electronic ocean of sound, of music and talk and music and talk coming in, coming in on the shore of her unsleeping mind." This is hardly a natural reverie of sea, since it is programmed by the media, and the fact that it is so unsatisfying in indicated by the fact that Mildred is unsleeping and suicidal: "There had been no night in the last two years that Mildred had not swum that sea, had not gladly gone down in it for the third time." Mildred is an expert at lip reading (ten years of study in this technique having been provided by the Seashell corporation) and when she has the Seashells in her ears, conversation is reduced to a kind of pantomime. The only thing Mildred seems to desire is the fourth parlor wall "to make the dream complete." If they had a fourth wall, she argues, then the room wouldn't be theirs anymore, but would belong to "all kinds of exotic people."

As Lasch has indicated, this is the pattern of pathological narcissism that advertising and consumer culture have reinforced through stimulating the desire to consume grandiose images of the self. Mildred's intrapsychic world is so thinly populated, consisting of these shadowy and specular images, that Montag in a moment of oneiric insight (derived, it is clear, from his dialogues with Clarisse,) senses the effect on Mildred's inner world of these mindless conversations emanating from the fantasy people who inhabit the T.V. walls. Mildred is the little girl of a fairy tale, lost, however, without the hope traditionally granted to heroines by the spirit-figures of this genre which Jung has identified (the anima herself, the wise old man, the archetype of the tree of life which Montag rediscovers at the novel's end). Mildred cannot find a way out of this insane asylum where the walls are always talking to her (where she is always talking to herself). Images of a real family have disappeared; fake images have taken their place. None of these "relatives" of the telescreen family will tell her a fairy tale, that traditional source of popular wisdom which, as Bettelheim indicates, offers a convincing view of the adult world to the child and which therefore builds a bridge to that world. And if fairy tales are the oldest form of utopian narrative, as Ernst Bloch suggests, then there is something sadly lacking in this "utopia" which feels it must burn those allegedly terrifying stories. The psychologistic age depicted in *Fahrenheit 451* has destroyed one of the primary means for assuring continuity of generations (since the child can come to feel, according to Bettelheim, that his parents do not inhabit a world that is totally alien to his own) and the memory of happy experiences. Recently, Ursula Le Guin has also written about the beneficial effects of these Jungian figures in fantasy and science fiction.

What this amounts to is that Mildred has no culture complex outside of a very primitive narcissism. Society has provided her with no means, however contradictory, to transform her inner psychic world, which is seen even more clearly from the narrator's perspective during her attempted suicide. In a cleverly staged scene in which two impersonal "operators" come to the rescue with a kind of vacuum cleaner mounted with an electronic eye, we are made acutely aware of the individual's dependence on a bureaucratized state and the "helping professions," those outside experts who intervene in family problems. The irony of the scene is that they are not even doctors, but "handymen," since suicide has become so common that it required the production of a new machine to deal specifically with the problem, and with a new job speciality. At the same time as we are working out for ourselves the depths of irony in which no one is really getting at the real problems behind Mildred's suicide (though of course the operators are efficient, practical and helpful), the narrator directly asks the reader a rhetorical question about the machine and its eye: "Did it drink of the darkness? Did it suck out all the poisons accumulated with the years?" On the oneiric level of material imagination, we must imagine through this critical negation of technology how time has stopped flowing toward the future for Mildred, how it has gathered in a "liquid melancholy" that cannot be sucked away by the machine, indeed that the "eye" of the machine cannot even see. Unlike the machine and its operators, we must give a full human response, cognitive and sublimative, if we are to grasp the significance of the scene.

Clarisse's disappearance brings about "vague stirrings of disease" in Montag and in a scene in the firehouse he recognizes that these men whose faces are sunburnt by a thousand real and ten thousand imaginary fires are "all mirror images of himself." Montag had stolen a book of fairy tales at the last fire; in a slip of the tongue which reveals the dominance of the anima in his mind he asks Fire Chief Beatty if "once upon a time" firemen put out fires instead of lighting them. This brings on a lesson in history of the Fireman of America which is nothing less than an illustration of the Freudian dreamwork, which distorts a basic content in order to represent a wish as fulfilled. Benjamin Franklin is the founding father who established the Firemen in the colonies to burn English-influenced books. The lives of the Firemen are governed by a series of five rules laid down by him that define a narrative circuit from alarm to fire to firehouse to alarm, the very instance of an anxiety mechanism.

In the next fire Montag witnesses a suicide that is undertaken deliberately with full knowledge of the consequences. An old woman chooses to die in the conflagration which destroys her library and home rather than be taken to the insane asylum. This action, while it horrifies Montag, also leads him to equate people with books and books with people. Fire Chief Beatty argues that the old woman was driven insane by the contradictions among the books ("a regular damned Tower of Babel"), but Montag begins to realize that their job is only to provide more spectacle, a show for the neighbors. In addition to this cognitive level of discovery, the oneiric level of significance emerges when books begin to pour out of the destroyed walls of the house onto Montag's shoulders: "A book lit, almost obediently, like a white pigeon, in his hands, wings fluttering. In the dim, wavering light, a page hung open and it was like a snowy feather, the words delicately painted thereon." This is a clear image of transcendence, the bird being symbolic of a proffered flight to the imaginary. The feather is snowy and of a very different climate from the burning world with which Montag is familiar. And the words of this book are not printed, making it a symbol of technology, but *painted,* which suggests the medieval illumination of manuscripts where words themselves come alive in ornate and painfully slow scriptive fantasy. Once one has seen one of these books, all other books, however produced, pale in comparison. Unfortunately, Montag loses this book of reveries, but not before reading a line in it: "Time has fallen asleep in the afternoon sunshine," which suggests an illuminator patiently reading and transcribing with love a sacred scripture, an occasion on which real time would seem to be transformed magically. It is nonetheless a powerful negation of Montag's sense of time as burning away the past and memory and history.

Beatty gives an artificial impression of being in command, but as he stares abstractedly into his eternal consumer lighter, we know that he is simply rationalizing. We must seek out, as Montag does, the true utopian wise man, Faber, who appears in the second part of the novel.

—William F. Touponce

It is no wonder then that Montag is not ready to accept Fire Chief Beatty's defense of the status quo, no matter how sympathetic he may seem. His perspective is undercut by all we and Montag have learned about books. They may indeed by contradictory, but that experience in itself is somehow valuable. Beatty wants a type of society that requires only enough mind to create and tend machines, which, of course, he thinks are marvelous labor-saving devices. He thinks that they have eliminated unhappiness: "The zipper displaces the button and a man lacks just that much time to think while dressing at dawn, a philosophical hour, and thus a melancholy hour." It is, of course, also an indication of his ambivalence towards the "doubleness" of philosophy whose terms seem to keep sliding despite the quest to embody truth, and an ironic indictment of him, that his own speech reveals more than he intends it to, that it is more than just the revelation that "Technology, mass exploitation, and minority pressure did the trick," in bringing about this "happy society." Beatty's language is an attempt to "sell" Montag on the idea of being a fireman, which is why it seems to be alienated from any connected meaning or attempt to think of a social totality. Just before he launches into his defense, we see him obsessively flicking his lighter:

> He examined his eternal matchbox, the lid of which said GUARANTEED: ONE MILLION LIGHTS IN THIS LIGHTER, and began to strike the chemical match abstractedly, blow out, strike, blow out, strike, speak a few words, blow out. He looked at the flame. He blew, he looked at the smoke. "When will you be well?"

This brief passage informs the reader about how to imagine the relationship between consciousness, language, and its objects during the course of Beatty's speech. It shows us the lighter as a practical technological device bearing a promise, but this object in turn shows us only the reified language of mass culture itself. The lighter is a fetish, an emblem of the eternal consumer, the ideal of this society of narcissists (in contrast, Faber tells Montag: "I don't talk *things*, sire . . . I talk the *meaning* of things.") So the structure of Beatty's language, and the reasons for its debasement, are here succinctly presented for the reader. As a symbol of our control over fire, with its promise of a million imaginary fires, it must be understood in a negative sense. Its ideal, the beauty in consumption, is a deception, based on repetition and sameness. It is this deception we must bear in mind throughout Beatty's defense and in the next part of the novel where we again see him talking about the "false promises" that literature offers.

Beatty's language has a quality difficult to capture in brief quotation. It seems to destroy previous stages of the argument without preserving anything for further thought. Although it is full of novelty and dynamic tempo (he invokes a film speeding faster and faster), it is really governed by a constant sameness, the rhythm of mechanical reproduction. It is a montage of superstructural effects which do not touch upon basic economic realities. Beatty's attitude towards the past (which he is supposed to be revealing) is obviously one in which there is no possibleexperience of an integrated tradition. Everything has to run incessantly to maintain the illusion of life:

> "Speed up the film, Montag, quick. *Click, Pic, Look, Eye, Now, Flick, Here, There, Swift, Pace, Up, Down, In, Out, Why, How, Who, What, Where, Eh?, Uh! Bang! Smack! Wallop, Bing, Bong, Boom!* Digests-digests, digest-digest-digests. Politics? One column, two sentences, a headline! Then, in midair, all vanishes! Whirl man's mind around so fast under the pumping hands of publishers, exploiters, broadcasters that the centrifuge flings off all unnecessary, time-wasting thought!

This is really a biting satire about the ways in which the culture industry turns the successes of enlightenment into mass deception. With the proliferation of magazines does not come more knowledge and power for the individual, but the absence of these things, and a brutalization and re-barbarization of language, a gradual descent into subhuman grunts. The lack of political discussion indicates that real freedom has been forfeited in order to preserve happiness (political candidates are chosen for their "winning images.") There is nothing left for the consumer to classify, no fundamental concepts that are evoked by these predigested tabloids. Beatty gives an artificial impression of being in command, but as he stares abstractedly into his eternal consumer lighter, we know that he is simply rationalizing. We must seek out, as Montag does, the true utopian wise man, Faber, who appears in the second part of the novel.

Part II, "The Sieve and the Sand," foregrounds the process of reading itself as a process of self-discovery. Once he begins reading in earnest, Montag is deeply worried that he will not be able to retain what he has read (hence the sieve), or understand it more deeply. He therefore seeks out an old retired school teacher, Faber. During this search the programmed fantastic is intensified as a threat to reading (especially in the subway). But finally Montag is equipped by Faber with an electronic transmitter which allows them to communicate their thoughts and especially for Faber to read to him unbeknownst to others. But Montag rashly thinks that he can reform his wife and her friends at one of their T.V. parlor parties by reading them a poem (Arnold's "Dover Beach"). This event marks the turning point of the novel, for Montag is now in open rebellion. Although he tries to cover up his mistake by burning the book in question, and even though he appears to lose another debate with Beatty, his wife decides to turn in the alarm on him. Part II ends with the fire engine arriving at Montag's own house. Again the oneiric level of the text provides us with instructions about how to imagine these events. In particular, Faber's demystifying of the programmed fantastic occurs before we are given a series of representations from it (earlier we were only given the fragmented experience of the self in such a fantasy, which provides us with the proper distantiation to effect a criticism of its inner mechanisms and the secret of its appeal).

Early on in this part Montag remembers or imagines Beatty telling him how to read a book:

> He could hear Beatty's voice. "Sit down, Montag. Watch. Delicately, like the petals of a flower. Light the first page, light the second page. Each becomes a black butterfly. Beautiful, eh? Light the third page from the second and so on, chain smoking, chapter by chapter, all the silly things the words mean, all the false promises, all the second-hand notions and time-worn philosophies." There sat Beatty, perspiring gently, the floor littered with swarms of black moths that had died in a single storm.

Beatty's reading is a kind of defloration, a perverse destruction that conserves nothing but depends on a total blank out of differences, lighting the third page from the second, never achieving synthesis but destroying past stages of history. The delicate nuances of meaning (color) produced by the flowering of reverie in the reader's mind (recall the flower image offered by the narrator of **"The Sea Shell"** here) are homogenized and made black by fire. Fire destroys those impurities and frictions, those irritants in reading that stimulate us to

discover new things. Fire destroys dialectical negation, the very principle of reading, as Iser has shown, and with it the labor of the concept and the fruitfulness of historical contradiction. The hallucination Beatty creates on the basis of the text is one of repetition and sameness. Each page becomes a black moth in the scattering storm of his reading. The butterfly, often a symbol of fantasy itself, or, in less capricious terms, of the soul's unconscious attraction towards light, here dies without the hope of ever rising up past the threshold of the unconscious, for Beatty's reading is a habituation, like chain smoking. Elsewhere, in a later perspective segment bearing on his fascination for fire, Beatty says:

> "What is there about fire that's so lovely? No matter what age we are, what draws us to it?" Beatty blew out the flame and lit it again. "It's perpetual motion; the thing man wanted to invent but never did. Or almost perpetual motion. If you let it go on, it'd burn our lifetimes out. What is fire? It's a mystery. Scientists give us gobbledegook about friction and molecules. But they don't really know. Its real beauty is that it destroys responsibility and consequences. A problem gets too burdensome, then into the furnace with it. Now, Montag, you're a burden. And fire will life you off my shoulders, clean, quick, sure; nothing to rot later. Antibiotic, aesthetic, practical."

Here Beatty's feeling for the beauty of fire, which mingles elements of both idolatry and ideology, belies his interest in its supposedly technological and practical effects. He is drawn to it (like a moth) because it destroys responsibility for his own life, his freedom. We note the persistence of a mythical attitude despite his claims to enlightenment. He even claims to know what the positivists do not know about fire with their "gobbledegook": fire as ideology is not brought about by friction with the real.

As Bachelard has shown, fire is an imaginative force that constantly distorts scientific inductions because it can explain anything—that is the secret of its ambivalence, which can never be entirely mastered, for human desires. It is both the subject (that which burns) and object (that which is burned); it is love, it is hate, comfort and torture, cookery and apocalypse. Beatty reveals his awareness of these contradictions when he says that fire is antibiotic, aesthetic, and practical, yet still a mystery, all at the same time. But if by ideology is meant a particular or relative discourse seeking to pass itself off as universal or absolute, then Beatty's discourse deserves this title, for it affirms only certain aspects of fire—those which stabilize a society of spectacles (the phoenix emblem on his uniform is a perfect example of this). Instead of proving our domination over nature, Beatty's discourse reveals an alienated nature's power over him, for man could never invent perpetual motion, the ideal of the consumer culture.

Beatty's complex thus is a true complex uniting the love of fire with the instinct for dying, felt as the appeal of the flames. At the center of his idolatry of fire is the Empedocles complex (Bachelard's name for it) containing the wish for the least lonely of deaths, one that would involve the entire universe in a conflagration (yes, Beatty also wants a cosmic reverie), but ironically he dies the most dehumanizing of deaths. In addition and most importantly, Beatty's idolatry of fire embraces the very principle of consumer culture: repetition and mechanical reproduction; once the reader discovers this, he has realized Bradbury's implicit oneiric criticism of our society.

It is Faber, however, who instructs Montag in the phenomenology of the reading process:

> "Number one: Do you know why books such as this are so important? Because they have quality. And what does the word quality mean? To me it means texture. This book has *pores*. It has features. This book can go under the microscope. You'd find life under the glass, streaming past in infinite profusion. The more pores, the more truthfully recorded details of life per square inch you can get on a sheet of paper, the more 'literary' you are. That's *my* definition anyway. *Telling detail. Fresh* detail. The good writers touch life often. The mediocre ones run a quick hand over her. The bad ones rape her and leave her for the flies.

> "So now do you see why books are hated and feared? They show the pores in the face of life. The comfortable people want only wax moon faces, poreless, hairless, expressionless. We are living in a time when flowers are trying to live on flowers, instead of growing on good rain and black loam. Even fireworks, for all their prettiness, come from the chemistry of the earth. Yet somehow we think we can grow, feeding on flowers and fireworks, without completing the cycle back to reality."

The forbidden and dangerous book that Faber is holding in his hands—the Bible—could well stand as a resonant symbol for the totality of literature, so many of the central myths and archetypal patterns of literature have come from it (including both patterns of utopia, the arcadian paradise and the heavenly city). According to Northrop Frye, the Bible is a total verbal order, the supreme example of how various myths can be integrated into a single vast vision of the world. Faber asserts almost the same thing earlier in this dialogue when he says the magic in the web of literature is texture: "How they stitched the patches of the universe into one garment for us."

Indeed, there is a striking resemblance between Faber's remarks on the function of literature and Frye's assertion that the reader himself is responsible for the moral quality of what he reads, that the cultivated response to culture is a redemptive if not a revolutionary act of consciousness. Faber is a kind of failed Northrop Frye, who has always insisted that we can get a whole liberal education simply by picking up one conventional poem and following its archetypes as they stretch out into the rest of literature. In the context of a study of romance (which Frye believes to be the structural core of all fiction) Frye remarks:

> When we study the classics of literature, from Homer on, we are following the dictates of common sense, as embodied in the author of Ecclesiastes: 'Better is the sight of the eye than the wandering of desire.' Great literature is what the eye can see: it is the genuine infinite as opposed to the phony infinite, the endless adventures and endless sexual stimulation of the wandering of desire.

This resemblance may seem all the more striking when we remember that Montag's moral response to this society, which stimulates the wanderings of desire, is, loving the wisdom of the preacher so much, to become the Book of Ecclesiastes among the itinerant book people.

Actually, Frye is ambivalent about the wanderings of desire, as of any centrifugal motion. Perhaps, he opines, literature would not exist without it, for the production of culture may be, like ritual, a half-involuntary imitation of organic rhythms or processes. But our response to *culture* remains nevertheless a formed response to human values. For Frye, literature is not mere wish-fulfillment; it provides not satisfaction of desire, but a realization of both its positive and negative moments (in *Fahrenheit 451,* for example, the reader discovers both the negative and positive dimensions of utopia). The literary universe is saturated with desire: its heroes incarnate the desirable, its villains the undesirable. The romance-world, and by extension the world of literature in general, is a paradise, then, not because our desires are always fulfilled there, but because they can in any case always be incarnated, brought to consciousness, formulated by the reader. For Faber also fiction is a genuine infinite, an imaginative vision that is also an ordering process, opposed by its very structure to the spectacles (fireworks) of the mass media.

But whereas Frye's visual imagination pertains more to a flash of insight, when we at a certain point in the narrative see a total design or unifying structure of converging significance, and nothing more, Faber's gives way to material imagination and our recessive desire in reading. People have lost touch with the earth, the principle of continuity and reality. They have lost the ability to ground their needs in the experience of satisfaction and real contentment. They have allowed the "helping professions"—psychiatrists, family counselors—to define their needs and psychic health for them. It is no wonder that those needs never seem to be satisfied: they are completely mediated by electronic images; flowers are trying to live on flowers.

Faber's reading complex appreciates images, telling details, but wants them to be part of the chemistry of the earth. Literature must also make us feel Bachelardian reverie, the texture of that good black loam. For him, books smell of nutmeg or some spice from a foreign land: "I loved to smell them when I was a boy." Even though he scoffs at Montag's naive request that he teach him to read, calling him a hopeless romantic for equating books with happiness (the archetypal wise old man always has some sobering truth for us!) he reveals through his reading complex that literature was for him as a boy the secular scripture, romance. Frye suggests that it is possible to look at secular stories as a whole, as forming a single integrated vision of the world, parallel to the Christian and Biblical vision. Faber shares this formal and visual imagination, telling Montag next a story from that other fabulous branch of now secular literature, classical mythology: the fable of Hercules and Antaeus; but the very presence of a book such as the Bible (which he has not held in his hands for so long) is enough to stir the material imagination of a better world.

Faber tells Montag, and us, how to read, by himself using suggestive details. Hercules was only able to defeat the giant wrestler, Antaeus (whose mother was Earth and who stands here for the force of the material imagination) by holding him rootless in the air. Each time Hercules threw Antaeus to the ground he grew stronger from contact with his source, so each time we read books of quality and texture we gain the experience of life—grainy, fibrous, woven and dimensional, as opposed to smooth, narcissistic, surface interests. Faber's Antaeus complex also tells us that as acts of consciousness and as lived experiences, images (flowers/fireworks) produced from the reading process must be sustained by an awareness of a historical dimension. In Iser's cognitive terms we would say that the text's repertoire of literary allusions suggest answers to the problems that the selection of norms and thought systems raises. Realistic texture (Faber's aesthetic is close to that of a realist) is therefore the imaginary correction of a deficient reality. It is an infinite profusion that is imaginatively real, not a false infinity of mere facts. By contrast, Beatty wants people crammed full of "noncombustible data," such as the fact, which every fireman and reader of the book should know, that book paper catches fire at 451°F.

Although this vision of a radiant literacy has failed, in another sense it has not entirely been disproved either, which is perhaps the reason why Montag chooses to read Matthew Arnold's "Dover Beach" to Mildred and her friends in a scene we will examine in a moment. The powers of literature exist apart from any attempt to theorize them, and theory may ultimately be a kind of defense against this power, as Geoffrey Hartman argues in connection with *Fahrenheit 451*. As readers we realize this also about Beatty's theorizing: he is secretly afraid of literature. When Montag is asked by one of Mildred's friends if the presence of the book in his hands is because he is reading up on fireman theory he responds: "Theory, hell . . . It's poetry." So we would be wise to keep our distance from theory as well in reading this book. Nevertheless, we can affirm that Faber, like Frye, still convinces us that we need a means to unite the world of nature with a total human form. Frye has argued that culture insists on totality—for whatever is excluded from culture by religion or state will get its revenge somehow. Faber exults in Montag's ruse of putting forbidden books he has stolen in the houses of firemen and then turning in the alarm: "The salamander devours his tail!" Faber's speech is didactic, but it leaves open paths of reverie and cognition by using the legend of Hercules and Antaeus for Montag to imagine and complete his own cycle back to reality. Books precisely are *not* completely real, although they allow the real to enter into them. They can be beaten down with reason, he says. On the other hand the programmed fantastic is so immediate that it rivals the real world: "It grows you any shape it wishes!"

Let us now consider, in the light of these discoveries made by the utopian reader, an example of the representations of the programmed fantastic:

> "Isn't this show *wonderful?*" cried Mildred.
>
> "Wonderful!"
>
> On one wall a woman smiled and drank orange juice simultaneously. How does she do both at once? thought Montag, insanely. In the other walls an x-ray of the same woman revealed the contracting journey of the refreshing beverage on its way to her delighted stomach! Abruptly the room took off on a rocket flight into the clouds, it plunged into a lime-green sea where blue fish ate red and yellow fish. A minute later, Three White Cartoon Clowns chopped off each other's limbs to the accompaniment of immense incoming tides of laughter. Two minutes more and the room whipped out of town to the jet cars wildly circling an arena, bashing and backing up and bashing each other again. Montag saw a number of bodies fly in the air.
>
> "Millie, did you *see* that!"
>
> "I saw it, I *saw* it!"
>
> Montag reached inside the parlor wall and pulled the main switch. The images drained away, as if the water had been let from a gigantic crystal bowl of hysterical fish.

In the five minutes during the showing of this fantasy, we see more action than in our slow moving world in many a day. It is, in fact, almost a perfect realization of Lasch's fears about the warlike social relations of a declining capitalist society where people are bashing and chopping each other to pieces for more consumer goods. First of all, we note the stimulation of infantile oral cravings. The x-ray provides the assurance (in this society which respects scientific images and facts it creates an aura of authenticity) that the shadowy and specular image of the ideal consumer's satisfaction is real. Then there follows a series of aggressive fantasy scenes, disconnected, and which entertain no relations of any kind with the reality principle. The action in these scenes completely defies the laws of gravitation, and seemingly all other known laws of nature. The room takes off on a rocket flight into the clouds and in the same sentence splashes into a lime-green sea where predation comically takes place. Weirdly artificial colors lend a kind of cartoon beauty to this scene that belies the obvious aggression of the fish; this is a reverie of the bright narcissistic surface of water, which quickly disperses without committing the imagination.

As the psychoanalytic critic Hans Sachs wittily observed on the subject of cartoons, this is animation with a vengeance (Sachs was punning on the regression of "animistic" thinking in cartoons). But interestingly, Sachs argued that the cartoon, unlike the fairy tale which does arouse anxiety and enable us to master it through its formal literary properties, is unable to eliminate or even diminish an anxiety situation (caused by the aggressive impulses of the spectator's projected id). This is so, Sachs argued, because in its pure form the cartoon is pure id, the overflowing vitality of libido. It offers us no coherence either of plot or of figures remotely resembling the human and through which we might identify.

How, then, does the cartoonist display so much aggression without arousing anxiety? Basically, says Sachs, it is "the amazing unreality of the world of cartoons which saves us from anxiety." In cartoons there really is no *form* by which we might master our fears (in Holland's sense of the transformation of fantasy), but everything is kept in constant motion (against the known laws of nature) so that our emotions seems sufficiently real, i.e., vivid. The cartoonist uses the unlimited despotic powers afforded to him by his medium to keep anxiety out of it. And as Lasch's social criticism here corroborates, in this type of fantasy Bradbury shows us that the modern propaganda of commodities has no need todisguise its id impulses—it gives us the illusion of a world full of vitality and force (in order to sell orange juice) and without the need for our imagination to engage itself. In the programmed fantastic, there are no novelistic techniques of illusion-building that might seek to simulate the reality of an action or a situation by having the reader use his own "free" imagination. Indeed, the very category of the real seems to be absent.

The Three White Clowns, who merrily chop each other's limbs off, are, of course, human figures, but the unreality of their gestures is rather emphasized by the fact that they are clowns. Anxiety is not supposed to be aroused here because they are not really losing their limbs (Sachs provides the example of Mickey Mouse, who in one instant is cut in half by a rolling wheel with a razor edge, and who in the next instant is reunited again, none the worse for his experience) in this unmistakably sadistic situation. It may of course arouse anxiety in the reader of *Fahrenheit 451,* but that is another matter. The spectators of this fantasy are perfectly assured that this violence is not real because the one technique for displacing anxiety that cartoons do in fact have is here effectively used: the Three White Clowns chop off each other's limbs to the accompaniment of immense incoming tides of *laughter.*

After unplugging the T. V. walls, Montag reads to Mildred and her friends Matthew Arnold's "Dover Beach." It is an indication of Bradbury's confidence in the power of literature to bring neglected states of mind to light, to convert passive knowledge into active, that he makes us feel in this scene, despite the obvious impracticality of Montag's gesture, that as long as we remember one poem from the repertoire of mankind's greatest poetry, the effects of habituation which threaten to devour, like fire, our families, friends, and even our fear of war, will find it more difficult to settle in. The last line about ignorant armies clashing by night rings particularly true for this society which indeed seems like a land of dreams, for none of the women seem to acknowledge the impending war. The poem provides also the idea of an alternative life in which people really speak to one another. Lovers communicate their deepest feelings, needs, and aspirations consequent on the very condition of being alive, knowing they have to die, needing love. This is decidedly not the happy ending which these women have come to expect, however, for it brings out uncontrollable sobbing in Mrs. Phelps and outright anger in Mrs. Bowles. Montag cannot help furiously throwing them out of his house when they attack him for arousing real emotions in them.

He realizes later that he has made a terrible error in acting so openly against the state and reproaches himself for being such a fool. Nevertheless, as Faber gradually reads to him he feels himself gently split into two people, one of whom is educating the other. On the oneiric level of experience, Montag is able to imagine himself as fire plus water, Montag-plus-Faber: "Out of two separate and opposite things, a third." That third thing brought about by dialectical sublimation is wine, for wine remembers, as it is put away and conserved, the earth from which it came. This newself will remember the past and will know the fool it once was.

It is only in part III, "Burning Bright," that technology is used directly against itself. Montag destroys the mechanical hound with a "single wondrous blossom" of fire, and Beatty as well, who dies like "a gibbering mannekin, no longer human or known." Montag also burns his own house, making everything once familiar seem strange. In a final nightmarish scene, Montag on the run has a vision of himself reflected in millions of T. V. sets, and imagines seeing himself killed on television by the hound, "a drama to be watched objectively." This vision of a fictive self and its false identification with society marks the climax of Montag's feelings of unreality and doubleness. From hence forth in the novel burning bright will mean the rediscovery of the utopian ideal. We need now to examine how this is presented to the reader:

> He felt as if he had left a stage behind and many actors. He felt as if he had left the great seance and all the murmuring ghosts. He was moving from an unreality that was frightening into a reality that was unreal because it was new.

The narrator relates these thoughts of Montage as he is "floating in a sudden peacefulness" downstream in a very real river he has plunged into in order to escape pursuit by the mechanical hound and the helicopters. They mark the beginning of a transition, a rebirth through water, a rite of passage that devests Montag entirely of his Fireman persona. This long water reverie symbolically puts out all the imaginary fires in Montag's mind. Montag's reverie becomes cosmic when he dreams of the sun and the burning of Time and the moon which shines by reflected light, discovering that he must never burn again in his life if human time is to be preserved.

When Montag drifts toward the shore, another reverie begins, organizing and transforming Montag's experience toward a utopian openness to the future. It has a highly organized, complexly layered, existential structure bearing the three dimensions of time (one indication that the programmed fantastic is so unreal is that it does not possess these existential temporal horizons): including the rediscovery of a happy childhood memory, events in the present, and a situation which is to emerge in the future, representing the fulfillment of a utopian wish as a broken promise.

The motion of the waters and the smell of hay from the shore awaken in Montag the memory of a farm he visited when he was "very young, one of the rare few times he discovered that somewhere behind the seven veils of unreality, beyond the tin moat of the city, cows chewed grass and pigs sat in warm ponds at noon, and dogs barked after white sheep on a hill." Obviously, he has transformed and idealized this memory through reverie into an arcadian utopia. Montag imagines sleeping in a hay loft on that farm. From this inhabited space he projects images of the future, utopian longings:

> During the night, he thought, below the loft, he would hear a sound like feet moving, perhaps. He would

tense and sit up. Thesound would move away. He would lie back and look out the loft window, very late in the night, and see the lights go out in the farmhouse itself, until a very young and beautiful woman would sit in an unlit window, braiding her hair. It would be hard to see her, but her face would be like the face of the girl so long ago in his past now, so very long ago, the girl who had known the weather and never been burnt by the fireflies, the girl who had known what dandelions meant rubbed off on your chin. Then, she would be gone from the warm window and appear again upstairs in her moon-whitened room. And then, to the sound of death, the sound of the jets cutting the sky in two black pieces beyond the horizon, he would lie in the loft, hidden and safe, watching those strange new stars over the rim of the earth, fleeing from the soft color of dawn.

Because of its oneiric level of meaning, this passage bears an experience of exceptional poignance. It may even approach the sublime. All the elements of its structure seem braided together like the girl's hair, with loving recollection. Clarisse has disappeared, and Montag hopes that she is not dead, projecting her face on that of the very beautiful young woman he imagines distantly in the window. That woman is clearly archetypal, however, being a Jungian spirit figure who symbolizes the free and sovereign image-making capacity of the mind. Clarisse had revealed Montag's unhappy being to him through the being of an image, a "dandelion test." She seems to him now the very spirit of utopia, innocent and inviolate, never burned by the sparks of any destructive fire, enabling him to master the sound of death with her fairy-tale stillness and beauty, helping him to watch with the ease of reverie the dawn chase away the apocalyptic stars.

For Freud, the utopian urge originates in the drive to restore an earlier state of gratification (mother-infant Eden-eternity), but Montag's reverie, from which we are forced to make only this brief selection, is actually what Ernst Bloch describes as a *Traum nach vorwarts,* a dreaming forward which fills the future with sublimated images of utopian desire. These images are certainly compounded of childhood wishes and desires, but reverie has so idealized them that they are uplifting and inspiring, quite unlike the images of satisfaction that can be found in the programmed fantastic, which are narcissistic and destructive. According to Bloch, the essence of the utopian principle is this: the interweaving of fear and wish (in our case, activated by the childhood image of the dawn) into a visionary future modeled on remembrance, imaginary or partially real, of the past. But Bloch stresses that utopian desire is not chaotic; it is *formed* wish. We would say that it is an imaginative existential structure open to the future: ". . . for the daydreaming 'I' persists throughout, consciously, privately, envisaging the circumstances and images of a desired, better life."

Montag's reverie is therefore a means for overtaking the future rather than a regression to the past. This scene resonates with what Bloch calls aurora archetypes which, when examined hermeneutically, reveal indications of utopian content like a glow on the horizon. For example, consider the open window lit by moonlight (which, we have already learned from Montag's cognitive reverie in Part 1, shines with a reflected light, reminding us of a source of light to come) where we can barely see the face of our ideal. Consider the girl herself who symbolizes utopian reverie and who remains forever young despite the fact that Montag knows that Clarisse is dead (hence the feeling of broken promise in the passage). And finally, there is the dawn itself, which we are certain is going to bring the apocalypse yet not entirely destroy our hopes for the future.

Objects too are transformed in this reverie, revealing their being to us. Montag's reverie is powered by distinctly oral images of happiness, yet paradoxically these objects are not there to be destroyed by eating; they are sings of a different relationship to the world:

> A cool glass of fresh milk, and a few apples and pears laid at the foot of the steps. This was all he wanted now. Some sign that the immense world would accept him and give him the long time he needed to think all the things that must be thought.

Imagining this scene, Montag steps from the river, having gained some notion of what the real satisfaction of human needs must be like ". . . a complete country night would have rested and slept him while his eyes were wide and his mouth, when he thought to test it, was half a smile." In the pink light of early morning when Montag has been made so aware of the world through his reverie, these objects appear as a "small miracle." But they are more than just the signs of a new composure towards things. Since they are no longer objects for consumption, allowing for their being to be revealed, Montag wants the time to "think all the things that need to be thought" in the hope of a poetic dwelling on the earth. Only when we let the thing *be* as the gathering together of the world in its "worlding" do we think, Heidegger says, of the thing as thing, how all that a thing is, is granted to it by the world. In terms of Heidegger's phenomenology, the fruit and the glass of milk a "thinging" things, not objects consigned to oblivion of being by technological thinking. These objects have lost their aura of commodity production and have taken on the power to reveal our being-in-the-world.

It is difficult to summarize the many levels of Montag's utopian aspirations in this long water reverie, and we have not even touched upon his dream of inhabiting the hayloft which stabilizes him long enough to participate in dramatic cosmic events, to represent to himself a world which is as yet to him unexplored and unfamiliar (he is floating on the surface of the water during the entire sequence). As an ontological structure relating self and world, however, we can affirm that it clearly manifests what Paul Tillich calls the transcendence of utopia: a structure of being wanting to transcend itself although at the same time wanting to remain within itself and protect itself. Montag's imaginary house-barn is a well-rooted being, so he does not fear climbing up to the loft where he can be open to the wind and the dawn, and to another house seen from outside at night.

Montag goes on, after he emerges from the river, to deeper reveries of a new autochthony in the forest world, where he imagines himself an animal attracted to a campfire, around which a group of the itinerant book-people have gathered to warm themselves. Montag is unfamiliar with this human use of fire and with the experience of language it gives rise to:

> There was a silence gathered all about the fire and the silence was in the men's faces, and time was there, time enough to sit by this rusting track under the trees and look at the world and turn it over with the eyes, as if it were held to the center of the bonfire, a piece of steel these men were all shaping. It was not only the fire that was different. It was the silence. Montag moved toward this special silence that was concerned with all of the world.

> And then the voices began and they were talking, and he could hear nothing of what the voices said, but the sound rose and fell quietly and the voices were turning the world over and looking at it; the voices knew the land and the trees and the city which lay down the track by the river. The voices talked of everything, there was nothing they could not talk about, he knew, from the very cadence and motion and continual stir of curiosity and wonder in them.

This description of campfire and silence at first breaks the pattern of narrative by putting the reader in a position of reverie, and therefore of reflection vis-à-vis himself. It is, in fact, a Bachelardian reverie of the forge which expresses the liberation of natural resources and the productive use of human energies. These men are intent on touching the world in material imagination, shaping it like a piece of metal in the sunset of their fire. Concern is the dominant mood. Even though we enter into a position of observing, we do not lose ourselves through technological domination of nature, because language and representation here arise from a conscious center (the bonfire). New worlds are being cast; language has the power to talk about anything but nothing is repressed. In the image of the campfire-forge, Bradbury shows us how the imagination (for it is clear that Montag has never before encountered such a "forge" in reality) can itself provide standards and values for our involvement with the world.

Even the nightmare of the telescreens has shrunk to a manageable proportion in this wilderness:

> Granger snapped the portable viewer on. The picture
> was a nightmare, condensed, easily passed from hand
> to hand in the forest, all whirring color and flight.

It is Granger who further enlightens Montag about the programmed fantastic by showing him how to view, without allowing hisimagination to take over, the death of someone who unfortunately looks like him on the telescreen. He exposes this society's carefully controlled scapegoating and murder of innocent victims. We realize that books have been the mock victims on an altar of fiery sacrifice all along. This society was not rational or enlightened, but had reverted to myth and ritual in order to control forces it no longer understood.

After the atomic war that has been building finally erupts, destroying the city, Granger also tells Montag a fable about the phoenix, who "must have been a first cousin to man." This is not symbolism, but allegory. The fabulous bird embodies our multi-colored dreams of the dominance of nature— our aspiration towards utopia—but also the destructive tendencies inherent in such a project which involves a forgetting of ourselves as part of nature. Yet it is also that within us which enables us to overcome the death of our dreams and to build again. *If* we understand it as allegory, we can effect some distance from this blind destructive cycle. The bird is only first cousin to man, and unlike the bird, we know the "damn silly things" we have done as Granger makes clear. We know temporal difference and irony, if we remember our past, our books. Beatty (whose very name suggests the ringmaster of a famous circus) was obsessed with the phoenix and the salamander as visionary images of atemporal authority and power that suppresses differences. We understand now that he was himself a frustrated romantic who believed, despite himself, in numinous symbols of nature.

Montag searches the faces of the book people for some trace of his ideal of radiant literacy, but finds none. The old romantic metaphor of the lamp is put away for Granger's idea of the book as a mirror. But we know this is not to be taken to mean simple identification, for we are to take a long hard look at ourselves. Besides, we are jokingly told not to judge a book by its cover. We must read it slowly and thoughtfully first, paying attention to its images and what it has to say. Montag is only partly sure that he has wisdom within him, but not from the tree of knowledge. As the book ends we are offered a quotation from Revelations that is itself a leaf from the tree of life, for the healing of nations. Knowledge must someday be converted back into life; through it the fruitfulness of utopia must come.

The complaint that utopian novels are more concerned with ideas than characters, and present characters who are simply one-dimensional spokesmen for the author's social hypothesis, is often voiced. I do not think that this change can be brought successfully against *Fahrenheit 451,* despite the fact that it uses the conventional figures of the utopian novel (Montag is himself the utopian traveller in disguise). Because it dramatizes the contradictions of books in a society where the reading of literature is forbidden, it motivates the reader easily and intensely to take up the quest for the utopian past. And because of its suggestive deployment of many different modes of reverie, it preserves the archetypes of utopian satisfaction as a criticism ofthe culture industry the reading subject has to work out for himself. Is it necessary to say that *Fahrenheit 451* continues to be relevant today, since the trends Bradbury projected in 1953 are unabated?

David Mogen (essay date 1986)

SOURCE: *"Fahrenheit 451,"* in *Ray Bradbury,* Twayne Publishers, 1986, pp. 105-11.

[*In the following excerpt, Mogen provides favorable analysis of* Fahrenheit 451, *citing Bradbury's use of satire, metaphor, and stylistic excellence to deliver social commentary.*]

If *The Martian Chronicles* (1950) established Bradbury's mainstream reputation as America's foremost science-fiction writer, publication of *Fahrenheit 451* three years later (1953) confirmed the promise of the earlier book. Indeed, these two science-fiction novels from the early fifties seem destined to survive as Bradbury's best-known and most influential creations, the most sustained expressions of his essentially lyrical treatment of science-fiction conventions. *The Martian Chronicles* presents the pioneering space romance in a distinctive tone of poignant irony and elegy; *Fahrenheit 451* counterpoises this ironic otherworldly drama with a searing vision of earthbound entrapment, evoking a painfully ambivalent poetry of incineration and illumination from the conventions of antiutopian fiction. Whereas *The Martian Chronicles* portrays entrapment in memory, the difficulty of accepting and adapting to an alien environment, *Fahrenheit 451* dramatizes entrapment in a sterile and poisonous culture cut off from its cultural heritage and imaginative life, vigilantly preserving a barren present without past or future. Though *Fahrenheit 451* has been accused of vagueness and sentimentality, it remains one of the most eloquent science-fiction satires, a vivid warning about mistaking, in Orville Prescott's phrase, "mindless happiness and slavish social conformity" for "progress."

Fahrenheit 451 fuses traditional themes of antiutopian fiction to focus satirically on the oppressive effect of a reductionist philosophy of "realism" translated into social policy. A very American satire, written in response to the cold war atmosphere after World War II, the novel's sarcasm is directed not at specific government institutions but at antiintellectualism and cramped materialism posing as social philosophy, justifying book burning in the service of a degraded democratic ideal. *Fahrenheit 451* depicts a world in which the American Dream has turned nightmare because it has been superficially understood. For all his burning eloquence Captain Beatty represents Bradbury's satirical target, not Big Brother but the potentially tyrannical small-mindedness of the common man, perverting the most basic community institutions to enforce conformity. The underground scholar Faber warns Montag that the captain's rhetoric, like the seductive brilliance of fire, destroys the foundations of true freedom in its leveling blaze: "Remember that the Captain belongs to the most dangerous enemy totruth and freedom, the solid unmoving cattle of the majority. Oh, the terrible tyranny of the majority."

Given this satirical target—the debased Americanism of McCarthyism—the ironically reversed role of the "firemen" serves admirably as Bradbury's central metaphor, since it represents both the charismatic seductiveness of demagoguery and a perversion of the community values of Green Town, Bradbury's symbol of the American tradition at its best. Indeed, the power of *Fahrenheit 451*'s imagery derives from this ironic inversion of values in an institution that once evoked Bradbury's boyish awe and respect. Writing of the personal memories that inform the novel, he recalls how like many boys he idolized local firemen prepared to battle the "bright monster" of fire:

> And I did pass the firehouse often, coming and going to the library, nights and days, in Illinois, as a boy, and I find among my notes many pages written to describe the red trucks and coiled hoses and clump-footed firemen, and I recall that night when I heard a scream from a part of my grandmother's house and ran to a room and threw open a door to look in and cry out myself.

> For there, climbing the wall, was a bright monster. It grew before my eyes. It made a great roaring sound and seemed fantastically alive as it ate of the wallpaper and devoured the ceiling.

In his memory, the firehouse is the protector of library and home. And this heroic image of the community firehouse, the curiously thrilling terror of fire, inspire the angry lyricism of Bradbury's vision of the American Dream gone awry: for in this appalling future the community firehouse has become the impersonal agent of fire itself, destroying rather than preserving the community institutions Bradbury cherishes above all others—family life, schools, and, most fundamentally of all, perhaps, the local library. As Donald Watt demonstrates in "Burning Bright: *Fahrenheit 451* as Symbolic Dystopia," ambivalent associations with fire, both destroyer and center of hearth and home, fundamentally structure

the novel. But the ambivalence evoked by fire metaphorically represents the ambivalent implications of American democracy, the possibility that the communal spirit of Green Town could become an American form of totalitarianism, a "tyranny of the majority" as fearful as the tyranny of Big Brother, founded on shallow misunderstanding of rationality, science, and the nature of "happiness."

[In Bradbury's] memory, the firehouse is the protector of library and home. And this heroic image of the community firehouse, the curiously thrilling terror of fire, inspire the angry lyricism of Bradbury's vision of the American Dream gone awry.

—David Mogen

Yet if *Fahrenheit 451* gains power and specificity from its American frame of reference, the satire also applies to patterns that can recur in all societies, whenever reductionist philosophies resultin the sacrifice of individuals and free play of imagination for the common good. Bradbury's satire is directed not at American ideals but at simplistic perversions of them, as well as at the American innocence that assumes totalitarianism can't happen here. However, horror at Hitler inspired the book's original conception, that to burn books is to burn people: "When Hitler burned a book I felt it as keenly, please forgive me, as burning a human, for in the long sum of history they are one and the same flesh." And though Hitler is defeated, and McCarthy's era finished, they will always have successors who will keep the firemen at work: "For while Senator McCarthy has been long dead, the Red Guard in China comes alive and idols are smashed and books are thrown to the furnace all over again. So it will go, one generation printing, another generation burning, yet another remembering what is good to remember so as to print again." Ultimately, *Fahrenheit 451* warns that tyranny and thought control always come under the guise of fulfilling ideals, whether they be those of Fascism, Communism, or the American Dream. Yet the cyclical pattern Bradbury describes also suggests the positive implications of one of the book's central symbols, the Phoenix: for, like the Phoenix, mankind always arises from ashes to rediscover and refashion a desecrated cultural heritage.

Though *Fahrenheit 451* has been compared frequently to Orwell's *Nineteen Eighty-four*—an obviously influential model—it actually combines the oppressive atmosphere of Orwell's police state with a cultural milieu derived from the other major model in the science-fiction antiutopian tradition, Huxley's *Brave New World*. Indeed, the novel's affinities with *Brave New World* are profound, since they establish the basic thrust of Bradbury's satire, which is not directed at authoritarianism but at a more characteristically American problem, a reductionist, materialist image of human nature and human culture reinforced through mass entertainment media. Though the novel's basic mechanics of thought control derive from Orwell, Bradbury's satirical vision does not focus primarily on government itself but on the potentially poisonous superficiality of mass culture, on whose behalf the firemen work. As in Huxley's satire (itself profoundly influenced by American culture in the twenties), the power of totalitarianism in *Fahrenheit 451* derives primarily from pleasure rather than pain, from addiction to mindless sensation rather than from fear of government oppression. The firemen work for the "people," not for an established hierarchy. Indeed, compared to Big Brother the firemen are haphazard and mild agents of repression.

Next to Orwell's vision of totalitarianism, Bradbury's appears vaguely defined, both ideologically and politically. Montag's entrapment generates nothing like the weight of despair that crushes Winston Smith's spirit. Yet understanding the American context in which Bradbury writes clarifies the logic of this political vagueness, since his major satirical target is the leveling impulse of mass culture, rather than the rigidity of ideology. As Kingsley Amis suggests, Bradbury's style is very different from Orwell's, working through key symbols rather thanthrough elaborately imagined detail. Yet the final effect is similarly impressive: "The book [*Fahrenheit 451*] emerges quite creditably from a comparison with *Nineteen Eighty-four* as inferior in power, but superior in conciseness and objectivity."

As is true of all Bradbury's best science fiction, *Fahrenheit 451* dramatizes its central extrapolations with lyrical intensity, creating an atmosphere of entrapment that originates in the mind-numbing addictiveness of mass culture as much as from the firemen themselves. The novel's most powerful scenes are not the sometimes tedious expositions in dialogue, but descriptive passages, asides, which capture the inarticulate spiritual desolation disguised by the busy, upbeat appearances of this world. As they burn, books and magazines appear as "slaughtered birds" drenched with kerosene, expiring with a dying fall: "A book lit, almost obediently, like a white pigeon, in his hands, wings fluttering." Montag sees himself in the mirror as "a minstrel man, burnt-corked" smiling a smile that "never ever went away, as long as he remembered." The single most powerful scene evoking this atmosphere of glazed entrapment, perhaps, is the description of Mildred dying of an overdose of sleeping pills in their bedroom, a "cold marbled . . . mausoleum after the moon has set." She is at her most appealing in this icy trance, like a princess cast under deathly enchantment by incantations from her "Seashell ear thimbles" and the hypnotic ritual activity of her television "walls," imaging forth in her "moonstone" eyes a despair she can never consciously acknowledge: "Two moonstones looked up at

him in the light of his small hand-held fire; two pale moonstones buried in a creek of clear water over which the life of the world ran, not touching them."

This icy alienation is the inner reality preserved by the fierce blaze of the firemen, a sterile desert of "happiness" within the widening circle of flames. Mildred's waking self, hungry only for distracting sensations, has irrevocably disassociated itself from her interior life, a subliminal meaning Truffaut artfully visualized by casting the same actress as both Mildred and Clarisse. Montag himself has never been able to distance himself so utterly from his inner self, that "subconscious idiot that ran babbling at times" inside his skull. It is this irrepressible inner self that projects his culture's hidden despair into cosmic imagery of alienation, imagining their noisy machines might leave them snowbound in stardust: "He felt that the stars had been pulverized by the sound of the black jets and that in the morning the earth would be covered with their dust like a strange snow. That was his idiot thought as he stood shivering in the dark, and let his lips go on and on, moving and moving."

Structurally, *Fahrenheit 451* moves from these early images of entrapment and alienation ("Part One: The Hearth and the Salamander"), through Montag's acknowledgement of and integration with the voice of his inner self (which becomes for a while the literal voice of Faber in "Part Two: The Sieve and the Sand"), to the final journey downriver to refuge in the wilderness ("PartThree: Burning Bright"). There those who have preserved their own inner life and man's cultural heritage quietly observe the final apotheosis of the culture that drove them out, as it finally consumes itself in flames. Thus, as the novel develops, the ambiguous connotations of Bradbury's central symbols express the emotional impact of his theme, the process of death and rebirth for Montag and the interior values he represents.

As the title suggests, fire provides the central metaphors for *Fahrenheit 451*. It opens and closes with contrasting images of fire and light, and the shifts in their symbolic associations illustrate how the novel's theme develops. In the opening description Montag revels in flame, like the mythical salamander, a blackened emblem of his culture's exhilaration in sensationalism and destruction: "It was a pleasure to burn. . . . While the books went up in sparkling whirls and blew away on a wind turned dark with burning." This fire is associated with darkness rather than light. But by the book's conclusion Montag has learned of the other fire of the "hearth," which warms and lights both "home" and "heart." Watching an old woman martyr herself in a pyre of her own books ignites a blaze of illumination inside him he cannot extinguish: "This fire'll last me the rest of my life." When he stumbles upon his first campfire in the wilderness, he finally comprehends fire's natural role in the "hearth," and he draws the moral himself: "It was not burning, it was warming."

In the campfire's glow Montag finally experiences the warmth of genuine human community, the slow lilt of relaxed conversation that in other contexts Bradbury identifies with talk at dusk on Green Town porches: "The voices talked of everything, there was nothing they could not talk about, he knew, from the very cadence and motion and continued stir of curiosity and wonder in them." And after the cities are scorched in the salamander's final revelry, the glow of the morning campfire blends into the light of a new day, as fire and light once again assume their roles in the natural cycle: "They finished eating and put the fire. The day was brightening all about them as if a pink lamp had been given more wick. In the trees, the birds that had flown away quickly now came back and settled down." Thus, the phoenix spirit of mankind regenerates new life from ashes, as Montag walks in the wilderness and savors the prophetic lines from Revelation: "*And the leaves of the tree were for the healing of the nations.*"

Like all of Bradbury's best fiction, *Fahrenheit 451* creates its best effects through vivid style. Yet it is also unique among his major writings for the sustained tautness of the narrative. Two of his other book-length fictions, *The Martian Chronicles* and *Dandelion Wine,* are not so much novels as patterned colleges of vignettes and short stories. And his other major novels, *Something Wicked This Way Comes* and *Death Is a Lonely Business,* are baggy monsters by comparison, in which the lyrical asides threaten to subvert the central narratives. But in *Fahrenheit 451* Bradbury achieved his central artistic objective, to rewrite the original novella, **"The Fireman,"** with the sustained intensity of his best short fiction: "I wanted to write a short novel and have it as 'truthful' as my stories. A novel, that is, with a skin around it and its own essence and being sacked up inside." This results, as Kingsley Amis describes it, in a "fast and scaring narrative" that successfully utilizes Bradbury's lyrical gifts to musically develop its disturbing theme.

An illustration of the fact that science fiction can comment eloquently on social problems, a story that translated effectively into Francois Truffaut's film, *Fahrenheit 451* deserves its reputation as one of the best American books of the post-war era. Willis McNelly calls it "in every way a magnificent achievement, perhaps his best book," and Mark Hillegas described it in the mid-sixties as "the archetypal anti-utopia of the new era in which we live." Fueled by Bradbury's lifelong passion for books and libraries, by his indignation at seeing American ideals defiled, *Fahrenheit 451* succeeds in warning of fire's seductive appeal while also affirming the power of man's phoenix-nature—the capacity to be warmed with inner illumination in desperate circumstances, to endure and rebuild new hearths in the ashes of history.

Susan Spencer (essay date 1991)

SOURCE: "The Post-Apocalyptic Library: Oral and Literate

Culture in *Fahrenheit 451* and *A Canticle for Leibowitz*," in *Extrapolation,* Vol. 32, No. 4, Winter, 1991, pp. 331-42.

[*In the following excerpt, Spencer examines oral tradition, textual knowledge, and their respective implications for memory and power as demonstrated in* Fahrenheit 451.]

At the dawn of widespread literacy in fourth-century Athens, Plato appended to the end of his *Phaedrus* a story that has often been perceived as, as Jacques Derrida puts it, "an extraneous mythological fantasy." Derrida argues in *Dissemination* that there is nothing extraneous about the myth at all, but rather it is an expression of an important and timely idea with which the classical Athenians were concerned. Recent orality/literacy theory, as outlined by Eric A. Havelock, Walter S. Ong, and others, would seem to back him up. The story is that of the discovery of the technology of writing, a tale that Socrates claims is traditional among the Egyptians. According to Socrates, the god Theuth invented this technology and offered it to the king of Upper Egypt as something that would "make the people of Egypt wiser and improve their memories." But the king scorned Theuth's gift, saying:

> by reason of your tender regard for the writing that is your offspring, [you] have declared the very opposite of its true effect. If men learn this, it will implant forgetfulness in their souls; they will cease to exercise memory because they rely on that which is written, calling things to remembrance no longer from within themselves, but by means of external marks. What you have discovered is a recipe not for memory, but for reminder. And it is no true wisdom that you offer your disciples, but only its semblance, for by telling them of many things without teaching them you will make them seem to know much, while for the most part they know nothing, and as men filled, not with wisdom, but with the conceit of wisdom, they will be a burden to their fellows.

The remark about "telling them . . . without teaching them" is evidently an expression of uneasiness with the idea of text as what Ong calls "unresponsive." In *Orality and Literacy: The Technologizing of the Word,* Ong sees one of Socrates's arguments as being "if you ask a person to explain his or her statement, you can get an explanation; if you ask a text, you get back nothing except the same, often stupid, words which called for your question in the first place." While this idea is so commonplace to us as to go practically unnoticed, except when we are frustrated by a particularly opaque text, it was new and frightening to the Greeks. According to Havelock in "The Oral Composition of Greek Drama," the late fifth and early fourth century B.C. was a period of relatively rapid change in literary style, as a direct result of the spread of popular literacy. Not only was an explanatory oral framework done away with, but also the old formulaic devices that helped oral composers keep their place and remember what they were talking about. "Compositionally, as plays began to be written with the expectation of being read, the composer would feel a reduced pressure to conform to certain mnemonic rules. The invented would be freer to prevail over the expected." This, Havelock hypothesizes, created some tension in the Greek theater—a tension that can be traced in Aristophanes's *Frogs,* where the more conservative, more "oral" Aeschylus wins a contest against the more "literary" and startlingly original Euripides; and, as we can see (although Havelock does not mention it here), in the inherent uneasiness in Plato's *Phaedrus.*

Although "The Oral Composition of Greek Drama" was first published in 1980, some theory of postliterary tension was working its way into the intelligentsia several decades before. To quote Havelock again, in his 1950 book *The Crucifixion of Intellectual Man,* the myth of the Fall in Genesis, as a direct result of eating of the tree of knowledge, "gives poignant expression to that conflict within the civilized consciousness of man, between his sense of intellectual power and his distrust and fear of that power. . . . All the warmth and the richness of man's nature demand that he live in the protection of certain illusions in order to be secure, happy, and peaceful." The "expected" rather than the "invented." The further the artificial "memory" created by textuality stretches back, and the more it can be built upon by an advancing science, the more that security fades away. Man becomes dangerous and also frightened. "Though our science may kill us, it will never allow us to retreat. Somehow we know that we would never burn enough books, nor eliminate enough intellectuals, to be able to return to the warm room" of blissful ignorance.

Within a decade of this assurance, two famous science fiction novels appeared dealing with the very attempt that Havelock had just pronounced futile: Ray Bradbury's ***Fahrenheit 451*** (1953) and Walter M. Miller's *A Canticle for Leibowitz* (1959). In ***Fahrenheit 451*** the protagonist, Guy Montag, is a "fireman"; that is, he burns forbidden books, and the houses that hide them, for a living. This is a busy job, considering the fact that just about all books are forbidden. There are a few rare exceptions, such as three-dimensional comic books, trade journals and, of course, rule books, those mainstays of any oppressive society. The rule book for the Firemen of America includes a brief history of the profession: "Established 1790, to burn English-influenced books in the Colonies. First Fireman: Benjamin Franklin." According to the only available text, and to the voice of political authority, this is a glorious and time-honored profession, an idea that gives the firemen a sense of continuity and security . . . and, perhaps, allows Bradbury to make a comment on the fact that textual knowledge is power, even—or perhaps especially—false knowledge. Power becomes unbreachable if textual information is monolithic. According to the sinister but brilliant

fire chief, Beatty, the main danger in books is that "none of those books agree with each other." Very true, but a danger to whom? Peace of mind, he argues repeatedly. To one lawbreaker, kneeling despairingly amid her kerosene-soaked illegal books, Beatty cries, "You've been locked up here for years with a regular damned Tower of Babel. Snap out of it!"

Inevitably, Montag becomes discontented with the status quo and curious about this nebulous "danger." Both his discontent and his curiosity are intensified when the woman mentioned above chooses to burn with her books rather than lose them. Beatty, seeing his distress when Montag feels "sick" and feigns illness, explains the real advent of the firemen in phrases that echo Havelock's concept of the loss of the "warm room" but takes it to its extreme limit:

> You always dread the unfamiliar. . . . We must all be alike. Not everyone born free and equal, as the Constitution says, but everyone *made* equal. Each man the image of every other; then all are happy, for there are no mountains to make them cower, to judge themselves against.

On the literary side, he also echoes Plato on the "conceit of wisdom," and just how far that can be taken as a sort of leveling device:

> Give the people contests they win by remembering the words to more popular songs or the names of state capitals or how much corn Iowa grew last year. Cram them full of noncombustible data, chock them so damned full of 'facts' they feel stuffed, but absolutely 'brilliant' with information. Then they'll feel they're thinking, they'll get a *sense* of motion without moving. And they'll be happy, because facts of that sort don't change. Don't give them any slippery stuff like philosophy or sociology to tie things up with. That way lies melancholy.

These things are written, but they are not literature. The classicist may be reminded here of the problems associated with Linear B, the proto-Greek script found at Mycenae and Knossos. All of the inscriptions are "bald counting-house dockets," "a text of the greatest interest" being a tablet that "lists amounts of barley against various classes of craftsmen." There is no literature *per se,* unless one were to use the standard eighteenth-century definition of literature as "anything written." As a result, it is difficult to get students interested in learning Linear B. There is simply nothing interesting to read. The situation is described by Havelock as one of preliteracy, in spite of the physical existence of written text: "whereas historians who have touched upon literacy as a historical phenomenon have commonly measured its progress in terms of the history of writing, the actual conditions of literacy depend upon the history not of writing but of reading." One needs an audience. Get the audience to lose interest, and you can do away with the literate civilization. In *Fahrenheit 451* the reader has the feeling of moving backward in time to a preliterate society, and the content of the society's "literature," although here it is for political ends, strengthens this impression.

The last phrase of Beatty's pronouncement, "That way lies melancholy," with its literary overtones—very different from the plainer common speech of his subordinates—is not unusual for Beatty. In keeping with the idea that knowledge is power, Bradbury gives us several hints that the fire chief has had frequent access to the forbidden texts and that this is either a cause or a result of his being made chief (just which one is unclear). Like Kurt Vonnegut, Jr.'s short story "Harrison Bergeron," set in another disturbing dystopia where "everybody [is] finally equal," some people are seen clearly to be more equal than others and thus enabled to wield power over their fellows. In Vonnegut's story, the ascendancy is physical: Diana Moon Glampers, the "Handicapper General," is the only citizen who isn't decked out in distorting glasses, distracting ear transmitters, and bags of birdshot to weaken her to the level of society's lowest common denominator. In *Fahrenheit 451,* the ascendancy is purely textual, but that is enough. Beatty's obnoxious confidence and habit of quoting famous works strikes the reader immediately and leads to a question that Bradbury never answers: why is this highly literate person permitted to survive, let alone hold a position of high authority, in an aggressively oral society? Something is rotten in the whole system. Evidently someone higher up, Beatty's shadowy superior, feels that there is some inherent value in a well-read man, in spite of all the political rhetoric. This probability is directly opposed to Beatty's frequent deprecation of texts (a protection of his own monopoly?) and claim that the eventual ban of almost all books was not a political coup accomplished by a power-hungry elite at one fell swoop. Beatty's explanation, which we are never called upon to doubt, is that an outraged people seeking complete equality called for more and more censorship as texts became more widely available to interest groups that might be offended by them: "It didn't come from the Government down. There was no dictum, no declaration, no censorship, to start with, no! Technology, mass exploitation, and minority pressure carried the trick." As Plato warned thousands of years earlier, well-read man had become anoffensive "burden to his fellows."

Bradbury closes the novel, however, with an optimistic view: the text *will* prevail, and man will be the better for it. This is shown symbolically in the escape from the city by Montag and Faber, the only two literate men in the story besides Beatty—who, also symbolically, perishes in the same manner as the many books he has burned. The ignorant oral-culture citizens, radios tamped securely in their ears, remain in the city to be blown up by an enemy they could easily have escaped, if it weren't for the fact that their monolithic media preferred to keep them ignorant and happy. Having taken up with a group of itinerant professors, haltingly trying to remember the text of Ecclesiastes, Montag takes the first steps toward realizing the dream he had as he blindly fled the government's persecution: "Somewhere the saving and the putting away had to begin again and someone had to do the saving and keeping, one way or another, in books, in records, in people's heads, any way at all so long as it was safe, free from moths, silverfish, rust and dry-rot, and men with matches."

The idea that it is safe only when locked away in memory is almost a startling one in this book that so privileges the literary text; it seems as if the author has come full circle to an oral culture and the need to circumvent the shortcomings of Theuth's invention. Yet Bradbury makes it clear that they will write everything down as soon as possible and will try to reconstruct a fully literate society again. This should not take long, and is certainly desirable. The concept of text is a progressive thing, not a cyclical, and as long as any remnants remain there is always a base, however small, on which to build a better and wiser world. . . .

Both *A Canticle for Leibowitz* and *Fahrenheit 451* end with a nuclear apocalypse and a new literacy springing from the ashes. Bradbury's positive, progressive view of literary history contrasts sharply with Miller's negative, cyclical view, just as Bradbury's depiction of a predominately oral culture as mind-numbing contrasts with Miller's depiction of orality as the preserver of ritual and collective human values. One might conclude this paper with the Unanswerable Question so popular with medieval bards at the ends of their stories: "Which point of view is the correct one?" And, as it has always been, the correct answer is "both."

Diane S. Wood (essay date 1992)

SOURCE: "Bradbury and Atwood: Exile as Rational Decision," in *The Literature of Emigration and Exile,* edited by James Whitlark and Wendall Aycock, Texas Tech University Press, 1992, pp. 131-42.

[*In the following essay, Wood compares* Fahrenheit 451 *with Margaret Atwood's* The Handmaid's Tale, *focusing on their historical context and respective treatment of conformity and institutionalized repression.*]

Ray Bradbury's *Fahrenheit 451* and Margaret Atwood's *The Handmaid's Tale* depict the rational decision to go into exile, to leave one's native land, that is, the pre-exile condition. These novels present horrifying views of the near future where societal pressures enforce rigid limitations on individual freedom. Their alienated characters find their circumstances repugnant. Justice and freedom are denied them, along with the possibility for enriching their lives through intellectual pursuits. These speculative novels like Orwell's *1984* are dystopian in nature, showing how precarious are today's constitutional rights and how necessary it is to preserve these liberties for future generations. They depict ordinary people, caught in circumstances that they cannot control, people who resist oppression at the risk of their lives and who choose exile because it *has* to be better than their present, unbearable circumstances. Voluntary exile necessitates a journey into the unknown as an alternative to the certain repression of the present.

Both novels offer a bleak possible future for the United States. Bradbury, writing in the McCarthy era of the 1950s, envisions a time when people choose to sit by the hour watching television programs and where owning books is a crime. Atwood, in the 1980s, foresees a time when, in the wake of changes begun during the Reagan Administration, women are denied even the most basic rights of working and owning property. Both novels thus present "political" stances in the widest sense of the word. . . .

In his 1966 Introduction to *Fahrenheit 451,* Bradbury expresses moral outrage concerning bookburning: "when Hitler burned a book I felt it as keenly, please forgive me, as his killing a human, for in the long sum of history they are one and the same flesh. Mind or body, put to the oven, is a sinful practice. . . ." He sees the necessity to guard constantly against such practices:

> For while Senator McCarthy has long been dead, the Red Guard in China comes alive and idols are smashed, and books, all over again, are thrown into the furnace. So it will go, one generation printing, another generation burning, yet another remembering what is good to remember so as to print again. . . .

The novels by Bradbury and Atwood examine the personal response of an individual who is in conflict with the majority in his society and whose occupation is abhorrent to him. *Fahrenheit 451* centers upon the personal crisis of Montag, a young fireman whose job consists of burning books. He finds his life increasingly meaningless and eventually comes to reject the too-simple, cliched values of his milieu. He experiences loneliness in a society where people are constantly entertained without time given to reflexion and personal development, activities often associated with the reading process. The more complicated nuances of the world of books are available to him only when he leaves his reductionistic society. . . .

In both novels the population is strictly regulated and the conduct of individuals is highly regimented. Indeed, in these repressive circumstances, it is not surprising that the protagonists would wish to flee, especially since, by the end of the

novels, they have broken laws which would bring the death penalty if they were apprehended. "Mechanical Hounds" use scent to hunt down lawbreakers in Bradbury's fiction. The hounds tear apart their prey. Montag narrowly escapes this fate but the police do not admit being outwitted. They stage his death for the benefit of the huge television audience which follows the developing story of his evasion. The authorities murder an innocent derelict in Montag's place, so as not to disappoint the viewers and appear ineffectual. The authorities are motivated by the desire to maintain power at any cost and blatantly violate human rights. . . .

In the world of *Fahrenheit 451* people have given up thinking for mindless pursuits. No revolution or *coup d'etat* brings about the loss of freedom. Rather, individual laziness precipitates a gradual erosion.

—*Diane S. Wood*

The major task of both Bradbury and Atwood is to portray convincingly in their futuristic novels how the abridgement of freedom evolved in the United States. As such, the novels are strong political statements warning of the consequences of what seem dangerous trends to the authors. One has only to look at the statistics for television watching, witness the decline of interest in reading among our students, and read current reports about ecological damage to verify the gravity of the dangers this country faces at the present time. In the world of *Fahrenheit 451* people have given up thinking for mindless pursuits. No revolution or *coup d'etat* brings about the loss of freedom. Rather, individual laziness precipitates a gradual erosion. This evolution takes place long before the birth of Montag, who grows up in a society where books are proscribed. His superior, a fireman, explains the trend of increasing simplification as the result of the influence of the mass media: "Things began to have *mass*. . . . And because they had mass, they became simpler. . . . Once, books appealed to a few people, here, there, everywhere. They could afford to be different. The world was roomy. But then the world got full of eyes and elbows and mouths. In a vast generalization which is itself a simplification, he tells how the modern era brought a movement to speed up and condense everything:

> Then, in the twentieth, century, speed up your camera. Books cut shorter. Condensations. Digests. Tabloids. Everything boils down to the gag, the snap ending. . . . Classics cut to fit fifteen-minute radio shows, then cut again to fill a two-minute book column, winding up at last as a ten- or twelve-line dictionary resume. . . . Do you see? Out of the nursery

into the college and back to the nursery; there's your intellectual pattern for the past five centuries or more.

The rich value of books is thus denied when they are reduced to brief summaries. Happiness to this fireman comes from eliminating all dissension, especially that caused by books: "'Colored people don't like Little Black Sambo. Burn it. White people don't feel good about Uncle Tom's Cabin. Burn it. Someone's written a book on tobacco and cancer of the lungs? The cigarette people are weeping? Burn the book. Serenity, Montag. Peace, Montag. Take your fight outside. Better yet, into the incinerator.'" Yet this society does not produce happiness. Montag is perpetually lonely and his wife attempts suicide.

Whereas Atwood's society ceremonializes violence, in Bradbury's book the society eliminates all cause for unhappiness and sweeps unpleasantness away, including those which are an integral part of the human condition: "'Funerals are unhappy and pagan? Eliminate them, too. Five minutes after a person is dead he's on his way to the Big Flue, the Incinerators serviced by helicopters all over the country. Ten minutes after death a man's a speak of black dust. Let's not quibble over individuals with memoriams. Forget them. Burn all, burn everything. Fire is bright and fire is clean.'" Television concerns itself with the ephemeral present and thus follows the trend toward forgetting the past. Books by their very essence preserve and memorialize those who have lived before. Bradbury would probably agree with Atwood's comments that all repressive governments eliminate authors because they are so dangerous. The fireman views fire as a means of purging and cleansing emotions in his society. Political dissension is eliminated by giving only one side of the argument. War is not even talked about. People are reduced to thinking about simple facts, meaningless data: "Cram them full of noncombustible data, chock them so full of 'facts' they feel stuffed, but absolutely 'brilliant' with information. Then they'll feel they're thinking, they'll get a *sense* of motion without moving. And they'll be happy, because facts of that sort don't change. Don't give them any slippery stuff like philosophy or sociology to tie things up with. That way lies melancholy." Through simplifying and reducing ideas, he feels that the firemen produce happiness for the society: "we're the Happiness Boys, the Dixie Duo, you and I and the others. We stand against the small tide of those who want to make everyone unhappy with conflicting theory and thought. We have our fingers in the dike. Hold steady. Don't let the torrent of melancholy and drear philosophy drown our world.'"

Balancing this reductionist apology are the views of another character in the novel, a retired English professor who "had been thrown out upon the world forty years ago when the last liberal arts college shut for lack of students and patronage." He traces the lack of reading to apathy: "Remember, the fire-

men are rarely necessary. The public itself stopped reading of its own accord. Your firemen provide a circus now and then at which buildings are set off and crowds gather for the pretty blaze, but it's a small sideshow indeed, and hardly necessary to keep things in line. So few want to be rebels anymore. And out of those few, most, like myself, scare easily." The professor's personal experience bears witness to the gradual nature of the transition from a reading to a non-reading culture. One day, there are simply no more students:

> That was a year I came to class at the start of the new semester and found only one student to sign up for Drama from Aeschylus to O'Neill. You see? How like a beautiful statue of ice it was, melting in the sun. I remember the newspapers dying like huge moths. No one *wanted* them back. No one missed them. And then the Government, seeing how advantageous it was to have people reading only about passionate lips and the fist in the stomach, circled the situation with your fire-eaters. . . .

In both novels books represent important artifacts of the past and the act of reading becomes a heroic gesture. This is not surprising since both authors are avid readers and have described the importance of books in their lives. In fact, *Fahrenheit 451* was written in the UCLA library. One of the most crucial passages in the novel shows a woman willing to die for her books. Montag is stunned when she sets fire to her library and immolates herself along with her precious volumes. This experience causes Montag to question what there is in books that is worth dying for and ultimately leads to his becoming a preserver of books instead of a destroyer. . . .

Each novel ends with the protagonist's escape and the beginning of his exile from repression. There is some ambiguity, however, since the alter native order is not elaborated on. Montag watches his city being destroyed by a nuclear explosion. He joins a group of vagabonds who memorize the books with which they have escaped. No attempt is made to follow his further development in these difficult circumstances or to predict the course the future holds for society or the survivors. The implication is clear, however, that intellectual freedom is worth the inconvenience of life outside the modern city. Because he left, Montag survives the death of the mindless masses who stayed behind. . . .

The appeal of these two highly acclaimed novels stems from the main characters' difficult situation in a repressive future United States. The plausible explanations given by both Bradbury and Atwood for the ghastly turn taken by American society in the futures they portray serves as a vivid reminder that freedom must be vigilantly guarded in order to be maintained. Apathy and fear create unlivable societies from which only a few courageous souls dare escape. "Ordinary" says one of the cruel Aunts of *The Handmaid's Tale* "is what you are used to." The main characters never are able to accept the "ordinariness" of the repression which surrounds them. They are among the few who are willing to risk the difficult path of exile.

FURTHER READING

Criticism

Jacobs, Robert. "The Writer's Digest Interview: Bradbury." *Writer's Digest* 56, No. 2 (February 1976): 18-25.

    Interview in which Bradbury discusses the writing profession and comments on his own work.

Additional coverage of Bradbury's life and career is contained in the following sources published by Gale Research: *Authors and Artists for Young Adults,* **Vol. 15;** *Authors in the News,* **Vols. 1, 2;** *Concise Dictionary of American Literary Biography, 1968-1988;* *Contemporary Authors,* **Vols. 1-4 rev ed.;** *Contemporary Authors New Revision Series,* **Vols. 2, 30;** *Contemporary Literary Criticism,* **Vols. 1, 3, 10, 15, 42;** *Dictionary of Literary Biography,* **Vols. 2, 8;** *DISCovering Authors; DISCovering Authors: British; DISCovering Authors: Canadian; DISCovering Authors Modules; Major 20th-Century Writers; Something about the Author,* **Vols. 11, 64;** *World Literature Criticism, 1500 to the Present.*

Joseph Mitchell
1908-1996

American journalist and nonfiction and fiction writer.

INTRODUCTION

A leading staff writer at the *New Yorker* magazine for over half a century, Mitchell became well known for his stories and sketches about a variety of eccentric and bizarre people he met while exploring New York City. Uninterested in the city's elite and famous and their activities, Mitchell preferred to write about the people and places of Harlem, Greenwich Village, the Bowery, and New York harbor. The subjects of his profiles are mainly oddballs and misfits, many of them homeless, who exist on the fringes of mainstream society— gypsies, drunks, bums, street preachers, strippers, panhandlers, carnies, clammers, oystermen. At the height of his creativity, from the late 1930s to the mid-1960s, Mitchell published five collections of his writings, all of which were enthusiastically received by critics and the public. Many critics labeled Mitchell the best reporter in the country in his chosen field, remarking upon his exceptional skills as an interviewer, photographic representation of his characters and their speech, deadpan humor, and graceful, unadorned prose style. These features of Mitchell's writing, combined with his respect and compassion for his subjects and his exploration of the themes of mortality, change, and the past, have led many commentators to credit Mitchell with transforming the craft of reporting into an art.

Biographical Information

Mitchell was raised on his family's cotton and tobacco farm in Fairmont, North Carolina. He enrolled at the University of North Carolina in 1925, leaving four years later without a degree to pursue a career as a journalist in New York City, with the ultimate aim of becoming a political correspondent. His first job was as a police reporter for the *New York World*. Initially assigned to the Brooklyn precinct, he was quickly transferred first to a district on the west side of Manhattan and then to Harlem. Although Mitchell stayed at the *World* for just a few months, his job there had an important influence on his career. It was while working the night shift in Harlem that Mitchell discovered his niche as a writer. He disliked writing crime stories, but he found life in Harlem fascinating; even when he was off duty, he would walk the streets, talking with the many unusual people he encountered. After leaving the *World*, Mitchell worked briefly for the *New York Herald Tribune*, where he began to write about the people he had met in Harlem. Later, as a feature interviewer for the

New York World-Telegram from 1931 to 1938, he specialized in writing about New York City's eccentric and obscure. Most of the forty articles included in Mitchell's first book, *My Ears Are Bent* (1938), were reprinted from the *Herald Tribune* and *World-Telegram*, but the collection also contains some pieces that first appeared in the *New Yorker*, where Mitchell worked from 1938 until shortly before his death from cancer on May 24, 1996.

Major Works

As its title indicates, *My Ears Are Bent* is comprised of articles about people who talked to Mitchell at length about their lives. In one portion of the book, Mitchell writes, "I have been tortured by some of the fanciest ear-benders in the world . . . and I have long since lost the ability to detect insanity." Among the people profiled in *My Ears Are Bent* are members of the United Fan, Bubble, and Specialty Dancers of America; a buxom blond Jewish woman who runs a dime movie theater in the Bowery and looks after the neighborhood drunks; an accomplished pickpocket; a man who sells racing cockroaches to the wealthy; and a lady boxer who claims to be a countess. Mitchell's subject matter and technique changed very little over the course of his career. Although he became increasingly interested in the activities on New York's waterfront and the old men who spent their time there, he continued to portray mainly loners, down-and-outers, and freaks. Few of Mitchell's characters are happy; some have had bad luck, others have succumbed to temptation, and many are old-timers whose lifestyles are threatened by progress and technology. Yet despite adversity, they fight to survive, aided in their struggle by their appreciation of life's absurdities and their enjoyment of simple pleasures, especially hearty eating and drinking, one of Mitchell's own frequent pastimes. Mitchell's approach to his work is objective and factual. He records detail upon detail about his subjects in simple, straightforward prose, and he allows his characters to speak for themselves, never passing judgment. He is equally precise when describing his favorite New York City landmarks. One of these was New York's oldest bar, McSorley's Old Ale House, which supplied Mitchell with the title for his second book, *McSorley's Wonderful Saloon* (1943). A collection of twenty stories and sketches, *McSorley's*, like all of Mitchell's later books, consists entirely of material that first appeared in the *New Yorker*. In the first piece in *McSorley's*, "The Old House at Home," Mitchell describes the atmosphere and clientele of the bar, relishing the fact that neither have changed much since the establishment's founding in 1854. Located on East Seventh Street near the edge of the Bowery, McSorley's is a men-only, working-class saloon. Cobwebs hang from the ceiling, gas lamps supply the only lighting, and there is no cash register—patrons drop coins in soup bowls to pay for their mugs of beer. "The Old House at Home" contrasts sharply with another sketch in *McSorley's*, "Obituary of a Gin Mill," in which Mitchell relates how Dick's Bar and Grill, a rowdy, low-class saloon, loses its charm and character when the owner moves it to a new location and equips it with chrome bar stools, a neon sign, and a mahogany bar. Other pieces in *McSorley's* are devoted to an array of New York personalities, including Cockeye Johnny Nikanov, a self-proclaimed leader of thirty-eight gypsy families with a five-quart-a-week gin habit; Jane Burnell, a bearded lady who travels with the freak shows; and Commodore Dutch, who subsists on the proceeds from an annual ball he gives for his own benefit. Mitchell's third book, *Old Mr. Flood* (1948), which he described as "stories of fish-eating, whiskey, death and rebirth," is unique among his writings because it deals with a fictional character. Hugh G. Flood, a ninety-three-year-old widower who believes he can live to be 115 by maintaining a strict diet of fresh fish untainted by modern chemicals, is a composite of several old men Mitchell met at the Fulton Fish Market. Mr. Flood and his aged friends are preoccupied with thoughts of death and the past, which to them was infinitely better that the present because of its simplicity, yet they pursue life with gusto, taking comfort in telling tall tales and overindulging in food and liquor. The theme of the past is also an important element in Mitchell's fourth book, *The Bottom of the Harbor* (1960). The six articles collected in *The Bottom of the Harbor* are entirely concerned with the waters around New York and the people who live and work nearby. Most of the people in these articles are old men, whose memories provide the reader with a history of New York as a seaport and its old fishing families. In one of the pieces, Mitchell describes what is literally at the bottom of the harbor; in another, he recounts a visit with one of the oldest surviving members of a nineteenth-century black village on Staten Island. The most frequently discussed piece in the collection, "Up in the Old Hotel," finds Mitchell at a waterfront fish restaurant, Sloppy Louie's, which is just across the street from the Fulton Fish Market. As Mitchell eats, the proprietor, Louie Morino, talks to him, and the two eventually decide to explore the four abandoned floors above the restaurant, the former site of the Fulton Ferry Hotel. Mitchell's next book, *Joe Gould's Secret* (1965), chronicles the life of a derelict bohemian eccentric who was well known in Greenwich Village from the 1920s to the 1940s. Gould, a member of the Harvard graduating class of 1911, crashed parties, sponged drinks at bars by imitating the cries of sea gulls, and claimed to be writing a book called *An Oral History of Our Time* that was eleven times longer than the Bible. Mitchell first profiled Gould in a 1942 *New Yorker* piece entitled "Professor Sea Gull," which was the outcome of several lengthy interviews during which Gould cadged large quantities of gin and beer. After the appearance of this article, Gould hounded

Mitchell, going so far as to use Mitchell's office as his mailing address. Exasperated by Gould's endless gabbing about himself and his legendary book, only a few paragraphs of which Gould had allowed anyone to see, Mitchell made repeated attempts to locate the manuscript of Gould's oral history. When Mitchell confronted Gould with his suspicion that the book did not really exist, Gould dropped out of his life and eventually ended up in a psychiatric hospital. Mitchell exposed Gould as a fraud in two *New Yorker* articles that ran in 1964, which, along with the 1942 profile, make up the contents of *Joe Gould's Secret*. Mitchell published no new material after the appearance of *Joe Gould's Secret*, although he continued to go to work at the *New Yorker* until shortly before his death. During these years, Mitchell closely guarded his privacy, avoiding interviews and refusing to allow his books to be reissued. However, he finally agreed to be anthologized, and in 1992 Pantheon Books brought out *Up in the Old Hotel*, a compendium of Mitchell's *New Yorker* writings including *McSorley's*, *Old Mr. Flood*, *The Bottom of the Harbor*, *Joe Gould's Secret*, and seven additional pieces. Modern Library editions of *The Bottom of the Harbor* (1994) and *Joe Gould's Secret* (1996) have since followed.

Critical Reception

By the time *Up in the Old Hotel* appeared, Mitchell's books had long been out of print. Welcomed by both die-hard *New Yorker* fans and readers unacquainted with Mitchell's writings, *Up in the Old Hotel* made it to the *New York Times* bestseller list. It was also widely reviewed in newspapers and magazines, where Mitchell was once again praised for his ear for dialogue and eye for detail, genuine interest in the lives of his subjects, and rhythmic, simple prose. Many commentators credited him with pioneering a new type of "literary journalism" that served as a model for later generations of nonfiction writers. Most critics of *Up in the Old Hotel* questioned why Mitchell had not published anything new for so many years. Some speculated that he had developed writer's block as a result of being hoodwinked by Gould. Others concluded that he had been deprived of his subject matter, noting that Mitchell's innocent world of lovable drunks and bums no longer existed. Mitchell offered his own explanation in a 1992 interview: "The city changed on me. . . . I can't seem to get anything finished anymore. The hideous state the world is in just defeats the kind of writing I used to do." Like the subjects of many of his profiles, Mitchell felt threatened by change and was saddened by the passage of time and the demise of long-standing traditions. While critics have remarked that the tone of Mitchell's writings became increasingly nostalgic, they also emphasize that Mitchell's melancholy is tempered by his earthy sense of humor and obvious delight in making new discoveries about New York. His writings are a testament to his insatiable interest in the city. As Noel Perrin observed, "Mitchell described the life and even the very soul of New York as perhaps no one else ever has."

PRINCIPAL WORKS

My Ears Are Bent (nonfiction) 1938
McSorley's Wonderful Saloon (nonfiction) 1943
Old Mr. Flood (fiction) 1948
The Bottom of the Harbor (nonfiction) 1960
Joe Gould's Secret (nonfiction) 1965
Up in the Old Hotel (nonfiction and fiction) 1992

CRITICISM

Robert Van Gelder (review date 23 January 1938)

SOURCE: "Some Talk That Bent a Reporter's Ears," in *The New York Times Book Review*, January 23, 1938, p. 5.

[*In the following review of* My Ears Are Bent, *Van Gelder describes the types of people Mitchell most liked to interview.*]

Mr. Mitchell is a sort of Stephen Crane of this generation's newspaper city rooms, a somber athlete with an exceptional writing talent who finds Harlem and the lower East Side the most interesting localities in town. The book's title [*My Ears Are Bent*] is his comment on the listening he has been obliged by his trade of daily newspaper interviewer to go through. He has become a connoisseur of talk and holds that the best talk is artless, made up of the wandering comments of people trying to reassure or comfort themselves. He particularly fancies the intimate confidences of those who might roughly be classified as "screwballs." For instance, there was a Mr. Samuel J. Burger who telephoned Mr. Mitchell's office to say that he was selling racing cockroaches to society people at 75 cents a pair. Mr. Mitchell went to interview him and found him in a Broadway delicatessen buying ham and cheese sandwiches for a couple of strip-tease women. Mr. Burger talked for a while about his cockroaches, and then mentioned a side line, the renting of monkeys. "I rent a lot of monkeys," he said. "People get lonesome and telephone me to send them a monkey to keep them company. After all, a monkey is a mammal, just like us."

Mr. Mitchell has decided that the most interesting human beings, so far as talk is concerned, are people whose occupations tend to restrain their own speech: anthropologists, farmers, prostitutes, psychiatrists, and an occasional bartender. The only people he does not care to listen to are society women, industrial leaders, distinguished authors, ministers, explorers, moving picture actors (except W. C. Fields and Stepin Fetchit), and any actress under the age of 35. His book is made up of interviews with fan dancers, Negro evangelists, taxi drivers, politicians, persons engaged in the conjure busi-

ness in one way or another, and people who own saloons. There are also some "atmosphere" sketches. The writing is always good and the book contains more of the strong, brash reds, yellows and blues that make New York the world's big town than any other book I ever have read.

Mr. Mitchell came here not many years ago at the age of 21. He had never lived in a town with a population of more than 2,699—he came from North Carolina. His first job was as a district reporter, which means that he was responsible for the coverage of all news of police activity in a set area. The district he liked best was Harlem, where he got to know a detective who sometimes took him on his rounds and showed him goings on that Mitchell hadn't quite believed possible. He also established talking terms with a few underworld figures.

After a few months on district he was brought into the main office of the newspaper for which he worked and for a time he specialized in writing crime stories. Then he moved to another paper and became a feature interviewer, a job that is so much what the reporter makes it that it is about as much strain on the conscience as is free-lancing. Mr. Mitchell has successfully fought off the temptation to let himself down when he goes out for a yarn, as the excellence of this book clearly proves.

Otis Ferguson (review date 2 March 1938)

SOURCE: "About People," in *The New Republic*, Vol. LXXXXIV, No. 1213, March 2, 1938, pp. 108-09.

[*In the following essay, Ferguson comments on Mitchell's creative approach to feature writing.*]

There are hundreds of fancy feature writers scattered through the newspaper business, but few of them ever show up as the creative people they hope to be (sufficient unto the day is the newsprint thereof). Joseph Mitchell is an exception, that writer's mirage of a man who can cover an angle of the news neither inspiring in itself nor congenital to him, get the stuff in for the home edition, and still be able to collect it for a second or third reading.

Mitchell covers several dozen news angles in the life of metropolitan New York, from freak to human interest, from behind the lines on headline sensations to strippers, reefer smokers, the life of a bar and grill. In doing it he has a perfect talent for hitting off the human equation. He is neither supercilious nor taken in; not a gawk, not a sob-sister; not Lucius Beebe nor a press agent, nor Winchell. He's got to make a story each time, but he makes it from the approach of a good novelist. His characters are realized in terms of how the world sees them and how they see the world revolving around themselves.

What with humor, kindness, straight candor, dramatic talent and the balance of a point of view being so infrequent in the supplements, and what with the fierce restrictions of time and subject under which such writers work clearly in mind, we lift a cheer for the publication of a book like *My Ears Are Bent*. But the questions still present themselves: Will Mr. Mitchell by his yeoman work help to elevate the craft of feature writing with its vitally larger audience? Or will all this news-must, deadline business merely serve to keep a man from writing in the more enduring literary forms? Joseph Mitchell's sympathy, eye and writing talents reveal themselves as among the things we really have to pay attention to.

Malcolm Cowley (review date 26 July 1943)

SOURCE: "The Grammar of Facts," in *The New Republic*, Vol. 109, No. 4, July 26, 1943, pp. 113-14.

[*In the following review of* McSorley's Wonderful Saloon, *Cowley comments on Mitchell's style, which he considers factual and repertorial.*]

In his own somewhat narrow field, which is that of depicting curious characters, Joseph Mitchell is the best reporter in the country. Some of his favorite subjects are Bowery angels, barflies, small-time Broadway sports, coffee-pot poets and Calypso singers. He writes about them with more sympathy and factual precision than you will find in the recent biographies of any famous authors or statesmen. In his new book, *McSorley's Wonderful Saloon,* there is not a trace of condescension. He says in an author's note, after explaining that these portraits were first written for *The New Yorker,* "The people in a number of the stories are of the kind that many writers have recently got into the habit of referring to as 'the little people.' I regard this phrase as patronizing and repulsive. There are no little people in this book. They are as big as you are, whoever you are."

They are in fact as big as life, because they are shown in perspective against their proper backgrounds. Mitchell's collection of portraits is the exact opposite of the books that choose an important subject, but are hastily written and have nothing much to say. These books, which form the bulk of current writing, always make you feel as if you had paid for looking into the wrong end of a telescope. Mitchell, on the other hand, likes to start with an unimportant hero, but he collects all the facts about him, arranges them to give the desired effects, and usually ends by describing the customs of a whole community.

Commodore Dutch, the subject of one portrait, "is a brassy little man who has made a living for the last forty years by giving an annual ball for the benefit of himself." Mitchell doesn't try to present him as anything more than a barroom scrounger; but in telling the story of his career, he also gives

a picture of New York sporting life since the days of Big Tim Sullivan. The story called **"King of the Gypsies"** is even better. It sets out to describe Cockeye Johnny Nikanov, the spokesman or king of thirty-eight gypsy families, but it soon becomes a Gibbon's decline and fall of the American gypsies; and it ends with an apocalyptic vision that is not only comic but also, in its proper context, more imaginative than anything to be found in recent novels. "I just can't wait for the blow-up of the whole entire world," says Cockeye Johnny. "It's going to bust wide open any day now, ask any gypsy, and I don't give a D-double-damn if it does." Still another portrait, that of my old friend, Joe Gould, has for its background "the cafeterias, diners, barrooms and dumps of Greenwich Village." Here the method is exactly that of the early Renaissance painters who, when depicting a rich landowner, liked to open a window and show the peasants working in the vineyards and olive fields of his estate.

> The people in a number of the stories [in *McSorley's Wonderful Saloon*] are of the kind that many writers have recently got into the habit of referring to as "the little people." I regard this phrase as patronizing and repulsive. There are no little people in this book. They are as big as you are, whoever you are.
>
> —*Joseph Mitchell*

Mitchell himself has a curious background for a man who specializes in genre pictures of metropolitan life. He was born on a cotton and tobacco farm in the North Carolina lowlands, not far from the Little Pee Dee River. As a boy he fished for blue bream in the swamps, hoed corn and chopped cotton in his bare feet. He still likes to go barefoot in his New York apartment, although the rug doesn't feel as cool and springy as the soil of a cornfield after a light rain. At the University of North Carolina, he wrote for the college paper and had a story accepted for publication in the third edition of *The American Caravan*—the same volume that contained the first published work of Erskine Caldwell and Robert Cantwell. It was a story in which the hero whispered to the cold winds, "Would to find a wine as wild as the boar is wild in the swamp deep in winter." He fell in love with a field woman, but you never heard her name or saw her face; in fact you weren't quite sure whether she was white or colored. Everything in the story was twilight, mood and strong lyrical feeling.

In the stories that Mitchell has been writing during the last few years, everything is action, factual statement and direct quotation. There are no moods or mysteries, no wraithlike women and no intrusions by the author, who now pretends to be merely arecording device. A good example of his behavioristic writing is the first paragraph of a portrait called **"Mazie"**:

> A bossy, yellow-haired blonde named Mazie P. Gordon is a celebrity on the Bowery. In the nickel-a-drink saloons and in the all-night restaurants which specialize in pig snouts and cabbage at a dime a platter, she is known by her first name. . . . She has a wry but genuine fondness for bums and is undoubtedly acquainted with more of them than any other person in the city. Each day she gives them between five and fifteen dollars in small change, which is a lot of money on the Bowery. "In my time I been as free with my dimes as old John D. himself," she says. Mazie has presided for twenty-one years over the ticket cage of the Venice Theatre, at 209 Park Row, a few doors west of Chatham Square, where the Bowery begins.

Mazie is a character who, allowing for a distance of three thousand miles and a hundred years, might have come straight out of Dickens. Almost all the subjects of Mitchell's portraits are essentially Dickens people, and therefore it is interesting to compare this paragraph with another in which Dickens introduces two of his favorite characters:

> Mr. and Mrs. Veneering were bran-new people in a bran-new house in a bran-new quarter of London. Everything about the Veneerings was spick and span new. All their furniture was new, all their friends were new, all their servants were new, their platewas new, their carriage was new, their harness was new, they themselves were new, they were as newly married as was lawfully compatible with their having a bran-new baby, and if they had set up a great-grandfather, he would have come home in matting from the Pantechnicon, without a scratch upon him, French polished to the crown of his head. [*Our Mutual Friend*]

After Dickens hit upon the phrase "bran-new" to describe the Veneerings—if he had been an American, he would have said "brand-new," which is etymologically sounder—everything else was a rhetorical development out of this one idea. None of it was observed or recorded, except possibly the baby; it was all the product of Dickens' inexhaustible verve. If Mitchell had been writing the paragraph, he would have started by saying, "The Veneerings were newly rich people with a brand-new baby"; then he would have gone on to tell how much they paid for their house, where they bought their furniture and the sort of polish used by their three housemaids to make it shine. The style would be businesslike and completely unobtrusive.

I am tempted to wonder whether this *New Yorker* method isn't typical of our age and whether we haven't entered a period when even authorship has become an impersonal and collective undertaking. In Mitchell's factual writing, it is hard not to see an image of the factual lives we lead, under the dictatorship of numbers, statistical averages and mass movements. Yet perhaps this impression of Mitchell is merely superficial. Reading some of hisportraits a second time, you catch an emotion beneath them that curiously resembles Dickens': a continual wonder at the sights and sounds of a big city, a continual devouring interest in all the strange people who live there, a continual impulse to burst into praise of kind hearts and good food and down with hypocrisy. Unlike Dickens, he represses this lyrical impulse, but it controls his selection of details. You might say that he tries—often successfully—to achieve the same effects with the grammar of hard facts that Dickens achieved with the rhetoric of imagination.

William S. Lynch (review date 31 July 1943)

SOURCE: "Raw Onions and No Ladies," in *Saturday Review of Literature*, Vol. XXVI, No. 31, July 31, 1943, p. 20.

[*In the following review of* McSorley's Wonderful Saloon, *Lynch praises Mitchell for his powers of observation and description, and especially for his compassion for his subjects.*]

A good saloon can be a lovely thing. The place where a man can join his fellows in free and easy camaraderie over a mug of ale or a pony of whiskey is an institution that deserves the literary and artistic recognition that so frequently it gets. New York has its share of such places, and they are not the chromium-plated cocktail bars of the post-Prohibition drinking age. Joseph Mitchell, the author of *My Ears Are Bent,* has a nice feeling for the friendly warmth of a Third Avenue saloon, and has selected as the title forhis new book of stories and sketches [*McSorley's Wonderful Saloon*] the name of one that lies just off the Avenue on Seventh Street, the oldest alehouse in New York, McSorley's. By now most literate Americans should be familiar with this historic shrine, for it has had frequent reference in recent American letters; and paintings of it hang on the walls of some of our best museums. Its apotheosis came with the inclusion in Thomas Craven's *A Treasury of Art Masterpieces,* of John Sloan's *McSorley's Bar.* Mitchell's account, which first appeared in *The New Yorker,* is one of the best brief descriptions of it. He has caught the fine flavor of this place of "good ale, raw onions, and no ladies," where, since 1854, hundreds and hundreds of New Yorkers, distinguished and otherwise, have drunk at the little bar beside the potbellied stove from earthenware mugs kept chilled in a washtub of ice water.

Mitchell knows other saloons than McSorley's, many of which

are settings for his stories. The people who live in them may seem queer and insignificant to the smug and respectable, but the author recognizes them for what they are—men and women fleeing desperately from the loneliness of the big city—men and women sometimes Homeric, sometimes craven, and frequently tormented by what his Professor Sea Gull calls "the 3-H's—homelessness, hunger, and hangovers."

Not all his stories are laid in New York. The only termagant he ever admired, Mrs. Copenhagen Calhoun, lives on a river bank watermelon farm in Black Ankle County; and Uncle Dockery, whose profound comments on the machine age might be summed up in his statement, "Son, the only inventions that make sense to me are the shotgun, the two-horse wagon, the butter churn, and the frying pan," is another denizen of that fabulous land.

Most of the stories do concern New York personalities. The author would protect this group of people from the patronizing and repulsive phrase "the little people." He says with truculent sentimentality, "There are no little people in this book. They are as big as you are, whoever you are." They range from Mazie, "a bossy, yellow-haired blonde," who is a celebrity in the Bowery, to the amazing Philippa Duke Schuyler, a gifted child with an IQ of 185, who at the tender age of nine "reads Plutarch on train trips, eats steaks raw, writes poems in honor of her dolls, plays poker, and is the composer of more than sixty pieces for the piano." There is a king of the gypsies whose greatest complaint is that "the entire country is overrun with private property." There is Commodore Dutch, the sporting man, who for forty years has been giving annual balls for the benefit of himself. There is even a bearded lady, Lady Olga, who is a student of society scandals and as a devoted reader of the Cholly Knickerbocker column observes "The Four Hundred is surely one cutting-up set of people."

Joseph Mitchell describes these and many others with great skill. His experience as feature writer for *The New York World-Telegram* and *The New Yorker* has added professional training to native perception. As a result, his studies are masterpieces of observation and description. Though they make one think of O. Henry and his "Four Million," it is not because of any imitative quality of treatment, but because of the similarity of subject matter. He does not try to be funny in a "pious friends and drunken companions" sort of way. Best of all, he has that quality which Fanny Hurst saw in his Mazie. "I admire Mazie," said Miss Hurst. "She is the most compassionate person I have ever known."

Stanley Walker (review date 1 August 1943)

SOURCE: "Historian of Queer—Not 'Little'—People," in *New York Tribune Weekly Book Review*, Vol. 19, No. 49, August 1, 1943, p. 5.

[*In the following review of* McSorley's Wonderful Saloon, *Walker ranks Mitchell as the best writer in his field, which Walker labels "low-life biography."*]

Joseph Mitchell is pretty generally accepted as the ablest practitioner of low-life biography, a field in which many talented writers have operated over the last few years. It has been said that he "must be about the best interviewer in the world," which may be true, although "interviewer" is not precisely the word. He is psychographer, historian and an extraordinarily acute observer of what some folk would call trivial. Whatever he is, there is little doubt that at the moment he is the Old Master of his particular type of stuff, which in his hands comes very near to being literature of a high order.

The sketches in this volume [*McSorley's Wonderful Saloon*] were printed originally in *The New Yorker* although some of them have been revised. For the most part they are portraits of persons who are generally regarded as of no importance; some, in fact, are downright vile. Some are amiable freaks. Some, in their way, achieve a sort of cockeyed heroic stature. In his note explaining and defending his choice of such characters the author says:

> The people in a number of the stories are of the kind that many writers have recently got in the habit of referring to as 'the little people.' I regard this phrase as patronizing and repulsive. There are no little people in this book. They are as big as you are, whoever you are.

A plausible defense, and almost perfect. The only trouble with it is that, on examination, it turns out to be not wholly true. Some of these people are smaller, and meaner, and dirtier than any group of citizens anywhere hereabouts.

There is no way of knowing what Mr. Mitchell could do if he turned his great talents to the examination of respectable and fairly normal people. Such dullards apparently hold little interest for him. In what he is trying to do, however, he has no superior. He is a remarkably competent, careful workman, and the apparently casual and effortless result comes from days and nights of research and toil which would flabbergast the ordinary reporter. There could be no greater fallacy than to assume that the people of Mr. Mitchell's chosen world are easy to write about.

"Literary taste" may be an odd phrase to use in connection with Mr. Mitchell and his unconventional heroes and heroines, and yet he has it. If there are any doubts, read his story of Lady Olga, the bearded lady. Here he set for himself a most difficult assignment: how to tell of the strange life of a woman of the sideshows, and tell it as fully and honestly as possible, without becoming either bathetic, sentimental, cruel or too funny. He succeeds magnificently. The tale has pathos, yes, but never too much; the reader must smile now and then, but it isn't a funny story.

The first piece in the book called **"The Old House at Home,"** is all about McSorley's old ale house on the East Side. This place has been the subject of many paintings, some of them excellent, but it remained for Mr. Mitchell to put it on paper. It is all here—the house customs and traditions, the smell of the establishment, and the old men who sit for hours in a curious state of half-life. There has been no finer picture of a saloon.

Other chapters include the career of Joe Gould, a far from attractive citizen, who also is known as Professor Sea Gull, who has filled 270 composition books with the talk, most of it unprintable which he has overheard; the life and times of Commodore Dutch who for many years has lived precariously by giving an annual ball for his own benefit; the goings-on of Mazie, the ticket-taker in a Bowery motion picture house, who in her off hours is a sort of Lady Bountiful to the bums of that area; the workings of Cockeye Johnny, one of the last of the Gypsy Kings, who drinks a vile mixture called "old popskull" and spends most of his time keeping his subjects out of trouble. There are also pieces on Mr. Colborne, "the don't swear man"; on Phillippa Duke Schuyler, the Negro child prodigy, and on Papa Houdini, the Calypso singer, who has a song entitled "I Like Bananas Because They Have No Bones." The piece on the gifted Schuyler girl is one of the few which deals altogether with respectable people, although even here the freakish aspects of the case give it its reason for being.

In the last part of the book Mr. Mitchell has three sketches of life in a place called Black Ankle County, in the Carolinas. They describe certain odd characters which he says he knew in his boyhood, and prove beyond doubt that eccentrics are by no means confined to New York. For good measure he throws in two New York barroom stories, which may or may not be fiction but which in any event are excellent.

It is probable that many of Mr. Mitchell's admirers and well wishers have at times hoped he could turn to a different field, on the ground that one can stand just so much of the lower depths without gagging. There may be something in this advice, but it probably is unsound. As long as he is enchanted by these people it seems a shame to divert him, for no one can do them so well.

Time (review date 2 August 1943)

SOURCE: "Bowery Botanist," in *Time*, Vol. XLII, No. 5, August 2, 1943, pp. 98, 100.

[*In the following review of* McSorley's Wonderful Saloon, *the critic describes the atmosphere of the bar and supplies thumbnail sketches of three of the people profiled in the book.*]

Joseph Mitchell is as gloomy as only a humorist can be. For years he has been studying, with the prying patience of a botanist, the queer human weeds he finds growing in the dingier interstices of Manhattan's bum-littered Bowery. But Mitchell is saddened when readers of *The New Yorker, Esquire* and other magazines chuckle at the results of his researches, these 20 profiles and stories, now collected for the first time in book form [in *McSorley's Wonderful Saloon*]. For Humorist Mitchell professes to find nothing comic in his wacky human jujubes. He says he does not caricature them. Instead, he describes them with a loving exactness which gives them an odd dignity. Such humor as they have, he implies, is incidental. It results from the lighting of an infallible eye on a fallible object.

Focus and locus of most of Author Mitchell's studies is the environs of McSorley's Old Ale House, which for 88 years has resisted change just off Cooper Square, where Manhattan's skidroad—the Bowery—ends. McSorley's has also provided a haven for Manhattan's literary transients—writers, newshawks, painters, poets (grateful Poet e. e. cummings once immortalized mcsorley's: "Inside snug and evil. . . . the Bar tinking luscious jigs dint of ripe silver with warmlyish wetflat splurging smells waltz the glush of squirting taps. . . ." The venerable saloon still has soup bowls instead of cash registers, gas lights over the bar, a rack of clay and corncob pipes for free smokes on the house. Under portraits of Lincoln, Garfield and McKinley is a brass plate: THEY ASSASSINATED THESE GOOD MEN THE SKULKING DOGS.

Once McSorley's was home to 18 cats. At feeding time, no matter how brisk business was, Bill McSorley would leave the bar and bang the bottom of a tin pan. "The fat cats would come loping up, like leopards, from all corners of the saloon." If Bill wanted to close up while customers were still drinking their ale, he would drum on the bar with both fists, shout: "Now, see here, gents! I'm under no obligoddamnation to stand here all night while you baby them drinks."

Women are still firmly excluded from McSorley's. Once a Greenwich Village feminist, disguised as a man, ordered an ale from Proprietor Bill McSorley. She downed first the ale, then her hair. Then she scrammed. Said the amazed McSorley between a moan and a bellow: "She was a woman! She was a goddamn woman!"

The city just outside McSorley's is less cozy but just as queer. It has yielded Author Mitchell specimens like:

—Mazie, who has a "genuine fondness for bums and is undoubtedly acquainted with more of them than any other person in the city." Every day Mazie gives away from $5 to $15 in small change to Bowery down-&-outers. Says Mazie: "I been as free with my dimes as old John D. himself."

For 21 years Mazie has presided at the ticket cage of the Venice Theater, on Park Row, where the Bowery begins. "Some days I don't know which this is, a movie-pitcher theater or a flophouse. . . . Pitchers with shooting in them are bad for business. They wake up the customers." But she adds with pride: "Nobody ever got loused up in the Venice."

—Joe Gould, "the last of the bohemians," otherwise known as Professor Sea Gull, Professor Bloomingdale, The Mongoose. Gould tells what it took to make him: "old Yankee blood, an overwhelming aversion to possessions, four years of Harvard, and 25 years of beating the living hell out of my insides with bad hooch and bad food." Joe professes never to be without his "three Hs"—homelessness, hunger, hangovers. On winter nights he sports a layer of newspapers between his shirt and undershirt. He is 5 ft. 4, weighs 95 lb., and trims his cinnamon beard every other Easter. Twenty-six years ago he began a mysterious work—*An Oral History of Our Time*—a chronicle composed entirely of chance conversations on the Bowery and elsewhere. He has been working on it ever since. The unfinished manuscript (the fruit of more than 20,000 conversations) contains 9,000,000 words in longhand, is eleven times wordier thanthe Bible. So far no publisher has nibbled.

—Cockeye Johnny, self-styled King of the Gypsies. Says Johnny: "To the Department of Welfare, I may not be no king and to the King of England, I may not be no king, but to those poor, persecuted gypsies that I run myself knock-kneed looking after their personal welfare, I am king." A gin drinker, Johnny mixes it with Pepsi-Cola, calls it old popskull, consumes five quarts of gin a week. Johnny believes there are but two kinds of merchandise: "lost and unlost. Anything that ain't nailed down is lost." Johnny gets easily worked up over the idea of a job. "I despise to work," he says. "Gypsy men ain't built like ordinary men. They ain't fitted for shovel work. They're high-strung and they rupture easy."

Jerome Mellquist (review date 14 August 1943)

SOURCE: "Mitchell's Wonderful McSorley," in *The Nation*, Vol. 157, No. 7, August 14, 1943, p. 190.

[*In the following essay, Mellquist likens the sketches and stories in* McSorley's Wonderful Saloon *to genre paintings.*]

Genre paintings resemble feature stories. They take a mellow, or raffish, or appetizing area of life and memorialize it by the affection they have for their subject. Too often, unfortunately, they remain ephemeral, registering but a moment of warmth. But John Sloan's painting of McSorley's, an old bar on East Seventh Street,in New York, is still remembered.

And other painters, though somewhat less impressively, have also inscribed their affection for the place. Now Joseph Mitchell, ex-newspaperman who contributes special features to the *New Yorker,* has assembled twenty of these pieces and put them in a book with the title of ***McSorley's Wonderful Saloon***.

He begins with McSorley's, recounting its sawdust career under four changes of management in the last eighty-nine years. Then he ambles over to the Bowery, where he describes Mazie, the brassy blonde who presides at the ticket window of the "bums'" favorite movie palace. He inspects gypsies and museum-keepers; glorifies Joe Gould, the Greenwich Village eccentric who has translated several of Longfellow's poems into Seagull; chats with Madame Olga, the Bearded Lady, and laments the lapse into respectability of a once boisterous gin mill. He sympathizes with old scrubbers from the skyscrapers and with cave-dwellers from Central Park. He finds a drinking reformer and a Times Square "sport" who arranges a yearly benefit ball for himself.

> **Joseph Mitchell, who is at all times a scrupulous and attentive writer, has contributed something comparable to the best of our twentieth-century genre painters.**
>
> —*Jerome Mellquist*

In the second section of his book, Mr. Mitchell celebrates beefsteak fests, clam-diggers, and terrapin-raisers; in a third hesuggests potentialities as a short-story writer (in **"Goodbye, Shirley Temple"** and in **"On the Wagon"**), while in the last he delineates both joys and depredations in his home community near the Little Pee Dee River, in North Carolina. For the most part he remains objective, assembling facts, measuring, limiting himself to exact data. This gives one the sense of an honest camera shot, deliberate but unmoving. Sometimes he chides city inhabitants for their lack of gumption, and then he seems to editorialize. At best, he touches some subterranean chord which puts us *en rapport* with the metropolitan community. Old McSorley—father and then son—draws the taps and eyes the aging men who harbor in the creaking chairs. Mazie, locking her wicket, paces the darker reaches of the Bowery, seeking the wastrels who might otherwise perish in the night. These moments are cherishable, and they give us something that O'Henry, in many ways the predecessor of Mitchell, could not convey.

This is the sympathetic penetration of life. Sloan had it in *McSorley's,* and certainly in his early etchings. The more smoldering George Luks—surely an American genre painter if there ever was one—all but entered the very marrow of his subjects. True, the density and the richness are not attained to the same degree as in the Dutch, such as Van Ostade, or the demoniac Jan Steen. But new affiliations have been made between man and his fellows. And in this sense, Joseph Mitchell, who is at all times a scrupulous and attentive writer, has contributed something comparable to the best of our twentieth-century genre painters.

George Conrad (review date 24 October 1948)

SOURCE: "Fish Every Day," in *New York Herald Tribune Weekly Book Review*, Vol. 25, No. 10, October 24, 1948, p. 20.

[*In the following essay, Conrad judges* Old Mr. Flood *to be an accurate representation of a rapidly disappearing phase of Manhattan life.*]

As a reporter of the New York scene whose integrity equals his human insight and his admirable command of a disciplined prose that is never loosely journalistic or falsely literary, Joseph Mitchell informs his readers that this portrait of Mr. Flood [in *Old Mr. Flood*] is not one man but the composite of several venerable Fulton Fish. Market habitues. His purpose has been to make the stories "truthful rather than factual." Having become acquainted with Mr. Flood when he first appeared in the pages of *The New Yorker* we are reluctant to accept a multiple image. In his person and his philosophies, in his speech and in every detail of his deportment, old Mr. Flood remains intact and indivisible.

Widowed Mr. Flood, ninety-three-year-old retired contractor domiciled in a drowsy waterfront hotel, has his sights set on seeing his 115th birthday, and he is reasonably optimistic about it: "he has his own teeth, he hears all right, he doesn't wear glasses, his mind seldom wanders, and his appetite is so good that immediately after lunch he begins speculating about what he will have for dinner." He knows definitely that dinner will be fish, for science has ruined vegetables and fruits, and fancy feeds for hens have done such damage that nowadays when you order scrambled eggs "you get a platter of yellow glue, Grade A."

His point—and he is eloquent and convincing in his argument—is that the flesh of finfish and shellfish haven't been—and in the nature of things cannot be—tampered with, enriched with vitamins, or given any other torture by chemists or cranks. On that faith in the wisdom of providence, he stakes his dream of longevity. We hope he realizes it. Just to be on the safe side he includes Scotch whisky in his diet.

Mr. Mitchell's book is a vignette of Manhattan of enduring worth and warm humor. It preserves a phase of the city's life

rapidly becoming a memory. In *Old Mr. Flood* even the smell of it is good.

Horace Sutton (review date 20 November 1948)

SOURCE: "Fish Fan," in *Saturday Review of Literature*, Vol. XXXI, No. 47, November 20, 1948, p. 18.

[*In the following review of* Old Mr. Flood, *Sutton commends Mitchell for faithfully capturing the atmosphere of the Fulton Fish Market.*]

Never let it be said that Mr. Joseph Mitchell is a social climber, that he hobnobs with the aristocracy, rubs elbows with mink. First he spent ten or more nights in a barroom and came up with a fine book called *McSorley's Wonderful Saloon*. I was in McSorley's Old Ale House on East Seventh Street once and, believe me, I'm glad I got back uptown with my whole hide.

And just where do you think Mr. Mitchell has been spending his time lately? Down, if you please, at the Fulton Fish Market, New York's original Aroma Corner. Somewhere amid the shad and the haddock, Mr. Mitchell has turned up a character name of Hugh G. Flood, a retired housewrecker of ninety-three years and some means. Mr. Flood's object in life is to live to be 115, and, as you can see, he has a few to go. He plans to make the grade by maintaining a strict diet of fish—sea urchins, blowfish tails, winkles, ink squids, and bardnoor skates. Whereas you or I might knock off a stack of wheat cakes, Mr. Flood's breakfasts are apt to consist of fried cod tongues, cheeks, and sounds. Sounds, Mr. Mitchell informs us, are gelatinous air bladders along the cod's backbone. I wish he hadn't.

Old Mr. Flood lives in the Hartford House, a waterfront hotel where his room, by personal choice, is decorated with signs issued by the Fishery Council reading, "Fresh Mackerel Is in Season at a Cost Within Reason." He takes most of his meals at Sloppy Louie Morino's, a place on South Street catering largely to wholesale fishmongers. He likes Louie's best because the cook is an old Genoese. Next to old Italians, Mr. Flood thinks the best fish cooks are "old colored men, then old mean Yankees, then old drunk Irishmen. . . . If the cook is an awful drunk so much the better. . . ."

So far, Mr. Flood's dietetic system for longevity is paying off. He hasn't had a cold since 1912, and he has a fairly valid excuse for catching that one:

> I went on a toot and it was a pouring-down rainy night in the dead of winter and my shoes were cracked and they let the damp in and I lost my balance a time or two and sloshed around in the gutter and somewhere along the line I mislaid my hat and I'd just

had a haircut and I stood in a draft in one saloon an hour or more and there was a poor fellow next to me sneezing his head off and when I got home I crawled into a bed that was beside an open window like a fool and passed out with my wet clothes on, and be-sides . . .

With his character and purpose thus firmly established, Mr. Mitchell takes his Mr. Flood through a number of typical day-to-day adventures with his friends in the fish market. There is Mrs. Birdie Treppel, the fish wife who is always cold and always talking about it:

> . . . if you went up to the North Pole in the dead of December and stripped to the drawers and picked out the biggest iceberg and dug a hole right down to the heart of it . . . and crawled in . . . and put a handful of snow under each arm and et a dish of ice cream why, you wouldn't be near as cold. . . .

Then there is the Savannah Negro, Mr. Ah Got Um, who walks through the fish stalls chanting, "Ah got pompanos! Ah got buffaloes! Ah got these! Ah got those! . . ." There is Mr. Murchison, who calls gourmets "goormys" and bouilla-baisse "booly-booze" and likes neither. And Matthew T. Cusack (Old Drop-Dead Matty), retired New York cop, now watchman for the Fulton Market Fishmongers Association. There is also Mr. Joseph Mitchell, who sits by quietly and faithfully photographs the wonderful words of his characters without ever getting his own thumb in the lens.

Old Mr. Flood originally appeared as a three-part *New Yorker* Profile, and my only complaint is that some of the explana-tions which were repeated for continuity in the magazine se-ries might have been edited out of the book. It is, really, a very short work, and you will, I'm sure, find yourself wish-ing there were more. Mr. Mitchell has written with such a pungency that you'll probably find the flavor of the Fulton Fish Market hanging over the house for a couple of days. Of course, that's nothing that a stiff control of your extrasensory perceptions and a fresh Air Wick can't cure.

Brooks Atkinson (review date 24 April 1960)

SOURCE: "The City's Dockside," in *The New York Times Book Review*, April 24, 1960, pp. 3, 36.

[*In the following essay, Atkinson praises* The Bottom of the Harbor *as both literature and as a travel guide.*]

Since Joseph Mitchell is an unselfconscious writer, readers of *The Bottom of the Harbor* are never distracted from the subject matter of his book. He is discussing and describing the natural phenomena of the waters around New York—

fish, clams, oysters and lobsters, and the natives who are equally indigenous.

Occasionally Mr. Mitchell, author of *McSorley's Wonderful Saloon* and other books, appears in his pages as the man talked to or the man who went somewhere to meet a riverman or waterman. His function is that of a guide. Under his guidance you learn a good deal about Louis Morino, temperamental proprietor of Sloppy Louie's restaurant at 92 South Street; George H. Hunter, 87, chairman of the board of trustees of the African Methodist Church in Sandy Ground, Staten Is-land; Andrew E. Zimmer, tireless Shellfish Protector who patrols the harbor in a sea skiff; Ellery Franklin Thompson, knowledgeable skipper of the dragger, Eleanor, out of Stonington, Conn.; Harry Lyons, 74, a shad fisherman who has lived all his life in Edgewater, N. J., and has never been diverted from his attendance on the Hudson River by the metropolis on the eastern bank.

There is a wary chapter on the unconquerable rats of the wa-terfront. But the memorable things in *The Bottom of the Harbor* are the portraits of men of strong character. Mr. Mitchell gives them his undivided attention. He does not criti-cize or evaluate them; he does not patronize them in any way.

If this book were a collection of feature articles, the character and technique of the author would not be a matter of impor-tance. But *The Bottom of the Harbor* is literature. It is origi-nal in the clarity of its focus on familiar though neglected things, and it is beautifully written. Although the author is the least described of its characters, his talent for self-efface-ment is creative. It represents enthusiasm that is muted in style but eloquent in understanding. It represents purity of perception.

Like many of New York's acolytes, Mr. Mitchell is an out-lander. He comes from the tobacco country of North Caro-lina. In New York he has been a reporter successively on *The Herald Tribune* and *The World-Telegram*. Since 1938 he has been a staff writer for *The New Yorker,* which published this material originally.

As a chronicler of the harbor he begins with a basic fact: the life of the harbor carries over into our sophisticated time the rhythms and forces of primeval nature. It exists independent of the shrill, gaudy, congested, filthy city centered here. De-spite the shipping, despite the pollution and the bottom sludge that discharges bubbles of noxious gas in warm weather, the shad swarm up the Hudson by the millions every spring, a few sea sturgeon still shoot upriver, clams, eels, lobsters breed inside the harbor, and outside the harbor commercial fishing flourishes.

Everything is against the continuance of marine life, and some branches of it have been destroyed by overfishing or by filth.

Butlooking under the steel and concrete rim of the city, the author realizes that the stream of life that began in primeval times continues.

He also knows that natives still live around the harbor in the tradition of their forebears, devoted to the harbor and river, uninterested in the city. To them the city is a separate world; it is a rank growth like the brush that springs up in uncultivated fields. Nor does Mr. Mitchell regard the river as a useful thoroughfare for commercial shipping; it is something "hushed and dark and secret and remote and unreal." It is a part of the nature that remains from the ages before Verrazano and Hudson.

Millions of people crowd the subways, choke the streets and fill the skyscrapers engaged in business and professional activities that have repercussions all over the world, and will extend into outer space eventually. But the riverman "not only works on the river or kills a lot of time on it or near it, he is also emotionally attached to it." Like Mr. Lyons, the shad fisherman, he feels the need of taking a glimpse of it at night although he has been beside it all day. Mr. Mitchell is not a riverman to that degree. But he is emotionally on the side of the river and harbor. Note that he refers to the "five Staten Island ports" (not "towns" or "cities"). He refers to the "coasts of Staten Island, Brooklyn and Queens." "Shores" is too much of a landsman's term for him.

The Bottom of the Harbor is full of homely, pungent detail andobservations. To Mr. Lyons, looking downriver at night toward the area of Times Square, "the glare in the sky looks like the Last Judgment is on the way, or the Second Coming, or the end of the world." Mr. Hunter, the patriarch of Sandy Ground, once looked up from the mud when he was searching for pokeweed in a Staten Island swamp: "I saw, away off in the distance. . . . the tops of the skyscrapers in New York shining in the morning sun. . . . It was like a vision in the Bible."

In a quiet, unassertive style Mr. Mitchell has written a glowing travel book.

Bennett Epstein (review date 8 May 1960)

SOURCE: "All Around This Area with J. Mitchell," in *New York Herald Tribune Book Review*, Vol. 36, No. 40, May 8, 1960, p. 4.

[*In the following review of* The Bottom of the Harbor, *Epstein considers the influence of Mitchell's prose style on his profiles of his subjects.*]

Half a dozen stories which appeared in *The New Yorker* from 1944 to 1959 make up the latest volume [*The Bottom of the Harbor*] designed to give a longer lease of life than guaran-teed by ephemeral magazine covers to some of its articles. Few of them have been worthier than Joseph Mitchell's of preservation.

The author of *McSorley's Wonderful Saloon* has poked around in out of the way corners in the city and its environs to dig up pursuits and the people who follow them that few New York inhabitants ever knew existed. In this collection Mr. Mitchell is interested in some traditional and still surviving activities in and about New York's rivers, harbor and Long Island Sound.

His first story tells about a waterfront fish restaurant, Sloppy Louie's, still flourishing in a mellow old brick building in Fulton Market. Mr. Mitchell is a meticulous reporter. He gives us the exact dimensions of the restaurant, the number, material and arrangement of the tables but he is mainly interested in the personality of the proprietor. Louis Moreno serves a larger variety of seafood than any restaurant in the country and he is also a wise, warm-hearted man with an alert philosophic curiosity. As in all the stories, from a mass of minute details emerges a lovable portrait of a dedicated man.

> **Each of the men pictured [in *The Bottom of the Harbor*] lives in a world of his own which, under Mr. Mitchell's perceptive and appreciative guidance, the reader is allowed to enter for a while and remember with warm pleasure long afterward.**
>
> —*Bennett Epstein*

Other pieces tell of the multitude of fish, shell and many other varieties, in the harbor and rivers and the teeming commerce that has been going on for decades and persists, mostly by descendantsof the old fishing families. **"Dragger Captain"** gives a picture of a stubbornly independent thinker with an ironic view of life. He owns the largest of a fleet of draggers, a type of trawler, which still operates out of Stonington, Connecticut, dragging the adjacent waters with large nets for flounders and lobsters for the New York market. They are the survivors of the whalers and sealers that sailed out of Stonington a century ago. When Ellery Thompson isn't on his dragger, fishing in the proper season or preparing his gear, he is doing oil paintings of boats and maritime scenes or studying oceanography. Another happy man doing exactly what he wants to do.

Harry Lyons owns a shad barge, largest of the few still operating out of Edgewater, New Jersey across from central New York City and surrounded by modern factories now in this community. Here is another affectionate portrait of a man contentedly following a calling traditional in his family for generations.

The gem of these fascinating stories is **"Mr. Hunter's Grave."** Roaming around the southern end of Staten Island searching for wild flowers Mr. Mitchell came upon a ghost town. Some houses, looking as though they had once been substantial, a church, an occasional ancient man or woman, a few children but no young or middle-aged men or women. Even before the Civil War the waters around this former garden spot of Staten Island and the kills between the island and New Jersey were teeming with oyster beds providing a flourishing commerce that attracted many free Negroes from Maryland. They prospered for years until the oysters became polluted by the shipping coming into the harbor. When the commerce died out the younger people went to New York City and elsewhere for jobs. One of the few remaining descendants of these fine old families is eighty-six-year-old George Hunter who knows many things including the history of all the original families, all the wild flowers and herbs in the surrounding woods and cemeteries, his Bible and how to cook. We meet him baking cakes and pies for a visiting gospel choir he has invited for dinner. With Mr. Mitchell's detailed reporting you can almost taste and smell these cakes and pies and, later, in the cemetery to which the old man takes him, his listing of the names of wild flowers and weeds makes a sort of tonal arrangement out of statistics.

Each of the men pictured lives in a world of his own which, under Mr. Mitchell's perceptive and appreciative guidance, the reader is allowed to enter for a while and remember with warm pleasure long afterward.

Harry C. Kenney (review date 12 May 1960)

SOURCE: "Waterfront Metropolis," in *The Christian Science Monitor*, Vol. 52, No. 142, May 12, 1960, p. 86.

[*In the following review of* The Bottom of the Harbor, *Kenney applauds Mitchell for giving readers a chance to experience the sights, sounds, smells, and noises of New York harbor.*]

Much of New York is exposed to view by its mighty sky-piercing buildings, its snarled traffic on the broad avenues, the roar of subways; the shifting of great greyhounds of the sea in the busy harbor; and even fishing in Central Park and sun browsing on the steps of the public library on Fifth Avenue.

But Joseph Mitchell, in *The Bottom of the Harbor,* has exposed off-the-track drama in New York. A drama that comes only to those who live here, walk the streets in sun, rain, fog, and at night. He intimately acquaints you with a personality, an activity, a smell, a noise, or an experience by making you a part of it all.

There is much suspense in the chapter **"Up in the Old Hotel."** This takes you to the Fulton Fish Market district and you learn about a cheerful market restaurant named Sloppy Louie's. Here, too, you will find the essence of New York and much of the flavor of it in a big, inexpensive, invigorating breakfast—a kippered herring and scrambled eggs, or a shad-roe omelet, or split sea scallops and bacon.

It is Louis Morino, born in Recco, Italy, who has the restaurant and the building. He also has a tremendous desire to know what secrets have been hiding in the upper stories of the structure over the many years that he has stayed below. Thus the suspense and the ultimate story of the "old hotel."

The author explores the bottom of the harbor and seems to have had a long and pleasurable acquaintance with the coming and going of oyster and clam beds, rotting shipwrecks, old-time fishermen, and even pollution.

Out of the harbor run ditchbanks, and it is in these areas where the story is sensitive to the resident and migratory wildlife in the marshes. This part of the book informs you well of pheasants, crows, marsh hawks, black snakes, muskrats, opossums, rabbits, rats, and field mice—all practically in the shadow of the Empire State Building.

I would suppose that most writers would avoid certain almost automatic pitfalls to a successful book. But Mr. Mitchell has a chapter on **"The Rats on the Waterfront"** that is so creepily written that it is positively captivating. You learn that the rats of New York are quicker-witted than those on farms, and they can out-think any man who has not made a study of their habits. But New York has the means to control them, and this means a good deal since ships from all over the world bring them here. In fact, none of the rats in New York are indigenous to this country.

The author says that the biggest fishing fleet in the vicinity of New York City is a fleet of 30 wooden draggers that works out of Stonington, Conn. It is the story of the **"Dragger Captain,"** that gives shine to the pieces in this book which have appeared in *The New Yorker* over the years since 1944.

It is in this story that the reader comes close to smelling the sea and shares the hazards of the draggers as they work with nets over the rocks, wrecks, mussel beds, sponge beds, bladder wrack, and even World War II bombs.

It is here, too, that the reader learns to love the most highly respected captain in the Stonington fleet—a sad-eyed, easy-going Connecticut Yankee named Ellery Franklin Thompson. He is a member of a family that has fished and clammed and crabbed and attended to lobster traps in these waters for 300 years. You will never hear him brag about it.

But the switch, and the surprise, and the delight come when—much to the captain's amazement—he becomes a successful painter. It was quite a "blow" to him for a while—until he recovered and got used to it.

If you like *The New Yorker,* you will like this collection of stories.

Noel Perrin (essay date Spring 1983)

SOURCE: "Paragon of Reporters: Joseph Mitchell," in *The Sewanee Review*, Vol. XCI, No. 2, Spring, 1983, pp. 167-84.

[*In the following essay, Perrin provides a detailed summary of Mitchell's career, attempting to show the development of his craft and the means by which he transformed reporting into an art.*]

There are, at a generous estimate, about a dozen North Carolinians who belong to American literature. That's not meant as a slur. There *are* states, my own included, where you'd be hard pressed to find five. North Carolina has Thomas Wolfe, of course. And it has O. Henry and Charles Chesnutt—the first important black novelist this country ever produced—and Doris Betts and Reynolds Price. It also has Joseph Mitchell—in some ways the least known of the whole dozen, and in some ways the most remarkable.

What is remarkable about Mitchell, or one of the things, is that he has taken that form of writing which has the very lowest claim to being art, and made an art of it. Some would say a high art.

When you start ranking literary genres in order of prestige, poetry still comes out on top. The very act of writing a poem, even a bad one, sets one on the olympian or parnassian slope, however far down. At least in America novelists come next—Wolfe, for example, and Chesnutt, Betts, and Price. Then come dramatists, short-story writers, including O. Henry, biographers, and so on down. Possibly on a separate mountain, but high up, lofty, with a splendid view, one finds critics. Indeed the promotion or self-promotion of critics to a position of equality with creative writers has been the great literary event of our time.

Joseph Mitchell was, and still is, a reporter. First on anewspaper, then on a magazine. Nobody has promoted reporters. New journalists, yes—but then, the new journalism specifically rejects old-fashioned or objective reporting in favor of something more imaginative. Joseph Mitchell is, in the sense of caring first and perhaps even second and third for accuracy, an old-fashioned reporter. He began his career in the classic old-reportorial style, covering a police beat for an urban newspaper. The year was 1929, he had left the University of North Carolina after four years but without a de-gree, and he got a job as the Brooklyn police reporter for the New York *World.* As he later put it, his job was to hang around Brooklyn "waiting for something violent to happen." When something did, he did not get to compose a story. He telephoned the facts in to a rewrite man, and then settled back to wait for the next act of violence. From Brooklyn he moved to a police precinct on the west side of Manhattan, and from there to Harlem, which is the point at which his career began to separate itself from those of a thousand other bright young cub reporters. He had been in New York three months.

He has now been there fifty-four years. He stayed with the *World* a few months, moved briefly to the *Herald Tribune,* then back to what was just becoming the *World-Telegram,* stayed there seven years (with a few months out when he worked as a seaman on a freighter bringing pulp logs from Russia), and moved to the *New Yorker,* where he has stayed ever since. *Stay* is the key word. All this time he has stayed a reporter, and though living so long in New York has stayed a North Carolinian, the kind who was born on a farm. (Hestill owns the farm.) Even when he began to get serious recognition, it was in old-journalism terms. "In his own somewhat narrow field," said Malcolm Cowley, "he is the best reporter in the country." The "paragon of reporters," Stanley Edgar Hyman called him—though Hyman, to be sure, went on to claim a good deal more for him that has nothing to do with journalism of any sort. Meanwhile, in five books and hundreds of articles, Mitchell described the life and even the very soul of New York as perhaps no one else ever has. In what follows I propose to summarize his career, and simultaneously to try to show by what means he converted reporting into an art.

The place to begin is back in North Carolina, because two of the qualities that distinguish Mitchell both as a person and as a writer are specifically southern ones that he brought with him when he came north.

One is a sense of the past—in Mitchell's case, as in Faulkner's, a strongly elegiac sense. Like Gail Hightower in *Light in August* Mitchell hears the hoofbeats of ghostly cavalry. Growing up in a country that was one-third white, one-third black, and one-third Indian, he knew even as a boy that America has had many avatars, that its present drags an immense past behind it, call this a new world or not. Growing up near a small town that had become the chief tobacco market of the region, he early got a sense not just of the excitement of the auctions, and of the little passing circuses and the black fishfry restaurants, but of the fact thatall this derived from local tradition and was threatened by national change. Growing up on a cotton farm, he could not even hear "Dixie" sung without an extra sense of poignancy. That he is a little embarrassed that in 1983 the farm produces mainly soybeans is typical of him. It is clear he feels this is a come-down—not for him as the absentee but frequently-visiting owner, but for the land itself. Former cotton fields are bound to look a little askance at soybeans.

The other quality Mitchell brought north is an enormous courtesy. In superficial southerners of his generation, that courtesy might be no more than habitual good manners, and a touch of formality that tended to confer dignity on any social transaction. In Mitchell's case it was and is something more. The ultimate courtesy is to accept people on their own terms—and more than accept them, which can be done *de haut en bas* or social-scientifically, but to take them seriously, to see them as they are or believe they are, and to value what you see.

There is no evidence that Mitchell specially valued what he saw in Brooklyn at the age of twenty-one—reporting violent crimes. (I have no doubt, though, that one form of his courtesy extended to Brooklyn thugs.) But when he was assigned to Harlem in the fall of 1929, something began to click. Mitchell had already discovered that he didn't like being a police reporter—"the only kind of crime I liked was gangster funerals," he wrote in his first book—and his conscious aim was to be graduated to political reporting. He might have wound up a White House correspondent.

In Harlem he found something more engaging than hanging around the White House waiting for a press release to happen. He found urban life. What first attracted him was its raffish side. Naturally, as a crime reporter working the night shift, Mitchell met a good many of the leading under-world figures in Harlem—and when he wasn't going to their funerals or reporting their indictments, he was sitting in black bars like the Broken Leg and Busted, talking to them. He was fascinated by what they had to say, and they found they had never had so good a listener before as this young southern white. The young white was so taken with the drama of Harlem at night, in fact, that even when he went off duty at 3 A.M. he couldn't bear to leave. He'd stay, walking the streets and visiting his friends, usually until dawn.

When, after four months on the *World-Telegram,* he began to be allowed to write his own stories, he found that what interested him most to write about were his new friends. He did a piece on Gilligan Holton, the owner of the Broken Leg and Busted. Another on uptown marijuana parties of 1930. Another on Elder Lightfoot Solomon Michaux, a former bartender turned revivalist and one of the three New York preachers he ever really warmed to. (The other two were Father Divine and the Rev. G. Spund, an East Side rabbi who specialized in low-priced but de luxe weddings. "When a couple gets married by the Rev. Dr. Spund it does not slip the mind," the rabbi told him.)

In these early articles the elegiac sense that he had brought north with him played no part. Mitchell was wholly caught up in the present, delighting in the variety of unselfconscious eccentrics, exotics, and frauds to be found in a great city. What had clicked in Harlem was the discovery that the double awareness with which he saw such people could be reflected in articles about them—seriously presenting Holton or Spund as a real if unusual person, and at the same time making full use of the comic and tragicomic aspects of their lives. In his own voice Mitchell seldom offers a judgment or a final truth about the people he portrays. Fairly often, though, as in Browning's dramatic monologues, the characters themselves wind up making a self-judgment, not always conscious. These tend to have great impact, since from the start Mitchell had a perfect ear for speech.

Within a year he had become his paper's specialist in the bizarre. He met exotics by the hundred. Here is his account of a typical working day:

> When I came in one morning at 9 I was assigned to find and interview an Italian bricklayer who resembled the Prince of Wales; someone telephoned that he had been offered a job in Hollywood. I tracked him to the cellar of a matzoth bakery on the East Side, where he was repairing an oven. I got into a fight with the man who ran the bakery; he thought I was an inspector from the Health Department. I finally got to the bricklayer and he would not talk much about himself but kept saying, "I'm afraid I get sued." I went back to my office and wrote that story and then I was assigned to get an interview with a lady boxer who was living at the St. Moritz Hotel. She had all her boxing equipment in her room. The room smelled of sweat and wet leather, reminding me of the locker-room of Philadelphia Jack O'Brien's gym on a rainy day. She told me she was not only a lady boxer but a Countess as well. Then she put on gloves to show me how she fought and if I had not crawled under the bed she would have knocked my head off. "I'm a ball of fire," she yelled. I went back to the office and wrote that story and then I was assigned to interview Samuel J. Burger, who had telephoned my office that he was selling racing cockroaches to society people at seventy-five cents a pair.

He had time to write that story, too (Burger really had sold a few cockroaches), before going home.

Even in this summary, which Mitchell wrote in 1937, one sees something of his early technique. The style is fast-paced, personal, and deadpan. The very punctuation tends to these effects. There is no exclamation point when the lady boxer yells; there are hardly any commas to slow the sentences down. All is motion.

In 1938 Mitchell published his first book, *My Ears Are Bent.*

To bend someone's ear is, in thirties slang, to talk to them, perhaps to talk to them quite a lot. The book contains forty accounts of people who had bent Mitchell's ear, mostly taken from the *Herald Tribune* and *World-Telegram,* along with a few from the *New Yorker,* for which he had gone to work in 1937. They are short, averaging 2000 to 2500 words, and mostly light-hearted. Countess Jeanne Vina La Mar, the lady boxer, is here; so is her intellectual counterpart, "Prince Childe Rohan d'Harcourt, a native of Guthrie, Oklahoma," now flourishing as a poet-guru in New York. So are Billy Sunday, two Tammany Hall politicians, and Mr. Andrew Piccirillo, proprietor of a dating service he called the National Social Register. (Entrance requirements were considerably less stringent than to the actual Social Register. "A woman Astor can get in for $1," Piccirillo said, "and a man Astor can get in for $2, just like anybody else.")

These people were deftly introduced. Mitchell had already established himself as the master of the equivocal lead. A piece on voodoo in New York begins "Sometimes a conjure doctor, a Brother Paul or Brother Daniel, mocks western civilization by drinking the blood of a crudely sacrificed bat in a tenement room on Lenox Ave., a room which contains electric lights and a radio." Is Mitchell about to give voodoo a friendly pat for managing to survive in the high-tech era? Is he going to expose it as a fraud? Impossible to tell from that sentence. He is, of course, going to do both—though the exposé will come not from Mitchell himself, but from the owner of a voodoo supply house (who also deals in candles and incense for ordinary Christian churches).

"Harry Lewis, an unobtrusive, well-mannered fellow from the lower East Side, has been one of the country's most accomplishedpickpockets for thirty-five years," another essay begins; and an arresting lead it is. The article does not go on to recommend stealing wallets as a career—Lewis himself says he would have preferred to be a bookmaker. Or if he had been born rich, he might just have been a heavy spender at casinos. He blows a good deal that way even as it is. "When I get a roll I am not a pickpocket any longer. I am a gambler then," he explains.

Without being wildly funny, like some of the interviews with the pretty naked girls who belong to that 1930s union The United Fan, Bubble, and Specialty Dancers of America, the article gets the full humor of Lewis's own view of his profession. Without granting him complete sympathy, such as is given to the title character in the piece called **"Except That She Smokes, Drinks Booze and Talks Rough, Miss Mazie Is a Nun,"** it hints at the sadness underneath. It is two-voiced articles like these that captured Malcolm Cowley's fancy, and led him to make the claim that I have not yet quoted in full. "In his somewhat narrow field, which is that of depicting curious characters, Joseph Mitchell is the best reporter in the country" is what Cowley actually said. It's a fair description of *My Ears Are Bent.*

It would not be an adequate description of Mitchell's next book. *McSorley's Wonderful Saloon* came out in 1943; it is that Mitchell title which people in 1983 are most likely to recognize. There are twenty pieces in it, averaging almost precisely twice as long as those in *My Ears Are Bent.* A mechanical explanation would be thatMitchell was now employed by the *New Yorker* and had more elbowroom. A better explanation would be—is—that the past has now entered his work. Usually it's the past of the people he is writing about, but there are occasional glimpses of the past of New York itself. It is not yet treated elegiacally; it is there to explain the present.

To some extent Mitchell's oeuvre resembles a set of Chinese boxes, with the smallest coming first. *McSorley's Wonderful Saloon* represents the first enlargement. In one case it's a literal enlargement. Miss Mazie Gordon appeared as a quick sketch in *My Ears Are Bent*: an eccentric secular saint who owned and ran a movie theater in the Bowery, personally selling tickets seven days a week from 9:30 A.M. until 11 P.M. "I do light house-keeping in here," she once told Mitchell, gesturing at her ticket booth. She also received callers at the booth, mostly bums looking for gin-money in the morning, a far more varied group in the afternoon, including the monsignor in charge of a nearby Catholic church, a young Chinese gambler, numerous nuns (she was friends with at least forty), and, at intervals over a twenty-year period, Mitchell himself.

All that was just a prelude to the last three hours of her day—that is, 11 P.M. to 2 A.M.—which she spent touring the Bowery with a pocketful of change and a flashlight, passing out small sums of money, on cold nights getting drunks safely to flophouses, calling ambulances for the injured ones. (Mitchell, who tends to learn theentire context of anyone he writes about, found that she summoned more ambulances than any other private citizen in New York.)

In *My Ears Are Bent* Mazie is indeed a curiosity: a bosomy blonde Jewish woman in her forties, rumored to have been a burlesque girl in her youth, now a tough-talking version of Mother Teresa. In *McSorley's Wonderful Saloon* she is a complete person. You get both a much fuller—and a wildly funny—account of the way she operates the movie theater, and the story of her life. A brilliant sketch has turned into a portrait full of light and shadow.

There are more important differences between the two books than the one of scale, however. In the five years between 1938 and 1943 Mitchell discovered his true vocation—to celebrate gusto, an immoderate relish for life. He had first approached that celebration through eccentrics—an eccentric, almost by definition, is someone who lives immoderately—and in *McSorley's Wonderful Saloon* there are still plenty of odd people, in whose oddity Mitchell delights. But there is a growing emphasis on immoderation in its common forms, such as hearty eating and drinking, or brawling, or telling tall tales. And hence on that stubborn, rowdy, peasant streak in many people which leads them to cling to life with both hands, to stuff themselves almost beyond belief at the kind of New York political dinner known as a "beefsteak," to scorn the temperate, delicate, fastidious pleasures of the highly civilized, to resist any change they see as diminishment—especially the change known as growing old. Among the peopleMitchell celebrates, no one goes gentle into any good night. (Nor *is* the night good. All pleasures that can be counted on are to be found right here on earth.)

McSorley's Wonderful Saloon **has no theme, . . . but if there were a theme, it would be the struggle between vulgar gusto on the one hand and anemic pretentiousness on the other.**

—*Noel Perrin*

The title piece and a later one called **"Obituary of a Gin Mill"** will illustrate this new emphasis. **"McSorley's"** is the triumphant form, **"Obituary"** the sad one. In **"McSorley's"** Mitchell writes a long loving account of a bar that has discovered how not to grow old. It has changed hardly at all from the youthful shape it had in 1854. It sold ale then; it was still selling ale—no whiskey, much less wine or liqueurs—in 1943. It was Men Only in 1854; it was still Men Only in 1943, even though now owned by a woman. There was no cash register in 1854; there still wasn't in 1943. The original line of bar snacks consisted of crackers, raw onions, and cheese; the current array was the same. The founder was addicted to three-pound steaks before bed; the current clientele remained heavy eaters. In short, Mitchell presented McSorley's as a completely unpretentious working-class saloon which has managed to stay uncorrupted for almost a century.

In sad contrast is the story of Dick's Bar and Grill, once an Italian parallel to McSorley's. When it was down by Washington Market, it was low-class and lively. On Fridays (payday for weekly workers) there was always a sort of bacchanal, in which Mitchell clearly used to take part. One regular customer was fond of jumping on the bar and preaching amateur sermons, including one which began, "Brothers and sisters! You full of sin! You full of gin! Youand the Devil are real close kin!" Dick himself had an even bigger appetite than old John McSorley. "Once," Mitchell writes, "I saw him stand at the bar and eat an eight-pound turkey the chef had cooked for the luncheon trade." ("The boss sure does have a passion for groceries," the head bartender remarked admiringly.)

Then, wanting a bigger kitchen, Dick moved to a new location. This meant buying new fixtures. Before the bar salesman got through with him, he had new ambiance as well. Now Dick's was "a big, classy place with a chromium and glass-brick front, a neon sign in four colors, a mahogany bar, a row of chromium bar stools with red-leather seats like those in the uptown cocktail lounges, a kitchen full of gleaming copper pots, a moody chef who once worked in Moneta's, a printed menu with French all over it, and seven new brands of Scotch. He told the bartenders they would have to shave every morning and made them put on starched white coats. For several days thereafter they looked clean and aloof, like people when they first get out of the hospital." No one jumped on the bar any more.

The term *gentrification* didn't exist yet, but of course that is what Mitchell is describing. He despises it. So, at heart, didDick, and so did most of the old customers. It was simply something that happened to them one prosperous year, taking not just the rowdiness but most of the life out of their bar. "Dick's old place was dirty and it smelled like the zoo, but it was genuine; his new place is as shiny and undistinguished as a two-dollar alarm clock." In middle-class terms immoderation is associated with death and danger. (Reckless poets and rock singers die young; bar fights lead to large dental bills, and eight-pound turkeys to coronaries.) In peasant terms it is simply a larger helping of life. *McSorley's Wonderful Saloon* has no theme, and many of the pieces do not fit the mold I have been describing. But if there were a theme, it would be the struggle between vulgar gusto on the one hand and anemic pretentiousness on the other.

Old Mr. Flood, Mitchell's third book, is something else again. This is his essay into new journalism, well before *that* concept existed. It came out in 1948.

The book, which is very short, consists of three sketches, almost stories, about Hugh G. Flood, a man of ninety-three. Mr. Flood lives in the Hartford House, a small waterfront hotel near the Fulton Fish Market, occupied by retired seamen and bargehands. He lives almost entirely on peculiar kinds of seafood, and believes that is one of the reasons he will make it to be one hundred and fifteen.

For the first time since Mitchell wrote (and published) a couple of short stories when he was still an undergraduate at Chapel Hill, we are dealing with a fictional character. More than that, a fictional character with literary overtones. Mitchell makes no reference in the book to another Flood—Eben Flood in a famous poem of Edwin Arlington Robinson's—but when you note that Robinson's poem is called "Mr. Flood's Party" and the third and final chapter of Mitchell's book is also called "Mr. Flood's Party," the allusion is unmistakable.

Mitchell's Hugh Flood is by no means pure fiction, but rather a composite of several old men Mitchell had really known around Fulton Fish Market. "I wanted these stories to be truthful rather than factual, but they are solidly based on facts," he writes in a prefatory note. Solidly indeed. The minor characters in the book, such as the proprietress of the Hartford House, are all real people, as are the settings, menus, dates, etc.

Inventing Mr. Flood seems to have given Mitchell the freedom to enter, when he himself was only forty, into the third phase of his celebration of rowdy life—the elegiac phase. At ninety-three Mr. Flood is by no means resigned to death, but he is very aware of death, as are the aged friends who come to his party. All confess that one of their keenest pleasures is hearing of the death of someone else. "You're in the funeral parlor, you old s. o. b.," one of them thinks on such an occasion, "and here I am, P. J. Mooney, esquire, eating a fine big plate of ham and eggs, and I'm not going to have two cups of coffee this morning, I'm going to have three."

The physical frailty of these old men and women, and their preoccupation with death and with the irretrievable past, gives a pathos to the zest with which they still go about eating and drinking and telling tall tales. There is much comedy in the book, notably in the long story Mr. Flood tells at his party about an ancient drayhorse named Sam, who pulls a seafood wagon. Sam is being secretly fed oysters by an oyster shucker who is curious to see what will happen. What happens, among much else, is that when Sam gets up to five dozen oysters a day, he bolts down Sixth Avenue "after a bay mare that was hauling a laundry wagon." A wish-fulfillment story, as both Mr. Flood and his listeners well know.

The dominant note of the book is a kind of sad gallantry, as in Robinson's poem. Death *is* inevitable, and the past is irretrievable. The past is also better than the present. One of Mr. Flood's friends, a retired policeman named Matthew Cusack, is the sort of man who only a few years ago could go to a picnic and eat "three hundred and sixty-six Great South Bay quahogs, one for every day in the year (it was a leap year), and put four rock-broiled lobsters on top of them." Now, from listening to health chats on the radio, he has become a hypochondriac, and hardly dares eat or drink at all. Cusack is the failed one, the man who lost his nerve and is going if not gentle then scared toward the night. None of the others have given up or gotten scared. But they know what they have lost.

The past was better, in this book, not just because all these people were younger then, but because technology was simpler and the country was smaller. "God damn the man that invented cellophane" is a kind of refrain that runs through the book, spoken by a friend of Mr. Flood's who used to deal in sheep intestines until he was put out of work by the spread of cellophane. God damn the radio is implicit in Mr. Cusack's story. God bless the way things were is implicit in the book.

Old Mr. Flood is Mitchell's first elegiac account of New York, but it is not his best. His best—his best book altogether, I think—is *The Bottom of the Harbor,* which came out in 1960. This means it took him twelve years to write it, and that, too, is part of a pattern. In his early days he was writing three newspaper pieces a day. Now it has taken twelve years to write six essays. They are far longer than the early stuff, to be sure—they average about twelve thousand words—but mainly they are much more complex, and they involve something like total knowledge of New York as a seaport, past and present.

In *The Bottom of the Harbor* Mitchell firmly returned to reporting. There are no composite characters here. Instead there are six of the most brilliant and moving essays or essay-stories I know: one literally on what is at the bottom of New York harbor; one on a fish restaurant in an old building; one on an ancient black community on Staten Island; one (the one someone else could most nearly have written) on the rats of New York; one on a trawlercaptain from Stonington, Connecticut, named Ellery Thompson; and one on the shad fishermen who live in Edgewater, New Jersey, on the other side of the Hudson from Manhattan between 94th Street and 164th Street. The best two—the one on Louie Morino's restaurant and the one on the shad fishermen—are the best reporting I have ever read.

Since there is not room to discuss both, I shall take the shorter and less complex of the two: the account of Louie Morino's restaurant called **"Up in the Old Hotel."** Three characters dominate the piece: Mitchell himself, Morino, and a six-story building called 92 South Street.

Mitchell begins with his own habit of occasionally getting up early and going down to the Fulton Fish Market (in those days supplied by boat, not by trailer-truck) around 5:30 in the morning. The market, just about to open for trading, is heaped with fish—fifty or sixty kinds. "The smoky riverbank dawn, the racket the fishmongers make, the seaweedy smell, and the sight of this plentifulness always give me a feeling of well-being, and sometimes they elate me," he writes on the first page of the article.

After wandering the market for an hour or two, he walks across the street to have breakfast at Louie Morino's. Before the reader meets Louie, though, he meets the building the restaurant is in. "Like the majority of the older buildings in the market district, it is made of hand-molded Hudson River brick, a rosy-pink and relativelynarrow kind that used to be turned out in Haverstraw and other kiln towns on the Hudson and sent down to the city in barges." It has a fine old slate roof. It is also dilapidated. Between the second floor and the roof there is nothing but boarded windows: the top four floors are not in use. It is a building with a past and with some mystery to it.

Now Louie enters the story, and for about fifteen hundred words Mitchell gives his history. He's a short, white-haired man, born in a north Italian village called Recco, where his ancestors had been fishermen for perhaps two thousand years. He came to New York as a boy of seventeen, worked for twenty-five years in restaurants, and then opened his own. It was in the Depression when Louie opened, and he could have got any of several premises in the style of Dick's Bar and Grill for very little. But he hears about an old rundown building by the fish market, and leases that instead. "The reason I did, Fulton Fish Market reminds me of Recco," he explains.

Now Mitchell and the reader enter the restaurant. There is a detailed account of what it looks like and of the rich variety of food it serves, such as cod cheeks, salmon cheeks, cod tongues, sturgeon liver, and blue-shark steak. The pace is leisurely. The reader learns, for example, that the cod cheeks are a delicacy that occasionally arrives in small shipments from Boston, "and the fishmongers, thinking of their own gullets, let Louie buy most of them."

Now Mitchell slowly approaches the true subject of the piece. He is having breakfast—probably a shad-roe omelet—and Louie sits down with him. They discuss the partial gentrification of the restaurant as people in the financial district "discover" it. Louie says regretfully that he'll have to put in some tables on the second floor to accommodate the growing lunch crowd. But then what will he do for storage?

"'That ought to be easy,' I said. 'You've got four empty floors up above.'"

"'They aren't empty,' he said."

It turns out that the building has stairs only to the second floor, and to get above that one must use a queer old hand elevator that hasn't been touched for fifty years. There are probably old hotel furnishings up there, or there may be hundreds of zinc-lined fish boxes with which a long-ago fishmonger hoped to make his fortune. No one knows.

Louie has wanted for years to find out, but all is dirt and darkness in that elevator shaft, and he has never found anyone who cared to go up with him. Once a representative of the company that manages the building almost did, but backed out; and once one of his customers who is a contractor got so far as to bring two hard hats before *he* backed out.

It also turns out that Louie knows a great deal about the his-

tory of 92 South Street; and though the building itself is not exceptionally old, it is linked not just with the early history of New York, but with New Amsterdam. When Louie was a waiter in Brooklyn, he got to know some of the old Brooklyn aristocracy, who were mainly of Dutch descent. He was particularly taken with the old ladies. "They all had some peculiarity, and they all had one foot in the grave, and they all had big appetites," he says approvingly. From them he learns a lot of early history of the city—and thus he knows what to make of it when he meets the actual owner of his building, a Mrs. Schermerhorn, the widow of a descendant of Jacob Schermerhorn, who came to New Amsterdam in the 1630s. As Louie puts it, "They go back so deep in Old New York that if you went any deeper you wouldn't find anything but Indians and bones and bears." Schermerhorns built 92 South Street, and have always owned it.

This building is as haunted by the past as the one further uptown that Henry James wrote about in "The Jolly Corner," and perhaps more.

Now comes the climax of the piece. Mitchell offers to go up in the elevator with Louie and see what's there. The trip is filthy and even dangerous, but they do make it to the third floor, wearing the hard hats and armed with flashlights. (No electricity above the second floor). They find themselves in the reading room of the old Fulton Ferry Hotel. There are things up there, all right, enough to take three pages to describe; but they are mostly rusted, and crumbled, and ruined. Once they find a square glass bottle with "two inches of colorless liquid" and some black sediment in it. Louie gets it open and smells it. "'It's gone dead,' he said. 'It doesn't smell like anything at all.'" Louie is so disgusted that he won't even go up to the fourth floor.

This climax is a tremendous let-down, and it is meant to be. They have broken through to the past, and all they find is trivial debris. For once the past had seemed retrievable—but when you reach out to seize it, you find nothing but dust and decay. Or to put it another way, both cities and cultures are mortal. Old New York had a longer life span than any individual Schermerhorn, or than old Mr. Flood; but what they find on the third floor is its corpse.

This is a fancy interpretation of a piece of reportage about an Italian seafood restaurant—though less fancy than the one by Stanley Edgar Hyman. He saw *The Bottom of the Harbor* as a deeply Freudian book, and he felt he could assign precise meaning to the details. The trip to the third floor of 92 South Street was an exploration of the depths of the unconscious, he said; and the line of hotel rooms that Mitchell and Louie Morino find stretching away beyond the reading room "are infantile experience." Just as, he added, all those rodents in **"The Rats on the Waterfront"** are Id wishes, and the wrecks and debris at the bottom of New York harbor are "festering failures and guilts."

Deep and complex as the book is, these are interpretations I would find quite easy to dismiss if Mitchell had not said a similar thing first. Back in 1952, in a note to go in a handbook of North Carolina authors being issued by the U.N.C. Extension Library, he wrote, "Without seeming to do so, I tried to make the reader conscious of parallels between the litter and the marine life down there [at the bottom of New York harbor]—the old wrecks and the eels and the polluted oyster beds—and the beauty and ugliness stored up in his own mind." Such a statement clearly licenses critics to make big claims of their own. I still have my doubts about the infantile experiences, but there is no doubt that 92 South Street, as Mitchell writes about it, is charged with meaning and emotion both. The whole book is.

Since *The Bottom of the Harbor* Mitchell has brought out just one more book, and it is a lesser work. *Joe Gould's Secret,* published in 1965, is the final Chinese box, and I suspect it is too large. But it is still a masterful piece of writing.

Twenty-two years earlier one of the pieces in *McSorley's Wonderful Saloon* had been called **"Professor Sea Gull,"** and it was about a Harvard graduate named Joe Gould, one of the leading characters in Greenwich Village in the 1920s and 30s. He got his nickname from his fondness for imitating seagull cries. (He liked to claim that seagulls had an actual language, which he could speak, and into which he had translated a considerable body of English poetry.) Gould, who was a professional drunk, divided his time about equally between cadging drinks in Greenwich Village bars and working on an enormous manuscript that he called *An Oral History of Our Time.* Though absurd and half-crazy he was not insignificant. One of the few things Gould actually published had a strong influence on the young William Saroyan; he himself was the subject of a poem by e. e. cummings.

Now Mitchell devotes a whole book to Gould, who is probably not quite worth it. First comes a slightly expanded version of **"Professor Sea Gull."** (It is typical of Mitchell's great concern for accuracy that the eighth sentence has been changed from "He is five feet four and he hardly ever weighs more than ninety-five pounds" to "He is five feet four and he hardly ever weighs more than a hundred pounds.") Then Mitchell spends a hundred and fifty pages telling Gould's later history, and recounting his own relationship with Gould. He is recounting it almost as a detective story, for it leads to his eventual discovery of the secret (which Gould was mostly able to keep even from himself) that there never was an *Oral History*—that Gould never wrote more than a few thousand of the nine million words everyone believed that he put down.

The unmasking of Gould has considerable drama, courteously

and even admiringly though Mitchell has done it. But more interesting are the necessary revelations that Mitchell makes about himself and his working methods. The one most impressive to me was the infinite patience he had. At one point when he was first preparing to write "**Professor Sea Gull,**" which is a nineteen-page article, he and Gould talked from 8 P.M. to about three in the morning on a Friday night—or, rather, Gould talked and Mitchell listened and paid for the drinks. Then on Saturday night they met again from six to twelve. Sunday they skipped. Then Monday six to midnight they talked, Tuesday 8 P.M. to 4 A.M., and so on through the week. And that was only one part of his preparation. "I had probably come to know more about his past than anybody else in the city and perhaps than anybody else in the world," Mitchell wrote in 1965. I should think only his old reportorial caution led him to put in the word *probably.* That is part of Joe Mitchell's secret—that whatever he writes about he tends to know better than anybody else in the world.

Another part is that he always had the judgment, at least until *Joe Gould's Secret,* to use only a minute fraction of what he knew in the finished work. His scholarship, which is on a par with his reportorial skill, he has taken care to hide entirely. One would never know, reading about the old building at 92 South Street, that the author is a semiprofessional student of architecture, a member of the Society of Architectural Historians, and so on. Similar invisible scholarship backs his writing on gypsies and on the Mohawk Indians.

But the greatest part will have to remain unsaid. Negative secrets like Joe Gould's can be revealed. The secrets of mastery are in the end inexplicable. No one writes as well as Joseph Mitchell bytaking trouble or by doing research. I can note his ear for dialogue, or speculate on his brooding sense of nostalgia over human loss and his delight in human appetite. But all I can say for sure is that in 1983 he remains the best reporter in the country—or at least the best that I have encountered. And I can continue to hope for the new book upon which he is working.

Roy Blount, Jr. (review date August 1992)

SOURCE: "Joe Mitchell's Secret," in *The Atlantic,* Vol. 270, No. 2, August, 1992, pp. 97-9.

[*In the following review of* Up in the Old Hotel, *Blount suggests reasons for Mitchell's decision to stop publishing after 1965, focusing on his experiences with Joe Gould.*]

If I could play around with time, I would make myself alive and literate on that week in 1940 when I could flip suspensefully through the latest *New Yorker* (whose table of contents in those days was minimal), come upon a piece titled **"Lady Olga,"** savor its first sentence ("Jane Barnell occasionally considers herself an outcast and feels that there is something vaguely shameful about the way she makes a living"), scan its first paragraph, jump ahead a number of pages to the byline, and exclaim:

"Oh, glory. Joseph Mitchell has profiled a bearded lady."

I did have the pleasure, in 1964, of devouring fresh out of that magazine Mitchell's series of articles about Joe Gould, a bizarre Greenwich Village character whose literary pretensions and hand-to-mouth subsistence Mitchell had first chronicled, more briefly, in 1942. Gould had continued to pester Mitchell over the years, in person or as a kind of specter (Gould sometimes referred to himself as Professor Sea Gull, and did eerie sea gull imitations that no one who heard them ever forgot), until Gould's death in a mental hospital. The closing revelation of this series was something Mitchell alone had been in a position to discover: that the fabled trove of notebooks in which Gould claimed to have recorded years and years of many people's talk, his life's work, his "Oral History of Our Time," had never in fact existed.

Except for his Gould articles collected in a book, *Joe Gould's Secret* (1965), Mitchell has published nothing since. He hasn't even allowed his four long-out-of-print collections to be reissued. For twenty-eight years his fans have been hearing that he continues to come to work at *The New Yorker,* and wondering what he's up to. We still don't know, but now we do have *Up in the Old Hotel,* a welcome one-volume edition of Mitchell's collected works: the collections (*McSorley's Wonderful Saloon, Old Mr. Flood, The Bottom of the Harbor,* and *Joe Gould's Secret*), seven pieces not included in those books, and a brisk introduction in which Mitchell, now in his eighties, confides little more than that he has always been inclined toward "graveyard humor."

"No matter how fat and sassy you may be," proclaims a street preacher in a 1943 piece titled **"A Spism and a Spasm,"** "you're living every second on the lip of the grave." The people Mitchell honored tended to derive enormous energy from that precariousness, to sing at great length from that lip. *Up in the Old Hotel*'s title piece concerns the boarded-up remnants of a long-abandoned hotel above Sloppy Louie's (now lamentably refurbished) restaurant. Mitchell and Louie venture up there and find—well, I won't spoil the details for you. They shudder and go back down. As it happened, that piece came out in 1952, the year Joe Gould was institutionalized for good.

J. D. Salinger, the other living *New Yorker* writer who stopped publishing in the mid-sixties, has remained in print and—thanks to his reclusiveness—has appeared sporadically in the news. A. J. Liebling, Mitchell's friend and fellow celebrant of drink, food, and raffishness, stopped writing in 1963, because that is when he died; but Liebling is still a familiar author and a journalistic legend. Mitchell has become

dismayingly obscure, except to those of us who are old enough and interested enough in a certain line of writing (he has been credited as a pioneer of the so-called New Journalism, but that suggests an inappropriate trendiness) to regard him as a master.

"People don't laugh at clowns anymore but they want to see them around," a circus official told Mitchell in 1940. If necessary, as a worst-case scenario, I was prepared to salute Mitchell on that basis when I began to read this volume, after not having actually looked at his stuff in some time. But his richly specific, levelly related sketches of mostly New York but sometimes outlying folk and ways—Mohawk high-steel workers, Gypsy swindlers, waterfront rat exterminators—are still funny, fluid, authoritative, tangy, and affecting. Five or six of this book's thirty-seven pieces are not marvelous (to use a word that I have never used before and that Mitchell would probably not be caught dead using). The rest are. I can't do them justice by quoting from them, because their best passages are built up to at length, but here is a description of Looba, the wife of Johnny Nikanov, whom Mitchell identified in 1942 as one of "at least one dozen gypsy kings" in New York:

> Looba is tall, gaunt, sad-eyed, and austere; in profile she looks exactly like the old Indian on Indian-head nickels. She goes to sleep at sundown and seldom gets up before 10 A.M., but she is constantly yawning, stretching, and grunting. Looba smokes a pipe. She is extremely irritable. Johnny says that she rarely refers to him by name; instead, using Romany, she calls him a ratbite, a sick toad, a blue-bellied eel, a black-yolked egg, a goat, a bat, a policeman, a gajo [a non-Gypsy], and various other loathsome things. He doesn't mind. "A gypsy woman that don't scream half the time, something is wrong with her," he says. "Screaming is their hobby."

A vigilant female or Gypsy reader today might find that portrait invidiously objectifying. A reader who is abreast of current food-chain consciousness might shudder at **"All You Can Hold for Five Bucks,"** Mitchell's 1939 study of old-style New York testimonial steak dinners, in which utensil-disdaining, greasy-to-their-ears gourmands merrily put away many, many animals' worth of steak and chops and kidneys while sloshing down gallons of beer. A reader who is up-to-date on dependency might have problems with all the drinking in these pieces. Many of Mitchell's favorite characters are zestfully bibulous, or else so eloquent in their demonizing of rum as to seem inversely intoxicated by it. Then there is the testimony of Mr. Flood, Mitchell's composite Fulton Fish Market character, who at his ninety-fifth birthday party reflects as follows:

> "I was lying in bed the other night . . . and I got to

thinking about death and sin and hell and God, the way you do, and a question occurred to me. I wonder what man committed the worst sin in the entire history of the human race. The man that invented whiskey, he's the one. When you stop and think of the mess and the monkey business and the fractured skulls and the commotion and the calamity and the stomach distress and the wife beating and the poor little children without any shoes and the howling and the hell raising *he*'s been responsible for down through the centuries—why, good God A'mighty! Whoever he was, they've probably got him put away in a special brimstone pit, the deepest, red-hottest pit in hell, the one the preachers tell about, the one without any bottom." He took a long drink. "And then again," he continued, "just as likely, he might've gone to heaven."

One of Mitchell's great gifts is for mixing humor with references to genuine misery while avoiding that great source of decay in comedy: facetiousness. A writer today could not present a Mr. Flood without shoring him up as regards substance-abuse awareness; but I would bet money that Mitchell's termagants, gluttons, and topers will outlast—if not indeed overwhelm the scruples of—any particular stripe of contemporarily fish-eyed reader.

So what has kept Mitchell silent since he put quits to the matter of Joe Gould in 1964? To see why Mitchell may not be inspired to write about contemporary New York, all you have to do is compare the old Fulton Fish Market, whose organic redolences Mitchell ventilated so well, with the deathly touristic South Street Seaport that incorporates what is left of it today. But there are other reasons why Mitchell's style of reporting is no longer, *o tempera, o mores,* state-of-the-art.

A couple of years ago I was asked to write the introduction to a reissue of one of Liebling's books. I took the occasion to ask Mitchell how his and Liebling's heyday differed from today.

"Back then," Mitchell said, "if you developed a character, the papers would mention him, but he was, you might say, your character. Nowadays fourteen different television programs would take him away from you, promise to pay him something—he'd wind up with about twelve dollars out of it. They just wear out and use up a character. Also, if you try to interview a character today you find that half the things they say they *heard* on television. Most of the quotes you hear today are pretty thin."

Also, Mitchell noted, "the disposition to sue wasn't as rampant then as it is now."

The quotations Mitchell delivered were so long and rich as to

take leave of naturalism. They stretch credibility rewardingly and so far as I know unimpeachably (in his introduction Mitchell says which of his pieces are fictional and which not), but probably not in a way that reporters today, who tend to use tape recorders defensively, can get away with. As we have seen in the case of Janet Malcolm versus Jeffrey Masson, the outraged psychiatrist she had profiled in *The New Yorker,* the question of fashioning text from transcript has become profoundly vexed.

There is another reason why characters aren't what they used to be: an honest writer today cannot avoid registering personality differently. Odd ducks today tend to fall under various sociological or psychological headings. They belong to marginalized groups for whom something should be, and probably isn't being,done. That bearded ladies are now preventable is a development no decent person can regret. I submit that the case of Joe Gould carried Mitchell reluctantly toward such thinking.

One of Mitchell's great gifts is for mixing humor with references to genuine misery while avoiding that great source of decay in comedy: facetiousness.

—Roy Blount, Jr.

Twenty-four of the pieces in this book were published from 1938 to 1942, the year Joe Gould entered Mitchell's life. Only thirteen—many of them, to be sure, among his best—appeared thereafter. Not content to be a one-piece character, Gould appropriated Mitchell's office as his mailing address, came painfully close to letting down his mask with him, and made Mitchell feel guilt and disgust. Mitchell's tone in *Joe Gould's Secret* is marred by uncharacteristic self-consciousness and exasperation.

Everyone who got to know the smelly, shamelessly freeloading Gould eventually dismissed him as impossible. Mitchell put up with a lot more from him than anyone else did. I don't think it is being fanciful to suppose that Gould wore Mitchell out. For one thing, Gould when drinking could talk even Mitchell under the table. More unsettling, Gould turned out to be a bad character for Mitchell's purposes. Pathetic. Dysfunctional.

Mitchell's style embraces austerely comic, independently cranky types. It renders downright inspirational their transcendence of hard times, of conventional people's scorn, and of their own intimations of mortality. In the 1942 profile Gould comes through as such a type. But in the end, unlike any other of Mitchell's leading characters, he dies as most people do today: disintegratedand in the hands of -ologists. Mitchell—who identified uncondescendingly with a hardheaded bearded lady, an unshakable religious haranguer, a rather unappealing but redoubtable child prodigy, and any number of fishwives, doomsayers, and cranks—couldn't seem to forgive the mortal weakness of his fellow conflicted writer. Professor Sea Gull, the messiest and most rounded person in this book, may have deconstructed Mitchell's sense of character.

If that is so, Mitchell's decades of reticence are a tribute to his integrity. And *his* oral history does exist, in *Up in the Old Hotel,* a book that should continue to inspire reporters who hope abidingly, as I do, to celebrate great talk of all kinds and to register such resounding mementos of historical orality as the one Mitchell espied on a hotel wall in 1944, a yellowed photograph of

> Buffalo Bill and some Indians in fringed buckskins eating lobsters at a family table in the dining room. Around the margin, in a crabbed hand, someone has written, "Col. Buffalo Bill and 1 doz. red Indians just off the Boston boat, stayed three days, big eaters, lobster every meal, up all night, took the place."

Malcolm Jones, Jr. (review date 10 August 1992)

SOURCE: "The Paragon of Reporters," in *Newsweek*, Vol. CXX, No. 6, August 10, 1992, pp. 53-4.

[In the following essay, Jones briefly summarizes Mitchell's career, discussing his style, the subjects of his profiles, and his association with the New Yorker.*]*

One recent balmy summer afternoon, Joseph Mitchell stood in the middle of New York's Fulton Fish Market and grinned like a schoolboy playing hooky. "As soon as I came down here in the '30s as a reporter, I felt at home," he said. Over a half century later, he is still prowling the market's cobbled streets. "It's so exciting, with the colors, the smells, the noise as the background to all that trading," he said. "Most markets now are abstract. It's stocks and bonds. But this is the real thing that those old Dutch painters painted. I think of it as the Dutchness of New York. I like that aspect of it, even the old Dutch names of the streets. If you come down here at 5 a. m. and walk around, you can't help leaving exhilarated."

Now 84, Mitchell has been writing about the people and places around New York that exhilarated him for more than 60 years, first as a newspaper reporter and, since 1938, as a staff writer for *The New Yorker.* But, as he says, "the city changed on me," and a lot of what he loved has gone. "There's an old country saying—from the cradle to the hearse, things are never so bad that they can't get worse—well, that's the way I see the world." The fish market was one of his first loves and now is his last. He has come to think of it as a microcosm of

the metropolis. "Every now and then, seeking to rid my mind of thoughts of death and doom, I get up early and godown to Fulton Fish Market," he wrote 40 years ago; today he still relies on it to repair his gloomy spirits.

Along with his *New Yorker* contemporaries A. J. Liebling, Lillian Ross and St. Clair McKelway, Mitchell transformed magazine writing in the '40s,' 50s and '60s. When Tom Wolfe and Truman Capote were still in knee pants, John McPhee points out, "Joe Mitchell was there, writing very artistic material in factual writing." Originally collected in such nonfiction classics as *McSorley's Wonderful Saloon* and *The Bottom of the Harbor,* Mitchell's darkly comic articles are models of literary journalism. "Mitchell is a reporter only in the sense that Defoe is a reporter," said the critic Stanley Edgar Hyman. Among his most ardent fans are William Kennedy and Calvin Trillin, who dedicated his book *Killings* "To the *New Yorker* reporter who set the standard—Joseph Mitchell."

A notoriously slow writer, Mitchell has not published anything in 27 years. "I can't seem to get anything finished anymore," he says. "The hideous state the world is in just defeats the kind of writing I used to do." And because he refused to let his books be reprinted until recently, a generation of readers has grown up ignorant of Mitchell's art. But this month Pantheon is publishing *Up in the Old Hotel,* an omnibus of all Mitchell's *New Yorker* writing. Seen in its entirety, his work is an epic of big-city life that shifts between unsentimental celebrations of human gumption and strangely elegiac meditations on death and the burdens of time.

Mitchell's colleague Brendan Gill thinks the timing of the book is perfect. It is coming out "not only at the crown of [Joe's] life but at a time when everybody's speculating on the change at *The New Yorker,*" Gill says, referring to the appointment of ex-*Vanity Fair* editor Tina Brown as editor—a move, say media-watchers, that spells the end of the old *New Yorker.* "Here's a kind of ideal summary of the intentions of *The New Yorker* in the work of one man. He was the model . . . the ideal."

The people in Mitchell's articles are tough old birds. There is Mazie P. Gordon, a blunt but kindly movie-theater ticket seller who looked after Bowery bums in the '30s. There is the bohemian barfly Joe Gould, "an odd and penniless and unemployable little man who came to the city in 1916 and ducked and dodged and held on as hard as he could for over 35 years." Though rarely happy, none of Mitchell's people is resigned to fate. They fight back, and their most common weapon is a mordant, earthy sense of the absurd that Mitchell has lately labeled "graveyard humor." He has immortalized gin mills (including the 138-year-old McSorley's, New York's oldest bar), a social club for deaf people, a terrapin farm near Savannah, Ga., and the rats on the New York waterfront. He has profiled everyone from calypso singers to the Mohawk

Indians who helped build New York's skyscrapers to a man who ran something called Captain Charlie's Museum for Intelligent People.

Mitchell is plainly awed by many of his subjects. One piece begins, "A garrulous old Southerner, the Reverend Mr. James Jefferson DavisHall, is the greatest and most frightening street preacher in the city." No matter how strange a person is, Mitchell's treatment is always delicately respectful. Of a bearded lady, he wrote, "Jane Barnell occasionally considers herself an outcast and feels that there is something vaguely shameful about the way she makes a living."

In an age when journalists have become stars who vie with their subjects for the spotlight, Mitchell is an anomaly. Private and self-effacing, he has for years politely turned down requests for interviews. "I always thought a reporter was supposed to ask the questions," he once said. For most of his life he has shuttled back and forth between New York and his family home in North Carolina. "Southerners feel like outsiders everywhere, even in the South sometimes, but when I go back I feel that I fit right in," he says. An avid naturalist, he is immersed in a reforestation project on the family farm.

The subjects who have intrigued him most—Gypsies, Indians, fishmongers—were members of clannish, hermetic worlds; by the late '40s he had begun to focus almost exclusively on the tightly knit denizens of the waterfront. The bustle of the trading and the community of ornery old men who hung around the market reminded him of the tobacco market in his hometown. "I didn't leave Fairmont," he says. "I found it up here in the fish market."

The prose of the fish-market stories is as graceful and unadorned as a Shaker chair, and its incantatory rhythms are as soothing as old hymns. "I read *Ulysses* in college and never got over it," says Mitchell of James Joyce, and the fish-market tales teem with images of death and regeneration. "In recent years, I have written mostly about what I guess could be called the unusual in the usual, such as a description of the bottom of the New York harbor, in which, without seeming to, I tried to make the reader conscious of parallels between the litter and the marine life down there—the wrecks and the eels and the polluted oyster beds—and the beauty and the ugliness stored up in his own mind," he once wrote. His accounts of an old seaman's hotel, rats and plague, the deep-sea fishermen of Connecticut and the shad fishermen of New Jersey are like what Joyce might have written had he gone into journalism.

Mitchell still goes into the office every day he is in New York and writes. Much of what he's at work on is about the fish market—and he's sanguine about his chances of completing the stories. "I'm on firmer ground . . . because I came out and said that graveyard humor is the way I look at the world . . .

In these things [pieces], I'm just going to say the future of the world looks horrible to me. I don't want to be gloomy, but that business about the cradle and the hearse just explains what I'm doing."

Jeffrey A. Trachtenberg (review date 14 August 1992)

SOURCE: "His Ears Are Bent on Hearing Talk of Town," in *The Wall Street Journal* (Eastern Edition), Vol. CCXX, No. 33, August 14,1992, p. A8.

[*In the following essay, Trachtenberg briefly describes the contents of the four books included in* Up in the Old Hotel.]

As media circles buzz over the naming of high-voltage Tina Brown to the top post at *The New Yorker,* Pantheon has released a collection of the best works of Joseph Mitchell, a *New Yorker* persona of a far more diffident stripe.

So shy was he that the author's photo for Mr. Mitchell's first book, *My Ears Are Bent* (1938), showed him seated on a couch, a newspaper covering his face. Eventually, he fairly disappeared altogether: He kept an office at *The New Yorker* but didn't publish another signed article these past 27 years.

Thanks to this new collection of his work, Mr. Mitchell, now 84 years old, is likely to attract another generation of fans. The anthology *Up in the Old Hotel* includes four previously published books, long out of print—*McSorley's Wonderful Saloon, Old Mr. Flood, The Bottom of the Harbor* and *Joe Gould's Secret*—and it should be immensely appealing to anyone interested in bearded ladies, child prodigies, oystermen and Indian steelworkers.

Rather than scrutinize the big names of the day, Mr. Mitchell wrote mostly about oddballs, dime-store philosophers and social misfits he plucked from obscurity. In rereading his earlier stories forthis book, Mr. Mitchell was surprised to discover how often the pieces were laced with what he describes as "graveyard humor." The realization gave him great pleasure, Mr. Mitchell adds in his brief introduction, because such humor "typifies my cast of mind."

Mr. Mitchell first gained prominence for *McSorley's Wonderful Saloon,* a collection of essays about ornery New Yorkers published in 1943. The title piece, a look at one of New York's oldest bars, reflects on the merits of a place where "bartenders never make a needless move, the customers nurse their mugs of ale, and the three clocks on the walls have not been in agreement for many years." It is a gem.

Such tenaciously unfancy places always seemed to attract Mr. Mitchell once he left the cotton and tobacco farm in Fairmont, N.C., where he was raised, and arrived in New York in 1929.

In **"Mr. Hunter's Grave,"** he wanders the south shore of Staten Island, where he stumbles across Sandy Ground, a small community founded by free blacks who worked in the oyster-planting business before the Civil War. In **"The Rivermen,"** he writes how new bridges and tunnels have isolated the once-bustling small Hudson River town of Edgewater, N.J.

Mr. Mitchell, in fact, had a strong penchant for fish, clams and all the creatures that live in, on or about the water. For his fictional ***Old Mr. Flood*** (1948), he brings to eccentric life Hugh G. Flood, a 93-year-old retired "house-wrecking contractor" determined to live until the age of 115. To that end, he has become what he proudly calls a "seafoodetarian," who never lets a meat morsel or a vegetable into the kitchen. "When I get through tearing a lobster apart, or one of those tender West Coast octopuses, I feel like I had a drink from the fountain of youth," he declares.

Mr. Mitchell's finest book may be ***The Bottom of the Harbor*** (1960), which includes a terrific, offbeat essay on hardy New York rats able to "outthink any man who made a study of their habits." But my own favorite has long been **"Up in the Old Hotel,"** the title piece for this collection. In it, Mr. Mitchell describes how he and Louis Morino, then the proprietor of Sloopy Louie's on the tip of lower Manhattan, explored the four abandoned floors above the restaurant. As they poke about, Mr. Mitchell takes us back in time to an old New York with merchant families and bustling docks.

In rereading Mr. Mitchell's previous book, ***Joe Gould's Secret*** (1965), I wondered if his epic case of writer's block wasn't in some way connected to his having being hoodwinked by one of his subjects—a secret terror of all journalists. Joe Gould was a Greenwich Village bohemian who claimed to be writing an oral history millions of words long. A cantankerous, ketchup-eating bum who enjoyed imitating sea gulls, Mr. Gould hovered on the periphery of what was once the demimonde of New York, cadging free drinks and crashing parties.

Mr. Gould's luck changed for the better after Mr. Mitchell published a long and sympathetic essay about him in 1942, transforming him into a celebrity of sorts. ***Joe Gould's Secret*** relates Mr. Mitchell's discovery that the oral history was a fraud. Although he later rebuked himself for it, Mr. Mitchell ultimately confronted Mr. Gould with his suspicions, and the relationship between the two men was never quite the same.

Mr. Gould is long gone. But Mr. Mitchell hasn't written a book since. This is too bad, for while Mr. Gould was a poseur, Mr. Mitchell, as this anthology shows, delivered the goods.

John Schulian (review date 16 August 1992)

SOURCE: A review of *Up in the Old Hotel*, in *Los Angeles Times Book Review*, August 16, 1992, pp. 1, 8.

[*In the following essay, Schulian uses the publication of* Up in the Old Hotel *as an opportunity to express his long-standing appreciation for Mitchell's work.*]

Getting hit on the head with a dead cow isn't necessarily a bad thing. Provided, of course, that you survive the experience, it can heighten your appreciation for the absurdities of life as well as for the people who revel in them. For the stalwart bearded lady and the saloon keeper who closes up because the joint's too crowded and the ticket taker who brags that nobody ever got fleas in her Bowery theater. For the homeless Harvard man who imitates sea gulls and the Gypsies who live on a mixture of gin and Pepsi called "popskull," and the street preacher who says, "The gutter is my pulpit and the roaring traffic is my pipe organ." For all the raving eccentrics Joseph Mitchell knew and loved and wrote about in *The New Yorker,* which, when you think about it, seems no less amazing than having the late Bossy come crashing down on your noggin.

Considering what a bore the magazine can be on any given week, it would be easy to assume that Mitchell risked being sent packing for admitting that a cow laid him low when it was supposedly hung for butchering. Too weird, too wonderful. But he had the great good fortune to arrive at *The New Yorker* in the late '30s, not long after A. J. Liebling had begun to spice its pages with tales of honest rainmakers and telephone-booth Indians. There was room for more madness, and Mitchell was only too happy to expand on the lessons he had learned in the subject down home in small-town North Carolina.

For the next 25 years, Liebling and he were 1 and 1A in *The New Yorker's* writing stable—two guys named Joe dueling in print, drinking in every bar that would give them a tab, and debating Liebling's contention that Christopher Marlowe was a better writer than Shakespeare. But after Liebling died in 1963, a strange and troubling thing happened: His work lived on, primarily because of his press criticism and boxing essays, while Mitchell, who is still alive, seemingly ceased to exist for all but the most passionate devotees of magazine journalism.

The only place I could learn anything about him was *Wayward Pressman,* Raymond Sokolov's biography of Liebling. Who else? Far more disturbing, however, was the fact that the four anthologies of Mitchell's prose—***McSorley's Wonderful Saloon, Old Mr. Flood, The Bottom of the Harbor*** and ***Joe Gould's Secret***—were nothing more than the stuff of used-book stores.

It took years, but I tracked them all down, and ever since, they have held an honored place on my bookshelf. Now I find that an editor at Pantheon shares my passion. Better yet, he has gathered Mitchell's books in this heavyweight volume called *Up in the Old Hotel,* complemented them with previously uncollected reportage and short stories, and even gotten the great man, at 84, to write an introduction. Part of me wishes Joseph Mitchell were still a secret treasure, known only to a few of us, but in my heart I know it is better this way.

To read these pieces, some written as long ago as 1938, none more recently than 1965, is to be taken back to a New York that is not America's answer to Calcutta, a New York where nocturnal drifters could sleep on park benches without being set on fire by kids with no hope, a New York where a thirsty man didn't have to fear being politically incorrect when he drank in a bar where the motto was "Good ale, raw onions and no ladies." There was joy in the city back then, and there was joy in the way Mitchell wrote about it.

He could look at a Fulton Fish Market restaurant, as he does in the title piece of this new anthology, and turn its walls into a story within a story: "Like the majority of office buildings in the market district, it is made of hand-molded Hudson River brick, a rosy-pink and relatively narrow kind that used to be turned out in Haverstraw and other kiln towns on the Hudson and sent down to the city in barges."

With grace and attention to detail, he could draw a word picture of the proprietor of Captain Charley's Private Museum for Intelligent People: "He is small, grimy, and surly. His eyes are always bleary. He wears a white, waxed mustache. He had on his customary outfit—ragged duck pants, a turtle-neck sweater, a pea jacket, a captain's cap, and tennis sneakers painted with silver radiator paint. He was decorating some seashells one day with the silver paint and decided it would look good on his sneakers."

What Mitchell did best, however, was listen. The man he listened to most was Joe Gould, Harvard, class of 1911, a lecherous, boozy, old poet-panhandler who imitated sea gulls—"Scree-eek! Scree-eek!"—and considered himself the last of the bohemians. "All the others fell by the wayside," he said. "Some are in the grave, some are in the loony bin, and some are in the advertising business." Mitchell kept going back to him because Gould claimed to be writing an oral history of his time that he estimated at 7.3 million words, then 8.8 million—until Mitchell simply called it "the world's longest unpublished book." But when he figured out what Professor SeaGull's oral history really was, he wasn't afraid to call a con a con.

After all, he was a reporter more than anything else, and he plied his trade with the acuity and elegance of his heroes,

Daniel Defoe, William Cobbett and William Hazlitt. Unlike the reportorial icons of a coming generation, Tom Wolfe and Hunter Thompson, he wrote with a style devoid of gimcracks. But that was only fitting, for he played everything right down the middle, even to the point of revealing that his Old Mr. Flood, age 93 and aiming for 115, was a composite drawn from an assortment of Fulton Fish Market characters. Funny how such distinctions eluded so many of the New Journalists who worked the same spiritual turf as Mitchell and acted as if he'd never been there.

If it seems that I'm holding Mitchell up as a measuring stick of journalistic integrity, I am. And the person I would most like to be aware of his high standards is Tina Brown, who has resigned as *Vanity Fair*'s high priestess to assume a similarly exalted position at the *New Yorker*. Someone should give fair Tina a copy of *Up in the Old Hotel* and if, after reading every word, she doesn't adopt it as the truth and the light, there is only one thing to do: Drop a dead cow on her head.

Verlyn Klinkenborg (review date 16 August 1992)

SOURCE: "This Was New York. It Was," in *The New York Times Book Review*, Vol. XCVII, No. 33, August 16, 1992, p. 7.

[*In the following review of* Up in the Old Hotel, *Klinkenborg emphasizes the historical value of Mitchell's writings.*]

There were many great eaters at *The New Yorker* in the 1940's, but surely the magazine's greatest eaters of that decade were A. J. Liebling and Joseph Mitchell. Their tastes differed. Liebling loved French food, as it was served in France before and between the world wars. He could describe a meal as if it were a procession of wise old courtesans. Joseph Mitchell had—perhaps still has, for he is 82 years old and divides his time between New York and a home in North Carolina—simpler tastes in food. He inclines to the beefsteak, the oyster and the clam. To his dining he brings a melancholic tinge.

"One Sunday afternoon in August, 1937," he writes in a story called **"A Mess of Clams,"** "I placed third in a clam-eating tournament at a Block Island clambake, eating 84 cherries. . . . I regard this as one of the few worthwhile achievements of my life." To readers of *Up in the Old Hotel,* a compendium of Mr. Mitchell's writing for *The New Yorker* between 1938 and 1965—stories, profiles and articles that have been out of print for years—this will seem like the most bilious kind of modesty. For among writers of nonfiction Mr. Mitchell has an extraordinary reputation, which has had to live in recent years by word of mouth.

A. J. Liebling and Joseph Mitchell shared a fondness for the eccentricities of life in New York City. The *New Yorker* has never again had such a pair of reporters when it comes to the subterranean, the aquatic, the twilit characters of the metropolis. But here again, their tastes differed. Liebling loved boxers, newspapermen and the men he called telephone booth Indians, whose language had a wry, idiosyncratic twist around which he could weave his own ineffably droll and florid wit. Of Liebling's characters you may safely say that they were the occasion for his prose.

But of Mr. Mitchell's characters—the bar owners, the Bowery preachers, the gypsies, the oystermen—you must say that he is the occasion for their prose. *Up in the Old Hotel* is a vast omnibus of Mr. Mitchell's writing, previously collected in four books—*McSorley's Wonderful Saloon* (1943), *Old Mr. Flood* (1948), *The Bottom of the Harbor* (1960) and *Joe Gould's Secret* (1965). In 718 pages, Mr. Mitchell only occasionally gets a word in edgewise. Joe Gould, whose derelict life was a kind of vermilion thread running through the weave of Mr. Mitchell's days, is emblematic of the men and women Mr. Mitchell was drawn to. Gould was the author of a work that turned out not to exist at all—"An Oral History of Our Time" some nine million words long. He also translated Longfellow's poetry into the language of sea gulls.

In the presence of a man like Gould, it is Mr. Mitchell's custom, in these stories at least, to sit almost mute and almost entirely rapt. His dictum might well have been something Joe Gould onceuttered while dining, no doubt, on his most frequent meal, a plate of ketchup. "What people say," Gould said, "is history."

Mr. Mitchell's art is to elicit history from an enormous range of people, and then to cause their words to fall into a shape that gives the reader none of the agony the unreconstructed reveries of these long-winded men might have done. In fact, the longer they talk, the more one admires them, something both Mr. Mitchell and his editors at *The New Yorker* had the wit to recognize.

Though Mr. Mitchell loves the Bowery preachers and the tavern owners and the gypsies of old New York, his favorite figures are the men who lived and worked on New York's waterfront. In presenting the people he wrote about—often homeless, always eccentric—Mr. Mitchell seems to me to be posing a tacit question about the character and value of his own life, of life itself. And it so happens that when he writes about the waterfront, that tacit inquiry overlaps with another question that is often in his mind: "What's for dinner?" And where a waterfront dinner is concerned, Mr. Mitchell has a geographical imagination. The oyster he eats calls to mind the bed in which it was raised, the market in which it was sold and the men whose livelihoods were earned raising and selling it.

At one point, the remarkable Mr. Flood—one of Mr. Mitchell's few fictional creations (borrowed from Edwin Arlington Robinson)—recites an epic catalogue of oysters: Shrewsburys, Maurice RiverCoves, Narragansetts, Wickfords, Cotuits, Lynnhavens, Pokomokes, Mobjacks, Bombay Hooks, Shinnecocks, Fire Island Salts, Blue Points, Saddle Rocks and so on. "I love those good old oyster names," says Mr. Flood. "When I feel my age weighing me down, I recite them to myself and I feel better. Some of them don't exist any more."

> **Mr. Mitchell's art is to elicit history from an enormous range of people, and then to cause their words to fall into a shape that gives the reader none of the agony the unreconstructed reveries of these long-winded men might have done. In fact, the longer they talk, the more one admires them.**
>
> —*Verlyn Klinkenborg*

It doesn't take an Aristotle to explain how a book full of people and places and customs that no longer exist could make a reader as happy as *Up in the Old Hotel* does. Mr. Mitchell always mediates the sadness such subjects bring—the loss of time, the life slipping by, the way the old manners fail to hang on—and he lets the reader feel only the pleasure that comes from his own very personal discoveries. He himself remains, in this prose at least, a melancholy man, wandering with a sandwich in his pocket among the wildflowers in abandoned cemeteries, seeking the company of solitary men who are gregarious only in the company of other isolates, sniffing out the odors of the Fulton Fish Market and its old hotels. And in such moments the reader gets a clear glimpse of Mr. Mitchell himself, even as he seems to disappear into the scenehe describes.

"The Fulton Market smell," he writes, "is a commingling of smells. I tried to take it apart. I could distinguish the reek of the ancient fish and oyster houses, and the exhalations of the harbor. And I could distinguish the smell of tar, a smell that came from an attic on South Street, the net loft of a fishing-boat supply house, where trawler nets that have been dipped in tar vats are hung beside open windows to drain and dry. And I could distinguish the oakwoody smell of smoke from the stack of a loft on Beekman Street in which finnan haddies are cured; the furnace of this loft burns white-oak and hickory shavings and sawdust. And tangled in these smells were still other smells—the acrid smoke from the stacks of the row of coffee-roasting plants on Front Street, and the pungent smoke from the stack of the Purity Spice Mill on Dover Street, and the smell of rawhides from The Swamp, the tannery district, which adjoins the market on the north."

That city, the one in which Joseph Mitchell finds his gloom lifted by the smoke itself, no longer exists. But a book like *Up in the Old Hotel*—in print forever, one hopes—will cause another melancholy soul, someone possessed by what Mr. Mitchell calls his "graveyard humor," to look in the waste places of the present city, listen to its lunatic ravings and report back to us, as amply and as sympathetically as Mr. Mitchell has done.

Luc Sante (essay date 5 October 1992)

SOURCE: "Heard on the Street," in *The New Republic*, Vol. 207, No. 15, October 5, 1992, pp. 43-6.

[*In the following essay, Sante describes the distinguishing features of Mitchell's stories and sketches, commenting on his characters, themes, and prose style. Sante also compares Mitchell's career to that of A. J. Liebling, his closest colleague at the* New Yorker, *and discusses the author's relationship with Joe Gould.*]

The title of this omnibus edition of Joseph Mitchell's books (four out of five of them) [*Up in the Old Hotel*] was an apt choice: it is both mysterious and deceptively cozy, and the 1952 piece from which it derives epitomizes a great deal about Mitchell's work. It opens with a sentence that is, again, ominous and deceptively reassuring: "Every now and then, seeking to rid my mind of thoughts of death and doom, I get up early and go down to Fulton Fish Market." Mitchell briefly evokes the sights, sounds, and smells of the place, then heads across the street for breakfast at Sloppy Louie's (still there, and still serving excellent fish, though rather gentrified nowadays). He spots the proprietor, Louis Morino, and listens to him talk.

Like all the people Mitchell listens to, Morino is voluble, plainspoken, sensuously articulate, so much so that you might suspect Mitchell's editorial hand, here as elsewhere, of turning raggedy ordinary speech into great prose—but never mind. Louie is from an Italian fishing village called Recco, and when he gets into why he bought this particular restaurant in 1930, when he had money saved up and the Depression had caused innumerable restaurants all over town to become available for bargain prices, he compares the fish market to his birthplace:

> . . . they're very much alike—the fish smell, the general gone-to-pot look, the trading that goes on in the streets, the roofs over the sidewalks, the cats in corners gnawing on fish heads, the gulls in the gutters, the way everybody's on to everybody else, the quarrelling and the arguing. There's a boss fishmonger down here, a spry old hardheaded Italian man who's got a million dollars in the bank and dresses as if he's on relief and walks up and down the fish pier

snatching fish out of barrels by their heads or their tails and weighing them in his hands and figuring out in his mind to a fraction of a fraction how much they're worth and shouting and singing and enjoying life, and the face on him, the way he conducts himself, he reminds me so much of my father that sometimes, when I see him, it puts me in a good humor, and sometimes it breaks my heart.

In between listening to Louie and filling in the rest of his story, Mitchell eats. By and by Louie gets around to the subject of expansion. He's been wanting to put tables on the second floor, but he's had to use it for storage, since waterfront houses don't have cellars. So, then, what about the floors above?

> "You mean those boarded-up floors," Louie said. He hesitated a moment.
>
> "Didn't I ever tell you about the upstairs in here?" he asked. "Didn't I ever tell you about those boarded-up floors?"

It is a fitting hook for a ghost story. Louie tells about the times he almost went up in the old hand-powered pulley elevator, and how he lost his nerve, and then he tells about how, now and then and in dribs and drabs and for reasons of curiosity and labyrinthine association, he researched the history of the building, and while he tells this he is interrupted by fishmongers going in and out and looking for other market workers. Finally Mitchell talks him into making the trip. The two of them proceed, wearing construction helmets and brandishing flashlights.

They yank their way up and find themselves in the old reading room of what had been the Fulton Ferry Hotel. "There was a thick, black mat of fleecy dust on the floor—dust and soot and grit and lint and slut's wool." In the rooms they find old iron bedsteads, broken crockery, mirror-topped bureaus, scattered playing cards, empty whiskey bottles, an old photograph, a sign saying "The Wages of Sin is Death." Mitchell is just getting started and wants to go on to the upper floors, but Louie hightails it for the elevator. "'Come on, pull the rope faster! Pull it faster! Let's get out of this.'"

Nearly all of Mitchell's hallmarks are present: a leading character with a good story to tell; the vernacular at its richest; the presence of plain but great food, seafood in particular; the bustle of people skilled at their trade; the spoor of the past, both the past that is irrevocably gone and the past that lives on, at least temporarily, in memories and places and crafts and traditions. Mitchell's pacing is deliberate. His prose appears simple, but it's about as simple as a suspension bridge, and anyway, as a character in another story says of fish cooks, "It takes almost a lifetime to learn how to do a thing simply."

There is his ability to convey masses of learning and lore offhandedly, by a kind of osmosis, while the reader's attention is diverted. There is his control of narrative dynamics, which allows him to balance a casual, almost conversational tone across dramatic ellipses through to clipped endings. And there is his humor, which is not always immediately apparent but is always there, lurking behind even, maybe especially, his grimmest and most melancholy passages—"graveyard humor," he calls it in a prefatory note, citing *Finnegans Wake* and the engravings of Posada, initially surprising choices that make increasing sense in the light of his work's course.

I first heard of Joseph Mitchell about six years ago, when I bought a battered paperback copy of his second book, *McSorley's Wonderful Saloon* (1943), from a peddler on Astor Place in Manhattan. I was getting interested in the history of the neighborhood, and from the cover design, featuring a beefy, bowtied, and mustachioedbartender, I expected a compilation of jocular and faded anecdotes about the venerable (1854) alehouse around the corner from my point of purchase. I was familiar with that sort of mildewed literature of nostalgia and had developed a perverse liking for it.

Here, though, I found something quite different. In the book's second piece, **"Mazie,"** a profile of a Bowery moviehouse ticket-taker, for example, there is a vignette of a poetically inclined bum called "Eddie Guest":

> At the Venice one night he saw "The River," the moving picture in which the names of the tributaries of the Mississippi were made into a poem. When he came out, he stopped at Mazie's cage, spread his arms, and recited the names of many of the walk-up hotels on the Bowery. "The Alabama Hotel, the Comet, and the Uncle Sam House," he said, in a declamatory voice, "the Dandy, the Defender, the Niagara, the Owl, the Victoria House and the Grand Windsor Hotel, the Houston, the Mascot, the Palace, the Progress, the Palma House and the White House Hotel, the Newport, the Crystal, the Lion, and the Marathon. All flophouses. All on the Bowery. Each and all my home, sweet home."

Surprise followed surprise in these profiles of fantastic, improbable, but undeniably real characters, and the whole shed new light on the street-level history of New York City. The writing was pure poetry, nothing purple about it, only the patient, accumulative poetry of names and the way people talk: not unlike"Eddie Guest," Mitchell composes rhapsodic lists of names, of shellfish and wildflowers and harbor traffic and Gypsy clans and traveling circuses and over-the-hill boxers. I set about finding his four other books, *My Ears Are Bent* (1938), *Old Mr. Flood* (1948), *The Bottom of the Harbor* (1959), and *Joe Gould's Secret* (1965).

Since the last named was his last published work, I assumed Mitchell was dead, until a stray item in the *Times* one day— an account of an expedition by preservation experts into the sealed City Hall subway station, the most beautiful in the system—noted his presence and quoted him. Although I knew how unfortunately easy it is for even the greatest writers to tumble into obscurity, even in their own lifetimes—look at Melville—I was nevertheless astonished that a living writer of such stature could be out of print and unknown to most people of my generation. Eventually I learned that he had long been at work on a memoir, or a book about markets (or maybe there were two books; accounts varied), and that he had been partly responsible for his earlier books remaining out of print, for reasons I did not know but could imagine, including pride, sadness, and obstinacy.

The publication of *Up in the Old Hotel* rights at least part of this wrong. It reprints the last four of Mitchell's books, as well as a number of previously uncollected pieces. All of its contents were first published in *The New Yorker*. Mitchell was born in 1908 on a tobacco farm in eastern North Carolina and came to New York to workas a reporter in 1929, arriving the day after the stock market crashed. After stints at the *World,* the *Herald-Tribune,* and the *World-Telegram,* he joined *The New Yorker* in 1938, and has had a cubicle there ever since.

> **Mitchell . . . remains conscious of the scythe and the clock even at his most ostensibly carefree. His work is haunted. Not only are his subjects aged more often than not, but mortality also shadows the traditions that they represent.**
>
> **—Luc Sante**

The New Yorker in the Depression years loosened its focus from the smart set that had preoccupied it in the '20s and adopted a more democratic vista, and Mitchell was one of a surge of experienced street reporters who realized this change. Another was A.J. Liebling, Mitchell's closest friend until Liebling's death in 1963. Both collected raffish characters, hung out with them, recorded their frequently inspired talk. They were fascinated by carnies and con artists and locality mayors, and they seldom failed to take notice of the food on hand. The two friends reflected the influence of such early nineteenth-century English journalists as George Borrow and William Cobbett, who wrote apparently effortless prose that flaunted its plainness through the avoidance of Latinate abstractions and the use of great chains of simple conjunctions in preference to complex clause structures. And their hearts were indisputably in their material: they were not slumming. The original edition of the McSorley book begins with a note:

> The people in a number of the stories are of the kind that many writers have recently got in the habit of referring to as "the little people." I regard this phrase as patronizing and repulsive. There are no little people in this book. They are as big as you are, whoever you are.

As their careers progressed, the differences between them became more visible. It was not just that Liebling, the native New Yorker, roamed far and wide in his choice of subjects, while the Southerner Mitchell wrote almost exclusively about the city and its near neighbors. Liebling was a gregarious bon vivant, by all accounts as much of a character as those he wrote about, and even when beset by depression himself or when writing about death and loss, as in his war pieces, he still manages to convey tremendous gusto and boisterous humor. Mitchell, on the other hand, remains conscious of the scythe and the clock even at his most ostensibly carefree. His work is haunted. Not only are his subjects aged more often than not, but mortality also shadows the traditions that they represent. *Up in the Old Hotel* has a necrological aspect. It is a record of the last days of beefsteak dinners and shad netting and a hundred specialized harbor trades and varieties of practical lore, as well as of kinds of individuality and of community that have been erased by technology and its social consequences.

That Mitchell was aware from the beginning of the moribund nature of the matters he celebrated can be seen, for example, in **"Obituary of a Gin Mill,"** from 1939. A saloonkeeper has closed up his old joint and moved to a new spot up the street, a place "so stylish that [the owner] did not, for good luck, frame the first dollar bill passed across the bar; he framed the first five-dollar bill." The old place was rude, anarchic, and comfortable. People sang and yelled and fought and played practical jokes. The "old place was dirty and it smelled like a zoo, but it was genuine; his new place is as shiny and undistinguished as a two-dollar alarm clock." Much of life has suffered the fate that a character in another story ascribes to vegetables, which "have been improved until they're down-right poisonous."

But nobody should get the idea that Mitchell is pulling a long face while relating these matters. His stories about old Mr. Flood (which he classifies as fiction; their main character is apparently a composite) are as much about obstinate survival as they are about ruinous change. Mr. Flood is well into his 90s and is determined to see the age of 115 by living near the fish market and consuming almost exclusively seafood. He is in sound health, hasn't had a cold since 1912:

> Only reason I caught that one, I went on a toot and it

was a pouring-down rainy night in the dead of winter and my shoes were cracked and they let the damp in and I lost my balance a time or two and I sloshed around in the gutter and somewhere along the line I mislaid my hat and I'd just had a haircut and I stood in a draft in one saloon an hour or more and there was a poor fellow next to me sneezing his head off and when I got home I crawled into a bed that was beside an open window like a fool and passed out with my wet clothes on, shoes and all. Also, I'd spent the night before sitting up on a train and hadn't slept a wink and my resistance was low.

In contrast to Mr. Flood there is his friend Matthew T. Cusack, an old retired cop who once possessed a boundless appetite for food and drink and life, until he was given a radio as a present. He started listening to health shows, whereupon he began exhibiting symptoms, and now he grimly awaits death. Mitchell, of course, is not editorializing against radios or public health or anything else so much as he is arguing for self-sufficiency and graveyard humor, as well as reminding his readers that every improvement in life, every gain, brings with it a corresponding loss. He can mourn the passing of the old ways, but elsewhere, as when he writes of the attempts to control the rat population around the harbor, he can show a dozen reasons why it is a good thing some of those old ways have passed. Civilization is often a bad bargain, and Mitchell documents again and again how progress is far from being a straightforward matter.

The book is densely populated by individualists, obsessives, strays, loners, freaks, operators, and keepers of various flames. Some of their voices, for example those of Jane Barnell, the bearded lady, or the Rev. Mr. James Jefferson "Daddy" Hall, the street preacher, are so compelling that it is difficult to keep from quoting them at length and nearly impossible to keep from reading them aloud. Of them all, the one who looms largest is Joe Gould, the New York bohemian eccentric otherwise known as Professor Sea Gull. Mitchell wrote a profile of him in 1942 but could not shake him, actually or figuratively, and finally reconsidered his case in a series of pieces published in 1964.

Gould was well known among the artistic and literary crowds and among people who went to bars in lower Manhattan from the '20s to the late '40s. He was a sponger, a soak, and a general nuisance, but he was also wildly imaginative. He owed his nickname to the seagull imitations he would launch into in bars, in part as a way of soliciting funds, and he claimed a special affinity with the birds, and to have mastered their language to the point of translating Longfellow into it. He was a member of the Harvard class of 1911. After graduation he joined an anthropological expedition, in which his duties consisted of measuring the heads of some 1,500 Chippewa and Mandan Indians in North Dakota. After that he moved to New

York City, worked for about a year as a police reporter, and then embarked on an Oral History of Mankind, which prevented him from doing any other kind of work for the rest of his life.

Excerpts from this project appeared in such literary journals as *Broom, Pagany,* and *The Dial.* For decades the work was legendary, and Gould gave varying estimates of its length, well into the millions of words. In the first profile, Mitchell summarized and quoted Gould's descriptions of some of its contents, which appearedto be fearsomely discursive, lodging chapters of complaint and reminiscence and speculation among verbatim transcriptions of innumerable life stories related to him by all kinds of people in speakeasies and cafeterias, on subway trains and park benches.

Gould was intermittently supported by a great many people, in large part on the strength of his project, which was widely believed on Gould's own word to be a masterpiece and an essential reference for generations of future scholars. Mitchell attempted at various times over the years to track down the bulk of the manuscripts, but Gould gave conflicting and elusive accounts of their whereabouts. Mitchell would hear of one Greenwich Village resident or another who was safeguarding a stack of notebooks, but whenever he actually located such a pile, their contents would inevitably consist of four or five complaining or reminiscent chapters copied again and again, with few variations.

Finally, after years of this, Mitchell guessed the truth: Gould's masterwork existed only in his head. When pressed, Gould didn't deny it, and Mitchell kept the secret until seven years after Gould's death. Telling this tale clearly caused Mitchell a great deal of discomfort. He summons up the ghost of his own unwritten youthful novel; he equivocates, citing the flood of unread books in the world and the probable commercial fate of the Oral History; he proposes that Gould had "created a character a good deal more complicated than most of the characters created by the novelists and playwrights of his time." What he doesn't mention is that he,Mitchell, came about as close as anybody has to fulfilling such a work, not a million words long (more's the pity), and not exactly "a great hodgepodge and kitchen midden of hearsay, a repository of jabber, an omnium-gatherum of bushwa, gab, palaver, hogwash, flapdoodle, and malarkey," but a shaped, seasoned, simmered, distilled account of a raft of people's stories that would otherwise have gone unrecorded. He made Gould himself live on, in a way that those excerpts in *Broom* and *The Dial* never would.

One reason for Mitchell's relative obscurity over the past few decades may be that he is uncommonly self-effacing in his work, even by the generally self-effacing standard of the classic *New Yorker* reporters, and this somehow manages to seem the case even when he is bringing himself into a story. In the

author's note at the back of the volume, he gives a one-paragraph autobiography, supplies a list of his ongoing enthusiasms, and briefly describes his visits back to the North Carolina countryside, where once

> he watched for an hour or so as a pileated woodpecker tore the bark off the upper trunk and limbs of a tall old dead black-gum tree, and he says he considers this the most spectacular event he has ever witnessed.

Joseph Mitchell's work is clear and strong and rich, and it also possesses a quality too seldom found in most writing of any sort: it is unreservedly generous.

William Zinsser (essay date Winter 1993)

SOURCE: "Journeys with Joseph Mitchell," in *The American Scholar*, Winter, 1993, pp. 132-33, 136-38.

[*In the following essay, Zinsser assesses the enduring worth of each of the four books collected in* Up in the Old Hotel, *basing his judgments on both Mitchell's technique and subject matter.*]

> Every now and then, seeking to rid my thoughts of death and doom, I get up early and go down to Fulton Street Fish Market. I usually arrive around five-thirty, and take a walk through the two huge open-fronted market sheds, the Old Market and the New Market, whose fronts rest on South Street and whose backs rest on piles in the East River. At that time, a little while before the trading begins, the stands in the sheds are heaped high and spilling over with forty to sixty kinds of finfish and shellfish from the East Coast, the West Coast, the Gulf Coast and half a dozen foreign countries. The smoky riverbank dawn, the racket the fishmongers make, the seaweedy smell, and the sight of this plentifulness always give me a feeling of well-being, and sometimes they elate me. I wander among the stands for an hour or so. Then I go into a cheerful market restaurant named Sloppy Louie's and eat a big, inexpensive, invigorating breakfast—a kippered herring and scrambled eggs, or a shad-roe omelet, or split sea scallops and bacon, or some other breakfast specialty of the place.

Any Joseph Mitchell fan would recognize that opening paragraph as his and nobody else's: the plain declarative sentences, the leisurely accretion of detail, the naggings of mortality, and the promise of renewal through the sight and smell and grateful consumption of food brought from the sea by old-fashioned toil and cooked by old-fashioned methods. The title of the piece, **"Up in the Old Hotel,"** is no less revealing of the author—a man drawn to old places and old people—and it also hints at a mystery. We are about to be taken on a journey.

These journeys with Joseph Mitchell, which ran in *The New Yorker* for more than a quarter of a century, from 1938 to 1965, were hugely influential on nonfiction writers of my generation—a primary textbook. They appeared with maddening infrequency, often two or three years apart. Sometimes I would ask friends who worked at the magazine when I might expect a new Mitchell piece, but they never knew or even presumed to guess. This was mosaic work, they reminded me, and the mosaicist was finicky about fitting the pieces together until he got them right. When at last a new article did appear, I saw why it had taken so long. It *was* exactly right.

Then, abruptly, everything stopped. After *Joe Gould's Secret,* in 1965, Mitchell didn't publish another word, though he continued to go to his *New Yorker* office, as he still does today, at eighty-four. What he has been writing is his own secret, as are his reasons for shutting the door on his career, refusing even to have his books reprinted. Only this year did he drop a clue, in an interview with the *New York Times*. "The luster of his best work became a kind of burden," the *Times* reporter wrote. "The past, which had always exerted a powerful pull on his imagination, exacted a kind of revenge as he grew older. His books and his reputation, he says, became 'an albatross around my neck.'"

One result was that Mitchell's work was unavailable by the early 1970s, when I became a writing teacher and wanted to pass him along to a new generation of students, believing that they would find in his writing—in his effortless style, his organization of enjoyable information, his humor and his humanity—much that they would need to know. Like all teachers who own the only copy in town of what they want to teach, I improvised, reading certain passages aloud, and over the years that introduction to Joseph Mitchell is what many students have especially thanked me for. But because the work was out of print, the legacy was snapped, and I took to steering students to his closest heirs in the next generation: Calvin Trillin, Mark Singer, and Ian Frazier.

Mitchell's interests didn't run to society's stable citizens, and the pieces [in the anthology *Up in the Old Hotel*] are still classic examples of writing about "ordinary" people without a tinge of condescension. That achievement is at the heart of all of Joseph Mitchell's work.

—*William Zinsser*

Now at last Joseph Mitchell has consented to be anthologized, his four principal books collected under one roof for the first time: *McSorley's Wonderful Saloon, Old Mr. Flood, The Bottom of the Harbor,* and *Joe Gould's Secret*. The anthology is called *Up in the Old Hotel,* and, again, the title struck me as apt, for as I opened the book I felt not unlike Mitchell himself and Louis Morino in that story, poking into the long-closed upper floors of Sloopy Louie's restaurant, which had once been a waterfront hotel for steamship passengers. I didn't know what ghosts I would rouse and what I would think of what I found.

The first half of the new anthology consists of *McSorley's Wonderful Saloon* (1943), the book about some marginal residents of downtown Manhattan that gave Mitchell his initial fame. For this collection he has added seven stories from the same period, including **"The Mohawks in High Steel,"** his piece about the Caughnawaga Indian construction workers, remarkable for having no fear of heights, that Edmund Wilson used as the introduction to his book *Apologies to the Iroquois*. The table of contents—**"King of the Gypsies," "Obituary of a Gin Mill," "Houdini's Picnic," "A Sporting Man"**—is ample warning that Mitchell's interests didn't run to society's stable citizens, and the pieces themselves are still classic examples of writing about "ordinary" people without a tinge of condescension.

That achievement is at the heart of all of Joseph Mitchell's work—a matter of both craft and character. **"Lady Olga"** catches the ultimate humanity of one of nature's ultimate freaks, a bearded lady. **"Mazie"** is about the resident ticket-taker at a dime movie house called the Venice Theater—a celebrity on the Bowery because "she has a genuine fondness for bums" and probably knows more of them than anyone in the city; every day she hands out money to them. "On the Bowery, cheap movies rank just below cheap alcohol as an escape, and most bums are movie fans. They go into the Venice early in the day and slumber in their seats until they are driven out at midnight." Mazie once told the manager that movies with a lot of shooting were bad for business because "they wake up the customers."

Just as **"Mazie"** is both one person's story and the larger story of the Bowery, **"King of the Gypsies"** is both about Johnny Nikanov and about all New York Gypsies; Mitchell is so genuinely curious and so dogged a listener that he eventually gets it all—the whole culture as well as a representative individual:

> They [gypsies] rent the cheapest flats in the shabbiest tenements on the worst blocks. Three or four families often share one flat. They move on the spur of the moment; in the last two years one family has given seventeen addresses to the Department of Welfare. They have nothing at all to do with gajo [non-gypsy]

neighbors. Even the kids are aloof; they play stick- and stoopball, but only with each other. The children are dirty, flea-ridden, intelligent and beautiful; one rarely sees a homely gypsy child. They are not par- ticularly healthy, but they have the splendid gutter hardihood of English sparrows.

"A gypsy gets to be a king by calling himself one," Mitchell writes, stating an outlandish fact in a sentence so simple that it goes by almost before we see how much it amuses him. Such deadpan sentences form a current of humor that runs through his work, and such is his control that nobody is pa- tronized. He never pokes us in the ribs to notify us that some- thing he has recorded is considerably odd; we are allowed the pleasure of realizing it on our own. Alternatingly, he uses his subjects' own words to supply a comic edge: "Johnny says that his gypsies are the poorest in the United States. 'If you was to turn them all upside down and give them a good shaking,' he says, 'you couldn't buy a quart of gin with what fell out.'" Mitchell has a sure ear for vernacular speech, and one of the pleasures of reading his work is to hear how en- gagingly Americans get things said in idiomatic and regional turns of phrase.

But a funny thing happened to me on the way back to *McSorley's Wonderful Saloon.* Though I still admired the craft, I wearied of the subject. Mitchell was writing about a world whose mother church was the Irish saloon, a time when drunks and bums were lovable and when garrulous mooch- ers like Joe Gould were amusing. Today there's no such thing as a picturesque alcoholic, and homeless people on the side- walks of our cities are a national shame and sorrow. Bums have lost their literary lovability. (So have hard-drinking writ- ers.)

It's not Mitchell's fault that our perception of his chosen mi- lieu has shifted after a half century of tumultuous social change and consciousness-raising. Nonfiction writers are captives of their given moment, and New York in the 1930s was still a small town; people knew their neighborhood bum. But I also couldn't help wondering how lovable all those drunks and bums and freaks were in the first place, or whether Mitchell romanticized them because they represented an American frontier type that he honored and perhaps even envied: the maverick, the outsider, the crazy individualist. Writers are in business to rattle the establishment, and Mitchell was only one of many *New Yorker* stars of his era who took loners and losers as their beat: the droll malefactors of St. Clair McKelway's "Annals of Crime," the raffish prizefighters of A. J. Liebling's boxing ring, the poetic dreamers of John McNulty's Irish bars.

I had the same problem with *Joe Gould's Secret,* the last of the four books collected here. Of all the half-mad misfits Mitchell met in a career that began as a young reporter on the

New York Herald Tribune and the *New York World-Telegram* when he arrived from North Carolina in 1929—interviews that constitute his earliest book, *My Ears Are Bent*—no ear- bender held him in such thrall as Gould, a legendary Green- wich Village bohemian who claimed to be writing a book called "An Oral History of Our Time" that was already eleven times as long as the Bible. "Gould's life is by no means care- free; he is constantly tormented by what he calls 'the three H's'—homelessness, hunger and hangovers," Mitchell wrote in his firstshot at Gould, a *New Yorker* profile and subse- quent chapter in *McSorley's* called **"Professor Sea Gull,"** so named because Gould cadged drinks by, among other things, doing sea gull imitations. He said he had translated many of Longfellow's poems into sea gull.

Returning to the subject twenty-one years later in *Joe Gould's Secret* (1964), Mitchell recapitulates the endless visits and monologues that the sea gull man inflicted on him. "I kept hoping that Gould would talk himself out," he recalls, "but the months went by and he showed no signs of doing so." One monologue lasted from 6:00 P. M. to 4:00 A. M. Even for a famously patient and courteous reporter, such forbearance goes well beyond normal limits, and it occurred to me, re- reading this valedictory book, that Gould just plumb wore Mitchell out. Untypically, the book skates close to the edge of exasperation. Finally unburdening himself of Gould's se- cret, finally coming to terms with all that manipulative be- havior and trying to maintain both Gould's dignity and his own, Mitchell may well have seen his whole professional life pass before his eyes, Gould being only the most tenacious of the hundreds of lost souls who trusted him to bear witness to their gallant but ultimately pathetic lives. It would be enough to give anyone terminal writer's block.

But lodged between the McSorley's book, in which Mitchell developed his craft, and the Gould book, in which he said good-bye to it, are two gems that have lost none of their bril- liance. With *Old Mr. Flood* and *The Bottom of the Harbor,* Mitchell grew beyond hisinfatuation with eccentrics and be- came a matchless chronicler of plain people doing plain work with integrity. The two books, however, are not the brothers they might appear to be.

Originally, the slender *Old Mr. Flood* took the form of three pieces in *The New Yorker,* and the opening paragraph is a pure concentrate of Mitchell's style:

> A tough Scotch-Irishman I know, Mr. Hugh G. Flood, a retired house-wrecking contractor, aged ninety- three, often tells people that he is dead set and deter- mined to live until the afternoon of July 27, 1965, when he will be a hundred and fifteen years old. "I don't ask much here below," he says. "I just want to hit a hundred and fifteen. That'll hold me." Mr. Flood is small and wizened. His eyes are watchful and icy-

blue, and his face is red, bony and clean-shaven. He is old-fashioned in appearance. As a rule, he wears a high, stiff collar, a candy-striped shirt, a serge suit, and a derby. A silver watch-chain hangs across his vest. He keeps a flower in his lapel. When I am in the Fulton Street Fish Market neighborhood, I always drop into the Hartford House, a drowsy waterfront hotel at 309 Pearl Street, where he has a room, to see if he is still alive.

Like most old people, Mitchell goes on to say, Mr. Flood "feels best when he is around things that have lasted a long time," and the book takes its tremendous gusto from the old men's recollections of the pulse of the Fulton Market and the golden age of restaurants like Still's, which had "a white marble bar for the half-shell trade, and there were barrels and barrels and barrels of oysters stood up behind this bar, and everything was nice and plain and solid—no piddling around, no music to frazzle your nerves, no French on the bill of fare; you got what you went for."

So full of exact detail were these "stories of fish-eating, whiskey, death and rebirth," as Mitchell called them, that when *Old Mr. Flood* was published as a book, in 1948, I was startled to read the author's prefatory note, which said: "Mr. Flood is not one man; combined in him are several old men who work or hang out in Fulton Fish Market, or who did in the past. I wanted these stories to be truthful rather than factual, but they are solidly based on facts." (In the new anthology, he calls the book "fictional.") I felt slightly betrayed by that admission and didn't know what to make of such tinkering with the rules of my craft. I now see that Mitchell anticipated by several decades the "New Journalism" that writers like Gay Talese and Tom Wolfe were hailed for inventing in the 1960s, using fictional techniques of imagined dialogue and emotion to give narrative flair to works whose facts they had punctiliously researched.

I also suspect that the obvious pleasure of writing about the waterfront in *Old Mr. Flood* told Mitchell that he had found his true subject—a world of dignified work that he could examine in depth, with no fictional fooling around. The result was *The Bottom of the Harbor* (1960), which still strikes me as perfect—one of the best of all American nonfiction books.

The Bottom of the Harbor consists of six long articles that appeared in *The New Yorker* over the space of twelve years. These were the pieces that I once awaited with so much impatience. Beginning with **"Up in the Old Hotel,"** they include **"The Bottom of the Harbor,"** an anatomy of what's under the city's waters—everything living and dead, from fish and clams and oysters to long-sunken wrecks; **"The Rats on the Waterfront,"** an enjoyable group portrait of the harbor's least enjoyable creatures; **"Mr. Hunter's Grave,"** a visit with one of the oldest survivors of a nineteenth-cen-

tury village of Negro oystermen on Staten Island; **"Dragger Captain,"** the story of an old salt in the fleet out of Stonington, Connecticut, that supplies the Fulton Fish Market with flounder; and **"The Rivermen,"** which is about the men of Edgewater, New Jersey, just below the George Washington Bridge, who fish the Hudson River for shad.

With this book the past becomes a major character in Mitchell's work, giving it a tone that is both elegiac and historical. Because the characters in *The Bottom of the Harbor* are mainly old men, they are custodians of memory, their stories a link with the history of a city that has always been mercantile at heart. My own family's shellac factory stood near the river on West 59th Street for well over a century—I'm a fourth-generation New Yorker—and I, too, was once a young reporter on the *Herald Tribune,* in love with the city and writing features about shad fishermen on the Hudson. My gratitude to Mitchell is therefore that of a native son. I got lucky that a man whose family has farmed in North Carolina since before the Revolutionary War came north, with his inborn respect for continuity and work, and caught my city's metabolism.

The mixture of themes in *The Bottom of the Harbor* is uniquely Joseph Mitchell's: specialized knowledge, pride of labor, enjoyment of the simple pleasures of the present, and mindfulness of the past and of the soon-to-be-joined dead. So organically are these themes woven through *The Bottom of the Harbor* that I could cite almost any page as evidence. One that comes to mind deals with the boats that take fishing parties out of Brooklyn's Sheepshead Bay. It comes to mind because my father spent his boyhood summers there, visiting his grandfather, who had been brought from Germany when *he* was a boy. Mitchell explains that there are hundreds of wrecks lying on the bottom of the approaches to New York harbor, some so close to shore that on sunny fall days it's possible to see schools of sea bass streaming in and out of their hulls, which provide shelter.

> Furthermore, [the hulls] are coated, inside and out, with a lush, furry growth made up of algae, sea moss, tube worms, barnacles, horse mussels, sea anemones, sea squirts, sea mice, sea snails, and scores of other organisms, all of which are food for fish. The most popular party boats are those whose captains can locate the fishiest wrecks and bridle them. Bridling is a maneuver in which, say the wreck lies north and south, the party boat goes in athwart it and drops one anchor to the east of it and another to the west of it, so that the party boat and wreck lie crisscross. Held thus, the party boat can't be skewed about by the wind and tide, and the passengers fishing over both rails can always be sure that they are dropping their bait on the wreck, or inside it. Good party-boat captains, by taking bearings on landmarks and lightships

and buoys, can locate and bridle anywhere from ten to thirty wrecks. A number of the wrecks are quite old; they disintegrate slowly. Three old ones, all sailing ships, lie close to each other near the riprap jetty at Rockaway Point, in the mouth of the harbor. The oldest of the three, the Black Warrior Wreck, which shelters tons of sea bass from June until November, went down in 1859. The name of the next oldest has been forgotten and she is called the Snow Wreck; a snow is a kind of square-rigged ship similar to a brig; she sank in 1886 or 1887. The third one is an Italian ship that sank in 1890 with a cargo of marble slabs. Her name has also been forgotten and she is called the Tombstone Wreck, the Granite Wreck, or the Italian Wreck. . . . Several of these wrecks have been fished steadily for generations, and party-boat captains like to say that they would be worth salvaging just to get the metal in the hooks and sinkers that have been snagged on them.

So insistent is the tug of the past—of long-gone ships and long-gone people—that *The Bottom of the Harbor* ought to be lugubrious. But it has a certain prevailing merriment. Since Mitchell and his subjects regard death as a normal part of life, his book has none of the self-indulgence common to the work of journalists confronted with aging and mortality. It's notsentimental, or maudlin, or strenuously colorful. It's Dickens without tears.

"Invariably, for some reason I don't know and don't want to know, after I have spent an hour or so in one of these cemeteries, looking at gravestone designs and reading inscriptions and identifying wild flowers and scaring rabbits out of the weeds and reflecting on the end that awaits me and awaits us all, my spirits lift, I become quite cheerful," Mitchell writes in **"Mr. Hunter's Grave,"** my favorite of all his pieces and the one I would commend to all nonfiction writers hoping to crack the secret. I still remember the exhilaration of reading it for the first time.

Mitchell meets the eighty-seven-year-old George H. Hunter—"one of those strong, self-contained old men you don't see much any more"—while exploring a settlement of dilapidated houses on Staten Island, called Sandy Ground, that has "an empty look, as if everybody had locked up and gone off somewhere." It's a relic of the oyster-planting business—a once-thriving community and a "garden spot"—founded before the Civil War by free Negroes from the Eastern Shore of Maryland and still inhabited by their descendants. Mr. Hunter, an elder of the African Methodist Church, spends an afternoon showing Mitchell around, and the day has the unhurried quality of actual time. Before it's over, Mr. Hunter, reflecting on the history of oyster farming in New York harbor, on the passing of generations in Sandy Ground, on families and family names, planting and cooking, wildflowers and

fruit, birds andtrees, churches and funerals, change and decay, has touched on much of what living is all about.

Near the end, in the old cemetery, not far from his own grave, he says: "To tell you the truth, I'm no great believer in gravestones. There's stones in here that have only been up forty or fifty years, and you can't read a thing it says on them, and what difference does it make? God keeps His eye on those that are dead and buried the same as He does on those that are alive and walking. . . . He knows the exact whereabouts of every speck of dust of every one of them. Stones rot the same as bones rot, and nothing endures but the spirit."

Joe Mysak (review date February 1993)

SOURCE: A review of *Up in the Old Hotel*, in *The American Spectator*, Vol. 26, No. 2, February, 1993, pp. 62-3.

[*In the following review, Mysak welcomes the publication of* Up in the Old Hotel *and briefly describes the subjects of some of Mitchell's best-known stories.*]

Joseph Mitchell, now 84, is the last of those great *New Yorker* writers of the magazine's heyday. Most of us got to know him through Brendan Gill's *Here at The New Yorker,* in which Gill profiled all the magazine's great stylists—White, Thurber, Benchley, Liebling, Gibbs, McNulty, Maloney, Edmund Wilson—and putMitchell at the top of the list. *Up in the Old Hotel* collects four Mitchell books: *McSorley's Wonderful Saloon* (1943), *Old Mr. Flood* (1948), *The Bottom of the Harbor* (1960), and *Joe Gould's Secret* (1965). For anyone who is not familiar with Mitchell—and his work has been out of circulation for so long that it is tough to see how many people could be—this collection is a feast, a staggering repast, a three-day bender.

As Mitchell told the *New York Times,* "I'm a ghost; everything's changed now." It is almost as if a hurricane roared through in the 1970s and blew out the picturesque, unthreatening city of Joseph Mitchell, replacing it with one that is almost pornographic. Yet Mitchell's tales can be appreciated even if the days of such gentle eccentrics as Old Mr. Flood, who lived in a venerable hotel downtown near Peck Slip, are long, long gone.

The art was in the writing; the craft was in the listening. Joseph Mitchell is a great eater and drinker, and a great listener. As he wrote in his first book, *My Ears Are Bent* (1938):

> The best talk is artless, the talk of people trying to reassure or comfort themselves, women in the sun, grouped around baby carriages, talking about their weeks in the hospital or the way meat has gone up, or men in saloons, talking to combat the loneliness everyone feels. The talk when you interview some-

one for a newspaper article is usually premeditated and usually artificial. Now and then, however, someone says something so unexpected it is magnificent.

There are a thousand stories in *Up in the Old Hotel,* most of them unexpected and magnificent, told by bartenders, gypsies, street preachers, a bearded lady, fishermen, boat captains, charlatans, cooks, Mohawk steelworkers, police detectives, and bricklayers. They are about life on the margin, desperation and endurance, living by one's wits. As Mitchell wrote in *My Ears Are Bent,* "I have been tortured by some of the fanciest ear-benders in the world . . . and I have long since lost the ability to detect insanity." And since many of these pieces date from the 1940s and 1950s, many of Mitchell's old-timers can just about remember Reconstruction and an East River filled with tall-masted ships.

"The Old House at Home" . . . hits all of the familiar Mitchell themes, and seems to me to be the finest piece about a saloon and its customers that has ever been penned.

—*Joe Mysak*

The first piece in this collection, **"The Old House at Home,"** about McSorley's Old Ale House, hits all of the familiar Mitchell themes, and seems to me to be the finest piece about a saloon and its customers that has ever been penned. Here is the lead:

> McSorley's occupies the ground floor of a red-brick tenement at 15 Seventh Street, just off Cooper Square, where the Bowery ends. It was opened in 1854 and is the oldest saloon in New York City. In eighty-eight years it has had four owners—an Irish immigrant, his son, a retired policeman, and his daughter—and all of them have been opposed to change.

Can there be any doubt that the reader will get to know each of these characters? Old John McSorley, for example, would keep a horse in a stable around the corner, with a nanny goat in the same stall,

> believing, like many horse-lovers, that horses should have company at night. During the lull in the afternoon a stable hand would lead the horse around to a hitching block in front of the saloon, and Old John, wearing his bar apron, would stand on the curb and groom the animal. A customer who wanted service would tap on the window and Old John would drop his currycomb, step inside, draw an ale, and return at once to the horse.

His son Bill's "principal concern was to keep McSorley's exactly as it had been in his father's time," and to that end, "if the saloon became crowded, he would close up early, saying, 'I'm getting too confounded much trade in here.'" His favorite poem was "The Man Behind the Bar." He especially liked the last verse:

> When St. Peter sees him coming he
>   will leave the gates ajar,
> For he knows he's had his hell on
>   earth, has the man behind the bar.

Contrast McSorley's with Dick's Bar & Grill, in **"Obituary of a Gin Mill,"** one of those saloons "within a few blocks of virtually every large newspaper in the United States . . . which also functions as a bank, as a sanitarium, as a gymnasium and sometimes as a home." The place apparently went downhill after Dick decided to move, and

> a salesman for a bar-fixtures concern got hold of him and sold him a bill of goods. I believe that bar-equipment salesmen have done more to destroy the independence and individuality of New York gin mills and their customers than Prohibition or repeal; there is nothing that will make a gin mill look so cheap and spurious as a modernistic bar and a lot of chairs made of chromium tubing.

Those who know the secret of Joseph Mitchell have their own favorites among the pieces here. Perhaps it is **"The Mohawks in High Steel,"** which tells why a group of Canadian Mohawk Indians became expert steel workers. Or **"Mr. Hunter's Grave,"** about a Staten Island community of black oystermen, and what happened after oystering died out in New York Harbor. Or perhaps it is the title piece, **"Up in the Old Hotel,"** a history of Sloppy Louie's restaurant near the Fulton Fish market. It might be the *Old Mr. Flood* stories, or the history of New York Harbor, or the profile of the rats on New York's waterfront.

For my money, though, nothing can top **"All You Can Hold for Five Bucks,"** a history of "the New York Steak Dinner, or 'beefsteak.'" Beefsteaks were thrown by clubs and lodges, and featured slices of steak served up on bread, double lamb chops, and pitchers of beer. "Knives, forks, napkins, and tablecloths never had been permitted; a man was supposed to eat with his hands," writes Mitchell. The eaters wiped their hands on butcher aprons, and wore chef's hats. Writing in 1939, the writer says that when women got the vote and began to be invited to beefsteaks, corruption set in:

> The life of the party at a beefsteak used to be the man who let out the most ecstatic grunts, drank the most beer, ate the most steak, and got the most grease on his ears, but women do not esteem a glutton, and at a

contemporary beefsteak it is unusual for a man to do away with more than six pounds of meat and thirty glasses of beer.

Mitchell, I hasten to add, is a normalsized, even smallish, man.

Richard Severo (essay date 25 May 1996)

SOURCE: "Joseph Mitchell, Chronicler of the Unsung and the Unconventional, Dies at 87," in *The New York Times*, May 25, 1996, p. 12.

[*In the following obituary, Severo provides an overview of Mitchell's career.*]

Joseph Mitchell, whose stories about ordinary people created extraordinary journalism in the pages of *The New Yorker,* died of cancer yesterday at Columbia-Presbyterian Medical Center in Manhattan. He was 87 and lived in Manhattan.

At the height of his creative powers, from the 1930's to the mid-60's, Mr. Mitchell tended to avoid the standard fare of journalists: interviews with moguls, tycoons, movie stars and captains of industry. Instead, he pursued the generals of nuisance: flops, drunks, con artists, panhandlers, gin-mill owners and their bellicose bartenders, at least one flea circus operator, a man who sold racing cockroaches, a bearded lady and a fast talker who claimed to have written nine million words of "An Oral History of Our Times" when, in fact, he had written no words at all.

Mr. Mitchell was also the poet of the waterfront, of the lime-light of New York's greatness as a seaport, of the Fulton Fish Market, of the clammers on Long Island and the oystermen on Staten Island: people who caught, sold and ate seafood and talked about it incessantly. One Sunday in August 1937, he placed third in a clam-eating tournament at Block Island after consuming 84 cherrystones. He regarded that, he said, as "one of the few worthwhile achievements" of his life.

For him, people were always as big as their dreams, as mellow as the ale they nursed in the shadows of McSorley's saloon off CooperSquare in the East Village. He wrote during a time when New Yorkers were mostly convinced that they were of good heart and that they had the best of intentions, whatever the rest of the world thought of their abrasiveness and contentiousness. Mr. Mitchell's articles offered evidence that they were right.

When somebody suggested that he wrote about the "little people," he replied that there were no little people in his work. "They are as big as you are, whoever you are," he said.

When Mr. Mitchell became a staff writer of *The New Yorker*

in 1938, the city had come through the Depression and was soon to send its sons and daughters off to fight a war. Even with the hard times and a jaded past, there was still an innocence of sorts, and an interest in the people Mr. Mitchell liked to write about as well as a tolerance for them. His nonfiction had grace and was rich with the sort of people a reader could find in Joyce or Gogol, two of the writers Mr. Mitchell admired. He was to letters what the Ashcan School had been to painting.

Mr. Mitchell arrived when the magazine's editor, Harold Ross, was giving its top nonfiction writers, among them St. Clair McKelway, A. J. Liebling and Philip Hamburger, more space and time than was available to reporters of the day. *The New Yorker* writers used their good fortune to advantage. In stories, "Profiles" and "Reporter at Large" articles, Mr. Mitchell helped to pioneer a special kind of reportage, setting standards to which latergenerations of reporters would aspire.

If his name is not as widely known as it might have been, that is mostly because for the last three decades of his life, he wrote nary a word that anybody got to see. For years, he would show up at his tiny office at *The New Yorker* every day and assure his colleagues that he was working on something, but that it was not quite ready.

"He told his pals he was writing about his roots in North Carolina," said Charles McGrath, who was deputy editor of *The New Yorker* and who is now the editor of *The New York Times Book Review*. "Then it became a book about his living in New York." Whatever it was, nothing of any substance emerged from his typewriter after 1965 and his friends came to think of it as an exceptionally bad case of writer's block. Mr. Mitchell had always been a perfectionist and Mr. McGrath said he suspected that Mr. Mitchell was raising his standards all the time. The janitor would find reams of copy in his waste-paper basket.

"I'm a ghost; everything's changed now," Mr. Mitchell said when he was in his 80's, adding that he had become used to being obscure.

Although Mr. Mitchell always had an extraordinary reputation among nonfiction writers and his out-of-print books were eagerly sought by collectors, he emerged from his obscurity in 1992 when the body of his work was reissued by Pantheon Books in a volume called *Up in the Old Hotel*. The book was a critical and commercial success, and Mr. Mitchell said he was pleased to learn that younger readers found merit in his prose.

The centerpiece of the book was the series of articles that appeared in *The New Yorker* in the late 1930's and early 40's, and then was published in 1943 as *McSorley's Wonderful Saloon*.

Mr. Mitchell had discovered McSorley's Old Ale House shortly after he joined *The New Yorker*. The saloon opened in 1854 and, as the oldest continuously run institution of its kind in New York, immediately endeared itself to Mr. Mitchell. He loathed most forms of progress and technology and so did the succession of people who drank in McSorley's.

> **His nonfiction had grace and was rich with the sort of people a reader could find in Joyce or Gogol, two of the writers Mr. Mitchell admired. He was to letters what the Ashcan School had been to painting.**
>
> —*Richard Severo*

"It is equipped with electricity," he wrote of it, "but the bar is stubbornly illuminated with a pair of gas lamps, which flicker fitfully and throw shadows on the low, cobwebby ceiling each time someone opens the street door. There is no cash register. Coins are dropped in soup bowls—one for nickels, one for dimes, one for quarters, and one for halves—and bills are kept in a rosewood cashbox."

And what of the service?

"It is a drowsy place; the bartenders never make a needless move, the customers nurse their mugs of ale, and the three clocks on the walls have not been in agreement for many years."

Who went to such a place?

"The backbone of the clientele is a rapidly thinning group of crusty old men, predominantly Irish, who have been drinking there since they were youths and now have a proprietary feeling about the place. Some of them have tiny pensions, and are alone in the world; they sleep in Bowery hotels and spend practically all their waking hours in McSorley's."

When Mr. Mitchell started writing such pieces about New York, the people who were then old could remember the draft riots of 1863, the various financial panics, the huzzahs that accompanied the end of the Spanish-American War in 1898 and the sorrow that attended the death of John McSorley, the original owner of the saloon, in 1910.

It is not possible to determine who the most memorable person was in Mr. Mitchell's stories, but there were many who rivaled the regulars of McSorley's.

There was Commodore Dutch, who somehow convinced rich and unrich alike that they should go to his annual charity ball, which he gave to benefit himself. "I haven't got a whole lot of sense," the Commodore told Mr. Mitchell, "but I got too much sense to work."

There was Arthur Samuel Colborne, who announced in 1941 that he had not uttered "a solitary profane word since a Sunday morning in the winter of 1886." He was so pleased with himself that he started the Anti-Profanity League and took to touring bars in Yorkville, preaching against the sin of swearing. "You start out with 'hell,' 'devil take it,' 'Dad burn it,' 'Gee whizz,' and the like of that, and by and by you won't be able to open your trap without letting loose an awful, awful blasphemous oath," Mr. Colborne told Mr. Mitchell. Mr. Colborne felt he had just about eliminated profanity in the saloons of Yorkville, but not without a price, since Mr. Colborne had to quaff a great deal of beer while spreading the word. His story, entitled **"The Don't Swear Man,"** ran in the magazine in 1941.

There was a ragged old man who said he was "John S. Smith of Riga, Latvia, Europe" who began hitchhiking around the United States in 1934, virtually penniless. Every time a benefactor gave him a free cup of coffee or a little soup, he would give him a check for hundreds, even thousands of dollars drawn on the Irving National Bank of New York, which had gone out of business in 1923. Mr. Mitchell wrote: "I began to think of the vain hopes he raised in the breasts of the waitresses who had graciously given him hundreds of meals and the truck drivers who had hauled him over a hundred highways, and to feel that about John S. Smith of Riga, Latvia, Europe, there is something a little sinister."

And there was Joseph Ferdinand Gould, who had graduated from Harvard in 1911 and come to New York, not long after he left an archeological expedition in which he measured the skulls of the remains of 1,500 Chippewa and Mandan Indians in North Dakota. He took to hanging around Greenwich Village coffee shops, where with no provocation he would do an imitation of a sea gull. Indeed, he claimed to have mastered sea gull language and had reached the point where he was about to translate Longfellow into it.

Joe Gould persuaded almost everybody who was anybody that he was writing an "Oral History of Our Times." He carried around paper bags that many believed contained his research but that, in reality, merely contained other paper bags and a few ratty newspaper clips. He lamented that he was the last bohemian and all the others he had known had fallen by the wayside. "Some are in the grave," he said, "some are in the loony bin and some are in the advertising business."

Malcolm Cowley admired him and so did E. E. Cummings. William Saroyan gave him alcohol and Ezra Pound trusted him.

It was not until 1964, 21 years since his first *New Yorker* profile of Mr. Gould and 7 years after Mr. Gould's death in a psychiatric hospital (death came as he was doing a sea gull imitation), that Mr. Mitchell told his readers the truth: that whatever the "Oral History" was, it reposed in Mr. Gould's noggin. Mr. Mitchell's first story about Mr. Gould, entitled **"Professer Sea Gull,"** ran in 1943. The final Joe Gould articles, which appeared in 1964, were Mr. Mitchell's last signed contributions to *The New Yorker*. Two of his books, ***The Bottom of the Harbor*** and ***Joe Gould's Secret,*** were recently published in Modern Library editions.

Reviewing *Up in the Old Hotel,* for *The New York Times Book Review,* Verlyn Klinkenborg wrote: "Mr. Mitchell always mediates the sadness such subjects bring—the loss of time, the life slipping by, the way the old manners fail to hang on—and he lets the reader feel only the pleasure that comes from his own very personal discoveries. He himself remains, in this prose at least, a melancholy man, wandering with a sandwich in his pocket among the wildflowers in abandoned cemeteries, seeking the company of solitary men who are gregarious only in the company of other isolates, sniffing out the odors of the Fulton Fish Market and its old hotels. And in such moments the reader gets a glimpse of Mr. Mitchell himself, even as he seems to disappear into the scene he describes."

Joseph Mitchell was born July 27, 1908, on his Parker grandparents' farm near Iona, N.C., the son of Averette Nance and Elizabeth A. Parker Mitchell. His family was in the cotton and tobacco trading business. Mr. Mitchell studied at the University of North Carolinafrom 1925 to 1929. He sent an article he had written on tobacco to *The New York Herald Tribune,* which liked it so much that it published it and summoned him to New York in 1929. Over the next nine years, he wrote for *The Herald Tribune, The Morning World* and *The World-Telegram,* the paper that first sent him to the Fulton Fish Market.

Mr. Mitchell married Therese Dagny Jacobsen in 1931. She died in 1980. He is survived by his companion, Sheila McGrath; two children from his first marriage, Nora Sanborn of Eatontown, N.J., and Elizabeth Curtis of Atlanta; three granddaughters; two grandsons, and one great-granddaughter.

Mr. Mitchell also wrote some fictional pieces about North Carolina, among them **"The Downfall of Fascism in Black Ankle County"** (1939); **"I Blame It All on Mama"** (1940), and **"Uncle Dockery and the Independent Bull"** (1939). A work of nonfiction, **"The Mohawks in High Steel,"** about American Indians who worked on steel bridges and skyscrapers, was published in *The New Yorker,* then used as the introduction to Edmund Wilson's *Apologies to the Iroquois.*

In a 1992 interview, Mr. Mitchell reminisced about New York and *The New Yorker* and how both had changed. He wasn't opposed to change, he said, but it was clear that his heart remained with the New York of Fiorello La Guardia and *The New Yorker* of Harold Ross.

"At the old *New Yorker,* the people were wonderful writers," hesaid. "A lot of us would go to lunch together: Liebling and Perelman and Thurber, who was idiosyncratic and funny. Now, everybody goes in and out. I go to lunch at the Grand Central Oyster Bar and eat by myself."

FURTHER READING

Criticism

Epstein, Joseph. "Joe Gould's Masterpiece." *The New Republic* 153, No. 17 (23 October 1965): 26-7, 30.

> Provides a brief sketch of Joe Gould's life and describes the circumstances surrounding the composition of *Joe Gould's Secret.*

———. "Talk of the Town." *The Times Literary Supplement*, No. 4666 (4 September 1992): 6-8.

> Discusses Mitchell's work in terms of the changing editors at the *New Yorker*, explains his failure to publish anything in the magazine for over twenty years, and compares his style to that of A. J. Liebling.

Ivry, Benjamin. "Joseph Mitchell's Secret." *New York* 20, No. 6 (9 February 1987): 20.

> A brief account of Mitchell's life as the *New Yorker*'s "elder statesman," focusing on his desire for privacy.

Additional coverage of Mitchell's life and career is contained in the following source published by Gale Research: *Contemporary Authors, Vols. 77-80.*

Clifford Odets
1906-1963

American playwright, scriptwriter, and film director.

The following entry provides an overview of Odets's career. For further information on his life and works, see *CLC,* Volumes 2 and 28.

INTRODUCTION

Odets was among the most prominent American playwrights of the 1930s. His early plays made him an overnight success for their realistic portrayal of Depression-era Americans searching for a place in modern society. Yet Odets never lived up to early critical acclaim that compared him favorably with Anton Chekhov and Eugene O'Neill, and he eventually settled into a financially successful, if lackluster, Hollywood scriptwriting career. His best plays retain historical significance for their portrayal of American—particularly Jewish-American—life after the Great Depression.

Biographical Information

Odets was born in Philadelphia and grew up in a Jewish section of the Bronx in New York. His middle-class family had a prosperous business in the 1920s and was financially secure during the Depression. Odets quit high school and pursued poetry writing for a time, provoking his father's anger and disappointment, but soon decided to become a stage actor, to which his parents gave their qualified approval. He joined an amateur company and from 1925 to 1927 performed in radio plays, vaudeville acts, and summer stock productions. In 1930 he joined the Group Theatre, founded by Harold Clurman, Cheryl Crawford, and Lee Strasberg and intended to be both a training ground for actors and an idealistic collective that would attempt to change society through the onstage presentation of alternative values. Odets gained little recognition in the organization as an actor, but with the production of his first play, *Waiting for Lefty* (1935), a leftist work centered around a taxi drivers' union preparing to take a strike vote, he became an immediate sensation. *Awake and Sing!* (1935) also garnered wide popular acclaim; in retrospect, it is seen as perhaps Odets's most important work. After the failure of *Paradise Lost* (1935), which was attacked by many critics for its stock characters and an optimistic closing speech that seemed to have little justification in the body of the play, Odets accepted an offer from Paramount Studios to work as a scriptwriter. Refuting charges that he was "selling out," he contended that his earnings could help finance the Group Theatre. He returned to the Group Theatre for the production of his next play, *Golden Boy* (1937), which became the great-

est commercial success of his career. The story of a young man trying to decide between careers as a violinist and a boxer, *Golden Boy* reflects Odets's love of music and anticipates his own idealistic turmoil as well. Following the failure of Odets's *Clash by Night* (1941), the Group Theatre disbanded, and Odets returned to Hollywood. Although he continued to work in theater and enjoyed another success with *The Country Girl* in 1950, his most acclaimed later works were the scripts for such films as *None but the Lonely Heart* and *Humoresque*. Odets alternately defended and spoke disparagingly of his film work, but he remained in Hollywood until his death.

Major Works

Odets's career as a playwright is often divided by critics into three phases. The first and most important of these encompasses his efforts as a proletarian dramatist. Odets joined the Communist Party in 1934, and *Waiting for Lefty, Awake and Sing!,* and *Paradise Lost* were all written during his brief association with that group. These plays confirm leftist principles while declaring archaic the values of middle-class America. Odets structured *Lefty* so that the personal problems of the characters reflect the conflict between the union and the taxi company. *Awake and Sing!* examines the aspirations of a Jewish working-class family that has become disillusioned by an oppressive economic system. In *Paradise Lost* a middle-class businessman and his family are destroyed by a series of disasters. Each character in this play represents a particular middle-class value, and the catastrophes that befall them symbolize the fall of these values during the 1930s. These plays also reflect the communal influence of the Group Theatre on Odets's writing style as well as the Jewish street idiom with which he was familiar. The second phase of Odets's career includes plays involving personal relationships rather than direct social criticism. *Golden Boy* portrays the quest for success and the tragedies suffered as a result of faulty decisions and changes in values. *Rocket to the Moon* (1938), *Night Music* (1940), and *Clash by Night* (1941) are love stories that focus more on plot and dialogue than on characterization and social commentary. The final phase of Odets's career comprises semi-autobiographical dramas with psychological overtones. Social commentary is nearly nonexistent in these late works. In *The Big Knife* (1949) a movie actor is offered a multimillion-dollar contract but wants to escape the corruption of the film industry and return to the New York stage. *The Country Girl* is about an alcoholic actor who attempts a comeback on Broadway with the help of his wife, upon whom he is totally dependent. Odets's last play, *The Flowering Peach* (1954), is an adaptation of the biblical story of Noah. It is unusual in Odets's work for combining elements of comedy, philosophy, and theology, and came in the wake of his testimony before the House Un-American Activities Committee in 1952.

Critical Reception

By the end of 1935, Odets's impressive first year as a playwright, many critics were praising him as a genius who spoke for the American people. Later critics, however, labeled Odets's early works as propaganda, with stereotypical characters and obvious messages. Recently critics have reappraised his plays, and his work is now appreciated for its dialogue—especially for its realistic capture of Jewish-American idioms—and for the author's belief in the nobility of humanity. The protagonists of Odets's plays are noted for relentlessly pursuing their dreams despite the often apparent futility of the quests. Once criticized for a lack of character development in his plays, Odets has won new praise for delivering emotional impact to his audiences while skillfully communicating the economic and spiritual insecurity of the American experience.

PRINCIPAL WORKS

*Waiting for Lefty (drama) 1935
*Awake and Sing! (drama) 1935
*Till the Day I Die (drama) 1935
*Paradise Lost (drama) 1935
The General Died at Dawn [adaptor; from the novel by Charles G. Booth] (screenplay) 1935
*Golden Boy (drama) 1937
*Rocket to the Moon (drama) 1938
Night Music (drama) 1940
Clash by Night (drama) 1941
The Russian People [adaptor; from the play by Konstantin Simonov] (drama) 1942
None but the Lonely Heart [adaptor; from the novel by Richard Llewellyn; director] (screenplay) 1944
Deadline at Dawn [adaptor; from the novel by William Irish] (screenplay) 1946
Humoresque [adaptor, with Zachary Gold; from the short story by Fannie Hurst] (screenplay) 1946
The Big Knife (drama) 1949
The Country Girl (drama) 1950
The Flowering Peach (drama) 1954
Sweet Smell of Success [adaptor, with Ernest Lehman; from the novella *Tell Me About It Tomorrow* by Lehman] (screenplay) 1957
The Story on Page One [director and screenwriter] (screenplay) 1960
Wild in the Country [adaptor; from the novel *The Lost Country* by I. R. Salamanca] (screenplay) 1961

*These works were collectively published as *Six Plays of Clifford Odets* (1939).

CRITICISM

Robert Warshow (essay date May 1946)

SOURCE: "Poet of the Jewish Middle Class: Clifford Odets Voices Its Conflicts and Frustrations" in *Commentary*, Vol. 1, No. 7, May, 1946, pp. 17-22.

[*Warshow was a Jewish-American editor, essayist, and film critic. In the following essay, he discusses Odets's* Awake and Sing! *and its realistic portrayal of the common Jewish-American experience of its time.*]

> Before migrating to America, all the ethnic groups of Yankee City possessed a family pattern of the patriarchal type in which the wife was subordinated to the husband and the children to the father. America has disrupted this pattern, increasing the wife's independence and making the children carriers of the new culture—a role that has brought them into open conflict with their parents. Among Jews these developments manifested themselves in their most extreme form. —"The Jews of Yankee City" (*Commentary*, January 1946)

The literary treatment of American Jewish life has always suffered from the psychological commitments of Jewish writers. Their motives are almost never pure: they must dignify the Jews, or plead for them, or take revenge upon them, and the picture they create is correspondingly distorted by romanticism or sentimentality or vulgarity. The romantic-sentimental picture, which endows the Jews with superior wisdom and an exaggerated spirituality, is typified in an earlier stage by the movie *The Jazz Singer.* It appears in more dignified form in Elmer Rice's *Street Scene* and most recently in the Hollywood biography of George Gershwin. The vulgar exploitation of the Jews is more common; the work of Milt Gross is carried on for a later audience in the self-conscious burlesques of Arthur Kober and the banality of Leonard Q. Ross. A more serious and more savage type of satire, focusing on the economic and social behavior of Jews, has appeared recently in the work of such writers as Jerome Weidman and Budd Schulberg, but their picture, if more honest, is still limited and superficial.

By a considerable margin, the most important achievement in the literature of the American Jews is that of Clifford Odets. No one else has been able to maintain that degree of confidence in the value of the exact truth which made his best work possible. His social understanding is limited, but he has been able to keep his eyes on reality and to set down his observations with great imagination and remarkable detachment. Jews are never commonplace to him—they are never commonplace to any Jew—but neither are they prodigies, either of absurdity or of pathos or of evil. He has perceived that they are human beings living the life which happens to be possible to them.

The elements that make up for most American Jews the image of their group are to be found in the Jewish culture of New York City; more specifically, in the culture of the Jewish lower middle class, in the apartment houses and two-family houses of the Bronx and Brooklyn, among those who all these years have had to think mainly about getting along. Not all Jews actually participate in this culture—perhaps most do not—but almost all are intimately connected with it. The New York pattern is the master pattern, repeated in its main outlines wherever there is a large Jewish population. What is especially characteristic of other areas of Jewish life is often simply the extension of this; what appears most sharply opposed to it, or furthest away from it, is often the expression of a deliberate struggle against it.

The crucial fact is that there are few who cannot immediately recognize and understand its smallest forms of behavior, its accepted attitudes, its language. If it is not "Jewish life," strictly speaking, it is for most American Jews the area of greatest emotional importance. It is what a Jew remembers, it is what he has in his mind when he experiences his more private emotions about being a Jew—affection, pity, delight,

shame. Just as the life of the small town can be said in some sense to embody the common experience of the older Americans, so the life of New York can be said at this particular stage in the process of acculturation to embody the common experience of the American Jews.

Clifford Odets is the poet of this life. In the body of his work so far, with its rather specious "development" and its persistent intellectual shallowness, the spectacular achievement which makes him a dramatist of importance is his truthful description of the New York Jews of the lower middle class.

Awake and Sing, his first full-length play, remains the most impressive. He has since become a more skillful dramatist, but his progress in theatrical terms has involved a loss in the simple observation of fact which is his greatest talent: he has become more superficial and more sentimental. His significant field of knowledge is among the Jews, and what he knows about the Jews is in *Awake and Sing*.

> The events of [*Awake and Sing*] are of little consequence; what matters is the words of the characters—the way they talk as much as the things they say. Odets employs consistently and with particular skill what amounts to a special kind of dramatic poetry.
>
> —*Robert Warshow*

In reading *Awake and Sing,* one is likely to be struck by its crudity: there is an illegitimate pregnancy and a hasty marriage, a life insurance policy, a suicide; the final curtain is brought down on a puerile note of "affirmation" (Odets has said, "New art works should shoot bullets"). But in the last analysis these crudities are of no great importance. The special experience of reading or seeing the play has nothing to do with the dramatics used to make it progress through its three acts.

For the Jew in the audience, at least, the experience is recognition, a continuous series of familiar signposts, each suggesting with the immediate communication of poetry the whole complex of the life of the characters: what they are, what they want, how they stand with the world.

It is a matter of language more directly than anything else. The events of the play are of little consequence; what matters is the words of the characters—the way they talk as much as the things they say. Odets employs consistently and with particular skill what amounts to a special type of dramatic poetry. His characters do not speak in poetry—indeed, they usually become ridiculous when they are made to speak "poetically"—but the speeches put into their mouths have the effect of poetry, suggesting much more than is said and depending for the enrichment of the suggestion upon the sensibility and experience of the hearer. Many of the things said on the stage are startling for their irrelevance; they neither contribute to the progress of the plot nor offer any very specific light upon the character of the participants: the hearer supplies a meaning.

The peculiarity of this poetic process is that it operates exclusively between the writer and the audience; it is not *in* the play. The characters are in a state of ignorance, always saying something different from what they think they are saying. This differs from dramatic irony in the usual sense by the fact that the ignorance of the characters is essential instead of accidental: they *do* know what is happening in the play; what they do *not* know is what they are. In a sense they are continually engaged in giving themselves away.

The effect of the method is to increase the distance between the audience and the specific facts of the play, while bringing before the audience more clearly than is usual the general facts about Jews and Jewish life which the play illustrates.

The young son, Ralph, puts into one sentence the history of his frustration: "It's crazy—all my life I want a pair of black and white shoes and can't get them. It's crazy!" The mother, Bessie, responds, betraying the bitterness of her relations with her children, the difficulty of her life, the general picture of what it must be like to live with her: "In a minute I'll get up from the table. I can't take a bite in my mouth no more." Demolishing an argument for the abolition of private property, she presents her concept of man's fate: "Noo, go fight City Hall!" She offers a scrap of worldly wisdom to justify her tricking a young man into marrying her daughter, already pregnant by another man: "Maybe you never heard charity begins at home. You never heard it, Pop?" The old man, Jacob, shows what his daughter is to him: "All you know, I heard, and more yet. . . . This is a house? Marx said it—abolish such families." Bessie's husband, Myron, demonstrates his ineffectuality: "This morning the sink was full of ants. Where they come from I just don't know. I thought it was coffee grounds . . . and then they began moving." A sentence exhibits his tenuous grasp on American culture: "My scalp is impoverished," he says, out of nowhere. Sam Feinschreiber, the unfortunate object of Bessie's choice for her daughter ("In three years he put enough in the bank . . ."), reacts to the news that the baby is not his own: "I'm so nervous—look, two times I weighed myself on the subway station." Uncle Morty, the successful dress manufacturer, replies to the suggestion that he might send a little more money to take care of his father: "Tell me jokes. Business is so rotten I could just as soon lay all day in the Turkish bath." Uncle Morty prepares to leave the house: "Where's my fur gloves?"

To the experienced ear, every speech tells again the whole story, every character presents over and over the image of his particular kind, the role of his kind in the culture which contains it. The characters are diminished as human beings in favor of their function as instruments of poetic evocation. Rich or poor, happy or not, they serve their purpose. The responses called forth by the play are responses to the life of the Jews, to the psychological roots of one's own life, never to the individual lives of the people on the stage.

In the end you really get something like a direct apprehension of sociological truth, the whole picture built up out of the words spoken on the stage, the tones of speech and thought, all is added to the knowledge already possessed by the audience.

It is not the whole picture of the Jews; there is no whole picture of the Jews. And even as a partial picture it calls for some reservations. Assuming all necessary reservations, the picture might be called: what happened to the Jews in New York.

The adult immigrant had some advantages. Whatever it was that drove him to come, he was able to carry with him a sense of his own dignity and importance. He had a kind of security though it is a strange thing to say of a Jew. In Europe, with the club over his head, he had nevertheless lived in a community which was in important ways self-sufficient, and which permitted him to think of himself as a man of value: he was a scholar, or a revolutionist, at the very least he knew himself to be a more serious man than his Gentile persecutors. To be a Jew was a continual burden, even a misfortune, but it could not have seemed to him a joke or a disgrace.

He came off a boat, he had to find a job the very next day, and for the rest of his life he was likely to be taken up by the numberless techniques of getting by: how to make a dollar, how to pursue the infinitesimal advantages which made it possible for him to survive from day to day. The humiliation of his poverty and impotence was tremendous, but he was already equipped with a mechanism for separating from it some of the needs of his personality. In his own mind, and in the semi-European atmosphere he created in the synagogues or the cafés and radical groups, he could contrive for his sad life the appearance of a meaning that went beyond the everlasting pettiness of which it actually consisted. He had a past.

For his children, helping after school with the family's piecework or going themselves to work in the shops, and often suffering in addition under a savage moral discipline with no apparent relevance to the real world, the pretensions of the father could be nothing but nonsense. He could create in the minds of his children only an entirely generalized ideal of moral and intellectual superiority absolutely without content. (Bessie Berger: "I raise a family they should have respect.")

If the parents had a great deal of love and wisdom, or if the family made money soon enough, the children could sometimes arrive at a tolerable balance between dignity and economic pressure. But the familiar pattern was not often to be avoided: the children holding before them the image of a suffering and complaining mother and of a father whose life went on outside the home, who was somehow responsible—with his "ideas"—for the family's hardships. It was remembered with undying resentment that he had given money to the synagogue or the Party—to "make a show"—while his family went hungry, and the things he believed in came to represent a wilful refusal to understand the principle that charity begins at home. ("Go in your room, Papa. Every job he ever had he lost because he's got a big mouth. He opens his mouth and the whole Bronx could fall in. . . . A good barber not to hold a job a week.") If he made money at last, then his demonstrations of allegiance to the things he thought valuable might be received with more tolerance, even with pride, but they still remained for his children outside the area of practical life.

For his part, he was always disappointed in his children and his sense of disappointment was often the only thing he could clearly communicate to them. He succeeded at least in becoming a reproach to them, and the bitterness of the personal conflict which ensued was aggravated by the fact that they could never quite see from what he derived his superiority or what it was he held against them.

The children took hold of what seemed to them the essential point—that they were living in a jungle. It would not be accurate to say that they failed to understand the rest; so far as they were concerned, the rest was not there to see, it had retired into the mind.

They tried to act reasonably. Every day they could see more clearly the basic truth: without a dollar you don't look the world in the eye. This truth was not for a moment welcome to them, they accepted it with all suitable reluctance, they doffed their hats continually in the direction of the "other things," but they really saw no alternative to following out the implications of what they knew. After all, their analysis of the situation was virtually a matter of life and death ("Ralphie, I worked too hard all my years to be treated like dirt. . . . Summer shoes you didn't have, skates you never had, but I bought a new dress every week. A lover I kept—Mr. Gigolo! . . . If I didn't worry about the family who would. . . . Maybe you wanted me to give up twenty years ago. Where would you be now? You'll excuse my expression—a bum in the park!")

Between the facts as they saw them and the burden of undefined moral responsibility laid upon them by the father, no decision was possible. Money was at least effective, it could really solve their worst problems. It was what they had to have. What they wanted was not money, but it was nothing

very definite. The best basis they could find for their life was a worldly compromise: money is filth, but money is all you'll ever get.

In general terms, the kind of life they established for themselves is not different from the characteristic life of the rest of their society: its primary concerns are economic security and social prestige; its daydreams are of unlimited economic security and unassailable social prestige. ("Ralph should only be a success like you, Morty. I should only live to see the day when he drives up to the door in a big car with a chauffeur and a radio. I could die happy, believe me.") Indeed, they were especially quick to perceive the underlying pattern of the society and to conform to it. Looking from the outside, and suffering from the hostility of those around them, they naturally understood the significant facts thoroughly; for Jews, that had always been one of the necessities of life.

But it was not merely a matter of a generation moving from one culture into another. As it happened, the newer culture had already come to a point where it was unable to provide much security or dignity even for those who indisputably belonged to it. Understanding was in this case a bar to adjustment, and the life of the Jews has been colored by their awareness of the terms of the compromise they have had to accept. Their frustration is part of a universal frustration, but their unhappiness is more acute because all along they have known what they were doing.

Sometimes their special situation gave them a kind of edge, as if they were a day older in history than everybody else. They were capable of phenomenal success. Errand boys made themselves into millionaires simply by shrewd and unremitting attention to the possibilities of capitalist enterprise. Entertainers, exploiting the contrast between what they were and what they wanted, found a huge audience suddenly ready to see the point. Hollywood became a gold mine, demonstrating that the Jews were not different from everybody else, only a little further along: they could feel the exact level to which culture had come.

Success made no essential difference. A million dollars was a great and wonderful thing—how can you refuse money if you don't know what would be better?- -but they could never believe that it was really enough to make a man important. Uncle Morty says "Where's my fur gloves?" not to impress the others but to remind himself of how far he has come.

They wanted also to be good and wise men. Having no frame of reference by which to attach a meaning to "good" and "wise," even a false meaning, they were forced to seek what assurance they could find in the tangible evidences they knew to be valueless: money, prestige, the intellectual superiority of one man to another. Thus from the complex of their fears and desires they evolved the three imperatives that govern them: be secure, be respected, be intelligent. In their world a dentist is better than a machinist, a doctor is better than a businessman, a college professor is best of all. But an unsuccessful intellectual is worse than an unsuccessful businessman: he should have known better than to try.

Their economic strength comes from their ability to act as the situation demands even though the situation is abhorrent to them. But the gap between moral man and the requirements of reality has seemed to them so wide that they have been able to function successfully only by imposing cynicism on themselves as a kind of discipline. They have gone further than most in the acceptance of reality, and this is perhaps the strongest kind of subversion—to take capitalism without sugar.

What it costs them is their characteristic mental insecurity a mixture of self-pity and self-contempt. Self-pity because their way of life was forced upon them, self-contempt because they can accept no excuse.

Awake and Sing is a depression play, and its picture of Jewish life is sharper and more brutal than it would have been a few years earlier. The hidden framework of need and compulsion had come out. If it had ever been possible for the Jews to lull themselves completely in the material benefits of capitalism, that possibility was gone. With the depression, their painfully built structure of defenses shook and fell, respectability itself was threatened, and they looked again into the abyss of poverty, all the more frightening because it was so familiar, because they had given so much to get out of it.

The characters contemplate the meaninglessness of their lives. The image of their failure is constantly before them; they cannot contain themselves, they must burst out every minute in a fury of bitterness and impotence, justifying themselves, calling for pity, enveloping themselves and the world in indiscriminate scorn. They have ceased to communicate; each confronts his own unhappiness, using language primarily as an instrument of self-expression and a weapon of defense.

 It is as if no one really listens to anyone else; each takes his own line, and the significant connections between one speech and another are not in logic but in the heavy emotional climate of the family.

> RALPH: *I don't know. . . . Every other day to sit around with the blues and mud in your mouth.*
> MYRON: *That's how it is—life is like that—a cake-walk.*
> RALPH: *What's it get you?*
> HENNIE: *A four-car funeral.*
> RALPH: *What's it for?*
> JACOB: *What's it for? If this life leads to a revolution it's a good life. Otherwise it's for nothing.*

> BESSIE: *Never mind, Pop! Pass me the salt.*
> RALPH: *It's crazy—all my life I want a pair of black and white shoes and can't get them. It's crazy!*
> BESSIE: *In a minute I'll get up from the table. I can't take a bite in my mouth no more.*
> MYRON: *Now, Momma, just don't excite yourself—*
> BESSIE: *I'm so nervous I can't hold a knife in my hand.*
> MYRON: *Is that a way to talk, Ralphie? Don't Momma work hard enough all day?*
> BESSIE: *On my feet twenty-four hours?*
> MYRON: *On her feet—*
> RALPH: *What do I do—go to night clubs with Greta Garbo? Then when I come home can't even have my own room? Sleep on a day-bed in the front room!*
> BESSIE: *He's starting up that stuff again. When Hennie here marries you'll have her room—I should only live to see the day.*
> HENNIE: *Me too.*

They live on top of one another, in that loveless intimacy which is the obverse of the Jewish virtue of family solidarity, and their discontentment is expressed in continual and undisguised personal hostility. The son, Ralph, is in love:

> BESSIE: *A girl like that he wants to marry. A skinny consumptive . . . six months already she's not working—taking charity from an aunt. You should see her. In a year she's dead on his hands. . . . Miss Nobody should step in the picture and I'll stand by with my mouth shut.*
> RALPH: *Miss Nobody! Who am I? Al Jolson?*
> BESSIE: *Fix your tie!*
> RALPH: *I'll take care of my own life.*
> BESSIE: *You'll take care? Excuse my expression, you can't even wipe your nose yet! He'll take care!*

Someone is slow about coming to the dining-room: "Maybe we'll serve for you a special blue-plate supper in the garden?" Morty responds to one of Jacob's dissertations on the class struggle: "Like Boob McNutt you know! Don't go in the park, pop—the squirrels'll get you."

In a brilliant climax, Bessie Berger reveals the whole pattern of psychological and moral conflict that dominates her and her family: when Ralph discovers that his sister's husband was trapped into marriage, Bessie, confronted inescapably with her own immorality, and trembling before her son's contempt, turns upon her *father*, who has said nothing, and smashes the phonograph records that are his most loved possessions and the symbol of his superiority. This act of fury is irrelevant only on the surface: one understands immediately that Bessie has gone to the root of the matter.

Purposeless, insecure, defeated, divided within themselves,

the Bergers made a life like a desert. The process which produced them was not ironbound; one way or another, there were many who escaped. But the Bergers are important. The luckiest is not out of sight of them; no consideration of the Jews in America can leave them out; in the consciousness of most of us they do in some sense stand for "Jew."

Michael J. Mendelsohn (interview date 1963)

SOURCE: "Odets at Center Stage," [Parts One and Two] in *Theatre Arts*, Vol. XLVII, Nos. 5 and 6, May and June, 1963, pp. 16-19, 74-76; pp. 28-30, 78-80.

[*Mendelsohn is an American educator, author, and critic. In the following interview conducted shortly before Odets's death, Odets comments on a wide range of topics, including theater, his influences, and his career in Hollywood.*]

[*Mendelsohn:*] *I have a number of general questions and some specific ones; do you have any preference as to where we begin?*

[Odets:] No, any way you choose to go is all right with me.

Well, let's begin with the idea that the playwright belongs to the theatre, rather than to the library.

Well, essentially there are two kinds of playwrights. Both can be excelling, but it would be necessary to make a distinction between the playwright who was essentially a theatre man and not a man of literature—not a man of the library, that is. If I talk about past and very great playwrights, it's obvious from the very style and form and cut and shape and pattern of their work that men like Moliere and Shakespeare were men of the theatre, not men of the library. And you see it on every page of their plays. They write with their feet solidly planted on the platform, and they write with a very knowing and frequently cunning theatrical knowledge, in the sense of what the audience is getting—they don't follow literary canon so much as they follow theatre canon.

At the same time, a piece of dramatic literature, when it is completed and bound between covers, can stand the test of good literature—if it is good literature.

Well, you have to admit that the two men I just mentioned, Molière and Shakespeare, wrote very great literature.

Let's go back to the 1930s. Do you feel the social protest plays accomplished something in themselves, or were they simply a dramatic manifestation in American society that would have taken place anyhow?

The plays undoubtedly came out of ascending values, out of positive values, out of the search of millions of American citizens for some way out of a horrifying dilemma—a dilemma which, by the way, I don't think is over. And the writer, or the playwright like myself, simply had to be alive and aware and partaking of this extraordinary ferment around him. The playwright then, as he always is, became the articulate voice of the aspiration of millions of people. If, for instance, you saw the opening night of *Waiting for Lefty,* you saw theatre in its truest essence. By which I mean that suddenly the proscenium arch of the theatre vanished and the audience and the actors were at one with each other.

You say that the proscenium disappeared, and I feel that this was something that you were trying to achieve in **Waiting for Lefty**—

Not consciously.

Not consciously? Well, I'm speaking of the theatrical concept of naturalism versus the Thornton Wilder type of presentational play. Consciously in your plays, it seems to me you are staying within the proscenium, in all of your plays except **Waiting for Lefty.** *Did you have that in mind?*

Well, sometimes there are formal ways in which one breaks down the proscenium arch and makes the audience a more active participant in what is going on on the stage. Formal ways consist, sometimes, in a new style for the writer, or sometimes in the physical construction of the theatre. We talk of "theatre in the round." These are all attempts to unify the acting material and the audience. They are, however, in my opinion, artificial ways. The real way to make the proscenium arch disappear, the thrilling and human way, what I should say is the *experienced* way, is to have your actors speak from your platform materials and values which are profoundly and *communally* shared with the audience.

And, if this happens, it doesn't matter whether they address the audience directly, as in **Waiting for Lefty,** *or talk to each other, as in* **Awake and Sing?**

It doesn't matter at all. When you have a community of values in the theatre (which is, of course, what we *don't* have), the proscenium arch disappears. The audience is not watching a play, and the actors are not playing to an audience which is seated passively somewhere in that dark pit which is the auditorium. Theatre in its profoundest sense—*all* literature in its profoundest sense—has come in periods when the plight or problem expressed by the actors was completely at one with the plight and problems and values or even moralities of the audience. This is why the literature of Homer and the Greek drama and the Bible, or, in music, works of composers like Bach have such size. It's because the artist, the composer, the writer, is not someone apart and inimical to his audience, not a man in *opposition* to the values he is expressing, but one who completely shares organically the very values of the audience for whom he is writing.

In other words; the specific type of "presentation" or "representation" doesn't make any difference at all?

Well, it does nowadays, when theatre consists, for the most part, of trifles, of weak slaps and gestures at something that you don't like. Or, for the most part, an acceptance of things around you. You take all of the light comedies. What are they about? How amusing adultery is. By the way, they constitute propaganda plays for adultery, whether we realize it or not. They have no positive values; they play upon the patterns of prejudice and the likes and dislikes of the audience. They do not lead the audience. They do not lift the audience.

Are you familiar with Waiting for Godot?

Yes.

This is a pretty good statement of a negative. I thought of that when you said "no positive values."

All you can say of a play like that—and, by the way, a small gem I should call it—all you can do is sit there sort of stunned and lament that the world is in a hell of a shape. You can be moved in a certain way. From that play I don't think you can be moved to try to lift yourself out of what it's saying into some higher living view of things. Unless, of course, you believe cutting your throat is a value!

Do you accept the label "optimist" that has very often been pinned on you?

"Optimist"? I would say that I have a *belief* in man and his possibilities as the measure of things, but I would not say that I was an optimistic writer. I would say that I have shown as much of the seamy side of life as any other playwright of the twentieth century, if not more.

It seems that many of your plays, even with the depiction of the seamy side of life, end on a hopeful note.

Sometimes the hopeful note is real, as, for instance, I believe it is in a play like **Rocket to the Moon,** and sometimes my critics are correct when they say that the optimistic note has been tacked on.

Awake and Sing*?*

No, not so much **Awake and Sing,** because I believe in the possibilities expressed in the last scene. I do believe that young people can go through an experience and have their eyes opened, and determine from it to live in a different way. I do believe that older and more crushed human beings can pass on some lifting values to the younger generation. I do believe that, as the daughter in that family does, she can make a break with the groundling lies of her life, and try to find happiness

by walking off with a man who is not her husband. I believed it then, and I believe it now. I think I believed it more *simply* then. I did not express roundly or fully the picture, but I don't think that ending is a lie.

What particular plays did you have in mind when you said that the optimistic ending was "tacked on"?

Well, there is a certain kind of subtle theatrical use that doesn't really ask too much. For instance, what did **Waiting for Lefty** ask? It asked really that you go out on strike and fight for better conditions. Well, the people did do that. Along came the C.I.O. But it is not enough to go out on strike and ask for better wages; it is much better to go out on strike and say, "Now we have made a *beginning*." Frequently, the simplicity of some of my endings comes from the fact that I did not say at the same time. "This is a beginning; this will give you the right to begin in a clean and simple way." But these things are not ends in themselves. A strike and a better wage is not an end in itself. It will give you the chance to begin. It will give you the chance, in a democracy, to find your place, to assume your place and be responsible for your growth and continued welfare and happiness in that place.

Why do you sometimes like to direct? Is there a particular reason?

Yes, there are several reasons. First of all, I think that, frankly, I can direct my plays almost as well as anyone I know. Therefore, why not do it myself? I am very capable with actors; I was an actor myself for about 14 years before I became a playwright. The stage, the acting platform, is my home. I am not a library writer. A library writer should not direct his plays, but should find a competent director who will say more or less what he wants to say.

As Archibald MacLeish did?

Yes, or as Maxwell Anderson did. Maxwell Anderson was my idea (and I mean no denigration), my idea of a library writer, although he had a great deal of theatre wisdom, let me say. So, since I can handle the materials of a play of my own, why talk it over with a director? Why not do it myself? Secondly, in a play like **The Country Girl,** which is relatively, in the body of my work, a superficial play, I knew just exactly how that play should become successful. I wanted to do a successful production. And in that case I trusted no one else, because it seems to me that that play walks on a tightrope and that if it is not done almost with a certain speed and tension, it would plunge right down into the abyss. It took us a year to cast the play. The final casting didn't satisfy me, but there it was. With all of these considerations, I trusted only myself to get the result I wanted to get, and I did get it. Another director, by the way, might have brought added dimension to some of the scenes. He might see things that I didn't see. That's always a danger when you direct your own play. On the other hand, in the case of *The Country Girl,* I was looking for a certain kind of—to say it vulgarly—a swift, tense strongly-paced production. And I simply didn't trust it to anyone else's hands.

Then, just as with the novelist, who has no one getting in the way, except perhaps an editor, you feel that the fewer people who get in the way of what comes out of your pen, the closer to the pure work it's going to end up?

Yes, there is such an aspect to directing one of my plays. But an even more important aspect is simply the stimulation. It stimulates me as a writer to keep my feet and my hands on the stage. It's not that I'm interested in giving or showing the definitive meaning of a play. That side doesn't bother me too much. The stimulation is very important. It keeps you *alive* with the script, until the opening night. I used to find that I lost all interest in the script when someone else was directing, even a director I trusted and a director I admired and liked—let's say, Harold Clurman at his best. The whole thing went dead on me, so that when I had to rewrite, it was almost like I was approaching a strange new subject. But when I, myself, am directing the play, although aliveness comes in a different sphere, that of directing, which is quite different from writing, nevertheless it keeps me alive as a *writer.* So that I can leave the stage when I am directing and go to my hotel room out of town, as I did in *The Country Girl,* and three or four nights before the New York opening, in Boston, rewrite the last 15 pages, which made the play successful. But if I hadn't been directing that play, I would have been dead on it, and I wouldn't have written those last 15 pages as well.

Your comment about the desire to have **The Country Girl** *be a commercial success suggests to me something else. Can you say that your early plays were written to push forward a certain point of view, and that your later plays were written for more artistic considerations, or for more financial considerations? Is there any way to separate these things?*

I can separate them. The result may not always be what I think it is, but I have only two times—I don't know, I think I've written 14 or 15 or 16 plays, 12 or 13 of which have been produced—only two times did I sit down with the goal of writing a play that would be successful on Broadway and have a long run. The other times, I simply sat down to express a "state of being." Sometimes an ache, sometimes an agony, sometimes an excitement, the excitement which comes out of some kind of conversion, emotional lift, a sudden *seeing* where before one felt blind, and a sudden strength, whereas before one felt weak and muscle bound. It was always to express an inner state of being. I think that any creative writer sits down to express that. Sometimes it's a sense, a very vague

sense of hurt, a vague mood, a vague sense of unhappiness, of, let me say, sometimes of disconnection. I don't think that any creative person in any craft or any medium can be creative unless he does sit down with that sense of expressing an inner state of being.

On the other hand I can see a certain shaped play dealing with certain materials, and I would like it to get across in a very successful way. So I will kind of put blinders on and not express the entire spread of what I feel about this material, but just make it theatrically viable, theatrically entertaining, and try to get across something that people will like, that will excite them. The first time I did that was once to keep the Group Theatre together in a play called *Golden Boy.* That was the other play, with *The Country Girl,* that I sat down deliberately to write a success. And, in both cases, let me say, "mission accomplished." As a matter of fact, I always held *Golden Boy* a little in contempt for that season, knowing how the seed had been fertilized. And it was maybe three years later that I saw the play had more quality than I gave it credit for. I don't, however, think I would change my mind about *The Country Girl.* It's a good show; it's a theatre piece. It does have about it a certain kind of psychological urgency, because if you are creative, things do creep in despite the conscious impulse. For instance, there crept into that play a central problem of my own life. And this did give a certain urgency and heat to much that went on in the script. I didn't *mean* for that problem to come out; I cannily and unconsciously disguised it. But that is unconsciously what came out in the writing of that play.

You wouldn't go so far as to attribute to **Golden Boy** *the sort of allegorical analysis that George Jean Nathan gave to it— of this being your entire career, and—*

I will tell you frankly that since the days of my youth were past—from those days on I have had no interest in what George Jean Nathan has written about me or has written about any other playwright dead or alive, or anything about the theatre. I think he was a first-class phony. I will always think so, and I don't miss him and never would miss him.

You've had 11 plays produced, aside from the translation in 1942—

Is it 11 plays?

So far as I've been able to keep track.

You've got me; I haven't counted them.

Eleven plus **The Russian People**—

Oh, let's not count that! They wouldn't let me do any work on it. It was forbidden to change a word. But Mrs. Litvinov, the Ambassador's wife, Ivy Litvinov—a very literate and charming woman—at the last moment got me permission to rewrite and change some of the scenes, but I said, "Mrs. Litvinov, it's too late." (We were opening in New York after, I think, two weeks in Washington, D.C.) "We're opening in New York City in three or four days, and I can't rewrite anything now." I did, here and there, enrich the texture, but no changes were permitted. This was a Soviet governmental order, you know.

Well, we won't worry about that one, but I was going to ask you—

Well, it's such a bad play; I shouldn't like to be responsible for it. I have the credit for adapting it.

Incidentally, how does one adapt a play from Russian? Do you get a literal—

Yes, you get a literal translation, and then you go to work on it. It's like you buy a chair made of raw wood, and you say now how shall I finish this chair? How shall I upholster it? The essential frame is there; you've bought the frame.

Well, I've counted 11 produced plays, anyhow, and—do you feel they move in a definite direction, from something to something, or is each one an individual expression of what you feel at the moment?

I don't think that I've written two plays alike. This makes trouble for me, because the materials of the play or its shape always seem to baffle not the audiences, but the critics. They seem to expect one thing. I don't do that consciously, but I write out of what interests me, and perhaps I'm still naive.

For instance, in my next group of plays, of which I have five laid out or written in part, I wanted to write the most serious play first. It's called *An Old-Fashioned Man,* and probably that title will stay. But then I think, if I write that play, and open it in New York—it's a big play, and necessarily will be densely textured—it will lay me open to all sorts of charges of immodesty, of lopsidedness. It's the kind of play you simply cannot get on one viewing. So I think, well, why not come in quietly with a much more modest play? And then when that one has its brief moment I would go to one a little heavier, from their point of view a little more immodest, because it will be attempting more and will be saying more. . . .

*Aside from **None But the Lonely Heart,** how many films would you want to have your name associated with along with your best plays?*

Well, let them stand for what they are. They are technically very adept. I have learned a great deal from making and shaping these scripts. I don't know; I suppose that by now I've

written—written or rewritten secretly for some friends of mine—fifteen or eighteen, close to twenty films. One need not be ashamed of them. I have not expressed anywhere any loss of standards. I haven't dehumanized people in them. I have even written a little picture that ended up being called **Deadline at Dawn.** I'm not ashamed of that. It's a little mystery thriller. I see it; it has its living moments. It's not merely that the dialogue is good. Or a picture that I rewrote called **Sweet Smell of Success.** It's professional work; I'm a professional writer. And I am never ashamed of the professional competence which is in these scripts. I have never downgraded human beings or a certain kind of morality. I'm not ashamed of any of them. . . .

Michael J. Mendelsohn (essay date Fall 1963)

SOURCE: "Clifford Odets and the American Family," in *Drama Survey*, Vol. 3, No. 2, Fall, 1963, pp. 238-43.

[*In the following essay, Mendelsohn traces a chronological progression in Odets's plays—from an early emphasis on anti-family social rebellion to a later integration and acceptance of the family into his plays' social landscapes. An editorial note states that this essay was in press when Odets died.*]

The drama of the Left in the Thirties was notorious for its redundancy in themes. Certain ones, such as championship of the laboring man, attacks on the evils or decadence of American society, pacifism, cropped up with great regularity until they began to sound to critics and playgoers alike monotonous as a broken record. The more skilled of the serious dramatists were satisfied to deal with one or two of these themes, while many of the others seemed to feel that a play was worth while if it contained all three subjects. Only a few playwrights, Clifford Odets among them, are remembered today among the score of social protest dramatists who were irretrievably ensnared by the trap that should have been apparent.

Many playwrights of the depression decade viewed the American stage more as a forum than as a place of entertainment. In the early part of his career, Odets was among those who could not completely escape the urge to propagandize even when the subject of the propaganda is unrelated to the main current of the play. Often this penchant halts the dramatic action. For instance, the trait shows up in a less than subtle way even in a relatively late play like *Clash By Night,* and the intrusion of the anti-fascist theme which threatens to take over the play is particularly jarring. Odets wants the reader to consider the events an allegory of the destruction of a simple, well-meaning individual by totalitarian forces too powerful to resist. But critics were not wrong in considering this aspect of the play to be forced, superimposed on a love-triangle melodrama.

Odets quickly outgrew the tendency to preach and to intrude

forced themes; what is more, even his early plays rise above that weakness through their superior craftsmanship. It is a tribute to Odets' integrity as a dramatist that he constantly strove for newer and more expressive insights to advance his themes. This integrity helped Odets to survive the decade that had fostered him and to go on writing excellent plays. *Awake and Sing* assumes a stature among the plays of 1935 not because the others were necessarily poor, but because Odets combined certain truths with effective dramaturgy in a manner that most other social protest writers found difficult to accomplish. Economic determinism is there, but so are real people. Marxist stock phrases are much in evidence in all his early plays, but so are rich and accurate colloquialisms. Melodramatic clichés abound in the plotting, but these, too, are outweighed by the great number of honest, natural moments. For Odets was—and is—much more than "the poet of the Jewish middle class" or "the little Jesus of the proletarian theatre." His plays remain valid because they deal with universals concretely realized.

Odets was more interested in depicting problems of inequality and repressed opportunity in American society than he was in dealing with more militant social protest themes. His principal medium for doing so was one often used by American dramatists—the family. Playwrights are fond of working within the milieu of domestic life; in American drama the range extends from the ugly Loman family of *Death of a Salesman* to the Norman Rockwell portraits offered by Eugene O'Neill in *Ah, Wilderness!* Since he deals almost exclusively with contemporary domestic dramatic situations, Odets naturally shows various pictures of family life in his plays. These include unsuccessful marriages (Libby and Ben in *Paradise Lost,* Mae and Jerry in *Clash By Night*), strained but workable ones (the Starks in *Rocket to the Moon,* the Elgins in *The Country Girl*), and some older couples, presumably past the point of disputes (the Gordons of *Paradise Lost,* the Bergers of *Awake and Sing*). The notable omission is a happy marriage among the younger characters. Perhaps Siggie and Anna in *Golden Boy* or Shem and Leah in *The Flowering Peach* come nearest to achieving some reasonable degree of contentment among Odets' younger couples, but they are in their respective plays for comic relief. Perhaps also Joe and Peggy in *Clash By Night* or Steve and Fay in *Night Music* are on their way toward happiness in marriage, but Odets does not depict that part of their lives. The suggested conclusions from the observation of all these couples are hardly very startling: marriage accompanied by economic distress is difficult, and marriage must be founded in compromise. This need for mutual understanding is suggested by the ending of *The Country Girl* and is implied as early as *Rocket to the Moon.*

But it is the family as a social organism (rather than specific marital problems) that most often occupies Odets' attention, and there seems to be a marked calming in the playwright's attitude on this subject that makes a comparison of his early and late plays interesting. In Odets' early dramas, the family mirrors society and the playwright's emphasis is on rebellion. The process can probably be translated into a simple axiom: the individual must liberate himself from the bonds of a repressive family; the people must liberate themselves from the bonds of a repressive society. Odets' basic attitude is not abnormal in a Western culture, where the emphasis has tended more and more toward individual achievement, less and less toward a family-oriented social structure. Still, Odets carries the idea to an extreme that is surprising, especially when viewed in the light of the traditional Jewish pattern of close family ties.

Few ties of love hold the Berger family together. Rather, according to the playwright in his note that precedes the listing of the characters, they are bound together because they "share a fundamental activity: a struggle for life amidst petty conditions." Odets follows this stark reflection with another important one. Describing Bessie he writes, "She knows that when one lives in the jungle one must look out for the wild life." This jungle morality extends to *Paradise Lost* as well, wherein Clara Gordon's eagerness to save the family by dishonest means is thwarted by Leo. But there is no Leo in the Berger family. This is a matriarchal group, and there is no one of Bessie's stature to check her activities.

Bessie's function seems almost exclusively to be repressive, leading one socially conscious critic to observe, "What Odets is also intent on pointing out is that the family, in circumstances of poverty and frustration, necessarily becomes an instrument of unjust coercion, even of unmorality, perpetuating false and outworn social values." Bessie's interference in Ralph's pitiable love affair is a minor matter; her concurrence in the plan to defraud the insurance company is worse; but her connivance in marrying Hennie to the unsuspecting Sam is a pure act of jungle warfare. The fact that Bessie has many moments of humor and affection, the fact that she acts in what she considers the best interests of the family, is insufficient excuse in Odets' eyes. Bessie is not evil; *Awake and Sing* is not *The Silver Cord*. It is her *objective* that is evil. Bessie is trying to preserve an outmoded institution—the family. Her father tells her so in plain language: "Marx said it—abolish such families."

A somewhat similar attitude is seen in other early Odets plays. In *Till the Day I Die* "the cause" is much more important than any feeling of family ties. Carl Tausig must dismiss any ideas of protecting his unfortunate brother when Ernst becomes a menace to the underground movement. Even Ernst's wife must reluctantly vote to isolate him from the other party members. Carl expresses the doctrine at the secret meeting:

> What are we fighting for? I need not answer the question. Yes, it is brother against brother. Many a com-

rade has found with deep realization that he has no home, no brother—even no mothers or fathers! What must we do here? Is this what you asked me? We must expose this one brother wherever he is met. Whosoever looks in his face is to point the finger. Children will jeer him in the darkest streets of his life! Yes, the brother, the erstwhile comrade cast out! There is no brother, no family, no deeper mother than the working class. Long live the struggle for true democracy!

And in *Waiting for Lefty* it is Edna, threatening to leave her husband, who is the spokesman for Odets' thesis that the family as well as the individual is of less importance than the solidarity of the working class.

The family of *Golden Boy* has a more pleasant relationship. Old Bonaparte, not nearly so dominant a character as Bessie Berger, is portrayed rather sympathetically because his wishes for Joe correspond to the reader's. If Joe's rebellion against family lacks the idealism of Ralph Berger's, the rebellion is there nonetheless. Turning his back on his father and his own better nature, Joe looks to his trainer and his manager for new ties: "Now I'm alone. They're all against me—Moody, the girl . . . you're my family now, Tokio—you and Eddie!" But Joe's rebellion is incomplete. After he kills Chocolate in his last fight, and even though he has not seen his family in months, his first reaction is, "What will my father say when he hears I murdered a man?"

The half-realized revolt of the golden boy is partially attributable to the fact that the Bonaparte family is not a repressive one and partially to the fact that Odets' own attitude seemed to be undergoing a moderation. In his plays of the late Thirties, the emphasis was gradually shifting from rebellion to search. Odets shows characters who are in search of something to call a family. Cleo Singer in *Rocket to the Moon* has a horrible home life that she is trying desperately to rise above: "Mom and Gert and two married sisters and their husbands and babies—eight in one apartment! I tell them I want to be a dancer—everybody laughs. I make believe they're not my sisters. They don't know anything—they're washed out, bleached . . . everybody forgets how to dream." Earl Pfeiffer in *Clash By Night* is much the same. The search is most pronounced in *Night Music* in which Steve and Fay represent not only their own yearnings but those of every character in the play. Harold Clurman's introduction clearly expresses the central theme: "The play stems from the basic sentiment that people nowadays are affected by a sense of insecurity; they are haunted by the fear of impermanence in all their relationships; they are fundamentally *homeless,* and, whether or not they know it, they are in search of a home." Hovering in the background of *Night Music* is the repressive family again. Fay's father makes a brief appearance to demonstrate her very good reasons for escaping Philadelphia. But in the main, Odets

pictures an essential groping for family by characters who are homeless.

> **[All of my plays] deal with homelessness in a certain way. . . . I've always *felt* homeless. I have never felt that I had a home. And if that is centrally true of me, and I know it is, that will necessarily come out in the work.**
>
> **—*Clifford Odets***

Odets moved into his late thirties during World War II, and the lost youths simultaneously disappeared from his plays. Beginning with the film *None But the Lonely Heart,* there is a further noticeable shift away from anti-family rebellion and toward pro-family solidarity. Ernie Mott is a wanderer like Steve Takis in *Night Music.* But when he learns that his mother is dying of cancer, he suddenly cements his family ties and wanders no more. When she is first introduced, Georgie Elgin (*The Country Girl*) has packed and is ready to leave Frank, but she, too, remains. And in *The Flowering Peach* the emphasis on unity reaches its logical end at the opposite pole from *Awake and Sing.* There is a great difference in the Berger family, where "everybody hates, nobody loves," and the family of Noah, which has love flowing in all directions. The unbending patriarch Noah is made to appear somehow less tyrannical than the resourceful matriarch Bessie, even when he resorts to force to convince Japheth that he should enter the ark. While it is not the dominant element of the play, the concept of family unity is frequently underscored. At the end of scene two Japheth stands outside the family circle as his father intones a Sabbath prayer: "Oh, Lord, our God, the soul is rejoiced in Thee and Thy wonders. Here the family . . . is united to serve You as You asked." The remainder of the play is partially a chronicle of Japheth's return to the family scene.

The central portrait of cohesive Jewish family life was partially explained by Odets in an interview before the opening of *The Flowering Peach:* "I have a favorite aunt and uncle in Philadelphia. This uncle of mine is very voluble, very human. It occurred to me that here was a man of flesh and blood who was the Noah of the play. . . . I said to myself, wait a minute, Noah had three sons, it was a family life, I know family life. There are children and parents, with ambitions, with disappointments, with anger and love." Noah's family is clearly the product of an older and wiser playwright.

Not long ago Harold Clurman attempted to sum up in a single sentence the essence of Odets' significance in American drama: "We should not forget that his contribution to our theatre does not lie in any intellectual or social position he has taken or may take but in the kindness and intuitive brother-feeling he brings to all the themes he treats." While this "intuitive brother-feeling" remains strongly imbedded in his heart and mind, Odets has calmed his anger sufficiently to keep the more obvious propaganda in check. I have attempted to demonstrate this tendency in his work by examining the playwright's changing attitude toward the American family. It is possible, of course, to read too much into this apparent movement. Superficially it seems that the playwright's feelings have undergone a change from rebellion *(Awake and Sing)* through search *(Night Music)* to cohesiveness *(The Flowering Peach),* but Odets himself denies any conscious move in this direction. He has said, on the contrary, that all his plays "deal with homelessness in a certain way. . . . I've always *felt* homeless. I have never felt that I had a home. And if that is centrally true of me, and I know it is, that will necessarily come out in the work." Yet it is somehow difficult to reconcile this statement with Odets' remarks before the opening of *The Flowering Peach* and even more with the events of that play.

Catharine Hughes (essay date 20 September 1963)

SOURCE: "Odets: The Price of Success," in *Commonweal,* Vol. LXXVIII, No. 21, September 20, 1963, pp. 558-60.

[*Hughes was an American playwright, editor, and critic. On the occasion of Odets's death, Hughes examines his reputation as a promising playwright who sold out to Hollywood.*]

> "What did I want? To be a great man? Get my picture on a postage stamp?"
> —*Clifford Odets, **Paradise Lost***

When Clifford Odets died on August 15 [1963], there were the usual paeans, the tributes in obituary and gossip columns, on stages and in drama sections. It was yet another testimony to the observation Albert Camus had recorded in his *Notebooks:* "a writer's death makes us exaggerate the importance of his work." Yet, running through all the lines of praise and retrospective evaluation, through all the reminiscences, there was an undercurrent, sometimes implicit, sometimes expressed. The obit writer for the New York *Times* took a stab at it when he noted Odets' "failure to outgrow the adjective 'promising' . . . the harsh criticism from many friends as a classic case of the artist who had 'sold out' to Hollywood."

Both of the observations in the *Times'* obituary happen to be true. Odets had become a symbol of literary prostitution long before the accusation—if accusation it be—was valid. He had also become something else, and it was much less noted.

When *Waiting for Lefty* opened as part of a New Theatre evening on January 5, 1935, and subsequently was reopened on Broadway by the Group Theatre, it was received with excitement by both audiences and the critics. Something new was going on in the theater, and the Depression theater badly needed it. Harold Clurman has termed it "the birth cry of the thirties," an indication that "our youth had found its voice."

It was not, of course, a very good play. A series of scenes, radiating from a meeting called to decide whether or not the taxi drivers' union is to go out on strike, with stereotyped characters: Harry Fatt, the union secretary; Miller, the lab assistant who stands on principle; Fayette, the industrialist; Benjamin, the idealistic Jewish physician: all were but briefly and perfunctorily sketched; all were there simply and solely to give voice to the author's thesis concerning the exploitation of the workingman and the revolutionary antidote.

Waiting for Lefty was a direct descendant—really, little more than a refinement—of the Communist and other left-wing agit-prop dramas of the thirties. Its importance lay not in any intrinsic merits, but in the fact that it was central to the appearance in the commercial theater of the socio-political drama. When the speaker turns to the audience with his exhortation, and all on stage shout "STRIKE, STRIKE, STRIKE!!!" at the curtain, he is only a step from the *Fifteen-Minute Red Revue. Lefty* was thus symptomatic of the efforts—and the partial success—of numerous writers and other artists who sought to bring their work into the mainstream of American life; to abandon the traditional Ivory Tower and assume roles in the rapidly evolving national scene. Its faults were those of any creative work which wears its Cause on its sleeve.

There is something more than usually ironic in the fact that Odets, starting out as the "symbol" of revolt in the American theater should ultimately have come to the point where, more than any other writer, he was singled out as the symbol of its opposite. Too often discussions of his work have failed to give due importance to the fact that the motion picture studios of the thirties were holding out not merely what were then fabulous salary offers, but also the promise of complete artistic freedom. Needless to say, Odets was far from alone in succumbing to this wooing. Indeed, it is probably accurate to say that a large percentage, if not most, of the successful writers of the period had their abortive fling. In Odets' case, however, the fling became habitual; the promises of a return to the theater, though sporadically and generally ineffectually fulfilled, but a preliminary to another junket West.

In the plays that followed *Waiting for Lefty—Awake and Sing, Golden Boy, Rocket to the Moon, Paradise Lost,* others—Odets was, consciously or otherwise, a romantic. He possessed little subtlety. If the ending was not happy, it was at least hopeful; it contained the promise of a future in which the sordid surroundings, the defeat and lethargy of the characters, might someday be surmounted. In one form or another, they proclaimed or whispered with young Ralph in *Awake and Sing*: "My days won't be for nothing. . . . I'm twenty-two and kickin'! I'll get along. Did Jake die for us to fight about nickels? No! 'Awake and Sing,' he said. . . . We're glad we're living."

Even in the anti-Fascist propaganda-piece *Till the Day I Die,* there is this element of affirmation. At the moment when he is about to commit suicide in order to avoid selling-out his comrades, Ernst feels called upon to assert that "we live in the joy of a great coming people! . . . Day must follow the night."

Odets was never fully able to avoid a sort of engaging naïveté. Perhaps more than anything else, it is what accounted for his later commercial failure. But, in its way "naïveté" is the wrong term; "sentimentality" would be more accurate. There *is* such a thing as love; there *are* such things as dreams. Tomorrow *will* come. They are sentiments increasingly out of place in the modern theater. Our "sophistication" has become too great. Odets said that an American playwright "shouldn't be afraid of being a bit corny." "Corn is part of American art," and he practiced what he preached.

"When I was twenty-one," Odets recalled, "I vowed I'd be famous. At twenty-eight I was—and found that fame isn't all it's cracked up to be." His comment—the theme of *Golden Boy*—was, to an extent considerably greater than his earlier revolutionary pronouncements, the most apt epitaph for one of our dominant literary attitudes. And, perhaps more than any other, it accounts for our failures.

To a considerable degree, Odets' sentiment—and his career—were almost an American prototype: the early overwhelming success and acclaim; the attempts to repeat it; the still-young relegation to the land of Whatever-Became-Of. We knew *what* had become of Odets; what we did not know was *why*. The American writer, with few exceptions, does not mature, he merely ages. His initial accomplishment is treated as *an accomplishment*. Under some all-seeing spotlight, he flails about in the fishbowl of his success. Sometimes, perhaps, it is easier to fail.

Odets, of course, knew what he had done, though not necessarily why he was doing it. In a sense, *Golden Boy* was his apologia; at least it was his search for one. As much as the Joe Bonaparte of that play, he was constantly seeking to reconcile two worlds. Where Joe, the violinist, attempts to sublimate his own sensitivities by an immersion in the promised quick success, the fame, the expensive cars and the like; where he, eventually—though accidentally—kills another man in the ring because of the necessity that he give vent to "the fury of a lifetime," Odets sought the reconciliation of his talent

with the demands of Hollywood. If he did not exactly admit it—and he came reasonably close—it provides the subsurface for many a speech and many an interview. And, in 1949, there was the play *The Big Knife,* with its idealistic and socially conscious young actor, so like the early Odets, who is destroyed by the easy fanfare, the quick buck of Hollywood.

As Harold Clurman, who knew him so well and directed several of his best plays, observed: "Perhaps what Charlie (Odets) wants most is not 'to do a job' but to be 'great'—just as everything and everyone must be 'great' in our country from our girl friends down to our symphonies, from our dramatists up to our refrigerators. If Charlie is to be taken literally, he is a pig prodded by Odets' conscience." And, it goes without saying, Odets *was* to be taken literally in nearly everything that he wrote. He was not given over to the veiled allusion, the needlessly—or even the need*fully*—obscure. In a career abundant with ironies, perhaps the greatest of all was the fact that, having made extensive notes on a half dozen future plays, he had, at his death, just completed the book for a musical version of *Golden Boy*.

In the thirties, Odets was writing for a theater which was far more relevant to its over-all social context than is the case today. Further, it was a theater which, for all its ventures in didacticism and overt propagandizing, was a majority, rather than minority, spokesman. Elmer Rice, in such plays as *Street Scene* and *The Adding Machine;* Sidney Kingsley in *Dead End;* Robert E. Sherwood in *Idiot's Delight,* along with much of Odets and numerous other writers, addressed themselves directly to the social and international problems of the time. To some extent, their plays assume the role almost of curiosities, museum pieces respectfully hauled out to say "that's the way it *was*." There is a strange, in some ways almost eerie feeling that hangs about discussions of the playwrights of the period. They were writing of a world unlike our own. And it all happened too quickly.

Through the scar tissue of our nostalgia, then, is the only way in which they are viewed. To a point, they were caretakers of a form. (Oddly, it is possible to forget fairly quickly that a *Waiting for Lefty,* a *Street Scene* or an *Adding Machine* was, and rightly, considered the experimental drama of the day.) Perhaps, a decade or two from now, we will find that they possessed more merit than our present myopia can envision. For the moment, though, it is a period decisively clothed in the past tense.

Since Odets was not a great writer—since, indeed, it is doubtful whether he was anything too far beyond a capable and occasionally exciting one—the eulogies proclaiming the "tragedy" of his wasted talent are more nostalgic than accurate. Like all groundbreakers, or all who achieve the reputation for having been such, his initial reputation was at least partially undeserved; also like them, his subsequent work was frequently unfairly and harshly judged against the background of what was thought—or hoped—to be rather than what was.

Perhaps Frank's description in *Golden Boy* of what he "gets out of life" was an expression of what Odets would later believe he was missing: "The pleasure of acting as you think! The satisfaction of staying where you belong, being what you are" . . . Then again, perhaps it was not; perhaps all the periodic disavowals that he had sold out were more true than anyone realized. It may be that they reflected merely an unconscious—and accurate—evaluation of his own talent; an acknowledgement of the fact that, all our misplaced values aside, few *are* great and that, for the rest, like Ralph in *Awake and Sing,* there's "a job to do," one which is in line with their own talents and, though we strive, can only infrequently reach beyond them. While this may not be an altogether flattering assessment of Odets the Dramatist, it may well be that it is a considerably more valid one of Odets the Man. While it is a truism that "some are born great and some achieve greatness," many others, incapable of either, are more the victim of their supporters' and detractors' aspirations than of their own defection from them. The "tragedy," if such it be, lies in the fact that one can never be *sure.* It is, of course, also the saving grace. For Clifford Odets, this tragedy was not in the fact of having missed greatness, but in the very norms and standards of the peculiar thing we insist on calling American Culture, where "good" is never good enough, where it is indeed a dirty word.

Clifford Odets (essay date September 1961)

SOURCE: "How a Playwright Triumphs," in *Harper's Magazine*, Vol. 233, No. 1396, September, 1966, pp. 64-70, 73-74.

[*In the following essay, drawn from a September 1961 interview, Odets recounts his genesis and progression as a playwright, with particular focus on his early days with the Group Theatre under Lee Strasberg and Harold Clurman.*]

> The following monologue—by one of the best American playwrights of the century—was originally a dialogue. It is drawn from an interview in Hollywood with Clifford Odets by Arthur Wagner of the Department of Theatre at Tulane University. The interview took place over a two-day period in September 1961, two years before Mr. Odets' death.

I had always wanted as a kid to be both an actor and a writer. For a while I thought I would be a novelist, but when I became a professional actor, my mind naturally began to take the form of the play as a means of saying something. I wasn't sure I had anything to say, because some of the other things I wrote were quite dismal. But being an actor. I began to think

in terms of three acts, divisions of acts, and scenes within the acts, and whatever technique I have has been unconsciously absorbed—almost through my skin—with all the kinds of acting I have done.

Before *Awake and Sing!* I wrote a whole very bad novel and a few short stories, all of which I later tore up. The question is really not one of knowing how to write so much as knowing how to connect with yourself so that the writing is, so to speak, born affiliated with yourself. Anybody can teach the craft of playwriting, just as I can teach myself how to make a blueprint and construct a house, on paper. But what cannot be taught, and what I was fortunate in discovering, was simply being myself, with my own problems and my own relationships to life.

Without the Group Theatre I doubt that I would have become a playwright. I might have become some other kind of writer, but the Group Theatre and the so-called "method" forced you to face yourself and really function out of the kind of person you are, not as you thought the person had to function, or as another kind of person, but simply using your own materials. The whole "method" acting technique is based on that. Well, after attempting to write for eight or ten years, I finally started a short story that made me really understand what writing was about in the sense of personal affiliation to the material.

I was holed up in a cheap hotel, in a kind of fit of depression, and I wrote about a young kid violinist who didn't have his violin because the hotel owner had appropriated it for unpaid bills. He looked back and remembered his mother and his hard-working sister, and although I was not that kid and didn't have that kind of mother or sister, I did fill the skin and the outline with my own personal feeling, and for the first time I realized what creative writing was.

A playwright who writes about things that he is not connected with, or to, is not a creative writer. He may be a very skilled writer, and it may be on a very high level of craft, but he's not going to be what I call an artist, a poet. We nowadays use the term creative arts, or a creative person, very loosely. A movie writer thinks of himself as a creative person who writes films or TV shows. Well, in the sense that I'm using the word, he's just a craftsman, like a carpenter. He has so many hammers, so many nails, so much dimension to fill, and he can do it with enormous skill. But the creative writer always starts with a state of being. He doesn't start with something outside of himself. He starts with something inside himself, with a sense of unease, depression, or elation, and only gradually finds some kind of form for what I'm calling that "state of being." He doesn't just pick a form and a subject and a theme and say this will be a hell of a show.

The form, then, is always dictated by the material; there can be nothing ready-made about it. It will use certain dramatic laws because, after all, you have to relate this material to an audience, and a form is the quickest way to get your content to an audience. That's all form is. Form is viability.

"MOST TALENTED"—BUT NO OPTION

I was twenty-six years old when I started *Awake and Sing!*, my first play. I wrote the first two acts, and six months later, in the spring of 1933, I went home to my folks' house in Philadelphia and finished the last act there. That summer the Group Theatre went to a place called Green Mansions Camp (in the Adirondacks), where we sang for our supper by being the social staff. After he read *Awake and Sing!* Harold Clurman announced one night at a meeting of the entire company that the Group Theatre idea—that we would develop from our ranks not only our own actors, but our own directors and perhaps our own playwrights—was really working out in practice. "Lo and behold!" he said, "sitting right here in this room is the most talented new young playwright in the United States." And everybody, including me, turned around to see who was in the room, and then with a horrible rush of a blush I realized he was talking about me.

But the Group Theatre didn't want to do the play. Although Harold Clurman, who was kind of the ideological head, liked it, he didn't have the strength to push it through to production against the wishes of the other two directors, Lee Strasberg and Cheryl Crawford. Lee Strasberg particularly didn't like the play. He kept saying, "It's a mere genre study." Strasberg and I were always on the outs. Although he has many other qualities, I could take just so much of his, let me call it now, authoritarian or dictatorial manner, his absolutism. And I, who was one of the humbler members of the acting company— even though I had been there practically from the start—would flare out at him and we would be shouting at each other like a pair of maniacs across the bowed heads of the entire company of thirty or so other persons.

I kept pleading with Clurman to do my play and he kept saying that it read so well he didn't know if it would act. I said it would act like a house on fire. And he said, "I don't know, I don't know," and I said, "Well, just take my word for it." I said it very fiercely. So he decided to try the middle act one night on the Green Mansions Camp audience—and it did just what I said. It played like a house on fire. I had felt sure it would, for I knew the theater very well by then. I'd been walking around on stages since I was a kid, putting on plays in high school, with amateurs, being a leading man and director of a company on the radio called "The Drawing Room Players." And when I saw that act up there on the stage I realized I had real writing talent, and right then I was not to be stopped or contained.

Well, now I thought surely that Group Theatre would do my play, but to my bitter disappointment they had not the slight-

est interest in it. Here was the Group Theatre with all its ideals, here was my own company with which I felt such a sense of brotherhood, and here was my play, which they could have just taken and done; I didn't want any money for it. Furthermore, it seemed to me better than the plays we were doing. The play we were rehearsing at this time (by Sidney Kingsley), called *Crisis*, seemed to all of us threadbare in texture. It turned out to be very successful—due chiefly to Lee Strasberg's extraordinary and beautiful production, and became very famous as *Men in White*. Well, I couldn't see why, if they could do *Men in White*, they couldn't do *Awake and Sing!*

However, just as *Men in White* was opening that fall on 46th Street at the Broadhurst Theater, a fellow I had acted with at the Theatre Guild, a nice man named Louis Simon, told me that he was now working with Frank Merlin in the Little Theatre right across the street. He said Merlin, who was looking for new American plays, had heard about *Awake and Sing!* and he suggested I give him a script for his boss. When I told him I didn't have any copies, he said, "Well, get some typed up and give me one and, who knows, next week you might have $500 advance royalties." I was very impressed with that possibility, so I had six scripts typed up for twelve bucks, which was one-third of my weekly salary of $35. And about five or six days later, I had a check for $500. I'd never seen so much money in my life. And since I had gone again before the Group Theatre and said, "Look, somebody wants to take an option on this play. You going to do it or not?" and they had practically thrown me out, it was with double satisfaction that I got my first option money.

Merlin was rhapsodic about *Awake and Sing!* He said, "This is the kind of play that America should be producing. It's the beginning of something new in the American theater." Then I thought, well, I'm going to get an immediate production here. But Merlin, poor man, made a fantastic blunder which changed his whole life. Now, Merlin had $50,000 to spend. A wealthy man had given his new wife $50,000 to play around with in the theater. She had walked in on Lee Strasberg and just said she wanted to hand this whole $50,000 over to the Group Theatre in exchange for a humble position as assistant stage manager, or whatever it was she wanted to learn. Well, Lee was such a kind of rabbinical student that he just turned and looked at her, kind of shrugged, and was silent. The woman felt very embarrassed and finally left and took the $50,000 to Frank Merlin at the Little Theatre.

Mr. Merlin, however, now made the sad mistake. He had another play, called *False Dreams Farewell*, which he said was an inadequate play, but a hell of a show. It had something to do with the sinking of the *Titanic* or the *Lusitania*— very expensive and elaborate. He put the play on first because he felt it was going to make money, and he didn't think my play would, and he lost about $40,000. If Mr. Merlin had done *Awake and Sing!* first—it was a small cast with one set and its operating cost would have run about $3,000 a week—it would have run for two or maybe three years. But he lost most of his money on this first venture.

This was now August or September of 1934, and the Group Theatre was determined, in the purity of its heart, that it would have to go away and do a new play when it might very well have continued the run of the very successful, and by this time Pulitzer Prize, *Men in White.* But purity prevailed and we went up to Ellenville, New York, to a big, rambling, broken-down hotel—don't forget, with its office and managerial staff the Group Theatre consisted of maybe thirty-six men and women and their children—and we had to find quite a large place to live in. We arrived practically when autumn was setting in at this old Saratoga-type wooden hotel, with all the bedding piled up, and we lived in an itchy and uncomfortable way there for about five or six weeks while we put into rehearsal a play by Melvin Levy, called *Gold Eagle Guy.* I had, perhaps unfairly, only scorn and contempt for the play because I thought *Awake and Sing!* was far superior as a piece of writing. Indeed, we all felt that *Gold Eagle Guy* was a stillborn script, and Luther Adler summed it up for us one morning at rehearsal when he said, kind of *sotto voce,* "Boys, I think we're working on a stiff." That morning we were almost improvising certain scenes, which we would later scale down to the playwright's words. Levy would get alarmed because the actors were not quite saying his words, and not using his punctuation. To this day there are playwrights who don't know their punctuation isn't very important in the recreation of the character they've written, or that, as we used to say in the Group Theatre, their script is only a series of stenographic notes.

THE WORDS GUSHED OUT

In any case, I had been given my own room at this old hotel, which gave me a certain lift. It's surprising how very important a small satisfaction can be in the life of one who is moving away from what I can only call illness to some kind of health or strength. (You must remember the background to all of this was that before I was twenty-five I had tried to commit suicide three times; once I stopped it myself and twice my life was saved by perfect strangers.) Before this I had always been quartered with one or two and sometimes three other actors, but when they gave me my own room, with clean, whitewashed walls, I began to feel they had some sense that I had some kind of distinction, and I was very happy.

I had by now started *Paradise Lost,* about a man, Leo, who was trying to be a good man in the world and meets raw, evil, and confused conditions where his goodness means nothing. Almost all of that play came out of my experiences as a boy in the Bronx. I saw people evicted, I saw block parties, I knew a girl who stayed at the piano all day, a boy who drowned, boys who went bad and got in trouble with the police. As a

matter of fact, two of the boys I graduated with ended up in the electric chair and another boy became a labor racketeer. Not too much of that play was invented; it was felt, remembered, celebrated.

One night I had the idea for the scene in the play which I call the Fire Bug Scene. It just impelled itself to be written, and since I had no paper I wrote the whole scene as fast as I could on the white wall. The words just gushed out; my hand couldn't stop writing. Then later, I copied it down on the typewriter, but to this day the scene may still be on the wall of that old hotel.

The next day, well, I had that advance money from Merlin, and I had always wondered what real liquor tasted like. Prohibition was over, and all I had ever had was bathtub gin and very phony rye whiskey. I went into a liquor store and bought two cases of mixed liquor—two bottles of everything—Scotch, gin and rye, applejack, sherry, red port, and something called white port which I have not seen again to this day. And I and my particular chums in the Group Theatre, Elia Kazan, Art Smith, Bud Bohnen, and one or two others, went to town on all that stuff. I got to know what real liquor, real Scotch, tasted like. There was booze in those two cases that I have not tasted since. We went down to the village one night, got drunk, and got arrested. We had a helluvatime.

During this time, however, I was extremely discontented about my acting. Many of us were fretful in those days, because we had higher hopes for ourselves than playing bits and walk-ons. I had been assigned to play two bits in *Gold Eagle Guy,* but I didn't have a part in *Success Story,* which we had done before and were now reviving out of town to keep us going while we were rehearsing *Gold Eagle Guy.*

John Howard Lawson's *Success Story*—a good play—had, by the way, a very decisive influence on me, by showing me the poetry that was inherent in the chaff of the street. I began to see that there was something quite elevated and poetic in the way the common people spoke. I understudied Luther Adler, who played the lead, and while I never got to play it, I came to understand that living quality in Lawson's play by studying the part and writing down how I thought I would approach it as an actor. Getting a part also meant that you would learn what the hell the technique was about. There wasn't time for too many technique classes, so there was more than an ego problem involved in our wanting good parts, for it was the only way we could really get the benefit of Strasberg's training.

THE STRASBERG-CLURMAN TEAM

Strasberg worked with a wide range, then, of techniques and things. There were times when you would do improvisation for a part—the sensation, for instance, for riding a train or boat. It would play only a small part in the play, but concentration was given to it. Or you would do exercises or improvisation for simply being cold, for re-creating winter on the stage. As a matter of fact, the Group Theatre built up a set of actors and actresses who were extraordinarily reliable in small parts as well as in leads. Say this woman is a nurse, and this actress would go away and she would be a nurse to the life. She thought about how a nurse waddled, and what kind of shoes she would wear, why she walks the way she does, and what her professional mannerisms are.

Anyway, one day I told Harold Clurman, who by then had become my particular friend among the three Group directors—he was a kind of older brother to me—I told him that since I had never got a part, I was leaving and was going to do something about playwriting. He pleaded with me to stay, promising he would see that I got a good acting part in the coming season, and indeed I think I was leading him on a bit because I wouldn't have known where to go. Where else could you go? All I really wanted was to have the Group Theatre do my plays. These early plays were made for the collective acting company technique. They're written for eight characters, with six or seven of the characters of equal importance. Well, this is purely from the Group Theatre ideal of a stage ensemble, and this so fetched me and so took me over that this was how I wrote. I don't think, still, that even today anyone could put together such a company with its very brilliant ensemble performance but Lee Strasberg. That was Lee Strasberg's baby and he was 100 per cent responsible for it. Later, with this perfected tool, this ensemble, anybody could direct them who had a common lingo, a common frame of reference. It was easy for Harold Clurman to direct *Awake and Sing!* or *Golden Boy* with this company that Lee Strasberg had put together—any actor could have directed it, by that time. And Lee Strasberg has never gotten enough credit for that.

Strasberg and Clurman were a unique team. The procedure was that the directors picked the plays—remember, though, that we didn't have our choice of dozens of plays. Strasberg and Clurman saw rather eye-to-eye about what was in a play. They wanted progressive materials, they wanted yea-saying rather than nay-saying materials. After the play was chosen Clurman would call the company together and would talk with extraordinary brilliance for anywhere from two to five hours, analyzing the meaning, talking from every point of view, covering the ground backwards and forwards. And if the actor's imagination was touched, somewhere, which was his intention, then the actor would catch something and begin to work in a certain way, with a certain image or vision of how the part should go, with here and there Clurman giving him a nudge. Strasberg would never say a word. He was the man who, in action, directing, would bring out the things which Clurman had abstracted. Strasberg understood the concrete elements which you give an actor. But the sense of the

play, its characters, its meaning, what it stood for, Clurman is most brilliant at this thing.

HOW THE ACTORS TOOK OVER

Well, now we move up to Boston in the late fall of 1934 to open *Gold Eagle Guy,* and that's when I wrote *Waiting for Lefty.* I now had behind me the practically completed *Awake and Sing!* and about half of *Paradise Lost,* but somehow *Waiting for Lefty* just kind of slipped itself in there. Its form and its feeling are different from the other two plays, and I actually wrote it in three nights in the hotel room in Boston after returning home from the theater about midnight. It just seemed to gush out, and it took its form necessarily from what we then called the agit-prop form, which, of course, stands for agitational propaganda.

I really saw the play as a kind of collective venture—something we would do for a Sunday night benefit in New York for the *New Theatre Magazine,* a Left magazine that was always in need of money. My demands were so modest that I tried to get two other actors in the Group Theatre who I thought had writing talent to assist me. One of them, Art Smith, came up with me one night to my hotel room and we talked around and around this thing, but he seemed rather listless about working with me, so I went ahead by myself.

As a matter of fact, the form of *Waiting for Lefty* is very rooted in American life, because what I semi-consciously had in mind was actually the form of the minstrel show. I had put on two or three minstrel shows in camp and had seen three or four other ones. It's a very American, indigenous form—you know, an interlocutor, end men, people doing their specialties, everyone sitting on the stage, and some of the actors sitting in the audience. There were a number of plays then, usually cheap and shoddy plays, that had actors in the audience. I had played in one called, I think, *The Spider,* in Camden, New Jersey, when I was in stock. I guess all these things conglomerated in my mind, but what's important for *Waiting for Lefty* is how it matched my conversion from a fellow who stood on the side and watched and then finally, with a rush, agreed—in this drastic social crisis in the early 'thirties—that the only way out seemed to be a kind of socialism, or the Communist party, or something. And the play represents that kind of ardor and that kind of conviction.

About ten days after the tryout in Boston we opened *Gold Eagle Guy* at the Morosco Theater in New York, and the play got very bad notices. In all New York theaters you automatically lose the theater when the play receipts fall below a certain figure, so we moved over to the Belasco. It happened that three or four or even five of my plays were done at that theater, which people thought was very glamorous, but I always thought it a rather crummy old joint, shabby, with uncomfortable seats. Anyway, to keep the play going the actors and the playwright took cuts in salary, but in a few weeks it closed and we were forced out into the cold winter. We had no new play to put into rehearsal and there was a sadness around the place.

In the meantime I'd gotten some of the actors together and had started to rehearse *Waiting for Lefty*. I gave Sandy Meisner, an actor friend of mine, some of the scenes to direct, and I directed the bulk of the play. Strasberg, who was quite resentful of it, told Harold Clurman, "Let 'em fall and break their necks." One of the main things about Strasberg was that he always hated to go out on a limb. He must save his face at all times. Almost Oriental. I suspect that the thing about Strasberg was that whenever the Group Theatre name was used or represented, it was as though his honor was at stake. He didn't like me, he didn't like what I had written, and he felt it would in some way be a reflection on him, on the entire Group Theatre. This man who could be so generous, sometimes could be so niggardly and begrudging. It was with great trepidation that I had proposed putting on this play at all, and when I asked him a few questions about handling a group, an ensemble, he'd answer me very curtly, and I thought to myself, "Oh, the hell with him. I'll just go ahead and do this myself."

And then, the night of the benefit, I had an enormous fight down at the old Civic Repertory Theatre on 14th Street to get my play put on last. They used to put on eight or nine vaudeville acts there for the Sunday night benefits and they wanted some dance group to close the show, but finally, because I threatened to pull it, they agreed to put *Waiting for Lefty* on last.

It was very lucky they did because there would have been no show after that. The audience stopped the show after each scene; they got up, they began to cheer and weep. There have been many great opening nights in the American theater but not where the opening and the performing of the play were a cultural fact. You saw a cultural unit functioning. From stage to theater and back and forth the identity was so complete, there was such an at-oneness with audience and actors, that the actors didn't know whether they were acting and the audience didn't know whether they were sitting and watching it, or had changed position. I was sitting in the audience with my friend, Elia Kazan, sitting next to me (I wouldn't have dared take on one of the good parts myself) and after the Luther Adler scene, the young doctor scene, the audience got up and shouted, "Bravo! Bravo!" I was thinking, "Shh, let the play continue," but I found myself up on my feet shouting, "Bravo, Luther! Bravo, Luther!" In fact, I was part of the audience. I forgot I wrote the play, I forgot I was in the play, and many of the actors forgot. The proscenium arch disappeared. That's the key phrase. Before and since, in the American theater people have tried to do that by theater-in-the-round, theater this way, that way, but here, psychologically and

emotionally, the proscenium arch dissolved away. When that happens, not by technical innovation, but emotionally and humanly, then you will have great theater—theater at its most primitive and grandest.

Of course, the nature of the times had a good deal to do with this kind of reaction. I don't think a rousing play today could have this kind of effect because there are no positive, ascending values to which a play can attach itself. My own new plays will never arouse that kind of enthusiasm, but they will have searched out and will express what has been happening here in the last fifteen years. And this isn't going to be anything to dance and shout about, because what happened here in fifteen years is really frightening. One of the new plays, *An Old-fashioned Man,* will almost cover the American scene from the time of FDR's death to today. I think the play is of considerable import, but really the kind of import that makes you sit there and think, rather than the kind that makes you get up and burn with zeal.

However, we now had to face the closing of *Gold Eagle Guy.* There was an emergency meeting and we were told we would have to disband. It was at this time that the actors took over and upset the applecart. We took the theater out of the hands of the three directors, especially Strasberg's, who was still extraordinarily resistant to the idea of doing *Awake and Sing!* What happened was that the Theatre Guild wanted to do *Awake and Sing!* for their last production of the season. So I rather timidly asked at this meeting whether the Group Theatre was or was not going to do my play because I had another offer.

Strasberg got up and pointed his finger at me and said, "I have told you a dozen times. I do not like your play. Your play will not be done by the Group Theatre." And it was Stella Adler who got up and said, "Well, is it better to disband, and those people who can get jobs will and the rest are going to be cold and hungry, as they have been many times before? And what's the matter with this play? Why shouldn't we do it?" And one or two other actors chipped in and Strasberg began to fight with them. Clurman says that he just sat letting things develop, and they did. Strasberg said, "But the play doesn't have a third act." I said, "It has a third act. It's not as good as it can be, but I can rewrite that." And, lo and behold, in a wave of what I call the Group Theatre spirit, it was voted, without the directors' interfering, that the next play we would do would be *Awake and Sing!* And Lee Strasberg kind of withdrew as the active director, so to speak, and Harold Clurman directed it.

When I rewrote the third act of *Awake and Sing!* I built up the boy to a kind of affirmative voice in the end, more affirmative than he had been in the original. There were technical reasons for this change, but the change had occurred in me, too—a growing sense of power and direction. If I was going up, everything had to go up with me. But as you see, it runs throughout the play. The boy is always resentful of who and what he is, of his position in the world. And he always wants to get married and he can't, because of, let me call it that economic factor in his mother, who is always very authoritarian, always making decisions for him. And the grandfather, as weak as he is, was always against the values by which his daughter and the household lives. He always sided with the boy. So tried and true, that play.

Awake and Sing! opened at the Belasco Theater in February 1935. The notices were legendary. In the meantime we had been playing benefit performances of *Waiting for Lefty* all around and it was getting more famous by the minute. Even the commercial managers, the Shubert office, had called me and asked to see a copy of it. In the general enthusiasm Strasberg jumped on the bandwagon and now suggested that we bring *Waiting for Lefty* uptown, and I said, yes, I would write another play to go with it, which later became *Till the Day I Die*. I had read in *The New Masses* what I thought was a letter that had been smuggled out of Europe, from a man to his brother in the (anti-Nazi) underground, and in a wave of enthusiasm I wrote, in three or four nights, a play based on that letter. That's how arrogant youth is, for it never occurred to me to clear it in any way with *The New Masses,* and it turned out that the letter was not a real letter at all, but a short story in letter form, and later I was approached and had to pay that man royalties. In any case, *Till the Day I Die* was paired with *Waiting for Lefty,* and the whole town wanted to see it. And the whole town wanted to see *Awake and Sing!* You know—"America has found a really important playwright"; "The Group Theatre has found its most congenial playwright within its own ranks. . . ."

For me, strangely enough, the success and fame was a source of acute discomfort. I didn't have the psychological strength to face this kind of onslaught. It had on me a strangely isolating effect, even more isolated and cut off from the very things I was trying to get to. Later on when I became really a successful playwright the Group Theatre acting members, my friends, started to treat me quite differently. However, that's ahead. All I wanted then in 1935 were some of the things that were mentioned in *Waiting for Lefty*—a room of my own, a girl of my own, a phonograph and some records. And I got 'em. Nothing more I wanted.

Then I ran into a nerve-racking period where I thought I was going to go to pieces, just out of emotional exhaustion. I understood in this period of my life how van Gogh felt. I understood the kind of insanity and frenzy of his painting. I almost couldn't stop writing. The hand kept going. It began to frighten me. With all this set in the matrix of an American success— nothing is more noisy and clamorous than that. There are enormous tensions and strains within it, because you don't want to change, you want to hold on. You want time to digest, but you're just kind of swept off your feet, with wire services and interviews and people telephoning you; the parties you're invited to, the people who just take you up. You want to savor these things, flavor them, but you'd like it on your own terms. You'd like the time to establish forms with which to deal with it, or else it will drive you cuckoo.

Some of it, though, was gentle and sweet, like my mother. This was in a way all she ever lived for, to see her son fulfilled. She hadn't been sick; she just lived another couple of months and died. My whole life changed in this period. Within three months I was not the same young man I used to be, but was trying to hold on to him.

In any case, I now began to finish up *Paradise Lost*. The play, with Harold Clurman directing it, was treated with dignity and importance, and the actors approached it in a very dedicated way. It opened on December 9, 1935. It's too jammed, too crowded, it spills out of its frame, but it is in many ways a beautiful play, velvety; the colors were very gloomy and rich. And no one who acted in it or saw it in that production will ever forget it. It got very bad notices from the working press, but from unexpected people like Clifton Fadiman it got quite extraordinary notices. But the play was by all means a practical failure, judging by the notices and the reception.

WHAT DAMAGED THE PLAYS

I was, by then, being offered all sorts of movie jobs. One man offered me $500 a week. He was then the head of Paramount; poor man, Budd Schulberg's father. I thought going to Hollywood was the most immoral thing I could do, and yet who wouldn't want to go to Hollywood? When I finally went it was with a sense of disgrace, almost. A man came from MGM and just to get rid of him I said I wanted $4,000 a week. He called the Coast and arranged to pay me $4,000 weekly. I didn't accept the offer, but the company was making their usual sacrifices trying to keep *Paradise Lost* going, and I thought finally I'd go to Hollywood and send back half my salary to the Group Theatre to keep the play going. So in the end I signed with Paramount for $2,500 a week and sent back half to the Group Theatre. That was really not enough to keep the show going, and it closed after another couple of weeks. I went out there and wrote a movie, *The General Died at Dawn,* which was full of good ideas, but in the end it was a set of clichés on which we made some good birthday decorations.

But I'm not really interested in talking about Hollywood. I am interested in investigating not so much why—I understand why—but how I tried to take some kind of real life I knew and tried to press it into an ideological mold. How, actually technically, I used to try many ways to make the materials of my plays say something that they really were not saying by tacking on a certain ideological posture. I think this did damage to the plays and the material, but I couldn't have done otherwise in that period. It's the one thing that really disturbs me about the early plays—that I would very easily, very fluently and naturally, give an expression of a certain kind of life, and then try to tell the audience what it meant.

I think very simply that the material was always richer than the ideational direction that I tried to superimpose upon it. It was just enough to give birth to the material and let it say what it had to say. And yet, still in all, the life which was expressed, was impelled by some ideological direction in which I was going. It's almost like not trusting the material to make a statement, but you have to add a comment that was not really indigenous to the material. Jack Lawson, for instance, was a distinguished playwright, but he ruined himself artistically by tailoring his materials to fit an ideological conception. The last play he wrote, *Marching Song,* was concepted along these lines, and it's dead as a nail. I think it's a crime to see what happened to this juicy, gifted playwright when he got an ideology. Fortunately, however, the Left movement didn't absorb too many good talents. When I started to write **Awake and Sing!** I didn't have a mission in life; I wasn't going to change society. When I came to rewriting it I was going to change the world—or help change it. I should have learned a lesson from Ibsen; that it's simply enough to present the question. "You in the audience think about it; maybe you have some answers."

Soon after I arrived in Hollywood I began working on a new play, *The Silent Partner,* which is a very sympathetic portrayal of a man from an old American family who is ousted from his plant when the new management takes over. His sons have kind of drifted off; one killed himself in Hollywood while drunk, by jumping into a pool which didn't have any water in it. I've never rewritten the last act, but five of the nine scenes in it are the best writing I've ever done. The Group Theatre was going to do the play but I didn't have it ready. I was kind of discontented with myself and with the way things were going. I had come out to Hollywood to do a movie and now I was getting mixed up with the woman who was going to be my first wife. Finally I rented a little house where I started to work on the play seriously but all the while I was beginning to resent being pushed into plays for the Group Theatre. A play, when I put it into rehearsal, would never be ready, but the Group Theatre needed it, for there was always the prospect of the actors going without work.

When the play was finally put into rehearsal I was not quite satisfied with it yet. I had to sacrifice some of what I call the poetic quality of the play, because the texture was very dense as originally written, and in attempting to make things more concrete the play suffered, but still it kept most of its virtue. By then, with the help of FDR's Administration, the strikers had won and had organized all over the country into the CIO, and the play was a little dated in the sense that these big strikes were now a year or two behind us. The play was also critical of the working class. Because the point was, you know, stop the foolishness. For God's sake, get serious or die. You're going to die for lack of seriousness.

After *The Silent Partner* was in rehearsal for three or four days Clurman said to me, "Look, we'll produce any play you write. But you know this will be a very heavy and expensive production. We budgeted it for $40,000." So I said, "Why are you telling me all this?" and he said, "Well, the play will fail. We'll be out all that money and the actors will be out of work. But if you want us to do the play we will."

So I said, "Well, when you put it that way you don't give me much choice. Pull the play, then; don't do it." And I was very hurt, but not intelligent or mature enough to say, "Stop the shit and do the play. It's necessary for me. And after all the sacrifices I've made, just do the play and lose $40,000. It's worth it to me." And I never even tried to publish the play. The production of that play was necessary for me, because nobody in the U.S. was writing that way. To this day nobody can write that way, including me. Everything was extremely heightened. You didn't know whether it was real, or mystic. Were these real human beings? Where was this happening? It was the beginning of a new striking out for me. You see, later, when I wrote a play that was successful, like **Golden Boy,** the Group Theatre had a treasury at last. It was quite all right for them to lose money, most of the time out of my pocket, on experimental things—to give Bobbie Lewis or Gadget Kazan a chance to direct something, to do trash by Irwin Shaw. But while it was necessary and good to help Gadget or Bobbie Lewis to become a director, or to do a special matinee performance of an Irwin Shaw play, I was the first necessity. I never put my mitts up. I just walked away.

"REALLY QUITE A GOOD PLAY"

And then the Group Theatre again was breaking up. Again there were no scripts. First of all, there was some impossible ideal. There was a time when we turned down plays like Maxwell Anderson's *Winterset* as not good enough for us. We realized later that we made a grave blunder there, but nobody was resourceful enough to go out and look for plays; the larder was always bare. This is why my plays always went on before they were finished.

Anyway, it looked like the Group Theatre was through. Strasberg and Cheryl Crawford had left; everybody kind of voluntarily disbanded for six months, and Harold Clurman came out here to Hollywood. It was very difficult for him to take the Group Theatre breakup. So I said, "I'll tell you what, Harold, I have an idea. You get the company together on October first and I'll have a new play." I told him in about two sentences what the play was about. I just said there was an Italian boy whose father wanted him to be a violinist and he has true gifts for that, but he wants to be a prizefighter. I had married Luise Rainer by then, and my bride of maybe six or eight months said, "What is that about? It's nothing. It sounds crazy." Harold said, "Let him alone, Luise. He knows what he's doing." She couldn't understand it and was rather bewildered. But he understood that something could come out of that; he knew how I worked.

I went back to the apartment in New York with my one page of notes for the new play, and Clurman set two or three actors to watch me to see that I didn't run off. All that summer I worked on *Golden Boy,* and it was ready I think before October first. I really wrote that play to be a hit, to keep the Group Theatre together. And it was a hit, my first really big hit. It pleased me, which was foolish on my part. It pleased me because now I was being accepted as a Broadway playwright. Before that I was kind of a nutty artist who had some kind of wild gift, and now, only now, was I a man with a ten-million-dollar arm who could really direct the ball just where I wanted it to go.

I must say, I think now that the circumstances under which I had written the play are what make me not like it. I feel the same way about *The Country Girl.* It doesn't mean anything to me; it's just a theater piece. I felt that way about *Golden Boy* for years afterwards, because it seemed to me to be really immoral to write a play for money. But I did see it once out here. Charlie Chaplin had never seen it, so the two wives, Charlie, and I jumped into a car and went to see it at the Pasadena Playhouse, and on seeing the play quite objectively, I thought, "Gee, this is really quite a good play." There's something written into it—a quality of American folk legend—that I really had nothing to do with. It was a much better play than I thought it was. So after that I made my peace with that play.

We revived it for ANTA in 1952. John Garfield always wanted to play the part and Lee Cobb played the father. By then, there were such accepted clichés for playing the parts that Garfield and Lee Cobb fell right into the stereotypes. Every once in a while Cobb would slouch onto the stage, very successful, at ease. Nobody can be so at home on a stage as Cobb, you know. And I'd say, "What are you playing? Are you playing a successful actor, or this rather humble, but perceptive old Italian father?" It was hard to try to break the stereotypes in four weeks.

One play I did like is *Rocket to the Moon.* It was based on an idea which I had for a long time, although I didn't know the real theme of it until I wrote it. I knew the play was going to take place in a dentist's office and that there was going to be a little dental secretary there who was going to take him away from his wife. But I didn't know that the play would be, so to

speak, about love in America, about the search for love, and all the things it turned out to be about.

Plenty of my ideas kind of germinated sometimes for two or three years. On the other hand, sometimes I get an idea and sit down and write from just one page of notes. I find that those things often come out best when I don't know what's going to happen, and in fact, most of the time I don't know what I know or what I think until I say it. Ask me what I think about the world, about the kind of morality in this country, oh, I can give you some intellectual talk about it, but it's not till I write a play that I know what I really think, that I know where I am in the whole mess and can really make a statement that I didn't know was in me to make. That's one of the reasons that keeps me writing plays.

Leslie Weiner (review date Winter 1975)

SOURCE: "Thinking about Odets," in *The Columbia Forum,* Vol. 4, No. 1, Winter, 1975, pp. 35-39.

[*Weiner is a playwright and a former student and acquaintance of Odets. In the following essay, he uses his familiarity with Odets and his works to offer insight into Odets's controversial career and life.*]

In the spring of 1960 I completed a draft of a play whose quality puzzled me. Not knowing quite what to do with it, I wrote a letter to Clifford Odets, asking if he'd be willing to read it. I had been one of twenty aspiring playwrights in a unique class given by Odets at the Actors Studio in 1951, but I hadn't been in touch with him in the almost nine years since the class disbanded. I addressed my letter to his agent in New York and the following week received a cheerful note from Beverly Hills. Odets was glad I was still writing plays, he had time on his hands because of a Hollywood strike, and if I'd care to send the script, he'd read it promptly. "Promptly" turned out to be a term of some elasticity, but after an exchange of letters and phone calls, he suggested I come to California for a day or two and hear what he had to say. He met me at the airport, insisted I stay at his home instead of a hotel, introduced me to his friends as "a playwright from New York" (I was then still unproduced), and the "day or two" became eleven fascinating days during which he discussed not only my play but his life. Our work sessions together consisted mainly of his talking and my laughing. I flew back home in a four-engine jet, but I could have made it without the plane.

This flow of memory has been stirred by the simplest of events: in moving my desk to another room, I came across my old, dog-eared copy of *Six Plays by Clifford Odets,* published in the Modern Library in 1939. The pages opened themselves to *Awake and Sing,* and immediately I was sucked into a Bronx apartment of forty years ago. All his life Ralphie wanted a pair of black and white shoes, I read, and the delight I once experienced upon hearing those words in the Belasco Theatre came rushing back with such intensity that I spent the rest of the weekend devouring all six plays. During the following week I got hold of the five later Odets plays beginning with *Night Music* and ending with *The Flowering Peach,* and for the first time I let myself make the connection between a motif in all his eleven plays and the man himself: all his characters, fool or knave, victim or victimizer, poet or peasant, are drawn with an expansive generosity, a genuine fellow-feeling; though viewed sharply and unsparingly, they are never rendered without a redeeming tolerance and good humor. We are all brother *schlemiels* in the human comedy, he seems to be saying, so let us try to be kind to one another. It is in this respect, in his loving attitude toward his gallery of creations from Bessie Berger to the Biblical Noah, and not in any penchant for plotlessness, that Odets is still our most Chekhovian playwright. The love which seems to be his special gift is manly and sympathetic and comes out of his awareness of the peculiar pain which American society, promising so much but delivering too little, inflicts on its hopeful middle class. But what was so winning and remarkable about Odets was that he didn't exhaust all his brotherly feeling on his fictional people; he was no less kindly and decent to the living people he went out of his way to know. How different he was from O'Neill, that instinctive recluse. Odets' readiness to offer a hand to me—whom he knew only in a most general way—was entirely consistent with the fraternal spirit which infuses his work and which, in my eyes, is one of the sources of its distinction.

[Odets'] most commercially successful creation, *Golden Boy,* ... is the single play which most directly mirrors Odets' own personal conflict between doing his work as an artist and "getting his name in the papers."

—Leslie Weiner

I feel I'm describing some prehistoric age when I say that for the generation that grew up in the Thirties, the Broadway theater was a glamorous and exciting institution. In addition to the great comics and Gershwin and Cole Porter and Rodgers and Hart, there were some twenty-odd talented dramatists working regularly, earning a good living from their plays. And the unchallenged star of them all, the playwright who had four productions running in 1935 alone, the face on the cover of *Time,* the darling of the galleries and the meal ticket of the idealistic Group Theatre was Clifford Odets. It wasn't puffery that made his reputation, nor was it the favor of the critics, who were never more than lukewarm. It was bestowed

on him by the audience who paid from 55¢ to $3 to see themselves on the stage for the very first time.

I had been going to the movies every Saturday afternoon since my fist was strong enough to hold a quarter. I was nurtured on American heroes—aviators, criminals, cowpokes, detectives, soldiers, lovers all. I never dreamed that I and my Jewish family could be the subject of drama—what bank did we ever rob, or cavalry outflank, or pretty thing rescue from an onrushing train? When in September of 1935 I saw my first Broadway play (two of them, in fact; *Awake and Sing* was running with *Waiting for Lefty*), I had no idea I was starting with the very best Broadway had to offer; I thought naively, well, this is the theater, this is what it's like. And what I saw was a bombshell, real, living, recognizable, ridiculous, passionate Jews, out of the closet at last! Father Coughlin regularly offered his fascist wisdom on the radio, and in the papers Hitler dominated European politics, and here before us came the object of their hatred, the Bergers and Benjamins and Starks of New York. And how they talked, these Odets characters! At a time when other playwrights wrote English, grammatical or otherwise, Odets employed a patois which was urban, sophisticated, funny, and apt. He moved the best of the street idiom from the streets to the stage and added his own joyous color and wordplay. The result was witty and exhilarating; even when he forced his metaphors and invited parody, it was *interesting* overwriting. Today, so many years later, it's amazing to me how vividly I recall the scene-by-scene progression of *Awake and Sing,* which, in a sense, is the most unwritten of Odets' work. The Bergers seem to tumble all over each other, writing their own lines, acting out their minor destinies without guidance from anybody, least of all the author. Odets was so full of the struggle of everyday living in a depressed city, he was so in sympathy with his embattled New Yorkers (he was a member in good standing), that he seemed to need very little theatrical artifice to render them lusty and whole. I spent a lot of time with Odets in the spring and fall of 1951 listening to him talk of his plays, and again in 1960 in California, but I don't recall him ever speaking of *Awake and Sing.* It was as though that play were a fact of nature, like a school of mackerel or a mountain; there wasn't really much to say about it.

The story of Clifford Odets' own life is almost classically American. His most commercially successful creation, *Golden Boy,* the tale of a gifted youth who had to choose between boxing and music, is the single play which most directly mirrors Odets' own personal conflict between doing his work as an artist and "getting his name in the papers." At three different stages of his working life, he left Broadway for Hollywood to make a bundle, and perhaps to spread his name; Hollywood was his fight game, the theater his fiddle. In his time, when practically all films made in Hollywood bore the flat, adulterated stamp of the studio, artistic work was not only not required, it was forthrightly regarded as an obstacle to production. Through two decades Odets was alternately able to doodle for the screen and to do some of his best work in the theater. But in 1955, after *The Flowering Peach* closed on Broadway, he turned for the third time to the Coast to raise his two motherless children and earn a livelihood from films. On my visit in 1960 he told me he had "ideas" for five plays. He never wrote them, but not because he was overwhelmed with movie work.

He filled a lot of his time optioning properties, proposing deals, fretting, waiting, waiting for the ponderous machinery of business to inch forward and give him the go-ahead on a screenplay. At that time I had a friend connected with Princeton University. I asked Odets if he would be interested in teaching for a year or two. His quick and emphatic interest surprised me. He would need a house and $25,000 a year and a limited schedule so he could write his plays. "Yes, I think I'd like to be a don," he said musingly, but he couldn't suppress a little laugh. I did try to make a marriage between Odets and Princeton, though I was doubtful he would actually come East. (He had earned $200,000 the previous year and was short of cash.) After mulling it over briefly, Princeton decided to let the matter drop; writers-in-residence, particularly expensive ones, were not yet in vogue.

There's no question that Odets' need for fame and fortune was real and enormous. We can understand Joe Bonaparte's sense of deprivation, his lust for a success that would take him out of the ranks of the nobodies. Joe, the Golden Boy, after all was 21, poor, a member of a despised ethnic minority and cockeyed to boot. But why was it important to Clifford Odets, an American playwright of international stature, that he always be welcome at Billy Rose's table? Or that he be seen in the company of Jascha Heifetz and Ava Gardner? Why did he have to earn $200,000? You don't permit yourself the indulgence of writing a Biblical parable for the stage when you're convinced you need that much "to live." (This was 1960, mind you; what's the equivalent figure today?) Odets knew only too well that in pursuing his art the chances of fashioning a popular success were just about what he had achieved: two hits in eleven tries. The fire to write was present all right, but it burned at a low flame; and if he did complete a play, who would produce it? The Group Theatre was no more, Dwight Deere Wiman was dead, and his experience with Robert Whitehead, who produced *The Flowering Peach,* was painfully unhappy. No wonder those five plays remained in his head.

He was more comfortable in Hollywood than he realized. He was regarded as a famous dramatist-doctor whose specialty was quick diagnosis and surgery for diseased films already shooting. His price was high, and he could work with energy and zest off the top of his head. He was a night person who enjoyed the social life of Los Angeles.

Tall and trim, he cut an imposing figure with his shrewd wide eyes and his wild half-a-head of reddish hair. He loved his bachelor freedom and took delight in dating the most beautiful women in the world. He was a brilliantly engaging companion and his generosity was excessive. The only thing he needed that he didn't possess was a proper respect for his talent, even though in his preface to his *Six Plays* he declared, speaking of himself, "Talent should be respected." He didn't even try to write good movies. "A good show" was what he aimed at, an elusive target when your heart's not really in it, as his last two movies proved. ("Did you see *Story on Page One*?" he asked. I had seen it, but said I hadn't. "See it, it's a good show.") The plain, sad fact is that he was not passionately committed to his work, as Charles Ives was to his music, as O'Neill was to his art; nor did he take Hollywood's money and run home to his desk as Faulkner did. He actually cared about the price he could command as against other screenwriters. That became his measure of respect.

His need for lots of money accounted for more than unwritten plays. It hurt him in the working out of a play which I've always found tremendously appealing and stageworthy, *The Country Girl*. It is the fashion to regard this play as superficial; even Odets, with enthusiastic reviews in his pocket and the play running strongly, joined in the general disparagement, referring to it as a mere "theater piece." *The Country Girl* is the story of two talented men of the theater who are dependent on the aid and comfort of a loving woman, Georgie Elgin. Georgie's defeated actor husband has a chance to regain his manhood in a comeback; though used and abused by both him and the director, Georgie sees her husband through his crisis successfully. By now the director has fallen in love with her, and so she has a choice: director, husband, neither. She opts for her husband, thereby satisfying the theme that an artist needs a "friend." Sure, why not, but what does the friend need? We have become convinced she is the only side of the triangle with the character to stand alone. She has paid and overpaid on her responsibility to these attractive but obtuse men; psychologically and dramatically, the way has been opened for her to walk out into the independent life she desires. The play appeared in 1950, two decades before the women's movement, but Odets had a clear chance to affirm in modern detail what Ibsen had dramatized seventy-odd years before in *A Doll's House*. Nothing holds Georgie back from a believable move to freedom but the playwright. Odets read the play to us in his Actors Studio class, read it proudly because he considered it "the best technical job of construction I ever did." At least five members of the class were so struck by Georgie's last-scene cave-in that they accused Odets of parental abandonment. To our surprise, Clifford made no attempt to defend himself. He said he had considered Georgie's solo exit very seriously, but inasmuch as his purpose in writing the play was to make some badly needed money, he was afraid a commercial audience wouldn't accept an "unhappy" ending. He was "sure" they would go for this more conventional windup.

How one can be "sure" about any new work in the theater is a question worth asking. What is still breathtaking, even discounting the degree to which he claimed he was conscious of the problem, is that an artist of Odets' gifts caught up in the production process—as intense and exhilarating an experience as one mind can deal with (he was his own director as well)—would deliberately debase the most important work of his life, which for a playwright is always the play he is currently working on. Can one imagine O'Neill trimming his sails this way? Last winter a television production of *The Country Girl* proved remarkably rich and complicated and touching—until that pallid, nerveless last scene.

But then, Odets was always doing things which would protect his flanks or, to be more exact, his earning power. In this sense too he was the playwright of the Thirties *par excellence.* He was haunted by the specter of the Depression, and he never lost his doubt and wonder that his ten fingers working on a typewriter could defend him from an economic cataclysm. Nor did he underestimate the toll in psychic energy that writing cost him. His life was a constant struggle between wanting to work and wanting to play. He felt guilty and oppressed when not working, but that didn't make him less reluctant to take a chance on something he might not get paid for. The idealism of the Thirties somehow came out in the Fifties as cynicism: all very well, *boychick,* for a single young man to say life shouldn't be printed on dollar bills, but when your wife is ill and the children require therapy, life turns out to be printed on nothing less than C-notes. More and more he made decisions according to the effect on his income.

At the same time, he was extravagant in the giving of what was indeed priceless: himself. Directly after *The Country Girl* opened in New York in November, 1950, Odets announced he would conduct a playwriting course, open to anyone interested, admission to be gained by submitting one playscript. Odets would read the scripts and determine the membership of the class. For the New Year of 1951 I quit my well-paying job and foolishly announced to my wife that henceforth I would be a writer. Suddenly with nothing but time on my hands, I couldn't think of anything to write. After a month of idleness I took sick, naturally. One afternoon when my wife and child were out and I was in bed with a fever, the phone rang. The caller identified himself as Clifford Odets. "Cut it out, Harold," I grumbled. "Quit horsing around. I have the flu." But it was Odets: he had read the play I had sent in and he invited me to join his class, clearing up my illness by nightfall. For more than three months, our group met twice a week through a hot muggy spring; Odets, punctual as a German, never missed a session. It was the best tutelage of my life.

In February, 1952, Odets was one of the speakers at a memorial for J. Edward Bromberg, who had been a member of the Group Theatre and the Uncle Morty of *Awake and Sing.* Odets was genuinely astonished at the huge turnout, the outpouring of affection for the dead blacklisted actor. He began to read what he had written out, but twice he interrupted himself, looked up, blinked at the crowd, and said haltingly, "I didn't realize so many cared, had no idea . . . I'll have to do some rethinking. . . ." It was clear he was moved and distressed, as though he were already wrestling with the summons from the House Un-American Activities Committee. In May of that year he appeared publicly at the Washington hearings and named the names which would give him absolution in the Committee's eyes but not in his own. He knew better than anyone that they were asking him to repudiate his *Paradise Lost* and *Waiting for Lefty*; he was caught in a ritual minuet and figured he might as well do the steps. He was the prize catch of the season for the Committee: the author of the "Communistic" *Awake and Sing* denouncing the communists.

Why did he cooperate with these petty political morons? Up until his appearance before them, no one had defied the Committee with impunity. The stubborn Hollywood Ten had been cited for contempt and were delaying their jail terms by litigation. The successful non-cooperation of Lillian Hellman and Arthur Miller came much later, after several court tests had delimited the Committee's power to punish. Odets was not going to break new ground and challenge "the government." Billy Rose, Jerry Wald, and the guys at "21" would not have understood, nor would they have approved. And the Committee had all the names anyway—what he told them wasn't *news.* Besides, giving out the names was a tiny fraction of his voluminous testimony. He was naively upset when the press quoted little else than that he had knuckled under; he thought they might have used *some* of his critical comments! Eight years later he still talked defensively about his testimony. I didn't particularly want to hear about it, for by that time I had resolved my own disappointment with him by deciding that his Committee appearance had really harmed no one but himself. Had he spectacularly challenged the Committee, it would have been exhilarating. But that would not have been the true Odets: for all his rhetoric, he was always more of a lover, in the Whitman sense, than a fighter. What did happen was that he spent many unhappy hours chewing over that experience. And the result of his rumination was his final play, *The Flowering Peach,* the story of Noah and the ark—Clifford Odets' expression of how, in times of catastrophe, one must be content to ride out the storm. As Rachel says to the character who represents the reflective side of Odets, "There is idealism now in just survival."

The play, begun as an idea for an opera to be written with Aaron Copland, suffered through a rocky shakedown tour before it settled into the Belasco in the last week of 1954. I saw that first production about a month into its run and thought the first half enchanting, the second a little less so, but I left the theater satisfied that I had seen a *play*. There was a cool mastery in the writing which suggested that, although Odets was certainly speaking of himself, he was telling about Noah at an honest arm's length. The writing in *The Flowering Peach* had a terseness, a wit, and a felicity of expression that may be superior to any of the other ten plays. Touching and suggestive of better things to come, it bespoke a wounded, chastened Odets immensely attractive even in guilt. It seems cruelly ironic that *The Flowering Peach* was his last work for the theater; to me, Odets stopping there is like O'Neill never having written *The Iceman Cometh, Long Day's Journey into Night,* and *A Moon for the Misbegotten.*

One afternoon during my Beverly Hills visit we'd had a particularly enjoyable session on my play, and later Odets expressed his confidence that I would soon find a producer for it. And then he said a little diffidently, "And listen, I think I'd like to direct it. Yes—I really would." I was delighted. I assured him nothing would make me happier. "I'd be good for the play," he said, trailing off, and then adding soberly, "and it would be good for me."

Movement in the theater being what it is, two years went by before my producer was ready to cast the play. He enthusiastically agreed that Odets should be the director and suggested I call and offer him $5,000. It happened that Clifford was free of movie commitments that fall, and he thanked me for my loyalty to him, but he simply couldn't afford to come East for that kind of money. I pointed out that he'd be receiving a fair percentage of the gross as director, we wouldn't necessarily die at the box office, we'd pick up his expenses, and so on. It was all terribly tempting, but no, thanks. A quarter-of-a-million dollars worth of Paul Klee on his walls, I thought bitterly, but he can't afford the theater! Where does he think he made that money, cutting velvet? In the end, we did die at the box office, but he might have delayed it.

The last time I saw Odets was February, 1963, in New York. He took me to dinner at the Plaza and was generously consoling about the failure of my play. I was blaming myself for the frantic rewriting I had done in Philadelphia and Boston which effectively drained off the strength of the original version. He assured me that it couldn't have been my fault, it was probably *them*. Depressed as I was, I couldn't help laughing.

When he signed on as script editor of *The Richard Boone Show*, he tried to get N.B.C. to approve an old script of mine which he had always liked. They turned it down, and he wrote me a note expressing his scorn and disgust with his TV *gauleiters*. That summer I fell into a spell of vivid dreams. I would wake in the morning remembering the dreams, something unusual for me. One night I dreamed that Clifford had died. In the morning I told my wife about it. That evening I received a call from a writer who had been my classmate in

Clifford's playwriting course. He told me that Odets was dead of cancer.

Jeanne-Marie A. Miller (essay date June 1976)

SOURCE: "Odets, Miller and Communism," in *CLA Journal*, Vol. XIX, No. 4, June, 1976, pp. 484-93.

[*In the following excerpt, Miller discusses Odets's* Till the Day I Die *and places it within the social and political contexts of its day.*]

Between the time of the October Revolution and the Stalin-Hitler Pact, many European and American literati were attracted to communism. Some chose communism at a definite time in history because they had lost faith in democracy and they wanted to defeat fascism. When Hitler came to power in Germany, the Soviet Union felt threatened, and out of this uneasiness came "a Russian foreign policy based on support of collective security measures against aggression." Communist parties then adopted the Popular Front, whose purpose was to create political coalitions of all anti-fascist groups. The Communists continued to be effective and consistent opponents of the rising power of Nazi Germany.

The conversion to communism of men of letters, often people of unusual sensitivity, expressed feelings sometimes shared by the inarticulate masses who felt that Russia was on the side of the working class. The compelling attraction of "an active comradeship of struggle involving personal sacrifice and abolishing differences of class and race"—was often too great to be resisted.

An American man of letters who joined the Communist party and used his pen to warn theatrical audiences against fascism was Clifford Odets. In 1935, in the midst of the Great Depression in America, *Till the Day I Die* was produced on Broadway and became one of the first serious anti-Nazi plays to reach the commercial theatre. This one-act play was suggested to Odets by a letter purporting to be from Nazi Germany. He had read this letter in *The New Masses*.

Using the expressionistic method, Odets divides his play into seven startling scenes. The action in *Till the Day I Die* takes place in Berlin in 1935, a time when Germany is undergoing economic distress. Ernst Tausig, a Communist working with the underground press, believes that the recently published leaflet will make the Nazis perspire once it gets into the workers' hands: "Workers might like to know the American embargo on German goods has increased 50% in the last six months." Wages are low, prices for vital foods have increased, and unemployment is widespread. The purpose of this underground newspaper is to inform the people of the *real* state of affairs in Germany. There is great distrust among the people, for the Nazis have infiltrated the ranks of the Communists, and Communist sympathizers, in turn, have joined the Nazi party.

The lives of the people in this troubled land have altered drastically. Ernst, once a violinist, has become an active member of the Communist underground in order to combat fascism. The party members, however, are full of hope. Ernst's dream of the world is for happy people everywhere:

> I ask for hope in eyes: for wonderful baby boys and girls I ask, growing up strong and prepared for a new world. I won't ever forget the first time we visited the nursery in Moscow. Such faces on those children! Future engineers, doctors; when I saw them I understood most deeply what the revolution meant.

Because the times are not conducive to marriage, he and his fiancee, Tillie, postpone theirs to a more favorable time. When the Secret Police enter their underground room, Tillie convinces them that she is a prostitute and Ernst is her customer. At the close of this scene, Odets employs the dramatic device of shrill whistles, variously pitched, which slow with hysterical intensity.

In a scene which takes place inside a Brown House where Ernst is taken as a prisoner, Odets shows some of the forms of Nazi brutality. Schlegel, the interrogator, asks Ernst, whom he knows to be a musician, to place his "sensitive hands" upon the desk, an action which is followed by the smashing of the prisoner's fingers with a rifle butt. This cruel act eventually results in the amputation of Ernst's right hand. The captured Communist, however, adamantly refuses to reveal the requested information to the Nazis. In the barracks the soldiers amuse themselves by seeing who, with the strongest blow to the head, can knock unconscious the unfortunate prisoners.

Major Duhring, a Nazi officer who is a Communist sympathizer, warns Ernst of the dangers he will encounter, for the Nazis are determined to obtain certain information from him, such as the names and addresses of party officials. They plan to beat Ernst savagely, nurse him back to health, and inform his comrades that he is a stool pigeon. They will place him next to the Nazi driver when they make raids and will stand him outside the courtroom when his friends are tried for treason. In order to carry out their plans, Ernst will be released immediately so that he can be followed by the Nazis who expect him to make contacts with other party members. Duhring advises Ernst to kill himself. Before long, Duhring and Schlegel have an encounter, and Schlegel is killed. Schlegel has investigated Duhring and found Jewish blood. Unknown to the others, Duhring has been destroying files containing valuable information. His parting words to Ernst

echo the philosophy of the Popular Front. He tells Ernst to let the people work for a united front in every capitalist country in the world. After Ernst leaves, the major removes his Nazi arm band, tears the Nazi flag from the wall, and kills himself.

When Ernst goes to Tillie, he learns that she is pregnant with his child. Despite the present gloom there is hope—hope that even if the two adults are not fortunate enough to live to see "strange and wonderful things," their unborn child will live in a better world.

The Nazis follow the procedure outlined by the sympathetic major. Even though Ernst is not guilty, the Communist underground cannot afford to take chances on his doubtful status. Ernst, then, is blacklisted by his group. His brother Carl states fervently the belief of the party: "There is no brother, no family, no deeper mother than the working class." As the scene ends, Tillie slowly raises her hand to be counted among the affirmative voters who expel her lover from the party.

In the final scene, a sick, lonely, and desperate Ernst comes to see his brother, who appears convinced that Ernst is working for the Nazis. Ernst, broken in mind and body, makes a final attempt to clear himself of the spy charges—to clear himself before his lover, his brother, and his comrades. His recitation is a tale of horror, and he begs his brother to kill him. Carl, of course, refuses but tells Ernst that if he destroys himself, the world will know that he is innocent. Before putting the gun into his mouth and firing the shot that ends his life, Ernst exclaims that although their agony is real, they live in the joy of a great and coming people:

> . . . The animal kingdom is past. Day must follow the night. Now we are ready: we have been steeled in a terrible fire, but soon all the desolate places of the world must flourish with human genius. Brothers will live in the soviets of the world! Yes, a world of security and freedom is waiting for all mankind!

Ernst remains faithful to his ideal, and the bitter drama closes on a note of hope.

Till the Day I Die met with disfavor from those who were not in sympathy with its theme. When the play was produced on the West Coast during the 1930's, Will Geer, who was affiliated with the production, was severely beaten by hoodlum sympathizers with the New Germany. In New York, Odets was forced to put a heavy lock on the door of his apartment. Some drama critics wrote unfavorable reviews of the play. Brooks Atkinson, for example, felt that Odets' communistic devotionals would best appeal to the party ear. If one wishes to register an emotional appeal against Nazi polity, declares Atkinson, Odets requires him to join the Communist party.

Despite its flaws, among them the scenes depicting Nazi brutality, Edith Isaacs writes that *Till the Day I Die* is "dramatic, honest, direct, mounting to its climax by a progress in characterization and a deepening of situation until there is no escape for either the man or the idea." When I reread the play after several years, I was touched by the poetic beauty of many of the lines in this otherwise stark drama.

Dissatisfaction with the economic and political situation in Germany caused the Communists to protest and engage in an active fight for a change. Increased military forces and the production of armaments were the basis of Hitler's economic recovery. Odets, in *Till the Day I Die,* implies that German Nazism, paralleled in capitalistic countries, was as great a threat to American hopes and integrity as it was to the German people. Odets felt that monopolistic capitalism was growing vicious or fascist. The struggle depicted in *Till the Day I Die* was for true democracy everywhere. As an artist as well as a social and political critic, Odets devised an expressionistic method that would arouse his audience to the dangers of fascism everywhere. . . .

Benjamin Appel (essay date Summer 1976)

SOURCE: "Odets University," in *The Literary Review*, Vol. 19, No. 4, Summer, 1976, pp. 470-75.

[*Appel was an American novelist, short story writer, poet, and one-time student of Odets. In the following essay, he relates his personal experience with Odets and discusses Odets's role at the House Un-American Activities Committee Hearings in the 1950's.*]

"Odets University" was my nickname for the playwrighting class Clifford Odets conducted for one memorable session in 1951 at the Actors Studio.

Everything was free. Tuition. Tickets to Broadway plays. Advice after class as well as free drinks in some nearby bar or at Odets' home in the East 60's. Quite a few of the "graduates" would see their plays produced—as Clifford Odets, president, dean and faculty had hoped—and with the cry of *Author! Author!* in effect be awarded their "degrees." William Gibson who had submitted a play on the life of the young Shakespeare (admission to "Odets University" depended on an approved script) would write *Two for the See-Saw*, and Louis Peterson would be acclaimed as an important playwright after the production of his *Take a Giant Step*. Leslie Wiener, Jack Levine, Jimmy McGee and four or five other students whose names skip me would make it to Broadway or Off-Broadway.

It so happened that I had written a play based on one of my novels and like a thousand—or were there ten thousand other would-be playwrights in New York?—I had read about the

projected class in the theatrical pages of the *New York Times*. I mailed mine in, it was accepted, and with some fifteen other successful applicants was admitted to the sessions. We met twice a week; each session lasted four hours with a break in the middle. Odets' theatrical knowledge, his patience, his generosity apparently had no limits. Once, he missed a class due to illness, to return, wrapped in a muffler with a bottle of medicine on his desk.

It was inevitable, however, as we smoked and chatted during the breaks for some of us to speculate about his motives. After all weren't we observers of mankind?

"Clifford's psychiatrist must've advised him to do good. . ."

"He's compensating for the money he made in Hollywood. . ."

We had no dearth of amateur psychiatrists. There were also one or two self-appointed commissars of culture:

"Clifford's full of guilt for the years he spent writing movie crap. . ."

The commissars had no use for *The Country Girl,* starring Uta Hagen, a Broadway hit. We had all seen it—those free tickets! and Odets had analyzed it in class, discussing the problems he had faced and their solutions. When he was done dissecting a scene he would throw the floor open for a general discussion.

Even his harshest critics in the class admitted that, "Clifford took it on the chin . . ." But one afternoon he exploded when his play was torn apart as being too commercial, too slick, too Hollywood. He reminded his leftist critics that he was a pro and that we were all beginners. The class was shocked. Hadn't Odets himself declared at the opening sessions that we were all peers, all students of the theatre?

He had been so unprofessionally open, so modest, answering every sort of question. Nothing was barred. Questioned about his politics he had unhesitatingly replied that he was a radical . . .

To me, Clifford Odets was a semi-legendary figure whose first plays *Waiting for Lefty, Awake and Sing, Rocket to the Moon* had given shape and voice to the 1930's, that decade of hunger and hope when so many writers, Odets among them, had, as the popular phrase put it, "gone left." His early plays made him famous. Airborne to Hollywood, the golden Olympus, he was soon a top writer of movie scripts. Perhaps, he would have remained there if the House Un-American Affairs Committee or HUAC hadn't pulled the curtain on a real-life drama that for all too many years would fascinate the nation. Like that epic of the silent movies, *The Perils of Pauline*, the HUAC production—it could be called The Red

Menace—was a non-stop serial running on and on, featured on the front pages of the national press.

The first scene of the first act—Time: 1947—starred the Hollywood Ten, among them Dalton Trumbo, Ring Lardner Jr., Albert Maltz, John Howard Lawson. Scene followed scene, involving still other alleged Communists, fellow travellers, left-wingers: a dazzling fireworks into which "unfriendly witnesses" (that is all who invoked the Fifth Amendment or so-called "Red Amendment") would be tossed. The show went on and on. If "unfriendly witnesses" defied the inquisitors, the "friendly witnesses" beat their once-upon-a-time red or pink breasts and hastily decked themselves out in red-white-and-blue brassieres. Some of the "friendlys" were genuinely sincere, genuinely disillusioned in—their once fervent faith in the haloed Josef Stalin, the Red Jesus. Still others, driven to the confessional box by plain sweaty fear, hoped to save their careers.

No use listing their names. All suffered. The men and women who resisted the pressures to conform, and the many whose principles had either changed or had never been more than skin-deep; red on top, white beneath, like the proverbial radish. HUAC purged Hollywood and when they moved on to other arenas, the blacklist remained. The movie moguls, of course, denied its existence but somehow or other if you weren't "friendly" you were, as they said in Hollywood, as good as dead.

There was also the gray list, so-called because the fate of the listees—writers, directors, actors—still had to be decided. Clifford Odets was one of the gray listees when he returned to New York in 1951 with his actress wife Betty Gray and their children, rented an apartment whose walls displayed his paintings: a mini-museum of Utrillos and Modiglianis.

My first meeting with Clifford Odets wasn't at the Actors Studio but at a party whose guests included Erwin Piscator and Mrs. Berthold Brecht, refugees from Hitler's Germany. Brecht himself had already returned to the eastern and Communist half. Odets, that evening was tense and uncommunicative. Only afterwards would I guess at some of his anxieties. There he was newly arrived in New York, a refugee himself, self-expelled from his native land—for Hollywood like some legendary kingdom has always belonged to its conquerors. He was no longer the young dramatic poet who had flashed like a revolutionary meteor over New York in the 1930's. Still youthful in appearance, the intelligence in his dark eyes like some invisible and preservative glue binding together mouth, chin, nose and high forehead, he was nevertheless in his middle forties. And no actor—and he had been an actor before becoming a playwright—can ignore the calendar reflected in his mirror.

He only came to life when Piscator criticized Odets' play,

The Big Knife, the first he had written since his early successes. I had seen it before meeting the playwright and hadn't cared for it. *The Big Knife* was one of those plays in which art and politics had been shaken together to make an unsatisfactory cocktail. The characters were Hollywood personalities typical of what might be called the HUAC 1950's; torn between their youthful beliefs and the pressures to keep silent, to conform, to betray. There was passion in the play and there was also hysteria as if *the big knife* had wounded Odets where no writer can afford to be wounded: his artistic vision. Piscator's barbs were sharp. Odets tried to defend his play, arguing that like a painting a play had to be seen more than once before a final judgement . . .

I have gone into some detail on my first meeting with Clifford Odets—offstage business so to speak—but necessary I feel in understanding the playwright who had left Hollywood and would soon found "Odets University." He had told us he was a radical, a man of the left . . . I would soon remember that statement of his. There is no doubt that he was already formulating what he would say when summoned by HUAC; rehearsing the role he would play when the lights came on full glare.

Several of his more intransigent critics dropped out of the class. The "off campus" gossip became more caustic. I found myself defending him. What difference did it make, I argued whether Odets felt guilty for his "wasted Hollywood years" or whether his psychoanalyst (if he had one) had told him to Do Good or whether *The Country Girl* was inferior to *Awake and Sing*. What mattered were his actions: the four-hour classes; the playdoctoring conferences at his home *including* weekends. We were lucky, I said, to have Clifford as our teacher.

At the occasional parties he gave at his home for his students and their wives or girl friends, Odets would sometimes ask me for my opinion about his venture. Perhaps, because I was more observer than active student; I hadn't done a thing with the play I had submitted, too busy preparing a new novel for publication—perhaps because like Odets himself I had come of literary age in the 1930's—anyway he was eager to know what I thought. And always I assured this unsure man of how much we appreciated the time, the energy, the knowledge that went into each session. He would visibly relax to hear me.

In the spring of 1951 "Odets University" shut down although he continued working with students at his home, reading their revised scripts and suggesting changes. Then, what he must have expected and feared came to pass. HUAC summoned him to Washington.

I followed the Hearings in the press and later read the full record issued by the Government Printing Office. It seemed to me that two different men had testified before the Committee. A defiant Odets who eloquently upheld the Constitution and the Bill of Rights. And a confused, worried Odets who eventually revealed the names of friends and associates who had once been Communists as Odets had been himself. He had "named names" and yet as I heard on the grapevine he didn't regard himself as an informer or as a "friendly witness." Hadn't all the names been named by previous witnesses? It was true. They had been named and Odets felt, it seemed, that he had divulged nothing new or incriminating.

All I was certain of was that I had no right to judge him. That right only belonged to those who themselves had faced the inquisitors. I hadn't been called to testify. I had never known— I could only imagine—the agonies of a man confronted by professional patriots who had the power to pin an updated scarlet letter on the chest of any witness they deemed to be unfriendly. What I did was write Clifford Odets a note in which I expressed my sympathy. I had to do that much. I couldn't forget his generosity, not only to me, but to all of us in that class of his.

This is his reply:

6/17/52

Dear Ben Appel—

I was glad to have your note. For the most part the judgements (so judgmental everyone is!) of what I did and said in Washington have been disgustingly mechanical, based on a few lines printed in newspapers, right or left, when actually there were three hundred pages of typed transcript. Personally, I find this a disturbingly immoral time and this immorality exists as much on the left as on the right. Personal clarity, in my opinion, is the first law of the day— that plus a true and real search for personal identity. I don't believe in any party or group doing my thinking or directing for me. When I find out what I mean it may in some small measure be what this country means and that I will say in play or plays. I hope you are well and writing as I am on the verge of being and doing.

Best regards,
Clifford Odets

He would return to Hollywood to write movie scripts. There would be no new plays. *The Big Knife, The Country Girl* and *The Flowering Peach*—this last written while he still lived in New York—completed what theatrical critics would call his opus. He died some years back but his plays, the last plays and the first plays, remain to tell his story.

Real writers like Clifford Odets always write their own auto-

biographies in their plays or novels. The formal biographies are necessary, of course, and no doubt they will appear.

Richard J. Dozier (essay date Fall 1978)

SOURCE: "Recovering Odets' *Paradise Lost*," in *Essays in Literature*, Vol. 5, No. 2, Fall, 1978, pp. 209-221.

[*In the following essay, Dozier examines* Paradise Lost, *a play originally criticized for being an inferior version of* Awake and Sing!, *Odets's first work. Dozier looks beyond superficial similarities between the two plays to analyze several distinct differences between them.*]

Paradise Lost has always occupied a special place in the Odets canon. For one thing neither the playwright nor his admirers ever quite gave up on the play. In the Preface to the 1939 *Six Plays* collection Odets described the piece as his "favorite" despite its poor reception as "a practical theatre work," and twenty years later he was still defending the play by admitting its faults but suggesting that they had somehow grown out of its virtues: "It's too jammed, too crowded, it spills out of its frame, but it is in many ways a beautiful play, velvety; the colors were very gloomy and rich. And no one who acted in it or saw it in that (original) production will ever forget it." So it would seem: when *Paradise Lost* was recently produced for public television, Harold Clurman, together with Luther and Stella Adler, stepped forward to praise Odets' achievement and to provide nostalgic comment on his first theatrical "failure." About some matters, at least, the Group could still be fervent.

Most of the critics who attended the December, 1935, opening of *Paradise Lost* were less enthusiastic. On the whole they discovered a play that by comparison with the earlier *Awake and Sing!* seemed "overwrought" and "confused." Indeed, the latter charge was made with numbing recurrency as reviewer after reviewer found fault with the play's sprawling characterization and plot structure. The new play was not of course without its defenders, even outside the ranks of the Group. John Gassner, who in January of the following year had already praised Odets' "realistic symbolism" in a long and thoughtful *New Theatre* article, in June reiterated his belief in the play's importance and suggested that it "involved a stylization and an abundance of content that laid the work open to misunderstanding." Nevertheless, in the years since it first appeared *Paradise Lost* has remained open to the kind of "misunderstanding" that characterized its initial reception in 1935. For the most part, it has continued to be regarded as a poorly managed reworking of material the author had dealt with more successfully in *Awake and Sing!* or an even more glaring example of the artistic collapse that could overtake a leftist playwright who forced ideological concerns on his art. The persistence of this view is most evident in Edward Murray's *Clifford Odets: The Thirties and After* (1968). In the long chapter he devotes to *Awake and Sing!* Murray provides us with the most thorough literary analysis of Odets' work to come out thus far, but in his zeal to establish Odets as a major playwright the author has felt it necessary to dismiss three of the early plays that made Odets famous. *Waiting for Lefty* is mentioned only briefly as an example of the playwright's misguided political militancy, and *Paradise Lost* is ignored along with *Till the Day I Die* since "neither," in Murray's opinion, "can add any luster to Odets' critical reputation."

Interestingly enough, there is less overt Marxism in *Paradise Lost* than in *Awake and Sing!* where Jacob's political platitudes are constantly at the mercy of Odets' ironies. Pike, the furnace man who serves as the play's resident revolutionary, remains as confused throughout as the other characters, and as someone nicely observes after one of his jeremiads, "all this radical stuff is like marrying the colored maid." But neither the presence nor absence of political theorizing in itself explains what happens in *Paradise Lost,* nor can such considerations ultimately dispel the objections lodged against Leo Gordon's hopeful speech at the play's close. Moreover, though the comparison with *Awake and Sing!* is both inevitable and instructive, the similarity between the two plays breaks down, for while the positive ending of *Awake and Sing!* is the result of a carefully sustained imagistic and gestural pattern, it is the abortiveness of this pattern that is everywhere emphasized in *Paradise Lost.* As Gerald Rabkin has noted, "the image is starker than that of *Awake and Sing!* because the seeds of redemption, although present in the play, are not allowed to flower." Odets' reluctance to establish this redemptive motif is the chief of the differences which separate *Paradise Lost* from his previous work, differences which suggest that in his final play of 1935 he was beginning to explore several new directions in his art. In order to appreciate Odets' achievement in *Paradise Lost* we must look beyond the similarity between Leo Cordon's and Ralph Berger's final speeches, as well as certain other elements common to both plays—we must even be prepared to admit that in the final act of *Paradise Lost* Odets' actual accomplishment may have run counter to his conscious intentions. But to do so is to be more fully aware of the "rich" and "gloomy" colors Odets was striving for in a work that represents a deeper, though more troubling, vision than that in *Awake and Sing!*

ii

Impatient with the Group's reluctance to produce *Awake,* Odets had already completed a considerable portion of his second full-length play before the first was produced. "My impulse," he later told interviewer Arthur Wagner, "was—well if they didn't like or think *Awake and Sing!* was good enough, I would in a certain sense try to write *Awake and Sing!* better." One consequence of this effort was the strong similarity between the two plays that disgruntled some of

Paradise Lost's reviewers. As the idiom in the Gordon household makes clear, theirs is still another urban Jewish family. Unlike the apartment-dwelling Bergers, the Gordons are part-owners of a small business and own their own home. The crash, however, has taken its toll, and the house has been mortgaged to keep the business going. The list of "boarders," which includes Leo's partner Sam Katz, has grown considerably over that in the earlier play, but the paradoxical situation created by the presence of so many "homeless" people under one roof is essentially the same as in *Awake.*

In both plays the press of economic conditions has either discouraged or deeply affected the romantic attachments of the young people. Like Ralph and Blanche, Pearl Gordon and her Felix reluctantly break off their engagement because of money; but no such misgivings prevent Ben Gordon, the one-time Olympic runner and pride of the family, from entering into a precipitous marriage with Libby Michaels that proves as unfortunate as the one in *Awake.* There are noticeable similarities between the lovers in the two plays. In her thwarted desire for happiness—"I want fun out of life!"—Libby appears to be a coarser, more calloused version of Hennie; and Ben's cuckoldry at the hands of his sidekick Kewpie recalls the fate of Sam Feinschreiber in *Awake.* Kewpie's attachment to a married woman, his illegitimate source of income, even his general philosophy—"In case you'd like to know, I'm sore on my whole damn life"—are traits obviously carried over from the character of Moe Axelrod.

Most of the other characters in the play also show traces of having been modelled on those in *Awake.* Libby's father, Gus Michaels, resembles *Awake's* Myron Berger both in his talk about movie stars and his preoccupation with the past; the blustery Sam Katz has replaced Uncle Morty as a spokesman from the capitalist class; and Pike, who takes over Jacob's function as political chorus to the action, is a not-too-distant relative of Schlosser, *Awake's* unhappy janitor. Finally, though there is more than a touch of Bessie Berger in Clara Gordon—her house, like Bessie's, is a matriarchy—it is the self-effacing Bertha Katz who, without any of Bessie's aggressive outer coating, eventually exercises the kind of control over her infantile husband that is practiced on Myron Berger.

More importantly, the Gordon household is another variation of the Odetsian "crazy house" whose inner disorder is designed to reflect the disarray in the world outside. As in *Awake,* that world is suffering from what Leo calls "a profound dislocation." "The whole world's fallin' to pieces, right under our eyes," Gus exclaims. One senses the disintegration in the physical impairments of the family members whom Clara repeatedly addresses as "lunatics." Leo Gordon is given to nose-bleeds at critical moments; Ben can no longer run because of a bad heart; and his brother Julie, who suffers from encephalitis, is a walking corpse. Perhaps the most ominous sign of conditions in the Gordon house is that the "ants" detected earlier by Myron Berger have now grown into "spiders" whose presence in the cellar of the building suggests that its very foundation is decayed and crumbling. Clara's warning to Leo that "The lock on the back door's broken again"—coming as it does on the heels of the call about Ben's death—contributes further to the overall impression that things are falling apart in Odets' symbolic house.

In *Paradise Lost* the emphasis is once again less on economics than on what Pike calls "the depression of modern man's spirit"; and the atmosphere in the Gordon house provides an appropriate setting for the distorted human relationships that constitute the pattern of Odets' particular wasteland vision. The reversal of parental and sexual roles, for instance, is occasionally more striking here than in the earlier play. In contrast to her shy and retiring husband, Clara Gordon takes the initiative when Sam Katz complains about the "bums" who move freely about the house, and her threat to "knock out his teeth" is almost made good when Katz attempts to prevent his wife from airing the truth about their life together. Near the end of the play when Phil Foley, the demagogic leader of the Nemo Democratic Club, demands that the Gordon furniture be removed from the sidewalk lest it interfere with his "prosperity block party," it is Clara who defies him, and she has to be restrained when Foley returns with two detectives. While she is always tolerant and indulgent toward Leo himself—"I found out many years ago I married a fool, but I love him"—her several references to playing "poker" with the "girls" are comic reminders that their relationship is not perhaps what it should be.

The most startling instance of the breakdown of conventional marital roles, however, is reserved for the scene in which Bertha finally reveals why the Katzes have no children. Prior to this Sam has always pretended that the fault lay with his wife, an explanation that has seemed plausible because of the wig a previous illness has forced her to wear. In fact, part of Sam's antagonism toward the shop delegation stems from his resentment that "A fly spot like Gerson should have a baby!" while "a man like an ox can't have a son." He still clings to this illusion, even on the brink of this confession to Leo: "In the circus they got a bearded lady . . . (and) in my house I got a baldy woman!" Pressured from all sides, however, Sam can no longer conceal either his theft of the company money or his sexual failure, and Gus Michaels' prophetic riddle about "a woman who sleeps with cats" is borne out in Bertha's disclosure of his impotency:

> BERTHA: All right, we can't have children.
> SAM: Tell everybody, tell the world!
> BERTHA: He didn't go out with girls. I never worried about that.
> SAM: No, no, no. . . . *(Falls on his knees in the outer hall and writhes in prayer on the lower step.)*

> BERTHA: We have upstairs a closet full of pills, medicine, electric machines. *For seven years Sam Katz didn't sleep with a girl*

Helped at last to his feet, the broken Katz makes his final exit, led away by a woman who turns out not to have been "childless" after all.

Although Sam Katz's collapse stands out in the play by virtue of its distressing suddenness, his predicament is not an isolated phenomenon in *Paradise Lost*. An imputation of childishness, sterility, or impotency—alike symbolic of the inability to order or direct their lives—hangs over most of the other males in the play. Leo, like Katz, cries in his sleep; Julie Gordon, Clara's "beautiful boy," asks his mother not to close her door at night; and Kewpie later tells Ben's parents that their elder son died because "He was a little kid in a man's world . . . you made him like that." More significantly, Sam Katz's references to his "baldy" wife form part of a pattern, reminiscent of the anecdote about the elder Feinschreiber in *Awake,* in which hair, beards, and barbering are associated with sexual or spiritual failure.

Despite his apparent fatherhood of Libby's child, Ben Gordon's ritual visits to the barbershop suggest that his "manhood" is in constant need of reassurance. Just such a stopover delays his initial appearance and the news of his and Libby's marriage. Asked to remove his hat, he at first refuses to do so: "Hear that? Pal o' my cradle days calling me a lunatic! Can't do it, Clara. Got to keep the haircomb in place. *(Shows hair)* Max worked an hour on it. But don't I make a bum out of a hat!" Later on in the play, when his dreams of a "berth on Wall Street" have shrunk to a corner toystand, Ben broods over his condition before making an unusual request of his father:

> BEN *(working the drumming toy):* Poor Mickey Mouse! That's it—always the army to join. Or the navy. Leo, if I wasn't afraid of missing Kewpie here, I'd ask a big favor.
> LEO: Ask it. . . .
> BEN: I'd ask to advance me a buck seventy-five and then go around to Harry's barber shop and get the whole works—haircut, massage and manicure. Believe you me, I'd like that feeling again.

The symbolic associations with which Odets invests Ben's behavior constantly interact with references elsewhere in the play. Felix, for example, confesses to Pearl that he is just "a worm in the ground," not "a wonderful guy—a musician with a big head of hair" (p. 182). And like Myron Berger—"The moment I began losing my hair I just knew I was destined to be a failure in life"—Gus Michaels, described in the stage directions as "*a small alert man with hair combed down to cover his baldness*" concludes: "I guess failure's gone to my head." Following his arrest over an incident involving a young girl, the man who has boasted that he is "sweet on the ladies" and has joked of having his own "harem" performs a ceremony that, like Myron's obsessive weighing, seems closely akin to Ben's visits to the barbershop:

> PIKE: Well, Gus is out there taking a shave.
> LEO: Two and three in the morning sometimes I find him shaving in front of the mirror.
> PIKE: He wants to look good.
> LEO: But three in the morning? For whom?
> PIKE: Man has to have something.

Characteristically, Odets draws together several strands of the pattern near the end of Act I where the play's three "fathers" gather to toast the newlyweds. Under the influence of the cognac which Leo has mistakenly poured for wine, the conversation turns from the young people to the speakers' recollections of their own fathers:

> PIKE: My father used to order sherry by the cask. He exorcised the devils by day, but at night, by George, they crawled all over him! . . .
> GUS: Ha, ha, ha.
> LEO: My father was a silent man. His hair was black as coal till the day he died. A silent man (maybe) he knew God intimately. I loved him like an idol.
> GUS: Why, he was a man with fur cuffs! Hair on his arms grew right down on his wrists—fur cuffs you would say.

The discussion does more than illustrate that the three are hopelessly tied to the past; the description of the elder Gordon is clearly calculated to evoke a comparison between the present "fathers" and the more vigorous beings who inhabit their childhood memories, a comparison that becomes immediately evident in Pike's adolescent show of strength with the bent coin. The elder Gordon may have known God "intimately," but as Clara pointedly reminds him, Leo doesn't even know his own business partner:

> LEO: Clara, I've trusted Sam for twenty-two years.
> CLARA: A lunatic can make a mistake.
> LEO (laughing): She's serious—a man I know intimately for thirty years.
> CLARA: Never mind! In business "intimately" don't grow hair on a bald men's head.

Moreover, the "idol" worshipped in the Gordon house not only possesses a weak heart—he is sexually suspect. When we first see them together, Kewpie is strangely incensed because someone at the barbershop has called Ben an "nance," and their intensely close relationship gradually casts doubt

on Kewpie's otherwise lustful attachment to Libby. In the midst of one of their reconciliations, Libby asks: "What's this, a love duet?" The hint of homosexuality here is fully realized elsewhere: the titular Milton of Odets' "Paradise Lost" is Phil Foley's lisping assistant (p. 167). Seen in this broad context, Ben's otherwise innocent tomfoolery at the picture-taking ceremony in which he holds the raccoon tail from Gus's motorcycle to his chin (p. 171) reveals more than the customary uncertainty about the step he and Libby have just taken.

As in the earlier play, the dilemma of the frustrated or failed artist is another symptom of the widespread unhappiness in Odets' crazy house. The situation of musicians Felix and Pearl comes readiest to mind, but the list includes others. Pike, for example, is reduced to employing his graphic skills in the depiction of dying men, and Ben Gordon's description of the exhilaration that comes with running suggests that his future inability to do so represents an even more alarming loss of self-expression: "Last night I couldn't sleep. All the way over to the new bridge, I walked. Stood there for a long time looking in the water. Then I began to run, down the street. I used to like to be out front. When I fell in that rhythm and knew my reserve—the steady driving forward—I sang inside when I ran. Yeah, sang like an airplane, powerful motors humming in oil. I wanted to run till my heart exploded . . . a funny way to die. . . ." Although Julie Gordon, unlike Jacob, rarely exhibits "*the flair of an artist*," it is significant that his "runs" on the billiard table, like his "runs" on the market, always go unnoticed. Leo's case is much clearer: "Mr. Gordon don't know!" Sam tells the shop delegation: "I run the business, he sits with artistic designs—."

In *Paradise Lost* images of entrapment, suffocation, and drowning appear in greater profusion than in *Awake*. "Under the roar of Niagara," Leo asks, "can a man live a normal life?" "There's your children, you, Sam Katz," Pike tells him, "—a big hand got itself around you, squeezin' like all hell gone on!" Kewpie calls Libby "A sleeping clam at the bottom of the ocean"; and when Clara asks, "How's business?" Ben cryptically replies: "Swimming without my water wings by now." Appropriately, it is Kewpie's alliance with "Joe the Shark" that momentarily permits him to thrive in an atmosphere that destroys Ben.

"Did you ever hear of a crazier proposition in all your born days?" Clara says of Leo's attempt to give away the German canary. The comic episode with which the play begins is not only Leo's first futile effort at repudiation; the birdcage, like the one that harbors Florrie in *Waiting for Lefty,* is also an image of physical and spiritual imprisonment. "Dope! You were sick in bed for two months!" Julie's mother tells him: "You expect to fly like an eagle the first week?" "Home is a prison," Sam Katz laments: "Sing Sing, my house—it's not different." Gus Michaels' pathetic "singing" appears to be an attempt to make his cage a pleasant place: "Goldfish and canary birds. I love to have them things around the house. *(Suddenly he is whistling vigorously like a canary)* I'm a son of a gun how he comes singin' out of me, this little bird!" "Don't you worry your head about them turtledoves," he says of Ben and Libby. By the end of the play, however, it is clear that Gus' optimistic stratagem has failed: "Leo, Clara, we had so much sorrow outa life, and now we want a good time! Sky rockets bustin' in the house! Ventriloquism! Beasts and birds!" *(Suddenly he is gloriously trilling like a bird. But the whistle ends in defeat.)* Ben's marriage to Libby and the announcement about his heart condition signal an end to the kind of "flight" he talks about. A moment or so before his own "song" for the cameraman, Post says to him: "I used to think you'd get married in an airplane." Libby is a "beautiful" but more earthbound "machine," however, than the metaphorical airplane of Ben's and Ralph Berger's reveries. Besides, as Kewpie later observes, Ben is a "burnt out spark plug."

Just as in the earlier play, images of escape exist alongside those of entrapment. Gus' desire to "go far away to the South Sea Isles and eat coconuts" obviously recalls the attractions of Moe Axelrod's "land of Yama Yama," but the expression of such hopes is muted in *Paradise Lost* and the paradisiacal retreats are even more suspicious:

> PIKE: Our country is the biggest and best pig-sty in the world!
> GUS: I don't know no better place, Mr. P.
> PIKE: I do. All picked out for me: the bottom of the ocean.

Ben Gordon's final run, we remember—both the one he describes, and the real one—ends in death.

The similarities between the two plays, however, have already taken us into the important differences between them. Even the overall structure they appear to have in common— the lyrical summation at the end of the first act, the announcement of death at the close of the second, and the "lifting" speech at the curtain—emphasizes the superficiality of their resemblance; for while young Ralph Berger is on his feet and singing at the end of *Awake,* the "Representative American youth" in *Paradise Lost* is dead before the final act begins.

iii

One of the major differences between Odets' first and second full-length play lies in the characterization. The difference in this case goes beyond the tendency toward allegory in *Paradise Lost* that led some critics to dismiss the characters as merely types or "case histories." In *Awake* the almost identical challenge facing the two sets of lovers was significant because of the way in which Odets' paired characters (Ralph-Moe, Blanche-Hennie) complemented each other. In *Paradise Lost* this kind of parallelism is more fully exploited, and the device of pairing characters is carried even further.

Nearly everyone in the Gordon household is provided with a "mate" or counterpart. Pike carries in his watch a picture of the two sons he has lost in the war. When Gus Michaels accidentally tunes the radio to an Armistice Day plea for rededication to "country" and "flag," the former recalls the hard times he and others have had to go through: "We lived on and hoped. We lived on garbage dumps. Two of us found canned prunes, ate them and were poisoned for weeks. One died. Now I can't die. But we gave up to despair and life took quiet years. We worked a little. Nights I drank myself insensible. Punched my own mouth." Several matters are worth noting here. First of all, Leo's situation will be much the same by the end of the play, for he will also have "lost" both his sons. Furthermore, Pike's self-flagellation during this speech suggests the peculiar love-hate relationship that exists between Kewpie and Ben. What is most interesting about Pike's outburst, however, is that the account of his poisoned friend implies that Pike himself is now only half alive, that part of him has somehow died in the past. When Clara tries to convince Julie that he will soon be back at his old post at the bank, the other knows better: "I don't believe it! In high school we had a kid named Gilbert. He had sleeping sickness, too. When he came back to school he began to get old. In two years . . . he died." A moment later, when Julie asks Gus if he likes "open-air cars," the latter is reminded of the picture he carries in his own watch: "No, I don't like open-air cars. Mrs. Michaels was killed like that. She was a very nervous woman and put her head out. . . . My wife had one blue eye and one grey eye—there's no use denyin' it, Julie . . . and if you want the whole truth, she was cockeyed; but I loved her very much." The circumstances of Mrs. Michaels' death provided us with a shocking correlate to Sam Katz's "baldy woman," and the condition of her eyes reminds us that we are once again in the "cockeyed world" against which *Lefty's* Agate Keller rebels. Near the end of the play when it is clear that Pearl's piano must be surrendered along with the house, Gus recalls the fate of still another acquaintance: "An old friend of mine, Harry Meyers, he used to be in the piano business. A fine and dandy man, but slow in the head. Then he went out on the ocean—April 1912. There was a marine disaster! The sinking of the *Titanic* . . . ." When we remember that Leo's business partnership as well as his marriage date from that year, it is clear that the story of Harry Meyers applies not only to Pearl, but to the "marine disaster" that is overtaking the other denizens of the Gordon house.

Just as the stories concerning off-stage characters often give the impression that the people in the play are only partially themselves, so several of the "pairings" within the play strongly suggest the disintegration of personality and purpose, and an inevitable drift towards death. From the division of responsibilities at the Cameo Shop it appears that the crisis that befalls Sam and Leo is the result of a fateful split between the material and moral consciousness. The "intimacy" of their relationship goes much deeper than their mutual rejection of the family pet; neither is willing to face the enormity of his incompleteness. What Leo finally fails to understand is that the childless Sam Katz's fate is his own and that he, too, "died . . . far back."

The tragic division of sensibility from which Leo suffers is also conspicuous in his son and daughter. Kewpie is more than Ben's "man Friday": "*I'm in you like a tape worm*," his friend tells him—"Yeah, a carbon copy who hates your guts," Libby warns. Though their outward personalities are different—Kewpie arouses Libby sexually, Ben "tells" her "poems"—the toy-doll metaphor in the play suggests that Odets' all-American and his would-be gangster are mirror images for the corrupting drives and lost idealism each perceives in the other. Their fatal kinship is made even more explicit in Ben's recollection of the drowning death of Danny, a childhood friend whose death-dress resembles the formal attire adopted by Ben's dying brother:

> We're still under the ice, you and me—we never escaped! Christ, Kewpie! Are we the same kids who used to go up to Whitey Aimer's roof and watch the pigeons fly? You and me and Danny? There's one old pal we know what happened to, where he is. The three of us under the ice with our skates on and not being able to get him out. Then sticking him dead in the box. Dressed in a blue serge suit and a stiff white collar . . . Christ, Kewpie, tell me, tell me—who died there—me or you or him or what?

"I'm just as proud as she is . . . ," Libby cries when Pearl scolds her brother for having had the "nerve" to get married. The contrast between them is established with brutal frankness in Pike's response to Pearl's complaints about being "homesick": "There she is alone in her room with the piano—the white keys banked up like lilies and she suckin' at her own breast. . . . You! Lay awake dreamin' at night. Don't you know it ain't comin' that land of your dreams, unless you work for it?" Nevertheless, Kewpie unwittingly calls attention to their common predicament when he tells Libby that her "shell's lined with pearls." In effect, Libby's pursuit of "fun" is merely a distorted reflection of Pearl's sterile embrace of her piano and refusal to seize hold of life. Like their male counterparts, Odets' two young women also appear to be doomed. Pike's funereal portrait of Pearl recalls the story Gus tells of Libby's birth: "She was a seven months' baby. Just imagine, we never thought she'd live."

Even a cursory glance at some of the other characters in the play reveals that most of them also share a "paired" existence. The apparent exception in the case of Clara, although hers and Bertha's situations are in many ways alike, seems

not so much an inconsistency as Odets' way of insisting on her "wholeness." On the other hand, both Phil Foley and Post ("*a dark man with a dead face*") are accompanied by "assistants," and in the final act Odets' "homeless men," as well as his detectives, arrive at the house in groups of two.

The dialogue in *Paradise Lost* is also noticeably different from that of the earlier play. In the exchanges between Ben and Kewpie, in the revelations provided by Sam and Bertha, and especially in Pike's terrifying address to Pearl, there is a psychological nakedness and a luxuriance of metaphor that is not present in *Awake.* The altered tone of the dialogue in *Paradise Lost* is evident, for instance, in the ease with which the author's editorial comment on Bessie Berger—"*She knows that when one lives in the jungle one must look out for the wild life*"—finds its way into one of Kewpie's speeches.

As if these and the other non-realistic elements in *Paradise Lost* did not sufficiently alert us to its expressionism, Odets' grotesques prowl through the rubble of their dreams upon a stage that is literally strewn with symbols. Even a partial list (the bird-cage, Ben's statue, his medals, the mechanical toys, Gus' motorcycle, his stamp collection, his aviator's cap, Pearl's unseen piano) indicates the depth of association Odets has built around these objects whose gradual disappearance or destruction signals the "fall" of the Gordon "house." In the closing moments of the play the stage has been stripped bare, except for a few pieces of furniture and Gus' useless motorcycle. Only Ben's statue remains intact, the pathetic embodiment of the golden calf in Clara's biblical "bed-time" story.

As Gassner has suggested, much of the "confusion" in the early notices of *Paradise Lost* probably resulted from a "misunderstanding" of the dramaturgical differences between it and *Awake and Sing!*, a misunderstanding that was natural enough, considering the resemblances between the two plays. Nevertheless, steps were taken in the production of the play to reflect the shift toward expressionism. In an April 1936 *Theatre Arts* piece entitled "The Director Takes Command," Morton Eustis recorded several of Clurman's observations about the approach he had taken in staging the play:

> *Paradise Lost,* he decided, after some contemplation, gave him the impression of "a crystal ball revolving in space, with various refracted lights and shadows revolving about it." [Relating] this feeling (now intellectual in character, as well as emotional) still further to the "production quality" of the play, he realized that the drama should have a "slightly circular movement meandering, no straight motion"; that the "visual element"—"the setting"—should be realistic and yet abstract, "the line of the ceiling not straight, the shape of the room not completely realistic and yet giving the impression of realism, the color of the walls

of varying degrees of light and shade"; that the light-ing should convey the same quasi-realistic impres-sion.

To judge by some of the reviews, this approach was not suf-ficiently pursued. In fact, the Eustis article contains an ad-mission by Clurman that "the designer's project erred on the realistic side. The abstract intention was not made clear enough." But it may be that no amount of stylization could have enabled Odets' 1935 audience to make the transition from "Longwood Avenue" to "Shakespeare Place."

iv

The most important difference between *Paradise Lost* and *Awake,* however, lies neither in the characterization nor the setting of the plays, but in Odets' treatment of the redemptive motif he had established in the earlier work. There Jacob's sacrificial death had forcefully illustrated Odets' fundamen-tal belief that "older and more crushed human beings" could bequeath "lifting values to the younger generation." What Gerald Rabkin has aptly called the "seeds of redemption" are indeed present in *Paradise Lost*: throughout the play there are unmistakable traces of the gestural pattern Odets had employed before. But the failure of this pattern to "flower" in the later play is an indication that, whatever the author's in-tentions may have been, Leo Gordon's final speech must not be viewed in the same light as Ralph Berger's. On the con-trary, the expression of hope at the end of *Paradise Lost* is plainly overshadowed by the somber framework in which it is delivered.

Aside from Pike, the character in *Paradise Lost* who most nearly resembles Jacob is Gus Michaels. "God," he tells Clara, "I would make the world jump if I was a young man again!!" And like his predecessor who had great plans but "drank in-stead a glass tea," Gus has considered suicide: "I have my troubles, Mrs. G. Be surprised how often I think about it—takin' my own life by my own hand. . . . But I turn the radio on instead of the gas. . . ." Despite Clara's insistence that the hobby is his "whole life," it is significant that Gus parts not with his life, but with his stamp collection. That such a ges-ture is intended to represent a symbolic break with the past is evident in the way in which it is associated with Leo's own resolve to "wake up" and face reality following the visit of the shop delegation:

> LEO: My brain has been sleeping. My mind is made up: our workers must have better conditions! Tomor-row I mean to start fresh. In life we must face certain facts.
> GUS: Yes. Only last night I was thinkin' about sell-ing my stamp collection. I figure she's easily worth a few thousand—but I guess I could just never do it. . . .

But as a redemptive gesture, Gus' action is only a feeble imi-tation of Jacob's sacrifice.

The futility of Gus' "sacrifice" is reinforced by the failure that attends similar gestures by others in the final act of the play. Kewpie's proffer of money, for instance, obviously rep-resents an effort to repudiate the sense of guilt he feels over Ben's death. And only moments later, Kewpie's frustrating experience is repeated in Leo's attempt to bestow the money on the two "bums" whom Pike has ushered into the house. Much to his surprise, Leo's hollow and somewhat conde-scending offer—"If it were within my power I would restore to you a whole world which is rightfully yours"—is rejected by Paul: "I look at you and see myself seven years back. I been there. This kind of dream paralyzes the will—confuses the mind. Courage goes. Daring goes . . . and in the nights there is sighing. . . . You had a sorta little paradise here. Now you lost this paradise. That should teach you something. But no! You ain't awake yet." It is the bird-cage episode all over again. By the end of the play Leo is just where he started. He is no more aware of his affinity with Paul than he was of his tie with Sam Katz.

The inadequacy of their gestures is finally evident in the in-ability of *Paradise Lost's* "older" and "more crushed" char-acters to pass on anything to the younger generation. The need for such a legacy is stronger here than in the earlier play:

> BEN: Orphans of the storm! We are low enough to crawl under a snake! Julie, Pearl, rise and shine! One of the living heirs must amount to something in this goddam family!
> JULIE: Let's shoot some billiards, Ben.
> BEN: Sure, why not? Anything to kill time. Tell the world we're down in the cellar pushing balls around. Coast to coast.

The trouble is that by the end of *Paradise Lost* the Gordon children, unlike their counterparts in *Awake,* are as "dead" as the cushions on their billiard table. Leo Gordon may pro-claim that "Heartbreak and terror are not the heritage of man-kind" and that "No fruit tree wears a lock and key," but for the "sleepers" in the Gordon house it is too late. "Finished," Felix says to Pearl: "I'll say good-bye and you'll say goodbye." "Finished!" Sam shouts to the shop delegation. "Finished!" Clara says of the idolaters in her story: "God blot-ted them out of the book." "You have been took like a bull-dog takes a pussycat!" Paul informs Leo: "Finished!" The phrase runs like a litany through *Paradise Lost*. It is a litany for the dead.

v

A few years before his death Odets appeared to side with

some of his critics in explaining the problems posed by his early plays: "I think very simply that the material was always richer than the ideational direction that I tried to superimpose upon it. It was just enough to give birth to the material and let it say what it had to say." It seems clear, however, that regardless of what ideological concerns may have prompted Odets to fashion the play as he did, *Paradise Lost* does "say what it has to say." That Odets built better than he knew becomes apparent if we attempt to replace the ending we have with another. No more patently pessimistic conclusion could have so effectively sustained the ironic pattern of Leo Gordon's previous false "awakenings" as the beleaguered hero's final desperate assertion that he at last sees life whole.

"Writing plays isn't like doing oil paintings," Odets once remarked. "You can't say if they don't get it now, then they'll get it forty years later; the play doesn't usually survive that long." Perhaps Odets was right. But free at last from the context in which it first appeared, *Paradise Lost* may yet justify the fervency of its admirers. In his recent full-length study of Odets' work, Gerald Weales has been kinder to the play than earlier critics and has suggested that "of all the Odets plays, it is probably the one that has most to gain from a revival," particularly "now that we are not so enamored of theatrical realism. . . ." *Paradise Lost* does occasionally "spill out of its frame," but with judicious editing and imaginative staging, it could challenge *Awake and Sing!* as the best of Odets' early work.

Harold Cantor (essay date 1982)

SOURCE: "Odets' Yinglish: The Psychology of Dialect as Dialogue," in *Studies in American Jewish Literature—From Marginality to Mainstream: A Mosaic of Jewish Writers*, State University of New York Press, Vol. 2, 1982, pp. 61-68.

[*Cantor is an American educator, editor, and non-fiction author. In the following essay, he examines Odets's use of Yinglish—a blend of Yiddish and English language—and its important function in his early plays.*]

Odets' Yinglish is only one facet in the development of what I have argued elsewhere was a rich poetic dialogue with roots in the Emersonian tradition. Like Emerson's disciple, Whitman, Odets created in his work a barbaric yawp (he used the word "yawping" in *The Big Knife*) that was original and distinctive enough to express his individual impressions of urbanized twentieth-century America—a rhythmic utterance capable of conveying precisely the myths and ethos of middle class life that previous playwrights, such as John Howard Lawson and Elmer Rice, had only approximated.

The first breakthrough in Odets' invention of a living, memorable dialogue was a discovery of the resources of Yiddish-

English and his willingness to seriously represent, not caricature, the speech rhythms and inflections of the American Jew on the stage. In the enclaves of Philadelphia and the Bronx where he grew up, Odets had ample opportunity to listen to the conversation of immigrant Jews. What he heard he remembered, and when he came to write of the Berger family—and, to a lesser extent, of the cabbies and their wives and sweethearts in *Waiting for Lefty*—he naturally turned to a language that would make the characters he wished to depict believable.

The Group Theater's productions of *Awake and Sing!* and the double bill of *Lefty* and *Till the Day I Die* were historic dramatic events. Before analyzing Odets' linguistic innovations, I should like to cite Alfred Kazan's description of the tremendous liberating effect of Odet's plays on a Jewish intellectual:

> . . . for it seemed to me, sitting high up in the second balcony of the Belasco Theater, watching Julie Garfield, J. Edward Bromberg, Stella and Luther Adler and Morris Carnovsky in Odets's *Awake and Sing,* that it would at last be possible for me to write about the life I had always known. In Odets's play there was a lyric uplifting of blunt Jewish speech, boiling over and explosive, that did more to arouse the audience than the political catchwords that brought the curtain down. Everybody on that stage was furious, kicking, alive—the words, always real but never flat, brilliantly authentic like no other theater speech on Broadway, aroused the audience to such delight that one could feel it bounding back and uniting itself with the mind of the writer.

Kazin's phrase, "the life I had always known," suggests how deeply Odets' language and the characters who spoke it evoked the Jewish experience. In Robert Warshow's interesting essay, "Clifford Odets: Poet of the Jewish Middle Class," we find the author reacting similarly:

> For the Jew in the audience, at least, the experience is recognition, a continuous series of familiar signposts, each suggesting with the immediate communication of poetry the whole complex of the life of the characters: what they are, what they want, how they stand with the world.

What are these familiar poetic "signposts" that Warshow sees and which allowed Odets to give a truthful description of the facts of Jewish life and, in turn, the entire immigrant experience and process of acculturation of New York City Jews? The historical and cultural artifacts of this experience—the *shtetl,* the East Side tenements and move to the Bronx, the struggle to make a dollar in the garment industry, the snatching of a laugh or a good cry at the thriving Yiddish theaters of from the *Forward's* "Bintel Brief" column, the revolt of the young against parental tradition and respectability—Bessie Berger: "I raise a family and they should have respect" (*Awake and Sing!*) —all these nourish and enrich Odets' early plays. He was both influenced by them, in the sense that he drew upon them for sources and prototypes, and critical of them, in the sense that he was aware of the limitations and ironies imposed by what Warshow describes as "the three imperatives" of Jewish life: "be secure, be respected, be intelligent."

Warshow also is on target in his recognition of the special tone of the play: "It is as if no one really listens to anyone else; each takes his own line, and the significant connections between one speech and another are not in logic but in the heavy emotional climate of the family." Some lines from the beginning of Act I are an apt illustration of this process:

> RALPH: I don't know . . . Every other day to sit around with the blues and mud in your mouth.
> MYRON: That's how it is—life is like that—a cake-walk.
> RALPH: What's it get you?
> HENNIE: A four-car funeral.
> RALPH: What's it for?
> JACOB: What's it for? If this life leads to a revolution it's a good life. Otherwise it's for nothing.
> BESSIE: Never mind, Pop! Pass me the salt.
> RALPH: It's crazy—all my life I want a pair of black and white shoes and can't get them. It's crazy!
> BESSIE: In a minute I'll get up from the table. I can't take a bite in my mouth no more.
> MYRON: Now, Momma, just don't excite yourself—
> BESSIE: I'm so nervous I can't hold a knife in my hand.

In this arrangement of indirect dialogue, Odets has the ear of a musician for the sharp turns and counterpoints of a verbal fugue.

But what of the jumble of Yiddish-English syntax and expressions poured into the verbal mix—what exactly are they and what do they contribute to the emotional tone? As Gerald Haslam has shown, an expression such as "I should live so long"—generally regarded as a Yiddish-English phrase forty years ago—today is an American cliche'. But Yiddishisms that today are colloquialisms were unfamiliar then, and the prepositional changes and omissions, inverted sentence order, and verb variations Odets employed were alien to non-Jewish (or non-Germanic) members of the audience. Examples from *Awake and Sing!* are:

> BESSIE: You were sleeping by a girl . . . ?
> BESSIE: Ralphie, bring up two bottles seltzer from Weiss.

> JACOB:. . . give me for a cent a cigarette.
> JACOB: It needs a new world.
> SAM: Once too often she'll fight with me, Hennie.

Merely to list these examples of Yiddishisms cannot begin to convey how they function within the play and their cumulative effect on an audience. Odets consciously attempted to create an art—language from Yiddish roots, and to do this he needed a profound knowledge of the psychology of Yiddish as a language. In addition, he had to be aware of its effect on a mixed audience of Gentiles and Jews (many of whom were second-generation sons and daughters of immigrants), and to avoid the extreme of heavy Yiddish dialect which would make his plays unintelligible or ludicrous. He solved the problem by seizing on the exact moment in the history of the Berger family (and later Noah's family, and individuals in other plays) when it was sufficiently acculturated to speak urban—Yiddish-English—an admixture which looks backwards to the *shtetl* and forward to Americanized urban slang. Here Odets brought into play his sensitivity to the psychological implications of words and phrases for both the older generation and the younger.

Some examples will help demonstrate the verbal signposts by which old and young in *Awake and Sing!* "give themselves away" (Warshow's phrase). When Bessie asks Jacob "You gave the dog eat?" and he replies, "I gave the dog eat," an entire complex of understandings is involved. On the dramatic level, we know that Bessie regards her father as a ne'er-do-well and relegates him to menial tasks in the household, But, on an additional level, Jews would appreciate Bessie's concern for feeding the animal, remembering the biblical and talmudic injunctions for the care and nourishment of cattle and sheep, which is an ancestral memory of a formerly nomadic people. Linguistically, Bessie's query and Jacob's reply in almost the exact words have a ritualistic quality to which an audience accustomed to incantations applied even to the slaughter of animals would respond. However, there is an irony in the fact that Bessie's concern is for a pet dog. In the *shtetl,* dogs and cats as pets were unheard of—that was a *goyish* custom—and Jewish children played with a young calf or ewe. No *proster Yid* (common Jew) would own a dog, although perhaps a *grosser gevir* (very rich man) might acquire a watchdog to guard his house and land. Thus, Bessie's concern for Tootsie is a sign of her Americanization; she, above all others, has accepted the status symbols of the new land. Her excessive pride is evinced moments later when she defends her pet to Schlosser, the janitor: "Tootsie's making dirty? Our Tootsie's making dirty in the hall? . . . Tootsie walks behind me like a lady, any time, any place."

Bessie's Yiddishisms also point up another psycho-linguistic effect of the language which Odets exploited for serio-comic overtones, namely, the Jewish tendency to identify verbally intense anguish and emotion with the digestive process. In the passage I have previously quoted, Bessie says: "In a minute I'll get up from the table. I can't take a bite in my mouth no more." In American-English, the equivalent phrase probably would be—"I'm leaving any minute. This is making me sick to my stomach." But the Yiddish-English expression is psychologically more acute because the specificity of "bite in my mouth" is tied up with hunger and underscores the preciousness of eating against a background of frequent famine and deprivation in "the old country." This would be apparent even to the younger Jewish members of the audience, who had heard this phrase from their parents; Gentiles could also appreciate its idiomatic verve. (They might even understand why the Bergers are constantly eating in this play.) Similarly, in the pregnancy-revelation dialogue with Hennie, Bessie exclaims, "My gall is bursting in me," and later, growing angry at Jacob, she says, "Your gall could burst from such a man." Bessie is translating her emotional state to a bodily state, but the interesting bit of synecdoche in which gall bladder is omitted and the secretion is stressed, is emblematic of the intensity with which Jews express anguish and anger. In the verbs "bursting" and "bust," one can hear the echo of the Yiddish *plotz*, as in "His heart will plotz from such suffering."

Finally, Bessie reveals linguistically a rather desperate effort to assimilate into her vocabulary words and phrases picked up from the mass media—"Another county heard from" and "A graduate from the B.M.T."—phrases which show the sarcastic usages by means of which Americanisms could be rendered into Yinglish, and Bessie's class-consciousness is demonstrated by her acidulous reference to Hennie as "Our society lady. . . ."

That Yinglish in Odets' plays involves a reciprocal relationship between young and old is evidenced by the fact that Hennie and Ralph, though for the most part they speak straight urban English, are influenced by speech patterns of their parents and grandparents. In the scene where she is "put down" by Bessie as "Our society lady," Hennie rejects her mother's suggestion that she marry San Feinschreiber: "I'm not marrying a poor foreigner like him. Can't even speak an English word. Not me! I'll go to my grave without a husband." A finely attuned ear would detect something foreign sounding in her last sentence, slyly mocking the sentiments she expresses. Instead of saying, "I'd rather die than marry that *mockie* (a pejorative meaning "greenhorn" or foreigner, which Hennie uses earlier to describe Sam), she will go to her grave without a husband. The sentence is formalized, and its concrete specificity suggests Yiddish rather than English, an outcry from *Tevye the Milkman,* or a phrase that Hennie might have picked up from some other melodrama at the Yiddish theater.

In the same way, Ralph's speech is overlaid by patterns learned from his family. The opening line of the play, "Where's ad-

vancement down the place?" contains an elision and prepositional omission that are typical of Yinglish. Even more significant is his use of the word "place" rather than "shop" or "factory." Here, the German word *platz* connotes a much richer meaning, since it is tied in with the Jewish idea of the value of having a place of work—not merely in the physical sense, but in the moral sense of the need to attain a position, a vocation, a useful status in society. Amusingly, Ralph mixes this Yiddish idiom with the very American word "advancement," which establishes at once an ironic link to the theme of a family in economic and linguistic transition. Yet in II, 1, Ralph reverts automatically to Bessie's emotional body language; describing Blanche's home, he says, "Every time I go near the place I get heart failure."

Yet another source of Yiddishisms in the play is Jacob, who represents the intellectual, bookish tradition of Judaism: "I'm studying from books a whole lifetime." He is the *melamed,* the unworldly teacher, and his words have a prophetic biblical cadence which Odets mixes with a smattering of Marxist-English diction Jacob probably picked up at the *Arbeiter Ring* (Workmen's Circle) on Manhattan's Lower East Side. Sometimes Jacob's mixed-up English is exploited for broad comic effect, as when he warns Ralph about the family's probable attitude toward Blanche: "Boychick . . . It's no difference—a plain bourgois prejudice—but when they find out a poor girl—it ain't so kosher." More often, there is a pathetic side to Jacob which, linguistically, is expressed by the juxtaposition of poetic prophecy with the cant Marxist terms which represent his process of acculturation. In a moving speech in II, 1, Jacob tells the assembled family:

> So you believe in God . . . you got something for it? You! You worked for all the capitalists. You harvested the fruit from your labor? You got God! But the past comforts you? The present smiles on you, yes? Did you find a piece of earth where you could live like a human being and die with the sun on your face? Tell me, yes, tell me. I would like to know myself. But on these questions, on this theme—the struggle for existence—you can't make an answer. The answer I see in your face . . . the answer is your mouth can't talk. In this dark corner you sit and die. But abolish private property!

The last sentence is totally incongruous and destroys the poetry by its platitudinous, soap-box quality. The audience would see the irony of a scholar who speaks Hebrew and quotes Isaiah being taken in by the cant terms of a then popular Americanized philosophy. (It could be assumed that Jacob had become a Marxist in the old country, but that it is hardly possible since, in Act III, Ralph examines his Marxist volumes and discovers "the pages ain't cut in half of them." We should remember that a subsidiary meaning for *melamed* is "an incompetent," and Jacob himself is aware that he is "a man who had golden opportunities but drank instead a glass of tea." The poignancy of that image is difficult to translate unless one has childhood memories of elderly Jews carefully lifting steaming glasses of hot brew to their mouths and smacking their lips in an almost obscene surrender to the exotic and sensually stimulating beverage. Although he is a failure, Jacob's role in the play is not to point the way to some Communist panacea for social ills (insofar as he does this, he is comic and pathetic), but to stand for older traditional Jewish values in opposition to Bessie and her cohorts. In II, 1, he tells Morty: "In my day the propaganda was for God. [Now] it's for success." Linguistically, Jacob's Yinglish reminds one of the moral authority and hortatory quality which was carried over syntactically into Yiddish-urban-English. One should not be told that one should make success. One should remember the words of Hillel: "If I am not for myself, who will be for me? And if I am only for myself, what am I . . . And if not now—when?"

It is remarkable how often Jacob uses the obligatory construction "it should." (used ironically); "My insurance policy. I don't like it should lay around. . . ." Both moral stricture and putative hope are expressed in his language. By contrast, the more assimilated characters in the play have lapsed into vulgar Yiddish: Uncle Morty says, "We'll give them strikes—in the kishkas (guts) we'll give them"; and in the same act, Moe Axelrod informs Ralph: "The insurance guys coming tonight. Morty 'shtupped' him." The vulgar materialists in the play add their minor notes to what I have referred to as a verbal fugue but, to continue the metaphor, the major counterpoints in the fugue are Jacob's Yinglish versus Bessie's— a contrast which Odets later would repeat in the language of the partriarchal, world-weary Noah and his practical, down-to-earth wife, Esther.

The overall effect of these foreign inflections and idiomatic phrases was threefold. For Gentiles (and even many Jews) it imparted a comic twist of fractured English that amused and provided some relief from the grim and gritty world of some of his plays. Indeed, *Awake and Sing!* proves Blake's adage: "Excess of sorrow laughs," and stands as the progenitor of Jewish "black humor" found in the works of dozens of later Jewish-American writers. Second, the Yiddish idiom conveyed a sense of family solidarity despite the family's conflicts and arguments and the "feel" of a social unit moving "up." Third, by this marvelous alchemy due to the addition of symbolic and metaphoric language and ironic, abrasive, cynical lines to the rhythmic foreign inflections, Odets transforms Yiddish-English into a rich poetic tongue. Many years ago Eleanor Flexner said of *Awake and Sing!*: "His dialogue displays what is little less than genius for sharp vivid phrasing which is unrealistic while it is still lifelike and human, a poetizing of speech that is nevertheless more realistic than poetic." And she added, "These (phrases from the play) are

the poet's transformation of a commonplace idiom into literature."

R. Baird Shuman (essay date 1983)

SOURCE: "Clifford Odets and the Jewish Context," in *From Hester Street to Hollywood*, edited by Sarah Blacher Cohen, Indiana University Press, 1983, pp. 85-105.

[Shuman is an American biographer, editor, and educator. In the following essay, he explores Odets's personal background and relates Odets's upbringing to the Jewish character of his work. He locates in Odets's plays several distinctly Jewish subjects, including Jewish mothers, exile and alienation, redemption, and idiomatic expression.]

Significant hazards lurk in any attempt to categorize a writer like Clifford Odets in terms of ethnic identity. Certainly Odets was not a Jew in the sense that he was a participating member of a religious group that practiced the rituals of the Jewish faith. Organized religion never played a significant part in his life. Nevertheless, the ethnicity that surrounded him in his formative years imprinted itself upon his writing, much of which has strong Jewish overtones.

ODETS'S EXPOSURE TO THE JEWISH EXPERIENCE

The early Odets, it must be remembered, was essentially and above all a spokesman for the proletariat, a propagandist writing in the first half of the 1930s about the depressed economic and social conditions that threatened the very fiber of American society. Coincidentally, some of the themes directly related to proletarian writing also had legitimate historical archetypes in the Jewish experience.

Odets was born into a Jewish-American family in Philadelphia in 1906. Both his parents had come to the United States as small children; his mother, Pearl Geisinger, came from Austria, his father, Louis, from Russia. For the first six years of Clifford's life, the Odets family lived in the so-called Northern Liberties area of Philadelphia, a section populated largely by German Jews, many of whom still spoke Yiddish, whose English was heavily accented, and whose speech patterns were primarily those of first- and second-generation Eastern European or German Jews.

The Odets family was essentially working class. However, the family was aspiring to the middle class, and in 1912 the Odetses moved to the Bronx, again settling in a largely Jewish neighborhood. They lived near Beck Street and Longwood Avenue in one of the better apartment buildings of the day. Louis Odets gradually advanced from his position as a feeder in a printery to become the owner of the shop. Soon he was able to buy a Maxwell automobile and to send his ailing wife to California to escape the cold of winter.

English was the only language spoken in the Odets house-hold. Both of Clifford's parents were near-native speakers of the language. They neither read nor spoke Yiddish. How-ever, Clifford's Aunt Esther and Uncle Israel Rosman, who were older when they immigrated to the United States than Odets's parents had been, spoke Yiddish and regularly read Yiddish newspapers. Odets recalls, ". . . while they were still my aunt and uncle, they were much more Jewish in their out-looks, and certainly in their language and customs, than my very American parents."

Odets grew up hearing and speaking English at home, but the dialect of English used there and in the neighborhoods where he grew up probably had in it many of the melodies, intona-tions, and speech patterns of Eastern European immigrants with strong Jewish religious ties. Such patterns come through even in recorded interviews with Odets, where a sentence like, "I want to show in David, who is pursued by a psychotic Saul, a young poet," illustrates a basic structure and cadence of Jewish-American speech. This phrase structure of indirect object followed by direct object, while common in some in-stances in Network Standard English where the preposition of the indirect object is omitted (e.g. "He gave her a book"), is uncommon where the preposition is expressed and is a speech pattern characteristic of many Jewish Americans.

But Jewishness enters into the writing of an author with Odets's upbringing and background in more subtle and sig-nificant ways than are found solely in speech patterns and intonations. Some of the underlying themes of Jewish cul-ture influenced his reactions to many of the social problems he treats in his plays, particularly the early ones, on both the literal and metaphoric levels. The very fabric of any writers' literary production is based upon the intricacies of his early, and in many cases, largely forgotten, experiences. For people raised in a Jewish family living in Jewish neighborhoods, whether the family appears acculturated or not, facets of the cultural heritage of the Jews come to be an ingrained part of their natures.

Guttmann, in answer to the question of how "Americans of-ten assume that the folkways of *Mitteleuropa* and of the Rus-sian *shtetl* are really the essentials of Jewishness," very rightly contends, "To answer such questions fully is to tell the story of the American Jews, but this much is certain: a minority that adopted many of the traits of its European neighbors is now distinguished in the eyes of its American neighbors by these adopted characteristics rather than by the fundamental differences that originally accounted for the minority status." It is, as Guttmann suggests, all too easy to identify as Jewish some characteristics that are essentially European or Slavic. Many Jewish immigrants to this country came from Eastern Europe or from Russia, so that the traditions which they brought with them to the New World represent a melding of two cultures, their traditional Jewish culture and the Euro-

pean or Slavic culture that their forefathers had long since adopted.

Certainly Jacob in *Awake and Sing!* is typical of the kind of Jew Guttmann alludes to. Much of the political and social philosophy of Eastern European revolutionaries is reflected in Jacob's thinking. He is the somewhat confused and muddled revolutionary living with a much more conservative younger generation (Bessie and Myron Berger) whose ideas are con-siderably more down-to-earth and conventional than his. If Jacob can say, "If this life leads to a revolution it's a good life. Otherwise it's for nothing." Bessie can provide the put-down by responding. "Never mind, Pop! Pass me the salt."

BIBLICAL INFLUENCES

In an interview with Michael Mendelsohn in 1961, two years before his death, Odets was asked about literary influences upon him and specifically about any influence the Bible might have had. He said,

> I like to read the Bible. I would like to read it more. I believe much that's in it. I want to write one more play—at least one more play that I know about—on a Biblical theme (that is after *The Flowering Peach,* which is about Noah and the Ark). I do want to write somewhere out of the two Books of Samuel, particu-larly the second book, I want to write about the life of Saul and David. I want to show in David, who is pursued by a psychotic Saul, a young poet.

The extent to which Odets wished to use this Old Testament story for any of its specific and inherent Jewish qualities is, indeed, questionable. Rather, he seemed to find in the story a reflection of some of his own most personal feelings about the role of the artist in society. The interview continues:

> . . . I want to show how the young poet becomes a very successful man—indeed, the most successful in his realm, because he becomes the King. And I want to show the life of Man from the time he is a poet until he dies an old man, unhappy, but somehow still a poet gnawing at his soul. I want to turn the various facets of his nature around so that you see what hap-pens to men of big success and how they meet the conflicting situations of their lives.

The theme of what success does to an artist, which Odets had earlier dealt with in both *The Country Girl* and *The Big Knife,* obviously fascinated him. Those two plays are certainly not prominently ethnic, nor is there any reason to suppose that in any dramatic version he might have done of the Saul/David story, Odets would have set out to write a play which would have been essentially ethnic in its impact. Nevertheless, a number of Odets's early plays, as well as his last play to be produced, *The Flowering Peach,* have a distinctly Jewish flavor and can legitimately be considered within the context of their Jewish ethnicity, as well as within a number of other contexts. Some of the less overtly Jewish plays can also be considered in terms of elements of the Jewish context that shaped Clifford Odets as a creative artist and as a person.

THE OVERTLY JEWISH PLAYS

Among Odets's early plays, both *Awake and Sing!* and *Paradise Lost* are about Jewish families. The Bergers in the former play are a lower-middle-class Jewish family struggling against the uncertainties of the economic depression of the 1930s. Three generations of the family live together and suffer the inevitable value confrontations that take place between people of different ages, backgrounds, and outlooks. The Gordons in *Paradise Lost* are an upper-middle-class Jewish family faced with economic and ethical problems growing out of the loss of the father's business through the dishonesty of his partner. The Gordons are more acculturated into American life, less obviously Jewish, than the Bergers. Indeed, they resemble Odets's own well-acculturated family.

Till the Day I Die focuses on the situation of a Communist in Nazi Germany. A tour de force in the *agitprop* tradition, it was written to accompany Odets's *Waiting for Lefty,* which first played at the Civic Repertory Theatre on Fourteenth Street, then was moved uptown to the Longacre Theater where it and *Till the Day I Die* played together for 136 performances. The protagonist of *Till the Day I Die,* Ernst Tausig, is a Jew as well as a Communist, so is doubly a target for inhumane treatment by the German SS.

THE LESS JEWISH PLAYS

Waiting for Lefty, Odets's first successful production, deals with the economic issues of the Depression. The only direct allusion to Jews in this play is in Scene 5, which concerns Dr. Benjamin, a physician who is discharged from his hospital position, presumably because of anti-Semitism on the part of those who run the hospital.

Golden Boy has an Italian protagonist, Joe Bonaparte, and the play is without strong Jewish overtones, although Joe's manager, Mr. Carp, is clearly Jewish. Roxy Gottlieb in this play is also presented as being Jewish, particularly in certain of his speech patterns. Similarly, *Rocket to the Moon, Night Music,* and *Clash by Night,* while they have Jewish characters in them, are not directly and primarily concerned with the Jewish experience, although numerous elements of Jewish life glimmer through them. Not until *The Flowering Peach* did Odets again deal with a subject as quintessentially Jewish as the depiction of the family in *Awake and Sing!*

PROMINENT THEMES IN THE JEWISH CULTURAL HERITAGE

The Jewish cultural heritage is stronger than a number of other heritages which are basically religious in their origins. Even Jews who shun the faith of their progenitors remain in many ways Jews. Karl Shapiro addresses this point in *Poems of a Jew:* ". . . a Jew who becomes an atheist remains a Jew. A Jew who becomes a Catholic remains a Jew." Harry Moore calls the Jewish heritage "environmental" and goes on to say "Granted, the environment of the Jews, usually clannish, sometimes produces physical characteristics that are fairly recognizable, yet these are intrinsically environmental. The young Jewish men often break with their community, leaving orthodoxy behind, yet many of them still marry Jewish girls, who understand their men's background, their early conditioning." While Moore's comments perhaps represent a genetic oversimplification, a Jewishness appears to exist which is independent of religiosity and which is identifiable by certain patterns of behavior, philosophical stances, and value systems. Many of these hark back to the traditional religious faith and doctrine of earlier generations of Jews, of course, but they exist also quite noticeably and prominently in modern Jews who may, indeed, have denied the religion of their forefathers.

Irving Malin contends that many modern Jewish-American writers are engaged in "the search for new images of divinity in the absence of orthodox belief." He continues, "Our best (Jewish) writers are 'mad crusaders,' hoping for a transcendent ideal—art, potency?- -to replace the tarnished ones they embraced in their youth." He considers Jewish stories to be "those that witness, even in distorted or inverted ways, traditional religious and literary moments." According to his definition, most of Odets's plays are not Jewish—the only ones that could be called Jewish are *The Flowering Peach,* most certainly *Awake and Sing!,* somewhat less certainly, and possibly *Paradise Lost.*

However, Malin identifies themes common to the Jewish heritage, and many of them are prominent in Odets's work, as well as that of many other writers, some of them Gentiles. In *Jews and Americans,* Malin organizes his material into chapters that deal with individual elements common to the Jewish heritage: exile, fathers and sons, time, head and heart, transcendence, irony, fantasy, and parable. In *Contemporary American-Jewish Literature,* Malin posits that the creators of Jewish tales "seek to escape from exile, to break old covenants, and to embrace transcendent ideals."

A part of the Jewish cultural heritage is the dominant, often overly protective mother. She will often be counterbalanced by the acquiescent father (like Myron in *Awake and Sing!*) and, in literature certainly, by the voluptuous, sexually tempting daughter (like Hennie, also in *Awake and Sing!*) . The hope of the future is vested in Jewish children, particularly in boy children, who are viewed as the precious heirs and prospective leaders of what ideally was to be a patriarchal Jewish society.

The mother, while dominant, is also a sufferer. She often is, as Auchincloss might call her, an "injustice collector." She must sacrifice in order to feel fulfilled. Robert Warshow, writing of *Awake and Sing!,* capsulizes the values of middle-class American Jews: "be secure, be respected, be intelligent." These are very much Bessie Berger's values in *Awake and Sing!,* Clara Gordon's in *Paradise Lost,* and Esther's in *The Flowering Peach.*

If Jewish society can be viewed as being ideally patriarchal. the Jewish family is in many ways matriarchal. The Jewish wife, when she becomes a mother, adopts a new role of dominance, particularly when she has sons whom she regards as the chief hope for the future. She becomes the beacon in an alien environment. She makes the home, which is because of her an impregnable fortress against all that might threaten it. With the birth of a son into a Jewish family, the father's dominance decreases and the mother's increases. In Odets's *Awake and Sing!* and *The Flowering Peach,* dominant women are the mortar that holds the family together in the most trying of times.

JEWISH MOTHERS

Some of Odets's plays have in them what might be called the conventional Jewish mother, the dominant female who suffers and serves, who is constantly urging food on her young, who assumes the responsibility for many of the necessary decisions within the family. Other of Odets's plays present in prominent roles women who, while they may be neither Jewish nor mothers, attempt to be surrogate mothers for weak husbands whom they treat as surrogate sons.

Among the former are Bessie Berger *(Awake and Sing!)* and Esther *(The Flowering Peach).* Somewhat midway between the two polarities is Clara Gordon in *Paradise Lost.* The surrogate mother type is represented by Bertha Katz in *Paradise Lost,* in a much more fully developed way by Belle in *Rocket to the Moon,* and in a somewhat different way by Georgie Elgin in *The Country Girl.*

In the list of characters preceding *Awake and Sing!,* Bessie Berger is described in more than twice the detail accorded to either her husband, Myron, her daughter, Hennie, or her son, Ralph. The description presents, it would seem, Odets's conception of what the prototypical Jewish mother is, although it must be remembered that Bessie Berger lives in the strained economic context of the Depression and that many of her characteristics are heightened by the pressures this context imposes. Odets calls her "not only the mother in this home

but also the father. She is constantly arranging and taking care of her family." He comments on her joy in living from day to day and on her resourcefulness.

Bessie is concerned with the here and now, with the day-to-day matters of human existence; her men, particularly Jacob, the grandfather, and Ralph, the son, are the dreamers, the philosophers in the family. Bessie deals with the mundane and revels in doing so. Odets writes of her, "She is a shrewd judge of realistic qualities in people in the sense of being able to gauge quickly their effectiveness. . . . She is naive and quick in emotional response. She is afraid of utter poverty. She is proper according to her own standards, which are fairly close to those of most middle-class families. She knows that when one lives in the jungle one must look out for the wild life." Bessie needs to be in control of things and she essentially is. The one threat to that control is the poverty she fears, because this could destroy her home and her family. Bessie alludes to this fear early in *Awake and Sing!:* "They threw out a family on Dawson Street today. All the furniture on the sidewalk. A fine old woman with gray hair." This concern is repeated toward the end of the play when Bessie warns, "A family needs for a rainy day. Times is getting worse. Prospect Avenue, Dawson, Beck Street—every day furniture's on the sidewalk."

Bessie's worst fears are the realities with which her counterpart Clara Gordon, in *Paradise Lost* must contend; Clara and Leo's furniture actually is put out into the street. They lose their business, their home, and indeed their hope for the future, which has been vested in their children—one is shot during a robbery, one is dying of encephalitis, and one is rapidly becoming a recluse.

If Bessie seems to some to be "instinctively dedicated to emasculating the men in the family," she is equally devoted to keeping the family intact when it is threatened from without. She is also concerned with projecting an image of respectability for her family even when to do so involves an act such as deceiving the gullible Sam Feinschreiber into marrying her daughter, Hennie, who is pregnant by another man. Through this marriage, Odets implies that the whole family cycle will recur; Sam will become the emasculated husband, Hennie the dominant wife and controlling mother.

Both Clara Gordon and Bessie Berger tend to be shrill much of the time, hypercritical, opinionated. They bicker. Granted they sometimes emasculate their men, but at the base of all this are love and concern such as that reflected in Clara's line, "I found out many years ago I married a fool, but I love him." Odets's Jewish mothers represent continuity and continuance. They are concerned with the survival of the Jewish tradition but equally, if not more so, with the economic and physical survival of the family. The Bergers in *Awake and Sing!* are under extreme financial pressures, but throughout the play they eat almost constantly. Bessie sees to that. The family survives and in Ralph's new beginning at the end of the play is the hope that both the Jewish tradition and the Berger family will continue.

The dramatic tensions in *Awake and Sing!*, *Paradise Lost*, *The Flowering Peach*, and to some extent in all of Odets's other plays, except perhaps his two agitprop dramas, *Waiting for Lefty* and *Till the Day I Die*, are part and parcel of the head-heart conflict which is developed through the interplay of practical, down-to-earth women who, in the last analysis, represent head, and impractical, idealistic men, who, in the last analysis, represent heart. Granted that Jacob, who reads books and listens to opera, is more the intellectual than Bessie; however, he functions according to emotion more than according to reason. Bessie, within her own value system, makes rational decisions that will preserve the family's appearance of respectability and improve its chances of survival. One must note that Odets, as his writing career progressed, came increasingly to side more often with the idealistic men than with the women.

As early as *Paradise Lost*, the play's last word is a long idealistic statement by Leo, whereas in *Awake and Sing!*, the idealistic Jacob commits suicide and there is less to suggest that Ralph is really going to be able to conquer new worlds despite his closing oratory. By the time of *The Flowering Peach*. written nearly two decades after *Awake and Sing!*, the Jewish mother, Esther, while somewhat carping and domineering. has mellowed a great deal. The idealism of Noah, her husband, who was commanded by God to build an Ark and did so despite the aspersions cast by others upon his judgment—indeed, upon his sanity—is, in the end, vindicated because his act saves the human race from total annihilation in the Flood. At the end of *The Flowering Peach*, Esther is dead, a victim of old age; but through Noah's idealistic following of God's word, future generations are saved and continuance is assured.

Toward the end of *Awake and Sing!*, Bessie has a speech that states very succinctly the head-heart conflict which exists in a Jewish mother like her: "'Mom, what does she know? She's old-fashioned!' But I'll tell you a big secret: My whole life I wanted to go away, too, but with children a woman stays home. A fire burned in my heart too, but now it's too late. I'm no spring chicken. The clock goes and Bessie goes." The theme of the worn-out mother recurs in *The Flowering Peach*. Esther says to Noah toward the end of the play, "Whatta you want from me, Noah? I'm a tired old woman . . . you're a young man." As the action nears its resolution, Esther still fights for the family while Noah stands as the patriarch who will preserve the laws of God, laws much more abstract than those of the family:

Esther: (to Noah) Marry the children . . . for the sake of happiness in the world . . .
Noah: Old friend, it hurts me to refuse you, but it stands in the books for a thousand years—
Esther: —But all the books are in the water now. . . . Marry the children before I go.

Just before Esther dies, Noah having denied her wish that he marry the children, she proclaims, "The children, their happiness . . . is my last promised land."

This is a curious reversal and represents Odets's coming far afield from *Awake and Sing!*; in *The Flowering Peach*, which begins with Esther representing head and Noah representing heart, Esther, in the end wants Noah to violate his conscience and to perform marriages among the children according to the dictates of her heart. Noah, by building the Ark, has assured the physical continuation of the human race; Esther now calls upon him to play God, as it were, and to help reestablish the conventions of the world which the Flood has destroyed. Esther, like Bessie Berger, remains concerned with the here and now; but Noah, with his more abstract philosophical concerns, really triumphs at the conclusion of *The Flowering Peach*.

SURROGATE MOTHERS

Some of the wives in Odets's plays are surrogate Jewish mothers. They are married to men of questionable strength and self-assurance. These men need strong women to tell them what to do (Ben Stark in *Rocket to the Moon*) or to keep them from vices that would destroy them (Frank Elgin in *The Country Girl*), wives who will suffer the abuse that stems from the husbands' own insecurities and inadequacies (Sam Katz in *Paradise Lost*). The first tentative step toward this kind of character is found in Tilly, Ernst Tausig's fiancee in *Till the Day I Die*. Tilly is the comforter, the one who understands and encourages Ernst after he has been interrogated, intimidated, and physically mutilated by the German SS. When Ernst returns to Tilly after the SS has crushed his hand, he is depicted as wincing in pain and Tilly tells him, "Sit down again. Don't be afraid of softness, of sorrow." She is the comforting mother type; but Ernst is not basically weak, as some male characters in other of Odets's plays have been. He has been victimized by a force much stronger than any man might be expected to resist.

Not until *Paradise Lost* did Odets develop to the utmost the surrogate mother type of character. Bertha Katz is childless, like Belle Stark in *Rocket to the Moon* and Georgie (a non-Jew) in *The Country Girl*. Being childless is particularly difficult for Jewish women, as Odets was well aware; they cannot obey the Biblical injunction, "Be fruitful and multiply." They are unfulfilled, and Odets turns their need for fulfillment toward their husbands. In *Paradise Lost*, where Odets really becomes concerned with this particular theme, it is Sam Katz, not his wife, who is responsible for their childlessness. Bertha tolerates Sam's abuse, both physical and verbal, dealing with him just as she might have with the children she has never had. He calls her "Momma," and she speaks the line, "Momma, he says, In the night he cried to God and no answer came. In my arms he cried, and no answer came." In the tense lines which follow, Bertha tells the Gordons of Sam's impotence, reveals to them that he has not slept with a girl in seven years, and then, like the good mother, she says, "He's a good boy—We'll go home Sam." The set directions here are especially revealing: "Goes up to Sam. Helps him up from the lower step. Wipes his face with handkerchief."

Belle Stark in *Rocket to the Moon* is Odets's next depiction of the surrogate mother type. She is by no means so sympathetic a character as Bertha Katz. She has miscarried in her first pregnancy and can have no more children. Her internalized anger reveals itself in sarcasm and often in outright nastiness. Odets suggests that Belle's mother was temperamentally very like Belle. He also intimates that Ben once had promise, but that during his marriage to Belle, his promise has remained unfulfilled. Ben reveals some of his past potential in the lines, "I was a pioneer with Gladstone in orthodontia, once. Now I'm a dentist, good for sixty dollars a week, while men with half my brains and talents are making their twenty and thirty thousand a year!" But Belle has now reduced him to the state where she does much of his thinking for him and says contemptuously, "Any day now I'm expecting to have to powder and diaper you."

Belle presumably does not want Ben to advance professionally, because she would then have difficulty controlling him. As Odets had originally conceived the play, Ben's affair with his receptionist, Cleo Singer, was to have given him strength through love, however, as the play finally appeared, the affair is fleeting, Ben is weak even in its midst, as is evidenced by his not even discouraging Cleo from going out with other men while it is going on; and when the affair is over, Ben presumably will return to the same trap in which he was before, except that Belle will have collected one more injustice to hold over him. Her longing for a child will continue, and she will use Ben as the child she cannot have, nagging him until the end of his days. There is a terrible irony in Ben's lines to Mr. Prince, his father-in-law, toward the end of the play: "For years I sat here, taking things for granted, my wife, everything. Then just for an hour my life was in a spotlight. I saw myself clearly, realized who and what I was. Isn't that a beginning? Isn't it?" And with these words, with this plaintive questioning, he seals his fate. Even at the close of the original play, ending as it does with the word "Awake," which is an allusion to Ben's earlier line, "A man falls asleep in marriage," there is little hope that Ben will ever be anything but emasculated, mothered and smothered by a woman who must control him through diminishing him as a person.

The relationship between Georgie and Frank Elgin in *The Country Girl* is somewhat different. Frank, a gifted actor whose alcoholism has all but ruined his career, is offered a last chance, an important role in a play. His wife, Georgie, who has suffered with him through the decline in his career caused by his alcoholism, has become his protectress. Georgie does not resemble the Jewish mother quite so much as she does the deeply concerned wife. Her mothering grows out of her concern, and much of it seems necessary to her husband's professional survival as well as to her own survival, which is closely allied to her husband's success. She protects his interests, sees that his rights and privileges are duly accorded. She says of him, "He doesn't like to make the slightest remark that might lose him people's regard and affection. I've simply grown into the habit of doing it for him." She then goes on to argue with Bennie Dodd, the play's director, about Frank's salary.

Georgie tells of having left Frank twice and of having twice resumed to him, largely, it would seem from the dialogue, in a motherly role: "Twice left, twice returned. He's a helpless child." Later she allows, "Yes, he has to be watched—he has to be nursed, guarded, and coddled." And she then adds the line, "But not by me, my very young friend (Bernie Dodd)!"

However, despite this proclamation, Georgie, talking to Bernie backstage on opening night about the congratulatory telegrams Frank received, clearly shows that she cannot stop mothering her husband:

> *Georgie:* It was sweet of you to send him all those wires.
> *Bernie: impassively:* Who told you?
> *Georgie:* Guessed. How many did you send?
> *Bernie:* Nine or ten. And you?
> *Georgie:* Four or five.

The husband-wife relationship in Odets's plays are often based upon sexual stereotypes current when he wrote. The Jewish mother and the surrogate mother present an interesting reversal of what was the usual role designation of Odets's era, i.e., the dominant male and the dependent female; but such role reversal is found in other plays which metaphorically presented the social and economic emasculation of their protagonists by a world which seems organized against them, characters like Willie Loman in *Death of a Salesman*.

EXILE AND ALIENATION

The story of the exodus as related in the Old Testament has long been with worldwide Jewry. As a cohesive ethnic group frequently in exile, Jews have been ghettoized throughout much of history. Those who have chosen to leave the ghetto have, nevertheless, been forced to bear all the kinds of discrimination visited upon Jews by many dominant cultures throughout history. Outbreaks of violent anti-Semitism through the history of the Western world have been sufficiently frequent and regular to remind Jews everywhere, particularly before the founding of the state of Israel, of their exile and to reinforce their feelings of alienation and homelessness. During Odets's early creative years, many Jews were exiling themselves from an insanely anti-Semitic Germany where, in many cases, they and their forefathers had lived for generations. Jews everywhere identified with these refugees, as today large numbers of Jews identify with their counterparts in the USSR.

Exiled and alienated as many Jews have been through the ages and were particularly during the Nazi era, there has always been a strong theme of redemption in their existence. Warshow writes,

> The adult immigrant had some advantages. Whatever
> it was that drove him to come (to the United States),
> he was able to carry with him a sense of his own
> dignity and importance. He had a kind of security,
> though it is a strange thing to say of a Jew. In Eu-
> rope, with the club over his head, he had neverthe-
> less lived in a community which was in important
> ways self-sufficient, and which permitted him to think
> of himself as a man of value: he was, a scholar, or a
> revolutionist; at the very least he knew himself to be
> a more serious man than his Gentile persecutors. To
> be a Jew was a continual burden, even a misfortune,
> but it could not have seemed to him a joke or a dis-
> grace.

A unique admixture of exile, alienation, and redemption exists among Jews and has so existed through much of their history.

It must be remembered that in Nazi German, anti-Semitism was directed against anyone with so-called "Jewish blood." Birth conferred the distinction of being Jewish in the Nazi view, and, as Ernest Van den Haag notes, "This was one part of the complicated truth which the Nazis grasped." The Jewish Americans by whom Odets was surrounded in his youth, both in the neighborhoods in which his parents lived and among his associates in the Group Theatre, were well aware of the historic persecution of the Jews; the rise of the Nazi party in Germany during the thirties only intensified their awareness of this long and unhappy history.

Superimposed upon the situation of Jews in Nazi Germany was the complication of a worldwide economic depression which, within Odets's own immediate frame of reference, threatened the economic security of large numbers of people by whom he was surrounded and made them feel alienated from their society. The threat of homelessness loomed large for working-class Americans. In his interview with Michael

Mendelsohn, Odets said. "Theatre in its profoundest sense— all literature in its profoundest sense—has come in periods when the plight or problem expressed by the actors was completely at one with the plight or problems and values or even moralities of the audience."

During his interview with Arthur Wagner, Odets, in speaking about how one writes, asserted, "The question is really not one of knowing how to write so much as knowing how to connect with yourself so that the writing is, so to speak, born affiliated with yourself." In the same monologue he acknowledges what he calls his "blood ties" with *Paradise Lost,* and indeed he could have established similar blood ties with most of his early plays.

Odets's immediate tie in a play like *Waiting for Lefty* was a tie with the working class caught up in the problems of the Depression. However, his blood ties to his material came out of his whole past, as they must in any author, and such ties reflect the way a Jewish-American writer reacts to the materials about which he is writing. Certainly Odets was not oblivious to the situation of Jews in Germany, as *Till the Day I Die* clearly illustrates. The "plights and problems" of which Odets speaks were the most legitimate plights and problems of his age and his Jewish background gave him a special competence to deal with them, "to connect with himself," as he put it.

Schaar suggests the pervasiveness of the exile motif and the attendant sense of alienation that accompanies it: "The motif of the eternal wanderer begins in the dawn of the Jewish tradition and weaves in and out of the whole subsequent history of Western religion. Abram is the prototype and universal symbol of alienated man." Rosenberg and Bergen contend, "In becoming an object-self, part of an objective social history, the person can come to feel that he has lost control over his own being." Many of Odets's characters, particularly those in *Waiting for Lefty* and *Till the Day I Die,* have lost control of their own destinies. Yet in both these early plays, the common Jewish motif of redemption is evident. Redemption for the cabbies in *Waiting for Lefty* comes after Lefty, who has been interpreted by some as being a Christ-like figure, is murdered and the men gathered in the union hall call for a strike, moved to fever pitch by their indignation over the murder. The same motif occurs in a different way in *Till the Day I Die.* Ernst Tausig kills himself at the conclusion of the play, but Tillie is pregnant with his child, the prospective leader, the precious heir. Tillie emphasizes this: "Let us hope we will both live to see strange and wonderful things. Perhaps we will die before then. Our children will see it then." Just before Ernst's suicide, his brother says to Tillie, "Let him die," but after the shot is heard, he utters the more redemptive, "Let him live."

Odets deals with the themes of exile (variations on the wandering Jew theme) and alienation throughout much of his writing. The concern is a central one for him. In *Waiting for Lefty,* the disparate group of people brought together by the economic uncertainties of their society are, for the most part, living unfulfilled lives—for example, the young hack and his girl cannot marry and Dr. Benjamin drives a taxicab rather than completing his hospital residency—and they are dealing with the "object-self." If they are to overcome the threat of complete alienation, they can do so only by joining together, and this is what they are forced into at the end of the play when they rally to strike after Lefty has been found dead behind the carbarns, a bullet in his head.

> **Many of Odets's characters, particularly those in *Waiting for Lefty* and *Till the Day I Die,* have lost control of their own destinies. Yet in both these early plays, the common Jewish motif of redemption is evident.**
>
> **—R. Baird Shuman**

Odets, during the uncertain years of the Depression, was a member of the close-knit Group Theatre, and in the unity of this association he felt less alienated personally than he might otherwise have felt. Deeper alienation came later in his life, first when he left the Group Theatre to go to Hollywood, an act which was in his eyes a prostitution of his talents and ideals, largely so he could earn money to help the Group Theatre stay afloat; and later when he began to rankle under the artistic pressures of Hollywood, where he experienced a significant loss of identity and self-esteem.

In *Awake and Sing!,* the threat of economic disaster always impends, but the family unit remains together, as it does in the face of great crisis in *The Flowering Peach.* Some hope remains in the Berger household, despite all its tribulations and discontent: Bessie, after protesting at Myron's wish to buy a fifty-cent Irish Sweepstakes Ticket from Moe Axelrod, says, "I'll give you money. Buy a ticket in Hennie's name. Say, you can't tell—lightning never struck us yet. If they win on Beck Street, we could win on Longwood Avenue." Bessie, reflecting a mentality which keeps exiles alive, always holds on to the hope of a better future.

Jacob in *Awake and Sing!* is the philosophical center of the play; Bessie Berger is the practical center. Jacob is the idealist whose immediate world is not threatened in quite the same way that Bessie's is, partly because Jacob has not so long to live as Bessie and partly because Bessie's concerns about security are more specific, focusing as they do upon her family, than Jacob's, whose concerns focus upon mankind more

broadly. Jacob has more philosophical detachment than Bessie, whose point of view is limited by the immediacy of assuring on a day-to-day basis her own survival and that of her family.

Bessie, struggling to preserve the family's respectability can pressure her pregnant daughter Hennie into marrying the unsuspecting Sam Feinschreiber, saying of him, "He's going to night school, Sam. For a boy only three years in the country he speaks very nice," followed by the crucial, "In three years he put enough money in the bank, a good living." She can first tell Moe Axelrod that Hennie is engaged to Sam, and then, upon hearing Moe, who is richer than Sam, say, ". . . maybe I'd marry her myself," can turn around and say, "why don't you, Moe? An old family friend like you. It would be a blessing on us all." Bessie is convinced that she is doing all this for the good and for the security of the family, which are her prime concerns; she can justify any deceit that will help her family to project an image of decency and respectability, to prevent an alienation of her family from its social milieu.

But Jacob's whole philosophical framework is different from Bessie's. He is sufficiently removed from the particulars of the immediate situation to be able to make a moral judgment about it and to be able to utter in disgust, "Marx said it—abolish such families." Their diverging viewpoints cause an estrangement between Bessie and Jacob, and the two are farthest apart when Hennie tells Sam that he is not the father of their child and Sam confronts Bessie with this information. Ralph tells his mother, "You trapped this guy," and Bessie's whole world is collapsing. Now, because of her efforts to keep up a respectable front, she is beginning to be alienated from her own family. At this point she turns to Jacob, venting her wrath upon him, saying, "You'll stand around with Caruso and make a bughouse. It ain't enough all day long. Fifty times I told you I'll break every record in the house," and she thereupon breaks Jacob's cherished recordings, and in so doing probably precipitates his suicide.

Of this tense scene Warshow writes, "Bessie Berger reveals the whole pattern of psychological and moral conflict that dominates her and her family. . . . (She) turns upon her father, who has said nothing, and smashes the phonograph records that are his most loved possessions and the symbol of his superiority." What remains to Bessie is the outer symbol of her superiority: respectability in the eyes of middle-class society, which probably scarcely knows she exists. In *Awake and Sing!,* redemption lies, albeit more facilely than artistically justifiable, not in Jacob's leaving Ralph three thousand dollars in insurance money—Ralph finally decides to "Let Mom have the dough"—but in Ralph's realization that Jacob's life and ultimately his death have perhaps given Ralph something on which to build a new beginning: "I'll get along. Did Jake die for us to fight about nickels? No! 'Awake and Sing,' he said. Right here he stood and said it. The night he died, I

saw it like a thunderbolt! *I saw he was dead and I was born!*"
(Italics mine). The cycle is repeated; Odets is suggesting that
continuance is assured.

Noah, in *The Flowering Peach,* is alienated from his society
for quite lofty reasons. God has come to him in a dream and
told him that the earth will be destroyed in a flood. He orders
him to build an ark and to take his family upon it along with
seven pairs of clean, and one pair of unclean, animals. Noah's
wife chides him for drinking too much and is, along with his
sons, quite skeptical of the validity of Noah's dream, attributing it to his drinking. But when God sends signs and por-
tents to Noah—first a gitka and then other animals arrive to
be put on the Ark, and a tired old Noah becomes young and
strong so that he can work at constructing the Ark—the family becomes more credulous. Yet even at this point, Noah is
shunned. He is stoned out of town when he goes for supplies.
He must refuse passage on the Ark to respected old friends,
because God's command is that he shall take only his family
on board. But Noah's oneness is with God, so his alienation
is not complete nor will his exile during the flood be permanent.

Odets's Noah story ends on a note of affirmation. Noah's
wife, Esther, has died on the Ark, but life will continue. Rather
than drinking himself into drunkenness at the end of the story,
as in the Biblical version, Odets's Noah asks God for a covenant: "You know what I want, Lord. Just like you guarantee
each month, with a woman's blood, that men will be born
. . . give such a sign that you won't destroy the world again,"
and at that point a rainbow appears in the sky. Although the
ending is again a bit facile, the theme of redemption is stronger in *The Flowering Peach* than in any of Odets's other
plays. Noah's alienation and his exile—his forty days on the
waters—have led him to be humble before God and obedient
to Him. Life will go on thanks to Noah's heeding of God's
command.

Night Music is a play about homelessness and alienation despite its bittersweet resolution. Writing of the theme of
homelessness in the play, Harold Clurman, its director, says,
"Odets does not state this (homelessness) as his theme in so
many words; he does not have to, since he has made it part of
every character, of every scene, almost of every prop. It is
not a thesis, it is the 'melody' that permeates the play. The
central character is made angry and adolescently belligerent
by his inability to take hold in society." This sort of alienation, this waste of human potential, had always angered
Odets: "Nothing moves me so much as human aspirations
blocked, nothing enrages me like waste. I am for use as opposed to abuse." The wasted human potential of the Depression provided him with material for his early plays, but he
was no less incensed by the waste and futility that he sometimes felt characterized his own endeavors in Hollywood.

In many ways his most acerbic play is *The Big Knife*; in it he
addresses directly the frustrations that had been gnawing away
at him during his first decade in California and makes an open
attack upon the motion picture industry. But these gnawings
actually had been festering in the writer for quite a long time.
Golden Boy addressed problems of unfulfillment that later
came to be a major part of the substance of *The Big Knife*.
Both plays can be viewed as escape-from-the-ghetto plays.
Joe Bonaparte escapes through his boxing ability, but the price
he pays is enormous; he is an accomplished violinist, but in
becoming a boxer, he sacrifices his hands. In the end, he kills
another boxer in the ring and then goes out in his new, expensive Duesenberg, a symbol of his success, and crashes it,
killing himself and his female companion, Laura. Similarly,
Charlie Castle moves from his humble background into a
successful career as an actor, only to be destroyed by the threat
of a disclosure that he has been involved in a fatal hit-and-
run accident for which he has allowed someone else to accept the blame and be punished. The threat drives Castle to
suicide.

The writing of both of these plays was a very self-searching
activity for their author and each in its own period grew out
of Odets's feelings of alienation and, in the case of *Golden
Boy* particularly, out of the sense of self-imposed exile which
he felt in deserting the Group Theatre for Hollywood, even
though the desertion was done in the best interests of the
Group. Cantor writes, "Indeed, it is difficult to disentangle
the work and the man in Odets' career, for Odets' major plays
on the subject of selling-out, *Golden Boy* and *The Big Knife,*
are rooted in his personal experience." The loss of identity
with which Charlie Castle had to deal in *The Big Knife* raises
again the object-self question; Charlie, like Joe Bonaparte in
Golden Boy, becomes a commodity to be haggled over. A
loss of identity, which begins with his having to change his
name at the studio's command, progresses to the point that
he has to sign a fourteen-year contract which he does not
wish to sign, has to sign away fourteen years of his life, as it
were, because the studio is blackmailing him. Well might he
utter such lines as "I'll bet you don't know why we all wear
these beautiful, expensive ties in Hollywood. . . . It's a military tactic—we hope you won't notice our faces," or "free
speech is the highest-priced luxury in this country today."

As Odets moved away from specifically Jewish settings for
his plays, he nevertheless imbibed deeply from his Jewish
heritage in their thematic development, and the intertwining
concerns with alienation and homelessness appear to be outgrowths of the exile motif which is pervasive in the whole of
Jewish history.

LANGUAGE

Reflecting on his early experience of seeing Odets's *Awake
and Sing!,* Alfred Kazin remarks, "In Odets' play there was

a lyric uplifting of blunt Jewish speech, boiling over and explosive, that did more to arouse the audience than the political catchwords that brought the curtain down." Odets probably had a better ear for language than any other playwright of his period. His early plays surge with the vitality of an authentic Yiddish-American which, as employed by Odets, is neither exaggerated nor burlesqued. He made such speech a legitimate idiom of the theater at a time when dialects were used so exaggeratedly in some other plays (*Abie's Irish Rose*), on the radio (*The Goldbergs* or *Amos and Andy*), or in comic strips (*The Katzenjammer Kids*) that they really demeaned the people portrayed as using them.

The Goldbergs was one of the more popular radio shows of the thirties; Weales notes that the dialect in the Goldberg scripts ("For vat is your fadder slaving for vat I'm esking you?" or "Maybe he got himself runned over by a cabsitac") uses "verbal humor at the expense of a real language, and it is used, perhaps unintentionally, to destroy any suggestion of validity in the characters and the situation." Weales continues, "Odets manages to find the humor in the language and retain the psychological truth of the family." For the first time in American drama, Jews were represented, through an honest recording of their language, in something other than caricature.

At times Odets deliberately employed the dialect of older, less acculturated Jews, particularly for such characters as Jacob, Bessie, and Myron in *Awake and Sing!*. However, elements of Yiddish-American appear in all of his plays and, indeed, quite tellingly, in his responses to questions in interviews. Even in situations where Odets is not striving to project a Jewish image, as he is with a character like Bessie Berger, for example, Yiddish-American word order and phrasing still are evident. Sid in *Waiting for Lefty* quite unselfconsciously speaks lines like, "If we went off together I could maybe look the world straight in the eye," naturally selecting a locution which is Jewish-American in its placement of the adverb *maybe*.

Cantor, who writes in detail about Odets's use of language, says of it, "It is Yiddish in its inflections (sometimes even when he is writing about the *goyish milieux*), and contains Yiddish-English expressions." Odets strove to establish a credible language for the people in his earlier plays and in so doing became the first American dramatist to use the Jewish-American dialect, with all of its humor, with all of its distinguishing cadences, for other than comic effects. Pochmann claims that while few Jews outside Palestine (and now Israel) speak Hebrew, Judaeo-German (Yiddish) has become more or less the tongue of the Jewish people throughout much of the world. From this Judaeo-German language Odets has borrowed so heavily.

One can open to any page of *Awake and Sing!* and find in it the most faithful representations of the Yiddish-American dialect. A few follow:

> *Bessie:* Go to your room, Papa. Every job he ever had he lost because he's got a big mouth. He opens his mouth and the whole Bronx could fall in. [In an editorial note, Shuman "finds the object of the sentence in the primary position (*Every job*) and also finds the exaggerated humorous cliché, 'the whole Bronx could fall in,' so common to Yiddish-English." He also notes "the third person singular aside."]
> *Myron:* I was a little boy when it happened—the Great Blizzard. [Shuman notes that in "this case the referent of the pronoun follows the pronoun."]
> *Bessie:* Myron, make tea. You'll have a glass tea. [Shuman notes: "Characteristic of Yiddish-English is the omission of the qualifier (*some* tea) and of the preposition (glass *of* tea)."]

Haslam, writing about Odets's use of language in *Awake and Sing!,* notes that Odets used "four major types of lexical or grammatical aberrations in constructing a believable stage Yiddish: (1) prepositional differences; (2) sentence order; (3) verb variations; and (4) Yiddish loans." He notes that an authenticity of dialect is achieved because Odets capitalizes on the difficulty that speakers like Jacob or Bessie have in translating words like the Yiddish *foon*, which can mean *of* or *from*; or *bei*, a more difficult preposition which can mean *at, by, among, beside, or with.*

In order to achieve believable Yiddish-American sentence structure, Haslam illustrates how Odets uses four specific techniques: (1) misplacement of modifiers; (2) the running together of some independent clauses without punctuation or conjunctions; (3) the misplacement of noun clusters used as objects; and (4) the omission of the objects of prepositions from the end of sentences. Haslam cites two types of verb variations that lend authenticity to Odets's dialogue, one which he identifies as mistranslation ("I won't stand he should make me insults") and the other as the frequent omission or addition of auxiliaries in verb clusters ("Wait, when you'll get married you'll know.")

Paradise Lost surges with the Yiddish-American idiom, despite the acculturation of the Gordons. Clara likes to begin speeches with "Do yourself a personal favor;" "Take a piece of fruit" is another staple of her conversation throughout the play, reminding one of the frequent allusions to fruit in *Awake and Sing!*. The well-ordered Jewish household will have fruit to offer guests. In the same play, one finds locutions like, "He's finished in ten minutes," rather than the more American. "He will be."

Odets tried to move away from his earlier idiom in plays like

Golden Boy, Night Music, Rocket to the Moon, and *Clash by Night,* but one still finds bits of the Jewish idiom creeping in: "Don't change the subject. Like my father-in-law here— he's always changing the subject when I get a little practical on him" or a typical Jewish wisecrack, "You can't insult me, I'm too ignorant" or a malapropism, "How do you like it with our boy for gratitude? He leaves us here standing in our brevities!"

Odets has been accused of abandoning his natural dialect as he became more successful and, indeed, of losing "his ear for this idiom." Cantor, however points out that Odets's ear did not fail him when he was writing *The Country Girl* and *The Big Knife,* but that in these plays he "is dealing with success and failure in the upper echelons of Hollywood and Broadway." *The Country Girl,* which Odets asserted "doesn't mean anything to me; it's just a theater piece," does not have the idiom of his other plays, nor is there any reason for this idiom. The cast of the play is not Jewish, nor does the play have overt ethnic characteristics. But Cantor makes a persuasive case for the idiom of *The Big Knife,* writing that in it "Yiddish-American dialect took a new turn when it went to Hollywood and incorporated a strain of what Charlie Castle called 'phony cathedral eloquence'; . . . Nat Danziger, Charlie Castle's agent, has 'all the qualities of the president of a synagogue,' though he is still capable of inverted Yiddish sentences and verb variants, such as 'Her I'm gonna talk to again' and 'a million dollars is got an awful big mouth' (I)."

If any doubt existed about Odets's ability to use the Yiddish-American idiom in his later productive years, *The Flowering Peach* should have erased it. In this play, Odets pulls out all the stops, borrowing Yiddish words like *tuchter,* the term Esther uses in addressing her daughter-in-law, using inverted word order, capitalizing on the comedy of Yiddish wisecracks and clichés much more than he ever had previously. *The Flowering Peach* is a comedy, and much of its comic character is found in its demotic language. When Noah tells a skeptical Esther that God has come to him in a dream and told of the impending flood Esther replies, "And all this God told you in one single dream?" to which Noah responds, "Told it to me in one dream, yeh! So now you know." When Esther wants Noah to urge their son Japheth to take himself a wife, Noah asks, "Such a boy, so strange, what could he offer a decent girl?" and Esther responds with the Yiddish humor of understatement "He could offer her a nice boat ride!" This sort of cynical litotes, characteristic of much Yiddish humor, blossoms in *The Flowering Peach* and grounds it in reality. Also the scatological is mingled with the idealistic to produce a similar comic effect in, for example, the scene where Noah discovers Shem has been making briquettes from manure and storing them on the Ark so that he can sell them at the flood's end: "On the Holy Ark he's makin' business! manure! With manure you want to begin a new world? Everybody's life he put in danger!"

Certainly in *Awake and Sing!* Odets strove most consciously to present the Yiddish-American dialect, using it as a means of building his characters and social setting. Cantor indicates how Odets manipulates the dialect: "That Yinglish in Odets' play involves a reciprocal relationship between young and old is evidenced by the fact that Hennie and Ralph, though for the most part they speak straight urban English, are influenced by the speech patterns of their parents and grandparents." The gradations of dialect by generation is particularly interesting in *Awake and Sing!*. Jacob, the least acculturated member of the family, speaks a clearly identifiable sort of Yinglish, using borrowed words, mistranslated prepositions, misplaced objects, and verb clusters without the auxiliary. The next generation, as represented by Bessie, Myron, and Uncle Morty, still clearly speaks Yiddish-American, and at times Bessie's dialect is stronger than Jacob's. However, Ralph and Hennie speak essentially an urban American English with only an occasional injection of Jewish locutions here and there. Haslam notes two sorts of borrowings from Yiddish: words taken over in toto such as *knish* or *shtupped* or the *chick* ending in *boychick,* or locutions which are translated directly into English from Yiddish such as the recurrent "by me," which comes from Yiddish *bei mir* or the frequent "already," which is translated from German and Yiddish *schon.*

ODETS AS A JEWISH WRITER

Odets will be remembered historically more as a proletarian playwright than as a Jewish playwright. Nevertheless, his background and upbringing imposed a Jewishness upon his work, a *Hébrewtude,* as I have called it elsewhere, in which were the roots of his depiction of characters (the dominant mother/wife, the acquiescent husband), his concern with the themes of homelessness and alienation which are outgrowths of the Jewish motif of the exile, his concern with redemption, and his use of language as found both in his depiction of Yiddish-American life and in his general use of a more conventional standard English.

Odets's social view in his early plays often suggested affirmation. Speaking of these plays, Odets said that they "undoubtedly came out of ascending values, out of positive values, out of the search of millions of American citizens for some way out of a horrifying dilemma—a dilemma which, by the way, I don't think is over." These final words ring very true today as the United States faces problems which seem even more threatening than those of the Great Depression of the 1930s. By focusing on the plight of Jews during the Depression, Odets was able to write about characters whom he understood from the inside out and was also able to build the dramatic tensions which vivified his productions. It can certainly be said that the social and economic circumstances of the 1930s provided him with the perfect dramatic material to write about and that his early exposure to Jewish society provided him with themes, language, and folkways which lent themselves perfectly to the kind of writing that accounted for his meteoric rise as a playwright.

Brendan Gill (review date 19 March 1984)

SOURCE: "Remaking Mankind," in *The New Yorker*, Vol. 60, March 19, 1984, p. 116.

[*Gill is an American novelist, short story writer, and critic. In the following review, he pans a modern production of Odets's* Awake and Sing! *and wonders if the work has been lost to history.*]

Innumerable plays have earned recognition in histories of the stage but are no longer readily producible on a stage, and I have the impression that Clifford Odets' *Awake and Sing!* may be one of them. I call it an impression, and not a conviction, because nobody could possibly judge the value of the play, either as a work deserving a certain place in history or as a source of entertainment to contemporary audiences, by the ramshackle version of it that is currently on view at the Circle in the Square. Odets finished the play when he was twenty-eight, early in 1935; that was his *annus mirabilis,* in the course of which he wrote three other plays as well, working in feverish, fruitful collaboration with the Group Theatre. What an assortment of gifted young radical idealists (if not quite revolutionaries) they were! Their aspiration was to change the entire world for the better, beginning—their idea of reasonableness—with America. The Bronx in the depths of the Great Depression was the setting of *Awake and Sing!,* and it was also a symbol: free the inmates of that grim gray prison house of the soul and mankind would take the hint and assume the heroic task of making itself over, in order that, among other welcome consequences, "life shouldn't be printed on dollar bills."

The cast of the first production of *Awake and Sing!* is worth noting, so we can remind ourselves of how distinguished the Group Theatre was from the very start: Art Smith, Stella Adler, Morris Carnovsky, Phoebe Brand, Jules Garfield, Roman Bohnen, Luther Adler, J. E. Bromberg, and Sanford Meisner. The scenery for the play was designed by Boris Aronson, and the director was Harold Clurman, Odets' close friend and, in Odets' phrase, "helpful obstetrician." Most of these people sprang from the same first- or second-generation Jewish American middle-class background, and they felt affection for and revulsion from the family life that Odets depicted. With the exception of Paul Sparer and Benjamin Hendrickson, the cast of the present production of *Awake and Sing!* seems as totally at sea as if the Bronx in the thirties were Tibet in the twelfth century; they are out of touch with the lilting, robust patois in which the play is written, and even with the way the characters ought to move about, embracing each other and recoiling from each other (what we nowadays call body En-

glish and in this case, looking back, we may risk calling body Yiddish). Odets describes Bessie Berger—the Stella Adler role—as a woman who "loves life, likes to laugh, has great resourcefulness, and enjoys living from day to day." Nancy Marchand plays Bessie as a bleak, stiff-jointed, scheming, and unaffectionate Protestant matron; her Jewish accent falters at every turn. The young hero, Ralph Berger, is played in the original production by Jules (later John) Garfield, is played by Thomas G. Waites; he brings innocence and ardor to the role, but he lacks the charm that would lead us to hope that the world will someday grant his ambition "to get to first base." We fear he will remain where he is, and that is not what the optimistic Odets, himself a prodigious hitter of home runs, wished Ralph's fate to be. Dick Latessa is touching as Myron Berger, the contented failed father of the family, and Harry Hamlin brings a necessary hardboiled vigor, but no Jewishness, to the role of Moe Axelrod. As Sam Feinschreiber, a classic lonely and unloved nebbish, fresh from the Old Country, Mr. Hendrickson works a trifle too hard for his own good but by doing so helps a dying play to stay alive. The calculated ugly Bronx-apartment setting is by John Conklin, the costumes are by Jennifer von Mayrhauser, the lighting is by Richard Nelson, and the heavy-handed direction is by Theodore Mann. We miss that jaunty, irrepressible Roman candle Harold Clurman on this occasion, as we do on so many others.

George L. Groman (essay date 1986)

SOURCE: "Clifford Odets's Musical World, The Failed Utopia," in *Studies in American Jewish Literature*, edited by Daniel Walden, State University of New York Press, Vol. 5, 1986, pp. 80-88.

[*Groman is an American educator, editor, and author. In the following essay, he examines the influence of music on Odets and his works. He finds that Odets's plays often equate music with an inner harmony that offers hope amidst the dissonance of the outside world.*]

In the 1935 production of *Paradise Lost,* playwright Clifford Odets had one of his major characters conclude the final act of the play with a lyrical affirmation of faith. "Everywhere now men are rising from their sleep," the character, Leo Gordon, asserts. "Men, men are understanding the bitter black total of their lives. Their whispers are growing to shouts! They become an ocean of understanding! *No man fights alone. . . . I tell you the whole world is for men to possess. Heartbreak and terror are not the heritage of mankind! The world is beautiful. No fruit tree wears a lock and key. Men will sing at their work, men will love. Ohhh, darling, the world is in its morning . . . and no man fights alone!*"

Leo Gordon, whose visionary statement ends the play, has

just lost his business through bankruptcy and the machina-tions of a dishonest, longtime partner; he has been evicted from his home, his furniture is on the street, and he and his family can look forward, in the depression year of 1935, to destitution, despair, and the gray anonymity that is the lot of those who mix bad judgment with seemingly idle dreams. The disparity described here between inner vision and exter-nal reality lies at the center of Odets's perception of the world. In America, even the America of the 1930s, men and women have the capacity for personal fulfillment, but are thwarted by political and social forces that leave few, if any, options for those without money or power. Odets's dilemma, like that of many another depression writer, was that he sought to make sense out of what appeared to be senseless and to account for those who were stubborn or courageous enough to seek sur-vival on their own terms—terms which at least some of the time encompassed independence of thought, group or family loyalty, and a belief in the sustaining power of artistic vision.

Odets, it is interesting to note, escaped many of the difficul-ties he so carefully described in his eleven plays and other writing efforts by gaining recognition as a writer and by earn-ing a good deal of money as a result of his work. The son of Central and East European Jewish immigrants and also a high school dropout, he resisted his father's efforts to involve him permanently in the family printing business and set about becoming first an actor and then a playwright. It will be re-called that the first play of Odets to be performed, *Waiting for Lefty,* in 1935, produced a sensation. Odets here described the attempts of a committee of workers to gain acceptance for a strike, and performances were so effective in moving audiences that even middle-aged matrons from Scarsdale got to their feet to yell "Strike!" along with the actors. According to Odets's most recent biographer, *Waiting for Lefty* has been the most widely produced and banned play in theatre history. Odets's *Awake and Sing!,* produced later in 1935 but in fact the first play Odets wrote, focused on the struggles of a Jew-ish-American family in the Bronx during the depression era. Undoubtedly the play which most closely paralleled Odets's own experience, it described, often by means of pungent dia-logue, the frustrations of people with essentially middle-class aspirations and strong personal needs, but an uncertain fu-ture. If the characters, in their search for material and emo-tional security, are sometimes crude and rude in their interactions with and treatment of one another, there is al-ways lurking somewhere beneath the surface Odets's vision of a more satisfying life, one which might in a better world ultimately be made whole through the redeeming power of art. In *Awake and Sing!* and in many other plays of Odets, the theme is sounded again and again. If art does not and cannot rule the world and banish despair, it nevertheless re-mains as a haunted utopia and a vision of what might be.

Of all the arts, it was music which made the most profound impression on Odets's imagination and thought. Indeed, this interest was widely noted even during the writer's lifetime. According to one early observer and friend, Odets used mu-sic like a drug, "experiencing a remarkable psychological intimacy with vanished composers—whom he called 'the mighty dead'" and "whose message he was always eager to impart to others." Odets's wife, Luise Rainer, the Viennese film actress and Academy Award winner who later divorced him, in fact considered his interest obsessional. She noted that although "their greatest relaxation had long been listen-ing to records," the steady intake of music and his insistence on playing it at top volume eventually created more of a wall than a bond between them. Odets himself often bemoaned the fact that he had not become a musician or composer. In a typical journal entry, he remarked that he had been "destined" in his "flesh and spirit to be a musician but somewhere the spirit clutched wrongly."

Odets did, however, continue to be fascinated by the artistic possibilities which music offered and spent a good deal of time thinking about the connections between music and the writing he was doing. In a *New York Times* article in April of 1951, Odets used a string quartet to illustrate the possibilities for plot development. Here he describes, in hypothetical terms, the playwright who is primarily a technician, who "fabricates," and the playwright who, though he may have "an equal tech-nical grasp," begins always by expressing "a personal state of being." To be sure, even the technician is able to manufac-ture a competent plot, one in which quartet members "func-tion as one man, are deeply content, socially useful, and without personal problems." Into this "minor" paradise, Odets suggests, comes a young woman, beautiful and destructive, who has just married the cellist, but who begins an affair with the handsome second violinist. Not content with such disrup-tion, she convinces her "uxorious husband" to leave the quartet in order to make "more money and splash as a solo artist. Q.E.D., paradise is lost and the quartet destroyed; farewell to a small, rich communal life dedicated to musical art."

The truly creative playwright, Odets believes, may utilize the same ideas, but will come at them another way. Odets imag-ines this second writer

> morosely suffering . . . from a sense of alienation,
> feeling cut off from other workers in the theatre, from
> men and women in all walks of life. His deepest be-
> lief has always been that men must work together,
> not apart; and now he feels that there is something in
> modern life (acutely and painfully reflected in him-
> self) which makes this not only difficult but impos-
> sible.

> Months and months of this mood until one night,
> without belaboring the point beyond patience, the
> writer attends a quartet concert and sees there on the
> stage a perfect image of four men who, by the very

nature of their art, must work together, dedicated, connected, humble and true.

Odets goes on to point out that many of the most prominent string quartets of the time have failed. Presumably, the truly creative artist might also make use of such information in shaping his play.

It is interesting to note that Odets uses essentially the same focus for both of the writers he conjures up. Indeed, both may envision a situation in which the artist is destroyed by urgent needs—lust, avarice, and the desire for social and artistic recognition. These needs, paradoxically, clash with the artist's ability to achieve that sublime inner harmony which brings with it the greatest human fulfillment.

Of all the composers Odets admired, it was Beethoven who meant the most to him. In fact, a number of early fictional works modeled on the composer portrayed young musical artists, either violinists or pianists, who are crippled by the loss of a hand or fall victim to the ministrations of an unscrupulous agent. Odets's Louis Brant (modeled on Beethoven) was also to be the central character in a historical play which he finally abandoned in favor of material closer to his own experience. Odets, nevertheless, continued to believe that the composer's lifelong struggles were much like his own. Both Beethoven and he "were shy, suspicious, essentially homeless, and parentless—negative elements that Beethoven had changed into a positive but embattled idealism, a reaching out for 'Bruderschaft.' In his creative work he embraced the entire world . . . making of it the home he never had."

Odets was also much concerned with the evolution of artistic form in Beethoven's work. Earlier composers like Bach had used the forms of their own time. Beethoven, however, was half master of those forms and half their servant. Beethoven "*began to make the forms serve him.* A fugue was no longer something to fill with content. Now, with him the fugue was shaped, pounded into serving his purpose in relation to a bigger thing—to the expression of his own individuality." Although later composers, particularly those after Wagner and Debussy, were free to explore themselves completely, they strayed too far away from "the roots and the nourishing earth of social form and life." The result, according to Odets, was sterility and a kind of "danse macabre" filled with "disease, hunger, neurotic pleading and searching, perhaps a complete lack of caring covered with childish cynicism, bitterness, often hatred, lostness, tearing down." Odets concluded, in 1931, that such individuality, what he now described as "sophistication," would die "a swift death" and that artists would come back to the "truth of root things" because of the spirit of artistic and social reform which filled the air. "Beethoven," Odets says, "is so much our man today." Although he was "the first great individualist in art," he also keenly felt "the lack of a group of his own kind of people who would be as intent as he

on building up for themselves the same kind of world." That world was soon to be achieved, Odets claimed, through such movements as communism and his own Group Theatre.

As indicated, Odets's creative output for the theatre and for films was heavily influenced by his absorption with music. This interest is clearly reflected in *Awake and Sing!,* his play about the fortunes and misfortunes of a Jewish-American family living in the Bronx during the 1930s. Bessie Berger, the matriarchal head of the family, much like Brecht's Mother Courage, will do anything she can to keep her family together and to provide whatever security may be available at the time. In contrast, the men in the family were weak or psychologically maimed. Grandfather Jacob Berger, who dreams of Marxian revolutions, settles for the charity of his children, Caruso records, and a "glass tea." The father and husband, Myron Berger, who had attended law school for two years, ekes out a living as a haberdashery clerk and always ends by accepting his wife's judgments and decisions. Ralph Berger, like his sister, Hennie, is under his mother's domination—though he broods about the childhood pleasures Bessie failed to provide (skates and black and white shoes). When he thinks of marrying, Bessie prevents him from doing so because his fiancee is an orphan and has no financial resources. Hennie's husband, Sam Feinschreiber (fine writer) is dominated by his wife as well as his mother-in-law. He broods about his wife's lack of interest in him and senses that he plays second fiddle to another man. (Bessie remarks to other members of the family that as far as she is concerned, he doesn't even belong in the orchestra.) Bessies' brother, Mort, has been successful in business, but cares for little else. Even the more vigorous Moe Axelrod, who was Hennie's first lover and who convinces her at the end of the play to go away with him, is crippled. He has lost a leg in World War I, and his bitterness and cynicism show him to be spiritually as well as physically maimed.

At the end of Act II, Ralph learns that Bessie has duped Sam Feinschreiber into marrying Hennie, knowing full well that her daughter is pregnant by another man. He also learns that his grandfather and father have done nothing to prevent the deception. When Ralph confronts his mother, the enraged Bessie marches into Grandfather Jacob's room and smashes his Caruso records—here asserting a symbolic reaffirmation of her own role as head of the family and denying values that are irrelevant to survival and vaguely subversive. Ralph picks up a fragment of one of the records which turns out to be "O Paradiso" from Meyerbeer's *L'Africaine.* Earlier in the play, Jacob had expressed pleasure in hearing the piece and had recalled that in the opera "a big explorer comes on a new land—'O Paradiso.'" Jacob imagines Caruso in the role (in Act IV of the opera) standing on the deck of a ship and looking on a Utopia. "Oh paradise! Oh paradise on earth! Oh blue sky, oh fragrant air," sings the legendary Caruso. Clearly for Jacob, the paradise is not to last. Although Ralph grieves for his grandfather's loss of the records, Moe Axelrod, the family friend and Hennie's onetime lover, does not. He begins to sing a popular ballad of the day, the "Yama Yama" song. If paradise is unavailable, at least some forms of comfort are readily at hand:

> Lights are blinking while you're drinking,
> That's the place where the good fellows go.
> Good-by to all your sorrows,
> You never hear them talk about the war,
> In the land of Yama Yama
> Funicalee, funicala, funicalo. . . .

It is worth noting that although classical music in Odets's writing is used to represent a realization of human potential, popular music usually is not. Here the trivialization of deeply felt experience underscores the inadequacy of the response.

Later that same evening, Jacob commits suicide by jumping off the roof of the house, and the money from his small insurance goes to Ralph. However, he turns over the money to Bessie. Although Odets suggests that Ralph has gained in new understanding and vitality, one suspects that Bessie will continue to prevail because her vision and even her denials are an enduring source of family strength.

It was in *Golden Boy,* first produced as a play in 1937 and later as a film, that Odets dealt most directly with the theme of the failed musical artist. His protagonist, Joe Bonaparte, exchanges one identity for another, giving up promising studies on the violin to become a boxer. He desperately wants to reach for the big prizes—money, fame, and power, but he discovers that the path he has chosen is not an easy one. The prizes somehow seem elusive and even when they come, fail to provide the satisfactions he had dreamed of. Those who work with and for him—Tom Moody, his problem- and debt-ridden manager, Lorna Moon, Moody's fiancée who comes to love Joe, the gangster Eddie Fuseli who dreams of "owning" the golden boy—all desperately seek something of their own through Joe's successes in the ring. Indeed, for all of them, life is little more than a succession of risks. As one earnest, if uneducated, backer of the golden boy says, in a burst of Odetsian humor, Joe must win or they will all be left in their "brevities."

For Joe himself, the issue is more complex than simple victory or loss in the ring because he discovers that he cannot escape his past after all. He confides to Lorna Moon that music has provided him with a special kind of support and well-being. "When I play music," Joe says, "nothing is closed to me. I'm not afraid of people and what they say. There's no war in music. It's not like the streets." However, Joe also makes clear that music is not enough. He says, "You can't get even with people by playing the fiddle. If music shot bullets I'd like it better. . . ."

That Joe continues to think of returning to music is made clear by the fact that in his early bouts he is careful to protect his hands. In one instance, he sees a man carrying a violin case and is so upset by it that he loses a bout scheduled for later the same day. Joe continues to box scientifically, and although he wins, his manager protests because scientific boxing does not give the crowds the kind of excitement that comes with seeing the losing fighter savagely beaten. Finally, the pressures on him are overwhelming, and he gives an important opponent a terrific beating. His hand broken, he has effectively shut the door on the past and become the "professional" who will destroy those who stand in his way.

Joe's father, Old Mr. Bonaparte, serves as a kind of moral center for the play. An Italian immigrant with a great love for music, he has encouraged Joe in his studies on the violin and even bought him a costly instrument for his twenty-first birthday. He disapproves of Joe's career as a fighter, but Joe, nevertheless, seems to need his support and asks him again and again for "the word." Finally, on the night of the fight in which Joe is to break his hand, Mr. Bonaparte gives his assent, but in a burst of anger and with the recognition that Joe will not and cannot turn back. He says, "Yeah . . . you fight. No I know . . . as'a too late for music. The men musta be free an' happy for music . . . not like-a you. Now I see whatta you are . . . I give-a you every word to fight. I sorry for you." That paradisical inner world with its serene and special harmonies, reserved for the "free an' happy," is lost forever. Indeed, it is the world outside which is out of tune and will eventually help to destroy the golden boy.

In his final fight, with the restraints removed, Joe puts "all of the fury of a lifetime" into a knockout punch and literally kills his opponent. Now he is at last made aware of what he has become, and he fears his father's response. Joe and Lorna speed into the night to meet death in a car crash—either through accident or design. Odets's melodramatic ending brings the story to its conclusion, but the dilemma posed by the playwright remains unresolved.

Other plays of Odets also make use of music for thematic and metaphorical purposes. In *Paradise Lost,* Pearl Gordon loses her fiancé, a violinist, because he can find no work, but she continues to play her piano and give lessons until the family falls victim to economic catastrophe. In *Till the Day I Die,* Ernst Tausig, an underground activist and former violinist, is imprisoned by the Nazis. When his interrogator learns of his career as a violinist, he asks Tausig if he is familiar with the Joachim Cadenza for Beethoven's Violin Concerto in D Major and then suddenly and angrily smashes Tausig's hand with a rifle butt. In *Night Music,* it is Steve Takis, a clarinet-playing Greek American who seeks a precarious foothold in the urban jungle. In *Clash by Night,* it is old Mr. Wilenski, a Polish immigrant who plays the accordion and dreams of better times long past. In Odets's last play, *The Flowering*

Peach, based on the story of Noah and the Ark, it is the mythical gitka, a creature with rare musical powers, that offers respite in the midst of turmoil. Clearly, music in Odets's plays continued to be pervasive and significant.

To be sure, other important American writers have also been drawn to music and used it in their work. One thinks of Willa Cather's *Youth and the Bright Medusa* where music fills a cultural void and forms a raison d'être when all else fails or, more recently, of William Styron's *Sophie's Choice* where a former concentration camp inmate and her mad lover reassert their basic humanity and reclaim a sense of dignity through the redeeming power of music. Clifford Odets's lifelong love of music also encompassed such broad understanding. For Odets as well, music continued to be the sustaining force. In the chaos of modern life, music could, finally, provide a sense of the good and the beautiful, and a special place for the soul.

Gerald Peary (essay date Winter 1986/1987)

SOURCE: "Odets of Hollywood," in *Sight and Sound*, Vol. 56, No. 1, Winter, 1986/1987, pp. 59-63.

[*In the following essay, Peary explores Odets's flirtation with and eventual immersion into Hollywood screenwriting.*]

Consider three contemporary playwrights. Sam Shepard becomes a movie star, a heartthrob, Harold Pinter turns out clever screenplays; David Hare directs films—and they do so without looking over their shoulders. Who today would criticise them for diminishing themselves as playwrights, squandering their talents, or just plain selling out? Selling Out—in capitals—the very notion is an anachronism. But in the 30s, for the theatre, the term still meant something. The stage was where 'real' dramatic artists made their stand. Eugene O'Neill never, ever went to Hollywood, Clifford Odets was reminded over and over again. And if Odets wished to be the next O'Neill—or maybe better than O'Neill—he must stay in New York and pump out plays. Some fifty-odd years ago, in 1935, MGM offered Odets $3,000 a week, or more, to write screenplays in Los Angeles. The playwright, though amazed, resisted. 'Like a conspirator, he whispered that he might be willing to consider it,' wrote Harold Clurman, co-founder of the Group Theatre, in *The Fervent Years.* The Group, however, kept its resident playwright in hand.

In Hollywood, riches awaited Odets. In New York, he remained almost as indigent as ever. He shared the heartfelt frustration of young Ralph in *Awake and Sing!*: 'He dreams all night of fortunes. Why not? Don't it say in the movies he should have a personal steamship, pyjamas for fifty dollars a pair, and a toilet like a monument. But in the morning he wakes up and for ten dollars he can't fix his teeth.' Odets

planned his escape to Hollywood. He was angered by the Group's righteous demands on him.

Ever the hopeful suitor, MGM invested $17,000 in Odets' play *Paradise Lost*—significantly, the Group Theatre didn't turn down this Hollywood financing. But the play faltered at the box-office, and the courtship abruptly ended. Though the MGM contract was lost, Odets adopted a new tack: he paid a money-raising visit to Hollywood on the Group's behalf. Conscience-stricken in the Beverly Wilshire Hotel, he bragged about the superiority of the Group Theatre back home in New York. He assured Lewis Milestone that his real interest was in the stage and the purpose of his trip was to keep *Paradise Lost* afloat; Milestone countered by asking Odets to produce a screenplay for *The General Died at Dawn,* from an unpublished China-set pulp novel which had landed on Ernst Lubitsch's desk at Paramount.

In February 1936, Odets signed a four-week contract with Paramount Pictures worth $2,500 a week. According to his biographer Margaret Brenman-Gibson, he felt respected 'as he had not since the opening of *Awake and Sing!*' It was as if, six months after the death of his own mother, Odets had achieved Bessie's most passionate hope for her son Ralph: 'I should only live to see the day when he rides up to the door in a big car with a chauffeur and a radio. I could die happy, believe me' (*Awake and Sing!*). Seemingly, Odets liked being in Hollywood. That was his guilt. How could he explain this to Clurman and the Group? The point can be made by jumping ahead for a moment, to Odets' autobiographical play about Southern California, *The Big Knife.* The play dissatisfied Clurman: the motivation for the protagonist's unhappiness was too shadowy. '"First you must show," I said, "how anxious the actor is to leave Hollywood how and why he hates it so much . . ." Odets suddenly blurted out, "He loves it."'

What could be more enjoyable than writing at Lewis Milestone's behest on *The General Died at Dawn*? Director of the uncompromisingly pacifist *All Quiet on the Western Front* (1930), Milestone was a European-born Jewish intellectual, a friend of the Group Theatre (he lent money for its production of *Johnny Johnson*), and he was a left-liberal—some might say, more politically conscious than Odets. When, under the influence of Malraux's novel *Man's Fate,* Odets edged his screenplay towards the recent revolutionary struggles in China, Milestone did not baulk. In fact, the director added (uncredited) a key political scene to the script: the opening, in which a high-handed colonialist is punched to the ground by the hero, O'Hara, an American fighting the Chinese revolution.

At night, Odets struggled with *The Silent Partner,* the labour play he had long promised the Group. The film script, however, progressed smoothly, at the rate of three or four pages a day. His hero's impoverished early life was modelled on that of the Group actor Jules (later John) Garfield. For the right-wing antagonist, General Yang, Odets used Hitler's oratory. For good measure he added fire-and-brimstone agitprop, Big Speeches attacking capitalists and dictators which could have been lifted verbatim from propagandist stands in *Waiting for Lefty*.

Had Odets managed to bite the hand which fed him $2,500 a week? By May he had finished the script and was so confident of its virtues, both aesthetic and political, that he told the *New York Times:* 'There is no attempt in Hollywood to stop anyone doing good writing . . . I believe that my ideas can be put over in pictures.' To prove his point, the shooting script of *The General Died at Dawn* found its way to the radical journal the *New Masses* for ideological inspection. In the magazine's July 1936 issue Sidney Kaufman endorsed the screenplay without reservation, praising Odets' instant mastery of cinematic technique. The *New Masses* also printed the text of two scenes, one in which O'Hara expounds on why he fights dictatorships ('You ask me why I'm for oppressed people? Because I got a background of oppression myself, and O'Hara and elephants don't forget'), and a second in which he rails against the warlord Yang for his self-serving philosophy ('Your belief is in your own very limited self-mine is in people! One day they'll walk on earth, straight, proud . . . men, not animals').

Both speeches survived in the release print. Why? Because here was evidence—to Paramount's glory—of the hand of Clifford Odets, the famous author of *Waiting for Lefty*: There is, however, evidence of post-production studio tampering. The lovers, Gary Cooper and Madeleine Carroll, are thrown together on a train in the middle of a complicated plot without introduction: the key meeting scene is simply missing. Surely Odets wrote it, and surely Milestone filmed it? Important political elements have also vanished. Kaufman alludes to a village laid ruin by Yang and a dead woman in a puddle: neither detail is in the movie. Yang's devastation is kept off screen entirely. Kaufman rejoiced that '150 million eyes and ears closely attentive' would heed the line, 'We who have been the anvil—will soon be the hammer.' But he rejoiced too soon: Odets' most overtly Marxist passage is not to be found in *The General Died at Dawn*.

O'Hara's radical speeches are in fact practically all that remains of 'leftist' content—and even these are undercut by Gary Cooper's delivery. Paramount Pictures was not the Group Theatre, and Gary Cooper, a political conservative, utters Odets' passionate words with the commitment of an actor under a multi-picture contract. Clurman wrote to Odets: 'Our greatest lesson was to hear lines so characteristic of you become almost imperceptible . . . when said by actors with no relation to them.'

The General Died at Dawn won no Academy Awards, nor

deserved to. Seen today, it seems a silly, toothless imitation of, in particular, *Shanghai Express* (Paramount, 1932), which was similarly located on an Oriental train to nowhere. General Yang is a brazen copy of the title character in Frank Capra's *The Bitter Tea of General Yen* (1932). (And, yes, Gary Cooper does say to Madeleine Carroll, 'We could have made wonderful music together.' That woeful line was written by Odets.) As for the film's politics, who can unravel the warring sides? When Paramount re-released the film in 1949, an opening title was added: 'Some time back in the early days of the Chinese government, the Chinese people, led by the great Chiang Kai-Shek, fought to rid themselves of the last of the warlords who preyed upon remote provinces. This picture is inspired by that battle and by its victorious conclusion.'

Odets never refuted this Cold War interpretation, which was undoubtedly the antithesis of his intentions: Chiang Kai-Shek, in fact, was probably the inspiration of General Yang. However, when Odets appeared voluntarily before the House Committee on Un-American Activities in 1952, he denied having inserted any social comment into the film, or even that he had told the *Daily Worker* in 1937 that 'I got away with some stuff' in the script. Odets confessed, perhaps disingenuously: 'I thought the whole matter was nonsense because *The General Died at Dawn* is a picture that starred Gary Cooper and (was) done by Paramount. There was nothing of any subversive or propaganda nature in it . . . I don't think Hollywood has ever made a movie with left propaganda in it. And I think the whole matter of social messages . . . cannot happen.'

Back in Hollywood, 1937, now married to the actress Luise Rainer, Odets was employed by Paramount on two projects, *Gettysburg* and *Castles in Spain*. Of *Gettysburg* Margaret Brenman-Gibson wrote: 'As soon would become his practice, Odets let this film script become longer and longer as he tried to improve it. He seemed unable to accomplish this, and the mammoth screenplay, with its torrent of colourful, lively dialogue, would soon be shelved . . .' *Castles in Spain*, an adaptation of Ilya Ehrenburg's *The Loves of Jeanne Ney*, switched to Loyalist Spain, went through two versions before the project was passed to another Group playwright, John Howard Lawson; his rewrite became the film *Blockade* (1938). Odets complained in public for the first time about the Hollywood screenwriting process. He told *World Film News:* 'When I saw (*Blockade*), I couldn't find one line left of what I'd written . . . I never sat through a film y'know without thinking to myself, "That's not true. It's a lie."'

Hollywood began to fill up with members of the Group Theatre seeking film work: Elia Kazan, Morris Carnovsky, Phoebe Brand, Ruth Nelson, Luther Adler and even Harold Clurman himself. The arrival of his colleagues did not free Odets' scenario-writing blocks, but it did ease the passage of his new play, *Golden Boy*. The critic Gerald Rabkin noted how Odets turned Hollywood subject matter and technique (the short scene and the fadeout) 'against itself, in order to combat the mythic Hollywood success story.' In *Golden Boy,* Odets, the insider, thumbed his nose at Hollywood. Unlike his pre-studio plays, which were sprinkled with references to cinema stars and visits to the local bijou, *Golden Boy* never directly mentions the movies. Joe Bonaparte punches his way through the boxing world without once thinking of Paramount Pictures. At the same time, Odets expected his audience to recognise that Bonaparte's rise to the top, in a plot full of stock film figures, follows the mythic, linear form of Hollywood at its streamlined best. Then Odets mocked Hollywood with the downbeat off-screen deaths of Joe and Lorna, as intentionally unmotivated as the most tacked-on studio ending.

Golden Boy was a Broadway hit and Odets was converted back to the theatre. He published a bilious attack on the cinema under the studio system in the *New York Times* (21 November 1937): 'It is sad to see what movies are doing to America's consciousness of itself . . . Hollywood has set our citizens examples of conduct and behaviour patterns fit only for lower animals.' Odets became obsessed with getting the Federal Theatre to produce *The Silent Partner* across America (that same play which had lain stillborn in Hollywood because of *The General Died at Dawn*). Meanwhile, his new play, *Rocket to the Moon,* maltreated and ridiculed its only Hollywood-tainted character, the movie dance director Willy Wax. On the East Coast, Wax is regarded as an interloper, practically a carpetbagger. Success, Odets wrote of this weakling and womanizer, had given him an 'unpleasant uneasiness'. He narrowly escapes death by strangulation.

Odets was asked on radio if serious-minded dramatists should try Hollywood. 'Flatly, the answer is they must stay where they are, myself included.' True to his new word, Odets declined Rouben Mamoulian's offer to write the script of *Golden Boy* for Columbia Pictures. In 1939, Hollywood took its revenge. The film of *Golden Boy,* written by Daniel Taradash and Lewis Meltzer stripped away Joe's brother Frank, the radical labour organiser, and also much of Odets' social-consciousness sermonising. Most serious, the unhappy ending was blithely repaired with a full life ahead for Joe and Lorna.

In 1940, unable to mount a Boston-to-New York production of *Night Music* without investment money from United Artists, Odets was lured to Los Angeles to try to write a *Night Music* screenplay for the producers Albert Lewin and David Loew. His efforts were unavailing. The dramatist's swift artistic comeback was the 1941 play *Clash by Night,* in which the villain, Earl, is a movie projectionist. Willy Wax was only threatened with death; Earl is actually strangled. He dies in his projection box ('a veritable picture of some minor hell') while a vapid Hollywood picture runs on, wedding bells on the soundtrack.

The keynote speech in *Clash by Night* echoes Odets' criticism of Hollywood in *Awake and Sing!* Motion pictures give false hope to America's Little People. Joe speaks for all the play's lost characters: 'Earl, Jerry, Mae, millions like them clinging to a goofy dream—expecting life to be a picnic. Who taught them that? Radio, songs, the movies . . .' *Clash by Night* failed as *Night Music* had failed. Odets returned to Hollywood in 1942 and again (with his new wife, Betty Grayson) in 1943: this time he stayed for five years. In 1948 he told the *New York Times*: 'I went West . . . because I wanted to shake out of my system the disappointments of two successive commercial failures in the theatre . . . I was looking for a period of "creative repose": money, rest, and simple clarity.' Again he turned about. 'I went to Hollywood and found much of interest there . . . The cinema medium, as the platitude goes, is a very great one: why not explore the possibilities? Why not mingle with and learn from some of the world's shrewdest theatre technicians, including writers?'

Odets was signed by Warner Brothers to write a life of George Gershwin, *Rhapsody in Blue.* Odets adored Gershwin and his script was 900 pages long. When he delivered it, Jack L. Warner promptly fired him, even though, according to Jean Negulesco, Odets begged to be allowed for no extra fee to compress the script to a more normal length. 'J. L. was adamant,' Negulesco remembered. 'He didn't want Odets in the studio. Another writer was called in to do a completely new job . . .'

The next studio to beckon Odets to Hollywood was RKO. In 1943 his agent arranged for Odets to write a movie version of *None But the Lonely Heart,* from the new novel by Richard Llewellyn. Odets liked the tale of a Cockney lad wandering in the bowels of between-the-wars London. He took the train West. On arrival at RKO, he learnt that Cary Grant was planned for the lead. 'There was silence for a moment and I asked if anyone read this book. It seemed no one had . . . When I met Cary for the first time, he said that he'd like me to direct the movie, too . . . (he) told me if I could write the words, I shall certainly be able to direct their use. Well, I did.'

Out of Clifford Odets' screenplays came the narrative technique for *Golden Boy*; out of his life in Hollywood came *The Big Knife*. At the centre of his career as a film-maker, however, is *None But the Lonely Heart*. Among its admirers were James Agee and Jean Renoir, and the reason is not far to seek. On his first time behind the camera, Odets took command. The result was assured, poetic and personal. Though there are compromises in the studio casting—an insufferably pixyish Barry Fitzgerald and a miscast Cary Grant—*None But the Lonely Heart* remains a small model of a successful literary transformation, rather than an adaptation.

The ambitious, overlong and overwritten novel is about a

working-class boy who never learns. Like his father, Ernie Mott aspires to be a painter; but he's sidetracked by flashy mobsters. Eventually, he stops talking about art and begins carting a gun. 'The gun felt like some old pal . . . kind of cool and steady, ready to do a job without no backchat or fuss.' As his mother lies dying of cancer, Ernie for a moment grows fearful of impending loneliness. 'Funny how the whole place was sort of dead cold without her . . . He started shaking so much he could hardly make a move, and the place was coming over dark with the grey of rain outside.' By the end, however, Ernie is back to oblivion: 'He was going to get a suit like Jim, and a tie pin, and proper look the part of The Smasher. He started feeling sorry for everybody going to work, because there was no need of it.'

Out of Clifford Odets' screenplays came the narrative technique for *Golden Boy*; out of his life in Hollywood came *The Big Knife*. At the centre of his career as a film-maker, however, is *None But the Lonely Heart*.

—Gerald Peary

The movie Ernie Mott is of a different, romantic breed: an instantly recognizable Odets dreamer, wishing for so much more than his assigned slum-life existence. As Cary Grant's Ernie Mott walks through London, a voice proclaims: 'The Story of Ernie Mott, who searched for a free, a beautiful and noble life in the second quarter of the twentieth century.' The conflict is pure Odets from the time of *Awake and Sing!*: the head-in-the-clouds son versus the materialistic mother. Ernie's mother wants her son in her second-hand shop. But he objects: 'I'm not in the business of sweating pennies out of devils poorer than myself.' In a patented Odets soliloquy, Ernie ponders his ambitions: 'Life is a piece of meat, when you know how . . . Take what you want? Right? Right! So that's what it's all about—either be a Victim or be a Thug. But suppose . . . suppose you don't want to be neither? Not a hare an' not a hound. Then what?'

Having discovered that his mother has cancer, Ernie decides for the time being to stay at home and help in the shop; and the movie's most tender scenes are those in which Ernie and his mother (Ethel Barrymore) come together as a true family. On the outside, however, Ernie chooses to run with the hounds: he joins a gang of thieves headed by Jim Mordinoy, having fallen in love with Mordinoy's girl, Ada. Odets takes Ernie through a swirl of London nightlife: it is a familiar film noir tale of the 40s, of the outsider whose love for a corroded woman weds him to a decadent and criminal, 24-hour-a-day nightclub life. The noir sections of the film are swift,

hardboiled and laced with tart dialogue. When Odets makes mistakes they are personal rather than generic, such as overplaying a Jewish pawnbroker, a sententious character who acts as Ernie's conscience, or making too much of the dichotomy between dark Ada and nice Aggie, who plays the cello at night and loves Ernie loyally despite his errant ways.

The last scenes of *None But the Lonely Heart* show Odets in the full flood of his romantic idealism, and they bear comparison with the final curtains of his best plays. The Cockney Orpheus has ascended from the underworld, given Ada back to the sharks and turned away from crime. London is about to be blitzed. He stands on a bridge and addresses his ageing pal, Twite: 'I'm dreaming, Dad, "a dream of a better man." Where's the decent, human life the books tell us about? When's the world coming out of its midnight? When's the human soul getting off its knees?' Twite reminds him that it sometimes takes a war. Ernie agrees: 'That's it, Dad, one thing is left. I see it plain as London town! Fight with the men who'll fight for a human way of life!' With that chivalrous pledge, Ernie descends from the bridge into the dark tentative city. The last shot is subdued: Ernie, all sobriety, standing at Aggie's door; he enters, but there is no shot of the lovers. Odets holds his camera on the street, keeping sentimentality at bay.

Ethel Barrymore won an Academy Award as Best Supporting Actress for her role in *None But the Lonely Heart* the film, however, did poorly at the box office, this being the reason, perhaps, why Odets' directing career was curtailed. What did follow, however, were numerous writing assignments in the 1940s and two screen credits.

Odets' 900-page *Rhapsody in Blue* was transformed into *Humoresque* (Warner, 1946). A new writer, Zachary Gold, cut the script down, eliminated the Gershwin biography, but kept Oscar Levant, Gershwin's pianist friend, as a major character; then he grafted what was left on to bits of Fanny Hurst's 1919 short story. That, at least, is director Jean Negulesco's version of how Odets and Zachary Gold came to share screen credit on *Humoresque*. But confusion arises from the number of *Humoresque* versions in the Warner Film Library housed at the University of Wisconsin's Center for Film and Theater Research. There are eight treatments by different people, plus scripts by Waldo Salt and Barney Glazer, but nothing from Zachary Gold. (Odets is represented by an anthology composite of *Rhapsody in Blue* scenes, seemingly compiled by a secretary.)

If Odets' career is to be measured by how shrewdly he subverted the studio system, then *Humoresque* is a meretricious project, the ultimate sellout. It is artificial, overripe, quintessentially Hollywood. But taken on its own terms, as a delirious John Garfield-Joan Crawford 'woman's picture', it often succeeds. It is played to the hilt by the dashing stars, and reaches a crescendo in a grand steal from *A Star Is Born*: Joan Crawford drowns herself in the ocean, in sacrifice, while violinist Garfield plays on, courtesy of Isaac Stern.

In 1946, Odets wrote **Deadline at Dawn** from a florid, amusing Cornell Woolrich thriller. It was directed at RKO by Harold Clurman, who at night in Hollywood wrote his masterly memoir of the 1930s, *The Fervent Years*. Clurman never particularly liked the movies, even when making one. Later he recalled, 'My almost casual attitude towards the job met with resentment, perhaps because I finished the film on time and it proved moderately profitable.' Clurman labelled **Deadline at Dawn** 'a run-of-the-mill RKO movie for which Clifford Odets as a favour to me wrote the screenplay.' Odets had a better opinion of it. 'I'm not ashamed of that,' he said in 1963. 'It's a little mystery thriller. l see it; it has its living moments.'

Between 1942-48, Odets was a prolific Hollywood scenarist. He planned a biography of Beethoven for Charles Laughton, though how much was written is unclear. Margaret Brenman-Gibson credits him with unproduced screenplays for projects called *All Brides Are Beautiful, April Shower* and *The Whispering Cup* and, interestingly, an adaptation of Dreiser's *Sister Carrie*. She also lists Odets working uncredited on *Sister Kenny* (1946) and Hitchcock's *Notorious* (1946). Unfortunately, there is no other record of Odets' involvement with the latter. And there is another project calling for further research: the complete Odets script for *It's a Wonderful Life* (1946). Although Frances Goodrich and Albert Hackett were hired for the final script, Frank Capra acknowledges in his autobiography, *The Name Above the Title,* that he retained Odets' early scenes.

Odets' West Coast days between 1942-48 exploded back on the New York stage as **The Big Knife** in 1949. The character of actor Charlie Castle is, unmistakably, a projection of the screen writer Odets. But what exactly troubles Castle? The second-rate movies he has worked on? All Hollywood pictures? The compromised work ethic of Southern California? The sterile life in the sun? Failed personal relationships? (The dissolution of the Group?) As its many critics have observed, **The Big Knife** is as muddled and contradictory as Odets' own vacillating opinions of Hollywood. (Regrettably, the 1955 film, directed by Robert Aldrich, was foggy and ill-motivated, probably because it was too loyal to the original script.)

In 1952, Odets appeared before HUAC, named names and then described his own non-subversive occupation: 'To speak generally, I go to Hollywood to make a living, not to write something . . . to demean or disgrace American people as I believe many people do. But to make an honest living, after writing entertaining scripts.' In 1955, after the death of his wife, Odets returned for good to Hollywood. He worried obsessively about having been a 'friendly' government witness. And he went back to writing screenplays.

Odets' chief disappointment in the years 1955-63 was that his monumental Biblical screenplay *Joseph and His Brethren* remained unproduced, even though Harry Cohn, president of Columbia, was an enthusiast. Frank Capra and Otto Preminger were asked to direct it, and Rita Hayworth was scheduled to star. Perhaps Odets' most challenging assignment in these years was to write (uncredited) the last scene of Nicholas Ray's *Bigger Than Life* (1956). What is to happen when James Mason wakes in hospital and realises, having suffered delusions of grandeur under a new wonder drug, that he tried to kill his son in imitation of Abraham's sacrifice of Isaac? Odets' solution was disappointingly conventional: Mason wakes up healed and normal, realises his mistake and embraces his wife and son in reaffirmation of the 1950s nuclear family.

The best of the later screenplays is **Sweet Smell of Success,** a patented Odets story about the heated symbiotic relationship between a Broadway press agent and a big-time gossip columnist. For this script, revised from an earlier one by Ernest Lehman, Odets could run free with zesty New York dialogue and non-stop Runyanisms. Here are none of the conscience-stricken characters of **The Big Knife. Sweet Smell of Success** wisely stays among the show-business shills and heels: Sidney Falco (Tony Curtis), *PR* man supreme, 'the boy with the ice-cream face', and J. J. Hunsecker (Burt Lancaster), the Walter Winchell-like gossip maven, who brags 'My right hand hasn't seen my left hand for thirty years.'

In 1960, Odets both wrote and directed a picture for the first time since **None But the Lonely Heart**. But **The Story on Page One** is two hours of tired and overacted courtroom drama which reveals, principally, that as Odets' politics grew more conservative, his vision of the working class grew more condescending. While Odets' films were claustrophobic, with their weak, compromised characters, the playwright himself began to speak out about the need for strong, uncontaminated national heroes. On 25 May 1952, six days after his final HUAC appearance, Odets eulogised John Garfield, who had just died aged 39, in a letter to the *New York Times:* 'He was as pure an American product as can be seen these days, processed by democracy, knowing or caring nothing for any other culture or race . . . His feeling never changed: that he had been mandated by the American people to go in there and "keep punching" for them.'

'One thing we need badly is heroes,' Odets told the *New York Herald Tribune* in 1958. 'As Emerson said, a hero must be a minority of one. He must be an ethical model who breaks the mould of conformity, but this is the age of conformity.' Four years later, he romanticised Marilyn Monroe in *Show* as a natural spirit who was ruined by the deprivations of her childhood, then callously treated by the studio system: 'That she could be sensitive, intuitive and with an animal wisdom far beyond them, most of the executives with whom she collided did not even dream.'

Odets' last screenplay was *Wild in the Country,* written for Elvis Presley in 1962. 'It pained me to hear him rationalise writing the screenplay,' Harold Clurman said, 'by declaring that Presley was something more than he seemed.' But was not Presley the perfect new Odets hero: the truck-driving country boy who keeps his Tennessee accent and Southern ways in homogenised Southern California? As the title suggests, the film is about a tearaway who keeps his rural integrity while all about him—bullying family, dishonourable townspeople—try to corrupt him, send him to jail, break his spirit. Yet there are echoes of that unmistakable Odets voice. Presley (Glenn Taylor): 'Don't let your Pa beat your wings down.' Tuesday Weld: 'Your aim is to fly above me. But if you ever come tumbling down, I can wait!' And the solution to the hero's burden of social problems? He is packed off to a safe university to become a writer. The last cinematic image Odets leaves us is of Glenn Taylor walking awed into the halls of learning: Elvis Goes to College.

In 1963, Clifford Odets became a writer for the *Richard Boone Show,* suddenly evincing the same enthusiasm for television that he had expressed, at various times, for the movies. He died of cancer that same year aged 57. Dead in Hollywood.

Were his years in movies worth it? His old Group Theatre friends, those still left after HUAC, remained as angry about the sacrifice of talent as they had been when Odets sidled off to Hollywood in 1935. In August 1963, Harold Clurman wrote in the *New York Times:* 'Now think of . . . the little floozie in *The Big Knife.* The girl is a confused victim of the Hollywood industry. She is both sordid and pathetic . . . She is Odets' female alter ego.' According to Margaret Brenman-Gibson, 'Elia Kazan said he could have forgiven Clifford anything except the grievous waste of . . . time and talent in writing films.'

None But the Lonely Heart, yes, and that splendid script for *Sweet Smell of Success.* Otherwise the Group Theatre was right from the start: one of America's major playwrights became only an intriguing footnote among film-makers. He sold out. Having gone merely to look round, he ended by becoming Hollywood. He was cremated, appropriately enough, at Forest Lawn cemetery. Odets' friend Jean Renoir understood the ties that bind. 'When Clifford Odets died,' Renoir said, 'I thought I wanted to leave Hollywood. He was a prince. Every gesture, every way of thinking was noble. Although I love Hollywood, I have to say it is without nobility. But I stayed, of course.'

David Denby (review date 29 September 1988)

SOURCE: "Odd Man In," in *The New York Review of Books*, Vol. XXXV, No. 14, September 29, 1988, pp. 37-42.

[*In the following excerpt, Denby reviews* The Time is Ripe: The 1940 Journal of Clifford Odets, *and comments on Odets's personal revelations at the beginning of a career slide.*]

Clifford Odets, [Elia] Kazan's friend and colleague in the Group, had such a mission [an artist's] and was ruined. In love with the theater but eager to make money, Odets dragged himself unhappily through long years in Hollywood, often working on screenplays never filmed or on anonymous re-writes of other men's work (at the end of his life. be was writing a television series for the actor Richard Boone). The journal he kept in 1940, now published by Grove Press as *The Time is Ripe,* suggests how much the movies attracted and shamed him. In the course of the year (he is thirty-three at the beginning of it) the Group, beginning to lose its way, failed with its New York production of his play *Night Music.* Odets then traveled to Los Angeles to write a screen adaptation of the play (never made). He was earning $2,500 a week. He was restless, with little to do but work, drink, and sleep with the actress Fay Wray, and he quickly came back.

The year was a turning point for him. No longer the famous young playwright whose picture had been on the cover of *Time* two years before, be had begun his excruciating career as a famous American has-been.

The Time is Ripe is an emotional record of Broadway, 1940, as a vale of soul-making. Fascinated by Casanova and Stendhal and Byron, Odets made breathless notation of his erotic triumphs, mixing rhapsodic ardor with homely notes of the bachelor life:

> Home I came to write on the trio play. And yet this goddam acute loneliness makes me leave the telephone on, hoping that by accident someone may call. And then the phone rang! . . . She came here in record time, whereupon we fell upon each other and slept and awoke and chatted and massacred each other again and again and then she fell asleep and I prowled around the house unable to sleep until past ten in the morning, she stained and scented beside me with all the exercises of the night.

There are many girls, some famous, some not; much re driving around the city late at night; and, on every pag the lyricism, descriptions of his friends and himse painful in their harshness. Idealistic, impassioned lacking in canniness, even routine common sens onstrates in this journal the intoxicating swe ousness of his famous conversation (by r one of the best talkers of his time). H autodidact, and he had caught art fe

Stendhal, Gide, Heine, and Strindberg, gearing himself up with long stretches of Beethoven on the record player—more than one beautiful young woman was forced to listen to the late piano sonatas before climbing into bed.

The journal details plans for projected plays about Van Gogh, Nijinsky, Woodrow Wilson, and reveals why he had so much trouble completing anything. Piety and frivolity were so ruinously mixed in Odets's nature that he could not begin to write without episodes of exaltation (Beethoven and more Beethoven) yet could not work seriously without stopping to run out and meet, say, Leonard Lyons or Walter Winchell at a nightclub. Returning home from the Stork Club at dawn, exhausted and guilty, he would write for an hour or so before falling asleep. Inspiration, raised in Odets's journal to a fetish, required the constant celebration of scribes and photographers.

He knew he was turning himself into a fool. "This living from the jowls and testicles is murderous for me. It engulfs me, a man with an essentially religious purpose and use in life, a sort of sunken cathedral of a person." The actor Lionel Stander said to him in a club one night: "You are a first-class man. What are you doing with these nitwits?" On the other hand, Odets got something useful out of the nitwits—the dialogue he added, years later, to Ernest Lehman's screenplay for *The Sweet Smell of Success,* an acrid portrait of columnists and press agents prowling the corrupt New York night world. But his own play about his Hollywood experience, *The Big Knife,* was overblown and self-pitying. Like many other serious writers, he thought the movies were childish but had great difficulty mastering the peculiar skill of screenwriting. At one of Dorothy Parker's cocktail parties, he sees the moldering figure of F. Scott Fitzgerald—"pale, unhealthy, as if the tension of life had been wrenched out of him." It is a meeting sad to imagine—one writer drawing near the end of his Hollywood martyrdom, the other beginning his long descent.

George L. Groman (essay date 1991)

SOURCE: "Clifford Odets and the Creative Imagination," in *Critical Essays on Clifford Odets*, edited by Gabriel Miller, G. K. Hall & Co., 1991, pp. 97-105.

[*In the following essay, Groman examines Odets's reverence for the inspired creativity of Victor Hugo, Ralph Waldo Emerson, Walt Whitman, and Ludwig van Beethoven. Groman then contrasts the high standards of heroism and idealism Odets found in these artists' works with the often hopeless and corrupt situations found in his own.*]

Clifford Odets, for all of his adult life as a playwright and screenwriter marveled at the gift of creativity, finding inspiration when that gift seemed within his grasp and enduring depression when it seemed beyond reach. His own experi-

ence operated as both a resource and an obstacle as he sought to resolve a number of personal crises—as a son whose father viewed his early acting and writing efforts with contempt, as a lover and husband whose stormy relationships ended in failure and bitterness, and as a creative artist whose need for privacy and discipline conflicted again and again with the temptations and demands of a public life and reputation. Yet whatever his own circumstances, Odets consistently sought fulfillment as a writer, viewing the creative act with reverence and continuing attention, and finding in the efforts of others inspiration as well as validation for his own creative identity.

Even as a boy, Odets was drawn to writers of powerful imagination whose heroes struggled with questions of identity and self-realization through social action or artistic effort. As a teenager Odets read Victor Hugo's *Les Misérables,* a book to which he would invariably return and comment on with great affection. Indeed, in his 1940 journal, he called Hugo "the rich love of my boyhood days" and went on to describe *Les Misérables* as "the most profound art experience I have ever had." The French author, as Odets noted, influenced him in ways that were to affect his later life as a writer and political activist: "Hugo . . . inspired me, made me aspire; I wanted to be a good and noble man, longed to do heroic deeds with my bare hands, thirsted to be kind to people, particularly the weak and humble and oppressed. From Hugo I had my first feeling of social consciousness. He did not make me a romantic, but he heightened in me that romanticism which I already had. I loved him and love him still, that mother (*sic*) of my literary heart."

For a boy entering adolescence, Hugo's clear division of right and wrong, his demarcation of heroes and villains, and the endless pursuits of the relentless Inspector Javert must have met the young Odets's need for suspense and adventure. More important, ultimately, was Hugo's gallery of characters who were capable of heroism *and* sacrifice—the saintly Bishop of Digne, whose every action is devoted to those in need; Fantine, who sells her hair and even her teeth, hoping to preserve the life of her daughter; the young radical and romantic Marius Pontmercy, who gives up an inheritance on political principle; and the hero of heroes, the solitary convict Jean Valjean, who benefits from the Bishop's generosity and repays him by pursuing a life of good works despite enormous personal sacrifice.

Odets was to continue his search for mentors of powerful and wide-ranging vision, and in the American writers [Ralph Waldo] Emerson and [Walt] Whitman he found new inspiration and direction. As he wrote to Harold Clurman in 1932, it was the business-oriented Louis Odets, the writer's father, who first encouraged him to consider Emerson seriously. Margaret Brenman-Gibson quotes from this letter, in which

Odets recalls his father leaving in his room "two volumes of a peculiar edition of Emerson 'made for business men.' In a gaily mocking account of this . . . (Odets) says, 'The devils quote and underline on every page glorious trumpet sounding maxims about success. They make Emerson the first Bruce Barton of his country. But I am reading with a clear brain and no interest in success.' Emerson is 'certainly the wisest American.'"

Reflecting further on Emerson's importance to him, Odets wrote in his 1932 journal, "I am glad that Emerson lived before I did. He has made life a richer thing for many (*sic*) of us. That is the function of all great men: that they reveal to us natural truths, ourselves and a realization of ourselves." Writing again in the same journal, he reflected on Emerson in a way that seemed to echo Hugo: "Emerson says somewhere that heroes are bred only in times of danger. I would add great artists are too bred in such times. Now I see the world is drifting into such times. I am waiting to see what heroes and artists will spring from the people."

Although Odets would come to share Emerson's belief that people are not fundamentally bad, he commented that few could or would rise to Emerson's call for "uncorrupted behavior." That he continued to brood over this loss of Emerson's faith in his fellow humans is amply demonstrated in his plays and elsewhere. Even near the end of his life, in a telecast interview, he would remember "what Emerson called 'uncorrupted behavior'" as a quality "with which all children are born . . . when nothing outside of yourself influences you, when you are in command of yourself with honor, without dishonesty, without lie, when you grasp and deal, and are permitted to deal, with exactly what's in front of you, in terms of your best human instincts."

To be sure, Odets could and did find many calls for "uncorrupted behavior" in Emerson's work and that of other writers but what he seems to have valued most in Emerson was his belief in the range of human potentialities despite the limitations of time, place, accident, or fate. It was Emerson who had emphasized in "Circles" that "there are no fixtures in nature. The universe is fluid and volatile," and in "Fate" that nature, rather than being limited to destructiveness, "solicits the pure in heart to draw on all its omnipotence." In "Circles" Emerson remarked that "the use of literature is to afford us a platform whence we may command a view of our present life, a purchase by which we may move it." Such statements were meant to clear the way to new horizons and did so for Odets and countless others.

Like Hugo and Emerson, Walt Whitman assumed heroic proportions for Odets, who even kept a plaster cast of the poet in his room. In 1940 he bought first editions of *November Boughs* and *Drum Taps,* as well as a collection of Whitman's letters

to his mother. In 1947, when Odets's only son was born, he named him Walt Whitman Odets.

If the large-scale models of Emerson and Whitman were encouraging, Odets nevertheless understood that American life might bring forth artists of quite different scope and temperament. In conversations with the composer Aaron Copland at Dover Furnace, the Group Theatre's summer retreat, Odets came to grips with this issue. He noted that "today the artists are not big, full, epic, and Aaron shows what I mean. They squeeze art out a thousandth of an inch at a time, and that is what their art, for the most part, lacks: bigness, vitality and health and swing and lust and charity. . . ." Odets concludes by asserting, "there I go to Whitman again. Of course that's what we need, men of Whitman's size."

In another entry in the 1932 journal, Odets suggests that Whitman "roars in your ears all the time. When you swing your arms and the muscles flex, they are Whitman's muscles too." Elsewhere Odets celebrates not only the strength that may come with well-being but also the sexuality and autoeroticism that made Whitman famous and, in the nineteenth century, generally disreputable: "I think with love o (*sic*) Whitman's lines, something like, 'Oh the amplitude of the earth, and the coarseness (*sic*) and sexuality of it and the great goodness and clarity of it.' And I myself feel that way with love for people and the earth and women and dark nights and being together and close to naked women, naked as I am naked."

Eventually, Odets's excitement and passion would cool—a result of hard living, many personal and professional disappointments, and, simply, aging. However, it may be that Whitman's imagery linked to a sense of purpose remained embedded in the playwright's consciousness, as suggested by a passage written a year before his death: "The whole fabric of my creative life I have built a room in which every corner there is a cobweb. They have mostly been swept away and I must begin again, *spinning out of myself* (italics mine) the dust and 'shroudness' of that room with its belaced and silent corners." The passage brings to mind Whitman's noiseless, patient spider involved in the act of creation, launching forth "filament, filament, filament, out of itself." Like the spider, the narrator's soul in the second verse of Whitman's poem (now personified) sends out "gossamer thread" to "catch somewhere," thereby hoping to end a pattern of isolation. If Odets, like the spider and soul of the poem, sought to reach out to others, he seemed also to be settling old scores here, undergoing a ritualistic purgation in a rather stifling atmosphere and, in doing so, readying himself for the task of creation, which Whitman's spider image so powerfully evokes.

Odets's search for heroic models extended to the musical world as well as to literature, and in the life and work of

Ludwig van Beethoven he found a source of inspiration that was to last until his death. Odets listened to Beethoven's music frequently and intensively, wrote on Beethoven's importance as a creative artist and man of his time, and would sometimes self-consciously compare and contrast Beethoven's problems and solutions with his own. In his early attempts at fiction and drama, Odets used the maimed musician or composer as a central figure. Indeed, in his unproduced play *Victory* he carefully modeled the hero, Louis Brant, on Beethoven himself. In later years in Hollywood, Odets also planned a screenplay on the composer's life, but the project was never completed.

Beethoven's early poverty, his difficult social relationships (often with women), and his dedication to his art (despite hearing problems and eventual deafness) greatly moved Odets. And in looking at W. J. Turner's biography of the composer, which Odets read while writing *Victory*, he would find one acquaintance of Beethoven remarking of him "that he loved his art more than any woman" and "that he could not love any woman who did not know how to value his art." Later, as Beethoven's hearing problems increased in severity and further isolated him, the composer thought of suicide but desisted, "art alone" restraining his hand. At other times he wrote of seizing "fate by the throat" to reach his goals. Clearly, for Odets, Beethoven was a truly courageous man and artist despite his personal difficulties.

Odets, in commenting on Beethoven's music, found the Eroica Symphony "an awesome and terrible piece of work' and his fourth piano concerto a composition in which the "characters of the orchestra never for a moment stop their exuberant conversation." As for Beethoven's Seventh Symphony, he noted, one must "be virgin of heart and spirit to write it. Beethoven did not lose the innocence," though ordinary mortals give it up simply "to survive." Odets's descriptions, quoted here, underscore the intensity of his feelings about Beethoven and sometimes suggest Emersonian parallels. They also indicate the kind of close thematic connections between music and literature the writer would make in his plays and films.

As Odets struggled with form, so did the Old Master, but Beethoven triumphed again and again. As Odets put it, "every time he found a form for his content he simultaneously found that his content had progressed in depth and a new form was necessary—a very Tantalus of life! He, however, had the hardheadedness to see it through to the bitter end—he obviously died looking for a new form—and he died having pushed music to a level which before had never been attained nor has yet been equalled. Great unhappy man!"

Finally, in Beethoven, Odets found a paradigm for the quintessential Romantic—a superman for all seasons—one who is "amazed, impressed, delighted, and enraged by the caprices of life." As Odets noted further, "It is the romantic who cries out that he is out of harmony with life—by which he means that life is not in harmony with his vision of it, the way he saw it as a youth with moral and idealistic hunger to mix his hands in it and live fully and deeply. The classic art is to accept life, the romantic to reject it as it is and attempt to make it over as he wants it to be." The man and his method were for Odets a means of perception, a symbol of hope, and possibly a basis for social action and change.

When we turn to Odets's own work, however, we find a curious paradox. The heroic models have disappeared, and in their place the protagonists of his plays respond at a primal level to a brutal, self-serving world; either they are (or become) corrupt or they are overwhelmed by an environment over which they have little or no control. Indeed, the America that Odets lived in and responded to was far different from the private and idealized world about which he wrote with such intensity and even affection and that he later abandoned with such regret. In *Waiting for Lefty,* Odets's first-produced and perhaps most well-known play, there is a rousing call for strike action by the rank and file of a taxi union after much indecision and argument. However, Lefty, the guiding spirit of the union, has already been murdered by unknown assailants, and even the ringing call to action at the end of the play suggests martyrdom as well as the benefits of solidarity. As Agate, one of the rallying strikers, puts it, "HELLO AMERICA! HELLO. WE'RE STORMBIRDS OF THE WORKING-CLASS. WORKERS OF THE WORLD. . . . OUR BONES AND BLOOD! And when *we die* they'll know what we did to make a new world! *Christ, cut us up to little pieces. We'll die* for what is right! put fruit trees *where our ashes are!"* (My italics.)

In *Awake and Sing!,* Odets's Depression-era play centered on an American-Jewish family in the Bronx, the Marxist Grandfather Jacob is ineffectual even in his own family and ends his life by suicide. His grandson Ralph Berger, who surrenders the insurance money Jacob had left him at his mother's insistence, will in all likelihood have little influence in times to come. As a number of critics have suggested, his optimism strikes a false note as he faces the future without a clear sense of purpose, training, or money. Indeed, as more than one character comes to understand, despite arguments to the contrary, life *is* "printed on dollar bills." The well-to-do Uncle Morty, a dress manufacturer, will continue to have the respect of Ralph's mother Bessie, he will continue to oppose strike action vigorously and probably successfully, and he will lead a personal life without personal responsibilities, sleeping with showroom models and seeking other creature comforts. Moe Axelrod, the World War One veteran and ex-bootlegger, has by the end of the play convinced Bessie's daughter Hennie to abandon her much-abused husband and infant to seek a life of pleasure with him. To be sure, arguments for social or family responsibility may be found in this often moving play, but the resolution nevertheless seems to suggest a definition of success devoid of commitment or love.

In *Golden Boy,* Joe Bonaparte, a violinist turned boxer, does become a hero *for his time*, defined by physical strength and a willingness to incapacitate or destroy his opponents in the prize ring. Although he has read the encyclopedia from cover to cover (perhaps fulfilling Ralph Berger's quest for learning) and "practiced his fiddle for ten years," the *private* world he has created is no longer sufficient for him. It cannot offer him the sense of power or perhaps the ability to dominate others for which he yearns. Indeed, he is seduced by the monied world that surrounds the prize arena and by the temptations offered by the gangster Eddie Fuseli, who seeks to remold the Golden Boy and turn him into a fighting machine— careless of others, indifferent to love, and irrevocably cut off from family ties and memories of the past. As the reborn Joe aggressively puts it, "When a bullet sings through the air it has no past—only a future—like me." Joe returns to his dressing room after what is to be his last fight, and his trainer, Tokio, notices that one eye is badly battered, symbolic of Joe's impairment of vision on a number of levels. The triumphant fighter learns that he has killed his opponent in the ring, and he must confront the implications of the disaster. In rejecting a personal integrity, he has betrayed his moral and spiritual center, and at the end of the play he dies, an apparent suicide. His personal tragedy is an awareness of the vacuity his life has become. He is trapped in a world that he himself has made, rejecting his father's simple but encompassing Old-World Italian version of what his personal struggle must lead to: fulfillment of a dream predicated on the yells of a mob over ten rounds, the quick buck, and tabloid headlines forgotten at a glance.

Both *The Big Knife* and *The Country Girl* are plays that show the failure of art and artists destroyed by a world that demands too much, too fast, too soon. In *The Big Knife,* Charlie Castle has given up a promising career in the theater and a somewhat vague belief in political and social action to become one of Hollywood's big stars. Like Joe Bonaparte or perhaps Odets himself, Charlie is plagued by the idea that he has betrayed his considerable talent in exchange for money and stardom. Early in the play, he argues that the theater is "a bleeding stump. Even stars have to wait years for a decent play." Now in the movie business, he cannot afford "acute attacks of integrity." In a succession of films, he reflects "the average in one way or another" or is at best "the warrior of the forlorn hope." As Hank Teagle, a family friend, puts it, "Half-idealism is the peritonitis of the soul. America is full of it."

Like Joe Bonaparte, Charlie understands only too well what he has become. He remarks that he has become an imitation of his old self, and young new actors now imitate—or parody—the imitation. However, it is Marion Castle, Charlie's estranged wife, who most emphatically reminds Charlie of his self-betrayal, warning that he acts against his own nature. She says to him, "Your passion of the heart has become a passion of the appetite. Despite your best intentions, you're a horror."

Indeed, Charlie has taken a downward path. He is on the way to becoming an alcoholic, he has been unfaithful to his wife, and he has avoided prosecution for an accident that occurred during an evening of drunken driving by allowing a studio employee to confess in his place and serve a prison term. Only when the studio management obliquely threatens to murder the woman companion turned blackmailer who was with him on the evening of the accident does Charlie assert himself by preventing a new crime. However, despite his one moment of decency, Charlie is lost. He has, over Marion's objections, signed a new contract with the studio moguls who have by turns enticed and threatened him. Too weak to face a loss of status poverty, and the unstable life of the theater, perversely attracted by the life he has been leading, and yet filled with self-loathing, Charlie takes his own life. Marion, his wife, leaves with Hank Teagle, the writer who has been faithful to his principles and whom Charlie had called his Horatio. Indeed, it is Teagle who will tell Charlie's story to the world—the tale of a man who was certainly not a Hamlet in depth or breadth, one who could understand and even dream but who could not change himself or the world, which paradoxically offered him so much and so little.

In *The Country Girl,* a play better structured and developed than *The Big Knife,* Broadway director Bernie Dodd is ready to take a chance on a new play starring a has been, an older actor named Frank Elgin. Dodd is "in love with art" and tells Elgin's wife Georgie that although he could "make a fortune in films," he intends to continue in the theater, where important work can still be done. Elgin's brilliant performances in two mediocre plays, based on his intuitive understanding of character and situation, had long ago inspired Dodd and now lead him to believe that the old actor can excel again. However, there are real problems. Elgin is weak and self-indulgent, he is an alcoholic, he is a liar, he needs constant reassurance, and like Arthur Miller's Willy Loman, he needs desperately to be well liked. As the play develops, Bernie Dodd and Georgie struggle with each other and with Frank. Each of the three seeks personal fulfillment, but finally the play becomes the all-consuming and all-important issue. Frank Elgin does succeed (with the help of the two closest to him) in rising to his full stature as an actor. He vindicates Bernie's judgment and justifies (or necessitates) Georgie's remaining with him—after years of failure and disappointment.

In this play about theater life, Frank Elgin's transgressions are forgiven in the name of art and artistry. Bernie discovers that Frank has lied about his wife's past. He has told Bernie that Georgie was once Miss America (possibly to enhance his own prestige), that she is an alcoholic, and that she is a depressive who has attempted suicide. Georgie learns that Frank has lied about her (his lies are partially based on a play in which he once appeared) and observes that he has begun to drink again. When the producer (Phil Cook), Bernie Dodd, and others in the company find out, there is turmoil, but there are no lasting repercussions. Because of Bernie's belief in Frank Elgin's talent, the actor is to continue in the play. Frank himself is simply following an old pattern. He has for much of his adult life drunk steadily, taken pills, and lied to relieve the pressures on him. When his and Georgie's only child dies, when he loses much of his money in producing a play, and when he begins to fail as an actor, the old remedies are close at hand. The conflict between the easy indulgence of the moment and the stern realities of working in a creative but uncertain world—with its quick rewards and even quicker condemnations—leads to the kind of disintegration Odets so often sought to depict. In this play, as in *The Big Knife,* intuitive understanding, talent, and artistry bring some forms of self-fulfillment and recognition, but are by themselves no protection against weakness or personal loss. In *The Big Knife,* Charlie Castle finds suicide the only way out. Frank Elgin is successful at the end of *The Country Girl,* but one suspects that his future success will depend on the continued availability of the long-suffering wife who mothers him, on directors and producers who excuse his frequent lapses, on unending applause, and on total self-involvement and self-delusion.

Odets, then, in his work revealed his fascination with the world of art and his belief that art may enhance our understanding of the human condition, though it cannot alter the environment or our responses to it. The romantic vision that Odets pursued so intensely in a personal way might seem ennobling or heroic, but in a world of shrunken values and failed personal lives, it offers only a sense, a resonance, of what might have been. Indeed, the romantic stance—as Odets portrayed it in the America of his time—was collateral to be called in, leaving only a shell without substance. Despite the excitements of the conflict, Odets's vision of the truth was profoundly pessimistic. That he portrayed it as he did often showed courage as well as artistry.

John Lahr (review date 4 April 1994)

SOURCE: "Ark Angels," in *The New Yorker,* April 4, 1994, pp. 94-6.

[*John Lahr is an American author of both fiction and nonfiction, a playwright, and a critic. In the following excerpt, he reviews a 1992 performance of* The Flowering Peach *and gives background on the play and Odets's reasons for writing it.*]

"Half-idealism is the peritonitis of the soul," says Hank Teagle,

a character in Clifford Odets' *The Big Knife*—a play about Hollywood, where Odets moved from New York in 1936, in search of a big audience and big bucks. He lived with a moral malaise every subsequent day of his professional life. Odets died, of cancer, on August 14, 1963, when he was fifty-seven, and on his writing desk were two copies of *Time.* One was the December 5, 1938, issue, which had Odets on the cover as a wunderkind (between 1935 and 1939 he wrote seven plays, including *Awake and Sing! Waiting for Lefty, Golden Boy,* and *Rocket to the Moon*) and bantered his famous battle cry "Down with the general fraud!" The other was a 1962 story announcing his appointment as script editor and chief writer on NBC's TV drama series *The Richard Boone Show.* In the intervening twenty-four years, Odets had had five more plays performed, and had created one major public sensation: in 1952, he testified as a "friendly witness" before the House Un-American Activities Committee. Odets had been one of the theatrical standard-bearers of the left, and his dialogue, with its pithy swagger, cut a raffish new figure on the American stage. But after that moment of compromise Odets' language, which had captured both the utopian thrill and the radical lament of the times, lost its moral purchase on the American experience. The true combative, lyric note of his literary voice was strangulated. Odets lapsed into a long period of inactivity, and when he emerged, in 1954, as the writer-director of *The Flowering Peach* (revived now by the National Actors Theatre, at the Lyceum), he spoke in a new voice and in a new way. Earlier, he had wanted to purge himself of Jewishness and be accepted as "a regular American playwright," but in *The Flowering Peach,* a retelling of the story of Noah and the Ark, he returned to his Jewish roots, and he also tried to rationalize his political volte-face. "There is idealism now in just survival," Rachel, Noah's daughter-in-law, says in the play, doing the author's special pleading. Noah, like Odets, was a true believer, but Odets turned Noah into someone like himself, whose values were confounded by the absurd turn of apocalyptic events. Out of God's awesome petulance ("I shall wipe off the face of the earth this human race which I have created") Odets created a comedy of righteousness in which Noah's ideals are sorely tested. Like Odets, he is forced to acknowledge the hard pragmatic fact of life: every dogma has its day.

Noah, the Bible tells us, was six hundred years old when the flood came, but the hoary-headed Eli Wallach, who bustles onto the Lyceum stage protesting to the heavens about being commanded to build an ark in the desert, doesn't look a day over a hundred. "I'm awake," he says, of his call to duty, "but I wish I was dead." Noah has been selected by God to repopulate the new and improved universe, but he is also that universe's first standup comic—a hostile sharpshooter loudly proclaiming his innocence. When his wife, Esther (Anne Jackson), kvetches about his drinking, he says, "You should be satisfied that I drink, otherwise I'd leave you." But age and drink—which are two large and endearing comic components of Noah's personality—are generally downplayed in Martin Charnin's sleepy production. It's a testament to the conviction in Odets' argument that *The Flowering Peach* holds the attention of the National Actors Theatre audience. (Jurors voted the play the Pulitzer Prize but were overruled by the advisory board, which gave it to Tennessee Williams' *Cat on a Hot Tin Roof.*) The debate between Noah, God, and Noah's recalcitrant family almost makes the audience forget some of the production's startling visual anomalies, like the impoverished prostitute Goldie (the curvaceous Molly Scott), who comes on board as Japheth's would-be wife, and, in her gold bangles and colorful pink and green silks, looks like a fugitive from *Kismet. The Flowering Peach,* in a sense, is the forerunner of Mel Brooks' *Two Thousand Year Old Man* ("Joan of Arc? I dated her"), with this difference: Noah is a test of faith, not of fun. To succeed, though, *The Flowering Peach* requires the eccentric conviction of great comic playing. The characters are a collection of ideas, not psychologies, and the play needs stars to bring their large personalities to bear on this sketchily drawn tribe which has been delegated to make the world over after God wipes it clean. But instead of comic cameos Charnin can manage only lacklustre cartoons. Noah's sons are a collection of isms for the new world order: idealism (Japheth), cynicism (Ham), and capitalism (Shem). Of this winded crew, only the enormous Josh Mostel, as Shem, finally gets into the swing of things, but not until the second act, when his stash of "dried manure briquettes" (his investment for the future) is discovered in the listing Ark. "With manure you want to begin a new world?" the outraged Noah says, ordering it dumped overboard, but not before Mostel's face has turned pink, his behemoth body wobbling with choked fury. "Poppa," he says. *"But what am I without my money?!"*

The play's original tryout included Washington and coincided with the Senate's censuring of Joseph McCarthy, and Robert Whitehead, the original producer, remembers that Odets was completely distracted by this political development. "Clifford would not come to terms with the end of the play," Whitehead recalls. "He kept saying to me, 'I'm locked in my room. I can't do anything, because you're forcing me to try (and write). I've got nothing but ashes in my mouth. You want poetry. I've got ashes.'"

The play still feels unresolved. When Noah's wife dies (Odets' last wife, Bette Grayson, died in 1954), he is weakened by grief and by his rigid adherence to his faith in the face of certain disaster. Japheth (played by David Aaron Baker) refuses to trust to God's will and let the leaking and rudderless Ark founder, and ultimately his faith in reason prevails over Noah's insistence on the will of God. "I have a strange feeling that God changed today," says Japheth, whose assertion of authority finally separates him from his father. When they reach land, Noah sends his offspring out to be fruitful and multiply. The flowering peach tree is an emblem, as plants

always were for Odets, of the universal potential for "perfect form." In the midst of this hope of perfection is the spectacle of man's imperfection. Noah blesses the unborn child of his favorite and idealistic son, Japheth, and his new bride, Rachel, but chooses to live with Shem and the status quo. "Why?" Noah says, as Shem exits ahead of him with his wheelbarrow piled high with booty from the trip, and he answers, "It's more comfortable." According to the Bible, Noah, after fulfilling his mission, lived three hundred and fifty years longer. But Odets lived only nine years more, hounded by a sense of incompleteness. "I may well be not only the foremost playwright manqué of our time but of all time," he wrote in his diary in 1961. "I do not believe a dozen playwrights in history had my natural endowment. . . . Perhaps it is not too late."

FURTHER READING

Biography

Brenman-Gibson, Margaret. "The Creation of Plays: With a Specimen Analysis." *Psychoanalysis, Creativity, and Literature: A French-American Inquiry*, edited by Alan Roland, pp. 178-230. New York: Columbia University Press, 1978
     Psychoanalysis of Odets and his works that includes substantial biographical information.

Odets, Nora and Walt Whitman. "Hollywood and its Discontents." *American Film* XIII No. 7 (May 1988): 28-34.
     Excerpt from Odets's 1940 journal that chronicles Odets in Hollywood and his thoughts on "selling out," the movie business, and his interactions with movie stars.

Criticism

Barbour, David, and Seward, Lori. "Waiting for Lefty." *The Drama Review* 28, No. 4 (Winter 1984): 38-48.
     Describes the genesis of Odets's first play and its production, with a complete summary of plot, action, and characters, and lists the original casts from the 1935 debut and subsequent Broadway run.

Bray, Bonita. "Against All Odds: The Progressive Arts Club's Production of Waiting for Lefty." *Journal of Canadian Studies* 25 No. 3 (Fall 1990): 106-122.
     Bray includes a social analysis of *Waiting for Lefty* in her recounting of a controversial 1935 production of the play during tense civil times in Canada.

Canby, Vincent. "Odets Waves An Olive Leaf in a Last Play." *The New York Times* (27 March 1994): Sec. 2, 5,32.
     In a review of a modern production of *The Flowering Peach*, Canby analyzes the play within the context of Odets's testimony before HUAC.

"Clifford Odets." *Educational Theatre Journal* 28 No. 4 (December 1976): 495-500.

Excerpt from an interview in which Odets discusses his early years as an actor and director in the Group Theatre and the influences he found there.

Devlin, Diana. "Period Pieces." *Drama* No. 151 (1984): 48.

Reviews the collection, *Clifford Odets: Six Plays,* and argues why Odets's plays are important only as period pieces.

Lahr, John. "Waiting for Odets." *The New Yorker,* (26 October 1992): pp. 119-22.

Review of a 1992 revival of *Awake and Sing!* that includes an examination of Odets's work and its current relevance.

Lal, Malashri. "The American Protest Theatre." *The Humanities Review* 2 No. 2: 16-21.

Places *Waiting for Lefty* and *Awake and Sing!* within the context of the protest theater movement of the 1930s.

Miller, Gabriel. "The Chekhovian Vision." In his *Clifford Odets,* pp. 29-61. New York: The Continuum Publishing Company, 1989.

Aligns *Awake and Sing!* and *Paradise Lost* with Anton Chekhov's plays on several points, then uses the comparisons to analyze Odets's plays thematically.

Pearce, Richard. "'Pylon,' 'Awake and Sing!' and the Apocalyptic Imagination of the 30's." *Criticism* XIII No. 2 (Spring 1971): 131-41.

Examines *Awake and Sing!* in the context of certain literature of the 1930s which reflected "a feeling of senselessness and a threat of apocalypse."

Shuman, R. Baird. "Thematic Consistency in Odets' Early Plays." *Revue des Langues Vivant* XXXV No. 4 (1969): 415-420.

Explores themes of "nonfulfillment, personal isolation, and loneliness," which permeate Odets's early plays and inform his later works.

Simon, John. "From Broadway to Berlin." *New York* 24, No. 3 (21 January 1991): 55-6.

Discussion of the plot and characters in *The Country Girl* in a review of a modern production of the play.

Mary Oliver
1935-

American poet.

The following entry provides an overview of Oliver's career through 1995. For further information on her life and works, see *CLC,* Volumes 19 and 34.

INTRODUCTION

An award-winning poet, Oliver is known for verses that celebrate nature and the lessons it holds. Her work explores with deceptive simplicity the mysteries of life, death, and regeneration. From an early identification with the poet Edna St. Vincent Millay, Oliver has since forged an individual alliance with nature that finds expression in an often rapturous lyricism. Her poems seek and speak of the unexpected beauty in nature, without ignoring its uglier truths.

Biographical Information

Oliver was born in Cleveland, Ohio, in 1935 to Edward William Oliver, a teacher, and Helen M. Vlasak Oliver. She studied at Ohio State University for one year, then moved east to attend Vassar College. Beginning in the early 1950s, Oliver occasionally stayed at Steepletop, the upstate New York farm of the poet Edna St. Vincent Millay, where she served as an assistant to Millay's sister. Millay's lyrical style and themes influenced Oliver's early work, and Oliver later found an artistic home in rural Provincetown, Massachusetts, just as Millay had. In the early 1980s Oliver served as Mather Visiting Professor at Case Western Reserve University. She went on to become poet in residence at Bucknell University in 1986 and, beginning in 1991, Margaret Banister Writer in Residence at Sweet Briar College in Virginia.

Major Works

Oliver's first poetry collection, *No Voyage, and Other Poems* (1963), established her reputation for treating nature in a direct, unsentimental, yet lyrical fashion. Subsequent publications, including *Twelve Moons* (1980) and *American Primitive* (1983), found her delving further and further into the natural world for subject matter while pulling farther away from human subjects. Thematically, the poems in these collections unflinchingly face nature and its continuous cycle of life and often vicious death to embrace the stark beauty of this process. Oliver shifted her perspective in *Dream Work* (1986) to feature certain human-centered themes of personal suffering and the past, including a poem dealing with the Holocaust, but returned in *House of Light* (1990) to a nature-based focus on isolation from human concerns and assimilation into various aspects and beings of nature. In her first book of prose, *A Poetry Handbook* (1994), Oliver brought her years of writing experience to bear on a close study of the processes of poetry writing.

Critical Reception

Critics have commended Oliver's poetry for its clarity, simplicity, and descriptive precision. *American Primitive,* which won the 1984 Pulitzer Prize for poetry, was highly acclaimed for its rendering of familiar objects and places in unique, refreshing ways. Some critics, however, noted that several poems contain, as Carolyne Wright asserted in *Prairie Schooner,* "conventional imagery and sentiments" that weaken the collection as a whole. Stylistically, critics have noted the lyrical beauty of Oliver's lines and turns of phrase, and the author has found favor for serving up her rapturous visions of nature without lapsing into sentimentality. While some feminist literature compilations have neglected her poetry because of her perceived status as a "woman in nature" poet, other critics have noted that Oliver forges outside of traditional Romantic poetry stereotypes to claim her own individual place in nature poetry. Critics have favorably reviewed *A Poetry Handbook* as an incisive guide to the mechanics of writing poetry. The book goes beyond mere instruction, said Susan Salter Reynolds in the *Los Angeles Times Book Review,* to "connect the conscious mind and the heart."

PRINCIPAL WORKS

No Voyage, and Other Poems (poetry) 1963
The River Styx, Ohio, and Other Poems (poetry) 1972
The Night Traveler (poetry) 1978
Twelve Moons (poetry) 1978
American Primitive (poetry) 1983
Dream Work (poetry) 1986
House of Light (poetry) 1990
New and Selected Poems (poetry) 1992
A Poetry Handbook (nonfiction) 1994
White Pine: Poems & Prose Poems (poetry) 1994

CRITICISM

Wallace Kaufman (review date Autumn 1966)

SOURCE: A review of *No Voyage, and Other Poems* in *Agenda,* Vol. 4, Nos. 5 & 6, Autumn, 1966, pp. 58-60.

[*Kaufman is an American educator and writer. In the following excerpt, he finds Oliver's poems in* No Voyage, and Other Poems *to be more personal than the work of Edna St. Vincent Millay.*]

In Mary Oliver's poems *No Voyage* one is tempted to look for the influence of Edna St. Vincent Millay, especially since Miss Oliver was secretary to the poet's sister and lived at the poet's estate. But as any writer knows influence is not so obvious as "What I like I follow".

The person, the mind, in Miss Oliver's poems seems to be a mind with the Millay sensitivity. But she is not cornered by the economics or social conditions that were the warp of so much of Millay's poetry. Miss Oliver's poems are more personal, yet move at a safer distance from the brink of sentimentality. Perhaps it is easier for a good poet to feel sorry for one's society than for one's self.

In tending to her personal life Miss Oliver usually treats herself as just an ordinary human being, though one who is aware of wanting to be more. As she writes one imagines the poet laughing at her subject as an adult laughs at a child dressing in old grown-up clothes and playing house. It is probably not comfortable to see life this way, so of course the poems are not comfortable—psychologically speaking. There are occasional streaks of feminine quaintness in description but over all *No Voyage* is a very tough minded, clear sighted woman struggling with a real sense of urgency to see some hope in the here and now. For instance these last lines from **"The Photograph"**:

> Ten years away and wondering what to do,
> I search my spirit for some flush of pain.
> But thought by thought the quiet moments fall.
> My heart, my heart is blank as hills of snow!—
> And all time leads us toward that last december . . .
> I stare upon your crumbling smile and keep you.
> I do not love you now. but I remember.

Carolyne Wright (review date Fall 1985)

SOURCE: A review of *American Primitive,* in *Prairie Schooner,* Vol. 59, No. 3, Fall, 1985, pp. 108-112.

[*Wright is an American poet and educator. In the following review, she finds in Oliver's Pulitzer Prize-winning collection both stunningly original and cliched elements.*]

This sixth volume of poetry by Mary Oliver is deceptively facile in its control of the language of the contemporary free-verse pastoral lyric. The book is often breathtaking—both in its luminous *apparent* simplicity (in the most successful poems), and in its seemingly narrow avoidance of triteness or flatness at times, especially in the final lines of the dozen or so weaker pieces. Some readers may object to the ordinariness of some poems here: haven't we all read too much of the conventional imagery and sentiments inspired by **"Spring"** or **"May"** or **"The Roses"**? And yet other poems—**"Mushrooms," "The Kitten," "An Old Whorehouse," "John Chapman"**—are stunning in the fresh ways in which they reveal the essential strangeness of the all-too-readily-taken-for-granted world. It may be odd to say, but I found these poems easy to read—not greatly demanding (as if making great demands on the reader's retrieval system of verbal echoes, literary allusions, and cultural phenomena were always a virtue), yet often amazing in the sudden turn of phrase, the unrehearsed conflation or dovetailing of perception:

> How sometimes everything
> closes up, a painted fan, landscapes and moments
> flowing together until the sense of distance—
> say, between Clapp's Pond and me—
> vanishes, edges slide together
> like the feathers of a wing . . . (**"Clapp's Pond"**)

Mary Oliver's voice is at once celebratory and elegiac; her subject matter is largely that of the primitive American landscape, the fragile realm in which human passions and needs, and the primordial cycles of nature, still meet and interact:

> I try to remember when time's measure
> painfully chafes, for instance when autumn
> flares out at the last, boisterous and
>   like us longing
> to stay—how everything lives, shifting
>
> from one bright vision to another, forever
> in these momentary pastures. (**"Fall Song"**)

The range of these poems—their movement from Ohio's forests and fields, the speaker's childhood country of the imagination, to Cape Cod's scrub pines, salt estuaries and views of the sea—is reminiscent at times of Roethke's "North American Cycle," although Oliver's voice is less sustained and her poems shorter, given more to immediate sensory experience than to extended meditations upon that experience. Perhaps it would be more accurate to liken her to Williams in her enumeration of sense impressions in short lines broken for dramatic effect:

>   I
> come down from Red Rock, lips streaked
> black, fingers purple, throat cool, shirt
> full of fernfingers, head full of windy
> whistling. It
>
> takes all day. (**"Blackberries"**)

Another poem, **"The Plum Trees,"** seems a response of sorts to Williams' famous "This is Just to Say." After a rather obvious play on the etymologies of root-words ("there's nothing / so sensible as sensual inundation") Oliver speaks with the same urgent directness as does Williams' note tacked to the refrigerator:

> Listen,
> the only way
> to tempt happiness into your mind is by taking it
>
> into the body first, like small
> wild plums.

But not all these poems are exultant in their "singing in the / heaven of appetite." There is a pervading undertone of loss and resignation to loss, of death and reconciliation to the world's ongoing processes, among which death is merely another turn of the great wheel. As do mushrooms "when they are done being perfect," Oliver knows that we, too, will all eventually "slide back under the shining fields of rain," and she evokes the unstudied beauty of the mushrooms' letting go. Instead of exploiting deformity's media potential, Oliver carries the "perfectly black" stillborn cyclopean kitten into a field and buries it, reminding us, and herself, what it in its perfect color and imperfect form really represents: not hideous error, but the fact that "life is infinitely inventive." Still, she's not entirely comfortable with her consolations, and must reiterate her rationale at poem's end:

> I think I did right to go out alone
> and give it back peacefully, and cover the place
> with the reckless blossoms of weeds.

Again, one thinks of Williams' obsession in *Paterson* with the "Beautiful Thing," the essence of loveliness persisting in the midst of violence, deformity and death—a loveliness not cosmetically superficial, but indwelling. Other poems address themselves to the flora and fauna of Oliver's surroundings, and evoke a sense of the fragility of species, even if they are not directly threatened by human predation (**"Egrets," "Ghosts," "Blossom," "The Fish," "Humpbacks"**).

Sometimes, however, the poet's elegiac vehicle veers dangerously close to the prosy clichés of "inspirational verse," and disappoints the reader who doesn't need to be told, after the imagery and tone have already implied their messages, that in the Mad River region, for example, "the wounds of the past / are ignored" (**"Tecumseh"**); or that the realization in **"May"** of our union with all things is a form of "spiritual honey" and is "as good / as a poem or a prayer"; or that because the wood hen calling her chicks at **"Little Sister Pond"** is "touching, feeling / good," the speaker and her companion are also "meanwhile / touching, feeling / pretty good / also." In this last example, the enjambments are melodramatic to

the point of silliness; the burden of the lines is not sufficiently profound or moving to bear the weighty emphasis that each line break would suggest. Some readers, especially the younger poets among them, may be disheartened by such falls in diction, wondering why *they* work so hard to make each image, each line, startlingly original and fresh, when (as too frequently happens) a mid-career poet with an established reputation, a battery of jacket blurbs from other "name" poets, and a standing contract with a major publisher, can content herself with the sort of unevenness that would only propel the manuscripts of the "unknowns" back over the transom more rapidly than otherwise. Perhaps it is true that "Suffering"—or at least the uncertainties and vicissitudes of publishing and job seeking—leads to Great Art; but must this truism always have appended the corollary that once the poet has struggled successfully to gain rightful recognition, she (or he) will abandon selectivity and self-criticism, be satisfied with less than earlier work shows her to be capable of? Mary Oliver is less subject to this corollary than many, however, and there are instances in which she employs direct statement or the didactic mode in a way that her readers can both identify with as emotive pronouncement, and assent to as workable poetry:

> To live in this world
>
> you must be able
> to do three things:
> to love what is mortal
> to hold it
>
> against your bones knowing
> your own life depends on it;
> and, when the time comes to let it go,
> to let it go.   (**"In Blackwater Woods"**)

In many of these poems, though, it is evident that the speaker has undergone some very real suffering; the losses referred to are personal and specific, but not subjected to direct autobiographical reportage. Although she could not properly be called a confessional poet, we sense that Oliver has earned the right to inner landscapes in which "the secret name / of every death is life again" (**"Skunk Cabbages"**). In **"University Hospital, Boston,"** the speaker visits a convalescing loved one, listens to the hopeful (but possibly self-deluded?) prognosis, then stands alone in an empty private room at visit's end, contemplating what the death of the room's previous occupant ("someone . . . here with a gasping face") and the vanishing of her own beloved, amidst the impenetrable impersonality of the institution, would mean. In **"Something,"** two lovers are very much aware of the voyeur outside their window, but "kiss / anyway"; in the fullness of their joy, they can extend a generosity of sentiment toward their "lonely brother." But then all changes: the voyeur, "a man who can no longer bear his life," commits suicide in the woods; and one of the lovers dies. The bereaved speaker, "no longer young," now "knows what a kiss is worth." In the face of such wisdom that can only be attained too late, Oliver offers no easy consolation: life goes on for the living, and time continues "reasonable and bloodless" in spite of the mourner's grief and need for something, anything, even if it be only "the dark wound / of watching"—vicarious or remembered fulfillment.

American Primitive most nearly warrants its title and its evocation of Williams in the poems that focus on the history of this country and its losses—primarily those of the Native Americans of Ohio's Mad River region (**"Tecumseh"**) or of the pioneers who eventually displaced them (**"The Lost Children"**). The most fully realized of these poems for me is **"John Chapman,"** the legal name of Johnny Appleseed, whom American folk legend has elevated into a sort of secular, arboreal-specific Saint Francis. Oliver's poem gains ironic depth by demythologizing the man who lived unharmed among Indians, settlers, and wild beasts, who had "apple trees [spring] up behind him lovely / as young girls." The trite simile here is ironically deliberate: we soon learn that despite Appleseed-the-hero's ostensible rendering of honor to "all God's creatures!" Chapman-the-man harbors fellow-feeling for all but the female of his own species:

> Mrs. Price, late of Richland County,
> at whose parents' house he sometimes lingered,
> recalled: he spoke
> only once of women and his gray eyes
> bristled into ice. "Some
> are deceivers," he whispered, and she felt
> the pain of it, remembered it
> into old age.

But the young woman (perhaps secretly attracted to her parents' guest?) who never forgets the force of Chapman's misogyny is an exception. Like so many from the realms of Paul Bunyan, George Washington and the Cherry Tree, and the Midnight Ride of Paul Revere, Chapman's human faults have been glossed over in history's canonization; he has become "the good legend," but his secrets and his pain have also left their mark on America:

> In spring, in Ohio,
> in the forests that are left you can still find
> sign of him: patches
> of cold white fire.

This is a book that we can read quickly, and therefore we run the risk of missing a great deal of it. It can also grow on us, unobtrusively—like the silence of the few forests left—and remind us that surface flash is not as enduring as "the unseen, the unknowable / center" toward which Mary Oliver's poetry is directed. *American Primitive* has won the Pulitzer Prize

for Poetry in 1984; it is an award that the poet's work to date certainly merits.

Alicia Ostriker (review date 30 August 1986)

SOURCE: A review of *Dream Work*, in *The Nation*, Vol. 243, No. 5, August 30, 1986, pp. 148-150.

[*Ostriker is an American poet, editor, and educator. In the following excerpt, she applauds the lyricism of* Dream Work *and notes a shift in emphasis from the natural world in Oliver's earlier works to more human-based themes in this collection.*]

Where [Donald] Hall's line is classically conversational and descriptive, Mary Oliver's is intensely lyrical, flute-like, slender and swift. Where he gathers detail, she will fling gesture. Her poems ride on vivid phrases: "the click of claws, the smack of lips" outside her tent turns out to be a bear's "shambling tonnage" in **"The Chance to Love Everything."** In a poem about an oncoming storm emblematic of human disaster, "the wind turns / like a hundred black swans / and the first faint noise / begins." She dreams the memory of past lives in the Amazonian landscape of **"The River,"** a poem of the soul's birth and rebirth:

> Once among the reeds I found
> a boat, as thin and lonely
> as a young tree. Nearby
> the forest sizzled with the afternoon
>   rain.

[Mary Oliver] is as visionary as Emerson, and is among the few American poets who can describe and transmit ecstasy, while retaining a practical awareness of the world as one of predators and prey.

—Alicia Ostriker

Behind Oliver's New England is Ohio—not the sorry Ohio of James Wright, but a frontier still untouched by cultivation and corruption, where you enter to find "your place / in the family of things," with a real hope of success if you work hard. Woodland and marsh are Oliver's kingdom, animals and plants her kin and alternative selves. There are some dazzling poems of deer, bear, geese, turtle, of trilliums and sunflowers. She is as visionary as Emerson, and is among the few American poets who can describe and transmit ecstasy, while retaining a practical awareness of the world as one of predators and prey, "the rapacious / plucking up the timid / like so many soft jewels."

Quite a number of the poems contain advice that is both right enough and rooted enough to be called (it's an old-fashioned term) wisdom. **"Dogfish,"** the opening poem of *Dream Work,* describes a dogfish with its chin "rough / as a thousand sharpened nails," coming in on the tide:

> And look! look! look! I think those
>   little fish
> better wake up and dash themselves
>   away
> from the hopeless future that is
> bulging toward them.
>
> And probably,
> if they don't waste time
> looking for an easier world,
>
> they can do it.

"One or Two Things" hovers between the mobility of a butterfly and the poet's own immobility, which feels to her like an iron hoof she can't lift from the center of her mind unless she has "an idea." The poem concludes:

> For years and years I struggled
> just to love my life. And then
>
> the butterfly
> rose, weightless, in the wind.
> "Don't love your life
> too much," it said,
>
> and vanished
> into the world.

Dream Work, coming after Oliver's 1984 Pulitzer-Prize-winning *American Primitive,* is an advance on her earlier writing in two ways, which are probably connected. Formally, her verse feels increasingly confident, smoother, and thus bolder—the work of someone able to take risks, take corners faster. At the same time she has moved from the natural world and its desires, the "heaven of appetite" that goes on without much intervention or possibility of control, further into the world of historical and personal suffering. In a half dozen or so poems she sketches a past burdened by trauma and breakdown, the temptation to die, the resolution to recover, the actual work of insisting on sanity: "I began to take apart / the deep stitches / of nightmares." In one poem the poet makes herself walk away, though the night is wild, from voices crying "Mend my life!" In another she is building a larger house, a daily labor.

She confronts as well, steadily, what she cannot change. In the climactic piece of *Dream Work,* a meditation on the Holocaust, there are two adjacent pictures linked by a half-re-frain. "Oh, you never saw / such a good leafy place" introduces an anecdote about meeting a fawn while walking with her dog; neither fawn nor dog knew "what dogs usually do," so they "did a little dance, / they didn't get serious." Then the line "Oh, you never saw such a garden!" brings a new picture, a Jamesian scene of a hundred kinds of flowers, cool shade, garden furniture and a man peacefully finishing lunch and lifting wine in a glass of "real crystal"—but "It is the face of Mengele." At the end of this poem the people have gone and the doe enters, sniffing the air where her fawn has been: "Then she knew everything." In her own garden of knowledge Mary Oliver moves by instinct, faith and determination. She is among our finest poets, and still growing.

Lisa M. Steinman (essay date Spring 1987)

SOURCE: "Dialogues Between History and Dream," in *Michigan Quarterly Review,* Vol. 36, No. 2, Spring, 1987, pp. 428-38.

[*In the following review, Steinman finds an "almost romantic lyricism" in* Dream Work *that floats over a deeper personal perspective of the past.*]

Mary Oliver's *Dream Work,* the last book reviewed here, stands out when placed next to the three books discussed above [*The Happy Man,* by Donald Hall, *The Walls of Thebes,* by David R. Slavitt, and *Thomas and Beulah,* by Rita Dove], precisely because it seems to take no notice of any past or history. True, the cover of one of Oliver's earlier volumes, *The Night Traveler,* showed a portrait of Virgil; but even there Oliver's Virgil came by way of Blake. *Dream Work,* in fact, opens with the poem **"Dogfish"** in which Oliver writes: "I wanted / the past to go away, I wanted / to leave it, like another country." Later in the same poem, the personal past is similarly discarded: "You don't want to hear the story / of my life, and anyway / I don't want to tell it, I want to listen / to the enormous waterfalls of the sun." As in *American Primitive,* there is a sort of trick here. In the earlier volume, the apparently unself-conscious celebrations of the present and of the natural world, presented as if in a picture with no perspective or depth, are quite self-consciously entitled primitives. In *Dream Work,* the past rejected is nonetheless felt loitering under the surface of many of the poems.

Yet in both volumes Oliver's best poems are those of an almost romantic lyricism. There are more references in *Dream Work* to the nightmare side of vision, to "the dark heart of the story" (**"The Chance to Love Everything"**), or to "the dark song / of the morning" after a night in which, we are told, "in your dreams you have sullied and murdered, / and dreams do not lie" (**"Rage"**). But despite the number of times darkness is mentioned, the dark is less detailed, less fully imagined, and less convincing than Oliver's primary subject, namely visionary experiences. If Slavitt's response to a flight of birds is to step back and explain he does not believe in redemption, here is Oliver on **"Wild Geese"**:

> Whoever you are, no matter how lonely,
> the world offers itself to your imagination,
> calls to you like the wild geese, harsh and excit-
> ng—
> over and over announcing your place
> in the family of things.

One might mistrust such epiphanic moments, wishing perhaps that Oliver had a bit more of Hall's restraint and a bit less of this yearning to merge with the world. Yet the poetry, in the iambs, in the careful mixture of statement and image, avoids sentimentality and is, in the final analysis, deeply moving. Here, in an epiphany built of the loss of such moments, is another equally powerful passage, from **"Whispers"**:

> Have you ever
> tried to
> slide into
> the heaven of sensation and met
>
> you know not what
> resistance but it
> held you back?

The poem ends:

> . . . have you stood,
>
> staring out over the swamps, the swirling rivers
> where the birds like tossing fires
> flash through the trees, their bodies
> exchanging a certain happiness
>
> in the sleek amazing
> humdrum of nature's design—
> . . . to which
> you cannot belong?

This is clearly not the humdrum world that most of us inhabit; there is no sign of Hall's Martha Bates Dudley and Mr. Wakeville, of Slavitt's eye tests, newspapers and books, or of Dove's couple, living through the Depression and company picnics. The other poets reviewed here let other people into their poetry, people who live and have jobs in a recognizable world. Oliver's more solitary landscapes are not even wholly of the natural world. As with romantic poetry generally, Oliver's "world" is centered in the self, or in the self's quests. **"The Journey"** admits:

> . . . there was a new voice,
> which you slowly

> recognized as your own,
> that kept you company
> as you strode deeper and deeper
> into the world,
>
> . . . .
>
> determined to save
> the only life you could
> save.

Finally, the world into which Oliver descends is not the physical world these poems at first appear to celebrate. *Dream Work* is notable in part because it explicitly acknowledges that sensuality is not what Oliver is after. In *American Primitive,* perhaps disingenuously, Oliver wrote: "the only way / to tempt happiness into your mind is by taking it / into the body first" (**"The Plum Trees"**). In *Dream Work,* we read: "The spirit / likes to dress up . . . it needs / the *metaphor* of the body" (**"Poem,"** emphasis added). It is admirable that *Dream Work* maintains the visionary lyricism of *American Primitive* while going on to examine its premises like this.

There are many ways in which Oliver's poems are the most immediately compelling of those reviewed here. And yet, by contrast, if Slavitt's over-explanatory discursiveness is irksome at times, it also seems to stem in part from an honest and tough-minded recognition, which we also admire, of what it means to be romantically inclined in 1986. The high romantic vein has always risked losing the world. For many of us, the poetry we want now will have to come (to borrow a phrase) from poets of reality. And we feel we have such poets when we read the way the seemingly unpoetic lives and language of Dove's couple or of Hall's awkwardly named, and precisely realized, individuals (Felix, Merle, Harvey) are given a place in poetry without being wrenched from history. At the same time, Oliver's poetry strikes a deep and seductive chord. It is, to quote Donald Hall from an early BBC interview, a poetry "that, if you leave yourself open to the language of dreams, is open to everyone. . . . You need not translate anything . . . you have to float on it." Perhaps, after all, the dialogue between history and dream—and between community and self—that we find when these poets are read together is what we really want from poetry.

Sandra M. Gilbert (review date May 1987)

SOURCE: "Six Poets in Search of a History," in *Poetry,* Vol. 150, No. 2, May, 1987, pp. 113-16.

[*Gilbert is an American editor, educator, and critic. In the following review, she applauds Oliver for mining the natural world to "learn the lessons of survival."*]

Compared to [Gail] Mazur's work, Mary Oliver's poems are deliberately impersonal, almost anti-confessional. Yet she too is haunted by history, by the private history of the oppressive father who is the subject of **"Rage"** ("in your dreams you have sullied and murdered, / and dreams do not lie") and by the public history of the holocaust that is the subject of **"1945-1985: Poem for the Anniversary,"** the history of Germany's "iron claw, which won't / ever be forgotten, which won't / ever be understood, but which did, / slowly, for years, scrape across Europe." Unlike the other poets in this group, however, Oliver finds a way to escape the rigors of human chronicles through attention to natural history. In doing so, she follows in the footsteps of such precursors as D. H. Lawrence, Marianne Moore, and Elizabeth Bishop, all of whom, at various times and in different modes, celebrated the intransigent otherness of birds, beasts, and flowers—of moose and jerboa, of snake and pomegranate and tortoise—in order to learn the lessons of survival taught by what Moore called "the simplified creature."

To my mind, Oliver is the most skillful of the six poets I am treating here: she is a writer who is never less than expert in her crafting of verse and her precision of language. Once in a while, the sense of structure that invariably leads her to point poems toward neat (and often brilliant) closures betrays her into excessive abstraction, even sententiousness, as in the ending of **"Starfish,"** where "I lay on the rocks, reaching / into the darkness, learning / little by little to love / our only world." But for the most part, her poems are wonderfully shapely, and there appears to be a connection between the aesthetic attentiveness that produces these elegantly articulated forms and their scrupulous anchoring in natural facts, in keen awareness of the history of lives that are other than human.

This is not to say, however, that Oliver is in any sense anti- or inhuman; on the contrary, like Mazur's, her voice is warmly human and open, even when, like Barnard, she is confronting the icy mystery of the constellations. I quote her **"Orion"** in its entirety:

> I love Orion, his fiery body, his ten stars,
> his flaring points of reference, his shining dogs.
> "It is winter," he says.
> "We must eat," he says. Our gloomy
> and passionate teacher.
>   Miles below
> in the cold woods, with the mouse and the owl,
> with the clearness of water sheeted and hidden,
> with the reason for the wind forever a secret,
> he descends and sits with me, his voice
> like the snapping of bones.
>   Behind him,
> everything is so black and unclassical; behind him
> I don't know anything, not even
> my own mind.

Still, impressive as this poem is, the pieces that impress me the most in Oliver's new collection are the ones in which—like Lawrence, Moore, and Bishop—she meditates on the alternative consciousness, the being in a perpetual present, that might liberate the lives of plants and animals from what human beings experience as the burden of the past.

In **"The Turtle,"** for instance, Oliver broods (as Lawrence once did) on the reproductive imperative that drives the shelled creature, laying her eggs:

> She's only filled
> with an old blind wish.
> It isn't even hers but came to her
> in the rain or the soft wind,
> which is a gate through which her life keeps
> walking.

Again, in **"Landscape,"** this poet looks at crows who

> . . . break off from the rest of the darkness
> and burst up into the sky—as though
>
> all night they had thought of what they would like
> their lives to be, and imagined
> their strong, thick wings.

And in **"Black Snakes,"** she engages, as Lawrence did in "Snake," the fearful yet historically sacred otherness of the reptile. Looking with Lawrentian awe at two terrifying snakes, Oliver confesses that

> . . . Once I had steadied,
> I thought: how valiant!
> and I wished
> I had come softly, I wished
> they were my dark friends.

It is, of course, daring, indeed risky, to rewrite Lawrence like this, as risky as it is for Mazur to rewrite Lowell. But to Oliver's credit she mostly brings the project off, perhaps because she not only revises but reshapes Lawrence, drawing on his poetical honesty while repudiating his political eccentricity. **"The Sunflowers,"** the closing poem in her collection, moralizes delicately on the other history we can learn from natural history. Beginning with a casual, friendly invitation—"Come with me / into the field of sunflowers. / Their faces are burnished disks, / their dry spines // creak like ship masts"—the piece moves toward a conclusion that summarizes the philosophy of history which might be said to underlie ***Dream Work:***

> Don't be afraid
>   to ask them questions!
>   Their bright faces,

which follow the sun,
    will listen, and all
        those rows of seeds—
            each one a new life!—

hope for a deeper acquaintance;
    each of them, though it stands
        in a crowd of many,
            like a separate universe,

is lonely, the long work
    of turning their lives
        into a celebration
            is not easy. Come

and let us talk with those modest faces,
    the simple garments of leaves,
        the coarse roots in the earth
            so uprightly burning.

Of course, Blake stands behind this poem, too, Blake whose sunflower was "weary of time" and yearned "after that sweet golden clime / Where the traveller's journey is done." But for Oliver, evidently, there is no chance of the journey being "done"; the journey is a difficult voyage toward celebration, and history is the history of survival. Rather than being "weary of time," Mary Oliver implies, we should, with Mary Barnard, be glad of time's dispensations and benedictions—blessings which allow us to reimagine history not as a nightmare from which we are trying to awake but as a story of "coarse roots in the earth / so uprightly burning."

Mary Oliver (essay date 1987)

SOURCE: "Some Thoughts on the Line," in *The Ohio Review,* Vol. 38, 1987, pp. 41-6.

[*In the following essay, Oliver discusses the mechanics of poetry and how length and tone variations can result in a wide range of effects.*]

1.

All manner of effects can be realized by the choices one makes concerning the line, and all choices are determined from a norm point, iambic pentameter.

The iamb is the paramount sound in any string of English words, thus it is the most fluid and natural sound. The pentameter line most nearly matches the breath capacity of our lungs, and is thus the line most suitable to our verse. By suitable I mean it fits without stress and yet makes a full phrase, so it gives off no particular message. It is the norm.

All deviations from the norm do emit messages. Excitement of all kinds, with its accompanying physical and psychic ten-

sion, "takes our breath"; any line shorter than pentameter indicates this. The reader is brought to attention as the shorter line reveals a situation which is in some way out of the ordinary. Tetrameter can release a felt agitation or restlessness, or on the other hand a gaiety, more easily and "naturally" than pentameter, and so on.

The longer line (longer than five feet) suggests a greater-than-human power. It can seem by its simple endurance—beyond ordinary lung capacity—grandiose, or prophetic. It can also indicate abundance, richness, a sense of joy. Underlying whatever freight of language (statement) it carries, it emits a sense of an unstoppable machine.

In free as in metered verse, a feeling of reliability and cohesion is important. In the opening lines of a piece—with whatever length of line and predominant kind of line-breaks or line-turns—an initial mood is created. Once this is set, the reader has a right to expect that the general tone and mood, created by these mechanical selections, will continue—or will change only for a purpose essential to the poem.

When the poet uses previous models (sonnets, blank verse, etc.), he or she is in charge of the arrangement of words and sounds within each line, and a rhyme scheme if it is called for, but the form dictates each turn. In the free-flowing, unmodelled poem, each turn is made according to the effects which the poet wants to achieve. Of these decisions, measurable length is only one. The point in syntax at which the line turns is another.

At the end of each line there exists—inevitably—a brief pause. This pause is part of the motion of the poem, as hesitation is part of dance. With it, the poet can do several things. Say the line is self-enclosed—not a sentence necessarily, but a phrase which is entire in terms of syntax, a logical unity. Here the pause works as an instant of inactivity, in which the reader is "invited" to weigh the information and pleasure of the line.

When the poet on the other hand enjambs the line—breaks syntax by turning the line before the phrase is complete at a natural point—it speeds the line for two reasons—curiosity about the missing part of the phrase impels the reader to hurry on, and the reader will hurry twice as fast over the obstacle of the pause *because it is there*—we leap with more energy over a ditch than over no ditch.

A third possibility is to repeat one type of line (say the self-enclosed) a number of times. Each line reinforces the reader's pace. A trusted rhythm, that primal pleasure, is swiftly achieved and the change, when it occurs, is therefore all the stronger.

Other or additional effects are achieved by the end sound at the point of turning. Feminine endings try to blur the pause;

masculine endings are forthright; mute-ended words slam a gate.

Complete units of logic or syntax make use of the pause as indicated above, with additional resonances playing off the aura of certainty which attaches to complete statements and the incantatory spell which comes from repeated gestures or rhythms of any sort. This mood asserts itself even if the lines are phrased as questions—when the conclusion of the line matches the conclusion of the sentence, authority is released.

All these mechanical selections, it seems to me, work as de-scribed. They are not magical of course, but illusionary. They are not the poem, but its crafty underpinnings.

2.

The tone of many contemporary lyric poems is that of per-sonal disclosure. Person to person, the poet is talking to some-one—often to *you,* the reader. Intimately, intensely, and smoothly. This being so, the sense of movement is crucial, and the poems flow on without a rattle—the line-turns are often chosen for important but small effects, like the changes of expression in conversation.

During the period when James Wright was letting books of bad poetry fall behind stones, when he and Robert Thy and others were investigating the "deep image," Wright's work changed significantly, as we know. Speaking now only of the mechanics of his changed work, I wonder if Wright did not discover during this time that a certain kind of language—heard all one's life but dismissed out-of-hand as anti-poetry exactly because it was so much a part of "real life"—could be incorporated with startling effect into the poem. I am think-ing of such passages as the following:

> I am hungry. In two more days
> It will be spring. So this
> Is what it feels like.
> > (**"Before a Cashier's Window in a Depart ment Store"**)

Or the seemingly casual, vernacular opening to **"Northern Pike"**:

> All right. Try this,
> Then. Every body
> I know and care for,
> And every body
> Else is going
> To die . . .

Or this passage:

> I had nothing to do with it. I was not here.
> I was not born.

> In 1862, when your hotheads
> Raised hell from here to South Dakota,
> My own fathers scattered into West Virginia
> And southern Ohio.
> My family fought the Confederacy
> And fought the Union.
> None of them got killed.
> But for all that, it was not my fathers
> Who murdered you.
> Not much.

> > (**"A Centenary Ode: Inscribed to**
> > **Little Crow, Leader of the Sioux**
> > **Rebellion in Minnesota, 1862"**)

Here is a winging back and forth between the manufactured literary line, and the simple, even humble, cadence of ver-nacular speech. Clearly the word "scattered" is a literary choice, and its appearance reminds us that this is not a con-versation though it sounds like one—it is still that formal thing, a poem. Yet the whole passage "works" because of the final two words, which are certainly not poetry—except in the con-text of the passage. What is forceful and gives pleasure is not just the use of the vernacular but its transformation. The un-assuming phrase, as familiar to us as our own name, is worked into the mechanical structure and literary body of the poem, it is resurrected; it is changed utterly.

The conversational tone is not without precedent. "I will teach you my townspeople how to hold a funeral," wrote William Carlos Williams, and a lot else besides which displays an af-finity, with rather than a difference from ordinary American speech, and thus invites us to listen with a natural rather than a separate kind of attention.

And now, what has happened to the line? It would be the devil's task to indicate strong and light stresses through the last quotation from Wright. The third sentence, the one con-taining "scattered," is fairly easy. But the others, difficult to scan, show different characteristics. So many words of one syllable, so much caesura, so many spondees. The rhythm is gone, the tension is all one stroke. By the old rules there is no determined result to such a line. We sense only a mood of intensity, and import. It is the unpretentious turned rhetori-cal, it is rhetoric that has unfolded as naturally as a leaf. It stretches the listening ear in a new way.

> My brother comes home from work
> and climbs the stairs to our room.
> I can hear the bed groan and his shoes drop
> one by one. You can have it, he says.
> > (**"You Can Have It"**)

Here is a more recent example from a poem by Philip Levine, a wonderful example because of the tightness of the stanza in which the final phrase blurts forth with utter weariness and yet uncommon resonance. We are being told a story, mostly in the cadence of iambs with no more variation than speech naturally holds; but the spondees in line three prepare us, though we don't know it, for the sustained almost unscannable effect of the fourth line, in which there is no emphasis, but the totality of gut eloquence.

What Wright did so often and so well I see practiced in many recent poems. I sometimes hear from poets (and am not without the feeling myself) of their wish to speak less personally and more on behalf of the "people entire." Whoever that is. It is an interesting and difficult wish, and without easy solution. The use of vernacular phrases, I imagine, is connected to this ambiguous but restless desire.

Additionally, I think the poetry reading has had a real influence on the line, and especially the kind of line I have been describing. As a matter of course the poet now takes on the role of reader as well as writer. In my experience, the audience finds great pleasure in poems which so use our "real language," and the poet of course senses this. The academic audience is stirred by something different, the more general audience is moved by phrases so familiar and yet infused with new energy.

> **Through the many possibilities of craft, the poem comes into its careful existence. And certainly the poet these days may thrill us still with finery, but just as likely with the simple cloth of plain speech which, in the conflagration of the poem, has also caught fire.**
>
> *—Mary Oliver*

And what does one hope the words on the page will be, as the eight o'clock reading begins? Not only an indication of what to say, but of how to say it. The vernacular line—which in truth is more spoken than read—is apt to appear on the page in just that way. And line-breaks on the page which will work for reading poems aloud will work that way for the attentive silent reader also. Through the many possibilities of craft, the poem comes into its careful existence. And certainly the poet these days may thrill us still with finery, but just as likely with the simple cloth of plain speech which, in the conflagration of the poem, has also caught fire.

Jean B. Alford (essay date 1988)

SOURCE: "The Poetry of Mary Oliver: Modern Renewal Through Mortal Acceptance," in *Pembroke Magazine,* Vol. 20, 1988, pp. 283-88.

[In the following essay, Alford discusses the positive, life-affirming aspects that Oliver's poetry uncovers in nature.]

Mary Oliver is a distinctive poet in the fashionably surreal and escapist world of contemporary verse. The message and craft of her poetry are valued by peers and critics alike despite her unfortunate neglect as potential critical review. According to Hyatt H. Waggoner, she lacks the representative qualities associated with contemporary aesthetic values. However, her real worth as a modern poet lies in these very atypical qualities. Representative contemporary poets gloomily doom modern man and his life in apprehensive responses to present political, social, economic, and moral uncertainties. Oliver instead passionately affirms their survival. Within them both, she exalts the natural—an inherently renewing and regenerative potential.

The theme of Oliver's poetry is revitalization. Through self-conscious denial, modern man must reconnect his roots with the natural cycles and processes of all life. As Oliver's poems engross the reader in a fully sensual union with nature, she urges him to recognize the universal joys, pains, beauties, and terrors experienced in such connectedness. She then celebrates his transforming potential—the loving acceptance of his mortality in the human and natural worlds.

Oliver's poetic technique will not be examined in this discussion. It is important to note, however, that it too is in keeping with her different contemporary stance. Rather than adopt the surreal escapism and the personal confessions of many peers, she uses the traditional lyric form to embrace her readers emotionally and intellectually. Her meticulous craft and her skilled use of language create poems that are seemingly effortless, sensual delights. She combines rich, musical lyrics with swift, taut meters; she uses illuminating images that seldom startle; and she produces a confident, yet graceful and serene, tone. According to Anthony Manousos, Oliver's craft is deceptively simple—an emotional intensity that speaks clearly and directly to the reader. More appropriately, James Dickey characterizes it as remarkable, creating richly complex poetry without throwing complexities in the way of the reader.

An analysis of Oliver's poetic message reveals that she begins her positive affirmation by seeking to reconnect modern man to his roots in the natural processes of all life. According to Waggoner, rather than despairing over the current separation and alienation of contemporary life, Oliver searches memory and present experiences. Through the world of nature, she finds those intrinsic meanings and values which can be retrieved, embraced anew, and celebrated in the modern world. To Manousos, then, her exploration of the natural world and its cycles elicits concurrent themes analogous to those which are deepest and most enduring in human experience.

In *Twelve Moons,* especially, Oliver celebrates the natural cycles of birth, decay, and death as flourishing in all life. More important, though, she reveals the companion dreams that motivate and drive the mortal existence. In **"The Fish,"** Oliver compares the salmon's exhaustive and painful battle upstream to reach her "old birth pond" with the efforts of "any woman come to term, caught / as mortality drives triumphantly toward / immortality / the shaken bones like/ cages of fire". **"Stark County Holidays"** describes a Christmas family reunion as the narrator's awareness of her mother's "wintering" decay; though the musical dream and desire persist, the "stiffened hands" on the "blasted scales" ensure that seasonally "the promise fades." In **"The Black Snake,"** the reptile found dead in the roadway is thrown into the bushes as "looped and useless as an old bicycle tire." Yet, it is remembered as "cool and gleaming as a braided whip," imbued with the "brighter fire" of all nature which " . . . says to oblivion: not me!"

Oliver identifies within these life cycles the continuous elements of change, sensual pleasure, and love. She reveals that they not only accompany the companion dreams but also necessarily involve experiencing both pain and pleasure. In **"Two Horses,"** Jack and Racket are wished from death into "Elysian fields . . . without fences" but realistically and sadly recognized as changed like all of life in "two graves big as cellar holes / At the bottom of the north meadow." In **"Worm Moon,"** the death of winter changes joyfully into spring's "love match that will bring forth fantastic children / . . . who will believe, for years, / that everything is possible." Celebrating sensual pleasure in **"Looking for Mushrooms,"** the poetic persona perceives the hunt and capture of the delectable "salvo of the forest" as "rich / and romping on the tongue" for man and beast alike. Yet, in the **"Bone Poem"** that follows, as she comes upon the "rat litter" at the bottom of the owl's tree, she recognizes the owl's most recent sensual delight not only as being part of the eternal food chain but also as eventually dissolving "back to the center" where "the rat will learn to fly, the owl / will be devoured." And, Oliver celebrates motherly love in both the human and animal world. In **"Snow Moon—Black Bear Gives Birth,"** the mother bear washes and snuggles her newborn, gives them the "rich river" of her nipples, and thus establishes each one as "an original." A mother's love changes, though, from joy to a pain that "lashes out with a cutting edge" in **"Strawberry Moon."** Elizabeth Fortune is not only left by "the young man / full of promises, and the face of the moon / a white fire" but also separated from the child born out of wedlock, being forced by society to "climb in the attic."

As Oliver celebrates the themes of birth, decay, death, dreams, change, sensual pleasure, and love, she asserts their equal and certain existence for both man and animal. In fact, she assures modern man of his survival because he is part of the natural world and its rejuvenating potential. This assurance, though, includes the experience of beauty, joy, and sensual pleasure as well as that of mystery, terror, and pain.

According to Joyce Carol Oates, Oliver relates these experiences to an essential tension and loneliness man experiences as he lives simultaneously in two worlds—the personal, familial, human world and the inhuman, impersonal, natural world. Within the human world, man essentially struggles alone to find a sense of identity, peace, and immortality. In the poem **"John Chapman,"** an eccentric, anti-social old man of the Ohio forests becomes a "good legend" by planting and giving away apple trees. He decides not to die to "the secret, and the pain" of unrequited love but "to live, to go on caring about something." In **"Dreams,"** the narrator compares a single rain-swollen creek's rushing drive and desire for "a new life in a new land / where vines tumble thick as ship-ropes, / The ferns grow tall as trees!" to two pioneering great-uncles who got lost in Colorado looking for the good life. With "pounding heart and pride," she celebrates them as "full of hope and vision; / . . . healthy as animals, and rich / as their dreams . . ."—at peace and immortalized before they died alone.

Manousos suggests that Oliver then counterbalances man's dream of immortality with man's struggle to survive mortality—his subjection to increasingly waning natural powers after birth. In **"Ice,"** the narrator painfully acknowledges her father's feverish distribution of ice grips as an attempt in his "last winter" to " . . . be welcomed and useful— / . . . Not to be sent alone over the black ice." In **"The Garden,"** the speaker pities the wealthy, good-mannered, defiant woman who spends her life alone working three gardeners around the clock to keep "the wilderness at bay." In the end, this self-sufficient matron terrifyingly discovers her wasted effort and struggle and loss—"how powerless she was / . . . like the least of us grew old and weedy. / Felt her mind crumble . . . / Heard the trees thicken as they stumbled toward her / And set their cracking weight upon her bones."

To Oliver, the reconciliation of man's desire for immortality and his experience of mortality depends on his willingness to recognize them as polarities. According to A. Poulin, Jr., the essential tension between them in Oliver's poetry " . . . defines the boundaries of all experience—whether in the physical world, in the realm of human relationships, or in the self." In her poems, she equates this reconciliation with the very sense of connectedness she celebrates in *Twelve Moons,* a unity existing between the human and natural worlds. Through a personal psychic journey, man must deny and eliminate the self-conscious "I" that seeks immortality and open his sensual perception to the mortal kinship between the human and the natural.

In **"Entering the Kingdom,"** the narrator expresses her desire to negate the "I" and become one with nature—"the dream of my life / Is to lie down by a slow river / And stare at the light in the trees— / To learn something of being nothing / A little while but the rich / Lens of attention." In **"Blackleaf Swamp,"** she asks whether being human negates her being "part bird, part beast" and queries if so, ". . . why does a wing in the air / Sweep against my blood / Like a sharp oar?" After her study of "darkness and trees and water," she confidently concludes that such selfless communion with nature "feels like the love of my mother." In **"The Plum Trees,"** as the poetic persona explores the sensual inundation of eating summer plums, she celebrates the "sensibility" or critical importance of increased sensual perception. For her, "joy / is a taste before / it's anything else . . ." and "the only way to tempt happiness into your mind is by taking it / into the body first, like small / wild plums." According to Manousos, Oliver's vision of man's sensual union with nature becomes celebratory and religious in the deepest sense. In **"The Fawn,"** the worshipper questions "what is holiness?" as she succumbs not to the ringing church bells but "to the woods instead," calling "blessed" a momentary touching of spirits between herself and a newborn fawn.

The results of a psychic journey which elevates man's sensual perception above his self-consciousness are still polar— eliciting both joy and pleasure, pain and terror. As man recognizes the oneness of all forms of life, he joyfully experiences glimpses of immortality and eternity. In **"Pink Moon the Pond,"** Oliver celebrates this moment:

> . . . the soul rises from your bones
> and strides out over the water . . .
> not even noticing
> You are something else . . .
> And that's when it happens—
> You see everything
> through their eyes,
> their joy, their necessity . . .
> And that's when you know
> You will live whether you will or not,
> one way or another,
> because everything is everything else,
> one long muscle.

Man finally sees his immortality as a self-denying mortal life in communion with the eternal processes of nature.

When man acknowledges his mortal participation in the natural cycles of life, he is also terrified by nature's total disregard for the individual, whether prey or predator. According to Oates, Oliver, in **"Winter in the Country,"** reveals the natural world's refusal to divide individuals or creatures into victims or oppressors. The narrator states, "the terror of the country / Is not the easy death . . ." but "Is prey and hawk together, / still flying, both exhausted, / In the blue sack of weather." Oliver insists that man must also take his place in this frightening, unsentimental, unpoliticized natural world, for he too is subject to waning natural powers. In **"Farm Country,"** the speaker criticizes the view that "life is chicken soup." She urges man to act as decisively and realistically as the farm wife does—"sharpening her knives, putting on the heavy apron and boots, crossing the lawn, and entering the hen house."

Because of this elevated yet terrifying sensual perception, man can be potentially renewed. When he denies the superiority of his own self-consciousness and acceptingly connects his own mortality to the world around him, he is different. No longer is he the "cruel but honest" one in **"Cold Poem."** Such a man keeps ". . . alive . . . taking one after another / the necessary bodies of others, the many / crushed red flowers" Neither can he be a part of the dispassionate news audience in **"Beyond the Snow Belt."** They "forget with ease each far mortality" because " . . . except as we have loved. / All news arrives as from a distant land."

Instead, contemporary man can be more loving, caring, and sensitive as he participates in his environment. His potential exists as surely as that of the narrator's ancestors in **"Stark Boughs on the Family Tree."** They "built great barns and propped their lives / Upon a slow heartbreaking care" as "they left the small / Accomplished, till the great was done." Like the niece in **"Aunt Mary,"** he may even long to know the hidden spirit of one so loud and fat. As he views the skinny child in the family album " . . . in a time before her glands / Grew wild as pumps, and fleshed her to a joke," he may even lament her death, learning "how wise we grow, / Just as the pulse of things slips from the hand."

As a different person, modern man can also recognize that facing, coping, and adapting to life's trials and disappointments are the only means of gaining inward peace and self-identity. In **"No Voyage,"** Oliver documents the human tendency to run away from the pain and unpleasantness experienced in life. The poem's narrator insists on the necessity to "inherit from disaster before I move / . . . To sort the weeping ruins of my house; / Here or nowhere I will make peace with the fact." To Oliver, as nature learns, so must man. In **"Storm,"** as the speaker seeks shelter from a deadly heaven "full of spitting snow," she marvels at "deer lying / In the pine groves," "foxes plunging home," "crows plump / As black rocks in cold trees." She concludes that "what saves them is thinking that dying / Is only floating away into / The life of the snow"—accepting their place and time in the natural cycle of life and fulfilling the complete potential of their being.

Poulin believes that the acceptance of the hard truths of mortal existence is epiphany for Oliver as well as for modern man himself—the essential nature or meaning of life. In **"Blackwater Wood,"** she asserts that living productively today is dependent on three measures of acceptance by man:

> to love what is mortal;
> to hold it
>
> against your bones knowing
> your own life depends on it;
> and, when the time comes to let it go,
> to let it go.

To Oliver, man's inward struggles to be immortal through art, work, or love do not cancel mortal existence but rather create a fleeting sense of stay. In **"Music Lessons,"** when the teacher takes over the piano, "sound becomes music" that flees "all tedious bonds: / supper, the duties of flesh and home, / the knife at the throat, the death in the metronome." The grand finale, though, is only a momentary transformation.

Contemporary man's acceptance of his mortality will benefit daily living in productive encounters of love, caring, and understanding. It allows him to look beyond the self to view death as in harmony with the recreative processes of nature In **"The Kitten,"** the narrator believes that she "did right" to give the stillborn "with one large eye / in the center of its small forehead" back peacefully to nature rather than to a museum. For she asserts, "life is infinitely inventive. / saying what other arrangements / lie in the dark seed of the earth . . ." In **"University Hospital, Boston,"** a family member reconciles the dying of a loved one. While she tells him "you are better," she sees other beds "made all new, / the machines . . . rolled away. . . ." And, she acknowledges, ". . . the silence / continues. deep and neutral, as I stand there, loving you"

The acceptance of the hard truths of mortality also provides a reforming perspective on daily dying—the progressive inward death of one's self-consciousness. As Oliver celebrates in **"Sleeping in the Forest,"** such daily extinctions allow man to "vanish into something better." In **"Sharks,"** as the narrator describes swimmers too soon forgetting the lifeguard's warning, she asserts: ". . . life's winners are not the rapacious but the patient; / What triumphs and takes new territory / has learned to lie for centuries in the shadows / like the shadows of the rocks."

Oliver's poetry, then, reminds modern man that accepting the dire consequences of mortal existence through a heightened sensual perception takes time and patience. It does not come easily like an automatic reflex but rather develops through a slow, painful transformation of self to selflessness. Its rewards, however, are as delectable and exciting as the red fox's appearance in **"Tasting the Wild Grapes"**—"lively

as the dark thorns of the wild grapes / on the unsuspecting tongue!"

Thus reviewed is the poetry of Mary Oliver—contemporarily non-representative, positive, traditional, conservative, deceptively simple, complex without throwing complexities in the way of the reader. As a modern poet, she is both distinctive and worthwhile. In her meticulous craft and loving insight into what endures in both the human and natural worlds, she gives us all not only hope but also the potential for salvation—a modern renewal through mortal acceptance.

Greg Kuzma (review date Spring 1989)

SOURCE: A review of *Dream Work*, in *Prairie Schooner*, Vol. 63, No. 1, Spring, 1989, pp. 111-12.

[Kuzma is an American poet. In the following review of Dream Work, *he praises Oliver's "purity of motive" in expressing the gracefulness of nature.]*

Mary Oliver's **Dream Work** sees in the earth everywhere evidence of a profound satisfaction. "Each pond," she tells us, "with its blazing lilies / is a prayer heard and answered . . ." (**"Morning Poem"**) or "The sea / isn't a place / but a fact, and / a mystery . . ." (**"The Waves"**). In all her various acts of defining or saying precisely what she knows, it is the earth's fact and mystery and beauty she is moving toward, a limit, a perfection. It is wiser than we are. It is more at peace. Even its humblest element surpasses us in virtue:

> Isn't it plain the sheets of moss, except that
> they have no tongues, could lecture
> all day if they wanted about
>
> spiritual patience?
>
> **("Landscape")**

Accordingly, most of the poems lend to Nature ear and eye. They notice the shark's "domed head," its "teeth / in the grin and grotto of its impossible mouth," the "stone eyes" of black snakes, "root-wrangle," "the moon staring / with her bone-white eye," "the smell of mud," "the crisp life-muscle" of the clam as she slashes through it with her knife, "the black anonymous roar" of the "turning tide." Fresh vigorous description characterizes the book, but it is also sufficient merely to name, to say what she's seen and done in the simplest terms, to enumerate the abundance. One finds always Oliver's purity of motive. Always the intent is to come close, and always it seems, one falls short. In what is perhaps her most thorough statement of theme, **"Whispers,"** she makes a series of proposals, all of which end in frustration. One tries to "slide into / the heaven of sensation" but meets a "resistance." One tries to imagine "pleasure, / shining like honey," but it is "locked in some / secret tree." And so on. Though the rivers swirl and the birds are "like tossing fires" and nature is "blood's heaven, spirit's haven," the message is clear—"you cannot belong."

Of course what is clear is that Oliver does belong, and that she comes as close as most of us are likely to get. While the poems are very good at dramatizing the aspiring soul in its restlessness, Oliver is all the while expressing harmony by means of her finely-tuned and lush language. If Nature confronts us with a gracefulness that is self-contained and self-sufficient, and needs nothing from us, not even our participation, our proper duty, Oliver seems to be saying, is to respond in kind through art. Flashes of marvelous language occur at almost every turn. In attempting to discover, for example, that "something" that lies at the, center of her responsiveness, she writes "something about the way / stone stays mute and put," where reiterations of consonants attest to the sturdiness that resides at the heart of experience. In "Trilliums," Nature's many voices and energies are embodied in the sequence of noun and verb combinations of stanza six:

> From the time of snow-melt,
>   when the creek roared
>   and the mud slid
>   and the seeds cracked . . .

Or when she describes our longing to understand the mysteries around us and within us (in **"Dreams"**), her use of falling meter in the third stanza beautifully expresses not only the ardor of the emotion and its confidence but also our doubt as to our ultimate success:

> if you could only remember
> and string them all together
> they would spell the answer . . .

These are all small touches, but deft ones, and take the poems well beyond mere flat assertion or statement, and, because rhythm is one of the ways voice becomes physical, we are taken toward a harmonizing of Nature and the human voice that sings its praises. Perhaps Oliver's most effective technique is her adoption in many of the poems of a short, breathy line. As in the quoted material, the poet is not cramped in these ordinarily tight confines. Instead she achieves rich parallels as well as generous and expansive postponements and delays, while also taking full advantage of the many surprises the short lines afford and hinge on, and the many returns. What one gets is a voice eager to speak of wonders and an urgency to get back line after line to further engagements. It is a mode altogether appropriate to her moods and represents, I think, a communion of form and content rare in contemporary poetry.

Janet McNew (essay date Spring 1989)

SOURCE: "Mary Oliver and the Tradition of Romantic Na-

ture Poetry," in *Contemporary Literature,* Vol. 30, No. 1, Spring, 1989, pp. 59-77.

[*In the following essay, McNew discusses why contemporary critics have difficulty analyzing Oliver's poetry within the framework of the romantic tradition.*]

> *The special puzzle of Romanticism is the dialectical role that nature had to take in the revival of the mode of romance. Most simply, Romantic nature poetry, despite a long critical history of misrepresentation, was an anti-nature poetry. . . . Romantic or internalized romance . . . tends to see the context of nature as a trap for the mature imagination.*
> —Harold Bloom, "The Internalization of the Quest Romance"

> *It is the destiny of consciousness . . . to separate from nature, so that it can finally transcend not only nature but also its own lesser forms.*
> —Geoffrey Hartman, "Romanticism and 'Anti-Self Consciousness'"

> *To become poets, women must shift form agreeing to see themselves as daughters of nature and as parts of the world of objects to seeing themselves as daughters of an Eve reclaimed for their poetry.*
> —Margaret Homans, *Women Writers and Poetic Identity*

To say that Mary Oliver is a visionary poet of nature is to place her in a modern poetic tradition that springs from the English romantics. Some of the best critical insights into modern mythopoeic lyricism have focused on this tradition as it moves from Wordsworth and Keats to Yeats and Stevens. A glittering company including Northrop Frye, Harold Bloom, M. H. Abrams, and Geoffrey Hartman have enriched readings of contemporary visionary poetry by revealing continuities with the romantic consciousness, yet this criticism also confuses readings of Mary Oliver—or H.D. or Audre Lorde—because of unexamined gender bias. Particularly in regard to mythic relations to nature, criticism that does not attend to differences in the psychology and visions of men and women slights the power of women poets. Susan Griffin in *Woman and Nature,* Carol Christ in *Diving Deep and Surfacing,* Alicia Ostriker in *Stealing the Language,* Estella Lauter in *Women as Mythmakers* all have begun to argue that revising myths about human relations to nature represents a crucial source of creative power for women, yet there remain extraordinary resistances in romantic criticism to valuing these specifically feminine myths. Even a feminist critic like Margaret Homans, whose first book, *Women Writers and Poetic Identity,* is the best and most sustained examination of women in the romantic tradition, insists that a "feminine tradition" in visionary poetry must turn away from myths that associate women with nature. Although Homans's second book, *Bearing the*

Word: Language and Female Experience in Nineteenth-Century Women's Writing, revises this formulation in ways that I will use later to evaluate Oliver's work, her early feminist work reflects her training in the Bloom-Hartman system of values. Why, we might ask, is so much important contemporary criticism in the romantic tradition unable to appreciate the kind of nature poetry that Mary Oliver writes?

The areas of dispute for these distinguished critics of romantic nature poetry usually involve boundaries—first, of course, between the self and nature, but also by extension between soul and body, consciousness and unconsciousness, subject and object, culture and nature, language and muteness, immortality and death, imaginative poet and immature child, transcendence and immanence. Hence, when we examine the archetypic situation of modern nature poetry and find a single human speaker considering his relation to a landscape (as in Wordsworth's "Tintern Abbey") or to another creature (as in Keats's "Ode to a Nightingale"), we also recognize the interplay of these mythologically opposed pairs. Furthermore, all of these dichotomies have also been philosophically and mythically related to that most pervasive pair, masculine and feminine. The usual sexual dynamic in romantic nature poetry assumes, therefore, a speaking male subject who explores his relation to a mute and female nature [McNew attributes this idea to Homans in *Women Writers and Poetic Identity*]. Finding an authentic place in this traditional pattern clearly presents challenges for women poets, but, I will argue, the mythological strategies of women poets are less bound by patriarchal strictures than is the literary criticism which evaluates them.

Mary Oliver won the 1984 Pulitzer Prize for *American Primitive,* and she has had five books of poetry printed and received with warm notices by important reviewers. Although in these circumstances it would be absurd to say that she is neglected, it is true that her work has not received sustained critical attention. Her poetry is neither a replication of romantic accomplishment nor is it, to use Bloom's term, a "belated" modern version of visionary romanticism as is, for instance, that of the much-attended John Ashbery. I suspect that her tones and dramatic situations are not of the sort to attract critics trained in the romantic tradition, for as M. H. Abrams has argued, "great Romantic poems were written . . . in the later mood of revolutionary disillusionment or despair."

Consider, by way of contrast, Oliver's poem **"Sleeping in the Forest"**:

> I thought the earth
> remembered me, she
> took me back so tenderly, arranging
> her dark skirts, her pockets
> full of lichens and seeds. I slept
> as never before, a stone
> on the riverbed, nothing

> between me and the white fire of the stars
> but my thoughts, and they floated
> light as moths among the branches
> of the perfect trees. All night
> I heard the small kingdoms breathing
> around me, the insects, and the birds
> who do their work in the darkness. All night
> I rose and fell, as if in water, grappling
> with a luminous doom. By morning
> I had vanished at least a dozen times
> into something better.

This poem is about comfort and a visionary experience that clearly continues to nourish the speaker even though the action of the poem is in the past tense. The first poem in *Twelve Moons,* the book published just before *American Primitive,* "Sleeping" exemplifies the dramatic concentration on a mystical closeness to the natural world which has become the major subject of Oliver's last three books. Taking the basic elements of a camping trip, Oliver suggests a ritual return to a maternal earth. The speaker's movement is earthward and toward immersion in a forest floor that so engulfs her that she feels "as if in water." The transformation she describes is the opposite of transcendence, as it associates her with "lichens and seeds." Though she sleeps as profoundly as "a stone / on the riverbed," her sleep is not a blankness but the route taken to a visionary dissolution of her human identity. She grapples "with a luminous doom" which is not a frightening end but rather a temporary vanishing "into something better." Short lines emphasize the lyrical simplicity in this celebration of the joy to be achieved in physical and imaginative unity with nature, but her spare form contains a world of mythic assumptions very different from those of her famous romantic precursors.

Because Oliver's poetry is not as well known as it deserves to be, I want to trace her visionary progress in more detail, but for now this one example will serve to associate her with what Estella Lauter sees as a widespread revision by women artists of "key elements of Western mythology," especially as they concern women's relationship to nature. With references to the work of Susan Griffin, Marge Piercy, and Audre Lorde, among others, Lauter finds a "degree of identification with nature, without fear and without loss of consciousness" which occurs in the works of "surprising numbers of women." Likewise, Carol Christ finds in her examination of spiritual quests "the themes of affirmation of women's bodies and women's connection to nature." Oliver clearly shares her vision with a growing group of women writers who assert with Susan Griffin that "We are nature seeing nature. We are nature with a concept of nature."

If we turn back now to the epigraphs from Bloom, Hartman, and Homans, the contrast is blatant. For the romantic visions these critics brilliantly and convincingly analyze, everything depends on a growth process that includes separating from and transcending nature and its attendant mortality. They reveal a paradoxical "romantic revolution" that began as an attempt to unify body and soul, subject and object, mind and nature but almost immediately became a poetry about the crises and imaginative reconstructions of an alienated consciousness which could regain only fleeting and ambiguous glimpses of union with body, objects, nature. Instead, these poets attempt to purchase new unities by leaving pantheistic pleasures in the past and by relocating faith in the transcendent imagination (Wordsworth's "years that bring the philosophic mind") or in a transcendent art that celebrates a creativity liberated from natural cycles (Yeats's "artifice of eternity').

In these terms Oliver might be associated with a line of female romantic figures like Blake's Thel or Wordsworth's Lucy who fail to pass through ecstatic childhood to the pains of an alienated consciousness and on to the freedom of a transcendent imagination. These mythic women either remain tragically childish or die tragically young and are merged with the mute and inert "rocks, and stones, and trees" of Wordsworth's elegy "A Slumber Did My Spirit Seal." Adult female figures associated with nature, like Keats's "La Belle Dame sans Merci," are given witchlike powers to ensnare male poetic questers in sensuous traps and stay them from progress to their transcendent goals. That Starhawk and Mary Daly, among other women writers, happily accept the once-dreaded association with the traditions of witchcraft can do little to allay suspicions that the vision of nature they share will not easily be subsumed into received patriarchal myths about the relation to nature. As witches, spinsters, crones, and nature-mothers begin to speak for themselves, they transvalue their romantic forefathers' mythic assessments as they defy the doom of muteness placed on all these female Others who inhabit masculine poetic landscapes.

Abrams (*Natural Supernaturalism*) and Hartman have shown that "The traditional scheme of Eden, fall, and redemption merges with the new [romantic] triad of nature, self-consciousness, imagination." Especially when nature is identified with mother and a transcendent God with father, it is easy enough to associate such a pattern with the Freudian version of the Oedipus myth which describes the child's progress from unity with the mother to separation and sexual yearning for renewed union with the mother and finally to a new resolution of identification with the father. That mythic third term, whether it be called Redemption, God the Father, or the Transcendent Imagination, has a distinctly masculine character. In short, the mythic pattern that contemporary criticism has valorized as the high modern poetic place of nature is built on a male model of development. Yet much important feminist theory accepts this valuation. Simone de Beauvoir agreed to a similar model when she celebrated the freedom gained by transcendence and denounced "immanence" as a doom that enmeshes woman in the biological prison house of nature

and her body. In her first book, Margaret Homans also assumed that some variation of this mythic pattern is the only way for women poets to come into their fullest powers. She disputed most directly with Adrienne Rich's "Transcendental Etude" because of its eventual refusal of transcendence and its association with nature in the form of a rock shelf. Homans could not credit a poetry that refuses to see human consciousness as necessarily involving transcendence of a maternal nature nor a visionary art that will not seek salvation at the price of alienation from what Oliver calls "the soft animal of your body."

Much, however, suggests that such a pattern for a woman would involve resignation to participation in a patriarchal plan that involves a repudiation of what is mythically female and maternal—the earth, natural cycles, the body. In a recent issue of *Critical Inquiry,* Sandra Gilbert speculated on ways that women novelists have encoded anxiety about laws of a patriarchal culture which preaches a horrible text to budding women artists: "You must bury your mother; you must give yourself to your father." Refusal to follow this patriarchal order puts a woman artist in a dangerously liminal position in relation to her culture, but it also holds the promise of regaining power lost to those who become what Gilbert calls good "literary daughter[s]." With all the strength of mythic association to body and to nature intact, Oliver and other "bad" daughters create mythic patterns unmarred by the shame of denied origins.

Several of Oliver's poems present the embrace of animals as a dreamlike regaining of original wholeness. **"Winter Sleep"** imagines crawling "under the hillside" with a "drowsy she-bear." She and her partner are "Two old sisters familiar to each other / As cups in a cupboard." And again, in a poem about remnants of lost prairie buffalo, she concludes with a dream of a buffalo cow giving birth:

> in the fragrant grass
> in the wild domains
> of the prairie spring, and I asked them,
> in my dream I knelt down and asked them
> to make room for me.

In terms of the romantic critical tradition I have outlined, these dreams would suggest a disturbing retreat from consciousness, a return to the preoedipal state that signals failure to achieve a mature poetic identity by successful separation from a maternal nature. Carol Christ, however, points out that because female patterns of development do not necessarily enforce so rigid a separation from the mother, the girl child's tendency to see the world in terms of sameness rather than difference may actually give her greater access to mystical experience. The re-embrace of an attachment to a woman has also, of course, become a standard theme of poets who see the necessity of woman-identification as a prerequisite to a strong womanly self. The best feminist psychology—like, for instance, that of Carol Gilligan—usually understands an integrated female identity to involve some version of Rich's "homesickness for a woman," which in her vision represents a recovery of lost maternal origins. Nowhere in her poetry is Oliver a programmatic feminist; nevertheless, her dreams of reunion with female creatures and with maternal nature receive the validation in feminist terms that male developmental theories and literary criticism built on them would deny.

"The Sea" takes this vision a step further and imagines the body crying for "the lost parts of itself— / fins, gills / opening like flowers into / the flesh." Her "legs / want to lock" and she can feel "the blue-gray scales." Her reverse phylogeny strongly suggests the backward ontogeny of a return to the womb:

> Sprawled
> in that motherlap,
> in that dreamhouse
> of salt and exercise,
> what a spillage
> of nostalgia pleads
> from the very bones!

The dive into the sea, "that / insucking genesis," allows her to "simply / become again a flaming body / of blind feeling." Nothing in the poem questions the ecstatic fulfillment of this vision. Indeed, in her mythic plot, immersion is revelation of a mystical consciousness and an experience of renewal. How strikingly different this attitude is from the most powerful masculine romantic myths can be seen in a few brief examples. Whitman in "Out of the Cradle Endlessly Rocking" and Crane in "Voyages" also express oceanic longings for immersion, yet there is a crucial difference in their ambivalent sense that returning to the womblike sea would be both vision and suicide. Almost echoing Whitman, Crane urges himself, "Hasten, while they are true—sleep, death, desire, / Close round one instant in one floating flower." This is the old lure of Keats's longing for union with the nightingale which is also a longing for an end to consciousness, "To cease upon the midnight with no pain," and of Whitman's cradle-rocking crone-mother, the sea, who hisses the "low and delicious word death."

Though Oliver's direction of desire is also toward dissolving individual consciousness, she lacks the male poet's mixture of finality and terror with her longing, perhaps because her sense of movement between her individual consciousness and oceanic immersion is more fluid. Her visionary unions belong neither to a lost childhood experience, as does Whitman's, nor to future ultimate death, as does Crane's. She often sleeps to dream of her unions, but she has none of Keats's torment over whether those dreams are the work of deceptive fancy. In **"Dreams"** as in **"White Night"** she recalls night

visions that tap a bodily consciousness hidden in the light of day and reason, one that reveals a blissful connection to the natural world. **"Dreams"** asserts that within the "dark buds of dreams" are truths:

> In the center
> of every petal
> is a letter,
> and you imagine
>
> if you could only remember
> and string them all together
> they would spell the answer.

As in **"Sleeping in the Forest,"** her relatively easy movement in and out of visionary physical immersion gives her less reason to find danger or ambiguity in these experiences. The less rigid boundaries to which Carol Christ refers allow her to avoid the anxious either / or questions which run through much male nature poetry: she is herself, human and finite, and in states that are a heightening of physicality and of vision, she is a part of a natural vastness that subsumes her human individuality. She crosses and recrosses those boundaries without anxiety. Nancy Chodorow has argued that this ease of movement back and forth into preoedipal modes represents a strength for maturing girls, who may therefore "come to experience themselves as less differentiated than boys, as more continuous with and related to the external object-world and as differently oriented to their inner object-world as well."

Something else, too, disinclines Oliver to tremble over boundaries between herself and nature, or subject and object, as philosophers would have it. She says in **"Humpbacks,"** "I know several lives worth living," and her imaginations of transformations into fish, fowl, and buffalo become dreams of other lives, other identities that are inhuman but neither unconscious nor mute. For her, almost nothing exists as unconscious object. In **"Winter Trees,"** she traces her gradual recognition that everything has consciousness and even language of some sort: "First it was only the winter trees—/ their boughs eloquent at midnight." But then, as spring comes on and "the ponds opened," she begins "to listen to them" and hears articulate sounds. Next, she even hears that most inert part of nature, "rocks / flicking their silver tongues all summer." Added to, then, Oliver's unpatrolled ego boundaries, her conviction that nature is also an articulate and conscious subject distinguishes her poetry from that built on the eventual recognition of nature as a mute and objective Other.

Perhaps I should pause here to insist, as Carol Gilligan did when she distinguished a moral development for some women that was different from but not inferior to that of Lawrence Kohlberg's men, that Oliver's difference does not necessarily diminish her visionary power. Gilligan and Chodorow have argued that the masculine emphasis on separation, individuation, and autonomy is not superior to the feminine emphasis on interdependence and attachment. For Oliver I have been arguing that this emphasis produces different myths of visionary progress and different concepts of maturity, but once schooled in masculine traditions, readers may find it dangerously easy to see only childish naivete in a celebratory sense of connection to nature. In poems such as **"Ghosts"** and **"Tecumseh,"** Oliver reveals a keen sense of the alienating effects of a white, imperialist culture that destroys the ecological balances of creatures and rivers, but she herself speaks as an outsider to this culture, as one who rejects its direction in order to join the "primitive" of her book title. As Sherry Ortner has argued, the primitive, the raw and natural, and prehistory all represent contexts within which women traditionally have been set apart from association with patriarchal culture.

> Oliver's visionary association with nature enables her to be truer to the original intentions of romanticism than were the great male poets who found themselves tugged toward solipsism and away from their original desires for a reconnection to nature.
>
> —*Janet McNew*

Neither ignorant nor immature, the choice of the primitive for Oliver represents choosing a life-affirming wisdom that our advanced culture has, to its detriment, forgotten. Especially in her newest book, *Dream Work,* Oliver confronts loathsome facts about father-daughter incest, the Holocaust, and starving children and sees them as cultural failures to grasp the simple truths of bodiliness, of our human connection to nature. The haughty businessman in **"Rage"** denies nightly dreams of his violated daughter as a "tree / that will never come to leaf"; Yeats, Whitman, and van Gogh all committed unforgivable sin when they created "exquisite poems" that celebrate solipsistic and life-hating visions. In her insistence on striving toward connections denied by her culture, then, Oliver's visionary association with nature enables her to be truer to the original intentions of romanticism than were the great male poets who found themselves tugged toward solipsism and away from their original desires for a reconnection to nature. Through the lens of feminist awareness, perhaps it is possible to read the re-emergence of Christian quest patterns that Abrams finds in romantic poetry as tragic failures of revolutionary intentions to break the grip of patriarchal imperatives. The beauty of "Tintern Abbey" or "Frost at Midnight" is beyond argument, but the valuation of their mythic order is not.

What Oliver does in her most intense visionary poetry is not so much to defy patriarchal boundaries as to ignore their defining powers. The terms "soul" and "body," for example, do appear in her poetry, but her mischievous phrasing often confuses the expected dichotomy. **"Pink Moon—The Pond"** begins with the thrilling call of the spring night at the pond, a calling so stirring that "your soul rises from your bones / and strides out over the water." The "bones," left desolate on the shore, shout for the soul to *"come back!"* but when the soul does not listen, "like a good friend, / you decide to follow." Ecstasy, vision, and transformation all occur when she steps bodily into the pond, wraps herself in "the darkness coming down / . . . called / a woman's body / as it turns into mud and leaves." As a matter of fact, then, she does not actually join that airy soul which skims lightly across the water. The transcendent soul floats "unfolding / like a pair of wings" above the pond, becoming a sort of illusory husk which lures her out but has nothing else to do with the vision and fulfillment which occur when she becomes pure body and sinks into the rhythms of nature's spring. Similarly, **"Humpbacks"** ends with this odd observation:

> Listen, whatever it is you try
> to do with your life, nothing will ever dazzle you
> like the dreams of your body,
>
> its spirit
> longing to fly while the dead-weight bones
>
> toss their dark mane and hurry
> back into the fields of glittering fire
>
> where everything,
> even the great whale,
> throbs with song.

Once again the "spirit" shows a tendency to move skyward while the "bones," often her image for bodily quintessence, dive downward into a singing, earthly communion. The odd thing about this body / soul configuration is that the soul's yearnings appear both foolish and less genuinely visionary than the wise dreams of the body.

In Oliver's "primitive" world, physicality thus becomes the most visionary spirituality. No less than sixteen poems in *American Primitive* use eating as a central, eucharistic symbol for mystical communion with nature. **"The Fish"** describes eating her catch:

> Now the sea
> is in me: I am the fish, . . .
> . . . .
>   Out of pain,
> and pain, and more pain
> we feed this feverish plot, we are nourished

by the mystery.

Three poems about eating honey depend on imagining the food as a link to wood, bees, and flowers, "a taste / composed of everything lost, in which everything / lost is found." Two poems about eating blackberries and one about eating plums confirm her assertion that when pursued with visionary intensity, a physical appetite for natural foods can become an agent of magical power, a nourishment for visionary knowledge:

>   Joy
> is a taste before
> it's anything else, . . .
>
> . . . .
>
>   Listen,
> the only way
> to tempt happiness into your mind is by taking it
>
> into the body first, like small
> wild plums

This mystical sensuality operates also through the sexual appetite which in **"Blossom"** presents the only viable alternative to despair in the face of time which "chops at us all like an iron / hoe." Only "our hunger" and "the burning" bring

>   . . . joy
> before death, nights
> in the swale—everything else
>   can wait but not
>   this thrust
>   from the root
> of the body.

"The Gardens" closes *American Primitive* in a Sapphic transport which imagines the lover as a "dark country / I keep dreaming of." Her lover's body becomes a landscape of "boughs," a deep forest of "trees," "white fields," and "rivers of bone" into which she plunges, running "toward the interior, / the unseen, the unknowable / center."

Intensely sensuous bodily experience represents for Oliver the human in the act of recovering a truth—that we are creatures. Memory of lost childhood sensuality, "splendor in the grass," led Wordsworth to a very different truth. In his "Ode: Intimations of Immortality," he demoted nature from mother to "homely nurse" because he wanted to claim a more divine parentage, a patriarchal one with "God, who is our home." Few romantic poets, even those like Wordsworth who wrote to recover a closer relation to nature, finally see themselves as entirely natural creatures, for natural creatures die, and poets, as Wordsworth's title indicates, must find an imaginative route to immortality. In the face of sober truths about mortality, Oliver remains faithful to her attachment to nature. Instead of forsaking the natural for supernatural eter-

nity, her poems follow the cycles of the seasons to image loss and the possibility for renewal. These vast natural cycles, which usually symbolize traps and prison houses for the romantic visionary, are strangely consoling for Oliver. Wedding herself to them holds her close to the deepest mysteries she knows, those of natural transformation. In a poem about the happiest month, **"May,"** she writes of her

>   deepest certainty that this existence too—
> this sense of well-being, the flourishing
> of the physical body—rides
> near the hub of the miracle that everything
> is a part of, is as good
> as a poem or a prayer . . .

She has also many meditations on crueler seasons which teach her lessons about necessity, survival, and limitation. **"A Poem for the Blue Heron"** is set in late November when the bird accepts the need for flight from the cold, and the speaker remembers someone telling her, "Not everything is possible; / some things are impossible." **"Cold Poem"** ends with a characterization of winter as a time for a necessary loss of illusion:

> In the season of snow,
> in the immeasurable cold,
> we grow cruel but honest; we keep
> ourselves alive,
> if we can, taking one after another
> the necessary bodies of others, the many
> crushed red flowers.

She codifies her visionary acceptance of the immanent truths of natural cycles most directly in **"In the Blackwater Woods"**:

> Every year
> everything
> I have ever learned
>
> in my lifetime
> leads back to this: the fires
> and the black river of loss
> whose other side
>
> is salvation,
> whose meaning
> none of us will ever know.
> To live in this world
>
> you must be able
> to do three things:
> to love what is mortal;
> to hold it

against your bones knowing
your own life depends on it;
and, when the time comes to let it go,
to let it go.

Perhaps the most surprising examples of her vision of the all-enveloping movement of natural cycles occur in a group of poems about the physical transformations occasioned by death. **"Bone Poem"** celebrates the eventual "equity" in the relation between raptor and victim that happens when bones decay into leaf meal and become food for other animals: "sooner or later / In the shimmering leaves / The rat will learn to fly, the owl / Will be devoured." **"Vultures"** celebrates the creatures who look for death "to eat it" and so to perform "the miracle: / resurrection." We are urged to overcome our revulsion and not to shrink from this gruesome demonstration of "the earth's / appetite, the unending / waterfalls of change." The poem that poses cyclical transformations in the largest and most positive way is **"Ghosts,"** an elegy for lost buffalo herds. While it mourns the wanton destruction of these beasts by "Passengers shooting from train windows," it also points to the golden eagle who "has a bit of heaviness in him; / moreover the huge barns / seem ready, sometimes, to ramble off / toward deeper grass." These clues, together with the grass which still grows lush over places where buffaloes once left "rich droppings," lead her to insist, "In the book of the earth it is written: / *nothing can die."* This vision of a natural immortality necessitates surrender of any belief in the supernatural life of an individual soul after death, yet the physical economy of the earth's large cycles does suggest comfort and endurance of a sort to her. Individuality diffuses into a kind of fertilizer for other plants and animals, and the soul does not transcend the body but rather travels with it in a cycle of change that affects other parts of nature through the agency of a physical transmigration. Golden eagles carry a bit of buffalo in them, rats become owls, and, presumably, humans too are carried in these "unending waterfalls of change." Even Whitman, who so robustly sings of the physical, writes in "This Compost" (in *Autumn Rivulets*) a much less enthusiastic description of this same earthly economy of decay and reconstitution. The thought of the many "carcasses" buried in the earth stirs him to horrified wonder that the ground itself "does not sicken" nor are the winds "infectious." Finally he confesses, "Now I am terrified at the Earth." Not Oliver, for whom this sense of joining the large cycles of the earth is far more comforting than a transcendent vision that will allow for the preservation of her individuality.

Oliver's visionary goal, then, involves constructing a subjectivity that does not depend on separation from a world of objects. Instead, she respectfully confers subjecthood on nature, thereby modeling a kind of identity that does not depend on opposition for definition. **"The Turtle"** and **"Moles"** thus become unlikely exemplars, indefatigable heroes who accomplish constantly what the poet achieves only in her most

intense dream visions: they have no self apart from their physical flourishing. Moles are "so willing to continue / generation after generation / accomplishing nothing / but their brief physical lives." **"The Turtle"** is a creature whose arduous climb toward the sands where she will lay eggs is a "greater thing" than a whole list of usual heroic virtues because

> She can't see
> herself apart from the rest of the world
> or the world from what she must do
> every spring.
>
> Crawling up the high hill,
> luminous under the sand that has packed against
>   her skin,
> she doesn't dream,
> she knows
>
> she is a part of the pond she lives in,
> the tall trees are her children,
> the birds that swim above her
> are tied to her by an unbreakable string.

It is perhaps no mistake that these enviable virtues of connectedness belong often to creatures who are also mothers. The ecstatic moments Oliver describes for herself are imitations of this turtle-state. In **"Crossing the Swamp,"** for instance, she enacts her typical immersion and ends with a vision of herself redeemed by the "rich / and succulent marrows" of swamp muck:

>   —a poor
>   dry stick given
>   one more chance by the whims
>   of swamp water—a bough
>   that still, after all these years,
>   could take root,
>   sprout, branch out, bud—
>   make of its life a breathing
>   palace of leaves.

The mythic direction pursued by Oliver has much in common with what Luce Irigaray calls "la mystérique," the mystical: "This is the place where 'she'—and in some cases he, if he follows 'her' lead—speaks about . . . 'subject' and 'Other' flowing out into an embrace of fire that mingles one term into another. . . . The walls of her prison are broken, the distinction between inside / outside transgressed." For Irigaray this mysticism is the most faithful women's vision because "any theory of the subject has always been appropriated by the 'masculine.' When she submits to (such a) theory, woman fails to realize that she is renouncing the specificity of her own relation to the imaginary." Toril Moi notes that Irigaray's formulation of mystical experience as "the loss of subjecthood . . . the disappearance of the subject / object opposition" holds "a particular appeal for women, whose very subjectivity is anyway being denied and repressed by patriarchal discourse."

At this point a return to Margaret Homans's work will clarify the situation of Oliver's mythmaking in feminist theory. In her first book, Homans designated as "daughters of an Eve reclaimed for their poetry" the sort of women poets who might eventually constitute an authentic "feminine tradition" by focusing even more insistently than their brother poets on the possibilities of "non-literal language" and their own "poetic subjectivity." As we have seen, Oliver could not take a place in such a tradition because her poems imagine an identity that does not depend on opposing and transcending the literal, natural creatures and things of the world. Identity matters less to her than consanguinity. Her vision involves not transforming nature into a more satisfactory imaginative realm but rather, paradoxically, using poetry to create a human who is more genuinely natural. Linda Gregerson, one of the most sensitive reviewers of *American Primitive,* notes, "She is not much moved by the works of man, and she somehow contrives to love the world more than she loves language, no common feat for an artisan who works in words." Put another way, Oliver gives primary emphasis not to the symbolic order of poetic language but to the more literal power of poetry to invoke inarticulate, intuitive experience itself. The frequent imperatives of her poems—all her urgings to "look!" or "listen!" —insist on moving outside art, into the lives of trees, damselflies, owls, and ponds.

In her second book, *Bearing the Word,* Homans implicitly revises her earlier standards for women's literary achievement. By means of a subtle and dazzling fusion of French and American feminist theory—of Kristeva, Irigaray, and Lacan with Chodorow, Showalter, and Froula-Homans explicates a revisionary and devalued "mother-daughter language" which has goals that almost coincide with those I have claimed for Oliver. Similar to Oliver's mode are the "revisionary myths of literal and figurative" which Homans sees as working "more through thematics than through the invention of new representational practices" such as those created by some French feminists. Homans writes, for instance, of feminine "literary situations and practices" which she terms "literalization" and observes in writers like Dorothy Wordsworth or Virginia Woolf who seek to associate themselves with the mythically female object-world which male literary discourse opposes to the subjectivity represented in the symbolic language of poetry. Homans praises Dorothy Wordsworth for her implicit criticism of her brother's representation of nature when she writes journal entries that offer "free parallels between human and natural, in which there is no order of hierarchy. Her parallels have meaning only if nature has as full a value as the human experience, and it can have that full value only if it is not portrayed as subordinate to the human." These "parallels" of Dorothy Wordsworth's also parallel the values I have attributed to Oliver when she

refuses cultural oppositions between a poetic and a natural identity. Thus Homans's new formulation of the feminine strategy of literalization by which women writers identify with things devalued by patriarchal culture—things particularly associated with the mythically feminine natural world—suggests a tradition that embraces Mary Oliver as surely as *Women Writers and Poetic Identity* denied her.

Finally to understand and properly to assess the poetry of Mary Oliver involves theoretical revisions at least as radical as those Homans is striving toward. Although Coleridge defined art as "the reconciler of nature and man," the best modern criticism has shown that most male romantic nature poetry is about achieving an identity that transcends nature. Unlike Keats, who famously characterized subsumption in natural cycles as becoming "a sod," Oliver finds comfort and joy in her dreams of dissolving into the forest floor. Unlike Wordsworth, who resigns himself to "the philosophic mind" when he becomes powerless to achieve the child's blissful absorption in nature, Oliver finds herself still able to enter a natural communion lost to the adult male poet:

> Every morning I walk like this around
> the pond, thinking: if the doors of my heart
> ever close, I am as good as dead.
>
> Every morning, so far, I'm alive.

At its most intense her poetry aims to peer beneath the constructions of culture and reason that burden us with an alienated consciousness to celebrate the primitive, mystical visions that reveal "a mossy darkness— / a dream that would never breathe air / and was hinged to your wildest joy / like a shadow," a dream of oneness with a maternal earth-womb. It would be presumptuous indeed to argue that her faithfulness to the original romantic project makes Oliver's poetry better than that of her great romantic precursors, but her difference from them may cause her vision to be misunderstood and undervalued by those who use male poets to define achievement in nature poetry. Although her mystical values are not those finally chosen by most romantic critics as the tenets of modern poetic faith, they are, I think, values celebrated by many feminist theorists and a burgeoning group of mostly women artists. Surely they and Mary Oliver are neither mistaken nor callow to turn to the web of natural connection to find the source, the sustenance, and the end of the human.

Eleanor Swanson (interview date April 1989)

SOURCE: "The Language of Dreams: An Interview with Mary Oliver," in *The Bloomsbury Review,* Vol. 10, No. 3, May/June, 1990, pp. 1, 6.

[In the following interview, Oliver discusses poetry criticism,

poetry workshops, and how her poetry has changed since her early work.]

Mary Oliver's poetry both celebrates the natural world and puts before us disturbing images of that world, in which we see reflections of ourselves. Her poetry leads us to question what it is that makes us human, what being "civilized" has given us—and what it has cost. She calls upon us as readers to be in her poetry, to "look!" and to "listen!" with all of our might. As Janet McNew wrote in *Contemporary Literature,* Oliver's poetry evidences a "mythical closeness to the natural world" and a "conviction that nature is . . . an articulate and conscious subject."

She has given us poetry in which the "power of the earth rampages" (**"Shadow,"** in *Dream Work*), poetry in which the "dark buds of dreams / open / richly" (**"Dreams,"** in *Dream Work*). As Donald Hall commented, hers is a poetry "that if you leave yourself open to the language of dreams, is open to everyone."

Born in 1935 in Ohio, Oliver attended Ohio State University and Vassar College. She now lives in Provincetown, Massachusetts. Her book *American Primitive* won the Pulitzer Prize for poetry in 1984, and she has won many other awards, including National Endowment for the Arts and Guggenheim fellowships. Oliver has four other books of poetry, including *Twelve Moons, Provincetown, Dream Work,* and her newest collection, *House of Light.*

[*The Bloomsbury Review:*] *Your poetic method has been compared to a number of other poets—Edna St. Vincent Millay, William Carlos Williams, Theodore Roethke, James Wright. I read a review of one of your books in which three of those names were mentioned in the same paragraph. Do you have a comment on this relentless pursuit of influences on the part of critics?*

[Mary Oliver:] What a compliment! And, yes, there is doubtless something about my work which is reminiscent of these poets who are in the American literary tradition. But, specifically, I don't think I have much to do now with Frost or Williams or Millay, or even Wright, whose work has been an important influence. Every poet learns by imitating other poets. We learn everything by imitation! And, as I tell students, there's no shame in this at all. It's a necessary period a writer goes through, a kind of discipleship. But there is finally a time when you begin to hear something new and different—something of your own—and that's the part of your work you want then to cherish, to make strong.

What do you think the critic's relationship is to the poet and poetry? I've read many reviews that reveal more about a critic's lack of knowledge of the poetry than anything else.

Today it seems that everyone wants to be a writer. No one wants to be "just" the reader, and few people are interested in being a critic. To read well is a worthy and not necessarily easy skill; and to criticize well—to be informative in terms of history, theory, background, so that you invite other people into the world of literature—is also a fine and difficult enterprise. A lot of critics don't really criticize, they review. And they review negatively with as much energy as they review positively. This is not very informative, or invitational. Of course there are exceptions—Peter Stitt, David Wojahn, Gregory Orr. Donald Hall is as good as anyone, and he's wonderful. He is in the way I mean, a mentor—more of an essayist really than a critic. Additionally, not many people write about why poets write, why they write about what they write about, etc., the really interesting questions.

I think this notion of the importance of reading well was implicit in my original question. I've sensed a superficiality— the critic doesn't seem to understand a new book, for instance, in the context of the poet's other work, or in the larger context, the much larger context out of which critical writing comes.

Well, yes. Good critical writing should and will illuminate beyond a single book. Criticism has a reputation for being kind of sour—rough and tough. I'll bet the word has some original sense of elucidating, or clarifying. That's one I'll have to look up. [In an editorial aside, Oliver adds: "From the *American Heritage Dictionary:* the word 'critic', derives from a Greek stem which means, simply, to separate, to choose."]

Your early work—and I'm thinking in particular of **The River Styx, Ohio***—is formalist. Is that fair, to call it "formalist"?*

It's fair to call it formalist, and it's also fair, once again, to call it derivative. *No Voyage* is my first book, it was published in this country in 1965. *The River Styx, Ohio* was published in 1972. They're the first two full collections, and they show the influence of all the people you mentioned earlier, plus others. They show the merit of admiring fine, American traditionalists, if you will: I was not concerned at that time about being "original." I was still learning how to write a poem. This was just before the passion for poetry workshops, and I worked alone. I knew very few people who wrote poetry. Today poetry is—can you bear this?—a "growth industry." So I have read, somewhere. But frankly, I'm not sure I didn't learn some things in those years of solitude—reading and writing every day for what . . . twenty years, twenty-five years—which a person working in company might not learn so well. I had to make my own decisions, without any social response. "In my craft or sullen art . . .," etc. I fear that sometimes, in workshops, fires are banked. After all, people enjoy a pleasant social response—that's why they join groups, isn't it? This pressure, if you will, could keep the writer a little tame. As well as ambitious for response. Prematurely.

What about Donald Hall and the "McPoem" and the whole workshop phenomenon, the consumer mentality he talks about in his essay "Poetry and Ambition." It's his point that people who come out of the workshop tradition, if that's the term for it, have a huge desire to win more prizes, publish more, possibly at the expense of the work. Would you like to elaborate on the whole workshop phenomenon?

Yes. I esteem Donald Hall greatly, as any sensible person would who knows his work, both his essays and his poetry. And, yes, he has worried over workshop procedures which give—heaven forbid!—"exercises." But now we're in the world of semantics. As I use the word, exercises are fine and useful. There are many mechanical aspects of writing which can be taught—which, in workshops, can be illustrated and practiced.

I go into the classroom like a magician, and I say here are some "tricks" which I have learned and which you can learn, just to have ready. Of course I am talking about language-skill, which, to tell the truth, is often in short supply, even among the most serious aspiring poets. "Tricks" are not poetry, but poetry does employ linguistic laws and acrobatics. So often I see that young writers are relying on luck for something to work—with more linguistic knowledge, they can begin to *make* the poem work. This, to me, is where a workshop can be helpful.

Remember too that workshops are run by individuals, and individuals have bias. There is no way around it, it's very difficult not to have a deeper affinity for some kinds of poems rather than for other kinds. Also, people try to get along. Two poets will try to get along, and so will twenty, or thirty. Additionally, it's very hard for writers in a workshop not to want, if only a little, to please the instructor. Everybody has to be very careful—writers can give up what is most strange and wonderful about their writing—soften their roughest edges—to accommodate themselves toward a group response.

The idea that something's lost in the process of "softening the rough edges" is an interesting one.

Yes. I think it can happen. I think criticism can come too soon and too harshly in workshops. And, also, the expressed aim of so much effort seems to be the publication of poems—right away, and for prizes. Of course this is almost always interconnected with the search for a teaching job.

One of the criticisms I've heard of Hall's views is that it's easy for someone who's already established to talk about there being no need to covet those awards and prizes, because there's a tremendous amount of competition for a very few jobs. I think that's a factor.

My life has been pretty singular, I guess. I mean, I never considered combining writing and teaching. Now they seem everywhere to go hand in hand. Yet I think they are not necessarily good friends to each other. I meet so many teachers who, in the first place, don't really want to be teaching and so they're kind of depressed people, and, in the second place, they are always trying to arrange for a "better" teaching position, meaning less teaching and more free time. What a sad attitude to have toward one's profession! Mostly, too, I find that people who want to be writers take on the usual joys and responsibilities—spouse, house, children—and so must plan their lives in a financial way. I can't argue with that. And it's too bad that creative people can't expect to make a decent living for years and years, but that's the way it is. If you put in the best part of every day, for years, writing, probably you're going to have a flat pocketbook. I certainly did! Teaching is such a fine profession. But writing is something else—a risk, and yet a necessity in certain spirits. What is the answer? Each of us must try to live a good life and a responsible life, whatever we decide that is. For myself, I do like to teach. But—not too much!

Over your several books, how to you feel your work has changed?

My first two books, *No Voyage* and *The River Styx, Ohio,* are out of print and, okay, they can sleep there comfortably. There may be a few poems I will someday want to salvage. But as I've said it's early work, derivative work. The books that follow, beginning with *Twelve Moons* and concluding with *House of Light,* I think of as a unit. I won't say much about them except that they all employ the natural world in an emblematic way, and yet they are all—so was my intent!—about the human condition. It's been said of *American Primitive* that it's a very joyous book. I hope *House of Light* will be seen in a similar way. What I write next will be quite different. Of course, writers always say this, don't they?

Can you elaborate a little on your ideas about the relationship between ego, the reader, and the world in light of how you feel your work has evolved? Why do you think it is evolving as it is? For example, in **Dream Work** *the human presence is consistently more dominant than in* **Twelve Moons** *or even in* **American Primitive.***

Yes, in both *American Primitive* and *Twelve Moons* there is one human presence, and that is the voice speaking in the poem, which should, or can, imaginatively, become the reader's inner voice. I was much involved in mechanics in those days. Flaubert says something wonderful: "Talent is long patience, and originality an effort of will and of intense observation." I lived for years with that, trying for intense observation, believing in it. Well, I still do!

Your poems that take us to that world are very different from the ones in which the human presence is more prominent.

What is the contrast between what is going on in the earliest of these four books and what is going on now in your writing?

What is going on, I suppose, is that I *am* a different person. It's often said that the lyric gift is the gift of the young—it comes with a tremendous amount of energy, it's tied in some deep way to the compulsive urge. I think it is so. Much of art is accomplished in the wonderful *fit* of compulsion! Sometimes, now, I think about such fits with utter longing! With age comes change. My commitment to art is as fierce now as my compulsion used to be. Of course I'm talking about the writer instead of the writing, but it amounts to the same thing. I think the poems run a little slower, I'm fonder of the longer line, wanting it to carry more. Issues are becoming more focused.

I sensed in your poem **"Singapore"** *(in* **House of Light***) the world. It's true that a very personal consciousness of death and of our own aging intrudes into our lives as human beings and writers. But I sensed in* **"Singapore"** *that the "impersonal" world—in the very best sense of that word—was pushing in too.*

Yes. I feel this way. When young poets talk about the confessional poem, I say to them, I should think you would *want* to represent something more than yourself. I feel the function of the poet—be it short-term or long-term—is to be representative, and under that heading to be political, or social, or anyway somehow instructive and opinionated and useful. Even if only as a devil's advocate. Poets who have no material but their own lives don't hold my interest long, no matter how good they may be. I want poetry to help clarify and enlarge my life, not just tell me, in whatever exquisite detail, about the poet's life. These poems, which speak of the world somewhat directly, please me very much. Of course, as I've said, I always felt I was using the natural world emblematically. But poems like **"Singapore"** or **"Acid"** or **"Tecumseh"** make me fairly happy.

Is it your practice to do a great deal of revision?

Oh yes, yes. I revise an awful lot, fifty, sixty drafts easily. I have an old electric typewriter, no computer, nothing like that. I use notebooks, pens and pencils, the old-fashioned stuff. I do a lot of drafts, and I usually don't keep for long any of the revisions. I *make* myself make the decisions and go on about it. A lot of writers keep their papers. I don't. I won't be found dead with a lot of papers!

You know, then, when a poem is finished.

When it works. I don't use the question, "Is it perfect?" I ask if it's the best I can do and if it works. And if those two things are so, then I go on to the next poem.

Do you go back and read your work, after it's in print?

I suppose, except for public readings, I wouldn't read very much of it. It's just that I'm that much involved in what isn't finished, or even begun! I think most writers are probably like this.

To go on to something else, I also believe my writing is influenced by the readings. I prefer poems with a narrative—or better yet, two or three stories. I like to switch from rhetoric to a sudden vernacular phrase, or a heavily lyric passage, or throw out a question. Such devices involve the listeners and draw them in. Of course this is all just so that you can soften them up and say what it is you really want to say. This sounds very programmatic, doesn't it? And yet, it's true. I do remember those "listeners" when I write. So all that old stuff—the various mechanics—still fascinates me thoroughly. How enjambed lines "feel" to the listener, as compared with end-stopped lines. All that good business.

That's something concrete, to tell students in workshops.

Yes, absolutely. You know, in every other discipline a student learns a little at a time. In the visual arts, you learn to draw, you learn perspective, you learn theories of color, you learn to use charcoal, and oil paints—all kinds of things. You train your eye and hand to paint a picture, finally. But in poetry you're given the huge responsibility of writing a whole poem, right from the first. And at that point I say the sad thing that happens is that someone says, "Okay, that's pretty good." So the person is encouraged to write exactly the same kind of poem the next time, to try to make it better but do it exactly the same way. Three or four poems down the line, the person is in an awful rut. When I operate a workshop I ask the writers to go back for a while to beginning things. To get some options they have missed. And to learn things from reading, as well as writing. To read, also, with "intense observation."

Perhaps there's something missing in the way students read today.

Well, they read for content, not for the felt experience which is also in the writing. The question asked today is: What does it mean? Nobody says, "How does it feel?" One of the things I like to suggest is for a student to take an especially admired poem—say Yeats' "Easter, 1916"—and read it every morning for thirty days or so. Read it slowly and carefully. As though it were the only poem in the world. Then, you begin to learn how to read.

That's a wonderful way, too, of defeating the notion that a poem will fall apart under close scrutiny.

Yes.

When we first corresponded about this interview, you were a bit reluctant to grant it. Do you feel interviews are invasive? Or have you been misrepresented in the past?

No, I've not been misrepresented, not seriously, but I feel interviews are opportunistic, and not every opportunity should be taken. Some company once wanted to do a videotape of me in my home—walk around and follow me—and wouldn't this be fine. And I said, thank you very much, no. They wrote and urged me again, suggesting that people who like my work would like to know more about me. And I wrote back and said that, if I've done my work well, I vanish completely from the scene. That's how I feel about it. I believe it is invasive of the work when you know too much about the writer, and almost anything is too much. I am trying in my poems to vanish and have the reader be the experiencer. I do not want to be there. It is not even a walk we take together. So, I don't do many interviews.

A reviewer of **American Primitive** *wrote that you find your primary subjects "outside the apparatus of the literary and high cultural heritage." Do you agree with that characterization?*

As opposed to what? Low-culture, or no-culture? Rather a negative way to go about it, don't you think? But it sounds like a lot of the world is left out of that statement, so I'll just take the chance and say: Okay, sure I do.

Eleanor Swanson (review date May/June 1990)

SOURCE: A review of *House of Light,* in *The Bloomsbury Review,* Vol. 10, No. 3, May/June, 1990, pp. 1, 28.

[*In the following review, Swanson finds* House of Light *to be a contemplative exploration of the paradoxes of nature to reveal the self.*]

We have come to expect images of the natural world in Mary Oliver's poetry: dark ponds and bears and lilies, deer, crows, and snakes. Never has the natural world been so pervasive as it is in her latest book, *House of Light;* never before have the human subjects—when they appear at all—been shown at such remove. Yet, each poem is a deep human cry, a search for a connection with nature that will relieve feelings of loneliness and isolation:

> I saw the heron shaking
> its damp wings—
> and then I felt
> an explosion—
> a pain—
> also a happiness
> I can hardly mention
> as I slid free—

> as I saw the world
> through those yellow eyes.

But loneliness stands at the edge of all the poet's imaginings, inevitable in a "difficult world." "I think I will always / be lonely / in this world," says the narrator of **"Lilies."** That is a given. Even moments of happiness are tempered, often through their very intensity, as the forest grows dark at its center and the pond yields nothing in its depths. Perhaps this is nature's essential message, that we live always at the mercy of our best experiences, of a thing; at an instant, turning into its opposite: "so long as you don't mind / a little dying how could there be a day in your whole life / that doesn't have its splash of happiness?"

Oliver sometimes seems to insist that despair be left outside the poems: "A person wants to stand in a happy place, in a poem," she says. But clearly the world intrudes, the world of "glass cities," "cold cities," the world of the poem **"Singapore"** in which a woman washes airport ashtrays in the public toilet. The trees and birds that "fill" this poem are not real; they are only the artifacts of poetry, a way of saying no to pain:

> If the world were only pain and logic, who would
>   want it?
> Of course, it isn't
> Neither do I mean anything miraculous, but only
> the light that can shine out of a life. I mean
> the way she unfolded and refolded the blue cloth,
> the way her smile was only for my sake; I mean
> the way this poem is filled with the trees, and birds.

The "house of light" is both the natural world and the poetry that celebrates that world. Familiar swans and lilies and owls have the power to affirm the meaning of the most difficult existence. Even darkness is not something to fear: "But my bones knew something wonderful / about the darkness." It is a source of knowledge:

> I thought of Da Vinci—
> the way he kept dreaming
> of what was inside the darkness—
> how it wanted to rise
> on its invisible muscle
> how it wanted to shine
> like fire.

Darkness is not light's opposite, but its complement on the continuum of experience. Darkness is related to light as birth is related to death, as fear is related to happiness. "How could anyone believe / that anything in this world / is only what it appears to be —" Oliver asks in **"What is it?"** Clearly these poems of paradox—which recall Taoism and Zen Buddhism—can give us a new perspective on our human trials.

We can learn much from the natural world; we need only know that "There are so many stories, / more beautiful than answers." But the most powerful lesson nature teaches is the acceptance of paradox in "the world / that is ours, or could be."

The tone of these poems is variously formal, elegiac, somber, rarely playful. The sense of loss, the experience, the objects of contemplation are delivered in the present moment, as if, indeed, we need know nothing but the present—nothing of personal history or current affairs, for example, nothing of an imperiled future. In **"Oak Tree at the Entrance to Blackwater Pond,"** each day the narrator passes an enormous oak felled many years ago by lightning. It reminds her of "a black boat / floating / in the tossing leaves of summer, / like the coffin of Osiris. . . ." She catches herself, then, and denies the power of the allusion. "But, listen," she says, "I'm tired of that brazen promise: / death and resurrection . . . what I loved, I mean, was that tree— / tree of the moment—tree of my own sad, mortal heart—."

This keen sense of mortality and immanence is what has come to matter more than anything.

Reading these poems is like taking a walk, deeper and deeper into the woods. We pass almost no people along our way, and when we do, such as in **"Singapore"** and **"Indonesia,"** these other humans stand at a distance that is troubling for its immensity or its silence. No human voices other than the narrator's disturb our retreat, the depth of our contemplation. The self seems the only subject; the introspection is privileged and sharply focused again and again, on a narrow landscape.

This seems Oliver's thematic intent, a close focus on self, on paradox in nature and the relationship between interior and exterior landscapes. As Oliver's poetry is crafted toward these thematic ends, so is it crafted for the ear. Sound and rhythm, short lines, and straightforward syntax work together to create poems of great power. This is not a style without risk, however, and the risk is that straightforwardness may lapse into banality, into assertions or conclusions that are pat or already contained within the details of the poem. Such lapses occur but rarely. The poetry in *House of Light* places us in the presence of beauty and mystery that we feel in our very bones. "Make of yourself a light," says the dying Buddha in **"The Buddha's Last Instruction,"** and this is what Oliver has done: She has illuminated many places of darkness and given us moments of "inexplicable value." Oliver is at her best in these poems: stepping onto the edge, dipping her hand into the dark water, standing in the "white fire," wanting to believe "that the light—is everything," that death "isn't darkness after all, but so much light / wrapping itself around us." This is a poetry in which wanting to believe is forged into belief, into faith:

I want to believe I am looking
into the white fire of a great mystery
I want to believe that the imperfections are
    nothing—
that the light is everything—
that it is more than the sum
of each flawed blossom rising and fading. And I
    do.

Robert Richman (review date 25 November 1990)

SOURCE: "Polished Surfaces and Difficult Pastorals," in *The New York Times Book Review,* November 25, 1990, sec. 7, p. 24.

[*In the following excerpt, Richman reviews* House of Light *and finds it to be an optimistic work concerned with the cycles of life.*]

Mary Oliver's work seems to inhabit an aesthetic domain unsullied by the bustle of human life. Indeed, her principal theme—"how to love this world," as she writes in **"Spring,"** a poem in her new volume, *House of Light*—often demands a poetic landscape that, brimming though it may be with lilies, herons, pipefish and crows, is devoid of human beings. Ms. Oliver would appear to think that if you take people as your subject, you will be forced to concentrate on their many hardships and misfortunes. Does she lack patience for such things? No: she's just not their poet.

When she does write about human suffering or nature's less benevolent side, it's usually to show how the agony might be soothed by the world's splendors. When the poet hears the death cries of an owl's victims, she admits that "it stabs my heart." "But isn't it wonderful," she then remarks,

what is happening
    in the branches of the pines;
        the owl's young,
            dressed in snowflakes,

are starting to fatten—
    they beat their muscular wings,
        they dream of flying
            for another million years
over the water,
    over the ferns,
over the world's roughage
    as it bleeds and deepens.

Ms. Oliver's shift from the imagery of death to the owl's brood "dressed in snowflakes" isn't an attempt to shirk whatever is repugnant. It's an attempt to make death more bearable by focusing on the endlessly recommencing life that surrounds it.

In **"Singapore,"** Ms. Oliver describes an encounter with a woman cleaning toilets in an airport washroom. Here too she tries to find something worth praising:

> I don't doubt for a moment that she loves her life.
> And I want her to rise up from the crust and the
>   slop
> and fly down to the river.
> This probably won't happen.
> But maybe it will.
> If the world were only pain and logic, who would
> want it?
>
> Of course it isn't
> Neither do I mean anything miraculous, but only
> the light that can shine out of a life. I mean
> the way she unfolded and refolded the blue cloth,
> the way her smile was only for my sake; I mean
> the way this poem is filled with trees, and birds.

Such a life asks the poet to find "the light that can shine out of" it. Ms. Oliver's optimistic point is strengthened by the self-reflexive touch at the end, where she compares the implausibility of the woman's flying to the river with the implausibility of poems "filled with birds and trees." Both express the vainest of hopes—or do they?

Mary Oliver's poems are thoroughly convincing—as genuine, moving, and implausible as the first caressing breeze of spring.

Dennis Sampson (review date Summer 1991)

SOURCE: "Poetry Chronicle," in *The Hudson Review,* Vol. 44, No. 2, Summer, 1991, pp. 333-42.

[*In the following excerpt, Sampson asserts that* House of Light *"yields . . . to everything in nature that is holy."*]

What does it mean to have a vision in our time, "in this century and moment of mania," as Robert Penn Warren called it? Is it possible to speak any more, as Whitman did, of humanity as a whole without sounding pompous or political?

Mary Oliver's new book yields, as did Thoreau, to everything in nature that is holy. Some may find seeming artlessness and obsession with birds, beasts, and flowers absurd in her new work; she is not a formalist and is drawn almost exclusively to what is not human in her poetry. Oliver is disarming in her innocence and deft at calling up brilliant similes, a thoughtful and thoroughly empathetic human being. Watching a heron, she says "A blue preacher / flew toward the swamp, / in slow motion," a swan is "a slim / and delicate ship" and "moves / on its miraculous muscles / as though time didn't exist." She describes an oak tree at the entrance to

a pond, "when the storm / laid one lean yellow wand against it, smoking it open / to its rosy heart," and, in **"The Summer Day,"** after watching the grasshopper in her hand "moving her jaws back and forth instead of up and down," she offers this final comment:

> I don't know exactly what prayer is.
> I do know how to pay attention, how to fall down
> into the grass, how to kneel down in the grass,
> how to be idle and blessed, how to stroll through
>   the fields,
> which is what I have been doing all day.
> Tell me, what else should I have done?
> Doesn't everything die at last, and too soon?
> Tell me, what is it you plan to do
> with your one wild and precious life?

One hears echoes of James Wright and Galway Kinnell, writers to whom Oliver would not resent being compared. Oliver risks sentimentality when love of the world almost gives in to emotions not won by the poem, but finally she is too wise to let this happen. **"Lilies"** ("I have been thinking about living / like the lilies / that blow in the fields") recalls Whitman's "I think I could turn and live with animals."

The poem concludes with this felicitous reference to a hummingbird:

> I think I will always be lonely
> in this world, where the cattle
> graze like a black and white river—
>
> where the ravishing lilies
> melt, without protest, on their tongues—
> where the hummingbird, whenever there is a fuss,
> just rises and floats away.

Pity sings a hideous and ultimately futile song to itself, as Oliver knows. "Make of yourself a light," says the Buddha in her **"The Buddha's Last Instruction"** before he dies. And Oliver does this. "Slowly, beneath the branches, / he raised his head. / He looked into the faces of that frightened crowd."

These may not be great poems, but they are awfully fine, wise even. Of the roses in **"Roses, Late Summer"** that "have opened their factories of sweetness / and are giving it back to the world," she scolds, as a Zen Master might:

> Fear has not occurred to them, nor ambition.
> Reason they have not yet thought of.
> Neither do they ask how long they must be roses,
>   and then what.
> Or any other foolish question.

Lee Upton (review date Summer 1991)

SOURCE: "Inside History," in *Belles Lettres,* Vol. 6, No. 4, Summer, 1991, pp. 42-4.

[*In the following review, Upton notes Oliver's connection of dissimilar images in* House of Light.]

Mary Oliver is yet another mature poet—one with whom many of us have much greater familiarity. While Eavan Boland works with domestic interiors, Mary Oliver sets her lens in nature. She writes of lilies and turtles and owls as if each possessed a soul and a singular identity. At times she echoes Walt Whitman, finding peace among animals for their very lack of consciousness, their inability to quarrel or irritate. Despite the note of horror and sudden menace in this book, she proceeds with near mystical love for her subjects.

For Oliver, every day must have "one splash of happiness." Her own happiness seems to arise from connecting images and actions that initially appear dissimilar and arbitrary.

Some of her virtues are immediately apparent in **"Looking for Snakes."** What is pretty and what is repulsive thrive in the same patch. Two snakes "rise / in a spit of energy / like dark stalks / among the wild, pink roses." The imagination is part of that same natural order.

What is the world but "hunger and happiness," Oliver asks. And she challenges her readers with what amounts to a fierce attention to the moment, "Tell me, what is it you plan to do / with your one wild and precious life?"

Ben Howard (review date September 1991)

SOURCE: "World and Spirit, Body and Soul," in *Poetry,* Vol. 158, No. 6, September, 1991, pp. 342-43.

[*In the following review of* House of Light, *Howard finds that Oliver's poems "evoke the fears, sorrows, and joys of the solitary spirit."*]

Mary Oliver's purpose is as rare as her austere, insistent voice. In **Dream Work** Oliver portrayed herself as the humble celebrant of natural enigmas, "learning / little by little to love / our only world." In the present collection, her eighth, she reaffirms that purpose, declaring flatly that there is "only one question: how to love this world." By turns retiring or demanding, self-effacing or peremptory, these new poems honor the otherness of the natural world, even as they contemplate "the white fire of a great mystery." Placing the self in the stream of natural change, these quiet but forceful poems evoke the fears, sorrows, and joys of the solitary spirit. At their most exuberant, they celebrate the spirit's light, whether it manifests itself in fish bones, lilies, snow, or a luminous vision of death—that "scalding, aortal light," wherein we are "washed and washed / out of our bones."

The world that Oliver would love is, for the most part, brutal, impermanent, and unpeopled. It reeks of death and impurity. Although a few of the forty-six poems in **House of Light** look compassionately at human subjects—laborers in Indonesia; a woman cleaning toilets in the Singapore airport—Oliver's attention turns most frequently to snakes, egrets, turtles, and other animals in the wild. What fascinates her about these creatures is at once their beauty and their unthinking, inhuman cruelty. "[D]eath / is everywhere," she reminds us, "even in the red swamp / of a flower." In the lion of Serengeti she finds an emblem of terror and awe, of grace and death conjoined:

> Can anyone doubt that the lion of Serengeti
> is part of the idea of God?
> Can anyone doubt that, for those first, almost-
> upright bodies
> in the shadow of Kilimanjaro,
>
> in the lush garden of Africa,
> in the continuation of everything beyond each
> individual thing,
>
> the lion
> was both the flower of life and the winch of
> death—
>
> the bone-breaker,
> and the agent of transformation?
> **"Serengeti"**

Here as elsewhere, Oliver's rhetoric is tendentious. In a secular age, one might well doubt the poet's theistic supposition. Insofar as one is convinced by these lines, the agent of persuasion is not Oliver's rhetorical questions so much as her singular vision, in which a carnivore becomes a vehicle of change, and the "individual thing"—be it the lion's prey or the human ego—is subjugated to the natural order.

Oliver is not indifferent to human concerns. On the contrary, her poems draw apt and surprising parallels between natural phenomena and the stirrings of the heart. Terns catching fish bring to mind "the heart blanching / in its fold of shadows / because it knows / someday it will be / the fish and the wave / and no longer itself—." The cry of an owl awakens spiritual longings: "I thought of Jesus, how he / crouched in the dark for two nights, / then floated back above the horizon." And the opening of lilies on the surface of a pond recalls the poet to her sadness:

> . . . they are
> devoid of meaning, they are
> simply doing,
> from the deepest

spurs of their being,
     what they are impelled to do
          every summer.
     And so, dear sorrow, are you.
"The Lilies Break Open Over the Dark Water"

Yet even in those poems which focus on human feeling, Oliver's stance is rarely self-regarding. She is well aware that the "flapping, blood-gulping crows" have their counterparts in the human psyche. But for Oliver, as for Robinson Jeffers, the natural world is primary. What engages her is not the psyche's inner conflicts but those numinous intersections of the self and the natural world, those meetings in the woods and by the ponds, which engender a sense of reverence and awe:

I was thinking:
so this is how you swim inward,
so this is how you flow outward,
so this is how you pray.
"Five A.M. in the Pinewoods"

Like D. H. Lawrence, Oliver likes to leap abruptly from the minute observation to the sweeping statement. And like Elizabeth Bishop, she is inclined to interrupt her narratives and descriptions with moral and metaphysical questions. When her statements drift toward the oracular ("Nothing's important // except that the great and cruel mystery of the world . . . not be denied") or when her questions sound naive ("Do you think there is any / personal heaven / for any of us?"), these techniques can be distracting. Within the context of selfless contemplation, they seem willful and intrusive. But in the best of these poems—**"Pipefish," "The Terns," "Fish Bones," "Praise"**—Oliver's comments ratify her perceptions, enhancing an atmosphere of awe and wonder. And in the last and finest poem of the collection, belief and image fuse in a moment of revelation:

          so I thought:
          maybe death
     isn't darkness, after all,
          but so much light
     wrapping itself around us—

          as soft as feathers—
     that we are instantly weary
of looking, and looking, and shut our eyes,
          not without amazement,
     and let ourselves be carried,
     as through the translucence of mica,
          to the river
that is without the least dapple or shadow—
     that is nothing but light . . .

"White Owl Flies Into and Out of the Field"

"Soft as feathers" is unfortunate, "so I thought" redundant. But has any recent collection ended with a more radiant vision—or a firmer affirmation?

David Baker (review date Winter 1991)

SOURCE: A review of *House of Light,* in *The Kenyon Review,* Vol. 13, No. 1, Winter, 1991, pp. 192-202.

[*In the following excerpt, Baker questions the "isolationist" and "righteous" tendencies in Oliver's poetry.*]

Like Stanley Plumly, Mary Oliver is a poet who reworks her passions. While Plumly's poems may have relatively few characters, Oliver's are downright isolated, hermetic; and while Plumly's phrasing is slow, severe, haunted, Mary Oliver's music is loose, humble, casual, innocent. I happen to like her work a good bit, and so find her new *House of Light* full of pleasures worth my repeated attention, but I also maintain a suspicion or two.

What I like most about Oliver's poems is their reverence for the natural world, their politics (usually implied rather than declared) of ecology, stewardship, and human connection. Her plain style and her persistent, nearly unvoiceable awe at the powerful beauty of nature are well-matched partners. She's in direct descent from the New England naturalists—Bartram and Thoreau, for instance—and, like them, is a rugged individualist. But at times she can seem more nearly an isolationist who prefers the company of herons, black bears, and oak trees to people:

I have been thinking
about living
like the lilies
that blow in the fields.

They rise and fall
in the wedge of the wind,
and have no shelter
from the tongues of the cattle,

and have no closets or cupboards,
and have no legs.
Still I would like to be
as wonderful

as that old idea.

These opening lines of **"Lilies"**—which echo the strategy and subject of a great many poems in this book—directly express Oliver's repeated struggle between the human and the natural, and perhaps purposely recall not only the Biblical lilies of the field but also Whitman's lovely section 32 of "Song of Myself": "I think I could turn and live with animals, they are so placid and self-contained. . . ." This is, of course, the wonderful old idea, that nature can serve as example and model for human behavior, if only we are unashamed enough, innocent enough, free enough—unhuman enough. And of course Oliver realizes the many reasons prohibiting her reaching such a state of naturalness. It's the age-old realization that the world is too much with us. Still, Oliver frequently wishes to transcend the human world, and the concluding lines of **"Lilies"** identify this ultimately mystical, more problematic, side of Oliver's vision:

> I think I will always be lonely
> in this world, where the cattle
> graze like a black and white river—
>
> where the ravishing lilies
> melt, without protest, on their tongues—
> where the hummingbird, whenever there is a fuss,
> just rises and floats away

To be "ravishing," of course is not only to be beautiful but also to be seized and carried away. Leaving the world of the human requires a death.

This is the point of one of my difficulties with Oliver. She persists in providing many poems with the same, perhaps too-easy solution—politically and aesthetically—merely to rise and float away from a troubling world, to erase it or to erase the self within that world. Occasionally Oliver seems just too good at deflecting blame or responsibility, good at accusing by implication or avoidance, but she's not quite so good at accepting her own share of guilt or involvement, and that is a central difference between her and one of her abiding influences, James Wright. Oliver often intones a rhetoric similar to Wright's voice in *The Branch Will Not Break,* wherein the human world is often a poor parody of the sublime, saving world of nature, and yet she seldom assumes the kind of participation that Wright demanded of himself. Only the fortunate few can afford to live in the luxury of expansive natural isolation. Her righteousness or piety is Oliver's least becoming quality: "And mostly I'm grateful that I take this world so seriously," she informs us in **"The Gift."** Too often, the only people we encounter in "this world" are the likes of Van Gogh, Buddha, Michelangelo, Jesus, Blake, Mahler—Oliver's preferred company of the misunderstood, the martyred, and (significantly) the absent.

Other times, though, Oliver seems to sense and question her own isolate habit. In what must be one of her most important and powerful poems, **"Singapore,"** Oliver directly addresses her naturalist's impulse:

> A poem should always have birds in it.
> Kingfishers, say, with their bold eyes and gaudy
> wings.

> Rivers are pleasant, and of course trees.

But here, as in a few other poems in **House of Light,** Oliver's speaker does not stand beside a pond or in a field; she is in the restroom of a Singapore airport, face to face with a woman who "knelt there, washing something in the white bowl." While Oliver's speaker longs for her familiar poetic—"a person wants to stand in a happy place, in a poem"—she cannot this time avoid or disregard the unpleasant, the human, as "disgust argued in [her] stomach." Oliver's poetry is quite persuasive when she allows herself to become politically, or merely personally, involved. In the second half of **"Singapore,"** she uses her love of nature to inform her growing sense of connection, of appreciation:

> She smiled and I smiled. What kind of nonsense is
>   this?
> Everybody needs a job.
>
> Yes, a person wants to stand in a happy place, in a
>   poem.
> But first we must watch her as she stares down at
>   her labor,
>   which is dull enough.
> She is washing the tops of the airport ashtrays, as
>   big as
>   hubcaps, with a blue rag.
> Her small hands turn the metal, scrubbing and
>   rinsing.
> She does not work slowly, nor quickly, but like a
>   river.
> Her dark hair is like the wing of a bird.

The deliberate similes "like a river" and "like the wing of a bird" signal the poem's leap, the poet's self-conscious insistence to make room for both the painfully human and the beautifully natural by answering her own earlier assertion (and confession) that a poem "should always have birds [and rivers and trees] in it." This poem is an example of Oliver working harder to justify the choices of other poems wherein nature is merely a place of private solace and comfort. Here the poet's own job is similar to the custodian's, to serve as caretaker to the human *and* the natural, to try to make the world clean again; in essence, for Oliver, not to ignore the world in the first place, since beauty and grace are characteristics of people as well as snowy owls. But, as Oliver admits in this poem, beauty and grace in people must come with the inevitable price of pain, toil, and involvement. The final two stanzas provide an example of Oliver's sympathy and artistry at work, at their best:

> I don't doubt for a moment that she loves her life.
> And I want her to rise up from the crust and the
>   slop and
>   fly down to the river.

This probably won't happen.
But maybe it will. If the world were only pain and
    logic, who would want it?

Of course, it isn't.
Neither do I mean anything miraculous, but only
the light that can shine out of a life. I mean
the way she unfolded and refolded the blue cloth,
the way her smile was only for my sake; I mean
the way this poem is filled with trees, and birds.

Stephen Dobyns (review date 13 December 1992)

SOURCE: "How Does One Live?," in *The New York Times Book Review,* December 13, 1992, sec. 7, p. 12.

[*In the following excerpt, Dobyns reviews* New and Selected Poems *and notes the consistency in tone and an "increased precision with language" over the thirty-year period featured.*]

Ever since Homer set Achilles brooding in his tent, poets have asked: how does one live? For Mary Oliver one lives by trying to learn how to love the world. For Carl Dennis one lives by learning how to reconcile one's hopes and ambitions with one's failures and shortcomings. For Stephen Berg, one lives by seeking redemption for one's adult nature: the frailty, fallibility and fear.

Mary Oliver's *New and Selected Poems,* just given a National Book Award, joins together poems written over 30 years. One of the astonishing aspects of her work is the consistency of tone over this long period. What changes is an increased focus on nature and an increased precision with language that has made her one of our very best poets. Her new poem, **"This Morning Again It Was in the Dusty Pines"** concludes with the description of the flight of the owl:

> as death
> rises up—
> god's bark-colored thumb—
> and opens the sheath of its wings
>
> and turns its hungry, hooked head
> upon me, and away,
> and softly,
> lamp-eyed,
>
> becomes the perfect, billowing instrument
> as it glides
> through the wind
> like a knife.

There are certain qualities in this poem that one has come to expect from Ms. Oliver: the startling yet precise modifiers (the owl is "lamp-eyed," it is "god's bark-colored thumb"),

the exact verbs (elsewhere in this poem the owl "pours itself / into the air) and the line breaks that move one along as easily as Tarzan used to swing from vine to vine. Much contemporary free verse strikes one as lazy. Ms. Oliver's lines and line breaks completely control the rhythm and the pacing. She forces us to read her poems as she meant them to be read. Perhaps only James Wright controlled the free verse line as well as she does.

Although Ms. Oliver's poems are mostly set in the natural world, it would be wrong to call her a nature poet. Nature for her is neither pretty nor nice. Beauty is to be found there, but it is a beauty containing the knowledge that life is mostly a matter of dying. The reason why the only true question is "how to love the world" is that the world is intrinsically unlovable, and one's temptation is to set down one's mortal burden and sink at last into the softness.

There is no complaint in Ms. Oliver's poetry, no whining, but neither is there the sense that life is in any way easy. As a result, many of her poems have as a subtext the teaching of how one lives. In my favorite of her single books, ***House of Light,*** she takes up the Buddha's last words to his followers: "Make of yourself a light." Her poems become her attempts to do just that, to make of herself a light.

This gives Ms. Oliver a public concern that differentiates her from many of her contemporaries. These poems sustain us rather than divert us. Although few poets have fewer human beings in their poems than Mary Oliver, it is ironic that few poets also go so far as to help us forward.

Robyn Selman (review date 12 January 1993)

SOURCE: "Natural History," in *Village Voice,* Vol. 38, No. 2, January 12, 1993, pp. 81-2.

[*In the following review of* New and Selected Poems, *Selman praises Oliver's composure, sincerity, and dedication to her subject.*]

It's a beautiful winter day—one can't help noticing the day when one reads Mary Oliver—a day on which she's won another prize, this time the National Book Award for her seventh book, *New and Selected Poems.* I think of her at home in Provincetown, where she has a reputation for being something of a recluse. I also think of Elizabeth Bishop, the other National Book Award-winning recluse, with whom Oliver has much in common. Like Bishop, Oliver doesn't go in much for politics, poetic or public. You won't see poems by either of them in women-only anthologies. And the similarities continue: Oliver's poems are not, strictly speaking, personal. She rarely teaches and gives readings far less often than her contemporaries. As Bishop was, Mary Oliver is shy.

But not on the page. She is one of a very few poets who declares her artistic intention boldly and unasked, usually right up front like a platform, or maybe a dedication. "When it's over, I want to say: all my life / I was a bride married to amazement. / I was the bridegroom, taking the world into my arms."

With the style of an Eve Arden character. Oliver's poetic composure is unflagging. She sets the tone of her poems straight off, but she keeps her voice gentle, articulate, and capable, as self-knowing as Eve's. Although, as Bishop did, Oliver often asks questions in her poems ("Is the soul solid, like iron?"), questions that make room for ambivalence and quarrel, the poems rarely fall into an impasse. They're solved a thousand times by beauty.

> Do you love this world?
> Do you cherish your humble
>   and silky life?
> Do you adore the green grass,
>   with its terror beneath?
> Do you also hurry, half-dressed
>   and barefoot, into the
>   garden.
> and softly,
> and exclaiming of their
>   dearness,
> fill your arms with the white
>   and pink flowers

Oliver's passionate medium is almost always the pastoral. Though one of her books, *Dream Work* contains meditations on the Holocaust and personal loss, the majority of her work, like D. H. Lawrence's, May Swenson's, Bishop's, and Marianne Moore's, focuses timelessly on the natural world. Unlike Moore and Bishop, Oliver doesn't anthropomorphize to quite the same effect. She is—and this isn't a negative comment, for I have none—less playful, more dogged, deadly sincere.

"One morning / the fox came down the hill, glittering and confident, / and didn't see me—and I thought: / so this is the world. / I'm not in it. / It is beautiful." Originally from Ohio, Oliver moved to New England, where she worked as a secretary to Edna St. Vincent Millay's sister Norma. She also brings to mind the sober side of Millay, with whom she shares New England and a penchant for poems that have as their underlying subject matter the inevitability of one's own death. And like the later Millay, and most obviously Blake, Oliver infuses her work with a touch of the ecstatic.

In her own time, Oliver has a contemporary in the ecstatic musician Van Morrison; I draw the comparison in part to say that Oliver has few contemporaries in current American poetry, as well as to say that she and Van share a connection to a pastoral life that seems far away (to say the least) from our collective urban grasp. "Every year, / and every year / the hatchlings wake in the swaying branches, / in the silver baskets, / and love the world. / Is it necessary to say any more? / Have you heard them singing in the wind, above the final fields? / Have you ever been so happy in your life?"

Mary Oliver is no guest in the woods. Her quotidian is made up of long walks, dog in tow, sleeping in a tent by a marsh, going out, not in, when a storm comes. At the outset of each poem, we are reminded of her daily task: testing the poet's vision. Her dedication to it is intense. For example, unlike other poets who use symbols from various mediums, Oliver keens her metaphors in the natural palette. Light of nature is never compared to the light of TV. ("When death comes / like an iceberg between the shoulder blades.")

In the vastness of *New and Selected Poems,* something new is unearthed about Oliver's insatiable hunger for the natural. The personal poems of *Dream Work,* which fall roughly halfway through the 250 pages, give off a centrifugal energy, drawing the reader in, throwing their power outward. But they're not confessional poems in the style to which we've grown accustomed. Personal moments appear like cloud formations, dense but in motion, throwing long, dark shadows of child abuse and breakdown as well as lightning bolts of blame, rage, and bitterness, all with only the lightest narrative detail. In the afterglow of these few pieces, one senses that for this poet nature is the parent, the companion, the hope, the boldly unselfconscious id riding the ego through the seasons.

> I was always running around,
>   looking
> at this and that.
> If I stopped
> the pain
> was unbearable.
> If I stopped and thought, maybe
> the world
> can't be saved,
> the pain
> was unbearable.
> Finally, I had noticed enough.
> All around me in the forest
> the white moths floated.

These new and selected poems; arranged newest to oldest, work, as you might expect, naturally—like memory, or the mind as it ages; true to a life of the imagination, strikingly declarative, and not at all shy.

Judith Kitchen (review date Spring 1993)

SOURCE: A review of *New and Selected Poems,* in *The Georgia Review,* Vol. 47, No. 1, Spring, 1993, pp. 145-59.

[*In the following review, Kitchen notes a disparity between earlier poems which feature a division between nature and narrator and later poems in which the narrator becomes one with nature.*]

Her [Oliver's] *New and Selected Poems* reminds us of the territory she has covered since her first publications in the early 1960's, and I am glad to see some old favorites in this larger context. For example, **"Ghosts"** mourns the loss of the buffalo by imagining a time when they were abundant; then, with its insistent question—"have you noticed?" —the poem forces the reader to examine the silence of extinction, the blissful oblivion of those who have inherited the land. From an earlier book **"Entering the Kingdom"** remains an excellent example of how human consciousness divides us from our own environment. The speaker of the poem goes out into the realm of the crows and is seen by them as "possibly dangerous." But the speaker wants only "to learn something by being nothing / a little while but the rich / lens of attention." The crows have the last word:

> They know me for what I am.
> No dreamer,
> No eater of leaves.

Or rather, she has the last word. The speaker is forced to articulate the crows' position; observation alone does not suffice. The division between the two realms remains. In spite of the promise of the title, she has failed to enter the kingdom on its terms.

The sharpened edge to Oliver's earlier work has been blunted in the intervening years. Her later poems began to celebrate through a kind of enraptured description; anything natural was a source of wonder. From there it was an easy step to grant to nature human emotions, and so it is that **"Spring"** can end with this image of a bear: "all day I think of her—/ her white teeth, / her wordlessness / her perfect love." Or that **"Roses, Late Summer"** can allow nature, instead of informing the human life, to become a substitute: "If I had another life . . . / I would be a fox, or a tree / full of waving branches. / I wouldn't mind being a rose / in a field full of roses." Even Oliver's questions seem to have presumptive answers: "Why should I have it [the soul], and not the camel?" Everywhere she exhibits an impulse toward fusion, toward discovering a place where the speaker can lay down her human burden and, quite literally, become one with the natural order.

Interestingly, in the thirty new poems which comprise the first section of the book, this essentially Romantic impulse is at war with her earlier vision of separation. If these poems by themselves comprised a single volume, I would be forced to note its radical divisions. Even as Oliver recognizes the inability of language to bridge the gap (referring to nature's "dumb dazzle" or its lack of "expression" or its "cold and

glassy eye"), she creates a space where nature's "green energy" can claim her in its "husky arms." She confronts the reader with a willed use of the pathetic fallacy. So it is that a deer can have "solicitude" before taking flight, that a waterfall can seem "surprised" by the "unexpected kindness of the air," that the gannet eating the fish is a beautiful thing because "nothing in this world moves / but as a positive power," that the owl can fill himself with a "red and digestible joy." The adjectives betray the stance: the natural is equated with the "good." The opposite is also implied: if something is not of nature, it is potentially bad.

> Aware that the natural world is actually indifferent to her, Oliver deliberately decides not to be indifferent to it. This gives rise to the ecstatic voice of many of the poems, and it is a voice that, because of its very excess, is most compelling.
>
> —*Judith Kitchen*

In **"Goldenrod,"** Oliver almost confronts her own dilemma: "And what has consciousness come to anyway, so far, // that is better than these light-filled bodies?" Well, for one thing, I want to answer, the ability to speak about them, to be able to note that it is "natural and godly" to bend in the wind. Aware that the natural world is actually indifferent to her, Oliver deliberately decides not to be indifferent to it. This gives rise to the ecstatic voice of many of the poems, and it is a voice that, because of its very excess, is most compelling. The reader is able to have reservations and still savor Oliver's ability to go with the rush of feeling. In **"Peonies"** she can gather the flowers with their "sweet sap" and "honeyed heaviness," exclaiming of their "dearness," and we willingly allow her this sensibility because it is so wholly hers. My favorite of such moments is at the end of **"Poppies"**:

> Inside the bright fields,
>
> touched by their rough and spongy gold,
> I am washed and washed
> in the river
> of earthly delight—
>
> and what are you going to do—
> what can you do
> about it—
> deep, blue night?

Frost characteristically recognizes the impenetrability of nature; Oliver defies it to shut her out.

Oliver's opposing impulse is toward a more objective depiction of nature—what happens is simply what happens—accompanied by a self-conscious awareness of human isolation. The last stanza of **"Rain"** begins "Where life has no purpose, / and is neither civil nor intelligent," and this reader sighs in recognition. In **"Hawk"** the bird turns into a white blade—and then the blade falls. The title of **"Lonely, White Fields"** reveals its deliberate slippage; the owl's nightly solitude is echoed by a speaker whose singular voice says, "I don't know / what death's ultimate / purpose is . . .." And the snow simply goes on falling, "flake after perfect flake."

Imagined death is at the heart of many of these new poems—and, for Oliver, death is the ultimate merger of the human and the natural. The section ends with just such an image:

> One morning
> the fox came down the hill, glittering and confi-
>   dent,
> and didn't see me—and I thought:
>
> so this is the world.
> I'm not in it.
> It is beautiful.

Oliver's failure to be adequate to her own epistemological questions makes many of these poems both interesting and irritating—how, for instance, is beauty to be perceived except through human eyes? By looking to nature as worthy of attention in its own right, Oliver acts as assessor. Her metaphors are often formulated in terms of coins, as if giving nature value in human terms. Similarly, her whole poetic endeavor to merge with nature through language reveals the contradiction (of which Oliver is painfully aware) implicit in the very phrase "nature writing."

Maxine Kumin (review date April 1993)

SOURCE: "Intimations of Mortality," in *Women's Review of Books,* Vol. 10, No. 7, April, 1993, p. 19.

[*In the following review of* New and Selected Poems, *Kumin praises Oliver for "reaching for the unattainable while grateful for its unattainability."*]

Mary Oliver is a patroller of wetlands in the same way that Thoreau was an inspector of snowstorms. She is without vanity or pretense in her celebrations of the lives of mussels, hermit crabs, hummingbirds and other creatures, including a few select people. Reading through her *New and Selected Poems,* I was struck again and again by the exactitude of her imagery, by her daring marriages of animal, vegetable and mineral kingdoms to the human condition, and by her slightly amended transcendentalism, which seems to allow for a stoical embrace of her own mortality. The book is composed of thirty new poems and generous selections from her eight earlier works, and was the winner of the 1992 National Book Award.

This splendid collection works backward from the most recently written poems to ones from Oliver's first collection, *No Voyage.* The early Ohio poems crisply delineate individuals ranging from Hattie Bloom, her uncle's lost love, to Miss Willow Bangs, the grammar-school teacher who bursts forth at the end of **"Spring in the Classroom"** "all furry and blooming . . . in the Art Teacher's arms." Here, too, are Mr. White, the tamed Indian of **"Learning About the Indians,"** Anne, said to be insane, "tending so desperately all / the small civilities," and Oliver's own relatives, evoked in poignant vignettes. We meet her father, who "spent his last winter / Making ice-grips for shoes / Out of strips of inner tube and scrap metal," and her grandmother, who "cooled and labeled / All the wild sauces of the brimming year."

Absent from Oliver's purview are poems we frequently encounter elsewhere today—about exotic triptychs come upon in Italian hill towns; rhapsodizing over glittering traffic rendered majestic by urban lighting; love poems, common or uncommon. But we do get, in among the early works, Aunt Elsie and Uncle William, and the poet as young girl sent out nightly to find the source of Elsie's hallucinatory night music. In this mental and visual landscape, we are in the time of the **"Wolf Moon,"** of "lean owls / hunkering with their lamp-eyes / in the leafless lanes / in the needled dark," in "the season / of the hunter Death; / with his belt of knives, / his black snowshoes . . .."

A three-part, wrenchingly spare and moving apostrophe to James Wright, Oliver's mentor at Ohio State, dates from 1980, the year of his death. She evokes the quintessential hooting lament of freight trains: "of course. I thought they would stop / when you did. I thought you'd never sicken / anyway, or, if you did, Ohio / would fall down too, barn / by bright barn . . .." Typically, she refuses to display sentiment: "I had a red rose to send you, / but it reeked of occasion."

Spanning her career in an orderly fashion, *New and Selected Poems* invites speculation about influences. James Wright is always mentioned as having influenced Oliver. Certainly she shares with him an attentiveness to the working-class world about her and a dogged determination to speak of it in simple diction. But it is also possible to point to May Swenson, who wrote delightful and witty "concrete" poems that assumed fitting shapes on the page.

Oliver dedicates a recent poem titled **"The Waterfall"** to Swenson, who died in 1989. The four-line stanzas indent in an orderly fashion, irregular longer lines alternating with brief ones, perhaps in imitation of "the water falling, / its lace legs and its womanly arms sheeting down. . . .." It concludes: "And maybe there will be, / after all, / some slack and perfectly balanced / blind and rough peace, finally, / in the deep and green and utterly motionless pools after all that falling?" It is impossible in this space to reproduce exactly the dance of many of Oliver's poems on the page, but the careful reader will also see patterns that enhance the text in, for example, **"The Swan," "White Flowers"** and **"The Egret."**

Swenson's irreverent anthropomorphism in such poems as **"News from the Cabin"**—"Hairy was here. / He hung on a sumac seed pod. / Part of his double tail hugged the crimson / scrotum under cockscomb leaves . . ."— may have reinforced Oliver's inclination to render fanciful a recognizable world. Although her early poems also display a startling ability to anthropomorphize (or engage in pathetic fallacy, as John Ruskin called it), in her later poems the vivid and often astonishing imagery actually comes to drive the narrative.

Nineteenth-century poets so overfilled the vessel with babbling brooks and sighing trees—Ruskin so effectively denounced the practice—that we modern writers are wary of trapping ourselves in unsubstantiated pathos. Mary Oliver, however, walks boldly into this terrain. She can afford to be fearless because she almost never stumbles. Her acuity is enviable. Her sun has "old, buttery fingers"; the turkey buzzards' beaks are "soft as spoons"; a skunk "shuffles, unhurried across the wet fields / in its black slippers . . . / and two bulbs of . . . diatribe under its tail. . . ." When the poet lights two lamps in her small house, they are "like two visitors with good stories. . . ." And an invented relative, a "great-great-aunt dark as hickory" is composed of "old twist of feathers and birch bark. . . ."

While we are pursuing influences, we might well ask if the work of Anne Sexton has played any part in shaping Oliver's poetry. Sexton wrote in "Jesus Cooks," one of nine poems in a series titled "The Jesus Papers," "Jesus multitudes were hungry / and He said, O Lord, / send down a short-order cook." Oliver's **"Sweet Jesus"** begins with this kind of wry dislocation—"Sweet Jesus, talking / his melancholy madness / stood up in the boat / and the sea lay downy silky and sorry"—but then moves away from Sexton's tongue-in-cheek blasphemy. In another poem, a sense of longing for innocence and order suggests Sexton: "I wouldn't mind being a rose / in a field full of roses. / Fear has not yet occurred to them, nor ambition."

Wherever we look we find Oliver reaching for the unattainable while grateful for its unattainability. She stands quite comfortably on the margins of things, on the line between earth and sky, the thin membrane that separates human from what we loosely call animal. Watching a grasshopper "gazing around with her enormous and complicated eyes," "lift[ing] her forearms and thoroughly wash[ing] her face," she declaims: "I don't know exactly what a prayer is. / I do

know how to pay attention, how to fall down / into the grass . . . how to be idle and blessed. . . ." She sees huge drama writ small in the things she observes. In **"White Owl Flies Into and Out of the Field,"** not only do the line placements suggest the swooping down onto the snow, the pounce, the lifting off with the prey in its talons—a small nightly drama of death and dismemberment—but the image opens out onto a disquisition on mortality: "[M]aybe death / isn't darkness, after all, / but so much light / wrapping itself around us / . . . scalding, aortal light. . . ."

We have our poets of ecstasy—Walt Whitman in the last century, Gerald Stern and Edna St. Vincent Millay in this one—and of threnody (too numerous to mention). But I think we do not have many poets like Oliver, who without apology affirms life everywhere she observes it. She is an indefatigable guide to the natural world, particularly to its lesser-known aspects: to turtles and owls, the spurned snake and abjured goldenrod and stagnant, reeking pond full of leeches and lilies. Perhaps because of her awareness of the precarious balance between life and death, she is willing to discard all the usual defenses, to risk the simple declaration: "Nobody knows what the soul is"; "There is only one question: / how to love this world"; "When it's over, I want to say: all my life / I was a bride married to amazement. / I was the bridegroom, taking the world into my arms."

Oliver's newer poems focus ever more trenchantly on the frail links between the human and the natural world, and on the passage from life into death. It is our misfortune that she has never shined the bright light of her introspection on human love. I trust whatever she tells me about moths and marsh marigolds, fingerlings and egrets, and am prepared to trust what she might have to say about passion. But I can hardly think of another book of poems that has moved me as deeply as this one.

David Barber (review date July 1993)

SOURCE: A review of *New and Selected Poems,* in *Poetry,* Vol. 162, No. 4, July, 1993, pp. 233-42.

[*In the following review, Barber praises Oliver for her unique presence in contemporary poetry, but finds that* New *and* Selected Poems *fails to adequately show her growth as a poet.*]

With apologies to Susan Mitchell, no poet of our day has more of a claim on the title *Rapture* than Mary Oliver. Many poets seek communion with nature; Oliver courts ravishment by wildness. Many write in the persona of a solitary; Oliver's projected extremity of isolation approaches that of an anchorite. None can match the singlemindedness with which she depicts states of grace and abandon, and none traffics so unironically in the sublime. A Midwesterner long transplanted to New England's rocky coast, Oliver has assimilated no

Yankee parsimony of utterance, and little of the flinty mindfulness that marks the Transcendentalist regard for leafy redoubts. One would have to reach back perhaps to [John] Clare or [Christopher] Smart to safely cite a parallel to Oliver's lyricism of radical purification and her unappeasable mania for signs and wonders.

How Oliver arrived at this far end of things, more mystic now than poet in certain respects, does not lie neatly exposed in her *New and Selected Poems.* Disconcertingly presented in reverse chronology, this ostensible assemblage of thirty years of Oliver's work is also heavily weighted toward the "new"—slightly more than half of the 132 poems have been published within the last decade. Such apportionment reflects, one must suppose, the poet's sense of conviction as well as coherence: the recent verse, evermore immoderate in its renunciations of the social and the civilized, stands squarely in the foreground as if to discourage an evolutionary perspective. As with a great many of Oliver's individual poems, so with this overview of her oeuvre: the setting is drastically foreshortened, the present tense predominates, the reader is hurtled precipitously into the here and the now.

Nonetheless, Oliver's thralldom does have a paper trail, and the stages and transitions of her poetic are here for the weighing. An instructive juncture can be found on facing pages in the selection drawn from her 1979 collection, *Twelve Moons.* "The dream of my life," Oliver declares in **"Entering the Kingdom,"** "Is to lie down by a slow river / And stare at the light in the trees—/ To learn something by being nothing / A little while but the rich / Lens of attention." What's appealing here is the delicate equilibrium between self-containment and self-surrender, an apprehension of temporality that points to the sharper temperings of the poem's final stanza: "But the crows puff their feathers and cry / Between me and the sun, / And I should go now. / They know me for what I am. / No dreamer, / No eater of leaves." The poem opposite, **"Buck Moon—From the Field Guide to Insects,"** also finds Oliver attempting to "enter the kingdom," this time by choreographing the mind's transit from disinterested scientific fact ("Eighty-eight thousand six-hundred / different species in North America. In the trees, the grasses / around us.") to devotional awe and wild surmise ("Maybe more, maybe / several million on each acre of earth. This one / as well as any other. Where you are standing / at dusk. . . / Where you feel / a power that is not you but flows / into you like a river").

All trace of mediation vanishes in Oliver's next collection, *American Primitive.* The field guide with its received knowledge has been banished; the lens of attention has given way to a whirlwind of sensation and exhilaration. The poet has taken up full-time residence in the kingdom:

> When the blackberries hang
> swollen in the woods, in the brambles

nobody owns, I spend

all day among the high
branches, reaching
my ripped arms, thinking

of nothing, cramming
the black honey of summer
into my mouth; all day my body

accepts what it is. In the dark
creeks that run by there is
this thick paw of my life darting among

the black bells, the leaves; there is
this happy tongue.

                                                        "August"

The headlong breathlessness of *American Primitive,* its delirious immersion in wood and swamp and creaturehood, staked out an exclusive poetic territory for Oliver. Her rambles in the wilds occasion none of the meditative rigor of A.R. Ammons strolls over dunes and shore; her extravagant embrace of the natural world wants nothing of Gary Snyder's Buddhistic vigilance and restraint. Her animals are not the allegorical, emblematic beasts of [Marianne] Moore or [Elizabeth] Bishop—when Oliver writes a poem titled **"The Fish"** the denouement is the devouring: "I am the fish, the fish / glitters in me, we are / risen, tangled together, certain to fall / back to the sea." With their explosive enjambments and jagged phrasing, their egrets that burst into "a shower / of white fire!" and their mushrooms that become "red and yellow skulls / pummeling upward / through leaves, / through grasses, / through sand," the poems in *American Primitive* hurl themselves into nature with a shuddering visceral intensity, each one another convulsive baptism in the primal and the wild.

No swinger of birches, then, but a seeker of blessings, Oliver has continued to write a breakneck visionary lyric ever since. Her marshes and meadows have become found shrines; her recurring owls and bears and snakes have turned totem. In the poems culled from *Dream Work* and *House of Light* one finds a smattering of portraits (**"Robert Schumann," "Stanley Kunitz"**) and exotic set pieces (**"Indonesia," "Singapore"**), but in the main we are planted squarely in Oliver's sensuous realm of earthly delights, a sanctified interior where **"The Lilies Break Open Over the Dark Water"** and **"White Owl Flies Into and Out of the Field."** Many of the poems are explicitly and overtly spiritual, throbbing with metaphysical questions ("Is the soul solid, like iron? / Or is it tender and breakable, like / the wings of a moth in the beak of the owl?") and prophetic expostulations ("the path to heaven / doesn't lie down in flat miles. / It's in the imagination / with which you perceive / this world, / and the gestures / with which you honor it"). Certain others, like **"Wild Geese,"** promise a grace that resides in our animal essence, so that "whoever you are, no matter how lonely, / the world offers itself to your imagination, / calls to you like the wild geese, harsh and exacting— / over and over announcing your place / in the family of things."

Any idiom of ecstasy, left to its own devices, faces almost certain exhaustion. Yet Oliver, judging by the thirty new poems at the head of the book, has only grown more heedless. While her general tenor is marginally suggestive of a "natural piety" that would align her with the revelatory Romanticism of Wordsworth and Blake—"When it's over, I want to say: all my life / I was a bride married to amazement. / I was the bridegroom, taking the world into my arms," she writes in **"When Death Comes"**—Oliver's repudiation of rational intellect and her retreat from sustained philosophical or moral inquiry has tended to produce something more accurately described as a poetry of noble savagery. Human nature, on Oliver's fierce terms, is but a corruption of what is "wild and perfect" or, variously, what is "perfect and shining." **"Whelks"** concludes with an altogether typical momentousness:

> When I find one
> I hold it in my hand,
> I look out over that shaking fire,
> I shut my eyes. Not often,
> but now and again there's a moment
> when the heart cries aloud:
> yes, I am willing to be
> that wild darkness,
> that long, blue body of light.

Altogether typical—and sore to say, all too predictable. However sincerely arrived at within the course of this single poem (and **"Whelks"** undeniably has a fine, briny urgency about it), that "not often" rings false. In these newest Oliver poems the epiphanies come thick and fast, and the exaltations are strictly routine. Even if one's sympathies lie, as mine do, with the spirit and scope of Oliver's undertaking, it's difficult not to mark with some dismay that, for all their reveling in unruly organic life, Oliver's poems are becoming increasingly mechanical. Most often composed across jaggedly indented quatrains or in tumbling verse paragraphs abristle with Dickinsonian dashes, their standard contract calls for them to open in riveted observation, shift abruptly as the speaker questions or comments upon the scene, and close, after a more or less uniform page and a half, with a burst of exclamation or a flash of immanence.

More damningly still, these formulaic tendencies point to thoroughgoing rhetorical weaknesses of the sort that call to mind Moore's caveat that "excess is the common substitute for energy." Oliver's language is increasingly beholden to humdrum adjectival intensifiers ("wonderful," "beautiful," "shin-

ing"), inert abstractions ("dream," "love," "darkness," "happiness," "wildness"), all-purpose figuration (the gullet of a gannet is a "black fire"; a thistle bud is "a coin of reddish fire"; consciousness is "a slow fire"), and sententious overstatement ("life is real / and pain is real, / but death is an impostor"; "in this world I am as rich / as I need to be"). Too often, a poem such as **"Poppies"** that begins in concentrated particulars ("The poppies send up their / orange flares swaying / in the wind, their congregations / are a levitation / of bright dust, of thin / and lacy leaves") lapses into editorialized pronouncements, the articulations of Oliver's triggering subject becoming fodder for oracular phraseology and inspirational sermonettes: "of course / loss is the great lesson. // But I also say this: that light / is an invitation / to happiness, / and that happiness, / when it's done right, / is a kind of holiness, / palpable and redemptive." Cutting away from her fixed gaze to her effusive "message," Oliver skates perilously close to the overweening rhetoric of the self-help aisle and the recovery seminar.

Reading these florid canticles against the more peopled and more prosodically alert work from early Oliver volumes like *No Voyage* and *The River Styx, Ohio,* I found myself longing for Oliver to recover a measure of her former solicitude for heritage and custom, to be impelled for old time's sake by fondness or wariness rather than joy or dread, to tarry awhile within the fold and the pale again. It's not that poems like **"Being Country Bred," "Spring in the Classroom"** or **"Learning About the Indians"** are necessarily more accomplished for being more couched in autobiography and hedged with home truths, but they do reinforce the impression that Oliver has rather overplayed her hand in recent years, devoting herself to nonce forms of druidic incantation at the expense of a greater, a more *generous* range of feeling and sensibility. Given that Oliver's sacramental regard for elemental nature is an indispensable counterweight to the painterly approach toward flora and fauna so prevalent in our period style, it is to be hoped that she will remain faithful to the mysteries she treasures by again writing poems driven by sustained attention and not overreaching emotion, poems entrusted to sight and insight somewhat more than to divination and vision.

Paul Oppenheimer (review date October-November 1993)

SOURCE: "The Innocence of a Mirror," in *American Book Review,* Vol. 15, No. 4, October-November, 1993, p. 11.

[*In the following excerpt, Oppenheimer reviews* New and Selected Poems *and praises Oliver for maintaining an honest balance in her portrayals of nature.*]

Mary Oliver's poetry regards nature with a pioneer's wary eye. Not for her the enthusiasm, which often looks like hysteria these days, of the nature-can-do-no-wrong school of thought, or the worship of natural forces by people who applaud the purity and balance of geological catastrophes, such as tidal waves and avalanches, while dismissing as corruption all valuable and even splendid human accomplishments, such as architecture. Oliver's poetry takes note of a natural murderousness. The lines report the slaughters to be found in any sylvan utopia. They limn a systematic violence. Her aptly horrific sketch of "the soft rope of a water moccasin," for instance, in **"Death at a Great Distance,"** shows it slipping into a tropical pool "where some bubbles / on the surface of that underworld announced / a fatal carelessness," and where "death blurted out of that perfectly arranged mouth." The idea of balance here is not ecology so much as a commonsensical honesty.

It is also that of a general solidity of aesthetic judgment. Oliver's poems demonstrate an awareness of themselves as art, acknowledging a drastic though often scanted difference between art and propaganda, to wit, that while art may affirm certain values, it cannot set about promoting them, no matter how excellent they maybe, without at once surrendering its very lifeblood to dullness, cliches, and pomposity. Pompous finger-wagging is almost entirely missing from these two volumes. If their larger theme is a rural, natural world, with wolves, crows, bears, roses, and ponds penned in vigorous portrait-poems, their method is an innocence of exploration. All is clean air among these stanzas, and the innocence is that of a style refreshingly unstained by sleight-of-hand messages to the reader, snobberies of doctrine, and scurrilities of self-pity. When this works well, what we are given is the innocence of a mirror, one that apprehends nature while shrinking from eccentric distortion—what Schiller may have meant by the smartly naive in art—and one that is devoid of the usual modernist and postmodernist contempt for the language of ordinary human beings.

In fact humanity is pretty nearly absent from Oliver's poetry, or at least this might be one's first impression. A rash judgment could even lead into assorting her with those trendy nature-poets who confuse art with advertising for some sort of save-the-planet campaign, though nothing could be more absurd. Through nine volumes to date, in a career stretching over almost three decades (her first volume appeared in 1963), she has implicitly urged that to reveal how "the crows break off from the rest of the darkness," or how a skunk "shuffles, unhurried, / across the wet fields / in its black slippers," is to clarify a set of essential, and utterly human, states of mind. In many of her poems, animals, flowers, and landscapes become gateways to human exploration. The unfrocking of a few of nature's mysteries exposes human conflicts. The passion of a vulture opens a sluice of human terror, while a glimpse of two does at dawn, as in **"Five A.M. in the Pinewoods,"** reveals "how you swim inward," "how you swim outward," and "how you pray."

The natural world is thus no mere objective correlative for this poet's emotions, nor, in the most acute of her poems, is a vivacious animal kingdom simply appropriated through false personification. Sentimentality is rejected, and observation continuously checks any maudlin subjectivity. A metallic hardness of phrasing, which results from reshuffling the usual contexts of words, but this with an intelligence that heeds the literal meanings of the words themselves, produces insights, and nature becomes, finally, a telescope through which to examine purely human sufferings, hopes, and madness. "The Deer," typically, focuses this telescope on what amounts to a spiritual quest, which is not necessarily religious, for "the earnest work" of the uncluttered soul:

> You never know.
> The body of night opens
> like a river, it drifts upward like white smoke,
>
> like so many wrappings of mist.
> And on the hillside two deer are walking along
> just as though this wasn't
>
> the owned, tilled earth of today
> but the past.
> I did not see them the next day, or the next,
>
> but in my mind's eye—
> there they are, in the long grass,
> like two sisters.
>
> This is the earnest work. Each of us is given
> only so many mornings to do it—
> to look around and love
>
> the oily fur of our lives,
> the hoof and the grass-stained muzzle.

The deer here go on to inspire a "terror of idleness, / like a red thirst," and a realization that "Death isn't just an idea":

> When we die the body breaks open
> like a river;
> the old body goes on, climbing the hill.

The hill may be the cemetery-hill of decay ("I never said / Nature wasn't cruel," Oliver recalls in another poem, **"The Foxes"**) or, equally, what she elsewhere terms a "turning into something of inexplicable value," but there are powerful hints in many of her poems that the "something" must be the universe itself, or nature, or God. An assumed harmony of a natural order of things, whatever the cruelty of nature and the miserable choices that human beings make, dominates such poems as **"What Is It?"** and **"Kingfisher."** Nature itself appears, in **"Nature,"** alternatively, as full of tact, as an ambassador of numinous repetitions and "bristling life" in which "nothing new / would ever happen." This freshness of perception throughout, together with an admirable coolness of diction—no doubt the result of Oliver's commitment to doing something "perfectly," as she puts it—is totally engaging. Yet there are serious risks in her affirmation of spiritual transcendence that one finds offered up so uncritically. The chief of these is that the poetry may slide off into mere eloquence. Allied with this is the risk of vapid generalizations. "Dreams do not lie," she writes in **"Rage,"** and one wonders, why not? What evidence is there of any moral superiority in dreams? Similarly, the poet's apparent belief that "light / is an invitation / to happiness" proves unconvincing: one recalls those occasions when light turns into an outright menace. as during the explosion of an atomic bomb. Sometimes, too, endings tend to be facile, a fact suggestive of another, subtler risk of her poetry's ultimately positive attitudes. In **"Morning,"** for example, after a series of effusive musings about a cat in a kitchen, we wind up with "what more could I do with wild words?" and "I stand in the cold kitchen, everything wonderful around me," lines that merely lounge, limply and senselessly, on the page.

Fortunately, there are few of these slips. "I am trying in my poems to vanish and have the reader be the experiencer," she has said in an interview. "I do not want to be there. It is not even a walk we take together." The aesthetic of impersonality attested to in these remarks, so reminiscent of T. S. Eliot (and also of his notion that only those with a great deal of personality will know how comforting it can be to escape from it), when it is achieved, and Oliver achieves it often, is surely a blessing: it promotes an artistic balance that allows nature and humanity their capacity for evil as well as good. How much intrinsic goodness can there be, after all, at least from the human point of view, in a natural system that annihilates every living creature, or that may have no compunction about blasting away at the planet with fissionable asteroids?

Susan Salter Reynolds (review date 12 June 1994)

SOURCE: A review of *A Poetry Handbook,* in *The Los Angeles Times Book Review,* June 12, 1994, p. 6.

[*In the following review, Reynolds applauds Oliver for going beyond a how-to format to "connect the conscious mind and the heart."*]

Most of us have a natural aversion to books that presume to tell us how to write poetry. [*A Poetry Handbook*] is not one of those books. Mary Oliver would probably never admit to anything so grandiose as an effort to connect the conscious mind and the heart (that's what she says *poetry* can do), but that is exactly what she accomplishes in this stunning little handbook, ostensibly written "to empower the beginning writer who stands between two marvelous and complex

things—an experience (or an idea of a feeling), and the urge to tell about it in the best possible conjunction of words." From here on in it's all straightforward work: Oliver gives us tools "for the listening mind," tools we need to write poetry, excavating them from centuries of embellishment and obfuscation. First, there is Sound, that link between experience and expression that has somehow come unhinged. Without it, there's hardly any pleasure in poetry. Oliver reminds us that there are not just vowels, but mutes *(b, d, k, p, t, q)* and aspirates *(c, f, g, h, j, s, x)* and liquids *(l, m, n, r)*! Then there is the Line: Why do we turn it when we do (a question often asked of poets, particularly writers of free verse)? Originally, Oliver reminds, the length of the line was linked to the regular English breath, for which the iambic pentameter is best suited. But there are other patterns which, by their very sound, convey anger or tension or melancholy, like notes and phrases in music: the dactyl, the anapest, the trochee, the caesura, all tools to reunite sound and meaning. And there are others: Imagery, Tone (much more intimate, writes Oliver, in contemporary poetry) and Diction. Perhaps my favorite, however, are the brief sections on "Revision," and "Workshops and Solitude," for it is here that Oliver gives some unobtrusive hints for caring for that part of the person that writes poetry: "Athletes take care of their bodies. Writers must simply take care of the sensibility that houses the possibility of poems." "Rise early," and "live simply and honorably," Oliver suggests. "Think of yourself," she writes, "as one member of a single, recognizable tribe."

Robert Hosmer (review date Summer 1994)

SOURCE: "Meditative Gazing on Contemporary Poetry," in *The Southern Review,* Vol. 30, No. 3, Summer, 1994, pp. 638-40.

[*In the following excerpt, Hosmer reviews* New and Selected Poems *and praises Oliver's work for its simplicity and clarity.*]

The work gathered in Mary Oliver's impressive ***New and Selected Poems*** spans three decades, from ***No Voyage and Other Poems*** to ***House of Light;*** in addition, it presents thirty new poems as well as five not previously included in any volume. And so this volume affords an opportunity to take the long view of this poet's fine work, savoring its many pleasures and assessing its considerable merits. This is a poet whose enduring preoccupation lies with posing apparently simple questions, the answers to which involve contemplation of the deepest mysteries of knowing and being. Though Oliver's verse echoes with the acerbic ironies of Dickinson, the singing cosmic consciousness of Whitman, and the serene playfulness of Edna St. Vincent Millay, her greatest kinship is with Elizabeth Bishop (neither one political or feminist or confessional) and William Blake, two poets whose deceptively simple questions provoked responses that often disclosed previously unnoticed realms; of the two, Blake's is the more powerful presence to emerge from *New and Selected Poems,* not because he is the only poet mentioned by name here but because his turning away "to a life of the imagination" (**"Spring Azures"**) led him to pose gentle interrogatives of shattering significance. His presence is often palpable in Oliver's work, particularly when, as in **"The Summer Day,"** she asks innocent questions ("Who made the world? / Who made the swan and the black bear? / Who made the grasshopper?") that generate even greater questions that, in turn, reflect scrupulously examined experience: "Doesn't everything die at last, and too soon?" From another poet, such conclusions would seem hopelessly trite and simple; from Oliver, they bear the simple and singular grace of the honest heart.

Even cursory study of Oliver's work reveals neither radical change nor startling departure (true, the narrative element diminishes, the landscape shifts from the Midwest to the Atlantic coast, and greater, though never radical, experiment with line breaks and stanzaic patterns emerges); rather, the panorama of Oliver's work exhibits an extraordinary and admirable consistency: simplicity, clarity, directness, sincerity (how dangerous to say it!), precision, discipline (her control of free verse is matched only by James Wright's mastery), a skilled use of repetition. Oliver achieves a rare, Zen-like clarity and economy; it can be no accident that so many of her poems bring traditions of Asian calligraphy and painting to mind.

Oliver's patient eye is trained on the natural environment where other creatures predominate, whether fauna (bears, owls, hawks, hummingbirds, swans) or flora (roses, lilies, marsh grass), and the effect is one of extraordinarily splendid profusion. Within such a landscape rests an unobtrusive poet who knows what another creature, the turtle, knows: "she is a part of the pond she lives in, / the tall trees are her children, / the birds that swim above her / are tied to her by an unbreakable string" (**"The Turtle"**). If Oliver's eye is patient, it is also fearless and far-ranging, scanning nature, unafraid of beauty that is harsh, unrelenting, and death-scented. In one of the earliest poems reprinted here, **"Morning in a New Land,"** the narrator's stance and attitude are emblematic of the poet's throughout this collection: "I stood like Adam in his lonely garden / On that first morning, shaken out of sleep, / Rubbing his eyes, listening, parting the leaves, / Like tissue on some vast, incredible gift." This is precisely what Mary Oliver has been doing all these years—looking and listening from a place within, marveling at the gift, perhaps living what she calls, in **"Entering the Kingdom,"** "the dream of my life": "to lie down by a slow river / And stare at the light in the trees."

With the passing of years and one collection after another, Oliver's voice has developed a deeper music, and her imag- ery has become more richly dense as she has sharpened the metaphysical edge of her questions (in **"Questions You Might Ask,"** from *House of Light,* she asks, "Is the soul solid, like iron?"). Though death remains an ever-present reality, Oliver has neither given way to a fashionable pessimism nor soared into a superficial, unconvincing spirituality: the poems from *House of Light* and the new poems here are bound together by a consciously chosen spirit of affirmation, expressed nowhere more clearly than in **"The Ponds"**: "I want to believe that the imperfections are nothing / —that the light is everything—that it is more than the sum / of each flawed blossom rising and fading. And I do."

The cumulative effect of Oliver's poems? Silence. The deep and embracing silence of amazed contemplation that graces the coda of **"When Death Comes,"** one of her latest, and best, poems:

> When it's over, I want to say: all my life
> I was a bride married to amazement.
> I was the bridegroom, taking the world into my
>   arms.
>
> When it's over, I don't want to wonder
> if I have made of my life something particular, and
>   real.
> I don't want to find myself sighing and frightened,
> or full of arguments.
>
> I don't want to end up simply having visited this
>   world.

There is about Mary Oliver's poetry "a deep and miraculous composure"—the words are hers (**"Three Poems for James Wright"**), the pleasure ours.

Vicki Graham (essay date Fall 1994)

SOURCE: "'Into the Body of Another': Mary Oliver and the Poetics of Becoming Other," in *Papers on Language and Literature,* Vol. 30, No. 4, Fall, 1994, pp. 352-72.

[In the following essay, Graham discusses Oliver's (and by extension, her readers') ability to "become" the various natural bodies she writes about.]

We belong to the moon, says Mary Oliver, and "the most / thoughtful among us dreams / of hurrying down . . . into the body of another." We dream, we long, and some of us believe that we can step outside of ourselves and enter the body of another. But Western culture discourages these yearnings and demands individualism and the formation of strong ego boundaries and stable identities. Unlike the traveller of Leslie Marmon Silko's "Story from Bear Country," we do not hear the bear's call; we do not see our "footprints / in the sand" become bear prints, nor do we see fur cover our bodies, "dark shaggy and thick." Yet we are conscious, too, of our potential not just to cross the boundaries between ourselves and others, but to be divided within ourselves. We encounter a variety of theories—feminist, psychoanalytic, cultural—that tell us identity is multiple and the boundaries of the self are unstable.

"Pull yourself together," my mother used to say, and I would grope wildly, hoping to catch even one of the selves that spun around me. But I have never been able to pull myself together, and works of art that tempt me to drop the fiction of singularity and invite me to enter the body of another fascinate me. Mary Oliver's *American Primitive* is one such work. The poems in this collection offer many bodies for us to inhabit; we can become, by turns, bear, fish, whale, swamp, and Pan. We can run with the fox, fly with the owl, dig with the mole, and finally, losing all outward form, dissolve into the totality of nature.

Oliver's celebration of dissolution into the natural world troubles some critics: her poems flirt dangerously with romantic assumptions about the close association of women with nature that many theorists claim put the woman writer at risk. But for Oliver, immersion in nature is not death: language is not destroyed and the writer is not silenced. To merge with the nonhuman is to acknowledge the self's mutability and multiplicity, not to lose subjectivity. But few feminists have wholeheartedly appreciated Oliver's work, and though some critics have read her poems as revolutionary reconstructions of the female subject, others remain skeptical "that identification with nature can empower women." [Graham attributes this quote to Diane S. Bonds in "The Language of Nature in the Poetry of Mary Oliver."]

Despite this implicitly proscriptive criticism, the desire to immerse oneself in and become part of the natural world persists in women's poetry and novels. Twenty years of feminist, deconstructive, and linguistic theory have not weaned writers like Oliver, Marilynne Robinson, and Susan Griffin (to name just a few) from what skeptics might label a naive belief in the possibility of intimate contact with the non-linguistic world of nature and a confidence in the potential of language to represent that experience. The persistence of this belief suggests to me that we might try reading these works differently. Rather than viewing them as dangerously regressive or as subtextually emancipatory, we might read—them as descriptions and enactments of what Walter Benjamin calls the "mimetic faculty."

According to Benjamin, the mimetic faculty is one of our most precious gifts. Important as sight or hearing, our capacity to mime, Benjamin explains, surpasses nature's, and is directly linked to our cultural activities:

Nature creates similarities. One need only think of mimicry. The highest capacity for producing similarities, however, is man's. His gift of seeing resemblances is nothing other than a rudiment of the powerful compulsion in former times to become and behave like something else. Perhaps there is none of his higher functions in which his mimetic faculty does not play a decisive role.

The speakers in Oliver's poems not only exhibit a "powerful compulsion . . . to become and behave like something else"; they also act out the process of becoming something else, inviting readers to join them.

In "The Mimetic Faculty," Benjamin asserts that the human capacity to mime has eroded in recent times, but in "The Work of Art in the Age of Mechanical Reproduction" he suggests that modern technology, particularly the moving picture camera, can help us recover that capacity, bringing us into a new kind of perceptual contact with the world through mechanical reproduction. He notes that "every day the urge grows stronger to get hold of an object at very close range by way of its likeness, its reproduction," and he suggests that moving pictures can stimulate the "optical unconscious," leading to increased perception. As Michael Taussig shows in *Mimesis and Alterity,* Benjamin's hopes were not realized. Poetry such as Oliver's suggests that this need to get hold of something—to touch it, taste it, smell it—has intensified rather than diminished in the last sixty years as technology moves us further and further from actual realities into virtual realities. Despite the stern schooling of postmodern theory, we continue to yearn, as Michael Taussig puts it, "for the true real." And what better way to get close to "the real"—which for Oliver means the natural world—than to become it through mimicry?

"Nature," claims Benjamin, "creates similarities." But so do poets. Word by word, image by image, they exercise their mimetic faculties, simulating the texture and weight of an object, the tenor and color of a feeling, the timbre of a voice. Words make copies of the world, but to say, merely, that these copies are constructions is to close discussion prematurely, as Taussig makes clear in his introduction to *Mimesis and Alterity.* Aware though we may be of "the constructed and arbitrary character of our practices" our mimetic faculty saves us, "suturing nature to artifice and bringing sensuousness to sense by means of what was once called sympathetic magic, granting the copy the character and power of the original, the representation the power of the represented." Similarly, to dismiss poems that celebrate merging with nature as naive projections is to ignore something crucial about the magical capabilities of language. Taussig offers a far more positive way to describe what Oliver is doing. In short, she is "miming the real into being."

But how does one mime the real into being? Taussig provides an answer immediately applicable to Oliver's poetry. Elaborating on Benjamin's theories, Taussig links mimesis to the sympathetic magic employed by healers and seers, and describes what Frazer distinguishes as the two classes of magic: contagious and imitative. Contact or contagious magic works because, as Frazer says, "things which have been in contact with each other continue to act on each other at a distance." Imitative magic works because "like produces like," or, as Taussig explains, the "copy, in magical practice, affect[s] the original to such a degree that the representation shares in or acquires the properties of the represented." Taussig suggests that often contact and copying overlap (as in an effigy made out of the effluvia of the victim), working together to conjure the presence of or to affect the other.

In Oliver's *American Primitive,* evoking and then becoming another depends on direct, sensuous contact with the other, on using the body rather than the mind to apprehend it. Over and over the speaker of Oliver's poems reminds herself to look, to touch, to taste, to see, and to smell.

—Vicki Graham

In Oliver's *American Primitive,* evoking and then becoming another depends on direct, sensuous contact with the other, on using the body rather than the mind to apprehend it. Over and over the speaker of Oliver's poems reminds herself to look, to touch, to taste, to see, and to smell. Only by yielding to her senses can she get close to the "real"—wild plums, egrets, the first light of morning. Contact leads to contagion; infected by what she has touched or tasted, she begins to copy it spontaneously, "miming [it] into being" through ecstatic identification. Oliver's poems allow us to trace this movement from sensuous contact to copying to becoming, and, in the process, offer a way back to nature, to the "real," from which language separates us. Because many of the poems are spoken in the second person, they also invite us to step outside the boundaries we draw around ourselves and become, not just another, but many others. The possibility of identifying or coming into contact with a "true real" is, of course, debatable, and Oliver's sense of merging with nature is shaped by her culture and by the language she uses to describe her experience, as I show later in this paper through a brief examination of two of Leslie Marmon Silko's poems. But the ways that we use language to describe the experience of stepping outside ourselves and getting to the real are worth studying; as contemporary enactments of sympathetic magic, the poems of *American Primitive* offer a chance to examine as

well as to participate in the process of miming the self "into the body of another."

For Oliver, becoming another begins with longing, a longing often tinged with sorrow, as though Oliver recognized and accepted the difficulties involved. *American Primitive* is permeated with verbs of desire; the speakers of the poems "want," "dream of," "strive," "long," and "cry for" contact with the natural world, but all too often that contact is blocked. In **"White Night,"** for example, the speaker longs to become one with the "black / and silky currents" of the moonlit pond and dreads the coming of day which will draw her back into the human world with its "difficult / and beautiful / hurricane of light." Half dreaming, she floats into the white night and wants, before day interrupts, to mingle herself with its dark waters:

> I want to flow out
> across the mother
> of all waters,
> I want to lose myself
> on the black
> and silky currents.

The speaker is caught between two worlds: the day world of language and logic and the night world of sensation and dissolution.

In **"The Sea,"** the speaker remembers and longs to return to a pre-rational, pre-human state of existence: "Stroke by / stroke my / body remembers that life . . ." Though the poem never clearly defines "that life," the images suggest that the speaker imagines herself as a pre-human, aquatic life-form or as an embryo arrested in the fish-stage of human embryonic development. Her "body cries for / the lost parts of itself—fins, gills":

> What a spillage
> of nostalgia pleads
> from the very bones! how
> they long to give up the long trek
> inland . . .

Here, as in **"White Night,"** the speaker longs to escape the difficulties of the rational and "to give up the long trek" towards becoming human, but remains fixed in the rational, human world.

Oliver habitually describes the desire to become another as originating in the body—it is the bones that long—but over and over, the mind—"what we know"—counters the body's impulse, bringing the speaker back to self-consciousness. Poems such as **"Blossom"** and **"The Plum Trees"** confront this battle between mind and body head on. **"Blossom"** describes the effect of spring and the moon on the body; aroused by the awakening of the natural world—the "frogs shouting / their desire"—the speaker longs to join in; But the poem is structured as a series of oppositions: "what we know"—that we are mortal and yet that "we are more / than blood"—is posed first against "what / we long for: joy / before death" and then against the "thrust / from the root / of the body." **"The Plum Trees"** works from the assumption that the mind (sense) and the senses oppose one another, but it reverses the traditional hierarchy, asking that we favor the body rather than the mind and give ourselves up to our senses:

> There's nothing
> so sensible as sensual inundation. Joy
> is a taste before
> it's anything else . . .
>
>   .   .   .
>
> the only way
> to tempt happiness into your mind is by taking it
>
> into the body first, like small
> wild plums.

Oliver insists that we return to the physical world, begin with the body rather than the mind, plums rather than ideas. Though the poem is almost didactic in its assertions, and its play on "sensible" is predictable, it illustrates, through sensuous images, Oliver's insistence on the body as the basis for abstract expression.

Letting her body rather than her mind guide her gives Oliver the contact with the natural world that she craves, but poems such as **"The Plum Trees"** do not examine the damaging effects of oppositional thinking. Split into a rigid duality, the self is not porous; it cannot take the other into itself nor can it flow outside its own boundaries. Privileging the body reinforces oppositional thinking and blocks rather than enables immersion in the other. In **"Humpbacks,"** for example, evading the mind leads to splitting the body itself into matter and spirit, as though oppositions were endlessly nested one in the other:

> . . . nothing will ever dazzle you
> like the dreams of your body,
>
> its spirit
> longing to fly while the dead-weight bones
>
> toss their dark mane and hurry
> back into the fields of glittering fire . . .

Again Oliver privileges the physical over the non-physical— the body's spirit "longs," while the bones simply "hurry back"—but now she has caught the body up in oppositional thinking; fissured, it plays out the original opposition between mind and body that Oliver wished to escape.

Occasionally, however, the natural world startles Oliver into forgetting that mind and body are split, and for a moment they move together. In **"Tasting the Wild Grapes,"** the joy of seeing the fox fills the speaker and she forgets not just the split between mind and body, but the gap between words and their referents. Seeing and naming become simultaneous acts:

> . . . And forgetting
> everything you will leap to name it
> as though for the first time, your lit blood
> rushing not to a word but a sound
> small-boned, thin-faced, in a hurry
> lively as the dark thorns of the wild grapes
> on the unsuspecting tongue.

The body, the "lit blood," not the mind, leaps to name the fox. A sound bursts from the body, but the sound is visual. The word "fox" is not onomatopoeic; rather, it looks like the fox, "small-boned, thin-faced, in a hurry." Sound becomes first visual, then tactile and glossal, "lively as the dark thorns of the wild grapes on the unsuspecting tongue." Taste, sound, sight, and touch merge into a word—"The fox! The fox!" — and the poem suggests that language comes from the body in imitation of the sensuous qualities of the thing perceived, not from a conscious decision to name. As the senses overlap, the distinction between sensuous and intellectual perception blurs, and the opposition between mind and body dissolves.

Once mind and body stop fighting, direct, sensuous contact with the other becomes possible, allowing an exchange of energy which leads to identification and then merging. In **"The Fish,"** Oliver describes the effects of contact through eating. Enchanted by the beauty of the first fish she ever caught, startled by its refusal, at first, to lie down in the pail and die, the speaker cleans and eats the fish. Eating transforms her:

> Now the sea
> is in me: I am the fish, the fish
> glitters in me.

Touching first lips, tongue, and throat, then entering the stomach and the bloodstream, the fish contacts every part of the speaker's body, and she not only becomes the fish, but the sea that it swims in. The poem suggests that this transformation is permanent: "*now* the sea / is in me" (emphasis mine), but subsequent poems in the collection suggest that this transformation, like the others, is temporary, and will have to be repeated.

"The Sea" describes the magical effects of contact through immersion of the other in the self; **"Crossing the Swamp"** describes the opposite, contact and transformation through immersion of the self in the other. The poem opens with a description of a swamp and the speaker's arduous trek across it. She enters the

> . . . endless
>   wet thick
>   cosmos, the center
>   of everything—the nugget
> of dense sap, branching
>   vines, the dark burred
>   faintly belching
>   bogs.

The speaker wallows, slips, scrambles for a "foothold, fingerhold, / mindhold over / such slick crossings." But here, the mind cannot get a hold and does not interrupt the process of physical contact with and immersion in the other. She sinks into:

> the black, slack
>   earthsoup. I feel
>   not wet so much as
>   painted and glittered
> with the fat grassy
>   mires, the rich
>   and succulent marrows
>   of earth—a poor
> dry stick given
>   one more chance . . .

Not wet, but painted, the speaker becomes a canvas. Covered with ooze, the swamp's effluvia, she first represents the swamp, as though she were a painting. Then she becomes the swamp, taking on its power with its image. Transformed, the "poor / dry stick" of her body sprouts, branches, and buds like the swamp whose life force it has acquired.

Contact leads to transformation, but it also leads to an even more powerful way of merging with nature—copying and taking on the power of the original. Several poems in *American Primitive* enact this imitative magic—in **"Music,"** for example, the speaker becomes Pan, and in **"Humpbacks"** she becomes a whale—but the most interesting examples are the poems which describe the process of imitating and becoming a bear. These poems form a sequence, moving from an indirect identification with a bear's essence to spontaneous, unmediated, almost "natural" imitation of and entering into the body of the bear. **"August,"** the first poem in the collection, introduces the bear through a synecdoche, subtly setting in motion a current that runs through the rest of the collection. The poem begins with a description of picking and eating blackberries; the speaker is

> thinking
>
> of nothing, cramming

> the black honey of summer
> into my mouth; all day my body
>
> accepts what it is.

Because she is not thinking, the speaker almost seems to be part of the natural world, to be more animal than human, and her "body / accepts what it is." "Accepts" can be read both literally—the body is content with itself—and figuratively—the body ingests (accepts) itself. The blackberries she eats, then, become emblems for the self as nature; taking them into her body reinforces and makes physical the connection she already has with the natural world. The poem ends with a reference to the bear's shadowy presence:

> . . . In the dark
> creeks that run by there is
> this thick paw of my life darting among
>
> the black bells.

Here, the bear is not simply another creature of the natural world; rather, it is the "thick paw of [her] life," and has special significance for her, a significance that Taussig's discussion of the Cuna belief in two worlds, an original and a copy, can help explain. According to Taussig, the Cuna believe in an "invisible counterpart" of the world we see, an "alter reality" for "all objects, animals, and places in the concrete world" which "is the creative life source of the object." The Cuna see this "spirit [as] superior to and causal of the concrete manifestation." Though Taussig questions, "which comes first, spirit or substance, original or copy?" he suggests that two worlds exist simultaneously, an original and a copy. In the last lines of **"August,"** Oliver, too, senses the presence of this "alter reality." For her, the spirit copy of her "life" takes the form of a bear, a presence that is "superior to and causal of the concrete manifestation." The presence of the bear in **"August"** suggests that the transformation of the speaker into a bear in later poems is natural; her own spirit copy, in the form of a bear, is already guiding her.

In **"Honey at the Table,"** the next bear poem in the collection, contact leads to copying, but the movement from one to the other is so fluid that it is difficult to pinpoint where contact ends and copying begins. Because the poem is spoken in the second person, it includes the reader in the process, inviting him or her to partake of the honey: "It fills you with the soft / essence of vanished flowers." Honey, like the fish, has the power to transform the speaker. But the honey itself metamorphoses, and starts to resemble, as the speaker eats, one of the "dark creeks" mentioned in **"August"**:

> . . . it becomes
> a trickle sharp as a hair that you follow
> from the honey pot over the table

and out the door and over the ground,
and all the while it thickens,

grows deeper and wider, edged
with pine boughs and wet boulders.

From flowers to trickle to creek, the honey of this poem calls up the bear before mentioning it. Honey also acts as a metonym for the bear; to taste it is to taste the bear. The transformation to bear occurs almost imperceptibly, the space between the third and fourth stanzas: the speaker has been following the honey-creek,

. . . edged
with pine boughs and wet boulders,
pawprints of bobcat and bear until

deep in the forest you
shuffle up some tree, you rip the bark,

you float into and swallow the dripping combs,
bits of tree, crushed bees—a taste
composed of everything lost, in which everything
lost is found.

No longer quite human, the speaker "shuffle[s] up some tree . . . rip[s] the bark." She becomes a bear in a tree eating honey, and has found everything she has lost. "Lost" here echoes "lost" in **"The Sea,"** where the speaker's body "cries for / the lost parts of itself." There, the speaker longs for a pre-human state which she cannot regain because she is blocked by the opposition between mind and body; here, she regains her spirit copy—the bear—through imitation, first by eating honey, then by shuffling up a tree and ripping the bark.

"Happiness," a bear poem that appears several pages later in the collection, sets up, in its first lines, a clear division between the speaker and the "she-bear," the watcher and actor: "In the afternoon I watched / the she-bear; she was looking / for the secret bin of sweetness." But the poem, which starts out matter-of-factly, veers suddenly into a description of the close tracking of a bear, raising questions about who this speaker is and where she is positioned:

Black block of gloom, she climbed down
tree after tree and shuffled on
through the woods. And then
she found it! The honey-house deep
as heartwood, and dipped into it
among the swarming bees.

Oliver as observer seems to have inserted herself into the natural world, getting closer to and becoming more intimately connected with the observed than is humanly possible, as though the bear she watches is herself. Telling the story of

the bear does more than evoke it; it also allows the speaker to identify with it, a process which resembles Taussig's account of the healer who evokes the spirit copy through detailed description. According to Taussig, detailed descriptions give one power over the thing described. He quotes the ethnographer Joel Sherzer: "The subsequent narration of actions and events, addressed to the spirit world, causes their simultaneous occurrence in the mirror image physical world." Taussig then exclaims, "Was ever Frazer's mimetic magic better expressed—except that the simulacrum here is created with words, not objects!" He goes on to say that "the spirits find pleasure in being told about themselves in a detailed and poetic way" and he cites chants in which "the chanter chants himself into the scene."

In **"Happiness"** Oliver creates a bear out of words. In **"The Honey Tree,"** the final bear poem in the collection, she chants herself into the scene, acting out what she claims to have observed:

And so at last I climbed
the honey tree, ate
chunks of pure light, ate
the bodies of bees that could not
get out of my way, ate
the dark hair of the leaves,
the rippling bark,
the heartwood. Such
frenzy!

The poem at once continues and revises **"Happiness."** The opening line, "And so at last," suggests that the poem takes up a prior activity, and the poem as a whole repeats many of the images of **"Happiness"**: in both, there is a frenzied tearing of bark and eating of honey. Both climax in an ecstatic moment of identification—the bear with the bees, the speaker with the bear. The bear hums and the speaker sings. The sequence of these two poems suggests that the detailing of the bear's activity in the earlier poem allows Oliver to mime it herself in the next, the first activity leading naturally to the second.

The last poem of the collection, **"The Gardens,"** moves from identification with the individual elements of nature—swamp, fish, bear, etc.—to identification with the totality of nature. Part one opens with an Edenic world, "the good / garden of leaves," where the speaker wanders, seeking "another / creature like me," and whispering, "Where are you?" It ends with the speaker's entrance into another world, as she leaves the "good garden" for the "garden / of fire." In the first lines of part two, the speaker is near to, but not yet in direct contact with the other she sought earlier:

This skin you wear
so neatly, in which

you settle
so brightly
on the summer grass, how
shall I know it?

She moves slowly through the garden, seeking, then gradually begins to understand that the contact she desires can be achieved by touching anything—everything—because the one she desires is everywhere:

How
shall I touch you
unless it is
everywhere?
I begin
here and there,
finding you,
the heart within you,
and the animal,
and the voice.

The last lines of the poem suggest that the "you" is not simply another person, but the ultimate Other, the natural world, personified, and this Other is everywhere; the speaker "trek [s] / wherever you take me, / the boughs of your body / leading deeper into the trees." This poem, like **"Happiness"** and **"The Honey Tree,"** climaxes with another ecstatic moment, but unlike these poems, **"The Gardens"** ends just before the speaker merges with the other. We leave her still moving towards it:

the shouting,
the answering, the rousing
great run toward the interior,
the unseen, the unknowable
center.

Clearly, Oliver meant to close the poem before this final merging; if the center is unseen and unknowable, it also must be outside of language.

American Primitive ends with fulfillment; the blank space at the end of **"The Gardens"** implies that Oliver has lost herself in the "body of another." But this loss of self is never permanent. Oliver becomes, in turn, a bear, a whale, a fish, but, as each poem and each subsequent transformation suggests, she returns again to human consciousness and must repeat the process of becoming another over and over. Rooted in the binary oppositions that structure Western thinking, Oliver can never fully escape the teaching of her culture that the mind is divided from the body and identity depends on keeping intact the boundaries between the self and others. Each of the selves Oliver becomes in this collection is self-contained and separate. A bear, like a human, has its own boundaries, and becoming bear as Oliver understands this

process involves moving back and forth across the boundaries between herself and the bear rather than dissolving the boundaries themselves.

Oliver's desire to become other through mimesis conflicts with a culturally instilled need to establish a single, unified self, but Oliver neither faces this problem head on nor articulates it clearly as another poet, Rainer Maria Rilke, does. Rilke, too, longs, to get inside the body of another creature, to "let [himself] precisely into the dog's center, the point from which it begins to be a dog, the place in it where God, as it were, would have sat down for a moment when the dog was finished." But unlike Oliver, Rilke articulates the consequences of staying there: "For awhile you can endure being inside the dog; you just have to be alert and jump out in time, before its environment has completely enclosed you, since otherwise you would simply remain the dog in the dog and be lost for everything else." It is that "everything else" that Oliver does not want to be lost for. She cannot resign herself to being just "the dog in the dog" because this would mean she could never be a bear or a fish. Giving up human subjectivity would mean, at least as Oliver perceives it, giving up the ability to mime herself into the body of another. It would also mean giving up self-consciousness, knowing who and what she is, as well as the ability to remember and write about the experience. Oliver's poems suggest that we need language and self-consciousness in order to experience stepping outside of language and the self. Over and over, Oliver lets herself into the whale, the fish, the bear, the Other, and over and over she jumps out in time, clinging to her humanity, to her individuality, and to her sense of the self as a unified subject with distinct boundaries.

Oliver's acceptance of this image of the self shapes her perception of what it means to become another. A different image of the self might have led her to a very different perception of this process. To clarify this point, I would like to turn briefly to some passages from Paula Gunn Allen's *The Sacred Hoop* and to two poems by Leslie Marmon Silko. According to Allen, Native Americans focus less on the individual than Westerners do; they see the individual as part of a whole which includes not just the community, but the natural world and the cosmic. All life is important; no hierarchies exist to separate humans from or elevate them above the rest of creation: "Tribal people allow all animals, vegetables, and minerals (the entire biota, in short) the same or even greater privileges than humans." Allen goes on to explain that

The American Indian sees all creatures as relatives .
. . as offspring of the Great Mystery, as cocreators,
as children of our mother, and as necessary parts of
an ordered, balanced, and living whole. This concept applies to what non-Indian Americans think of
as the supernatural, and it applies as well to the more
tangible (phenomenal) aspects of the universe. Ameri-

can Indian thought makes no such dualistic division, nor does it draw a hard and fast line between what is material and what is spiritual. . . .

Allen's description suggests that the contact and exchange between the self and nature that Oliver longs for so urgently is part of the everyday lives of Native Americans because they do not separate the human world from the natural.

Speaking from her Laguna Pueblo perspective, Leslie Marmon Silko examines specific occurrences of this contact and exchange between human and non-human and the effects on the individual and the community. In her poems "Story from Bear Country" and "He was a small child," she describes what happens to people who join the bears. Because her culture thinks differently from Western culture about the construction of the self and the relationship between the self and others, Silko's account differs radically from Oliver's.

In "Story from Bear Country," Silko speaks to a solitary traveller, telling him that when he walks in bear country, he will know, and will hear the bears calling. She tells him to listen; dares him to follow; but warns him:

> The problem is
> you will never want to return
> Their beauty will overcome your memory.

If he does follow the call, the "bear priests" will try to get him back, but they may not succeed:

> When they call
> faint memories
> will writhe around your heart
> and startle you with their distance.

The poem ends with a dare:

> Go ahead
> turn around
> see the shape
> of your footprints
> in the sand.

The poem is followed by another bear poem, this time told in third person. It describes a child who wanders away from his family and joins the bears. The family calls a medicine man who knows "how to call the child back again." "They couldn't just grab the child"; rather, the medicine man had to bring him back "step by step." However, the child "wasn't quite the same / after that / not like the other children." This same poem appears in Silko's novel *Ceremony,* and is used to suggest why the medicine man's helper, Shush (which means bear), is "strange." Betonie, the medicine man, then explains

that "it is very peaceful with the bears; the people say that's the reason human beings seldom return."

The attitudes embedded in Silko's work differ significantly from Oliver's. The loss of the traveller and the child is a communal rather than a personal loss; in both poems, it is not the person who becomes a bear who is missing something, but the people he left behind. Bringing him back also involves the community, whose presence is part of the ceremony. Second, the person who has gone to join the bears does not want to return; he must be coaxed back carefully, and if he returns, he will be altered. Third, there doesn't seem to be any question at all about the possibility of joining the bears. One simply answers a call; there is no yearning, no searching, as we see in so many of Oliver's poems.

Both Oliver and Silko assume that contact between the human and non-human world is possible, but the way that each experiences and describes this contact differs. At first, Silko's poems seem to suggest that becoming a bear means giving up human consciousness entirely: "Human beings who live with the bears. . . . are naked and not conscious of being different from their bear relatives." But Allen's description of Native American culture suggests that Western concepts of individual human consciousness are not applicable to Native American culture, where rigid distinctions between the self and others, the human and non-human, do not exist. Since all creatures are related and the boundaries between them are fluid, there is a continuous interplay and communication between the human and non-human. Human consciousness is not rigidly separated from other consciousness. For Oliver, the distinction between human and non-human never ceases to exist. Miming and becoming another is a willed artistic act that carries her across boundaries that she nonetheless remains conscious of.

Drawn though she is to the possibility of losing herself in the body of another, Oliver comes to her writing with her cultural assumptions about the self and individuality intact, assumptions that are highly valued and fostered, particularly in American culture. Thinking oppositionally, Oliver sees the boundaries between human and non-human as something that can be crossed but not erased. She perceives nature always as an other which she elevates over the human. The chief value of "entering the body of another" lies, for Oliver, in the temporary loss of human consciousness. She wants to cast off what writers like Silko and Allen see as part of creation, something that cannot be cast off without destroying the balance of the whole.

Oliver's *American Primitive* is "primitive" in that Oliver has introduced into her poetry the sympathetic magic that Taussig finds in "primitive" cultures, a magic that allows an exchange between things that imitate or have been in contact with each other. Through contact and copying, Oliver envisions and then creates a cosmic order in which she can cross the boundaries between human and non-human and become another, at least momentarily. Oliver does with her imagination what Benjamin thought the moving picture camera could do and what Taussig shows that sympathetic magic can do. Through her writing she can "get hold of an object at very close range by way of its likeness, its reproduction" (**"The Work of Art"**). She immerses herself, however briefly, in the natural world, perceives it sensuously, and becomes part of it. The poems she writes allow us to become part of this world with her, letting us cross the boundaries we draw around ourselves and flowing, for a few moments, "into the body of another."

Thomas R. Smith (review date July-August 1995)

SOURCE: A review of *A Poetry Handbook* and *White Pine* in *Bloomsbury Review,* Vol. 15, No. 4, July-August, 1995, p. 28.

[*In the following review, Smith praises* A Poetry Handbook *for providing an incisive guide for students of poetry and notes an emphasis on storytelling and mythmaking in* White Pine.]

I have before me on the desk a stack of books nearly the height of my coffee mug, Mary Oliver's combined output for the past 15 years and all of her work she has chosen to keep in print. By most poets' productivity standards—a collection every five years or so is standard—this is prodigy. The titles—*Twelve Moons, American Primitive, Dream Work, House of Light,* and *New and Selected Poems*—evoke for the reader who has consistently followed Oliver's trail some of the most radiant moments in American poetry in recent decades. To that bright stack, we can now add *White Pine,* Oliver's new volume of poems, and *A Poetry Handbook,* her first prose work.

Imagine, if you will, the absurdity of completing a medical education without having attained a thorough knowledge of the parts of the human body—yet poetry students are not expected to learn the parts of the poem's body. *A Poetry Handbook* is Mary Oliver's response to this increasingly prevalent situation.

While students preparing for careers in music and the visual arts accept as routine "a step-by-step learning process" familiarizing them with the elements and vocabulary of their art, students of poetry are encouraged in the belief that they can write fully realized poems with little or no technical or historical understanding of poetry. Beginning to write in such a milieu, the student does not forge a true style, but

> falls into a manner of writing, which is not a style but only a chance thing. Vaguely felt and not understood, or even probably intended.

In its mission to educate the student of poetry, whether reader or writer, beginning or advanced, Oliver's handbook lays down for a new generation basic principles of sound, tone diction, and form, and stands honorably beside earlier guides to prosody, including Babette Deutsch's *Poetry Handbook*, Harvey Gross's *Sound and Form in Modern Poetry,* and Paul Fussell's *Poetic Meter and Poetic Form.*

Oliver's prose is crisp and authoritative. Her discussion of Frost's sound-work in "Stopping by Woods on a Snowy Evening" is fresh and satisfying, and an excellent chapter on imagery can help poets of varying degrees of accomplishment sort the living image from the cliche in their own work. Her testimony to the awesome truth—as stated by Donald Hall—that "the new metaphor is a miracle, like the creation of life," is inspiring.

While intellectually admirable throughout, some passages in *A Poetry Handbook* are less passionate and lively than others. It may be fair to demand of Oliver's prose those qualities we expect of her poetry, yet comparisons are inevitable. A trio of closing chapters, on revision, workshops, and solitude, come as close as any in this book to Oliver's poetic fervor:

> Poetry is a life-cherishing force. And it requires a vision—a faith, to use an old-fashioned term. . . . For poems are not words, after all, but fires for the cold, ropes let down to the lost, something as necessary as bread in the pockets of the hungry.

The reader hungers for more, as well as a bibliography for further study.

Oliver remarks in *A Poetry Handbook,*

> If the poem is thin, it is likely so not because the poet does not know enough words, but because he or she has not stood long enough among the flowers—has not seen them in any fresh, exciting, and valid way.

Indeed, one of Mary Oliver's special gifts as a poet is the ability to awaken us to the beauty of the world and the responsibility that vision costs us.

The 40 poems in *White Pine* extend in often surprising ways Oliver's meditations on the appropriate relationship of human beings with nature, the rewards of attentiveness toward the world, and the inseparability of beauty and terror. As a practitioner of the "nature" poem, she is currently without rival; no poet in recent times has honored deer, pine trees, hummingbirds, spiders, and owls with the intense, sustained, and loving scrutiny she brings to even the least of her poems.

From the porcupine's dazzling, dark "gown of nails" to the breathtaking glimpse of an owl's open beak "clean and wonderful / like a cup of gold," Oliver's is a landscape distinctly feminine in tone, transformative and pagan, subtly touched all over by the hands of the Goddess, where hummingbirds wear "pale green dresses" and "sea-green helmets," where a doe startled in the pine woods on the hottest day of summer is "a beautiful woman" who rises up "on pretty hooves."

While *White Pine* is marked by a certain formal restlessness and experimentation (a third of the poems are prose poems), Oliver doesn't break faith or continuity with the line of reckless vision that flashes through her earlier books. If anything, she lives more deeply and riskily the questions that provoke sleeplessness at the end of the 20th century, as she writes in **"Snails"**: "Who are we? What are our chances? Where have we made the terrible mistake we must turn from, or perish?"

The question of how to live, of course, raises the question of how to die, and some of the best poems here, such as **"The Sea Mouse"** and **"I Found a Dead Fox,"** face the necessity and awful beauty of death with a fearless gaze. In **"Williams Creek,"** we witness the dismembering of a buck's corpse by neighborhood dogs:

> . . . it must be done—
> perfectly,
> without levity or argument—
> as though it were a dance —
>
> the only one
> that could outwit winter—
> as though the life of everything
> were in it.

These are not comforting observations or thoughts, yet responsible membership in the community of the living depends on our making peace with them. If we necessarily make claims on the world's beauty and abundance, then the world necessarily claims of us a conscious and moral recognition of

> . . . the hard
> and terrible truth
> we live with,
> feeding ourselves
> every day.
> ("**Blue Heron**")

In this view (which is also the view of indigenous cultures), we are both eater and eaten; each death buys food, water, a place in the sunlight for a new life. Oliver's appreciation of the essential sacredness of the world's edible and voracious body aligns her with the planet's most enduring religious traditions.

In her prose poem about a boy, **"William,"** Oliver applies the logic of that tradition to her own life: "Whatever he does,

he'll want the world to do it in." In a time when the clinging selfishness of the old amounts to an undeclared war on the young, Oliver's generosity is bracing and much-needed:

> But he is irresistible! Whatever he wants of mine—
> my room, my ideas, my glass of milk, my socks and
> shirts, my place in line, my position, my world—he
> may have it.

A persistent theme in *White Pine,* and in Oliver's work generally, is that of necessity—the human necessity of wrestling with questions of death and beauty, desire and surrender, and the animal necessity, to which we also must yield, of eating and being eaten. Yet it must be noted that a part of Oliver hesitates to accept such necessities as absolute. In the lovely title poem, she asks, "Isn't everything, in the dark, too wonderful to be exact, and circumscribed?"

William Stafford distinguished between the darkness of evil and the darkness of nature—in that second, good darkness things are not nearly as "exact" and "circumscribed" as the rational, disenchanted scientific intellect's fantasy of them. In nature at its most profound level, we apprehend the marvelous and inexplicable, to which story, religion, and myth are appropriate human responses. Finally, it is toward storytelling and mythmaking, those ancient disciplines of veneration, that the poems in *White Pine* lean:

> . . . what happens
> next we say what happens
> next and why does it
> happen and what happens
> then because that has happened
> lifting up the darkness
> by that much.
> ("**Stories**")

In the prose poem **"December,"** a deer with leaves growing from its antlers is Oliver's emblem of a world stranger and more sacred than we know: "The great door opens a crack, a bit of the truth is given—so bright it is almost a death, a joy we can't bear . . ."

Richard Tillinghast (review date August 1995)

SOURCE: "Stars and Departures, Hummingbirds and Statues," in *Poetry,* Vol. 166, No. 5, August, 1995, pp. 288-90.

[*Tillinghast is an American poet and educator. In the following review, he praises Oliver for handling "description with a satisfying, jeweler's precision" in* White Pine.]

Reading Mary Oliver's new book, *White Pine,* I was reminded of the cover of the old *Petit Larousse Illustre,* which shows a girl blowing on a white dandelion blossom, with the caption,

"Je sème à tout vent." Oliver's poetry, pure as the cottony seeds of the dandelion, floats above and around the schools and controversies of contemporary American poetry. Her familiarity with the natural world has an uncomplicated, nineteenth-century feeling. In the poem **"Work,"** for instance, Pasture Pond "had lain in the dark, all night, / catching the rain / on its broad back." She handles description with a satisfying, jeweler's precision. Two chicks in the poem **"Hummingbirds"** are pictured ready "to fly, for the first time, / in their sea-green helmets, / with brisk, metallic tails."

In the first poem quoted above, the poet's own work, given a deliberately feminine connotation in the way it is described, "with the linen of words / and the pins of punctuation," is contrasted to the serene obliviousness of the pond:

> all day I hang out
> over a desk
>
> grinding my teeth
> staring.
> Then I sleep.

In **"Hummingbirds"** Mary Oliver depicts her comings and goings, the flux of her emotional life, with an almost mythic but still light-fingered touch that, mysteriously, acknowledges a strange kinship with the birds she has just encountered:

> Alone,
> in the crown of the tree,
>
> I went to China,
> I went to Prague;
> I died, and was born in the spring;
> I found you, and loved you, again.

The last quatrain of the poem summarizes almost offhandedly:

> Likely I visited all
> the shimmering, heart-stabbing
> questions without answers
> before I climbed down.

Oliver's innocent-looking adverb, "likely," which introduces the poem's delicate endgame, slyly and modestly undercuts the hovering, balancing play of emotional coloring between "shimmering" and "heart-stabbing."

Though Oliver unapologetically focuses the only awareness she possesses—i.e., her human awareness—on the natural world, nature is not, in the jargon of the day anthropomorphized in the world of *White Pine.* Its otherness is acknowledged. **"Toad,"** for instance, depicts the odd spectacle, which somehow escapes being comical, of the poet squatting down beside a toad she encounters on a walk, and talking to him:

> I began to talk. I talked about summer, and about
> time. The pleasures of eating, the terrors of the night.
> About this cup we call a life. About happiness. And
> how good it feels, the heat of the sun between the
> shoulder blades.

The toad becomes an emblem of a sort of dumb grace that belongs to the world of inarticulate creatures—lacking the complexity of human awareness, immune to its sorrows:

> He might have been Buddha—did not move, blink
> or frown, not a tear fell from those gold-rimmed eyes
> as the refined anguish of language passed over him.

FURTHER READING

Criticism

Bonds, Diane S. "The Language of Nature in the Poetry of Mary Oliver." *Women's Studies* 21, No. 1 (1992): 1-15.
    Discusses whether Oliver's identification with nature in her poetry echoes traditional poetic stereotypes of women and nature.

Fast, Robin Riley. "Moore, Bishop, and Oliver: Thinking Back, Re-Seeing the Sea." *Twentieth Century Literature* 34, No. 3 (Fall 1993): 364-79.
    Analyzes the poetry of Oliver, Marianne Moore, and Elizabeth Bishop to see how they use their poetry to relate to their female poet predecessors and successors.

Additional coverage of Oliver's life and career is contained in the following sources published by Gale Research: *Contemporary Authors,* **Vol. 21-24;** *Contemporary Authors New Revision Series,* **Vol. 9;** *Contemporary Literary Criticism,* **Vols. 19, 34;** *Dictionary of Literary Biography,* **Vol. 5.**

Mary Robison
1949-

American short story writer and novelist.

The following entry provides criticism of Robison's work through 1991. For further information on her life and works, see *CLC,* Volume 42.

INTRODUCTION

Robison is considered a primary proponent of the so-called "minimalist" school of short fiction, which includes such writers as Ann Beattie, Raymond Carver, and Frederick Barthelme, among others. In her stories seemingly mundane yet absurd events are illuminated by a terse, laconic style that often relies on humor. Commended for her skill with dialogue, Robison is admired for her keen perception of the idiosyncrasies of contemporary American life. Remarking on Robison's career, a commentator for the *Virginia Quarterly Review* stated: "Acetylene bright, hip as any talk show host, greatly gifted, and flaky enough in her writing to be a role model for new talents . . . [Robison] has written some of the finest stories of our time, stories which will stand the test of time."

Biographical Information

Born January 14, 1949, in Washington, D.C., Robison is the daughter of an attorney and a psychologist. She attended Johns Hopkins University, where she earned a master's degree in 1977. A 1980 Guggenheim fellow and the recipient of other grants, Robison has taught English at Harvard University since 1981 and was named writer-in-residence at various universities during the mid-1980s. Her stories have appeared in such periodicals as *Esquire* and the *New Yorker* and were first collected in *Days* (1979). Following the publication of the novel *Oh!* in 1981, Robison wrote *An Amateur's Guide to the Night* (1983), her second collection of short fiction. In an interview she claimed that the combination of teaching and writing "doesn't work at all," so her writing career took a five-year hiatus before the publication of *Believe Them,* another short story collection, in 1988. Robison's latest book is the short novel *Subtraction* (1991).

Major Works

The stories in *Days* are full of characters who are apparently oblivious to both the bizarre and ordinary incidents of their lives. This collection is marked by a deadpan narrative tone that reflects the languor in the characters' lives. *Oh!,* Robison's

first novel, centers on the internal dynamics of the Clevelands—an eccentric, wealthy family of alcoholics and drug abusers—and comically portrays the absurdity and alienation prevalent in contemporary American life. Notable among the stories featured in *An Amateur's Guide to the Night* are "The Wellman Twins," which concerns the vicious honesty shared by the twins, and "Yours," in which a dying man and his wife carve pumpkins. Each of the stories in *Amateur's Guide* are set in the Midwestern United States and feature such distinctly American venues as fast-food restaurants and convenience stores. *Believe Them* juxtaposes several vignettes illuminating the foibles of the upper middle class with tales revealing the surrealistic dimensions of ordinary events. The novel *Subtraction* is a love story involving an irresponsible husband and his devoted wife.

Critical Reception

Robison's fiction is often discussed in terms of "minimalism," a recent trend in American letters characterized by a pronounced emphasis on perception, visuality, and attention to minute detail. Described by Anne Tyler as "stripped, incisive," Robison's writing style has earned praise for its sparseness and innovative technique. Art Seidenbaum wrote that Robison "plays with words and people in a spare, almost ascetic way." This acclaimed detachment from her work, however, has also provoked persistent criticism. Larry McCaffery observed that Robison's "restraint and refusal to supply her incidents with a more conventionally dramatic shape occasionally produces stories that evoke a sense of 'So what?'" Yet most critics have applauded Robison's dexterity with dialogue and her ability to convince the reader that her characters and situations are indeed real. Others have detected the influence of television media in Robison's fiction, often likening it to turning the television on and off with a program in progress. "She is a master of line and texture," commented Joseph Coates, "who gets maximum information out of the glittering and intentionally deceptive surfaces of our image-dominated culture." Richard Eder concluded that Robison "is a powerful writer, and her best books have used a disciplined minimalism to emit, by constriction, some powerfully shaped emotions."

PRINCIPAL WORKS

Days (short stories) 1979
Oh! (novel) 1981
An Amateur's Guide to the Night (short stories) 1983
Believe Them (short stories) 1988
Subtraction (novel) 1991

CRITICISM

Kirkus Reviews (review date 1 April 1988)

SOURCE: A review of *Believe Them,* in *Kirkus Reviews,* Vol. LVI, No. 7, April 1, 1988, p. 487.

[*In the following review, the critic finds "some hints of Robison's comic gift" in* Believe Them.]

Seven oh-so-trendy stories [in *Believe Them*] by a writer who, with Beattie, Carver, et al., has helped set the (mono) tone for hip contemporary fiction.

Most of these pieces are just that—snippets in search of context, of something to give them resonance and meaning. As they are, the only messages come from bumper stickers, T-shirts, and bathroom graffiti. And these bits of wacky wisdom seldom touch on the actual events at hand, if you can really call them events, since nothing much happens here. **"Trying"** strings together bits about an odd sort of girl (the daughter of liberal poverty lawyers) whose weirdness—mostly wisecracking outbursts during class—seems to be indulged by the nuns at her suburban Catholic school. Another

spoiled young woman (in **"Mirror"**) recalls the reason she's been friends all her life with the unmarried, pregnant girl she's visiting: they "remembered the same stuff." Robison displays a certain fondness for suburban family life: the brother recuperating back home after an unsuccessful foray to Hollywood (**"While Home"**); the children who turn the house upside down one night while the parents usher in yet another sibling at the hospital (**"Seizing Control"**); the young mother of three who "gets by" after her husband dies in a plane accident. The one excellent piece here, **"Again, Again, Again,"** picks up the story—is there a novel gestating?—of **"The Coach"** from Robison's last collection (*An Amateur's Guide to the Night*). The quick wit that she flashed in her novel *Oh!* glimmers also in this saga of a college football coach, his artist wife, and their smart-lipped teen daughter as they settle into yet another new town. Remaining stories include two tales of soured affairs, and three of crumbling marriages.

Mostly drab and disposable stuff, with some hints of Robison's comic gift.

Richard Eder (review date 19 June 1988)

SOURCE: "Hidden Pictures of Sorrow and Pain," in *Los Angeles Times Book Review,* June 19, 1988, pp. 3, 12.

[*Eder is an American critic who has won a citation for excellence in reviewing from the National Book Critics Circle as well as a Pulitzer Prize for criticism. In the review below, he considers the "hidden messages" in the stories from* Believe Them, *concluding that the stories are "boundless in their emotion."*]

Mary Robison's characters need to grieve and lament but they can't. They can only smile, be kind, be recklessly witty, and push enlightened self-mockery to suicidal extremes.

Sorrow and pain are underground messages in these finely made stories [in *Believe Them*]. They are hidden pictures, as in the children's books where, if you look hard—but not too hard or it won't work—you see a giant concealed in a peaceable barnyard.

Behind Robison's intelligent and decent faces—with ruefulness and irony as the limits of expression—there is a face of anguish.

Why should the message be hidden? Why must pain take an Aesopian form; like dissent under a dictatorship, where fables are quietly slipped into a film or a play under the eyes of the State? Does our state—lower-case—make unfeasible, as situation comedies do, a howl of despair? And how sick does this render our buoyancy?

These are the kinds of questions that Robison points to, without ever quite pointing. The minimalist authors do not separate their voices from those of their characters; they do not point. Only once does Robison, who is a minimalist in some respects though not in others, wave to us directly.

In **"Your Errant Mom,"** a woman who has left home for an older and richer man is trying to hold on to her old life even while abandoning it. At the end, after realizing that she has lost her involvement with her husband's and daughter's affairs, and perhaps her own identity as well, she says:

"I would sleep on my stomach now, without a pillow, and with no sustained thoughts. I wanted what I wanted. Before bed, I had read stories with I-narrators who could've been me."

They *are* "her," of course; the stories are by Robison. The author's wave is jaunty and cramped. Waving *and* drowning.

All of the stories in *Believe Them* are written with a mastery of the surface. Whether the narrative voice is calm and matter-of-fact, cheerful, or mildly overwrought, we are presented with a world where matters are proceeding, perhaps not terribly well, but at least under some kind of reasonable control. What makes the difference between the merely well-written and the genuinely moving is the quality of the hidden picture that emerges.

In **"While Home,"** the exchanges among a father, an adult son who is having trouble getting his life started, and a younger son who is still at home are affectionate and marked by evident good will. Underneath is something rawer: the older son's shock at finding that the world is not easy, and the father's fear for a child he can no longer help. The contrast does not really come off, though; the tones are too subdued.

"Adore Her" is about a young man who has settled for a decently paying job, a comfortable apartment and a pretty girlfriend. Finding a stranger's wallet that contains a small chamber of horrors—pictures of 15 different women and an address that identifies the owner as a settled, middle-class householder—the young man realizes he has settled too easily. His apartment is tacky; he hates his job; his girlfriend uses him as a convenience. Again, the hidden picture is almost as flat as the one on the surface.

"For Real" is much stronger. The narrator is a young woman who presents an afternoon B-movie show on a small TV station. Her commentary is derisive and comical, and she wears a clown's outfit to deliver it.

Between camera sessions, she thinks of the man she's been living with. He is a German; she had intended to marry him to help him get resident status, even though she doesn't love him. But he has just told her that he may not need her help and won't marry her because she might fall in love with someone "for real."

All this while, she is adjusting her floppy shoes, her purple gloves, her clown's wig. They mock her thoughts. It is as if Hamlet delivered his soliloquies standing on his head. What is "for real" to someone who faces the world in disguise? Perhaps she does love the German; perhaps she has no way of distinguishing.

The picture emerges, painful and moving. So it does in **"Trying,"** one of the best stories in the collection. The narrator is Bridey, a knowing, irrepressible teen-ager. She is the bright eccentric in her convent school—arguing with her teachers, making speeches when called on instead of answering questions, sneaking out of class, giving agit-prop lectures on nuclear disarmament in the locker room, and eternally in detention.

It is amiable detention. The nuns are exasperated but loving. Her parents are unconventional and loving. Bridey bursts with charm, originality, promise. And Robison suggests her peril. She may literally burst. She is at the naked, unarmed hinge of growing up. The grown-ups are all too understanding; she has nothing to butt her head against or to contain her flights.

Another of the best stories is **"Seizing Control."** Five children spend a night alone at home. Their father is at the hospital where their mother is giving birth. The neighbors are available, if necessary; it is perfectly safe.

It *is* safe, in fact, and nothing terrible happens; only a few minor mishaps and disorders. The children play in the snow rather too long. They do forbidden things: Terrence, who is 17, has a glass of wine; the others split a bottle of beer; they make coffee. They put Sarah, the baby, in bed with Hazel, who is the oldest but feeble-minded. In her sleep, Hazel punches Sarah, making her nose bleed. Terrence drives them slowly through the snow to the hospital. It's nothing serious, and afterwards, they stop for pancakes. "We'd been through an emergency," the narrator explains solemnly.

It is true: Nothing serious, but everything has slipped a little. With the parents away, the walls are gone; the world's wind—a tiny breeze, really—has blown through. The ending is brilliant and heartrending. Next day, when the parents ask what has gone on, Hazel tries to answer. All she can get out are the phrases she's been taught; the phrases of parental protection:

> Don't pet strange animals. . . . It is never all right to hit. . . . We have Eastern Standard Time. . . . Put baking soda on your bee stings. . . . Whatever Mother and Father tell you, believe them. . . .

The most powerful stories in *Believe Them* tend to touch upon children and adolescents. Robison uses a minimalist discipline and barely ruffled surfaces, but her hidden pictures of childhood and other states of vulnerability can be boundless in their emotion.

Larry McCaffery (review date 31 July 1988)

SOURCE: "Errant Mom Hits Road," in *New York Times Book Review,* July 31, 1988, p. 12.

[*Below, McCaffery discusses the strengths of Robison's stories in* Believe Them.]

Certain reviewer catch phrases have become so closely associated with Mary Robison's writing that her work now rather resembles one of those boats at anchor whose surfaces have become indistinguishable under a mass of barnacles. And since it is the highly *particularized* surface features of her work that make Ms. Robison's fiction so distinct, the distorting effect of these critical buzzwords—"dispassionate voice," "stripped-down delivery," "deadpan" and, of course, the m-word ("minimalism")—has been especially acute, just as it has been in the cases of the equally distinctive authors with whom Ms. Robison has frequently been compared (Raymond Carver, Ann Beattie and Frederick Barthelme).

In fact, what is striking about the 11 stories that make up *Believe Them*—Ms. Robison's third story collection and first in five years—is not their similarities (to one another or to works by other writers) but their variety of voices and texture, and the subtle range of emotional effects that Ms. Robison is able to create through her exquisitely controlled presentation of details. Several of these stories retain Ms. Robison's familiar focus on the lives of disaffected, upwardly mobile men and women who are shown in moments of quiet desperation; she conjures up this world with remarkable economy and precision. We instantly know these people by the clothes they wear (Nike running shoes), the cars they drive (Saabs, Alfa Romeos), their topics of casual conversation (John Mitchell, Mary Steenburgen, Claude Lévi-Strauss, Kurt Schwitters), even their names (Jay, Shane, Bridie, Jonathan, Lolly).

On the other hand, the effectiveness of several of the most memorable stories here results less from Ms. Robison's eye for the telling realistic detail than from her fascination with the grotesque and darkly comic, her characterizations of quirky people possessing odd tics of speech and behavior—in short, her intuitive feel for the surrealistic dimensions of American life that lie barely concealed under the ordinary. For example, the collection's opening story, **"Seizing Control,"** presents Hazel, a retarded child who has never been awake when the television wasn't on. Left suddenly unattended one night when Dad follows Mom to the hospital delivery room, Hazel and her brothers and sisters "seize control"

of the television, family car, telephone, liquor cabinet and all the other emblems of adult life they've been dying to try out for themselves. **"For Real"** is narrated by Boffo, a "girl clown" who runs old, bad movies on Channel 22's "Midday Matinee" and is in the process of deciding not to marry Dieter, a West German youth whose overly meticulous hairstyle and failure ever to get the in-joke reference to Charlton Heston or Claude Rains mark him as a dullard. In **"Trying,"** we witness an eerily suspended moment of confrontation between a freckle-faced member of an all-girl band and her monstrously oversized homeroom teacher, Sister Elspeth, who suffers from giantism.

The longest and funniest piece in the collection, **"Again, Again, Again,"** displays the same instincts for farcical domestic comedy and vicious (but somehow good-natured) social satire that Ms. Robison demonstrated in her novel, *Oh!* Loosely describing the period of adjustment undergone by a town and its new college football coach, **"Again"** presents suburban life in all its demented banality and absurdist splendor.

> **Robison's methods allow the careful reader an honest perspective into lives usually dealt with either melodramatically or contemptuously by other authors.**
>
> *—Larry McCaffery*

These occasional forays into the familiarly bizarre are balanced by stories in which Ms. Robison does what she is best known for—creating understated vignettes that dissect and illuminate the foibles and secret anxieties of the upper middle class. In **"Your Errant Mom,"** a woman who refuses to take refuge within the fragile comfort of a marriage that is crumbling seeks out her high school art teacher before she leaves (because "it's necessary to say goodbye to *someone*"). Eventually she accepts that failure in her two biggest roles to date (wife and mother) at least allows her the chance to explore other roles. Her concluding observation, "I wanted what I wanted," provides a good example of the complex resonances Ms. Robison sometimes generates from eloquent simplicity. In **"Mirror,"** two longtime girlfriends sit side by side in a hair salon near the Watergate, exchanging a series of remarks that reveal the undercurrents of difference and larger patterns of similarity in the lives they've come to inhabit. Another splintered marriage leads the female narrator of **"In the Woods"** to her sister's Indiana farm, where the summer heat and the insistent bugs, together with tractor sounds and the rich smells of animals and flowers, combine to refocus her anger and to lead her out on daily horseback rides, during one of which she experiences a thrilling, epiphanic moment:

"It was as though the world had died but not quite yet bothered to topple. Blades of grass, bugs, blank sky . . . were all cast in glass. I was alone in it and feeling suddenly afloat, as if I had bolted a lot of champagne."

That this woman can suddenly see herself "afloat" in the midst of her miseries and self-doubts is a small but significant personal triumph that doesn't prevent her from sobbing into the phone the next several nights; and the truth her sister tells her at the story's end—"Being so selfish and wrong often brings with it a sort of strength. You know?"—is similarly measured, with the sources of its comfort lying not in its grand profundity but in its simple applicability. These notes of quiet but insistent affirmation occur frequently in *Believe Them*, but they are not meant to be resolutions in the traditional sense. Ms. Robison recognizes that disquieting self-doubts and fears produced by what one character calls "the big things" are never as easily resolved as most story writers would lead us to believe.

This sort of restraint and refusal to supply her incidents with a more conventionally dramatic shape occasionally produces stories that evoke a sense of "So what?"; more often, however, Ms. Robison's methods allow the careful reader an honest perspective into lives usually dealt with either melodramatically or contemptuously by other authors. Throughout this collection, Ms. Robison asks us to believe that people possessing six-figure bank accounts and ranch-style suburban homes feel much the same confusions, resentments and longings as everyone else; she asks us to believe that they exist in a milieu in which the denial or sublimation of anguish and raw emotion is expected. Believe her? We do.

Ann-Marie Karlsson (essay date 1990)

SOURCE: "The Hyperrealistic Short Story: A Postmodern Twilight Zone," in *Criticism in the Twilight Zone: Postmodern Perspectives on Literature and Politics,* edited by Danuta Zadworna-Fjellestad and Lennart Bjork, Almqvist & Wikell International, 1990, pp. 144-53.

[*In the following essay, Karlsson discusses the features of "minimalism" as represented in the short stories of several writers, including Robison.*]

In 1983 the British literary magazine *Granta* announced the birth of a new American writing which appeared to occupy territories yet unknown, a literary twilight zone. Bill Buford, the editor of *Granta,* proclaimed: "a new fiction seems to be emerging from America and it is a fiction of a peculiar and haunting kind." Since then a wave of exciting new fiction by young American writers has washed over America and Europe, a wave which began even a decade before *Granta*'s recognition.

The labels assigned to the recent writing are already in abundance and the various names all point to different characteristics. In Britain *Granta* coined the name "Dirty Realism," which suggests a writing focused on the sordid aspects of life, the dark side of contemporary America. "Minimalist fiction" or just "Minimalism" are probably the most common labels used in the United States to describe the fiction of such writers as Jayne Anne Phillips, Frederick Barthelme, Raymond Carver, Bobbie Ann Mason, and Ellen Gilchrist. Together with more imaginative epithets, such as "K-mart Realism," "Hick Chic," and "Post-Vietnam, post-literary, post-modernist blue-collar neo-early-Hemingwayism," these labels indicate some, but by no means all characteristic qualities of this recent trend in American writing.

Apart from those already mentioned, writers like Ann Beattie, Richard Ford, Lorrie Moore, Tobias Wolff, and Mary Robison are often considered to belong to the main core of the literary group. In reality there is naturally no such clearly defined group or school of writers—some of them have also publicly expressed their discontent with any kind of literary categorization and have declared their independence and individuality as writers—but it is still possible to talk about typical tendencies, features uniting rather than separating the writers. Although this paper will only deal with short stories from the last two decades, during which there has been a virtual renaissance of the American short story, it must be emphasized that the tendencies can also be found in longer fiction by these and other writers. The focus on short stories in the present paper is therefore not an indication of a trend exclusively committed to short stories, but is rather a choice based on a personal interest in a dynamic genre as well as a question of practicality.

The first major category of principal textual tendencies or strategies, the latent rebellion against realism, is exercised within a representational writing: it is not an overt dismissal of fictional representation, but neither does it seem to be traditional realism. [In "On Being Wrong: Convicted Minimalist Spills Bean," *New York Times Book Review* (3 April 1988)] Frederick Barthelme explains how he rejected this established realism, since, among other things "it was full of lies, falsifications of experience for the sake of drama" and because "in constructing the 'see-through' prose, writers too often overlooked the prose itself, the result being cat food." Instead he suggests another type of writing, devoid of customary conventions. He draws a distinction between realism, which according to Barthelme stands for a whole system of literary artifice, and representation, which stands for only one part of the system. Barthelme himself chooses a representational writing:

> What you figured was you could try some of this representation stuff . . . and see what happened. So suddenly you had characters that looked as if you

just slowed for them in the parking lot outside the K&B drugstore, but instead of waiting patiently and driving off, as you would in life, now you were talking to them and they were talking back—not in conventional "realist" fashion or as people might in life, but like some characters in trees, or somebody discovering ice, or some other artificial beings in some other artificial text—very careful, very clear, achingly pristine and precise. But because you'd put them right down on an ordinary planet that looked strikingly like ours, the readers were reading right along as if what you'd written was some kind of one-for-one depiction of the real world.

The attack on realism is consequently not a visible one, but rather an invisible subversion. Although Barthelme's world seems real, it becomes conspicuously real and, paradoxically, remarkably artificial—a quality his fiction shares with many of the new writers' works. This deliberately peculiar and intriguing quality sometimes manifests itself in the recent short stories as a sense of absence in characters, events and setting.

The characters in the new American writing are so-called "ordinary people," people who make up the mass culture of blue-collar America; who work as waitresses, truck drivers, secretaries or are unemployed drifters without aims or motives. They are secretive and reticent, and the complexity and richness of their dreams and difficulties can merely be surmised. Painful memories from the Vietnam War, previous marriage disasters, failures in their personal and professional lives seem to loom in their minds, but never surface to a level of communication. These characters are surrounded by silences that tell us more about the absence that permeates their lives than any spoken word could ever communicate.

In Mary Robison's brief story **"Yours"** the reader is told very little about the characters, how they live and what they think and feel, but the few sketches fully bring out the tragedy of the situation. In the two pages of the story we find out that Allison, who is thirty-five years old, tall and wears a blond natural-hair wig, volunteers afternoons at a children's day-care centre and that this night she and her seventy-year-old husband are sitting up late making jack-o'-lanterns for the children. The expressive faces of the pumpkins are seemingly innocuously described, as is the couple's mutual admiration for each other's work, and yet a feeling of menace creeps in between the lines, only to emerge in the surprising ending:

> That night, in their bedroom, a few weeks earlier in her life than had been predicted, Allison began to die. "Don't look at me if my wig comes off," she told Clark. "Please."

> Her pulse cords were fluttering under his fingers. She raised her knees and kicked away the comforter. She

said something to Clark about the garage being locked.

At the telephone, Clark had a clear view out back and down to the porch. He wanted to get drunk with his wife once more. He wanted to tell her, from the greater perspective he had, that to own only a little talent, like his, was an awful, plaguing thing; that being only a little special meant you expected too much, most of the time, and liked yourself too little. He wanted to assure her that she had missed nothing.

He was speaking into the phone now. He watched the jack-o'-lanterns. The jack-o'-lanterns watched him.

In general, the events in the characters' lives are uneventful, trivial. The characters watch the Johnny Carson show on television, go shopping at Safeways, eat cheeseburgers at McDonalds, play bingo, go fishing or get drunk. But most of the time they just wait for something to happen, for a change they cannot realize or verbalize, only sense and anticipate.

In Raymond Carver's short story "Fat" the female narrator is telling her friend Rita about an extremely fat man who once came into the restaurant where she and her husband Rudy work. But the story about the fat man's excessive meal has no punch-line, no climax. The narrator goes on to tell Rita about the couple's dull evening at home, and Carver's story ends:

> I can't think of anything to say, so we drink our tea and pretty soon I get up to go to bed. Rudy gets up too, turns off the TV, locks the front door, and begins his unbuttoning.

> I get into bed and move clear over to the edge and lie there on my stomach. But right away, as soon as he turns off the light and gets into bed, Rudy begins. I turn on my back and relax some, though it is against my will. But here is the thing. When he gets on me, I suddenly feel I am fat. I feel terrifically fat, so fat that Rudy is a tiny thing and hardly there at all.

> That's a funny story, Rita says, but I can see she doesn't know what to make of it. I feel depressed. But I won't go into it with her. I've already told her too much. She sits there waiting, her dainty fingers poking her hair.

> Waiting for what? I'd like to know.

> It is August.

> My life is going to change. I feel it.

As for the setting, these "low-rent tragedies," as Raymond Carver puts it, often take place in small towns in for example Oregon, Montana or Kentucky, or in drab suburbs of cities like Memphis or New Orleans. The characters' world appears to be familiar, since supermarkets and bars, sales girls and newspaper deliverers, Big Macs and Ivory soap are recognised by the reader as a part of his/her everyday reality. The stories are filled with objects and brand-names, which take on a sharpened intensity contrasted with the unadorned style of the rest of the story. In "Safeways" Frederick Barthelme writes:

> She doesn't stop, only pushes on toward the front of the store. You race in the opposite direction, trying to get the waffles and the *TV Guide* and find her checkout line for a last look, but the store is out of the waffles you want, Kellogg's, so you take the house brand—small squares in a clear plastic bag.

> Only three checkers are working; the woman is not in any of the lines. You linger at the magazine mini-rack on the end of one of the unused counters, thumb through a current *People,* waiting, feeling foolish.

> She arrives unexpectedly out of the aisle behind you—soaps and toiletries—and as she gets in line behind two men, you catch a trace of her scent, delicate and flowerlike, almost jasmine.

> You drop *People* into its wire slot and pick up *TV Guide,* then push your basket into line behind hers. You stare at the back of her head, the glistening hair, and at her shoulders, noticing, where the fabric is tight to her skin, the precise, shallow relief of straps.

That objects are important to the character of the stories and to the reactions of the reader is clearly underlined by Raymond Carver: "it is possible, in a poem or a short story, to write about commonplace things and objects using commonplace but precise language, and to endow those things—a chair, a window curtain, a fork, a stone, a woman's earring—with immense, even startling power" ["On Writing," in *Fires, Essays, Poems, Stories,* 1986]. Details of setting have traditionally been minimized in short stories and devised to carry maximum significance, to reveal as much as possible about the characters' lives. In the new fiction, however, the overwhelming profusion of details, objects and brand-names does not deepen our knowledge or understanding of characters or plot. Despite their prominent presence these details do not communicate but conversely display uncommunicativeness. They act as physically present tokens of absence, silence and secretiveness. These tokens are present in material while absent in substance, refusing to voice signification in favour of an expression of silence.

Indeed the whole text seems enigmatic and reticent, with-holding resolution, revelation and completion. What we expect to be communicated is left out, remains silent, and what we encounter is insufficient, incomplete, gives neither an opening nor a closure. The triviality of action helps to build up suspense, since we are awaiting a climax which will compensate for the uneventful development of the plot; we, like the characters, are awaiting a build-up or a break-down, which remains unexpressed and unknown.

Let us now turn to the second important category of textual strategies, the stress on immediacy, which primarily is represented in narrative tense (the present tense, the future and the imperative), and in brevity of form (short words, short sentences, short units, short short stories).

It may seem curious that a fiction so filled with absence should require presence in the present, in the moment existing right here and now. Critics have commented on and sometimes expressed disapproval of the contemporary stress on the present: they claim that fictional characters lack history and live only in the present, short story writers are said to be only preoccupied with themselves and their immediate problems, and readers are charged with having too short attention spans to be able to concentrate on longer, more elaborate fiction. We are told that this is a sign of the times, a phenomenon which can be explained by pop culture, television, films, videos, Reaganism, overload of information, declining reading skills, university writing programs, and the belief that we are rapidly approaching the end of the world (cf. Barth, Dunn, Gass).

Yet it may be natural that the present tense should dominate these stories where the characters are trapped in the present, surrounded by inertia and emptiness, but also find refuge in the present, since their past remains unspeakable and their future unimaginable. Nevertheless the future tense occasionally appears, as for example in Lorrie Moore's short stories, expressed with the great uncertainty of "mights" and "mays" and "maybes," together with the imperative, to achieve the effect of immediate experience.

This imperative can also be seen as an effacement of the subject, since the direct instructions or prompts seem to delete the presence of the subject. Yet the irrepressible subject always reasserts him/herself in the end, insisting on the necessity of his/her existence, however marginal that position may be. Lorrie Moore's "How to Be an Other Woman" begins in the imperative, giving instructions to an unknown subject:

> Meet in expensive beige raincoats, on a pea-soupy night. Like a detective movie. First, stand in front of Florsheim's Fifty-seventh Street window, press your face close to the glass, watch the fake velvet Hummels inside revolving around the wing tips; some white shoes, like your father wears, are propped up with

garlands on a small mound of chemical snow. All the stores have closed. You can see your breath on the glass. Draw a peace sign. You are waiting for a bus.

But what looks like directives in the imperative, could in fact be a first or third-person narrative in the present tense, where the subject has been erased: "(We/They) Meet in expensive beige raincoats . . . First, (I/She) stand(s) in front of Florsheim's Fifty-seventh Street window . . . ." Furthermore, what is initially suppressed emerges later on in the text when the subject is restored in the shape of the second-person: "You can see your breath on the glass . . . You are waiting for a bus." The ambiguity as regards point of view is further emphasized in the frequent employment of this second-person point of view: "you" is neither the viewpoint of a private first-person nor an objective third-person, or the perspective of the "real" reader. "You" implies an immediate identification with the reader, but simultaneously avoids it by referring to a specific character. It seems to occupy an indeterminate gap, the void between the reader and the character, referring to both but relying on neither.

Finally the brevity of form also expresses a sometimes disturbing sense of immanence or immediacy. The short words and sentences do not only reflect the characters' inarticulateness but also a directness, a closer distance between the word and the action. The brief unit, the fragment and the surrounding ellipses, frustrates the linear narrative, juxtaposing series of frozen images, separated presents in time. The short short story, again a celebrated form, implies a certain uneasiness: it is devoted to a glimpse rather than a vision, a glimpse which promises access to new lives and vistas, but abruptly breaks the promise when the curtain suddenly drops and the reader finds him/herself excluded from the everlasting Never Never Land. I let the short story writer Robert Kelly sum up the emphasis on immediacy in the short stories: "this is the short fiction, the insidious, sudden, alarming, stabbing, tantalizing, annihilating form. . . ."

The short stories' concern with perception and visuality is acknowledged by several literary reviewers who compare the stories to other arts and media. Mary Robison's short stories, for example, have been compared to Hyper- or Superrealistic painting: "Mary Robison's stories recall those '70s superrealistic airbrush paintings of Chevy convertibles, gas stations, hamburger stands and other pop Americana: they dwell on the common, making art of it, with the same unrelenting blown-up detail. . ." [E. Innes-Brown, "Mary Robison, 'Days'," *Fiction International* (1980)].

Moreover, the short stories are similar to hyperrealistic painting and sculpture (the prefixes "hyper-," "super-," "photo-," "radical," and "sharp-focus" are alternately used to describe this group of artists) in more than choice of technique and motifs. Just like the writers, the hyperrealistic painters and sculptors of the 1970s (among others Ralph Goings, John Salt, Robert Cottingham, Richard Estes and Duane Hanson) were accused of wanting to take art back to where it was before modernism and even impressionism. The artists were claimed to be interested in a perfection of technique alone, in creating a glossy surface without substance, despite the fact that the "Documenta 5" exhibition in 1972, where the art movement emerged in a fully fledged style, was devoted to the theme of "questioning reality." Extreme verisimilitude was their way of questioning reality; "the photorealists . . . produce a reality so real that it proclaims its artificiality from the rooftops," as Umberto Eco puts it [in *Travels in Hyperreality,* 1987]. Initially photorealism seemed to be a return to representation and figuration, "until it became clear that its objects were not to be found in the 'real world' either," as Fredric Jameson explains [in "Postmodernism or Cultural Logic of Late Capitalism," *New Left Review* (1984)], "but were themselves photographs of that real world, this last now transformed into images, of which the 'realisms' of the photorealist painting is now the simulacrum."

The intense vision of reality achieved by exaggerated verisimilitude and emphasis on immediate experience might also suggest a film-like quality of this fiction. However, the recent short stories do not resemble the metonymic conventional narrative film, but rather the "underground movies" of the sixties or the rock videos of the eighties. [In *The Modes of Modern Writing,* 1979] David Lodge points out that underground movies deviated from the metonymic norm either by montage or "by parodying and frustrating the syntagm, setting the naturally linear and 'moving' medium against an unmoving object." In underground movies like Andy Warhol's *Sleep* and *Empire* from the early sixties, action is replaced by stillness, communication by silence, and plot by perception, which is also the case with many of Frederick Barthelme's and Raymond Carver's stories. In rock videos series of images are brought together according to themes and visual association rather than to a regular plot, and bear some resemblance to fragmentary stories like "Talk Show" by Charles Baxter (1985) and Lorrie Moore's "How" (1985).

Significantly, television plays an important role in the new writing where it becomes a tool for questioning such concepts as "reality" and "origin." In the short stories TV dissolves into life and life dissolves into TV, breaking down distinctions between sender and receiver, subject and object, medium and message. The characters often speak of the TV stars as old friends and feel as close to them as to members of their own family. In Jayne Anne Phillip's "Home" the mother of the family worries about the news announcer Walter Cronkite's health and refers to him as "Walter"; in "Next Door" by Tobias Wolff, a couple are watching "Johnny," i.e. the Johnny Carson show. In the short story, the male character would like to take the announcer of the show, Ed

McMahon, with him on a long voyage since "he is always so cheerful." The difference between the artificial image of people on the TV screen and their real flesh-and-blood existence becomes even more evidently blurred in Frederick Barthelme's short story "Violet," in which the protagonist taps on the TV screen to straighten a lock of a newsreader's hair:

> A lock of Kathleen's hair has gotten crosswise with her part. I crouch in front of the set, tap the glass, and say, "Kathleen, Kathleen," but she goes on talking. I advance the color intensity and twist the hue knob to change the color of her lips to crimson. "That's better," I say to the television.

Television often occurs in the new fiction as an example of how an image of reality outside is brought into everybody's home and there perceived as more real than its origin. When the newscaster in "Violet" starts to work for another channel and therefore changes her clothes and hair style, she does not seem real any more: "A caller who says his name is Toby, from Tennessee, says that he doesn't think that she's the real Kathleen Sullivan, that the real Kathleen must've gone to heaven." The truly real Kathleen, the woman behind the image, has ceased to exist; what is perceived as "real" is the image on the TV screen, and if that image changes, the "original" image also ceases to exist and there is now a new "real" Kathleen in the form of a new image. This separation and independent relationship between the copy and its origin can be seen as a phenomenon typical of the age of mass media and mass communication—the age of simulacrum.

The media are no longer identifiable as such, but now function, in Jean Baudrillard's words, as "a sort of genetic code which controls the mutation of the real into the hyperreal" ["The Precession of Simulacra," in *Art After Modernism,* edited by B. Wallis, 1984]. The hyperreal, which Baudrillard defines as "the generation by models of a real without origin or reality," in its turn, makes distinctions between the real and the imaginary inoperative. In "an America of furious hyperreality," as Eco writes, "absolute unreality is offered as real presence."

Since the new American short fiction has the same dismantling quality as the hyperreal, I suggest that we call it a *Hyperrealistic fiction,* rather than Dirty Realist or Minimalist. The recent writing is hyperrealistic in the sense that its extreme verisimilitude creates an "over-realism" also apparent in the motifs and techniques of hyperrealist art. The minimal, "clean" style of the writing corresponds to the clean, stylish surfaces of the airbrush paintings, and the sharp focus on details of American pop culture features in both literature and art. Hyperrealism has in all its forms often been accused of simplicity, since meaning appears to be found only on the surface. And yet its meaning tantalizingly evades the reader/

spectator and the fiction and paintings become emotionally and intellectually disturbing, as the objects of the representation continually dissolve into images, or models, of yet another real in an endless process of simulation. Hyperrealistic fiction is therefore hyperrealistic by virtue of form, content and, above all, inherent ideas; the new name moves the stress to the intriguing and disintegrating, the ingenious and disingenuous qualities of the writing, and shifts the focus to wider, more comprehensive spheres of interest.

The final questions then concern the status of the Hyperrealistic short story; whether it can be seen as a natural sequel to or a reaction against its literary forbear, and in which direction Hyperrealism will lead contemporary fiction.

Could the short stories be a retreat to modernist values and traditional realism, and the story writers be the sullen nephews of Hemingway and Chandler? The reticence of the characters, the impersonal narration (perhaps most apparent in Raymond Carver's short stories) and the enigmatic plots, which seem to thrive on Hemingway's famous omissions, are all points that seem to speak for this alternative.

But it is also obvious that the recent short stories are different from for example Hemingway's early short stories in subject matter and underlying ideas. So perhaps Hyperrealism is an extension of realism, a continuation with a new perspective generated by contemporary American society? [In "A Few Words about Minimalism," *New York Times Book Review* (28 December 1986)], Barth enumerates several political and social factors to account for the current literary trend and mentions, among other things, the "national hangover from the Vietnam war, felt by many to be a trauma literally and figuratively unspeakable," the energy crises of 1973-76 and the subsequent reaction against excess and wastefulness, and the resistance to political and commercial advertising.

Have the slender short stories emerged as a reaction against the "maximalist" metafiction or fabulation by such writers as Robert Coover, Donald Barthelme, John Barth, William Gass and Thomas Pynchon? From this point of view the differences are more emphasized than the similarities: matter-of-fact detachment replaces ironic black humour and low-brow reticence replaces academic intellectuality in a development perceived to be a decline in literary standard.

Or is Hyperrealistic fiction a development of metafiction, in which the new writers deal with essentially the same basic literary and philosophical issues as their predecessors, of playing against reading conventions and standard norms and expectations, as well as of questioning and probing the language of fiction and the fictional "reality" within a representational writing? Frederick Barthelme acknowledges his debts to "the four big guys" (Barth, Gass, Hawkes, and Donald Barthelme), but also points out how his own writing took a different direction in the mid-seventies, when he decided not to become another poor imitator of the four postmodern writers:

> So then if you were a trained post-modern guy, sold on the primacy of the word, on image, surface, sound, connotative and denotative play, style and grace, but short on sensitivity to the representational, what you did was drive from Texas to Mississippi and realize . . . that people were more interesting than words. That idea . . . was joined by the sense that ordinary experience—almost *any* ordinary experience—was essentially more complex and interesting than a well-contrived encounter with big-L Language. Then you remembered that experience was itself a language, even if it was a language mostly unknowable, in the sense *irreducible* . . . Understandably, you wanted to put these things together—the heightened sense of the valences of words on the one hand, new-up people-interest on the other. ["On Being Wrong"]

So maybe we are dealing with a writing which is partly a socially committed literature, which expresses a concern for the "shopping mall generation" of ordinary blue-collar workers or drifters on the edge of society, and partly an experimental avant-garde fiction, which is attempting to find new means of expression beyond traditional realism and postmodern fiction. Hyperrealistic fiction could also be a fiction of effacement, influenced by contemporary literary criticism and philosophy as well as earlier fiction, but which has internalized ideas of marxism, feminism and post-structuralism and chooses to express the ideas implicitly in its silences rather than explicitly; a strange fiction of absence, which seems to erase itself in its self-assertion, and yet hinges on the obsessive, disturbing persistence of the marginal self.

Whatever it is, it is a literature which raises questions, as yet unanswerable questions of whether it is the faint light of a closing postmodern era or the first glimmer of a new day that is twinkling in the Twilight Zone.

Joseph Coates (review date 10 February 1991)

SOURCE: "Deceptive Surfaces," in *Chicago Sunday Tribune,* February 10, 1991, p. 13.

[*In the review below, Coates praises Robison's achievement in* Subtraction, *calling her "a master . . . who gets maximum information out of the glittering and intentionally deceptive surfaces of our image-dominated culture."*]

Mary Robison's *Subtraction* adds up either to the model novel of the '90s or one of the funniest, most erotically charged and satirically observant failed novels since those of the late Donald Barthelme, whose title of Maximum Minimalist she hereby inherits.

From the standpoint of the reader's enjoyment, it doesn't much matter which of these Robison has accomplished, nor is it easy or especially important to decide whether the cultural stigmata brought to fiction by her generation—the first to have lived with television from infancy—is an asset or a brilliant liability. Either way, she is a master of line and texture who gets maximum information out of the glittering and intentionally deceptive surfaces of our image-dominated culture.

Robison raises sitcom wit to the level of real emotional situations, real comedy and real art.

—Joseph Coates

Robison raises sitcom wit to the level of real emotional situations, real comedy and real art with much the same perspicacity as Henry James did a century ago in *The Reverberator,* his romantic satire on American media madness and the first novel to isolate the wisecrack or one-liner as the basic unit of American courtship conversation. But where James' use of the wisecrack satirized his innocents abroad in the 1880s, Robison makes the one-liner emblematic of her characters' '90s hipness at home against a background of baffled emotional and intellectual drift.

Subtraction is, among other things, a romantic "road" novel, and the various quests pursued by the three main characters extend across a continent where restless movement in search of vanished personal frontiers substitutes for a sense of purposeful life.

Paige Deveaux is a poet in her early 40s who uses a year's sabbatical from teaching at Harvard to follow a trail of credit-card telephone calls (*Subtraction* is part detective novel) to track her alcoholic husband, Raf.

Raf's latest bender has taken him from Brookline, Mass., to Washington, D.C., then on to Charlottesville, Va.; Birmingham, Ala.; Oxford, Miss.; Thibodaux, La., New Orleans and finally Houston. There Paige enlists his most recent unwilling host, a cowboy/construction worker and Princeton classmate of Raf's named Raymond Hamilton, to help find her roving and lecherous husband.

After Raymond tells Paige that she is "as tall as I thought you'd be . . . I never saw Raf with a woman wasn't one of your stretch jobs," she asks, "How many women have you seen Raf *with*?"—to which Raymond replies, "Umm. However many there are. . . .

"He crashed your car, drank your liquor, ate your food?," Paige continues. "Jumped your wife? Borrowed money? Ate your parakeet?" "Some of those," says Raymond. "Yes, ma'am."

An instant physical attraction springs up between Raymond and Paige, who decides that "the rank steam heat of this city must knock its people sideways" as Raymond guides her like Vergil through the various circles of "Raf's type of territory— of the spirit and mind": Mexican bars and dance halls and "THE NEW TEXAS MOTEL—WE HAVE HOURLY RATES—XXX-PLUS MOVIES!"

With the additional help of a bisexual B-girl named Jewels, who tries to seduce her, Paige locates Raf, totally wasted to the point of paralysis but, back in her motel room, still enjoying his chronic affliction of manic satyriasis:

"*This* is the moment all those grueling months of *training* were for. . . . The hours on the practice mattress . . . The work on technique . . . All that is over. Right now, right here, it's just a question of pride and character; a question of will."

An erotic quadrangle develops among Raf, Paige, Raymond and an environmentalist stripper named Pru, while leaving Raymond's wife, Luisa, pretty much out of the equation. But it is questions of pride and character that the novel ambiguously tries to settle, with rather intriguing results.

The mystery of Raf's character, motivation and even occupation is built up by means of a delayed entrance nearly as prolonged as Ahab's—and indeed he is a kind of updated, amorous Ahab with, as they say in show biz, some great lines.

It seems that Raf thinks as well as drinks, while making his living at any kind of manual labor that allow him to drink on the job ("the kinds they build beer ads around"), from lobster fisherman to wildcat oil-rigger.

The note he left Paige when he left on his latest drunk was a quote from Nietzsche: "Whither are we moving? Away from all suns? . . . Are we not straying through infinite nothing? . . ."

Touring a squalid barrio with Paige, he concludes "that's eighty percent of the . . . world. The palace is surrounded. . . ." And he seems to seek the condition described in a passage from E.M. Cioran's "The Trouble with Being Born" that Paige finds him reading: "We should have abided by our larval condition, dispensed with evolution, . . . delighting in the elemental siesta and calmly consuming ourselves in an embryonic ecstasy."

All this is rendered with brilliant conviction—Raf is believable as both barrio bum and former Rhodes scholar—but a certain TV shallowness manifests itself in the ending. As in a sitcom, the best man (Raymond) doesn't get the girl; the funniest one (Raf) does—or at least he does after a fashion.

Paige callously (and vainly) has an affair with Raymond to make Raf jealous, and Raf takes off again. Then, after a hallucinogenic road trip north, Paige ends up at a snowed-in Atlantic coastal inn managed by her mother, where Raf has promised to meet her and where Raymond follows her for a dramatic confrontation.

It's difficult to say whether Robison shares the class smugness we see in Paige's dismissal of Raymond. "You should've been different with me, Paige," he tells her as she drives him to the airport. "You got a nice inn to go to, and a sit-down . . . job, and Raf's got your dad backin' him up, but what I do sort of counts." The reader tends to agree.

We last see Paige embarking with Raf on yet another aimless auto trip and idolizing him as he studies a road map: "I thought: generic man, perfect man. I thought how even when Raf was dead-still, he had an intensity out of which someone could interpret a world."

Well, maybe. But it's a world that's not big enough for anyone else.

Richard Eder (review date 17 February 1991)

SOURCE: "Parodies Lost," in *Los Angeles Times Book Review,* February 17, 1991, p. 3.

[*In the following review, Eder argues that* Subtraction *is an "unsteady" parody in which Robison has "lost control of her material and emptied out along with it."*]

All we know about Minnie is that she loves Mickey. But if all we know about Mickey is that Minnie loves him, then we know nothing about Mickey. And so we know nothing about Minnie.

The two lovers in **Subtraction** are pretty much what the title suggests. They are two empty parcels. They are wrapped expensively, and labeled with a note of self-parody. So we are not sure whether what we are getting from the author, Mary Robison, is a joke or a gyp.

Even Paige's name is expensive. She is a poet with four published volumes, and an arts grant big enough to let her take off a year from teaching at Harvard. The publishers' blurb makes her out to be a Harvard professor; the text doesn't claim quite that. Maybe she's only a Harvard lecturer; still, that's quite classy, and besides, she has sexy legs.

So one of her two lovers tells her. Both are Princeton graduates, and one of them, who is married to her, was a Rhodes scholar as well. His name is pretty expensive, too; it is Raf. At least, that is what everyone thinks it is. In a moment of despair, in the book's only genuinely raw moment, Paige discloses that it is really Walter.

That was cruel. But Raf has given cause. While Paige has been turning out poems and aspiring poets, doing the household bills and taking care of their apartment in Brookline, Raf has been cutting a swath.

He is darkly handsome, we learn, and has "a crinkly smile." He is formidably promising; there must be a film or a play in him, if he could only get it out. Instead, he has gone from job to job, suitably chosen to suggest *wild, lost, romantic.* He has hung plasterboard, worked as a bouncer, a foundryman, a lobster fisherman; anything, he explains, that will allow him to drink Jack Daniels on the job.

He drinks a lot of it. He is generous in his thirsts and his appetites. He shares them with many women, and takes them periodically on the road. Yet he always comes back. He and Paige would not know what to wear or what to do alone, she says.

Emily Dickinson loves Jack Kerouac? Not quite. At the book's start, he is gone and she traces him, through the telephone bills, to Houston, where he has gone to see an old college mate and fellow vagrant. She flies down, rents a convertible, puts up at a motel, finds Raf—he is nuzzling a brunette in a bar, but swears he'll go straight and dry out—and his friend Ray.

With Raf and Ray, Paige plunges into the dives and strip joints on the scuzzy side of town. She drinks beer, lounges around in the torpid heat, goes for rides with Ray and, after considerable wanting to, has sex with him. She meets their friends: Jewels, a bisexual blonde who invites her to scrub her back in the tub, and Pru, a post-modern stripper.

Feminism is dead, Pru explains, so she is into shame. She strips, sleeps around, goes on bulimic junk-food orgies out of "contempt." Self-contempt? Paige wonders, Harvard-like. Not a bit, says Pru.

It is Paige's walk on the wild side. When she is not low-lifing, she curls up in bed with *Granta* and *American Poetry Review.* She breaks off now and then to scribble a tercet or add to the 16-page poem she has brewing on her laptop. Raf, trying to go straight, jogs, reads Schopenhauer and makes love, mightily but exclusively, to Paige. The strain is too much; he disappears once more. Paige works her way north, motel by motel, quatrain by quatrain, pickup—casual but sexless—by pickup.

Eventually, at a Cape Cod beach hotel run by her mother,

they are all reunited in a raging blizzard: the lovesick Ray, the wandering Raf, and both halves of Paige—high-culture poet and All American Road Queen. After considerable wavering, she decides to follow her muse, but the last thing we see, she is driving west with Raf and admiring his profile:

"I thought: generic man, perfect man. I thought how even when Raf was dead-still, he had an intensity out of which someone could interpret a world."

Robison is a powerful writer, and her best books have used a disciplined minimalism to emit, by constriction, some powerfully shaped emotions.

—Richard Eder

With such lines, such characters and such stances, it is tempting to take *Subtraction* for parody. If it is parody, the targets are widely scattered. Pretentiousness of some sort, of course, but which sort? Certainly, Paige's scribbling of exotic poetic forms amid the breakfast bacon or upended beer bottles suggests the modern poetry academic.

The couple's high-cult-pop-cult mishmash spreads in all directions. There are music-video touches in the posturings and deliberate cliche-ing. And sometimes the book suggests a party whose guest list mixes the post-orgasmic denizens of the Guess Jeans ads with Seagrams' tidy have-it-and-do-it-alls.

But the parody is unsteady. It keeps slipping indistinguishably into itself. It lacks the wit and detachment to fix its subjects. And perhaps it is not what Robison is intending.

She is a powerful writer, and her best books have used a disciplined minimalism to emit, by constriction, some powerfully shaped emotions. Here everything goes slack and indistinct.

Somehow, in trying to convey the mutual emptinesses of American high and low cult, Robison lost control of her material and emptied out along with it.

Douglas Bauer (review date 24 February 1991)

SOURCE: "New Scars, New Stories, No Excuses," in *New York Times Book Review,* February 24, 1991, p. 10.

[*Below, Bauer offers a mixed review of* Subtraction.]

Mary Robison's fiction, with all its consistent strengths, seems to divide itself into two distinct categories. Much of her work offers trademark displays of formal daring, an idiosyncratic descriptive precision and a stylized conversational wit. But additionally, in such stories as **"I Get By," "In the Woods"** and the powerful **"Seizing Control,"** a strong moral focus is apparent in the telling (a focus that does not come, it should be stressed, at the expense of her verbal snap and humor).

In these examples of Ms. Robison's fiction, one reads of people openly struggling and, if not achieving a rescuing clarity, then at least glimpsing ways to distinguish among different types of behavior in the great societal murk. But in several other stories—and in her first novel, *Oh!*—one finds the same wit, formal ingenuity and wacky angle used seemingly to sanction worlds in which people are unable or cynically unwilling to act, or are frozen in states of abdicating adolescence (whether they be 25 or 60). One finds them displaying, in other words, what Wayne Booth, in *The Rhetoric of Fiction,* has called "'beliefs' or 'attitudes'. . . that we cannot adopt even hypothetically as our own."

The good news regarding Ms. Robison's second novel, *Subtraction,* is that it seems, at its conclusion, to move away from that sanctioning of a resigned, self-pitying refusal to grow up. Unfortunately it's an awfully modest and peripheral gesture, and it occurs long after we've stopped caring whether Ms. Robison's confused narrator will reclaim or reject her supposedly charming rake of a husband.

As the novel opens, Raf Deveaux has vanished. For his wife, Paige, a poet and a teacher of poetry writing at Harvard, this is nothing new. "He'd be gone a week, ten days," she tells us. "Then he'd be back, and he'd have new scars, new stories, no excuses." Paige learns that Raf is in Houston, and she flies there to track him down. She finds him, whispering drunkenly into the ear of a beautiful young woman in a derelict bar. (Ms. Robison's descriptions of Houston's seedier neighborhoods convey a splendid sense of dissolute torpor.) "Paige," he says blithely upon spotting her. "Someone said you might be in town." She plans to remain in Houston a couple of days, but her stay turns instead into a couple of months—for things get complicated.

First of all, Raf is especially deep in drunkenness and angst. "One uncomplicated dream is all I ask," he moans. But now he launches a massive effort to restore himself: five-mile runs at dawn, drinking fruit juices, reading Schopenhauer—all the mean astringents. He explains to Paige that they can't leave Houston because "we haven't served out our sentences yet."

And then there's Raf's Houston friend Raymond, the ultimate hunk as Marlboro Man: frayed denims, red Texas mud on the heels of his boots. He quickly finds Paige irresistible. And she finds him the same. So another reason they can't

leave Houston, Raf explains to Paige, is "your being in love with Raymond."

And finally there's Paige herself, who justifies her desperate efforts to make a life with her husband by saying: "We need each other. Otherwise we can't feed or dress ourselves. We don't know what to think next." Of all these folks, Paige seems most to belong among the permanent juveniles of Ms. Robison's *Oh!* It's not so much Paige's acceptance of the terms Raf's delinquency sets for her, but rather the stunted immaturity of her interior life, that makes her the least convincing character in *Subtraction*. Here is a woman, near or at the age of 40, who thinks, not atypically, when she hears the sound of another woman's "tinkling laugh," that it "sent me back to junior high, slumber parties, night whispers, the TV with the sound off, homemade cake."

Having told Paige why they cannot leave Houston, it is Raf who eventually does, falling spectacularly off the wagon and once more dropping out of sight. This sends everyone back across the country to a round of final conversations, mostly at a Cape Cod inn run by Paige's dope-smoking mother. And it is here that Raymond speaks the chastening sentiments we've been waiting for one of the characters—and, most of all, the novel's own narrative sensibility—to suggest. It is good that he does. But it is Paige and Raf who are the story's central figures, presumably the ones whose lives readers are supposed to care about. Yet at the book's end one feels only—past any interest and without the least concern—that they deserve each other.

This reader, at least, unable to become the kind of reader *Subtraction* asks him to be, wishes that Ms. Robison had posited the guiding moral intelligence of her finest short stories in plainer and more integral fashion here—right along with her humor and her wondrous eccentricity.

Donna Rifkind (review date 17 May 1991)

SOURCE: "Highbrows and Lowlifers," in *Book World—The Washington Post,* May 17, 1991, p. 4.

[*In the following review, Rifkind contends that* Subtraction *"would have had more narrative punch in a shorter form," concluding that the novel "does not manage to add up to much at all."*]

Paige Deveaux is a Harvard professor and poet whose current work-in-progress is a long poem titled "Enantiotropy" (don't ask what it means—it doesn't matter). Her husband, Raf, is nothing but trouble: a faithless alcoholic who runs away from home whenever things get rough. When Paige leaves her cozy Cambridge house to search for Raf in his latest hideout, a seedy section of Houston, passions explode in the steamy July heat like a battered pinata.

Or so Mary Robison would like us to believe. These characters, the stars of her second novel, *Subtraction,* are more remarkable for their peculiar combination of the highbrow and the lowdown than for their passion. Raf, whose latest farewell note to Paige was a quotation from Nietzsche, is a former Princeton philosophy student who has held jobs as a foundry worker, a lobster fisherman, a Las Vegas bouncer and a construction worker. Paige, who narrates the story, is known to write tercets in times of crisis but has no problem swigging beer and playing cards with the women from a local Houston slum.

Slumming, in fact, seems to be the real subject of this novel. These are characters who, despite their Ivy League credentials, insist on living on the edge. Why else would Robison introduce Pru, a rich girl turned stripper, who claims she dances nude in a nightclub out of "contempt" for mankind, buys only "politically correct beverage products," and delivers sermonettes to anyone who will listen about feminism, the rain forests and government censorship?

To round out this high-toned group, we are given Raymond, an old Princeton friend of Raf's, whom Robison portrays as a Marlboro Man from somewhere in the Southwest, with "blond, metal-bright hair" and the ability to make profound observations in an irresistibly sexy drawl.

It is Raymond who helps Paige track Raf down in a Hispanic dance hall on the outskirts of Houston. But although Paige's apparent willingness to rescue her husband from the sleaziest depths is arresting at first, after a while her devotion begins to strain the reader's credulity.

Though all the other characters in *Subtraction* are constantly remarking on Raf's attractiveness and charm, Robison fails to make his so-called charisma convincing. Here, for example, is her first description of Raf: "He did look handsome in his way, in his loose black suit, although there was a badge-sized bruise on his left cheekbone below his glass eye, and he seemed far along in his drunk. Just moving back and forth along the bar he stumbled twice."

While this is hardly an enticing portrait, when Robison adds the fact that Raf is the kind of self-hating alcoholic who is fond of making such smart-alecky statements as "It's not an authentic day for me unless I degrade myself in so many ways," it is hard to imagine what Paige and others in the book find so winsome about this creature.

Paige herself, who brags of having "an arts grant bigger than my Harvard salary," is all fancy credentials with barely any depth. She is that late-1980s phenomenon, the Smart Woman Who Makes Foolish Choices, whining to her mother that "Raf's a bad husband. I deserve a good husband. Why do I still want Raf?" To which her mother responds: "He's an

awfully good time." But Robison never gives her protagonist enough complexity to expand beyond this kind of superficial dialogue, so that Paige remains not so much a character as a cliche.

Raymond and Pru, for their part, fade in and out of the narrative at random, as do Paige's thinly sketched parents, Dottie and Mario. Since they seem to exist primarily as temporary distractions from the wearisome cat-and-mouse game that Raf is playing with Paige, these peripheral characters are allowed to develop very little life of their own.

Mary Robison is primarily known as a writer of short stories (she has published three collections, titled *Days, An Amateur's Guide to the Night,* and *Believe Them*), and perhaps *Subtraction*—a curious title, never explained—would have had more narrative punch in a shorter form. Stretched out to fit the roomier dimensions of a novel, neither the plot nor the characters have enough strength to sustain themselves over nearly 200 pages. In the end, *Subtraction* does not manage to add up to much at all.

Virginia Quarterly Review (review date Summer 1991)

SOURCE: A review of *Subtraction,* in *Virginia Quarterly Review,* Vol. 67, No. 3, Summer, 1991, p. 96.

[*In the following review, the critic finds* Subtraction *funny at times but "not funny enough" at others.*]

Mary Robison, author of three highly regarded and highly praised collections of stories and one novel, *Oh!* (1981), may or may not be the muses darling, but has been, for sure, a greatly admired member-in-good-standing of the contemporary literary establishment. Acetylene bright, hip as any talk show host, greatly gifted, and flaky enough in her writing to be a role model for newer talents like Amy Hempel and Lorrie Moore, she has written some of the finest stories of our time, stories which will stand the test of time. Robison, like Paige Deveaux, splits her time between teaching jobs at Harvard and Houston. Most of [*Subtraction*], the center of it, takes place in Houston where Paige's husband, Raf, an alcoholic, has washed up after his latest disappearing act. (The sense of place, the evocation of Houston, in detail and in general, is simply superb.) As Paige tries to put their life together again, they become involved with a crew of eccentric characters, chiefly two—Raf's buddy, Raymond, an urban cowhand and former Princetonian, and Pru, a wonderfully acrobatic exotic dancer. Mostly their story is played out in a variety of high- and low-class honky-tonks, where, as Raf (a sharp-tongued fellow) puts it: "Assorted wretchednesses ensue." The story is overwhelmingly told in dialogue, clever talk if no match for Noel Coward or, for that matter, George Higgins. Many a zinger flies like an arrow in humid Houston air or chilled out air-conditioning. The wrap-up, a sort of happy ending, reconciliation, anyway, takes place against a major snowstorm in New England. At many places it's very funny writing; at others not funny enough. Maybe you had to be there. Allowing for everything, however, it's good to have a new book from Mary Robison, written in what her fan Frederick Barthelme defines as "the peculiar squinted view she has."

FURTHER READING

Criticism

Hooper, Brad. Review of *Believe Them,* by Mary Robison. *Booklist* 84, No. 20 (15 June 1988): 1709.
> Claims that while "some readers may find her tedious; others will proclaim her brilliant."

Review of *Subtraction,* by Mary Robison. *Kirkus Reviews* LVIII, No. 24 (15 December 1990): 1703.
> Finds *Subtraction* "a funny, beautifully written novel, dry and bubbly as good champagne."

Review of *Believe Them,* by Mary Robison. *Publishers Weekly* 233, No. 15 (15 April 1988): 76.
> Describes Robison's prose as "carefully honed," but detects a "zany, fast-talking sameness" throughout the collection.

Review of *Subtraction,* by Mary Robison. *Publishers Weekly* 237, No. 51 (21 December 1990): 42.
> Concludes that Robison's spare prose is an exact fit for her novel.

Saari, Jon. Review of *Subtraction,* by Mary Robison. *The Antioch Review* 49, No. 3 (Summer 1991): 469.
> Comments briefly on the style and themes of *Subtraction.*

Seaman, Donna. Review of *Subtraction,* by Mary Robison. *Booklist* 87, No. 10 (15 January 1991): 1008.
> Describes *Subtraction* as "a haunting existential love story . . . sharply funny, sad, sexy, and acute."

Additional coverage of Robison's life and career is contained in the following sources published by Gale Research: *Contemporary Authors,* Vols. 113, 116; and *Dictionary of Literary Biography,* Vol. 130.

Nelly Sachs
1891-1970

German poet, playwright, and translator.

The following entry presents criticism of Sachs' writing from 1966 through 1994. For further information on her life and works, see *CLC*, Volume 14.

INTRODUCTION

As a German Jew who narrowly escaped the concentration camps of the Holocaust, Sachs built her body of poetry as a monument to the sufferings of the Jews. Her work is lyrical and often psalm-like, drawing much of its inspiration from both Jewish and Christian mysticism. Death, redemption, and the search for peace are important themes throughout her work, which Stephen Spender called "apocalyptic hymns rather than 'modern poetry.'" Sachs was awarded the Nobel Prize for Literature in 1966.

Biographical Information

Sachs was raised in an upper-class neighborhood of Berlin, Germany, the only child of well-to-do parents, and received a well-rounded education including literature, music, and dance. Little else is known of her life before the age of forty-nine, when she and her widowed mother escaped the Nazis and orders to report to a concentration camp through the intervention of a friend, the Swedish author Selma Lagerlöf, who arranged for their escape to Stockholm in the summer of 1940. By the time the two arrived, Lagerlöf had died, but she had made provisions for their care. Sachs's mother died several years later, leaving Sachs alone in her exile. The terrifying experience of her escape and later, safe in Sweden, the agony of hearing of the deaths of those left behind, consumed Sachs's life thereafter and provoked the writings that she is known for today.

Major Works

All of Sachs's writing, with the exception of some light-hearted pre-war poems that she later requested remain out of print, can be seen as a struggle for catharsis in the wake of the horrors of the Holocaust. She stated that she felt compelled to write, describing the creation of her first post-Holocaust works, the poetry collection *In den Wonungen des Todes* (*In the Houses of Death*) and the verse play *Eli,* as a brutally painful process which she was powerless to stop. All of her work is concerned with the themes of sin (particularly human brutality), redemption or atonement, and death as a re-

lease from the suffering of life. Her poetry is characterized by rich symbolic imagery, often violent and often drawn from the Bible or the Zohar, and concerned with the phenomenon of voicelessness in an individual, an artist, or a people. Many critics identify this preoccupation with silence as stemming from the Nazi interrogation Sachs endured before her escape, during which she became mute, unable to answer questions or defend herself. She described the experience in a prose piece entitled "Living under a Threat" as five days during which she "lived without speech in a witches' trial. My voice fled to the fish. Fled without caring about the remaining limbs fixed in the salt of terror." Sachs's devotion to serving as the voice of those murdered in the Holocaust is rooted in this experience.

Among Sachs's most studied poems is "O die Schornsteine" ("O the Chimneys"), the first piece in *In the Houses of Death* and a monument to the victims of the Holocaust whose ashes and souls traveled through the chimneys to freedom. Critics have praised the poem for its multilayered symbolism and its emotional impact as Sachs shows readers first the innocuous chimney stacks, then the thresholds beyond which death was certain, and finally the release from suffering demonstrated by the dispersal of "Israel's body in smoke through the air." Also collected in *In the Houses of Death* are the many "chorus" poems, each of which speaks for a silenced group—the "Chorus of Things Left Behind," "Chorus of Orphans," and "Chorus of Stars," among others. In her second collection, *Sternverdunkelung* (*Eclipse of Stars*), Sachs broadened her scope, including some poems that are unrelated to the Holocaust and exploring further the themes of Israel and Jewish history. The first collected edition of her work, entitled *Fahrt ins Staublose* (*Journey into Dustlessness*), was published in 1961 on the occasion of her seventieth birthday. Sachs's final collection, published posthumously and entitled *Teile dich Nacht*, demonstrates the multiple layers of meaning and the themes of terror and helplessness inherent in her body of work.

Critical Reception

As awareness of the atrocities of the Holocaust grew over the years, so did interest in Sachs's work. First published in Sweden during her exile and later in post-war Germany, Sachs's work found critical acclaim and sympathy in both countries. Interest in her writings grew in the United States after 1966, the year she shared the Nobel Prize for Literature with S. Y. Agnon. Sachs's poetry has been extensively analyzed, with many critics drawing parallels between Sachs and authors including Franz Kafka and Paul Celan. As a body of work, her writings are considered among the most important interpretive reactions to the Holocaust. A number of critics have remarked that in her poetry Sachs succeeded in "describing the indescribable," although others maintain that the attempt should never be made—that creative works which take the events of the Holocaust as their subject invariably do a disservice to the victims. Rather than criticize her undertaking of the task, however, most critics applaud Sachs's stated purpose: "I will not stop following step by step the path of fire and flame and star of our people and I will bear witness with my poor being."

PRINCIPAL WORKS

In den Wohnungen des Todes (poetry) 1946
Sterverdunkelung (poetry) 1949
Eli: Ein Mysterienspiel vom Leiden Israels (play) 1951
Und niemand weiss weiter (poetry) 1957
Flucht und Verwandlung (poetry) 1959
Fahrt ins Staublose: Die Gedichte der Nelly Sachs (poetry) 1961
Ausgewählte Gedichte (poetry) 1963
Glühende Rätsel (poetry) 1964
O the Chimneys: Selected Poems, Including the Verse Play, Eli (poetry) 1967
The Seeker and Other Poems (poetry) 1970
Teile dich Nacht (poetry) 1971

CRITICISM

Gertrude Schwebell (essay date 10 December 1966)

SOURCE: "Nelly Sachs," in *Saturday Review,* Vol. XLIX, December 10, 1966, pp. 46-7.

[*Schwebell is an author and translator. In the following essay, she traces Sachs' poetry career from its beginnings in Sweden, noting the gradual growth of her popularity in Sweden and Germany and its culmination in the Nobel Prize for Literature.*]

"Let us walk together into the future to seek again and again a new beginning; let us try to find the good dream that wants be realized in our hearts." This is Nelly Sachs, who just received the Nobel Prize for Literature.

Born in 1891, the only child of a well-to-do manufacturer, she grew up in the Tiergartenviertel, the most distinguished neighborhood of Berlin. She studied music and dancing and, at the age of seventeen, started to write poetry—pretty, highly polished verse in the traditional manner. In accordance with her wish, this poetry was not included in her collected work.

With the Nazi rise to power, Nelly Sachs's world collapsed, but she stayed on in Berlin until 1940, when she and her ailing mother were taken to Sweden, where, acting on the request of Selma Lagerlöf, Prince Eugene of Sweden had interceded on her behalf. They arrived in Stockholm, shaken and afraid, for Selma Lagerlöf had died. However, a friend of the novelist welcomed the fugitives. By then almost fifty years old, Nelly Sachs started to write the sweeping poetry that has now brought her worldwide renown.

She wrote during the night to find herself again, wrote about **"The Houses of Death"** where her friends were perishing, wrote **"Eclipse of Stars," "And No One Knows Where to Go."** She wrote in German: her mother tongue was the only home left. Nevertheless, Nelly Sachs studied Swedish, and soon she was translating Swedish poetry into German, perhaps to find a way into the new world that had received her. Here Miss Sachs's sensitive language penetrates the innermost confines "into the mysterious that blurs all boundaries." Her first anthology of Swedish poetry, **Welle und Granit** ("Wave and Granite"), was published in West Berlin in 1947; **Aber auch diese Sonne ist heimatlos** ("But Even This Sun Has No Home") followed in 1957. Such books brought well-deserved recognition to Swedish poets: Gunnar Ekelöf, Johannes Edfelt, Karl Vennberg, Erik Lindgren, to name only a few. In 1958 Miss Sachs received the Prize of the Swedish Poets' Association.

Neither the first collection of her own verse, *In the Houses of Death* (*In den Wohnungen des Todes*), printed in West Berlin in 1946, nor her second volume, *Eclipse of Stars* (*Sternverdunkelung*), printed in Amsterdam in 1949, received much attention since there was no communication within Germany in those years. Life was but a bleak struggle for survival. In 1950, Swedish friends had published 200 copies of her *Eli: A Miracle Play of the Sufferings of Israel* in a private edition. A copy found its way to West Germany, where it was read over the radio station Süddeutscher Rundfunk in the same year. Later *Eli* was turned into a radio play and became widely known in West Germany.

Nelly Sachs's next two books, *Und Niemand weiß weiter* ("And No One Knows Where to Go"), published in 1957, and *Flucht und Verwandlung,* ("Flight and Metamorphosis"), which came out two years later, brought her deserved acclaim as a lyric poet. Rainer Gruenter writes in a review in *Neue Deutsche Hefte,* "Her poetic voice descends from Luther down to Trakl, yet is entirely the speech of today. There also is a sisterly echo of the Lamentations of Jeremiah. . . . Miss Sachs does not have the attitude of Job, who in his misery ascertains the Lord's love in testing him, nor does she feel the security in God that the Prophets have, which rests on their knowing about good and evil, about guilt and punishment. . . ."

Hugo von Hoffmannsthal said that suffering is the only business we shy away from, but suffering is our lot. Nelly Sachs accepts in her poetry the suffering of creatures for nothing but suffering's sake, a conception which raises her beyond conventional morality—with good and evil for touchstones—into the realm of a cosmic trust. "Man," she wrote in *Nightwatch,* "will always become guilty. Wherefore? Therefore. This is his tragedy on earth. This most terrible question, one of the essential questions of mankind, permeates the whole: why is evil necessary to create the saint, the martyr? No one will ever be able to answer this—Mars and the Moon would rather give up their secrets before this eternal sigh of mankind will find an answer." Miss Sachs is not speaking of revenge and of the wrath of the angry God, nor is she using the word forgiveness. She does not feel that she has to forgive the horrors of our apocalyptic times, but she accepts the forces of evil that live on forever in our bipolar world. This is her greatness.

The arc of Nelly Sachs's poetry reaches from **"The Houses of Death"** over **"Metamorphosis"** to the **"Journey Into the Beyond"** (*Fahrt ins Staublose*), the title she gave to her collected poetry. ". . . Strictly speaking, she has been writing one book," says H. M. Enzensberger in his introduction to *Ausgewählte Gedichte* (**"Selected Poems"**). "This priority of the whole over the detail is not just a formal feature, it is not just implied in the composition, as a cyclic or an epic structure: its roots are deeper. The idea on which her work is based is of religious origin." Her bond with the fate of the

Jewish people, with their and with Germany's literary tradition is the source of her work, a psalmodic lyric in free rhythm, austere and rich in metaphors.

In a time when lyrics are not meant to have moving qualities, the stirring poetry of Nelly Sachs has great impact. It is not easy reading; one must have patience and the will to enter into her poems. But they are not written in a code, calculated or estranged. Her metaphors come naturally: "Butterflies / over the burning bush / feeling the weight of life / and death / on their wings." At times she uses simple sentences, shimmering with transparency: "How light / the earth will be / only a cloud / of evening-love." "Someone / will come / who will take the ball / from the hands of the terrible players. . . ." "Where ever man is / under the sun / the shadow lily guilt / is cast upon the sand." "We, who were saved / —Death was ready to cut his flutes from our hollow bones / Death was ready to use as chords our sinews / —our bodies are still aching / with their mutilated music." But in spite of anguish and dread she finds words like these: "We, the mothers / who guard in the cradles / light memories / of the Day of Creation— / The rhythm of breath / is our love song's melody. / We, the mothers / are rocking the heart of the world: / the melody of Peace."

Great and powerful is her gesture of a new beginning. Nelly Sachs has risen beyond our time, and her lyrics cross the boundaries of one people and one time and one language. This has enabled the youth of Germany to receive the poet as their own. "The young Germans are coming to me in Stockholm," she told Erika Guetermann during an interview in 1960. "Young people, the young poets; they say: You are speaking our language. I received marvelous letters! Paul Celan, Max Frisch, Ingeborg Bachmann, Hermann Kasack— they all held me in their arms. All the dear people. It was like a dream. I do not know how I ever shall be able to earn this. This youth—that they want me! It was almost a shock. I live quite secluded in Sweden. . . . Certainly, I have a small circle of friends, and young Swedish poets used to visit me. But I had no access to modern German poetry. I was so completely by myself. . . ."

In contrast to the language in her poems, that in Nelly Sachs's *Szenische Dichtungen* (scenic poetry, as she calls her plays) initially had the simplicity of the medieval miracle plays of the Christian church, especially the first three: *Eli, Abram in the Salt,* and *Nightwatch,* written between 1940 and '44. Ten years later she wrote eleven more of these plays, some of them very short sketches. Her language now is more complicated, fraught with ambiance—but her attitude towards suffering and sufferance never changes. Especially remarkable are *Simon Plunges Through Thousands of Years: A Dramatic Happening in Fourteen Scenes* (1955) and *Beryll Gazes Into the Night, or the Lost and Refound Alphabet* (1961). In the appendix to the latter she writes, "The German mystic, Jakob Böhme (1575-1624) said: 'Nothing is the search for Something.' He knows about the inexhaustibility of the creative forces. So does the magnificent Sohar, the book of Hebrew mysticism. . . . I have always endeavored to raise the unspeakable onto the transcendental level to make it bearable thus, and to let a glow of the holy darkness fall into this night of nights."

In a time when lyrics are not meant to have moving qualities, the stirring poetry of Nelly Sachs has great impact. It is not easy reading; one must have patience and the will to enter into her poems. But they are not written in a code, calculated or estranged. Her metaphors come naturally.

—Gertrude Schwebell

In a discussion of her scenic poetry with Erika Guetermann Nelly Sachs explained: "I tried to say in a dramatic form what cannot be expressed in lyrics. . . . I was a dancer, once. I try to let the world develop into movement and back into the new word, as in the choruses of the dramatic poetry of antiquity."

During the excavations at Ur in Chaldea the archeologists found impressions in the earth left by objects that had completely turned to dust. In *Abram in the Salt* Miss Sachs tries to bring back to life this handwriting of that which has become invisible. The scene takes place in post-Flood time in Ur, where the cult of Zin, God of the Moon, demands human sacrifice. Abram, the fifteen-year-old, returns from the cave of the dead—the first human being to long for an invisible god. "Longing born of thirst" might be the topic of this play. In her stage directions she says, "The stage-design should always seem to be far away, only outlines like the hunting scenes in the caves of the Ice Age. The salt landscape should be abstract—a skeleton in white—the left-over after the Flood (and in the salt originates the thirst of mankind). The choruses of the thirsty, the mothers, the possessed shall accompany the scenes like Greek choruses. There is also a touch of the Japanese Noh play in the musical themes; these themes come from far away, as from the faraway past."

When Nelly Sachs received the Nobel Prize in Literature she was virtually unknown beyond Germany and Sweden. Nevertheless, her poetry had received a number of previous awards. The first was the West German *Kulturkreis,* given by German industry, in 1959; then came the *Annette von Droste Hülshoff Preis* in 1960, when for the first time she returned to Germany; she was the initial recipient of the *Nelly Sachs Preis* established in her honor by the city of Dortmund in 1961. On the occasion of Miss Sachs's seventieth birthday

the publishing house Suhrkamp Verlag brought out her collected work—*Fahrt ins Staublose,* her poetry, and *Zeichen im Sand,* her plays, as well as *Nelly Sachs zu Ehren,* a volume of poetry, articles, and memories about her by such writers as Ilse Aichinger, Beda Allemann, Ingeborg Bachmann, Paul Celan, Hilde Domin, Günter Eich, Hans Magnus Enzensberger, and others. In 1964 Miss Sachs received the prize of the Börsenverein; in 1965, the *Friedenspreis des Deutschen Buchhandels.* When she received the peace prize at the Paulskirche in Frankfurt in October 1965, Nelly Sachs addressed her acceptance especially to the young German generation: "In spite of all the horrors of the past, I believe in you. . . . Together, full of grief, let us remember the victims, and then let us walk together into the future to seek again and again a new beginning—maybe far away, yet ever-present; let us try to find the good dream that wants to be realized in our hearts."

Paul Konrad Kurz (essay date 1967)

SOURCE: "Journey into Dustlessness: The Lyrics of Nelly Sachs," in his *On Modern German Literature,* University of Alabama Press, 1967, pp. 194-215.

[*In the following essay, Kurz presents a deep analysis of Sachs's poetry, concentrating on her use of biblical imagery and of symbols including the butterfly.*]

Klaus Nonnenmann does not even mention Nelly Sachs in his *Schriftsteller der Gegenwart* ("Present-Day Writers"). The *Kleines Lexikon der Weltliteratur* ("Small Lexicon of World Literature") allots her only a third as much space as has been allotted the biography of Ingeborg Bachmann. Michael Landmann, a Berlin professor of philosophy closely connected with the ivory tower of Stefan George's former circle of disciples [the *Georgekreis*], complained in 1963: "Even today, fashionable abuse allows poems to be written—not certainly for the sake of musicality, but rather from extreme aversion to what can be rationally comprehended—which, like those of Nelly Sachs or Perse, either say disturbingly little—are little more than emoted printer's ink—or else remain so inaccessible to even the most genuine attempt to understand them, that one longs for a return to banal clarity." Hans Magnus Enzensberger, who trumpeted his *Landessprache* ("Vernacular") angrily across the land, knew her as early as 1961, when he wrote: "In the center of Stockholm . . . between the neat Paalsundpark and the little grocery stores opposite, the visitor could, if he were so minded, meet at certain hours of the afternoon a dainty, friendly, shy, elderly woman: the greatest poetess who is writing in German today." And he continues, "Don't utter it, that superlative! Go past, stranger! For the little dwelling . . . is a refuge, the sanctuary of a woman who has been persecuted." There, in this little dwelling, Rolf Italiaander visited her in the first of his postwar visits. He reports: "Nelly Sachs' kitchen was her bedroom, living room, and workroom, as well as her reception room for visitors. In the other room, her old mother lay in great pain. When I arrived, Nelly Sachs took off her kitchen apron. I was surprised to see how small and frail she was. I found her manner typically Berlinish. I . . . was enchanted by her cordial simplicity. Even as she was pushing the peeled potatoes to one side, we began to talk about literature."

Nelly Sachs has been called "Kafka's sister." But her experience and linguistic expression are structurally different from Kafka's. For her, darkness does, indeed, hold a painful meaning, but it is one that illumines existence. Grief can be transformed. The way of flight stands open, not from here to there, but from here upwards, from immanence to transcendence. For her, God has not disintegrated, as He had for the merchant's son Kafka; for her He is ever present as He was for the elect of the Old Covenant. With more justice, she has been called "a sister of Job." She is, indeed, a sister of Job, separated from him by two and a half millennia, but not by any difference in the intensity of her experience of suffering, in her enduring of earthly losses, in gnawing doubt, in attachment to Yahweh-God, in searching for God in grief and finding Him in hope. Not by accident is the exemplary figure of the suffering and believing people of Israel the main theme of Nelly Sachs' poetry.

Job

O thou weathervane of suffering!
Lashed by primeval tempests
into this storm's course and that;
even thy South is called loneliness.
Where thou standest is the navel of pain.

Thine eyes are sunk deep into thy head
like cave doves in a night
that the hunter brings out blindly.
Thy voice has become silent
for it has too often queried *why*.

Thy voice has gone to rest among the worms and fish.
Job, thou hast wept through all the watches of the night.
But there will come a time when constellations of thy blood
will cause all rising suns to pale.

Suffering comes from every direction of the wind to surround the sufferer. There is no possibility of avoiding it in time or space. Wherever he stands, there "is the navel of pain." Escape is impossible—but not transformation. In *Glühende Rätsel* ("Glowing Riddles") the last cycle of her poems thus far published, the poetess dared to write: "Thine anxiety has issued into the light."

Nelly Sachs was born in Berlin on December 10, 1891, the only child of a Jewish manufacturer, William Sachs. She grew up in a villa in the Zoo Section, in a cosmopolitan atmosphere. She was taught by private tutors. As a girl, she enjoyed her father's musical efforts. In his library, she found books on German Romanticism, which fascinated her. She herself soon began to play an instrument, to dance, and to write. At the age of fifteen, she read Selma Lagerlöf. Later, she dedicated her own first work, *Legenden und Erzählungen* ("Legends and Tales"), to the Swedish authoress. In the 1920s, Stefan Zweig became her first literary mentor. Her first poems appeared in 1929 in the *Vossische Zeitung.* In 1932, Leo Hirsch printed the verses of the still unknown poetess in the *Berliner Tageblatt.* Her works were printed even in the formerly well-known Munich journal, *Jugend.* Soon, however, only *Der Morgen,* journal of the Jewish cultural group, was open to her. She could no longer publish in Aryan Germany. After 1938-1939, when the extermination of the Jews was rigorously pursued, her life was in danger. In the summer of 1939, in response to the pleading of a friend, Selma Lagerlöf in conjunction with the Swedish royal house, intervened on behalf of Nelly Sachs and her mother. In June 1940, they fled by plane from Berlin to Stockholm. In the meantime, Selma Lagerlöf had died. It seemed a miracle to Nelly Sachs that her rescue had been so successful. Her relatives were being put to death in the concentration camps of the Third Reich. With all the ardor of her thinking and loving soul, she suffered the murder of those dear to her and the systematic extermination of her people in the gas chambers.

From this suffering there arose, after 1940, her verses *In den Wohnungen des Todes* ("In the Dwellings of Death"). They appeared first in 1947 in the Aufbau-Verlag in East Berlin. The cycles in the volume *Sternverdunkelung* ("Eclipse of the Stars") were written from 1944 on. She meditated on the figures of the Old Testament and inquired unceasingly into the meaning of life and death in this world. In 1949, the poetess was able to have her verses published by the Bermann-Fischer Publishing Company, which was then located in Amsterdam. The greater part of this printing had to be destroyed. No one knew her or wanted to buy her poems. No literary journal presented her to the public. Her next volume, *Und niemand weiß weiter* ("And No One Knows Anything More") contains elegies on the death of her mother and further Biblical reflections. The Hamburg publisher Heinrich Ellermann printed this collection in 1957. Two years later, the Deutsche Verlags-Anstalt in Stuttgart published her new cycle, *Flucht und Verwandlung* ("Flight and Metamorphosis"). The later cycles, *Fahrt ins Staublose* ("Journey into Dustlessness") and *Noch feiert der Tod das Leben* ("Death Is Still Celebrating Life"), as well as the earlier poems, appeared in the Suhrkamp Verlag in Frankfurt in 1961. The collected edition of her poems bears the title *Fahrt ins Staublose.* A selection, to which has been added the first part of the cycle *Glühende Rätsel* from the year 1962, was brought out in a Suhrkamp edition in 1963. It offers a kind of lyrical summary of her work. Parts 2 and 3 of *Glühende Rätsel*—her last publication to date—appeared in *Späte Gedichte* ("Late Poems").

> **Nelly Sachs has been called "Kafka's sister." But her experiences and linguistic expression are structurally different from Kafka's.**
>
> —*Paul Konrad Kurz*

Nelly Sachs also wrote dramatic scenes. *Eli,* a mystery play about the sufferings of Israel, became well known. Eli is an eight-year-old shepherd boy in a small Jewish city in Poland that was destroyed during the last war. German soldiers drag his parents from their beds. In his nightshirt, Eli runs after them, raises his shepherd's flute, and with it calls God to their assistance. One of the soldiers fears that it is a signal and strikes the boy dead with the butt of his rifle. Samuel, the old grandfather, who had also run after them, is struck dumb with fear. Later, the soldier suffers and dies from pangs of conscience.

As a sign of gratitude to her host-land, Sweden, Nelly Sachs translated modern Swedish lyrics into German. For this work, she received her first public honor, the Literature Prize of the Association of Swedish Lyricists. There followed in 1959 a presentation from the Cultural Committee of the Federal Association of German Industry. A year later, she accepted the Droste-Prize in Meersburg. In her speech of acceptance, she pleaded: "My brothers and sisters, bestow on me more of this courage with which you help me today to overcome my weakness. I have nothing to forgive: I am a human being, like all the rest." Had they read her poetry? Or did they want to make "restitution"? In 1961, she was honored again, this time with the Literature Prize of the city of Dortsmund. The last token of esteem from Germany came to her in the Paulskirche in Frankfurt on October 17, 1965 when the Peace Prize of the German Book Trade was bestowed upon her. A disinterested observer noticed that, as the cameras flashed, the prizewinner assumed no pose. Where speakers were eloquent, she was silent. Heroes and stars, even writer-stars, are corruptible. But hymns of praise could not corrupt Nelly Sachs. The show, the bustle, the fawning publicity had no effect on her. What unadorned sincerity, what a sign, what a consolation in this world! She had chosen suffering as her lot. Her work is "inconceivable without the additional notion of substitution. . . . Out of her mouth speaks more than just herself." On October 20, 1966, Nelly Sachs, together with the Jewish novelist Samuel J. Agnon, was awarded the Nobel Prize for literature.

After the war, Theodor W. Adorno, a man who had himself experienced exile, expressed a thought that has subsequently often been quoted: Since Auschwitz, it is impossible to write a poem. Nelly Sachs has written poems not only since Auschwitz but even about it. She proves Adorno right in that she has been unable to produce specimens of the post-Romantic or of the Expressionist "Clang-and-Bang" tradition. But she disproves the philosopher's contention by her own concentrated, prophetically astringent, religious tone, which has been purified by her encounter with death and is radically suited to an age of horror.

In the Dwellings of Death is the title she gave the four verse-cycles in which she meditated on, prayed over, and conjured up the incomprehensible occurrences in the concentration camps. They are dedicated "To my Dead Brothers and Sisters." The first part pertains to the Jewish people as a whole; the second contains the **"Gebete für den toten Bräutigam"** ("Prayers for a Dead Bridegroom"); the third, a series of **"Grabschriften in die Luft geschrieben"** ("Epitaphs Written into the Air"); the fourth, **"Chöre nach Mitternacht"** ("Choruses After Midnight"). Several of the poems have epigraphs from the Bible, Hasidism, and the Cabala. The speaker belongs to the tradition of the believer, of the devout Jew.

The epigraph of the first poem—it supplied the title of the first volume—is taken from the Book of Job, where the context implies an "invocation of the Muse," but not the Muse of antiquity, nor a new mythic Muse, nor even a Muse of Job's own making. In his fifth reply, Job pleads with his accusers and friends for pity, wishes that his words might be written down, inscribed on rock, because they confess his experience, document his belief in the counsel of Yahweh, and reveal his endurance of the incomprehensible, his reaching out to the Savior-God. The poetess—Gottfried Benn would have said "the lyrical I"—chose the central verse as a pertinent motto, an epigraph. It reads: "Even after my skin is flayed, without my flesh I shall see God" (Job 19:26). The title poem reads as follows:

> *O the chimneys*
> On the ingeniously conceived dwellings of death,
> When Israel's body released in smoke went forth
> Through the air—
> A star, like a chimney sweep, received him
> And became black
> Or was it a sunbeam?
>
> O the chimneys!
> Paths to freedom for Jeremiah and the dust of
> Job—
> Who conceived and built you stone on stone
> The path for fugitives from smoke?
>
> O the dwellings of death,

Invitingly constructed
For the master of the house who formerly was
guest—
O you fingers,
Laying the threshold at the entrance
Like a knife between life and death—

O you chimneys,
O you fingers,
And Israel's body in smoke through the air!

The situation presented here is the murder of the Jews and their cremation in the extermination camps of the Third Reich. The verses are a lament for the dead. The anonymous killing and dying seek a memorial—a direction with meaning. The murder is done to "Israel's body." It is the Jewish people in its visible, earthly form, regarded from the standpoint of religion, not of race. The occurrence is not so much described as invoked, evoked, and expounded. Its brutal and monstrous shape is subsumed by invocation, evocation, and suggestive query into the person who commemorates it.

In the "dwellings of death," the descendants of Israel were put to death. Through the chimneys of the cremation ovens, they were pursued into the air. What irony in the word "dwellings." These are dwellings, not to dwell and live in, but to be killed in. And what perversion of thought, what reversal of meaning, that these dwellings, these murder-factories, are "ingeniously conceived." The cosmos grieves. The "star" that shone "like a chimney sweep" down the chimneys of the cremation factories was "black"—black from soot, black from smoke, black from grief. "Or was it a sunbeam?" queries the last line of the strophe—participation has been added from the direction of the supernatural. Star and sunbeam are lament, lamenter, and consoler in one. The murderers wanted literally to pursue "Israel's body" into the air and destroy it. But "Israel's body released in smoke went forth / *Through* the air," through the beyond. Whither? Into what dwellings? Into cosmic, supernatural realms. "Star" and "sunbeam" did more than turn black, did more than endure the situation passively. They, too, inaugurated an action: against banishment, reception; against annihilation, rescue. They "received" Israel's body. A higher, lighter irony answers the wicked irony of the "ingeniously conceived dwellings." It surpasses the wickedness but is unable—and therein lies, for man, the incomprehensible darkness—to hinder the earthly course of annihilation. The supernatural realms receive only what is left, what is immortal.

One who ponders in faith recognizes (strophe 2) the chimneys of death as "paths to freedom for Jeremiah and the dust of Job." "Dust" belongs to the basic vocabulary of the poetess. It defines one pole of human existence. The definition is rooted in the Biblical formula of experience: Dust thou art and unto dust thou shalt return (Genesis 3:19). But the lyrical

work of Nelly Sachs continues the Biblical sentence in a manner that is Biblical: and thou shalt return *through* dust. The dust is at the same time the "ashes of resurrection"—and as such the point of departure for the last metamorphosis. From this perspective, the experience of dust ("Disinherited, we bemoan the dust," *Späte Gedichte*) and the becoming dust, in whatever forms, become stations on what the later lyrics have called the ***Journey into Dustlessness.*** All this has not been said expressly in the poem, but it has been intimated. The poem inquires expressly into the identity of the one who conceived and built the chimneys that became, though their innovator had not intended it, "paths to freedom." "Who conceived and built you stone on stone / The path for fugitives from smoke?" As opposed to him who conceived and built the "chimneys," the poem recognizes him who conceived and built the "paths to freedom"; as opposed to the dispositions below, it recognizes in wonder the dispositions from above. The paths to annihilation built by murderers are at the same time "paths to freedom"; the paths to freedom are "paths for fugitives"; the paths of flight—so says the later work—are paths of "metamorphosis." There is no express answer here to the query as to who conceived and built the paths of freedom. It has already been given in the context. It is the God "of Israel," the God of Jeremiah and of Job. It had also been expressly stated in the epigraph: "Even after my skin is flayed, without my flesh I shall see God."

In sharp contrast to the interpretation of death as victorious escape for the slain, the third strophe speaks insistently of the remembrance of what has happened and of lamentation. What language, what pathos would be adequate to portray this death? The primeval movement of lament cries out: "O the dwellings of death." In a combination of euphemistic understatement and irony, the simple lament is commented upon in a verse heavy with antithetical tension: "Invitingly constructed / For the master of the house who formerly was guest." This master is death. The use of the present participle *einladend* (here translated in its adverbial form, *invitingly*) makes the event more graphic. And just as the first strophe apostrophizes the ingenious thought of the manufacturers of death, so now the perpetrators are represented in shuddering memory by their "fingers" (*pars pro toto*). "O you fingers / Laying the threshold at the entrance / Like a knife between life and death." That such a thing existed can be proclaimed only with lamentation, only in a form that is at once as simple and as intensive as possible.

The last strophe is a summary. It conjures up the whole poem with the utmost brevity and condensation: one verse each for the place, the perpetrators, the dead; report and reflection, lamentation and consolation combined:

O you chimneys,
O you fingers,
And Israel's body in smoke through the air!

Here is utmost economy of words, a great poem, a unique statement.

In quite a different way, Paul Celan, in his famous "Todesfuge" ("Fugue of Death"), has made the same occurrence the object of a poem. As a "Fugue," his poem is not only more artistically constructed; it is also linguistically richer. Instead of the primitively simple, faltering tone of lament in Nelly Sachs' poem, Celan has employed a swifter, lighter, almost dancing rhythm and a magically whirling tone. He makes no attempt to interpret the occurrence. In long, artistically constructed lines, he offers a visionary presentation unsurpassed for power of imagery and suggestion. But there is no search for meaning, no ascent to religious transcendence. Celan's poem is tremendously beautiful; Nelly Sachs' verses are reflective, prophetical, and simple.

The cycle **"Dein Leib im Rauch durch die Luft"** ("Thy Body in Smoke Through the Air"), whose title poem has just been interpreted, was followed by the **"Gebete für den toten Bräutigam"** ("Prayers for a Dead Bridegroom"). These are at once love poems and prayers. The all-pervasive pain of separation at the threshold of death, the address to the absent one, the speaking to God and to creatures about the beloved dead, this directness of address and compact consciousness, this unity between the experience of suffering and the contemplation that penetrates its meaning—all this is unique as well as completely personal, religious, and cosmic in tone. One might say that no one else since Dante has achieved such intensity, purity, or transcendent power of longing. Like "dust," "longing" is one of the words most frequently used by the poetess. If "dust" defines man in the existence that has been predetermined for him, "longing" defines him in his character as wayfarer and in his freedom to transcend it.

> *But perhaps* God needs longing,
> or where else would she be found,
> She who with kisses and tears and sighs
> fills the mysterious spaces of the air—
> Perhaps it is the invisible kingdom of earth
> from which the glowing roots of stars emerge—
> And the radiant voice over the fields of separation
> that summons to reunion?
> O my beloved, perhaps our love
> has already borne worlds in the heaven of long-
> ing—
> As our breathing in—and out
> builds a cradle for life and death?
> Grains of sand, we two, dark from parting
> and lost in the golden secret of births,
> And perhaps already lighted round about
> by future stars and moons and suns.

The words seem conventional; any one of them might have been written two generations earlier. Whence comes, then, their undeniable power to convince? From the purity, the interiority, the spiritualization of love and pain, from the mystic consciousness of the omnipresence of the beloved and of cosmic and personal union.

The "Prayers for a Dead Bridegroom" were followed by **"Grabschriften in die Luft geschrieben"** ("Epitaphs Written in the Air"). They are epitaphs for the individual acquaintances designated in the headings by professional title or initials. The memorial words are written in the air because these people have no grave and no gravestone. They all belong to "Israel's body released in smoke . . . through the air."

The last cycle in the volume *In den Wohnungen des Todes* is formed by the **"Chöre nach Mitternacht"** ("**Choruses After Midnight**"): a "**Chorus of Things Left Behind**"; a "**Chorus of the Saved**"; a "**Chorus of Wanderers**"; a "**Chorus of Orphans**"; a "**Chorus of the Dead**" and a "**Chorus of Shades**"; a "**Chorus of Stones**" and a "**Chorus of Stars**"; a "**Chorus of Clouds**" and a "**Chorus of Trees**"; a "**Chorus of Invisible Things**"; and a "**Chorus of the Unborn.**" All the choruses reflect a real world and time: the cosmic, historical, interpreted, present time of the world. It is the "time after midnight," after the great murder, after the war; the time when a new day is dawning. It is not improbable that the midnight of Jeremiah is concealed in the midnight-cipher of the poetess. In Jeremiah, the "energy of chaos and creation [bears] its own name. This is midnight. Midnight is primarily a place: the region of the North where darkness and night reign. All harmful powers are concentrated around midnight. When the portals of midnight are opened, evil wins free course. It is impossible to predict the physiognomy of evil—neither its degree nor the duration of its harmfulness can be known in advance. But midnight is also the exciting hour into which—with Jeremiah—all men are plunged. Jeremiah saw the portals of midnight open." In Nelly Sachs' works, midnight is also the time of inner confidence, as witness the later verses: "und nach Mitternach / reden nur Geschwister" ("After midnight, only brothers and sisters speak"). The **"Chorus of the Saved"** pleads: "Lasst uns das Leben leise wieder lernen" ("Let us learn life gently once again"). The "dead of Israel" speak: "Wir reichen schon einen Stern weiter / In unseren verborgenen Gott hinein" ("We have progressed one star farther / Into our hidden God"). The "unseen things" console the "separated loved ones" and rise up, conscious of their strength, against the **"Klagemauer Nacht"** ("Wailing Wall, Night"):

> *Wailing wall,* night,
> Thou canst be shattered by the lightning of a prayer
> And all who have missed God in sleep
> Awaken unto Him behind
> Thy falling walls.

Lastly, there speaks the "voice of the holy land" (does not this name spring from the Christian domain?). She speaks: "O meine Kinder / Der Tod ist durch eure Herzen gefahren / Wie durch einen Weinberg—" ("O my children, / Death rode through your hearts / As through a vineyard—]. She queries further: "Wo soll die kleine Heiligkeit hin / Die noch in meinem Sande wohnt?" ("Whither the little holiness / That still dwells in my sand?") And she answers admonishingly: In forgiveness.

> Lay upon the plowed fields your weapons of
> revenge
> That they may become gentle—
> For even iron and grain are brother and sister
> In the bosom of the earth—

Who could utter these words today and be believed? A Christian? What Christian? But the Jewess Nelly Sachs can and does. In the poem **"Auf dass die Verfolgten nicht die Verfolger werden"** ("That the Persecuted May Not Become the Persecutors"), she admonishes her brothers and sisters to renounce the spirit of revenge.

According to all current theories about the lyric, from Benn to Brecht and from Höllerer to Heissenbüttel, this kind of speech is old-fashioned; themes of Biblical import are not admissible. At least, they never occur to the programmatic mind of the programmatic poet. They have all defined knowledge and wisdom after their own fashion. They omit the greater reality. They seem to know nothing of mystic community.

The very first poem in the ***Wohnungen des Todes*** mentioned the key word "flight." The fact that those exiled to the gas chambers are received supernaturally, that the most radical restraint upon them is recognized as a possibility of utmost freedom, points to a metamorphosis. The cycle **Glühende Rätsel** is still concerned with the puzzle of her own existence as flight and metamorphosis. Flight and metamorphosis are themes in all of Nelly Sachs' poems. The cycle published in 1959 bears this title. It is concerned with the same radical, inescapable, and indestructible existence which, in a later formulation, was called **"Fahrt ins Staublose."** Man's life begins in the birth of dust. It ends in dustlessness. Between lies the journey, with its many stations of farewells, of death, of metamorphoses, of gradual, often violent, birth. Man, "dark from parting," but "lost in the golden secret of births"; man "exploding," charged with the "stuff of longing", is always "the ashes of resurrection":

> Upward from daily destructions
> his prayers have winged their way
> seeking the eyes' inner thoroughfares.
>
> Craters and dry seas

> filled with tears
> traveling through the starry stations
> on the journey into dustlessness.

The "journey into dustlessness" is a flight from and a flight toward something: a flight from the "dwellings of death" in this world, with their "breath of Sodom" and their "burden of Nineveh"; a flight from the world that has slain the "bridegroom" and affords no "homeland" ("Heimat,"); a flight from this world that is nourished on the "shrub of despair." But whither? In the very concretely recognizable, personal "refugee" situation on the "pavement of a strange city," where the show windows present their "picture-book heaven," the "survivors" (***Überlebende,*** title of one cycle) protest: "World, do not ask those who have been snatched from death / whither they are going, / they are always going to their grave." In the cycle *Von Flüchtlingen und Flucht* "[On Fugitives and Flight)", this experience is portrayed: "That is the flight that draws fugitives with it / into epilepsy, into death!" The lyrical "I" of these verses knows that it is "fleeing the land / with the heavy baggage of love." Fleeing the land to go where? Into the other world, into the world of the bridegroom and of God, for it is one world. "Always on your luminous trail," i.e., the trail of the dead bridegroom. In accordance with strict Israelite reverence before the absolute spirituality and infinity of the totally Other, God is not addressed as "Thou" in these verses. He is the God of "creation,", of "births," of the "source," of "what is hidden," of "resurrection," of "salvation." Despite the teleological role of His world, the "trails" to it and to Him are again and again "darkened in epilepsy." In June 1961, the poetess confessed in a letter: "The poems that I write from time to time—in the beginning it was done to be able to breathe—are now tumbling as though epileptic to their end." The intensity of the ecstatic flight compels the fugitive at times almost into madness.

> Flight from the black-bloodied constellation
> of farewell,
> Flight into the lightning-tapestried
> inns of insanity.
>
> Flight, flight, flight
> into the coup-de-grâce of flight
> from the ruptured arteries
> of a brief stopping place.

Since the days of "Abraham," Israel's fate has been flight. Nelly Sachs' personal flight has its place within the larger exodus of her people. But even this larger exodus of her people must be understood as encompassing more than just the one most obvious and visible exodus in a movement of flight that is actually cosmic. For Nelly Sachs, the whole world is proceeding endlessly toward the start of flight and its goal. The whole universe is putting on a new condition, a new birth.

Whither o whither
thou universe of longing
who, even in the caterpillar bewitched yet dimly
surmised,
unfurl thy wings,
and with the fishes' fins
incessantly describe thy origin
in depths of water that
a single heart
can measure with the plummet
of grief.
Whither o whither
thou universe of longing
with the lost kingdoms of dreams
and the ruptured arteries of the body;
as the curled soul awaits
its new birth
under the ice of the death mask.

The poem seems to be a parallel to the eighth chapter of the Epistle to the Romans: "For the eager longing of creation awaits the revelation of the sons of God," St. Paul says. "For creation was made subject to vanity . . . in hope, because creation itself also will be delivered from its slavery to corruption into the freedom of the glory of the sons of God . . . And not only it, but we ourselves . . . groan within ourselves, waiting for the adoption as sons, the redemption of our bodies" (Rom. 8:19-21; 23 passim).

In the poem **"Wohin,"** the poetess develops for the first time her great image of the transformation of the caterpillar into the butterfly. It is one of the central images in the mysticism of both Orient and Occident and is even found in a secular form in Goethe's poem "Selige Sehnsucht" ("Blessed Longing") in the *West-Östlicher Divan.* For the "flight and metamorphosis" that she had both experienced and understood in faith, Nelly Sachs found an objective correlative in the image of the butterfly. The caterpillar has many metamorphoses before it; the butterfly has already experienced them: from caterpillar to chrysalis to flying lepidopteron—each one a process of dying and of being reborn. Nelly Sachs sees—and this is the fruit of her reflections on Hasidism and the Cabala—the "origin" of the butterfly's wings as implicit in the "fishes' fins." For her, fish are creatures that lie farther back in creation, farther below in longing, nearer the beginning. They, too, are objective correlatives, namely of the soul's "consciousness of water."

Repeated reflection reveals in the aspect of the butterfly yet another level of comparison. An otherworldly splendor has been painted onto the dust of its wings. The image of metamorphosis becomes an image of promise and transcendence. Unlike Mörike in his poem "Im Weinberg," Nelly Sachs portrays, even at the outset, a butterfly that is diaphanous, and so allows a glimpse of transcendence. In Mörike's poem, the

lyric "I," sitting in the vineyard, recognizes the butterfly first as a shimmering natural being, as a charming sylph, as an aesthetic encounter. Only as a second step and from without does the lyric observer, who holds the New Testament in his hands, draw any connection between the butterfly and the Word of God—and even then only in the narrowest sense. For Nelly Sachs, the butterfly is, itself, an image of promise.

> *Butterfly*
> *What* beautiful otherworldness
> has been painted on thy dust.
> Through the fiery core of earth,
> through its stony crust
> thou wert passed,
> farewell web in the measure of mortality.
>
> Butterfly
> the good night of all creatures!
> The weights of life and death
> sink down with thy wings
> upon the rose
> that wilts as the light ripens homeward.
>
> What beautiful otherworldness
> has been painted on thy dust.
> that a symbol of royalty
> in the secret of the air.

The butterfly is neither described naturalistically nor regarded in the manner of Goethe or Mörike. From the beginning, its image is viewed from the horizon of that transcendental knowledge that comes from faith, its symbolical character is recognized, and it is depicted in precisely this referential character. This kind of writing existed in the Middle Ages and in the Age of Baroque. Transcendental faith seeks its symbolical analogue; existence that is but dimly directed to the world beyond seeks its objective correlative. Everything visible must serve faith; the whole representational world must serve the nonrepresentational world. To the degree that a rationalistic and scientific point of view was declared the only legitimate one, such a contemplative attitude was rejected as unscientific. It found its natural sphere among the mystics. In the poem here quoted, the butterfly is understood a priori as the sign of an existence that is subject to change, but whose goal is not of this world, and whose return home is through the portals of death. This attitude does not turn the butterfly into a thin allegory or a formal emblem. On the contrary, presentation from the standpoint of faith intensifies it until it becomes most truly what it is in the plan of creation, a being that points beyond itself.

The poem begins with an exclamation of astonishment: "What beautiful otherworldness has been painted on thy dust." In the dust that the wings have accumulated in flight is concealed all the transitoriness of all dust, the birth of the dust of created beings. But it bears also the traces of immortality, the beauty of the world beyond—in the polar tension between the world beyond and dust. The beautiful flaming structure of the wings passed, as the poem says, "through the fiery core of earth." It springs from the fire that is innermost, strongest; from the creative fire. But then it passes "through [earth's] stony crust," through the limiting and limited confines of earth. The regions from which the butterfly emerges, to which it is bound by its origin, are named. The last line of the first strophe identifies the butterfly itself. What is it then? A "farewell web in the measure of mortality." What a definition! What a metaphor! What a combination of image and concept! Whose "farewell web" is meant? In the first place, of course, that of the butterfly itself. In its own development from caterpillar to chrysalis and from chrysalis to butterfly, the web of wings is the last web to be formed, the farewell garment. As such, the web is, at the same time, a cosmic sign of farewell for the one who beholds it, a *memento mori* in the fullness of its beauty and in the fragility of its design. Therefore, it is "the *good* night of all creatures"; it is not only the sign of night and the night of death, but a promise that both of these will be turned to good. This promise is based on the butterfly's own being, whose process of becoming and dying rises in a single direction, from lower to higher, from the heaviness of the cocoon to the lightness of air. It is, by definition, a being between "life and death." In this role, the weightless "weights" of its wings "sink down . . . upon the rose." The rose is the second correlative, the second sign of the human soul. Even in bloom, it is on its way home; it attains the high point of its existence in the face of encroaching death. Between butterfly and rose there exists, then, an inner relationship. They attract one another mutually, show themselves to one another, and, as the butterfly sinks to rest upon the rose, speak to one another the word of love and of farewell. This is also an image of man and wife, together an intensified sign of "light ripening homeward."

The poem begins with a statement. It ends with a proof. It is astonishment at a higher level, the fruit of meditative reflection, when the poetess repeats at the end: "What beautiful otherworldness has been painted on thy dust." In conclusion, explicit reference is made to the symbolic character of image and event. "What a symbol of royalty in the secret of the air." *Symbol of royalty*—the highest among signs. The poetess uses the metaphor of royalty frequently. She speaks, for instance, of "the fish with the purple gills torn out / a king of sorrows"; of "this chain of riddles / laid around the neck of night / a royal word written far away"; and she knows about the "royal road of secrets." The metaphor of royalty points beyond what is highest and most worthy on earth and into the regions of the divine kingdom of Yahweh, i.e., once more into transcendence. This word, too, is a cipher in the Jewish Cabala. In the poem we have been discussing, the sign of royalty is the butterfly, the rose, the meeting of the two: a "secret" in a double sense. Not everyone heeds the image in its character as a sign.

They see and do not see. But the process remains a "secret" even for those who do see. There is no definitive interpretation for the process of living and dying. The referential function of the image empties into infinity.

The penetrating experience of the "I" that speaks out of all these verses is flight—flight as destiny and freedom, as necessity and grace; flight as both the potentiality and the predestination of life; as "epilepsy" and "pursuit." Compelled to flee, the "I" prays "for the blinking of an eye: / Rest upon the flight." The prayer is heard. The "hearing" is depicted in the following lines:

> *During the flight*
> what a great reception
> on the way—
>
> Wrapped
> in the winding cloth of wind
> feet in the prayer of the sand
> that can never say Amen
> for it muse be transformed
> from fin to wing
> and further—
>
> The sick butterfly
> will soon have knowledge of the sea again—
> This stone
> with the inscription of the fly
> has come into my hand—
>
> In place of a homeland
> I hold the metamorphoses of the world—

The man forced into flight is accorded not only a "brief stopping place," as in an earlier poem, but "a great reception." In what does the reception consist? Who grants it? The reception "during the flight" (an echo of "upon the flight") consists in becoming aware of an image, more specifically, of the poetess's great image of metamorphosis. She recognizes at once its character as a sign, as an objective correlative, as the reflection of her own condition. In the encounter with the image of the butterfly, the "I" experiences rest during the flight, confirmation, direction, hope, and consolation. The butterfly is a "sick butterfly" at rest. It, too, is on its way—on its way to the sea. What is its sickness? We are not told explicitly, only implicitly. It is sick from weariness, from longing, from flight, from the long journey.

"Wrapped / in the winding cloth of wind / feet in the prayer of the sand," it stands, sits, and lies there. "Wrapped in the winding cloth of wind" is an ironic euphemism, for it means not wrapped in the winds, but exposed to them. "But the wind is no home / it only licks, like the animals, / the wounds of the body," we read in the poem **"Jäger, mein Sternbild"** ("Huntsman, my Constellation"). The wind is no house, no covering, no vis-à-vis. And yet it is a kind of place, of covering, of vis-à-vis: a place *sui generis,* i.e., the place in which "flight and metamorphosis" occur, where the barriers of space are removed—a kind of unpredictable "being-spoken-to" from all sides. It indicates her symbolic and cosmic view of the butterfly, her extraordinary awareness of this removal of barriers, as well as of space, person, and transcendence, when the poetess says that the butterfly's "feet [are] in the prayer of the sand." That is, of course, a mystic interpretation. The butterfly is understood as the reflection of the speaking "I." But that does not exclude the possibility that the butterfly achieves, precisely through this recognition by another, its own cosmic individuality. It stands in the sand "that can never say Amen." If we tried to count the grains of sand, we would never come to an end. In this not-coming-to-an-end, the sand is like the endless sea toward which the butterfly is moving. To the objective endlessness of the goal there corresponds the subjective endlessness of the "I's" own condition, of prayer. It is not only the sand "that can never say Amen," it is also (stylistically, this is the figure of enallage, of extension of the basic reference of a word) the butterfly; it is also man "during the flight": "it (the butterfly) must be transformed / from fin to wing / and further." "Fin" and "wing" are formally shortened expressions. We have already seen that, in the imaginative world of the poetess, longing—the necessity of flight and the task of metamorphosis—has its origin in the "fishes' fins." In man, flight and metamorphosis begin "back among the stars in memory / borne on the waters of sleep." The way, "the vein of gold in mortals / sinks under the awareness of water / and works for God." From this state in which it has fins and is aware of water, the creature that is subject to flight and metamorphosis must be transformed into "the cocoon of the silkworm," into "wing / and further." But even the winged state is not a final state. As a winged creature of dust, man must—the "sick butterfly" must—be further transformed until the last metamorphosis of "death" has been completed by the "resurrection" from "the ashes of the resurrection."

At present, the sick butterfly has lost its awareness of the sea and therewith its inner compulsion toward the goal. The loss is part of its sickness. But it "will soon have knowledge of the sea again," of the nearness of what it seeks and the goal of its predestination. Surprisingly, the poem offers a second image of encounter: "This stone / with the inscription of the fly / has come into my hand," says the lyric "I." This is no egotistical grasping for the object seen, but a reverent contemplation, which comprehends the stone as a gift, the gift as a sign. What kind of stone is it? Probably a piece of amber found in the sands on the beach, in which an insect has been embedded. Far from being valued for the sake of adornment, the amber is a sign for faith. Was not the slain Christ entombed in the rock as the insect is in this stone? The stone thus found is an image of death. "Job's four-winds-cry / and the cry hidden in the Garden of Olives / like an insect in crys-

tal overcome by weakness," so reads the poem **"Landschaft aus Schreien"** ("A Landscape of Cries"). As the Christ of Easter, the Christ entombed is the sign of a "resurrection in stone." The stone with the "inscription of the fly" is, for the believing "I" who contemplates it, a sign of its own death and its own resurrection.

Butterfly and stone-enclosed fly are, symbolically, forms of the "metamorphoses of the world." The rest during the flight, the reception, the contemplation, the gift—all consist in this: that they reveal to the lyric "I" both its own inner condition and its own state. The point of departure for the poem was a situation of flight. The two middle strophes showed two images of metamorphosis. On the basis of these strophes, the final one points, on a higher level, to the flight of the "lyric I," a flight transformed by the sign of death and resurrection. The final verses read: "Instead of a homeland / I hold the metamorphoses of the world." Critics have recognized in them the lyrical interpretation of the poetess herself, the sum of her existence incorporated in a poetic formula. It is no accident that not only the word "flight" but also the word "reception" appeared in Nelly Sachs' first poem, "In the dwellings of death." Star and sunbeam received there the "fugitives from smoke." In this poem, the "sick butterfly" and the "fly" in stone receive the fugitive. Unlikely hosts give a "great reception," behind which stands the God of Israel. The "sea" is a sign of Him; the "metamorphoses" are paths to Him. The man who is in flight throughout his existence possesses no home. He cannot cling to anything, cannot rest; he is not rooted in what we generally call a "homeland." What is a "homeland" for other men is for him the "metamorphoses of the world." What poverty! What a presentation of life—an exceedingly challenged and symbolical existence—the most exposed path to the God of creation and of resurrection.

In the twentieth century, destiny has replaced the medieval pilgrim with the refugee. Yet we refuse to recognize his existence. Regarded from its brighter side, flight means "journey." Whatever is found on the journey: fish, butterfly, rose, or loved ones; whoever "comes from the earth" is, in the language of the Bible, "dust"; born in dust, perishable dust, dust of metamorphosis, "dust, that stands open to a blessed encounter." The man who is completely and finally transformed, the resurrected man, will be the "dustless" man—goal of all flight and of all metamorphosis. Surpassing all the definitions of man that have been hurled at us in recent times, Nelly Sachs defines man out of her Biblical faith as one "on the journey into dustlessness." What definition could be more necessary for us? Technical man wants to change; mystical man lets himself be changed.

Robert L. Kahn (essay date 1968)

SOURCE: "Nelly Sachs: A Characterization," in *Dimension,* Vol. 1, No. 2, 1968, pp. 377-81.

[*In the following essay, Kahn explores Sachs's unique place among modern poets.*]

In its treatment of recent poetry literary history likes to employ the term "modern" to emphasize the deep gulf that separates the old and the new trends in the development of the genre. Baudelaire, Rimbaud, Mallarmé, T. S. Eliot, Garcia Lorca are "modern" poets, whereas Goethe and the Romantics belong to the old tradition.

Nelly Sachs, who was born in Berlin in 1891 and is now living in Stockholm, in many ways is a "modern" poet. She, too, is lonely and fearful in an apparently empty and chaotic world; she, too, in her work destroys reality and the logical and effective order of normal existence; she, too, increasingly breaks down the form of her poem, and operates instead with the irrational force of the word; she, too, relies on suggestiveness rather than rationality; she, too, communicates—if at all—by evocation rather than by precise meaning; she, too, is conscious of living at a time of civilization which is approaching its end.

But in contrast to Gottfried Benn, for instance, her work is emotional and inspirational in character; in contrast to Georg Trakl her views are founded on humanistic values; in contrast to Karl Krolow her imagination is nonintellectual; in contrast to Rainer Maria Rilke her symbols are not entirely private; in contrast to Stefan George she prefers the lyrical voice of the "I" or "we"; in contrast to all of these she is a deeply engaged writer, she is a confessional author, and she does not appear to glory in her loneliness. Nelly Sachs is thus a unique phenomenon in "modern" poetry.

Her uniqueness, one is tempted to think, is explained largely by the fact that she has her roots in a mystic, indeed "secret," tradition: that of Jewish mysticism and religion. She therefore reaches a transcendence which is not broken or empty, as is the case with Stephane Mallarmé's "Nothingness," for instance, but is alive, though shrouded in mystery. This mystic tradition is her firm basis of operation and permits her to resolve her earthly problems—psychological, autobiographical, historical, spatial, temporal—within a larger and ideal framework. In her work we witness a marvelous integration of the individual and personal elements with those of an objective order, the latter by definition being in constant flux and regeneration (of which more shall be said later). As an individual she questions existence and death, suffering and salvation with as much if not more genuine anguish and sincerity than do the rest of the "modern" poets, but her poetry is lifted onto an entirely different plane: that of hope and redemption in another dimension which is totally absent in the non-believing poets. The process of transmutation, here alluded to, is not an escape from the human condition. It allows her, however, to discover a purpose for her existence and her writing outside of herself.

This kind of poet, whom here we shall refer to as the modern mystic writer is, nevertheless, in an unenviable position. While the "modern" poets despair as humans on all levels and find solace only in their own creation, the mystic author—at the deepest level of his psyche—considers not only his life transient, but also his work, which calls forth a degree of despair unequalled in the other poets. The poem to the mystic writer offers but isolated glimpses of the other world. The "mystic union," in the final analysis, is beyond words. That, in part, explains the frequent occurrence of the term "silence" in Nelly Sachs' poetry, as well as that of "door" and related images.

> **Death was my teacher. How could I have occupied myself with anything else, my metaphors are my wounds. Only through this can my work be understood.**
>
> —*Nelly Sachs*

The modern mystic has to have an awakening or an illumination at one particular time in his life. Generally speaking it occurs at a period of utter distress and disillusionment. In Miss Sachs' case we can reconstruct that moment. It appears to have been an unforgettable and shattering experience, for she refers to it by implication in many of her poems and her few occasional statements. Central to that experience are the themes of death, exile, and injury: The word "wound" occurs as frequently as "death" and the terms for "wandering" in her work. But these images only describe the pre-existent critical condition, not the moment of truth itself, about which she is almost silent, as are all mystics, since it cannot be described in words. Let me be specific. The forty-nine-year-old poetess and her bed-ridden mother were saved from the Nazis as if by a miracle in 1940. Previous to their escape to Sweden, Miss Sachs' father died, while several years later her mother passed away after a long illness. In the winter of 1943-1944 Nelly Sachs wrote a letter to Walter A. Behrendson which is most revealing and reads in part:

> A dreadful piece of news came my way—a person very close to me had died a genuine martyr's death. We had arrived here completely exhausted ["zu Tode gehetzt"]. My mother lived through the terror every night. Poverty, sickness, complete despair! Still don't know how I survived. But love for the beloved last human being whom I called my own gave me courage. Thus originated *In the Habitations of Death* [her first collection of poems, Berlin] and almost at the same time *Eli* [subtitled *ein Mysterienspiel vom Leiden Israels*, her first play, Stockholm]. It revealed itself in three nights under such circumstances that I believed myself torn in pieces.

It makes very little difference if the "It" mentioned in this letter (in German "Er") refers to the play *Eli* or to the word "courage" ("Mut"), the experience described here is her moment of poetical inspiration, which will be repeated again and again. Obviously, it was a traumatic rather than a happy experience, a breakthrough which is described on another occasion as follows: "Death was my teacher. How could I have occupied myself with anything else, my metaphors are my wounds. Only through this can my work be understood." By her own request none of her verses which had appeared before this time have since been printed. Psychologically speaking, then, death and exile are the inspirational basis for her new poetry. Her mystic moment is rooted in despair, it still is and will always be, and that is her tragedy and that of "modern" mysticism. The happy released mystic is a figure of a primarily Christian past. I suspect that Miss Sachs' predominantly Old Testamentary theology as well as her highly emancipated, i.e. civilized and controlled religious background, prevented her from that experience. Our age is doomed to suffer.

The key for an understanding of Nelly Sachs' poetry is to be found in Jewish mysticism. Every line of hers is filled with suggestions and allusions to this secret treasure of Judaic lore which extends through the Bible, particularly the Book of Genesis and the Prophets (especially Jeremiah, Isaiah, and Ezekiel); it runs on through the Midrash, the Aggadoth, the apocryphal writings (particularly the Books of Enoch and Abraham) and the Books Bahir and Yetzira; it flows on the Chassidim of Germany and France of the eleventh century, in the Kabbalists of Spain of the thirteenth century (particularly in the Book of Sohar of Moses de Leon), in the teachings of Isaac Luria in the sixteenth century, those of Sabbatai Zwi in the seventeenth and of the East European Chassidim in the succession of Baal Shem in the eighteenth century.

It is impossible to do justice to or to exhaust the subject of the Kabbala, i.e., of Jewish mysticism. It is sufficient here perhaps if mention is made of the fact that Jewish mysticism, like any other, seeks the union of its living god on the basis of its tradition (Kabbala means law or tradition), that it has fastened especially on the story of creation, and that it awaits the divine revelation without mediator. In its later stages in Luria, Zwi, and Baal Shem the role of the mediator, i.e. of the Messiah, was emphasized, but that proved to be an illusion and false hope. All of these facets appear in Nelly Sachs' work.

Although Nelly Sachs' view of death is steeped in traditional Jewish thought, it can be understood by everyone. Lines, such as the following, in spite of the peculiarly Jewish emphasis on "listening to the voice" ("Hakol") and the "last breath" ("Haodom"), demonstrate the truth of this assertion:

> And you shall hear, cleaving your slumber

> You shall hear
> How in death
> Life begins.

> (Und ihr werdet hören, durch den Schlaf hindurch
> Werdet ihr hören
> Wie im Tode
> Das Leben beginnt.)

> But death is ordained for us all
> Patiently wait for the last breath
> It sings for you too.

> (Aber es ist ja Tod für uns alle bestimmt
> Wartet den Atemzug aus
> Er singt auch für euch.)

From these two quotations we can deduce her characteristic outlook and mode of expression. Miss Sachs' personal history has led her back to a faith which affirms the value of human life, of compassion, and of justice coupled with mercy. She does not equate the universe with absurdity. To her death and suffering, exile and loss are impermanent. Life finds its solution and resolution in passing away, in change, in changing, in being lifted to a higher stage. Exile and wandering are necessary phases of all of nature.

> **The key for an understanding of Nelly Sachs' poetry is to be found in Jewish mysticism. Every line of hers is filled with suggestions and allusions to this secret treasure of Judaic lore which extends through the Bible, particularly the Book of Genesis and the Prophets.**
>
> **—*Robert L. Kahn***

Miss Sachs' language is musical and evocative of the hymn-like tone of the Bible and the Jewish psalmists. She is not afraid to use the first person singular and plural or to address others. Her tone is thus emotional and hortative, although deeply elegiac. There are people in her poems; she does not present a dehumanized world. Miss Sachs likes to pose puzzles of mystic connotation (her last volume bears the characteristic title *Glowing Riddles* [*Glühende Rätsel*]) and she employs humor, not satire or irony. The words are chosen carefully by sound, rhythm, elevation. They have magic properties.

Her world is dualistic, infinite, cosmic; yet at the same time it is unified and symbolic because of the sacred bond and presence in even the lowliest object. The abstract concepts are personified and objectified ("death," "love," etc.), the concrete things are given abstract values ("sand," "stone," "earth," etc.). All nature lives in various stages; all objects breathe and are not dead precisely because of the divine element in them; but all can expect their liberation through death which is the "door" to God, even though they may not know it. This essential tension, which is to be released in the hereafter, is at the basis of her contrasting compound formulations (principle of alienation), such as "invisible objects," "psalms of silence," "secret of a sigh," "black moss," "the unsung song," "torn-apart lovers," "murdered child," "warm darkness," "lightning of prayer."

Everywhere in her poetry there is movement. In her most power-filled famous poem, **"O the Chimneys,"** we find the verbs "drifted," "welcomed," "turned," "devised," "laid," "appointed," ending in the line (without verb!): "And Israel's body as smoke through the air!" Time and space are hurried through; they have become almost meaningless attributes on the road towards fulfillment.

Miss Sachs has formulated some wonderful images for her world, such as the bloody gills of fish (the higher hieroglyphics), that of the calf torn from its mother, of the approaching steps (of the hunter), of the fingers (pointing the way), of the hunter and the hunted. In this mystical and poetic world a human being of our period has found her truth and salvation. It is a unique and great poetess who has voiced her and our terror, her and our longing. She will not be forgotten.

Hayden Carruth (review date September 1968)

SOURCE: A review of *O the Chimneys,* in *Poetry,* Vol. CXII, No. 6, September, 1968, pp. 418-19.

[In the following excerpt from a review of several authors' work, Carruth describes O the Chimneys *as deeply moving, and notes the influence of the Nobel Prize in bringing Sachs's work to the attention of English-speaking readers.]*

I shall begin with the translations among the books assigned me, because in the whole range of my assignment, the book that has moved me most deeply, without any doubt, is *O the Chimneys,* by Nelly Sachs; a good and generous selection of poems from all her books, translated by various hands. With poetry like this we are hesitant to say whether our response is primarily to the generalized emotional context or to the particular qualities of the poems themselves; but does it matter? Not, at any rate, as much as we once thought. Nelly Sachs fled from Germany to Sweden in 1940, taking with her nothing but her heart and her language; meager tools with which to confront the murder of her people; yet bravely and bitterly she did it. Using the merest rudimentary poetic tokens—the butterfly and the chrysalis, sun, stone, smoke, wind, the ideas of dust and distance—she worked ever more deeply into her

feelings, in short compressed poems; until finally, from beginnings perhaps not promising, great poems emerged. Naturally she took what help she could from whatever sources she found, mostly from the Jewish tradition, Isaiah to the *Sohar* to Martin Buber, all present to her and in her continually; so that her book is both a great emblem at the head of the procession and a camera through which we look backward along the ranks. And it is a procession: these poems winding through our consciousness as those interminable lines of people wind across the sands and snows. Do not think these are easy poems to read, for they will break your heart. As to the translations, nowadays it is fashionable to argue heatedly about translating methods, but I do not think many people will argue about these. Granted, here and there one finds lines, or whole poems, which one would have done differently oneself; but given the difficulties of translation, they are good enough; many are much better. And the German is there on the facing pages. Certainly this is one case in which I urge everyone to read it, whether you know the language or not; read it, puzzle it out, then sing it, chant it—quickly you will find yourself inside the poems. Then you will see that as the poems become more forceful, the translations fall into line, as it were, until, in the bitterest, most sorrowful of them, the literal translation is also poetically the best. Thus Michael Hamburger, whose translations in the past have seemed wooden to me, comes splendidly alive here in his selections from the three series of *Glowing Enigmas,* and Christopher Holme has done even better with the verse play, *Eli.* Indeed, this play by itself would almost be enough, the summation of all Nelly Sachs's feeling and vision. It is a strange mixture in some respects, for one sees in it bits of Lorca, bits of Brecht, the traditions of morality and Hasidic theatre; yet they are fused indissolubly in this grieving, tortured, humorous work, which is like a ritual so full of feeling that it exceeds itself without destroying itself; the iris bud unfolding. I ended it with sensations neither Brechtian nor Lorca-esque, as a matter of fact, nor Euripidean either (though this would be closer), but proto-formal, as if this work were prior to all esthetic localizations, alone in the world. I do wish some film-maker in this country would take it, in Holme's translation, for his next scenario; it is a natural. Incidentally, *O the Chimneys* shows the real value of the Nobel Prize. How many Americans knew Nelly Sachs or her work before 1966, when she shared the prize with S. Y. Agnon of Israel? Certainly not I. And without the prize would we ever have had this full-scale presentation of her work here? For me, this goes a long way toward making up the deficiencies of the prize in other years.

Times Literary Supplement (review date 21 November 1968)

SOURCE: A review of *Selected Poems,* in *Times Literary Supplement,* Vol. 67, No. 3482, November 21, 1968, p. 1304.

[In the following review, the critic praises Selected Poems *in*

spite of some "signs of hurry" evident in the translation of the poems from German to English.]

Nelly Sachs was almost unknown to English-speaking readers until she won the 1966 Nobel Prize for Literature. Younger Germans had discovered her poems only a few years before . . . , and even then such transcendental treatment of suffering and violence, specifically genocide, must have seemed, to many, a lofty irrelevance. With the award of the Nobel Prize, Nelly Sachs has been rushed into English: Christopher Holme's version of her play *Eli* was sent for, Michael Hamburger was commissioned to translate poems, Ruth and Matthew Mead contributed their share, as did Michael Roloff (who had made the capture).

The translations do show some signs of hurry. These are highly volatile and precarious poems, in which the German words may carry seven shades of meaning to every three carried by their English counterparts. It is also, in many respects, an esoteric poetry which relies heavily on metaphor, yet the metaphors seldom allow strong visualization (which is likely to vex English readers). Perhaps the translations might have been no better even if the haste had been more decent:

> Earth, old man of the planets, you suck
> at my foot
> which wants to fly . . .

"du saugst an meinem Fuss" *is* less purely physical than the English, and "which wants to fly" *is* a lot thicker than "der fliegen will". But what alternatives exist?

The many genitive metaphors are another problem. These are even multiplied in English, because Nelly Sachs can substitute compound nouns which often have to be spelled out in English. Here would be an object of study for structuralists. The "world as metaphor"—as transformational process—may be Nelly Sachs's theme, but her (genitive) metaphors are so overworked that one wonders if such a macrocosmic vision can balance on such a delicate pivot (a pivot, moreover, which Rilke's excesses, and those of his imitators, have already undermined). One also wonders if such total relativity does not abolish all substance; which is a useful fiction for poetry, if nothing more. Miss Sachs is a visionary of an ontological realm between death and birth (not vice versa), and the genitive metaphor is her vehicle for exploring that transcendental region: what, though, if one decides that this vehicle is rickety, because arbitrary (or just "literary")? Where, then, is the guarantee that her vision has authenticity, and that her flight actually occurred?

The grand cosmic themes—love, life, death, transformation—are ventured with a single-mindedness which takes the breath away. Miss Sachs has been through the hells of knowledge, of poverty, of suffering with her tormented and slaughtered Jewish people. Yet her work is haunted by a paradisal levity; seldom do the drifting skeins of metaphors catch the actual scream, the phenomenon itself happening in the instant of articulation. The poem becomes an image of total relativity, supernalizing everything it touches, even the most horrific banal evils of humankind:

> I do not know the room
> where exiled love
> lays down its victory
> and the growing into the reality
> of visions begins
> nor where the smile of the child
> who was thrown as in play
> into the playing flames is preserved
> but I know that this is the food
> from which earth with beating heart
> ignites the music of her stars—

From any other poet, the indefiniteness of the word "this" ("dieses") in line 9 would be profoundly shocking (it seems to sanctify the murder of the child). The poem in its context is, however, one of a cycle of variations on the life of the four elements, celebrating the elemental life, and there the poem, "this" included, is (in the smug old terminology) "satisfying". After some time spent reading these poems, ranging from the icy horror of the **"Landscape of Screams"** and **"Night of the Weeping Children"**, to the melisma of the later **"Glowing Enigmas"**, one ends up asking if this art is not an improbable compound of Käthe Kollwitz and Vieira da Silva. Such extremes of darkness and delicate abstraction are, at least, within its range, perceptible among the ingrained elements of traditional wisdom and modern poetic vision which German critics have already descended upon (Cabala, Sohar, Novalis, Rilke). Yet another question might be put as follows: the images in these poems, pregnant as they are, undergo transformation and serial development at a velocity which is not matched by rhythmic movement. The rhythmic invention seems too slight to sustain these lightning shifts of perspective. The rhythms do not change one's sense of time, however much the skeins of imagery may change one's sense of space. One is aware of momentous moments rather than of a synchronistic organization or "eternity" in the poem. This is one way in which the poems move with a somewhat old-fashioned air through their interstellar space.

This reviewer's doubts are, in Prospero's language, questions which the tale demands. Nelly Sachs is definitely a saint of the inner revolution. Her work carries the holy fire in a sealed vessel, nursing it through the bad days. Christoph Meckel's prose poem in *Nelly Sachs zu Ehren* suggested something similar:

> Poems from deep, holy, and profaned Biblical
> darknesses. Stars in an eclipse of the stars. Wailing

Wall poems. Poems placed on graves, half scream, half silence. Songs of the Beyond, quiet and hard with sounds of pain, but containing a few flashes of green lightning.

Ehrhard Bahr (essay date May 1972)

SOURCE: "Shoemaking as a Mystic Symbol in Nelly Sachs' Mystery Play *Eli*," in *German Quarterly,* Vol. XLV, No. 3, May, 1972, pp. 480-83.

[*In the following essay, Bahr explains the elements of Jewish mysticism in* Eli.]

Nelly Sachs' *Eli: Ein Mysterienspiel vom Leiden Israels,* one of her *Szenische Dichtungen,* as she has called her verse plays, has received much attention by the critics. Nevertheless, some important features of the play, such as the figure of the protagonist Michael, the motif of his trade as a shoemaker, and the central image of the joining of the upper leather to the sole of a shoe, have so far remained unexplained. This omission may be due to the fact that any meaningful interpretation of Nelly Sachs' lyric and scenic poetry cannot ignore certain basic concepts of Jewish mysticism (Kabbalism and Hasidism), especially with reference to religious promise and fulfilment. Analyzed in the light of these concepts, some of the problematical symbolism of *Eli* emerges in clearly understandable form.

Nelly Sachs' mystery play concerns the murder of Eli, an eight-year-old boy, a God child, as indicated by the Hebrew name. The action takes place in a small town in Poland, the home of Hasidism, "the latest phase of Jewish mysticism," as Gershom Scholem has called it. The time of the play is defined symbolically rather than historically, as the period "Nach dem Martyrium." Eli was killed by a guard when his parents were led through the streets of their little town for deportation. Trying to follow them, Eli blew his shepherd's pipe as a call to God for help:

> den Kopf hat er geworfen nach hinten,
> wie die Hirsche, wie die Rehe,
> bevor sie trinken an der Quelle.
> Zum Himmel hat er die Pfeife gerichtet,
> zu Gott hat er gepfiffen, der Eli, . . .

reminiscent of the words of the 42nd Psalm: "As the hart panteth after the water brooks, so panteth my soul after thee, O God. My soul thirsteth for God, for the living God. When shall I come and appear before God." In a postscript to *Eli,* Nelly Sachs interprets the shepherd's pipe with which the boy, in his despair, calls to God, as a "versuchter Ausbruch des Menschlichen vor dem Entsetzen."

At this moment, when Eli is piping his call to God, one of the guards turns around and, assuming the pipe to be a secret signal, he kills Eli with his rifle butt. The soldier's fear of a secret signal is explained by the poet as a symbol of unbelief.

After the war a new city is being built outside the gates of the old town. But the townspeople continue to grieve about the murder of their loved ones, especially about Eli, the God child. Michael, the shoemaker, who has the eyes of the Baal Shem, the saint-mystic of Hasidism, cannot find peace. Shoemaking traditionally is a mystic trade. Jacob Böhme, for instance, the German mystic at the beginning of the seventeenth century, who was strongly influenced by Kabbalism, was a shoemaker. It was Böhme who became a source of inspiration for Nelly Sachs, in whose work these two parallel strands, Jewish and German mysticism, are united.

Another mystic cobbler may be found in the figure of the patriarch Enoch "who . . . was taken from the earth by God and transformed into the angel Metatron," according to a Hasidic story told by Martin Buber. "At every stitch of his awl he not only joined the upper leather with the sole, but all upper things with all lower things. In other words, he had accompanied his work at every step with meditations which drew the stream of emanation down from the upper to the lower (so transforming profane into ritual action)." Similarly, in Nelly Sachs' *Eli,* the other characters say of Michael:

> Näht er auch Sohle an Oberleder fest,
> weiss er doch mehr als nur Wandern zum Grabe

In the terminology of the *Zohar,* the "Book of Splendor," the most important book of Jewish mysticism, the words "lower" and "upper" frequently denote the distinction between men and God, earth and heaven, this world and the world to come.

Michael is also one of the Thirty-Six Pious or Just Men for whose sake the world was saved by God. Nelly Sachs here draws on the same legend as André Schwarz-Bart in his novel *Le Dernier des justes* (1959). As one of the Thirty-Six, Michael takes his people's grief into his own heart, so that they are relieved of the burden of their sorrow and thus are able to build the new town without grief. Taking with him Eli's pipe—the instrument for invoking God—Michael leaves the town and goes into the world in search of Eli's murderer. Wherever he meets people, he takes their sorrows, too, unto himself, so that they can live or die in peace.

Finally, Michael finds work in a village "in the West, beyond the border," where Eli's murderer lives. Again, the direction is indicated symbolically rather than geographically or politically. Michael works at his shoemaker's trade, but he cannot mend the murderer's shoes:

> Die Sohle ist nicht mehr zu flicken,
> ein Riß geht in der Mitte—

It is impossible for Michael to connect the "lower" and the "upper," because the murderer has split the "lower world" into two pieces.

When the murderer's child comes to Michael's shop with his father, he wants to blow on the pipe of Eli, the God child, but the father will not permit it. Denied the whistle, the child is overcome by a strange, powerful yearning for the toy which the father tries to ridicule. In his harshness the murderer prevents his child from establishing a relationship with God through an instrument giving voice to longing. Instead, he promises the child the flute of the Pied Piper, expressing worldly domination and demagogy:

> Wenn du sie hast,
> so folgen dir alle Kinder
> und geben dir ihr Spielzeug—

He does not allow his child to blow the shepherd's pipe whose sound reaches God. The child dies, not because of the sins of his father but because of the denial of his yearning for God. The killer thus repeats his murderous act. In his innocence this child, too, dies, as Eli did, both victims of evil, as Nelly Sachs explains.

Confronting the murderer, Michael now becomes the guardian angel of Israel. A primordial light shines from a symbolical embryo in the sky, representing the original God child. The murderer crumbles into dust—a picture of remorse, as the poet interprets this scene. The primordial light now fastens onto Michael's brow. His mission has been fulfilled, and he is taken to God, just as "the earthly Enoch" was transfigured "into the transcendent Metatron."

Now the town can be built again. The New Year liturgy which forms the central part of the play, offering a promise of the Lord's return, is fulfilled in the last scene.

Jewish mysticism thus provides Nelly Sachs with "objective correlatives" to describe the unfathomable, the mystery of religious promise and fulfilment. The torn sole of a shoe which cannot be repaired symbolizes the destruction of the world by the murderer and the inability of the killer to relate to God, even through his own child. The sole and the upper leather cannot be joined, just as the evil on this earth cannot be embraced by the heavenly powers. But the mystic shoemaker, in his quest for justice, is led to his goal, thus redeeming the town of its evil past.

Hamida Bosmajian (essay date Spring 1973)

SOURCE: "'Landschaft aus Schreien': the Shackled Leaps of Nelly Sachs," in *Bucknell Review*, Vol. XXI, No. 1, Spring, 1973, pp. 43-62.

[*In the following essay, Bosmajian presents a deep analysis of "Landschaft aus Schreien," emphasizing Sachs's use of imagery and symbolism.*]

Nelly Sachs's poems disprove and confirm Theodor Adorno's statement that "after Auschwitz we cannot write poetry." The conjunction of Auschwitz and poetry seems an obscenity, for what has the cruel reality of the camp to do with lyricism?

The poems of Nelly Sachs do not reproduce that reality with documentary exactness; they fail to reveal the essence of evil. This failing is not new, for the makers of verbal universes have always revealed little about the essences with which they have concerned themselves. Dante envisioned the essence of evil as a corporeal and grotesque image of a trinity immobilized in the icy pit of hell, and he could do no more than humbly sing the praises of the eternal moving light of goodness. Nelly Sachs knows that evil is real and manifests itself in millions of grotesque examples which in aggregation reach cosmic if not metaphysical dimensions. Again and again her poems come to a point of demonic epiphany beyond which beckons the glimmer of a very uncertain hope. This is the case in **Zahlen** (**"Numbers"**) where she describes the future of the numbers that were branded into the arms of the condemned:

> erhoben sich Meteore aus Zahlen
> gerufen in die Räume
> darin Lichterjahre wie Pfeile sich strecken
> und die Planeten
> aus den magischen Stoffen
> des Schmerzes geboren werden—
>
> (meteors of numbers arose
> beckoned into spaces
> wherein light-years expand like arrows
> and the planets
> are born of the magic matter
> of pain—)

Her whole work is a search for the reason of suffering, for the source of peace, and it is also a struggle against the forgetfulness of man. In her poems, suffering and the need for transformation and liberation extend into time and space, but the simple and comforting belief in an afterlife is not part of her faith, which rests primarily on what Martin Buber has called "holy insecurity." Perhaps death is no more than a liberation from physical agony, as in her famous poem

> O ihr Schornsteine,
> O ihr Finger,
> Und Israels Leib im Rauch durch die Luft!
>
> (O you chimneys,
> O you fingers,

And Israel's body in smoke through the air!)

There is a yearning for spatial expansion in her poetry, a desire for an energy that would lift her upward and away from a gruesome reality. The speaker of her poems is often like the dreamer in a nightmare who wants to fly but is pulled back by what he fears. The condition is well expressed in the agonized cry of Marlowe's Faustus: "I'll leap up to my God, who pulls me down?" Nelly Sachs also yearns for a peace that surpasses understanding, but she is shackled by the knowledge that to have such a peace in one's lifetime would be wrong: "Erde, Planetengreis, du saugst an meinem Fuss / der fliegen will." (Earth, senile man of planets, you suck at my foot / that wants to fly). Her commitment to life is stated in a letter to Walter A. Berendson, (May 15, 1946): "I will not stop following step by step the path of fire and flame and star of our people and I will bear witness with my poor being." Only the dead are free, while the living must restrain their desire for flight. Her act of faith and her only escape lie in the tracing of the crooked line of suffering through the use of a language that she hopes will be free from the corruption of her time.

[Sachs'] whole work is a search for the reason of suffering, for the source of peace, and it is also a struggle against the forgetfulness of man.

—*Hamida Bosmajian*

Nelly Sachs, however, made one great flight. The order to report for a camp was already in her pocket when she flew with her mother to Stockholm on May 16, 1940, after she had been granted asylum there through the intercession of Selma Lagerlöf. She had thus lived under the Hitler regime for quite some time until she was sorted to the "Chor der Geretteten," the chorus of the rescued "aus deren hohlem Gebein der Tod schon seine Flöten schnitt" (from whose hollow bones death already whittled his flutes). She had seen much of the nightmare spectacle created by the "schrecklichen Marionettenspieler," the terrible puppeteer who moved

> Arme auf und ab,
> Beine auf und ab
> Und die untergehende Sonne des Sinaivolkes
> Als den roten Teppich unter den Füssen.
>
> (Arms up and down
> Legs up and down
> And the setting sun of Sinai's people
> As a red carpet under their feet.)

For the living there remained "am ziehenden aschgrauen Horizont der Angst / Riesengross das Gestirn des Todes / Wie die Uhr der Zeiten stehend" (on the receding ash-grey horizon of fear / The constellation of death gigantic / Looming like the clock face of ages.) The names of the murderers and even their particular deeds are not found in her poetry; what is emphasized is the feeling of the sufferer. She said: "We have to believe that suffering is meaningful, this has nothing to do with 'faith.' It is simply necessary." There is an absurdity in her belief that almost seems to justify it. Besides, her survival leads her to a sense of guilt and the need to assuage that guilt by suffering spiritually and by recording the suffering she had escaped. She shares the paradox of all writers who survived the Nazi terror: the silenced victim of terror cannot bear witness, but the witness can only imaginatively project himself into the ultimate reality of the victim.

Like Job, whom she much admired, she is caught between two extreme forces that reduce her to helplessness and at the same time wrench from her a passionate elemental outcry. Beda Alleman has pointed out that "the scream as the ultimate utterance and its opposite silence are the boundaries of her use of language." These boundaries are often fused in what Kenneth Burke has termed the "mystic oxymoron": the silent scream, the insect in crystal, the stone angel, the shackled leap—each combining yearning and restraint. When she does mention documentary material such as the shoes of the dead, the buckle of the executioner, or the wind that blows over the hair of dead children she usually links such details to a transcending vision. Many of her poems combine the effects of the fearful grotesque and the terrifying sublime, as is evident in the puppets, red carpet, and sunset of the above quoted lines. Though the grotesque and the sublime seem opposites, they both point to something beyond the natural. The seeming nonsensical distortion of the grotesque is akin to the nonsense of the sublime. The grotesque in her work springs from a shattered world, from an intensely real yet unnatural and artificial nightmare. When she adds to this terror an energy toward transcendence, the terror takes on aspects of the sublime that leads at times to the mystic's vision of divine No-Thingness. Her poem **"Landschaft aus Schreien"** (landscape of screams) is such a fusion of the grotesque and the sublime. We rarely find the sublime in contemporary literature that deals with historical events, for the modern writer tends to portray the atrocities of man either with documentary exactness or as grotesque allegories of the "banality of evil." Nelly Sachs's use of the sublime is justified by her infinite yearning into infinite space.

There is much in her poetry that reminds the reader of the poetry of Blake, and this is not surprising since she shared with Blake an admiration for the Christian mystic Jakob Boehme, whose vision is akin to that of the Zohar, the Judaic work that began to exert its influence on her when a friend gave her a copy of Gershom Scholem's *Jewish Mysticism*.

Her study of the Zohar not only enriched her use of symbols but also showed her the need for the preservation and regeneration of language, as can be seen in her poem "Da schrieb der Schreiber des Sohar."

"Landschaft aus Schreien" is a forceful and even aggressive poem about the universality of suffering written in a language that forces the reader to meditate on the symbolic essences of the words. On one level the poem is a horizontal journey through a landscape of pain that extends from Genesis to the New Testament, from Hiroshima to Maidanek. From this horizon of pain and fear, however, the scream moves vertically upward into infinity. Though the poem is steeped in the tradition of Jewish and Christian mysticism, it is also a very modern poem, especially in its openendedness, which reminds one at times of the Orphic vision of Rilke in the *Duino Elegies,* where we also see no end to the wanderer's yearning in the landscape of pain. Before I discuss **"Landschaft aus Schreien"** in detail, I will quote the poem in its entirety since the arrangement of lines and the grotesqueness of the German compounds create a visual impact that aids the reader in understanding this poem.

> In der Nacht, wo Sterben Genähtes zu trennen
> beginnt,
> reisst die Landschaft aus Schreien
> den schwarzen Verband auf,
>
> Über Moria, dem Klippenabsturz zu Gott,
> schwebt des Opfermessers Fahne
> Abrahams Herz-Sohn-Schrei,
> am grossen Ohr der Bibel liegt er bewahrt.
>
> O die Hieroglyphen aus Schreien,
> an die Tod-Eingangstür gezeichnet.
>
> Wundkorallen aus zerbrochenen Kehlenflöten.
>
> O, o die Hände mit Angstpflanzenfinger,
> eingegraben in wildbäumende Mähnen
> Opferblutes—
>
> Schreie, mit zerfetzten Kiefern der Fische
> verschlossen,
> Weheranke der kleinsten Kinder
> und der schluckenden Atemschleppe der Greise,
>
> eingerissen in versengtes Azur mit brennenden
> Schweifen.
> Zellen der Gefangenen, der Heiligen,
> mit Albtraummuster der Kehlen tapezierte,
> fiebernde Hölle in der Hundehütte des Wahnsinns
> aus gefesselten Sprüngen—
>
> Dies ist die Landschaft aus Schreien!

> Himmelfahrt aus Schreien,
> empor aus des Leibes Knochengittern,
> Pfeile aus Schrein, erlöste
> aus blutigen Köchern.
>
> Hiobs Vier-Winde-Schrei
> Und der Schrei verborgen im Ölberg
> wie ein von Ohnmacht übermanntes Insekt im
> Kristall.
>
> O Messer aus Abendrot, in die Kehlen geworfen
> wo die Schlafbäume blutleckend aus der Erde
> fahren,
> wo die Zeit wegfällt
> an den Gerippen in Maidanek und Hiroshima.
>
> Ascheschrei aus blindgequältem Seherauge—
>
> O du blutendes Auge
> in der zerfetzten Sonnenfinsternis
> zum Gott-Trocknen aufgehängt
> im Weltall—

> In the night where dying begins to sever all seams
> the landscape of screams
> tears the black bandage open,
>
> Above Moria, the cliffs falling off to God,
> hovers the flag of the sacrificial knife
> Abraham's Heart-Son-Scream
> caught at the great ear of the Bible.
>
> O hieroglyphs of screams,
> carved into the entrance gate of death.
>
> Wound-corals of broken throat flutes.
>
> O, o hands with finger plants of dread
> dug into wildly rearing manes of sacrificial
> blood—
>
> Screams, locked in the tattered mandibles of fish,
> woe tendrils of smallest children
> and the gulping train of breath of the old,
>
> slashed into burned azure with burning tails.
> Cells of prisoners, of saints,
> tapestried with the nightmare patterns of throats,
> feverish hell in the doghouse of madness
> of shackled leaps—
>
> This is the landscape of screams!
> Transfigured ascension of screams
> from the bony grate of the body,

Arrows of screams
freed from bloody quivers.

Job's Four-Wind-Scream
and the scream concealed in Mount Olive
like a powerless insect caught in crystal.

O knife of sunset tossed into throats,
where the trees of sleep surge blood-licking from
the earth,
where time falls off
the skeletons in Maidanek and Hiroshima.

Ashen scream from the seer's eye tortured blind—

O thou bleeding eye
in the tattered eclipse of the sun
hung up for God-drying
in the cosmos—

The deepest irony of the poem is that we never hear and see one creature screaming in the direct sense of "he screams." The poem itself, in spite of the violent images and the repetition of the word *Schrei,* is a stifled scream of protest and agonized longing. The auditory image of *Schrei* is communicated through the visual image of *Landschaft,* a place that exists in the expanse of the universe and in the horizontal nightmare of each human life. The landscape of screams "acts" in an ambiguous state of darkness that pervades the poem. This ambiguous darkness can be partially explained through Gershom Scholem's description of the Zoharic concept of God: "The hidden God, the innermost Being of Divinity so to speak, has neither qualities nor attributes." This innermost being is the *En-Sof,* the infinite, which is likened to a coal. The latent power of the coal is manifest only through the flame. Therefore, we can know about God only through his emanations, through his symbols. The origin of such symbols is imagined in the Zohar's description of Genesis: "'In the beginning, when the will of the King began to take effect, he engraved signs in the divine aura. A dark flame sprang forth from the innermost recesses of the Infinite.'" In **"Landschaft aus Schreien"** the inexpressible agony of the sufferer is extended to a landscape manifesting itself through the scream which bursts forth like a dark flame and is in that sense a creative act (II. 1-3). Whoever causes suffering wants it to remain hidden in mysterious darkness, but the scream bears witness by tearing through the darkness like a comet or by emanating from it like the corona around an eclipsed sun, both important images in this poem.

Darkness, then, is associated with mystery, but it is also a symbol of evil. The scribe of the Zohar saw evil as one of the manifestations of God, for when God does not temper the quality of stern judgment with mercy, then judgment becomes the source of evil: "When it ceases to be tempered, when in its measureless hypertropical outbreak it tears itself loose from the quality of mercy, then it breaks away from God altogether and is transformed into the radically evil, into Gehenna and the dark world of Satan." In this state evil is dead and comes to life only if the faint light of God falls upon it or if it is quickened by the sinfulness of man. The source of creation and destruction is thus the same, but the motivation of the source remains a mystery which neither the author of the Zohar, nor Jakob Boehme, nor Nelly Sachs can explain.

Images of violence establish, in the first three lines of the poem, an inextricable relationship between creation and destruction: "In the night where dying begins to sever all seams, / the landscape of screams tears / the black bandage open." Implicit in these lines is the image of the comet (also in I.15) and the black hole(s) of the mouth(s) from which the upward surge of the scream meets the downward motion of the death-bringing comet. Death and scream are both flashes that expose mystery. Like a fine knife or a pair of scissors, the comet-death cuts the threads of what has been sewn together. In contrast to the scream which tears the bandage that hid the wound, death's action seems quite gentle, yet it is more cruel in its slowness: 'Wo Sterben Genähtes zu trennen *beginnt.*' A further meaning of the comet is that of the aberrant star, an active force that breaks loose in a "hypertropical outbreak" from the harmonious rhythm of the heavens. The death-comet is thus a severing apocalyptic force, and as such it is creative in its destructiveness. The third line ends with the word *auf,* which with its meanings of *up* and *open* indicates the exposure of evil, the yearning for salvation, and the structurally important openendedness of the poem.

The next stanza individualizes the cosmic scream through the figure of Abraham, the first suffering Israelite, who is here envisioned in the moment of suspension between deepest agony and relief. This stanza repeats the pattern of the first. Over Mount Moria the sacrificial knife flashes like a triumphant flag that points downward to bring death to the victim. This image is echoed in "dem Klippenabsturz zu Gott" (I.4), the cliffs that fall down to God. Both images reflect the traditional initiation pattern where the *agon* and *sparagmos* of the hero eventually lead to his triumph. Nelly Sachs, however, alludes nowhere to the angel who announces that God does not wish human sacrifice. We see the moment of extreme tension when Abraham, the potential murderer, recognizes his beloved son, in the victim, and when Isaac realizes that his father will be his killer. Love makes these two beings one at this moment and each grants the other release through a scream rising from the heart's agony. "Abrahams Herz-Sohn-Schrei" does not, however, rise in an infinite line but is caught "am grossen Ohr der Bibel" (I.7), the great ear of the Bible that like a vessel stores the verbal record of man's suffering. Here suffering is *bewahrt,* it is stored safely as well as proved true, as the double meaning of the German word implies. The Bible, then, is a true and meaningful record in which future generations will recognize themselves.

The need to sound or to record suffering is restated in the next two lines through the image of Egyptian pictographs: "O die Hieroglyphen aus Schreien, / an die Tod-Eingangstür gezeichnet" (O hieroglyphics of screams / drawn into the entrance gate of death). Egypt, Israel's ancient enemy, also records the suffering of man in images that are riddles which fascinate and demand contemplation, for the inexplicable cannot be communicated through easy rationalism. Nelly Sachs uses hieroglyphics in almost all of her poems as she does in the next line, which is set off as a forceful and compact enigma: "Wundkorallen aus zerbrochenen Kehlenflöten" (Wound corals of broken throat flutes). An ancient folk motif, the bleeding tree is usually an enchanted human being awaiting liberation and the bleeding is the first sign of that liberation, for through it the tree makes its hidden nature known. Literally, red coral is a tree-like structure composed of the skeletons of marine animals; its branches are used for jewelry. Coral and necklace are symbols in Nelly Sachs's poems. She says in **"Diese Kette von Rätseln":**

> Diese Kette von Rätseln
> um den Hals der Nacht gelegt
> Königswort weit fort geschrieben
> Unlesbar
> vielleicht in Kometenfahrt
> wenn die aufgerissene Wunde des Himmels
> schmerzt

> (This chain of riddles
> laid around the neck of night
> King's word written far away
> illegible
> perhaps in comet journeys
> when the open, torn wound of the sky
> hurts)

Kette means both chain and ornament and is thus appropriate for her work, which reveals the bondage of suffering and offers a relief, a means of coping with suffering by giving it lasting form in the work of art, the jewel. In her poem **"Und wir die ziehen"** she describes Sweden as the land of ice where she lives in the deadness of winter, but she evokes in that frozen state the memory of her dead beloved, whom she immortalizes as a wounded coral, the artifact made out of the stuff of life: "Hier an dieser Stelle / aussetzte ich die Koralle, / die blutende, / deiner Botschaft." (Here at this place / I exposed the coral, / the bleeding one, / of your message.)

Like corals and chains, her poems form a *Korallenkette,* the redness of which suggests a wound around the neck. In **"Landschaft aus Schreien"** the wounded corals are made of shattered throat-flutes. When properly functioning, the hu-

man throat emits a harmonious sound, but in a fallen world that sound becomes a scream, which at its worst is the stifled broken scream of Gehenna. Her poems are tunes similar to the tune played by Eli, the martyred boy in her mystery play on the suffering of Israel. When the child saw how his parents were driven away to death, he raised his pipe to heaven; he piped to God. His beautiful song is a demanding and despairing call and the soldier is quite right when he assumes that it is a secret message, except that he does not know that the message remains simply an infinitely ascending line. Then, the "soldier marching with the procession / looked round and saw Eli / piping to high heaven / struck him down with his rifle butt." The throat-flute is broken, the sound has been stifled and its sole receptacle is the ear of the poem.

The sweeping comet, the cosmic night, and the scream are sublime, but the hieroglyphics of Nelly Sachs evoke a nightmarish and grotesque effect. The great ear of the Bible, the throatflutes, the *Angstpflanzenfinger* fuse the nonhuman with significantly isolated parts of the human body into metaphysical grotesques. The tearing apart and strange joining of living and non-living not only illustrates the paradox of life in art, but also mirrors the shattered state of the world. The poem is a string of such images, each one repeating and reinforcing variables of the same idea just as documentary photographs of glasses, boots, or hair heaped in a concentration camp say the same thing and point to something beyond thingness.

The danger of hieroglyphics is that the reader will become too concerned with the unraveling of their mystery and forget that the poem is about very real pain. Nelly Sachs is aware of that danger and therefore returns to specific human agonies which she introduces through the image of a cosmic nightmare horse and rider: "O, o Hände mit Angstpflanzenfinger / eingegraben in wildbäumende Mahnen Opferblutes—" (O, o hands with fear-plant-fingers / dug into wildly rearing manes of sacrificial blood). To whom do these hands belong? They are plants of fear, but they also plant fear as the ambiguity of the compound indicates: *die Finger pfanzen Angst.* As they dig themselves into the manes, they plant fear while at the same time they are holding on tightly to their victims who carry them through the *Nachtmar* (night*mare*) of evil and suffering. The hands then belong to the murderers who bear their victims no love and yet are strangely united to them. As the fingers of death bear downward, the victims rise with rearing manes—doomed to die; they die not passively. Yet there is no scream of relief here as there was for Abraham, who bore great love for his only son.

The next two sections also contain examples of stifled screams (II.13-20). We see first three examples of silent suffering beginning with "Schreie, mit zerfetzten Kiefern der Fische verschlossen" (Screams, locked within the shredded mandibles of fish). Olof Lagercrantz points out that Nelly Sachs compares herself in her mute fear of death with the mute fish (she actually suffered a paralysis of the throat for five days after she had been questioned by the Gestapo), and she gave the fish an important place in her work. "The hunter shoots to kill, but the fisher with hook and net wants to keep his catch alive. The fish with its long silent agony is for Nelly Sachs a foremost symbol of martyrdom." She is, of course, also aware of the fish as a Christ symbol, for Christ's scream too was stifled in the Garden of Olives (I.27). Thus, the mute creation suffers and the old and young cannot give expression to the horror of events that come upon them. The smallest children raise only their "Weheranke" (woe tendril) in a tiny parallel of protest to the "Angstptlanzenfinger," while the ancient ones swallow and drag their breath like a chain (I.15). The stanza begins with the word *Schreie,* but from fish, child, and old man comes no scream; instead the screams are "eingerissen in versengtes Azur mit brennenden Schweifen" (slashed into seared azure with burning tails). Now the screams do exactly what the death-comet did in the first stanza, except that the screams cut into azure that has been burned, a cosmic wound brought about by the violence of an unnatural death.

The poem reaches at this point a frantic pace through a series of violent images that end in frustration (II.16-20). The landscape shrinks to the claustrophobic cells of prisoners and saints where the walls are tapestried with the nightmare pattern of throats; the hieroglyphics of screams are now microscopic rather than cosmic. The line "mit Albtraummuster der Kehlen tapezierte" can refer to the walls of the cells as well as to the feverish hell in the doghouse of madness, for both are metaphors of the human brain. As man encounters evil and its ensuing agony, he grows mad and must be controlled like a mad dog: "Fiebernde Hölle in der Hundehütte des Wahnsinns / aus gefesselten Sprüngen" (feverish hell in the doghouse of madness / of shackled leaps). These lines also refer to the poet and her dilemma: she wants to express the inexpressible but nears insanity in her attempt. The insane matter must be controlled by an artifact constructed of "shackled leaps." Having reached this pitch of desperate intensity, the poet can either stop the poem or introduce a shift in tone.

Nelly Sachs does the latter in the next line, which opens the second part of the poem with the declaration: "Dies ist die Landschaft aus Schreien" (This is the landscape of screams). Three sections divide the second part: the release and frustration of screams, the sunset of Maidanek and Hiroshima, the function of the poet-visionary and his relation to God.

The first section (II.21-28) shows the release of screams from "des Leibes Knochengittern" (the body's grate of bones) and from the "blutigen Köchern" (the bloody quivers) as well as the frustrated screams of the living Job and Christ. Only the dying are granted the "Himmelfahrt aus Schreien," the freedom that comes with the final scream. The use of the word *Himmelfahrt,* which refers specifically to Christ's transfigured ascension, contrasts ironically with the ascension of "or-

dinary" sufferers. The grate of bones suggests also the image of a ladder and a lyre upon which the screams ascend and by doing so form a cacophonous tonal ladder. There is, however, no last rung in that ladder, as there was in the one of Jacob's dream where the Lord stood at the top and promised: "I am with thee, and will keep thee in all places whither thou goest" (Genesis 28:15). The terror and the deep modernity of Nelly Sachs's poem lies in her concept of an infinitely ascending line. The image of the arrows released from the bloody quivers repeats this concept of ascending desire with a goal denied.

In the examples of Job and Christ, the poet-seer finds once more the frustrated and stifled scream. Job's scream is scattered to the winds and loses through this diffusion the aggressiveness of the scream as arrow or comet, "for the speeches of one that is desperate are as the wind" (Job 6:26). Yet, by naming Job, the poet as recorder fulfills that sufferer's wish: "O that my words were now written! Oh that they were recorded in a book." Christ, though always an archetype of the sufferer in her poems, is not named directly in any of her poems during and after the Hitler regime. Names held a magical quality for her, and the name of Christ had been soiled and abused by the persecutors. As Lagercrantz points out: "The Jews were marked as God's murderers, which meant that they bore the guilt of the crucifixion of Christ. In her youth she had published a collection of legends in which Christ is present everywhere. . . . Now Christ is prohibited to her, but he returns in mysterious ways." Job's scattered scream and the scream stifled in the Garden of Olives are powerless like the insect caught in crystal, but they are really no more powerless than the screams that trace the line of suffering through the infinite. The insect caught in crystal is another parallel to Abraham's scream caught at the ear of the Bible; it is again an image of pain controlled in form. Once again the poet visionary does not mention the triumphant and peaceful ending of the lives of Job and Christ, for in her world there seems to be no evidence for such an ending.

Human existence reaches its nadir in the vision of twentieth-century horror:

> O Messer aus Abendrot, in die Kehlen geworfen,
> wo die Schlafbäume blutleckend aus der Erde
> fahren,
> wo die Zeit wegfällt
> an den Gerippen in Maidanek und Hiroshima.

> (O knife of sunset tossed into the throats,
> where trees of sleep surge blood-licking from the
> ground,
> where time falls off
> the skeletons in Maidanek and Hiroshima.)

Black and red dominate the landscape of screams where a

fierce sunset-death cuts the throats before the screams can escape. The motion of the sun is countered by another of Nelly Sachs's hieroglyphic: "die Schlafbäume," the trees of sleep. They quicken the nightmare atmosphere of the stanza, but the sudden aggressiveness with which they surge from the ground also suggests the sudden terror of the mushrooming atomic blast which resembles a tree as well as the shape of the human skull and neck. The metaphor bears a striking resemblance to the tree image in "The Human Abstract," by Blake, another Boehme admirer:

> The Gods of the earth and sea
> sought thro' nature to find this Tree;
> But their search was all in vain:
> There grows one in the Human Brain.

We must not forget that the knife tossed by the evening red is presented in terms of a human action and that the trees have bloodthirsty and human desires which lead to Maidanek and Hiroshima and ultimately to timeless skeletons, "wo die Zeit wegfällt." This timelessness leads not to God but turns the skeletons into hieroglyphics that demand an interpreter who then faces the task of giving meaning to a suffering that cannot be put into words. For this reason the poem concludes with a description of the failure and desire of the poet-visionary.

His dilemma is imagined by means of another hieroglyphic: "Ascheschrei aus blindgequältem Seherauge," the ashen scream of the visionary eye tortured blind. The lucid ball of the eye—mythically it may be the eye of the seer who beheld what no man should see; psychologically it may be the soul that has meditated too long on man's inhumanity to man—this eye is blind. As a living organism it could not contain the suffering the way the crystal contains the insect or the ear of the Bible the scream of Abraham. From its darkened socket, however, comes the ashen scream as a variation of the stifled and the infinite scream. As an impotent (*ohnmächtig*) scream, it is contained in and composed of inorganic matter, but it rises from the blinded yet all-perceiving eye into eternity, as the punctuation indicates. A line exists between the scene of suffering, the seer's eye, and the infinite.

In the last stanza we see the bleeding eye hung "in der zerfetzten Sonnenfinsternis" (in the tattered eclipse of the sun). With this image of literal suspension that implies a cloth as well as a crucified body, the poem reaches the point of demonic epiphany: within the darkness of the universal eye the poet's eye-scream-poem is hung in the cosmos "zum Gott-Trocknen," meaning that either a god will dry its wound or that it will dry the suffering god and receive his imprint as Veronica received the true ikon on her cloth. In retrospect we find that the night, the bandage, the scream, the shredded

mandibles of fish, Job's scattered scream, Christ's stifled scream, the bleeding eye of the poet in the tattered eclipse of the sun, present as a unit one true ikon of suffering: the poem.

Nelly Sachs's mystic vision has to be understood in the relationship of the tortured eye to the tattered, eclipsed sun whose corona suggests the crown of thorns and the crown of glory. In discussing modern man's relation to God, Martin Buber points out that "an eclipse of the sun is something that occurs between the sun and our eyes, not in the sun itself." It is interesting that this something, the moon, is never used by Nelly Sachs as a positive image. Buber argues that the eclipse metaphor implies "the tremendous assumption that we can glance up to God with our . . . being's eye, and that something can step between our existence and His as between the earth and the sun." It is the I-It relationship which has replaced the I-Thou and has thus stepped between God and man. Nevertheless, "the eclipse of the light of God is no extinction; even tomorrow that which has stepped in between may give way."

That moment is not reached in Nelly Sachs's **"Landschaft aus Schreien."** The willingness for an I-Thou relationship is there, for the eye wants to comfort cosmic suffering and it also wants comfort for itself. But the last words "im Weltall" hint that the waiting, the moment of suspension, may be eternal. In spite of this painful recognition, Nelly Sachs does not want to communicate bitterness, desperation, or even anger in her work. Her omission of an angry poem from the cycle *Sternverdunkelung* proves this. The poem reads in part:

> Welt, wie kannst du deine Spiele weiterspielen
> und die Zeit betrügen—
> Welt, man hat die kleinen Kinder wie
> Schmetterlinge,
> flügelschlagend in die Flamme geworfen—
>
> und deine Erde ist nicht wie ein fauler Apfel
> in den schreckaufgejagten Abgrund geworfen
> worden
>
> Und Sonne und Mond sind weiter
> spazierengegangen—
> zwei schieläugige Zeugen, die nichts gesehen
> haben.
>
> (World, how can you continue your games
> and deceive time—
> World, small children, like butterflies flapping
> their wings, have been tossed into the flame
>
> and your earth was not thrown like a rotten apple
> into the terrified abyss—
>
> And sun and moon went

on with their walk
two cross-eyed witnesses who saw nothing.)

She does not forget and forgive; her poems tear again and again the black bandage, but she also longs for the moment of love that could heal the wound. In **"Landschaft aus Schreien"** she shows her readiness for that moment, though her yearning leap remains shackled in suspension. She comes closest to peace and fulfillment in those poems wherein she describes the true death, the gentle dissolution willed and welcomed in the rhythm of existence:

Nicht zu landen
auf den Ozeanen des süchtigen Blutes
nur zu wiegen sich
in Lichtmusik aus Ebbe und Flut
nur zu wiegen sich
im Rhythmus des unverwundeten
Ewigkeitszeichen:

            Leben-Tod—

(Not to land
on the oceans of lustful blood
only to sway
in the light-music of ebb and flood
only to sway
in the rhythm of the unwounded
sign of eternity:

            Life-Death—)

Perhaps she found this rhythm on May 12, 1970, in Stockholm.

Dinah Dodds (essay date January 1976)

SOURCE: "The Process of Renewal in Nelly Sachs' *Eli,*" in *German Quarterly,* Vol. XLIX, No. 1, January, 1976, pp. 50-8.

[*In the following essay, Dodds examines* Eli *as a work representative of the influence of Hasidism on Sachs's writing. The piece includes a concise explanation of Hasidism and its place within Judaism.*]

In 1940 Nelly Sachs fled Germany for Sweden, leaving behind her the country of her German-Jewish heritage. The war years 1943 and 1944 saw the composition of the verse drama *Eli* and of many poems, which appeared in 1946 as *In den Wohnungen des Todes.* Here almost her sole poetic theme was death. . . . This preoccupation with the images of war manifests itself in *Eli* and in the poems of *In den Wohnungen des Todes.* The same tone, the same metaphors and symbols permeate both works. In the poems of the volume *Sternverdunklung,* published in 1949, death continues to be the prominent theme.

Nelly Sachs' work transcends, however, this brief period of history. Having been uprooted from her native tradition, she sought to reestablish ties with a much older tradition, with that found in Hasidism. For her, the years 1939-1945 were not linear history but rather constituted one revolution of a repeating cycle. In addition, they became part of a myth which, although resting on the basis of Hasidism, represented her own attempts to come to terms with her new life. Working within the myth of Hasidism, she created her own myth. In doing so she suspended the sensation of historical time and replaced it with mythic time.

What is mythic time? W. F. Otto states: "Der eigentliche Mythos ist immer Göttermythos. Zu ihm gehört auch der Heroenmythos." The gods and heroes of myth are seen by Mircea Eliade to have existed at the beginning of time, and enact a "sacred history, that is, a primordial event." For the man who believes in it, this primordial act becomes present reality during his religious ceremonies. Here man actually re-creates original acts of the gods, thus reactivating sacred time. Ernesto Grassi summarizes: "Mythos ist das Ordnende, das in einer unvergänglichen, stets gegenwärtigen Zeit ruht." Mythic time, then, is past and present, is timelessness, or is eternally repeating time. For us, as products of the Enlightenment and of a technological revolution, myth is a story, and the past is history. For Nelly Sachs, however, myth was alive through Hasidism, a myth which had begun with the events of the First Book of Moses and would end with the destruction of the world.

Hasidism itself was formed around the myth of the Baal Shem in eighteenth century Poland, and thus constitutes a relatively recent religious development within Judaism. Martin Buber characterized Hasidism as a combination of mysticism and saga in which tradition joined with folktale to produce a viable religion. Buber found further that "the Jews are a people that has never ceased to produce myth. . . . The religion of Israel has at all times felt itself endangered by this stream [of myth], but it is from it, in fact, that Jewish religiousness has at all times received its inner life."

It is through new or revitalized myth that religion endures. If myth is not constantly renewed by the individual, it turns stagnant and petrifies. "Living" myth is so only because it has become virtually an organic part of the believer. For Buber, Hasidism is the most viable form of Judaism since it is "the latest form of the Jewish myth that we know." Buber further states: "the Hasidic teaching is the proclamation of rebirth. No renewal of Judaism is possible that does not bear in itself the elements of Hasidism." Hasidism took mythic elements from the past and centered them around a new figure, its founder Israel ben Eliezer, who then came to be called the Baal Shem and provided believers with a renewed faith.

A careful reading of Nelly Sachs' work reveals a similar process of renewal occurring artistically. The existing body of Hasidic faith brings forth a new personal religion, which process is perhaps best illustrated by the verse play *Eli.* In *Eli,* Nelly Sachs never explicitly states the time of the action. The time is designated "Nach dem Martyrium," which could be taken to mean any of the countless times that Jews have been driven from their homes. Nelly Sachs only implies the present time of World War II, for this present is also a renewal of the past into which she slips repeatedly and almost unnoticeably. Similarly the words "deutsch" or "Deutschland" are never mentioned, for the persecutors of the Jews have had many names. Significantly, *Eli* takes place in Poland, the country in which Hasidism originated.

The play revolves around an event which had occurred earlier: the killing of eight-year-old Eli by a guard who thought he heard in Eli's pipe-playing a secret signal. Indeed, Eli was sounding a signal. He was calling to God to prevent the soldiers from taking away his parents. Michael, the town cobbler, arriving too late to save Eli, seeks out the guard upon whom divine justice is finally carried out.

The process of mythic renewal described by Buber is encountered in *Eli* on various levels. The most obvious renewal is the rebuilding of the town, which is depicted in ruins. This physical rebuilding can be seen to have a metaphysical parallel represented by the fountain, which occupies the central position on the stage. The fountain has been damaged, and Samuel, Eli's grandfather, struck dumb at the sight of his grandson's murder, is repairing it. The time is the New Year, for which the fountain will be ready: . . . with the advent of a New Year, life will start afresh in a renewal of the cycle of time. The fountain symbolizes this new life. Standing at the fountain, two women are deep in conversation about the recent events and the "Schritte" of the invading soldiers which still echo in their ears. . . . At the end of the scene the fountain begins to flow. . . . The *Bäckerin* thus appeals to the fountain for renewed life.

The water which is drawn from the fountain is also used for the building bricks of the town. . . . The buildings are renewed, as is the spiritual state of the people. As the fountain is repaired, optimism grows among the people, as evidenced in the words of the *Bäckerin* as well as in the prayer of one of the *Beter.* . . . His prayer for the reinstatement of lost unity with God may now, at this time of renewal, be heard. . . . Nelly Sachs has chosen a traditional image, the fountain of life, to express the revitalizing of this town. With the coming of the New Year, life also begins anew.

The fountain imagery has a deeper meaning, as it does also in a poem from *Sternverdunklung.* . . . In the first strophe, Nelly Sachs suggests that the fountain can be read as a chronicle of the Jewish people. Each time the Jews have moved to a new spot in their desert wanderings, they have dug a new well.

And each time, this well has been a vital source: it has cut away a slice of death from the whole body of life. The phrase "Wieviel Münder" suggests the uncountable number of such new fountains. . . . Where they thirsted, they dug new wells. This thirst can be seen as a drive for life.

In the figure of Eli himself a mythic renewal can be seen. Just as Buber saw Hasidism spring out of the small streets in Poland and form around the figure of the Baal Shem, so one can witness the origins of a myth centering around Eli. Eli's death is related in the manner of a myth: by word of mouth. The *Wäscherin* retells the story which *die Witwe Rosa* had told her before she died. Eli's tale, already told at two removes, will eventually become a vital and integral part of the Hasidic tradition as it exists within the fictional context of this small Polish town.

> **For us, as products of the Enlightenment and of a technological revolution, myth is a story, and the past is history. For Nelly Sachs, however, myth was alive through Hasidism, a myth which had begun with the events of the First Book of Moses and would end with the destruction of the world.**
>
> **—*Dinah Dodds***

Furthermore, Eli's flute-playing can be seen as a repetition of an act which occurred thousands of years ago—the exact time is irrelevant—at the foot of Mt. Sinai. In a poem from ***In den Wohnungen des Todes,*** we read:

> Einer war,
> Der blies den Schofar—
> Warf nach hinten das Haupt,
> Wie Rehe tun, wie die Hirsche
> Bevor sie trinken an der Quelle.

Almost identical words describe Eli in the play. One can assume that Eli, in playing his flute, was symbolically blowing the shofar, the rams' horn that was sounded when God revealed himself on Mt. Sinai. Later, in the eighth scene, the shofar sounds as part of the New Year's celebration. One of the *Beter* cries:

> Das Heimholerhorn hat geblasen.
> Er vergass uns nicht!

Although this reference is specifically to the New Year's ceremony, which has been in progress since the beginning of the scene, it is possible to interpret it to include Eli's pipe-blowing. For through Eli there has been direct communication between God and Israel. . . . The people feel hope that God has been called "home" and that the covenant has been renewed.

Buber relates a tale of a foolish man who climbed the Mount of Olives and blew the shofar, and a "rumor spread that this was the shofar blast which announced the redemption." The shofar, then, signals the hope for redemption as well as redemption itself. Eli, through a symbolic ritual act united the past of Mt. Sinai, the present of World War II and the future.

It is no accident that Eli is a child. Children occur often in Nelly Sachs' poetry. They are close to their origins, unspoiled by materialism and mundane life, and still in contact with God, especially in their dreams. . . . But Eli is no ordinary child. As the Hebrew name indicates, he is a God child. Thus it is appropriate that Eli should attempt to contact God directly with his pipe in a time of need: for Nelly Sachs, Eli's piping was a "versuchter Ausbruch des Menschlichen vor dem Entsetzen." It is also fitting that Eli's slayer be sought out by a figure who, like Eli, has mythic overtones: Michael.

Michael is one of the "sechsunddreissig Gerechte" (*Zaddikim*), who, according to Hasidic tradition, directly receive the light of God. Gershom Scholem cites a fourth century Babylonian teacher Abbaye who stated: "The world is never without thirty-six just men who daily receive the Divine Countenance." In her notes to *Eli* Nelly Sachs writes "Nach der chassidischen Mystik ist er [Michael] einer der geheimen Gottesknechte, die, sechsunddreissig an der Zahl—und ihnen gänzlich unbewusst—, das unsichtbare Universum tragen." And Buber writes in his *Hasidism* that the *Zaddik* leads the community in God's stead, acting as mediator between God and the people. He is the man "in whom the metaphysical responsibility of human beings steps out from mere consciousness and takes on an organic existence." It is he who performs the decisive, renewing movement of the world. . . .

The concept of "Scherben sehen," a plight in which man finds himself with his handcrafted world, is found often in Nelly Sachs' work and reflects her concern for man's loss of awareness of the basis of his existence which is rooted deeply in his beginnings and in God. The Baal Shem, in unity with God, has "den ungebrochenen Blick," which sees the whole, "von einem Ende der Welt zum anderen.". . . Michael is a second Baal Shem figure in the play. As the avenger of Eli's death, he can also be seen as Eli's spiritual father; in addition to God child, the name Eli in Hebrew also carries the meaning of "foster son." The name Michael means literally "who is like God" and carries connotations of "the loving one," and of the Biblical archangel who fought and defeated the devil.

Michael is also the guardian angel of Israel. Michael, like Eli, performs a priestly function. In communication with God, he carries out God's mission.

He is in addition, a cobbler, as was Jakob Böhme, whose mystical thought influenced Nelly Sachs. Hasidic legend also tells of a certain patriarch Enoch, who was a shoemaker: "At every stitch of his awl he not only joined the upper leather with the sole, but all upper things with all lower things, until he himself was transfigured from earthly Enoch into the transcendent Metatron, who had been the object of his meditation." As Ehrhard Bahr has pointed out, the words "lower" and "upper" occur frequently in the *Zohar,* the "Book of Splendor" and the testament of faith of Hasidism, to indicate the "lower" and "upper" realms of man God, of this life and the next. . . . Thus, Michael takes Eli's shoes with him on his search for the soldier. These shoes simultaneously embody Israel's past. . . .

Through his shoes, Eli is linked to the Sinai sand of his ancestors. His shoes are not of the present, rather "von noch früher." Herein is further evidenced his mythic existence. In these same shoes Moses wandered, and every other Jew of the Bible as well as all the wandering Jews of the future.

Samuel gives Michael Eli's pipe which, like a Mozartian Magic Flute, leads him to the goal of his quest. Michael's quest is ostensibly for Eli's slayer. But in fact Michael reaches the ultimate goal of life's quest in a mystic union with God. His union is not restricted to himself as an individual: he is "einer, der Israels Wanderschuhe zu Ende trägt."

The murder is also broadened into a re-enactment of the archetypal murder of Cain. . . .

By creating on multiple levels, Nelly Sachs effects a suspension of historical time and replaces it with mythic time where past, present and future are indistinguishable. And she sees in this leveling ability of mythic time the potential salvation not only of Judaism but of mankind in general. . . .

Eli ends with the transfiguration of Michael: a strong light and the image of an embryo appear above his head. The embryo signifies Michael's return to his beginnings as well as a rebirth of all. It is a sign of hope, denying the finality of death and reaffirming the presence of God.

This hope and faith lie at the very basis of the process of renewal. Like the fountain in *Eli* which, when not seen on the stage can still be heard splashing in the background, hope can be heard in all of Nelly Sachs' work. As the town is rebuilt with water from the fountain, so Nelly Sachs' life is rebuilt and renewed through her faith. Perhaps this is seen nowhere more clearly than in one of the poems of the cycle **"Gebete für den toten Bräutigam"**:

O mein Geliebter, vielleicht hat unsere Liebe in
den Himmel der
 Sehnsucht schon Welten geboren—

Wie unser Atemzug, ein—und aus, baut eine
Wiege für Leben
und Tod?

Sandkörner wir beide, dunkel vor Abschied, und in
das goldene
Geheimnis der Geburten verloren,
Und vielleicht schon von kommenden Sternen,
Monden und Sonnen umloht.

Lawrence L. Langer (essay date April 1976-77)

SOURCE: "Nelly Sachs," in *Colloquia Germanica,* Vol. 10,
April, 1976-77, pp. 316-25.

[*In the following essay, Langer discusses Sachs's treatment
of divine and human justice in her writings.*]

One of the last poems Nelly Sachs wrote before her death is
called **"Teile dich Nacht"** (the name also given to her last
volume of poems by its editor). Her first collection of verse
was called ***In den Wohnungen des Todes.*** It should come as
no surprise to us that the two words used most often in her
poems, according to the count of a diligent scholar, are "Tod"
and "Nacht". For in the twentieth century, we have lived in
the habitations of death as no previous generation has been
compelled to, and no matter how we "divide" night in our
search for greater light, we only seem to encounter the memory
of more corpses. "Death" and "night" are not merely metaphors for Nelly Sachs, they literally describe the reality of
her experience, the history of her time—and ours. They define the terrain which the imagination must cross in its search
for a vision to restore to men a sense of justice and a justification for human life. For without that sense, how can men tolerate their pain, or endure their existence? Night and death
are powerful masters that challenge the poet to find counter
images to resist their dominion. We survive the threat of annihilation only by "seeing", and the poet's images are indispensable beacons toward such insight.

Earlier poets have faced similar challenges, but their task
seems to have been more simple. The literary imagination
has addressed itself to the problem of divine and human justice—and injustice—from the beginning. Near the outset of
the *Odyssey,* Zeus complains: "Oh, for shame, how the mortals put the blame upon us gods, for they say evils come from
us, but it is they, rather, who by their own recklessness win
sorrow beyond what is given." Milton is even more explicit,
for the opening words of *Paradise Lost* sing of "man's first
disobedience", placing the responsibility for human suffering firmly in the hands of the human chooser. The author of
the Book of Job offers a vision potentially more tragic, for
here it is difficult to reconcile divine displeasure with human
agency. Unlike Adam and Odysseus, Job has not consciously
transgressed divine ordinance; if, as the magisterial Voice
from the Whirlwind chastises him, he was not present when
the morning stars sang together, the fault can hardly be Job's.
Beyond the assertion of his moral innocence lies the melancholy fact that we live in a universe where men often "win
sorrow beyond what is given", even when the recklessness of
their behavior is not to blame. Job's comforters would have
preferred Zeus's version.

What would Nelly Sachs have preferred? As a Jewish writer,
she inherited an ancient tradition of suffering far in excess of
comprehensible cause, but still compatible with spiritual aspiration and a tragic view of existence. As a Jewish writer
who lived through the Holocaust (though not a literal survivor), she inherited a modern tradition of suffering so far in
excess of comprehensible cause that it is not compatible with
any view of existence hitherto available to the human imagination. The Holocaust has so complicated the question of justice that some have suggested the temporary withdrawal of
divine presence from human affairs. But Nelly Sachs wrote
as a poet, not as a philosopher or theologian, and once having
accepted the challenge of finding a language to express the
paradox of inexplicable Jewish suffering (which gradually
merges with the larger idea of inexplicable human suffering), she was faced with the task of locating images to ani-
mate this paradox.

Nelly Sachs has been called one of the great language healers
of our time. George Steiner and Alexander Solzhenitsyn,
among others, have commented on how an age of atrocity
has wounded the word and thus victimized both art and the
artist. For Nelly Sachs, the dilemma is not merely restoring
health to the word, as if language could be cured of corruption by a stroke of the imaginative pen, but recognizing that
some words are incurable—"Wahrheit" and "Recht", for example, scarcely appear in her poems—while others, like "Tod"
and "Nacht", achieve a resonance that resembles no familiar
refrain. Just as music is politically suspect to Mann's
Settembrini, all nominatives are untrustworthy for Nelly
Sachs, including the commonest nouns in our vocabulary.
Indeed, she argues that one must return to the separate letters
of the alphabet if one is to re-establish a link between words
and spiritual reality. "The alphabet is the land where the spirit
settles and the holy name blooms", she says in a note to one
of her dramatic pieces. "It is the lost world after every deluge. It must be gathered in by the somnambulists with signs
and gestures." The poet plays a major role in restoring connection with the spiritual powers, thereby saving the drowned
word.

Sometimes it seems as if Nelly Sachs has narrowed her artistic goal to rehabilitating the purity of the noun. Her poems are signs and gestures in tribute to this part of speech, not to verbs, and least of all to adjectives, as if for her, poetry were no more than a renaming of the items of creation, a sanctification of reality by a reassertion of the noun. Forty-eight of the fifty commonest words in her poems are nouns. One would like to say that she uses them precisely, so that the reader might define their meaning unmistakably. She *chooses* words precisely, but their echo, the reverberations they cause when we drop them like shining pebbles in the pool of the imagination—these are less clear. We know what "night" and "death" mean, but she refuses to use them in familiar contexts, we must guess at their allusions, while remaining only half-convinced of our solutions to their shadowy enigmas. It is not just that reality is enigmatic, but that language, having been shaken loose from its usual moorings, continues to float on an ocean of uncertainty. Her nouns, unencumbered by descriptive epithets, are like new-baked bricks thudding on the pavement of the mind. Death, love, time, night, star, earth, blood—those favorite words of Emily Dickinson too—seek to reconstruct a reality out of the void, solid blocks of experience that will rebuild the continuity of our lives while reminding us what we have paid for the spare architecture of her vision.

> As a Jewish writer who lived through the Holocaust (though not a literal survivor), [Sachs] inherited a modern tradition of suffering so far in excess of comprehensible cause that it is not compatible with any view of existence hitherto available to the human imagination.
>
> *—Lawrence L. Langer*

That very continuity, however, requires an unprecedented revision of the vision of reality that makes it possible in the first place. The dilemma, the abyss between God's will and man's fate, is exposed in the initial poem of *In den Wohnungen des Todes*—**"O die Schornsteine"**. The epigraph to this poem from Job is both paradox and affirmation: "Und wenn diese meine Haut zerschlagen sein wird, so werde ich ohne mein Fleisch Gott schauen" ("And though after my skin worms destroy this body, yet in my flesh shall I see God."—Job, 19:26). It reminds us that man's longing for continuity is eternally contradicted by his physical suffering, and that when such suffering exceeds the bounds of moral reason—as it did in Job, and even more, during the Holocaust—the issue is not merely a simple test of one man's faith, but the hope of a people, and the survival of a feeling for spiritual reality. How, asks Nelly Sachs, shall that feeling

endure? Not, she replies, by returning to the terms offered by the Book of Job. For Job still thinks of a personal God, demands a confrontation, while Nelly Sachs introduces her epigraph only to warn us against false expectations: a Voice from the Whirlwind would be choked by the smoke from crematorium chimneys.

The New English Bible translation of this passage from Job shifts the emphasis to judicial metaphor, making it an even stronger testament of faith, but the last such unequivocal statement we will find in Nelly Sachs's poems; its irrelevance to her imaginative world confirms the need for a new version of justice, human and divine: "But in my heart I know my vindicator lives, and that he will rise last to speak in court. And I shall discern my witness standing at my side, and see my defending counsel, even God himself. Whom I shall see with my own eyes, I myself and no other." (Job, 19:25-27.) The poem **"O the Chimneys"** and its successors eschew such affirmations for questions; to the question, "Wer erdachte euch und baute Stein auf Stein / Den Weg für Flüchtlinge aus Rauch?" ("Who devised you and laid stone upon stone / the road for refugees of smoke?"), we are left with anguish in place of an answer, the perplexing fact of extermination of "Israels Leib" ("Israel's body") but no vindicator to justify or transcend that awful human fate.

Uncertainty looms between grief and consolation in most of Nelly Sachs's early poems. In a climate of justice, one knows one's loss, even if the reasons for it are obscure. But in a poem like **"Wenn ich nur wüßte"** (**"If I only knew"**), there is a gulf between mourner and victim, an ineradicable scar on the memory, forbidding any reconciliation between justice and suffering:

> Wenn ich nur wüßte
> Worauf dein letzter Blick ruhte.
> War es ein Stein, der schon viele letzte Blicke
> Getrunken hatte, bis sie in Blindheit
> Auf den Blinden fielen?
>
> (If I only knew
> On what your last look rested.
> Was it a stone that had drunk
> So many last looks that they fell
> Blindly upon its blindness?)
>
> ....
>
> Oder sandte dir diese Erde
> Die keinen ungeliebt von hinnen gehen läßt
> Ein Vogelzeichen durch die Luft,
> Erinnernd deine Seele, daß siezuckte
> In ihrem qualverbrannten Leib?
>
> (Or did this earth,

Which lets no one depart unloved,
Send you a bird-sign through the air,
Reminding your soul that it quivered
In the torment of its burnt body?)

We are not in search of new images, but of new ways to assimilate the old ones: earth and air, body and soul are not alien to our ears, but appear strange to our imagination because of the uses to which the human form has been put in their behalf.

This was the quandary Nelly Sachs faced as a poet, as normal human relationships disintegrated and men lacked a frame for reshaping the ensuing chaos into a usable form. This is the lament of **"Chor der Waisen"** (**"Chorus of the Orphans"**):

> Welt warum hast du die weichen Mütter
> genommen
> Und die Väter, die sagen: Mein
> Kind du gleichst mir!
> Wir Waisen gleichen niemand mehr
> auf der Welt!
> O Welt
> Wir klagen dich an!
>
> (World, why have you taken our soft mothers from
> us
> And the fathers who say: My child, you are like
> me!
> We orphans are like no one in this world anymore!
> O world
> We accuse you!)

Once again we are faced with unanswered and perhaps unanswerable questions, and no voice to speak with majesty *or* vindication as witness for man. Nelly Sachs is more concerned with recognizing the alienation which such unprecedented violations of justice have imposed on the human spirit. At least this is a necessary first step. In **"Chor der Sterne"** (**"Chorus of the Stars"**), she makes clear that man must be his own witness, that only man can incorporate the catastrophe of the Holocaust into a cosmic vision which includes and reaches beyond disaster:

> Erde, Erde, bist du eine Blinde
> geworden
> Vor den Schwesternaugen der Plejaden
> Oder der Waage prüfendem Blick?
> Mörderhände gaben Israel einen Spiegel
> Darin es sterbend sein Sterben
> erblickte—
>
> Erde, o Erde
> Stern aller Sterne

> Einmal wird ein Sternbild Spiegel heißen.
> Dann o Blinde wirst du wieder sehn!
>
> (Earth, earth, have you gone blind
> Before the sister eyes of the
> Pleiades
> Or Libra's examining gaze?
> Murder hands gave Israel a mirror
> In which it recognized its death
> while dying
>
> Earth, O earth
> Star of stars
> One day a constellation will be
> called *mirror.*
> Then, O blind one, you will see again.)

But if, to restore the lost connection between earth and stars, men and constellations, a mirror reflecting not man's destiny but his murdered past must ascend into the heavens as a permanent fixture in the divine cosmology, then a reordering of how we perceive our fate is crucial. For if "they" recognized their death while dying, *we* must renew acquaintance with their death while living, gazing into the skies of the mind to see their murdered past each time we seek a token of our eternal future. We pay a painful price for the right to "see again". The unborn in **"Chor der Ungeborenen"** (**"Chorus of the Unborn"**) offer promise for the past dead "Wir kommenden Lichter für eure Traurigkeit" ("We future lights for your sorrow")—but mourning is now indistinguishable from hope, and if Nelly Sachs were to join two nouns to urge on us a fresh way of perceiving, she might call it "Trauerhoffnung".

In a world where "tears mean eternity", as Nelly Sachs writes in **"Stimme des Heiligen Landes"** (**"The Voice of the Holy Land"**), abstractions like justice and injustice lose their vigor as part of a poetic vocabulary. Night was once an interval between twilight and dawn, but atrocity has permanently altered its symbolic possibilities, as the following lament confirms:

> Nacht, Nacht,
> einmal warst du der Geheimnisse
> Braut
> schattenliliengeschmückt—
>
> (Night, night,
> Once you were the bride of mysteries
> adorned with lilies of shadow—)
>
> ....
>
> Nacht, Nacht
> jetzt bist du der Friedhof

für eines Sternes schrecklichen
Schiffbruch geworden—
sprachlos taucht die Zeit in dir
unter mit ihren Zeichen:
Der stürzende Stein
und die Fahne aus Rauch!

(Night, night
now you are the graveyard
for the terrible shipwreck of a
star—
time sinks speechless in you
with its sign:
The falling stone
and the flag of smoke.)

Time sinks speechless into night as a kind of requiem to the fate of humanity at the hands of history. It will reemerge, as in the poem **"Auf daß die Verfolgten nicht Verfolger werden"** (**"That the persecuted may not become persecutors"**), but accompanied by images that do not coalesce, that threaten disorder, and disrupt the harmony which once enabled good and evil to achieve some kind of balance in a divine plan. The murdered past furnishes a different measure for time, while the clock hours of man and the eternity of God are stained by a violence that will not conform to old visions of order:

Schritte
die Zeit zahlend mit Schreien,
Seufzern,
Austritt des Blutes bis es gerinnt,
Todesschweiß zu Stunden häufend—

Schritte der Henker
Uber Schritten der Opfer,
Sekundenzeiger im Gang der Erde,
von welchem Schwarzmond
schrecklich gezogen?

In der Musik der Sphären
wo schrillt euer Ton?

(Footsteps
measuring time with screams, groans
the seeping of blood until it congeals,
heaping up hours of sweaty death—

Steps of hangmen
over the steps of victims,
what black moon pulled with such terror
the sweep-hand in earth's orbit?

Where does your note shrill
in the music of the spheres?)

The "Schwarzmond" ("black moon") of Nelly Sachs is comparable to the "Schwarze Milch" ("black milk") of Paul Celan's *Todesfuge*, emotional opposites that fuse into a single image what once was a polarity. Our challenge is to find in the music of the spheres a note to harmonize with the steps of *such* victims and *such* hangmen. God's will, in this matter, if it exists, is to be discovered, not revealed; one commentator speaks of Nelly Sachs's need to pierce the "Ungeist" of the world, and goes on to describe this world in terms of Jakob Böhme and the Zohar that would have been familiar to the poet: "God is unreachable. He is the holy Nothing . . . God has no qualities, no desires. He is eternal silence, eternal night. In this abyss of infinity life begins in that a will or longing arises, like light when it is born out of darkness." But silence and night are eternal, and the light and life which may be reborn from their womb possess only a fragile and tentative strength. Although she longs for recovery herself, Nelly Sachs is never certain how much is possible, as the following lines suggest:

Wenn die Propheten
mit den Sturmschwingen der Ewigkeit
hineinführen
wenn sie aufbrächen deinen Gehörgang mit den
Worten:
Wer von euch will Krieg führen gegen ein
Geheimnis
wer will den Sterntod erfinden?

Wenn die Propheten aufständen
in der Nacht der Menschheit
wie Liebende, die das Herz des
Geliebten suchen,
Nacht der Menschheit
würdest du ein Herz zu vergeben
haben?

(If the prophets
rushed in with the storm-pinions
of eternity
If they broke open your acoustic
duct with the words:
Which of you wants to make war
against a mystery
who wants to invent the star-death?

If the prophets stood up
in the night of mankind
like lovers who seek the heart of
the beloved,
night of mankind
would you have a heart to offer?)

Neologisms like "Schwarzmond" and "Sterntod" represent attempts to use a process of linguistic annealing to squeeze fresh vision out of weary words and wearier men. To invent a "star-death" is to revise the relationship between heaven and earth, and even if the prophets, inspired by eternity, have the strength to embrace a destiny that includes the Holocaust, is the human heart strong enough to endure such an encounter? The entire poem is written in the subjunctive mood, a conditional interrogative. If divinity tried to restore justice, offer love anew, would the human longing for justice be vital enough for revival, the heart still have enough blood to respond? Again the night of mankind looms between past and future, extinction and renewal, a negation so pervasive that it may have withered the arteries of feeling through which once flowed the blood of faith and love.

But Nelly Sachs hopes that the withered arteries of Israel's body are flexible. Out of the unpromising matter of a tainted blood, a vital future may yet flow, though its origin must not be suppressed. The Dajan, a sober voice in the play *Eli,* cautions his more optimistic fellow-survivors:

> Der neue Pentateuch, sage ich Euch
> der neue Pentateuch,
> steht mit dem Schimmel der Angst
> geschrieben
> auf den Wänden der Todeskeller!
>
> (The new Pentateuch, I tell you, the
> new Pentateuch
> is written in mildew, the mildew of
> fear
> on the walls of the death cellars.)

If men are to return to the beginning to recreate their universe and reconstitute its holiness, they must acknowledge the difference between the post-Holocaust era and the original moment of creation. Adam's was the innocence of not-yet-having-lived. Nelly Sachs's survivors are heirs of annihilation, vessels of memory who seek equilibrium between an unaccountable past and an indefinable future. "Alle Zeit", says Beryll in Nelly Sachs's brief dramatic piece called *Beryll sieht in der Nacht* (*Beryll Sees in the Night*), "ist Sieger- und Besiegten-Zeit" ("All time is conqueror- and conquered-time"), while another character announces: "Immer das Reine aus Unreinem" ("Always the pure from the impure"). One is reminded of Elie Wiesel's new formulation of the old tragic dilemma: "The problem is not: to be or not to be. But rather: to be and not to be." Whatever principle of justice emerges from this chaos, good will always reflect the shadow of evil, while the *Urlicht* or primal light will shine *through,* not in opposition to the darkness. Beryll is Hamlet-like in his uncertainty, as he gazes at a stone floating in the twilight of space and fails to perceive how little it takes to transform this "Stein" into a "Stern":

> Ist das die Erde—ist das ein Totenschädel?

> Ich zweifle—ich zweifle—
> Im traumhaften Raum des Wortes leben wir
> Schlafen wir oder wachen wir?
> oder im Nichts—
> Ich lausche an einem Totenschädel—
>
> (Is that the earth—is that a skull?
> I waver—I waver—
> In the dreamlike space of the word we live
> Do we sleep or do we wake?
> or in nothingness—
> I listen to a death's head—)

For also swimming in space are the letters of the alphabet, and another figure in this mystery play combines them into words, which light up in a message: "Nichts—ist die Sucht nach Etwas" ("Nothing—is the passion for Something"). This echo of Böhme makes even more meaningful Nelly Sachs's dictum that the "alphabet is the land where the spirit settles and the holy name blooms."

For though Beryll wavers between earth and skull, the poet is more secure. "Gesang ist Leiden" ("song is suffering") says the voice of Night in this mystery play. Poems renew life by forming letters into songs, letters that peer "aus dem Fenster der Einsamkeit" ("from the window of loneliness") in a continuing "Sucht nach Etwas", not in light or eternal being but "im dunklen Stoff der Nacht" ("in the dark substance of night"). Divine and human justice are replaced by a darkness that threatens to engulf even as it encourages insight, while the conquering and conquered word is man's chief weapon against nothingness. Men are totally responsible for making something out of it. Nelly Sachs's verse is *her* contribution to this passion for Something that was once called Order or Justice, a Something that comes into being in the very process of creation, celebrating the human imagination which conquers through art even as it is conquered itself by time and night and death.

William H. McClain (essay date Autumn 1980)

SOURCE: "The Imaging of Transformation in Nelly Sachs's Holocaust Poems," in *Hebrew University Studies in Literature,* Vol. 8, No. 2, Autumn, 1980, pp. 281-300.

[*In the following essay, McClain examines the "images of transformation" in Sachs's Holocaust poems, and discusses poems which provide insight into the personal losses the Holocaust imposed on her.*]

One of Nelly Sachs's most revealing comments about her writing is her statement in an early letter to her friend Walter Berendsohn that her aim as a poet was ". . . die Verwandlung der Materie in das uns jenseitig Verborgene" ("the transmutation of the material into that which is hidden from us in the beyond"). One of the ways in which she sought to realize this aim technically was to transpose into various images of transformation her intuitions of the connections between the visible world and an invisible higher reality. She created several of these images for the holocaust poems and dramas which she wrote during her first exile-years in Sweden. Because she employed them again and again in modified form in later poetic works, however, they gradually became fundamental modes of expression in her poetic vocabulary, as several scholars have pointed out. In this paper I have attempted to show how in the poems for which they were initially created these images fulfill not only a representational function but also function in a subtle way as rhetorical devices. To make clear this dual function I have selected from Nelly Sachs's two collections of holocaust poems, *In den Wohnungen des Todes* [*In the Houses of Death*] in 1947 and *Sternverdunkelung* [*Star's Darkening*] in 1949, six poems in which the images of transformation serve both as a means of evoking the aspect of the holocaust experience with which the poem deals and of persuading the reader to accept the point of view from which the experience is represented.

For Nelly Sachs the only way of living with the anguish of witnessing the holocaust as an outsider was, as she told her Swedish friend Olof Lagercrantz, to write about it. Although her holocaust poems are rooted in profound emotion, their tone is restrained and controlled. Geneviève Bianquis aptly characterized the attitude reflected in them as "la plus noble inquiétude," and it is beautifully exemplified by the first poem in *In den Wohnungen des Todes,* **"O die Schornsteine" ("O the chimneys"):**

> Und wenn diese meine Haut zerschlagen sein wird,
> so werde ich ohne mein Fleisch Gott schauen
> —Hiob

> (And after my skin has thus been destroyed,
> then without my flesh I shall see God
> —Job)

O die Schornsteine

O die Schornsteine
Auf den sinnreich erdachten Wohnungen des
Todes,
Als Israels Leib zog aufgelöst in Rauch
Durch die Luft—
Als Essenkehrer ihn ein Stern empfing
Der schwarz wurde
Oder war es ein Sonnenstrahl?

O die Schornsteine!
Freiheitswege für Jeremias und Hiobs Staub—

Wer erdachte euch und baute Stein auf Stein
Den Weg für Flüchtlinge aus Rauch?
O die Wohnungen des Todes,
Einladend hergerichtet
Für den Wirt des Hauses, der sonst Gast war—
O ihr Finger,
Die Eingangsschwelle legend
Wie ein Messer zwischen Leben und Tod—
O ihr Schornsteine,
O ihr Finger,
Und Israels Leib im Rauch durch die Luft!

(O the chimneys/ On the ingeniously conceived houses of death, / When Israel's body rose as smoke / Through the air— / Was welcomed as a chimney-sweep by a star / That was blackened, / Or was it a ray of sun? // O the chimneys! Ways to freedom for the dust / of Jeremiah and Job— / Who conceived of you and built, stone upon stone, / The way for refugees turned into smoke? // O the houses of death, / Prepared invitingly / For the host who was formerly a guest— / O fingers, / Laying the thresholds / Like a knife between life and death— // O chimneys, / O fingers / and Israel's body as smoke through the air!)

The prefatory verses from Job [19.26], which recall the inscrutable ways of God toward man as exemplified by one of the most perplexing episodes in the Bible, dispose us to read **"O die Schornsteine"** more dispassionately than we otherwise might by encouraging us to think of the events in it in relation to earlier examples of seemingly meaningless suffering. In keeping with this seeming desire to put us in a dispassionate frame of mind the speaker in the poem softens the initial impact of the crematoria by first directing our line of vision upwards to the chimneys and the smoke coming from them rather than to the doors through which the corpses were passed. Like the prefatory verses, the mention of Jeremiah and Job also causes us to think of the most recent Jewish suffering in relation to earlier times of persecution and anguish. Only in the fifteenth verse does the speaker finally focus attention on the doorways. Here, too, however, the emotional impact is lessened by the use of metonymy in referring to the builders of the houses of death simply as "Finger". Also conciliatory is the earlier reference to "Freiheitswege" which suggests that in designing these ingenious structures the persecutors unwittingly provided access to a higher, spiritual form of existence.

In spite of its grim subject matter **"O die Schornsteine"** might be said to offer a vision of the holocaust which is at least in a limited sense hopeful. This sense of hopefulness is communicated mainly by what we might call its "positive" images of transformation, which collectively suggest that the smoky remains of the victims ascend from the chimneys of the crematoria into a space which is redeeming space, as the startling metaphor of the chimney-sweep welcomed by a star so strongly implies. By thus evoking an impression of a process of transfiguration the images of transformation also become a means of suggesting that the mass suffering in the houses of death may have an as yet inscrutable meaning. Their power to persuade us to share the vision of the speaker in the poem stems mainly from their vividness and their dynamism, which enable the poem as a whole to generate momentarily the illusion that the mysterious process of transformation of which it speaks may actually be happening before our very eyes.

One of Nelly Sachs's most shattering exile-experiences was the news that the man with whom she had been in love as a young woman had died in a concentration camp. The most direct expression of her grief are the ten poems in *In den Wohnungen des Todes* entitled *Gebete für den toten Bräutigam* [*Prayers for the Dead Betrothed*]. The third of these prayers strikingly exemplifies her ability even in her early poems to evolve boldly original images of transformation:

> Vielleicht aber braucht Gott die Sehnsucht, wo
> sollte sonst sie auch bleiben,
> Sie, die mit Küssen und Tränen und Senfzern füllt
> die geheimnisvollen Räume der Luft—
> Vielleicht ist sie das unsichtbare Erdreich, daraus
> die gluhenden Wurzeln der Sterne treiben—
> Und die Strahlenstimme über die Felder der
> Trennung, die zum Wiedersehn ruft?
> O mein Geliebter, vielleicht hat unsere Liebe in
> den Himmel der Sehnsucht schon Welten
> geboren—
> Wie unser Atemzug, ein—und aus, baut eine
> Wiege für Leben und Tod?
> Sandkorner wir beide, dunker vor Abschied, und in
> das goldene Geheimnis der Geburten, verloren,
> Und vielleicht schon von kommenden Sternen,
> Monden und Sonnen umloht.

(But perhaps God needs the longing, where else should it stay / The longing that fills the secret spaces of air with kisses, tears, and sighs— / perhaps it is the invisible earth-realm from which the glowing roots of stars grow— / Or the light-voice that summons to reunion over fields of separation? / O my beloved, perhaps our love has already brought forth entire worlds into the heaven of longing— / As our breath, in—and out, forms a cradle for life and death? / We are both grains of sand, dark because of our leaving, and who have already lost their way into the golden secret of births / And perhaps already reflect the light of coming stars, moons, and suns.)

Because of the long lines, the subtly shifting rhythms, and the many dashes, the regular ab ab cd cd rhyme-scheme of the prayer may not at first be noticed. Structurally, however, the rhyme-scheme fulfills an important function by linking and thus emphasizing keywords. In form the prayer might be

likened to a mystical monody about the possibility that longing, in this case the longing of a living lover for a dead beloved, might perhaps form a spiritual bridge between the visible world and the invisible beyond. No rational reason is offered for believing in such a possibility. The poem opens with a conjecture which is supported only by a second one in the form of a question. With these two as their sole logical foundation three further conjectures are proposed. A sense of the speaker's uncertainty is also imparted by the long, slowly progressing lines, the recurrent dashes, and the frequent repetitions of "vielleicht." Only in the seventh verse does the speaker indicate assurance with the assertion that she and her dead betrothed are "Sandkörner" and that both are "dunkel vor Abschied." This latter enigmatic formulation suggests both that the speaker looks forward to her departure and that it may be imminent; and it also intimates her awareness that her dead betrothed shares her anticipation of the journey, which will ostensibly take them deeper into the realm in which the dead beloved waits, and in which the union they could not enjoy on earth will be perfectly consummated as a spiritual union.

As an expression of longing for supra-earthly existence, through its central theme of reciprocal longing of living and dead as a possible means of bridging the gap separating this world from the beyond, and also as an anticipatory vision of the afterlife, Nelly Sachs's third prayer recalls the final stanzas of Novalis's sixth hymn to the night and thus offers an opportunity to compare one of her early exile-poems with a major work by the poet who, as she herself admitted, was one of her most important literary models. When one compares the two works, however, one discovers differences that are even more striking than the similarities.

In the sixth of the *Hymnen an die Nacht* the speaker longs for death because it promises reunion with his dead betrothed; and, as though in response to the intensity of his longing, he receives reassuring signs of various kinds from the beyond, as he ecstatically proclaims in the closing stanzas:

> Unendlich und geheimnisvoll
> Durchströmt uns süsser Schauer—
> Mir däucht, aus tiefen Fernen scholl
> Ein Echo unsrer Trauer.
> Die Lieben sehnen sich wohl auch
> Und sandten uns der Sehnsucht Hauch.
>
> Hinunter zu der süssen Braut,
> Zu Jesus, dem Geliebten—
> Getrost, die Abenddämmrung graut
> Den Liebenden, Betrübten.
> Ein Traum bricht unsre Banden los
> Und senkt uns in des Vaters Schoss.

(Infinite and mysterious, / A sweet shudder courses through

us— / It seems as though from afar resounds / An echo of our grief. / Doubtless our loved ones long for us too / And send us the breath of their longing. // Downward to the sweet bride, / To Jesus, the beloved— / be consoled, the twilight grows gray / For lovers and those who grieve. / A dream bursts our bonds asunder / And lowers us into our Father's arms.)

From Novalis's use here of the present tense, from his inclusion of the reader in the speaker's experience through the use of the first person plural pronoun, from his direct appeals to the reader's visual and auditory senses, and also from his speaker's final exhortation, we may conclude that he wished to impart in these final verses the impression of a moment of higher revelation as it is taking place. The images of transformation,—the striking oxymoron portraying the beginning of eternal night as dawning twilight and the dream of release from earthly bonds,—also seem to have been designed to impart a sense of the immediacy of the mysterious events taking place. The speaker's obvious confidence in the validity of his epiphanic experience, which recalls noetic experiences of mystics, is even reflected in the metrical pattern of alternating masculine and feminine rhymes which communicates a sense of certainty on the sound level of the poem by generating a rhythmical impression of movement toward a point where dissonances will be harmonized and dichotomies overcome.

In Nelly Sachs's prayer, on the other hand, the long, slowly moving lines, the silences indicated by the frequent dashes, and the tentative qualities of the formulations are more suggestive of a groping toward meaning than of meaning apprehended. Even more striking than these differences, however, is the fact that Nelly Sachs's persona receives no reassuring echo from the beyond. This silence is significant as a reminder that a century and a half after Novalis poets like Nelly Sachs were no longer able to acquire the same degree of understanding of self in relation to the larger process of being.

Although tentative in its formulations and conclusions, Nelly Sachs's third prayer to the dead betrothed reflects poetic skill comparable to Novalis's; and because of the unique way in which it combines lament and affirmation it is also comparable to his sixth hymn in affective power. Because it is far more a meditation on the possibility of belief than an expression of belief, it is not surprising that the persona speaking in it makes no attempt to involve us in her experience or to persuade us of its validity. And if we feel consoled by what she says, it is only because it recalls the solace that hope can offer.

Death and transfiguration is also the main theme of the third of Nelly Sachs's *Grabschriften in die Luft geschrieben* (*Epitaphs written on Air*) in *In den Wohnungen des Todes,* and for this poem, too, she created striking images of transformation to portray the experience:

Die Tänzerin [D.H.]

Deine Füsse wussten wenig von der Erde,
Sie wanderten auf einer Sarabande
Bis zum Rande—
Denn Sehnsucht war deine Gebärde.

Wo du schliefst, da schlief ein Schmetterling
Der Verwandlung sichtbarstes Zeichen,
Wie bald solltest du ihn erreichen
Raupe und Puppe und schon ein Ding

In Gottes Hand.
Licht wird aus Sand

(Your feet knew but little of earth, / They wandered in a sarabande / Up to the very edge— / For longing was your gesture. // Where you slept there slept a butterfly / Most visible sign of metamorphosis. / How soon you were to reach Him / Larva, pupa, and already a thing // In God's hand. / Sand is transmuted into light.)

The epitaph, in memory of a young dancer who died in the holocaust and who is identified simply by the initials D.H., conjures up before the imagination a space filled briefly by a dancing figure who exists now only in the memory of others. As remembered here by the speaker, however, she seems almost to live again for a moment. Her dancing, as she moves through the carefully planned choreography of the poem, expresses the intense love of life which artists with the potential of becoming fine performers often manifest; and the affective power of the poem as a lamentation stems mainly from this impression of a gifted individual of great potential who is cut off prematurely. The sadness thus evoked is alleviated, however, by the assurance in the final verses that the young dancer lives on in transfigured form in the beyond.

On the sound-level the rhyme-scheme serves as a means of conveying a sense of connections between visible and invisible reality by linking keywords associated with both domains ("Schmetterling" and "Ding" and "Hand" and "Sand"). The short, rapidly moving lines function equally effectively as a means of creating a rhythmical impression of the young dancer's speedy attainment of transfiguration.

The initial image of dancing feet scarcely touching earth and the characterization of dancing as longing enable Nelly Sachs to convey in a few words the impression that the dead girl's dedication to her art and also the nature of that art itself may have facilitated her transition from material to spiritual existence. The image of the butterfly vividly expresses the idea that the longing for transfiguration is a universal longing present in all creatures. And by thus recalling the longing of all living forms to become something higher and more beautiful, the image prepares us for the final mysterious image of sand transmuted into light by means of which the poem conveys an actual impression of the process of transfiguration which has recently taken place. Again, as in **"O die Schornsteine"** and the third prayer for the dead betrothed, the experience of transfiguration is expressed verbally in the form of an image which is an oxymoron, as though to imply that the paradox may be the only means of conceptualizing the ineffable.

To express the mass suffering of the holocaust victims, Nelly Sachs wrote a series of poems in choral form. Because of their dramatic quality and the point of vantage from which the speakers comment in them on the holocaust experience many of these *Chöre nach der Mitternacht* (*Choruses after Midnight*) recall the choruses of Greek tragedies. Particularly reminiscent of the choral laments in Greek tragedy is the *Chorus of the Stars*:

Wir Sterne, wir Sterne
Wir wandernder, glänzender, singender Staub—
Unsere Schwester die Erde ist die Blinde geworden
Unter den Leuchtbildern des Himmels—
Ein Schrei ist geworden
Unter den Singenden
Sie, die Sehnusuchtvollste
Die im Staube begann ihr Werk: Engel zu bilden
Sie, die die Seligkeit in ihrem Geheimnis trägt
Wie goldführendes Gewässer
Augeschüttet in der Nacht liegt sie
Wie Wein auf den Gassen
Des Bösen gelbe Schwefellichter hüpfen auf ihrem Leib.

O Erde, Erde
Stern aller Sterne
Durchzogen von den Spuren des Heimwehs
Die Gott selbst begann
Ist niemand auf dir, der sich erinnert an deine Jugend?
Niemand, der sich hingibt als Schwimmer
Den Meeren von Tod?
Ist niemandes Sehnsucht reif geworden
Dass sie sich erhebt wie der engelhaft fliegende Samen
Der Löwenzahnblüte?

Erde, Erde, bist du eine Blinde geworden
Vor den Schwesteraugen der Plejaden
Oder der Waage prüfendem Blick?

Mörderhände gaben Israel einen Spiegel
Darin es sterbend sein Sterben erblickte—

Erde, o Erde
Stern aller Sterne

Einmal wird ein Sternbild Spiegel heissen.
Dann, o Blinde wirst du wieder sehn!

(We stars, we stars / We wandering, glistening, singing dust— / Earth, our sister, has gone blind / Among the constellations of heaven, / She has become a strident cry / Among the singers— / She, richest in longing, / Who began in dust her task of forming angels, / She who carries bliss as a secret within her / Like streams bearing gold— / Now lies in the night / Like wine spilled on the streets— / And over her body evil's yellow lights flicker. // O earth, earth / Star of stars / Veined by the traces of homesickness / Initiated by God Himself— / Have you no one who remembers your youth? / No one who will surrender himself as the swimmer / To the oceans of death? / Has no one's longing ripened / So it will rise like the angelically flying seed / Of the dandelion? // Earth, earth, have you gone blind/ Before the sister eyes of the Pleiades / Or Libra's scrutinizing gaze? // Murderers' hands gave Israel a mirror / In which it saw its own death as it died— // Earth, o earth / Star of stars / One day a constellation will be called mirror. / Then, o blind one, you will see again!)

The intricate pattern of accented and unaccented syllables in the opening lines conveys on the sound-level the impression that the stars are moving through space along their orbital paths as they lament over their fallen sister. The frequent dashes, on the other hand, suggest that they are at times so overwhelmed by distress that they cannot speak for a while. To the reader familiar with Nelly Sach's poetic vocabulary and ontological outlook, the stars' initial reference to themselves as glistening, singing dust indicates that in contrast to earth they are not fallen planets, but are still close to the state of things at Creation when all was bright and harmonious. Their mention of their sister's blindness suggests, by recalling well-known instances of individuals blinded for their transgressions, that her present affliction may be a form of punishment. In speaking of her as a dissonant cry, however, they also move us to pity her by causing us to visualize her as deranged and unhappy as well as helpless. Their startling simile likening their fallen sister to wine spilled on dark streets, a striking example of Nelly Sachs's use of grotesque combinations to evoke the distorted world of the holocaust, conjures up ugly images of violence, depravity, and shame. To these impressions is added that of perdition by the mention of the yellow lights of evil which flicker on earth's fallen body.

The unusual metaphor of earth's body veined by vestiges of homesickness midway in the poem is reassuring, on the other hand, in that it suggests the possibility of redemption as long as a vestige of earth's longing for God remains. The questions which follow imply that an agent of salvation must be found, as in past instances when the earth was in need of redemption. They also imply that, like the redeemers of the past he will have to be a human being who "remembers" past innocence.

Through its bold negative images of transformation, the chorus of stars communicates an unforgettable impression of the holocaust as an event which reduced fallen earth to the point where all hope of redemption seemed futile. The final prophecy of metamorphosis encourages us to hope nevertheless by suggesting that those who died so horribly at the hands of murderers may have paid through their suffering the price for the redemption of all of us.

Nelly Sachs's second collection of poems, ***Sternverdunkelung,*** also includes poems that deal with the holocaust. The character of the volume as a whole, however, is different from that of *In den Wohnungen des Todes* because three of the five sections in the volume contain poems which are either unrelated to the holocaust or touch upon it only indirectly. Among the latter are eleven poems on Biblical subjects in the second section and six poems on the newly founded state of Israel in the fourth section.

Poems cannot explain the holocaust any better than history can. But they can evoke its atmosphere in such a way as to compel us, as Nelly Sachs's holocaust poems do, to try to discover for ourselves the implications of the terrible events they recall.

—*William H. McClain*

In the group of poems on Biblical subjects "Hiob" (Job) is a striking example of Nelly Sachs's skill in adapting received material to her own poetic purpose:

Hiob

O du Windrose der Qualen!
Von Urzeitstürmen
in immer andere Riehtungen der Unwetter gerissen;
noch dein Süden heisst Einsamkeit.

Wo du stehst ist der Nabel der Schmerzen.
Deine Augen sind tief in deinen Schädel gesunken
wie Höhlentauben in der Nacht
die der Jäger blind herausholt.
Deine Stimme ist stumm geworden,
denn sie hat zuviel *Warum* gefragt.

Zu den Würmern und Fischen ist deine Stimme
eingegangen.

Hiob, du hast alle Nachtwachen durchweint
aber einmal wird das Sternbild deines Blutes
alle aufgehenden Sonnen erbleichen lassen.

(O Windrose of suffering! / Continually buffeted by primordial storms / into different zones of bad weather; / even your South means loneliness. / The navel of suffering is wherever you stand. // Your eyes are sunken in your skull like cavebirds in the night / which the hunter fetches out blind. / Your voice has become silent, / from asking "why" too often. // Your voice has diminished to the muteness of worms and fishes, / Job, you have wept through all nightly vigils / but one day the constellation of your blood / will cause all rising suns to pale.)

The speaker's manner of deploring Job's wretchedness in the opening verses causes it to seem present rather than past. These lines impart an impression of total exposure to suffering. The magnitude of his misery is then vividly evoked by the startling metaphor of the navel of pain, which suggests that it is equivalent to the totality of the pain experienced by all human beings at birth. While the navel-metaphor recalls the Biblical Job's cursing the day of his birth, the bold simile likening his sunken eyes to cave-dwelling birds tracked down by hunters stirs recent memories by recalling that holocaust victims were sometimes hunted down in similar manner. The abjectness and passivity of Nelly Sachs's Job and also his muteness in consequence of having too often asked "why?", also evoke associations with contemporary history by recalling drawings and paintings of "Moslems" by concentration camp artists.

Because Nelly Sach's Job is mute he needs an interpreter. And in her poem, significantly, it is not God speaking from the whirlwind, but this spokesman who proclaims that Job's descendants will be transformed into a constellation in compensation for his suffering. Like the cryptic reference to sand transformed into light in the epitaph to the dancer D.H., this prophecy is also expressed in the form of a *contradictio in adjecto* which in this poem, too, seems to have been employed as a means of suggesting the ineffable mystery of cosmic justice.

Through the final prophecy of transformation, which is entirely her own invention, Nelly Sachs creates in her poem a new Job-myth. Like the Biblical Job, hers too is a man whom we can visualize as a kind of epitome of suffering; but unlike his Biblical counterpart, who demonstrates his faith at the end of his trials by humbly acknowledging God's infinite power and wisdom, her Job remains to the last silent and passive. His only consolation (and ours in reading the poem) is the final prophecy, but even that consolation seems hollow when we reflect that the only authority on which the prophecy rests is that of the voice that proclaims it.

From the six poems on Israel in *Sternverdunkelung* one might easily conclude that Nelly Sachs was as strongly influenced by Martin Buber's views on Zionism and on Israel's obligations as a state as by his poetic-philosophical writings. For from the poems it would seem that for her, too, the larger meaning of Zionism was the opportunity it offered the Jewish people to renew the historical Judaic tradition. Her hope that the new state would set an example for others by the ethical quality of its nationalism is expressed in the first of her *Land Israel* poems:

> Land Israel,
> deine Weite, ausgemessen einst
> von deinen, den Horizont übersteigenden Heiligen.
>
> Deine Morgenluft besprochen von den Erstlingen
> Gottes,
> deine Berge, deine Büsche
> aufgegangen im Flammenatem
> des furchtbar nahegerückten Geheimnisses.
>
> Land Israel,
> erwählte Sternenstätte
> für den himmlischen Kass!
>
> Land Israel,
> nun wo dein vom Sterben angebranntes Volk
> einzieht in deine Täler
> und alle Echos den Erzvätersegen rufen
> für die Rückkehrer,
> ihnen kündend, wo im schattenlosen Licht
> Elia mit dem Landmanne ging zusammen am
> Pfluge,
> der Ysop im Garten wuchs
> und schon an der Mauer des Paradieses—
> wo die schmale Gasse gelaufen zwischen Hier und
> Dort
> da, wo Er gab und nahm als Nachbar
> und der Tod keines Erntewagens bedurfte.
>
> Land Israel,
> nun wo dein Volk
> aus den Weltenecken verweint heimkommt
> und die Psalmen Davids neu zu schreiben in deinen
> Sand
> und das Feierabendwort *Vollbracht*
> am Abend seiner Ernte singt—
>
> steht vielleicht schon eine neue Ruth
> in Armut ihre Lese haltend
> am Scheidewege ihrer Wanderschaft.

(Land of Israel, / your expanse measured formerly / by your saints who stood out on your horizon. / Your morning air named by the first creatures of God, / your hills, your bushes / consumed in the fiery breath / of the mystery that came so frighteningly near. // Land of Israel / starry spot chosen / for the celestial kiss! // Land of Israel, / where your people, singed by death, / is now moving into your valleys / and all echoes call down the ancestral blessings / on those returning, / making known to them where in the shadeless light / Elijah walked on the side of the farmer as he ploughed, / where hyssop grew in the garden / and already at the wall of Paradise— / where the narrow lane ran between Here and There / where He gave and received as neighbor / and Death had no need of a harvest-wagon. // Land of Israel, / now that your people / having cried all their tears, come home from all corners of the earth / to inscribe the psalms of David anew in your sand / and sing, as they prepare to rest, the word: *accomplished* / on the evening of their harvest— // perhaps another Ruth already stands / gleaning in her poverty / at the crossroads of her wanderings.)

Although we are supposed to imagine the landscape in the poem as a present landscape to which people are returning, the speaker's manner of characterizing it as a place hallowed by history almost causes us to stop thinking of it as a present reality. Of the present expanse of Israel we learn, for example, only that it has been measured by saints who walked there in the past; and its atmosphere is characterized only as air named by the first creatures of God. Its bushes and mountains seem significant only because they recall God's covenants and His nearness to his people in the early days of their history. The past seems present everywhere to those coming to live and work in the new state. As they pass through its valleys they hear in the echoes ancestral blessings, and the echoes also remind them of hallowed regions in their new country, such as the place where hyssop grew, or where Elijah sought out Elisha. A sense of the continuity between past, present, and future is imparted by the assertion that the new inhabitants of Israel have come to inscribe the psalms of David anew in its sands. The reference to peaceful harvests suggests that the new psalms will also be songs of thanksgiving. That they may be songs of thanksgiving for deliverance from the holocaust is implied as well by the earlier allusion to the diaspora, the mention of the returning survivors singed by death, and the touching assurance that in the new homeland Death will no longer need a harvest-wagon. The allusion to the new Ruth in the final verses is an effective way of recalling that the divine plan of salvation was from the beginning a plan requiring the cooperation of human beings. For we are reminded here that Ruth, as the grandmother of Jesse, became the ancestress of David, and through him of Christ. With this suggestion that Israel's future may be a time of peace like that portrayed in the Book of Ruth **"Land Israel"** concludes on a hopeful note. What makes it profoundly moving, however, is its implication that the people who in our time have borne the heaviest afflictions may have founded the nation which will restore to a darkened world the light of humanitarian values.

In the holocaust poems for which many of them were initially evolved, and also in the later poems in which they recur, Nelly Sachs's images of transformation offer striking evidence of the richness of her poetic imagination and of the boldness of her experiments with poetic language and poetic effects. With these images as her main poetic means she succeeds in evoking for, and hence, in sharing with the readers of her holocaust poems the intuitive perception of the possible higher meaning of human existence which had helped her overcome the near despair to which she was reduced by the experience of the holocaust. And if we assess rhetorical effectiveness in terms of the ability to stir our psyches as well as in terms of suasive power, we must also conclude in light of the examples considered above that her images of transformation are not only powerfully evocative but also highly efficacious as rhetorical devices. For they touch deep-seated longings in us. Doubtless it is this latter capacity that prompts us to consider them indispensable. Without them, we feel, her poems would not be able to offer, as they do, the kind of creative experience we have come to expect of poetic works of high quality, that of inducing us to conceive of new possibilities. Poems cannot explain the holocaust any better than history can. But they can evoke its atmosphere in such a way as to compel us, as Nelly Sachs's holocaust poems do, to try to discover for ourselves the implications of the terrible events they recall.

As a poet Nelly Sachs may be said to have realized an important aim of the Hassidic mystics in whose writings she found such strong spiritual support during her exile-experience, that of learning the secret melody, "the holy song that merges the lonely, shy letters into the singing of the spheres." Out of the lonely letter of the language she took with her into exile, she created poetic works in which, even while they lament the darkening of the world during the time of the holocaust, one can hear, even though only faintly, the singing of the spheres. For while her works sadden us, they also hearten us by encouraging us to hope that the infinite capacity of life to renew itself may enable the fallen world of the present to regain one day the place it lost so long ago in the harmonious order of the heavens.

Burghild O. Holzer (essay date 1985)

SOURCE: "Concrete (Literal) versus Abstract (Figurative) Translations in Nelly Sachs's Poetry," in *Translation Review*, No. 18, 1985, pp. 26-9.

[*In the following excerpt from her dissertation entitled "Nelly Sachs and Kabbala," Holzer discusses the problem of conveying in other languages the multiple meanings created in Sachs's highly symbolic poetry.*]

During the process of translating [Nelly Sachs's] *Teile Dich Nacht,* I frequently came across individual words that seemed of key importance within a poem but resisted translation. Upon closer inspection of such an obstacle, I would often find that the word functioned both on a literal and a figurative level, and that the English language forced me to make a choice between the two. In German both possibilities would clearly echo within the context of the poem, but in English I would lose that echo. I would then try to comb the poem for clues that would support either a literal or a more figurative translation of the word, but would find myself unable to determine either. During this search, however, I would become extremely sensitive to all the nuances between these concrete and abstract poles. I finally decided that this was precisely the "function" of such a word—to echo between these two poles. However, this function can rarely be translated. While in the German original the concrete and the abstract echo within the same word, in English they are often represented by several different words. This is, of course, a problem which translators have to confront frequently. But when I am translating a poet who is influenced by the Kabbala, this function of the Word—the representation of concrete and abstract poles of language—can be a significant part of *how* the poem means. The following poem will illustrate one example of such a translation problem.

> Wieder Mitte geworden
> für *abgezogene* Musikskelette
> im Gehörraum
> die Hölle gegründet
> mit Bienensang
> verirrt im Ohr—
> Oasen wo Tod die Raumräuber
> Schweigen lehrt
> Ihr göttlichen Verstecke
> schlagt die Augenlider auf—   (II, 131)

The difficult word here is "abgezogen." On the most literal level this could be translated as "peeled" or "skinned." This interpretation would be supported by "Musik*skelette,*" suggesting the image of musical instruments that have been "scraped," "stripped," "blanched," "pared." All of these are literal translations of "abgezogen," which would work in the context of the poem. They suggest pain and torture, which is reinforced by the next two lines "im Gehörraum / die Hölle gegründet." The "musical skeletons" now are connected to the "inner ear" and the sense of torture is reinforced by "mit Bienensang / verirrt im Ohr —."

On a somewhat less concrete level "abgezogene Musikskelette" could be translated as "departed musical skeletons." This is the translation I intuitively chose when I first translated the poem, perhaps because of the effective contrast it establishes in the first two lines, of "becoming a center" for something that has "departed." This interpretation seems to be supported by the last four lines of the poem which, in contrast to the previous lines, have a soothing effect: "Oasen wo Tod die Raumräuber / schweigen lehrt / Ihr göttlichen Verstecke / schlagt die Augenlider auf —." Both "Oasen" and "Verstecke" seem to function as names for something that has been mentioned earlier in the poem. They are plural nouns, and the only thing they could grammatically refer to in the previous lines is "Musikskelette." One would thus have to interpret that "abgezogene Musikskelette" are later in the poem called "Oasen" and "göttlichen Verstecke."

On a third and more abstract level "abgezogen" can be translated as "subtracted." This seems a most unlikely and rather awkward possibility for "abgezogene Musikskelette." I would, however, like to point out that this poem appears in Part II of *Teile Dich Nacht,* and that it is the first poem in that attempted cycle which was later interrupted by Sachs's illness. Sachs seems to do battle with the Word in these poems, that this battle takes place at the border of "Nothing," that the realm of Nothing is often signified by inverted concepts, and that many metaphors in these poems function as signs of inversion, indicating movement toward a strange realm. Thus "abgezogene" could conceivably indicate "subtracted" in the sense of "inverted."

The interpretation, and therefore the translation of this poem hinges for the most part on determining "abgezogene." Let us assume that I interpret "Musikskelette" as "words." Are these words which have left for a while and are now back, causing pain? Or are they stripped words, reduced to skeletons, thus causing pain? Or are they subtracted (or inverted) words causing a hell in the ear? And how do these interpretations connect to the last four lines of the poem? Can "Oasen" and "göttliche Verstecke" refer to "Musikskelette" if "abgezogene Musikskelette" indicate painful words? Perhaps the last four lines of the poem do not refer to anything in the previous lines, but form a separate statement. If so, then the poem falls into two statements. One, that the poet has become a center for flayed, absent or subtracted words. Two, that she also experiences oases of silence which she addresses as "divine hiding places."

Finally I realize that the difficult word, which refuses determination and therefore balks at translation, demands of the reader a careful excavation of word content. It makes the reader sensitive to the nuances between the concrete and abstract poles of language. As a translator, one would like to make this experience available to the reader in the translated language but is only rarely able to do so. Thus, I failed with "abgezogene Musikskelette," since I could neither determine its specific meaning nor recreate its function as an indeterminate linguistic unit. I finally returned to my original intuition

and translated it as "departed," hoping that the contrast between "become center" and "departed" would cause the reader some thought. "Departed" is also close enough to the literal translation to allow, in the Kabbalistic tradition, some revelation through the structure of the word.

In the poem **"Früh die Meere,"** which follows the poem **"Wieder Mitte geworden"** in part II of *Teile Dich Nacht,* we find again a word which functions both on the literal and figurative level and which seems of key importance in the poem.

> Früh die Meere
> mit ihren versteckten Echos
> eingeschlingen in Muscheln
> sendest du mir
> Erde
> versunkenes Mutterland
> Fremde Säer streuen
> *entsetzte* Zeichen
> verwunden das Licht
> Abend—Morgenrot—
> sind Waisen geworden
> verwunschen in blutiger Hand
> Aber "Niemand"
> reisst der Blitz der fällt—   (II, 132)

At first glance the word "entsetzte" may not demand attention in the context of this poem. It conveys a sense of terror, and depending on the amount of terror the context suggests, it would normally be translated as "startled," "shocked," or "terrified." Thus "Alien sowers cast / terrified signs." This figurative translation of "entsetzt" produces a vivid image. The signs become personified, and one sees them with terrified faces. The sense of terror is reinforced by "Fremde Säer" in the previous line and by "verwunden das Licht" in the following line. Assuming, however, that I interpret "Zeichen" in the Kabbalistic tradition as letters (or numbers, or code), and that I know from that tradition that these "Zeichen" are the powerful elements of the universe, the question arises: why should they be terrified? Suddenly the literal translation of "entsetzt" seems much more appropriate. "Entsetzt" literally means—"displaced" and the nuances of displacement can go all the way from "depose" (unseat, dethrone) to "shocked" (losing one's composure, being beside oneself). In this literal sense the *"entsetzte* Zeichen" could have been dislocated, or placed wrongly by the alien sowers. The reverence in the Kabbalistic tradition for each letter of the alphabet stems from the belief that a mishandling of the "Zeichen" could have catastrophic results in the universe.

> To mutilate a single word in the Torah, to set it in the wrong order, might be to imperil the tenuous links between fallen man and the Divine presence. Already the Talmud had said: "the omission or the addition

of one letter might mean the destruction of the whole world." Certain illuminati went so far as to suppose that it was some error of transcription, however minute, made by the scribe to whom God had dictated holy writ, that brought on the darkness and the turbulence of the world.

This belief that an improper handling of the letters may result in catastrophe must be taken into account when interpreting the function of *"entsetzte* Zeichen" in Sachs's poem.

Reading the German poem over, I find that both the sense of *terror* and *dislocation* are echoed in the rest of the poem, and that the word "entsetzt" has both a literal and a figurative function in the poem. If I were to attempt a true translation of form into form, I would have to be able to recreate how the Word does what it means, or *how* I came to the insight that terror has to do with dislocation. But I am unable to find a word in English which reveals its concrete and abstract roots in the same way. This, however, means that I am unable to translate how the Word witnesses for language. It does so by revealing its own structure. I finally translated "displaced signs" following the Kabbalistic practice of literal interpretation and hoping that the literal (and rarely used) form would provoke insights for those readers who had some access to the original. In this way some revelation of structure would take place. For those readers who have no access to the original, the translation "displaced signs" functions to emphasize my Kabbalistic interpretation of the poem. The question is, of course: is this interpretation supported by the entire poem? Or perhaps the question should be: is what the word "entsetzt" reveals about itself reflected in the entire poem? To answer this question, it is again necessary to demonstrate how Kabbalistic belief entered into even the formal aspects of Sachs's poetic language.

I mentioned in the previous section that the Kabbala tells of an accident that happened during the process of creation which resulted in the spilling of divine light. I mentioned that the process of collecting the scattered sparks of divine light and the re-integration of the original whole, can be aided by man. It is what is behind Benjamin's argument for the "pure language." This belief also demands an extreme reverence towards letters, since they represent the forces of the universe as well as the names of God. But this process of re-integration can also be reversed, with catastrophic results, by an improper handling of the letters. In Sachs's poem we see "Alien sowers cast / displaced" (and therefore) "terrified signs." The word "entsetzt," when the literal and the figurative are both heard, reveals that terror and dislocation have the same root—when letters are cast about by "alien sowers" they "injure the light." What these central lines in the poem express, Nelly Sachs experienced in her own life. The German language was cast about by "Fremde Säer" with disastrous effects. The world which she had known as home

became "verwunschen in blutiger Hand." But while the historical background of Sachs's life is certainly reflected in these lines, is this the subject of the entire poem? How are we to understand the last two lines of the poem?

> Aber "Niemand"
> reisst der Blitz der fällt—

These two lines present us with two translation problems. One involves the recognition of a mystical code, the other involves syntax and punctuation.

In the original poems . . . semantic doubling is a language gesture that is a significant part of *how* a poem means. But a translation is rarely able to duplicate this effect. Thus, while the original reveals itself through its entire language structure, the translation often has to make do with partial revelations.

—*Burghild O. Holzer*

The first problem, that of recognizing and appropriately translating a mystical code word, is not especially difficult in this case. Nelly Sachs herself tries to help us by capitalizing the word and putting it in quotation marks, thus identifying it as a name. "Niemand" is a mystical term for God, equivalent to Nothing or "Nichts." In the Kabbala it signifies the first Sefirah, the first divine emanation before the Word. It is also the mystical realm which is the goal of the mystic on his way back through the Path of the Sefiroth. This path starts with our world (the tenth Sefirah) and ends up in Nothing (the first Sefirah). In this context it is not insignificant that the first line in Sachs's poem contains a code word for the tenth Sefirah.

> Früh die *Meere*
> mit ihren versteckten Echos
> eingeschlichen in Muscheln
> sendest du mir
> Erde
> versunkenes Mutterland

With the code word "Meer" in the first line of the poem, and the code word "Niemand" at the end of the poem, the poem can be read as a journey back, through the broken state of the universe, back to the primal cause, the first accident.

> Aber "Niemand"
> reisst der Blitz der fällt—

The syntax is broken in this sentence, it does not make sense as is. It does not establish cause and effect. The German verb "reissen" (to tear, to rend) can be transitive or intransitive. It can be used to portray a situation where the subject acts upon (tears) the object. In this case the sentence would have to be: "Aber Niemand reisst *den* Blitz der fällt—." Or "reissen" can be used to show that the subject itself tears. Then the sentence would have to be: "Aber *Niemand reisst,* der Blitz der fällt—." In this case the tearing of "Niemand" is a separate action, but it could be the cause for the stroke of lightning. However, Sachs deliberately breaks the line after "Niemand," placing the verb on the next line where it does not establish cause and effect. There is a tearing, a dislocation in the language of these last two lines of the poem. The realm of "Niemand" cannot be entered with reason, and the primal cause cannot be figured out. (It is also of interest that "reissen" is related to "ritzen"—to scribe, draw, *design—zeichnen.*)

> Early the oceans
> with their hidden echoes
> snuck into shells
> you send me
> earth
> sunken motherland
> Alien sowers cast
> displaced signs
> injure the light
> Dusk—dawn
> have become orphans
> spell of a bloody hand
> But "No-one"
> rends the stroke it falls —

What the word "entsetzt" reveals about itself is reflected in the structure of the entire poem. Moreover, when its concrete and abstract poles are understood, the word reveals something about the universe. The function of this type of semantic doubling is to testify for a "divine etymology." "The Ur-Sprache had a congruence with reality such as no tongue has had after Babel. . . . In the original poems such semantic doubling is a language gesture that is a significant part of *how* a poem means. But a translation is rarely able to duplicate this effect. Thus, while the original reveals itself through its entire language structure, the translation often has to make do with partial revelations. This, however, is of considerable consequence when translating a poet who tells us that she is "searching for the language of home / at the beginning of words—." The language that she is seeking is precisely one where abstract and concrete are not separated, an unsplintered, divine language. Her attempt to show this and actualize it in her poetic language may therefore represent an attempt at restitution of a broken language. A translation can, however, stunt or even reverse this process, since it is forced to choose between one or the other term. My literal translation of "entsetzt" cannot actually recreate Sachs's language act, but

it can, in the Kabbalistic tradition of literalness—that is, revelation of word content—point to the mystical process behind that act.

Eleonore K. Cervantes (essay date Spring 1986)

SOURCE: "A Woman's View of the Holocaust: The Poetry of Nelly Sachs," in *Rendezvous,* Vol. XXI, No. 2, Spring, 1986, pp. 47-50.

[*In the following essay, Cervantes discusses Sachs's role as the "voice of the silenced victims" of the Holocaust.*]

In her exhaustive study, *Accounting for Genocide,* Helen Fein takes note of the historical fact underlying her social history: Two thirds of European Jews alive in 1930—in the territories later to experience the dominance of Nazi terror—had been killed by 1945. And the majority of the victims were women and children. All of poet Nelly Sachs' published oeuvre is indelibly marked by the nightmarish experience of the Nazis' extermination policies and practices against Jewish people, what we have come to know as the Holocaust. Earlier in the twentieth century Jewish writers, such as Franz Kafka, had turned visionary nightmares into masterful prose. In the 1940's, when Sachs began writing about her people's fate, the nightmare had become a physical reality that the Jewish writer could no longer ignore and had to grapple with for understanding.

Sachs' point of view is that of the victim facing her end in the isolation of "l'univers concentrationnaire." Though she herself managed to escape to the Swedish exile of her later life in 1940, she had previously experienced the welling up of terror during a Nazi interrogation. It is this intense fear, experienced while confronting the inevitability of a violent death, that renders Sachs' victims speechless, forcing them to swallow their last screams while breathing in death with locked throats. In her short prose piece, **"Living under a Threat,"** Sachs declares that it is her "greatest wish on earth: to die without being murdered" and recalls her own inarticulate terror. "For five days I lived without speech in a witches' trial. My voice fled to the fish. Fled without caring about the remaining limbs fixed in the salt of terror."

With metaphorical precision Sachs labels all extermination camp murder as the "Golem Death," the false manufactured death of mass proportion that inspires the utmost horror. [The author adds in a footnote: "The golem, in Jewish folklore, is an artificially created being endowed with supernatural strength."]

> Golem death!
> A scaffold is prepared
> and the carpenters have come

and like a pack of hounds
slavering,
they track your shadow-spiral.

Golem death!
Navel of the world,
your skeleton spreads its arms
in false blessing!
You lay your ribs along earth's latitudes
fitting exactly!

(*Seeker*)

Sachs understands her function as poet to be the voice of the silenced victims, to provide their common existence with some measure of permanence. "Forgive me my sisters / I have taken your silence into my heart / There it lives and suffers the pearls of your suffering" (*Chimneys*). She writes epitaphs for individuals—many women among them—who are simply identified by a common trait and their initials, such as "The Market Woman (B.M.)". "You fingers, touching the bleeding mystery and red with leaving-taking, / Carried the little deaths into one gigantic death." (*Seeker*). Other examples are "The Imbecile Woman (B.H.)," "The Adventuress (A.N.)": "But your last adventure— / Hush; a soul left the fire," (*Seeker*) and "The Woman Who Forgot Everything (A.R.)."

But in old age all drifts in blurred immensities.
The little things fly away like the bees.

You forgot all the words and forgot the object too;
And gave your enemy your hand where roses and
nettles grew.

(*Seeker*)

Sachs' feminine perspective is evident here in the nurturing care she takes to retrieve bits of memory of simple women who became nameless victims of the "Golem Death." Elsewhere in her poetry it expresses itself in a number of recurrent motifs of which the mother who mourns the loss of her child is both common and poignant. Here we find the poet's conviction that love is the pervasive creative force, that love beyond death constitutes an act of re-creation, and that life and death are ultimately one in the mystic's conception.

Already embraced by the arm of heavenly solace
The mad mother stands
With the tatters of her torn mind
With the charred tinders of her burnt mind
Burying her dead child,
Burying her lost light,
Twisting her hands into urns,
Filling them with the body of her child from the
air,
Filling them with his eyes, his hair from the air,

And with his fluttering heart—

Then she kisses the air-born being
And dies!

(*Chimneys*)

Laboring at the edge of insanity the poet herself enters the poems as its female persona. Her mental torment at facing the enormity of her task imbues these poems with the tension of her struggle to find the appropriate metaphors for the unspeakable horror that has overtaken her existence.

Doing nothing
perceptible wilting
My hands belong to the wingbeat stolen and
carried off
With them I am sewing around a hole
but they sigh before this open abyss—

(*Chimneys*)

The guilt and resultant pain of the survivor permeates these poems with existential dread and ultimately with a longing for her own death, not a false death but a natural one that is mysterious and incomprehensible to the living yet full of mystical potential.

The contorted line of suffering
retracing the supernally ignited geometry
of the cosmos
always on the gleaming tracer path to you
and obscured again in the epilepsy
of this impatience to reach the end—

And in these four walls here nothing
but the painting hand of time
eternity's embryo
with primordial light on the brow
and the heart the shackled fugitive
leaping out of its calling: to be a wound—

(*Chimneys*)

Such poetry is neither pleasant nor elevating. The poet is shaping the inexpressible into contorted language, trying to make concrete the mysteries of arbitrary suffering that she cannot comprehend. Such irony defines the essence of Sachs' poetry.

This internalized, self-destructive struggle, this exhausting labor to bring back to life the countless dead and instilling them, the survivors, the impassive witnesses of the gargantuan crime, and the executioners with human qualities might be considered an almost heroic effort. Perhaps it is this consideration that prompted the statement that writing poetry after Auschwitz is barbaric. And George Steiner, who continued the debate, emphatically declares, "Auschwitz lies outside speech as it lies outside reason." Taking the reality, the atrocities, and transferring them to the realm of aesthetics may be seen as an act of trivializing the horror and of minimizing the dread in the face of unfeeling human brutality by means of stylization. But one cannot accuse Sachs of exploiting or manipulating the garrish historical reality for aesthetic ends. In all of her writing she is motivated by the need to find meaning in the snuffed-out lives of her people, in the eternal and universal game between hunter and hunted, hangman and victim.

The irony of German Jewish poets using the language of the "master race," the murderers, to distill the essence of the infernal world of the Holocaust from the victims' perspective into works of art was not lost on Sachs. There is an element of schizoid pathology in the poetry's imagery. On the one hand she relies on the concrete metaphors of the earthly realm to focus clearly the dreadful victimization, on the other she insists on the existence of a spiritual realm, her cosmos, which tends to provide a haven for the souls of those released from their material selves and earthly torture. But Sachs does not dogmatically stipulate a religious answer; it is the mystic's search for answers that is her central theme. She is the "seeker" in her poetry who knows that finding is always "elsewhere," and she tries to express this by use of paradox, the "language of silence."

Steiner's dictum concerning Auschwitz may not be the entire truth after all. Fein's reversal of Steiner's categorization presents the justification for her social history of twentieth century genocide. "Although one may be able to grasp the essence and entirety of the Holocaust only through art, there is no intrinsic reason to assume that what we do not yet understand cannot be understood by reason." Sachs is most sincerely trying to grasp this essence in her poetry, all the time imploring her readers to make use of all their faculties in their search for an answer.

Elisabeth Strenger (essay date 1994)

SOURCE: "Nelly Sachs and the Dance of Language," in *Bridging the Abyss: Reflections on Jewish Suffering, Anti-Semitism, and Exile,* edited by Strenger and Amy Colin, Wilhelm Fink Verlag, 1994, pp. 225-36.

[In the following essay, Strenger examines Sachs's use of the body as a symbol in her work.]

The Hasidic tales collected by Martin Buber constituted part of Nelly Sachs's initial significant intellectual and poetic contact with Jewish culture. The following anecdote, entitled "Silence and Speech," evokes the historical reasons Sachs had for maintaining the struggle for her poetic voice, at first as the memorializer, then as the singer, of her people:

A man had taken upon himself the discipline of silence and for three years had spoken no words save those of the Torah and of prayer. Finally the Yehudi sent for him. "Young man," he said, "how is it that I do not see a single word of yours in the world of truth?" "Rabbi," said the other to justify himself, "why should I indulge in the vanity of speech? Is it not better just to learn and to pray?" "If you do that," said the Yehudi, "not a word of your own reaches the world of truth. He who only learns and prays is murdering the word of his own soul. . ."

In her own poetry, Nelly Sachs locates the poetic voice in the throat, *die Kehle,* at times, more specifically—the nightingale's throat. In the nightingale, we recognize the romantic icon of Brentano and Eichendorff's poetry and also the Baroque emblem of the German metaphysical poets. One is reminded especially of Friedrich von Spee's devotional "Trutz Nachtigall." The conscious use of the nightingale reveals Sachs's continuing interest in the Baroque and Romantic poetic traditions. In addition to these intertextual possibilities, the throat, as a physiognomic feature, signifies the frailty of the voice and of the material aspect of life. This constellation of associations, juxtaposed with the biographical incidence of Nelly Sachs's loss of voice occasioned by a Gestapo interrogation ("Fünf Tage lebte ich ohne Sprache unter einem Hexenprozeß."), underscores her dual vulnerability as a Jewish woman and her awareness of that vulnerability.

As a German Jew, exile and exodus determined the poles of Nelly Sachs's experience of culture and history. Her fate exemplifies how question of identification was intensified for all Jews writing in the German cultural context. The equation was solved differently by each individual: either the Jewish or German side is weighted with varying degrees of assimilation or commitment to Judaic tradition in response to historical, political, or personal pressures. The Nuremberg laws forced a realignment, a re-evaluation of points of orientation. The content of German culture, now radically shifted to a position of "otherness," was called into question. In Nelly Sachs's case, this shift manifests itself in her rejection of the literary norms of German Romanticism and her subsequent exploration of Hasidic mysticism and the adaptation of its ontological and semiotic systems.

Sachs's metamorphosis into a Jewish poet acknowledges her continuous development of Jewish issues and motifs that exist in a symbiotic relationship with the German language, for, as a modernist poet, her poetry's formative theme is language and its ability to bear meaning. The German language was discredited as a system encouraging meaning because it had been the language of the disruptive oppressors. She developed a strategy for salvaging her means of expression and communication—her system of metaphors, which is, in effect, a reinvention of language. Her system affirms the existence of bonds between words and their meanings, while opening up a new range of meanings, and it challenges words to describe what has been termed the indescribable.

To reject completely the German language would imply the loss of her poetic voice and the structuring element of her personal and cultural experience. For Sachs, inspired by the theological and linguistic precepts of Kabbalistic and Hasidic mysticism, the agent that initiates and sustains the creation and the creative process is language. Her poetic and semiotic experiments are conducted in German, on German, and through these she attempts to transform the language of the oppressors ("die Jäger") and reclaim it on behalf of the oppressed ("die Gejagten"). Two pieces that illustrate the process by which she appropriates and reshapes German as a medium to express the Jewish experience are **"Chassidische Schriften"** from the collection *Sternverdunkelung* and the scenic poem **"Der magische Tänzer."** **"Chassidische Schriften"** represents the initial stage of this process where she begins to develop a metaphoric system based primarily on the *Book of the Zohar,* one of the central Kabbalistic texts from thirteenth-century Spain. The dramatic poem **"Der magische Tänzer"** with its evocation of Kleist's *Uber das Marionettentheater* reveals the deeply problematic relationship between the German and Jewish cultural spheres. It questions the possibility of reconstituting the language and posits two extensions to the traditional poetic medium: silence and dance.

Within the Jewish mystical tradition we find a perception of human language that emphasizes the ambivalence of language itself as a possible system of access to divine understanding. Human language is opposed to the immanent Creative, Divine Word. Medieval German Hasidism delivers perhaps the most unequivocal faith in the power of language. In this movement with its belief in mystic ascent, as Gershom Scholem describes, "the emphasis is no longer on the approach of the mystic himself to God's throne, but on that of his prayer. It is the word, not the soul, which triumphs over fate and evil." But when commenting on Jewish mysticism's relationship to language, Scholem asks, "how can words express an experience for which there is no adequate simile in this finite world of man?" There is a strong sense that we can only know by analogy or association. The Kabbalistic tradition also operated within metaphors—these being the only means by which to "name" the "deus absconditus": "that which is infinite, that which is not conceivable by thinking. At best these are words with close approximations." Sachs extends the limitations of language so that it can form a bridge between experiential "Bezogenheit" and the place in which language has its source—the place before language.

Fashioning one's own language is in keeping with the great Jewish mystic traditions, from the secret passwords for pro-

tection on ecstatic journeys to the *Zohar's* artificially reproduced Aramaic. So too Nelly Sachs seeks to transform her language into one that can express the inexpressible. Her transformed language includes non-verbal communication strategies. Her highly visual metaphors become emblems in the reader's eye. The human body itself is pressed into service—gestures and dance are summoned to convey meaning both to the reader, and, in prayer, to God.

A consideration of the physical, sensual aspect of her imagery and communicative strategy, as represented by description and inclusion of gesture, reads 'to the observation of how verbal and non-verbal communication merge in the image of having the word, or sign, inscribed upon the body. Even in transcendent poems describing mystic projections, the reader finds Sachs's attention on the intersection between the material and spiritual. In the **"Magischer Tänzer,"** the body becomes the word: first in dance, and then, finally, when the heart is torn from the body. Unmediated communication via the body takes place as the Hasidic mystic completes his journey to the place before language.

If we continue to interpret Sachs's poetry as attempts at transcending the strictures of the material world, we will only focus on the abstract qualities of her metaphorical system which, as Ruth Dinesen points out, is one of the obstacles to her critical reception. At the core of her transcendent impulses lies an acute awareness and understanding of the materiality that constitutes the human experience of one's surroundings, of history, and of self. In the reading and the speech of bodies are found occasions not only for vertically channeled contact between the divine and human spheres, but her poems also record the touching between bodies as a means of establishing lateral bonds, or community. Sometimes the simple human or animal gestures echo contact between man and God. A mother stroking her child's hip in **"Ein totes Kind spricht"** parallels Jakob's encounter with the angel: "And there was one that wrestled with him until daybreak who, seeing that he could not master him, struck him in the socket of his hip. . . (Gen. 32:26). Sachs's lines transform the blow to the hip:

> Die Mutter löste ihre Hand aus der meinen,
> Damit es mich nicht träfe.
> Sie aber berührte noch einmal leise meine Hüfte—
> Und da blutete ihre Hand—

Feminist questions, on the identification of a woman through her body and with her body, arise in relation to certain aspects of Sachs's poetry. She concretizes the body in her poetry, and though this body is not always a feminine body, hers, the poet's, is, and feminist implications, especially in evaluating the link between biography and poetry should not be overlooked. Johanna Bossinade began the feminist exploration of Sachs's work. She discusses the importance of the feminine identity for her poetics in terms of Freud's theory of the female wound, the wounded female. She too has noted that many of Sachs's images of separation or loss are opposed to metaphors of maternal security or "Geborgenheit."

Throughout her oeuvre we find the cosmos, that same starry realm that represents the patriarchal promise to Abraham, associated with feminine terms: the milky way, if we wish, becomes the mother's milk way. We find umbilical cords binding us to the divine in the form of crystalline wombs. And pervasive is the blood, not always the blood of victims or death, but the blood of exuberant, painful, beginning life. Sachs gives birth to language renewed, and this metaphorical feminine presence is far more pervasive than is warranted by traditional Jewish mysticism and the limited role it ascribes to the *Shekinah,* that feminine manifestation of God.

Sachs lets her body, the body, be heard, but not in a manner easily accounted for by a single theoretical model. And for Sachs, it is not just a question of what the body says, but what the body hears. What experiences does the body react to, testify to? Mystics transcend the body, but the locus of their experience remains the body, and their bodies are said to bear signs of light or blood in response to that experience. It is significant that the strongest statements we have about Sachs and the production of her poems is that she felt them burning within her. One can read these either as the signs of a changing woman's body or the searing ecstasy of a mystic. Her epoch has seen the fragility of the body—she writes against this thoughtless, horrific waste. Her epitaphs for the Holocaust's nameless victims collected in *Wohnungen des Todes* contain detailed descriptions of their bodies or gestures, of their physical existence, as well as testimonies to their spiritual presence.

The poem **"Chassidische Schriften"** serves as a significant marker in Nelly Sachs's quest to transform language. Blomster, Klingman and Weissenberger have viewed this poem as a poetic / mystic manifesto and have discussed it in terms of how systematic her analysis and integration of Kabbalism and Hasidism have been. Sachs's mysticism is not a system of abstractions. She poetically transforms personal memory into an evocation of the cosmos and fate of a people. In this poem, she seeks to produce her own Hasidic text: a mystical contemplation on the opening passages of the Kabbalistic *Book of the Zohar.* But whereas the *Zohar's* author was inspired to seek for the layers of illumination contained within each word of the Creation narrative, Sachs's meditation telescopes the entire Torah as it moves from Creation through Exodus.

The poem's epigram reads: "Es heißt: die Gebote der Thora entsprechen der Zahl der Knochen des Menschen, ihre Verbote der Zahl der Adern. So decks das ganze Gesetz den ganzen Menschenleib." It invites us to contemplate the convergence of word and body although the dynamics of this convergence remain a mystery, a mystery which the poem goes on to invoke as the space in which all is whole and intact, and for which all creatures long.

The epigram is echoed within the poem: "Und die Knochen leben die magische Zahl der Gebote / und die Adern bluten sich zu Ende." The poet's eye transgresses the boundaries of the body, passes through the permeable barrier of skin. The skeletal and bleeding body, the bones and open veins, transcend their conventional association with death to connote life as well, a life encompassed by, or more accurately stated, circumscribed by the Laws of the Torah. The body, an object of death and genocide in the *Wohnungen des Todes,* functions here primarily as the living symbol of a god's covenant with his people. The gender specific sign of circumcision is replaced by the whole inscribed body. In a fashion reminiscent of Christianity's saints who bore stigmata as signs of mystical union, the body becomes the sign of God's Covenant with his people. It can be "read" according to Kabbalistic numerology and one perceives the possibility of an unmediated experience of divinity.

The poem places the reader at the beginning of creation as light is born of darkness in the protective, nurturing matrix of the universe. The entire process is distilled into the elemental images of night, stars, water and sand that we find recurring in Sachs's poetry. The agent which initiates and sustains the creation is language: "und das Wort lief aus / . . . Namen bildeten sich / wie Teiche im Sand." In as much as man participates in the naming activity he participates in creation, as Blomster has elaborated in his essay on Sachs's theosophy of the creative word.

In this poem, darkness and light have universal significance, but Sachs expresses her hopeful belief in transformation when she imagines the night giving birth to the stars. Dark and light are not in perpetual conflict, rather one can engender the other. Similarly she transforms the image of the stone, (hard, lifeless matter and symbolic of exile in the barren desert), into a petrified darkness that still contains the promise of divine movement and light. Even threatening quicksand becomes a metaphor for the potential for change on the most elemental level.

In conjunction with the final images of fertile seeds and stars, sand assumes yet another dimension inspired by the Bible (Genesis 22:17). God promises Abraham, "I will shower blessings on you, I will make your descendants as many as the stars in heaven and the grains of sand on the seashore." The poem closes with the image of another stigmatized figure: Jacob, whose injured hip bore the trace of his encounter with his deity. No longer the Jew victimized by history, Jacob is the emblem for an Israel which continues to sleep with the stars that betoken the promise to engender a people. If we can "read" God's presence in or on our bodies, then the possibility exists that we might reverse the direction of communication in accordance with the mystics' belief that the path to God is the reversal of the path from God. For the Psalmist David, for the Hasidic pious, and for Nelly Sachs, the body could then speak back to God, in dance.

Hellmut Geissner has attempted to describe the nature of dance as it is understood and applied by Nelly Sachs according to anthropological categories of ritualistic dance. He defines it as "enthusiasmic" dance which is at once inward and outward turning, seeking both to conjure the god and to join with him. Such an ethnographical definition ignores both the communal and personal / psychological aspects of dance. These other forces operating on dance are represented in Sachs's work by Hasidic dance and by the expressive / interpretative dance of her childhood. Only when one considers dance within this triad of contexts can one understand the complex dynamics of dance as an act of communication.

Critical interpretations measure carefully the weight of autobiography in her works. Bahr describes her symbolic autobiography: "Sie wollte hinter ihrem Werk verschwinden, wollte anonym bleiben." Her individuality may have been suppressed, but not her humanity. Of the few facts that can be gleaned from her self-representations, her autobiographical sketches or references in letters, the most consistently mentioned by biographers and critics is her fascination with dance. . . .

As a mature poet she still feels that dance is her natural element, not the word. In the scenic poem **"Magischer Tänzer"** dance is the return to cosmic harmony, harmony with the breath which animates the universe. . . .

Besides the desire to recover a lost harmony, a desire strongly associated with nostalgic attachment to her father, Sachs's autobiographical reflections on dance contain another mystical aspect which illuminates her relationship to language. Of her dancing as her father played she writes: "Ich folgte ihm weit hinweg, um die Fernen zu erreichen, beugte mich hinaus in ein sprachloses Gebiet."

One more piece of biographical evidence suggests that dance had not lost its attraction as a means of personal expression for the mature poet. Lili Simon reports Ingeborg Drehwitz's anecdote that tells of Sachs dancing with abandon when she saw the Berlin Tiergarten again for the first time after twenty-five years. She had returned to Germany to receive the Friedenspreis des Deutschen Buchhandels, Frankfurt, 1965. In light of her constant experimentation with mime and movement that accompanied her poetic endeavors, we cannot easily dismiss this interest's childhood origins.

Theorists of dance and of its essential component—move-

ment—emphasize the developmental aspects of kinesthetic awareness. Kinesthetics has been defined as:

> the sensual discrimination of the position and movement of body parts based on information other than visual, auditory, verbal. . . . Sensors in muscles, tendons, joints, as well as the vestibular apparatus of the inner ear . . . provide a constant, though subliminal, knowledge of the arrangement of body parts. This awareness is enhanced by the sense of touch—the contact and pressure sensors.

In infancy, kinesthesis and physical contact with the external environment are instrumental in helping the individual "begin to conceptualize the world as an orderly and understandable place."

Conceptualization then is grounded in movement. Isadora Duncan and the proponents of dance education / dance therapy insisted that the relationship between movement and the conceptualization of the self and the world extends throughout one's life. Isadora Duncan writes in her essay "Dancing in Relation to Religion and Love": "a child can understand many things through the medium of the body which would be impossible for it to comprehend by the medium of the written or spoken word."

Beyond the tactile exploration of one's own body, movement is incorporated early into a pattern of communication strategies. For infants there are the touches, gestures and facial expressions of caregivers. This stage of kinesthesis is found in many moments in Nelly Sachs's poetry: the cow licking her calf, the mother stroking her child's hip, the old women combing their hair. These gestures, seen as either direct expression of emotion or as symbolic, establish the communal matrix onto which language (verbal communication) is grafted.

The power of Hasidic dance is best observed in its communal implications. For the Hasid, dance is much more than the expression of a single individual's encounter with God; the message the dancer conveys to his pious observers is an equally important function. Through dance, the hasid teaches and inspires. The Hasidic Tales contain many reports of the infectiousness of dance; strangers, passersby, skeptics are drawn into a communal ecstasy. Their oral tradition also tells of rabbis who communicated their enlightenment through dance: The Baal Shem Tov, founder of Eastern European Hasidism, danced with the Torah, and when he set it down in the midst of the dance one of his disciples proclaimed, "Now our master has laid aside the visible, dimensional teachings, and has taken the spiritual teachings into himself." And of a nameless, pious grandfather is remarked, "You may believe me: he has made all his limbs so pure and so holy, that with every step he takes, his feet accomplish holy unifications."

Nelly Sachs emblematizes the Hasidic dancer in her scenic poem **"Der Magische Tänzer."** The stage directions for the first scene describe impoverished surroundings hung with laundry. Marina, who has devoted her life to David, the former stage-dancer turned mystic, struggles to support him by taking in washing. The scene's opening dialogue between Marina and her neighbor is about a head of cauliflower. This portrayal of quotidian life reminds one of the lack of disjuncture between daily and mystical / religious experience advocated by the Eastern European Hasids.

The figure of David gives the impression of being a large wounded bird ("den Eindruck eines großen angeschossenen Vogels"), and in this posture are suggested his vulnerability as a hunted object, his ungainliness and his interrupted flight. His metaphoric association with the bird indicates that he is not completely earthbound, he occupies a space between the material and celestial realms. David sits with his head dropping down until it hangs between his knees in the contemplative position of the early Merkabah or throne mystics. After fasting this position was required for the soul's mystic journey through the gates to the throne of God. It is a position many religions have in common: it influences the blood's progress to the brain—induces physical and psychological "symptoms." The rushing heard in the ears, the play of light against the eyelids, the changing body temperatures are all translated into different aspects of the ecstatic experience.

In the first scene the entire onus of David's functioning (as a subject as well as an object of our gazes, as someone who interprets or configures reality as well as someone who invites interpretation) is placed on his postures, gestures and movements. He is speechless, and the only way he communicates his mystical experience is through dance. His utterances during the second scene mark the stages of his spiritual journey through history and the cosmos. His seeking for the doorway into the night parallels experiences of the Merkabah mystics who confronted gatekeepers at each stage of their ascendancy to God's throne.

An ironic juxtaposition to this silent yet expressive figure is created by the figure of the neighbor, who is represented by a marionette with a built in tape for a voice. Through this figure Sachs dehumanizes the subject. This dehumanization is appropriate for the neighbor who, completely focussed on material reality, is lacking in sympathy for David's ecstatic re-enactment among the clotheslines of King David's dance before the Ark. This David's Ark is Marina's keepsake chest. Of course, the saint appears as crazed to the neighbor, to someone representing society's norm, just as King David's dance was derided by his wife, Michal.

For the second scene, the stage is transformed by lighting techniques into a crystalline globe in which the figures of David and Marina are encased. The crystalline globe creates the effect of a cosmic womb and indicates the return to a pre-creation state. The visualization of the womb pierced by light parallels the *Book of the Zohar*'s Creation myth in which the male ray enters the female womb.

David's somnambulistic dance continues and a cosmic wind, the breath of the universe, sets the clotheslines into movement. The magic dancer, portrayed by a marionette, appears and the stage retains an enormous amount of kinetic energy until the piece concludes. David's somnambulism indicates the movements of one who has no self consciousness.

The marionette's presence on stage and David's unself-conscious movements stand in an interesting relationship to Heinrich von Kleist's critical musings *Uber das Marionettentheater*. This connection may serve as yet more evidence of Sachs's continuing connection to the German Romantic literary heritage. The most striking parallel with Sachs's understanding of dance is the reason given for preferring marionettes over the self-conscious, hence distorted movements of dancers, because they have the advantage of being anti-gravitational, or defying some of the rules of materiality. Kinetic energy overcomes considerations of mass and gravity. . . .

Dance, pure movement, for Kleist and Sachs presents the possibility of transcending materiality. Sachs's dancer takes on some of the characteristics of Kleist's marionettes in order to problematize the paradox of achieving transcendence of the body, through the body.

The magic dancer serves as guide along the mystical journey; he assists in preparing David for his ecstatic encounter. In a stark counterpoint to the scene of cultic, ritual preparations in Euripides' *Bacchae* where Dionysius suggests transformative actions to Pentheus, who dons the costume of a Bacchante, the magic dancer, by means of naming, shapes David's perception of the process in which he is engaged. Urged to burst from his skin, David flings off his coat; a belt is perceived as a tonguing snake. While the magic dancer's kinetic energy dismantles the world projected on the hanging linens and unravels the meridians hence negating the distinctions, divisions and confinements imposed by man upon the geos, David continues stripping until, in his shredded undergarments, he bares his chest.

The mention of the snake, its mouth open, winding about David's waist introduces the thematic of Eden and the Fall of Man which figures in Kleist's deliberations on the causes of man's loss of physical grace: "Anmut und Grazie." This loss is associated with Adam and Eve's shame upon becoming conscious of their nakedness. If we superimpose a mystic's reading of this scriptural passage, the awareness of nakedness represents a distinct separation from God. Kleist couches the idea of retracing our steps to God in satirical wit: "Mithin sagte ich ein wenig zerstreut, müßten wir wieder von dem Baum der Erkenntnis essen, um in den Stand der Unschuld zurückzufallen? Allerdings antwortet Herr C; das ist das letzte Kapitel von der Geschichte der Welt."

David continues his dance, unwinding the confining threads, unraveling the cocoon so that he can undergo his final metamorphosis. The butterfly, that royal sign, Sachs's metaphor of transformation, is here embodied in David's dance. The concluding gesture of his dance is to tear the heart from his bared chest. With this, the interior becomes the exterior, expression occurs through the body, since the living heart, not the work, becomes the bearer of the self, and ultimately, of meaning.

For Nelly Sachs, the human capacity to communicate, to express, to configure reality includes both verbal and non-verbal languages. The rhythmic movement of dance can overreach the body's boundaries of space, time, and gravity. Jewish mystical voices cry out over the uninitiated language of the German oppressors. Sachs's German dances in a new rhythmical ascendance to spiritual freedom. She explores and acknowledges the paradoxical nature of the mystic journey to God: the body is both the starting point of that journey and the vehicle through which the goal of transcendence is attained.

> On every sabbath eve Rabbi Hayyim of Kosov, the son of Rabbi Mendel, danced before his assembled disciples. His face was aflame and they all knew that every step was informed with sublime meanings and effected sublime things. Once while he was in the midst of dancing, a heavy bench fell on his foot and he had to pause because of the pain. Later they asked him about it. "It seems to me," he said, "that the pain made itself felt because I had interrupted the dance."

FURTHER READING

Criticism

Blomster, W. V. "A Theosophy of the Creative Word: The *Zohar*-Cycle of Nelly Sachs." *Germanic Review* XLIV (1969): 221-27.
> Presents an investigation of Sachs's concern with the word of God in her poetry, particularly the poems of the *Zohar* cycle.

Bosmajiam, Hamida. "Towards the Point of Constriction: Nelly Sachs's "Landschaft aus Schreien" and Paul Celan's "Engführung." In his *Metaphors of Evil: Contemporary German Literature and the Shadow of Nazism*, pp. 183-228. Iowa City: University of Iowa Press, 1979.
> Compares "Landschaft aus Schreien" and "Engführung," describing them as "hermetic poems forged by the imagination of two survivors who internalized the chaos of history and struggled with it until their deaths in 1970."

Foot, Robert. *The Phenomenon of Speechlessness in the Poetry of Marie Luise Kaschnitz, Günter Eich, Nelly Sachs and Paul Celan.* Bonn: Bouvier Verlag Herbert Grundmann, 1982, 415 p.
> Examines the phenomenon of "Verstummen," or speechlessness, in twentieth-century poetry, a condition brought on by the poet's lack of faith in his abilities and subsequent "attitude of self-defeat," and provoked in Sachs' work by her difficulty verbalising both "the unspeakable cruelty of the human world" and the "metaphysical aspects of existence."

Margetts, John. "Nelly Sachs and 'Die Haargenaue Aufgabe': Observations on the Poem-Cycle 'Fahrt ins Staublose'." *Modern Language Review* 73, No. 3 (July 1978): 550-62.
> Offers an analysis of the nine poems in the cycle *Fahrt in Staublose,* highlighting the "unity of the individual poems in dealing with the central poetological theme of the cycle."

☐ Contemporary Literary Criticism

Indexes

**Literary Criticism Series
Cumulative Author Index
Cumulative Topic Index
Cumulative Nationality Index
Title Index, Volume 98**

How to Use This Index

The main references

Camus, Albert
1913-1960 . . **CLC 1, 2, 4, 9, 11, 14, 32, 69; DA; DAB; DAC; DAM DRAM, MST, NOV; DC2; SSC 9; WLC**

list all author entries in the following Gale Literary Criticism series:

BLC = Black Literature Criticism
CLC = Contemporary Literary Criticism
CLR = Children's Literature Review
CMLC = Classical and Medieval Literature Criticism
DA = DISCovering Authors
DAB = DISCovering Authors: British
DAC = DISCovering Authors: Canadian
DAM = DISCovering Authors Modules
  DRAM = dramatists; **MST** = most-studied
  authors; **MULT** = multicultural authors; **NOV** =
  novelists; **POET** = poets; **POP** = popular/genre
  writers; **DC** = Drama Criticism
HLC = Hispanic Literature Criticism
LC = Literature Criticism from 1400 to 1800
NCLC = Nineteenth-Century Literature Criticism
PC = Poetry Criticism
SSC = Short Story Criticism
TCLC = Twentieth-Century Literary Criticism
WLC = World Literature Criticism, 1500 to the Present

The cross-references

See also CA 89-92; DLB 72; MTCW

list all author entries in the following Gale biographical and literary sources:

AAYA = Authors & Artists for Young Adults
AITN = Authors in the News
BEST = Bestsellers
BW = Black Writers
CA = Contemporary Authors
CAAS = Contemporary Authors Autobiography Series
CABS = Contemporary Authors Bibliographical Series
CANR = Contemporary Authors New Revision Series
CAP = Contemporary Authors Permanent Series
CDALB = Concise Dictionary of American Literary Biography
CDBLB = Concise Dictionary of British Literary Biography

DLB = Dictionary of Literary Biography
DLBD = Dictionary of Literary Biography Documentary Series
DLBY = Dictionary of Literary Biography Yearbook
HW = Hispanic Writers
JRDA = Junior DISCovering Authors
MAICYA = Major Authors and Illustrators for Children and Young Adults
MTCW = Major 20th-Century Writers
NNAL = Native North American Literature
SAAS = Something about the Author Autobiography Series
SATA = Something about the Author
YABC = Yesterday's Authors of Books for Children

Literary Criticism Series
Cumulative Author Index

Alcala-Galiano, Juan Valera y
See Valera y Alcala-Galiano, Juan

Alcott, Amos Bronson   1799-1888 .. **NCLC 1**
See also DLB 1

Alcott, Louisa May
   1832-1888 ..... **NCLC 6, 58; DA; DAB;
      DAC; DAM MST, NOV; WLC**
See also CDALB 1865-1917; CLR 1, 38;
   DLB 1, 42, 79; DLBD 14; JRDA;
   MAICYA; YABC 1

Aldanov, M. A.
See Aldanov, Mark (Alexandrovich)

Aldanov, Mark (Alexandrovich)
   1886(?)-1957 .... **TCLC 23**
See also CA 118

Aldington, Richard   1892-1962 ...... **CLC 49**
See also CA 85-88; CANR 45; DLB 20, 36,
   100, 149

Aldiss, Brian W(ilson)
   1925- .... **CLC 5, 14, 40; DAM NOV**
See also CA 5-8R; CAAS 2; CANR 5, 28;
   DLB 14; MTCW; SATA 34

Alegria, Claribel
   1924- .... **CLC 75; DAM MULT**
See also CA 131; CAAS 15; DLB 145; HW

Alegria, Fernando   1918- .... **CLC 57**
See also CA 9-12R; CANR 5, 32; HW

Aleichem, Sholom .... **TCLC 1, 35**
See also Rabinovitch, Sholem

Aleixandre, Vicente
   1898-1984 .... **CLC 9, 36; DAM POET;
      PC 15**
See also CA 85-88; 114; CANR 26;
   DLB 108; HW; MTCW

Alepoudelis, Odysseus
See Elytis, Odysseus

Aleshkovsky, Joseph   1929-
See Aleshkovsky, Yuz
See also CA 121; 128

Aleshkovsky, Yuz .... **CLC 44**
See also Aleshkovsky, Joseph

Alexander, Lloyd (Chudley)   1924- .. **CLC 35**
See also AAYA 1; CA 1-4R; CANR 1, 24,
   38; CLR 1, 5; DLB 52; JRDA;
   MAICYA; MTCW; SAAS 19; SATA 3,
   49, 81

Alexie, Sherman (Joseph, Jr.)
   1966- .... **CLC 96; DAM MULT**
See also CA 138; NNAL

Alfau, Felipe   1902- .... **CLC 66**
See also CA 137

Alger, Horatio, Jr.   1832-1899 ..... **NCLC 8**
See also DLB 42; SATA 16

Algren, Nelson   1909-1981 .... **CLC 4, 10, 33**
See also CA 13-16R; 103; CANR 20;
   CDALB 1941-1968; DLB 9; DLBY 81,
   82; MTCW

Ali, Ahmed   1910- .... **CLC 69**
See also CA 25-28R; CANR 15, 34

Alighieri, Dante   1265-1321 .... **CMLC 3, 18**

Allan, John B.
See Westlake, Donald E(dwin)

Allen, Edward   1948- .... **CLC 59**

Allen, Paula Gunn
   1939- .... **CLC 84; DAM MULT**
See also CA 112; 143; NNAL

Allen, Roland
See Ayckbourn, Alan

Allen, Sarah A.
See Hopkins, Pauline Elizabeth

Allen, Woody
   1935- .... **CLC 16, 52; DAM POP**
See also AAYA 10; CA 33-36R; CANR 27,
   38; DLB 44; MTCW

Allende, Isabel
   1942- .... **CLC 39, 57, 97; DAM MULT,
      NOV; HLC**
See also AAYA 18; CA 125; 130;
   CANR 51; DLB 145; HW; INT 130;
   MTCW

Alleyn, Ellen
See Rossetti, Christina (Georgina)

Allingham, Margery (Louise)
   1904-1966 .... **CLC 19**
See also CA 5-8R; 25-28R; CANR 4;
   DLB 77; MTCW

Allingham, William   1824-1889 ... **NCLC 25**
See also DLB 35

Allison, Dorothy E.   1949- .... **CLC 78**
See also CA 140

Allston, Washington   1779-1843.... **NCLC 2**
See also DLB 1

Almedingen, E. M. .... **CLC 12**
See also Almedingen, Martha Edith von
See also SATA 3

Almedingen, Martha Edith von   1898-1971
See Almedingen, E. M.
See also CA 1-4R; CANR 1

Almqvist, Carl Jonas Love
   1793-1866 .... **NCLC 42**

Alonso, Damaso   1898-1990 .... **CLC 14**
See also CA 110; 131; 130; DLB 108; HW

Alov
See Gogol, Nikolai (Vasilyevich)

Alta   1942- .... **CLC 19**
See also CA 57-60

Alter, Robert B(ernard)   1935- ...... **CLC 34**
See also CA 49-52; CANR 1, 47

Alther, Lisa   1944- .... **CLC 7, 41**
See also CA 65-68; CANR 12, 30, 51;
   MTCW

Altman, Robert   1925- .... **CLC 16**
See also CA 73-76; CANR 43

Alvarez, A(lfred)   1929- .... **CLC 5, 13**
See also CA 1-4R; CANR 3, 33; DLB 14,
   40

Alvarez, Alejandro Rodriguez   1903-1965
See Casona, Alejandro
See also CA 131; 93-96; HW

Alvarez, Julia   1950- .... **CLC 93**
See also CA 147

Alvaro, Corrado   1896-1956 ...... **TCLC 60**

Amado, Jorge
   1912- .... **CLC 13, 40; DAM MULT,
      NOV; HLC**
See also CA 77-80; CANR 35; DLB 113;
   MTCW

Ambler, Eric   1909- .... **CLC 4, 6, 9**
See also CA 9-12R; CANR 7, 38; DLB 77;
   MTCW

Amichai, Yehuda   1924- ...... **CLC 9, 22, 57**
See also CA 85-88; CANR 46; MTCW

Amiel, Henri Frederic   1821-1881 .. **NCLC 4**

Amis, Kingsley (William)
   1922-1995 ..... **CLC 1, 2, 3, 5, 8, 13, 40,
      44; DA; DAB; DAC; DAM MST, NOV**
See also AITN 2; CA 9-12R; 150; CANR 8,
   28, 54; CDBLB 1945-1960; DLB 15, 27,
   100, 139; INT CANR-8; MTCW

Amis, Martin (Louis)
   1949- .... **CLC 4, 9, 38, 62**
See also BEST 90:3; CA 65-68; CANR 8,
   27, 54; DLB 14; INT CANR-27

Ammons, A(rchie) R(andolph)
   1926- .... **CLC 2, 3, 5, 8, 9, 25, 57;
      DAM POET; PC 16**
See also AITN 1; CA 9-12R; CANR 6, 36,
   51; DLB 5, 165; MTCW

Amo, Tauraatua i
See Adams, Henry (Brooks)

Anand, Mulk Raj
   1905- .... **CLC 23, 93; DAM NOV**
See also CA 65-68; CANR 32; MTCW

Anatol
See Schnitzler, Arthur

Anaya, Rudolfo A(lfonso)
   1937- .... **CLC 23; DAM MULT, NOV;
      HLC**
See also CA 45-48; CAAS 4; CANR 1, 32,
   51; DLB 82; HW 1; MTCW

Andersen, Hans Christian
   1805-1875 .... **NCLC 7; DA; DAB;
      DAC; DAM MST, POP; SSC 6; WLC**
See also CLR 6; MAICYA; YABC 1

Anderson, C. Farley
See Mencken, H(enry) L(ouis); Nathan,
   George Jean

Anderson, Jessica (Margaret) Queale
   .... **CLC 37**
See also CA 9-12R; CANR 4

Anderson, Jon (Victor)
   1940- .... **CLC 9; DAM POET**
See also CA 25-28R; CANR 20

Anderson, Lindsay (Gordon)
   1923-1994 .... **CLC 20**
See also CA 125; 128; 146

Anderson, Maxwell
   1888-1959 ...... **TCLC 2; DAM DRAM**
See also CA 105; 152; DLB 7

Anderson, Poul (William)   1926- .... **CLC 15**
See also AAYA 5; CA 1-4R; CAAS 2;
   CANR 2, 15, 34; DLB 8; INT CANR-15;
   MTCW; SATA 90; SATA-Brief 39

Anderson, Robert (Woodruff)
   1917- .... **CLC 23; DAM DRAM**
See also AITN 1; CA 21-24R; CANR 32;
   DLB 7

Anderson, Sherwood
   1876-1941 .... **TCLC 1, 10, 24; DA;
      DAB; DAC; DAM MST, NOV; SSC 1;
      WLC**
See also CA 104; 121; CDALB 1917-1929;
   DLB 4, 9, 86; DLBD 1; MTCW

Andier, Pierre
See Desnos, Robert

Andouard
See Giraudoux, (Hippolyte) Jean

Andrade, Carlos Drummond de . . . . . . **CLC 18**
See also Drummond de Andrade, Carlos

Andrade, Mario de 1893-1945 . . . . . **TCLC 43**

Andreae, Johann V(alentin)
1586-1654 . . . . **LC 32**
See also DLB 164

Andreas-Salome, Lou 1861-1937 . . . **TCLC 56**
See also DLB 66

Andrewes, Lancelot 1555-1626 . . . . **LC 5**
See also DLB 151, 172

Andrews, Cicily Fairfield
See West, Rebecca

Andrews, Elton V.
See Pohl, Frederik

Andreyev, Leonid (Nikolaevich)
1871-1919 . . . . **TCLC 3**
See also CA 104

Andric, Ivo 1892-1975 . . . . **CLC 8**
See also CA 81-84; 57-60; CANR 43;
DLB 147; MTCW

Angelique, Pierre
See Bataille, Georges

Angell, Roger 1920- . . . . **CLC 26**
See also CA 57-60; CANR 13, 44; DLB 171

Angelou, Maya
1928- . . . . **CLC 12, 35, 64, 77; BLC; DA;
DAB; DAC; DAM MST, MULT, POET,
POP**
See also AAYA 7; BW 2; CA 65-68;
CANR 19, 42; DLB 38; MTCW;
SATA 49

Annensky, Innokenty Fyodorovich
1856-1909 . . . . **TCLC 14**
See also CA 110

Anon, Charles Robert
See Pessoa, Fernando (Antonio Nogueira)

Anouilh, Jean (Marie Lucien Pierre)
1910-1987 . . . . . . **CLC 1, 3, 8, 13, 40, 50;
DAM DRAM**
See also CA 17-20R; 123; CANR 32;
MTCW

Anthony, Florence
See Ai

Anthony, John
See Ciardi, John (Anthony)

Anthony, Peter
See Shaffer, Anthony (Joshua); Shaffer,
Peter (Levin)

Anthony, Piers 1934- . . **CLC 35; DAM POP**
See also AAYA 11; CA 21-24R; CANR 28;
DLB 8; MTCW; SAAS 22; SATA 84

Antoine, Marc
See Proust, (Valentin-Louis-George-Eugene-)
Marcel

Antoninus, Brother
See Everson, William (Oliver)

Antonioni, Michelangelo 1912- . . . . . **CLC 20**
See also CA 73-76; CANR 45

Antschel, Paul 1920-1970
See Celan, Paul
See also CA 85-88; CANR 33; MTCW

Anwar, Chairil 1922-1949 . . . . **TCLC 22**
See also CA 121

Apollinaire, Guillaume
1880-1918 . . . . **TCLC 3, 8, 51;
DAM POET; PC 7**
See also Kostrowitzki, Wilhelm Apollinaris
de
See also CA 152

Appelfeld, Aharon 1932- . . . . **CLC 23, 47**
See also CA 112; 133

Apple, Max (Isaac) 1941- . . . . **CLC 9, 33**
See also CA 81-84; CANR 19, 54; DLB 130

Appleman, Philip (Dean) 1926- . . . . . **CLC 51**
See also CA 13-16R; CAAS 18; CANR 6,
29

Appleton, Lawrence
See Lovecraft, H(oward) P(hillips)

Apteryx
See Eliot, T(homas) S(tearns)

Apuleius, (Lucius Madaurensis)
125(?)-175(?) . . . . **CMLC 1**

Aquin, Hubert 1929-1977 . . . . **CLC 15**
See also CA 105; DLB 53

Aragon, Louis
1897-1982 . . . . . **CLC 3, 22; DAM NOV,
POET**
See also CA 69-72; 108; CANR 28;
DLB 72; MTCW

Arany, Janos 1817-1882 . . . . **NCLC 34**

Arbuthnot, John 1667-1735 . . . . **LC 1**
See also DLB 101

Archer, Herbert Winslow
See Mencken, H(enry) L(ouis)

Archer, Jeffrey (Howard)
1940- . . . . **CLC 28; DAM POP**
See also AAYA 16; BEST 89:3; CA 77-80;
CANR 22, 52; INT CANR-22

Archer, Jules 1915- . . . . **CLC 12**
See also CA 9-12R; CANR 6; SAAS 5;
SATA 4, 85

Archer, Lee
See Ellison, Harlan (Jay)

Arden, John
1930- . . . . . **CLC 6, 13, 15; DAM DRAM**
See also CA 13-16R; CAAS 4; CANR 31;
DLB 13; MTCW

Arenas, Reinaldo
1943-1990 . . . . . . **CLC 41; DAM MULT;
HLC**
See also CA 124; 128; 133; DLB 145; HW

Arendt, Hannah 1906-1975 . . . . . **CLC 66, 98**
See also CA 17-20R; 61-64; CANR 26;
MTCW

Aretino, Pietro 1492-1556 . . . . **LC 12**

Arghezi, Tudor . . . . **CLC 80**
See also Theodorescu, Ion N.

Arguedas, Jose Maria
1911-1969 . . . . **CLC 10, 18**
See also CA 89-92; DLB 113; HW

Argueta, Manlio 1936- . . . . **CLC 31**
See also CA 131; DLB 145; HW

Ariosto, Ludovico 1474-1533 . . . . **LC 6**

Aristides
See Epstein, Joseph

Aristophanes
450B.C.-385B.C. . . . . **CMLC 4; DA;
DAB; DAC; DAM DRAM, MST; DC 2**

Arlt, Roberto (Godofredo Christophersen)
1900-1942 . . . . . **TCLC 29; DAM MULT;
HLC**
See also CA 123; 131; HW

Armah, Ayi Kwei
1939- . . . . **CLC 5, 33; BLC;
DAM MULT, POET**
See also BW 1; CA 61-64; CANR 21;
DLB 117; MTCW

Armatrading, Joan 1950- . . . . **CLC 17**
See also CA 114

Arnette, Robert
See Silverberg, Robert

**Arnim, Achim von (Ludwig Joachim von
Arnim)** 1781-1831 . . . . **NCLC 5**
See also DLB 90

Arnim, Bettina von 1785-1859 . . . . **NCLC 38**
See also DLB 90

Arnold, Matthew
1822-1888 . . . . . **NCLC 6, 29; DA; DAB;
DAC; DAM MST, POET; PC 5; WLC**
See also CDBLB 1832-1890; DLB 32, 57

Arnold, Thomas 1795-1842 . . . . . . **NCLC 18**
See also DLB 55

Arnow, Harriette (Louisa) Simpson
1908-1986 . . . . **CLC 2, 7, 18**
See also CA 9-12R; 118; CANR 14; DLB 6;
MTCW; SATA 42; SATA-Obit 47

Arp, Hans
See Arp, Jean

Arp, Jean 1887-1966 . . . . **CLC 5**
See also CA 81-84; 25-28R; CANR 42

Arrabal
See Arrabal, Fernando

Arrabal, Fernando 1932- . . . **CLC 2, 9, 18, 58**
See also CA 9-12R; CANR 15

Arrick, Fran . . . . **CLC 30**
See also Gaberman, Judie Angell

Artaud, Antonin (Marie Joseph)
1896-1948 . . . **TCLC 3, 36; DAM DRAM**
See also CA 104; 149

Arthur, Ruth M(abel) 1905-1979 . . . . **CLC 12**
See also CA 9-12R; 85-88; CANR 4;
SATA 7, 26

Artsybashev, Mikhail (Petrovich)
1878-1927 . . . . **TCLC 31**

Arundel, Honor (Morfydd)
1919-1973 . . . . **CLC 17**
See also CA 21-22; 41-44R; CAP 2;
CLR 35; SATA 4; SATA-Obit 24

Arzner, Dorothy 1897-1979 . . . . **CLC 98**

Asch, Sholem 1880-1957 . . . . **TCLC 3**
See also CA 105

Ash, Shalom
See Asch, Sholem

Ashbery, John (Lawrence)
1927- ..... CLC 2, 3, 4, 6, 9, 13, 15, 25,
41, 77; DAM POET
See also CA 5-8R; CANR 9, 37; DLB 5,
165; DLBY 81; INT CANR-9; MTCW

Ashdown, Clifford
See Freeman, R(ichard) Austin

Ashe, Gordon
See Creasey, John

Ashton-Warner, Sylvia (Constance)
1908-1984 .... CLC 19
See also CA 69-72; 112; CANR 29; MTCW

Asimov, Isaac
1920-1992 ..... CLC 1, 3, 9, 19, 26, 76,
92; DAM POP
See also AAYA 13; BEST 90:2; CA 1-4R;
137; CANR 2, 19, 36; CLR 12; DLB 8;
DLBY 92; INT CANR-19; JRDA;
MAICYA; MTCW; SATA 1, 26, 74

Assis, Joaquim Maria Machado de
See Machado de Assis, Joaquim Maria

Astley, Thea (Beatrice May)
1925- .... CLC 41
See also CA 65-68; CANR 11, 43

Aston, James
See White, T(erence) H(anbury)

Asturias, Miguel Angel
1899-1974 .... CLC 3, 8, 13;
DAM MULT, NOV; HLC
See also CA 25-28; 49-52; CANR 32;
CAP 2; DLB 113; HW; MTCW

Atares, Carlos Saura
See Saura (Atares), Carlos

Atheling, William
See Pound, Ezra (Weston Loomis)

Atheling, William, Jr.
See Blish, James (Benjamin)

Atherton, Gertrude (Franklin Horn)
1857-1948 .... TCLC 2
See also CA 104; DLB 9, 78

Atherton, Lucius
See Masters, Edgar Lee

Atkins, Jack
See Harris, Mark

Attaway, William (Alexander)
1911-1986 .... CLC 92; BLC;
DAM MULT
See also BW 2; CA 143; DLB 76

Atticus
See Fleming, Ian (Lancaster)

Atwood, Margaret (Eleanor)
1939- ..... CLC 2, 3, 4, 8, 13, 15, 25, 44,
84; DA; DAB; DAC; DAM MST, NOV,
POET; PC 8; SSC 2; WLC
See also AAYA 12; BEST 89:2; CA 49-52;
CANR 3, 24, 33; DLB 53;
INT CANR-24; MTCW; SATA 50

Aubigny, Pierre d'
See Mencken, H(enry) L(ouis)

Aubin, Penelope 1685-1731(?) .... LC 9
See also DLB 39

Auchincloss, Louis (Stanton)
1917- .... CLC 4, 6, 9, 18, 45;
DAM NOV; SSC 22
See also CA 1-4R; CANR 6, 29, 55; DLB 2;
DLBY 80; INT CANR-29; MTCW

Auden, W(ystan) H(ugh)
1907-1973 ..... CLC 1, 2, 3, 4, 6, 9, 11,
14, 43; DA; DAB; DAC; DAM DRAM,
MST, POET; PC 1; WLC
See also AAYA 18; CA 9-12R; 45-48;
CANR 5; CDBLB 1914-1945; DLB 10,
20; MTCW

Audiberti, Jacques
1900-1965 ...... CLC 38; DAM DRAM
See also CA 25-28R

Audubon, John James
1785-1851 .... NCLC 47

Auel, Jean M(arie)
1936- .... CLC 31; DAM POP
See also AAYA 7; BEST 90:4; CA 103;
CANR 21; INT CANR-21; SATA 91

Auerbach, Erich 1892-1957 ...... TCLC 43
See also CA 118

Augier, Emile 1820-1889 .... NCLC 31

August, John
See De Voto, Bernard (Augustine)

Augustine, St. 354-430 ...... CMLC 6; DAB

Aurelius
See Bourne, Randolph S(illiman)

Aurobindo, Sri 1872-1950 .... TCLC 63

Austen, Jane
1775-1817 ..... NCLC 1, 13, 19, 33, 51;
DA; DAB; DAC; DAM MST, NOV;
WLC
See also AAYA 19; CDBLB 1789-1832;
DLB 116

Auster, Paul 1947- .... CLC 47
See also CA 69-72; CANR 23, 52

Austin, Frank
See Faust, Frederick (Schiller)

Austin, Mary (Hunter)
1868-1934 .... TCLC 25
See also CA 109; DLB 9, 78

Autran Dourado, Waldomiro
See Dourado, (Waldomiro Freitas) Autran

Averroes 1126-1198 .... CMLC 7
See also DLB 115

Avicenna 980-1037 .... CMLC 16
See also DLB 115

Avison, Margaret
1918- .... CLC 2, 4, 97; DAC;
DAM POET
See also CA 17-20R; DLB 53; MTCW

Axton, David
See Koontz, Dean R(ay)

Ayckbourn, Alan
1939- ...... CLC 5, 8, 18, 33, 74; DAB;
DAM DRAM
See also CA 21-24R; CANR 31; DLB 13;
MTCW

Aydy, Catherine
See Tennant, Emma (Christina)

Ayme, Marcel (Andre) 1902-1967 ... CLC 11
See also CA 89-92; CLR 25; DLB 72;
SATA 91

Ayrton, Michael 1921-1975 .... CLC 7
See also CA 5-8R; 61-64; CANR 9, 21

Azorin .... CLC 11
See also Martinez Ruiz, Jose

Azuela, Mariano
1873-1952 ..... TCLC 3; DAM MULT;
HLC
See also CA 104; 131; HW; MTCW

Baastad, Babbis Friis
See Friis-Baastad, Babbis Ellinor

Bab
See Gilbert, W(illiam) S(chwenck)

Babbis, Eleanor
See Friis-Baastad, Babbis Ellinor

Babel, Isaak (Emmanuilovich)
1894-1941(?) ...... TCLC 2, 13; SSC 16
See also CA 104

Babits, Mihaly 1883-1941 .... TCLC 14
See also CA 114

Babur 1483-1530 .... LC 18

Bacchelli, Riccardo 1891-1985 ..... CLC 19
See also CA 29-32R; 117

Bach, Richard (David)
1936- ...... CLC 14; DAM NOV, POP
See also AITN 1; BEST 89:2; CA 9-12R;
CANR 18; MTCW; SATA 13

Bachman, Richard
See King, Stephen (Edwin)

Bachmann, Ingeborg 1926-1973 ..... CLC 69
See also CA 93-96; 45-48; DLB 85

Bacon, Francis 1561-1626 .... LC 18, 32
See also CDBLB Before 1660; DLB 151

Bacon, Roger 1214(?)-1292 ...... CMLC 14
See also DLB 115

Bacovia, George .... TCLC 24
See also Vasiliu, Gheorghe

Badanes, Jerome 1937- .... CLC 59

Bagehot, Walter 1826-1877 ...... NCLC 10
See also DLB 55

Bagnold, Enid
1889-1981 ...... CLC 25; DAM DRAM
See also CA 5-8R; 103; CANR 5, 40;
DLB 13, 160; MAICYA; SATA 1, 25

Bagritsky, Eduard 1895-1934 ..... TCLC 60

Bagrjana, Elisaveta
See Belcheva, Elisaveta

Bagryana, Elisaveta .... CLC 10
See also Belcheva, Elisaveta
See also DLB 147

Bailey, Paul 1937- .... CLC 45
See also CA 21-24R; CANR 16; DLB 14

Baillie, Joanna 1762-1851 .... NCLC 2
See also DLB 93

Bainbridge, Beryl (Margaret)
1933- .... CLC 4, 5, 8, 10, 14, 18, 22, 62;
DAM NOV
See also CA 21-24R; CANR 24, 55;
DLB 14; MTCW

Baker, Elliott 1922- .... CLC 8
See also CA 45-48; CANR 2

Baker, Jean H. .... TCLC 3, 10
See also Russell, George William

Baker, Nicholson
1957- .... CLC 61; DAM POP
See also CA 135

Baker, Ray Stannard 1870-1946 ... TCLC 47
See also CA 118

Baker, Russell (Wayne) 1925-...... **CLC 31**
See also BEST 89:4; CA 57-60; CANR 11,
41; MTCW

Bakhtin, M.
See Bakhtin, Mikhail Mikhailovich

Bakhtin, M. M.
See Bakhtin, Mikhail Mikhailovich

Bakhtin, Mikhail
See Bakhtin, Mikhail Mikhailovich

Bakhtin, Mikhail Mikhailovich
1895-1975 .... **CLC 83**
See also CA 128; 113

Bakshi, Ralph 1938(?)-............ **CLC 26**
See also CA 112; 138

Bakunin, Mikhail (Alexandrovich)
1814-1876 .... **NCLC 25, 58**

Baldwin, James (Arthur)
1924-1987 ...... **CLC 1, 2, 3, 4, 5, 8, 13,
15, 17, 42, 50, 67, 90; BLC; DA; DAB;
DAC; DAM MST, MULT, NOV, POP;
DC 1; SSC 10; WLC**
See also AAYA 4; BW 1; CA 1-4R; 124;
CABS 1; CANR 3, 24;
CDALB 1941-1968; DLB 2, 7, 33;
DLBY 87; MTCW; SATA 9;
SATA-Obit 54

Ballard, J(ames) G(raham)
1930- .... **CLC 3, 6, 14, 36; DAM NOV,
POP; SSC 1**
See also AAYA 3; CA 5-8R; CANR 15, 39;
DLB 14; MTCW

Balmont, Konstantin (Dmitriyevich)
1867-1943 .... **TCLC 11**
See also CA 109

Balzac, Honore de
1799-1850 .... **NCLC 5, 35, 53; DA;
DAB; DAC; DAM MST, NOV; SSC 5;
WLC**
See also DLB 119

Bambara, Toni Cade
1939-1995 ...... **CLC 19, 88; BLC; DA;
DAC; DAM MST, MULT**
See also AAYA 5; BW 2; CA 29-32R; 150;
CANR 24, 49; DLB 38; MTCW

Bamdad, A.
See Shamlu, Ahmad

Banat, D. R.
See Bradbury, Ray (Douglas)

Bancroft, Laura
See Baum, L(yman) Frank

Banim, John 1798-1842 .... **NCLC 13**
See also DLB 116, 158, 159

Banim, Michael 1796-1874 ...... **NCLC 13**
See also DLB 158, 159

Banks, Iain
See Banks, Iain M(enzies)

Banks, Iain M(enzies) 1954-....... **CLC 34**
See also CA 123; 128; INT 128

Banks, Lynne Reid .... **CLC 23**
See also Reid Banks, Lynne
See also AAYA 6

Banks, Russell 1940- .... **CLC 37, 72**
See also CA 65-68; CAAS 15; CANR 19,
52; DLB 130

Banville, John 1945-............. **CLC 46**
See also CA 117; 128; DLB 14; INT 128

Banville, Theodore (Faullain) de
1832-1891 .... **NCLC 9**

Baraka, Amiri
1934- .... **CLC 1, 2, 3, 5, 10, 14, 33;
BLC; DA; DAC; DAM MST, MULT,
POET, POP; DC 6; PC 4**
See also Jones, LeRoi
See also BW 2; CA 21-24R; CABS 3;
CANR 27, 38; CDALB 1941-1968;
DLB 5, 7, 16, 38; DLBD 8; MTCW

Barbauld, Anna Laetitia
1743-1825 .... **NCLC 50**
See also DLB 107, 109, 142, 158

Barbellion, W. N. P. .... **TCLC 24**
See also Cummings, Bruce F(rederick)

Barbera, Jack (Vincent) 1945-...... **CLC 44**
See also CA 110; CANR 45

Barbey d'Aurevilly, Jules Amedee
1808-1889 .... **NCLC 1; SSC 17**
See also DLB 119

Barbusse, Henri 1873-1935 .... **TCLC 5**
See also CA 105; 154; DLB 65

Barclay, Bill
See Moorcock, Michael (John)

Barclay, William Ewert
See Moorcock, Michael (John)

Barea, Arturo 1897-1957 .... **TCLC 14**
See also CA 111

Barfoot, Joan 1946- .... **CLC 18**
See also CA 105

Baring, Maurice 1874-1945 .... **TCLC 8**
See also CA 105; DLB 34

Barker, Clive 1952- ... **CLC 52; DAM POP**
See also AAYA 10; BEST 90:3; CA 121;
129; INT 129; MTCW

Barker, George Granville
1913-1991 ..... **CLC 8, 48; DAM POET**
See also CA 9-12R; 135; CANR 7, 38;
DLB 20; MTCW

Barker, Harley Granville
See Granville-Barker, Harley
See also DLB 10

Barker, Howard 1946-............ **CLC 37**
See also CA 102; DLB 13

Barker, Pat(ricia) 1943-........ **CLC 32, 94**
See also CA 117; 122; CANR 50; INT 122

Barlow, Joel 1754-1812 .... **NCLC 23**
See also DLB 37

Barnard, Mary (Ethel) 1909-....... **CLC 48**
See also CA 21-22; CAP 2

Barnes, Djuna
1892-1982 ... **CLC 3, 4, 8, 11, 29; SSC 3**
See also CA 9-12R; 107; CANR 16, 55;
DLB 4, 9, 45; MTCW

Barnes, Julian (Patrick)
1946-.................... **CLC 42; DAB**
See also CA 102; CANR 19, 54; DLBY 93

Barnes, Peter 1931- .... **CLC 5, 56**
See also CA 65-68; CAAS 12; CANR 33,
34; DLB 13; MTCW

Baroja (y Nessi), Pio
1872-1956 .... **TCLC 8; HLC**
See also CA 104

Baron, David
See Pinter, Harold

Baron Corvo
See Rolfe, Frederick (William Serafino
Austin Lewis Mary)

Barondess, Sue K(aufman)
1926-1977 .... **CLC 8**
See also Kaufman, Sue
See also CA 1-4R; 69-72; CANR 1

Baron de Teive
See Pessoa, Fernando (Antonio Nogueira)

Barres, Maurice 1862-1923 .... **TCLC 47**
See also DLB 123

Barreto, Afonso Henrique de Lima
See Lima Barreto, Afonso Henrique de

Barrett, (Roger) Syd 1946- .... **CLC 35**

Barrett, William (Christopher)
1913-1992 .... **CLC 27**
See also CA 13-16R; 139; CANR 11;
INT CANR-11

Barrie, J(ames) M(atthew)
1860-1937 .... **TCLC 2; DAB;
DAM DRAM**
See also CA 104; 136; CDBLB 1890-1914;
CLR 16; DLB 10, 141, 156; MAICYA;
YABC 1

Barrington, Michael
See Moorcock, Michael (John)

Barrol, Grady
See Bograd, Larry

Barry, Mike
See Malzberg, Barry N(athaniel)

Barry, Philip 1896-1949.......... **TCLC 11**
See also CA 109; DLB 7

Bart, Andre Schwarz
See Schwarz-Bart, Andre

Barth, John (Simmons)
1930-...... **CLC 1, 2, 3, 5, 7, 9, 10, 14,
27, 51, 89; DAM NOV; SSC 10**
See also AITN 1, 2; CA 1-4R; CABS 1;
CANR 5, 23, 49; DLB 2; MTCW

Barthelme, Donald
1931-1989 ...... **CLC 1, 2, 3, 5, 6, 8, 13,
23, 46, 59; DAM NOV; SSC 2**
See also CA 21-24R; 129; CANR 20;
DLB 2; DLBY 80, 89; MTCW; SATA 7;
SATA-Obit 62

Barthelme, Frederick 1943-........ **CLC 36**
See also CA 114; 122; DLBY 85; INT 122

Barthes, Roland (Gerard)
1915-1980 .... **CLC 24, 83**
See also CA 130; 97-100; MTCW

Barzun, Jacques (Martin) 1907- .... **CLC 51**
See also CA 61-64; CANR 22

Bashevis, Isaac
See Singer, Isaac Bashevis

Bashkirtseff, Marie 1859-1884 ... **NCLC 27**

Basho
See Matsuo Basho

Bass, Kingsley B., Jr.
See Bullins, Ed

Bass, Rick 1958-................. **CLC 79**
See also CA 126; CANR 53

Bassani, Giorgio 1916-............ **CLC 9**
See also CA 65-68; CANR 33; DLB 128;
MTCW

Bastos, Augusto (Antonio) Roa
See Roa Bastos, Augusto (Antonio)

Bataille, Georges 1897-1962 .... **CLC 29**
See also CA 101; 89-92

Bates, H(erbert) E(rnest)
1905-1974 .... **CLC 46; DAB;**
DAM POP; SSC 10
See also CA 93-96; 45-48; CANR 34;
DLB 162; MTCW

Bauchart
See Camus, Albert

Baudelaire, Charles
1821-1867 .... **NCLC 6, 29, 55; DA;**
DAB; DAC; DAM MST, POET; PC 1;
SSC 18; WLC

Baudrillard, Jean 1929-.......... **CLC 60**

Baum, L(yman) Frank 1856-1919 ... **TCLC 7**
See also CA 108; 133; CLR 15; DLB 22;
JRDA; MAICYA; MTCW; SATA 18

Baum, Louis F.
See Baum, L(yman) Frank

Baumbach, Jonathan 1933-...... **CLC 6, 23**
See also CA 13-16R; CAAS 5; CANR 12;
DLBY 80; INT CANR-12; MTCW

Bausch, Richard (Carl) 1945- ...... **CLC 51**
See also CA 101; CAAS 14; CANR 43;
DLB 130

Baxter, Charles
1947- .... **CLC 45, 78; DAM POP**
See also CA 57-60; CANR 40; DLB 130

Baxter, George Owen
See Faust, Frederick (Schiller)

Baxter, James K(eir) 1926-1972 .... **CLC 14**
See also CA 77-80

Baxter, John
See Hunt, E(verette) Howard, (Jr.)

Bayer, Sylvia
See Glassco, John

Baynton, Barbara 1857-1929 ..... **TCLC 57**

Beagle, Peter S(oyer) 1939-......... **CLC 7**
See also CA 9-12R; CANR 4, 51;
DLBY 80; INT CANR-4; SATA 60

Bean, Normal
See Burroughs, Edgar Rice

Beard, Charles A(ustin)
1874-1948 .... **TCLC 15**
See also CA 115; DLB 17; SATA 18

Beardsley, Aubrey 1872-1898 ..... **NCLC 6**

Beattie, Ann
1947- .... **CLC 8, 13, 18, 40, 63;**
DAM NOV, POP; SSC 11
See also BEST 90:2; CA 81-84; CANR 53;
DLBY 82; MTCW

Beattie, James 1735-1803 .... **NCLC 25**
See also DLB 109

Beauchamp, Kathleen Mansfield 1888-1923
See Mansfield, Katherine
See also CA 104; 134; DA; DAC;
DAM MST

Beaumarchais, Pierre-Augustin Caron de
1732-1799 .... **DC 4**
See also DAM DRAM

Beaumont, Francis
1584(?)-1616 .... **LC 33; DC 6**
See also CDBLB Before 1660; DLB 58, 121

Beauvoir, Simone (Lucie Ernestine Marie
Bertrand) de
1908-1986 .... **CLC 1, 2, 4, 8, 14, 31, 44,**
50, 71; DA; DAB; DAC; DAM MST,
NOV; WLC
See also CA 9-12R; 118; CANR 28;
DLB 72; DLBY 86; MTCW

Becker, Carl 1873-1945 .... **TCLC 63:**
See also DLB 17

Becker, Jurek 1937-............ **CLC 7, 19**
See also CA 85-88; DLB 75

Becker, Walter 1950-............. **CLC 26**

Beckett, Samuel (Barclay)
1906-1989 ...... **CLC 1, 2, 3, 4, 6, 9, 10,**
11, 14, 18, 29, 57, 59, 83; DA; DAB;
DAC; DAM DRAM, MST, NOV;
SSC 16; WLC
See also CA 5-8R; 130; CANR 33;
CDBLB 1945-1960; DLB 13, 15;
DLBY 90; MTCW

Beckford, William 1760-1844 .... **NCLC 16**
See also DLB 39

Beckman, Gunnel 1910-.......... **CLC 26**
See also CA 33-36R; CANR 15; CLR 25;
MAICYA; SAAS 9; SATA 6

Becque, Henri 1837-1899........ **NCLC 3**

Beddoes, Thomas Lovell
1803-1849 .... **NCLC 3**
See also DLB 96

Bede c. 673-735.............. **CMLC 20**
See also DLB 146

Bedford, Donald F.
See Fearing, Kenneth (Flexner)

Beecher, Catharine Esther
1800-1878 .... **NCLC 30**
See also DLB 1

Beecher, John 1904-1980........... **CLC 6**
See also AITN 1; CA 5-8R; 105; CANR 8

Beer, Johann 1655-1700............. **LC 5**
See also DLB 168

Beer, Patricia 1924-.............. **CLC 58**
See also CA 61-64; CANR 13, 46; DLB 40

Beerbohm, Max
See Beerbohm, (Henry) Max(imilian)

Beerbohm, (Henry) Max(imilian)
1872-1956 ....**TCLC 1, 24**
See also CA 104; 154; DLB 34, 100

Beer-Hofmann, Richard
1866-1945 .... **TCLC 60**
See also DLB 81

Begiebing, Robert J(ohn) 1946-..... **CLC 70**
See also CA 122; CANR 40

Behan, Brendan
1923-1964 .... **CLC 1, 8, 11, 15, 79;**
DAM DRAM
See also CA 73-76; CANR 33;
CDBLB 1945-1960; DLB 13; MTCW

Behn, Aphra
1640(?)-1689 ...... **LC 1, 30; DA; DAB;**
DAC; DAM DRAM, MST, NOV,
POET; DC 4; PC 13; WLC
See also DLB 39, 80, 131

Behrman, S(amuel) N(athaniel)
1893-1973 .... **CLC 40**
See also CA 13-16; 45-48; CAP 1; DLB 7,
44

Belasco, David 1853-1931 .... **TCLC 3**
See also CA 104; DLB 7

Belcheva, Elisaveta 1893- .... **CLC 10**
See also Bagryana, Elisaveta

Beldone, Phil "Cheech"
See Ellison, Harlan (Jay)

Beleno
See Azuela, Mariano

Belinski, Vissarion Grigoryevich
1811-1848 .... **NCLC 5**

Belitt, Ben 1911-.................. **CLC 22**
See also CA 13-16R; CAAS 4; CANR 7;
DLB 5

Bell, Gertrude 1868-1926......... **TCLC 67**
See also DLB 174

Bell, James Madison
1826-1902 .... **TCLC 43; BLC;**
DAM MULT
See also BW 1; CA 122; 124; DLB 50

Bell, Madison Smartt 1957-........ **CLC 41**
See also CA 111; CANR 28, 54

Bell, Marvin (Hartley)
1937- .... **CLC 8, 31; DAM POET**
See also CA 21-24R; CAAS 14; DLB 5;
MTCW

Bell, W. L. D.
See Mencken, H(enry) L(ouis)

Bellamy, Atwood C.
See Mencken, H(enry) L(ouis)

Bellamy, Edward 1850-1898 ...... **NCLC 4**
See also DLB 12

Bellin, Edward J.
See Kuttner, Henry

Belloc, (Joseph) Hilaire (Pierre Sebastien
Rene Swanton)
1870-1953 ... **TCLC 7, 18; DAM POET**
See also CA 106; 152; DLB 19, 100, 141,
174; YABC 1

Belloc, Joseph Peter Rene Hilaire
See Belloc, (Joseph) Hilaire (Pierre Sebastien
Rene Swanton)

Belloc, Joseph Pierre Hilaire
See Belloc, (Joseph) Hilaire (Pierre Sebastien
Rene Swanton)

Belloc, M. A.
See Lowndes, Marie Adelaide (Belloc)

Bellow, Saul
1915-...... **CLC 1, 2, 3, 6, 8, 10, 13, 15,**
25, 33, 34, 63, 79; DA; DAB; DAC;
DAM MST, NOV, POP; SSC 14; WLC
See also AITN 2; BEST 89:3; CA 5-8R;
CABS 1; CANR 29, 53;
CDALB 1941-1968; DLB 2, 28; DLBD 3;
DLBY 82; MTCW

Belser, Reimond Karel Maria de   1929-
See Ruyslinck, Ward
See also CA 152

Bely, Andrey . . . . TCLC 7; PC 11
See also Bugayev, Boris Nikolayevich

Benary, Margot
See Benary-Isbert, Margot

Benary-Isbert, Margot   1889-1979 . . . CLC 12
See also CA 5-8R; 89-92; CANR 4;
CLR 12; MAICYA; SATA 2;
SATA-Obit 21

Benavente (y Martinez), Jacinto
1866-1954 . . . . . TCLC 3; DAM DRAM,
MULT
See also CA 106; 131; HW; MTCW

Benchley, Peter (Bradford)
1940- . . . . . CLC 4, 8; DAM NOV, POP
See also AAYA 14; AITN 2; CA 17-20R;
CANR 12, 35; MTCW; SATA 3, 89

Benchley, Robert (Charles)
1889-1945 . . . . TCLC 1, 55
See also CA 105; 153; DLB 11

Benda, Julien   1867-1956 . . . . TCLC 60
See also CA 120; 154

Benedict, Ruth   1887-1948 . . . . TCLC 60

Benedikt, Michael   1935- . . . . . . CLC 4, 14
See also CA 13-16R; CANR 7; DLB 5

Benet, Juan   1927- . . . . CLC 28
See also CA 143

Benet, Stephen Vincent
1898-1943 . . . . . . TCLC 7; DAM POET;
SSC 10
See also CA 104; 152; DLB 4, 48, 102;
YABC 1

Benet, William Rose
1886-1950 . . . . . . TCLC 28; DAM POET
See also CA 118; 152; DLB 45

Benford, Gregory (Albert)   1941- . . . . CLC 52
See also CA 69-72; CANR 12, 24, 49;
DLBY 82

Bengtsson, Frans (Gunnar)
1894-1954 . . . . TCLC 48

Benjamin, David
See Slavitt, David R(ytman)

Benjamin, Lois
See Gould, Lois

Benjamin, Walter   1892-1940 . . . . . TCLC 39

Benn, Gottfried   1886-1956 . . . . TCLC 3
See also CA 106; 153; DLB 56

Bennett, Alan
1934- . . . CLC 45, 77; DAB; DAM MST
See also CA 103; CANR 35, 55; MTCW

Bennett, (Enoch) Arnold
1867-1931 . . . . TCLC 5, 20
See also CA 106; CDBLB 1890-1914;
DLB 10, 34, 98, 135

Bennett, Elizabeth
See Mitchell, Margaret (Munnerlyn)

Bennett, George Harold   1930-
See Bennett, Hal
See also BW 1; CA 97-100

Bennett, Hal . . . . CLC 5
See also Bennett, George Harold
See also DLB 33

Bennett, Jay   1912- . . . . CLC 35
See also AAYA 10; CA 69-72; CANR 11,
42; JRDA; SAAS 4; SATA 41, 87;
SATA-Brief 27

Bennett, Louise (Simone)
1919- . . . . . CLC 28; BLC; DAM MULT
See also BW 2; CA 151; DLB 117

Benson, E(dward) F(rederic)
1867-1940 . . . . TCLC 27
See also CA 114; DLB 135, 153

Benson, Jackson J.   1930- . . . . CLC 34
See also CA 25-28R; DLB 111

Benson, Sally   1900-1972 . . . . CLC 17
See also CA 19-20; 37-40R; CAP 1;
SATA 1, 35; SATA-Obit 27

Benson, Stella   1892-1933 . . . . TCLC 17
See also CA 117; 154; DLB 36, 162

Bentham, Jeremy   1748-1832 . . . . . NCLC 38
See also DLB 107, 158

Bentley, E(dmund) C(lerihew)
1875-1956 . . . . TCLC 12
See also CA 108; DLB 70

Bentley, Eric (Russell)   1916- . . . . CLC 24
See also CA 5-8R; CANR 6; INT CANR-6

Beranger, Pierre Jean de
1780-1857 . . . . NCLC 34

Berdyaev, Nicolas
See Berdyaev, Nikolai (Aleksandrovich)

Berdyaev, Nikolai (Aleksandrovich)
1874-1948 . . . . TCLC 67
See also CA 120

Berendt, John (Lawrence)   1939- . . . . CLC 86
See also CA 146

Berger, Colonel
See Malraux, (Georges-)Andre

Berger, John (Peter)   1926- . . . . . . CLC 2, 19
See also CA 81-84; CANR 51; DLB 14

Berger, Melvin H.   1927- . . . . CLC 12
See also CA 5-8R; CANR 4; CLR 32;
SAAS 2; SATA 5, 88

Berger, Thomas (Louis)
1924- . . . . CLC 3, 5, 8, 11, 18, 38;
DAM NOV
See also CA 1-4R; CANR 5, 28, 51; DLB 2;
DLBY 80; INT CANR-28; MTCW

Bergman, (Ernst) Ingmar
1918- . . . . CLC 16, 72
See also CA 81-84; CANR 33

Bergson, Henri   1859-1941 . . . . TCLC 32

Bergstein, Eleanor   1938- . . . . CLC 4
See also CA 53-56; CANR 5

Berkoff, Steven   1937- . . . . CLC 56
See also CA 104

Bermant, Chaim (Icyk)   1929- . . . . . . CLC 40
See also CA 57-60; CANR 6, 31

Bern, Victoria
See Fisher, M(ary) F(rances) K(ennedy)

Bernanos, (Paul Louis) Georges
1888-1948 . . . . TCLC 3
See also CA 104; 130; DLB 72

Bernard, April   1956- . . . . CLC 59
See also CA 131

Berne, Victoria
See Fisher, M(ary) F(rances) K(ennedy)

Bernhard, Thomas
1931-1989 . . . . CLC 3, 32, 61
See also CA 85-88; 127; CANR 32;
DLB 85, 124; MTCW

Berriault, Gina   1926- . . . . CLC 54
See also CA 116; 129; DLB 130

Berrigan, Daniel   1921- . . . . CLC 4
See also CA 33-36R; CAAS 1; CANR 11,
43; DLB 5

Berrigan, Edmund Joseph Michael, Jr.
1934-1983
See Berrigan, Ted
See also CA 61-64; 110; CANR 14

Berrigan, Ted . . . . CLC 37
See also Berrigan, Edmund Joseph Michael,
Jr.
See also DLB 5, 169

Berry, Charles Edward Anderson   1931-
See Berry, Chuck
See also CA 115

Berry, Chuck . . . . CLC 17
See also Berry, Charles Edward Anderson

Berry, Jonas
See Ashbery, John (Lawrence)

Berry, Wendell (Erdman)
1934- . . . . CLC 4, 6, 8, 27, 46;
DAM POET
See also AITN 1; CA 73-76; CANR 50;
DLB 5, 6

Berryman, John
1914-1972 . . . . . . CLC 1, 2, 3, 4, 6, 8, 10,
13, 25, 62; DAM POET
See also CA 13-16; 33-36R; CABS 2;
CANR 35; CAP 1; CDALB 1941-1968;
DLB 48; MTCW

Bertolucci, Bernardo   1940- . . . . CLC 16
See also CA 106

Bertrand, Aloysius   1807-1841 . . . . NCLC 31

Bertran de Born   c. 1140-1215 . . . . . CMLC 5

Besant, Annie (Wood)   1847-1933 . . . TCLC 9
See also CA 105

Bessie, Alvah   1904-1985 . . . . CLC 23
See also CA 5-8R; 116; CANR 2; DLB 26

Bethlen, T. D.
See Silverberg, Robert

Beti, Mongo . . . . CLC 27; BLC; DAM MULT
See also Biyidi, Alexandre

Betjeman, John
1906-1984 . . . . CLC 2, 6, 10, 34, 43;
DAB; DAM MST, POET
See also CA 9-12R; 112; CANR 33;
CDBLB 1945-1960; DLB 20; DLBY 84;
MTCW

Bettelheim, Bruno   1903-1990 . . . . . . CLC 79
See also CA 81-84; 131; CANR 23; MTCW

Betti, Ugo   1892-1953 . . . . TCLC 5
See also CA 104

Betts, Doris (Waugh)   1932- . . . . CLC 3, 6, 28
See also CA 13-16R; CANR 9; DLBY 82;
INT CANR-9

Bevan, Alistair
See Roberts, Keith (John Kingston)

Bialik, Chaim Nachman
1873-1934 . . . . TCLC 25

Bogosian, Eric 1953- . . . . **CLC 45**
See also CA 138

Bograd, Larry 1953- . . . . **CLC 35**
See also CA 93-96; SAAS 21; SATA 33, 89

Boiardo, Matteo Maria 1441-1494 . . . . **LC 6**

Boileau-Despreaux, Nicolas
1636-1711 . . . . **LC 3**

Bojer, Johan 1872-1959 . . . . **TCLC 64**

Boland, Eavan (Aisling)
1944- . . . . **CLC 40, 67; DAM POET**
See also CA 143; DLB 40

Bolt, Lee
See Faust, Frederick (Schiller)

Bolt, Robert (Oxton)
1924-1995 . . . . . . **CLC 14; DAM DRAM**
See also CA 17-20R; 147; CANR 35;
DLB 13; MTCW

Bombet, Louis-Alexandre-Cesar
See Stendhal

Bomkauf
See Kaufman, Bob (Garnell)

Bonaventura. . . . . **NCLC 35**
See also DLB 90

Bond, Edward
1934- . . . **CLC 4, 6, 13, 23; DAM DRAM**
See also CA 25-28R; CANR 38; DLB 13;
MTCW

Bonham, Frank 1914-1989 . . . . **CLC 12**
See also AAYA 1; CA 9-12R; CANR 4, 36;
JRDA; MAICYA; SAAS 3; SATA 1, 49;
SATA-Obit 62

Bonnefoy, Yves
1923- . . . . . . **CLC 9, 15, 58; DAM MST,**
POET
See also CA 85-88; CANR 33; MTCW

Bontemps, Arna(ud Wendell)
1902-1973 . . . . **CLC 1, 18; BLC;**
DAM MULT, NOV, POET
See also BW 1; CA 1-4R; 41-44R; CANR 4,
35; CLR 6; DLB 48, 51; JRDA;
MAICYA; MTCW; SATA 2, 44;
SATA-Obit 24

Booth, Martin 1944- . . . . **CLC 13**
See also CA 93-96; CAAS 2

Booth, Philip 1925- . . . . **CLC 23**
See also CA 5-8R; CANR 5; DLBY 82

Booth, Wayne C(layson) 1921- . . . . . **CLC 24**
See also CA 1-4R; CAAS 5; CANR 3, 43;
DLB 67

Borchert, Wolfgang 1921-1947 . . . . . **TCLC 5**
See also CA 104; DLB 69, 124

Borel, Petrus 1809-1859 . . . . **NCLC 41**

Borges, Jorge Luis
1899-1986 . . . . . . **CLC 1, 2, 3, 4, 6, 8, 9, 10,**
13, 19, 44, 48, 83; DA; DAB; DAC;
DAM MST, MULT; HLC; SSC 4; WLC
See also AAYA 19; CA 21-24R; CANR 19,
33; DLB 113; DLBY 86; HW; MTCW

Borowski, Tadeusz 1922-1951 . . . . . . **TCLC 9**
See also CA 106; 154

Borrow, George (Henry)
1803-1881 . . . . **NCLC 9**
See also DLB 21, 55, 166

Bosman, Herman Charles
1905-1951 . . . . **TCLC 49**

Bosschere, Jean de 1878(?)-1953 . . . **TCLC 19**
See also CA 115

Boswell, James
1740-1795 . . . . . . **LC 4; DA; DAB; DAC;**
DAM MST; WLC
See also CDBLB 1660-1789; DLB 104, 142

Bottoms, David 1949- . . . . **CLC 53**
See also CA 105; CANR 22; DLB 120;
DLBY 83

Boucicault, Dion 1820-1890 . . . . . . **NCLC 41**

Boucolon, Maryse 1937(?)-
See Conde, Maryse
See also CA 110; CANR 30, 53

Bourget, Paul (Charles Joseph)
1852-1935 . . . . **TCLC 12**
See also CA 107; DLB 123

Bourjaily, Vance (Nye) 1922- . . . . **CLC 8, 62**
See also CA 1-4R; CAAS 1; CANR 2;
DLB 2, 143

Bourne, Randolph S(illiman)
1886-1918 . . . . **TCLC 16**
See also CA 117; DLB 63

Bova, Ben(jamin William) 1932- . . . . **CLC 45**
See also AAYA 16; CA 5-8R; CAAS 18;
CANR 11; CLR 3; DLBY 81;
INT CANR-11; MAICYA; MTCW;
SATA 6, 68

Bowen, Elizabeth (Dorothea Cole)
1899-1973 . . . . . . **CLC 1, 3, 6, 11, 15, 22;**
DAM NOV; SSC 3
See also CA 17-18; 41-44R; CANR 35;
CAP 2; CDBLB 1945-1960; DLB 15, 162;
MTCW

Bowering, George 1935- . . . . **CLC 15, 47**
See also CA 21-24R; CAAS 16; CANR 10;
DLB 53

Bowering, Marilyn R(uthe) 1949- . . . **CLC 32**
See also CA 101; CANR 49

Bowers, Edgar 1924- . . . . **CLC 9**
See also CA 5-8R; CANR 24; DLB 5

Bowie, David . . . . **CLC 17**
See also Jones, David Robert

Bowles, Jane (Sydney)
1917-1973 . . . . **CLC 3, 68**
See also CA 19-20; 41-44R; CAP 2

Bowles, Paul (Frederick)
1910- . . . . **CLC 1, 2, 19, 53; SSC 3**
See also CA 1-4R; CAAS 1; CANR 1, 19,
50; DLB 5, 6; MTCW

Box, Edgar
See Vidal, Gore

Boyd, Nancy
See Millay, Edna St. Vincent

Boyd, William 1952- . . . . **CLC 28, 53, 70**
See also CA 114; 120; CANR 51

Boyle, Kay
1902-1992 . . . . . **CLC 1, 5, 19, 58; SSC 5**
See also CA 13-16R; 140; CAAS 1;
CANR 29; DLB 4, 9, 48, 86; DLBY 93;
MTCW

Boyle, Mark
See Kienzle, William X(avier)

Boyle, Patrick 1905-1982 . . . . **CLC 19**
See also CA 127

Boyle, T. C. 1948-
See Boyle, T(homas) Coraghessan

Boyle, T(homas) Coraghessan
1948- . . . . . **CLC 36, 55, 90; DAM POP;**
SSC 16
See also BEST 90:4; CA 120; CANR 44;
DLBY 86

Boz
See Dickens, Charles (John Huffam)

Brackenridge, Hugh Henry
1748-1816 . . . . **NCLC 7**
See also DLB 11, 37

Bradbury, Edward P.
See Moorcock, Michael (John)

Bradbury, Malcolm (Stanley)
1932- . . . . **CLC 32, 61; DAM NOV**
See also CA 1-4R; CANR 1, 33; DLB 14;
MTCW

Bradbury, Ray (Douglas)
1920- . . . . . **CLC 1, 3, 10, 15, 42, 98; DA;**
DAB; DAC; DAM MST, NOV, POP;
WLC
See also AAYA 15; AITN 1, 2; CA 1-4R;
CANR 2, 30; CDALB 1968-1988; DLB 2,
8; INT CANR-30; MTCW; SATA 11, 64

Bradford, Gamaliel 1863-1932 . . . . . **TCLC 36**
See also DLB 17

Bradley, David (Henry, Jr.)
1950- . . . . . **CLC 23; BLC; DAM MULT**
See also BW 1; CA 104; CANR 26; DLB 33

Bradley, John Ed(mund, Jr.)
1958- . . . . **CLC 55**
See also CA 139

Bradley, Marion Zimmer
1930- . . . . **CLC 30; DAM POP**
See also AAYA 9; CA 57-60; CAAS 10;
CANR 7, 31, 51; DLB 8; MTCW;
SATA 90

Bradstreet, Anne
1612(?)-1672 . . . . . . **LC 4, 30; DA; DAC;**
DAM MST, POET; PC 10
See also CDALB 1640-1865; DLB 24

Brady, Joan 1939- . . . . **CLC 86**
See also CA 141

Bragg, Melvyn 1939- . . . . **CLC 10**
See also BEST 89:3; CA 57-60; CANR 10,
48; DLB 14

Braine, John (Gerard)
1922-1986 . . . . **CLC 1, 3, 41**
See also CA 1-4R; 120; CANR 1, 33;
CDBLB 1945-1960; DLB 15; DLBY 86;
MTCW

Brammer, William 1930(?)-1978 . . . . **CLC 31**
See also CA 77-80

Brancati, Vitaliano 1907-1954 . . . . . **TCLC 12**
See also CA 109

Brancato, Robin F(idler) 1936- . . . . . **CLC 35**
See also AAYA 9; CA 69-72; CANR 11,
45; CLR 32; JRDA; SAAS 9; SATA 23

Brand, Max
See Faust, Frederick (Schiller)

Brand, Millen 1906-1980 . . . . **CLC 7**
See also CA 21-24R; 97-100

Branden, Barbara . . . . **CLC 44**
See also CA 148

Brown, George Mackay
1921-1996 .... **CLC 5, 48**
See also CA 21-24R; 151; CAAS 6;
CANR 12, 37; DLB 14, 27, 139; MTCW;
SATA 35

Brown, (William) Larry 1951- ..... **CLC 73**
See also CA 130; 134; INT 133

Brown, Moses
See Barrett, William (Christopher)

Brown, Rita Mae
1944- ..... **CLC 18, 43, 79; DAM NOV,**
POP
See also CA 45-48; CANR 2, 11, 35;
INT CANR-11; MTCW

Brown, Roderick (Langmere) Haig-
See Haig-Brown, Roderick (Langmere)

Brown, Rosellen 1939- .... **CLC 32**
See also CA 77-80; CAAS 10; CANR 14, 44

Brown, Sterling Allen
1901-1989 .... **CLC 1, 23, 59; BLC;**
DAM MULT, POET
See also BW 1; CA 85-88; 127; CANR 26;
DLB 48, 51, 63; MTCW

Brown, Will
See Ainsworth, William Harrison

Brown, William Wells
1813-1884 .... **NCLC 2; BLC;**
DAM MULT; DC 1
See also DLB 3, 50

Browne, (Clyde) Jackson 1948(?)- ... **CLC 21**
See also CA 120

Browning, Elizabeth Barrett
1806-1861 ..... **NCLC 1, 16; DA; DAB;**
DAC; DAM MST, POET; PC 6; WLC
See also CDBLB 1832-1890; DLB 32

Browning, Robert
1812-1889 .... **NCLC 19; DA; DAB;**
DAC; DAM MST, POET; PC 2
See also CDBLB 1832-1890; DLB 32, 163;
YABC 1

Browning, Tod 1882-1962 .... **CLC 16**
See also CA 141; 117

Brownson, Orestes (Augustus)
1803-1876 .... **NCLC 50**

Bruccoli, Matthew J(oseph) 1931- .. **CLC 34**
See also CA 9-12R; CANR 7; DLB 103

Bruce, Lenny .... **CLC 21**
See also Schneider, Leonard Alfred

Bruin, John
See Brutus, Dennis

Brulard, Henri
See Stendhal

Brulls, Christian
See Simenon, Georges (Jacques Christian)

Brunner, John (Kilian Houston)
1934-1995 ...... **CLC 8, 10; DAM POP**
See also CA 1-4R; 149; CAAS 8; CANR 2,
37; MTCW

Bruno, Giordano 1548-1600 .... **LC 27**

Brutus, Dennis
1924- ..... **CLC 43; BLC; DAM MULT,**
POET
See also BW 2; CA 49-52; CAAS 14;
CANR 2, 27, 42; DLB 117

Bryan, C(ourtlandt) D(ixon) B(arnes)
1936- .... **CLC 29**
See also CA 73-76; CANR 13;
INT CANR-13

Bryan, Michael
See Moore, Brian

Bryant, William Cullen
1794-1878 ..... **NCLC 6, 46; DA; DAB;**
DAC; DAM MST, POET
See also CDALB 1640-1865; DLB 3, 43, 59

Bryusov, Valery Yakovlevich
1873-1924 .... **TCLC 10**
See also CA 107

Buchan, John
1875-1940 .... **TCLC 41; DAB;**
DAM POP
See also CA 108; 145; DLB 34, 70, 156;
YABC 2

Buchanan, George 1506-1582 .... **LC 4**

Buchheim, Lothar-Guenther 1918- ... **CLC 6**
See also CA 85-88

Buchner, (Karl) Georg
1813-1837 .... **NCLC 26**

Buchwald, Art(hur) 1925- .... **CLC 33**
See also AITN 1; CA 5-8R; CANR 21;
MTCW; SATA 10

Buck, Pearl S(ydenstricker)
1892-1973 .... **CLC 7, 11, 18; DA; DAB;**
DAC; DAM MST, NOV
See also AITN 1; CA 1-4R; 41-44R;
CANR 1, 34; DLB 9, 102; MTCW;
SATA 1, 25

Buckler, Ernest
1908-1984 .. **CLC 13; DAC; DAM MST**
See also CA 11-12; 114; CAP 1; DLB 68;
SATA 47

Buckley, Vincent (Thomas)
1925-1988 .... **CLC 57**
See also CA 101

Buckley, William F(rank), Jr.
1925- .... **CLC 7, 18, 37; DAM POP**
See also AITN 1; CA 1-4R; CANR 1, 24,
53; DLB 137; DLBY 80; INT CANR-24;
MTCW

Buechner, (Carl) Frederick
1926- ...... **CLC 2, 4, 6, 9; DAM NOV**
See also CA 13-16R; CANR 11, 39;
DLBY 80; INT CANR-11; MTCW

Buell, John (Edward) 1927- .... **CLC 10**
See also CA 1-4R; DLB 53

Buero Vallejo, Antonio 1916- ... **CLC 15, 46**
See also CA 106; CANR 24, 49; HW;
MTCW

Bufalino, Gesualdo 1920(?)- .... **CLC 74**

Bugayev, Boris Nikolayevich 1880-1934
See Bely, Andrey
See also CA 104

Bukowski, Charles
1920-1994 .... **CLC 2, 5, 9, 41, 82;**
DAM NOV, POET
See also CA 17-20R; 144; CANR 40;
DLB 5, 130, 169; MTCW

Bulgakov, Mikhail (Afanas'evich)
1891-1940 .... **TCLC 2, 16;**
DAM DRAM, NOV; SSC 18
See also CA 105; 152

Bulgya, Alexander Alexandrovich
1901-1956 .... **TCLC 53**
See also Fadeyev, Alexander
See also CA 117

Bullins, Ed
1935- .... **CLC 1, 5, 7; BLC;**
DAM DRAM, MULT; DC 6
See also BW 2; CA 49-52; CAAS 16;
CANR 24, 46; DLB 7, 38; MTCW

Bulwer-Lytton, Edward (George Earle Lytton)
1803-1873 .... **NCLC 1, 45**
See also DLB 21

Bunin, Ivan Alexeyevich
1870-1953 .... **TCLC 6; SSC 5**
See also CA 104

Bunting, Basil
1900-1985 .... **CLC 10, 39, 47;**
DAM POET
See also CA 53-56; 115; CANR 7; DLB 20

Bunuel, Luis
1900-1983 .... **CLC 16, 80;**
DAM MULT; HLC
See also CA 101; 110; CANR 32; HW

Bunyan, John
1628-1688 ...... **LC 4; DA; DAB; DAC;**
DAM MST; WLC
See also CDBLB 1660-1789; DLB 39

Burckhardt, Jacob (Christoph)
1818-1897 .... **NCLC 49**

Burford, Eleanor
See Hibbert, Eleanor Alice Burford

Burgess, Anthony
. **CLC 1, 2, 4, 5, 8, 10, 13, 15, 22, 40, 62,**
81, 94; DAB
See also Wilson, John (Anthony) Burgess
See also AITN 1; CDBLB 1960 to Present;
DLB 14

Burke, Edmund
1729(?)-1797 ...... **LC 7, 36; DA; DAB;**
DAC; DAM MST; WLC
See also DLB 104

Burke, Kenneth (Duva)
1897-1993 .... **CLC 2, 24**
See also CA 5-8R; 143; CANR 39; DLB 45,
63; MTCW

Burke, Leda
See Garnett, David

Burke, Ralph
See Silverberg, Robert

Burke, Thomas 1886-1945 .... **TCLC 63**
See also CA 113

Burney, Fanny 1752-1840 .... **NCLC 12, 54**
See also DLB 39

Burns, Robert 1759-1796 .... **PC 6**
See also CDBLB 1789-1832; DA; DAB;
DAC; DAM MST, POET; DLB 109;
WLC

Burns, Tex
See L'Amour, Louis (Dearborn)

Burnshaw, Stanley 1906- ..... **CLC 3, 13, 44**
See also CA 9-12R; DLB 48

Burr, Anne 1937- .... **CLC 6**
See also CA 25-28R

Capote, Truman
1924-1984 ...... **CLC 1, 3, 8, 13, 19, 34, 38, 58; DA; DAB; DAC; DAM MST, NOV, POP; SSC 2; WLC**
See also CA 5-8R; 113; CANR 18; CDALB 1941-1968; DLB 2; DLBY 80, 84; MTCW; SATA 91

Capra, Frank 1897-1991 .... **CLC 16**
See also CA 61-64; 135

Caputo, Philip 1941- .... **CLC 32**
See also CA 73-76; CANR 40

Card, Orson Scott
1951- ...... **CLC 44, 47, 50; DAM POP**
See also AAYA 11; CA 102; CANR 27, 47; INT CANR-27; MTCW; SATA 83

Cardenal, Ernesto
1925- .... **CLC 31; DAM MULT, POET; HLC**
See also CA 49-52; CANR 2, 32; HW; MTCW

Cardozo, Benjamin N(athan)
1870-1938 .... **TCLC 65**
See also CA 117

Carducci, Giosue 1835-1907 ...... **TCLC 32**

Carew, Thomas 1595(?)-1640 .... **LC 13**
See also DLB 126

Carey, Ernestine Gilbreth 1908- .... **CLC 17**
See also CA 5-8R; SATA 2

Carey, Peter 1943- .... **CLC 40, 55, 96**
See also CA 123; 127; CANR 53; INT 127; MTCW

Carleton, William 1794-1869 ...... **NCLC 3**
See also DLB 159

Carlisle, Henry (Coffin) 1926- ...... **CLC 33**
See also CA 13-16R; CANR 15

Carlsen, Chris
See Holdstock, Robert P.

Carlson, Ron(ald F.) 1947- .... **CLC 54**
See also CA 105; CANR 27

Carlyle, Thomas
1795-1881 .... **NCLC 22; DA; DAB; DAC; DAM MST**
See also CDBLB 1789-1832; DLB 55; 144

Carman, (William) Bliss
1861-1929 .... **TCLC 7; DAC**
See also CA 104; 152; DLB 92

Carnegie, Dale 1888-1955 .... **TCLC 53**

Carossa, Hans 1878-1956 .... **TCLC 48**
See also DLB 66

Carpenter, Don(ald Richard)
1931-1995 .... **CLC 41**
See also CA 45-48; 149; CANR 1

Carpentier (y Valmont), Alejo
1904-1980 .... **CLC 8, 11, 38; DAM MULT; HLC**
See also CA 65-68; 97-100; CANR 11; DLB 113; HW

Carr, Caleb 1955(?)- .... **CLC 86**
See also CA 147

Carr, Emily 1871-1945 .... **TCLC 32**
See also DLB 68

Carr, John Dickson 1906-1977 ...... **CLC 3**
See also CA 49-52; 69-72; CANR 3, 33; MTCW

Carr, Philippa
See Hibbert, Eleanor Alice Burford

Carr, Virginia Spencer 1929- .... **CLC 34**
See also CA 61-64; DLB 111

Carrere, Emmanuel 1957- .... **CLC 89**

Carrier, Roch
1937- ... **CLC 13, 78; DAC; DAM MST**
See also CA 130; DLB 53

Carroll, James P. 1943(?)- .... **CLC 38**
See also CA 81-84

Carroll, Jim 1951- .... **CLC 35**
See also AAYA 17; CA 45-48; CANR 42

Carroll, Lewis .... **NCLC 2, 53; WLC**
See also Dodgson, Charles Lutwidge
See also CDBLB 1832-1890; CLR 2, 18; DLB 18, 163; JRDA

Carroll, Paul Vincent 1900-1968 .... **CLC 10**
See also CA 9-12R; 25-28R; DLB 10

Carruth, Hayden
1921- ...... **CLC 4, 7, 10, 18, 84; PC 10**
See also CA 9-12R; CANR 4, 38; DLB 5, 165; INT CANR-4; MTCW; SATA 47

Carson, Rachel Louise
1907-1964 .... **CLC 71; DAM POP**
See also CA 77-80; CANR 35; MTCW; SATA 23

Carter, Angela (Olive)
1940-1992 ...... **CLC 5, 41, 76; SSC 13**
See also CA 53-56; 136; CANR 12, 36; DLB 14; MTCW; SATA 66; SATA-Obit 70

Carter, Nick
See Smith, Martin Cruz

Carver, Raymond
1938-1988 .... **CLC 22, 36, 53, 55; DAM NOV; SSC 8**
See also CA 33-36R; 126; CANR 17, 34; DLB 130; DLBY 84, 88; MTCW

Cary, Elizabeth, Lady Falkland
1585-1639 .... **LC 30**

Cary, (Arthur) Joyce (Lunel)
1888-1957 .... **TCLC 1, 29**
See also CA 104; CDBLB 1914-1945; DLB 15, 100

Casanova de Seingalt, Giovanni Jacopo
1725-1798 .... **LC 13**

Casares, Adolfo Bioy
See Bioy Casares, Adolfo

Casely-Hayford, J(oseph) E(phraim)
1866-1930 .... **TCLC 24; BLC; DAM MULT**
See also BW 2; CA 123; 152

Casey, John (Dudley) 1939- .... **CLC 59**
See also BEST 90:2; CA 69-72; CANR 23

Casey, Michael 1947- .... **CLC 2**
See also CA 65-68; DLB 5

Casey, Patrick
See Thurman, Wallace (Henry)

Casey, Warren (Peter) 1935-1988 ... **CLC 12**
See also CA 101; 127; INT 101

Casona, Alejandro .... **CLC 49**
See also Alvarez, Alejandro Rodriguez

Cassavetes, John 1929-1989 .... **CLC 20**
See also CA 85-88; 127

Cassill, R(onald) V(erlin) 1919- ... **CLC 4, 23**
See also CA 9-12R; CAAS 1; CANR 7, 45; DLB 6

Cassirer, Ernst 1874-1945 .... **TCLC 61**

Cassity, (Allen) Turner 1929- .... **CLC 6, 42**
See also CA 17-20R; CAAS 8; CANR 11; DLB 105

Castaneda, Carlos 1931(?)- .... **CLC 12**
See also CA 25-28R; CANR 32; HW; MTCW

Castedo, Elena 1937- .... **CLC 65**
See also CA 132

Castedo-Ellerman, Elena
See Castedo, Elena

Castellanos, Rosario
1925-1974 ...... **CLC 66; DAM MULT; HLC**
See also CA 131; 53-56; DLB 113; HW

Castelvetro, Lodovico 1505-1571 ..... **LC 12**

Castiglione, Baldassare 1478-1529 ... **LC 12**

Castle, Robert
See Hamilton, Edmond

Castro, Guillen de 1569-1631 .... **LC 19**

Castro, Rosalia de
1837-1885 ...... **NCLC 3; DAM MULT**

Cather, Willa
See Cather, Willa Sibert

Cather, Willa Sibert
1873-1947 .... **TCLC 1, 11, 31; DA; DAB; DAC; DAM MST, NOV; SSC 2; WLC**
See also CA 104; 128; CDALB 1865-1917; DLB 9, 54, 78; DLBD 1; MTCW; SATA 30

Catton, (Charles) Bruce
1899-1978 .... **CLC 35**
See also AITN 1; CA 5-8R; 81-84; CANR 7; DLB 17; SATA 2; SATA-Obit 24

Catullus c. 84B.C.-c. 54B.C. ..... **CMLC 18**

Cauldwell, Frank
See King, Francis (Henry)

Caunitz, William J. 1933-1996 ..... **CLC 34**
See also BEST 89:3; CA 125; 130; 152; INT 130

Causley, Charles (Stanley) 1917- .... **CLC 7**
See also CA 9-12R; CANR 5, 35; CLR 30; DLB 27; MTCW; SATA 3, 66

Caute, David 1936- .... **CLC 29; DAM NOV**
See also CA 1-4R; CAAS 4; CANR 1, 33; DLB 14

Cavafy, C(onstantine) P(eter)
1863-1933 .... **TCLC 2, 7; DAM POET**
See also Kavafis, Konstantinos Petrou
See also CA 148

Cavallo, Evelyn
See Spark, Muriel (Sarah)

Cavanna, Betty .... **CLC 12**
See also Harrison, Elizabeth Cavanna
See also JRDA; MAICYA; SAAS 4; SATA 1, 30

Cavendish, Margaret Lucas
1623-1673 .... **LC 30**
See also DLB 131

Childress, Alice
    1920-1994 .... **CLC 12, 15, 86, 96; BLC;
        DAM DRAM, MULT, NOV; DC 4**
    See also AAYA 8; BW 2; CA 45-48; 146;
    CANR 3, 27, 50; CLR 14; DLB 7, 38;
    JRDA; MAICYA; MTCW; SATA 7, 48,
    81

Chislett, (Margaret) Anne 1943- .... **CLC 34**
    See also CA 151

Chitty, Thomas Willes 1926- .... **CLC 11**
    See also Hinde, Thomas
    See also CA 5-8R

Chivers, Thomas Holley
    1809-1858 .... **NCLC 49**
    See also DLB 3

Chomette, Rene Lucien 1898-1981
    See Clair, Rene
    See also CA 103

Chopin, Kate
    .... **TCLC 5, 14; DA; DAB; SSC 8**
    See also Chopin, Katherine
    See also CDALB 1865-1917; DLB 12, 78

Chopin, Katherine 1851-1904
    See Chopin, Kate
    See also CA 104; 122; DAC; DAM MST,
    NOV

Chretien de Troyes
    c. 12th cent. - .... **CMLC 10**

Christie
    See Ichikawa, Kon

Christie, Agatha (Mary Clarissa)
    1890-1976 ...... **CLC 1, 6, 8, 12, 39, 48;
        DAB; DAC; DAM NOV**
    See also AAYA 9; AITN 1, 2; CA 17-20R;
    61-64; CANR 10, 37; CDBLB 1914-1945;
    DLB 13, 77; MTCW; SATA 36

Christie, (Ann) Philippa
    See Pearce, Philippa
    See also CA 5-8R; CANR 4

Christine de Pizan 1365(?)-1431(?) .... **LC 9**

Chubb, Elmer
    See Masters, Edgar Lee

Chulkov, Mikhail Dmitrievich
    1743-1792 .... **LC 2**
    See also DLB 150

Churchill, Caryl 1938- ... **CLC 31, 55; DC 5**
    See also CA 102; CANR 22, 46; DLB 13;
    MTCW

Churchill, Charles 1731-1764 .... **LC 3**
    See also DLB 109

Chute, Carolyn 1947- .... **CLC 39**
    See also CA 123

Ciardi, John (Anthony)
    1916-1986 .... **CLC 10, 40, 44;
        DAM POET**
    See also CA 5-8R; 118; CAAS 2; CANR 5,
    33; CLR 19; DLB 5; DLBY 86;
    INT CANR-5; MAICYA; MTCW;
    SATA 1, 65; SATA-Obit 46

Cicero, Marcus Tullius
    106B.C.-43B.C. .... **CMLC 3**

Cimino, Michael 1943- .... **CLC 16**
    See also CA 105

Cioran, E(mil) M. 1911-1995 .... **CLC 64**
    See also CA 25-28R; 149

Cisneros, Sandra
    1954- ..... **CLC 69; DAM MULT; HLC**
    See also AAYA 9; CA 131; DLB 122, 152;
    HW

Cixous, Helene 1937- .... **CLC 92**
    See also CA 126; CANR 55; DLB 83;
    MTCW

Clair, Rene .... **CLC 20**
    See also Chomette, Rene Lucien

Clampitt, Amy 1920-1994 .... **CLC 32**
    See also CA 110; 146; CANR 29; DLB 105

Clancy, Thomas L., Jr. 1947-
    See Clancy, Tom
    See also CA 125; 131; INT 131; MTCW

Clancy, Tom ..... **CLC 45; DAM NOV, POP**
    See also Clancy, Thomas L., Jr.
    See also AAYA 9; BEST 89:1, 90:1

Clare, John
    1793-1864 .... **NCLC 9; DAB;
        DAM POET**
    See also DLB 55, 96

Clarin
    See Alas (y Urena), Leopoldo (Enrique
    Garcia)

Clark, Al C.
    See Goines, Donald

Clark, (Robert) Brian 1932- .... **CLC 29**
    See also CA 41-44R

Clark, Curt
    See Westlake, Donald E(dwin)

Clark, Eleanor 1913-1996 .... **CLC 5, 19**
    See also CA 9-12R; 151; CANR 41; DLB 6

Clark, J. P.
    See Clark, John Pepper
    See also DLB 117

Clark, John Pepper
    1935- .... **CLC 38; BLC; DAM DRAM,
        MULT; DC 5**
    See also Clark, J. P.
    See also BW 1; CA 65-68; CANR 16

Clark, M. R.
    See Clark, Mavis Thorpe

Clark, Mavis Thorpe 1909- .... **CLC 12**
    See also CA 57-60; CANR 8, 37; CLR 30;
    MAICYA; SAAS 5; SATA 8, 74

Clark, Walter Van Tilburg
    1909-1971 .... **CLC 28**
    See also CA 9-12R; 33-36R; DLB 9;
    SATA 8

Clarke, Arthur C(harles)
    1917- .... **CLC 1, 4, 13, 18, 35;
        DAM POP; SSC 3**
    See also AAYA 4; CA 1-4R; CANR 2, 28,
    55; JRDA; MAICYA; MTCW; SATA 13,
    70

Clarke, Austin
    1896-1974 ...... **CLC 6, 9; DAM POET**
    See also CA 29-32; 49-52; CAP 2; DLB 10,
    20

Clarke, Austin C(hesterfield)
    1934- .... **CLC 8, 53; BLC; DAC;
        DAM MULT**
    See also BW 1; CA 25-28R; CAAS 16;
    CANR 14, 32; DLB 53, 125

Clarke, Gillian 1937- .... **CLC 61**
    See also CA 106; DLB 40

Clarke, Marcus (Andrew Hislop)
    1846-1881 .... **NCLC 19**

Clarke, Shirley 1925- .... **CLC 16**

Clash, The
    See Headon, (Nicky) Topper; Jones, Mick;
    Simonon, Paul; Strummer, Joe

Claudel, Paul (Louis Charles Marie)
    1868-1955 .... **TCLC 2, 10**
    See also CA 104

Clavell, James (duMaresq)
    1925-1994 .... **CLC 6, 25, 87;
        DAM NOV, POP**
    See also CA 25-28R; 146; CANR 26, 48;
    MTCW

Cleaver, (Leroy) Eldridge
    1935- ..... **CLC 30; BLC; DAM MULT**
    See also BW 1; CA 21-24R; CANR 16

Cleese, John (Marwood) 1939- ..... **CLC 21**
    See also Monty Python
    See also CA 112; 116; CANR 35; MTCW

Cleishbotham, Jebediah
    See Scott, Walter

Cleland, John 1710-1789 .... **LC 2**
    See also DLB 39

Clemens, Samuel Langhorne 1835-1910
    See Twain, Mark
    See also CA 104; 135; CDALB 1865-1917;
    DA; DAB; DAC; DAM MST, NOV;
    DLB 11, 12, 23, 64, 74; JRDA;
    MAICYA; YABC 2

Cleophil
    See Congreve, William

Clerihew, E.
    See Bentley, E(dmund) C(lerihew)

Clerk, N. W.
    See Lewis, C(live) S(taples)

Cliff, Jimmy .... **CLC 21**
    See also Chambers, James

Clifton, (Thelma) Lucille
    1936- .... **CLC 19, 66; BLC;
        DAM MULT, POET**
    See also BW 2; CA 49-52; CANR 2, 24, 42;
    CLR 5; DLB 5, 41; MAICYA; MTCW;
    SATA 20, 69

Clinton, Dirk
    See Silverberg, Robert

Clough, Arthur Hugh 1819-1861 .. **NCLC 27**
    See also DLB 32

Clutha, Janet Paterson Frame 1924-
    See Frame, Janet
    See also CA 1-4R; CANR 2, 36; MTCW

Clyne, Terence
    See Blatty, William Peter

Cobalt, Martin
    See Mayne, William (James Carter)

Cobbett, William 1763-1835 ..... **NCLC 49**
    See also DLB 43, 107, 158

Coburn, D(onald) L(ee) 1938- ...... **CLC 10**
    See also CA 89-92

Cocteau, Jean (Maurice Eugene Clement)
    1889-1963 .... **CLC 1, 8, 15, 16, 43; DA;
        DAB; DAC; DAM DRAM, MST, NOV;
        WLC**
    See also CA 25-28; CANR 40; CAP 2;
    DLB 65; MTCW

Codrescu, Andrei
1946- . . . . CLC 46; DAM POET
See also CA 33-36R; CAAS 19; CANR 13,
34, 53

Coe, Max
See Bourne, Randolph S(illiman)

Coe, Tucker
See Westlake, Donald E(dwin)

Coetzee, J(ohn) M(ichael)
1940- . . . . . . CLC 23, 33, 66; DAM NOV
See also CA 77-80; CANR 41, 54; MTCW

Coffey, Brian
See Koontz, Dean R(ay)

Cohan, George M.   1878-1942 . . . . . TCLC 60

Cohen, Arthur A(llen)
1928-1986 . . . . CLC 7, 31
See also CA 1-4R; 120; CANR 1, 17, 42;
DLB 28

Cohen, Leonard (Norman)
1934- . . . . CLC 3, 38; DAC; DAM MST
See also CA 21-24R; CANR 14; DLB 53;
MTCW

Cohen, Matt   1942- . . . . CLC 19; DAC
See also CA 61-64; CAAS 18; CANR 40;
DLB 53

Cohen-Solal, Annie   19(?)- . . . . CLC 50

Colegate, Isabel   1931- . . . . CLC 36
See also CA 17-20R; CANR 8, 22; DLB 14;
INT CANR-22; MTCW

Coleman, Emmett
See Reed, Ishmael

Coleridge, Samuel Taylor
1772-1834 . . . . . NCLC 9, 54; DA; DAB;
DAC; DAM MST, POET; PC 11; WLC
See also CDBLB 1789-1832; DLB 93, 107

Coleridge, Sara   1802-1852 . . . . NCLC 31

Coles, Don   1928- . . . . CLC 46
See also CA 115; CANR 38

Colette, (Sidonie-Gabrielle)
1873-1954 . . . . TCLC 1, 5, 16;
DAM NOV; SSC 10
See also CA 104; 131; DLB 65; MTCW

Collett, (Jacobine) Camilla (Wergeland)
1813-1895 . . . . NCLC 22

Collier, Christopher   1930- . . . . CLC 30
See also AAYA 13; CA 33-36R; CANR 13,
33; JRDA; MAICYA; SATA 16, 70

Collier, James L(incoln)
1928- . . . . CLC 30; DAM POP
See also AAYA 13; CA 9-12R; CANR 4,
33; CLR 3; JRDA; MAICYA; SAAS 21;
SATA 8, 70

Collier, Jeremy   1650-1726 . . . . LC 6

Collier, John   1901-1980 . . . . SSC 19
See also CA 65-68; 97-100; CANR 10;
DLB 77

Collingwood, R(obin) G(eorge)
1889(?)-1943 . . . . TCLC 67
See also CA 117

Collins, Hunt
See Hunter, Evan

Collins, Linda   1931- . . . . CLC 44
See also CA 125

Collins, (William) Wilkie
1824-1889 . . . . NCLC 1, 18
See also CDBLB 1832-1890; DLB 18, 70,
159

Collins, William
1721-1759 . . . . LC 4; DAM POET
See also DLB 109

Collodi, Carlo   1826-1890 . . . . NCLC 54
See also Lorenzini, Carlo
See also CLR 5

Colman, George
See Glassco, John

Colt, Winchester Remington
See Hubbard, L(afayette) Ron(ald)

Colter, Cyrus   1910- . . . . CLC 58
See also BW 1; CA 65-68; CANR 10;
DLB 33

Colton, James
See Hansen, Joseph

Colum, Padraic   1881-1972 . . . . CLC 28
See also CA 73-76; 33-36R; CANR 35;
CLR 36; MAICYA; MTCW; SATA 15

Colvin, James
See Moorcock, Michael (John)

Colwin, Laurie (E.)
1944-1992 . . . . CLC 5, 13, 23, 84
See also CA 89-92; 139; CANR 20, 46;
DLBY 80; MTCW

Comfort, Alex(ander)
1920- . . . . CLC 7; DAM POP
See also CA 1-4R; CANR 1, 45

Comfort, Montgomery
See Campbell, (John) Ramsey

Compton-Burnett, I(vy)
1884(?)-1969 . . . . . . CLC 1, 3, 10, 15, 34;
DAM NOV
See also CA 1-4R; 25-28R; CANR 4;
DLB 36; MTCW

Comstock, Anthony   1844-1915 . . . . TCLC 13
See also CA 110

Comte, Auguste   1798-1857 . . . . NCLC 54

Conan Doyle, Arthur
See Doyle, Arthur Conan

Conde, Maryse
1937- . . . . CLC 52, 92; DAM MULT
See also Boucolon, Maryse
See also BW 2

Condillac, Etienne Bonnot de
1714-1780 . . . . LC 26

Condon, Richard (Thomas)
1915-1996 . . . . CLC 4, 6, 8, 10, 45;
DAM NOV
See also BEST 90:3; CA 1-4R; 151;
CAAS 1; CANR 2, 23; INT CANR-23;
MTCW

Confucius
551B.C.-479B.C. . . . . CMLC 19; DA;
DAB; DAC; DAM MST

Congreve, William
1670-1729 . . . . LC 5, 21; DA; DAB;
DAC; DAM DRAM, MST, POET;
DC 2; WLC
See also CDBLB 1660-1789; DLB 39, 84

Connell, Evan S(helby), Jr.
1924- . . . . . . CLC 4, 6, 45; DAM NOV
See also AAYA 7; CA 1-4R; CAAS 2;
CANR 2, 39; DLB 2; DLBY 81; MTCW

Connelly, Marc(us Cook)
1890-1980 . . . . CLC 7
See also CA 85-88; 102; CANR 30; DLB 7;
DLBY 80; SATA-Obit 25

Connor, Ralph . . . . TCLC 31
See also Gordon, Charles William
See also DLB 92

Conrad, Joseph
1857-1924 . . . . TCLC 1, 6, 13, 25, 43, 57;
DA; DAB; DAC; DAM MST, NOV;
SSC 9; WLC
See also CA 104; 131; CDBLB 1890-1914;
DLB 10, 34, 98, 156; MTCW; SATA 27

Conrad, Robert Arnold
See Hart, Moss

Conroy, Donald Pat(rick)
1945- . . . CLC 30, 74; DAM NOV, POP
See also AAYA 8; AITN 1; CA 85-88;
CANR 24, 53; DLB 6; MTCW

Constant (de Rebecque), (Henri) Benjamin
1767-1830 . . . . NCLC 6
See also DLB 119

Conybeare, Charles Augustus
See Eliot, T(homas) S(tearns)

Cook, Michael   1933- . . . . CLC 58
See also CA 93-96; DLB 53

Cook, Robin   1940- . . . . CLC 14; DAM POP
See also BEST 90:2; CA 108; 111;
CANR 41; INT 111

Cook, Roy
See Silverberg, Robert

Cooke, Elizabeth   1948- . . . . CLC 55
See also CA 129

Cooke, John Esten   1830-1886 . . . . . NCLC 5
See also DLB 3

Cooke, John Estes
See Baum, L(yman) Frank

Cooke, M. E.
See Creasey, John

Cooke, Margaret
See Creasey, John

Cook-Lynn, Elizabeth
1930- . . . . CLC 93; DAM MULT
See also CA 133; NNAL

Cooney, Ray . . . . CLC 62

Cooper, Douglas   1960- . . . . CLC 86

Cooper, Henry St. John
See Creasey, John

Cooper, J. California
. . . . CLC 56; DAM MULT
See also AAYA 12; BW 1; CA 125;
CANR 55

Cooper, James Fenimore
1789-1851 . . . . NCLC 1, 27, 54
See also CDALB 1640-1865; DLB 3;
SATA 19

Coover, Robert (Lowell)
1932- . . . . CLC 3, 7, 15, 32, 46, 87;
DAM NOV; SSC 15
See also CA 45-48; CANR 3, 37; DLB 2;
DLBY 81; MTCW

Copeland, Stewart (Armstrong)
    1952- .... CLC 26

Coppard, A(lfred) E(dgar)
    1878-1957 .... TCLC 5; SSC 21
    See also CA 114; DLB 162; YABC 1

Coppee, Francois 1842-1908 ...... TCLC 25

Coppola, Francis Ford 1939-........ CLC 16
    See also CA 77-80; CANR 40; DLB 44

Corbiere, Tristan 1845-1875 ..... NCLC 43

Corcoran, Barbara 1911-.......... CLC 17
    See also AAYA 14; CA 21-24R; CAAS 2;
    CANR 11, 28, 48; DLB 52; JRDA;
    SAAS 20; SATA 3, 77

Cordelier, Maurice
    See Giraudoux, (Hippolyte) Jean

Corelli, Marie 1855-1924........ TCLC 51
    See also Mackay, Mary
    See also DLB 34, 156

Corman, Cid....................... CLC 9
    See also Corman, Sidney
    See also CAAS 2; DLB 5

Corman, Sidney 1924-
    See Corman, Cid
    See also CA 85-88; CANR 44; DAM POET

Cormier, Robert (Edmund)
    1925- .... CLC 12, 30; DA; DAB; DAC;
                       DAM MST, NOV
    See also AAYA 3, 19; CA 1-4R; CANR 5,
    23; CDALB 1968-1988; CLR 12; DLB 52;
    INT CANR-23; JRDA; MAICYA;
    MTCW; SATA 10, 45, 83

Corn, Alfred (DeWitt III) 1943-.... CLC 33
    See also CA 104; CAAS 25; CANR 44;
    DLB 120; DLBY 80

Corneille, Pierre
    1606-1684 .... LC 28; DAB; DAM MST

Cornwell, David (John Moore)
    1931- .... CLC 9, 15; DAM POP
    See also le Carre, John
    See also CA 5-8R; CANR 13, 33; MTCW

Corso, (Nunzio) Gregory 1930-... CLC 1, 11
    See also CA 5-8R; CANR 41; DLB 5, 16;
    MTCW

Cortazar, Julio
    1914-1984 ..... CLC 2, 3, 5, 10, 13, 15,
             33, 34, 92; DAM MULT, NOV; HLC;
                                       SSC 7
    See also CA 21-24R; CANR 12, 32;
    DLB 113; HW; MTCW

CORTES, HERNAN 1484-1547..... LC 31

Corwin, Cecil
    See Kornbluth, C(yril) M.

Cosic, Dobrica 1921- .... CLC 14
    See also CA 122; 138

Costain, Thomas B(ertram)
    1885-1965 .... CLC 30
    See also CA 5-8R; 25-28R; DLB 9

Costantini, Humberto
    1924(?)-1987 .... CLC 49
    See also CA 131; 122; HW

Costello, Elvis 1955-............. CLC 21

Cotter, Joseph Seamon Sr.
    1861-1949 .... TCLC 28; BLC;
                               DAM MULT
    See also BW 1; CA 124; DLB 50

Couch, Arthur Thomas Quiller
    See Quiller-Couch, Arthur Thomas

Coulton, James
    See Hansen, Joseph

Couperus, Louis (Marie Anne)
    1863-1923 .... TCLC 15
    See also CA 115

Coupland, Douglas
    1961- .... CLC 85; DAC; DAM POP
    See also CA 142

Court, Wesli
    See Turco, Lewis (Putnam)

Courtenay, Bryce 1933-........... CLC 59
    See also CA 138

Courtney, Robert
    See Ellison, Harlan (Jay)

Cousteau, Jacques-Yves 1910-...... CLC 30
    See also CA 65-68; CANR 15; MTCW;
    SATA 38

Coward, Noel (Peirce)
    1899-1973 .... CLC 1, 9, 29, 51;
                              DAM DRAM
    See also AITN 1; CA 17-18; 41-44R;
    CANR 35; CAP 2; CDBLB 1914-1945;
    DLB 10; MTCW

Cowley, Malcolm 1898-1989 .... CLC 39
    See also CA 5-8R; 128; CANR 3, 55;
    DLB 4, 48; DLBY 81, 89; MTCW

Cowper, William
    1731-1800 ...... NCLC 8; DAM POET
    See also DLB 104, 109

Cox, William Trevor
    1928- .... CLC 9, 14, 71; DAM NOV
    See also Trevor, William
    See also CA 9-12R; CANR 4, 37, 55;
    DLB 14; INT CANR-37; MTCW

Coyne, P. J.
    See Masters, Hilary

Cozzens, James Gould
    1903-1978 .... CLC 1, 4, 11, 92
    See also CA 9-12R; 81-84; CANR 19;
    CDALB 1941-1968; DLB 9; DLBD 2;
    DLBY 84; MTCW

Crabbe, George 1754-1832....... NCLC 26
    See also DLB 93

Craddock, Charles Egbert
    See Murfree, Mary Noailles

Craig, A. A.
    See Anderson, Poul (William)

Craik, Dinah Maria (Mulock)
    1826-1887 .... NCLC 38
    See also DLB 35, 163; MAICYA; SATA 34

Cram, Ralph Adams 1863-1942.... TCLC 45

Crane, (Harold) Hart
    1899-1932 .... TCLC 2, 5; DA; DAB;
               DAC; DAM MST, POET; PC 3; WLC
    See also CA 104; 127; CDALB 1917-1929;
    DLB 4, 48; MTCW

Crane, R(onald) S(almon)
    1886-1967 .... CLC 27
    See also CA 85-88; DLB 63

Crane, Stephen (Townley)
    1871-1900 ...... TCLC 11, 17, 32; DA;
           DAB; DAC; DAM MST, NOV, POET;
                               SSC 7; WLC
    See also CA 109; 140; CDALB 1865-1917;
    DLB 12, 54, 78; YABC 2

Crase, Douglas 1944-.............. CLC 58
    See also CA 106

Crashaw, Richard 1612(?)-1649...... LC 24
    See also DLB 126

Craven, Margaret
    1901-1980 .... CLC 17; DAC
    See also CA 103

Crawford, F(rancis) Marion
    1854-1909 .... TCLC 10
    See also CA 107; DLB 71

Crawford, Isabella Valancy
    1850-1887 .... NCLC 12
    See also DLB 92

Crayon, Geoffrey
    See Irving, Washington

Creasey, John 1908-1973.......... CLC 11
    See also CA 5-8R; 41-44R; CANR 8;
    DLB 77; MTCW

Crebillon, Claude Prosper Jolyot de (fils)
    1707-1777 .... LC 28

Credo
    See Creasey, John

Creeley, Robert (White)
    1926- ..... CLC 1, 2, 4, 8, 11, 15, 36, 78;
                              DAM POET
    See also CA 1-4R; CAAS 10; CANR 23, 43;
    DLB 5, 16, 169; MTCW

Crews, Harry (Eugene)
    1935-.................... CLC 6, 23, 49
    See also AITN 1; CA 25-28R; CANR 20;
    DLB 6, 143; MTCW

Crichton, (John) Michael
    1942- .... CLC 2, 6, 54, 90; DAM NOV,
                                       POP
    See also AAYA 10; AITN 2; CA 25-28R;
    CANR 13, 40, 54; DLBY 81;
    INT CANR-13; JRDA; MTCW; SATA 9,
    88

Crispin, Edmund .... CLC 22
    See also Montgomery, (Robert) Bruce
    See also DLB 87

Cristofer, Michael
    1945(?)- .... CLC 28; DAM DRAM
    See also CA 110; 152; DLB 7

Croce, Benedetto 1866-1952 ...... TCLC 37
    See also CA 120

Crockett, David 1786-1836 .... NCLC 8
    See also DLB 3, 11

Crockett, Davy
    See Crockett, David

Crofts, Freeman Wills
    1879-1957 .... TCLC 55
    See also CA 115; DLB 77

Croker, John Wilson 1780-1857 .. NCLC 10
    See also DLB 110

Crommelynck, Fernand 1885-1970 .. CLC 75
    See also CA 89-92

Davies, (William) Robertson
  1913-1995 ..... **CLC 2, 7, 13, 25, 42, 75,
  91; DA; DAB; DAC; DAM MST, NOV,
  POP; WLC**
  See also BEST 89:2; CA 33-36R; 150;
  CANR 17, 42; DLB 68; INT CANR-17;
  MTCW

Davies, W(illiam) H(enry)
  1871-1940 .... **TCLC 5**
  See also CA 104; DLB 19, 174

Davies, Walter C.
  See Kornbluth, C(yril) M.

Davis, Angela (Yvonne)
  1944- .... **CLC 77; DAM MULT**
  See also BW 2; CA 57-60; CANR 10

Davis, B. Lynch
  See Bioy Casares, Adolfo; Borges, Jorge
  Luis

Davis, Gordon
  See Hunt, E(verette) Howard, (Jr.)

Davis, Harold Lenoir 1896-1960.... **CLC 49**
  See also CA 89-92; DLB 9

Davis, Rebecca (Blaine) Harding
  1831-1910 .... **TCLC 6**
  See also CA 104; DLB 74

Davis, Richard Harding
  1864-1916 .... **TCLC 24**
  See also CA 114; DLB 12, 23, 78, 79;
  DLBD 13

Davison, Frank Dalby 1893-1970 ... **CLC 15**
  See also CA 116

Davison, Lawrence H.
  See Lawrence, D(avid) H(erbert Richards)

Davison, Peter (Hubert) 1928- ..... **CLC 28**
  See also CA 9-12R; CAAS 4; CANR 3, 43;
  DLB 5

Davys, Mary 1674-1732............. **LC 1**
  See also DLB 39

Dawson, Fielding 1930- .... **CLC 6**
  See also CA 85-88; DLB 130

Dawson, Peter
  See Faust, Frederick (Schiller)

Day, Clarence (Shepard, Jr.)
  1874-1935 .... **TCLC 25**
  See also CA 108; DLB 11

Day, Thomas 1748-1789............. **LC 1**
  See also DLB 39; YABC 1

Day Lewis, C(ecil)
  1904-1972 .... **CLC 1, 6, 10;
  DAM POET; PC 11**
  See also Blake, Nicholas
  See also CA 13-16; 33-36R; CANR 34;
  CAP 1; DLB 15, 20; MTCW

Dazai, Osamu .... **TCLC 11**
  See also Tsushima, Shuji

de Andrade, Carlos Drummond
  See Drummond de Andrade, Carlos

Deane, Norman
  See Creasey, John

de Beauvoir, Simone (Lucie Ernestine Marie
  Bertrand)
  See Beauvoir, Simone (Lucie Ernestine
  Marie Bertrand) de

de Brissac, Malcolm
  See Dickinson, Peter (Malcolm)

de Chardin, Pierre Teilhard
  See Teilhard de Chardin, (Marie Joseph)
  Pierre

Dee, John 1527-1608 .... **LC 20**

Deer, Sandra 1940-.............. **CLC 45**

De Ferrari, Gabriella 1941-........ **CLC 65**
  See also CA 146

Defoe, Daniel
  1660(?)-1731 .... **LC 1; DA; DAB; DAC;
  DAM MST, NOV; WLC**
  See also CDBLB 1660-1789; DLB 39, 95,
  101; JRDA; MAICYA; SATA 22

de Gourmont, Remy(-Marie-Charles)
  See Gourmont, Remy (-Marie-Charles) de

de Hartog, Jan 1914-............. **CLC 19**
  See also CA 1-4R; CANR 1

de Hostos, E. M.
  See Hostos (y Bonilla), Eugenio Maria de

de Hostos, Eugenio M.
  See Hostos (y Bonilla), Eugenio Maria de

Deighton, Len .... **CLC 4, 7, 22, 46**
  See also Deighton, Leonard Cyril
  See also AAYA 6; BEST 89:2;
  CDBLB 1960 to Present; DLB 87

Deighton, Leonard Cyril 1929-
  See Deighton, Len
  See also CA 9-12R; CANR 19, 33;
  DAM NOV, POP; MTCW

Dekker, Thomas
  1572(?)-1632 ..... **LC 22; DAM DRAM**
  See also CDBLB Before 1660; DLB 62, 172

Delafield, E. M. 1890-1943 .... **TCLC 61**
  See also Dashwood, Edmee Elizabeth
  Monica de la Pasture
  See also DLB 34

de la Mare, Walter (John)
  1873-1956 .... **TCLC 4, 53; DAB; DAC;
  DAM MST, POET; SSC 14; WLC**
  See also CDBLB 1914-1945; CLR 23;
  DLB 162; SATA 16

Delaney, Franey
  See O'Hara, John (Henry)

Delaney, Shelagh
  1939- .... **CLC 29; DAM DRAM**
  See also CA 17-20R; CANR 30;
  CDBLB 1960 to Present; DLB 13;
  MTCW

Delany, Mary (Granville Pendarves)
  1700-1788 .... **LC 12**

Delany, Samuel R(ay, Jr.)
  1942- .... **CLC 8, 14, 38; BLC;
  DAM MULT**
  See also BW 2; CA 81-84; CANR 27, 43;
  DLB 8, 33; MTCW

De La Ramee, (Marie) Louise 1839-1908
  See Ouida
  See also SATA 20

de la Roche, Mazo 1879-1961 ...... **CLC 14**
  See also CA 85-88; CANR 30; DLB 68;
  SATA 64

Delbanco, Nicholas (Franklin)
  1942- .... **CLC 6, 13**
  See also CA 17-20R; CAAS 2; CANR 29,
  55; DLB 6

del Castillo, Michel 1933- .... **CLC 38**
  See also CA 109

Deledda, Grazia (Cosima)
  1875(?)-1936 .... **TCLC 23**
  See also CA 123

Delibes, Miguel .... **CLC 8, 18**
  See also Delibes Setien, Miguel

Delibes Setien, Miguel 1920-
  See Delibes, Miguel
  See also CA 45-48; CANR 1, 32; HW;
  MTCW

DeLillo, Don
  1936- ..... **CLC 8, 10, 13, 27, 39, 54, 76;
  DAM NOV, POP**
  See also BEST 89:1; CA 81-84; CANR 21;
  DLB 6, 173; MTCW

de Lisser, H. G.
  See De Lisser, H(erbert) G(eorge)
  See also DLB 117

De Lisser, H(erbert) G(eorge)
  1878-1944 .... **TCLC 12**
  See also de Lisser, H. G.
  See also BW 2; CA 109; 152

Deloria, Vine (Victor), Jr.
  1933- .... **CLC 21; DAM MULT**
  See also CA 53-56; CANR 5, 20, 48;
  MTCW; NNAL; SATA 21

Del Vecchio, John M(ichael)
  1947- .... **CLC 29**
  See also CA 110; DLBD 9

de Man, Paul (Adolph Michel)
  1919-1983 .... **CLC 55**
  See also CA 128; 111; DLB 67; MTCW

De Marinis, Rick 1934-........... **CLC 54**
  See also CA 57-60; CAAS 24; CANR 9, 25,
  50

Dembry, R. Emmet
  See Murfree, Mary Noailles

Demby, William
  1922- ..... **CLC 53; BLC; DAM MULT**
  See also BW 1; CA 81-84; DLB 33

Demijohn, Thom
  See Disch, Thomas M(ichael)

de Montherlant, Henry (Milon)
  See Montherlant, Henry (Milon) de

Demosthenes 384B.C.-322B.C. .... **CMLC 13**

de Natale, Francine
  See Malzberg, Barry N(athaniel)

Denby, Edwin (Orr) 1903-1983..... **CLC 48**
  See also CA 138; 110

Denis, Julio
  See Cortazar, Julio

Denmark, Harrison
  See Zelazny, Roger (Joseph)

Dennis, John 1658-1734........... **LC 11**
  See also DLB 101

Dennis, Nigel (Forbes) 1912-1989.... **CLC 8**
  See also CA 25-28R; 129; DLB 13, 15;
  MTCW

De Palma, Brian (Russell) 1940-.... **CLC 20**
  See also CA 109

De Quincey, Thomas 1785-1859 ... **NCLC 4**
  See also CDBLB 1789-1832; DLB 110; 144

Eichendorff, Joseph Freiherr von
1788-1857 .... **NCLC 8**
See also DLB 90

Eigner, Larry .... **CLC 9**
See also Eigner, Laurence (Joel)
See also CAAS 23; DLB 5

Eigner, Laurence (Joel) 1927-1996
See Eigner, Larry
See also CA 9-12R; 151; CANR 6

Einstein, Albert 1879-1955 .... **TCLC 65**
See also CA 121; 133; MTCW

Eiseley, Loren Corey 1907-1977 ..... **CLC 7**
See also AAYA 5; CA 1-4R; 73-76;
CANR 6

Eisenstadt, Jill 1963- .... **CLC 50**
See also CA 140

Eisenstein, Sergei (Mikhailovich)
1898-1948 .... **TCLC 57**
See also CA 114; 149

Eisner, Simon
See Kornbluth, C(yril) M.

Ekeloef, (Bengt) Gunnar
1907-1968 .... **CLC 27; DAM POET**
See also CA 123; 25-28R

Ekelof, (Bengt) Gunnar
See Ekeloef, (Bengt) Gunnar

Ekwensi, C. O. D.
See Ekwensi, Cyprian (Odiatu Duaka)

Ekwensi, Cyprian (Odiatu Duaka)
1921- ...... **CLC 4; BLC; DAM MULT**
See also BW 2; CA 29-32R; CANR 18, 42;
DLB 117; MTCW; SATA 66

Elaine .... **TCLC 18**
See also Leverson, Ada

El Crummo
See Crumb, R(obert)

Elia
See Lamb, Charles

Eliade, Mircea 1907-1986 .... **CLC 19**
See also CA 65-68; 119; CANR 30; MTCW

Eliot, A. D.
See Jewett, (Theodora) Sarah Orne

Eliot, Alice
See Jewett, (Theodora) Sarah Orne

Eliot, Dan
See Silverberg, Robert

Eliot, George
1819-1880 ..... **NCLC 4, 13, 23, 41, 49;**
DA; DAB; DAC; DAM MST, NOV;
WLC
See also CDBLB 1832-1890; DLB 21, 35, 55

Eliot, John 1604-1690 .... **LC 5**
See also DLB 24

Eliot, T(homas) S(tearns)
1888-1965 ..... **CLC 1, 2, 3, 6, 9, 10, 13,**
15, 24, 34, 41, 55, 57; DA; DAB; DAC;
DAM DRAM, MST, POET; PC 5;
WLC 2
See also CA 5-8R; 25-28R; CANR 41;
CDALB 1929-1941; DLB 7, 10, 45, 63;
DLBY 88; MTCW

Elizabeth 1866-1941 .... **TCLC 41**

Elkin, Stanley L(awrence)
1930-1995 ...... **CLC 4, 6, 9, 14, 27, 51,**
91; DAM NOV, POP; SSC 12
See also CA 9-12R; 148; CANR 8, 46;
DLB 2, 28; DLBY 80; INT CANR-8;
MTCW

Elledge, Scott .... **CLC 34**

Elliot, Don
See Silverberg, Robert

Elliott, Don
See Silverberg, Robert

Elliott, George P(aul) 1918-1980 ..... **CLC 2**
See also CA 1-4R; 97-100; CANR 2

Elliott, Janice 1931- .... **CLC 47**
See also CA 13-16R; CANR 8, 29; DLB 14

Elliott, Sumner Locke 1917-1991 ... **CLC 38**
See also CA 5-8R; 134; CANR 2, 21

Elliott, William
See Bradbury, Ray (Douglas)

Ellis, A. E. .... **CLC 7**

Ellis, Alice Thomas .... **CLC 40**
See also Haycraft, Anna

Ellis, Bret Easton
1964- .... **CLC 39, 71; DAM POP**
See also AAYA 2; CA 118; 123; CANR 51;
INT 123

Ellis, (Henry) Havelock
1859-1939 .... **TCLC 14**
See also CA 109

Ellis, Landon
See Ellison, Harlan (Jay)

Ellis, Trey 1962- .... **CLC 55**
See also CA 146

Ellison, Harlan (Jay)
1934- ...... **CLC 1, 13, 42; DAM POP;**
SSC 14
See also CA 5-8R; CANR 5, 46; DLB 8;
INT CANR-5; MTCW

Ellison, Ralph (Waldo)
1914-1994 .... **CLC 1, 3, 11, 54, 86;**
BLC; DA; DAB; DAC; DAM MST,
MULT, NOV; WLC
See also AAYA 19; BW 1; CA 9-12R; 145;
CANR 24, 53; CDALB 1941-1968;
DLB 2, 76; DLBY 94; MTCW

Ellmann, Lucy (Elizabeth) 1956- .... **CLC 61**
See also CA 128

Ellmann, Richard (David)
1918-1987 .... **CLC 50**
See also BEST 89:2; CA 1-4R; 122;
CANR 2, 28; DLB 103; DLBY 87;
MTCW

Elman, Richard 1934- .... **CLC 19**
See also CA 17-20R; CAAS 3; CANR 47

Elron
See Hubbard, L(afayette) Ron(ald)

Eluard, Paul .... **TCLC 7, 41**
See also Grindel, Eugene

Elyot, Sir Thomas 1490(?)-1546 ..... **LC 11**

Elytis, Odysseus
1911-1996 .... **CLC 15, 49; DAM POET**
See also CA 102; 151; MTCW

Emecheta, (Florence Onye) Buchi
1944- .. **CLC 14, 48; BLC; DAM MULT**
See also BW 2; CA 81-84; CANR 27;
DLB 117; MTCW; SATA 66

Emerson, Ralph Waldo
1803-1882 ..... **NCLC 1, 38; DA; DAB;**
DAC; DAM MST, POET; WLC
See also CDALB 1640-1865; DLB 1, 59, 73

Eminescu, Mihail 1850-1889 ..... **NCLC 33**

Empson, William
1906-1984 .... **CLC 3, 8, 19, 33, 34**
See also CA 17-20R; 112; CANR 31;
DLB 20; MTCW

Enchi Fumiko (Ueda) 1905-1986.... **CLC 31**
See also CA 129; 121

Ende, Michael (Andreas Helmuth)
1929-1995 .... **CLC 31**
See also CA 118; 124; 149; CANR 36;
CLR 14; DLB 75; MAICYA; SATA 61;
SATA-Brief 42; SATA-Obit 86

Endo, Shusaku
1923-1996 .... **CLC 7, 14, 19, 54;**
DAM NOV
See also CA 29-32R; 153; CANR 21, 54;
MTCW

Engel, Marian 1933-1985 .... **CLC 36**
See also CA 25-28R; CANR 12; DLB 53;
INT CANR-12

Engelhardt, Frederick
See Hubbard, L(afayette) Ron(ald)

Enright, D(ennis) J(oseph)
1920- .... **CLC 4, 8, 31**
See also CA 1-4R; CANR 1, 42; DLB 27;
SATA 25

Enzensberger, Hans Magnus
1929- .... **CLC 43**
See also CA 116; 119

Ephron, Nora 1941- .... **CLC 17, 31**
See also AITN 2; CA 65-68; CANR 12, 39

Epsilon
See Betjeman, John

Epstein, Daniel Mark 1948- .... **CLC 7**
See also CA 49-52; CANR 2, 53

Epstein, Jacob 1956- .... **CLC 19**
See also CA 114

Epstein, Joseph 1937-............. **CLC 39**
See also CA 112; 119; CANR 50

Epstein, Leslie 1938- .... **CLC 27**
See also CA 73-76; CAAS 12; CANR 23

Equiano, Olaudah
1745(?)-1797 .... **LC 16; BLC;**
DAM MULT
See also DLB 37, 50

Erasmus, Desiderius 1469(?)-1536.... **LC 16**

Erdman, Paul E(mil) 1932- .... **CLC 25**
See also AITN 1; CA 61-64; CANR 13, 43

Erdrich, Louise
1954- .... **CLC 39, 54; DAM MULT,**
NOV, POP
See also AAYA 10; BEST 89:1; CA 114;
CANR 41; DLB 152; MTCW; NNAL

Erenburg, Ilya (Grigoryevich)
See Ehrenburg, Ilya (Grigoryevich)

Feinstein, Elaine 1930-............ **CLC 36**
See also CA 69-72; CAAS 1; CANR 31;
DLB 14, 40; MTCW

Feldman, Irving (Mordecai) 1928-.... **CLC 7**
See also CA 1-4R; CANR 1; DLB 169

Fellini, Federico 1920-1993..... **CLC 16, 85**
See also CA 65-68; 143; CANR 33

Felsen, Henry Gregor 1916-....... **CLC 17**
See also CA 1-4R; CANR 1; SAAS 2;
SATA 1

Fenton, James Martin 1949-....... **CLC 32**
See also CA 102; DLB 40

Ferber, Edna 1887-1968........ **CLC 18, 93**
See also AITN 1; CA 5-8R; 25-28R; DLB 9,
28, 86; MTCW; SATA 7

Ferguson, Helen
See Kavan, Anna

Ferguson, Samuel 1810-1886..... **NCLC 33**
See also DLB 32

Fergusson, Robert 1750-1774....... **LC 29**
See also DLB 109

Ferling, Lawrence
See Ferlinghetti, Lawrence (Monsanto)

Ferlinghetti, Lawrence (Monsanto)
1919(?)-............ **CLC 2, 6, 10, 27;**
DAM POET; PC 1
See also CA 5-8R; CANR 3, 41;
CDALB 1941-1968; DLB 5, 16; MTCW

Fernandez, Vicente Garcia Huidobro
See Huidobro Fernandez, Vicente Garcia

Ferrer, Gabriel (Francisco Victor) Miro
See Miro (Ferrer), Gabriel (Francisco
Victor)

Ferrier, Susan (Edmonstone)
1782-1854 .... **NCLC 8**
See also DLB 116

Ferrigno, Robert 1948(?)-......... **CLC 65**
See also CA 140

Ferron, Jacques 1921-1985 ... **CLC 94; DAC**
See also CA 117; 129; DLB 60

Feuchtwanger, Lion 1884-1958..... **TCLC 3**
See also CA 104; DLB 66

Feuillet, Octave 1821-1890 ...... **NCLC 45**

Feydeau, Georges (Leon Jules Marie)
1862-1921 ..... **TCLC 22; DAM DRAM**
See also CA 113; 152

Ficino, Marsilio 1433-1499 .... **LC 12**

Fiedeler, Hans
See Doeblin, Alfred

Fiedler, Leslie A(aron)
1917-.................. **CLC 4, 13, 24**
See also CA 9-12R; CANR 7; DLB 28, 67;
MTCW

Field, Andrew 1938-............. **CLC 44**
See also CA 97-100; CANR 25

Field, Eugene 1850-1895 .... **NCLC 3**
See also DLB 23, 42, 140; DLBD 13;
MAICYA; SATA 16

Field, Gans T.
See Wellman, Manly Wade

Field, Michael .... **TCLC 43**

Field, Peter
See Hobson, Laura Z(ametkin)

Fielding, Henry
1707-1754 ...... **LC 1; DA; DAB; DAC;**
DAM DRAM, MST, NOV; WLC
See also CDBLB 1660-1789; DLB 39, 84,
101

Fielding, Sarah 1710-1768 .... **LC 1**
See also DLB 39

Fierstein, Harvey (Forbes)
1954-..... **CLC 33; DAM DRAM, POP**
See also CA 123; 129

Figes, Eva 1932-................. **CLC 31**
See also CA 53-56; CANR 4, 44; DLB 14

Finch, Robert (Duer Claydon)
1900-...................... **CLC 18**
See also CA 57-60; CANR 9, 24, 49;
DLB 88

Findley, Timothy
1930-...... **CLC 27; DAC; DAM MST**
See also CA 25-28R; CANR 12, 42;
DLB 53

Fink, William
See Mencken, H(enry) L(ouis)

Firbank, Louis 1942-
See Reed, Lou
See also CA 117

Firbank, (Arthur Annesley) Ronald
1886-1926 .... **TCLC 1**
See also CA 104; DLB 36

Fisher, M(ary) F(rances) K(ennedy)
1908-1992 .... **CLC 76, 87**
See also CA 77-80; 138; CANR 44

Fisher, Roy 1930-................ **CLC 25**
See also CA 81-84; CAAS 10; CANR 16;
DLB 40

Fisher, Rudolph
1897-1934 .... **TCLC 11; BLC;**
DAM MULT
See also BW 1; CA 107; 124; DLB 51, 102

Fisher, Vardis (Alvero) 1895-1968.... **CLC 7**
See also CA 5-8R; 25-28R; DLB 9

Fiske, Tarleton
See Bloch, Robert (Albert)

Fitch, Clarke
See Sinclair, Upton (Beall)

Fitch, John IV
See Cormier, Robert (Edmund)

Fitzgerald, Captain Hugh
See Baum, L(yman) Frank

FitzGerald, Edward 1809-1883 .... **NCLC 9**
See also DLB 32

Fitzgerald, F(rancis) Scott (Key)
1896-1940 .... **TCLC 1, 6, 14, 28, 55;**
DA; DAB; DAC; DAM MST, NOV;
SSC 6; WLC
See also AITN 1; CA 110; 123;
CDALB 1917-1929; DLB 4, 9, 86;
DLBD 1; DLBY 81; MTCW

Fitzgerald, Penelope 1916-... **CLC 19, 51, 61**
See also CA 85-88; CAAS 10; DLB 14

Fitzgerald, Robert (Stuart)
1910-1985 .... **CLC 39**
See also CA 1-4R; 114; CANR 1; DLBY 80

FitzGerald, Robert D(avid)
1902-1987 .... **CLC 19**
See also CA 17-20R

Fitzgerald, Zelda (Sayre)
1900-1948 .... **TCLC 52**
See also CA 117; 126; DLBY 84

Flanagan, Thomas (James Bonner)
1923-.................. **CLC 25, 52**
See also CA 108; CANR 55; DLBY 80;
INT 108; MTCW

Flaubert, Gustave
1821-1880 .... **NCLC 2, 10, 19; DA;**
DAB; DAC; DAM MST, NOV; SSC 11;
WLC
See also DLB 119

Flecker, Herman Elroy
See Flecker, (Herman) James Elroy

Flecker, (Herman) James Elroy
1884-1915 .... **TCLC 43**
See also CA 109; 150; DLB 10, 19

Fleming, Ian (Lancaster)
1908-1964 ..... **CLC 3, 30; DAM POP**
See also CA 5-8R; CDBLB 1945-1960;
DLB 87; MTCW; SATA 9

Fleming, Thomas (James) 1927- .... **CLC 37**
See also CA 5-8R; CANR 10;
INT CANR-10; SATA 8

Fletcher, John 1579-1625...... **LC 33; DC 6**
See also CDBLB Before 1660; DLB 58

Fletcher, John Gould 1886-1950... **TCLC 35**
See also CA 107; DLB 4, 45

Fleur, Paul
See Pohl, Frederik

Flooglebuckle, Al
See Spiegelman, Art

Flying Officer X
See Bates, H(erbert) E(rnest)

Fo, Dario 1926-..... **CLC 32; DAM DRAM**
See also CA 116; 128; MTCW

Fogarty, Jonathan Titulescu Esq.
See Farrell, James T(homas)

Folke, Will
See Bloch, Robert (Albert)

Follett, Ken(neth Martin)
1949-...... **CLC 18; DAM NOV, POP**
See also AAYA 6; BEST 89:4; CA 81-84;
CANR 13, 33, 54; DLB 87; DLBY 81;
INT CANR-33; MTCW

Fontane, Theodor 1819-1898 ..... **NCLC 26**
See also DLB 129

Foote, Horton
1916-....... **CLC 51, 91; DAM DRAM**
See also CA 73-76; CANR 34, 51; DLB 26;
INT CANR-34

Foote, Shelby
1916-...... **CLC 75; DAM NOV, POP**
See also CA 5-8R; CANR 3, 45; DLB 2, 17

Forbes, Esther 1891-1967......... **CLC 12**
See also AAYA 17; CA 13-14; 25-28R;
CAP 1; CLR 27; DLB 22; JRDA;
MAICYA; SATA 2

Forche, Carolyn (Louise)
1950-.... **CLC 25, 83, 86; DAM POET;**
PC 10
See also CA 109; 117; CANR 50; DLB 5;
INT 117

Ford, Elbur
See Hibbert, Eleanor Alice Burford

Garrett, George (Palmer)
1929- .... **CLC 3, 11, 51**
See also CA 1-4R; CAAS 5; CANR 1, 42;
DLB 2, 5, 130, 152; DLBY 83

Garrick, David
1717-1779 .... **LC 15; DAM DRAM**
See also DLB 84

Garrigue, Jean 1914-1972 .... **CLC 2, 8**
See also CA 5-8R; 37-40R; CANR 20

Garrison, Frederick
See Sinclair, Upton (Beall)

Garth, Will
See Hamilton, Edmond; Kuttner, Henry

Garvey, Marcus (Moziah, Jr.)
1887-1940 .... **TCLC 41; BLC;**
DAM MULT
See also BW 1; CA 120; 124

Gary, Romain .... **CLC 25**
See also Kacew, Romain
See also DLB 83

Gascar, Pierre .... **CLC 11**
See also Fournier, Pierre

Gascoyne, David (Emery) 1916- .... **CLC 45**
See also CA 65-68; CANR 10, 28, 54;
DLB 20; MTCW

Gaskell, Elizabeth Cleghorn
1810-1865 .. **NCLC 5; DAB; DAM MST**
See also CDBLB 1832-1890; DLB 21, 144,
159

Gass, William H(oward)
1924- ... **CLC 1, 2, 8, 11, 15, 39; SSC 12**
See also CA 17-20R; CANR 30; DLB 2;
MTCW

Gasset, Jose Ortega y
See Ortega y Gasset, Jose

Gates, Henry Louis, Jr.
1950- .... **CLC 65; DAM MULT**
See also BW 2; CA 109; CANR 25, 53;
DLB 67

Gautier, Theophile
1811-1872 ...... **NCLC 1; DAM POET;**
SSC 20
See also DLB 119

Gawsworth, John
See Bates, H(erbert) E(rnest)

Gay, Oliver
See Gogarty, Oliver St. John

Gaye, Marvin (Penze) 1939-1984 ... **CLC 26**
See also CA 112

Gebler, Carlo (Ernest) 1954- .... **CLC 39**
See also CA 119; 133

Gee, Maggie (Mary) 1948- .... **CLC 57**
See also CA 130

Gee, Maurice (Gough) 1931- .... **CLC 29**
See also CA 97-100; SATA 46

Gelbart, Larry (Simon) 1923- ... **CLC 21, 61**
See also CA 73-76; CANR 45

Gelber, Jack 1932- .... **CLC 1, 6, 14, 79**
See also CA 1-4R; CANR 2; DLB 7

Gellhorn, Martha (Ellis) 1908- .. **CLC 14, 60**
See also CA 77-80; CANR 44; DLBY 82

Genet, Jean
1910-1986 ...... **CLC 1, 2, 5, 10, 14, 44,**
46; DAM DRAM
See also CA 13-16R; CANR 18; DLB 72;
DLBY 86; MTCW

Gent, Peter 1942- .... **CLC 29**
See also AITN 1; CA 89-92; DLBY 82

Gentlewoman in New England, A
See Bradstreet, Anne

Gentlewoman in Those Parts, A
See Bradstreet, Anne

George, Jean Craighead 1919- ...... **CLC 35**
See also AAYA 8; CA 5-8R; CANR 25;
CLR 1; DLB 52; JRDA; MAICYA;
SATA 2, 68

George, Stefan (Anton)
1868-1933 .... **TCLC 2, 14**
See also CA 104

Georges, Georges Martin
See Simenon, Georges (Jacques Christian)

Gerhardi, William Alexander
See Gerhardie, William Alexander

Gerhardie, William Alexander
1895-1977 .... **CLC 5**
See also CA 25-28R; 73-76; CANR 18;
DLB 36

Gerstler, Amy 1956- .... **CLC 70**
See also CA 146

Gertler, T. .... **CLC 34**
See also CA 116; 121; INT 121

gfgg .... **CLC XvXzc**

Ghalib .... **NCLC 39**
See also Ghalib, Hsadullah Khan

Ghalib, Hsadullah Khan 1797-1869
See Ghalib
See also DAM POET

Ghelderode, Michel de
1898-1962 .... **CLC 6, 11; DAM DRAM**
See also CA 85-88; CANR 40

Ghiselin, Brewster 1903- .... **CLC 23**
See also CA 13-16R; CAAS 10; CANR 13

Ghose, Zulfikar 1935- .... **CLC 42**
See also CA 65-68

Ghosh, Amitav 1956- .... **CLC 44**
See also CA 147

Giacosa, Giuseppe 1847-1906 ...... **TCLC 7**
See also CA 104

Gibb, Lee
See Waterhouse, Keith (Spencer)

Gibbon, Lewis Grassic .... **TCLC 4**
See also Mitchell, James Leslie

Gibbons, Kaye
1960- .... **CLC 50, 88; DAM POP**
See also CA 151

Gibran, Kahlil
1883-1931 .... **TCLC 1, 9; DAM POET,**
POP; PC 9
See also CA 104; 150

Gibran, Khalil
See Gibran, Kahlil

Gibson, William
1914- .... **CLC 23; DA; DAB; DAC;**
DAM DRAM, MST
See also CA 9-12R; CANR 9, 42; DLB 7;
SATA 66

Gibson, William (Ford)
1948- .... **CLC 39, 63; DAM POP**
See also AAYA 12; CA 126; 133; CANR 52

Gide, Andre (Paul Guillaume)
1869-1951 .... **TCLC 5, 12, 36; DA;**
DAB; DAC; DAM MST, NOV; SSC 13;
WLC
See also CA 104; 124; DLB 65; MTCW

Gifford, Barry (Colby) 1946- .... **CLC 34**
See also CA 65-68; CANR 9, 30, 40

Gilbert, W(illiam) S(chwenck)
1836-1911 ..... **TCLC 3; DAM DRAM,**
POET
See also CA 104; SATA 36

Gilbreth, Frank B., Jr. 1911- .... **CLC 17**
See also CA 9-12R; SATA 2

Gilchrist, Ellen
1935- .... **CLC 34, 48; DAM POP;**
SSC 14
See also CA 113; 116; CANR 41; DLB 130;
MTCW

Giles, Molly 1942- .... **CLC 39**
See also CA 126

Gill, Patrick
See Creasey, John

Gilliam, Terry (Vance) 1940- .... **CLC 21**
See also Monty Python
See also AAYA 19; CA 108; 113;
CANR 35; INT 113

Gillian, Jerry
See Gilliam, Terry (Vance)

Gilliatt, Penelope (Ann Douglass)
1932-1993 .... **CLC 2, 10, 13, 53**
See also AITN 2; CA 13-16R; 141;
CANR 49; DLB 14

Gilman, Charlotte (Anna) Perkins (Stetson)
1860-1935 .... **TCLC 9, 37; SSC 13**
See also CA 106; 150

Gilmour, David 1949- .... **CLC 35**
See also CA 138, 147

Gilpin, William 1724-1804 .... **NCLC 30**

Gilray, J. D.
See Mencken, H(enry) L(ouis)

Gilroy, Frank D(aniel) 1925- .... **CLC 2**
See also CA 81-84; CANR 32; DLB 7

Ginsberg, Allen
1926- ...... **CLC 1, 2, 3, 4, 6, 13, 36, 69;**
DA; DAB; DAC; DAM MST, POET;
PC 4; WLC 3
See also AITN 1; CA 1-4R; CANR 2, 41;
CDALB 1941-1968; DLB 5, 16, 169;
MTCW

Ginzburg, Natalia
1916-1991 .... **CLC 5, 11, 54, 70**
See also CA 85-88; 135; CANR 33; MTCW

Giono, Jean 1895-1970 .... **CLC 4, 11**
See also CA 45-48; 29-32R; CANR 2, 35;
DLB 72; MTCW

Giovanni, Nikki
1943- ...... **CLC 2, 4, 19, 64; BLC; DA;
DAB; DAC; DAM MST, MULT, POET**
See also AITN 1; BW 2; CA 29-32R;
CAAS 6; CANR 18, 41; CLR 6; DLB 5,
41; INT CANR-18; MAICYA; MTCW;
SATA 24

Giovene, Andrea 1904- .... **CLC 7**
See also CA 85-88

Gippius, Zinaida (Nikolayevna) 1869-1945
See Hippius, Zinaida
See also CA 106

Giraudoux, (Hippolyte) Jean
1882-1944 .... **TCLC 2, 7; DAM DRAM**
See also CA 104; DLB 65

Gironella, Jose Maria 1917- .... **CLC 11**
See also CA 101

Gissing, George (Robert)
1857-1903 .... **TCLC 3, 24, 47**
See also CA 105; DLB 18, 135

Giurlani, Aldo
See Palazzeschi, Aldo

Gladkov, Fyodor (Vasilyevich)
1883-1958 .... **TCLC 27**

Glanville, Brian (Lester) 1931- ...... **CLC 6**
See also CA 5-8R; CAAS 9; CANR 3;
DLB 15, 139; SATA 42

Glasgow, Ellen (Anderson Gholson)
1873(?)-1945 .... **TCLC 2, 7**
See also CA 104; DLB 9, 12

Glaspell, Susan 1882(?)-1948 ...... **TCLC 55**
See also CA 110; 154; DLB 7, 9, 78;
YABC 2

Glassco, John 1909-1981 .... **CLC 9**
See also CA 13-16R; 102; CANR 15;
DLB 68

Glasscock, Amnesia
See Steinbeck, John (Ernst)

Glasser, Ronald J. 1940(?)- .... **CLC 37**

Glassman, Joyce
See Johnson, Joyce

Glendinning, Victoria 1937- .... **CLC 50**
See also CA 120; 127; DLB 155

Glissant, Edouard
1928- .... **CLC 10, 68; DAM MULT**
See also CA 153

Gloag, Julian 1930- .... **CLC 40**
See also AITN 1; CA 65-68; CANR 10

Glowacki, Aleksander
See Prus, Boleslaw

Gluck, Louise (Elisabeth)
1943- .... **CLC 7, 22, 44, 81;
DAM POET; PC 16**
See also CA 33-36R; CANR 40; DLB 5

Gobineau, Joseph Arthur (Comte) de
1816-1882 .... **NCLC 17**
See also DLB 123

Godard, Jean-Luc 1930- .... **CLC 20**
See also CA 93-96

Godden, (Margaret) Rumer 1907- ... **CLC 53**
See also AAYA 6; CA 5-8R; CANR 4, 27,
36, 55; CLR 20; DLB 161; MAICYA;
SAAS 12; SATA 3, 36

Godoy Alcayaga, Lucila 1889-1957
See Mistral, Gabriela
See also BW 2; CA 104; 131; DAM MULT;
HW; MTCW

Godwin, Gail (Kathleen)
1937- .... **CLC 5, 8, 22, 31, 69;
DAM POP**
See also CA 29-32R; CANR 15, 43; DLB 6;
INT CANR-15; MTCW

Godwin, William 1756-1836...... **NCLC 14**
See also CDBLB 1789-1832; DLB 39, 104,
142, 158, 163

Goethe, Johann Wolfgang von
1749-1832.......**NCLC 4, 22, 34; DA;
DAB; DAC; DAM DRAM, MST,
POET; PC 5; WLC 3**
See also DLB 94

Gogarty, Oliver St. John
1878-1957 .... **TCLC 15**
See also CA 109; 150; DLB 15, 19

Gogol, Nikolai (Vasilyevich)
1809-1852 .... **NCLC 5, 15, 31; DA;
DAB; DAC; DAM DRAM, MST; DC 1;
SSC 4; WLC**

Goines, Donald
1937(?)-1974 .... **CLC 80; BLC;
DAM MULT, POP**
See also AITN 1; BW 1; CA 124; 114;
DLB 33

Gold, Herbert 1924- .... **CLC 4, 7, 14, 42**
See also CA 9-12R; CANR 17, 45; DLB 2;
DLBY 81

Goldbarth, Albert 1948- .... **CLC 5, 38**
See also CA 53-56; CANR 6, 40; DLB 120

Goldberg, Anatol 1910-1982 .... **CLC 34**
See also CA 131; 117

Goldemberg, Isaac 1945- .... **CLC 52**
See also CA 69-72; CAAS 12; CANR 11,
32; HW

Golding, William (Gerald)
1911-1993 .... **CLC 1, 2, 3, 8, 10, 17, 27,
58, 81; DA; DAB; DAC; DAM MST,
NOV; WLC**
See also AAYA 5; CA 5-8R; 141;
CANR 13, 33, 54; CDBLB 1945-1960;
DLB 15, 100; MTCW

Goldman, Emma 1869-1940 ...... **TCLC 13**
See also CA 110; 150

Goldman, Francisco 1955- .... **CLC 76**

Goldman, William (W.) 1931- .... **CLC 1, 48**
See also CA 9-12R; CANR 29; DLB 44

Goldmann, Lucien 1913-1970 ...... **CLC 24**
See also CA 25-28; CAP 2

Goldoni, Carlo
1707-1793 .... **LC 4; DAM DRAM**

Goldsberry, Steven 1949- .... **CLC 34**
See also CA 131

Goldsmith, Oliver
1728-1774 ...... **LC 2; DA; DAB; DAC;
DAM DRAM, MST, NOV, POET;
WLC**
See also CDBLB 1660-1789; DLB 39, 89,
104, 109, 142; SATA 26

Goldsmith, Peter
See Priestley, J(ohn) B(oynton)

Gombrowicz, Witold
1904-1969 .... **CLC 4, 7, 11, 49;
DAM DRAM**
See also CA 19-20; 25-28R; CAP 2

Gomez de la Serna, Ramon
1888-1963 .... **CLC 9**
See also CA 153; 116; HW

Goncharov, Ivan Alexandrovich
1812-1891 .... **NCLC 1**

Goncourt, Edmond (Louis Antoine Huot) de
1822-1896 .... **NCLC 7**
See also DLB 123

Goncourt, Jules (Alfred Huot) de
1830-1870 .... **NCLC 7**
See also DLB 123

Gontier, Fernande 19(?)- .... **CLC 50**

Goodman, Paul 1911-1972.... **CLC 1, 2, 4, 7**
See also CA 19-20; 37-40R; CANR 34;
CAP 2; DLB 130; MTCW

Gordimer, Nadine
1923- .... **CLC 3, 5, 7, 10, 18, 33, 51, 70;
DA; DAB; DAC; DAM MST, NOV;
SSC 17**
See also CA 5-8R; CANR 3, 28;
INT CANR-28; MTCW

Gordon, Adam Lindsay
1833-1870 .... **NCLC 21**

Gordon, Caroline
1895-1981 ... **CLC 6, 13, 29, 83; SSC 15**
See also CA 11-12; 103; CANR 36; CAP 1;
DLB 4, 9, 102; DLBY 81; MTCW

Gordon, Charles William 1860-1937
See Connor, Ralph
See also CA 109

Gordon, Mary (Catherine)
1949- .... **CLC 13, 22**
See also CA 102; CANR 44; DLB 6;
DLBY 81; INT 102; MTCW

Gordon, Sol 1923-................ **CLC 26**
See also CA 53-56; CANR 4; SATA 11

Gordone, Charles
1925-1995 ..... **CLC 1, 4; DAM DRAM**
See also BW 1; CA 93-96; 150; CANR 55;
DLB 7; INT 93-96; MTCW

Gorenko, Anna Andreevna
See Akhmatova, Anna

Gorky, Maxim......... **TCLC 8; DAB; WLC**
See also Peshkov, Alexei Maximovich

Goryan, Sirak
See Saroyan, William

Gosse, Edmund (William)
1849-1928 .... **TCLC 28**
See also CA 117; DLB 57, 144

Gotlieb, Phyllis Fay (Bloom)
1926- .... **CLC 18**
See also CA 13-16R; CANR 7; DLB 88

Gottesman, S. D.
See Kornbluth, C(yril) M.; Pohl, Frederik

Gottfried von Strassburg
fl. c. 1210-................. **CMLC 10**
See also DLB 138

Gould, Lois .... **CLC 4, 10**
See also CA 77-80; CANR 29; MTCW

Griffin, Gerald 1803-1840 .... **NCLC 7**
See also DLB 159

Griffin, John Howard 1920-1980.... **CLC 68**
See also AITN 1; CA 1-4R; 101; CANR 2

Griffin, Peter 1942- .... **CLC 39**
See also CA 136

Griffiths, Trevor 1935- .... **CLC 13, 52**
See also CA 97-100; CANR 45; DLB 13

Grigson, Geoffrey (Edward Harvey)
1905-1985 .... **CLC 7, 39**
See also CA 25-28R; 118; CANR 20, 33;
DLB 27; MTCW

Grillparzer, Franz 1791-1872...... **NCLC 1**
See also DLB 133

Grimble, Reverend Charles James
See Eliot, T(homas) S(tearns)

Grimke, Charlotte L(ottie) Forten
1837(?)-1914
See Forten, Charlotte L.
See also BW 1; CA 117; 124; DAM MULT,
POET

Grimm, Jacob Ludwig Karl
1785-1863 .... **NCLC 3**
See also DLB 90; MAICYA; SATA 22

Grimm, Wilhelm Karl 1786-1859 .. **NCLC 3**
See also DLB 90; MAICYA; SATA 22

Grimmelshausen, Johann Jakob Christoffel
von 1621-1676 .... **LC 6**
See also DLB 168

Grindel, Eugene 1895-1952
See Eluard, Paul
See also CA 104

Grisham, John 1955- .. **CLC 84; DAM POP**
See also AAYA 14; CA 138; CANR 47

Grossman, David 1954- .... **CLC 67**
See also CA 138

Grossman, Vasily (Semenovich)
1905-1964 .... **CLC 41**
See also CA 124; 130; MTCW

Grove, Frederick Philip .... **TCLC 4**
See also Greve, Felix Paul (Berthold
Friedrich)
See also DLB 92

Grubb
See Crumb, R(obert)

Grumbach, Doris (Isaac)
1918- .... **CLC 13, 22, 64**
See also CA 5-8R; CAAS 2; CANR 9, 42;
INT CANR-9

Grundtvig, Nicolai Frederik Severin
1783-1872 .... **NCLC 1**

Grunge
See Crumb, R(obert)

Grunwald, Lisa 1959- .... **CLC 44**
See also CA 120

Guare, John
1938- .... **CLC 8, 14, 29, 67;**
DAM DRAM
See also CA 73-76; CANR 21; DLB 7;
MTCW

Gudjonsson, Halldor Kiljan 1902-
See Laxness, Halldor
See also CA 103

Guenter, Erich
See Eich, Guenter

Guest, Barbara 1920- .... **CLC 34**
See also CA 25-28R; CANR 11, 44; DLB 5

Guest, Judith (Ann)
1936- .... **CLC 8, 30; DAM NOV, POP**
See also AAYA 7; CA 77-80; CANR 15;
INT CANR-15; MTCW

Guevara, Che .... **CLC 87; HLC**
See also Guevara (Serna), Ernesto

Guevara (Serna), Ernesto 1928-1967
See Guevara, Che
See also CA 127; 111; DAM MULT; HW

Guild, Nicholas M. 1944- .... **CLC 33**
See also CA 93-96

Guillemin, Jacques
See Sartre, Jean-Paul

Guillen, Jorge
1893-1984 ...... **CLC 11; DAM MULT,**
POET
See also CA 89-92; 112; DLB 108; HW

Guillen, Nicolas (Cristobal)
1902-1989 .... **CLC 48, 79; BLC;**
DAM MST, MULT, POET; HLC
See also BW 2; CA 116; 125; 129; HW

Guillevic, (Eugene) 1907- .... **CLC 33**
See also CA 93-96

Guillois
See Desnos, Robert

Guillois, Valentin
See Desnos, Robert

Guiney, Louise Imogen
1861-1920 .... **TCLC 41**
See also DLB 54

Guiraldes, Ricardo (Guillermo)
1886-1927 .... **TCLC 39**
See also CA 131; HW; MTCW

Gumilev, Nikolai Stephanovich
1886-1921 .... **TCLC 60**

Gunesekera, Romesh .... **CLC 91**

Gunn, Bill .... **CLC 5**
See also Gunn, William Harrison
See also DLB 38

Gunn, Thom(son William)
1929- .... **CLC 3, 6, 18, 32, 81;**
DAM POET
See also CA 17-20R; CANR 9, 33;
CDBLB 1960 to Present; DLB 27;
INT CANR-33; MTCW

Gunn, William Harrison 1934(?)-1989
See Gunn, Bill
See also AITN 1; BW 1; CA 13-16R; 128;
CANR 12, 25

Gunnars, Kristjana 1948- .... **CLC 69**
See also CA 113; DLB 60

Gurganus, Allan
1947- .... **CLC 70; DAM POP**
See also BEST 90:1; CA 135

Gurney, A(lbert) R(amsdell), Jr.
1930- .... **CLC 32, 50, 54; DAM DRAM**
See also CA 77-80; CANR 32

Gurney, Ivor (Bertie) 1890-1937 ... **TCLC 33**

Gurney, Peter
See Gurney, A(lbert) R(amsdell), Jr.

Guro, Elena 1877-1913.......... **TCLC 56**

Gustafson, Ralph (Barker) 1909-.... **CLC 36**
See also CA 21-24R; CANR 8, 45; DLB 88

Gut, Gom
See Simenon, Georges (Jacques Christian)

Guterson, David 1956- .... **CLC 91**
See also CA 132

Guthrie, A(lfred) B(ertram), Jr.
1901-1991 .... **CLC 23**
See also CA 57-60; 134; CANR 24; DLB 6;
SATA 62; SATA-Obit 67

Guthrie, Isobel
See Grieve, C(hristopher) M(urray)

Guthrie, Woodrow Wilson 1912-1967
See Guthrie, Woody
See also CA 113; 93-96

Guthrie, Woody .... **CLC 35**
See also Guthrie, Woodrow Wilson

Guy, Rosa (Cuthbert) 1928-........ **CLC 26**
See also AAYA 4; BW 2; CA 17-20R;
CANR 14, 34; CLR 13; DLB 33; JRDA;
MAICYA; SATA 14, 62

Gwendolyn
See Bennett, (Enoch) Arnold

H. D. .... **CLC 3, 8, 14, 31, 34, 73; PC 5**
See also Doolittle, Hilda

H. de V.
See Buchan, John

Haavikko, Paavo Juhani
1931- .... **CLC 18, 34**
See also CA 106

Habbema, Koos
See Heijermans, Herman

Hacker, Marilyn
1942- .... **CLC 5, 9, 23, 72, 91;**
DAM POET
See also CA 77-80; DLB 120

Haggard, H(enry) Rider
1856-1925 .... **TCLC 11**
See also CA 108; 148; DLB 70, 156, 174;
SATA 16

Hagiosy, L.
See Larbaud, Valery (Nicolas)

Hagiwara Sakutaro 1886-1942 .... **TCLC 60**

Haig, Fenil
See Ford, Ford Madox

Haig-Brown, Roderick (Langmere)
1908-1976 .... **CLC 21**
See also CA 5-8R; 69-72; CANR 4, 38;
CLR 31; DLB 88; MAICYA; SATA 12

Hailey, Arthur
1920- .... **CLC 5; DAM NOV, POP**
See also AITN 2; BEST 90:3; CA 1-4R;
CANR 2, 36; DLB 88; DLBY 82; MTCW

Hailey, Elizabeth Forsythe 1938-... **CLC 40**
See also CA 93-96; CAAS 1; CANR 15, 48;
INT CANR-15

Haines, John (Meade) 1924-....... **CLC 58**
See also CA 17-20R; CANR 13, 34; DLB 5

Hakluyt, Richard 1552-1616........ **LC 31**

Haldeman, Joe (William) 1943-..... **CLC 61**
See also CA 53-56; CAAS 25; CANR 6;
DLB 8; INT CANR-6

Haley, Alex(ander Murray Palmer)
    1921-1992 .... **CLC 8, 12, 76; BLC; DA;**
        DAB; DAC; DAM MST, MULT, POP
    See also BW 2; CA 77-80; 136; DLB 38;
    MTCW

Haliburton, Thomas Chandler
    1796-1865 .... **NCLC 15**
    See also DLB 11, 99

Hall, Donald (Andrew, Jr.)
    1928- .. **CLC 1, 13, 37, 59; DAM POET**
    See also CA 5-8R; CAAS 7; CANR 2, 44;
    DLB 5; SATA 23

Hall, Frederic Sauser
    See Sauser-Hall, Frederic

Hall, James
    See Kuttner, Henry

Hall, James Norman   1887-1951 ... **TCLC 23**
    See also CA 123; SATA 21

Hall, (Marguerite) Radclyffe
    1886-1943 .... **TCLC 12**
    See also CA 110; 150

Hall, Rodney   1935- .... **CLC 51**
    See also CA 109

Halleck, Fitz-Greene   1790-1867 .. **NCLC 47**
    See also DLB 3

Halliday, Michael
    See Creasey, John

Halpern, Daniel   1945- .... **CLC 14**
    See also CA 33-36R

Hamburger, Michael (Peter Leopold)
    1924- .... **CLC 5, 14**
    See also CA 5-8R; CAAS 4; CANR 2, 47;
    DLB 27

Hamill, Pete   1935- .... **CLC 10**
    See also CA 25-28R; CANR 18

Hamilton, Alexander
    1755(?)-1804 .... **NCLC 49**
    See also DLB 37

Hamilton, Clive
    See Lewis, C(live) S(taples)

Hamilton, Edmond   1904-1977 .... **CLC 1**
    See also CA 1-4R; CANR 3; DLB 8

Hamilton, Eugene (Jacob) Lee
    See Lee-Hamilton, Eugene (Jacob)

Hamilton, Franklin
    See Silverberg, Robert

Hamilton, Gail
    See Corcoran, Barbara

Hamilton, Mollie
    See Kaye, M(ary) M(argaret)

Hamilton, (Anthony Walter) Patrick
    1904-1962 .... **CLC 51**
    See also CA 113; DLB 10

Hamilton, Virginia
    1936- .... **CLC 26; DAM MULT**
    See also AAYA 2; BW 2; CA 25-28R;
    CANR 20, 37; CLR 1, 11, 40; DLB 33,
    52; INT CANR-20; JRDA; MAICYA;
    MTCW; SATA 4, 56, 79

Hammett, (Samuel) Dashiell
    1894-1961 .... **CLC 3, 5, 10, 19, 47;
        SSC 17**
    See also AITN 1; CA 81-84; CANR 42;
    CDALB 1929-1941; DLBD 6; MTCW

Hammon, Jupiter
    1711(?)-1800(?) .... **NCLC 5; BLC;
        DAM MULT, POET; PC 16**
    See also DLB 31, 50

Hammond, Keith
    See Kuttner, Henry

Hamner, Earl (Henry), Jr.   1923- ... **CLC 12**
    See also AITN 2; CA 73-76; DLB 6

Hampton, Christopher (James)
    1946- .... **CLC 4**
    See also CA 25-28R; DLB 13; MTCW

Hamsun, Knut .... **TCLC 2, 14, 49**
    See also Pedersen, Knut

Handke, Peter
    1942- .... **CLC 5, 8, 10, 15, 38;
        DAM DRAM, NOV**
    See also CA 77-80; CANR 33; DLB 85,
    124; MTCW

Hanley, James   1901-1985 ... **CLC 3, 5, 8, 13**
    See also CA 73-76; 117; CANR 36; MTCW

Hannah, Barry   1942- .... **CLC 23, 38, 90**
    See also CA 108; 110; CANR 43; DLB 6;
    INT 110; MTCW

Hannon, Ezra
    See Hunter, Evan

Hansberry, Lorraine (Vivian)
    1930-1965 ...... **CLC 17, 62; BLC; DA;
        DAB; DAC; DAM DRAM, MST,
            MULT; DC 2**
    See also BW 1; CA 109; 25-28R; CABS 3;
    CDALB 1941-1968; DLB 7, 38; MTCW

Hansen, Joseph   1923- .... **CLC 38**
    See also CA 29-32R; CAAS 17; CANR 16,
    44; INT CANR-16

Hansen, Martin A.   1909-1955 ..... **TCLC 32**

Hanson, Kenneth O(stlin)   1922- .... **CLC 13**
    See also CA 53-56; CANR 7

Hardwick, Elizabeth
    1916- .... **CLC 13; DAM NOV**
    See also CA 5-8R; CANR 3, 32; DLB 6;
    MTCW

Hardy, Thomas
    1840-1928 ...... **TCLC 4, 10, 18, 32, 48,
        53; DA; DAB; DAC; DAM MST, NOV,
            POET; PC 8; SSC 2; WLC**
    See also CA 104; 123; CDBLB 1890-1914;
    DLB 18, 19, 135; MTCW

Hare, David   1947- .... **CLC 29, 58**
    See also CA 97-100; CANR 39; DLB 13;
    MTCW

Harford, Henry
    See Hudson, W(illiam) H(enry)

Hargrave, Leonie
    See Disch, Thomas M(ichael)

Harjo, Joy   1951- ... **CLC 83; DAM MULT**
    See also CA 114; CANR 35; DLB 120;
    NNAL

Harlan, Louis R(udolph)   1922- ..... **CLC 34**
    See also CA 21-24R; CANR 25, 55

Harling, Robert   1951(?)- .... **CLC 53**
    See also CA 147

Harmon, William (Ruth)   1938- ..... **CLC 38**
    See also CA 33-36R; CANR 14, 32, 35;
    SATA 65

Harper, F. E. W.
    See Harper, Frances Ellen Watkins

Harper, Frances E. W.
    See Harper, Frances Ellen Watkins

Harper, Frances E. Watkins
    See Harper, Frances Ellen Watkins

Harper, Frances Ellen
    See Harper, Frances Ellen Watkins

Harper, Frances Ellen Watkins
    1825-1911 .... **TCLC 14; BLC;
        DAM MULT, POET**
    See also BW 1; CA 111; 125; DLB 50

Harper, Michael S(teven)   1938- .. **CLC 7, 22**
    See also BW 1; CA 33-36R; CANR 24;
    DLB 41

Harper, Mrs. F. E. W.
    See Harper, Frances Ellen Watkins

Harris, Christie (Lucy) Irwin
    1907- .... **CLC 12**
    See also CA 5-8R; CANR 6; DLB 88;
    JRDA; MAICYA; SAAS 10; SATA 6, 74

Harris, Frank   1856-1931 .... **TCLC 24**
    See also CA 109; 150; DLB 156

Harris, George Washington
    1814-1869 .... **NCLC 23**
    See also DLB 3, 11

Harris, Joel Chandler
    1848-1908 .... **TCLC 2; SSC 19**
    See also CA 104; 137; DLB 11, 23, 42, 78,
    91; MAICYA; YABC 1

Harris, John (Wyndham Parkes Lucas)
        Beynon   1903-1969
    See Wyndham, John
    See also CA 102; 89-92

Harris, MacDonald .... **CLC 9**
    See also Heiney, Donald (William)

Harris, Mark   1922- .... **CLC 19**
    See also CA 5-8R; CAAS 3; CANR 2, 55;
    DLB 2; DLBY 80

Harris, (Theodore) Wilson   1921- .... **CLC 25**
    See also BW 2; CA 65-68; CAAS 16;
    CANR 11, 27; DLB 117; MTCW

Harrison, Elizabeth Cavanna   1909-
    See Cavanna, Betty
    See also CA 9-12R; CANR 6, 27

Harrison, Harry (Max)   1925- ...... **CLC 42**
    See also CA 1-4R; CANR 5, 21; DLB 8;
    SATA 4

Harrison, James (Thomas)
    1937- .... **CLC 6, 14, 33, 66; SSC 19**
    See also CA 13-16R; CANR 8, 51;
    DLBY 82; INT CANR-8

Harrison, Jim
    See Harrison, James (Thomas)

Harrison, Kathryn   1961- .... **CLC 70**
    See also CA 144

Harrison, Tony   1937- .... **CLC 43**
    See also CA 65-68; CANR 44; DLB 40;
    MTCW

Harriss, Will(ard Irvin)   1922- ...... **CLC 34**
    See also CA 111

Harson, Sley
    See Ellison, Harlan (Jay)

Hart, Ellis
    See Ellison, Harlan (Jay)

Hemingway, Ernest (Miller)
1899-1961 .... **CLC 1, 3, 6, 8, 10, 13, 19,
30, 34, 39, 41, 44, 50, 61, 80; DA; DAB;
DAC; DAM MST, NOV; SSC 1; WLC**
See also AAYA 19; CA 77-80; CANR 34;
CDALB 1917-1929; DLB 4, 9, 102;
DLBD 1; DLBY 81, 87; MTCW

Hempel, Amy 1951- .... **CLC 39**
See also CA 118; 137

Henderson, F. C.
See Mencken, H(enry) L(ouis)

Henderson, Sylvia
See Ashton-Warner, Sylvia (Constance)

Henley, Beth .... **CLC 23; DC 6**
See also Henley, Elizabeth Becker
See also CABS 3; DLBY 86

Henley, Elizabeth Becker 1952-
See Henley, Beth
See also CA 107; CANR 32; DAM DRAM,
MST; MTCW

Henley, William Ernest
1849-1903 .... **TCLC 8**
See also CA 105; DLB 19

Hennissart, Martha
See Lathen, Emma
See also CA 85-88

Henry, O. .... **TCLC 1, 19; SSC 5; WLC**
See also Porter, William Sydney

Henry, Patrick 1736-1799 .... **LC 25**

Henryson, Robert 1430(?)-1506(?).... **LC 20**
See also DLB 146

Henry VIII 1491-1547............. **LC 10**

Henschke, Alfred
See Klabund

Hentoff, Nat(han Irving) 1925- ..... **CLC 26**
See also AAYA 4; CA 1-4R; CAAS 6;
CANR 5, 25; CLR 1; INT CANR-25;
JRDA; MAICYA; SATA 42, 69;
SATA-Brief 27

Heppenstall, (John) Rayner
1911-1981 .... **CLC 10**
See also CA 1-4R; 103; CANR 29

Herbert, Frank (Patrick)
1920-1986 ...... **CLC 12, 23, 35, 44, 85;
DAM POP**
See also CA 53-56; 118; CANR 5, 43;
DLB 8; INT CANR-5; MTCW; SATA 9,
37; SATA-Obit 47

Herbert, George
1593-1633 .... **LC 24; DAB;
DAM POET; PC 4**
See also CDBLB Before 1660; DLB 126

Herbert, Zbigniew
1924- .... **CLC 9, 43; DAM POET**
See also CA 89-92; CANR 36; MTCW

Herbst, Josephine (Frey)
1897-1969 .... **CLC 34**
See also CA 5-8R; 25-28R; DLB 9

Hergesheimer, Joseph
1880-1954 .... **TCLC 11**
See also CA 109; DLB 102, 9

Herlihy, James Leo 1927-1993 ...... **CLC 6**
See also CA 1-4R; 143; CANR 2

Hermogenes fl. c. 175- .... **CMLC 6**

Hernandez, Jose 1834-1886 ...... **NCLC 17**

Herodotus c. 484B.C.-429B.C..... **CMLC 17**

Herrick, Robert
1591-1674 ..... **LC 13; DA; DAB; DAC;
DAM MST, POP; PC 9**
See also DLB 126

Herring, Guilles
See Somerville, Edith

Herriot, James
1916-1995 .... **CLC 12; DAM POP**
See also Wight, James Alfred
See also AAYA 1; CA 148; CANR 40;
SATA 86

Herrmann, Dorothy 1941- .... **CLC 44**
See also CA 107

Herrmann, Taffy
See Herrmann, Dorothy

Hersey, John (Richard)
1914-1993 .... **CLC 1, 2, 7, 9, 40, 81, 97;
DAM POP**
See also CA 17-20R; 140; CANR 33;
DLB 6; MTCW; SATA 25;
SATA-Obit 76

Herzen, Aleksandr Ivanovich
1812-1870 .... **NCLC 10**

Herzl, Theodor 1860-1904 .... **TCLC 36**

Herzog, Werner 1942- .... **CLC 16**
See also CA 89-92

Hesiod c. 8th cent. B.C.- .... **CMLC 5**

Hesse, Hermann
1877-1962 .... **CLC 1, 2, 3, 6, 11, 17, 25,
69; DA; DAB; DAC; DAM MST, NOV;
SSC 9; WLC**
See also CA 17-18; CAP 2; DLB 66;
MTCW; SATA 50

Hewes, Cady
See De Voto, Bernard (Augustine)

Heyen, William 1940- .... **CLC 13, 18**
See also CA 33-36R; CAAS 9; DLB 5

Heyerdahl, Thor 1914- .... **CLC 26**
See also CA 5-8R; CANR 5, 22; MTCW;
SATA 2, 52

Heym, Georg (Theodor Franz Arthur)
1887-1912 .... **TCLC 9**
See also CA 106

Heym, Stefan 1913- .... **CLC 41**
See also CA 9-12R; CANR 4; DLB 69

Heyse, Paul (Johann Ludwig von)
1830-1914 .... **TCLC 8**
See also CA 104; DLB 129

Heyward, (Edwin) DuBose
1885-1940 .... **TCLC 59**
See also CA 108; DLB 7, 9, 45; SATA 21

Hibbert, Eleanor Alice Burford
1906-1993 .... **CLC 7; DAM POP**
See also BEST 90:4; CA 17-20R; 140;
CANR 9, 28; SATA 2; SATA-Obit 74

Hichens, Robert S. 1864-1950 ..... **TCLC 64**
See also DLB 153

Higgins, George V(incent)
1939- .... **CLC 4, 7, 10, 18**
See also CA 77-80; CAAS 5; CANR 17, 51;
DLB 2; DLBY 81; INT CANR-17;
MTCW

Higginson, Thomas Wentworth
1823-1911 .... **TCLC 36**
See also DLB 1, 64

Highet, Helen
See MacInnes, Helen (Clark)

Highsmith, (Mary) Patricia
1921-1995 .... **CLC 2, 4, 14, 42;
DAM NOV, POP**
See also CA 1-4R; 147; CANR 1, 20, 48;
MTCW

Highwater, Jamake (Mamake)
1942(?)- .... **CLC 12**
See also AAYA 7; CA 65-68; CAAS 7;
CANR 10, 34; CLR 17; DLB 52;
DLBY 85; JRDA; MAICYA; SATA 32,
69; SATA-Brief 30

Highway, Tomson
1951- ..... **CLC 92; DAC; DAM MULT**
See also CA 151; NNAL

Higuchi, Ichiyo 1872-1896 ...... **NCLC 49**

Hijuelos, Oscar
1951- .... **CLC 65; DAM MULT, POP;
HLC**
See also BEST 90:1; CA 123; CANR 50;
DLB 145; HW

Hikmet, Nazim 1902(?)-1963 ...... **CLC 40**
See also CA 141; 93-96

Hildesheimer, Wolfgang
1916-1991 .... **CLC 49**
See also CA 101; 135; DLB 69, 124

Hill, Geoffrey (William)
1932- ... **CLC 5, 8, 18, 45; DAM POET**
See also CA 81-84; CANR 21;
CDBLB 1960 to Present; DLB 40;
MTCW

Hill, George Roy 1921- .... **CLC 26**
See also CA 110; 122

Hill, John
See Koontz, Dean R(ay)

Hill, Susan (Elizabeth)
1942- .. **CLC 4; DAB; DAM MST, NOV**
See also CA 33-36R; CANR 29; DLB 14,
139; MTCW

Hillerman, Tony
1925- .... **CLC 62; DAM POP**
See also AAYA 6; BEST 89:1; CA 29-32R;
CANR 21, 42; SATA 6

Hillesum, Etty 1914-1943 .... **TCLC 49**
See also CA 137

Hilliard, Noel (Harvey) 1929- ...... **CLC 15**
See also CA 9-12R; CANR 7

Hillis, Rick 1956- .... **CLC 66**
See also CA 134

Hilton, James 1900-1954 .... **TCLC 21**
See also CA 108; DLB 34, 77; SATA 34

Himes, Chester (Bomar)
1909-1984 .... **CLC 2, 4, 7, 18, 58; BLC;
DAM MULT**
See also BW 2; CA 25-28R; 114; CANR 22;
DLB 2, 76, 143; MTCW

Hinde, Thomas .... **CLC 6, 11**
See also Chitty, Thomas Willes

Hindin, Nathan
See Bloch, Robert (Albert)

Hine, (William) Daryl 1936- . . . . **CLC 15**
See also CA 1-4R; CAAS 15; CANR 1, 20;
DLB 60

Hinkson, Katharine Tynan
See Tynan, Katharine

Hinton, S(usan) E(loise)
1950- . . . . **CLC 30; DA; DAB; DAC;
DAM MST, NOV**
See also AAYA 2; CA 81-84; CANR 32;
CLR 3, 23; JRDA; MAICYA; MTCW;
SATA 19, 58

Hippius, Zinaida . . . . **TCLC 9**
See also Gippius, Zinaida (Nikolayevna)

Hiraoka, Kimitake 1925-1970
See Mishima, Yukio
See also CA 97-100; 29-32R; DAM DRAM;
MTCW

Hirsch, E(ric) D(onald), Jr. 1928- . . . **CLC 79**
See also CA 25-28R; CANR 27, 51;
DLB 67; INT CANR-27; MTCW

Hirsch, Edward 1950- . . . . **CLC 31, 50**
See also CA 104; CANR 20, 42; DLB 120

Hitchcock, Alfred (Joseph)
1899-1980 . . . . **CLC 16**
See also CA 97-100; SATA 27;
SATA-Obit 24

Hitler, Adolf 1889-1945 . . . . **TCLC 53**
See also CA 117; 147

Hoagland, Edward 1932- . . . . **CLC 28**
See also CA 1-4R; CANR 2, 31; DLB 6;
SATA 51

Hoban, Russell (Conwell)
1925- . . . . **CLC 7, 25; DAM NOV**
See also CA 5-8R; CANR 23, 37; CLR 3;
DLB 52; MAICYA; MTCW; SATA 1,
40, 78

Hobbes, Thomas 1588-1679 . . . . **LC 36**
See also DLB 151

Hobbs, Perry
See Blackmur, R(ichard) P(almer)

Hobson, Laura Z(ametkin)
1900-1986 . . . . **CLC 7, 25**
See also CA 17-20R; 118; CANR 55;
DLB 28; SATA 52

Hochhuth, Rolf
1931- . . . . . **CLC 4, 11, 18; DAM DRAM**
See also CA 5-8R; CANR 33; DLB 124;
MTCW

Hochman, Sandra 1936- . . . . **CLC 3, 8**
See also CA 5-8R; DLB 5

Hochwaelder, Fritz
1911-1986 . . . . . . **CLC 36; DAM DRAM**
See also CA 29-32R; 120; CANR 42;
MTCW

Hochwalder, Fritz
See Hochwaelder, Fritz

Hocking, Mary (Eunice) 1921- . . . . . **CLC 13**
See also CA 101; CANR 18, 40

Hodgins, Jack 1938- . . . . **CLC 23**
See also CA 93-96; DLB 60

Hodgson, William Hope
1877(?)-1918 . . . . **TCLC 13**
See also CA 111; DLB 70, 153, 156

Hoeg, Peter 1957- . . . . **CLC 95**
See also CA 151

Hoffman, Alice
1952- . . . . **CLC 51; DAM NOV**
See also CA 77-80; CANR 34; MTCW

Hoffman, Daniel (Gerard)
1923- . . . . **CLC 6, 13, 23**
See also CA 1-4R; CANR 4; DLB 5

Hoffman, Stanley 1944- . . . . **CLC 5**
See also CA 77-80

Hoffman, William M(oses) 1939- . . . **CLC 40**
See also CA 57-60; CANR 11

Hoffmann, E(rnst) T(heodor) A(madeus)
1776-1822 . . . . **NCLC 2; SSC 13**
See also DLB 90; SATA 27

Hofmann, Gert 1931- . . . . **CLC 54**
See also CA 128

Hofmannsthal, Hugo von
1874-1929 . . . . **TCLC 11; DAM DRAM;
DC 4**
See also CA 106; 153; DLB 81, 118

Hogan, Linda
1947- . . . . **CLC 73; DAM MULT**
See also CA 120; CANR 45; NNAL

Hogarth, Charles
See Creasey, John

Hogarth, Emmett
See Polonsky, Abraham (Lincoln)

Hogg, James 1770-1835 . . . . **NCLC 4**
See also DLB 93, 116, 159

Holbach, Paul Henri Thiry Baron
1723-1789 . . . . **LC 14**

Holberg, Ludvig 1684-1754 . . . . **LC 6**

Holden, Ursula 1921- . . . . **CLC 18**
See also CA 101; CAAS 8; CANR 22

Holderlin, (Johann Christian) Friedrich
1770-1843 . . . . **NCLC 16; PC 4**

Holdstock, Robert
See Holdstock, Robert P.

Holdstock, Robert P. 1948- . . . . **CLC 39**
See also CA 131

Holland, Isabelle 1920- . . . . **CLC 21**
See also AAYA 11; CA 21-24R; CANR 10,
25, 47; JRDA; MAICYA; SATA 8, 70

Holland, Marcus
See Caldwell, (Janet Miriam) Taylor
(Holland)

Hollander, John 1929- . . . . . . **CLC 2, 5, 8, 14**
See also CA 1-4R; CANR 1, 52; DLB 5;
SATA 13

Hollander, Paul
See Silverberg, Robert

Holleran, Andrew 1943(?)- . . . . **CLC 38**
See also CA 144

Hollinghurst, Alan 1954- . . . . **CLC 55, 91**
See also CA 114

Hollis, Jim
See Summers, Hollis (Spurgeon, Jr.)

Holly, Buddy 1936-1959 . . . . **TCLC 65**

Holmes, John
See Souster, (Holmes) Raymond

Holmes, John Clellon 1926-1988 . . . . **CLC 56**
See also CA 9-12R; 125; CANR 4; DLB 16

Holmes, Oliver Wendell
1809-1894 . . . . **NCLC 14**
See also CDALB 1640-1865; DLB 1;
SATA 34

Holmes, Raymond
See Souster, (Holmes) Raymond

Holt, Victoria
See Hibbert, Eleanor Alice Burford

Holub, Miroslav 1923- . . . . **CLC 4**
See also CA 21-24R; CANR 10

Homer
c. 8th cent. B.C.- . . . . . **CMLC 1, 16; DA;
DAB; DAC; DAM MST, POET**

Honig, Edwin 1919- . . . . **CLC 33**
See also CA 5-8R; CAAS 8; CANR 4, 45;
DLB 5

Hood, Hugh (John Blagdon)
1928- . . . . **CLC 15, 28**
See also CA 49-52; CAAS 17; CANR 1, 33;
DLB 53

Hood, Thomas 1799-1845 . . . . **NCLC 16**
See also DLB 96

Hooker, (Peter) Jeremy 1941- . . . . . . **CLC 43**
See also CA 77-80; CANR 22; DLB 40

hooks, bell . . . . **CLC 94**
See also Watkins, Gloria

Hope, A(lec) D(erwent) 1907- . . . . **CLC 3, 51**
See also CA 21-24R; CANR 33; MTCW

Hope, Brian
See Creasey, John

Hope, Christopher (David Tully)
1944- . . . . **CLC 52**
See also CA 106; CANR 47; SATA 62

Hopkins, Gerard Manley
1844-1889 . . . . **NCLC 17; DA; DAB;
DAC; DAM MST, POET; PC 15; WLC**
See also CDBLB 1890-1914; DLB 35, 57

Hopkins, John (Richard) 1931- . . . . . . **CLC 4**
See also CA 85-88

Hopkins, Pauline Elizabeth
1859-1930 . . . . **TCLC 28; BLC;
DAM MULT**
See also BW 2; CA 141; DLB 50

Hopkinson, Francis 1737-1791 . . . . . . **LC 25**
See also DLB 31

Hopley-Woolrich, Cornell George 1903-1968
See Woolrich, Cornell
See also CA 13-14; CAP 1

Horatio
See Proust, (Valentin-Louis-George-Eugene-)
Marcel

Horgan, Paul (George Vincent O'Shaughnessy)
1903-1995 . . . . . . **CLC 9, 53; DAM NOV**
See also CA 13-16R; 147; CANR 9, 35;
DLB 102; DLBY 85; INT CANR-9;
MTCW; SATA 13; SATA-Obit 84

Horn, Peter
See Kuttner, Henry

Hornem, Horace Esq.
See Byron, George Gordon (Noel)

Hornung, E(rnest) W(illiam)
1866-1921 . . . . **TCLC 59**
See also CA 108; DLB 70

Horovitz, Israel (Arthur)
1939- . . . . **CLC 56; DAM DRAM**
See also CA 33-36R; CANR 46; DLB 7

Horvath, Odon von
See Horvath, Oedoen von
See also DLB 85, 124

Horvath, Oedoen von 1901-1938... **TCLC 45**
See also Horvath, Odon von
See also CA 118

Horwitz, Julius 1920-1986. . . . . **CLC 14**
See also CA 9-12R; 119; CANR 12

Hospital, Janette Turner 1942- . . . . . **CLC 42**
See also CA 108; CANR 48

Hostos, E. M. de
See Hostos (y Bonilla), Eugenio Maria de

Hostos, Eugenio M. de
See Hostos (y Bonilla), Eugenio Maria de

Hostos, Eugenio Maria
See Hostos (y Bonilla), Eugenio Maria de

Hostos (y Bonilla), Eugenio Maria de
1839-1903 . . . . **TCLC 24**
See also CA 123; 131; HW

Houdini
See Lovecraft, H(oward) P(hillips)

Hougan, Carolyn 1943- . . . . **CLC 34**
See also CA 139

Household, Geoffrey (Edward West)
1900-1988 . . . . **CLC 11**
See also CA 77-80; 126; DLB 87; SATA 14;
SATA-Obit 59

Housman, A(lfred) E(dward)
1859-1936 . . . . . **TCLC 1, 10; DA; DAB;**
DAC; DAM MST, POET; PC 2
See also CA 104; 125; DLB 19; MTCW

Housman, Laurence 1865-1959 . . . . . **TCLC 7**
See also CA 106; DLB 10; SATA 25

Howard, Elizabeth Jane 1923- . . . **CLC 7, 29**
See also CA 5-8R; CANR 8

Howard, Maureen 1930- . . . . . **CLC 5, 14, 46**
See also CA 53-56; CANR 31; DLBY 83;
INT CANR-31; MTCW

Howard, Richard 1929- . . . . . . **CLC 7, 10, 47**
See also AITN 1; CA 85-88; CANR 25;
DLB 5; INT CANR-25

Howard, Robert Ervin 1906-1936... **TCLC 8**
See also CA 105

Howard, Warren F.
See Pohl, Frederik

Howe, Fanny 1940- . . . . **CLC 47**
See also CA 117; SATA-Brief 52

Howe, Irving 1920-1993. . . . . **CLC 85**
See also CA 9-12R; 141; CANR 21, 50;
DLB 67; MTCW

Howe, Julia Ward 1819-1910 . . . . . **TCLC 21**
See also CA 117; DLB 1

Howe, Susan 1937- . . . . **CLC 72**
See also DLB 120

Howe, Tina 1937- . . . . **CLC 48**
See also CA 109

Howell, James 1594(?)-1666 . . . . **LC 13**
See also DLB 151

Howells, W. D.
See Howells, William Dean

Howells, William D.
See Howells, William Dean

Howells, William Dean
1837-1920 . . . . **TCLC 7, 17, 41**
See also CA 104; 134; CDALB 1865-1917;
DLB 12, 64, 74, 79

Howes, Barbara 1914-1996 . . . . **CLC 15**
See also CA 9-12R; 151; CAAS 3;
CANR 53; SATA 5

Hrabal, Bohumil 1914- . . . . **CLC 13, 67**
See also CA 106; CAAS 12

Hsun, Lu
See Lu Hsun

Hubbard, L(afayette) Ron(ald)
1911-1986 . . . . **CLC 43; DAM POP**
See also CA 77-80; 118; CANR 52

Huch, Ricarda (Octavia)
1864-1947 . . . . **TCLC 13**
See also CA 111; DLB 66

Huddle, David 1942- . . . . **CLC 49**
See also CA 57-60; CAAS 20; DLB 130

Hudson, Jeffrey
See Crichton, (John) Michael

Hudson, W(illiam) H(enry)
1841-1922 . . . . **TCLC 29**
See also CA 115; DLB 98, 153, 174;
SATA 35

Hueffer, Ford Madox
See Ford, Ford Madox

Hughart, Barry 1934- . . . . **CLC 39**
See also CA 137

Hughes, Colin
See Creasey, John

Hughes, David (John) 1930- . . . . **CLC 48**
See also CA 116; 129; DLB 14

Hughes, Edward James
See Hughes, Ted
See also DAM MST, POET

Hughes, (James) Langston
1902-1967 . . . . . **CLC 1, 5, 10, 15, 35, 44;**
BLC; DA; DAB; DAC; DAM DRAM,
MST, MULT, POET; DC 3; PC 1;
SSC 6; WLC
See also AAYA 12; BW 1; CA 1-4R;
25-28R; CANR 1, 34; CDALB 1929-1941;
CLR 17; DLB 4, 7, 48, 51, 86; JRDA;
MAICYA; MTCW; SATA 4, 33

Hughes, Richard (Arthur Warren)
1900-1976 . . . . . . **CLC 1, 11; DAM NOV**
See also CA 5-8R; 65-68; CANR 4;
DLB 15, 161; MTCW; SATA 8;
SATA-Obit 25

Hughes, Ted
1930- . . . . **CLC 2, 4, 9, 14, 37; DAB;**
DAC; PC 7
See also Hughes, Edward James
See also CA 1-4R; CANR 1, 33; CLR 3;
DLB 40, 161; MAICYA; MTCW;
SATA 49; SATA-Brief 27

Hugo, Richard F(ranklin)
1923-1982 . . . . **CLC 6, 18, 32;**
DAM POET
See also CA 49-52; 108; CANR 3; DLB 5

Hugo, Victor (Marie)
1802-1885 . . . . **NCLC 3, 10, 21; DA;**
DAB; DAC; DAM DRAM, MST, NOV,
POET; WLC
See also DLB 119; SATA 47

Huidobro, Vicente
See Huidobro Fernandez, Vicente Garcia

Huidobro Fernandez, Vicente Garcia
1893-1948 . . . . **TCLC 31**
See also CA 131; HW

Hulme, Keri 1947- . . . . **CLC 39**
See also CA 125; INT 125

Hulme, T(homas) E(rnest)
1883-1917 . . . . **TCLC 21**
See also CA 117; DLB 19

Hume, David 1711-1776. . . . . **LC 7**
See also DLB 104

Humphrey, William 1924- . . . . **CLC 45**
See also CA 77-80; DLB 6

Humphreys, Emyr Owen 1919- . . . . . **CLC 47**
See also CA 5-8R; CANR 3, 24; DLB 15

Humphreys, Josephine 1945- . . . . **CLC 34, 57**
See also CA 121; 127; INT 127

Huneker, James Gibbons
1857-1921 . . . . **TCLC 65**
See also DLB 71

Hungerford, Pixie
See Brinsmead, H(esba) F(ay)

Hunt, E(verette) Howard, (Jr.)
1918- . . . . **CLC 3**
See also AITN 1; CA 45-48; CANR 2, 47

Hunt, Kyle
See Creasey, John

Hunt, (James Henry) Leigh
1784-1859 . . . . . . **NCLC 1; DAM POET**

Hunt, Marsha 1946- . . . . **CLC 70**
See also BW 2; CA 143

Hunt, Violet 1866-1942 . . . . **TCLC 53**
See also DLB 162

Hunter, E. Waldo
See Sturgeon, Theodore (Hamilton)

Hunter, Evan
1926- . . . . **CLC 11, 31; DAM POP**
See also CA 5-8R; CANR 5, 38; DLBY 82;
INT CANR-5; MTCW; SATA 25

Hunter, Kristin (Eggleston) 1931- . . . **CLC 35**
See also AITN 1; BW 1; CA 13-16R;
CANR 13; CLR 3; DLB 33;
INT CANR-13; MAICYA; SAAS 10;
SATA 12

Hunter, Mollie 1922- . . . . **CLC 21**
See also McIlwraith, Maureen Mollie
Hunter
See also AAYA 13; CANR 37; CLR 25;
DLB 161; JRDA; MAICYA; SAAS 7;
SATA 54

Hunter, Robert (?)-1734. . . . . **LC 7**

Hurston, Zora Neale
1903-1960 . . . . **CLC 7, 30, 61; BLC; DA;**
DAC; DAM MST, MULT, NOV; SSC 4
See also AAYA 15; BW 1; CA 85-88;
DLB 51, 86; MTCW

Huston, John (Marcellus)
1906-1987 . . . . **CLC 20**
See also CA 73-76; 123; CANR 34; DLB 26

Levine, Norman 1924- . . . . **CLC 54**
See also CA 73-76; CAAS 23; CANR 14;
DLB 88

Levine, Philip
1928- . . . . **CLC 2, 4, 5, 9, 14, 33;**
DAM POET
See also CA 9-12R; CANR 9, 37, 52;
DLB 5

Levinson, Deirdre 1931- . . . . **CLC 49**
See also CA 73-76

Levi-Strauss, Claude 1908- . . . . **CLC 38**
See also CA 1-4R; CANR 6, 32; MTCW

Levitin, Sonia (Wolff) 1934- . . . . **CLC 17**
See also AAYA 13; CA 29-32R; CANR 14,
32; JRDA; MAICYA; SAAS 2; SATA 4,
68

Levon, O. U.
See Kesey, Ken (Elton)

Lewes, George Henry
1817-1878 . . . . **NCLC 25**
See also DLB 55, 144

Lewis, Alun 1915-1944 . . . . **TCLC 3**
See also CA 104; DLB 20, 162

Lewis, C. Day
See Day Lewis, C(ecil)

Lewis, C(live) S(taples)
1898-1963 . . . . . **CLC 1, 3, 6, 14, 27; DA;**
DAB; DAC; DAM MST, NOV, POP;
WLC
See also AAYA 3; CA 81-84; CANR 33;
CDBLB 1945-1960; CLR 3, 27; DLB 15,
100, 160; JRDA; MAICYA; MTCW;
SATA 13

Lewis, Janet 1899- . . . . **CLC 41**
See Winters, Janet Lewis
See also CA 9-12R; CANR 29; CAP 1;
DLBY 87

Lewis, Matthew Gregory
1775-1818 . . . . **NCLC 11**
See also DLB 39, 158

Lewis, (Harry) Sinclair
1885-1951 . . . . . **TCLC 4, 13, 23, 39; DA;**
DAB; DAC; DAM MST, NOV; WLC
See also CA 104; 133; CDALB 1917-1929;
DLB 9, 102; DLBD 1; MTCW

Lewis, (Percy) Wyndham
1884(?)-1957 . . . . **TCLC 2, 9**
See also CA 104; DLB 15

Lewisohn, Ludwig 1883-1955 . . . . . . **TCLC 19**
See also CA 107; DLB 4, 9, 28, 102

Leyner, Mark 1956- . . . . **CLC 92**
See also CA 110; CANR 28, 53

Lezama Lima, Jose
1910-1976 . . . . **CLC 4, 10; DAM MULT**
See also CA 77-80; DLB 113; HW

L'Heureux, John (Clarke) 1934- . . . . **CLC 52**
See also CA 13-16R; CANR 23, 45

Liddell, C. H.
See Kuttner, Henry

Lie, Jonas (Lauritz Idemil)
1833-1908(?) . . . . **TCLC 5**
See also CA 115

Lieber, Joel 1937-1971 . . . . **CLC 6**
See also CA 73-76; 29-32R

Lieber, Stanley Martin
See Lee, Stan

Lieberman, Laurence (James)
1935- . . . . **CLC 4, 36**
See also CA 17-20R; CANR 8, 36

Lieksman, Anders
See Haavikko, Paavo Juhani

Li Fei-kan 1904-
See Pa Chin
See also CA 105

Lifton, Robert Jay 1926- . . . . **CLC 67**
See also CA 17-20R; CANR 27;
INT CANR-27; SATA 66

Lightfoot, Gordon 1938- . . . . **CLC 26**
See also CA 109

Lightman, Alan P. 1948- . . . . **CLC 81**
See also CA 141

Ligotti, Thomas (Robert)
1953- . . . . **CLC 44; SSC 16**
See also CA 123; CANR 49

Li Ho 791-817 . . . . **PC 13**

Liliencron, (Friedrich Adolf Axel) Detlev von
1844-1909 . . . . **TCLC 18**
See also CA 117

Lilly, William 1602-1681 . . . . **LC 27**

Lima, Jose Lezama
See Lezama Lima, Jose

Lima Barreto, Afonso Henrique de
1881-1922 . . . . **TCLC 23**
See also CA 117

Limonov, Edward 1944- . . . . **CLC 67**
See also CA 137

Lin, Frank
See Atherton, Gertrude (Franklin Horn)

Lincoln, Abraham 1809-1865 . . . . . **NCLC 18**

Lind, Jakov . . . . **CLC 1, 2, 4, 27, 82**
See also Landwirth, Heinz
See also CAAS 4

Lindbergh, Anne (Spencer) Morrow
1906- . . . . **CLC 82; DAM NOV**
See also CA 17-20R; CANR 16; MTCW;
SATA 33

Lindsay, David 1878-1945 . . . . **TCLC 15**
See also CA 113

Lindsay, (Nicholas) Vachel
1879-1931 . . . . **TCLC 17; DA; DAC;**
DAM MST, POET; WLC
See also CA 114; 135; CDALB 1865-1917;
DLB 54; SATA 40

Linke-Poot
See Doeblin, Alfred

Linney, Romulus 1930- . . . . **CLC 51**
See also CA 1-4R; CANR 40, 44

Linton, Eliza Lynn 1822-1898 . . . . **NCLC 41**
See also DLB 18

Li Po 701-763 . . . . **CMLC 2**

Lipsius, Justus 1547-1606 . . . . **LC 16**

Lipsyte, Robert (Michael)
1938- . . . . **CLC 21; DA; DAC;**
DAM MST, NOV
See also AAYA 7; CA 17-20R; CANR 8;
CLR 23; JRDA; MAICYA; SATA 5, 68

Lish, Gordon (Jay) 1934- . . **CLC 45; SSC 18**
See also CA 113; 117; DLB 130; INT 117

Lispector, Clarice 1925-1977 . . . . . . **CLC 43**
See also CA 139; 116; DLB 113

Littell, Robert 1935(?)- . . . . **CLC 42**
See also CA 109; 112

Little, Malcolm 1925-1965
See Malcolm X
See also BW 1; CA 125; 111; DA; DAB;
DAC; DAM MST, MULT; MTCW

Littlewit, Humphrey Gent.
See Lovecraft, H(oward) P(hillips)

Litwos
See Sienkiewicz, Henryk (Adam Alexander
Pius)

Liu E 1857-1909 . . . . **TCLC 15**
See also CA 115

Lively, Penelope (Margaret)
1933- . . . . **CLC 32, 50; DAM NOV**
See also CA 41-44R; CANR 29; CLR 7;
DLB 14, 161; JRDA; MAICYA; MTCW;
SATA 7, 60

Livesay, Dorothy (Kathleen)
1909- . . . . **CLC 4, 15, 79; DAC;**
DAM MST, POET
See also AITN 2; CA 25-28R; CAAS 8;
CANR 36; DLB 68; MTCW

Livy c. 59B.C.-c. 17 . . . . **CMLC 11**

Lizardi, Jose Joaquin Fernandez de
1776-1827 . . . . **NCLC 30**

Llewellyn, Richard
See Llewellyn Lloyd, Richard Dafydd
Vivian
See also DLB 15

Llewellyn Lloyd, Richard Dafydd Vivian
1906-1983 . . . . **CLC 7, 80**
See also Llewellyn, Richard
See also CA 53-56; 111; CANR 7;
SATA 11; SATA-Obit 37

Llosa, (Jorge) Mario (Pedro) Vargas
See Vargas Llosa, (Jorge) Mario (Pedro)

Lloyd Webber, Andrew 1948-
See Webber, Andrew Lloyd
See also AAYA 1; CA 116; 149;
DAM DRAM; SATA 56

Llull, Ramon c. 1235-c. 1316 . . . . . **CMLC 12**

Locke, Alain (Le Roy)
1886-1954 . . . . **TCLC 43**
See also BW 1; CA 106; 124; DLB 51

Locke, John 1632-1704 . . . . **LC 7, 35**
See also DLB 101

Locke-Elliott, Sumner
See Elliott, Sumner Locke

Lockhart, John Gibson
1794-1854 . . . . **NCLC 6**
See also DLB 110, 116, 144

Lodge, David (John)
1935- . . . . **CLC 36; DAM POP**
See also BEST 90:1; CA 17-20R; CANR 19,
53; DLB 14; INT CANR-19; MTCW

Loennbohm, Armas Eino Leopold 1878-1926
See Leino, Eino
See also CA 123

Loewinsohn, Ron(ald William)
1937- . . . . **CLC 52**
See also CA 25-28R

MacCarthy, (Sir Charles Otto) Desmond
1877-1952 .... TCLC 36

MacDiarmid, Hugh
.... CLC 2, 4, 11, 19, 63; PC 9
See also Grieve, C(hristopher) M(urray)
See also CDBLB 1945-1960; DLB 20

MacDonald, Anson
See Heinlein, Robert A(nson)

Macdonald, Cynthia 1928- ..... CLC 13, 19
See also CA 49-52; CANR 4, 44; DLB 105

MacDonald, George 1824-1905 .... TCLC 9
See also CA 106; 137; DLB 18, 163;
MAICYA; SATA 33

Macdonald, John
See Millar, Kenneth

MacDonald, John D(ann)
1916-1986 .... CLC 3, 27, 44;
DAM NOV, POP
See also CA 1-4R; 121; CANR 1, 19;
DLB 8; DLBY 86; MTCW

Macdonald, John Ross
See Millar, Kenneth

Macdonald, Ross..... CLC 1, 2, 3, 14, 34, 41
See also Millar, Kenneth
See also DLBD 6

MacDougal, John
See Blish, James (Benjamin)

MacEwen, Gwendolyn (Margaret)
1941-1987 .... CLC 13, 55
See also CA 9-12R; 124; CANR 7, 22;
DLB 53; SATA 50; SATA-Obit 55

Macha, Karel Hynek 1810-1846 .. NCLC 46

Machado (y Ruiz), Antonio
1875-1939 .... TCLC 3
See also CA 104; DLB 108

Machado de Assis, Joaquim Maria
1839-1908 ..... TCLC 10; BLC; SSC 24
See also CA 107; 153

Machen, Arthur.......... TCLC 4; SSC 20
See also Jones, Arthur Llewellyn
See also DLB 36, 156

Machiavelli, Niccolo
1469-1527 .... LC 8, 36; DA; DAB;
DAC; DAM MST

MacInnes, Colin 1914-1976 ...... CLC 4, 23
See also CA 69-72; 65-68; CANR 21;
DLB 14; MTCW

MacInnes, Helen (Clark)
1907-1985 ..... CLC 27, 39; DAM POP
See also CA 1-4R; 117; CANR 1, 28;
DLB 87; MTCW; SATA 22;
SATA-Obit 44

Mackay, Mary 1855-1924
See Corelli, Marie
See also CA 118

Mackenzie, Compton (Edward Montague)
1883-1972 .... CLC 18
See also CA 21-22; 37-40R; CAP 2;
DLB 34, 100

Mackenzie, Henry 1745-1831 .... NCLC 41
See also DLB 39

Mackintosh, Elizabeth 1896(?)-1952
See Tey, Josephine
See also CA 110

MacLaren, James
See Grieve, C(hristopher) M(urray)

Mac Laverty, Bernard 1942- .... CLC 31
See also CA 116; 118; CANR 43; INT 118

MacLean, Alistair (Stuart)
1922-1987 .... CLC 3, 13, 50, 63;
DAM POP
See also CA 57-60; 121; CANR 28; MTCW;
SATA 23; SATA-Obit 50

Maclean, Norman (Fitzroy)
1902-1990 .... CLC 78; DAM POP;
SSC 13
See also CA 102; 132; CANR 49

MacLeish, Archibald
1892-1982 .... CLC 3, 8, 14, 68;
DAM POET
See also CA 9-12R; 106; CANR 33; DLB 4,
7, 45; DLBY 82; MTCW

MacLennan, (John) Hugh
1907-1990 .... CLC 2, 14, 92; DAC;
DAM MST
See also CA 5-8R; 142; CANR 33; DLB 68;
MTCW

MacLeod, Alistair
1936- ...... CLC 56; DAC; DAM MST
See also CA 123; DLB 60

MacNeice, (Frederick) Louis
1907-1963 ...... CLC 1, 4, 10, 53; DAB;
DAM POET
See also CA 85-88; DLB 10, 20; MTCW

MacNeill, Dand
See Fraser, George MacDonald

Macpherson, James 1736-1796 ...... LC 29
See also DLB 109

Macpherson, (Jean) Jay 1931- ...... CLC 14
See also CA 5-8R; DLB 53

MacShane, Frank 1927- .... CLC 39
See also CA 9-12R; CANR 3, 33; DLB 111

Macumber, Mari
See Sandoz, Mari(e Susette)

Madach, Imre 1823-1864 .... NCLC 19

Madden, (Jerry) David 1933- .... CLC 5, 15
See also CA 1-4R; CAAS 3; CANR 4, 45;
DLB 6; MTCW

Maddern, Al(an)
See Ellison, Harlan (Jay)

Madhubuti, Haki R.
1942- .... CLC 6, 73; BLC;
DAM MULT, POET; PC 5
See also Lee, Don L.
See also BW 2; CA 73-76; CANR 24, 51;
DLB 5, 41; DLBD 8

Maepenn, Hugh
See Kuttner, Henry

Maepenn, K. H.
See Kuttner, Henry

Maeterlinck, Maurice
1862-1949 ...... TCLC 3; DAM DRAM
See also CA 104; 136; SATA 66

Maginn, William 1794-1842 ...... NCLC 8
See also DLB 110, 159

Mahapatra, Jayanta
1928- .... CLC 33; DAM MULT
See also CA 73-76; CAAS 9; CANR 15, 33

Mahfouz, Naguib (Abdel Aziz Al-Sabilgi)
1911(?)-
See Mahfuz, Najib
See also BEST 89:2; CA 128; CANR 55;
DAM NOV; MTCW

Mahfuz, Najib .... CLC 52, 55
See also Mahfouz, Naguib (Abdel Aziz
Al-Sabilgi)
See also DLBY 88

Mahon, Derek 1941- .... CLC 27
See also CA 113; 128; DLB 40

Mailer, Norman
1923- ...... CLC 1, 2, 3, 4, 5, 8, 11, 14,
28, 39, 74; DA; DAB; DAC; DAM MST,
NOV, POP
See also AITN 2; CA 9-12R; CABS 1;
CANR 28; CDALB 1968-1988; DLB 2,
16, 28; DLBD 3; DLBY 80, 83; MTCW

Maillet, Antonine 1929- ...... CLC 54; DAC
See also CA 115; 120; CANR 46; DLB 60;
INT 120

Mais, Roger 1905-1955 .... TCLC 8
See also BW 1; CA 105; 124; DLB 125;
MTCW

Maistre, Joseph de 1753-1821 .... NCLC 37

Maitland, Frederic 1850-1906 ..... TCLC 65

Maitland, Sara (Louise) 1950- ...... CLC 49
See also CA 69-72; CANR 13

Major, Clarence
1936- .... CLC 3, 19, 48; BLC;
DAM MULT
See also BW 2; CA 21-24R; CAAS 6;
CANR 13, 25, 53; DLB 33

Major, Kevin (Gerald)
1949- .... CLC 26; DAC
See also AAYA 16; CA 97-100; CANR 21,
38; CLR 11; DLB 60; INT CANR-21;
JRDA; MAICYA; SATA 32, 82

Maki, James
See Ozu, Yasujiro

Malabaila, Damiano
See Levi, Primo

Malamud, Bernard
1914-1986 ...... CLC 1, 2, 3, 5, 8, 9, 11,
18, 27, 44, 78, 85; DA; DAB; DAC;
DAM MST, NOV, POP; SSC 15; WLC
See also AAYA 16; CA 5-8R; 118; CABS 1;
CANR 28; CDALB 1941-1968; DLB 2,
28, 152; DLBY 80, 86; MTCW

Malaparte, Curzio 1898-1957 ..... TCLC 52

Malcolm, Dan
See Silverberg, Robert

Malcolm X................. CLC 82; BLC
See also Little, Malcolm

Malherbe, Francois de 1555-1628 ..... LC 5

Mallarme, Stephane
1842-1898 .... NCLC 4, 41;
DAM POET; PC 4

Mallet-Joris, Francoise 1930- ...... CLC 11
See also CA 65-68; CANR 17; DLB 83

Malley, Ern
See McAuley, James Phillip

Mallowan, Agatha Christie
See Christie, Agatha (Mary Clarissa)

McCauley, Stephen (D.) 1955- ..... **CLC 50**
See also CA 141

McClure, Michael (Thomas)
1932- .... **CLC 6, 10**
See also CA 21-24R; CANR 17, 46;
DLB 16

McCorkle, Jill (Collins) 1958-..... **CLC 51**
See also CA 121; DLBY 87

McCourt, James 1941-............ **CLC 5**
See also CA 57-60

McCoy, Horace (Stanley)
1897-1955 .... **TCLC 28**
See also CA 108; DLB 9

McCrae, John 1872-1918........ **TCLC 12**
See also CA 109; DLB 92

McCreigh, James
See Pohl, Frederik

McCullers, (Lula) Carson (Smith)
1917-1967 .... **CLC 1, 4, 10, 12, 48; DA;
DAB; DAC; DAM MST, NOV; SSC 24;
WLC**
See also CA 5-8R; 25-28R; CABS 1, 3;
CANR 18; CDALB 1941-1968; DLB 2, 7,
173; MTCW; SATA 27

McCulloch, John Tyler
See Burroughs, Edgar Rice

McCullough, Colleen
1938(?)- .... **CLC 27; DAM NOV, POP**
See also CA 81-84; CANR 17, 46; MTCW

McDermott, Alice 1953- .... **CLC 90**
See also CA 109; CANR 40

McElroy, Joseph 1930- .... **CLC 5, 47**
See also CA 17-20R

McEwan, Ian (Russell)
1948- .... **CLC 13, 66; DAM NOV**
See also BEST 90:4; CA 61-64; CANR 14,
41; DLB 14; MTCW

McFadden, David 1940-.......... **CLC 48**
See also CA 104; DLB 60; INT 104

McFarland, Dennis 1950- .... **CLC 65**

McGahern, John
1934- .... **CLC 5, 9, 48; SSC 17**
See also CA 17-20R; CANR 29; DLB 14;
MTCW

McGinley, Patrick (Anthony)
1937- .... **CLC 41**
See also CA 120; 127; INT 127

McGinley, Phyllis 1905-1978 ...... **CLC 14**
See also CA 9-12R; 77-80; CANR 19;
DLB 11, 48; SATA 2, 44; SATA-Obit 24

McGinniss, Joe 1942-............ **CLC 32**
See also AITN 2; BEST 89:2; CA 25-28R;
CANR 26; INT CANR-26

McGivern, Maureen Daly
See Daly, Maureen

McGrath, Patrick 1950-.......... **CLC 55**
See also CA 136

McGrath, Thomas (Matthew)
1916-1990 .... **CLC 28, 59; DAM POET**
See also CA 9-12R; 132; CANR 6, 33;
MTCW; SATA 41; SATA-Obit 66

McGuane, Thomas (Francis III)
1939- .... **CLC 3, 7, 18, 45**
See also AITN 2; CA 49-52; CANR 5, 24,
49; DLB 2; DLBY 80; INT CANR-24;
MTCW

McGuckian, Medbh
1950- .... **CLC 48; DAM POET**
See also CA 143; DLB 40

McHale, Tom 1942(?)-1982....... **CLC 3, 5**
See also AITN 1; CA 77-80; 106

McIlvanney, William 1936-........ **CLC 42**
See also CA 25-28R; DLB 14

McIlwraith, Maureen Mollie Hunter
See Hunter, Mollie
See also SATA 2

McInerney, Jay
1955- .... **CLC 34; DAM POP**
See also AAYA 18; CA 116; 123;
CANR 45; INT 123

McIntyre, Vonda N(eel) 1948- ..... **CLC 18**
See also CA 81-84; CANR 17, 34; MTCW

McKay, Claude
.... **TCLC 7, 41; BLC; DAB; PC 2**
See also McKay, Festus Claudius
See also DLB 4, 45, 51, 117

McKay, Festus Claudius 1889-1948
See McKay, Claude
See also BW 1; CA 104; 124; DA; DAC;
DAM MST, MULT, NOV, POET;
MTCW; WLC

McKuen, Rod 1933-............. **CLC 1, 3**
See also AITN 1; CA 41-44R; CANR 40

McLoughlin, R. B.
See Mencken, H(enry) L(ouis)

McLuhan, (Herbert) Marshall
1911-1980 .... **CLC 37, 83**
See also CA 9-12R; 102; CANR 12, 34;
DLB 88; INT CANR-12; MTCW

McMillan, Terry (L.)
1951- .... **CLC 50, 61; DAM MULT,
NOV, POP**
See also BW 2; CA 140

McMurtry, Larry (Jeff)
1936- .... **CLC 2, 3, 7, 11, 27, 44;
DAM NOV, POP**
See also AAYA 15; AITN 2; BEST 89:2;
CA 5-8R; CANR 19, 43;
CDALB 1968-1988; DLB 2, 143;
DLBY 80, 87; MTCW

McNally, T. M. 1961-............ **CLC 82**

McNally, Terrence
1939- ... **CLC 4, 7, 41, 91; DAM DRAM**
See also CA 45-48; CANR 2; DLB 7

McNamer, Deirdre 1950-......... **CLC 70**

McNeile, Herman Cyril 1888-1937
See Sapper
See also DLB 77

McNickle, (William) D'Arcy
1904-1977 ...... **CLC 89; DAM MULT**
See also CA 9-12R; 85-88; CANR 5, 45;
NNAL; SATA-Obit 22

McPhee, John (Angus) 1931- ...... **CLC 36**
See also BEST 90:1; CA 65-68; CANR 20,
46; MTCW

McPherson, James Alan
1943- .... **CLC 19, 77**
See also BW 1; CA 25-28R; CAAS 17;
CANR 24; DLB 38; MTCW

McPherson, William (Alexander)
1933- .... **CLC 34**
See also CA 69-72; CANR 28;
INT CANR-28

Mead, Margaret 1901-1978 .... **CLC 37**
See also AITN 1; CA 1-4R; 81-84;
CANR 4; MTCW; SATA-Obit 20

Meaker, Marijane (Agnes) 1927-
See Kerr, M. E.
See also CA 107; CANR 37; INT 107;
JRDA; MAICYA; MTCW; SATA 20, 61

Medoff, Mark (Howard)
1940- .... **CLC 6, 23; DAM DRAM**
See also AITN 1; CA 53-56; CANR 5;
DLB 7; INT CANR-5

Medvedev, P. N.
See Bakhtin, Mikhail Mikhailovich

Meged, Aharon
See Megged, Aharon

Meged, Aron
See Megged, Aharon

Megged, Aharon 1920-............. **CLC 9**
See also CA 49-52; CAAS 13; CANR 1

Mehta, Ved (Parkash) 1934-....... **CLC 37**
See also CA 1-4R; CANR 2, 23; MTCW

Melanter
See Blackmore, R(ichard) D(oddridge)

Melikow, Loris
See Hofmannsthal, Hugo von

Melmoth, Sebastian
See Wilde, Oscar (Fingal O'Flahertie Wills)

Meltzer, Milton 1915- .... **CLC 26**
See also AAYA 8; CA 13-16R; CANR 38;
CLR 13; DLB 61; JRDA; MAICYA;
SAAS 1; SATA 1, 50, 80

Melville, Herman
1819-1891 ..... **NCLC 3, 12, 29, 45, 49;
DA; DAB; DAC; DAM MST, NOV;
SSC 1, 17; WLC**
See also CDALB 1640-1865; DLB 3, 74;
SATA 59

Menander
c. 342B.C.-c. 292B.C......... **CMLC 9;
DAM DRAM; DC 3**

Mencken, H(enry) L(ouis)
1880-1956 .... **TCLC 13**
See also CA 105; 125; CDALB 1917-1929;
DLB 11, 29, 63, 137; MTCW

Mercer, David
1928-1980 .... **CLC 5; DAM DRAM**
See also CA 9-12R; 102; CANR 23;
DLB 13; MTCW

Merchant, Paul
See Ellison, Harlan (Jay)

Meredith, George
1828-1909 .. **TCLC 17, 43; DAM POET**
See also CA 117; 153; CDBLB 1832-1890;
DLB 18, 35, 57, 159

Meredith, William (Morris)
1919- .. **CLC 4, 13, 22, 55; DAM POET**
See also CA 9-12R; CAAS 14; CANR 6, 40;
DLB 5

Merezhkovsky, Dmitry Sergeyevich
1865-1941 .... **TCLC 29**

Merimee, Prosper
1803-1870 .... **NCLC 6; SSC 7**
See also DLB 119

Merkin, Daphne 1954- .... **CLC 44**
See also CA 123

Merlin, Arthur
See Blish, James (Benjamin)

Merrill, James (Ingram)
1926-1995 .... **CLC 2, 3, 6, 8, 13, 18, 34,**
91; DAM POET
See also CA 13-16R; 147; CANR 10, 49;
DLB 5, 165; DLBY 85; INT CANR-10;
MTCW

Merriman, Alex
See Silverberg, Robert

Merritt, E. B.
See Waddington, Miriam

Merton, Thomas
1915-1968 .. **CLC 1, 3, 11, 34, 83; PC 10**
See also CA 5-8R; 25-28R; CANR 22, 53;
DLB 48; DLBY 81; MTCW

Merwin, W(illiam) S(tanley)
1927- ...... **CLC 1, 2, 3, 5, 8, 13, 18, 45,**
88; DAM POET
See also CA 13-16R; CANR 15, 51; DLB 5,
169; INT CANR-15; MTCW

Metcalf, John 1938- .... **CLC 37**
See also CA 113; DLB 60

Metcalf, Suzanne
See Baum, L(yman) Frank

Mew, Charlotte (Mary)
1870-1928 .... **TCLC 8**
See also CA 105; DLB 19, 135

Mewshaw, Michael 1943- .... **CLC 9**
See also CA 53-56; CANR 7, 47; DLBY 80

Meyer, June
See Jordan, June

Meyer, Lynn
See Slavitt, David R(ytman)

Meyer-Meyrink, Gustav 1868-1932
See Meyrink, Gustav
See also CA 117

Meyers, Jeffrey 1939- .... **CLC 39**
See also CA 73-76; CANR 54; DLB 111

Meynell, Alice (Christina Gertrude Thompson)
1847-1922 .... **TCLC 6**
See also CA 104; DLB 19, 98

Meyrink, Gustav .... **TCLC 21**
See also Meyer-Meyrink, Gustav
See also DLB 81

Michaels, Leonard
1933- .... **CLC 6, 25; SSC 16**
See also CA 61-64; CANR 21; DLB 130;
MTCW

Michaux, Henri 1899-1984 ..... **CLC 8, 19**
See also CA 85-88; 114

Michelangelo 1475-1564 .... **LC 12**

Michelet, Jules 1798-1874 .... **NCLC 31**

Michener, James A(lbert)
1907(?)- .... **CLC 1, 5, 11, 29, 60;**
DAM NOV, POP
See also AITN 1; BEST 90:1; CA 5-8R;
CANR 21, 45; DLB 6; MTCW

Mickiewicz, Adam 1798-1855 ..... **NCLC 3**

Middleton, Christopher 1926- ...... **CLC 13**
See also CA 13-16R; CANR 29, 54;
DLB 40

Middleton, Richard (Barham)
1882-1911 .... **TCLC 56**
See also DLB 156

Middleton, Stanley 1919- .... **CLC 7, 38**
See also CA 25-28R; CAAS 23; CANR 21,
46; DLB 14

Middleton, Thomas
1580-1627 .... **LC 33; DAM DRAM,**
MST; DC 5
See also DLB 58

Migueis, Jose Rodrigues 1901- ..... **CLC 10**

Mikszath, Kalman 1847-1910 ..... **TCLC 31**

Miles, Josephine (Louise)
1911-1985 .... **CLC 1, 2, 14, 34, 39;**
DAM POET
See also CA 1-4R; 116; CANR 2, 55;
DLB 48

Militant
See Sandburg, Carl (August)

Mill, John Stuart 1806-1873 .. **NCLC 11, 58**
See also CDBLB 1832-1890; DLB 55

Millar, Kenneth
1915-1983 .... **CLC 14; DAM POP**
See also Macdonald, Ross
See also CA 9-12R; 110; CANR 16; DLB 2;
DLBD 6; DLBY 83; MTCW

Millay, E. Vincent
See Millay, Edna St. Vincent

Millay, Edna St. Vincent
1892-1950 ...... **TCLC 4, 49; DA; DAB;**
DAC; DAM MST, POET; PC 6
See also CA 104; 130; CDALB 1917-1929;
DLB 45; MTCW

Miller, Arthur
1915- .... **CLC 1, 2, 6, 10, 15, 26, 47, 78;**
DA; DAB; DAC; DAM DRAM, MST;
DC 1; WLC
See also AAYA 15; AITN 1; CA 1-4R;
CABS 3; CANR 2, 30, 54;
CDALB 1941-1968; DLB 7; MTCW

Miller, Henry (Valentine)
1891-1980 .... **CLC 1, 2, 4, 9, 14, 43, 84;**
DA; DAB; DAC; DAM MST, NOV;
WLC
See also CA 9-12R; 97-100; CANR 33;
CDALB 1929-1941; DLB 4, 9; DLBY 80;
MTCW

Miller, Jason 1939(?)- .... **CLC 2**
See also AITN 1; CA 73-76; DLB 7

Miller, Sue 1943- ..... **CLC 44; DAM POP**
See also BEST 90:3; CA 139; DLB 143

Miller, Walter M(ichael, Jr.)
1923- .... **CLC 4, 30**
See also CA 85-88; DLB 8

Millett, Kate 1934- .... **CLC 67**
See also AITN 1; CA 73-76; CANR 32, 53;
MTCW

Millhauser, Steven 1943- .... **CLC 21, 54**
See also CA 110; 111; DLB 2; INT 111

Millin, Sarah Gertrude 1889-1968 .. **CLC 49**
See also CA 102; 93-96

Milne, A(lan) A(lexander)
1882-1956 .... **TCLC 6; DAB; DAC;**
DAM MST
See also CA 104; 133; CLR 1, 26; DLB 10,
77, 100, 160; MAICYA; MTCW;
YABC 1

Milner, Ron(ald)
1938- ..... **CLC 56; BLC; DAM MULT**
See also AITN 1; BW 1; CA 73-76;
CANR 24; DLB 38; MTCW

Milosz, Czeslaw
1911- .... **CLC 5, 11, 22, 31, 56, 82;**
DAM MST, POET; PC 8
See also CA 81-84; CANR 23, 51; MTCW

Milton, John
1608-1674 ...... **LC 9; DA; DAB; DAC;**
DAM MST, POET; WLC
See also CDBLB 1660-1789; DLB 131, 151

Min, Anchee 1957- .... **CLC 86**
See also CA 146

Minehaha, Cornelius
See Wedekind, (Benjamin) Frank(lin)

Miner, Valerie 1947- .... **CLC 40**
See also CA 97-100

Minimo, Duca
See D'Annunzio, Gabriele

Minot, Susan 1956- .... **CLC 44**
See also CA 134

Minus, Ed 1938- .... **CLC 39**

Miranda, Javier
See Bioy Casares, Adolfo

Mirbeau, Octave 1848-1917 ...... **TCLC 55**
See also DLB 123

Miro (Ferrer), Gabriel (Francisco Victor)
1879-1930 .... **TCLC 5**
See also CA 104

Mishima, Yukio
.... **CLC 2, 4, 6, 9, 27; DC 1; SSC 4**
See also Hiraoka, Kimitake

Mistral, Frederic 1830-1914 ...... **TCLC 51**
See also CA 122

Mistral, Gabriela .... **TCLC 2; HLC**
See also Godoy Alcayaga, Lucila

Mistry, Rohinton 1952- ...... **CLC 71; DAC**
See also CA 141

Mitchell, Clyde
See Ellison, Harlan (Jay); Silverberg, Robert

Mitchell, James Leslie 1901-1935
See Gibbon, Lewis Grassic
See also CA 104; DLB 15

Mitchell, Joni 1943- .... **CLC 12**
See also CA 112

Mitchell, Joseph (Quincy)
1908-1996 .... **CLC 98**
See also CA 77-80; 152

Mitchell, Margaret (Munnerlyn)
1900-1949 ...... **TCLC 11; DAM NOV,**
POP
See also CA 109; 125; CANR 55; DLB 9;
MTCW

Mitchell, Peggy
See Mitchell, Margaret (Munnerlyn)

Mitchell, S(ilas) Weir 1829-1914 .. **TCLC 36**

Author Index

Morris, William   1834-1896 . . . .   **NCLC 4**
See also CDBLB 1832-1890; DLB 18, 35, 57, 156

Morris, Wright   1910-. . .   **CLC 1, 3, 7, 18, 37**
See also CA 9-12R; CANR 21; DLB 2; DLBY 81; MTCW

Morrison, Chloe Anthony Wofford
See Morrison, Toni

Morrison, James Douglas   1943-1971
See Morrison, Jim
See also CA 73-76; CANR 40

Morrison, Jim . . . .   **CLC 17**
See also Morrison, James Douglas

Morrison, Toni
1931- . . . .   **CLC 4, 10, 22, 55, 81, 87;**
BLC; DA; DAB; DAC; DAM MST,
MULT, NOV, POP
See also AAYA 1; BW 2; CA 29-32R; CANR 27, 42; CDALB 1968-1988; DLB 6, 33, 143; DLBY 81; MTCW; SATA 57

Morrison, Van   1945- . . . .   **CLC 21**
See also CA 116

Mortimer, John (Clifford)
1923- . . . . . .   **CLC 28, 43; DAM DRAM,**
POP
See also CA 13-16R; CANR 21; CDBLB 1960 to Present; DLB 13; INT CANR-21; MTCW

Mortimer, Penelope (Ruth)   1918-. . . .   **CLC 5**
See also CA 57-60; CANR 45

Morton, Anthony
See Creasey, John

Mosher, Howard Frank   1943-. . . . . .   **CLC 62**
See also CA 139

Mosley, Nicholas   1923-. . . . .   **CLC 43, 70**
See also CA 69-72; CANR 41; DLB 14

Mosley, Walter
1952- . . . . .   **CLC 97; DAM MULT, POP**
See also AAYA 17; BW 2; CA 142

Moss, Howard
1922-1987 . . . .   **CLC 7, 14, 45, 50;**
DAM POET
See also CA 1-4R; 123; CANR 1, 44; DLB 5

Mossgiel, Rab
See Burns, Robert

Motion, Andrew (Peter)   1952-. . . . . .   **CLC 47**
See also CA 146; DLB 40

Motley, Willard (Francis)
1909-1965 . . . .   **CLC 18**
See also BW 1; CA 117; 106; DLB 76, 143

Motoori, Norinaga   1730-1801 . . . .   **NCLC 45**

Mott, Michael (Charles Alston)
1930- . . . .   **CLC 15, 34**
See also CA 5-8R; CAAS 7; CANR 7, 29

Mountain Wolf Woman
1884-1960 . . . .   **CLC 92**
See also CA 144; NNAL

Moure, Erin   1955- . . . .   **CLC 88**
See also CA 113; DLB 60

Mowat, Farley (McGill)
1921- . . . . . .   **CLC 26; DAC; DAM MST**
See also AAYA 1; CA 1-4R; CANR 4, 24, 42; CLR 20; DLB 68; INT CANAR-24; JRDA; MAICYA; MTCW; SATA 3, 55

Moyers, Bill   1934-. . . . .   **CLC 74**
See also AITN 2; CA 61-64; CANR 31, 52

Mphahlele, Es'kia
See Mphahlele, Ezekiel
See also DLB 125

Mphahlele, Ezekiel
1919- . . . . .   **CLC 25; BLC; DAM MULT**
See also Mphahlele, Es'kia
See also BW 2; CA 81-84; CANR 26

Mqhayi, S(amuel) E(dward) K(rune Loliwe)
1875-1945 . . . .   **TCLC 25; BLC;**
DAM MULT
See also CA 153

Mrozek, Slawomir   1930-. . . . .   **CLC 3, 13**
See also CA 13-16R; CAAS 10; CANR 29; MTCW

Mrs. Belloc-Lowndes
See Lowndes, Marie Adelaide (Belloc)

Mtwa, Percy   (?)-. . . . .   **CLC 47**

Mueller, Lisel   1924-. . . . .   **CLC 13, 51**
See also CA 93-96; DLB 105

Muir, Edwin   1887-1959 . . . .   **TCLC 2**
See also CA 104; DLB 20, 100

Muir, John   1838-1914 . . . .   **TCLC 28**

Mujica Lainez, Manuel
1910-1984 . . . .   **CLC 31**
See also Lainez, Manuel Mujica
See also CA 81-84; 112; CANR 32; HW

Mukherjee, Bharati
1940- . . . .   **CLC 53; DAM NOV**
See also BEST 89:2; CA 107; CANR 45; DLB 60; MTCW

Muldoon, Paul
1951- . . . .   **CLC 32, 72; DAM POET**
See also CA 113; 129; CANR 52; DLB 40; INT 129

Mulisch, Harry   1927-. . . . .   **CLC 42**
See also CA 9-12R; CANR 6, 26

Mull, Martin   1943-. . . . .   **CLC 17**
See also CA 105

Mulock, Dinah Maria
See Craik, Dinah Maria (Mulock)

Munford, Robert   1737(?)-1783 . . . .   **LC 5**
See also DLB 31

Mungo, Raymond   1946-. . . . .   **CLC 72**
See also CA 49-52; CANR 2

Munro, Alice
1931- . . . . . .   **CLC 6, 10, 19, 50, 95; DAC;**
DAM MST, NOV; SSC 3
See also AITN 2; CA 33-36R; CANR 33, 53; DLB 53; MTCW; SATA 29

Munro, H(ector) H(ugh)   1870-1916
See Saki
See also CA 104; 130; CDBLB 1890-1914; DA; DAB; DAC; DAM MST, NOV; DLB 34, 162; MTCW; WLC

Murasaki, Lady. . . . .   **CMLC 1**

Murdoch, (Jean) Iris
1919- . . . . . .   **CLC 1, 2, 3, 4, 6, 8, 11, 15,**
22, 31, 51; DAB; DAC; DAM MST,
NOV
See also CA 13-16R; CANR 8, 43; CDBLB 1960 to Present; DLB 14; INT CANR-8; MTCW

Murfree, Mary Noailles
1850-1922 . . . .   **SSC 22**
See also CA 122; DLB 12, 74

Murnau, Friedrich Wilhelm
See Plumpe, Friedrich Wilhelm

Murphy, Richard   1927-. . . . .   **CLC 41**
See also CA 29-32R; DLB 40

Murphy, Sylvia   1937-. . . . .   **CLC 34**
See also CA 121

Murphy, Thomas (Bernard)   1935-. . .   **CLC 51**
See also CA 101

Murray, Albert L.   1916- . . . .   **CLC 73**
See also BW 2; CA 49-52; CANR 26, 52; DLB 38

Murray, Les(lie) A(llan)
1938- . . . .   **CLC 40; DAM POET**
See also CA 21-24R; CANR 11, 27

Murry, J. Middleton
See Murry, John Middleton

Murry, John Middleton
1889-1957 . . . .   **TCLC 16**
See also CA 118; DLB 149

Musgrave, Susan   1951- . . . .   **CLC 13, 54**
See also CA 69-72; CANR 45

Musil, Robert (Edler von)
1880-1942 . . . .   **TCLC 12; SSC 18**
See also CA 109; CANR 55; DLB 81, 124

Muske, Carol   1945- . . . .   **CLC 90**
See also Muske-Dukes, Carol (Anne)

Muske-Dukes, Carol (Anne)   1945-
See Muske, Carol
See also CA 65-68; CANR 32

Musset, (Louis Charles) Alfred de
1810-1857 . . . .   **NCLC 7**

My Brother's Brother
See Chekhov, Anton (Pavlovich)

Myers, L. H.   1881-1944. . . . .   **TCLC 59**
See also DLB 15

Myers, Walter Dean
1937- . . . . .   **CLC 35; BLC; DAM MULT,**
NOV
See also AAYA 4; BW 2; CA 33-36R; CANR 20, 42; CLR 4, 16, 35; DLB 33; INT CANR-20; JRDA; MAICYA; SAAS 2; SATA 41, 71; SATA-Brief 27

Myers, Walter M.
See Myers, Walter Dean

Myles, Symon
See Follett, Ken(neth Martin)

Nabokov, Vladimir (Vladimirovich)
1899-1977 . . . . .   **CLC 1, 2, 3, 6, 8, 11, 15,**
23, 44, 46, 64; DA; DAB; DAC;
DAM MST, NOV; SSC 11; WLC
See also CA 5-8R; 69-72; CANR 20; CDALB 1941-1968; DLB 2; DLBD 3; DLBY 80, 91; MTCW

Nagai Kafu.   **TCLC 51**
See also Nagai Sokichi

Nagai Sokichi 1879-1959
See Nagai Kafu
See also CA 117

Nagy, Laszlo 1925-1978............ CLC 7
See also CA 129; 112

Naipaul, Shiva(dhar Srinivasa)
1945-1985 ..... CLC 32, 39; DAM NOV
See also CA 110; 112; 116; CANR 33;
DLB 157; DLBY 85; MTCW

Naipaul, V(idiadhar) S(urajprasad)
1932- .... CLC 4, 7, 9, 13, 18, 37; DAB;
DAC; DAM MST, NOV
See also CA 1-4R; CANR 1, 33, 51;
CDBLB 1960 to Present; DLB 125;
DLBY 85; MTCW

Nakos, Lilika 1899(?)-............ CLC 29

Narayan, R(asipuram) K(rishnaswami)
1906- ...... CLC 7, 28, 47; DAM NOV
See also CA 81-84; CANR 33; MTCW;
SATA 62

Nash, (Frediric) Ogden
1902-1971 .... CLC 23; DAM POET
See also CA 13-14; 29-32R; CANR 34;
CAP 1; DLB 11; MAICYA; MTCW;
SATA 2, 46

Nathan, Daniel
See Dannay, Frederic

Nathan, George Jean 1882-1958 ... TCLC 18
See also Hatteras, Owen
See also CA 114; DLB 137

Natsume, Kinnosuke 1867-1916
See Natsume, Soseki
See also CA 104

Natsume, Soseki .... TCLC 2, 10
See also Natsume, Kinnosuke

Natti, (Mary) Lee 1919-
See Kingman, Lee
See also CA 5-8R; CANR 2

Naylor, Gloria
1950- ..... CLC 28, 52; BLC; DA; DAC;
DAM MST, MULT, NOV, POP
See also AAYA 6; BW 2; CA 107;
CANR 27, 51; DLB 173; MTCW

Neihardt, John Gneisenau
1881-1973 .... CLC 32
See also CA 13-14; CAP 1; DLB 9, 54

Nekrasov, Nikolai Alekseevich
1821-1878 .... NCLC 11

Nelligan, Emile 1879-1941....... TCLC 14
See also CA 114; DLB 92

Nelson, Willie 1933-.............. CLC 17
See also CA 107

Nemerov, Howard (Stanley)
1920-1991 .... CLC 2, 6, 9, 36;
DAM POET
See also CA 1-4R; 134; CABS 2; CANR 1,
27, 53; DLB 5, 6; DLBY 83;
INT CANR-27; MTCW

Neruda, Pablo
1904-1973 ..... CLC 1, 2, 5, 7, 9, 28, 62;
DA; DAB; DAC; DAM MST, MULT,
POET; HLC; PC 4; WLC
See also CA 19-20; 45-48; CAP 2; HW;
MTCW

Nerval, Gerard de
1808-1855 ..... NCLC 1; PC 13; SSC 18

Nervo, (Jose) Amado (Ruiz de)
1870-1919 .... TCLC 11
See also CA 109; 131; HW

Nessi, Pio Baroja y
See Baroja (y Nessi), Pio

Nestroy, Johann 1801-1862...... NCLC 42
See also DLB 133

Neufeld, John (Arthur) 1938- ...... CLC 17
See also AAYA 11; CA 25-28R; CANR 11,
37; MAICYA; SAAS 3; SATA 6, 81

Neville, Emily Cheney 1919-....... CLC 12
See also CA 5-8R; CANR 3, 37; JRDA;
MAICYA; SAAS 2; SATA 1

Newbound, Bernard Slade 1930-
See Slade, Bernard
See also CA 81-84; CANR 49;
DAM DRAM

Newby, P(ercy) H(oward)
1918- .... CLC 2, 13; DAM NOV
See also CA 5-8R; CANR 32; DLB 15;
MTCW

Newlove, Donald 1928- .... CLC 6
See also CA 29-32R; CANR 25

Newlove, John (Herbert) 1938-..... CLC 14
See also CA 21-24R; CANR 9, 25

Newman, Charles 1938-.......... CLC 2, 8
See also CA 21-24R

Newman, Edwin (Harold) 1919- .... CLC 14
See also AITN 1; CA 69-72; CANR 5

Newman, John Henry
1801-1890 .... NCLC 38
See also DLB 18, 32, 55

Newton, Suzanne 1936-........... CLC 35
See also CA 41-44R; CANR 14; JRDA;
SATA 5, 77

Nexo, Martin Andersen
1869-1954 .... TCLC 43

Nezval, Vitezslav 1900-1958 ...... TCLC 44
See also CA 123

Ng, Fae Myenne 1957(?)-......... CLC 81
See also CA 146

Ngema, Mbongeni 1955- .... CLC 57
See also BW 2; CA 143

Ngugi, James T(hiong'o) .... CLC 3, 7, 13
See also Ngugi wa Thiong'o

Ngugi wa Thiong'o
1938- ..... CLC 36; BLC; DAM MULT,
NOV
See also Ngugi, James T(hiong'o)
See also BW 2; CA 81-84; CANR 27;
DLB 125; MTCW

Nichol, B(arrie) P(hillip)
1944-1988 .... CLC 18
See also CA 53-56; DLB 53; SATA 66

Nichols, John (Treadwell) 1940- .... CLC 38
See also CA 9-12R; CAAS 2; CANR 6;
DLBY 82

Nichols, Leigh
See Koontz, Dean R(ay)

Nichols, Peter (Richard)
1927- .... CLC 5, 36, 65
See also CA 104; CANR 33; DLB 13;
MTCW

Nicolas, F. R. E.
See Freeling, Nicolas

Niedecker, Lorine
1903-1970 .... CLC 10, 42; DAM POET
See also CA 25-28; CAP 2; DLB 48

Nietzsche, Friedrich (Wilhelm)
1844-1900 .... TCLC 10, 18, 55
See also CA 107; 121; DLB 129

Nievo, Ippolito 1831-1861 .... NCLC 22

Nightingale, Anne Redmon 1943-
See Redmon, Anne
See also CA 103

Nik. T. O.
See Annensky, Innokenty Fyodorovich

Nin, Anais
1903-1977 ...... CLC 1, 4, 8, 11, 14, 60;
DAM NOV, POP; SSC 10
See also AITN 2; CA 13-16R; 69-72;
CANR 22, 53; DLB 2, 4, 152; MTCW

Nishiwaki, Junzaburo 1894-1982 .... PC 15
See also CA 107

Nissenson, Hugh 1933-........... CLC 4, 9
See also CA 17-20R; CANR 27; DLB 28

Niven, Larry .... CLC 8
See also Niven, Laurence Van Cott
See also DLB 8

Niven, Laurence Van Cott 1938-
See Niven, Larry
See also CA 21-24R; CAAS 12; CANR 14,
44; DAM POP; MTCW

Nixon, Agnes Eckhardt 1927-...... CLC 21
See also CA 110

Nizan, Paul 1905-1940.......... TCLC 40
See also DLB 72

Nkosi, Lewis
1936- ..... CLC 45; BLC; DAM MULT
See also BW 1; CA 65-68; CANR 27;
DLB 157

Nodier, (Jean) Charles (Emmanuel)
1780-1844 .... NCLC 19
See also DLB 119

Nolan, Christopher 1965-.......... CLC 58
See also CA 111

Noon, Jeff 1957-................. CLC 91
See also CA 148

Norden, Charles
See Durrell, Lawrence (George)

Nordhoff, Charles (Bernard)
1887-1947 .... TCLC 23
See also CA 108; DLB 9; SATA 23

Norfolk, Lawrence 1963-.......... CLC 76
See also CA 144

Norman, Marsha
1947- .... CLC 28; DAM DRAM
See also CA 105; CABS 3; CANR 41;
DLBY 84

Norris, Benjamin Franklin, Jr.
1870-1902 .... TCLC 24
See also Norris, Frank
See also CA 110

Norris, Frank
See Norris, Benjamin Franklin, Jr.
See also CDALB 1865-1917; DLB 12, 71

Norris, Leslie 1921- .... CLC 14
See also CA 11-12; CANR 14; CAP 1;
DLB 27

North, Andrew
See Norton, Andre

North, Anthony
See Koontz, Dean R(ay)

North, Captain George
See Stevenson, Robert Louis (Balfour)

North, Milou
See Erdrich, Louise

Northrup, B. A.
See Hubbard, L(afayette) Ron(ald)

North Staffs
See Hulme, T(homas) E(rnest)

Norton, Alice Mary
See Norton, Andre
See also MAICYA; SATA 1, 43

Norton, Andre 1912- .... **CLC 12**
See also Norton, Alice Mary
See also AAYA 14; CA 1-4R; CANR 2, 31;
DLB 8, 52; JRDA; MTCW; SATA 91

Norton, Caroline 1808-1877...... **NCLC 47**
See also DLB 21, 159

Norway, Nevil Shute 1899-1960
See Shute, Nevil
See also CA 102; 93-96

Norwid, Cyprian Kamil
1821-1883 .... **NCLC 17**

Nosille, Nabrah
See Ellison, Harlan (Jay)

Nossack, Hans Erich 1901-1978 ..... **CLC 6**
See also CA 93-96; 85-88; DLB 69

Nostradamus 1503-1566............ **LC 27**

Nosu, Chuji
See Ozu, Yasujiro

Notenburg, Eleanora (Genrikhovna) von
See Guro, Elena

Nova, Craig 1945-.............. **CLC 7, 31**
See also CA 45-48; CANR 2, 53

Novak, Joseph
See Kosinski, Jerzy (Nikodem)

Novalis 1772-1801 .... **NCLC 13**
See also DLB 90

Nowlan, Alden (Albert)
1933-1983 .. **CLC 15; DAC; DAM MST**
See also CA 9-12R; CANR 5; DLB 53

Noyes, Alfred 1880-1958 .... **TCLC 7**
See also CA 104; DLB 20

Nunn, Kem 19(?)-................ **CLC 34**

Nye, Robert
1939- .... **CLC 13, 42; DAM NOV**
See also CA 33-36R; CANR 29; DLB 14;
MTCW; SATA 6

Nyro, Laura 1947- .... **CLC 17**

Oates, Joyce Carol
1938- ...... **CLC 1, 2, 3, 6, 9, 11, 15, 19,
33, 52; DA; DAB; DAC; DAM MST,
NOV, POP; SSC 6; WLC**
See also AAYA 15; AITN 1; BEST 89:2;
CA 5-8R; CANR 25, 45;
CDALB 1968-1988; DLB 2, 5, 130;
DLBY 81; INT CANR-25; MTCW

O'Brien, Darcy 1939-............. **CLC 11**
See also CA 21-24R; CANR 8

O'Brien, E. G.
See Clarke, Arthur C(harles)

O'Brien, Edna
1936- .... **CLC 3, 5, 8, 13, 36, 65;
DAM NOV; SSC 10**
See also CA 1-4R; CANR 6, 41;
CDBLB 1960 to Present; DLB 14;
MTCW

O'Brien, Fitz-James 1828-1862... **NCLC 21**
See also DLB 74

O'Brien, Flann....... **CLC 1, 4, 5, 7, 10, 47**
See also O Nuallain, Brian

O'Brien, Richard 1942-........... **CLC 17**
See also CA 124

O'Brien, Tim
1946- .... **CLC 7, 19, 40; DAM POP**
See also AAYA 16; CA 85-88; CANR 40;
DLB 152; DLBD 9; DLBY 80

Obstfelder, Sigbjoern 1866-1900... **TCLC 23**
See also CA 123

O'Casey, Sean
1880-1964 ...... **CLC 1, 5, 9, 11, 15, 88;
DAB; DAC; DAM DRAM, MST**
See also CA 89-92; CDBLB 1914-1945;
DLB 10; MTCW

O'Cathasaigh, Sean
See O'Casey, Sean

Ochs, Phil 1940-1976............. **CLC 17**
See also CA 65-68

O'Connor, Edwin (Greene)
1918-1968 .... **CLC 14**
See also CA 93-96; 25-28R

O'Connor, (Mary) Flannery
1925-1964 .... **CLC 1, 2, 3, 6, 10, 13, 15,
21, 66; DA; DAB; DAC; DAM MST,
NOV; SSC 1, 23; WLC**
See also AAYA 7; CA 1-4R; CANR 3, 41;
CDALB 1941-1968; DLB 2, 152;
DLBD 12; DLBY 80; MTCW

O'Connor, Frank........... **CLC 23; SSC 5**
See also O'Donovan, Michael John
See also DLB 162

O'Dell, Scott 1898-1989........... **CLC 30**
See also AAYA 3; CA 61-64; 129;
CANR 12, 30; CLR 1, 16; DLB 52;
JRDA; MAICYA; SATA 12, 60

Odets, Clifford
1906-1963 .... **CLC 2, 28, 98;
DAM DRAM; DC 6**
See also CA 85-88; DLB 7, 26; MTCW

O'Doherty, Brian 1934-........... **CLC 76**
See also CA 105

O'Donnell, K. M.
See Malzberg, Barry N(athaniel)

O'Donnell, Lawrence
See Kuttner, Henry

O'Donovan, Michael John
1903-1966 .... **CLC 14**
See also O'Connor, Frank
See also CA 93-96

Oe, Kenzaburo
1935- ..... **CLC 10, 36, 86; DAM NOV;
SSC 20**
See also CA 97-100; CANR 36, 50;
DLBY 94; MTCW

O'Faolain, Julia 1932-....... **CLC 6, 19, 47**
See also CA 81-84; CAAS 2; CANR 12;
DLB 14; MTCW

O'Faolain, Sean
1900-1991 .... **CLC 1, 7, 14, 32, 70;
SSC 13**
See also CA 61-64; 134; CANR 12;
DLB 15, 162; MTCW

O'Flaherty, Liam
1896-1984 .... **CLC 5, 34; SSC 6**
See also CA 101; 113; CANR 35; DLB 36,
162; DLBY 84; MTCW

Ogilvy, Gavin
See Barrie, J(ames) M(atthew)

O'Grady, Standish James
1846-1928 .... **TCLC 5**
See also CA 104

O'Grady, Timothy 1951- .... **CLC 59**
See also CA 138

O'Hara, Frank
1926-1966 .... **CLC 2, 5, 13, 78;
DAM POET**
See also CA 9-12R; 25-28R; CANR 33;
DLB 5, 16; MTCW

O'Hara, John (Henry)
1905-1970 .... **CLC 1, 2, 3, 6, 11, 42;
DAM NOV; SSC 15**
See also CA 5-8R; 25-28R; CANR 31;
CDALB 1929-1941; DLB 9, 86; DLBD 2;
MTCW

O Hehir, Diana 1922- .... **CLC 41**
See also CA 93-96

Okigbo, Christopher (Ifenayichukwu)
1932-1967 .... **CLC 25, 84; BLC;
DAM MULT, POET; PC 7**
See also BW 1; CA 77-80; DLB 125;
MTCW

Okri, Ben 1959- .... **CLC 87**
See also BW 2; CA 130; 138; DLB 157;
INT 138

Olds, Sharon
1942- ..... **CLC 32, 39, 85; DAM POET**
See also CA 101; CANR 18, 41; DLB 120

Oldstyle, Jonathan
See Irving, Washington

Olesha, Yuri (Karlovich)
1899-1960 .... **CLC 8**
See also CA 85-88

Oliphant, Laurence
1829(?)-1888 .... **NCLC 47**
See also DLB 18, 166

Oliphant, Margaret (Oliphant Wilson)
1828-1897 .... **NCLC 11**
See also DLB 18, 159

Oliver, Mary 1935-........ **CLC 19, 34, 98**
See also CA 21-24R; CANR 9, 43; DLB 5

Olivier, Laurence (Kerr)
1907-1989 .... **CLC 20**
See also CA 111; 150; 129

Olsen, Tillie
1913- ..... **CLC 4, 13; DA; DAB; DAC;
DAM MST; SSC 11**
See also CA 1-4R; CANR 1, 43; DLB 28;
DLBY 80; MTCW

Olson, Charles (John)
1910-1970 ..... **CLC 1, 2, 5, 6, 9, 11, 29;
DAM POET**
See also CA 13-16; 25-28R; CABS 2;
CANR 35; CAP 1; DLB 5, 16; MTCW

Olson, Toby 1937- .... **CLC 28**
See also CA 65-68; CANR 9, 31

Olyesha, Yuri
See Olesha, Yuri (Karlovich)

Ondaatje, (Philip) Michael
1943- .... **CLC 14, 29, 51, 76; DAB;**
DAC; DAM MST
See also CA 77-80; CANR 42; DLB 60

Oneal, Elizabeth 1934-
See Oneal, Zibby
See also CA 106; CANR 28; MAICYA;
SATA 30, 82

Oneal, Zibby .... **CLC 30**
See also Oneal, Elizabeth
See also AAYA 5; CLR 13; JRDA

O'Neill, Eugene (Gladstone)
1888-1953 ...... **TCLC 1, 6, 27, 49; DA;**
DAB; DAC; DAM DRAM, MST; WLC
See also AITN 1; CA 110; 132;
CDALB 1929-1941; DLB 7; MTCW

Onetti, Juan Carlos
1909-1994 .... **CLC 7, 10; DAM MULT,**
NOV; SSC 23
See also CA 85-88; 145; CANR 32;
DLB 113; HW; MTCW

O Nuallain, Brian 1911-1966
See O'Brien, Flann
See also CA 21-22; 25-28R; CAP 2

Oppen, George 1908-1984 .... **CLC 7, 13, 34**
See also CA 13-16R; 113; CANR 8; DLB 5,
165

Oppenheim, E(dward) Phillips
1866-1946 .... **TCLC 45**
See also CA 111; DLB 70

Origen c. 185-c. 254............ **CMLC 19**

Orlovitz, Gil 1918-1973........... **CLC 22**
See also CA 77-80; 45-48; DLB 2, 5

Orris
See Ingelow, Jean

Ortega y Gasset, Jose
1883-1955 ..... **TCLC 9; DAM MULT;**
HLC
See also CA 106; 130; HW; MTCW

Ortese, Anna Maria 1914-........ **CLC 89**

Ortiz, Simon J(oseph)
1941- .... **CLC 45; DAM MULT, POET**
See also CA 134; DLB 120; NNAL

Orton, Joe........... **CLC 4, 13, 43; DC 3**
See also Orton, John Kingsley
See also CDBLB 1960 to Present; DLB 13

Orton, John Kingsley 1933-1967
See Orton, Joe
See also CA 85-88; CANR 35;
DAM DRAM; MTCW

Orwell, George
..... **TCLC 2, 6, 15, 31, 51; DAB; WLC**
See also Blair, Eric (Arthur)
See also CDBLB 1945-1960; DLB 15, 98

Osborne, David
See Silverberg, Robert

Osborne, George
See Silverberg, Robert

Osborne, John (James)
1929-1994 ..... **CLC 1, 2, 5, 11, 45; DA;**
DAB; DAC; DAM DRAM, MST; WLC
See also CA 13-16R; 147; CANR 21;
CDBLB 1945-1960; DLB 13; MTCW

Osborne, Lawrence 1958- .... **CLC 50**

Oshima, Nagisa 1932- .... **CLC 20**
See also CA 116; 121

Oskison, John Milton
1874-1947 ..... **TCLC 35; DAM MULT**
See also CA 144; NNAL

Ossoli, Sarah Margaret (Fuller marchesa d')
1810-1850
See Fuller, Margaret
See also SATA 25

Ostrovsky, Alexander
1823-1886 .... **NCLC 30, 57**

Otero, Blas de 1916-1979......... **CLC 11**
See also CA 89-92; DLB 134

Otto, Whitney 1955-.............. **CLC 70**
See also CA 140

Ouida .... **TCLC 43**
See also De La Ramee, (Marie) Louise
See also DLB 18, 156

Ousmane, Sembene 1923- .... **CLC 66; BLC**
See also BW 1; CA 117; 125; MTCW

Ovid
43B.C.-18(?) ... **CMLC 7; DAM POET;**
PC 2

Owen, Hugh
See Faust, Frederick (Schiller)

Owen, Wilfred (Edward Salter)
1893-1918 ...... **TCLC 5, 27; DA; DAB;**
DAC; DAM MST, POET; WLC
See also CA 104; 141; CDBLB 1914-1945;
DLB 20

Owens, Rochelle 1936-............. **CLC 8**
See also CA 17-20R; CAAS 2; CANR 39

Oz, Amos
1939- .... **CLC 5, 8, 11, 27, 33, 54;**
DAM NOV
See also CA 53-56; CANR 27, 47; MTCW

Ozick, Cynthia
1928- .... **CLC 3, 7, 28, 62; DAM NOV,**
POP; SSC 15
See also BEST 90:1; CA 17-20R; CANR 23;
DLB 28, 152; DLBY 82; INT CANR-23;
MTCW

Ozu, Yasujiro 1903-1963 .... **CLC 16**
See also CA 112

Pacheco, C.
See Pessoa, Fernando (Antonio Nogueira)

Pa Chin .... **CLC 18**
See also Li Fei-kan

Pack, Robert 1929-.............. **CLC 13**
See also CA 1-4R; CANR 3, 44; DLB 5

Padgett, Lewis
See Kuttner, Henry

Padilla (Lorenzo), Heberto 1932-... **CLC 38**
See also AITN 1; CA 123; 131; HW

Page, Jimmy 1944-.............. **CLC 12**

Page, Louise 1955-.............. **CLC 40**
See also CA 140

Page, P(atricia) K(athleen)
1916- .... **CLC 7, 18; DAC; DAM MST;**
PC 12
See also CA 53-56; CANR 4, 22; DLB 68;
MTCW

Page, Thomas Nelson 1853-1922.... **SSC 23**
See also CA 118; DLB 12, 78; DLBD 13

Paget, Violet 1856-1935
See Lee, Vernon
See also CA 104

Paget-Lowe, Henry
See Lovecraft, H(oward) P(hillips)

Paglia, Camille (Anna) 1947-...... **CLC 68**
See also CA 140

Paige, Richard
See Koontz, Dean R(ay)

Pakenham, Antonia
See Fraser, (Lady) Antonia (Pakenham)

Palamas, Kostes 1859-1943 .... **TCLC 5**
See also CA 105

Palazzeschi, Aldo 1885-1974....... **CLC 11**
See also CA 89-92; 53-56; DLB 114

Paley, Grace
1922- .... **CLC 4, 6, 37; DAM POP;**
SSC 8
See also CA 25-28R; CANR 13, 46;
DLB 28; INT CANR-13; MTCW

Palin, Michael (Edward) 1943- ..... **CLC 21**
See also Monty Python
See also CA 107; CANR 35; SATA 67

Palliser, Charles 1947-............ **CLC 65**
See also CA 136

Palma, Ricardo 1833-1919........ **TCLC 29**

Pancake, Breece Dexter 1952-1979
See Pancake, Breece D'J
See also CA 123; 109

Pancake, Breece D'J.............. **CLC 29**
See also Pancake, Breece Dexter
See also DLB 130

Panko, Rudy
See Gogol, Nikolai (Vasilyevich)

Papadiamantis, Alexandros
1851-1911 .... **TCLC 29**

Papadiamantopoulos, Johannes 1856-1910
See Moreas, Jean
See also CA 117

Papini, Giovanni 1881-1956....... **TCLC 22**
See also CA 121

Paracelsus 1493-1541.............. **LC 14**

Parasol, Peter
See Stevens, Wallace

Parfenie, Maria
See Codrescu, Andrei

Parini, Jay (Lee) 1948- .... **CLC 54**
See also CA 97-100; CAAS 16; CANR 32

Park, Jordan
See Kornbluth, C(yril) M.; Pohl, Frederik

Parker, Bert
See Ellison, Harlan (Jay)

Parker, Dorothy (Rothschild)
1893-1967 .... **CLC 15, 68;**
DAM POET; SSC 2
See also CA 19-20; 25-28R; CAP 2;
DLB 11, 45, 86; MTCW

Parker, Robert B(rown)
1932- . . . . . . CLC 27; DAM NOV, POP
See also BEST 89:4; CA 49-52; CANR 1,
26, 52; INT CANR-26; MTCW

Parkin, Frank 1940-. . . . . CLC 43
See also CA 147

Parkman, Francis, Jr.
1823-1893 . . . . NCLC 12
See also DLB 1, 30

Parks, Gordon (Alexander Buchanan)
1912- . . . CLC 1, 16; BLC; DAM MULT
See also AITN 2; BW 2; CA 41-44R;
CANR 26; DLB 33; SATA 8

Parnell, Thomas 1679-1718 . . . . LC 3
See also DLB 94

Parra, Nicanor
1914- . . . . . . CLC 2; DAM MULT; HLC
See also CA 85-88; CANR 32; HW; MTCW

Parrish, Mary Frances
See Fisher, M(ary) F(rances) K(ennedy)

Parson
See Coleridge, Samuel Taylor

Parson Lot
See Kingsley, Charles

Partridge, Anthony
See Oppenheim, E(dward) Phillips

Pascal, Blaise 1623-1662 . . . . LC 35

Pascoli, Giovanni 1855-1912 . . . . . . TCLC 45

Pasolini, Pier Paolo
1922-1975 . . . . CLC 20, 37
See also CA 93-96; 61-64; DLB 128;
MTCW

Pasquini
See Silone, Ignazio

Pastan, Linda (Olenik)
1932- . . . . CLC 27; DAM POET
See also CA 61-64; CANR 18, 40; DLB 5

Pasternak, Boris (Leonidovich)
1890-1960 . . . . . . CLC 7, 10, 18, 63; DA;
DAB; DAC; DAM MST, NOV, POET;
PC 6; WLC
See also CA 127; 116; MTCW

Patchen, Kenneth
1911-1972 . . . CLC 1, 2, 18; DAM POET
See also CA 1-4R; 33-36R; CANR 3, 35;
DLB 16, 48; MTCW

Pater, Walter (Horatio)
1839-1894 . . . . NCLC 7
See also CDBLB 1832-1890; DLB 57, 156

Paterson, A(ndrew) B(arton)
1864-1941 . . . . TCLC 32

Paterson, Katherine (Womeldorf)
1932- . . . . CLC 12, 30
See also AAYA 1; CA 21-24R; CANR 28;
CLR 7; DLB 52; JRDA; MAICYA;
MTCW; SATA 13, 53

Patmore, Coventry Kersey Dighton
1823-1896 . . . . NCLC 9
See also DLB 35, 98

Paton, Alan (Stewart)
1903-1988 . . . . . . CLC 4, 10, 25, 55; DA;
DAB; DAC; DAM MST, NOV; WLC
See also CA 13-16; 125; CANR 22; CAP 1;
MTCW; SATA 11; SATA-Obit 56

Paton Walsh, Gillian 1937-
See Walsh, Jill Paton
See also CANR 38; JRDA; MAICYA;
SAAS 3; SATA 4, 72

Paulding, James Kirke 1778-1860. . NCLC 2
See also DLB 3, 59, 74

Paulin, Thomas Neilson 1949-
See Paulin, Tom
See also CA 123; 128

Paulin, Tom. . . . . CLC 37
See also Paulin, Thomas Neilson
See also DLB 40

Paustovsky, Konstantin (Georgievich)
1892-1968 . . . . CLC 40
See also CA 93-96; 25-28R

Pavese, Cesare
1908-1950 . . . . . TCLC 3; PC 13; SSC 19
See also CA 104; DLB 128

Pavic, Milorad 1929- . . . . CLC 60
See also CA 136

Payne, Alan
See Jakes, John (William)

Paz, Gil
See Lugones, Leopoldo

Paz, Octavio
1914- . . . . . . CLC 3, 4, 6, 10, 19, 51, 65;
DA; DAB; DAC; DAM MST, MULT,
POET; HLC; PC 1; WLC
See also CA 73-76; CANR 32; DLBY 90;
HW; MTCW

p'Bitek, Okot
1931-1982 . . . . CLC 96; BLC;
DAM MULT
See also BW 2; CA 124; 107; DLB 125;
MTCW

Peacock, Molly 1947-. . . . . CLC 60
See also CA 103; CAAS 21; CANR 52;
DLB 120

Peacock, Thomas Love
1785-1866 . . . . NCLC 22
See also DLB 96, 116

Peake, Mervyn 1911-1968 . . . . CLC 7, 54
See also CA 5-8R; 25-28R; CANR 3;
DLB 15, 160; MTCW; SATA 23

Pearce, Philippa . . . . CLC 21
See also Christie, (Ann) Philippa
See also CLR 9; DLB 161; MAICYA;
SATA 1, 67

Pearl, Eric
See Elman, Richard

Pearson, T(homas) R(eid) 1956- . . . . CLC 39
See also CA 120; 130; INT 130

Peck, Dale 1967- . . . . CLC 81
See also CA 146

Peck, John 1941- . . . . CLC 3
See also CA 49-52; CANR 3

Peck, Richard (Wayne) 1934- . . . . . . CLC 21
See also AAYA 1; CA 85-88; CANR 19,
38; CLR 15; INT CANR-19; JRDA;
MAICYA; SAAS 2; SATA 18, 55

Peck, Robert Newton
1928- . . CLC 17; DA; DAC; DAM MST
See also AAYA 3; CA 81-84; CANR 31;
JRDA; MAICYA; SAAS 1; SATA 21, 62

Peckinpah, (David) Sam(uel)
1925-1984 . . . . CLC 20
See also CA 109; 114

Pedersen, Knut 1859-1952
See Hamsun, Knut
See also CA 104; 119; MTCW

Peeslake, Gaffer
See Durrell, Lawrence (George)

Peguy, Charles Pierre
1873-1914 . . . . TCLC 10
See also CA 107

Pena, Ramon del Valle y
See Valle-Inclan, Ramon (Maria) del

Pendennis, Arthur Esquir
See Thackeray, William Makepeace

Penn, William 1644-1718 . . . . LC 25
See also DLB 24

Pepys, Samuel
1633-1703 . . . . . LC 11; DA; DAB; DAC;
DAM MST; WLC
See also CDBLB 1660-1789; DLB 101

Percy, Walker
1916-1990 . . . . CLC 2, 3, 6, 8, 14, 18, 47,
65; DAM NOV, POP
See also CA 1-4R; 131; CANR 1, 23;
DLB 2; DLBY 80, 90; MTCW

Perec, Georges 1936-1982 . . . . CLC 56
See also CA 141; DLB 83

Pereda (y Sanchez de Porrua), Jose Maria de
1833-1906 . . . . TCLC 16
See also CA 117

Pereda y Porrua, Jose Maria de
See Pereda (y Sanchez de Porrua), Jose
Maria de

Peregoy, George Weems
See Mencken, H(enry) L(ouis)

Perelman, S(idney) J(oseph)
1904-1979 . . . . . . CLC 3, 5, 9, 15, 23, 44,
49; DAM DRAM
See also AITN 1, 2; CA 73-76; 89-92;
CANR 18; DLB 11, 44; MTCW

Peret, Benjamin 1899-1959 . . . . TCLC 20
See also CA 117

Peretz, Isaac Loeb 1851(?)-1915 . . . TCLC 16
See also CA 109

Peretz, Yitzhok Leibush
See Peretz, Isaac Loeb

Perez Galdos, Benito 1843-1920 . . . TCLC 27
See also CA 125; 153; HW

Perrault, Charles 1628-1703 . . . . LC 2
See also MAICYA; SATA 25

Perry, Brighton
See Sherwood, Robert E(mmet)

Perse, St.-John . . . . CLC 4, 11, 46
See also Leger, (Marie-Rene Auguste) Alexis
Saint-Leger

Perutz, Leo 1882-1957. . . . . TCLC 60
See also DLB 81

Peseenz, Tulio F.
See Lopez y Fuentes, Gregorio

Pesetsky, Bette 1932-. . . . . CLC 28
See also CA 133; DLB 130

Peshkov, Alexei Maximovich   1868-1936
See Gorky, Maxim
See also CA 105; 141; DA; DAC;
DAM DRAM, MST, NOV

Pessoa, Fernando (Antonio Nogueira)
1888-1935 . . . . TCLC 27; HLC
See also CA 125

Peterkin, Julia Mood   1880-1961. . . . CLC 31
See also CA 102; DLB 9

Peters, Joan K.   1945-. . . . . CLC 39

Peters, Robert L(ouis)   1924-. . . . . . . CLC 7
See also CA 13-16R; CAAS 8; DLB 105

Petofi, Sandor   1823-1849. . . . . . . NCLC 21

Petrakis, Harry Mark   1923-. . . . . . . CLC 3
See also CA 9-12R; CANR 4, 30

Petrarch
1304-1374 . . . . CMLC 20; DAM POET;
PC 8

Petrov, Evgeny . . . . TCLC 21
See also Kataev, Evgeny Petrovich

Petry, Ann (Lane)   1908- . . . . . . CLC 1, 7, 18
See also BW 1; CA 5-8R; CAAS 6;
CANR 4, 46; CLR 12; DLB 76; JRDA;
MAICYA; MTCW; SATA 5

Petursson, Halligrimur   1614-1674 . . . . LC 8

Philips, Katherine   1632-1664. . . . . . . LC 30
See also DLB 131

Philipson, Morris H.   1926-. . . . . CLC 53
See also CA 1-4R; CANR 4

Phillips, Caryl
1958-. . . . . CLC 96; DAM MULT
See also BW 2; CA 141; DLB 157

Phillips, David Graham
1867-1911 . . . . TCLC 44
See also CA 108; DLB 9, 12

Phillips, Jack
See Sandburg, Carl (August)

Phillips, Jayne Anne
1952-. . . . . CLC 15, 33; SSC 16
See also CA 101; CANR 24, 50; DLBY 80;
INT CANR-24; MTCW

Phillips, Richard
See Dick, Philip K(indred)

Phillips, Robert (Schaeffer)   1938-. . . CLC 28
See also CA 17-20R; CAAS 13; CANR 8;
DLB 105

Phillips, Ward
See Lovecraft, H(oward) P(hillips)

Piccolo, Lucio   1901-1969. . . . . CLC 13
See also CA 97-100; DLB 114

Pickthall, Marjorie L(owry) C(hristie)
1883-1922 . . . . TCLC 21
See also CA 107; DLB 92

Pico della Mirandola, Giovanni
1463-1494 . . . . LC 15

Piercy, Marge
1936-. . . . . CLC 3, 6, 14, 18, 27, 62
See also CA 21-24R; CAAS 1; CANR 13,
43; DLB 120; MTCW

Piers, Robert
See Anthony, Piers

Pieyre de Mandiargues, Andre   1909-1991
See Mandiargues, Andre Pieyre de
See also CA 103; 136; CANR 22

Pilnyak, Boris . . . . TCLC 23
See also Vogau, Boris Andreyevich

Pincherle, Alberto
1907-1990 . . . . . CLC 11, 18; DAM NOV
See also Moravia, Alberto
See also CA 25-28R; 132; CANR 33;
MTCW

Pinckney, Darryl   1953-. . . . . CLC 76
See also BW 2; CA 143

Pindar   518B.C.-446B.C. . . . . CMLC 12

Pineda, Cecile   1942-. . . . . CLC 39
See also CA 118

Pinero, Arthur Wing
1855-1934 . . . . . TCLC 32; DAM DRAM
See also CA 110; 153; DLB 10

Pinero, Miguel (Antonio Gomez)
1946-1988 . . . . CLC 4, 55
See also CA 61-64; 125; CANR 29; HW

Pinget, Robert   1919-. . . . . CLC 7, 13, 37
See also CA 85-88; DLB 83

Pink Floyd
See Barrett, (Roger) Syd; Gilmour, David;
Mason, Nick; Waters, Roger; Wright,
Rick

Pinkney, Edward   1802-1828 . . . . . NCLC 31

Pinkwater, Daniel Manus   1941-. . . . CLC 35
See also Pinkwater, Manus
See also AAYA 1; CA 29-32R; CANR 12,
38; CLR 4; JRDA; MAICYA; SAAS 3;
SATA 46, 76

Pinkwater, Manus
See Pinkwater, Daniel Manus
See also SATA 8

Pinsky, Robert
1940-. . CLC 9, 19, 38, 94; DAM POET
See also CA 29-32R; CAAS 4; DLBY 82

Pinta, Harold
See Pinter, Harold

Pinter, Harold
1930-. . . . . CLC 1, 3, 6, 9, 11, 15, 27, 58,
73; DA; DAB; DAC; DAM DRAM,
MST; WLC
See also CA 5-8R; CANR 33; CDBLB 1960
to Present; DLB 13; MTCW

Piozzi, Hester Lynch (Thrale)
1741-1821 . . . . NCLC 57
See also DLB 104, 142

Pirandello, Luigi
1867-1936 . . . . . . TCLC 4, 29; DA; DAB;
DAC; DAM DRAM, MST; DC 5;
SSC 22; WLC
See also CA 104; 153

Pirsig, Robert M(aynard)
1928-. . . . . CLC 4, 6, 73; DAM POP
See also CA 53-56; CANR 42; MTCW;
SATA 39

Pisarev, Dmitry Ivanovich
1840-1868 . . . . NCLC 25

Pix, Mary (Griffith)   1666-1709. . . . . . LC 8
See also DLB 80

Pixerecourt, Guilbert de
1773-1844 . . . . NCLC 39

Plaidy, Jean
See Hibbert, Eleanor Alice Burford

Planche, James Robinson
1796-1880 . . . . NCLC 42

Plant, Robert   1948-. . . . . CLC 12

Plante, David (Robert)
1940-. . . . . . . CLC 7, 23, 38; DAM NOV
See also CA 37-40R; CANR 12, 36;
DLBY 83; INT CANR-12; MTCW

Plath, Sylvia
1932-1963 . . . . . CLC 1, 2, 3, 5, 9, 11, 14,
17, 50, 51, 62; DA; DAB; DAC;
DAM MST, POET; PC 1; WLC
See also AAYA 13; CA 19-20; CANR 34;
CAP 2; CDALB 1941-1968; DLB 5, 6,
152; MTCW

Plato
428(?)B.C.-348(?)B.C. . . . . CMLC 8; DA;
DAB; DAC; DAM MST

Platonov, Andrei . . . . TCLC 14
See also Klimentov, Andrei Platonovich

Platt, Kin   1911-. . . . . CLC 26
See also AAYA 11; CA 17-20R; CANR 11;
JRDA; SAAS 17; SATA 21, 86

Plautus   c. 251B.C.-184B.C. . . . . DC 6

Plick et Plock
See Simenon, Georges (Jacques Christian)

Plimpton, George (Ames)   1927-. . . . . CLC 36
See also AITN 1; CA 21-24R; CANR 32;
MTCW; SATA 10

Plomer, William Charles Franklin
1903-1973 . . . . CLC 4, 8
See also CA 21-22; CANR 34; CAP 2;
DLB 20, 162; MTCW; SATA 24

Plowman, Piers
See Kavanagh, Patrick (Joseph)

Plum, J.
See Wodehouse, P(elham) G(renville)

Plumly, Stanley (Ross)   1939- . . . . . . CLC 33
See also CA 108; 110; DLB 5; INT 110

Plumpe, Friedrich Wilhelm
1888-1931 . . . . TCLC 53
See also CA 112

Poe, Edgar Allan
1809-1849 . . . . NCLC 1, 16, 55; DA;
DAB; DAC; DAM MST, POET; PC 1;
SSC 1, 22; WLC
See also AAYA 14; CDALB 1640-1865;
DLB 3, 59, 73, 74; SATA 23

Poet of Titchfield Street, The
See Pound, Ezra (Weston Loomis)

Pohl, Frederik   1919-. . . . . CLC 18
See also CA 61-64; CAAS 1; CANR 11, 37;
DLB 8; INT CANR-11; MTCW;
SATA 24

Poirier, Louis   1910-
See Gracq, Julien
See also CA 122; 126

Poitier, Sidney   1927-. . . . . CLC 26
See also BW 1; CA 117

Polanski, Roman   1933-. . . . . CLC 16
See also CA 77-80

Poliakoff, Stephen   1952-. . . . . CLC 38
See also CA 106; DLB 13

Ray, Satyajit
1921-1992 . . . **CLC 16, 76; DAM MULT**
See also CA 114; 137

Read, Herbert Edward 1893-1968. . . . **CLC 4**
See also CA 85-88; 25-28R; DLB 20, 149

Read, Piers Paul 1941- . . . . . . **CLC 4, 10, 25**
See also CA 21-24R; CANR 38; DLB 14;
SATA 21

Reade, Charles 1814-1884 . . . . **NCLC 2**
See also DLB 21

Reade, Hamish
See Gray, Simon (James Holliday)

Reading, Peter 1946- . . . . **CLC 47**
See also CA 103; CANR 46; DLB 40

Reaney, James
1926- . . . . . . **CLC 13; DAC; DAM MST**
See also CA 41-44R; CAAS 15; CANR 42;
DLB 68; SATA 43

Rebreanu, Liviu 1885-1944 . . . . **TCLC 28**

Rechy, John (Francisco)
1934- . . . . **CLC 1, 7, 14, 18;
DAM MULT; HLC**
See also CA 5-8R; CAAS 4; CANR 6, 32;
DLB 122; DLBY 82; HW; INT CANR-6

Redcam, Tom 1870-1933 . . . . **TCLC 25**

Reddin, Keith . . . . **CLC 67**

Redgrove, Peter (William)
1932- . . . . **CLC 6, 41**
See also CA 1-4R; CANR 3, 39; DLB 40

Redmon, Anne . . . . **CLC 22**
See also Nightingale, Anne Redmon
See also DLBY 86

Reed, Eliot
See Ambler, Eric

Reed, Ishmael
1938- . . . . **CLC 2, 3, 5, 6, 13, 32, 60;
BLC; DAM MULT**
See also BW 2; CA 21-24R; CANR 25, 48;
DLB 2, 5, 33, 169; DLBD 8; MTCW

Reed, John (Silas) 1887-1920 . . . . . . **TCLC 9**
See also CA 106

Reed, Lou . . . . **CLC 21**
See also Firbank, Louis

Reeve, Clara 1729-1807 . . . . **NCLC 19**
See also DLB 39

Reich, Wilhelm 1897-1957 . . . . **TCLC 57**

Reid, Christopher (John) 1949- . . . . . **CLC 33**
See also CA 140; DLB 40

Reid, Desmond
See Moorcock, Michael (John)

Reid Banks, Lynne 1929-
See Banks, Lynne Reid
See also CA 1-4R; CANR 6, 22, 38;
CLR 24; JRDA; MAICYA; SATA 22, 75

Reilly, William K.
See Creasey, John

Reiner, Max
See Caldwell, (Janet Miriam) Taylor
(Holland)

Reis, Ricardo
See Pessoa, Fernando (Antonio Nogueira)

Remarque, Erich Maria
1898-1970 . . . . **CLC 21; DA; DAB; DAC;
DAM MST, NOV**
See also CA 77-80; 29-32R; DLB 56;
MTCW

Remizov, A.
See Remizov, Aleksei (Mikhailovich)

Remizov, A. M.
See Remizov, Aleksei (Mikhailovich)

Remizov, Aleksei (Mikhailovich)
1877-1957 . . . . **TCLC 27**
See also CA 125; 133

Renan, Joseph Ernest
1823-1892 . . . . **NCLC 26**

Renard, Jules 1864-1910 . . . . **TCLC 17**
See also CA 117

Renault, Mary . . . . **CLC 3, 11, 17**
See also Challans, Mary
See also DLBY 83

Rendell, Ruth (Barbara)
1930- . . . . **CLC 28, 48; DAM POP**
See also Vine, Barbara
See also CA 109; CANR 32, 52; DLB 87;
INT CANR-32; MTCW

Renoir, Jean 1894-1979 . . . . **CLC 20**
See also CA 129; 85-88

Resnais, Alain 1922- . . . . **CLC 16**

Reverdy, Pierre 1889-1960 . . . . **CLC 53**
See also CA 97-100; 89-92

Rexroth, Kenneth
1905-1982 . . . . . . **CLC 1, 2, 6, 11, 22, 49;
DAM POET**
See also CA 5-8R; 107; CANR 14, 34;
CDALB 1941-1968; DLB 16, 48, 165;
DLBY 82; INT CANR-14; MTCW

Reyes, Alfonso 1889-1959 . . . . **TCLC 33**
See also CA 131; HW

Reyes y Basoalto, Ricardo Eliecer Neftali
See Neruda, Pablo

Reymont, Wladyslaw (Stanislaw)
1868(?)-1925 . . . . **TCLC 5**
See also CA 104

Reynolds, Jonathan 1942- . . . . **CLC 6, 38**
See also CA 65-68; CANR 28

Reynolds, Joshua 1723-1792 . . . . **LC 15**
See also DLB 104

Reynolds, Michael Shane 1937- . . . . **CLC 44**
See also CA 65-68; CANR 9

Reznikoff, Charles 1894-1976 . . . . **CLC 9**
See also CA 33-36; 61-64; CAP 2; DLB 28,
45

Rezzori (d'Arezzo), Gregor von
1914- . . . . **CLC 25**
See also CA 122; 136

Rhine, Richard
See Silverstein, Alvin

Rhodes, Eugene Manlove
1869-1934 . . . . **TCLC 53**

R'hoone
See Balzac, Honore de

Rhys, Jean
1890(?)-1979 . . . . **CLC 2, 4, 6, 14, 19, 51;
DAM NOV; SSC 21**
See also CA 25-28R; 85-88; CANR 35;
CDBLB 1945-1960; DLB 36, 117, 162;
MTCW

Ribeiro, Darcy 1922- . . . . **CLC 34**
See also CA 33-36R

Ribeiro, Joao Ubaldo (Osorio Pimentel)
1941- . . . . **CLC 10, 67**
See also CA 81-84

Ribman, Ronald (Burt) 1932- . . . . **CLC 7**
See also CA 21-24R; CANR 46

Ricci, Nino 1959- . . . . **CLC 70**
See also CA 137

Rice, Anne 1941- . . . . . **CLC 41; DAM POP**
See also AAYA 9; BEST 89:2; CA 65-68;
CANR 12, 36, 53

Rice, Elmer (Leopold)
1892-1967 . . . . **CLC 7, 49; DAM DRAM**
See also CA 21-22; 25-28R; CAP 2; DLB 4,
7; MTCW

Rice, Tim(othy Miles Bindon)
1944- . . . . **CLC 21**
See also CA 103; CANR 46

Rich, Adrienne (Cecile)
1929- . . . . **CLC 3, 6, 7, 11, 18, 36, 73, 76;
DAM POET; PC 5**
See also CA 9-12R; CANR 20, 53; DLB 5,
67; MTCW

Rich, Barbara
See Graves, Robert (von Ranke)

Rich, Robert
See Trumbo, Dalton

Richard, Keith . . . . **CLC 17**
See also Richards, Keith

Richards, David Adams
1950- . . . . **CLC 59; DAC**
See also CA 93-96; DLB 53

Richards, I(vor) A(rmstrong)
1893-1979 . . . . **CLC 14, 24**
See also CA 41-44R; 89-92; CANR 34;
DLB 27

Richards, Keith 1943-
See Richard, Keith
See also CA 107

Richardson, Anne
See Roiphe, Anne (Richardson)

Richardson, Dorothy Miller
1873-1957 . . . . **TCLC 3**
See also CA 104; DLB 36

Richardson, Ethel Florence (Lindesay)
1870-1946
See Richardson, Henry Handel
See also CA 105

Richardson, Henry Handel . . . . **TCLC 4**
See also Richardson, Ethel Florence
(Lindesay)

Richardson, John
1796-1852 . . . . **NCLC 55; DAC**
See also DLB 99

Richardson, Samuel
1689-1761 . . . . . . **LC 1; DA; DAB; DAC;
DAM MST, NOV; WLC**
See also CDBLB 1660-1789; DLB 39

Saura (Atares), Carlos 1932- . . . . **CLC 20**
See also CA 114; 131; HW

Sauser-Hall, Frederic 1887-1961. . . . **CLC 18**
See also Cendrars, Blaise
See also CA 102; 93-96; CANR 36; MTCW

Saussure, Ferdinand de
1857-1913 . . . . **TCLC 49**

Savage, Catharine
See Brosman, Catharine Savage

Savage, Thomas 1915- . . . . **CLC 40**
See also CA 126; 132; CAAS 15; INT 132

Savan, Glenn 19(?)- . . . . **CLC 50**

Sayers, Dorothy L(eigh)
1893-1957 . . . . . **TCLC 2, 15; DAM POP**
See also CA 104; 119; CDBLB 1914-1945;
DLB 10, 36, 77, 100; MTCW

Sayers, Valerie 1952- . . . . **CLC 50**
See also CA 134

Sayles, John (Thomas)
1950- . . . . **CLC 7, 10, 14**
See also CA 57-60; CANR 41; DLB 44

Scammell, Michael . . . . **CLC 34**

Scannell, Vernon 1922- . . . . **CLC 49**
See also CA 5-8R; CANR 8, 24; DLB 27;
SATA 59

Scarlett, Susan
See Streatfeild, (Mary) Noel

Schaeffer, Susan Fromberg
1941- . . . . **CLC 6, 11, 22**
See also CA 49-52; CANR 18; DLB 28;
MTCW; SATA 22

Schary, Jill
See Robinson, Jill

Schell, Jonathan 1943- . . . . **CLC 35**
See also CA 73-76; CANR 12

Schelling, Friedrich Wilhelm Joseph von
1775-1854 . . . . **NCLC 30**
See also DLB 90

Schendel, Arthur van 1874-1946 . . . **TCLC 56**

Scherer, Jean-Marie Maurice 1920-
See Rohmer, Eric
See also CA 110

Schevill, James (Erwin) 1920- . . . . **CLC 7**
See also CA 5-8R; CAAS 12

Schiller, Friedrich
1759-1805 . . . . **NCLC 39; DAM DRAM**
See also DLB 94

Schisgal, Murray (Joseph) 1926- . . . . . **CLC 6**
See also CA 21-24R; CANR 48

Schlee, Ann 1934- . . . . **CLC 35**
See also CA 101; CANR 29; SATA 44;
SATA-Brief 36

Schlegel, August Wilhelm von
1767-1845 . . . . **NCLC 15**
See also DLB 94

Schlegel, Friedrich 1772-1829 . . . . **NCLC 45**
See also DLB 90

Schlegel, Johann Elias (von)
1719(?)-1749 . . . . **LC 5**

Schlesinger, Arthur M(eier), Jr.
1917- . . . . **CLC 84**
See also AITN 1; CA 1-4R; CANR 1, 28;
DLB 17; INT CANR-28; MTCW;
SATA 61

Schmidt, Arno (Otto) 1914-1979 . . . . **CLC 56**
See also CA 128; 109; DLB 69

Schmitz, Aron Hector 1861-1928
See Svevo, Italo
See also CA 104; 122; MTCW

Schnackenberg, Gjertrud 1953- . . . . . **CLC 40**
See also CA 116; DLB 120

Schneider, Leonard Alfred 1925-1966
See Bruce, Lenny
See also CA 89-92

Schnitzler, Arthur
1862-1931 . . . . **TCLC 4; SSC 15**
See also CA 104; DLB 81, 118

Schopenhauer, Arthur
1788-1860 . . . . **NCLC 51**
See also DLB 90

Schor, Sandra (M.) 1932(?)-1990 . . . **CLC 65**
See also CA 132

Schorer, Mark 1908-1977 . . . . **CLC 9**
See also CA 5-8R; 73-76; CANR 7;
DLB 103

Schrader, Paul (Joseph) 1946- . . . . . . **CLC 26**
See also CA 37-40R; CANR 41; DLB 44

Schreiner, Olive (Emilie Albertina)
1855-1920 . . . . **TCLC 9**
See also CA 105; DLB 18, 156

Schulberg, Budd (Wilson)
1914- . . . . **CLC 7, 48**
See also CA 25-28R; CANR 19; DLB 6, 26,
28; DLBY 81

Schulz, Bruno
1892-1942 . . . . **TCLC 5, 51; SSC 13**
See also CA 115; 123

Schulz, Charles M(onroe) 1922- . . . . **CLC 12**
See also CA 9-12R; CANR 6;
INT CANR-6; SATA 10

Schumacher, E(rnst) F(riedrich)
1911-1977 . . . . **CLC 80**
See also CA 81-84; 73-76; CANR 34

Schuyler, James Marcus
1923-1991 . . . . . **CLC 5, 23; DAM POET**
See also CA 101; 134; DLB 5, 169; INT 101

Schwartz, Delmore (David)
1913-1966 . . . **CLC 2, 4, 10, 45, 87; PC 8**
See also CA 17-18; 25-28R; CANR 35;
CAP 2; DLB 28, 48; MTCW

Schwartz, Ernst
See Ozu, Yasujiro

Schwartz, John Burnham 1965- . . . . **CLC 59**
See also CA 132

Schwartz, Lynne Sharon 1939- . . . . . **CLC 31**
See also CA 103; CANR 44

Schwartz, Muriel A.
See Eliot, T(homas) S(tearns)

Schwarz-Bart, Andre 1928- . . . . **CLC 2, 4**
See also CA 89-92

Schwarz-Bart, Simone 1938- . . . . **CLC 7**
See also BW 2; CA 97-100

Schwob, (Mayer Andre) Marcel
1867-1905 . . . . **TCLC 20**
See also CA 117; DLB 123

Sciascia, Leonardo
1921-1989 . . . . **CLC 8, 9, 41**
See also CA 85-88; 130; CANR 35; MTCW

Scoppettone, Sandra 1936- . . . . **CLC 26**
See also AAYA 11; CA 5-8R; CANR 41;
SATA 9

Scorsese, Martin 1942- . . . . **CLC 20, 89**
See also CA 110; 114; CANR 46

Scotland, Jay
See Jakes, John (William)

Scott, Duncan Campbell
1862-1947 . . . . **TCLC 6; DAC**
See also CA 104; 153; DLB 92

Scott, Evelyn 1893-1963 . . . . **CLC 43**
See also CA 104; 112; DLB 9, 48

Scott, F(rancis) R(eginald)
1899-1985 . . . . **CLC 22**
See also CA 101; 114; DLB 88; INT 101

Scott, Frank
See Scott, F(rancis) R(eginald)

Scott, Joanna 1960- . . . . **CLC 50**
See also CA 126; CANR 53

Scott, Paul (Mark) 1920-1978 . . . . **CLC 9, 60**
See also CA 81-84; 77-80; CANR 33;
DLB 14; MTCW

Scott, Walter
1771-1832 . . . . **NCLC 15; DA; DAB;**
DAC; DAM MST, NOV, POET; PC 13;
WLC
See also CDBLB 1789-1832; DLB 93, 107,
116, 144, 159; YABC 2

Scribe, (Augustin) Eugene
1791-1861 . . . . **NCLC 16; DAM DRAM;**
DC 5

Scrum, R.
See Crumb, R(obert)

Scudery, Madeleine de 1607-1701 . . . . . **LC 2**

Scum
See Crumb, R(obert)

Scumbag, Little Bobby
See Crumb, R(obert)

Seabrook, John
See Hubbard, L(afayette) Ron(ald)

Sealy, I. Allan 1951- . . . . **CLC 55**

Search, Alexander
See Pessoa, Fernando (Antonio Nogueira)

Sebastian, Lee
See Silverberg, Robert

Sebastian Owl
See Thompson, Hunter S(tockton)

Sebestyen, Ouida 1924- . . . . **CLC 30**
See also AAYA 8; CA 107; CANR 40;
CLR 17; JRDA; MAICYA; SAAS 10;
SATA 39

Secundus, H. Scriblerus
See Fielding, Henry

Sedges, John
See Buck, Pearl S(ydenstricker)

Sedgwick, Catharine Maria
1789-1867 . . . . **NCLC 19**
See also DLB 1, 74

Seelye, John 1931- . . . . **CLC 7**

Seferiades, Giorgos Stylianou 1900-1971
See Seferis, George
See also CA 5-8R; 33-36R; CANR 5, 36;
MTCW

Sheridan, Richard Brinsley
1751-1816 .... **NCLC 5; DA; DAB;
DAC; DAM DRAM, MST; DC 1; WLC**
See also CDBLB 1660-1789; DLB 89

Sherman, Jonathan Marc .... **CLC 55**

Sherman, Martin 1941(?)- .... **CLC 19**
See also CA 116; 123

Sherwin, Judith Johnson 1936-... **CLC 7, 15**
See also CA 25-28R; CANR 34

Sherwood, Frances 1940-.......... **CLC 81**
See also CA 146

Sherwood, Robert E(mmet)
1896-1955 ...... **TCLC 3; DAM DRAM**
See also CA 104; 153; DLB 7, 26

Shestov, Lev 1866-1938 .... **TCLC 56**

Shevchenko, Taras 1814-1861 .... **NCLC 54**

Shiel, M(atthew) P(hipps)
1865-1947 .... **TCLC 8**
See also CA 106; DLB 153

Shields, Carol 1935-......... **CLC 91; DAC**
See also CA 81-84; CANR 51

Shields, David 1956-.............. **CLC 97**
See also CA 124; CANR 48

Shiga, Naoya 1883-1971... **CLC 33; SSC 23**
See also CA 101; 33-36R

Shilts, Randy 1951-1994 .... **CLC 85**
See also AAYA 19; CA 115; 127; 144;
CANR 45; INT 127

Shimazaki, Haruki 1872-1943
See Shimazaki Toson
See also CA 105; 134

Shimazaki Toson .... **TCLC 5**
See also Shimazaki, Haruki

Sholokhov, Mikhail (Aleksandrovich)
1905-1984 .... **CLC 7, 15**
See also CA 101; 112; MTCW;
SATA-Obit 36

Shone, Patric
See Hanley, James

Shreve, Susan Richards 1939-...... **CLC 23**
See also CA 49-52; CAAS 5; CANR 5, 38;
MAICYA; SATA 46; SATA-Brief 41

Shue, Larry
1946-1985 ...... **CLC 52; DAM DRAM**
See also CA 145; 117

Shu-Jen, Chou 1881-1936
See Lu Hsun
See also CA 104

Shulman, Alix Kates 1932-...... **CLC 2, 10**
See also CA 29-32R; CANR 43; SATA 7

Shuster, Joe 1914-.............. **CLC 21**

Shute, Nevil .... **CLC 30**
See also Norway, Nevil Shute

Shuttle, Penelope (Diane) 1947-..... **CLC 7**
See also CA 93-96; CANR 39; DLB 14, 40

Sidney, Mary 1561-1621 .... **LC 19**

Sidney, Sir Philip
1554-1586 ..... **LC 19; DA; DAB; DAC;
DAM MST, POET**
See also CDBLB Before 1660; DLB 167

Siegel, Jerome 1914-1996 .... **CLC 21**
See also CA 116; 151

Siegel, Jerry
See Siegel, Jerome

Sienkiewicz, Henryk (Adam Alexander Pius)
1846-1916 .... **TCLC 3**
See also CA 104; 134

Sierra, Gregorio Martinez
See Martinez Sierra, Gregorio

Sierra, Maria (de la O'LeJarraga) Martinez
See Martinez Sierra, Maria (de la
O'LeJarraga)

Sigal, Clancy 1926-.............. **CLC 7**
See also CA 1-4R

Sigourney, Lydia Howard (Huntley)
1791-1865 .... **NCLC 21**
See also DLB 1, 42, 73

Siguenza y Gongora, Carlos de
1645-1700 .... **LC 8**

Sigurjonsson, Johann 1880-1919... **TCLC 27**

Sikelianos, Angelos 1884-1951 .... **TCLC 39**

Silkin, Jon 1930- .... **CLC 2, 6, 43**
See also CA 5-8R; CAAS 5; DLB 27

Silko, Leslie (Marmon)
1948- .... **CLC 23, 74; DA; DAC;
DAM MST, MULT, POP**
See also AAYA 14; CA 115; 122;
CANR 45; DLB 143; NNAL

Sillanpaa, Frans Eemil 1888-1964... **CLC 19**
See also CA 129; 93-96; MTCW

Sillitoe, Alan
1928- .... **CLC 1, 3, 6, 10, 19, 57**
See also AITN 1; CA 9-12R; CAAS 2;
CANR 8, 26, 55; CDBLB 1960 to
Present; DLB 14, 139; MTCW; SATA 61

Silone, Ignazio 1900-1978 .... **CLC 4**
See also CA 25-28; 81-84; CANR 34;
CAP 2; MTCW

Silver, Joan Micklin 1935-........ **CLC 20**
See also CA 114; 121; INT 121

Silver, Nicholas
See Faust, Frederick (Schiller)

Silverberg, Robert
1935- .... **CLC 7; DAM POP**
See also CA 1-4R; CAAS 3; CANR 1, 20,
36; DLB 8; INT CANR-20; MAICYA;
MTCW; SATA 13, 91

Silverstein, Alvin 1933-........... **CLC 17**
See also CA 49-52; CANR 2; CLR 25;
JRDA; MAICYA; SATA 8, 69

Silverstein, Virginia B(arbara Opshelor)
1937-..................... **CLC 17**
See also CA 49-52; CANR 2; CLR 25;
JRDA; MAICYA; SATA 8, 69

Sim, Georges
See Simenon, Georges (Jacques Christian)

Simak, Clifford D(onald)
1904-1988 .... **CLC 1, 55**
See also CA 1-4R; 125; CANR 1, 35;
DLB 8; MTCW; SATA-Obit 56

Simenon, Georges (Jacques Christian)
1903-1989 .... **CLC 1, 2, 3, 8, 18, 47;
DAM POP**
See also CA 85-88; 129; CANR 35;
DLB 72; DLBY 89; MTCW

Simic, Charles
1938- .... **CLC 6, 9, 22, 49, 68;
DAM POET**
See also CA 29-32R; CAAS 4; CANR 12,
33, 52; DLB 105

Simmel, Georg 1858-1918 .... **TCLC 64**

Simmons, Charles (Paul) 1924-..... **CLC 57**
See also CA 89-92; INT 89-92

Simmons, Dan 1948-... **CLC 44; DAM POP**
See also AAYA 16; CA 138; CANR 53

Simmons, James (Stewart Alexander)
1933-..................... **CLC 43**
See also CA 105; CAAS 21; DLB 40

Simms, William Gilmore
1806-1870 .... **NCLC 3**
See also DLB 3, 30, 59, 73

Simon, Carly 1945-.............. **CLC 26**
See also CA 105

Simon, Claude
1913- .... **CLC 4, 9, 15, 39; DAM NOV**
See also CA 89-92; CANR 33; DLB 83;
MTCW

Simon, (Marvin) Neil
1927- .... **CLC 6, 11, 31, 39, 70;
DAM DRAM**
See also AITN 1; CA 21-24R; CANR 26,
54; DLB 7; MTCW

Simon, Paul (Frederick) 1941(?)- ... **CLC 17**
See also CA 116; 153

Simonon, Paul 1956(?)- .... **CLC 30**

Simpson, Harriette
See Arnow, Harriette (Louisa) Simpson

Simpson, Louis (Aston Marantz)
1923- .... **CLC 4, 7, 9, 32; DAM POET**
See also CA 1-4R; CAAS 4; CANR 1;
DLB 5; MTCW

Simpson, Mona (Elizabeth) 1957-... **CLC 44**
See also CA 122; 135

Simpson, N(orman) F(rederick)
1919-..................... **CLC 29**
See also CA 13-16R; DLB 13

Sinclair, Andrew (Annandale)
1935-..................... **CLC 2, 14**
See also CA 9-12R; CAAS 5; CANR 14, 38;
DLB 14; MTCW

Sinclair, Emil
See Hesse, Hermann

Sinclair, Iain 1943-.............. **CLC 76**
See also CA 132

Sinclair, Iain MacGregor
See Sinclair, Iain

Sinclair, Mary Amelia St. Clair 1865(?)-1946
See Sinclair, May
See also CA 104

Sinclair, May .... **TCLC 3, 11**
See also Sinclair, Mary Amelia St. Clair
See also DLB 36, 135

Sinclair, Upton (Beall)
1878-1968 ...... **CLC 1, 11, 15, 63; DA;
DAB; DAC; DAM MST, NOV; WLC**
See also CA 5-8R; 25-28R; CANR 7;
CDALB 1929-1941; DLB 9;
INT CANR-7; MTCW; SATA 9

Singer, Isaac
See Singer, Isaac Bashevis

Strummer, Joe 1953(?)- . . . . **CLC 30**

Stuart, Don A.
See Campbell, John W(ood, Jr.)

Stuart, Ian
See MacLean, Alistair (Stuart)

Stuart, Jesse (Hilton)
1906-1984 . . . . **CLC 1, 8, 11, 14, 34**
See also CA 5-8R; 112; CANR 31; DLB 9,
48, 102; DLBY 84; SATA 2;
SATA-Obit 36

Sturgeon, Theodore (Hamilton)
1918-1985 . . . . **CLC 22, 39**
See also Queen, Ellery
See also CA 81-84; 116; CANR 32; DLB 8;
DLBY 85; MTCW

Sturges, Preston 1898-1959 . . . . . . **TCLC 48**
See also CA 114; 149; DLB 26

Styron, William
1925- . . . . **CLC 1, 3, 5, 11, 15, 60;
DAM NOV, POP**
See also BEST 90:4; CA 5-8R; CANR 6, 33;
CDALB 1968-1988; DLB 2, 143;
DLBY 80; INT CANR-6; MTCW

Suarez Lynch, B.
See Bioy Casares, Adolfo; Borges, Jorge
Luis

Su Chien 1884-1918
See Su Man-shu
See also CA 123

Suckow, Ruth 1892-1960 . . . . **SSC 18**
See also CA 113; DLB 9, 102

Sudermann, Hermann 1857-1928 . . **TCLC 15**
See also CA 107; DLB 118

Sue, Eugene 1804-1857 . . . . **NCLC 1**
See also DLB 119

Sueskind, Patrick 1949- . . . . **CLC 44**
See also Suskind, Patrick

Sukenick, Ronald 1932- . . . . . **CLC 3, 4, 6, 48**
See also CA 25-28R; CAAS 8; CANR 32;
DLB 173; DLBY 81

Suknaski, Andrew 1942- . . . . **CLC 19**
See also CA 101; DLB 53

Sullivan, Vernon
See Vian, Boris

Sully Prudhomme 1839-1907 . . . . . . **TCLC 31**

Su Man-shu . . . . **TCLC 24**
See also Su Chien

Summerforest, Ivy B.
See Kirkup, James

Summers, Andrew James 1942- . . . . **CLC 26**

Summers, Andy
See Summers, Andrew James

Summers, Hollis (Spurgeon, Jr.)
1916- . . . . **CLC 10**
See also CA 5-8R; CANR 3; DLB 6

**Summers, (Alphonsus Joseph-Mary Augustus)
Montague** 1880-1948 . . . . **TCLC 16**
See also CA 118

Sumner, Gordon Matthew 1951- . . . . **CLC 26**

Surtees, Robert Smith
1803-1864 . . . . **NCLC 14**
See also DLB 21

Susann, Jacqueline 1921-1974 . . . . **CLC 3**
See also AITN 1; CA 65-68; 53-56; MTCW

Su Shih 1036-1101 . . . . **CMLC 15**

Suskind, Patrick
See Sueskind, Patrick
See also CA 145

Sutcliff, Rosemary
1920-1992 . . . . **CLC 26; DAB; DAC;
DAM MST, POP**
See also AAYA 10; CA 5-8R; 139;
CANR 37; CLR 1, 37; JRDA; MAICYA;
SATA 6, 44, 78; SATA-Obit 73

Sutro, Alfred 1863-1933 . . . . **TCLC 6**
See also CA 105; DLB 10

Sutton, Henry
See Slavitt, David R(ytman)

Svevo, Italo . . . . **TCLC 2, 35**
See also Schmitz, Aron Hector

Swados, Elizabeth (A.) 1951- . . . . **CLC 12**
See also CA 97-100; CANR 49; INT 97-100

Swados, Harvey 1920-1972 . . . . **CLC 5**
See also CA 5-8R; 37-40R; CANR 6;
DLB 2

Swan, Gladys 1934- . . . . **CLC 69**
See also CA 101; CANR 17, 39

Swarthout, Glendon (Fred)
1918-1992 . . . . **CLC 35**
See also CA 1-4R; 139; CANR 1, 47;
SATA 26

Sweet, Sarah C.
See Jewett, (Theodora) Sarah Orne

Swenson, May
1919-1989 . . . . **CLC 4, 14, 61; DA; DAB;
DAC; DAM MST, POET; PC 14**
See also CA 5-8R; 130; CANR 36; DLB 5;
MTCW; SATA 15

Swift, Augustus
See Lovecraft, H(oward) P(hillips)

Swift, Graham (Colin) 1949- . . . . **CLC 41, 88**
See also CA 117; 122; CANR 46

Swift, Jonathan
1667-1745 . . . . . . **LC 1; DA; DAB; DAC;
DAM MST, NOV, POET; PC 9; WLC**
See also CDBLB 1660-1789; DLB 39, 95,
101; SATA 19

Swinburne, Algernon Charles
1837-1909 . . . . . . **TCLC 8, 36; DA; DAB;
DAC; DAM MST, POET; WLC**
See also CA 105; 140; CDBLB 1832-1890;
DLB 35, 57

Swinfen, Ann . . . . **CLC 34**

Swinnerton, Frank Arthur
1884-1982 . . . . **CLC 31**
See also CA 108; DLB 34

Swithen, John
See King, Stephen (Edwin)

Sylvia
See Ashton-Warner, Sylvia (Constance)

Symmes, Robert Edward
See Duncan, Robert (Edward)

Symonds, John Addington
1840-1893 . . . . **NCLC 34**
See also DLB 57, 144

Symons, Arthur 1865-1945 . . . . **TCLC 11**
See also CA 107; DLB 19, 57, 149

Symons, Julian (Gustave)
1912-1994 . . . . **CLC 2, 14, 32**
See also CA 49-52; 147; CAAS 3; CANR 3,
33; DLB 87, 155; DLBY 92; MTCW

Synge, (Edmund) J(ohn) M(illington)
1871-1909 . . . . **TCLC 6, 37;
DAM DRAM; DC 2**
See also CA 104; 141; CDBLB 1890-1914;
DLB 10, 19

Syruc, J.
See Milosz, Czeslaw

Szirtes, George 1948- . . . . **CLC 46**
See also CA 109; CANR 27

Tabori, George 1914- . . . . **CLC 19**
See also CA 49-52; CANR 4

Tagore, Rabindranath
1861-1941 . . . . **TCLC 3, 53;
DAM DRAM, POET; PC 8**
See also CA 104; 120; MTCW

Taine, Hippolyte Adolphe
1828-1893 . . . . **NCLC 15**

Talese, Gay 1932- . . . . **CLC 37**
See also AITN 1; CA 1-4R; CANR 9;
INT CANR-9; MTCW

Tallent, Elizabeth (Ann) 1954- . . . . . **CLC 45**
See also CA 117; DLB 130

Tally, Ted 1952- . . . . **CLC 42**
See also CA 120; 124; INT 124

Tamayo y Baus, Manuel
1829-1898 . . . . **NCLC 1**

Tammsaare, A(nton) H(ansen)
1878-1940 . . . . **TCLC 27**

Tan, Amy (Ruth)
1952- . . . . . **CLC 59; DAM MULT, NOV,
POP**
See also AAYA 9; BEST 89:3; CA 136;
CANR 54; DLB 173; SATA 75

Tandem, Felix
See Spitteler, Carl (Friedrich Georg)

Tanizaki, Jun'ichiro
1886-1965 . . . . . . **CLC 8, 14, 28; SSC 21**
See also CA 93-96; 25-28R

Tanner, William
See Amis, Kingsley (William)

Tao Lao
See Storni, Alfonsina

Tarassoff, Lev
See Troyat, Henri

Tarbell, Ida M(inerva)
1857-1944 . . . . **TCLC 40**
See also CA 122; DLB 47

Tarkington, (Newton) Booth
1869-1946 . . . . **TCLC 9**
See also CA 110; 143; DLB 9, 102;
SATA 17

Tarkovsky, Andrei (Arsenyevich)
1932-1986 . . . . **CLC 75**
See also CA 127

Tartt, Donna 1964(?)- . . . . **CLC 76**
See also CA 142

Tasso, Torquato 1544-1595 . . . . **LC 5**

Tate, (John Orley) Allen
1899-1979 . . . . **CLC 2, 4, 6, 9, 11, 14, 24**
See also CA 5-8R; 85-88; CANR 32;
DLB 4, 45, 63; MTCW

Tate, Ellalice
  See Hibbert, Eleanor Alice Burford

Tate, James (Vincent) 1943- ... **CLC 2, 6, 25**
  See also CA 21-24R; CANR 29; DLB 5, 169

Tavel, Ronald 1940- .... **CLC 6**
  See also CA 21-24R; CANR 33

Taylor, C(ecil) P(hilip) 1929-1981... **CLC 27**
  See also CA 25-28R; 105; CANR 47

Taylor, Edward
      1642(?)-1729 .... **LC 11; DA; DAB;
                  DAC; DAM MST, POET**
  See also DLB 24

Taylor, Eleanor Ross 1920- .... **CLC 5**
  See also CA 81-84

Taylor, Elizabeth 1912-1975 ... **CLC 2, 4, 29**
  See also CA 13-16R; CANR 9; DLB 139;
  MTCW; SATA 13

Taylor, Henry (Splawn) 1942- ...... **CLC 44**
  See also CA 33-36R; CAAS 7; CANR 31;
  DLB 5

Taylor, Kamala (Purnaiya) 1924-
  See Markandaya, Kamala
  See also CA 77-80

Taylor, Mildred D. .... **CLC 21**
  See also AAYA 10; BW 1; CA 85-88;
  CANR 25; CLR 9; DLB 52; JRDA;
  MAICYA; SAAS 5; SATA 15, 70

Taylor, Peter (Hillsman)
      1917-1994 ..... **CLC 1, 4, 18, 37, 44, 50,
                                71; SSC 10**
  See also CA 13-16R; 147; CANR 9, 50;
  DLBY 81, 94; INT CANR-9; MTCW

Taylor, Robert Lewis 1912- .... **CLC 14**
  See also CA 1-4R; CANR 3; SATA 10

Tchekhov, Anton
  See Chekhov, Anton (Pavlovich)

Teasdale, Sara 1884-1933. .... **TCLC 4**
  See also CA 104; DLB 45; SATA 32

Tegner, Esaias 1782-1846. .... **NCLC 2**

Teilhard de Chardin, (Marie Joseph) Pierre
      1881-1955 .... **TCLC 9**
  See also CA 105

Temple, Ann
  See Mortimer, Penelope (Ruth)

Tennant, Emma (Christina)
      1937- .... **CLC 13, 52**
  See also CA 65-68; CAAS 9; CANR 10, 38;
  DLB 14

Tenneshaw, S. M.
  See Silverberg, Robert

Tennyson, Alfred
      1809-1892 .... **NCLC 30; DA; DAB;
                  DAC; DAM MST, POET; PC 6; WLC**
  See also CDBLB 1832-1890; DLB 32

Teran, Lisa St. Aubin de .... **CLC 36**
  See also St. Aubin de Teran, Lisa

Terence 195(?)B.C.-159B.C. ...... **CMLC 14**

Teresa de Jesus, St. 1515-1582 ...... **LC 18**

Terkel, Louis 1912-
  See Terkel, Studs
  See also CA 57-60; CANR 18, 45; MTCW

Terkel, Studs .... **CLC 38**
  See also Terkel, Louis
  See also AITN 1

Terry, C. V.
  See Slaughter, Frank G(ill)

Terry, Megan 1932- .... **CLC 19**
  See also CA 77-80; CABS 3; CANR 43;
  DLB 7

Tertz, Abram
  See Sinyavsky, Andrei (Donatevich)

Tesich, Steve 1943(?)-1996. ..... **CLC 40, 69**
  See also CA 105; 152; DLBY 83

Teternikov, Fyodor Kuzmich 1863-1927
  See Sologub, Fyodor
  See also CA 104

Tevis, Walter 1928-1984 .... **CLC 42**
  See also CA 113

Tey, Josephine. .... **TCLC 14**
  See also Mackintosh, Elizabeth
  See also DLB 77

Thackeray, William Makepeace
      1811-1863 .... **NCLC 5, 14, 22, 43; DA;
                  DAB; DAC; DAM MST, NOV; WLC**
  See also CDBLB 1832-1890; DLB 21, 55,
  159, 163; SATA 23

Thakura, Ravindranatha
  See Tagore, Rabindranath

Tharoor, Shashi 1956- .... **CLC 70**
  See also CA 141

Thelwell, Michael Miles 1939- ..... **CLC 22**
  See also BW 2; CA 101

Theobald, Lewis, Jr.
  See Lovecraft, H(oward) P(hillips)

Theodorescu, Ion N. 1880-1967
  See Arghezi, Tudor
  See also CA 116

Theriault, Yves
      1915-1983 .. **CLC 79; DAC; DAM MST**
  See also CA 102; DLB 88

Theroux, Alexander (Louis)
      1939- .... **CLC 2, 25**
  See also CA 85-88; CANR 20

Theroux, Paul (Edward)
      1941- .... **CLC 5, 8, 11, 15, 28, 46;
                                DAM POP**
  See also BEST 89:4; CA 33-36R; CANR 20,
  45; DLB 2; MTCW; SATA 44

Thesen, Sharon 1946- .... **CLC 56**

Thevenin, Denis
  See Duhamel, Georges

Thibault, Jacques Anatole Francois
      1844-1924
  See France, Anatole
  See also CA 106; 127; DAM NOV; MTCW

Thiele, Colin (Milton) 1920- .... **CLC 17**
  See also CA 29-32R; CANR 12, 28, 53;
  CLR 27; MAICYA; SAAS 2; SATA 14,
  72

Thomas, Audrey (Callahan)
      1935- .... **CLC 7, 13, 37; SSC 20**
  See also AITN 2; CA 21-24R; CAAS 19;
  CANR 36; DLB 60; MTCW

Thomas, D(onald) M(ichael)
      1935- .... **CLC 13, 22, 31**
  See also CA 61-64; CAAS 11; CANR 17,
  45; CDBLB 1960 to Present; DLB 40;
  INT CANR-17; MTCW

Thomas, Dylan (Marlais)
      1914-1953 ... **TCLC 1, 8, 45; DA; DAB;
              DAC; DAM DRAM, MST, POET;
                          PC 2; SSC 3; WLC**
  See also CA 104; 120; CDBLB 1945-1960;
  DLB 13, 20, 139; MTCW; SATA 60

Thomas, (Philip) Edward
      1878-1917 ...... **TCLC 10; DAM POET**
  See also CA 106; 153; DLB 19

Thomas, Joyce Carol 1938- .... **CLC 35**
  See also AAYA 12; BW 2; CA 113; 116;
  CANR 48; CLR 19; DLB 33; INT 116;
  JRDA; MAICYA; MTCW; SAAS 7;
  SATA 40, 78

Thomas, Lewis 1913-1993 .... **CLC 35**
  See also CA 85-88; 143; CANR 38; MTCW

Thomas, Paul
  See Mann, (Paul) Thomas

Thomas, Piri 1928- .... **CLC 17**
  See also CA 73-76; HW

Thomas, R(onald) S(tuart)
      1913- .... **CLC 6, 13, 48; DAB;
                                DAM POET**
  See also CA 89-92; CAAS 4; CANR 30;
  CDBLB 1960 to Present; DLB 27;
  MTCW

Thomas, Ross (Elmore) 1926-1995 .. **CLC 39**
  See also CA 33-36R; 150; CANR 22

Thompson, Francis Clegg
  See Mencken, H(enry) L(ouis)

Thompson, Francis Joseph
      1859-1907 .... **TCLC 4**
  See also CA 104; CDBLB 1890-1914;
  DLB 19

Thompson, Hunter S(tockton)
      1939- .... **CLC 9, 17, 40; DAM POP**
  See also BEST 89:1; CA 17-20R; CANR 23,
  46; MTCW

Thompson, James Myers
  See Thompson, Jim (Myers)

Thompson, Jim (Myers)
      1906-1977(?) .... **CLC 69**
  See also CA 140

Thompson, Judith .... **CLC 39**

Thomson, James
      1700-1748 ..... **LC 16, 29; DAM POET**
  See also DLB 95

Thomson, James
      1834-1882 ..... **NCLC 18; DAM POET**
  See also DLB 35

Thoreau, Henry David
      1817-1862 ..... **NCLC 7, 21; DA; DAB;
                  DAC; DAM MST; WLC**
  See also CDALB 1640-1865; DLB 1

Thornton, Hall
  See Silverberg, Robert

Thucydides c. 455B.C.-399B.C. .... **CMLC 17**

Thurber, James (Grover)
1894-1961 .... **CLC 5, 11, 25; DA; DAB; DAC; DAM DRAM, MST, NOV; SSC 1**
See also CA 73-76; CANR 17, 39; CDALB 1929-1941; DLB 4, 11, 22, 102; MAICYA; MTCW; SATA 13

Thurman, Wallace (Henry)
1902-1934 .... **TCLC 6; BLC; DAM MULT**
See also BW 1; CA 104; 124; DLB 51

Ticheburn, Cheviot
See Ainsworth, William Harrison

Tieck, (Johann) Ludwig
1773-1853 .... **NCLC 5, 46**
See also DLB 90

Tiger, Derry
See Ellison, Harlan (Jay)

Tilghman, Christopher 1948(?)-..... **CLC 65**

Tillinghast, Richard (Williford)
1940-...................... **CLC 29**
See also CA 29-32R; CAAS 23; CANR 26, 51

Timrod, Henry 1828-1867 .... **NCLC 25**
See also DLB 3

Tindall, Gillian 1938-.............. **CLC 7**
See also CA 21-24R; CANR 11

Tiptree, James, Jr. .... **CLC 48, 50**
See also Sheldon, Alice Hastings Bradley
See also DLB 8

Titmarsh, Michael Angelo
See Thackeray, William Makepeace

Tocqueville, Alexis (Charles Henri Maurice Clerel Comte) 1805-1859..... **NCLC 7**

Tolkien, J(ohn) R(onald) R(euel)
1892-1973 .... **CLC 1, 2, 3, 8, 12, 38; DA; DAB; DAC; DAM MST, NOV, POP; WLC**
See also AAYA 10; AITN 1; CA 17-18; 45-48; CANR 36; CAP 2; CDBLB 1914-1945; DLB 15, 160; JRDA; MAICYA; MTCW; SATA 2, 32; SATA-Obit 24

Toller, Ernst 1893-1939 .... **TCLC 10**
See also CA 107; DLB 124

Tolson, M. B.
See Tolson, Melvin B(eaunorus)

Tolson, Melvin B(eaunorus)
1898(?)-1966 .... **CLC 36; BLC; DAM MULT, POET**
See also BW 1; CA 124; 89-92; DLB 48, 76

Tolstoi, Aleksei Nikolaevich
See Tolstoy, Alexey Nikolaevich

Tolstoy, Alexey Nikolaevich
1882-1945 .... **TCLC 18**
See also CA 107

Tolstoy, Count Leo
See Tolstoy, Leo (Nikolaevich)

Tolstoy, Leo (Nikolaevich)
1828-1910 ...... **TCLC 4, 11, 17, 28, 44; DA; DAB; DAC; DAM MST, NOV; SSC 9; WLC**
See also CA 104; 123; SATA 26

Tomasi di Lampedusa, Giuseppe 1896-1957
See Lampedusa, Giuseppe (Tomasi) di
See also CA 111

Tomlin, Lily.................... **CLC 17**
See also Tomlin, Mary Jean

Tomlin, Mary Jean 1939(?)-
See Tomlin, Lily
See also CA 117

Tomlinson, (Alfred) Charles
1927-.............. **CLC 2, 4, 6, 13, 45; DAM POET**
See also CA 5-8R; CANR 33; DLB 40

Tonson, Jacob
See Bennett, (Enoch) Arnold

Toole, John Kennedy
1937-1969 .... **CLC 19, 64**
See also CA 104; DLBY 81

Toomer, Jean
1894-1967 ...... **CLC 1, 4, 13, 22; BLC; DAM MULT; PC 7; SSC 1**
See also BW 1; CA 85-88; CDALB 1917-1929; DLB 45, 51; MTCW

Torley, Luke
See Blish, James (Benjamin)

Tornimparte, Alessandra
See Ginzburg, Natalia

Torre, Raoul della
See Mencken, H(enry) L(ouis)

Torrey, E(dwin) Fuller 1937-....... **CLC 34**
See also CA 119

Torsvan, Ben Traven
See Traven, B.

Torsvan, Benno Traven
See Traven, B.

Torsvan, Berick Traven
See Traven, B.

Torsvan, Berwick Traven
See Traven, B.

Torsvan, Bruno Traven
See Traven, B.

Torsvan, Traven
See Traven, B.

Tournier, Michel (Edouard)
1924-..............CLC 6, 23, 36, 95
See also CA 49-52; CANR 3, 36; DLB 83; MTCW; SATA 23

Tournimparte, Alessandra
See Ginzburg, Natalia

Towers, Ivar
See Kornbluth, C(yril) M.

Towne, Robert (Burton) 1936(?)-.... **CLC 87**
See also CA 108; DLB 44

Townsend, Sue 1946-.. **CLC 61; DAB; DAC**
See also CA 119; 127; INT 127; MTCW; SATA 55; SATA-Brief 48

Townshend, Peter (Dennis Blandford)
1945-.................... **CLC 17, 42**
See also CA 107

Tozzi, Federigo 1883-1920....... **TCLC 31**

Traill, Catharine Parr
1802-1899 .... **NCLC 31**
See also DLB 99

Trakl, Georg 1887-1914.......... **TCLC 5**
See also CA 104

Transtroemer, Tomas (Goesta)
1931-........ **CLC 52, 65; DAM POET**
See also CA 117; 129; CAAS 17

Transtromer, Tomas Gosta
See Transtroemer, Tomas (Goesta)

Traven, B. (?)-1969............. **CLC 8, 11**
See also CA 19-20; 25-28R; CAP 2; DLB 9, 56; MTCW

Treitel, Jonathan 1959- .... **CLC 70**

Tremain, Rose 1943-.............. **CLC 42**
See also CA 97-100; CANR 44; DLB 14

Tremblay, Michel
1942-...... **CLC 29; DAC; DAM MST**
See also CA 116; 128; DLB 60; MTCW

Trevanian..................... **CLC 29**
See also Whitaker, Rod(ney)

Trevor, Glen
See Hilton, James

Trevor, William
1928-..... **CLC 7, 9, 14, 25, 71; SSC 21**
See also Cox, William Trevor
See also DLB 14, 139

Trifonov, Yuri (Valentinovich)
1925-1981 .... **CLC 45**
See also CA 126; 103; MTCW

Trilling, Lionel 1905-1975 .... **CLC 9, 11, 24**
See also CA 9-12R; 61-64; CANR 10; DLB 28, 63; INT CANR-10; MTCW

Trimball, W. H.
See Mencken, H(enry) L(ouis)

Tristan
See Gomez de la Serna, Ramon

Tristram
See Housman, A(lfred) E(dward)

Trogdon, William (Lewis) 1939-
See Heat-Moon, William Least
See also CA 115; 119; CANR 47; INT 119

Trollope, Anthony
1815-1882 ..... **NCLC 6, 33; DA; DAB; DAC; DAM MST, NOV; WLC**
See also CDBLB 1832-1890; DLB 21, 57, 159; SATA 22

Trollope, Frances 1779-1863 ..... **NCLC 30**
See also DLB 21, 166

Trotsky, Leon 1879-1940........ **TCLC 22**
See also CA 118

Trotter (Cockburn), Catharine
1679-1749 .... **LC 8**
See also DLB 84

Trout, Kilgore
See Farmer, Philip Jose

Trow, George W. S. 1943-......... **CLC 52**
See also CA 126

Troyat, Henri 1911-.............. **CLC 23**
See also CA 45-48; CANR 2, 33; MTCW

Trudeau, G(arretson) B(eekman) 1948-
See Trudeau, Garry B.
See also CA 81-84; CANR 31; SATA 35

Trudeau, Garry B.................. **CLC 12**
See also Trudeau, G(arretson) B(eekman)
See also AAYA 10; AITN 2

Truffaut, Francois 1932-1984....... **CLC 20**
See also CA 81-84; 113; CANR 34

Trumbo, Dalton 1905-1976 .... **CLC 19**
See also CA 21-24R; 69-72; CANR 10; DLB 26

Trumbull, John 1750-1831 . . . . . . **NCLC 30**
See also DLB 31

Trundlett, Helen B.
See Eliot, T(homas) S(tearns)

Tryon, Thomas
1926-1991 . . . . . **CLC 3, 11; DAM POP**
See also AITN 1; CA 29-32R; 135;
CANR 32; MTCW

Tryon, Tom
See Tryon, Thomas

Ts'ao Hsueh-ch'in 1715(?)-1763. . . . . . **LC 1**

Tsushima, Shuji 1909-1948
See Dazai, Osamu
See also CA 107

Tsvetaeva (Efron), Marina (Ivanovna)
1892-1941 . . . . **TCLC 7, 35; PC 14**
See also CA 104; 128; MTCW

Tuck, Lily 1938- . . . . **CLC 70**
See also CA 139

Tu Fu 712-770. . . . . **PC 9**
See also DAM MULT

Tunis, John R(oberts) 1889-1975 . . . **CLC 12**
See also CA 61-64; DLB 22, 171; JRDA;
MAICYA; SATA 37; SATA-Brief 30

Tuohy, Frank . . . . **CLC 37**
See also Tuohy, John Francis
See also DLB 14, 139

Tuohy, John Francis 1925-
See Tuohy, Frank
See also CA 5-8R; CANR 3, 47

Turco, Lewis (Putnam) 1934- . . . **CLC 11, 63**
See also CA 13-16R; CAAS 22; CANR 24,
51; DLBY 84

Turgenev, Ivan
1818-1883 . . . . **NCLC 21; DA; DAB;
DAC; DAM MST, NOV; SSC 7; WLC**

Turgot, Anne-Robert-Jacques
1727-1781 . . . . **LC 26**

Turner, Frederick 1943- . . . . **CLC 48**
See also CA 73-76; CAAS 10; CANR 12,
30; DLB 40

Tutu, Desmond M(pilo)
1931- . . . . . **CLC 80; BLC; DAM MULT**
See also BW 1; CA 125

Tutuola, Amos
1920- . . . . **CLC 5, 14, 29; BLC;
DAM MULT**
See also BW 2; CA 9-12R; CANR 27;
DLB 125; MTCW

Twain, Mark
. . . . . **TCLC 6, 12, 19, 36, 48, 59; SSC 6;
WLC**
See also Clemens, Samuel Langhorne
See also DLB 11, 12, 23, 64, 74

Tyler, Anne
1941- . . . . **CLC 7, 11, 18, 28, 44, 59;
DAM NOV, POP**
See also AAYA 18; BEST 89:1; CA 9-12R;
CANR 11, 33, 53; DLB 6, 143; DLBY 82;
MTCW; SATA 7, 90

Tyler, Royall 1757-1826. . . . . **NCLC 3**
See also DLB 37

Tynan, Katharine 1861-1931 . . . . . . **TCLC 3**
See also CA 104; DLB 153

Tyutchev, Fyodor 1803-1873 . . . . . **NCLC 34**

Tzara, Tristan
1896-1963 . . . . . . **CLC 47; DAM POET**
See also Rosenfeld, Samuel; Rosenstock,
Sami; Rosenstock, Samuel
See also CA 153

Uhry, Alfred
1936- . . . . . **CLC 55; DAM DRAM, POP**
See also CA 127; 133; INT 133

Ulf, Haerved
See Strindberg, (Johan) August

Ulf, Harved
See Strindberg, (Johan) August

Ulibarri, Sabine R(eyes)
1919- . . . . **CLC 83; DAM MULT**
See also CA 131; DLB 82; HW

Unamuno (y Jugo), Miguel de
1864-1936 . . . **TCLC 2, 9; DAM MULT,
NOV; HLC; SSC 11**
See also CA 104; 131; DLB 108; HW;
MTCW

Undercliffe, Errol
See Campbell, (John) Ramsey

Underwood, Miles
See Glassco, John

Undset, Sigrid
1882-1949 . . . . **TCLC 3; DA; DAB;
DAC; DAM MST, NOV; WLC**
See also CA 104; 129; MTCW

Ungaretti, Giuseppe
1888-1970 . . . . **CLC 7, 11, 15**
See also CA 19-20; 25-28R; CAP 2;
DLB 114

Unger, Douglas 1952- . . . . **CLC 34**
See also CA 130

Unsworth, Barry (Forster) 1930- . . . . **CLC 76**
See also CA 25-28R; CANR 30, 54

Updike, John (Hoyer)
1932- . . . . . . **CLC 1, 2, 3, 5, 7, 9, 13, 15,
23, 34, 43, 70; DA; DAB; DAC;
DAM MST, NOV, POET, POP;
SSC 13; WLC**
See also CA 1-4R; CABS 1; CANR 4, 33,
51; CDALB 1968-1988; DLB 2, 5, 143;
DLBD 3; DLBY 80, 82; MTCW

Upshaw, Margaret Mitchell
See Mitchell, Margaret (Munnerlyn)

Upton, Mark
See Sanders, Lawrence

Urdang, Constance (Henriette)
1922- . . . . **CLC 47**
See also CA 21-24R; CANR 9, 24

Uriel, Henry
See Faust, Frederick (Schiller)

Uris, Leon (Marcus)
1924- . . . . **CLC 7, 32; DAM NOV, POP**
See also AITN 1, 2; BEST 89:2; CA 1-4R;
CANR 1, 40; MTCW; SATA 49

Urmuz
See Codrescu, Andrei

Urquhart, Jane 1949- . . . . **CLC 90; DAC**
See also CA 113; CANR 32

Ustinov, Peter (Alexander) 1921- . . . . **CLC 1**
See also AITN 1; CA 13-16R; CANR 25,
51; DLB 13

Vaculik, Ludvik 1926- . . . . **CLC 7**
See also CA 53-56

Valdez, Luis (Miguel)
1940- . . . . . **CLC 84; DAM MULT; HLC**
See also CA 101; CANR 32; DLB 122; HW

Valenzuela, Luisa
1938- . . . **CLC 31; DAM MULT; SSC 14**
See also CA 101; CANR 32; DLB 113; HW

Valera y Alcala-Galiano, Juan
1824-1905 . . . . **TCLC 10**
See also CA 106

Valery, (Ambroise) Paul (Toussaint Jules)
1871-1945 . . . . **TCLC 4, 15;
DAM POET; PC 9**
See also CA 104; 122; MTCW

Valle-Inclan, Ramon (Maria) del
1866-1936 . . . . . **TCLC 5; DAM MULT;
HLC**
See also CA 106; 153; DLB 134

Vallejo, Antonio Buero
See Buero Vallejo, Antonio

Vallejo, Cesar (Abraham)
1892-1938 . . . . **TCLC 3, 56;
DAM MULT; HLC**
See also CA 105; 153; HW

Vallette, Marguerite Eymery
See Rachilde

Valle Y Pena, Ramon del
See Valle-Inclan, Ramon (Maria) del

Van Ash, Cay 1918- . . . . **CLC 34**

Vanbrugh, Sir John
1664-1726 . . . . **LC 21; DAM DRAM**
See also DLB 80

Van Campen, Karl
See Campbell, John W(ood, Jr.)

Vance, Gerald
See Silverberg, Robert

Vance, Jack . . . . **CLC 35**
See also Vance, John Holbrook
See also DLB 8

Vance, John Holbrook 1916-
See Queen, Ellery; Vance, Jack
See also CA 29-32R; CANR 17; MTCW

**Van Den Bogarde, Derek Jules Gaspard Ulric
Niven** 1921-
See Bogarde, Dirk
See also CA 77-80

Vandenburgh, Jane . . . . **CLC 59**

Vanderhaeghe, Guy 1951- . . . . **CLC 41**
See also CA 113

van der Post, Laurens (Jan) 1906- . . . **CLC 5**
See also CA 5-8R; CANR 35

van de Wetering, Janwillem 1931- . . **CLC 47**
See also CA 49-52; CANR 4

Van Dine, S. S. . . . . **TCLC 23**
See also Wright, Willard Huntington

Van Doren, Carl (Clinton)
1885-1950 . . . . **TCLC 18**
See also CA 111

Van Doren, Mark 1894-1972. . . . . **CLC 6, 10**
See also CA 1-4R; 37-40R; CANR 3;
DLB 45; MTCW

Van Druten, John (William)
1901-1957 .... **TCLC 2**
See also CA 104; DLB 10

Van Duyn, Mona (Jane)
1921- .... **CLC 3, 7, 63; DAM POET**
See also CA 9-12R; CANR 7, 38; DLB 5

Van Dyne, Edith
See Baum, L(yman) Frank

van Itallie, Jean-Claude 1936-....... **CLC 3**
See also CA 45-48; CAAS 2; CANR 1, 48;
DLB 7

van Ostaijen, Paul 1896-1928 ..... **TCLC 33**

Van Peebles, Melvin
1932- .... **CLC 2, 20; DAM MULT**
See also BW 2; CA 85-88; CANR 27

Vansittart, Peter 1920-............ **CLC 42**
See also CA 1-4R; CANR 3, 49

Van Vechten, Carl 1880-1964 ...... **CLC 33**
See also CA 89-92; DLB 4, 9, 51

Van Vogt, A(lfred) E(lton) 1912-..... **CLC 1**
See also CA 21-24R; CANR 28; DLB 8;
SATA 14

Varda, Agnes 1928- .... **CLC 16**
See also CA 116; 122

Vargas Llosa, (Jorge) Mario (Pedro)
1936- .... **CLC 3, 6, 9, 10, 15, 31, 42, 85;**
DA; DAB; DAC; DAM MST, MULT,
NOV; HLC
See also CA 73-76; CANR 18, 32, 42;
DLB 145; HW; MTCW

Vasiliu, Gheorghe 1881-1957
See Bacovia, George
See also CA 123

Vassa, Gustavus
See Equiano, Olaudah

Vassilikos, Vassilis 1933-......... **CLC 4, 8**
See also CA 81-84

Vaughan, Henry 1621-1695 .... **LC 27**
See also DLB 131

Vaughn, Stephanie................ **CLC 62**

Vazov, Ivan (Minchov)
1850-1921 .... **TCLC 25**
See also CA 121; DLB 147

Veblen, Thorstein (Bunde)
1857-1929 .... **TCLC 31**
See also CA 115

Vega, Lope de 1562-1635........... **LC 23**

Venison, Alfred
See Pound, Ezra (Weston Loomis)

Verdi, Marie de
See Mencken, H(enry) L(ouis)

Verdu, Matilde
See Cela, Camilo Jose

Verga, Giovanni (Carmelo)
1840-1922 .... **TCLC 3; SSC 21**
See also CA 104; 123

Vergil
70B.C.-19B.C...... **CMLC 9; DA; DAB;**
DAC; DAM MST, POET; PC 12

Verhaeren, Emile (Adolphe Gustave)
1855-1916 .... **TCLC 12**
See also CA 109

Verlaine, Paul (Marie)
1844-1896 .... **NCLC 2, 51;**
DAM POET; PC 2

Verne, Jules (Gabriel)
1828-1905 .... **TCLC 6, 52**
See also AAYA 16; CA 110; 131; DLB 123;
JRDA; MAICYA; SATA 21

Very, Jones 1813-1880.......... **NCLC 9**
See also DLB 1

Vesaas, Tarjei 1897-1970......... **CLC 48**
See also CA 29-32R

Vialis, Gaston
See Simenon, Georges (Jacques Christian)

Vian, Boris 1920-1959 .... **TCLC 9**
See also CA 106; DLB 72

Viaud, (Louis Marie) Julien 1850-1923
See Loti, Pierre
See also CA 107

Vicar, Henry
See Felsen, Henry Gregor

Vicker, Angus
See Felsen, Henry Gregor

Vidal, Gore
1925- ..... **CLC 2, 4, 6, 8, 10, 22, 33, 72;**
DAM NOV, POP
See also AITN 1; BEST 90:2; CA 5-8R;
CANR 13, 45; DLB 6, 152;
INT CANR-13; MTCW

Viereck, Peter (Robert Edwin)
1916-...................... **CLC 4**
See also CA 1-4R; CANR 1, 47; DLB 5

Vigny, Alfred (Victor) de
1797-1863 ...... **NCLC 7; DAM POET**
See also DLB 119

Vilakazi, Benedict Wallet
1906-1947 .... **TCLC 37**

Villiers de l'Isle Adam, Jean Marie Mathias
Philippe Auguste Comte
1838-1889 .... **NCLC 3; SSC 14**
See also DLB 123

Villon, Francois 1431-1463(?) .... **PC 13**

Vinci, Leonardo da 1452-1519...... **LC 12**

Vine, Barbara .... **CLC 50**
See also Rendell, Ruth (Barbara)
See also BEST 90:4

Vinge, Joan D(ennison)
1948- .... **CLC 30; SSC 24**
See also CA 93-96; SATA 36

Violis, G.
See Simenon, Georges (Jacques Christian)

Visconti, Luchino 1906-1976....... **CLC 16**
See also CA 81-84; 65-68; CANR 39

Vittorini, Elio 1908-1966...... **CLC 6, 9, 14**
See also CA 133; 25-28R

Vizinczey, Stephen 1933-......... **CLC 40**
See also CA 128; INT 128

Vliet, R(ussell) G(ordon)
1929-1984 .... **CLC 22**
See also CA 37-40R; 112; CANR 18

Vogau, Boris Andreyevich 1894-1937(?)
See Pilnyak, Boris
See also CA 123

Vogel, Paula A(nne) 1951-......... **CLC 76**
See also CA 108

Voight, Ellen Bryant 1943-........ **CLC 54**
See also CA 69-72; CANR 11, 29, 55;
DLB 120

Voigt, Cynthia 1942- .... **CLC 30**
See also AAYA 3; CA 106; CANR 18, 37,
40; CLR 13; INT CANR-18; JRDA;
MAICYA; SATA 48, 79; SATA-Brief 33

Voinovich, Vladimir (Nikolaevich)
1932-.................... **CLC 10, 49**
See also CA 81-84; CAAS 12; CANR 33;
MTCW

Vollmann, William T.
1959- ...... **CLC 89; DAM NOV, POP**
See also CA 134

Voloshinov, V. N.
See Bakhtin, Mikhail Mikhailovich

Voltaire
1694-1778 ..... **LC 14; DA; DAB; DAC;**
DAM DRAM, MST; SSC 12; WLC

von Bingen, Hildegard
1098(?)-1179 .... **CMLC 20**

von Daeniken, Erich 1935- .... **CLC 30**
See also AITN 1; CA 37-40R; CANR 17,
44

von Daniken, Erich
See von Daeniken, Erich

von Heidenstam, (Carl Gustaf) Verner
See Heidenstam, (Carl Gustaf) Verner von

von Heyse, Paul (Johann Ludwig)
See Heyse, Paul (Johann Ludwig von)

von Hofmannsthal, Hugo
See Hofmannsthal, Hugo von

von Horvath, Odon
See Horvath, Oedoen von

von Horvath, Oedoen
See Horvath, Oedoen von

von Liliencron, (Friedrich Adolf Axel) Detlev
See Liliencron, (Friedrich Adolf Axel)
Detlev von

Vonnegut, Kurt, Jr.
1922- ...... **CLC 1, 2, 3, 4, 5, 8, 12, 22,**
40, 60; DA; DAB; DAC; DAM MST,
NOV, POP; SSC 8; WLC
See also AAYA 6; AITN 1; BEST 90:4;
CA 1-4R; CANR 1, 25, 49;
CDALB 1968-1988; DLB 2, 8, 152;
DLBD 3; DLBY 80; MTCW

Von Rachen, Kurt
See Hubbard, L(afayette) Ron(ald)

von Rezzori (d'Arezzo), Gregor
See Rezzori (d'Arezzo), Gregor von

von Sternberg, Josef
See Sternberg, Josef von

Vorster, Gordon 1924-............ **CLC 34**
See also CA 133

Vosce, Trudie
See Ozick, Cynthia

Voznesensky, Andrei (Andreievich)
1933- ...... **CLC 1, 15, 57; DAM POET**
See also CA 89-92; CANR 37; MTCW

Waddington, Miriam 1917-........ **CLC 28**
See also CA 21-24R; CANR 12, 30;
DLB 68

Wagman, Fredrica 1937-.......... **CLC 7**
See also CA 97-100; INT 97-100

Wagner, Richard 1813-1883...... **NCLC 9**
See also DLB 129

Wagner-Martin, Linda 1936-...... **CLC 50**

Wagoner, David (Russell)
1926-................... **CLC 3, 5, 15**
See also CA 1-4R; CAAS 3; CANR 2;
DLB 5; SATA 14

Wah, Fred(erick James) 1939-..... **CLC 44**
See also CA 107; 141; DLB 60

Wahloo, Per 1926-1975 .... **CLC 7**
See also CA 61-64

Wahloo, Peter
See Wahloo, Per

Wain, John (Barrington)
1925-1994 .... **CLC 2, 11, 15, 46**
See also CA 5-8R; 145; CAAS 4; CANR 23,
54; CDBLB 1960 to Present; DLB 15, 27,
139, 155; MTCW

Wajda, Andrzej 1926-............. **CLC 16**
See also CA 102

Wakefield, Dan 1932-.............. **CLC 7**
See also CA 21-24R; CAAS 7

Wakoski, Diane
1937-........... **CLC 2, 4, 7, 9, 11, 40;**
DAM POET; PC 15
See also CA 13-16R; CAAS 1; CANR 9;
DLB 5; INT CANR-9

Wakoski-Sherbell, Diane
See Wakoski, Diane

Walcott, Derek (Alton)
1930- .... **CLC 2, 4, 9, 14, 25, 42, 67, 76;**
BLC; DAB; DAC; DAM MST, MULT,
POET
See also BW 2; CA 89-92; CANR 26, 47;
DLB 117; DLBY 81; MTCW

Waldman, Anne 1945- .... **CLC 7**
See also CA 37-40R; CAAS 17; CANR 34;
DLB 16

Waldo, E. Hunter
See Sturgeon, Theodore (Hamilton)

Waldo, Edward Hamilton
See Sturgeon, Theodore (Hamilton)

Walker, Alice (Malsenior)
1944-....... **CLC 5, 6, 9, 19, 27, 46, 58;**
BLC; DA; DAB; DAC; DAM MST,
MULT, NOV, POET, POP; SSC 5
See also AAYA 3; BEST 89:4; BW 2;
CA 37-40R; CANR 9, 27, 49;
CDALB 1968-1988; DLB 6, 33, 143;
INT CANR-27; MTCW; SATA 31

Walker, David Harry 1911-1992.... **CLC 14**
See also CA 1-4R; 137; CANR 1; SATA 8;
SATA-Obit 71

Walker, Edward Joseph 1934-
See Walker, Ted
See also CA 21-24R; CANR 12, 28, 53

Walker, George F.
1947- .... **CLC 44, 61; DAB; DAC;**
DAM MST
See also CA 103; CANR 21, 43; DLB 60

Walker, Joseph A.
1935- .... **CLC 19; DAM DRAM, MST**
See also BW 1; CA 89-92; CANR 26;
DLB 38

Walker, Margaret (Abigail)
1915- .... **CLC 1, 6; BLC; DAM MULT**
See also BW 2; CA 73-76; CANR 26, 54;
DLB 76, 152; MTCW

Walker, Ted..................... **CLC 13**
See also Walker, Edward Joseph
See also DLB 40

Wallace, David Foster 1962-....... **CLC 50**
See also CA 132

Wallace, Dexter
See Masters, Edgar Lee

Wallace, (Richard Horatio) Edgar
1875-1932 .... **TCLC 57**
See also CA 115; DLB 70

Wallace, Irving
1916-1990 ..... **CLC 7, 13; DAM NOV,**
POP
See also AITN 1; CA 1-4R; 132; CAAS 1;
CANR 1, 27; INT CANR-27; MTCW

Wallant, Edward Lewis
1926-1962 .... **CLC 5, 10**
See also CA 1-4R; CANR 22; DLB 2, 28,
143; MTCW

Walley, Byron
See Card, Orson Scott

Walpole, Horace 1717-1797......... **LC 2**
See also DLB 39, 104

Walpole, Hugh (Seymour)
1884-1941 .... **TCLC 5**
See also CA 104; DLB 34

Walser, Martin 1927-............. **CLC 27**
See also CA 57-60; CANR 8, 46; DLB 75,
124

Walser, Robert
1878-1956 .... **TCLC 18; SSC 20**
See also CA 118; DLB 66

Walsh, Jill Paton................. **CLC 35**
See also Paton Walsh, Gillian
See also AAYA 11; CLR 2; DLB 161;
SAAS 3

Walter, Villiam Christian
See Andersen, Hans Christian

Wambaugh, Joseph (Aloysius, Jr.)
1937- .... **CLC 3, 18; DAM NOV, POP**
See also AITN 1; BEST 89:3; CA 33-36R;
CANR 42; DLB 6; DLBY 83; MTCW

Ward, Arthur Henry Sarsfield 1883-1959
See Rohmer, Sax
See also CA 108

Ward, Douglas Turner 1930-....... **CLC 19**
See also BW 1; CA 81-84; CANR 27;
DLB 7, 38

Ward, Mary Augusta
See Ward, Mrs. Humphry

Ward, Mrs. Humphry
1851-1920 .... **TCLC 55**
See also DLB 18

Ward, Peter
See Faust, Frederick (Schiller)

Warhol, Andy 1928(?)-1987........ **CLC 20**
See also AAYA 12; BEST 89:4; CA 89-92;
121; CANR 34

Warner, Francis (Robert le Plastrier)
1937- .... **CLC 14**
See also CA 53-56; CANR 11

Warner, Marina 1946-............ **CLC 59**
See also CA 65-68; CANR 21, 55

Warner, Rex (Ernest) 1905-1986.... **CLC 45**
See also CA 89-92; 119; DLB 15

Warner, Susan (Bogert)
1819-1885 .... **NCLC 31**
See also DLB 3, 42

Warner, Sylvia (Constance) Ashton
See Ashton-Warner, Sylvia (Constance)

Warner, Sylvia Townsend
1893-1978 .... **CLC 7, 19; SSC 23**
See also CA 61-64; 77-80; CANR 16;
DLB 34, 139; MTCW

Warren, Mercy Otis 1728-1814... **NCLC 13**
See also DLB 31

Warren, Robert Penn
1905-1989 .... **CLC 1, 4, 6, 8, 10, 13, 18,**
39, 53, 59; DA; DAB; DAC; DAM MST,
NOV, POET; SSC 4; WLC
See also AITN 1; CA 13-16R; 129;
CANR 10, 47; CDALB 1968-1988;
DLB 2, 48, 152; DLBY 80, 89;
INT CANR-10; MTCW; SATA 46;
SATA-Obit 63

Warshofsky, Isaac
See Singer, Isaac Bashevis

Warton, Thomas
1728-1790 .... **LC 15; DAM POET**
See also DLB 104, 109

Waruk, Kona
See Harris, (Theodore) Wilson

Warung, Price 1855-1911........ **TCLC 45**

Warwick, Jarvis
See Garner, Hugh

Washington, Alex
See Harris, Mark

Washington, Booker T(aliaferro)
1856-1915 .... **TCLC 10; BLC;**
DAM MULT
See also BW 1; CA 114; 125; SATA 28

Washington, George 1732-1799...... **LC 25**
See also DLB 31

Wassermann, (Karl) Jakob
1873-1934 .... **TCLC 6**
See also CA 104; DLB 66

Wasserstein, Wendy
1950-................. **CLC 32, 59, 90;**
DAM DRAM; DC 4
See also CA 121; 129; CABS 3; CANR 53;
INT 129

Waterhouse, Keith (Spencer)
1929-..................... **CLC 47**
See also CA 5-8R; CANR 38; DLB 13, 15;
MTCW

Waters, Frank (Joseph)
1902-1995 .... **CLC 88**
See also CA 5-8R; 149; CAAS 13; CANR 3,
18; DLBY 86

Waters, Roger 1944-.............. **CLC 35**

Watkins, Frances Ellen
See Harper, Frances Ellen Watkins

Watkins, Gerrold
See Malzberg, Barry N(athaniel)

Watkins, Gloria   1955(?)-
See hooks, bell
See also BW 2; CA 143

Watkins, Paul   1964-.............. **CLC 55**
See also CA 132

Watkins, Vernon Phillips
1906-1967 .... **CLC 43**
See also CA 9-10; 25-28R; CAP 1; DLB 20

Watson, Irving S.
See Mencken, H(enry) L(ouis)

Watson, John H.
See Farmer, Philip Jose

Watson, Richard F.
See Silverberg, Robert

Waugh, Auberon (Alexander)   1939-.. **CLC 7**
See also CA 45-48; CANR 6, 22; DLB 14

Waugh, Evelyn (Arthur St. John)
1903-1966 ..... **CLC 1, 3, 8, 13, 19, 27,**
44; DA; DAB; DAC; DAM MST, NOV,
POP; WLC
See also CA 85-88; 25-28R; CANR 22;
CDBLB 1914-1945; DLB 15, 162; MTCW

Waugh, Harriet   1944- .... **CLC 6**
See also CA 85-88; CANR 22

Ways, C. R.
See Blount, Roy (Alton), Jr.

Waystaff, Simon
See Swift, Jonathan

Webb, (Martha) Beatrice (Potter)
1858-1943 .... **TCLC 22**
See also Potter, Beatrice
See also CA 117

Webb, Charles (Richard)   1939-...... **CLC 7**
See also CA 25-28R

Webb, James H(enry), Jr.   1946-.... **CLC 22**
See also CA 81-84

Webb, Mary (Gladys Meredith)
1881-1927 .... **TCLC 24**
See also CA 123; DLB 34

Webb, Mrs. Sidney
See Webb, (Martha) Beatrice (Potter)

Webb, Phyllis   1927-.............. **CLC 18**
See also CA 104; CANR 23; DLB 53

Webb, Sidney (James)
1859-1947 .... **TCLC 22**
See also CA 117

Webber, Andrew Lloyd............. **CLC 21**
See also Lloyd Webber, Andrew

Weber, Lenora Mattingly
1895-1971 .... **CLC 12**
See also CA 19-20; 29-32R; CAP 1;
SATA 2; SATA-Obit 26

Webster, John
1579(?)-1634(?) ...... **LC 33; DA; DAB;**
DAC; DAM DRAM, MST; DC 2; WLC
See also CDBLB Before 1660; DLB 58

Webster, Noah   1758-1843 .... **NCLC 30**

Wedekind, (Benjamin) Frank(lin)
1864-1918 ...... **TCLC 7; DAM DRAM**
See also CA 104; 153; DLB 118

Weidman, Jerome   1913-............ **CLC 7**
See also AITN 2; CA 1-4R; CANR 1;
DLB 28

Weil, Simone (Adolphine)
1909-1943 .... **TCLC 23**
See also CA 117

Weinstein, Nathan
See West, Nathanael

Weinstein, Nathan von Wallenstein
See West, Nathanael

Weir, Peter (Lindsay)   1944- .... **CLC 20**
See also CA 113; 123

Weiss, Peter (Ulrich)
1916-1982 .... **CLC 3, 15, 51;**
DAM DRAM
See also CA 45-48; 106; CANR 3; DLB 69,
124

Weiss, Theodore (Russell)
1916- .... **CLC 3, 8, 14**
See also CA 9-12R; CAAS 2; CANR 46;
DLB 5

Welch, (Maurice) Denton
1915-1948 .... **TCLC 22**
See also CA 121; 148

Welch, James
1940- ..... **CLC 6, 14, 52; DAM MULT,**
POP
See also CA 85-88; CANR 42; NNAL

Weldon, Fay
1933- .... **CLC 6, 9, 11, 19, 36, 59;**
DAM POP
See also CA 21-24R; CANR 16, 46;
CDBLB 1960 to Present; DLB 14;
INT CANR-16; MTCW

Wellek, Rene   1903-1995........... **CLC 28**
See also CA 5-8R; 150; CAAS 7; CANR 8;
DLB 63; INT CANR-8

Weller, Michael   1942-........ **CLC 10, 53**
See also CA 85-88

Weller, Paul   1958-............... **CLC 26**

Wellershoff, Dieter   1925-.......... **CLC 46**
See also CA 89-92; CANR 16, 37

Welles, (George) Orson
1915-1985 .... **CLC 20, 80**
See also CA 93-96; 117

Wellman, Mac   1945- .... **CLC 65**

Wellman, Manly Wade   1903-1986 .. **CLC 49**
See also CA 1-4R; 118; CANR 6, 16, 44;
SATA 6; SATA-Obit 47

Wells, Carolyn   1869(?)-1942 ...... **TCLC 35**
See also CA 113; DLB 11

Wells, H(erbert) G(eorge)
1866-1946 .... **TCLC 6, 12, 19; DA;**
DAB; DAC; DAM MST, NOV; SSC 6;
WLC
See also AAYA 18; CA 110; 121;
CDBLB 1914-1945; DLB 34, 70, 156;
MTCW; SATA 20

Wells, Rosemary   1943-............ **CLC 12**
See also AAYA 13; CA 85-88; CANR 48;
CLR 16; MAICYA; SAAS 1; SATA 18,
69

Welty, Eudora
1909- ...... **CLC 1, 2, 5, 14, 22, 33; DA;**
DAB; DAC; DAM MST, NOV; SSC 1;
WLC
See also CA 9-12R; CABS 1; CANR 32;
CDALB 1941-1968; DLB 2, 102, 143;
DLBD 12; DLBY 87; MTCW

Wen I-to   1899-1946 .... **TCLC 28**

Wentworth, Robert
See Hamilton, Edmond

Werfel, Franz (V.)   1890-1945 ..... **TCLC 8**
See also CA 104; DLB 81, 124

Wergeland, Henrik Arnold
1808-1845 .... **NCLC 5**

Wersba, Barbara   1932-............ **CLC 30**
See also AAYA 2; CA 29-32R; CANR 16,
38; CLR 3; DLB 52; JRDA; MAICYA;
SAAS 2; SATA 1, 58

Wertmueller, Lina   1928- .... **CLC 16**
See also CA 97-100; CANR 39

Wescott, Glenway   1901-1987....... **CLC 13**
See also CA 13-16R; 121; CANR 23;
DLB 4, 9, 102

Wesker, Arnold
1932- .... **CLC 3, 5, 42; DAB;**
DAM DRAM
See also CA 1-4R; CAAS 7; CANR 1, 33;
CDBLB 1960 to Present; DLB 13;
MTCW

Wesley, Richard (Errol)   1945-....... **CLC 7**
See also BW 1; CA 57-60; CANR 27;
DLB 38

Wessel, Johan Herman   1742-1785 .... **LC 7**

West, Anthony (Panther)
1914-1987 .... **CLC 50**
See also CA 45-48; 124; CANR 3, 19;
DLB 15

West, C. P.
See Wodehouse, P(elham) G(renville)

West, (Mary) Jessamyn
1902-1984 .... **CLC 7, 17**
See also CA 9-12R; 112; CANR 27; DLB 6;
DLBY 84; MTCW; SATA-Obit 37

West, Morris L(anglo)   1916-..... **CLC 6, 33**
See also CA 5-8R; CANR 24, 49; MTCW

West, Nathanael
1903-1940 ..... **TCLC 1, 14, 44; SSC 16**
See also CA 104; 125; CDALB 1929-1941;
DLB 4, 9, 28; MTCW

West, Owen
See Koontz, Dean R(ay)

West, Paul   1930- .... **CLC 7, 14, 96**
See also CA 13-16R; CAAS 7; CANR 22,
53; DLB 14; INT CANR-22

West, Rebecca   1892-1983 .. **CLC 7, 9, 31, 50**
See also CA 5-8R; 109; CANR 19; DLB 36;
DLBY 83; MTCW

Westall, Robert (Atkinson)
1929-1993 .... **CLC 17**
See also AAYA 12; CA 69-72; 141;
CANR 18; CLR 13; JRDA; MAICYA;
SAAS 2; SATA 23, 69; SATA-Obit 75

Westlake, Donald E(dwin)
1933- .... **CLC 7, 33; DAM POP**
See also CA 17-20R; CAAS 13; CANR 16,
44; INT CANR-16

Westmacott, Mary
See Christie, Agatha (Mary Clarissa)

Weston, Allen
See Norton, Andre

Wetcheek, J. L.
See Feuchtwanger, Lion

Zhukovsky, Vasily 1783-1852 . . . . **NCLC 35**

Ziegenhagen, Eric . . . . **CLC 55**

Zimmer, Jill Schary
  See Robinson, Jill

Zimmerman, Robert
  See Dylan, Bob

Zindel, Paul
    1936- . . . . . **CLC 6, 26; DA; DAB; DAC;**
        DAM DRAM, MST, NOV; DC 5
  See also AAYA 2; CA 73-76; CANR 31;
    CLR 3; DLB 7, 52; JRDA; MAICYA;
    MTCW; SATA 16, 58

Zinov'Ev, A. A.
  See Zinoviev, Alexander (Aleksandrovich)

Zinoviev, Alexander (Aleksandrovich)
    1922- . . . . **CLC 19**
  See also CA 116; 133; CAAS 10

Zoilus
  See Lovecraft, H(oward) P(hillips)

Zola, Emile (Edouard Charles Antoine)
    1840-1902 . . . . . . **TCLC 1, 6, 21, 41; DA;**
        DAB; DAC; DAM MST, NOV; WLC
  See also CA 104; 138; DLB 123

Zoline, Pamela 1941- . . . . **CLC 62**

Zorrilla y Moral, Jose 1817-1893 . . **NCLC 6**

Zoshchenko, Mikhail (Mikhailovich)
    1895-1958 . . . . **TCLC 15; SSC 15**
  See also CA 115

Zuckmayer, Carl 1896-1977 . . . . **CLC 18**
  See also CA 69-72; DLB 56, 124

Zuk, Georges
  See Skelton, Robin

Zukofsky, Louis
    1904-1978 . . . . **CLC 1, 2, 4, 7, 11, 18;**
                DAM POET; PC 11
  See also CA 9-12R; 77-80; CANR 39;
    DLB 5, 165; MTCW

Zweig, Paul 1935-1984 . . . . **CLC 34, 42**
  See also CA 85-88; 113

Zweig, Stefan 1881-1942 . . . . **TCLC 17**
  See also CA 112; DLB 81, 118

Literary Criticism Series
Cumulative Topic Index

This index lists all topic entries in Gale's *Classical and Medieval Literature Criticism, Contemporary Literary Criticism, Literature Criticism from 1400 to 1800, Nineteenth-Century Literature Criticism,* and *Twentieth-Century Literary Criticism.*

Topic Index

Topic Index

Cumulative Nationality Index

Nationality Index

Nationality Index

Nationality Index

Nationality Index

Nationality Index

CLC-98 Title Index

CLC VOL 98

ISBN 0-7876-1062-3
90000

9 780787 610623